THE JOURNAL OF

ARNOLD BENNETT

PORTRAIT OF ARNOLD BENNETT BY EDWARD WOLFE

THE JOURNAL OF

ARNOLD BENNETT

1896–1928

NEW YORK

THE VIKING PRESS

MCMXXXIII

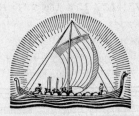

PUBLISHERS' FOREWORD

TO THE AMERICAN EDITION

Beginning in 1896, and continuing until shortly before his death, Arnold Bennett kept Journals in which he set down sometimes from day to day, sometimes at longer intervals, his comments on people seen, books read, places visited, his thoughts and observations on the varied life of which he was a part. Sometimes he was consciously collecting material for use in his books; more often he was simply compiling the intimate record of his personal development. He died in London on March 27, 1931.

The Journals, containing over a million words, were preserved in his own distinguished longhand in a series of notebooks. The task of editing such a mass of material and of reducing it no more and no less than necessary to make publication practicable, was not an easy one. It was found upon examination, however, that a certain amount of extraneous matter could be sacrificed easily—matter which Arnold Bennett had written in accordance with his dutiful habit of recording even the minor details of how he lived on 24 hours a day. A few passages could be spared because they duplicated ideas or subject-matter already included. Still others, personal references, were omitted because their allusions have no meaning to us today. But nothing has been withheld which would distort the true picture of the author's character; nothing changed except obvious mechanical errors; nothing added except footnotes. The editors have been guided by the belief that the interest of the Journals lies in their revelation of the author's mind and opinion as it was at the time of writing, rather than as he might have wished it to appear if he himself had edited them at some later date. The footnotes—which in some cases will seem supererogatory—have been prepared with an eye to future as well as to immediate readers.

Enoch Arnold Bennett was born at Shelton near Hanley in North

Staffordshire, one of his "Five Towns," on May 27, 1867. He was educated at Newcastle Middle School and became a lawyer's clerk in London in 1889; but after a few years he threw up his position in favour of journalism. He became sub-editor on a paper called *Woman,* and it is at this point, in 1896, that he began his Journal. Of his personal traits, it need only be said that he suffered from stammering; his search for a cure will come out in the course of this volume.

The Journals were first published in three independent volumes. The first, covering the period 1896–1910, revealed the details of the early and formative years of Arnold Bennett's career. The second volume, 1911–1920, opened with the extremely interesting record of his first visit to America; it then became primarily a War Diary and showed the impress of a great international happening on the sensitive mind of the author, and his attitudes to the undercurrents of which he became aware. The third volume, 1921–1928, carried the Journal down through the eventful post-war years and is a record of men and movements that may still be called contemporary. The publishers now take pleasure in presenting the entire Journal, without changes or deletions from its original published form, in one volume.

The Journal provides a complete picture of Arnold Bennett's working life, the autobiography of a craftsman in whom the impulse to write was so strong that he produced over a million words in 34 years as a mere sideline to his large literary output. What he thought, he was impelled to write down; what he saw—the drama or the humour of countless little episodes in life—he had to record, and usually in the form of a perfect pen-picture in miniature. The Journal is a legacy of anecdote, criticism, narrative, and thoughtful comment, a rich account of his outward and inward life. Its interest as a study of the processes of literary creation is second only to its interest as a personal record of the literary and artistic world during the eventful years of his life.

On the death of Arnold Bennett, the Journals became the property of Dorothy Cheston Bennett, who asked Newman Flower of Cassell and Company, the English publisher, to edit them for England, and sent copies of the original to the Viking Press for the American edition. The American editors make grateful acknowledgment to Mr. Flower for his work of selection and for his invaluable help in identifying obscure references; at the same time they wish to point out that he is in no way responsible for the omissions they have made, or the many items they have seen fit to reinstate, in preparing the edition for American readers.

NOTE

It was the Author's intention to add to parts of the Journal. Had this been done, some of his earlier opinions might have been altered or modified, although the later Arnold Bennett, when reading the earlier Arnold Bennett, generally found himself in agreement with his younger self.

Unaltered as these Journals remain in their present form (although selection was necessary owing to their great length) they are pure autobiography, and the development of character and mind is subtly revealed at first hand.

Speaking generally, it could be said that the first third of the Journals (1896–1910) shows Arnold Bennett interested in his own mind and its development, in study and the acquisition of all sorts of knowledge. People in this period interest him in relation to their impact on himself more than later on, although his imagination forces him always to see them from their own point of view.

In the ten middle years (1911–1920) the effect of success upon him is revealed and a more and more objective observation of the world and of people shown.

The last part (1921–1928) records his more personal and social life, his interest in the next generation.

D. C. B.

THE JOURNAL

1896-1914

1896

April 27th.

A fire engine was trotting down Chandos Street and in front of it two women in a victoria excitedly implored their coachman to draw to the side of the road. I walked on, and then, guessing that the fire must be near at hand, turned round, and hurrying as others hurried, found myself at the edge of a loosely packed crowd in Villiers Street.

Three fire brigade vehicles, two of them steamers, and all three pair-horsed, were standing in line. Smoke and steam curled out idly from the glittering brass funnels of the steamers; the firemen talked and laughed in groups, unconcerned; and one or two idlers stroked the glossy flanks of the magnificent grey horses. No sign of a fire anywhere!

Then I saw people turning in under one of the arches beneath Charing Cross Station, and I went to explore further. From an open door towards the middle of the arch, guarded by a policeman, a thin smoke exuded into the faces of a ring of spectators. Beyond doubt the outbreak had been successfully dealt with before the engines arrived. At the other end of the arch was a fire-escape (looking curiously out of place, having regard to the locality of the fire), officiously watched by three street loiterers who had presumably helped to bring it there. "Come along, lads," said a fireman to them, "we'll be getting off home."

A fire under Charing Cross Station might have proved a brilliant and exciting event, if circumstances had given it a chance.

At the Comedy Restaurant, to which I seldom go without overhearing an interesting or an instructive duologue, were two soberly dressed young women—perhaps actresses. One, about 28, a girl with a small, self-contained face, with two "ruts" from either side the nostrils indicating a disposition towards fastidiousness in all things. The other had her back to me; she was older, plainer, and less assertive. They were evidently discussing some domestic calamity in which the second was concerned. The first spoke continually in a pained, compassionate voice, using frequently the phrase, "your mother," "your dear mother." Her tones were modulated cleverly, and yet the effect was one of monotony. The second said little, beyond an occasional assenting "Yes."

"And yet I don't know," the first said. "I think I *will* go with you to see Mrs. ——. You would wish it, dear, would you not? Yes, it might do good. . . ." And she went on talking, and on, and on, in the same superior, pained, and consciously compassionate voice. She called the waiter authoritatively, quietly. They went out, and I heard the commissionaire whistle for a hansom.

Somehow, I felt sorry for No. 2.

April 29th.

Last night Eugène d'Albert [1] made his first appearance in England after an absence of many years in Europe and America. Sharpe [2] called, on his way to the concert, and talked about him. His father's father was a Frenchman and his father's mother a German. His mother was a Scotswoman, and he was born in Glasgow, where his father was a dancing-master. Both parents, said Sharpe, who knew them, were nice people, amiable, upright, and sober as to manner—though the father composed much very bad dance music. Mrs. d'Albert was a quiet, reserved woman, with a shy pride in her son.

Sharpe, who frequently visited their house in order to play duets with Eugène, used to tell her that he thought her son was a great artist. "You really think so, Mr. Sharpe?" she would answer, with a slight smile—and that was all. D'Albert is said to have treated all his English friends in a rather strange manner. "But," said Sharpe, who has before now told me that in his opinion d'Albert was a greater pianist when he left the College of Music than Paderewski is now, "let him play one move-

---

[1] The pianist and composer; died 1932.
[2] Arnold Bennett was an intimate and lifelong friend of the Sharpe family, all of whom were musical. *Anna of the Five Towns* was dedicated to Herbert Sharpe. Of the younger generation, Cedric Sharpe became later a well-known 'cellist.

ment, and all that will be forgotten!" And the prophecy was curiously fulfilled, if the reports of the concert in today's papers are not exaggerated. D'Albert was received with marked coldness, but the audience was wildly enthusiastic when he left the platform.

Thursday, April 30th.

This morning (it being the second day of the press view) I spent an hour at the Academy. The number of portraits seems to increase year by year. For a man who is engrossed in a single art, this comprehensive selection of portraits of celebrities cannot fail to have a moral value. They remind him that there are several other arts and several hundred other occupations besides his own in which men of genius and men of talent can actually and deeply interest themselves: a fact he is in danger of forgetting. And they do this quite independently of their artistic worth, which in the majority of cases is nearly nil. To study these faces of men and women brings one in contact with activities, ideals, ambitions, of which otherwise one would know little besides the mere names.

The attitude of the general public towards a picture—by which apparently they regard it as a story first and a work of art afterwards—is not so indefensible as it seems, or at least not so inexcusable. In the attitude of the perfectly cultured artist himself, there is something of the same feeling—it must be so. Graphic art cannot be totally separated from literary art, nor vice versa. They encroach on each other.

Friday, May 1st.

In the course of conversation today, a man said to me, *apropos* of the question whether he or I was the more energetic: "I get up at 6, go out for a walk; breakfast at 8; then an hour's work, and afterwards to the office; half an hour for lunch . . ." The detailed programme, made up of alternated work and exercise, stretched out to 11 P.M.

"Well," I said, "that's very good indeed. How long have you been doing that?"

"Oh!" he said, "I'm going to start in the morning!"

Alcock [1] maintained to me at tea that to practise a musical instrument as it should be practised was as fatiguing as creative composition. I deny it.

---

[1] Arnold Bennett was friendly with several members of this family.

Monday, May 4th.

Gardner [1] told me that 1,200 people sat down to Charles Wyndham's [2] "celebration-of-managerial-majority" supper at the new Hotel Cecil on Friday last. The contract price for the supper was £1,000. Far finer than any other part of the entertainment was the sight of the sunrise across the Thames. But the faces of the actresses when daylight came . . . !

Wednesday, May 6th.

Eugène d'Albert played tonight at the Philharmonic concert. A little, round-shouldered man, with diminutive legs and a shrewd face, who looked as if nature had intended him to wear a large white apron and be a chemist and druggist. He was coldly received, but when Liszt's notoriously difficult E-flat concerto was finished, the audience had aroused itself, and an encore was inevitable.

It appears that when Sullivan [3] heard that the Philharmonic had engaged d'Albert, he threatened not only to remove his own name from the membership, but to do all he could to induce the Queen and the Prince of Wales to withdraw their patronage. However, he was persuaded to alter his plans. Sullivan helped d'Albert in every possible way when he was a student; obtained engagements for him at the Popular Concerts, the Crystal Palace, etc.; and when d'Albert went to the Continent gave him introductions to all the Courts. Yet on his return, a year afterwards, d'Albert not only refused to call on Sullivan but threw contempt on him and all Englishmen. In the meantime Liszt had heard him play and spoken enthusiastically of him, dubbing him "the young Tausig." D'Albert, by the way, once (seriously?) claimed to be a (natural) son of Tausig, though there cannot be a shadow of justification for such a claim.

Friday, May 8th.

Tonight I heard Yvette Guilbert sing five songs—including "La Soularde," Béranger's "Grand'mère," "Her golden hair was hanging down her back," and "I want you, ma honey" (alternate verses in French and English). The performance took about 23 minutes, and she receives £70 per night (10 nights). My father, who had seen her on

---

[1] Fitzroy Gardner, formerly editor of *Woman* and subsequently manager for Sir Herbert Tree, the actor.

[2] The well-known actor, opened Wyndham's Theatre in 1899, and was knighted in 1902.

[3] Sir Arthur Sullivan, the composer.

the previous evening, said to me at dinner at Gatti's, "I can't see £70 in what she does." "No," I said, "perhaps *you* can't; but you can see it in the audience which pays to listen to her."

I think I never saw the Empire so full. Yvette wore a gown of bluish green flowered silk, and the unchangeable black gloves. To the back of the pit, where I stood, her voice came as if from an immense distance, attenuated, but clear and crisp.

Monday, May 11th.

I read through in the typewritten copy some of the later chapters of my novel,[1] and they seemed to be ineffective and sketchy. Which severely depressed me, and to recover myself I had to read certain other chapters which I knew would not come out badly. I happened to see in an old *Idler* today "Q's"[2] article on his first book. In it he says that he wrote *Dead Man's Rock* without a trace of feeling. His view is that if on *revision* the work moves its author, then there is surely some good in it. Amen! Parts of my novel have had that blessed effect on me.

In "Vailima Table-Talk," an article by Isobel Strong (Stevenson's step-daughter and amanuensis) in May *Scribner's,* it is said: "He dictates with great earnestness, and when particularly interested unconsciously acts the part of his characters. When he came to the description of the supper Anne has with Flora and Ronald (*St. Ives*), he bowed as he dictated Anne's polite speeches, and twirled his moustache . . ." I do that sort of thing myself, but not unconsciously—rather because it amuses me, and deceives me into a belief that I can see the scene which I am describing. But I never *can* see the scene, or even a single character. Yet (thanks be to Gawd!) it needs a constant, or at least a repeated, mental effort to grasp the fact that certain stories which I have written, and the novel I am now finishing, aren't really true. I frequently have to say to myself, as it were, "But of course it's not true, really!"

Wednesday, May 13th.

I dipped into *Adam Bede,* and my impression that George Eliot will never be among the classical writers was made a certainty. Her style, though not without shrewdness, is too rank to have any enduring vitality. People call it "masculine." Quite wrong! It is downright, aggressive,

---

[1] *In the Shadow.*
[2] Sir Arthur Quiller-Couch, who signs himself "Q."

sometimes rude, but genuinely masculine, never. On the contrary it is transparently feminine—feminine in its lack of restraint, its wordiness, and the utter absence of feeling for form which characterizes it. The average woman italicizes freely. George Eliot, of course, had trained herself too well to do that, at least formally; yet her constant, undue insistence springs from the same essential weakness, and amounts practically to the same expedient. Emily and Charlotte Brontë are not guiltless on this count, but they both had a genuine, natural appreciation of the value of words, which George Eliot never had.

Jane Austen, now, is different. By no chance does she commit the artistic folly of insisting too much. Her style has the beauty and the strength of masculinity and femininity combined, and, very nearly, the weakness of neither.

In May *Chapman's,* there is a story by Henry James. His mere ingenuity, not only in construction, but in expression, is becoming tedious, though one cannot but admire. Also his colossal cautiousness in statement is very trying. If he would only now and then contrive to write a sentence without a qualifying clause!

Friday, May 15th.

At noon precisely I finished my first novel, which was begun about the middle of April last year; but five-sixths of the work at least has been performed since the 1st October. Yesterday, I sat down at 3 P.M. to write, and, with slight interruptions for meals etc., kept at it till 1 A.M. this morning. The concluding chapter was written between 9 and 12 today.

My fears about *In the Shadow* are (1) that it is not well knit, (2) that it is hysterical, or at any rate strained in tone. Still, I should not be surprised if it impressed many respectable people. The worst parts of it seem to me to be in front of my *Yellow Book* story,[1] which came in for a full share of laudation.

At a matinée at the Prince of Wales's the sisters Esmé and Vera Beringer played respectively Romeo and Juliet in a very creditable performance indeed of *Romeo and Juliet.* . . . It is quite true; all Shakespearean actors speak their blank verse much too slowly.

---

[1] "A Letter Home" appeared under the name of Enoch Arnold Bennett in the *Yellow Book* for July, 1895. Reprinted in *Tales of the Five Towns.*

A lady talking to old Joe Knight in the foyer said, in answer presumably to a protest of his against the part of Romeo being taken by a woman, "If Mrs. Patrick Campbell is allowed to play Juliet, there is no earthly reason why Esmé Beringer should not play Romeo." Joe Knight shook with laughter in every part of his immense frame.

Wednesday, May 20th.

I regard it as a serious and disquieting symptom that, now that my novel is finished, I have a positive *wish* to work. No man healthy in mind and body ever *wants* to work. He knows that work is good for him and will probably produce happiness, but that he should actually want to *work* is incredible, except of course after a too-protracted holiday.

During a rehearsal of *The Pompadour,* one of Tree's ancient failures at the Haymarket and almost if not quite the first piece in which Mrs. Tree came out as a serious, professional actress, she managed clumsily to give Tree a blow in the face while embracing him. "Maud, Maud," he exclaimed, stopping the rehearsal, "here have I been teaching you to act all this time, and the best you can do is to put your thumb in my eye! Begone, Maud! Begone!" And the rehearsal concluded—so Gardner told me today.

Thursday, May 21st.

Stevenson's *Weir of Hermiston, An Unfinished Romance,* appeared yesterday. Chap. VI, "A Leaf from Christina's Psalm-Book," contains about 40 pages of the subtlest, surest, finest psychological analysis that I can remember. I am quite sure that there exists nowhere a more beautiful or more profoundly truthful presentation of the emotional phenomena (both in the man and in the woman) which go to the making of "love at first sight." On p. 178 Stevenson, with secret pride I swear, says, "Thus even that phenomenon of love at first sight, which is so rare and seems so simple and violent, like a disruption of life's tissue, may be decomposed into a sequence of accidents happily concurring." . . . Yes, it may, by a Stevenson; perhaps by a Meredith; but by none else of modern writers. *Weir of Hermiston* is as far beyond anything that Hardy, for example, could compass, as *The Woodlanders* is beyond *In the Shadow*. Which is to say much! The mere writing of *Weir of Hermiston* surpasses all Stevenson's previous achievement.

Thursday, May 28th.

John Lane [1] showed me John Buchan's report on my novel. It was laudatory and kind, but not (I thought) critically appreciative. He had no fault whatever to find with the novel *qua* novel, but he said it would probably not be popular and that the same sort of thing had often been done before. Although it probably will not be popular, the same sort of thing has not been often done before; it has never been done before— in England. I can recall no novel of which either the essential material or the treatment is at all similar. The man is most honest, and anxious to do justice, but he clearly has not been able quite to sympathize with the latest disciple of the Goncourts. Lane said, "I will publish it," and I said, "That is very good of you," or something like that, and that was really all that passed in the matter of the book.

(*Margin Note*.) I find on reading more carefully a copy of the report that Buchan said no such thing.—*June 6th.*

Wednesday, June 3rd.

First night of *Magda*,[2] at the Lyceum—Mrs. Patrick Campbell as Magda, Fernandez as Schwartze, and Forbes-Robertson as the Pastor. *Apropos* of the so-called foolishness of allowing oneself to be moved by a story which one knows not to be "true, after all," it occurred to me tonight that a work of dramatic art moves us precisely because we know that it *is* real. If those particular events depicted did not actually happen, others essentially similar to them did . . . we feel it; we feel that they must have happened. And so we cry, perhaps, not on account of the misery presented to us, but on account of the wider, cruder misery of which the presented misery demonstrates to us the existence . . . existence perhaps hitherto unsuspected or but dimly guessed by us. Thus Mrs. M's rebuke to her husband when he cried at *Faust*, "Don't be so silly, Fred; you know it's not real," was singularly inapt. "Fred" cried just because the reality of the thing was only too clear.

Friday, June 5th.

The *Meistersinger*, Covent Garden. From a side box on the top tier I could see all the furtive activities which in an opera performance are hidden from the bulk of the audience: Screened by his wooden hood, the

---

[1] The publisher.
[2] By Hermann Sudermann.

prompter's head appears just above the level of the stage; he follows the score untiringly with his left hand while beating time, giving cues, gesticulating with his right; he is never for a moment at rest; he seems to know instinctively when an actor will be at fault, and his low, clear voice is heard exactly at the second when its help is imperative, and not till then. Compared to the prompter the conductor seems almost insignificant. In the wings a couple of chorus-masters with book in hand direct and inspire the sheep-like masses of men and women who cluster round the principals. Several other men, one in a straw hat, move mysteriously to and fro in the wings. A fireman and a footman stand guard over the curtain ropes. Right at the back of the stage dim shadows with lamps pass and repass. High up, even higher than the top tier, are men in their shirt sleeves moving amid a multitude of ropes, winches, and blocks. . . .

Consider the order and discipline which is necessary to the harmonious interworking of all these different forces for an hour and a half at a time. A slight forgetfulness on the part of any one of them might bring the performance to a standstill and cover the entire organization with disgrace. When once the first chord of the *Vorspiel* has been sounded, the boats are burned, as it were, and all depends on courage and presence of mind. In an opera like the *Meistersinger* systematization must indeed be carried to extremes. Now and then even the audience gets a hint of this; as witness the first and second bells for the raising of the curtain, each struck firmly and decisively at a particular bar of the score; with what marvellous obedient promptitude the immense stretch of canvas vanished into the ceiling on the stroke of the second bell!

At the end of an act, while the "principal" principals are taking their calls, all sorts of people crowd into the wings to watch their demeanour; even the principals of the second rank (Corsi, Gilibert, de Bars, etc.) press forward with childish curiosity to watch the Reszkes, Plançon, Eames, Bispham, etc., receive the adoration of the audience. This is surely a significant manifestation of what may be called the "operatic temperament."

Sunday, June 14th.

It is amazing what curious ideas even educated women have where statistics are concerned. Mrs. Devereux [1] was positive today that women

---

[1] She and her sister, Mrs. Laye, were long friends of Arnold Bennett.

outnumbered men by 3 to 1. When I corrected her, 17 to 16, she said, "But surely there are a million women in the country who can't possibly find husbands?" And her man said, "Yes, but that is because so few men will marry nowadays!" Mrs. Devereux accepted the explanation(!). Her sister put the preponderance of women at 7 to 1. From a sea of talk about dress, I rescued one curious theory of Mrs. Devereux's: "A woman with a turned-up nose must be most simple in her attire, and especially careful to avoid frocks that attract attention. A woman with a really good nose may wear anything. Thus the whole subject of woman's dress resolves itself into a question of noses."

A sprightly article might be written under the title, "Confessions of a Young Reviewer." Mrs. Devereux expressed the opinion that, provided one had to do only one review of it, half an hour was amply sufficient to spend in reading a book.

Monday, June 15th.

Mr. Johnson, the art editor of the *Ladies' Home Journal,* the richest and widest circulated monthly in the world, is a good-natured and conceited young Yankee of about 28 years. He told me something about prices he paid to artists, mentioning that Howard Pyle received $250 for a full-page drawing.

"Ah!" I said, "Pyle is your greatest man."

"Ye-es," he said, "a great man"—hesitatingly.

"Who greater?" I asked.

"Well," he said, stroking his shaven chin, "I guess I should put Alice Barber Stephens a shade higher" (!!).

He said that *Harper's* did not pay good prices unless the artist had a great name; they argued that the advertisement of having pictures in their magazine was in itself good payment.

"And it is, you know," he added. "I worked for them for 3 years, and got little besides advertisement out of it. But then it paid. It is to that, in fact, that *I owe my present position.*" This with a gesture of ineffable self-satisfaction. Nevertheless Mr. Johnson is what may be called "a good fellow." . . . He told me, in further reference to *Harper's,* that he had known instances in which they had offered an artist $75 for a drawing, the price to be reduced to $50 if they printed his name.

Sarah Bernhardt was stout last year. This season she is positively obese. But most of the women in her company have waists even larger than hers. Query: Is this an accident or has she carefully engineered it in order to soften the effect of her own enormous proportions?

Wednesday, June 17th.

Louis Rhead, "the leading American designer of posters," came to supper: a diminutive man, loosely jointed, carelessly dressed in good clothes; rough hair, and two days' growth of hair on his chin; large, glaring eyes which sometimes give him an appearance almost uncanny; the lower part of his face is monkey-like, and the habit of a slightly affected, simian smile, has worn a curved crease in the cheek on either side of the mouth. He is a good specimen of "the man who has succeeded," perfectly self-possessed under any circumstance, accustomed to be the centre of a group, and to relate his experiences, which he knows by heart. He talks quietly, soothingly, even caressingly at times; and there is a certain hard sense in all he says. He is proud of himself and of his own importance; now and then he makes praiseworthy but ineffectual attempts to efface himself, to step down from the chair of honour. He has artistic feeling, and a good deal of it; his description of the American night was genuinely poetical; yet he apparently views his own art strictly from the business point of view; and when discussing their work with other artists, he is full of worldly advice about the necessity of "having a plan," of "following up a success." He criticized English, American, and French art comparatively, in a way that proved his breadth; also with a subtle condescension to all and sundry. He told me how in the New York summer he had worked stark naked in his studio with the temperature at 104.

Tuesday, June 23rd.

At John Lane's I met John Buchan, just now principal "reader" to the Bodley Head. A very young, fair man; charmingly shy; "varsity" in every tone and gesture. He talks quietly in a feminine, exiguous voice, with the accent of Kensington tempered perhaps by a shadow of a shade of Scotch (or was that my imagination?). Already—he cannot be more than 23—he is a favourite of publishers, who actually seek after him, and has published one book.[1] He told me that his second novel, a long Scotch romance, was just finished, and that he had practically sold the serial rights. . . . A most modest, retiring man, yet obviously sane and shrewd. Well disposed, too, and anxious to be just; a man to compel respect; one who "counts."

Saturday, June 27th.

In the afternoon we rowed lazily up the river, from Richmond to Kingston—Brown[2] and I, and two little girls, Daisy and Georgie, whom Brown in a moment of inspiration had invited to complete the party. Tall little girls for their 12 or 13 years, with wide straw hats, white blouses, and long foal-like legs showing below their short blue skirts; shy at first, but gradually expanding and unfolding before our efforts to be utterly, absurdly foolish, and laughing loyally at far-fetched allusive jokes which they could not possibly have understood; always in doubt whether or not to believe what we said, and in any case accepting or rejecting it with cautious reservations. Georgie, the eldest, was a spoilt girl, and both spoke with an alarming cockney accent, yet the unique charm characteristic of just their age made the worst sins of behaviour delightful. They rowed till they were tired, labouring hard and willingly, anxious to do their best, and when questioned admitted without shame that they *were* tired—"a bit." We camped and brewed tea on an island, and Georgie ate so many sardines and strawberries that she was sick on the way home and had to be quiet in the bows till the colour came back to her cheeks. In the evening at the corner of the street, Brown kisses them, and I shake hands with a profound bow, and they walk off sedately side by side to their home a few yards away. A quite new and tickling sensation, this intimate companionship with very young girls!

Wednesday, July 8th.

Miss Symonds[3] lamented the decadence of the novel since Thackeray and George Eliot, and I retorted that in future years the present would be regarded as a golden age of fiction. She regretted the lapse of that custom which made it lawful for authors to intersperse their narratives

---

[1] *Sir Quixote* was published in 1895; *Scholar-Gipsies* in 1896.

[2] An artist friend.

[3] E. M. Symonds, under the name of George Paston, is the author of various novels and plays.

by personal reflections, opinions, moralizings. In the case of a great author, she said, these constituted for her frequently the chief charm of a novel.

Which shows that sensible people are capable of holding the most bizarre views.

Friday, July 24th.

How rarely does one find people unaffectedly content with themselves and their social status; keeping well within that status; not deigning in any way to ape the attire of a superior class or to attempt any other similar deception of *manner;* and yet attaining to dignity! On the bus I met two of these scarce creatures: a rather ugly but pleasant-featured young man of 30, dressed, with a suspicion of carelessness, in roughly-cut clothes of good material; a girl of 24 or 25, with high cheek-bones and a face which, while indicating firmness of character, was eager to smile; she wore a neat green-and-yellow dress, with a low hat to match, plain and well made, but clearly inexpensive. Both belonged to what is called the lower middle class, and both were well-to-do, in that their means were obviously more than sufficient for their needs. They talked with a Northern accent, quietly, confidentially, about domestic affairs, and were certainly in love with each other—probably engaged to be married.

On neither side was there any affectation of conventional *manners,* nor a trace of that low instinct to pose which one encounters so frequently in public vehicles. They got off without stopping the bus; the man jumped down first, and running along gave his hand to the girl, who sprang lightly forward into the air, and smiled victoriously to find herself safe on the ground. . . . I very nearly said to the conductor, "Isn't that pretty?"

Monday, August 3rd.

Stratford-on-Avon is a simple, straightforward, unaffected town—sane and serene like Shakespeare's last plays and last years.[1] Even the exterior of the Shakespeare Memorial Institute, which was built in 1877 on the banks of the Avon, looks distinguished—by moonlight.

The town is well furnished with mellow old inns—inns honeycombed

---

[1] In later years Bennett reversed his judgment and would not go near Stratford-on-Avon on account of its affectedness.

with crimson-carpeted oak staircases and long tortuous corridors with old prints on the walls. In the low-ceiled parlours, of which in some inns there are two, of different degrees of privacy, are merry, respectable, well-dressed women of middle age or verging thereon, who serve old and tried customers on terms of perfect and amiable equality, to the accompaniment of shrewd, slow conversation. In the stable-yards at the rear, obese ostlers move awkwardly about, and the soft noises of horses moving amid straw are heard through red walls and over wooden half-doors.

August 20th.

At Ostende:

The Quai des Pêcheurs, where one lands, is a street of houses that look like lanky overgrown cottages. Nearly every dwelling is an *estaminet,* in the sanded, pine-dressed taproom of which fat, *enceinte,* good-humoured women move loosely and languidly to serve sailors and quay loafers with bock and cheap tobacco.

Along the front lounge sailors in English blue (looking precisely like English sailors in face, gait, manner, and dress); children clatter their loose *sabots;* fishwives are carrying fish from a brown and yellow tangle of smacks to waiting carts; occasionally a woman porter goes by, sweating in the sunshine, with her elongated barrow curving downwards to one little wheel at the extremity.

In the afternoon Brown squatted down on his stool, *en pleine rue,* to paint the smacks and lighthouse behind. He had no water. We interrogated small boys and afterwards men in French, but only Flemish is spoken on this quay. At last a sailor comes who can speak French, and he sends a child for a glass of water. But the child never returns, and the French-speaking sailor has gone. Then a boy takes off his *sabot,* holds it up to me suggestively, rushes off with a clack-thud, clack-thud, and comes back with the *sabot* full of water.

Brown's audience gets larger, and it is difficult to keep them in order. Then he discovers that German is near enough to Flemish to be understood, and begins to talk to a short, thick-set young sailor with an honest, amiable face, who thereupon constitutes himself policeman of the crowd. We make friends with the sailor, and when the picture is done take him to an *estaminet* for bock. In the corner of the taproom is a primitive bagatelle-table; we play and beat him easily, while the fat and pregnant women of the establishment, three in number, look on good-humouredly and yet with a distant air of tolerance.

Turning to the left at the end of the Quai des Pêcheurs, one is on the Digue—a vast, straight expanse of promenade paved with small, diamond-shaped, corrugated brown tiles, and dedicated to pedestrians and cyclists only. This promenade, overlooking the immense sands and the dazzling sea, is flanked by lofty buildings of florid modern architecture, painted white or yellow—lodging-houses, restaurants, hotels, and the white Kursaal (all curves) in the centre—flashing in the brilliant sun so that one can scarcely bear to look on them.

The lodging-houses are peculiar, and seem to be all made to one pattern. The front room of the *rez-de-chaussée* has a sliding glass front, giving by a broad flight of steps directly on to the street. At the top of the steps is invariably mounted a large brass telescope, polished to blindingness. This front room is furnished with garish theatrical magnificence: highly decorated walls, elaborately carved furniture, a chandelier fit for a ballroom scene at the Haymarket, gaudy transparent paper screens. In the rear of this room wide doors folded back disclose another room— the *salle-à-manger*—treated in the cool shadow of drawn blinds. One's impression is that the occupiers of these apartments conduct their existences for the delectation of the public eye. After lunch, during the siesta, one observed stout men, carefully attired in flannels, smoking or drowsing in the front rooms, while further back in the picture fashionably dressed women with closed or half-shut eyes waved their fans dreamily.

All day, visitors perambulate the promenade and treat each other punctiliously.

This part of the town reaches the very summit of artificiality. The back streets and market-places are different in character, quaint, with Flemish signboards, dog-carts, bargaining wives, and a free, unhampered stir and movement of old, mellow colours—amidst all which the visitors, whose natural resting-place is the Digue, seem out of key.

August 23rd.
At Bruges:
The difference between Bruges and other cities is that in the latter

you look about for the picturesque, while in Bruges, assailed on every side by the picturesque, you look curiously for the unpicturesque, and don't find it easily.

Monday, September 21st.

A not unknown journalist, finding himself prospering with an income of from £8 to £10 a week, took for paramour a lady barber out of Chancery Lane. Then he wrote a book, and having decided upon the publisher who he thought ought to take it, sought a personal introduction to the man of his choice, who happened to be Mr. John Lane. Only one person of his acquaintance knew Mr. Lane at all well, and he, after some parleying, agreed to give the introduction—for a consideration. It was arranged: the journalist got his introduction, and the acquaintance was allowed to take the lady barber for a week's holiday.

The book was refused.

Tuesday, September 29th.

Tonight I am to begin my new novel, *Sir Marigold,* a study of paternal authority. All the old timidities, banished for a time by the prompt acceptance of my first book, have returned, have crept back again imperceptibly, until misgivings, intensified perhaps by experimental knowledge of the difficulties to be overcome, seem to hem me in on every side. My one chance of security lies in fixing attention solely on the first chapter and ignoring all else. Enthusiasm, after a week of suppressed expectant anxiety and wakeful nights, has stealthily withdrawn itself, or fallen away and left me naked. I have no desire to write, and at intervals an impulse arises to put off the beginning till another day. And yet through it all, I know that I shall somehow accomplish a sketch, more or less unsatisfactory, of the first chapter tonight—delve it up from somewhere. And then the rest will be easier for a time.

The main outline of the book is well settled, and appears to me to be safe and good. But not a vestige of material useful for incident presents itself. I have hold of nothing but the bare leading facts. I suddenly realize that I know none of the five principal characters—neither by face nor voice. I have forgotten all the maxims and rules of technique carefully evolved during the last few months. Moreover, I have unwisely been reading books by George Meredith and Mrs. Humphrey Ward, and at first my work will certainly reflect their methods—methods which—the one splendidly fantastic, the other realistic by dint of laborious and carefully ordered detail—are both at variance with my natural instincts towards a *synthetic impressionism*. I ought during the past month to have read nothing but Goncourt.

10.30 P. M. After an hour of miserable hesitation, quite fruitless, I began to read bits of the manuscript of my first novel, and found it not unimpressive. This heartened me. I searched for an old sketch which I thought might be useful for my opening chapter; found it, and was not disappointed. Then at last I began to write. When I had done only 200 words, my spirits suddenly rose to positive vocal gaiety. Incidents began to present themselves in fitting order. I knew I was going on well. When I had sketched out 900 words, Kennerley [1] called, and though I was ready to continue writing, I was glad enough to be interrupted. I had done enough (2 hours) to reassure myself.

Afterwards, alone, I read the "death of Jules" in the *Journal des Goncourts,* and the spirit of the brothers took hold of me; Meredith and Mrs. Humphrey Ward were effectually forgotten.

I have commenced work again: what joy!

Saturday, October 3rd.

William Morris died.

Monday, October 5th.

Nearly every paper, except the *Chronicle,* is content with a brief notice of William Morris's life. The *Pall Mall* had a leader, and half a column or less of biography. The *Chronicle* had special articles by Shaw and another.

Thursday, October 8th.

The *Chronicle* has had more special articles and a large portrait. George du Maurier [2] died. Long article in the *Pall Mall*—cool and just, on the whole.

---

[1] W. W. Kennerley (brother of Mitchell Kennerley of New York) was born in Burslem and was an intimate of the Bennett family from childhood. He preceded Arnold Bennett to London by a few months. He later married Bennett's sister Tertia and is the "W.W.K." to whom *The Old Wives' Tale* is dedicated.

[2] Long famed for his drawings in *Punch,* he surprised the public, late in life, by writing the very successful *Trilby* and *Peter Ibbetson.*

Sunday, October 11th.

A week of sluggish liver and disordered kidneys; restless nights; ill-tempered mornings. An evening of strong contrasts: At 8 o'clock, I left the musical, emotional atmosphere of Sharpe's, where Sharpe, Weist Hill, Mrs. Sharpe, Werge, and Alcock were playing to a very mixed audience, Cherubini, Saint-Saëns, Stanford, and Schumann; raced home on my bicycle, rushed out again, took the bus, and was having supper with Miss Symonds and her mother at Thurloe Square in exactly half an hour. At Putney, music, loud laughter, undiluted emotionalism, and sincere artistic purpose. At South Kensington, literature, quietude, the restraint of an eighteenth-century demeanour—and sincere artistic purpose, too. Miss Symonds is a frank worshipper of the eighteenth century. Her mother, an ample little lady, with a quick cheerful laugh and a most pleasant manner, is ready to enjoy anything. She recalled the pleasure with which, at 19, she read *Monte Cristo,* and joyfully accepted my offer to lend her the *Vicomte de Bragelonne* so that she might renew the "Dumas sensations."

Miss Symonds, on the whole the most advanced and intellectually fearless woman I have met, stuck to the old formula that a woman should marry a man 10 years her senior. "Ten or 15 years," she corrected herself. Her reasons: that a woman matures earlier than a man, and that at 40 a woman is middle-aged, while the man . . . etc. The old reasons, which I combated, with cases in point to support my view.

I ventured to mention that I have never learnt to be enthusiastic about the work of her celebrated cousin, John Addington Symonds. To my astonishment, both she and her mother confessed that they had read very little of it, and did not care for it.

I have noticed several times lately that when young boys run whooping and leaping along the street, from sheer effervescence of animal spirits, they do not ever smile. On the contrary their faces are sternly set, and have a rapt, intent expression, as though they were thinking out some difficult problem.

Monday, October 12th.

I have been re-reading *Virgin Soil,* and it occurs to me, is indeed forced on me, that I know practically nothing yet of *development* of character.

In drawing character, Turgenev generally begins by sketching the previous history of the person almost from birth, with piquant gossipy detail. The reader, therefore, is made personally acquainted with the character to start with. A simple trick this, in essence. Yet what perfect art Turgenev puts into the composition of these little biographies! There is no doubt in my mind that he is the greatest master of the modern novel. I can divine, even through a mediocre translation, that his style was simple, natural, graceful, and effective. Probably he took no pleasure in the mere arrangement and nice choice of words—I mean no "technical" pleasure in the labour itself of composition—such as Flaubert, the Goncourts, Stevenson, and Pater found.

Tuesday, October 13th.

If people only had the gift of knowing when they were bored and the courage to admit the fact openly when it was discovered, how many novelists, poets, playwrights, musicians, and entertainers would be compelled to join the ranks of the unemployed! ... The cleverest and frankest of us is bored sometimes without knowing it or without daring to confess it.

Thursday, October 15th.

The appearance today of the first volume of a new edition of Boswell's *Johnson,* edited by Augustine Birrell, reminds me once again that I have read but little of that work. Does there, I wonder, exist a being who has read all, or approximately all, that the person of average culture is supposed to have read, and that not to have read is a social sin? If such a being does exist, surely he is an old, a very old man, who has read steadily that which he ought to have read 16 hours a day, from early infancy. I cannot recall a single author of whom I have read everything —even of Jane Austen. I have never seen *Susan* and *The Watsons,* one of which I have been told is superlatively good. Then there are large tracts of Shakespeare, Bacon, Spenser, nearly all Chaucer, Congreve, Dryden, Pope, Swift, Sterne, Johnson, Scott, Coleridge, Shelley, Byron, Edgeworth, Ferrier, Lamb, Leigh Hunt, Wordsworth (nearly all), Tennyson, Swinburne, the Brontës, George Eliot, W. Morris, George Meredith, Thomas Hardy, Savage Landor, Thackeray, Carlyle—in fact every classical author and most good modern authors, which I have never even overlooked. A list of the masterpieces I have *not* read would fill a volume. With only one author can I call myself familiar, Jane Austen. With Keats and Stevenson, I have an acquaintance. So far of English. Of foreign authors I am familiar with Maupassant and the Goncourts. I have yet to finish *Don Quixote!*

Nevertheless I cannot accuse myself of default. I have been extremely fond of reading since I was 20, and since I was 20 I have read practically nothing (save professionally, as a literary critic) but what was "right." My leisure has been moderate, my desire strong and steady, my taste in selection certainly above the average, and yet in 10 years I seem scarcely to have made an impression upon the intolerable multitude of volumes which "everyone is supposed to have read."

Essential characteristic of the really great novelist: a Christ-like, all-embracing compassion.

Saturday, October 17th.

Foyer of the Haymarket Theatre. First night of *Under the Red Robe.*[1] Newnes[2] and Harmsworth,[3] chiefs of the two greatest "popular" journalistic establishments in the kingdom, each controlling concerns which realize upwards of £100,000 net profit per annum, talking together. Newnes, the very type of the middle-aged prosperous bourgeois, with full, flamboyant brown-grey beard and greying hair; a pleasant, comfortable face, not strikingly shrewd. Harmsworth (director of 14 weeklies reaching 3,300,000 copies, and three daily papers) with the head of a poet and thinker; blond hair; quiet, acute, self-contained; a distinguished look about him. One would take him for a *Saturday Reviewer* or the editor of some *Yellow Book,* a young lion of the people-despising kind, a contemner of popular taste and of everything that caught the public fancy. Never did a man's appearance so belie his true character. He cannot be more than 30. He too had a pleasant, good-natured face. One felt that it would be good to talk to him.

---

[1] From the novel by Stanley Weyman.

[2] Sir George Newnes in 1896 founded the penny *Courier* which lasted only a few weeks.

[3] On the same day as the *Courier* there first appeared the halfpenny *Daily Mail,* founded by Alfred C. Harmsworth, later Viscount Northcliffe.

Monday, October 26th.

In the bus tonight were two women of the upper (rural) working class, whose manner of talking seemed usefully characteristic. They were sisters: the younger, about 30 but looking older; feathered hat, and jacket; face almost ugly, and very shapeless; a pleasant reliable look about the eyes, and a certain fading attractiveness in the infrequent smile; she was suffering from the usual complaint, a surfeit of sordid domesticity, and the symptoms were the common ones—subdued peevishness, a hopeless expression of being beaten, and a general attitude which implied that suffering and inconveniences were the natural heritage of her class and her sex. I judge that her character, though far from fine, had its virtues, and that suffering had done something to brighten and enhance these.

She carried a sleeping baby, and her elder child, a silent, queer-tempered little boy of 5, sat on the other side of the bus with his aunt. This aunt, the younger woman's sister, was about 50, or perhaps less, with a black shawl round her shoulders, parcels on her knee and parcels at her feet. She had a radiant face, a face which no trouble could darken, the face of one who naturally and inevitably looks on the bright side of things; with the high prominent cheek-bones that seem invariably to indicate strength of character.

The two women talked across the crowded bus to each other in the tones of ordinary conversation, quickly, confusedly, saying the same thing over and over again in slightly different words. In their ignorance, their naïveté, they were like children, but not like children in their passive, almost bland submission to the misfortunes which had beset them that day. The younger woman had committed some indiscretion—"I was worried, I was worried," she kept on saying, and her sister murmured sympathetic replies. Their accent was soft, drawling, and Southern, especially in the case of the younger woman; the elder had lived some time in London.

Presently this latter began to converse with a stranger at her side, and the story came out. The mother of the children had travelled 50 miles to London to bring the silent boy to a throat hospital for an operation. When she got there, the bed which had been promised was said to be occupied, and she was told to come again in 4 days. And so the 4 days were to be spent at her sister's. The mischief was that she had paid

10/6 for a week's keep for the child in the hospital, and had learnt since that he would only be kept there 3 days; that she had foolishly parted with her "letter" and had "nothing to show"; and that her home in the country was unkempt and uncared-for during her absence. The elder sister told the tale with a great quantity of minute detail, and many "of courses" and commiserating glances; and during the recital, the object of the glances observed an absolute silence, unless it was to entreat her boy not to go to sleep.

Wednesday, November 4th.

Last night, in order to enliven a drowsy liver, I walked the streets of the West End, for 3 hours, 8.30 to 11.30, from Tottenham Court Road to Hyde Park Corner; and noted nothing beyond the extraordinary number of policemen, stationed every few score yards on either side the road, in Coventry Street and neighbouring thoroughfares. Everything was quiet and I puzzled in vain to account for them. Only the fear of a snub prevented me from inquiring of one of them direct. Except the fact as to the policemen, I collected nothing of any interest whatever. For over a week I had noticed nothing, made not a single useful observation. And this in spite of the fact that I have been going through experiences at the office,[1] have been writing hard, have been staying at Brown's with George Sturt,[2] and have had Sturt over here for an evening.

Thursday, November 5th.

Two ideas for new books have occurred to me:

1. A novel of which a character drawn mainly and fully from Emily Brontë shall be the heroine. In reading Clement Shorter's *Charlotte Brontë and Her Circle,* the sombre splendours of Emily's character have again attracted me, and I seem to see in the short and vague history of her life the most superb material for fiction.

2. *My Adventures in London:* a sentimental, Leigh Hunt sort of book. Short, about 25,000 words; dealing with a dozen "adventures."

Today was published Kipling's *The Seven Seas.* Red-letter day.

---

[1] He was then sub-editor of the journal *Woman.*
[2] Author of various books, under pseudonyn of G. Bourne.

Sunday, November 8th.

Dr. Farrar [1] said that the difficulties of diagnosis were much greater than most people imagined. As an instance he stated in certain cases it was impossible for a doctor to say whether a patient was suffering from consumption or typhoid fever, widely and essentially different though these two diseases were. He was called (he had said before this) to attend a girl engaged in a house of business. Her temperature was 104° and he treated her for influenza. She went on well, except that her temperature refused to go below 101°. At the end of a fortnight her employers wished her either to get better or to leave the premises, and she was taken in an ambulance to St. George's Hospital. The doctors there failed to diagnose the symptoms at all. She was quite comfortable, but the temperature stuck at 101°. At length, after another fortnight, just as they were about to put her on ordinary diet, she was taken with diarrhœa, hæmorrhage of the bowels, and other unmistakable symptoms of typhoid fever.

Speaking of typhus fever, he said that it had practically died out; he himself had never known a case of it. I, however, remember a case at Burslem, 10 or 12 years ago.

Friday, November 13th.

At the Press View of the New English Art Club, Egyptian Hall. About 10 people, half women, in the one gallery sparsely hung with eccentric landscapes imitative of early Italian and Dutch work, a few soft hazy portraits, a few intelligent originalities, a few sterile meaningless absurdities, and one striking, shouting, insistent, dominant nude by Wilson Steer. In the centre of the gallery a table with sandwiches, wines, and cigarettes, which everyone carefully avoided in spite of whispered invitations from a middle-aged male attendant.

Seated in front of the nude—a slim woman of 30, with full breasts and red cheeks sitting up in a very large bed—were a man and a woman talking in loud Kensingtonian tones which outraged the prim silence of the gallery. Near them an old and shabby art critic, to be seen everywhere, was writing in a notebook, his red nose and small peering eyes bent down close to the page. After a long time he joined in the conversation of the other two, and they began even more loudly to discuss the nude,

---

[1] Bennett's doctor at this period, and a life-long friend.

dispraising it in a few light easy sentences of condemnation. It certainly was not a masterpiece with its hard, laboured, unreal flesh-painting, but the manner of this condemnation almost made me like it.

When I next turned round, the art critic had withdrawn and the other man was elaborately raising a silk hat from his grey head to the departing woman. She left him to talk to another woman in a corner, and then stood alone staring round the gallery. She was a well-developed woman of 34 or less, with the face and bearing of a Sunday-school teacher; her thick mouth worked in that calculating contemplative way that I have noticed in Sunday-school teachers with a passion for gossip at sewing meetings. To see her in the street none would have dreamt that she was a professed art critic, capable of discussing—however foolishly—an uncompromising nudity with her male acquaintance for half an hour at a time.

The total conglomerate effect—loud voices falling coarsely on the silence; untouched sandwiches; silk-hatted man; dowdyish self-possessed woman; inured, quiet art critic practising his trade in the spirit of a tradesman; and the rank, calm, supercilious, harsh nudity—the effect was bizarre and memorable.

Tuesday, November 17th.

Today a business crisis which has been active for a fortnight ended with a definite arrangement that I should accept the editorship of *Woman*. A fortnight of secret conclaves suddenly hushed at the sound of a door opening; of poring over figures and lists of names and correspondence; of devising schemes, each one superseded by a better, a more perfect one; of planning and counter-planning; of saying the same thing over and over again to a colleague merely because it was impossible to leave the subject and impossible to say anything fresh; of publicly expressed hopes and private pessimism; of forced jocularities; of feverish incessant *thinking* by day and night, awake and asleep, walking or sitting, silent or speaking. Almost my first real task of a strictly business, personal anxiety! A few years of such anxiety (the lot of many men), even a year of it, even a month, would drive me, I fancy, to clerkhood again, just for the sake of being free from responsibility and worry.

Edith Evors, my new secretary, is the first genuine middle-class bachelor woman, living alone in London lodgings, that I have been intimately familiar with. A tall woman, slightly under 30, with big limbs and a large, honest, red-cheeked face, and a quiet, *intense* voice. Transparently conscientious; with little self-reliance, but a capacity for admiring self-reliance in others. She lives in Bloomsbury, and at nights goes to socialist and anarchist lectures. "It is dreadful," she said to me today, "to think how *little* one can do!" She cannot make her own clothes, though her earnings are only 30/- a week, and she grudges "every moment spent in their repair." But personally she is neat enough in an unadorned, aggressively simple way. She is serious, earnest, practical in small affairs, and visionary in great ones. Full of easily aroused pity and indignation. Physically strong and healthy.

Friday, November 20th.

At the Empire—"Monte Cristo" ballet. In this most gorgeous spectacle perhaps ever seen on the modern stage, it appeared to me that a fine and catholic taste in form and colour had used its last endeavour in order to neutralize the effect of an unparalleled expenditure. Mere costliness had been tortured and beaten into a semblance of artistic simplicity and parsimony in the use of material. It was as though two opposing intentions had been deliberately set to war with each other—the intention to be lavish and the intention to be artistic—and the result of the affray remained uncertain.

Friday, November 27th.

Last night, Young,[1] who is an amateur palmist, examined my hand. He diagnosed my character with considerable accuracy; and, prying into the future, found there wealth but not a long existence. The "life-line," indeed, puzzled him.

Friday, December 4th.

As we were finishing dinner, there was a knock at the front door, and presently Mrs. Shepherd burst into the room. "Delighted!" exclaimed the Marriotts,[2] with their little inarticulate cries of surprise. "You'll have something to eat?"

---

[1] C. Young was manager of Messrs. Lamley & Co., who published some of Bennett's early books.

[2] Very early London friends of Arnold Bennett; Mr. and Mrs. Frederick Marriott are artists.

"Yes—but it's bad news that brings me—Oswald's in the hospital . . . operation." Here she began to cry and laugh, and we all felt suddenly awkward and self-conscious.

"Is he worse, then?"

" 'Fraid so. . . . And we thought he was getting on so nicely at Margate. But the doctor there frightened me so much—a *horrid* man he is—that I brought Ossie up to London at once to see a specialist. They said at the hospital that the Margate doctor was very clever and a good doctor. But I told them he might be, but he was a very nasty man—no, I said, nor a good doctor either. Why, he wanted to stick a needle into Ossie's chest, and I had to stand between them to prevent him. Yes, and he said all the time he didn't know anything about the chest. . . . The specialist didn't want to stick a needle into Ossie's chest. 'No,' he said, 'I've never had a death yet in my surgery, and I don't intend to have one' . . . as much as to say, you see, that it would be so dangerous as that . . . you see . . . a regular horrid man the Margate doctor is. . . . The specialist said there would have to be an operation, but whether it was a tumour or merely water he couldn't say. . . . It's just where his heart ought to be, and his heart is on the right side—pushed it right away, ye see. . . . I didn't think we should be able to get in at the hospital: I brought Ossie on the chance, and as luck would have it we did. . . . Yes, a bit of bread and cheese or anything. I've got to be back again in an hour, or the porter will lock me out. And I want to borrow a knife and fork and spoon for Ossie. He has to have them, and us coming away in such a hurry. . . . Now there's Maggie (Mrs. Marriott) gone getting me a regular dinner, and I only want a bit of bread and cheese. . . . Maggie! . . . Maggie!" (She went out of the room and to the top of the kitchen steps.) "I only want a bit of bread and cheese."

Mrs. Marriott, her eyes all wet, had hurried away immediately after the first news to prepare a meal from the remains of ours.

Wednesday, December 9th.

I have just finished reading J. M. Barrie's account of his mother, *Margaret Ogilvy*. This book is a picture of a grave, mighty, passionate family of men and women. Instinctively, and all the time, I was comparing it with my own, and in particular comparing Margaret Ogilvy and J. M. Barrie with my mother and myself. Again and again, I had to acknowledge inferiority—inferiority of essential "character," apart from inessential talent—a lack of bigness, and a presence of certain littlenesses. Yet at the same time, I found us sturdy enough not to be ashamed of shortcomings. What we are, we are! "I exist as I am, that is enough." To hold such a creed religiously is in one way to be great.

A proud, self-unconscious self-esteem: that is what few people have. If at times it deserts me and mine, it always returns the stronger for having retreated. We are of the North, outwardly brusque, stoical, undemonstrative, scornful of the impulsive; inwardly all sentiment and crushed tenderness. We are of the North, incredibly, ruthlessly independent; and eager to say "Damn you" to all the deities at the least hint of condescension.

When I was only an assistant editor, on leaving the office I could forget the office with absolute certainty and effectiveness. Now that I am editor, do what I will, watch myself as I may, the office dogs me everywhere, night and day.

Wednesday, December 16th.

During these busy days, I go through my existence continually getting dim, pale impressions, but when I try to recall them at night, they have faded away—because I have had neither time nor inclination to "fix" them as they came.

1897

Tuesday, January 5th.

I was reading in *The Trumpet-Major*. What an excessively slow method of narration Hardy employs! In this he is as old-fashioned (*mutatis mutandis*) as Richardson. Much of his humour, too, is obvious and Dickens-like, character-y, in quality. Yet somehow his persons have individuality.

Monday, January 11th.

The novelist of contemporary manners needs to be saturated with a sense of the picturesque in modern things. Walking down Edith Grove this afternoon, I observed the vague, mysterious beauty of the vista of houses and bare trees melting imperceptibly into a distance of grey fog. And then, in King's Road, the figures of tradesmen at shop doors, of children romping or stealing along mournfully, of men and women each totally different from every other, and all serious, wrapt up in their own thoughts and ends—these seemed curiously strange and novel and wonderful. Every scene, even the commonest, is wonderful, if only one can detach oneself, casting off all memory of use and custom, and behold it (as it were) for the first time; in its right, authentic colours; without making comparisons. The novelist should cherish and burnish this faculty of seeing crudely, simply, artlessly, ignorantly; of seeing like a baby or a lunatic, who lives each moment by itself and tarnishes the present by no remembrance of the past.

Tuesday, January 12th.

Reading *Mike Fletcher,*[1] I felt inclined to give up my new project of taking a house, and instead to take rooms in Grays Inn or the Temple, and cultivate carefully the art of being a bachelor in comfort . . . to dine regularly at the same secluded, excellent restaurant, to know the byways of town life, to accomplish slowly the right and rare furnishing of one's rooms, to be utterly independent. . . . The sound of these words is attractive, and such employments might give content till one was 45, say; but afterwards?

I took up my neglected novel *Sis Tellwright,*[2] and sketched out a chapter, with difficulty re-creating the atmosphere. The portions already drafted seemed good, more than satisfactory, as the result of the "first process" in the manufacture of my fiction. The "first process" (imagine the building of a house on a hill) is to get the materials, pell-mell, intermixed, anyhow, to a certain height. Having carried them there, I have found that what remains to be done is somewhat less difficult, at any rate requires less *brute power of brain.*

Wednesday, January 20th.

At *The Mikado,* now nearing the close of its fourth or fifth revival. Half-empty house; band apathetic and playing with eyes anywhere but on the music. Seated near the stage, I could realize what at the theatre one realizes so seldom, that the actors are ordinary human beings acting a part for a livelihood; I could see beneath the mask the evolutions of the real person, his lassitudes, excitements, pleasures, wearinesses. Never before have I seen these things so plainly, this under-life. Yet the excellence of *The Mikado* is such that as the evening passed, the piece took hold of the players, and lifting them out of their monotony, did away with the *ennui* that disclosed their humanity.

Friday, January 22nd.

In this week's *Woman* is one of those mistakes that must inevitably occur now and then when a man edits a woman's paper. Under some

---

[1] By George Moore. Bennett made a footnote that it was "vicious, meretricious, and—delicious."

[2] Published in 1902 under the title of *Anna of the Five Towns.*

designs for a layette outfit is the legend *"Cut to measure* patterns supplied."* Nine men out of nine would never observe the blunder.

Wednesday, January 27th.

At a City branch of a certain bank yesterday morning two golden-haired girls, with large feathered hats, presented a piece of paper bearing a penny stamp and the words, "Please pay bearer £2 10/-. Henry T. Davies." The cashier consulted his books and had to inform the ladies that Henry T. Davies had no account there. "I don't know about that," said one of them, "but he slept with me last night, and gave me this paper because he hadn't any cash. Didn't he, Clara?" "Yes," said Clara, "that he did, and I went out this morning to buy the stamp for him." The cashier commiserated them, but they were not to be comforted.

Thursday, January 28th.

I cannot conceive that any author should write, as the Goncourts say they wrote, "for posterity." An artist works only to satisfy himself, and for the applause and appreciation neither of his fellows alive nor his fellows yet unborn. I would not care a bilberry for posterity. I should be my own justest judge, from whom there was no appeal; and having satisfied him (whether he was right or wrong), I should be content—as an artist. As a *man,* I should be disgusted if I could not earn plenty of money and the praise of the discriminating.

During these weeks of indolence (in the matter of creative work) I can feel, with a sense of satisfaction, the tide of *unexpressed sensation* rising higher and higher; soon, I know, it will break the dam of inactive habit which circumstances and a somewhat weak purpose have erected, and pour forth over a thousand sheets. It grows and rises of itself, and I watch it lazily.

Saturday, January 30th.

Tonight I met the typical respectable Clerk and his wife. The Clerk: a short man, with a merry, half-boyish face, and a good moustache; keen in looks, yet every feature disclosing a narrow habit of mind; at first good-naturedly *too* courteous and deferential, afterwards assuming his natural manner of unaffected pleasantness. His wife: a woman of about 35, apparently older than the clerk, dressed plainly in red and grey; a broad face of peculiar shape, with long, censorious lips that came together in a straight line, and remained so; a sensible, sober face, full of what is called character. One felt that while her husband supplied the motive power of their existence, the wife furnished the steadying ballast. She was very restrained till late in the evening when at the sight of some comic drawings she laughed immoderately and long, repeating, "I do think that's funny." . . . After this, the Clerk began to give us his volunteering experiences, and over his quietly vivacious talk I heard a conversation begin between the wife and Gertie Kennerley: "Are you fond of reading?" "Yes," said Gertie. "Read Charlotte Brontë's books? *Jane Eyre? Villette? Shirley?*—I like *Shirley* the best. And George Eliot's? And Mrs. Henry Wood's[1]? I think —— is the best of *hers.*" Here the Clerk broke in to say he hadn't read that: hadn't read anything of Mrs. Henry Wood's. "I don't think *you'd* care for them," she turned to him. "There isn't much *in* them, you know." So, though clearly the stronger character, she looked up to him, wondering from below to what heights his intellect reached.

Both were skilful, experienced, alive, in the things which lay within their own segment of life's circle, and lost and awed, like babes in the wood, if they happened to stray outside that segment. Example: Though the husband was above Mrs. Henry Wood and read Lamb, and had a distant interest in Stevenson, he asked, "What is this *Yellow Book,* Mr. Bennett?" as if he were inquiring into the nature of the differential calculus or bimetallism. But both of them know all about latchkeys, burglars, the programmes at the Empire and the Alhambra, and so on. The Clerk was fond of horses. He liked riding, because there was "a lot of danger in it—you might get thrown off." Then he explained the difficulties.

They made several attempts to go, and finally left at 11.05, the Clerk with genial smiles and punctilious salutations, the wife rather stiffer, but breaking out into a warm, genuine smile and a "We've had *such* a pleasant evening," for Mrs. K.

Monday, February 1st.

Today I took up my novel again, and after roughly scribbling 2,300 words in 3 hours, began actually to have a dim vision of some of the

---

[1] Among her thirty-five novels, *East Lynne* is best remembered.

characters—at last. To "get way on," there is nothing like seizing the
pen and writing something, anything, about one's characters.

If I could spend every day as I have spent today, happiness would
almost be within grasp. A couple of hours' editorial work at the office
in the morning. After dinner I read myself to sleep with d'Annunzio's
Annales d'Anne, and when I awoke I went to pay some money into the
bank. Then I schemed out in my head the next chapter of my novel.
Before tea, Mrs. Sharpe came upstairs for a talk, a talk which continued
till some time after tea was over. From 6 to 9 I worked fairly easily at
my novel, drafting 2,300 words—a complete chapter. After supper, I
opened a new copy of Arnold's *Essays in Criticism* (second series) and
read the essay on Tolstoy. I shall read myself to sleep (for the second
time today) with Maria Edgeworth's *Belinda.* In spite of the laziest liver
in the world, I am well-nigh content with myself tonight.

February 13th.

In either 1893 or 1894 I heard a Wagner opera for the first time with
understanding. It was at Drury Lane and we sat in the balcony. There
was no crush on entering; not more than a dozen people had collected
when the doors opened. At most 40 people occupied the balcony, and
the other parts of the immense building were similarly forlorn. Nevertheless it was an excellent performance with Alvarez and (I think)
Klafsky as chief stars.

Contrast: Tonight with Frank [1] I went to a Wagner orchestral concert
(promenade) at Queen's Hall, under Henry J. Wood. We got there a
quarter of an hour before the commencement and already the entrance
hall was packed with an eager tumultuous mass (excited by expectation),
struggling to get at the ticket offices. At eight o'clock the vast floor
(promenade) and the upper circle were crowded in every part, and in
the balcony only a few reserved seats were left, which in turn were
taken before the second piece on the programme had been played. The
audience was enthusiastic, keenly anticipatory; and the orchestra under
the magnetic influence of the occasion played in a fashion which steadily
increased the exquisite nervous tension of its hearers. At the opening
bars of the *Flying Dutchman* overture I felt those strange tickling sensa-

[1] His younger brother, who later edited an Arnold Bennett Calendar.

tions in the back which are the physical signs of æsthetic emotion. The mysterious effects of orchestral colour contrast dazed and dazzled Frank's willing ears till he existed simply as a "receiver"—receiver of a microphone or other phonetic instrument. . . . The waves of sound swallowed him up, and at the end he emerged, like a courageous child from the surf of a summer sea, dripping wet, breathless, and enraptured.

Tuesday, February 16th.

When I saw Miriam Clements as the Princess of Pannonia in *My Friend the Prince* at the Garrick tonight, I realized for the first time that the story of Helen of Troy was potentially if not actually true. For the first few moments I was inclined to think the report of her extraordinary beauty somewhat exaggerated. Then I began to appreciate. Then shortly I could think of nothing else but her face and figure. She was dressed in a regal outdoor costume of blue velvet, with a large waving hat. Her dark hair, carried down from the forehead in a slight curve so as to cover most of the ear, half hid the most wonderful woman's face I have ever seen—not a face with regular classic features, but one finely, bafflingly irregular, full of lovely lines and firmly marked character, and the eyes with a strange, sad, imperious expression. . . . The sight of her gave me an understanding sympathy with the man who "goes mad" about a woman, dishonours himself to possess her, and continues to worship her, let her be as contemptuous or as vile as she may. Previously I had only a sneer for such "madness."

Wednesday, February 17th.

I came home in the train tonight with two acquaintances who were relating stories of their facile transitory passions. Strange how such men, whose steadfast aim seems to be to acquire possession of attractive, "sympathetic," yielding girls, can, without any hypocrisy or false shame, cast a garment of sentiment round the narrative of their easy conquests—a narrative, too, filled full of minute physical detail! Strange also what importance they attach to the girl's being *simpatica!* More strange still, with what calm suddenness they will pass from the pseudo-romance of actual possession to the description of the strange secret diseases which at intervals result therefrom!

Saturday, February 20th.

Another promenade Wagner concert. At the interval, when the Wagner music was finished, Brown and I tortuously picked our way to the orchestra room, where he has many acquaintances. From a little conversation with Busby, the horn player, I learned a lot about rehearsals, the *personnel* of the band, and the conductor's popularity. Then we went into the orchestra and sat down by the drums. The serious part of the programme was now over, and both conductor and orchestra were larkish for the *Pinafore* fantasia. The conductor raps, consults each leader of a section in turn with a questioning nod and wink, and then, lifting both arms, he starts the great machine. The mere noise is cosmic! The booming of the tympani shakes the floor, the brass splits your ears, and the heavy, piercing crepitation of the (kettle)drum almost frightens you into running away. It seems as if the unfortunate conductor had created suddenly a monster impossible to control. . . . Then someone makes an utterly wrong attack, and a loud wave of laughter unsubdued runs across the orchestra. One wonders that the audience isn't shocked, but the audience can't hear it. Even the conductor laughs, winking at the delinquent—this piece is only fun. Yet it won't do to be too slack, and one sees the men bracing their faces to seriousness. They are at work, earning a livelihood. Beneath the mirth of Sullivan's music, there is a perceptible under-effect of solid workaday endeavour by industrious and capable men. When the end came, with a prodigious rattle of kettle-drums, a bassoon player said to the kettledrummer, "You enjoy yourself, no mistake."

"I do," was the answer, in great broad tones, "and I work hard."

"No one seemed to know where anybody was that time!" another player said, passing me to leave the orchestra; he was charging a pipe.

Monday, March 1st.

Sturt said: "Too much importance is attached to intellect. None of us have yet recovered from the surprise of discovering that we are animals who can think."

Wednesday, March 10th.

In the noon omnibuses, I notice more and more frequently the well-dressed, well-bred unattended woman of from 20 to 35. She is typically and finely English; fresh, fair complexion, clear eyes, glossy hair, and (for the most part) comely—at worst—as to face; generally quite pretty. Her clothes had been cut to fit exactly her neat, firm figure, and they are well made, of excellent material, and quiet in style. She is *bien gantée,* and when she happens to lift her skirt, one sees that she is also *bien chaussée,* and carries irreproachable *lingerie.* She holds her small purse easily, and selects a penny from its contents with a most businesslike precision; she knows exactly where the bus must stop for her, and gives her orders to the conductor with all the air of a seasoned commercial traveller at a large railway terminus. In a word, she knows as much about bus-riding as may be known; an escort would merely be a useless embarrassment. Sometimes she finds herself without money for the fare, and she is by no means nonplussed. Either she offers a stamp, or calmly asks the conductor to wait while she gets financial assistance from a shop where she happens to be known. I have seen this occur—and no trace of embarrassment in the lady's demeanour either. A man in such a predicament would certainly betray his perplexity.

And yet the very faces of these women, unwrinkled, unconcerned, almost childlike in comparison to the men's, indicate that they are the carefully nurtured, sheltered, supposed-to-be-fragile creatures their mothers were. . . . At least in essentials. I judge from the mere faces of these women that the "woman's emancipation" etc. movement has yet penetrated but slightly into the ranks of the middle class. These women are unacquainted with the realities of existence. Someone—never seen in that bus where she is, but rather in the underground railway carriage at 9.30 and 6, someone who wears a silk hat and comes home at night self-important for dinner—protects the woman in the bus, apparently so free —protects her, commands her, gives her money to spend, bullies her, spoils her, perhaps ruins her happiness. . . .

A different style of woman is to be seen in the bus going townwards at night. As I was on my way to the first night of *Saucy Sally* [1] at the Comedy this evening, a woman got in the bus (empty save for myself), went quickly past me, and sat down at the far end, with her face carefully turned from the door. Curious, I took an opportunity to change my seat for one that enabled me to see her face. I glanced furtively at her over my newspaper. Soon she caught my eye, and returned the glance

---

[1] By F. C. Burnand.

with a cold, questioning stare, as who should say, "Now do you mean business or not?" I looked at her again, and again her eye was a half-inviting question. As other passengers arrived, she edged up the bus, till she was sitting exactly opposite to me, and our eyes almost carried on a conversation. She was a woman over 30, with a face pretty enough (unless seen in profile, when a long crease in the cheek cast an unpleasant shadow) and the full, only slightly accentuated bosom which many light women seem to affect. Had it not been for the cold calculation expressed occasionally in her glance, I should have judged her not much spoilt—as to disposition—by her profession. After a time she gathered that my intentions were not serious, and ignored me.

Among the other occupants of the bus were two young girls, stagily pretty, with large lustrous eyes, darkened eyebrows, and dolls' mouths. They wore large waving hats and talked in crudest cockney to a man who looked like a scene-shifter. As one watched their unreserved demeanour, one instinctively contrasted them with the women who had filled that bus a few hours earlier in the day. No doubt they were chorus girls, and without stain, but no one had sheltered, protected them. They knew as much as most men. They knew what the woman opposite me was; they detected her instantly and furtively, whispered to each other, smiling, and then dismissing the matter.

Thursday, March 18th.

There can be no knowledge without emotion. We may be aware of a truth, yet until we have felt its force, it is not ours. To the cognition of the brain must be added the experience of the soul. Because her instinct has told her, or because she has been reliably informed, the faded virgin knows that the supreme joys are not for her; she knows, by a process of the intellect; but she can feel her deprivation no more than the young mother can feel the hardship of the virgin's lot. Of all the inhabitants of the Inferno, none but Lucifer knows that hell is hell, and the secret function of purgatory is to make of heaven an effective reality.

But to the artist is sometimes granted a sudden, transient insight which serves in this matter for experience. A flash, and where previously the brain held a dead fact, the soul grasps a living truth! At moments we are all artists.

Thursday, May 20th.

Bicycle accident. Sunday morning, 21 Mch.

Dislocation of the elbow.

Chloroform operation 22 Mch.

I carried my arm in splints for a month, and in a sling for six weeks. For three weeks I dictated all articles and letters.

The orderliness of my existence was never so deranged before. Since the middle of March neither of my books now in progress has been touched.

At the Press Club yesterday I met Eden Phillpotts, a man of 35, quiet, restrained, with a kind face and voice, and a peculiarly flattened yet sturdy nose.

Tuesday, June 15th.

Never since first I came to London has the West End been so crowded with sightseers, so congested by the business of pleasure: lines of women, gay and perspiring in the hot sun, recklessly ruffling their light thin frocks in scrambles for seats on the tops of buses; straw-hatted and waist-coatless men continually discussing the prices of seats to view the processions,[1] and the fortunes made and lost thereby; the thoroughfares packed with vehicles six and eight deep, and the drivers in their grey felt hats as imperturbable as ever, save for a stronger tendency to quarrel cynically among themselves for right of way. On all sides the sound of hammers on wood, and the sight of aproned carpenters working with the leisurely content of men earning eighteenpence an hour. In all the gutters poles springing up, decorated with muslins and streamers and gilt apexes, and here and there patches, daily growing bigger, of red and blue draperies covering the yellow wood of jubilee stands. Everything, taken separately, ugly and crude, yet in combination, by sheer immensity and bold crudity, certain in the end to produce a great spectacular effect.

Imagine, for instance, the view of that part of Fleet Street which includes St. Clement Dane's Church, upon whose walls, right to the summit, are hung pendant stands for hundreds of people, the highest seemingly halfway to heaven.

No one has talked of anything but Jubilee till this morning, when the suicide of Barney Barnato brought about a diversion which a bad rail-

---

[1] On the occasion of Queen Victoria's Diamond Jubilee.

way accident, a treacherous mutiny in India, and an earthquake in Calcutta, had all failed to accomplish.[1]

This afternoon I had closed my office windows and drew the blinds in order to review books in quiet and cool, when someone came in to say that a man who was fixing an electric wire had fallen out of the second-floor window (next below me) on his head on the pavement. I was so busy that I scarcely noticed what was said. Then another came to say that the man had been carried away in an ambulance to the hospital, with a hole in his forehead into which one could put three fingers. And then later came the report that he was slowly sinking, and in a very short while would certainly be dead. The thing had happened within a few feet of me, and I had not troubled even to open my window and look out into the street. Only the catch in Miss Evor's voice as she spoke to me gave warning that not everyone was unmoved.

I had finished my work, and I ran out into Fleet Street to get a bus home. The crowds were still increasing; there was a pleasant thrill and rumour of excited expectancy in the air. Soon I forgot the man in the hospital, who a couple of hours before had been full of skilled strength and had had his own private hopes and expectations. The streets this evening were full of dowdy matrons, wives of toil, both of London and the country, going about with the naïve child-look of surprise which the housewife cooped up in kitchen and parlour for months together always exhibits on her infrequent outings. This inspection of the mere preliminaries of a great festival was their high holiday; they enjoyed the same sensations as the man free to roam will enjoy in witnessing all the splendid magnificence of Jubilee Day itself.

Stands seem to have been *flung* round some of the churches like a scarf, swathing them from tower to lowest buttress with almost the curves of drapery, clinging to the stonework like drapery pressed against it by a strong wind.

Friday, June 18th. Felixstowe.

We rode out of Ipswich at dusk, with rain coming on, a high wind whistling behind us in the telegraph wires, and every sign of a stormy

---

[1] The South African mining magnate threw himself overboard on the return voyage from Cape Town; an excursion train left the rails at Oswestry on June 11, causing 11 deaths; 22 officers and men had been killed in a Waziri rising; the Calcutta earthquake had caused over 1,500 deaths.

night. We had scarcely climbed the hill from the town, when an incoming cyclist warned us of bad roads; and indeed the roads proved worse than his account of them. Nevertheless we rode every foot of the 12 miles to this place. Soon after 9.30 it was quite dark, the rain was coming down steadily, the wind (fortunately at our backs) had increased, and we were riding warily across a wild, naked country on a road of which the narrow cart-ruts formed the only rideable surface; all else was loose sand, sticky and dangerous with rain.

For miles we rode on hardened strips of the road scarcely a foot wide, the wheels of the bicycles continually grating amongst sand and pebbles as we groped our way forward. The rain gradually penetrated our cloth-ing and settled in our shoes, till my feet at least were stone cold. At every few yards we started a rabbit or a stoat or some unrecognizable creature of the night. There were no houses or cultivated ground till we passed through a village only two miles from Felixstowe. After this we lost our way, having left Felixstowe on the right. My lamp went out, and on dismounting I found that my invalid right arm was useless, and so we walked the last mile to a hotel in the pouring rain.

Marriott vowed he enjoyed the ride thoroughly. I was anxious, un-comfortable in my saddle, and nervous. Clearly my nerves had not yet recovered from my accident in March. I imagined every possible sort of accident, in each case following out a train of circumstances to the direst possible climax. In particular, I dreaded a puncture, and that I might take a cold, to be followed by rheumatic fever. Yet, underneath this surface discontent, discomfort, and sick imagination, there was a sense of deep satisfaction, the satisfaction of facing and overcoming difficulties, of slowly achieving a desired end, in spite of obstacles.

Saturday, June 19th. Southwold.

We sat out the evening in the bar parlour of the Crown Hotel, a typical room with a long low corner window, dark woodwork, and sporting pictures. Five or six men of the district present, including the proprietor, a rough, bluff, good-humoured fat fellow. We were all served by a girl of about 22, dressed like a shopgirl, fairly tall and thin, with high cheek-bones, quick-handed, and with the quick docile smile of one accustomed to serve. In age, sex, bearing, and appearance she was an extreme and piquant contrast to the men on whom she waited. Her presence supplied a perfume of refinement, neatness, and above all femininity, which the most callous man in the world could not but appreciate with pleasure more or less conscious.

I have noticed exactly the same phenomena in many inn parlours; and doubtless it is partly accountable for the popularity of inn parlours; but this was a specially fine instance, the young girl's interesting wistful face showed such sweet feminine docility, and all the men, even the oldest and even the youngest, were so plainly affected by her environment of them.

Riding in rural parts, the country seems a network of roads dominated by signposts, which dominate also the rider. One is obsessed by signposts; they become the chief institution, the witness of civilization—forbidding here, and there reassuring and urging on.

Sunday, June 20th. Ipswich.

With what reluctance one leaves the sea!

Ipswich is a closely-knit town, reminding one in its contours and large masses of the eighteenth-century parts of Bruges. Many of the streets were crudely decorated with the primary colours of flags, and the continual clashing of church bells indicated that this was the Day of Thanksgiving for the Queen's long reign.

Tonight we "lie" at the Great White Horse, Pickwick's inn, and by good fortune have been allotted the Pickwick bedroom, No. 36, an immense apartment, accommodating three and labelled outside "Pickwick." On the walls an extremely bad oil painting of a Pickwick banquet. "A facsimile of this hotel was erected at the World's Fair, Chicago, as one of the celebrated old inns of this country." In many ways it has been modernized, but still it keeps the air of the ancient hostelry.

Tuesday, June 29th.

I wonder if women realize the acute pleasure which men derive from the sight of them in their fresh, cool, clean, summer toilettes—openwork stockings, diaphanous sleeves, and general impression of *muslin-ness*.

Saturday, July 3rd.

At Earl's Court Exhibition.[1] It is good to bear in mind that all these

---

[1] The Victorian Era Exhibition, promoted by Imre Kiralfy, who, with his brother, was once active in the New York theatre.

vast vulgarized crowds of people are being subjected to the same influences which one feels oneself—the influences of bright colour and
music, al fresco gaiety, and sex; that all the men enjoy more or less the
close presence of these thousands of girls in their summer attire and
white shoes, the smiles and light laughter coming from behind veils of
spotted muslin; that this assemblage has not got itself together simply
to provide a pleasurable humanizing sensation for *you,* but that each unit
of it revels in just the same sensation and will go away the better and
the happier for it.

Sunday, July 4th.

I rode up to the Tower Bridge, starting at 6.30 A.M. The streets, not
yet cleansed, had a sallow look in the strong hot sunlight. In the course
of an hour the description of the occupants of stray hansoms changes
from people who have obviously been awake all night to people who
are away on some excursion with all the fresh energy of morning.

In Piccadilly; two Rothschild servants starting out for a bicycle ride;
the older, a woman of 45, brisk, alert, who smiled profusely and self-
consciously on the policeman at the corner, the other a young thin girl.

Woman cleaner unlocking a church door.

In Newgate St.; the night guard of soldiers returning from the Bank
to their quarters.

Soho, with all its side alleys and lanes, was quite deserted; littered with
the refuse of Saturday night.

By seven o'clock there were plenty of people about with provision
baskets and hampers, setting forth for a day on the river and elsewhere.

Monday, July 12th.

At Her Majesty's Theatre—

Mademoiselle de Belle-Isle, by Dumas *père,* advertised as *The Silver
Key,* by Sydney Grundy. At the Haymarket opposite, another of Dumas's
plays, *Un Mariage de Convenance,* also translated by Sydney Grundy, is
in the midst of a successful run. It is the character of Gabrielle in *The
Silver Key* which shows Dumas at his best. Gabrielle is worthy to stand
by Diane de Méridor, Olympe de Clèves, and Marguerite de Valois; and
she is worthy to stand by the Shakespearean women—even the best. She
has the *royal* bearing, the freedom from any sort of littleness, which

mark all Dumas's characters, and which make his kings so kingly. She is above nature. Dumas knew better than nature. So did Wagner. And between these two came no one with the same large strong knowledge. It was curious to watch an audience of over-civilized weaklings weakly enjoying the work of this immense creator who was never civilized, who worked and ate and slept like a savage, and always was a savage—a "noble savage"—the only "noble savage." This evening was the triumph of sheer innate force over delicate refined skill without force. Gabrielle made one forget all the creations of Dumas *fils,* of Donnay,[1] of Ibsen, of Pinero. At the beginning of the second act, Dumas in ten sentences paints a woman more adorable than any of his successors could paint in ten acts, and he does it roughly, curtly, ignoring base verisimilitude and all the trickery of art. Evelyn Millard appreciated her part to a nicety, acting in the true Dumas vein and spirit.

Tuesday, July 13th.

I lunched at the Rainbow, a type of City restaurant which is passing away. A large dark room, sombrely furnished in mahogany, and gas-lighted, even in the sunshine of a hot July day. In the centre a table at which a stout carver in white cap coat and apron carves the saddle of mutton and the sirloin of beef—dishes which are never varied, and of which the customers seem never to tire. Here come lawyers and other *hommes d'affaires* of middle age to whom luncheon is a serious meal, not to be ordered without minute instructions to the obsequious waiter. "Do you call this underdone?" a portly customer asks sharply. "Yes, sir." "Well, I don't. Take it back." "Yes, sir." Here one drinks either stout from a tankard, or some sound wine; but if one orders wine, one gives the waiter directions as to the temperature. It is *de rigueur.* The door leading into the dining-room is labelled "coffee room," and there is a significant notice: "Ladies' dining-room upstairs." Ladies are not willingly admitted to the ground floor, and those women, if any, who dared to pass that door labelled "coffee room" would be requested to leave, or at least pointed at as unwomanly. This is one of the last strongholds of the conservative male. Yet here we males respect ourselves; we have a regard for the decencies. "Gentlemen are requested not to smoke pipes in this establishment."

---

[1] Charles Maurice Donnay's most famous play was *Amants.*

Friday, July 16th.

Mrs. Penrose [1] gave me a lovely scrap of a conversation which had passed between an aunt of hers and Marie Corelli.

M.C. Do you like tennis?

The aunt makes a perfunctory answer.

M.C. The only tennis I like is Tennyson.

Pause.

M.C. The dear old man sent me a beautiful letter once.

"I tried to look," said the excellent aunt afterwards, "as if Tennyson had been in the habit of sending me a letter every day."

Friday, July 30th.

I started with Sharpe and Alcock to cycle to Halifax.

The Ivel hotel at Biggleswade is kept by a man named Allbone, whom Alcock called "the father of the North Road"; a mild-mannered, well-built man of 35 or so, but with peculiar involuntary movements of the hands and head which seemed to indicate some sort of paralysis. Alcock and he were exchanging reminiscences of racing in the old cycling days, before the safety came into use. They decided that real racing belonged only to the past. In those days a man would ride from London to Oxford, win a cup, and ride back the same evening with the pot under his arm. Now, the crack cyclist, "trained to the minute," is taken to the railway station in a perambulator (so to say) and carefully escorted from the carriage to the sports ground. He has one man to attend to tires, another to attend to bearings, another to attend to himself.

Saturday, July 31st.

Watson, the late registrar of the Royal College of Music, went to get shaved in a provincial town. "How easy it would be for me to cut your throat, sir!" said the barber as he was stropping the razor. Watson considered a moment and fled. The next day the barber did cut a customer's throat. He had become a homicidal maniac.

Sunday, August 1st. Lincolnshire.

Riding through the heart of England, the general impression is one of decent prosperity and content. One sees nothing of that agricultural

---

[1] Author of *The Modern Gospel* and a number of other novels.

distress of which one reads so much in towns. It is an endless succession of picturesque and cleanly rural activities punctuated by neat towns, where old-fashioned inns seem to dominate and represent the municipal architecture. The worst roads are passable, and every village has the air of being well tended. But then one rides only in summer and fair weather.

Thursday, September 2nd. Ouistreham.[1]

A pile of letters and papers which had been following me about France arrived today. Among them were two from my mother, which I saved till the end of my reading. The last one was as follows:

> Barmouth,
> 9 Marine Terrace,
> August 30/ '97.
> 10.30 A.M.

My Dear Arnold,

How ever am I to tell you of the dreadful calamity that has come over us: after breakfast on Sunday morning the four boys went out to bathe, and poor Billy[2] has not returned: how we managed to live through it I can't tell: Billy the strongest swimmer of the four: I knew one was missing, but I was sure it was our Frank, indeed we all thought the same: but Frank came out the third: and the fourth has gone: poor Billy: Sep and Frank Boulton came on Saturday afternoon: we are hoping the body will come in with the tide: there is a very high sea on the last day or two: they walked out on the sands for a long way, the water scarcely up to their waists: and they must suddenly have got into the current, which is very strong: but why don't they put notices up to say it is dangerous? Oh why? Pa rushed for a boat, but they are a long way off: and all day yesterday we were waiting, waiting, waiting: hoping to hear something: we could not telegraph to Boultons yesterday, but Pa wrote a letter to Mr. Dodds, our minister, to ask him to go in first thing this morning, and break it to his father and mother: so far we have not had a telegram from

---

[1] On the coast of Calvados, at the head of the deep-water canal from Caen.
[2] Willie Boulton, who was engaged to his sister, Tertia Bennett.

them: so we are waiting, waiting, waiting again. You can't have any idea what fearfully hard work it is: killing work: Tertia takes it bravely: she and Florrie were out on the beach when he disappeared: Pa was there too, he went out with the boys and stood by their mackintoshes, etc.: they bathed from the beach, as no vans were out at the time: Pa rushed for a boat when he knew something was wrong, but he thought it was our Frank that was in danger. Tertia was hysterical after she came in from the beach: several times when we have missed her from the room she has been found lying on Willie's bed hugging the clothes that he took off just before bathing; and the cap that he used to wear, a brown check one, never leaves her hands, she clasps it to her tightly and paces backwards and forwards in the room: scarcely any sleep for anybody: no appetite though the meals are served as usual, and go away practically untasted: Our Frank feels it fearfully: he was the last to speak to him: the three were fearfully exhausted: one gentleman took Sep in the next house to his, Sep would have fallen going up the steps, but the gentleman caught him; gave him a big dose of brandy and came here and put him in bed: another one brought Frank Boulton in, took him to his bedroom, rubbed him well down, and put his feet in hot water: everybody was very good: the people in this house as well: but alas! he is gone, he is gone: poor Billy! Poor Tertia! Whatever sort of a house is there at Grange Cottage?

I have not heard anything from you except Sissie's p.c.

Your very sorrowful mother.

We don't know how soon we can get from here, I suppose we shall have to wait longer: they say if he doesn't turn up by tomorrow, it may be a week.

I can't read the letter through, please excuse mistakes.

I threw the letter over to Kennerley to read, and walked away to the lock. Presently Kennerley came up, and putting the letter into my hand whispered, "Thank you."

"Shall you go home tonight?" he asked.

"Oh, no," I said. "What's the use?"

In a few minutes it occurred to me that of course I was going by the Newhaven steamer that night. Nothing else was possible.

As the time approached for the appearance of the steamer, little groups of people collected round the darkness of the lock, in which small craft had already encamped. At some distance on the other side of the channel were a few electric lights where some earthworks had begun to be thrown up. Save for these and one or two other scattered lamps, all was mysterious gloom. At last the hoot of the steamer came eerily down the canal, and as the vessel rounded the last corner its electric head-light, like a great eye dropping a tear in the still water, illuminated the vista of the canal, and though it was yet a mile away, threw a deep black shadow behind our figures.

Then suddenly I felt that this passage of a channel steamer through Ouistreham lock was going to be an impressive transaction.

I was filled with the presence of an inexorable power. With tremendous majesty the great ship crept gradually forward to the accompaniment of hoarse calls and hoots, and so at last into the lock. It was an hour before the water of the lock had subsided and her bulwarks were level with the sides of the lock. She moved out silently, save for the pilot's call, and with the same dignity as she appeared, disappeared with us into the wind and blackness of the sea.

Such scenes as this are the poetic apotheosis of machinery. The spectacle accorded with and soothed my feelings.

Friday, September 3rd.

I went into the breakfast-room at home, scene of a thousand love-makings. Tertia, dressed in black, sat in the easy chair in front of the fire. It was cold. She got up.

"Poor old girl!" I said, as I kissed her. She cried a moment. Then we others began to talk of common affairs. Tertia sat silent.

Afterwards in the dining-room Pater recounted his version of the accident; how Sep had struggled out of the water, and running towards him had shouted something which the high wind carried away. "Pa, if you don't get a boat quick you'll never see our Frank again"; Pater's run of over 500 yards of loose sand to the nearest boat, and the long-drawn delay of launching; the appearance of Tertia and Florrie on the beach, and the altercation between him and Tertia as to whether it was Frank or Willie who was in danger—an altercation of dreadful pathos; how all the boys had remained cool throughout, and how Willie had

struck out strongly, after our Frank had told the others to leave him
to float on the current till a boat could overtake him; how Frank had
somehow contrived to reach land, and how he thought till long afterwards that Willie was safe, taking it for granted. . . .

Friday, September 10th.

During this week, when I have been taking early morning walks with
Tertia, and when I have been traversing the district after dark, the grim
and original beauty of certain aspects of the Potteries, to which I have
referred in the introduction to *Anna Tellwright,* has fully revealed itself
for the first time. Before breakfast, on the heights of Sneyd Green, where
the air blows as fresh and pure (seemingly) as at the seaside, one gets
glimpses of Burslem [1] and of the lands between Burslem and Norton,
which have the very strangest charm. The stretch of road on which one
stands, used by men and young women on their way to work, is sufficiently rural and untouched to be intrinsically attractive. It winds through
pretty curves and undulations; it is of a good earthy colour and its
borders are green and bushy. Down below is Burslem, nestled in the
hollow between several hills, and showing a vague picturesque mass of
bricks through its heavy pall of smoke. If it were an old Flemish town,
beautiful in detail and antiquely interesting, one would say its situation
was ideal. It is *not* beautiful in detail, but the smoke transforms its
ugliness into a beauty transcending the work of architects and of time.
Though a very old town, it bears no sign of great age—the eye is never
reminded of its romance and history—but instead it thrills and rever-
berates with the romance of machinery and manufacture, the romance
of our fight against nature, of the gradual taming of the earth's secret
forces. And surrounding the town on every side are the long straight
smoke and steam wreaths, the dull red flames, and all the visible evi-
dences of the immense secular struggle for existence, the continual striv-
ing towards a higher standard of comfort.

This romance, this feeling which permeates the district, is quite as
wonderfully inspiring as any historic memory could be.

And if the effects of morning are impressive, what shall be said of the

---

[1] The town in Staffordshire where the Bennett family continued to live after Arnold
Bennett went to London. Burslem was "Bursley," one of the "Five Towns" of his most
famous books.

night scenes—of the flame-lit expanses bearing witness to a never-ceasing activity; the sky-effects of fire and cloud; and the huge dark ring of hills surrounding this tremendous arena.

Monday, September 13th.

We were all seated in the chapel. A dozen apprentice boys had carried in armfuls of wreaths and piled them about the communion-rail. Then entered the great oak coffin, borne shoulder high by four men from Boulton's works, and on it two solitary wreaths, Tertia's and that of the Boulton family. The solitariness of these wreaths would have made me cry had I continued to look at them. Yet I had placed them there myself while the coffin was yet on the bier in the chapel yard.

Of all the thousands of people congregated in the streets to witness the funeral processions, I saw two only who removed their hats as we passed.

Tuesday, September 14th.

This affair is now over. The Goncourt brothers would in my place have noted every item of it, and particularly watched themselves. I had intended to do as much, but the various incidental distractions proved too strong for my resolution.

Thursday, September 30th.

This morning John Lane gave a definite undertaking to publish my novel *A Man from the North,* on or before the 1st of February next.

As an excuse for delay, he said that the past season had been incredibly bad for publishers, and that he had been obliged to postpone publication of so many volumes that everything was in arrears.

Speaking of his approaching marriage, he said: "I want it to come; I want it to be soon; I must settle down; one needs a woman in the house. I am tired of my present life, have been tired of it for a long time."

This from a bachelor aged *circa* 40.

Tuesday, October 5th.

To wake up at midnight, after an hour's sleep, with a headache, slight but certainly indicative of the coming attack; to hear the clock strike, every note drilling a separate hole into your skull; to spend the rest of the night uneasily between sleeping and waking, always turning over the pillow, and tormented intermittently by idiotic nightmares, crowded with action, which fatigue the brain: this is a disturbed liver. Towards morning comes the hope, caused by the irregularity of the pain, that the headache will pass away on getting up. But it never does so. Then one comes downstairs, eyes as it were in red-hot sockets, and gulps some effervescing saline. One rises from breakfast with a mouth full of reminiscences—butter, cocoa, porridge; and the headache remains. One walks to the office in the fresh autumn air; the headache remains. Towards noon, one seeks the last remedy, a draught which weakens the action of the heart. It is effective, and after half an hour's somnolence in a chair, one recovers, half dazed, but without the headache; weak, silly, nerveless, but without the headache. The impulse to work is alive again, and one accomplishes an hour. But after lunch and dinner one has a consciousness that a new headache is lying in wait, and, one's resolves worn away by the constant sense of fatigue in the eyes and of rapid pulsation round the back of the head, one weakly lapses into idleness, trusting that tomorrow will be different.

I found myself at the Wagner promenade concert. It seems to me that Henry J. Wood lacks the repose and reticence of a great conductor. He continually endeavours to express the music to his band in curves of the arm, sudden contractions of all the muscles, frowns and smiles. If such procedure is to be effective, it can only be effective at rehearsal. At the performance, the conductor knowing what the band can do and the band knowing what the conductor desires, gestures should be unnecessary. At the performance the band needs, not an interpretation of the music, but merely control and reminders.

Steindl,[1] the pianist aged 6 or 7, played a Schubert Impromptu (No. 4) and Raff's "Fabian." He is not more than 7, and has the pale face and vast skull of the typical precocious genius. He runs on to the platform, takes his seat, and then stares down at the audience with calm reproachful expression. Then he turns to his father for the signal to begin. He is not lost in his performance, but rather (as it were) preoccupied with something else, seldom looking at the keyboard and constantly directing upon the audience that reproachful stare. During the

---

[1] The appearance of Bruno Steindl, the prodigy pianist, aged 7, created a stir in the musical world.

performance his father exchanged looks of pride and pleasure with members of the orchestra, every man in which followed the child's movements with a sort of paternal wistfulness. At the end, when Steindl stood bowing and bobbing to the applause, my body shook and my eyes filled with tears, in spite of myself.

Wednesday, October 6th.

At times, and in some fortunate aspects, London will look as quaint, picturesque, and medieval, as any old-world continental city. But it must be regarded with a "fresh" eye, an eye unprejudiced by custom and associations. When I catch the town in such an aspect, I understand how the inhabitants of these old-world continental cities can be oblivious to the attractiveness which surrounds them, as they certainly are, and I suddenly see eye to eye with the appreciative foreigner in London.

This morning, as I walked through the Green Park in an October mist, it occurred to me that the sheep grazing there and the soldiers practising flag-signals would, if seen by me in an unfamiliar city, have constituted for me a memorable picture of pure quaintness. Then, walking in the Strand as the sun overpowered the fog, what mellow picturesque was there in the vista of churches, backed by the roofs of the Law Courts, and further away a tower for all the world like the Beffroi at Bruges. Observed five hundred miles away, a scene less striking than this would be one to talk about and grow enthusiastic over, one to buy photographs of. . . . But it happens to be in London.

At moments the pathos of Willie's death suddenly seizes one tightly, and one wonders that any of those immediately concerned in the scene itself should have come sane out of such an ordeal. Then, as suddenly, the sensation departs, and one forgets it utterly till some little word or other trifle evokes it once more.

Thursday, October 7th.

On Tuesday my father called on me at Fetter Lane,[1] and afterwards a lady inquired from me whether he was my brother, thus carrying on the tradition of youthfulness to which his appearance long ago gave rise.

---

[1] The offices of *Woman*, 10–11 Fetter Lane.

But today I noticed, I think for the first time, the approaches of middle age upon him. I felt acutely that he and I were of different generations; that parent and child, be they never so willing, can never come intellectually together, simply because one time of life differs crudely and harshly from another. He has now the physical and mental deliberativeness which characterizes the aging. I chafe under this slowness, but I need not do so: it is a sign not of decay, but of natural development. He balances argument against counter-argument with an evident pleasure in the process of balancing, not as a means to an end, but for the sake of so balancing. The other day he said sarcastically to Emily, "How my children do patronize me!" And a few weeks ago when I laughingly referred to my "aged parents," he seized the phrase, repeated it, and recounted it to callers in the evening—jokingly, but I could see that it occupied his thoughts.

Criterion Theatre. Whenever I see Charles Wyndham in a new part,[1] I come away from the theatre full of a desire to conduct my life as invariably he conducts his, on the stage: with good humour, kind cynicism, adaptability, and at back of these a strain of real faith in the "ultimate decency of things"; but perhaps most of all I envy his *savoir faire,* his equality to any *contretemps* that may arise, and his unfailing presence of mind. Whatever his dramatists may have intended, Charles Wyndham always plays exactly the same character, a character which has the qualities I have named and which sets me buzzing with insane aspirations.

Monday, October 11th.

At the Symonds's. As I listened to this mother and daughter recounting their deeds and wanderings since I last saw them, I was struck by their faculty for extracting from life pleasure and amusement. They read everything that appears, travel during several months in the year, gamble soberly when gambling is to be had, and generally make it a duty to go through life with as much pleasantness and change as will not fatigue them. Both are witty, and neither is afraid of criticizing her friends, or of

---

[1] He was playing Sir Christopher Deering in H. A. Jones's *The Liars,* produced at the Criterion, October 6.

getting fun out of idols. The daughter writes clever novels, and exhibits a good-humoured, railing tolerance for all "missions," including her own.

They live alone, and love to throw a dart at "men." They are cultured and latitudinarian. They are never shocked, or very seldom, and then instead of showing it, they faintly sneer at the objectionable thing. Backed by a certain income, they know they can hold their own in any way against anybody, and the thought gives them a fine sense of security. No struggle for them! They are among the conquerors, for they have brains and wit, as well as money, and they are philosophers enough to value all three accurately. They see all sides and appreciate all. They know how to live, calmly, reticently, yet gaily, and sometimes with abandon. They have attained wisdom, in that they accept the world as it is, endeavour to improve it according to their talents, eschew impossible ideals, and look after themselves.

Tuesday, October 19th.

I called on Gardner at the Avenue Theatre to pay a visit of sympathy. His brief venture there closed abruptly last night because (immediately) the Gas Company had cut off the gas.

At the stage door I had to wait while the commissionaire satisfied himself that I was not a lawyer's clerk and took Gardner's pleasure as to seeing me. A little group of minor stage-folk were round the door asking for various officials and being put off by the commissionaire. Occasionally someone appeared, out of a maze of scenery, from the interior and said, "Morning, old boy, what can I do for you?" Then followed a colloquy, a pat on the back, and the applicant departed, temporarily appeased.

Gardner received me in the saloon of the theatre, which I reached through dark, very narrow passages varied by sudden short flights of steps; I had to light myself with a match. The end of a cigarette stuck to his lower lip throughout the interview. As we talked I could see now and then the cold pallid interior of the theatre with the stage set.

He told me a wonderful story of the failure of backers to back, of the hostility or stupidity of the press, of the prosperity that was coming at the very moment when he was compelled to close. "Can't be helped," he said at the end; "fortune of war." The expenses of the production had been at the rate of £400 a week, and the takings at the rate of £70.

Thursday, October 21st.

Lunch with Eden Phillpotts, H. D. Lowry,[1] Bayly, and another. The conversation came round to author's receipts. Phillpotts said that he, one of the original band of contributors, was suing the *Idler* for (I think) twelve guineas, and that he had recently lost fifteen guineas due from the *Minster Magazine*.[2] The fifth man told how G. A. Sala[3] had got him to work for six months without paying a penny.

Referring to defaulting journals, I told them that I had only lost money once. For years the *Star* has owed me 3/6 for a paragraph, which I have never been able to obtain.

Friday, October 22nd.

Rankin, formerly American journalist, now college professor and connoisseur of early Italian art, told me some stories of the unscrupulousness which characterizes American journalism. He said that the *New York Journal* was once nearly extinguished by its rivals through the agency of the Associated Press of New York. The latter, by arrangement, refused on any terms to supply the *Journal* with the ordinary service of news, and the *Journal,* in order to avert complete stoppage and disaster, took the only course open; namely, bought up, at enormous cost, another newspaper which had a contract for the news service.

He said that the *New York Herald* existed simply as an advertising medium. The *World,* perhaps, had a larger acreage of advertisements, but the *Herald* was the leading vehicle. No one by any chance ever paid the slightest attention to the editorial utterances of the *Herald*.

Pulitzer of the *World* was known in press circles as "the Jew." A renowned special correspondent, whose Chicago stuff about the Bryan candidature was being paid for by the *Journal* but not printed, wired to that paper, "If you don't print my stuff, the Jew will." The *Journal* printed it.

Asked about the status of the *Tribune,* which I had always understood to be the one paper in New York at once fearless, influential, and respectable, he said: "No sale; no influence; no nothing. As a force it simply doesn't exist.

---

[1] Leader writer of the *Morning Post.*

[2] This magazine ceased publication in March, 1896.

[3] George Augustus Sala (d. 1895) was one of England's famous journalists, and had at one time founded his own *Sala's Journal,* a failure.

"To my mind," he said, "the Philadelphia *Ledger* is the best paper in America."

Apropos: When Cléo de Mérode was dancing recently in New York, she one day told her managers that on that night she should change her coiffure, abandoning for the time her method of brushing the hair straight down from the centre of the forehead over the ears. Posters were immediately issued:

> TONIGHT
>
> CLÉO DE MÉRODE
>
> WILL SHOW
>
> HER EARS

Saturday, October 23rd. Paris.

As the train swaggered through Dulwich, we[1] caught a glimpse of a platform full of city men and city clerks and a few girls, waiting for an up local. It was impossible not to feel uplifted by a feeling of superiority. In the minds of how many on that platform is not the Continental train, as it thunders past every morning, the visible symbol of pleasure, adventure and romance! . . . I remembered my emotions years ago at Hornsey, as I stood on the platform there and saw the Edinburgh express sweep swiftly and smoothly by. . . . And the Edinburgh express was not the Continental boat train, though it moved more proudly with its gorgeous Pullman in the centre of it.

Dover and Calais. What mean, amorphous entrance portals to great kingdoms! Mere grimy untended back doors!

As we left Dover harbour, the lines of greyish-yellow official buildings on the grey-green hillside spread out clear, and then disappeared in the vague distance. The sea was rough. I closed my eyes and prepared to be uncomfortable.

---

[1] Arnold Bennett was accompanied to Paris by his friend, Edwin Rickards, the architect.

Paris train: The carriage was full of silent Frenchmen, and as we flew along through a flying sea of yellow leaves glinting in the sunlight, I remembered tales of the sociability of Frenchmen—how, unlike Englishmen, they beguiled their journeys by courteous and cheerful dialogue. Perhaps on this line the native public has suffered by the example of our insular manners.

For màny miles the landscape was bare, greyish and uninteresting. Then, as we increased our distance from the sea southwards a change of temperature and of atmosphere became more and more perceptible, until the warmth and brightness made almost an English summer. Presently the character of the landscape altered. Water was everywhere in large quiet pools bordered by trees delightfully tinted, and we passed by picturesque towns with fine churches and wonderful crooked white streets.

We entered Paris, as one enters London, by boring a way into the city through ravines with windowed walls. On the right was a single impressive feature, the hill of Montmartre surmounted by a great cathedral under scaffolding.[1]

It was dusk as we drove to the hotel through traffic less crowded than that of London, but noisier, more gesticulating, and far more bewilderingly mazy.

On my first evening in Paris, it was proper that I should see *Faust* at the Opéra. We arrived 20 minutes before the curtain, and found a vast interior honeycombed with corridors in which people, by comparison insignificant as ants, were rushing wildly about, arguing, gesticulating, and quarrelling with the harpy-like *ouvreuses*.

This was the 1099th performance of *Faust* at the Opéra, and it was listened to with all the rapt attention of a première. It is true that *Faust* still draws an average of over 20,000 francs per performance, and is still the most popular work in the répertoire, but this was a special occasion, and the audience larger and more interested even than usual.

As we came out of the Opéra, men were crying the *Journal,* with the first *feuilleton* of Zola's *Paris*. Zola and the *Journal* and Steinlen's poster thereof seem just now to flame in the forehead of the City.

---

[1] The Sacré Cœur was begun in 1875.

Sunday, October 24th.

Walking from the Trocadéro to the Bois de Boulogne, and so to the Arc de Triomphe and down the Champs-Elysées, I search for the formula which should express Paris—in vain. The great central difference—the phrase which is to disclose the gulf between the Latin and the Teutonic, eludes and evades the effort of the mind to seize it; only the obvious, the palpable, the little discrepancies show forth: the grandeur of the streets, the large vision of the architects who made them, monopolize attention and thought, and with the tail of the eye one notes slight peculiarities—ribboned costumes of nursemaids, coachmen's hats, toy balloons of children, cyclists' cowbells, and a thousand other trifles. One tries to get behind and below them, but without success.

Strange how in a foreign city one will take trouble to see things not deemed worth seeing at home! I went to the Folies-Bergère with the expressed intention of studying the audience. The main part of the performance was a weak imitation of the Empire, with two well-known Empire stars, Loïe Fuller and Cinquevalli, to give distinction. Yet I stood on tiptoe most of the evening in the midst of a tightly pressed crowd in order to get a mere occasional glimpse of the stage.

Monday, October 25th.

Ascended the tower of Notre Dame in order to see the devils, which surpassed expectations. It struck me that these twelfth-century devils gazed over Zola's Paris with a certain benign satisfaction.

Gardens of the Luxembourg. It is here that Bohemian Paris takes the air. This part of the city has an effective significance which is missing in the neighbourhood of the cosmopolitan Boulevard des Italiens. Here is some Doing. People are less self-conscious and more purposeful; more truly lighthearted and yet more earnest. . . . A beautiful afternoon, absolutely cloudless sky, gentlest breeze just moving out of the perpendicular the high fountain-spray in front of the Palace. . . . A large, apparently but not really shapeless space, gravelled and sown with brown trees and yellow chairs, and untidy with autumn leaves.

As to the people:

Nursemaids, whose large white or blue aprons and white caps seem to strike the *note* of the scene; scores of children, many just able to walk, others learning to skip or clumsily trundling hoops, others in arms; the last seemed always to be receiving clean napkins from their plump, comfortable nurses.

Students in fine black hats and vast neckties, walking about or sitting in groups.

The chair woman, a buxom young woman, capless, with a large black apron. She goes to a group of young students who are talking and laughing among themselves. Without apparently noticing her, they throw her a few words, still laughing, a colloquy ensues, and then for some reason she goes away without exacting pennies from them.

Young women carelessly *chic,* some powdered, all talkative, sitting about in pairs, with looks on their faces of invitation.

Here and there a few sedater groups, well dressed; *papa, maman et bébé,* or perhaps several old women full of volubility and gesture.

A few inquisitive dogs.

In the distance, the tooting of tram cars, and the vague roar of traffic.

The traveller, however virginal and enthusiastic, does not enjoy an unbroken ecstasy. He has periods of gloom, periods when he asks himself the object of all these exertions, and puts the question whether or not he is really experiencing pleasure. At such times he suspects that he is not seeing the right things, that the characteristic, the right aspects of these strange scenes are escaping him. He looks forward dully to the days of his holiday yet to pass, and wonders how he will dispose of them. He is disgusted because his money is not more, his command of the language so slight, and his capacity for enjoyment so limited. His mind goes forward to speculate as to his future career, which seems one of but narrow possibilities, and he foresees failure. The newness of things grows monotonous; he desires the known, the expected.

Tuesday, October 26th.

Curious, the frequency of *maisons d'accouchement* of vast size with large gilt signs in a city whose population is said to be, if not actually falling, stationary.

One house had a pictorial sign, showing a young girl, in modern costume, looking at an opening bush from which rises a baby.

Wednesday, October 27th.

With infinite labour and fatigue I casually inspected one little corner, perhaps the fiftieth part, of the Louvre: Italian and Flemish pictures; and came forth again exhausted.

Musée Cluny: the Musée Plantin over again, but less complete in detail and less realistic as a redintegration of renaissance life.

Luxembourg Gallery. I was a little disappointed with Watts, Stevens, Sisley, Manet, and Monet. It seems to me that the last two have been extinguished by several painters of the present generation.

The *Journal* stated today that last Saturday 100 *voitures-réclames* visited every place within 20 kilometres of the fortifications, to distribute Steinlen's *affiche* of Zola's *Paris;* also that 30 *voitures-réclames* had been circulating continuously for 10 days previously; also that the cost of launching the novel had been 150,000 francs.

12 rue Feydeau.

I walked the length of the Champs-Elysées and back again tonight between 10 and 11. The immense thoroughfare had a depressing deserted appearance. In the side alleys under the trees a light mist hung low, and through this the forms of empty chairs were made spectrally visible by the gas lamps. Down the road at intervals passed cyclists with Chinese lanterns, swiftly overtaking the few fiacres. Occasionally the light of a flying lantern lit up the face of a girl pedalling hardily in her neat knickerbockers over the perfect surface of the gloomy thoroughfare.

At the beginning of the Place de la Concorde I trod on a dead cat, its limbs all spread abroad and its cheek on the roadway. In the rue de Rivoli and the rue de la Paix all was obscure, save for a few small bright squares of illumination, marking shops which vended obscenities for the convenience of travelling Englishmen.

Thursday, October 28th.

By steamer to Saint-Cloud, where the chief attraction was a number of stiff-limbed shrewd old philosophic Frenchmen of the well-to-do lower middle class, playing a rude sort of bowls in the alleys of trees in the park. It seemed to me that their class represented the spinal column of the nation.

Tonight, owing to the inaccuracy of a map, I walked straight out of Paris, in search of the Casino. Up one long street with no turning, the rue Saint-Martin, miles of gas-lit resounding monotony. There were cafés all the way, thickly strewn on both sides the way; at first large and lofty and richly decorated, with vast glazed façades, and manned by waiters in black and white; then gradually growing smaller and less busy; the black and white waiters gave place to men in blouses, and men in blouses gave place to women and girls, short, fat women and girls, who chattered among themselves and to customers; once I passed a café quite deserted save for the waiter and the waitress, who sat, head on arms, side by side over a table, asleep. I saw deserted *cafés concerts,* only open on Sundays and fête days. The shops got smaller and busier; they were filled apparently by the families of the proprietors. At length I crossed over a canal, and here the street widened out to an immense width, and it was quiet and deserted under the gas lamps. I went under railway bridges, and saw in the distance great termini, silent in their blue hazes of electric light. Then came the city barriers and the *octroi,* and I knew then that the map was wrong about the location of the Casino of Paris. But the straight street, darker now, still stretched in front of me, and I followed it a little while for curiosity, till I passed another *octroi* and was in a township outside Paris. At last I turned back, and as soon as I was again within the barriers, I called a fiacre:

"*Cocher, le Casino de Paris.*"

Friday, October 29th.

The Panthéon.

Aux grands hommes. La Patrie reconnaissante.

This legend, stretching its gold letters across the face of the building, has in it something wonderfully moving. It breathes piety in the true sense.

Rickards told me a story of George Llewellyn Morris, the architect and journalist, who used to lodge with him. R. lent to Morris the Whitman which he had had from me. Morris had read nothing of Whitman before, and the effect on him was prodigious. He was found in odd corners talking to himself, and when interrogated replied that he was "loafing, inviting his soul." From being a practical, hard-headed man, he became unpractical, visionary. His earnings during the ensuing year fell to £80. Moreover, he could not keep Whitman out of his articles. An article on Philip Webb in a recent number of the *Architectural Review* was full of Whitman, and the editor wrote to Morris advising him to keep future articles clear of Whitman. Whereupon Morris got himself into a terrible rage, and went to ask the editor what he meant by such an insult; finally the sub-editor interfered and separated the two.

Saturday, October 30th.

Montmartre. "Cabaret, du Conservatoire (Ancienne abbaye de la Butte—12th cent.)."

There was an attractiveness in the simple exterior of this café of the Boulevard Rochechouart. When we went in, the *salle du concert* was not yet opened. While waiting we ordered cognacs, and looked at the very clever pencilled portraits which covered the walls. The café proper, or outer court, was a long low narrow room, narrowing still more at the back to the door giving on the *salle du concert*. There were perhaps a dozen *consommateurs,* none of them apparently different from the *consommateurs* of any other café. At about 9.30 it was quietly announced that the concert would commence at once, and we went forward, rather surprised at the charge of 2 francs for entrance to the show. The *salle* was a room of irregular shape, roughly painted to represent a crypt, with a groined roof. Down the middle of it were three narrow trestle-tables with seats at either side of them. In one corner a clumsy tapestry arrangement of a proscenium, very small and toy-like, and near this a piano. At the back were several toy *loges,* a comical imitation of a theatre. The walls were hung with copies of ancient standards and with old brass musical instruments, and here and there they were frescoed.

The pianist came and moved his fingers lightly over the keyboard and drifted into a march. Then the proprietor at the back announced *"mon bon camarade"* So-and-so. A dark little man of about 35 with a keen pleasant face, dressed in blue serge, came forward, and leaning negligently on the piano, sang very prettily, in a thin voice, a sentimental song about Venice. His tone suited the small room (which 80 people filled) to perfection. Then another *"bon camarade"* was announced, an older heavier man, very dark and self-contained, and with a face something like Verlaine's in its torpor and pallor. He sang a humorous song, and in the last verse, after 3 verses of utter impassivity, disclosed a twinkle and a smile to show that he also was enjoying the joke. The applause was immense. This man sang twice, and each time hoisted himself on to the low platform by clinging to the piano. Others followed him, all roughly dressed—one man had brown gloves sticking up from the breast pocket of an old frock coat, and among them two women ("*ma bonne camarade*"), both charmingly unaffected and good-natured and clever, dressed in black or dark blue, with none of the conventional stage airs. Before the entertainment had proceeded 10 minutes, the artistic feeling which permeated it was most apparent. The audience was of the lower middle class, seemingly quite ordinary, but nevertheless appreciating what was set before them. One woman, not at all fashionably dressed, wore an exquisitely embroidered stomacher in blues and purples.

The songs were varied by some scenes from the little *théâtre de l'ombre,* in which cardboard figures throw a shadow against a background thrown from a magic lantern. Then, after more songs, came the piece of the evening, for *théâtre de l'ombre, pièce en dix tableaux,* entitled *La Marche à l'Etoile.* The lights were turned down, and the *auteur-compositeur,* looking like an intelligent carpenter, came forward to sing the lyric accompaniment to his shadow-drama. The play proved to be a rendering of the story of the Cross, and, as rendered, it was remarkably effective, even moving; certainly the theme was treated with singular poetic breadth. I could not judge either the words or the music, but there could not be a doubt that the intelligent carpenter was some sort of an artist. . . . After this, we left, agreed that this was the most artistic show that we had encountered in Paris. We wondered how the affair was based as regards finance. At most the room held £5, and very little drink was sold, and that at quite a cheap rate. The *chansonniers* could not possibly have been adequately paid, and moreover they had not the look of professional performers; yet they surely would not sing regularly night after night *con amore.*

As we went home past the Moulin Rouge and met crowds of carriages going towards it, each told the other that he had no desire to go there, and each lied. However, we did not call at the Moulin Rouge, but only for cognac at a café in the Boulevard des Italiens.

Sunday, October 31st.

I left Paris. None of my deepest impressions about it seems to have been set down at all.

Saturday, November 13th.

A fortnight of industry. Hence nothing noted. Lately I have been depressed by apprehensions as to the future—the future of the paper, and of my scheme for renting a house at Fulham. I have imagined all possible misfortunes and calamities.

Thursday, November 18th.

Dr. Farrar once told me that my heart and lungs were absolutely perfect, but that my stomach would always be a trouble to me. On Monday morning I ate, irregularly, an apple. Only this evening did I recover from the headache and general derangement caused by that apple.

Monday, November 22nd.

At the Grieg concert, St. James's Hall. A crowded house, mainly filled with hordes of those idle, well-dressed, supercilious, unintelligent women who inhabit the West End and the more expensive suburbs; their hats, though it is autumn, made a garden.

Grieg came on in a short jacket of black velvet which served to decrease still further his short stature. He has a large head with white hair and a bald patch, and the shrewd wrinkled face of a thinker. A restless man, weary and yet the victim of an incurable vivacity. The concussion of his hands on the keys jerked back his head at every loud chord. Between the movements of a sonata he bowed almost imperceptibly and wiped his face every time with the same mechanical movement. He looked like one who has exhausted the joys of fame and of being adored.

In the orchestra, full of hero-worshippers, I noticed particularly two girls, friends, who must have stood hours at the door to gain their unique position in the first row. One smiled ecstatically and showed her teeth (I think she was American) throughout the concert. The other had a fixed and mournful face. She never stirred and seldom spoke; she did not join in the applause, which was frantic in those seats. Her thin lips were set, and her dark eyes set. She was the Serious Student, never happy, never even passably content, always reaching for the unattainable; without doubt she had little talent, but an immense purpose and energy. I fancied I could see her in her daily existence, secretive, self-contained, and occasionally, only occasionally, opening the gates of her soul to some companion in a sudden abandonment.

Round about me a group of newspaper critics exchanged the childish babble of daily journalism.

As I went out, I thought that in another hour or so a thousand pianos in a thousand suburban homes would echo to the chords of that Grieg sonata and suite.

Thursday, November 25th.

Last night, as I sat alone in the house, reviewing, there was a strange knock. I went to the door, and saw old Mr. Boulton [1] in the fog; a hansom was just driving away. He came in, and sat down in my easy chair: a tall, slightly bent figure, with a creased benevolent large face, and the whitest, silkiest hair and long beard: the most venerable and dignified person that has ever sat in this room of mine. I felt proud of the slight connection between us. He began to talk to me about the technique of writing, making naïve, original observations—the thoughts of a gifted child; you could see the strong working of the mind that by means of machinery has revolutionized an entire craft. "I don't know anything about writing," he said, "but give me a bit of machinery, and I could go to bed with it."

I told him I had just bought a folio Bible printed at Burslem by John Tregortha, and asked if he would like to see it. "Ay," he said, "I should. It's a book I'm rather partial to." So he got it over his knees, and putting his spectacles on, spelt out the interminable title page. I directed him to the family register which had been kept according to custom between the Old and the New Testaments. When he came to the date 1786 he said, "My father was alive then," and at 1826, "I was born just a year before that." Afterwards he examined with the same minuteness my Tregortha Hymn Book and Herbal.

At a quarter to ten he must go. He said he always went to bed between 10.30 and 10.45, and answered 20 or 30 letters before breakfast. I asked him how he proposed to get to Bloomsbury. "Oh," he said,

---

[1] The father of Tertia Bennett's fiancé who had been drowned.

"I shall go up this street, turn to the right, and pick up what I can—cab or bus." I had a mind to set him on his way, but he seemed so alert, so equipped, with his 71 years and his magnificent white hair and his tall stooping figure, that to offer to do so would have been an insult.

Afterwards, I wondered to myself if he had taken the trouble to sum me up quickly. I felt always with him that he spoke about the hundredth part of what he thought, and I have noticed that he never contradicts.

A lone and wonderful genius, if ever there was one, existing in the world of his own brain, and passing over the earth as if in a dream. Yet shrewd in earthly things and never to be fooled. . . . The force of his character radiates from him a certain fine influence sensible enough to those delicate enough to see it. . . . I regarded his visit as an event in my life, though he had not come to see me but Tertia, and was disappointed at missing her.

Saturday, November 27th.

Indirectly I heard news of Simeon Solomon through a picture dealer in Regent Street, via Marriott. Simeon Solomon was once one of the lights of the Pre-Raphaelite School, the friend of Rossetti and of Burne-Jones, who both had sincere admiration for his work.[1] The dealer said that he was now in a lunatic asylum. "At one time," he said, "I gave him £2 a week and took his sketches. The money was paid daily, for he was always penniless." Marriott asked where Solomon lived in those days. "He didn't live anywhere," the dealer said; "he had no home. If he could afford it, he slept at a common lodging-house; if not, on the Embankment."

Marriott said that Solomon had really been mad for years, and that many years ago, it was stated that he was reduced to doing sketches for pots of beer.

Sunday, November 28th.

Talking about things uncanny, Webster said that the weirdest thing of all was the vibrating cry of the snipe on the moors at night—a cry

---

[1] Solomon's best work was done between 1858 and 1872, when he ceased to exhibit. He died in 1905.

which you hear, faint and wavering, in the distance, and which the next second has shot past your ears in the darkness. This bird is also called the bog-bleater; Webster said that its cry had been termed "the wail of a lost soul," and that the name was justified. There is nothing more horribly scaring, and the awfulness of it cannot be conceived by those who have not heard it. He described it effectively as "the *last cry on earth*," and related how, as a child, he had been lost all night on the Westmoreland moors; his terror of the invisible snipes shooting across the waste with their awful cries; and his terror of stepping into a bog.

Then he told me of his sole experience of ghosts. On a hill near Milnthorpe is a ruined cottage, said to be haunted. A man and his wife had lived there, and one night the man being called away gave a gun into his wife's hands for her protection, and told her to shoot anything that appeared. Before he had proceeded far, he recollected that he had left something behind him, and returning to his cottage was shot by his wife. Hence the ghost.

It seems that Webster was walking late in a dark lane near the ruin— a lane with a dreadful reputation for spirits—when he saw a sombre figure in front of him. It advanced to within a few paces of him, and then grew large and wide, till it towered above him. Then it collapsed and Webster was standing in the middle of it. At last it edged away from him, face upwards, with a curious backward motion on hands and feet. As soon as it had moved Webster turned and ran two miles to the nearest humanity. . . . He was a child, and thinks now the appearance was merely a subjective hallucination, but at the time nothing could have been more real to him.

Webster related these stories with extraordinary graphic effectiveness. As he spoke of the terrors of the bog-bleater and his night on the moor, I had one of those periodical glimpses which are vouchsafed to me occasionally, of the vast crowd of wonderful sensations and experiences that a dweller in towns, like myself, is debarred from. . . . A night on the moors, alone, with the snipe winging and crying about one. . . . The townsman can scarcely imagine it!

Monday, November 29th.

Byways of literature! To Barnum and Bailey's circus, which has just arrived in London from America, is attached a professional descriptive writer—"Tody Hamilton, Barnum's cyclone press-agent and descriptive epigrammatist. America's representative word-smith! A wild, whirling tornado of breathless adjective! ! An inexhaustible mine of glittering epithet! ! !" The Goncourts would have been interested in Tody Hamilton.

Wednesday, December 1st.

Fitzroy Gardner told me what he knew about the cult of Lesbianism in Europe and America *apropos* of a veiled statement in the *Pelican* concerning an actress and a marchioness. He said that just at present one theatrical company talked of nothing else but the doings of the actor-manager's wife, the marchioness (mentioned in the *Pelican*), and a young and beautiful girl who had recently joined the company. Also that Charles Wyndham had had great difficulty in saving from the Lesbians a young girl in his own company, and had only succeeded by one night standing sentry over the stage door, and carrying off the girl by force in a cab to sup with himself and his wife. The grand organizer of Lesbianism throughout the world, said Gardner, in his most synthetic poetic manner, is ——.

He averred that within his own knowledge, Lesbians from Paris, Berlin, Vienna, New York, etc., had secret appointments and ways of meeting. To finish with this sort of thing, he told me a tale, also within his own knowledge, of an actress and a poodle, which could only be written down in a foreign tongue.

It appears that Lesbianism is not a criminal offence in any country, but that efforts are being made in America to make it so.

Wednesday, December 15th.

I was talking to a woman who for a number of years has been a working journalist, attached to the staff of a reputable ladies' paper, and producing an average of 4 or 5 or 6,000 words per week. She said to me:

"Tell me, Mr. Bennett, what is the way to learn to write properly? I am absolutely ignorant of the subject."

Characteristic of the woman journalist of today, whom I have lashed with scorpions in my just-finished book on journalism! [1]

---

[1] *Journalism for Women.*

Thursday, December 16th.

At my dentist's, a strangely Bohemian cockney, who called me "mate" at the second interview, and referred intimately to the missus and the kids. Nevertheless a good dentist. In his own jargon he said, "I have put in two uppers and a lower today." He told me also of a curious domestic custom: "My missus," he said, "has extraction money and tooth-powder money for 'er perks."

Friday, December 17th.

I had imagined that leader-writers on the morning dailies received munificent salaries. But at lunch today, discussing with Lowry the murder of Terris,[1] on which the previous evening he had written a column leader in 70 minutes, I learnt otherwise. Lowry is on the *Morning Post,* and he is paid by the piece, receiving 2 guineas for a column, 1 guinea for half a column, and half a guinea for a quarter column.

Sunday, December 19th.

A story told to me today reminded me of a conference of my aunt's, made some years ago, concerning my maternal grandfather. It was given in the horrified tones of a daughter whose Puritan susceptibilities had been lacerated. My grandfather, it appears, at the age of 70 and odd, and after having been a long time a widower, began to pursue servant girls upon the outskirts of Burslem; and not all the shocked remonstrances of his daughters could bring him back to the narrow path. He never succeeded in enchanting any of these girls, but the intention was, I was told, only too obvious. It is curious that at such a time of life, the long-repressed instincts of a man who had lived as a strict Wesleyan Methodist should at last have become unmanageable. Shortly after the episodes of the servant girls he married a buxom woman 40 years his junior, a plump-faced pleasant woman who had the greatest difficulty not to call me *"Mr.* Arnold."

Tuesday, December 21st.

The constant unsleeping watchfulness for verbal mistakes and slips

---

[1] William Terris, the actor, was fatally stabbed by a discharged "super" as he was entering the stage-door of the Adelphi Theatre, December 16, 1897.

and clumsiness in composition, necessitated by my post as editor of women's journalism, has sharpened and exasperated my susceptibilities to such a point that only by a great effort can I read anything now without noting such slips, however trifling. In spite of myself, my mind registers them as they occur, in no matter what writer's work. Such preposterous attention to the superficialities of style seriously interferes with the enjoyment of literature. There is scarcely an author—unless it be Henry James—whom I find flawless, and whom, therefore, I can read in perfect comfort.

Tuesday, January 11th.

During the period of unproductiveness which has followed the completion of my book on journalism for women, I have been thinking about a history of the English novel in the nineteenth century. I believe in the course of a few years I could write such a history as would cast a new light on English fiction considered strictly from the craftsman's standpoint. As regards fiction, it seems to me that only within the last few years have we absorbed from France that passion for the artistic shapely presentation of truth, and that feeling for words as words, which animated Flaubert, the Goncourts, and Maupassant, and which is so exactly described and defined in Maupassant's introduction to the collected works of Flaubert. None of the (so-called) great masters of English nineteenth-century fiction had (if I am right) a deep artistic interest in form and treatment; they were absorbed in "subject"—just as the "anecdote" painters of the Royal Academy are absorbed in subject, and in my view they are open to the same reproach as these. Certainly they had not the feeling for words to any large degree, though one sees traces of it sometimes in the Brontës—never in George Eliot, or Jane Austen, or Dickens, or even Thackeray or Scott.

Yet that this feeling for words existed independently in England is proved by the prose of Charles Lamb and John Ruskin. The novelists cared little for form, the *science* of construction—*Composition*. They had not artistic taste; they lacked this just as Millais lacked it. Millais may have been a great painter; these novelists may have been great writers, but neither (to use Maupassant's distinction) was a great artist in the sense in which I understand the word. An artist must be interested

71

primarily in presentment, not in the thing presented. He must have a passion for technique, a deep love for form. . . . And so on.

Wednesday, January 12th.

In accordance with an urgent message from Lane, I called this morning to see him about my second book, *Journalism for Women: a Practical Guide.* He was unwell and in bed, and the interview passed in his bedroom. He beamed on me, made attentive inquiries about my affairs, and sent for cigarettes. Then he showed me the glowing report made by Miss Evelyn Sharpe upon my book, and said that he wanted to publish it at once—within 3 weeks. He offered me a 10 per cent. royalty; I suggested 15 per cent., and he agreed at once. Title, shape, type, paper, and price were settled there and then and Chapman received instructions to draw the contracts. In another 5 minutes the contracts were signed and exchanged, and the manuscript was made up to go to the printers that morning—within the hour.

How different the reception of this book from the frigid welcome given to *A Man from the North!* The latter, a serious and laborious work, has waited, after acceptance, nearly two years for publication. *Journalism for Women,* thrown off in about 8 weeks, is to be printed and published in less than a month.

Phillpotts today told me that my paragraph criticism of his *Lying Prophets* had given him more pleasure than any other criticism upon the book; and was, in fact, the best he had had. He urged me to write exhaustive critical articles upon some of the classics. I said I wanted to deal thoroughly with Turgenev, and he approved.

Thursday, January 13th.

Lever Tillotson, of Tillotson and Sons, the literary agents, called to offer me some serials for *Woman.* He gave me some interesting details as to current "prices per thousand." Thomas Hardy is being outstripped by some of the younger men. He stands now only equal with H. G. Wells, at 12 guineas per thousand, which is also the price of the blood-and-thunder William Le Queux.[1] Stanley Weyman,[2] because of his large following in America, can only be bought at 16 to 18 guineas per thou-

---

[1] Author of many novels dealing with espionage and secret service.
[2] Author of *Under the Red Robe* and other romances dealing with French history.

sand. Kipling stands solitary and terrible, at £50 per thousand, £200 being his minimum for his shortest short story. What surprised me most was a statement that W. W. Jacobs (quite a new man, who has published only two small books of a quietly humorous nature) recently refused an offer of £500 for six short stories.

Wednesday, January 19th.

At lunch I met Robert Barr the novelist, and his brother James Barr,[1] of the *Pall Mall Gazette*. Robert Barr is a short sturdy greyish Yankee who has conquered Yankee prejudices but not the Yankee accent. His freckled bluff features and his short beard indicate a man who has seen most things and has learnt to tolerate most things; plenty of rough, very dry wit; an honest and plain-spoken man. I do not suppose that Barr has much, if any at all, feeling for literature, but he is an admirable specimen of the man of talent who makes of letters an honest trade; has no self-complacences, and does not pose. A man one could soon like very much indeed!

Sunday, January 23rd.

After an interval of about 9 months I sit down again to the composition of serious fiction; and though I make slow progress, finding myself out of practice, I experience a satisfaction deeper than I can get from any other sort of labour.

At Lowry and Eckhardt's studio for tea. As I went down their street I perceived Lowry and a rather pretty girl buying muffins from a muffin man. It was dusk and a mist rising. Several men in the studio, which is large, with a good collection of antique furniture, Japanese prints, and French posters; the posters are even visible in the obscurity of the ceiling. Eckhardt, with all the appearance of a simple good-natured unaffected schoolboy, was at work in his shirt-sleeves on a black and white sketch. The girl presently re-appeared and began to prepare afternoon tea. Everyone called her Marie. A girl about 25, dressed in black; red-gold hair, large expressive eyes; and a certain intense ecstatic expression which was matched by the low voice; obviously a favourite model of Eckhardt's.

---

[1] Both were novelists and editors. They were Canadians, living in England. Robert Barr was co-editor of the *Idler* with Jerome K. Jerome.

After tea, Lowry being laid flat on the floor in front of the stove, she made the grave moody leader-writer of the *Morning Post* go through his tricks of catching and throwing a cushion with his feet.

Sunday, January 30th.

Marriott said that to enjoy the *earth* there was nothing like following a plough at early morning. The smell of the newly turned soil was fresh, fragrant, and piquant beyond imagination.

Tuesday, February 1st.

The Silver Fox, by Martin Ross and E. Œ. Somerville, is, within its limit, a perfect novel. The style exhibits a meticulous care not surpassed by that of Henry James. It actually repays a technical analysis. It is as carefully worded as good verse. There is a reason for every comma, and the place of every preposition and conjunction. All prose which pretends to be artistic should be as meticulous as this. Yet in fact the quality is almost unknown. Except in Henry James and Pater, I know of no modern prose of which it can be said that the choice and position of *every* word and stop has been the subject of separate consideration.

Tuesday, February 15th.

The preoccupation of removing to a new house (9 Fulham Park Gardens) is now almost over and after 3 days of incessant manual work, arranging books, clothes, furniture, and pictures. A householder for the first time, I find myself wandering without aim through the house, staring at finished rooms, and especially at the terra cotta effects of my new study, with a vague satisfaction. But stronger, more insistent than this satisfaction, is the feeling of graver and complicated responsibilities, and a sort of anxiety for the future.

And I wonder, at the age of 30, whether the great game is worth the candle. I return with regretful fancy to the time when, with the lighter cares and the highest hopes that ignorance could induce, I lived in Raphael Street, and in Cowley Street, on about 15s. a week.

Tonight I have set to work on a long criticism of George Moore.

Wednesday, February 16th.

As I opened the front door this morning to leave for the office, the postman put a parcel in my hand. It was from John Lane, and it contained the first copy of my first book.[1] I untied it hastily, and after glancing at the cover, gave it to Tertia to read. Tonight I looked through the tale, picking out my favourite bits. The style seemed better than I had hoped for.

Sunday, February 20th.

Mrs. Clozier, charwoman, who seeks a separation from her husband, is a rather shrivelled creature. She said to Mrs. Marriott: "When I first came to London, I had fat red cheeks, and my bosoms"—making a large round movement with her hands—"stuck out like that. I tell ye I was a fine woman in those days."

The contingency of a war with France [2] has worried me yesterday and today, just as if it were a personal matter. I have wakened up to puzzle out all its possible unpleasantness and bother and material loss.

Wednesday, February 23rd.

Sitting with me in his dark little office at *Black and White* after lunch, Eden Phillpotts, heavily wrapped up and pale after a long attack of influenza, told me something of his life. After leaving school at 17, he came to London and entered an insurance office. His first idea was to be an actor. He studied elocution etc. at the School of Dramatic Art, and after 2 years found he was unfitted entirely for acting. Then, having already written a little, he turned to literature with seriousness. For 8 years he wrote from 6 to 9 in the evening. At the end of that time he could earn £400 a year by his pen. He left the insurance office, married, and lived by his pen comfortably till *Black and White* offered him, through his agent, the post of assistant editor. As this meant an assured revenue, he accepted it. He works 3 days a week, machine-writing, free from responsibility, and the rest of his time he gives to novels and short stories.

Today is published my first book, *A Man from the North*. I have seen it mentioned in several papers among "books received." Beyond that, I have scarcely thought of it. The fact has not at the moment interested

---

[1] *A Man from the North.*
[2] Over Far Eastern difficulties.

me. But during the last few days I have been several times naïvely surprised that some of my friends are not more awake and lively to the fact than they seem to be.

Sunday, February 27th.

My housewarming. When supper is nearly over, and at the third bottle of champagne, Marriott gets up and begins a speech by pulling out of his sleeve a huge pantomime cuff on which are written the notes of his oration. For 25 minutes he keeps us wildly laughing, and winds up with a series of comic couplets setting forth my vices and virtues. I laughed all through, but after it was over I felt horribly self-conscious, and opened a bottle with an air of awful gravity.

Tuesday, March 1st.

A lady who wished to write a palmistry column for *Woman* read my hands. She was very accurate in describing my character, and told me several facts about my past. She said that I should live long, make money, and enjoy much domestic happiness; that Friday was a lucky day for me; that I should marry "soon," but not till after some difficulty as regards the lady had been smoothed over; that I should have a prescience of coming disaster or good fortune. Also—most remarkable—that I had not long since suffered a shock through some female relative. She seemed a clever and capable woman, and it was difficult for me not to believe that her predictions had not some reasonable foundation. She gave me some particulars, marvellous enough, about the healing of nervous diseases by will-power, in which subject she is interested, and invited me to investigate one case.

Tea at an A.B.C. shop in Westminster, where the waitresses offer an inexhaustible field for the study of character. They are so naïve, unveiling the secrets of their natures in every trifling action.

Wednesday, March 2nd.

Dunn [1] brought to lunch Charles Robinson, who has designed the cover of *Journalism for Women*: a very young unkempt pale nervous

---

[1] James N. Dunn was editor of *Black and White* from 1895 to 1897 and of the *Morning Post* 1897–1905.

man, with a poor chin, and sensuous, tremulous eyes. One could see
that not long since he had been more nervous than he is today. Contact
with the world was making him less like a startled faun. He told me
that his design for my book had been so much liked that it had resulted
in orders for 20 other covers.

Phillpotts was extremely enthusiastic about the merits of *A Man from
the North*. It seemed strange and unreal to be treated by this finely
serious novelist as an artist of the same calibre with himself.

Wednesday, March 9th.

At lunch Dunn and Bayly suddenly began to talk about the chances
of war. I was astonished at their eagerness for it, and the certainty with
which they predicted where and between whom it would occur. They
said England would engage France and Russia, while Germany and
U.S.A. would remain absolutely neutral. We might have the help of
Japan, possibly also of Italy. The war would be wholly naval, and would
occur round our own coasts. It would be over in ten days. Every month
of delay, they said, lessened our chances. We ought to have fought the
U.S.A. a year or two ago, when they wanted a war. We should have
thrashed them easily, and that would have cleared the air of the war
cloud.

Saturday, March 12th.

On my way to seeing Mrs. L., I called at a bread-shop in Holborn. To
judge from the exterior one could desire no place of refreshment more
fastidiously neat and dainty. But when I was inside I found the shop
and the room at the back occupied by women and girls in various conditions of *déshabillé*. The place was being cleaned, and the hour being
only 11 A.M. customers were clearly not expected. The girls all looked up
surprised, and with a show of indifference I picked my way amongst
kneeling figures into the inner room. When I had sat down, I heard a
rummaging noise under the table, and presently a fat young girl appeared therefrom. She hurried away laughing, but came back shortly
and produced from under the table a tin bowl of dirty water which she
carried away, with a giggle. I ordered a glass of milk and a sandwich,
and then waited. A girl, tall, thin, and vacuous, ran upstairs and came

down soon afterwards, pinning on an apron at the back. She brought me my food. I ate it, while looking at a dirty newspaper placed to protect the newly washed floor, and at the crimson petticoat showing through the placket-hole of a girl who was washing the floor behind the counter. I could feel about me the atmosphere of femininity. The dirt and untidiness spoilt the taste of my food, and I thought, "This is a bad omen for the result of my interview with Mrs. L."

The room into which I was shown in Gower Street was, I think the ugliest, the most *banal,* I have seen. From the twisted columns of the furniture to the green rep of the upholstering, everything expressed Bloomsbury in its highest power. This was a boarding-house. My hopes sank, and they were not raised by the appearance of Mrs. L., who combines the profession of a landlady with that of a "mental healer." She looks the typical landlady, shabbily dressed, middle-aged, and with that hardened, permanently soured expression of eyes and lips which all landladies seem to acquire. She fitted with and completed the room.

She asked me about my stammering and my health generally, talking in a quiet, firm, authoritative voice. I noticed the fatigue of her drooping eyelids and the terrific firmness of her thin lips. She told me how she had been cured of nervousness by Dr. Patterson of America, and gave a number of instances of his success and her own in "mentally treating" nervous and physical disorders. Some of them were so incredible that I asked myself what I, notorious as a sane level-headed man, was doing in that galley. However, as Mrs. L. talked I was rather impressed by her sincerity, her strong quietude, and her sagacity. I asked what the patient had to do. "Nothing," she said. I explained my attitude towards "mental healing"—that I neither believed nor disbelieved in it, that certainly I could not promise her the assistance of my "faith." She said sympathy on the part of the patient always helped, but was by no means necessary, and she went on to relate several cases where she had cured people who had absolutely declined to believe in her powers.

"Can you cure me of my stammering?"

"I am quite sure I can," she answered with quiet assurance, "but it will take some time. This is a case of a lifelong habit, not of a passing ailment."

"Shall you want to see me often?"

"I shall not want to see you at all; but if you feel that you want to see me, of course you can do so. I shall look after your general health too. If you have a bad headache, or a liver attack, send me a word and I will help you."

I nodded acquiescence, but I was nearly laughing loud, and telling her that I preferred to dispense with these mysterious services. As I was arranging terms with her I marvelled that I should be assisting at such an interview. And yet—supposing there were after all something in it! I was not without hope. She had distinctly impressed me, especially by odd phrases here and there which seemed to indicate a certain depth of character in her. I went away smiling—half believing that the whole business was a clever fraud, and half expecting some happy result.

Tonight I sent her a cheque. I wondered, as I wrote it out, whether 12 months hence I should be wanting to burn these pages which recorded my credulity, or whether with all the enthusiasm of my nature I should be spreading abroad the report of Mrs. L.'s powers.

Friday, March 25th.

During the past fortnight I have been overworked at the office, and very busy at home with a long article on George Moore. And so several impressions have been lost.

Monday, April 18th.

What with a long article of 8,000 on George Moore, a short story for *Black and White,* the Easter holidays, and a serious fire at our printers' resulting in the loss of all "copy," proofs, and blocks, I have been too much occupied to attend to this book for some weeks past.

Today as I walked among all the nursemaids and mothers and babies and loungers by the riverside in Bishop's Park—it was a beautiful sunny afternoon—I was specially struck by the immense quantity of fine material which the novelist must ignore or only peep at, in order to develop and utilize effectively his own particular chosen little titbit.

I had intended to take up my novel *Anna Tellwright* again, but left it for a critical article on *Our Illiterate Novelists,* which needed less brain-energy.

Sunday, April 24th.

Tonight Sharpe played and sang through *Das Rheingold*. Afterwards he gave us some reminiscences of Wagner which he had recently had from Wagner's friend Dannreuther.

Wagner told Dannreuther that before he had begun to write *Tristan* he had seen the complete score, as it were, in a vision before him. The writing cost him no trouble.

One of Wagner's greatest faculties was his reading of Shakespeare, which Dannreuther said was better than any acting of Shakespeare that he had ever seen. In this connection Dannreuther referred to Wagner's habit during rehearsals of running on to the stage and showing the singers how to act their parts. He said that Wagner's acting was transcendently fine.

As to Wagner's piano-playing, it was "damned bad."

Friday, May 6th.

Leonard Goddard, who is manager of a firm of insurance brokers at Lloyds, told me that the rate against there being war between England and France within 6 months was 5 guineas per cent. He also said that tradesmen regularly insured the life of the Queen at 10 guineas per cent. for the season.

Tuesday, May 10th.

Phillpotts, who has just finished a novel, *Children of the Mist*, told me that his publisher was moaning about the length of it—180,000 words. He said that he had cut a lot out of the typewritten copy, and should probably cut more from the slip proofs. He appeared to see nothing extraordinary in this. To me it was very extraordinary. Having finished a novel I could not cut it down, because I should have satisfied myself that it contained nothing inessential. Phillpotts admitted that he was uncertain whether some parts of the book were not redundant. If I cut out I should be obliged to rewrite. The notion that anything can be taken from a finished work of art without leaving a gap seems to me monstrous.

Some details of Kitchener the Sirdar, from René Bull, war artist of *Black and White*, just returned from the Soudan. Kitchener is deeply disliked both by generals and his army. Gatacre will not speak to him.

His severity is terrible, and for days at a time during the recent campaign he spoke to no one. Yet he always saw well after himself; none of the Spartan soldier about him.

Sunday, May 15th.

Sharpe played the last two acts of *Siegfried*.

In another fortnight, he will have played and sung through the whole of the *Ring*.

It occurred to me that the reason of Nietzsche's defection from Wagner was that he expected a different kind of beauty in the *Ring* from what he found there. Only that. The philosophic account of the defection could have amounted to nothing but that. The worst of critics is that they will not allow artists to choose their own kind of beauty. Those critics are excessively rare who have learnt that the kind of beauty is immaterial, and who have had the wit and restraint not to pledge themselves to any particular kind. Critics who *have* so pledged themselves, and who are excellent critics of their chosen kind of beauty, are common enough.

Wednesday, June 8th.

Apropos of the marriage of G. B. Shaw and Miss Payne-Townshend, Nolan [1] told me that every few years some prominent member of the Fabian Society contrived to marry an heiress whose wealth and energies were subsequently devoted wholly to the cause. Thus Sidney Webb married Beatrice Potter; B. F. Costelloe married Miss Pearsall Smith; and J. R[amsay]. MacDonald married Miss M. E. Gladstone. Nolan assured me as a fact that G. B. Shaw some months ago discussed with certain other members of the Fabian Society as to whose "duty" it was to marry the heiress.

Thursday, June 9th.

While reading George Moore's new novel, *Evelyn Innes*, I was struck by the magnificence of the career of a prima donna as a theme for fiction. In Moore's book the vocal side of the prima donna, her triumphs etc., is scarcely more than incidental. I would make it central. There is noth-

---

[1] J. J. Nolan, journalist and editor, at that time assistant editor of *Hearth and Home*, subsequently editor of *Woman*.

ing more marvellous, more all-compelling, more inscrutable in the world than a great soprano voice. And the emotions of the prima donna in the hour when she dominates her audience must be unique. Probably I shall never be able to write such a novel—from lack of material. But if I could wander about Covent Garden stage during a season, and could have a few afternoon teas with a prima donna, I would attempt the book. The old age of the prima donna and her death might make a superbly cruel contrast to the rest of the story—astringent, chilling, unbearably hopeless, and bitter with reminiscence.

Friday, June 24th.

When Lewis Hind[1] gave me George Moore's *Evelyn Innes* to review for the *Academy* I was careful to explain to him my attitude of admiration towards George Moore, and he told me to write exactly what I thought, without considering him. He explicitly gave me *carte blanche*. For once, therefore, I *expressed myself* as regards fiction in general and George Moore in particular. I sent in the article 11 days ago. Today Hind writes me that "while fully acknowledging the excellence" of the article he will not use it, though he will pay for it! The timidity of people in the matter of George Moore's work is almost incredible. My article was indeed an excellent one, and I was intensely annoyed that it should be lost to the public. For the sake of English fiction such articles are sadly needed.

Talking to Webster about sex in fiction tonight, I convinced him and myself that no serious attempt had yet been made by a man to present essential femininity; also that the chasm between male and female was infinitely wider and deeper than we commonly realized—in fact an absolutely unpracticable chasm.

A woman might draw, and probably has drawn, woman with justice and accuracy for her own sex. But a woman's portrait of a woman is not of much use to a man. Either it is meaningless to him—a hieroglyphic— or it tells him only things which he knew. A woman is too close to woman to observe her with aloofness and yet with perfect insight—as we should do if we had the insight. Observation can only be conducted from the outside. A woman cannot possibly be aware of the things in

---

[1] C. Lewis Hind (1862–1927) was editor of the *Academy,* 1896–1903. He lived in New York for a number of years after the War.

herself which puzzle us; and our explanations of our difficulties would simply worry her. The two sexes must for ever remain distant, antagonistic, and mutually inexplicable.

Monday, September 12th.

It is so long since I wrote anything here that I have forgotten the circumstances under which I abandoned this book for a while. But no doubt the habit of writing in it—always irksome to some extent—was interfered with by some temporary pressure of work, and then the summer and the heat and the holiday feeling conspired against its resumption.

In the meantime, partly owing to the influence of Phillpotts, I have decided very seriously to take up fiction for a livelihood. A certain chronic poverty had forced upon me the fact that I was giving no attention to money-making, beyond my editorship, and so the resolution came about. Till the end of 1899 I propose to give myself absolutely to writing the sort of fiction that sells itself. My serious novel *Anna Tellwright,* with which I had made some progress, is put aside indefinitely— or rather until I have seen what I can do. To write popular fiction is offensive to me, but it is far more agreeable than being tied daily to an office and editing a lady's paper; and perhaps it is less ignoble, and less of a strain on the conscience. To edit a lady's paper, even a relatively advanced one, is to foster conventionality and hinder progress regularly once a week. Moreover I think that fiction will pay better, and in order to be happy I must have a fair supply of money.

Also I have decided very seriously to aim at living in the country, to the entire abandonment of London. A year ago I could not have contemplated the idea of leaving London, but I have developed since then.

Saturday, September 17th.

Young, Kennerley, and I rode from Farnham to Witley to inspect the house which Young and I are to rent for the next 3 years. About 4 centuries old, this house for the last hundred years had been called The Fowl House, until it was named by its present occupants Godspeace. These occupants are four: C. E. Dawson, a young artist; Morris, a journalist who writes on the connection between Whitman and architecture; Gertrude Dix, the novelist, and Esther Wood, a writer on art. I saw all but Gertrude Dix. They are vegetarians and teetotallers—and they wear sandals. They have an air of living the higher life. All of us were pleased with Esther Wood, but I said she was too earnest, and Sturt supported me. He said she yearned. Kennerley—this was at supper at Young's afterwards—was angry, and said she didn't yearn. I made no secret of my contempt for cranks, and I called these people cranks. I admitted it was Philistinic and I gloried in being a Philistine so far. I was glad that both the Sturts had the same feeling. Kennerley, of course, with his immensely wide sympathies, cursed us heartily for narrow-minded stupids. Nevertheless, preserve me from all peculiar people, high self-conscious people, vainly *earnest* people..

Sunday, September 18th.

Last night I dreamt that I wore sandals and was ashamed. Since seeing the house at Witley I have been quite depressed in anticipation of the time which must elapse before I can leave London permanently for the country. It is as though the next year or two in London will be unbearable.

Saturday, October 22nd.

This is my idea of fame:

At an entertainment on board H.M.S. *Majestic,* Rudyard Kipling, one of the guests, read *Soldier and Sailor Too,* and was encored. He then read *The Flag of England.* At the conclusion a body of subalterns swept him off the stage and chaired him round the quarterdeck, while "For he's a jolly good fellow" was played by the massed bands of the Fleet and sung by 200 officers assembled.

Tuesday, November 8th.

Last Wednesday I was arguing with Phillpotts, that it would be simpler and more lucrative for him to do serials than short stories, as hitherto. Before we parted he decided to do one by way of experiment. Today I asked him, "Well, what about that serial?"

"I've written 12,000 words of it," he said; "started on Friday, and have done 3,000 words a day. It's disgustingly easy. I've no trouble with plots, you know, and the rest is mere writing." He then explained the plot for me, and it was decidedly a proper "popular" plot.

"And what is the *dénouement?*" I asked.

"Haven't the least idea. But there's a brass ornament with mysterious signs on it that I expect will do great things towards the end."

Later he said, "I shall finish it in a month—70,000 words. And if anyone would make it worth my while, I wouldn't mind betting that I could do twelve such serials in a year—easily."

Telling me about his early life, he mentioned that though he was 36, his mother was only 53. She married an Indian Army officer at 16, and went out with him on a transport. Eden was born exactly ten months after the marriage. She was left a widow at 21, with three children.

1899

Sunday, January 1st.

During the last quarter of 1898 I produced about twice as much work as in any previous similar period. I wrote two-thirds of a serial story, 4 or 5 short stories, a lot of reviews for the *Academy,* and all my usual stuff for *Woman* and *Hearth and Home.*

Mrs. Kennerley was here today to have tea with Ma. She said, speaking of the diseases of children: "We never used to *think* of having the doctor for measles. I had all my children down at once. We kept them in the sitting-room during the day, and carried them upstairs at night. They went on quite well. It is different now. People seem to be more afraid, but we never used to *think* of the doctor in those days."

"Those days" would be 15 or 16 years ago.

Monday, January 2nd.

If I gained nothing else last year, I gained facility. In the writing of sensational fiction I made great strides during the last few months, and with ordinary luck I could now turn out a complete instalment (about 4,000 words) after 3 o'clock in an afternoon. For critical work too, I have become much faster and more adroit.

Tannhäuser, the opening night of the reconstructed Carl Rosa Opera Company at the Lyceum. Jacobi,[1] late of the Alhambra. I was more impressed by the music than ever before, and more disgusted by the performance itself. A rough orchestra, a nervous chorus, nervous principals,

---

[1] Georges Jacobi, conductor and composer. He died in 1906.

and a general atmosphere of provincialism enveloping everything. I was specially amazed by the Venus, as grossly and unvoluptuously fat as Tannhäuser Venuses, by sacred tradition, invariably are. She was as fat as Adini. The whole show depressed me. But it must have reached a very fair level of excellence. The fact is that the Covent Garden orchestra and principals have spoilt us for any opera less good in these respects. Although the season of grand opera at Covent Garden lasts only 10 weeks, it makes other operas impossible during the remainder of the year. Any other operatic enterprise is bound to fail unless it resolves to shine where Covent Garden is dull; say by an intelligently chosen répertoire with good novelties, or by a well-trained chorus, or by fine stage management. Without undue expense, the Carl Rosa might do, say, *The Marriage of Figaro,* as it is done at Munich, and cover themselves with glory.

Tuesday, January 3rd.

At the Burne-Jones Exhibition; I was much impressed by the whole thing, and especially by the superb richness and spirituality of the early *Annunciation* (two panels) and *The Adoration of the Magi,* all 3 pictures being dated 1861. In some ways these surpass, or at least equal, any subsequent work.

The sight of Burne-Jones's aloofness, of his continual preoccupation with the spiritual, to the ignoring of everyday facts, served to complete in me a modification of view which has been proceeding now for a year or two. The day of my enthusiasm for "realism," for "naturalism," has passed. I can perceive that a modern work of fiction dealing with modern life may ignore realism and yet be great. To find beauty, which is always hidden—that is the aim. If beauty is found, then superficial facts are of small importance. But they are of *some* importance. And although I concede that in the past I have attached too high a value to realism, nevertheless I see no reason why it should be dispensed with. My desire is to depict the deeper beauty while abiding by the envelope of facts. At the worst, the facts should not be ignored. They might, for the sake of more clearly disclosing the beauty, suffer a certain *distortion*—I can't think of a better word. Indeed they cannot be ignored in the future. The achievements of the finest French writers, with Turgenev and Tolstoy, have set a standard for all coming masters of fiction.

What the artist has to grasp is that there is no such thing as ugliness in the world. This I believe to be true, but perhaps the saying would sound less difficult in another form: All ugliness has an aspect of beauty. The business of the artist is to find that aspect.

Thursday, January 5th.

You can find a certain wide romance even in the January sales at the draper's shop. My mother bought some very large unbleached linen sheets today for our cottage at Milford. They cost 1s. 11½d. each, and are 3¾ yards in length. She was told that these sheets are woven by Russian peasants by hand. They are sold to the French War Office, used during the annual military manoeuvres, and after the wear of a month or so, are sold by the French Government to English traders. So it comes that I may sleep between linen that has passed through the hands of the most miserable and unhappy people in Europe—Russian peasants and French conscripts.

Friday, January 6th.

Today during breakfast, I happened to collect some ideas for that book on modern fiction which I am to do when I have time. I would call it *Our Novelists*. There would be chapters on "conscious pleasure in technique," which was apparently unknown to the earlier generation; illiteracy among our leading writers; the real position of Dickens, Thackeray, George Eliot, and others whom every one has (ridiculously) agreed are above criticism; Turgenev, and the relation of English to Continental fiction; the courageous exploitation of the author's personality in fiction, with special reference to George Moore; an essay on Eden Phillpotts, the greatest of our younger writers, yet very imperfectly recognized at present; the conjuncture of realism with idealism.

Monday, January 9th.

The "beach" (for it is not a wharf) on the Surrey side of the Thames at Putney Bridge presents one of the most genuinely picturesque sights in London. Moored side by side in rows are a number of barges with their immense brown mainsails furled on the masts. Their rigging, seen as I see it against the panorama of a sunset sky, makes a forest of cordage, above which the little coloured pennants flutter. At all states of the tide the barges are being busily unloaded of their cargoes of yellow bricks and road metal. Shovelfuls of stones and little cubes of bricks pass ceaselessly from the enormous holds into the, by comparison, tiny carts, and as each cart is fitted a tip-horse attaches itself to it, and with cracking of whips the animals dash up the steep incline to the street.

This seems to go on all day and every day. At high tides the water is over the hubs of the wheels and washing against the chests of the motionless horses. . . . It is a scene of rapid and healthy activity, and the blue smoke from the cabins of the sailing barges suggests other activities than those seen from the bridge.

In time no doubt all this building and road material will reach Putney by railway or by steamer; at any rate a wharf will be built and served by a steam crane; and then this singular survival of an old activity will pass away in its turn, and we shall tell young people that we remember it.

Monday, January 16th.

Looking through some short stories in old volumes of a weekly paper today, I was astonished at the old-fashioned air of them. Mediocre work must age very rapidly. These tales appeared in 1893, and they were positively antique.

Tuesday, January 17th.

Roche [1] told me today some stories of James Gordon Bennett of the *New York Herald;* he used to be on the staff of that paper. Most of the points depended on the exact slang used, and this I forget.

Bennett one day had dismissed his financial editor—all the staff were liable to instant dismissal and might leave without notice—and he was sitting in the reporters' room when one of the reporters entered; he had a hooked nose.

"What's your name?" asked Bennett.

"So-and-so."

"You're a Jew, aren't you?"

"Yes, sir."

"What salary d'you get?"

"Fifty dollars a week."

"I'll give you $125. All Jews know about money. Go on to Wall Street and do the finance report."

---

[1] A journalist friend, at that time obituary writer to a daily paper.

Saturday, January 21st.

In the midst of a literary discussion this morning, George Sturt and I began to talk about the curious savage custom, *la couvade*. He said he had known cases in which the husband actually was ill during his wife's pregnancy. One of his acquaintances had said to him, "I'm not feeling well, and I begin to suspect that my wife must be in the family way—I am always queer while she is pregnant."

Tuesday, January 24th.

Last night I finished my sensational novel, *The Curse of Love*,[1] 50,000 words in exactly 3 months, with all my other work. The writing of it has enormously increased my facility, and I believe that now I could do a similar novel in a month. It is, of the kind, good stuff, well written and well contrived, and some of the later chapters are really imagined and, in a way, lyrical. I found the business, after I had got fairly into it, easy enough, and I rather enjoyed it. I could comfortably write 2,500 words in half a day. It has only been written once, and on revision I have scarcely touched the original draft. Now I want to do two short sensational stories—and then to my big novel.

Friday, January 27th.

A few nights ago—we had been to the Empire, Sharpes, Mater, Sep, and I—there was a gale. In the usual midnight altercation at Piccadilly Circus for the inside seats of omnibuses we had suffered defeat; we sat on the inclement top of the vehicle, a disconsolate row of four, cowering behind the waterproof aprons (which were not waterproof), and exchanging fragments of pessimistic philosophy.

We knew we were taking cold; at first we were annoyed, but with increasing numbness came resignation. We grew calm enough to take an interest in the imperturbable driver, who nonchalantly and with perfect technique steered his dogged horses through the tortuous mazes of traffic, never speaking, never stirring, only answering like an automaton to the conductor's bell. Some drivers will gossip, but this one had apparently his own preoccupations. We could see only his hat, some grey hairs, his rotund cape, and his enormous gloved hands, and perhaps we began to wonder what sort of man he was. For mile after mile he drove forward in a Trappist silence till we were verging upon Putney, and the

---

[1] Subsequently called *For Love and Life*. See pp. 93, 116, 175.

rain-washed thoroughfares reflected only the gas lights and the forbidding façades of the houses. Then at last, but without moving his head, he suddenly joined the conversation.

"I've been out in worse," he said. "Yes, we gets used to it. But we gets so that we *has* to live out of doors. If I got a indoor job I should die. I have to go out for a walk afore I can eat my breakfast."

A pause, and then:

"I've driven these roads for eight-and-twenty year, and the only pal I've found is cod liver oil. From September to March I takes it, and I never has rheumatism and I never has colds nor nothing o' that sort. I give it my children ever since they was born, and now I'm blest if they don't cry for it."

He finished; he had imparted his wisdom, delivered his message, and with the fine instinct denied to so many literary artists, he knew when to be silent. We asked him to stop, and he did so without a word. "Good night," we said; but he had done with speech for that evening, and gave us no reply. We alighted. The bus rolled away into the mirror-like vista of the street.

Saturday, January 28th.

The hypnotized audience, crowded tier above tier of the dark theatre, held itself strained and intent in its anxiety not to miss one gyration, one least movement, of the great dancer [1]—that dancer who had enslaved not only New York and St. Petersburg but Paris itself. Swaying incorporeal, as it were within a fluent dazzling envelope of endless drapery, she revealed to them new and more disturbing visions of beauty in the union of colour and motion. She hid herself in a labyrinth of curves which was also a tremor of strange tints, a tantalizing veil, a mist of iridescent light. Gradually her form emerged from the riddle, triumphant, provocative, and for an instant she rested like an incredible living jewel in the deep gloom of the stage. Then she was blotted out, and the defeated eye sought in vain to penetrate the blackness where but now she had been. . . .

It was a marvellous and enchanting performance. Even the glare of the electric clusters and the gross plush of the descending curtain could not rob us all at once of the sense of far-off immaterial things which it

---

[1] Adeline Genée.

had evoked in our hearts. We applauded with fury, with frenzy; we besieged the floor with sticks and heels, and clapped till our arms ached. . . . At length she came before the footlights, and bowed and smiled and kissed her hands. We could see she was a woman of 30 or more, rather short, not beautiful. But what dominion in the face, what assurance of supreme power! It was the face of one surfeited with adoration, cloyed with praise.

While she was humouring us with her fatigued imperial smiles, I happened to look at a glazed door separating the auditorium from the corridor. There, pressed against the glass, was another face, the face of a barmaid, who, drawn from her counter by the rumour of this wonderful novelty, had crept down to get a glimpse of the star's triumph.

Of course I was struck by the obvious contrast between these two creatures. In a moment the barmaid had departed, but the wistfulness of her gaze remained with me as I listened to legends of the dancer— her whims, her diamonds, her extravagances, her tyrannies, her wealth. I could not banish that pale face; I could not withhold from it my sentimental pity.

Later, I went up into the immense gold refectory. Entrenched behind a magnificent counter of carved cedar flanked on either side by mirrors and the neat apparatus of bottles and bonbons, the barmaid stood negligently at ease, her cheek resting in the palm of one small hand as she leaned on the counter. I noticed that she had the feeble prettiness, the voluptuous figure, the tight black bodice inexorably demanded of barmaids. In front of her were 3 rakish youths whom I guessed to be of the fringe of journalism and the stage. They talked low to her as they sipped their liqueurs, frankly admiring, frankly enjoying this brief intimacy. As for her, confident of her charms, she was distantly gracious; she offered a smile with a full sense of its value; she permitted; she endured. These youths were to understand that such adulation was to her an everyday affair.

In the accustomed exercise of assured power her face had lost its wistfulness, it was the satiated face of the dancer over again, and so I ventured quietly to withdraw my sentimental pity.

Thursday, February 2nd.

It is curious how authors arrive at pseudonyms. Phillpotts, having finished the sensational serial which he did partly at my suggestion, desires a pseudonym. A couple of months ago he told me he thought the name "ought to have 'wolf' in it." Now I hear from him that he has fixed on "Wolfe Pollexfen." He writes that *The Golden Fetish* is 80,000 words long, and took him 30 days.

Wednesday, February 22nd.

On Friday I went down to Torquay to spend the week-end with Eden Phillpotts.

I found him settled in a decently large house (with several rooms about 20 feet square), with a charming wife, and 2 children, with whom he must play every evening in the nursery from 6 to 7, inventing new games, etc.

On Saturday Phillpotts and I went for a walk in the February mist. In a country lane, seeing some primrose roots lying in the road, he got suddenly angry with a person unknown, and carefully replanted the roots under the hedge. Both he and his brother ask nothing better than to potter about garden and greenhouse, diagnosing the case of every plant, noting minute changes, and discussing methods of treatment. For 2 days a rumour that a camellia was growing in the hedge of a certain garden in a certain street excited them until they proved to themselves satisfactorily that the rumour was wrong and the camellia only a rhododendron.

Talking of venereal disease and its propagation one night (he had lent me a pipe), Eden told me of an authentic case in which a man had contracted syphilis through drinking after another man at Holy Communion.

Phillpotts said he had contrived another pseudonym for his sensational serial, namely "Samson Death." I said this was better than "Wolfe Pollexfen," and he said he should adopt it.

Today Tillotsons offered me £60 for the serial rights of *For Love and Life*. I have asked them for £80, but £60 was the price I had myself thought of.

I left Phillpotts full of a desire to live in the country in a large house with plenty of servants, as he does, not working too hard, but working when and how one likes, at good rates. It can only be done by means of fiction. Perhaps the sale of this my first serial may be considered as a step in the desired direction.

Thursday, March 2nd.

I accepted £75 from Tillotsons for the serial, and have adopted the pseudonym, "Sampson King."

It is 10 years ago today since I came to London. Tonight I had a large party, 26 people, to celebrate the anniversary. And my first play, a little duologue called *The Music Lesson,* was performed by Mr. and Mrs. Hazell. Intense and genuine enthusiasm and applause about it.

Tuesday, April 18th.

I finished the draft of *Anna Tellwright* just before Easter—having written it at the rate of 8 or 10,000 words a week—and till that was done I had no leisure for keeping a journal or spare energies for observation. I went home at Easter in order to collect facts useful for the novel, and I got what I wanted. The novel, however, is to rest till after Whitsuntide. In the meantime I am doing a one-act farce, *The Arrival,* and some short stories—one called *Marooned in London,* and a great deal of work for the *Academy.*

As the draft of my novel progressed I got thoroughly interested in it, and I finished it with good hopes of the excellence of the complete thing. It was with difficulty that I resisted the temptation to proceed with the second writing immediately after Easter.

Today I sat on a coroner's jury at Fulham and heard four cases, including one suicide through religious mania. I was struck by several things:

The decency of people in general.

The common sense and highly trained skill of the coroner.

The dramatic quality of sober fact. In two instances, the deceased persons had died from causes absolutely unconnected with the superficial symptoms. Thus a woman who had brought on a miscarriage and died, had died from heart disease.

The sinister influence of the ugliness amid which the lower classes carry on their lives.

The enormous (as it were) underground activity of the various charitable and philanthropic agencies which spread themselves like a network over London. It would seem that nothing could happen among a certain class of society without the cognizance of some philanthropic agency.

The dullness and the conscientiousness of a jury.

The absolute thoroughness with which suspicious deaths are inquired into.

Tuesday, May 30th.

I went to the Ysaye concert this afternoon. Ysaye, aged apparently about 45, has the unkempt, bleary, depraved look of a well-seasoned music-hall comedian. From my distance, I could not detect any sign of distinction in his head or face. His hair was neither long nor short; there were queer little locks, over the ears, which waved constantly to and fro as he played. To me he was the greatest of all violinists.

Balzac thoroughly enjoyed building up the social atmosphere of a place—and taking his full time over the business. Witness *Ursule Mirouet,* in which a third and more of the book is "preparation." *The Country Doctor* contains, strictly speaking, no "story"; the sole concern is a change of atmosphere.

Monday, July 3rd.

I have bought the hundred books which Bells allow you to select from the 600 volumes of Bohn's Libraries. They stand in a long beautiful row, houseless on the top of my shelves. Arriving late last night from Witley, eager to view them—they had been delivered in my absence—I cut several of them and looked through Juvenal, Suetonius, and da Vinci. I found that the celebrated and marvellous passage in Beaumont and Fletcher's *Philaster,* about marrying "a mountain girl," in which occurs the line

> And bear at her big breasts
> My large coarse issue

must certainly be based on a passage in Juvenal's Sixth (?) Satire.[1]

---

[1] *Sed potanda ferens infantibus ubera magnis.* . . .
Juvenal, *Satire VI,* line 9.

Today I began to read Benvenuto Cellini. He seems to have been less absolutely reprobate than I had imagined. The mark of the truly great man is on every page. I was enchanted with a phrase attributed to Benvenuto's father. Benvenuto was in trouble with the magistrates, and his father was defending him with moral support. "My father, in answer to these menaces, said, 'You will do what God permits you, and nothing more.' The magistrate replied that nothing could be more certain than that God had thus ordered matters. My father then said boldly to him, *My comfort is that you are a stranger to the decrees of Providence!*"

What strikes me, regarding the book technically, is its literary naïveté and lack of art. It must have been written without any prearranged plan, *currente calamo.* Evidently much of primary interest has been left out— some by design, but more by accident.

Thursday, August 10th.

I have just remembered a saying of Mrs. Dunmer, our new house-keeper at Witley. She said to me: "There's a lot of old maids in this village, sir, as wants men. There was 3 of 'em after a curate as we had here; a very nice young gentleman he was, sir. No matter how often the church was opened those women would be there, sir, even if it was 5 times a day. It's a sign of a hard winter, sir, when the hay begins to run after the horse."

Saturday, August 12th.

Two ideas for books:
The City Clerk, natural history and psychology.
I could do this well.

A novel with, for hero, an artist moulded after the character of Benvenuto Cellini. Such a character is magnificently suited to evoke drama in fiction. Moreover, in Cellini's memoirs, the character is drawn ready to hand.

Monday, August 21st.

I rode up from Witley to Hindhead with Ravenshaw on his motor-car. He said that he did not have pneumatic tires on his wheels because a set cost £40 and would only last 3,000 miles. The cost for tires alone would therefore be over 3d. per mile. In 20 years this fact will acquire quaintness.

Tuesday, August 22nd.

Finished memoirs of Cellini. What it leaves most clearly on my mind is an impression of the intense interest which princes and people showed in the fine arts in the sixteenth century. Of course Cellini sees nothing extraordinary in this interest.

I called on Dr. Farrar and had to wait for him to come in. He said when he saw me, "I hope you aren't in the family way, because I've had enough of that today."

Talking of midwifery among the very poor, he said that in one-room tenements, he had met one instance where the mother had had the decency to screen her own bed by a temporary curtain. It was her sixth confinement; a small room about 12 by 10 at most, 3 beds in it, and scarcely space to move about. In the other 2 beds were the 5 children. Just as the infant was being born Farrar happened to look up for a second, and he saw a row of 5 small heads peeping curiously under the curtain which the woman had hung up for privacy's sake.

Thursday, August 24th.

In an article of mine on d'Annunzio in last week's *Academy,* there is a passage which seems to me, now, such beautiful English that I can't help repeating it over and over, in my mind. Perhaps in 10 years' time I may come to despise it in favour of a more severe, ascetic style. Here it is:

"These rare creatures, sad with the melancholy of a race about to decay, radiant with the final splendour which precedes dissolution, wistful by reason of a destiny never to be satisfied, move through the drama with a feminine perfection of bodily and spiritual elegance seldom equalled and certainly never surpassed in any previous prose fiction."

Wednesday, October 18th.

Today I made an arrangement with Bayly by which I am only to attend at the office 4 half days and 1 whole day in the week. As I never count office work as real work, this means that I can do 5 full days of my own work at home, excluding Sunday. It is a great stroke of business, well managed by me, and I feel like a man suddenly enriched who is not quite ready with a scheme for spending. I hope to devote at least 3 whole days a week to *Anna Tellwright* and to resume this journal with regularity. I shall cease now to work at such high pressure as I have been driving at during the last 6 months.

Saturday, October 21st.

This morning, leisurely reading up for a 3,000-word article with which I am to celebrate for the *Academy* the approaching completion of Mrs. Garnett's translation of the works of Turgenev, I spent 4 hours in what seemed to me almost an ideal way. I was not hurried; I had books heaped about me; and I allowed ideas slowly to germinate in my head. It was calmer, less exciting than creative composition. Tonight, for a change, I composed the crudest funny song which Marriott is to sing at Christmas to make us laugh at Burslem—a lyric about Sissie's baby.

Tuesday, October 24th.

Richter Concert. I sat in the orchestra, between the kettle-drums and the side-drum. You can't be too close to an orchestra. The sound is quite different, more voluptuous, more significant, when you are in the middle of it. Everything takes on a new aspect. The orchestra becomes a set of individuals delicately interrelated, instead of one huge machine.

Richter has all the air of a great man. He seems to exist in an inner world of his own, from which, however, he can recall himself instantly at will. He shows perfect confidence in his orchestra, and guides them by little intimate signs, hints, suggestions. When pleased he shows it in a gay half-childlike manner; smiling, nodding, and a curious short wave of the fore-arm from the elbow. Having started his men, he allowed them to go through the second movement of Tchaikovsky's "Pathétique" symphony without conducting at all (I understand this is his custom with this movement). They played it superbly. At the end he clapped delightedly, and then turned to the audience with a large gesture of the arms to indicate that really he had had nothing to do with that affair.

Friday, October 27th.

I went down to Torquay to spend a week-end with Phillpotts. I had not been long with him before I found my own creative ideas begin to flow under the impulsion of his companionship.

Saturday, October 28th.

We walked by the coast to Teignmouth, and thence up the Teign to Newton Abbot, and back to Torquay by train. I was struck by Phillpotts's minute botanical knowledge, and his unfailing eye for a rare flower. Talking of dreams, he said that he had once kept a dream diary, with probable causes of the dream in opposite pages. But it was useless. He agreed with me that dreams, as works of art, were an utter failure. He had only had one dream that was of the least use to him.

Sunday, October 29th.

Every night we have had long literary talks, in which I did rather more than half of the talking, while Mrs. Phillpotts sat between us, quiet but apparently interested. Phillpotts often spoke of these "shoppy" talks with the greatest pleasure. He said they were a sharp stimulant—a stimulant he seldom got. He said, among dozens of other little personal statements, that as regards style De Quincey had influenced him most. What he chiefly admired was stateliness, the stately management of a *long* sentence. He remarked how few men cared to attempt a long and elaborate sentence. He admitted, as a defect in himself, that he could not tolerate the romantic convention: he could *not* tolerate it, it was so false. He went on to contrast the heroine of the usual historical novel (even Scott) with the actual coarse, ignorant, crude-thinking, rough-mouthed maiden of past times. He said he had been influenced by Hardy ("Talking about your god, are you?" said his wife, coming in) and, distantly, by Fielding, for whom he has an intense admiration.

"The hero of my next book," he said (*The Pagan*), "has better ideas about Dartmoor than any person I ever met. He seems to me to have the *proper* ideas, the only right attitude. He knows much more of Dartmoor than I do, and has taught me a lot." This, almost seriously, of a creature of his own brain.

Looking through Mrs. Phillpotts's collection of autographs, I was a little surprised at the warmth and spontaneity of the tributes sent by well-known men. A letter from James Payn [1] about *Lying Prophets,* and another from R. D. Blackmore [2] about *Children of the Mist,* pleased me

---

[1] Editor of *Chambers's Journal* and the *Cornhill Magazine,* and author of various books of essays and novels.

[2] The author of *Lorna Doone.*

particularly, so natural and large-hearted and fine. I had no idea that well-known men put themselves out to do these things.

Tuesday, October 31st.

Mr. and Mrs. Phillpotts and I walked down into Torquay. Mild, with flowers blooming everywhere. It seemed to me to be a place of retired military officers, rich and stiff dowagers, and spoiled overfed dogs led about by servant maids. Phillpotts said that for its size, it was the second richest place in England, Tunbridge Wells being first. There were scarcely any poor. Nearly every house stood in its own garden. There were very few children, as the inhabitants were mainly retired and old. Also, but few young men. If a young man above the tradesman's class grew up in Torquay, he could not stay there, because there was nothing for him to do. The whole town consisted of rich households and the people who fed them and waited on them.

I left Torquay in the afternoon for London, and I left it with the main idea that in 10 years Phillpotts would be one of the biggest, if not the biggest, novelist in England and America.

At Exeter I heard of the British defeat in the Transvaal.[1]

Thursday, November 2nd.

This is an authentic instance of the amazing habit of mind to which religious mania, even in a mild form, will lead. A young couple, married 3 or 4 years, have had no children. They are probably rather more than average amorous, and their reasons for dispensing with offspring are no doubt sternly practical. The husband is the only son of his mother, who, having had one child, requested, from religious motives of purity, to be relieved of any further conjugal duties. The request was granted, her spouse possibly sympathizing with the motives. Now this mother, discussing with her daughter-in-law the fact that the latter has had no children, expresses the opinion that doubtless her son is like herself, has a distaste for the impurity of sexual intercourse, and that this explains why her son is not a father.

Secret wild laughter of the son and his wife.

---

[1] At Nicholson's Nek.

Today I wrote 5 articles; 2 reviews, 2 articles on *The Black Tulip* play,[1] and my weekly "household notes."

Saturday, November 4th.

I have just remembered that Phillpotts told me an authentic story about an old man of 90. For 30 years one or other of his aged daughters had always been at the old man's side. He had never been left. One day both daughters happened, under very special circumstances, to be away together for a quarter of an hour. They left the old man apparently quite well, but he took advantage of their absence to die. When they returned he had passed away.

Sunday, November 5th.

I have now decided, acting on Phillpotts's advice, to write a short story *every* month. I finished my November story this morning: *The Phantom Sneeze,* a humorous ghost tale, 4,500 words.

Tuesday, November 7th.

Yesterday and today I have been reading through the draft of *Anna Tellwright.* It came fresh to me. Some involutions of the plot I had quite forgotten. On the whole I was pleased with it. Much of it impressed me to a surprising extent, but the end will have to be approached more slowly; it needs to be "prepared"; and when it comes it must be described with much greater detail.

I was talking to Cranstorm Metcalfe today, Colles's[2] head man, about the commercial aspect of my MS. He advised me, as regards magazines, to turn out humorous stories, for which, he said, the demand was keen and constant. Speaking of authors' prices generally, he said: "It is editors themselves who fix prices. When the psychological moment arrives and an author is for the first time *in demand,* then his price rises, and it is the editors who raise it—not the author, nor the author's agent."

I tried very hard to make a satisfactory beginning of the final writing of *Anna Tellwright* this afternoon, and could do absolutely nothing, couldn't get down a sentence that wasn't drivel.

---

[1] By Alexandre Dumas; then appearing at the Haymarket Theatre.
[2] In 1890 W. M. Colles founded the Authors' Syndicate; he was a leading authors' agent.

Friday, November 10th.

After cogitating off and on all through the night I decided upon what will probably be the first sentence of my novel: "Bursley, the ancient home of the potter, has an antiquity of a thousand years"—and also upon the arrangement of the first long paragraph describing the Potteries.[1]

This evening, at his request, I called to "have a chat" with Cyril Maude at the Haymarket Theatre.[2] I saw him in his dressing-room, a small place with the walls all sketched over by popular artists. Round the room was a dado-border of prints of Nicholson's animal drawings. Although the curtain would not rise for over half an hour, Maude was made up and dressed. He was very kind and good-natured about my one-act play, *The Stepmother,* without overflowing into that gush which nearly all actors give off on all occasions of politeness. He said that he and Harrison [3] would certainly consider seriously any 3- or 4-act play of mine. He advised me against doing any more curtain-raisers. He suggested that any man, not perfectly familiar with the stage, who wished to write a play, should study Dumas and—Boucicault.

Speaking of Phillpotts, he asked me if he was doing well.

"Very well indeed for a novelist," I said, "but a novelist never makes much money compared with you folks."

"Except," interrupted Maude, "when he writes a good play. I have a vivid recollection of sending Barrie a cheque for over £1,000 for the first 6 weeks of the provincial tour of *The Little Minister.*"

As I was leaving, he said, "Shall you begin the play at once?"

"I can't," I said; "I've too much on hand, but I shall do it within a year from now. Good-bye."

"And let us see it?" he called out anxiously. If it was acting, it was incredibly fine acting. If it wasn't, he is really anxious to consider a piece of mine.

Thursday, November 16th.

Today is published my third book, *Polite Farces.* (Lamley & Co, 2/6 net.) And tonight, by a coincidence, I made the first real start of the final writing of *Anna Tellwright.* I worked from 5 to 12 P.M. and wrote 1,000 words, first-rate stuff.

---

[1] This idea is not actually used in *Anna of the Five Towns* until Chapter VIII.

[2] When *The Black Tulip* was on.

[3] Cyril Maude and Frederick Harrison managed the Haymarket in partnership from 1896 to 1905.

Thursday, December 14th.

I am rather dissatisfied with Balzac's *Illusions Perdues* (but I have not yet read the part dealing with Lucien de Rubempré in Paris). This highly praised and renowned work seems to me rather second-rate in imaginative power, and often tedious.

In the whole range of literature familiar to me, the one thing that recurs most frequently to my mind, and on which I dwell with the most constant and equable pleasure, is Baudelaire's sonnet *La Géante*.

A. E. Housman's *A Shropshire Lad* contains verse which must be immortal. I am entranced by it.

Sunday, December 24th.

Thomas Arrowsmith called on John Beardmore for a subscription to the Burslem Wesleyan Chapel. Beardmore declined to contribute, and explained how he was losing money on all hands and had in fact had a very bad year. He went to such lengths of pessimism that Arrowsmith at last interrupted:

"If things are so bad as that, Mr. Beardmore," he said, "we'll have a word of prayer," and without an instant's hesitation he fell on his knees.

Beardmore began to stamp up and down the room.

"None o' that nonsense," he shouted. "None o' that nonsense. Here's half a sovereign for ye."

Sunday, December 31st.

This year I have written 335,340 words, grand total; 228 articles and stories (including 4 instalments of a serial of 30,000—7,500 words each) have actually been published.

Also my book of plays—*Polite Farces*.

I have written 6 or 8 short stories not yet published or sold.

Also the greater part of a 55,000-word serial—*Love and Life*—for Tillotsons, which begins publication about April next year.

Also the whole draft (80,000 words) of my Staffordshire novel, *Anna Tellwright.*

My total earnings were £592 3s. 1d., of which sum I have yet to receive £72 10s.

1900

Friday, January 5th.

My father, in a mood of reminiscence, told us of an incident which, he said, happened when he was about 8. (He seemed fairly sure about the date, but I should say he would more probably be 10 or 12; anyhow he still wore pinafores.) At the time, being highly precocious, he taught in a sort of night school and earned 2d. a night for so doing. One day he was fetched out of day-school by an older boy, who had just begun to work in the office of Sneyd Colliery. This boy had embezzled certain small sums—my father did not know this till afterwards—and was itching to spend. They took train to Stone, and there bought a lop-eared rabbit. Returning to Burslem, they walked with a third boy (George Wigley) to Mow Cop, and bought there a donkey for 12s. The Sneyd boy drove the donkey home, while Pater and Wigley carried the lop-eared rabbit in a basket.

Pater reached home about midnight. My grandmother had sent the town crier round to "cry" him. By a lie he managed to escape immediate consequences. But on the third day my grandfather entered his bedroom carrying a pair of braces. In the meantime the whole adventure had revealed itself. My grandfather set himself specially against the lying. First of all he knelt down and prayed, and then he thrashed the Pater with the braces till neither of them could very well stand. My father remembers how his mother afterwards, with tears, displayed his bruised back for the commiseration of a neighbour. At that time my father was accustomed daily to strip everything but his trousers and wash in the yard at the rear of the house. The Bennetts then lived in Pitt Street.

Saturday, January 6th.

Finished Balzac's *A Start in Life*. Though the first half is an amazing example of Balzac's superb digressiveness—the description of the coaching system is *impudent* in its utter impertinence—the story as a whole must be put among his best, and it contains more laughter than most. Some of the coaching stuff was like Hardy in *A Few Crusted Characters*, where the same machinery of a carrier's vehicle is used . . . like, but of course vehemently different.

Tuesday, January 9th.

I finished Balzac's *A Second Home* in the middle of last night, being sleepless, and thought it among his very best short stories, though absurd here and there with its Byronic flavours—"the stranger," "the unknown," and the whole attitude of Roger de Granville towards his mistress. The last two pages are great—a superb example of Balzac's instinctive knowledge of how to leave out everything but essentials. The relations between the Comte and his children are not explained at all, but the first words between father and son in the former's room explain what these relations have been in an instant. . . . One phrase struck me as comic: "The babe awoke and craved its limpid nourishment."

Friday, February 9th.

Last week I wrote my best short story up to now, *A Feud in the Five Towns:* a Staffordshire story, and I propose to stick to Staffs, at the rate of one story per month.

Yesterday I finished the first act and the outlines of Acts 2, 3, and 4, of *The Chancellor*, the play which I am writing at Cyril Maude, in collaboration with Arthur Hooley.[1]

Sunday, February 11th.

At Maldon (Essex). We stood on the bridge over the Blackwater at the bottom of the town. There was snow everywhere, a very keen frost, and a bright moon approaching the full. On either side the river, the wharves and warehouses were silhouetted in deep tones. The tide was coming in, and we could hear a faint continuous crackling or mysterious

---

[1] An early friend of Bennett's. They wrote plays together which were never produced. Hooley came to America in 1908 as literary adviser for Mitchell Kennerley and wrote under the pseudonym of "Charles Vale." He died in 1928.

rustling as the ice, constantly forming, was crunched and crumbled gently against the projecting piles of the wharves. We stood quite still in the silent town and listened to this strange soft sound. Then we threw tiny pebbles over the bridge and they slid along the surface of the river. The water froze in broad areas as it passed under the bridge. . . . We saw a very fat and aged woman walking home, very carefully. The road was extremely slippery, and a fall would have been serious to one of her age and weight. To me she seemed rather a pathetic figure, balancing herself along. . . . And yet, if I have learnt anything, it is not to be spendthrift of pity. She would be all right.

Tuesday, February 20th.

At their request I went up to see Harrison and Maude at the Haymarket Theatre as to the draft of our play, *The Chancellor.* Maude said he did not "see himself" in the principal part, and that he had done with making love on the stage—especially with his wife. They both said, with apparent sincerity, that we had shown more talent for and grasp of the stage technique than many playwrights of long experience. In the end I said I would consider the possibility of "writing in" another part for Maude. Harrison asked me to "have a shot at" a short play which they were immediately in need of. I was distinctly impressed by Harrison's suave and courtly kindliness.[1]

Tuesday, February 27th.

I saw Harrison and Maude at the Haymarket Theatre tonight at 9.30, and subject to two alterations, they accepted my curtain-raiser, *The Post Mistress,* for production before Easter. It was the very hour when Lord Dundonald entered Ladysmith.

Sunday, March 4th.

At the musical evening at Marriott's last night, Sharpe led a great demonstration of patriotism, *apropos* of Ladysmith—flag-waving, portrait of Buller,[2] reading aloud of a leading article from the *Telegraph,* cheering, singing of "Rule Britannia." It was distinctly an exhibition of insularity. I must say that I have been quite unable to join with any

---

[1] The play was eventually taken by Julia Neilson. See p. 112.
[2] Sir Redvers H. Buller commanded the South African Field Force in the Boer War.

sincerity in the frantic and hysterical outburst of patriotic enthusiasm of the last few days. Such praise of ourselves as a nation, such gorgeous self-satisfaction and boastfulness, are to me painful.

Tuesday, March 6th.

This evening I arranged finally with Harrison and Maude for the production of *The Post Mistress* at the Haymarket.

Thursday, March 22nd.

At his request I lunched with Stanley Service, manager of Pearson's book-publishing department, at the Bath Club, and we entered into a temporary arrangement for a year, under which I am to become the literary adviser of the firm.

Monday, April 2nd.

I had an interval with Harrison and Maude at the Haymarket. They said they could not run my play with *The Rivals,* and they were full of contrition. We arranged terms upon which it should be held over.

Tuesday, April 10th.

Morris Colles urged me this morning to try to write a serial "about the masses for the masses"—for *Lloyd's Newspaper.* . . . Colles said that the precise thing that Catling, the editor, was searching for did not exist at present.

I discussed with the Pater last night the advisability of my leaving *Woman.* He was thoroughly in favour of my doing so, and the stroke was then and there finally decided on in my own mind.

[From this date Arnold Bennett ceased to make any further entries in his journal during 1900, but resumed the entries with the coming of the New Year. During the period for which no entries exist he gave up his editorial work on *Woman* and went to live with his father and mother at Hockliffe.—Editor.]

1901

TRINITY HALL FARM,
HOCKLIFFE, BEDFORDSHIRE.

Tuesday, January 1st.

Last year I wrote 3 plays.

The Postmistress (1 act).

Children of the Mist (4 acts—in collaboration with Eden Phillpotts).

The Chancellor (4 acts—in collaboration with Arthur Hooley).

Also a serial, *The Grand Babylon Hotel,* of 70,000 words.

Also the draft of my Staffordshire novel, *Anna Tellwright,* 80,000 words, and part of the final writing.

Also half a dozen short stories.

I also wrote and published 196 articles of various length.

I also collected, revised, and wrote a preface for a series of my articles from the *Academy,* to be called *Fame and Fiction, an Inquiry into Certain Popularities.*[1]

I also edited *Woman* till 30th Sept.—when I resigned, and came to live in the country with Pater, Mater, and Tertia.

I also advised Pearsons on 50 MS. books.

From April till the third week in December I was working almost continuously at very high pressure, and had no energy to spare for this journal. Since I came here I wrote both *Children of the Mist* and *The Chancellor* in collaboration; and I was, moreover, very much preoccupied and fretted in the superintendence of the repairs to this house.

---

[1] Published in September, 1901.

On the completion of *The Chancellor*, I vowed never again to work so hard, but in future to find time to read poetry regularly, to gather materials for a work on the fiction of the nineteenth century, and—?—to study Latin.

I made £620 last year; more than ever I made in any previous year. This year, unless something goes wrong with *The Chancellor*, I hope to make much more.

Thursday, January 3rd.

As we drove through Battlesdon Park this misty moist morning, Kennerley and Tertia in front, and Sharpe and I cramped and pinched behind, I had a sense of a constantly unrolling panorama of large rounded meadows, studded with immense bare cedars, also of a formal and balanced shape; bulls and sheep, all of fine breeds, wandered vaguely about; sometimes a house; often a gate to be opened, and Spot gallivanting tirelessly around the trap; in one distant clump of trees, we saw a rook perched on an invisible twig on the top of a high elm; in the mist he seemed enormous, an incredible motionless fowl; at length he stretched his wings slowly, sank gently forward, and beat heavily away into the distance. Everything was a vague green and dark grey in the fog—everything except the red hips and the staring white of Spot's coat.

On the way home we called for a dead snipe that had been given to us; the first snipe I had ever seen; I was naïvely astonished at its small proportions, and the impossible length of its thin bill.

Monday, January 7th.

I came back from the Potteries to the country, and found it under snow, and every room dazzlingly white with the reflected light. This is the first time in my life that I have been in *and of* the country under snow, and there is something very exhilarating and cleanly in the sensation aroused.

Friday, January 11th.

It was a misty morning, and I walked across the fields behind the house, to see what they looked like in a fog. In the middle of the first big field I gradually descried the bald-headed youth, Giffen, perched on a haystack cutting fodder and dropping it into a cart underneath him.

The composition was very effective, and the sense of isolation caused by the mist added to it a sort of lone drama.

"Hello," I said to him. "How's that cow getting on?"

"Adams's?" he queried.

"Yes," I said. "She's dead, isn't she?"

"I think so," he admitted, with habitual caution. "You see, she slipped calf a month or two ago, and never got over it." The cow, as a matter of fact, dropped dead in the road yesterday, and Giffen knew it quite well.

I walked on and came into another large field, that seemed to be too carefully tended to belong to Adams. Only a very narrow path was left under the hedge, and the dogs had to follow me in Indian file. An old man and a boy were ploughing the field. "Who's field is this?" I shouted at the man. "Hey?" he called, and called "Wo!" to the horses, and the ponderous affair pulled up. It never occurred to me before how great is the inertia of a plough and horses, and that to start and stop it is not like starting a pony-trap.

"Is this Adams's field?" I asked.

"No," the man said, "that's one of Adams's fields other side the hedge."

"Whose is this?"

He seemed to answer reluctantly, "This is Gwynett's."

"What are you going to put here?" I asked.

"Oats, I think," he said, with still more reluctance.

Then, as I turned away, he called out, as if repentant, in a sociable tone, "Rather a heavy morning." The plough went on again.

Saturday, January 12th.

I was out again this morning in a thick mist. The appearance of two teams ploughing a large field, and looming vaguely with large, slow, dignified movements, was as picturesque as that of vessels coming into harbour early on a misty morning. I think that never before have I regarded a land movement as being equal in picturesqueness to a sea movement.

Monday, January 14th.

Balzac is said to have had a feeling for the art of music. But it is doubtful whether he had much genuine musical taste. In *Gambara*, a story overloaded with references to the keys in which various compositions are written, he speaks with solemn awe of Beethoven's C minor symphony, but it is also plain that he thinks Meyerbeer's *Robert le Diable* a superb work of art.

Willison, the man who combines the function of tailor and horse-dealer, told me a story of old Adams, now over 80, and still a "character." It was an early-morning dialogue between Adams and an old farm-hand:

Adams. What's this mean, Dick? It's a quarter past 6, and you but just come.

Man. Yes, but I was late last night; it was nigh on 8 before I left this yard last night.

Adams. Oh! Ah! But it's a quarter past 6, Dick. I won't have this. You can go home, Dick.

Man (surprised). Go home?

Adams. You can go back home, Dick. Go to hell, Dick.

Man (recovering himself). If I do go to hell, damned if I don't tell your old father how badly you're farming his land.

I can't recall the exact phrase of the last sentence which Willison used in telling me. I can only preserve the point.

Friday, January 18th.

Last night I read and re-read a lot of Dr. John Brown's *Horae Subsecivae,* and was much impressed by it. The pictures of Scottish character give one to see why the Scots prevail everywhere; and what a number of great men there are in the world who never achieve wide fame. The *Letter to Dr. Cairns* is one of the best biographical sketches I have ever read; the records in it of fine scholarship in humble places are amazing, and humiliating to one who has been forced into the habit of taking seriously the facile reputations of literary London. Dr. Brown himself was a passably big man, but his father, grandfather, great-grandfather, uncle, and great-uncle were at least as big, if not bigger. He is the best known of all the family, by reason of these essays and sketches which have been popular for 30 or 40 years, but perhaps he marks the beginning of the decline of a great family; he was a light *littérateur,* an amuser and diverter.

What a difference between that and his father's immense and erudite work *On Civil Obedience*—of which I had never heard before!

With the history of the Browns fresh in my mind this morning, I was able to estimate at its proper unimportance the circular which the *Graphic* people have issued about my serial, *The Grand Babylon Hotel,* to appear in the *Golden Penny,* which they sent me this morning, and which in a whirl of adjectives describes the thing as "the most original, amusing, and thrilling" serial written this decade—the best thing of the sort since *The Mystery of a Hansom Cab*.[1] Fancy writing a story as good as *The Mystery of a Hansom Cab!*

Sunday, January 27th.

Today I heard from R. G. Legge finally accepting *The Chancellor* on behalf of Julia Neilson and Co., for production. In the first year of our play-writing partnership Arthur Hooley and I have got 2 plays accepted for production by first-class managers, and have received £220 in actual cash.

Saturday, February 2nd.

This morning I saw what I could, over the heads of a vast crowd, of the funeral procession of the Queen.[2] The people were not, on the whole, deeply moved, whatever journalists may say, but rather serene and cheerful.

Afterwards, Legge, Fred Terry,[3] and Hooley lunched with me at the Golden Cross Hotel, and all was very agreeable and merry. Terry explained that they wished the third act of *The Chancellor* altered somewhat, but not at all radically.

Wednesday, February 20th.

As I was walking down Watling Street today a man accosted me with the words: "Can I show you some horse recipes this morning, sir? I've got a very good recipe for quietening a horse, sir, and that's always useful."

---

[1] Fergus Hume's famous story appeared in 1896.
[2] Queen Victoria died January 22.
[3] Brother of Ellen Terry, and himself an actor.

Tuesday, February 26th.

The latter half of *The Queen's Necklace* is one of the finest examples of Dumas's skill, supreme skill, in handling a purely artificial intrigue. The complexity of it is only equalled by its perfect clearness, its diversity only by its unity and coherence. Beginning with a Dromio-like similarity of face between Marie Antoinette and a country girl of loose morals, he gradually builds up a dazzling erection of misunderstanding, and, what is more, his sheer creative power is such that he forces you to believe in the gigantic impossibility.

I have been reading Gaboriau's *Lecoq* and its sequel (which is not a sequel but the solution of the problem) for the *Academy*. It struck me as among the best of all detective stories. And the sequel had a touch of Dumas at his most melodramatic and "plotty."

Monday, May 13th.

We were talking of the neighbourhood of Macclesfield, and *apropos* of the visit of Gregory Hill. My mother said: "We (that is herself, sister, and brother) were all baptized at Mellor Church, near Marple. Grandfather had a farm there. Father and his 3 brothers were all born there, and he brought each of us over from Glossop to be baptized at the church. There were 4 Longson brothers, James, John, Robert, and Henry."

"All dead, I suppose?" I said.

"Eh, bless ye, yes. Long and long ago."

This evocation by my mother of these farming, Puritanical ancestors, dust now, was rather touching, in a way. It gave me larger ideas of the institution of "the family." When I thought also of my mother's mother's side (the Claytons), my father's father's side (the Bennetts, descended illegitimately, as my Uncle John once told me, from "Schemer" Brindley the engineer [1]), and my father's mother's side (the Vernons, of whom several, I believe, are living now in Burslem, ignored by my father and us)— when I thought of all these 4 stocks gathered together and combined to produce me . . . a writer, an artist pure and simple, yet with strong mercantile instincts, living on a farm after two generations of town life,

---

[1] The engineer of the Bridgewater and Grand Trunk Canals.

I wondered. It is strange that though all my grandparents worked with their hands—weavers, potters, farmers, etc.—I have a positive aversion for any manual labour; the sole relic of all that manual dexterity left in me is a marked gift for juggling with balls.

Friday, May 17th.

I finished *Anna Tellwright* (*Anna of the Five Towns*) this morning at 2.45 A.M., after 17 hours' continuous work, save for meals, on the last 5,000 words. I was very pleased with it; slept well for 4 hours, got up with a frightful headache, and cycled through Hemel Hempstead to St. Albans, lunched at the George, and home—42 miles. *A.T.* is 74,000 in length.

Wednesday, May 22nd.

Rickards and I, in the evening, went over the vast, unfinished Roman Catholic cathedral in Victoria Street, and found it distinguished, impressive, a work of great and monumental art. Bentley, the architect, was wandering under the dome, examining and enjoying his mighty production, the realization of a conception which must live for many centuries. It was an impressive sight to see him, an impressive thought to think that one has seen him so, this magnificent artist, who started life as a stonemason, and is now slowly dying of cancer on the tongue.[1] He wore a frock-coat and silk hat, but a necktie of black silk tied in a loose bow.

Sunday, May 26th.

Talking about the Potteries with me, Billy Bennett told me that his father had once pointed out to him that no potting firm except Wedgewoods had survived to the third generation. The first generation was of the people, industrial, simple; the second, though raised in the social grade, was still plodding and energetic and kept the business together; the third was a generation of wastrels coming to grief. He said that the usual condemnatory phrase of potters for bad clay was "nowt but moss-muck."

[Arnold Bennett now ceased to keep his journal for nearly two years, during which time he lived chiefly in Paris.—EDITOR.]

---

[1] He died the following year.

1903

Monday, September 28th.

Illustration of the *sans-gêne* of Montmartre. As I was sitting on the
terrace of the Café de la Place Blanche, a *voiture* drove up containing two
men, two women, and a white puppy. One of the men was clearly an
actor or singer of some sort; he had the face and especially the mouth;
one of the women, aged perhaps 25, short, getting plump, and dressed
with a certain rough style, especially as to the *chic* hat and the *jupon,* was
evidently his *petite amie;* the other woman was a servant, *nu-tête,* and
wearing a white apron; the other man had no striking characteristic. The
two men and the *petite amie* got out and sat near me. The driver turned
away.

"*Où allez-vous?*" the *petite amie* shouted curtly in a hoarse, vulgar
voice. Whereupon the driver gave a shout of laughter, and the servant,
who was nursing the puppy, laughed too. "*Oh! Il tourne,*" murmured
the *petite amie,* grimly enjoying the joke at her expense. The driver was
only turning round to a quiet corner where he might wait without im-
peding the traffic. Having drawn up his vehicle, he got down and sat in
the carriage and produced a coloured comic paper, and shared his amusement over it with the servant. From time to time the *petite amie* from her
table shouted remarks to the servant.

Afterwards, I dined with the Schwobs.[1] First night of Jean Aicard's
drama in verse, *La Légende du Cœur,* at the Théâtre Sarah Bernhardt,
in which Mme. Schwob[2] plays the hero troubadour. Schwob ill and very

---

[1] Marcel Schwob, general writer and bibliographer, wrote much under the pseudonym of
Loyson-Bridet. He died in 1905.
[2] Marguerite Moréno, a member of the Comédie Française.

pale and extremely gloomy and depressed. Neither of them could eat, and each grumbled at the other for not eating. Before dinner Schwob had described to me the fearful depression of spirit accompanied by inability to work, which has held him for several months. Every morning he got up feeling, "Well, another day, and I can do nothing, I have nothing to look forward to, no future." And speaking of my novel, *Leonora,* he said, "You have got hold of the greatest of all themes, the agony of the older generation in watching the rise of the younger." Yet he is probably not 40.

Tuesday, September 29th.

Last night, in talking of the waning of Kipling's power, Marcel Schwob said that an artist could not do as he liked with his imagination; it would not stand improper treatment, undue fatigue, etc., in youth; and that a man who wrote many short stories early in life (Schwob seemed to think short-story-writing very exhausting to the imaginative power) was bound to decay prematurely. He said that he himself was going through this experience. He was in a very black and despondent mood when he said this. The observation seemed to me to be interesting, but it did not convince me.

Thursday, October 1st.

Leonora appeared, my tenth book, and my fifth published novel. But Chatto has two novels in hand, *Love and Life* [1] and *Teresa,* which, I hope, never will be published.

Sunday, October 4th.

I walked up to Sacré Cœur, and took the funicular up to the portals of the church. Environs of church: memento shop, image shop, church accessory shop. Tickets for entrance to crypt, belfry, and tower. The horrible unfinished look of the front, with *aged* hoardings and scaffolding. I was not much impressed by the interior. Mass was just finishing. I noticed the small-boy acolyte, dressed up and murmuring at the altar. Concentration of lights etc. round about main altar. Sparse congregation. Woman collecting at door, and regularly shaking her bag at two-second intervals. Meanly dressed clerks taking holy water at door and crossing

---

[1] This was the title of the serial he had written for Tillotson's under the pen name of Sampson King. See p. 90.

themselves. Curious effect, both interior and exterior, of church being built of large blocks of stone; it looked as if these stones were imitation stones in wall-paper, like the old-fashioned wall-paper in halls of small houses in England. The effect of the dome was goodish, akin to that of St. Paul's, but marred by the new yellowish-cream tint of the masonry.

I then came out and surveyed Paris from the front. I could distinguish most of the landmarks—Notre Dame, Panthéon, Invalides, Gare d'Orléans, Saint-Sulpice, and Louvre. Never before had I had such a just idea of the immense size of the Louvre. I could also see the Opéra (that centre of *Paris qui s'amuse*) with its green roof (? copper). And it looked so small and square and ordinary. And I thought of the world-famed boulevards and resorts lying hidden round about there. And I thought: Is that all it is? For a moment it seemed impossible to me that, as the result of a series of complicated conventions merely, that collocation of stones, etc. (paving-stones and building-stones) could really be what it is—a synonym and symbol for all that is luxurious, frivolous, gay, vicious, and artistic. I thought, "Really, Paris is not Paris after all; it is only a collocation of stones." The idea, though obvious enough, was very striking for a minute or two.

In the afternoon Schwob called unexpectedly. We went up to the Moulin de la Galette, which he said was the last genuine *bal* of the lower classes left in Paris, and even that genuine only on Sunday afternoons. In the evenings it was the resort of whores like the other *bals*. A tremendous climb (we had a difficulty in getting a driver to take us). Inside: stuffy. All the walls seemed to be covered with trellis work on which creepers grew very sparsely. Crowded dancing hall, with a sort of aisle for drinking on either side. The *monde ouvrier* was certainly there, dancing clumsily and perspiringly, and colliding with itself. Not nearly so graceful as the Bal Bullier. Band very brassy. Schwob said there were plenty of scoundrels—*maquereaux,* thieves, *apaches,* till-robbers, etc.—but I doubt it. The company looked innocent on the whole, though I thought I saw a few wrong 'uns (men). Afterwards we climbed up into the garden, and I saw the old wooden windmill (with its date 1295) garlanded with electric light apparatus. A solitary gendarme up there was glad to talk to Schwob. He began by saying that the weather was turning colder; he did not disguise that he was bored, but *"On est tranquille,"* he said, shrugging his shoulders. He was a rather cynical philosopher, and referred slightingly to the clients of the *moulin,* and dashed the respectability of the women with a single grimace. But when the cake-walk began he descended part of the stairs to get a glimpse of it.

All this part of Montmartre (north of the *boulevard extérieur,* that is to say) had a character of its own. It was like a place by itself, a self-contained village. Not many cabs got up into those steep picturesque streets, nor omnibuses. Schwob said it was "old Paris."

Monday, October 5th.

You can divide the restaurants of Paris, roughly, into two classes, those where the customers eat to live, and those where the customers eat to enjoy themselves. The Duvals are the great type of the former. Everything is stern, business-like, sharp, and no extra-food luxuries at all. In the second class there is always leisure, and the waiters seem to be in a charming conspiracy to anticipate your wishes, and everything is done for you (quite apart from eating) that you could desire. In a word, the attitude of the restaurant to its customer is: "You are here to enjoy yourself. Do so. Command us in anything. We will do all we can to produce an atmosphere of gaiety."

Sunday, October 11th.

The same thing has happened again that has happened many times before. Immediately I begin seriously on creative work, my journal ceases. It seems as if I cannot do both. I have nearly written the first of my series of 6 stories for the *Windsor Magazine.* I started the actual writing on Thursday, and since then I have had no literary ideas beyond the scope of the story. I must have seen plenty of interesting things, but they have not in the least impressed themselves on my mind.

Monday, October 12th.

I finished *The Fire of London,* the first of 6 stories for the *Windsor Magazine,* commissioned.

Wednesday, October 14th.

We went to see *Faust* at the Opéra. A performance exquisitely free from any sort of distinction. But between the acts, from the balcony, we had amazingly good views of the illumination of the Avenue de l'Opéra for the King and Queen of Italy. It was only a trial illumination and was "out" at 11 P.M. I noted the effect of the masts lighted perpendicularly. The only part of the opera that we enjoyed was the ballet. I noted the business-like air and habits of the *corps de ballet;* how they calmly tested shoes and hair in the middle of the stage; and the enormous potential activity of their legs—strong, muscular, and elegant, but not exactly pretty, animals. And how the whole "convention" of the piece was changed, and cleared of all sentimentality and make-believe, and sickliness, while the ballet lasted. As if the corps said: "Now understand, no mistake, no pretence, this is a ballet and nothing else, a thing by itself, complete in itself, and we shall execute it regardless of everything except the rules and conventions of the ballet. You must forget *Faust* for a while." I was much struck with this.

Friday, October 16th.

From Sharpe, through Frank, story of the girl with money, who was forbidden by her parents to marry a certain man. The latter afterwards became engaged to a poor girl. The rich girl bought *lingerie* for the poor girl, and generally looked after her trousseau, even to inserting blue ribbon into the neck of the bride's nightgown, in order that "she might look nice for him." Finally the rich girl took a cab to the wedding.

When George, not loving Eva, is loved by Eva, he finds her caresses and endearments nice but rather a bore. He finds them rather a tie. But when, by chance, Eva's manner becomes cold for a space, he resents (privately) the absence of warmth; he feels its loss, and wants the warmth again. Note this. His attitude is fundamentally egotistic. He likes a creature to be absolutely wrapped up in him; he likes to be the centre of a creature's whole existence, but is always resenting the tie; always wanting to be both free and bound at the same time.

Monday, October 19th.

Yesterday there were two alarms of fire (false) at French theatres, the Opéra Comique and the Français. A reporter of the *Débats* stated that, at the latter, nearly every one ran for the doors, and that when they came back some were still *tout émus.* One lady was sure that the auditorium was full of smoke. "Can't you see it, Monsieur?" she said to him. "You can see it very well." Another had *seen* flames round the chandelier. Yet

there had been no fire at all. The alarm had been caused thus: A spectator, feeling ill, had gone out into the *couloir* of the fourth gallery to take
the air. He fainted, fell against the door of a *loge,* and the door being
forced open had upset some chairs.

Tuesday, October 20th.

Talking about wages in Paris, C. said that every one was badly paid
and that every one was "on the make." She told me that when she was
in the chorus at the Variétés, the fines were simply an organized swindle
by the *régisseur* at the expense of the choristers. Fines were levied for the
most absurd trifles, and her month's bill for fines would sometimes
amount to 30 francs, out of a total of 90 francs wages.

I began to read Boswell again, sixth volume, and couldn't leave it.

Wednesday, October 21st.

Mrs. Devereux, talking of her study of Myers's book on *Human Personality,* spoke of a series of incarnations, and said she was *quite sure* she
had been an oriental in a previous state, probably a priest. When I
naturally objected, against her argument that the ego persisted, that if
one could not recall past states in this present state, there was no reason
why one should recall this present state in a future state, and that really
the persistence of the ego was a question of memory—when I argued
thus, she said that some people could recall, that she could recall vaguely;
that anyhow the faculty was there, if dormant, and could be developed.
It is not the fact that intelligent people should hold views about future
and past states that surprises me, but that they should be so precise and
sure of them.

In the reviews of *Leonora,* what strikes me most is the inability of the
reviewers to perceive that the life therein described (with its "meat teas"
—which they always fasten on to) is no more vulgar than any other sort
of life. The *Scotsman* says, "The smug prosperity of the home, with its
six-o'clock 'meat-teas' and its subservient attitude to the blustering head
of the house." As if that kind of thing was not tremendously prevalent
everywhere in England and Scotland. No, what really abrades them is
not the life described but what the *Scotsman* calls "the fearless strength
of description" of it.

C. told me that, by an order of police, gas was forbidden on the stage in Paris. All lighting must be done by electricity. Also that there was a decree against cigarettes or matches in the dressing-rooms. When I told her that I had seen smoking in dressing-rooms, she said: "Oh, yes, of course. Every one does it. But there is an official search of all dressing-rooms etc. once a month by the firemen, and before that, an attendant comes round and says to the artists, 'Kindly hide your matches etc., as the *pompiers* will be here directly.'" The extraordinary humour of this did not seem to occur to her. *"C'est bien Parisien, ça!"* I said, and she cynically and bitterly agreed that it was. But she could not see the joke.

Saturday, October 24th.

I could not work today. I think I find my nerves more sensitive every day, really. I wish letters came just before dinner instead of just after breakfast; then they could not interfere with and disarrange the general "lay" of one's thoughts for the day's work.

Sunday, October 25th.

This afternoon, instead of proceeding with fiction, I suddenly wrote the 52nd and last of my *Savoir Faire Papers* for *T.P.'s Weekly*—the second of 2 articles on marriage.

I went out to intercept Mrs. Devereux on her way from the Lamoureux concert, and caught her in a *voiture* with some Italian countess or other to whom I was introduced and who then drove off, while we took another cab to Schwob's. We found the Schwobs sitting alone together, and Schwob more depressed and ill than ever. He had been reading G. B. Shaw's plays, and broke out into invective against Shaw and all his works. He could see nothing in them at all. He said he could see what *we* saw and took for *esprit,* and what to us *was esprit,* but to the French mind it was nothing but foolishness. He denied that the characters had any reality, even the reality of fantasy, and said that Barrie's plays were much better. I was much inclined to agree with him, but then I always find French criticism of English work very instructive, disconcerting, and tonic.

Mme. Schwob told us of a curious and highly obscene theatrical venture called the Théâtre Naturaliste, of a man named Ch., and a play in which the characters actually *did* on the stage all the actions described in the dialogue. She would not tell us what these were, but one gathered that they were pretty awful. In one scene the actors were about to portray something quite impossibly awful, and the audience broke out into protests. Ch. came forward and said, "Ladies and Gentlemen, if you make this noise we cannot proceed; we will recommence the scene." The scene was recommenced—same protests at same point. Ladies merely got up and left. Mme. Schwob described the night as wildly and incredibly mad. In the result Ch. was imprisoned—I suppose for an offence against public morals and decency.

Monday, October 26th.

I read the last pages of Boswell, and was sorry I had not brought over more volumes to re-read. Tonight I worked till midnight at the second of the *Windsor* stories.

Tuesday, October 27th.

I worked very late again, though with an incipient headache and much dissatisfaction with the work done. You may perceive intellectually that a sensational story may also be artistic, but it does not follow that you can sit down and produce the thing, unless you have a natural bent for it. I have been under the mistaken idea that, because I saw the possibility of its being done, therefore I could do it.

Friday, October 30th.

Opéra Comique. *Pelléas and Mélisande.* This thing made a profound impression on me, as a play. I thought the music neither helped nor spoilt the piece; it did not offend me and at times it seemed rather good; it was "always" in the key! But the play! I thought that nothing could be more simple and more profound in its presentation of the essential quality of "life." The whole performance was a triumph (and this in spite of bad seats).

Saturday, October 31st.

At last I finished the second story for the *Windsor*. Really, it is no good; because the plot is nothing but a concoction without a central idea. But I wrote it all out 3 times, and it has the superficial air of being good.

Casino de Paris. Plenty of stylish *cocottes* here, in whom Tertia and Lizzie were tremendously interested. Which reminded me of C.'s saying about the married woman's way of remarking, "*Ça doit être une cocotte.*"

But Tertia and Lizzie now confess their interest, and insist on going to another music-hall on Monday night in order to see more *cocottes*. Yet when I told them of the idea I had discussed with Frank, of writing a handbook or practical guide *for cocottes*, for the private joy of friends, they were certainly startled. I can always tell when they are *really* a little shocked.

Monday, November 2nd.

I received a long letter from Whitten [1] last Thursday with his idea for my new series in *T.P.'s Weekly*, to be called *A Novelist's Notebook*, and today I began the first article or rather the planning of it.

"I never study style," Darwin wrote to Mr. J. Scott in 1863; "all that I do is to try to get the subject as clear as I can in my own head, and express it in the commonest language that occurs to me. But I generally have to think a good deal before the simplest arrangement and words occur to me."

Tuesday, November 3rd.

I was told today that, as I thought, the most distinguished of the music-hall *cocottes* went to the Casino de Paris; and also that they did business comparatively infrequently, but what they did was very remunerative. This latter statement I regarded with suspicion, as also the following: that a particular woman, tall, very distinguished, and well dressed and well jewelled, whom I had often admired in various resorts, had an absolute minimum of 250 francs. It seems she goes about in a pair-horse carriage in the evening, by some sort of arrangement with the coachman. I was told that many *cocottes* pay their coachmen either partly or wholly in love. This woman, by the way, sometimes brings to the Casino her young child, of 7 or 8 years old perhaps, I have seen them together there, and the effect was certainly effective.

Wednesday, November 4th.

At the Montmartre Fair, now in progress, I was much struck by the charming effect of the roundabout opposite the Moulin Rouge: The machine in full swing, the pigs galloping one way and the ceiling of the machine going the other, brilliantly lit by electric light in clusters and in

---

[1] Wilfred Whitten, editor of *T.P.'s Weekly*.

single arc lamps. Two young, fair, and pretty *cocottes* with red lips and white teeth, brilliantly dressed, sitting *sans gêne* in one of the cars, in the full glare, showing well against red velvet cushions of the car, and throwing those peculiarly French coloured paper streamers into the crowd; these streamers have the effect of fireworks, rockets, in the sky— a line of fire. The whole machine is gradually covered with them, and becomes a sort of cocoon, and they stream round after it in thousands and lie thick in the road.

I had an idea, for my Hotel Continental novel, of doing the Covent Garden Fancy Dress Ball as a carnival scene, and making it seem as though nothing could surpass it, in the way of the abandon of decadence; and then afterwards doing the Bal des Quatz' Arts here, knocking the Covent Garden affair all to smithereens.

Bought Kipling's *Five Nations*. I thought *Bridge Guard* quite excellent. I was not much struck with *Recessional*. But a lot of *The Islanders* seemed legitimate and fine invective.

Thursday, November 5th.

I had a chill, and all day I failed to concentrate my thoughts on my third *Windsor* story. But I had one good idea in the night.

In the afternoon I walked down the whole length of the Fête de Montmartre as far as La Chapelle, and then back on the other side of the road, incidentally inspecting the immense shop of Dufayel. I only saw one episode that interested me—a horse falling down as it turned too sharply from the boulevard into one of the steep streets north. This accident, like many others here, was due to the practice of balancing really large and heavy carts (the cart was loaded with bricks) on two wheels only. The strain on the shaft-horse must sometimes be enormous. The leader had stumbled several times on to his knees in the boulevard, but he got round the corner in safety. It was the shaft-horse that fell. The teamster gave a little fatalistic nod. The horse, after a brief struggle, resigned himself. Of course, a crowd gathered immediately; a busy, interfering, wishful-to-help crowd. I was much struck by the stink of the crowd, the low type of face, the squints, the bullet-heads, the misshapen features. The getting up of the horse was mismanaged for a long time; but in the end it was accomplished without injury to the horse or cart. No gendarme appeared until just before the end, and then he stood amiably smiling and watching—an

oldish man. At least a dozen men gave active assistance, and dozens ges-
ticulated and shouted advice. It was rather melancholy, this exhibition in
the mass of the French *man's* ineptitude. A crowd of French *women*
would have managed it better. I was out an hour and a half, and at the
end, as I came in, the noise of the scores of sham orchestras had got
fearfully on my nerves.

Friday, November 6th.

Dined at the celebrated Café Foyot, and found it rather ordinary.

C. told me that between 8 and 9 years ago only, at Orléans, she had
actually seen a little shrunken old lady arrive at the cathedral there in a
sedan chair. She was carried up the steps, but dismounted in the portico,
and entered the cathedral on foot.

C. also told me that the front row of the chorus at the big music-halls
were usually *femmes entretenues,* and very *exigeantes* with the *perruquier*
and other officials, who dared not cross them. She also told me about
rehearsals of ballets, and of the rows thereat, and how the *régisseur* would
throw up the thing in disgust and retire to his den, and then all the
women would follow and kiss and cajole him to come back again. Then
a pause, and one could hear his step descending the stairs, and peace was
restored.

I did no work again today. Couldn't concentrate.

Saturday, November 7th.

The *domestique* says it froze last night. I have a cold, caught in the
omnibus last night.

Couldn't work again today. But in the afternoon I was determined to
do something, and I cleared off all my correspondence etc., which always
accumulates in my periods of idleness; it is only when I am busy that I
can find time to write letters. This business took nearly 3 hours, and after
it I felt rather more virtuous. I dined at Mrs. D.'s, and her sister Mrs. L.
was there.

They were talking about an old lady who had fallen violently in love
with a young man, really very violently. He wouldn't marry her, because
he was too proud to have it said that he, a poor young man, had married
a rich old woman for her money. On the other hand she wouldn't have
an irregular liaison. So they live together platonically in the same house.

It was understood that if he left her the desertion would kill her. At the moment the old lady is dying, not expected to recover.

They both said that they could see no more objection to a man taking money from a woman than a woman taking it from a man. They could not understand (*façon de parler*) a man marrying a *girl;* it was too disgusting, cruel, etc. For "girl" read "young virgin." (I said nothing would induce me to marry a girl.) Yet Mrs. L. told me that at 16½ she had run away with her present husband, she being then engaged to another man. She said: "Passion and all that sort of thing has vanished long since. All I can say, with regard to my feeling for my husband, is that when he comes into the room I always feel soothed. I could not imagine myself being able to live with any other man." I met Mr. L. at Mrs. D.'s some months ago, and I was quite sure that intellectually and imaginatively, he is decidedly his wife's inferior.

Sunday, November 8th.

Today I managed to concentrate pretty nearly all day, till 9.30 P.M., on my story, and I collected a few decent ideas for it. I saw no one to speak to except my *domestique,* in the morning, and the waitresses at my restaurants. Last thing, I began to read *Don Quixote.*

Today I spent such a day as ought to satisfy a man of letters. Having done my correspondence, I went out at 10.15 for a walk and to consider the plot of my story. I strolled about the Quartier de l'Europe till 11.30, and then lunched at my usual restaurant, where I am expected, and where my maternal waitress advised me in the selection of my lunch. During lunch I read *Le Journal.* I came home, finished *Le Journal,* read *Don Quixote,* and fell asleep. Then at 1.30 I amused myself on the piano. At 2 I began, in my Bruges chair, to ponder further on my story, and the plot seemed to be coming. At 3.30 I made my afternoon tea, and then read more *Don Quixote,* and fell asleep for about a minute. The plot was now coming faster and faster, and at 5 I decided that I would, at any rate, begin to sketch the story. At 6.45 I had done a complete rough draft of the whole story.

Then I dressed and went to dine at my other restaurant in the Place Blanche, where the food and wine are good, and the waiters perfect models, and the *chasseur* charming, where men bring their mistresses, and where occasionally a "mistress" dines alone, and where the atmosphere is a curious mixture of discretion and *sans gêne* (the whole place seems to say, "You should see what fun we have here between midnight and 3 A.M. with our Hungarian music and our improvised dancing, and so on and so on"). I *dined* slowly and well, while reading *Le Temps* and *The Pilot,* and also while watching the human life of the place. Then I took coffee and a cigar. I returned home at 8.30, and played the piano. The idea of writing my *chronique* for *T.P.'s Weekly* a day earlier than usual came into my head, the scheme of the article presented itself, and at 9.30 I suddenly began to write it, finishing it at 11.35. I then went to bed and read *Don Quixote* till 12.15.

Tuesday, November 10th.

Of course I did not have a very good night.

Wednesday, November 11th.

I worked all day yesterday, except between 4 and 6, when I paid a call, till 1 o'clock this morning. I lunched on 2 francs and dined on 2 francs at the Duval, and took coffee at the Café Terminus Saint-Lazare, a big place with an orchestra. And I noticed how even Donizetti came out strong and alive amongst the mass of Czibulkas, Métras, and other common composers of light music.

Again today I worked the whole day, till 10.40, and I finished the third *Windsor* story. *A Bracelet at Bruges;* 5,100 words complete in 2 days. Already, after a period of slackness, I have a sort of wild hope of being able to finish the 6 stories by the end of the month.

Tonight I had 2 letters from Eden, both of them about our play and our holiday next spring on the Riviera. He says that Jerome [1] has written asking him to collaborate in a big serious play! Eden says that my recent letters indicate a tendency to cynicism, and that my recent articles in *T.P.'s W.* seemed to "throw distrust, not to say contempt, on love of women." He goes on: "Some natures are self-contained and don't want it—some can't do without it. Golden Rule in the matter: *To keep the mouth shut and go one's own way.*"

---

[1] Jerome K. Jerome, best known for his *Three Men in a Boat* and *The Passing of the Third Floor Back.*

Thursday, November 12th.

I am still reading *Don Quixote,* and was much struck with the perfect narrative style of the inserted story, *The Ill-Advised Curiosity.* It is simply charming. And I am with the licentiate who, after censuring the improbabilities, said, "With the manner of the telling I have no fault to find." I should like sometime to write a few stories in that simple style— pure narration, very little dialogue, and what there is, arranged conventionally in long speeches. Hardy's *A Group of Noble Dames* must have been composed under some such influence, I imagine.

Friday, November 13th.

Less than 3 weeks ago, Alice Woods wrote me that she was suffering from nervous prostration, and asked me to call round one day. I did not succeed in going till yesterday. Mrs. Woods greeted me. "I suppose my daughter has written you," she said. "No," I said. "Well," she said, "she's married and gone off, a week ago. It was a great surprise to me," she added. The figure of this middle-aged American woman, hating France and the French character, all alone there in that Paris flat, was of course pathetic. I heard how her daughter's health had at last necessitated a doctor. She didn't like French doctors, but they had heard of a doctor at Brussels. And Alice went to Brussels, and came back and just said, "Mother, I'm going to marry Ullman." And they were married at once, and went away honeymooning, perhaps to London. Mrs. Woods said that Mr. Ullman was a rich young painter, associate of the Salon, with a beautiful apartment, and they had known him for years and years—but she had had no idea. . . . Then she began to talk about herself, how her arrangements were upset; she had taken the flat for a year; and now she was going back to America, and she wanted some one to go with, in December, and she wanted a big boat, and not a fast one, because the fast ones pitched so. She had an unmarried son in America, very well off, and she had her own property in Indianapolis. She wished to spend part of each year with her son and part with her daughter. "My daughter will keep her maiden name, Alice Woods Ullman, because she's pretty well known all over America. My husband was on the United States Bench" (Illinois Court of Appeal, I think). Talking of travelling, she said English people amused her, the way they talked. She said she used to think nothing of going up to Chicago (7 hours) to see her dressmaker one day, and coming back the next. "I'm glad to have met you," she said when I left. Every time I have seen her she has used that phrase. I left her sewing there all alone, a little sort of a camp bed made up in a corner.[1]

Saturday, November 14th.

Yesterday I did nothing but think, very vaguely and loosely, about the plot of my next two *Windsor* stories. And I want to have them both finished by the 22nd!

I had an excellent idea for the next two stories this morning, one of those big ideas, heroic sort of things, that only come now and then. I meant to work it out further this afternoon, but while I was asleep after lunch Davray[2] called. I told him I wanted to buy some books, so we went off by omnibus to the quays to get a Casanova, a dictionary, and other things. He took me first into the shop of Honoré Champion. It was like a bookshop in a story by Anatole France, exactly. We were greeted first by a young man who spoke well and vivaciously, and then in a corner at a desk I saw a venerable and beaming white-haired man in a skull-cap. This was the father. He said little, but smiled affectionately at all of us. The understanding between father and son was rather fine. The large shop was full of books that no one but a bibliophile would buy, and it appeared that the young Champion was learned and had published something of his own.

Then we went to another shop close by, where the bookseller was a little pinched man, not distinguished—walled in with books. Then we went across to the quay (Voltaire) and had a learned conversation with one of the stall keepers, who grasped exactly what we wanted and said we couldn't get it second hand.

After this Davray lost the scent of books, and remembered that he had to go to the Bon Marché for his wife. We reached the Bon Marché. He couldn't get the patterns for his wife, but he got some gloves for himself. Then I cried out for tea. We walked off. I said it would rain. He said it wouldn't. I bet the price of tea it would rain within 5 minutes; it rained within a minute. We had tea at Foyot's.

We were close to the bookshops at the Odéon, at Foyot's, so we ran

---

[1] George Ullman and his wife later became very close friends of Arnold Bennett. See page 182.

[2] Henry D. Davray translated into French novels by Bennett, Conrad, etc. From 1898 he edited the Collection of Foreign Authors for *Le Mercure de France*.

across, and I bought Casanova, 2 Maupassants, and an Anatole France, and Davray carried off the parcel to have it despatched from the office of the *Mercure de France*. I found this periodical established in an old *hôtel* once belonging to I forget what historic family. Fine large rooms, and good woodwork. I was introduced to the *directeur* (who was not sitting in his own chair because the cat had taken it) as the "hope of English fiction."

Sunday, November 15th.

I sketched out plot of story No. 4 for *Windsor*. Lunched and dined alone.

I read over 200 pages of *Bel-Ami*,[1] which I bought yesterday. It must be 10 years since I read it. The opening chapter or two I found rather stiff and forced, especially as to Duroy's first conquests of Rachel and of Little Laurine, for instance; and I seemed to feel a certain absence of ease in the "undulation" of the narrative. But it gradually got hold of me and soon held me thoroughly.

People might easily say that in *A Man from the North* I had plagiarized from it: the scene at the Folies-Bergère, the handing of her purse to Duroy by Clotilde de Marelli at the dinner, etc., etc. But I am not conscious, now, of having imitated. There are things in it superlatively good: for example, Norbert de Varenne's long monologue to Duroy about death and about the old age of a bachelor in lodgings (p. 160 etc. of illustrated edition). And the death scene of Forestier at Cannes. The duel is also good.

I also read the preface to Casanova's *Mémoires*.

Monday, November 16th.

Today I wrote the whole of my fourth *Windsor* story, *A Solution of the Algiers Mystery*, 5,100 words. I have written as many words in a day before, but never a complete short story of that length. I began at 9.40 A.M. and finished at 12.40 A.M. with about 4 hours off for meals and sleep.

Tuesday, November 17th.

Then I read *Bel-Ami* till 1.30. I woke up this morning fatigued but well.

---

[1] By Guy de Maupassant.

I received a letter from Sharpe about *Leonora*. He says, *inter alia,* "I think Leonora was tired of her husband and merely wanted another man; there seems to be no tragedy reached." But on the whole he is immensely enthusiastic.

Bel-Ami. This book stands re-reading very well. There are dozens of sudden fine flashes in it. The scenes after the death of the Comte de Vaudrec (beginning with Georges's sensations when he is told that the Count is dying) are superb. And the description of Mme. Walter's clumsy ways of making love is ferociously great.

But the political part (beginning Chap. 7, Part II) about the conquest of Morocco and the enrichment of Walter and Co. is decidedly clumsy and ill advised. It doesn't convince because it defies history too crudely. It seems to be a feeble imitation of one of Balzac's coups with *Rentes*.

Wednesday, November 18th.

Last night, when I went into the Duval for dinner, a middle-aged woman, inordinately stout and with pendent cheeks, had taken the seat opposite to my prescriptive seat. I hesitated, as there were plenty of empty places, but my waitress requested me to take my usual chair. I did so, and immediately thought, "With *that* thing opposite to me my dinner will be spoilt!" But the woman was evidently also cross at my filling up her table, and she went away, picking up all her belongings, to another part of the restaurant, breathing hard. Then she abandoned her second choice for a third one. My waitress was scornful and angry at this desertion, but laughing also. Soon all the waitresses were privately laughing at the goings-on of the fat woman, who was being served by the most beautiful waitress I have ever seen in any Duval. The fat woman was clearly a crotchet, a *maniaque,* a woman who lived much alone. Her cloak (she displayed on taking it off a simply awful light puce flannel dress) and her parcels were continually the object of her attention and she was always arguing with her waitress. And the whole restaurant secretly made a butt of her. She was repulsive; no one could like her or sympathize with her. But I thought—she has been young and slim once. And I immediately thought of a long 10 or 15 thousand words short story, *The History of Two Old Women.*[1] I gave this woman a sister

---

[1] This idea was afterwards developed into *The Old Wives' Tale*. See also p. 154.

fat as herself. And the first chapter would be in the restaurant (both sisters) something like tonight—and written rather cruelly. Then I would go back to the infancy of these two, and sketch it all. One should have lived ordinarily, married prosaically, and become a widow. The other should have become a whore and all that; "guilty splendour." Both are overtaken by fat. And they live together again in old age, not too rich, a nuisance to themselves and to others. Neither has any imagination. For "tone" I thought of *Ivan Ilyitch*,[1] and for technical arrangement I thought of that and also of *Histoire d'une Fille de Ferme.* The two lives would have to intertwine. I saw the whole work quite clearly, and hope to do it. But I expect I shall have to do my humorous novel, *A Great Man,* first, not to mention other things.

Thursday, November 19th.

Yesterday I had a nervous dyspeptic headache, due to the labours of Monday. I did nothing but perambulate the city, and collected a few ideas for my next story. I did well to collect any at all.

I certainly ought to have been sure from the first that my waitress at the Duval, fat, 50, and apparently the image of shrewd content, was really a *névrosée,* given to crises and sudden violent feelings of an irrational character. I ought to have known it from the day when, after a few days' absence from the restaurant, she greeted me bluntly with the question, "Is she prettier than I am, then?" I only made sure of her nervous temperament yesterday, when she cried violently about some undisclosed thing, at lunch. One meets an extraordinary large number of *névrosés* of all sorts in Paris.

Friday, November 20th.

I worked till 10.30 last night, on the fifth *Windsor* story, but the following words from Whitten's review of *Leonora* in *T.P.'s Weekly,* which I received by the last post, pleased and excited me so much that I had some difficulty in recommencing work in the evening: "His claim as an artist is drawn from the source of all art—life itself. And from the standpoint of art it is significant that one naturally refers this book, not to the fleeting fashions of the circulating library, but to the great stand-

---

[1] By Leo Tolstoy.

ards themselves—to Tolstoy, to Flaubert, to Thomas Hardy." This is the sort of thing I want.

Sunday, November 22nd.

I was invited last night to the annual banquet of *La Plume* at the restaurant of the Sociétés Savants. About 200 guests, I should imagine, including a dozen or so "movement-y" women, sloppy, of the sort that I detest—Stage Society, Fabian Society sort, almost exactly as in London. A big, badly arranged, too crowded banquet, mediocre as a meal. I was with Davray and Kozakiewicz, a Pole, who translated Sienkiewicz, and is now running H. G. Wells in France. I was introduced to a lot of people. I saw Paul Adam, handsome and not as old as I expected, but I was not introduced to him. I believe Octave Mirbeau was there but I did not see him.[1] Besnard, the painter, was there. I was introduced to Auguste Rodin, a little man with a fine long grey beard and a big nose over it, and very vivacious. He was in evening dress (against the rule) with the rosette. He seemed a simple man; he talked to me for a few minutes quite naturally and without any sort of pose. Afterwards I came home with Kozakiewicz, and found him an ardent Wagnerian. He told me he had sold 300,000 copies of the French translation of Sienkiewicz, and had paid the author over 80,000 francs. He is a cultivated man, and seems to combine a financial faculty with genuine taste in art.

Monday, November 23rd.

I called on the Schwobs yesterday afternoon and found Davray and his wife there. Schwob a little better, but very listless, and those terrible piercing eyes which he has when he is ill. They were talking of Remy de Gourmont's new book on the sexual instinct.[2] Moréno[3] said she supposed she ought not to admit that she had read it, and she forbade me to read it. She said that all the pornography was interlarded with reflections in the style of *Paul and Virginia*.

Davray got talking about another book dealing with sexual intercourse between animals, and they both laughed tremendously. *"Oh!*

---

[1] Paul Adam was a French novelist and writer on sociology. He died in 1920. Octave Mirbeau (1850–1917) was author of many novels, including *Journal d'une Femme de Chambre*.

[2] *Physique de l'Amour: Essai sur l'Instinct Sexuel.*

[3] Mme. Schwob. See p. 115.

Davray! Des choses inouies! . . . Oh! Davray! Les tortues! Quinze jours! ! !" Moréno said that the book ought to be on every *table de nuit.* "Yes," said Davray, "and afterwards *dans un lieu commun."*

Les Trois Filles de M. Dupont, by Brieux, at the Comédie Mondaine. House packed. I found this well-known piece interesting enough. Thoroughly serious, and marked by great "justice of observation." But of course clumsily constructed. Too much "means" for too little "end," and the big situation between the three sisters at the close, where even unsuccessful marriage is justified, and one sister persuades Julie against a life of solitary industry and the other against a life of vice—this situation is badly "forced." But the play is the sort of play that makes you think. It made the audience think. It angered them and it pleased them, and on coming out they discussed the problems raised. It is not a good work of art, but it is a serious work of art. I thought of it so much on coming out that I quite forgot that I had meant to go to a café at midnight to meet a friend. I went straight to bed.

Tuesday, November 24th.

Yesterday I walked a great deal about Paris.

Moréno told me on Sunday, when I complained about the Théâtre des Variétés, that it was the dearest-rented theatre on the Boulevard; also that it was a *théâtre à femmes,* and that the entr'actes were made long in order that the men might have time to scribble notes to, and receive answers from, the women. I didn't take this latter quite seriously. When I visited the theatre the audience was most dowdy, and there is absolutely no provision whatever in the way of a foyer.

Wednesday, November 25th.

It was a thoroughly wet and rotten day yesterday. After noon the streets became impossible. I did not work at all, couldn't concentrate in the least. I had to go out and lunch with a companion, and to suffer all sorts of sentimental worries, and to argue closely in French, and to write a long letter in French. Afterwards I played Bach's preludes and fugues till I couldn't play them any longer. I read Casanova, *L'Etui de Nacre,*[1] Maupassant's *La Vie Errante,* and *Le Mercure de France.* I went to bed at 10.15 and arose at 8.30 this morning thoroughly well in all ways.

---

[1] By Anatole France.

After a sluggish beginning, the ideas for my sixth and last *Windsor* story, *Lo! 'Twas a Gala Night,* came with much freedom this afternoon and evening. It occurs to me that I am almost happy, strolling about Paris, and calling in at a café occasionally, working out the ideas for my fiction. Tonight also I sleep early, preparatory to writing 3,000 words tomorrow.

Thursday, November 26th.

I wrote over 3,000 words of my last *Windsor* story, dined at a nice Duval on the Boulevard, smoked a cigar at the Globe, and then went to the Théâtre Antoine and saw Ibsen's *Ghosts.* This is not after all a good play. It is vitiated by the symbolism of the asylum. And the fire at the asylum is "prepared" in a way worthy of Sardou. The defect, fatal defect, of the play is that it is "stagy." It has not the air of being quite sincere. It is too clever. All this I can see quite clearly. The "curtain" of every act is dreadfully "stagy." There are moments in the first and second acts, however, which are poignantly dramatic.

Also *La Paix Chez-soi,* a new one-act piece by Georges Courteline. Very good, funny, and at the same time bitterly true, in its essence, to real life. How such an idea would have been ruined by sentimentality in an English play! But I think I could write a play as good.

I returned home after 12, and after reaching my *étage* dropped my box of matches, which fell right down the well of the stairs to the bottom. I had to return and find them. Vile weather.

Friday, November 27th.

This morning I finished the 6 *Windsor* stories. They will probably be issued as a book under the title *The Loot of Cities,*[1] and I shall make out of them, first and last, from £200 to £250—probably the smaller sum. They have occupied rather less than 2 months of my time. I began well, languished in the middle, and fired up tremendously towards the end. Indeed I wrote the last 3 stories in 12 days. And if I had really tried I could have done the whole 6 in a month. I have learnt a lot about the technique of construction while writing them. And on the whole have not been bored. But once or twice I have been terribly bored.

At the restaurant in the Hippodrome I saw the notorious "Pipe-en-

---

[1] This book appeared in June, 1905.

bois" with two young and naïve and rather ugly girls, sisters. "Pipe-en-bois" is a corset-maker in a large and successful way of business, and a shareholder in many Parisian theatres. He is a perfectly ordinary common-looking man, quite without *chic,* a long spreading auburn beard, and bad neckties; rough hair, short of stature. He has keen eyes. He is a *coureur;* enjoys himself every night. Known in all the *coulisses,* of which he has the run; favourite of all the chorus girls. He gets hold of beginners, dines and sups them, and loves them without further payment. I should say, very shrewd and *rusé* under that frank air of simple joyousness. They say he is extremely keen in business, and a grudging taskmaster. His wife takes a large share in the management of the business. They understand each other, these two, and go their own separate ways. Certainly a "type," this man. Age between 45 and 50.

Saturday, November 28th.

Mrs. D. dined with me at the Place Blanche. Talking of women's internal complaints, she told me she was once in a drawing-room where a number of women were discussing the subject, and one very old lady on being appealed to said sharply, "In my time, no woman *had* a womb, except the Virgin Mary."

Monday, November 30th.

Yesterday I wrote a 4,000-word tale for Tillotsons complete, and had finished it before 7 P.M. Moreover I slept perfectly after it, from 12 to 8.15 without a break, which is extraordinary for me.

The weather is worse and worse. After raining all day it began to snow in the evening. I dined well and came in after dinner for an hour, meaning to go later to a music hall. But once inside, I could not persuade myself to go out again.

This morning when I woke up it was still snowing, the roofs all white, and the streets all water.

This last few days I have begun to make my luncheons about half their usual size—two poached eggs, a roll, and a cup of chocolate; with excellent results.

Reading Anatole France, Jules Renard,[1] Casanova.

---

[1] French caricaturist whose work appeared under the pseudonyms "Draner" and "Paf."

Tuesday, December 1st.

I wrote my fourth and last Tillotson short story yesterday afternoon, 2,000 words. This year I have written 12 short stories, and as some of my stories are apt to disappear from view absolutely in the files of the periodical press, I will make a list of them:

> *The Hungarian Rhapsody* (*T. P.'s Weekly*), good.
> *Midnight at the Great Babylon* (Tillotsons).
> *The Clock*   (Tillotsons).
> *Phantom* (*Hearth and Home*, Xmas No.), fairly good.
> *Loot of Cities* series

| All good on their plane | { | *The Fire of London* *Comedy on the Gold Coast* *A Bracelet at Bruges* *A Solution of the Algiers Mystery* *The Capital of the Sahara* *Lo! 'Twas a Gala Night* | } | (*Windsor.*) |

> *The Railway Station* (Tillotsons), facetious.
> *Saturday to Monday* (Tillotsons), fairly good.

Besides these, several stories have appeared this year which I wrote last year—but I cannot remember all their titles—in *Sphere, Queen, T.P's Weekly,* and elsewhere.

Wednesday, December 2nd.

It snowed all yesterday morning. I walked out 3 miles in it to make purchases; amongst other things the *Mercure de France,* where I found 3 pages concerning myself by Davray—all that was most amiable and appreciative, and yet sober too.

I dined with C.L. at Maire's, corner of Boulevard de Strasbourg, and really enjoyed myself. The place is very *chic,* and I hit on a Burgundy at 3.50 which was really fine. Naturally I drank too much of it. I finished the dinner with *fruits rafraîchis,* refreshed, that is, with abundant liqueurs such as kirsch; I also had a little cognac. The consequence was that I was extremely unwell in the night. However, the attack, which in other days would have lasted 48 hours, cleared away this morning, and I was able to go out and buy a closed French stove—45 francs, second hand, a bargain. I now hope to get, and keep, the *appartement* warm.

After the dinner, Antoine's. And I saw for the first time Henri Becque's famous *La Parisienne*. A play perfectly simple, but exquisitely constructed. Only one important character—played really with genius by Mme. Devoyod. Yes, genius. The play is well entitled. This *is the* Parisienne, even *the* woman. And it is human nature with all its sins presented without the slightest ethical or didactic tendency—with an absolute detachment from morals. It is certainly one of the great plays of the period. I learnt a lot from it, not only in technique, but in the matter of fundamental attitude towards life.

I have spent a good part of today in staring at my new stove.

I hate, now, having any evening quite free, with no society. It is on these evenings, although I amuse myself with writing letters and reading, that I feel "out of it." And that phrase expresses the whole thing. "Out of *it*." What *it* is I don't exactly know.

Thursday, December 3rd.

I had a fine example this morning of the instinctive opposition of the industrial intelligence to any new machine which it doesn't understand. My grand new stove had extinguished itself early this morning, and the *domestique* had to light it. She had been expecting me to buy another sort of stove, simpler. In about 5 minutes she had almost lost her head. After a few days she will have settled down to the novelty and will praise it to her friends.

Friday, December 4th.

Last night *Pelléas et Mélisande,* at the Opéra Comique. This time I thought Debussy's music very good. Sometimes really powerful.

The day before yesterday, or a bit earlier, two children were born in the streets of Paris the same day. C. explained to me that the thing occurred not infrequently. Accouchement in a *maison* was an expensive affair, comparatively. Hence women, at the very last moment, went to the *poste de police* and demanded the assistance which the law binds itself to give.

It is extraordinary how the leading cafés of Montmartre are absolutely crammed at midnight. Till a day or two ago I had scarcely known of the existence of the Café Graff. I was in there last night, and at 12.15 there was not a seat empty. I came home and found my stove gone out.

I lighted it, at 1 p.m., but it would not "take." This trifling thing annoyed me wonderfully. It got on my nerves. I could not sleep and was extremely depressed about everything. The cold continues, and this morning it is even more severe.

Saturday, December 5th.

Dined at Mrs. Devereux's last night. Frank Hurd, Mrs. Richard Le Gallienne,[1] and a Maurice F——(I forget the name—son of one of Napoleon III's generals and an English mother); also Blanche Devereux. Hurd, who seemed to know Italy very well, gave a lot of interesting details about the "keeping up of appearances" there by the reduced aristocracy, which he said far surpassed anything in the same line of effort in England. He told how in Naples a number of families will join in a carriage, and each have their own emblazoned doors, for fitting on to the carriage on their day for using it. But the most curious thing he related was the story of a carriage accident in Rome (I think), where a lady occupying one of the carriages concerned absolutely declined to get out, although the wheels were inextricably locked. Eventually she was pulled out, and it appeared that though she was magnificently dressed as far down as the carriage-rug, below that she wore a ragged old skirt and a pair of bedroom slippers.

Mrs. Le Gallienne made some sensible remarks to the effect that the high architecture of New York and Chicago was only ugly because it was strange to us, and that there was no reason why it should not have a fine character of its own. She said it had that fine character. She told me her husband got 10 times the price in America that he could get in England, and that he loved America, and she gave some details of life in apartments and clubs on fifteenth and twenty-second stories.

The young Maurice F——, whose father was in the very middle of the Boulangist movement, told us how he himself drove the cab containing the General on a famous occasion and how the populace insisted on getting on the roof of the cab. And he gave particulars of the General's *liaison* with Mme. Bonnemain, and how his father predicted the ruin of the "cause" from the moment Madame went into the General's *appartement,* and how she telegraphed to him to leave Paris when he

---

[1] The second wife of the English writer, *née* Julie Norregaard.

certainly ought to have stayed and how generally she ruined a thing which might have succeeded. Wise remarks from the company to the effect that a clever woman in (irregular) love may make a man's fortune, while a stupid one is certain to ruin it.

After more snow the frost turned to rain yesterday.

Monday, December 7th.

I cured my depression yesterday by slaving all day at our play. I did the sketch of it complete and posted it to Eden last night. I only went out to eat, and for quite a short walk of about 20 minutes. Today I approach the humorous novel.

Tuesday, December 8th.

I succeeded far beyond my hopes in planning out *A Great Man* yesterday, and in making a detailed sketch of the first chapter. I was, however, and I remain, extremely dissatisfied and discontented with my general condition. I suppose I shall always be more or less like this. I cannot think of any device or policy by which I could change my condition with any prospect of improvement. I want to be free and fettered at the same time, and it can't be done.

I read the first act of *Othello* last night, and it did me good.

Friday, December 11th.

Yesterday I worked from 10 A.M. to 11 P.M., chiefly on *A Great Man*.

There was a long article in *Le Temps* on Herbert Spencer, which confirmed the view which Wells expressed to me about him in the early part of last year; namely, that as a thinker, he was "woolly."

I meant to go and see Brieux's *Robe Rouge* at the Théâtre du Peuple, but as I was busy, and as they had allotted 500 seats to *midinettes* last night, I refrained. Three plays of Brieux's are being done in Paris this week: the new *Maternité* at Antoine's, *Le Berceau* at the Comédie Mondaine, and the *Robe Rouge*.

Sunday, December 13th.

After buying papers and tea yesterday I lunched at the little creamery in the Place de la Trinité. Then I came home and read various papers and periodicals and Casanova, and fell asleep, sleeping uncomfortably.

Then I tried seriously to find the ideas for Chapter II of new novel; I had been more or less asking for them all morning; no success. Then I went out for a walk, and felt tired even in starting. I walked through the Saint-Lazare quarter to the Madeleine and turned along the *grands boulevards* to the Grand Café. I like the interior of this café. It is as much like the respectable ugliness of an English club as anything in Paris. I ordered a cup of chocolate because I felt empty.

I thought steadily for one hour over this chocolate, and I seemed to leave the café with one or two germs of ideas. I walked home, cogitating. When I arrived, there was a telegram from Whitten requiring my weekly article 2 days earlier than usual. This upset my plans somewhat. I felt so tired—I had taken a chill—that I lay down under the eiderdown on the bed and went to sleep again, reading Casanova.

When I awoke it was dark. I made tea and felt better. A leading notion for the chapter had now formed itself. I went to the Comédie Mondaine to book a seat for Brieux's *Berceau,* and then to the Duval to dine, where I read *Le Temps* all through. Then I bought a cigar and had coffee in the Place Clichy. I cogitated at the café for an hour, and then I had the whole chapter clearly outlined in my head. This is a fair specimen of one of my cogitating days.

Monday, February 14th.

Talking about *Nana,* Moréno confirmed C.'s statement that the theatre portrayed there was the Vaudeville. She also said that Nana was drawn from Hortense Schneider, the famous Offenbach singer. In response to another of my numerous questions she said there *was* a prompter at the Théâtre Sarah Bernhardt but he was stuck away in a corner and couldn't be heard except for the most urgent occasion.

Thursday, December 17th.

I went into a rather select little café for coffee last night in the Place Clichy, and was more than ever struck by the "intimity" of this kind of café. The place amounted to a club. Nearly every one who entered shook hands with the *demoiselle de comptoir.* An aged couple came in, aged between 60 and 70. The man was reading *La Presse,* and the woman, big and bony, called for *Paris-Sport* and busied herself in the day's racing until they were joined by another man, also old and very mannered. All three were intensely respectable and dignified, though not in the least *chic*. I had meant to see Sudermann's *L'Honneur* at the Théâtre du Peuple, but being interested in my novel, I came home at 8.30 and worked till 11 P.M.

I finished *Sapho*.[1] Chapter XII, describing Jean's management of the rupture with Fanny, is very great indeed. No general accusation of sentimentality can be brought against the book. As a whole it is great and terrible. Now I can go back to my Casanova, having read *all* the absolutely first-class French novels of the nineteenth century.

This morning the weather is exactly London weather, gloomy and muggy, and not very cold.

Friday, December 18th.

The most singular thing that I have heard from C. about Paris is that in the night (? after 12) one cannot legitimately ring up a doctor without the presence of a gendarme. You get the gendarme to go with you to the doctor's; then the doctor is bound to come. The gendarme enters with the doctor, remains in an adjoining room, and afterwards the doctor fills up the gendarme's *feuille*.

Sunday, December 20th.

Yesterday I finished Chapter II. I went to Cook's in the morning and began the business of departing to England by drawing out all the money I could and getting my ticket, and the clerk asked me if I was going to England, and I said I was, and he wished me a happy Christmas. At night I didn't feel very hungry; so I had to tempt myself with a "nice little dinner" at Sylvain's, which cost me 6 francs. Then I came home, played Beethoven's two sonatas, Op. 49, perfectly charming, finished reading *Le Temps* all through, and went to bed at 10.30. I slept till 8.10 this morning.

Wednesday, December 23rd.

I had a smooth passage over on Monday.

Yesterday I saw Pinker [2] twice, and after some hesitations on his part, arranged that he should pay me £50 a month certain during 1904.

---

[1] By Alfonse Daudet.
[2] The literary agent.

Pinker, Barry Pain,[1] and I lunched together. But Pain hadn't many new stories. I heard that Mrs. Humphrey Ward had £10,000 from *Harper's* for serial rights of *Lady Rose's Daughter,* and that the book sold 400,000 in America alone.

Woke up this morning at 4.30. Read Maupassant, myself, and the *Telegraph;* but couldn't sleep again till 8.30.

Thursday, December 24th.

I came to Burslem yesterday evening with Tertia and William and a headache. Went out this morning and saw numbers of people. Walking to Hanley this afternoon, I was struck by the orange-apple *cold* Christmas smell of the greengrocers' shops.

Saturday, December 26th.

Yesterday, Christmas Day, I was reading *Falk* in Conrad's *Typhoon,* and then several stories by Wells. Also Mérimée's famous *Mateo Falcone,* which is nothing special except in the extraordinary cruelty of the plot.

I went to bed at 1.30 and was kept awake till 4.30 by a barking dog. Then at 7.15 Mater knocked on the wall. She was in the middle of a bilious crisis caused by overnight hare and bilberries. She stays in bed. Hence the whole atmosphere of the house becomes special, and "sick-roomy," and I can't proceed with my novel today, as I had meant.

---

[1] Humorous writer best known for his "Eliza" stories.

1904

Sunday, January 3rd.

I came to Paris yesterday, and wrote letters all the way over on the boat.

Monday, January 4th.

Today, with difficulty, I resumed *A Great Man* and wrote rather less than 1,000 words.

I read some Emerson, and found much in common between him and Walt Whitman. I also made the acquaintance—I had almost quite forgotten it—of Beethoven's sonata, Op. 10 No. 3. I played it in instalments during the afternoon.

Wednesday, January 6th.

All yesterday I was ill—probably owing to mussel soup at Sylvain's on Monday night, but I do not feel sure. Rawson called for his lunch, and I was obliged to send him away again. C. came in the evening and stayed till midnight. I had slept nearly all day. As curiously illustrating the customs of costume—she cannot go out to do household shopping in a hat. She must go *nu-tête*. I couldn't read anything yesterday but newspapers. I read Stead's [1] new paper, *The Daily Paper,* first number, all through. It made me admire the man, but if the paper succeeds I shall be surprised.

Although feeble I did a good day's work.

Davray called, and handed me the half-price ticket for Mentone which

---

[1] W. T. Stead, the famous journalist and vice-crusader.

he obtained for me through the *Mercure de France*. Rhoden gave me an excellent Viennese dinner at an Austrian restaurant in the Rue d'Hauteville. Afterwards at the Grand Café he enlarged on his international experiences as an insurance man. He explained to me how various circumstances relating to my King of Bosnia in *The Grand Babylon Hotel* coincided with the case of the King of Serbia; so much so that when he read the book he thought I had been down there and knew the facts. However, I knew nothing whatever, and the coincidence was purely accidental. When I outlined to him the plot of the *Algiers Mystery* in my forthcoming *Windsor* stories, and told him that I had had the St. George at Algiers in view, he replied that an attempt (by natives) to rob the Hotel St. George on a grand scale took place some years ago. Of this I had no knowledge whatever.

Friday, January 8th.

I finished third chapter of *A Great Man.*

In the afternoon I went to see Rhoden at the offices of the New York *Life* on the boulevard, and I was much surprised at the vast magnificence of the interior—great staircases, immense corridors, numberless large rooms, and all highly and profusely decorated, in the manner of a palace, with marble, silks, gold, and fancy carved panellings. The place, as a place of business, is really impressive. Rhoden showed me all over it, including the President's room, a gorgeous empty chamber, and through a half-open door I saw into another gorgeous chamber, where the Lord God of the European section was working at a desk. Never before had I seen a real American magnate in his den. I noticed how heavy was the lower part of his face. Stuck about all the offices are printed incentives to commercial activity, such as "Do it now" in white letters on red. I saw also a poster addressed to the French employees of the company, pointing out that the company's business in France was now equal to that in Germany, but that if the French employees didn't work hard . . . The thing was made humorously effective by means of typographical tricks.

I forgot to set down, on the 1st, the brief record of last year. I wrote five-sixths of *Leonora,* and 12 short stories. Four books of mine were published, *The Gates of Wrath, The Truth about an Author, How to Become an Author,* and *Leonora.* The great fact illustrating my commercial progress was that the *Windsor Magazine* gave me a commission for 6 short stories. I did nothing in the way of drama except the sketch of the play which I am now about to write with Phillpotts. I did practically no work between January 15 and March 15, when I was travelling in Algeria, etc. I returned from Algeria March 1 and spent a fortnight or so in England preparatory to settling in Paris. Then between April 1 and June 30 I wrote nearly all *Leonora*.

On June 29 I went to England, and messed about England till September 18, doing scarcely any work—a summer cut to pieces and wasted and therefore not a pleasant one. I came to Paris about September 18, spent 10 days in taking and furnishing a flat; then I started to work, and I have worked ever since. I propose to work almost without intermission, at any rate till July 30.

I bought *The Gates of Wrath* (Tauchnitz edition) and read some of it. Its smartness and clarity prevent me from being quite honestly ashamed of it.

The recital of Marmeladoff's domestic history in one of the early chapters of *Crime and Punishment* is one of the finest instances of the mingling of tragedy and humour that I can call to mind.

Wednesday, January 13th.

Horrible muddy weather yesterday. I did nothing but prepare to depart for Mentone. I bought two Stevensons and read a lot of *Island Nights*. Good sound work, but, strictly judged, decidedly mediocre—though marked by the most charming justice of "values," as they say in painting.

Thursday, January 14th.

I left the Rue de Calais yesterday, depressed, at 5 P.M., after having lunched with C. The drive to the Gare de Lyon along the interminable length of the Rue de Rivoli got on my nerves. And I was decidedly excited and "wrought up" when the train *de grand luxe* came up and I saw Phillpotts. Much talking and mutual satisfaction. (I have a sore throat now.) The train left sharp at 6 P.M. and arrived here at Mentone sharp at 9.56 A.M. this morning. On the whole a really good, sound train. It would be almost perfect if it had a drawing-room car, as it certainly ought to have. The ceaseless noise and jolting did not noticeably affect me much. I took a sedative and slept very well, though mostly conscious of the action and the din. Coming along the coast, I had my first glimpse of Monte Carlo and the salons thereof. I was duly impressed by the beauty of the coast, and of Mentone in particular. But my thoughts were chiefly occupied with the idea of the train, that luxurious complete entity—running through a country and ignoring it. I seldom had the least idea where the train was. Space, as a notion, had vanished for me. I might have been in the void.

Friday, January 15th.

I woke up this morning just before dawn, and there was a red streak of light along the horizon, and the sea smoke-colour, and the lamps and the riding-lights of the vessels just beginning to be ghostly. On either side the hills with their bare rocky tops. Then, when I woke up again, the strong sun was shining brilliantly on to my balcony and almost into my face. There must be a fairly strong off-shore wind blowing, but this place is very sheltered and the sea seems quite calm. However, one can *hear* the wind. The beauty of the landscape and of the old Italianate town to the right, with its red flat-square conical roofs, and the delicate softness of the air, make a deep impression on one.

I took my tea and *croissant* out on the balcony in the 8.30 A.M. sun, wrapped in my largest overcoat, and in the sunshine. It was tremendous, after the bed breakfasts of a Paris flat.

Night. The beauty of this place even grows on one. The afternoon and dusk were simply miraculous for colour. Before lunch I went for a walk up on the hill and then down again and along the coast. I walked into Italy in about a quarter of an hour. Most of the morning I spent on the balcony thinking out Chapter V, and before dinner I wrote 700 words.

As a curious form of eroticism, Eden told me: The Misses F., aged 40, went to Oxford, and came back and said how fine it was to hear the tramping of *men* in the streets after Torquay. There is a good deal in this, and I ought not to forget it. It is a sort of touch that couldn't be invented.

Saturday, January 16th.

I wrote 2,500 words of *A Great Man* today, and it's impossible to work hard at a novel and appreciate a new environment at the same time.

Beyond a walk to the centre of the town and the bandstand, I made no excursion. But I breakfasted on the balcony in dressing-gown and overcoat, and all day I have had the atmosphere, perfectly wonderful, and the magnificent views from the balcony.

Before dinner Eden and I discussed and settled certain outstanding preliminary points in our play. It took about half an hour. I expect to begin the actual writing on Tuesday, and the actual detailed constructive thinking on Monday.

Sunday, January 17th.

I was much disquieted today by Tertia's letter in which she said twice that the Mater was "extremely ill." Deep down in every one's mind will be the idea that I am "enjoying myself on the Riviera" while she is extremely ill. It is the address of the absent son that matters on these occasions. But I should be a fool to go to London unless she was much worse than she is. However, I managed to do a good day's work, and finished Chapter V of *A Great Man*, 5,500 words.

Hanbury, of Allen and Hanbury's foods, and the great botanist, editor of the *London Catalogue*, came to lunch. He is staying with his cousin Sir Thomas Hanbury, the Lord God of these parts. Sir Thomas has the finest private garden in the world, 100 acres, 5,000 species (some absolutely unique), and 46 gardeners. Speaking of Monte Carlo, he told us how he was at the tables 30 years ago and saw two Russian princesses there losing heavily, but keeping stoical silence, the tears streaming down their cheeks. He is emphatically not a man of the world, and his Russian princesses were probably French whores; but nevertheless his picture of the women playing and losing, in silent, irrepressible, hopeful-despairing tears, was an effective one. He is far from an ordinary man, and I rather liked something at the root of him, but soon after lunch I stole away to sleep.

Monday, January 18th.

Breakfast again on the balcony, while the fishing-boats went out one by one straight into the dazzle of the sun, with an extraordinary *sentimental* effect. A highly dandiacal yacht, with fittings all brass and mahogany apparently, had been at anchor since we came: she was moored by two ropes to the jetty, and by two anchors from the stern. I noticed a detail of actualness which might be brought into a scene with great effect. The yacht swung from side to side on the jetty ropes, lifting first the starboard and then the port rope clear of the water, and as each rope came clear of the still water, the drops from it fell into the water in hundreds for a few seconds, making a wonderfully pretty pattering sound. On first catching this sound I did not perceive how it was caused.

Tuesday, January 19th.

I finished reading *Jekyll and Hyde* before breakfast. It is not bad. I thought less than ever of the writing, which is never more than dignified. As regards the scientific part, after Wells it comes feeble. No future novelist will be able to "fudge" science now that Wells has shown how it can be done without fudging. All the potion business in Jekyll's final document is childish and unconvincing, and mars what is otherwise the strongest part of the book. The psychology of the last chapter is indeed really good and subtle.

Thursday, January 21st.

This afternoon I heard from Tertia that the Mater was considerably better. I had been fearing a fatal conclusion.

Two hard days' work on *A Credit to Human Nature*. I wrote more than two-thirds of the first act—4,300 words; and shall finish it tomorrow. I had a long yarn with Eden tonight about the plot, and cleared up sundry more points and improved sundry others. It is wonderful how two brains working together on a piece of pure concoction are worth so much more than twice one brain.

Sunday, January 24th.

Mr. and Mrs. C. N. Williamson [1] came over from Monte Carlo to lunch; she very bright, sincere, and well dressed, and he very smart, quick, and generally decent. Mrs. Williamson explained to me how she had come to use a plot similar to the *Grand Babylon Hotel* in a story for the *Strand*. She assured me that a number of people did make a regular income by gambling at the tables, and that the authorities allowed it because it was a good advertisement. She said that it was not systems that were wrong,

---

[1] C. N. and A. M. Williamson are known chiefly for their popular detective stories. Their books include *The Princess Passes, The Lightning Conductor,* etc.

but the fallible humanness of the people who, in using them, were not content to stick to them absolutely.

Tuesday, January 26th.

The first visit to Monte Carlo must be a sort of an event in the life of any one with imagination. I went there yesterday afternoon from Mentone by tram. The ride is very diversified, and here and there fine views are obtained.

On the whole I was disappointed by the exterior aspects of the town. It lacks spaciousness, and since it is in the absolute control of one autocratic authority, spaciousness is what it ought not to have lacked. Some of the villas, however, with their white paint and general air of being toys, are *excessivement chic*. The casino is all right in its florid, heavy way—but what a chance for an architect, on that site over the sea! The whole town had an air of being Parisian, but not quite Parisian enough. I could distinguish courtesans among the wayfarers long before the tram reached the Casino gardens.

Inside the gaming-saloons (4 o'clock) I found a large crowd and many tables in full work. The crowd not so distinguished in appearance as I had (foolishly) expected. Scores and scores of prostitutes, and of course a number of really "classy" people. I saw few signs at the tables of suppressed or *ex*pressed excitement, though quite a large proportion of the people seemed to be gambling seriously. I had no intention of betting, but after I had watched several tables and grasped the details of roulette (30 and 40 I didn't attempt to grasp) I remained at one table as if hypnotized; without knowing it I began to finger a 5-franc piece in my pocket, and then I became aware that I was going to bet. I knew I should bet some seconds before I formally decided to. I staked a 5-franc piece on an even chance and won. Like a provincial up from the country, who has heard tales of metropolitan rascality, I stood close to a croupier and kept a careful eye on my coin, and picked up the winnings without an instant's delay. I kept on playing, carefully, and always on even chances, for some time, and stopped when I had made a little money, and went and had some tea. I didn't play again.

The idea of gambling quite absorbed all my thoughts; obsessed me; and I had schemes—such as that it would be experientially worth while to go there with, say, 5,000 francs, and deliberately become a regular system-using gambler for a time. There is no doubt that the human spectacle of the gaming saloons is tremendous; unequalled; the interest of it could not easily fail for an observer. To a stranger, of course, one of the most curious things is the sight of large sums of money in notes and gold constantly being flung about the tables. I am told that the Casino employs 1,800 people altogether. The croupiers work 6 hours a day each; so I estimate there must be about 200 croupiers altogether. I just missed a tram in coming home and had half an hour to wait; all that time I thought of gaming, gaming. And I look forward to going again on Friday.

Thursday, January 28th.

Two long and hard days' work on the play, and a thundering bad night's rest in between. But beautiful weather, superlatively beautiful. Mediterranean like a duck pond, and cloudless sunshine both days. I am getting interested again in *Crime and Punishment,* after deserting it in the middle for *M. Bergeret à Paris.*[1]

Saturday, January 30th.

I went over with the Phillpottses to lunch with the Williamsons at the Royal Hotel at Monte Carlo yesterday. Mrs. Williamson had all sorts of material for wild and whirling plot, which she had gathered at Monte Carlo, and she gave it away with the utmost freedom.

Afterwards we went to the Casino. I began on my system at once, and made 45 francs in ¾ of an hour, when Eden and the rest wished to go out for tea. Eden was very interested in the place, but took no pleasure in it, as I expected. We had tea at the Café de Paris, next to the Russian grand duke who lately "broke the bank." Then we came home in the car, and Mrs. Phillpotts was too tired to utter a word, and Eden's chest had been much disturbed by the foul air of the rooms. I learned that the tables are lighted by oil lamps because once a great raid was attempted which began with the cutting off of the electric light.

Today I finished Act II of *A Credit to Human Nature.*

Sunday, January 31st.

Having nothing to do yesterday afternoon, and Eden being at work,

---

[1] By Anatole France.

and two others being out, and the day wet, I could not resist going over to Monte Carlo in the tram. I lost money at the tables, and came home depressed. In the evening I played billiards, practically for the first time, Eden teaching me.

Today, bad weather again. I wrote an excellent *T.P.* article on Monte Carlo.

But at present my interest in this journal is not what it was. Monte Carlo and other things have disturbed it.

Wednesday, February 3rd.

The ideas of the average decently informed person are so warped, and out of perspective, and ignorant, and entirely perverse and wrong and crude, on nearly every mortal subject, that the task of discussing anything with him seriously and fully and to the end is simply appalling. This has struck me several times recently in this hotel, and I have recoiled from a discussion. The state of that average person's mind can scarcely be contemplated by me, in certain moods.

The funeral feast given by Catherine Ivanovna in *Crime and Punishment* is a magnificent piece of work, both as serious accurate observation and as brutal humour.

Today I began Act III of the play, and wrote about 2,000 words.

Friday, February 5th.

I finished the play. All that remains to be done to it now is Eden's revise. In 3 weeks exactly, we have written, between us, (1) the play, (2) 2 short stories, (3) 3 articles, (4) a long chapter of my novel. This is what may be called the industry of genuine craftsmen. Nothing has been scamped except this journal, which doesn't count. The play is 19,000 words in length—about 2,000 words too long.

Saturday, February 6th.

Yesterday being wet, I went over to Monte Carlo, and lost money, and was depressed by that and the weather, and more particularly by my lack of sense in playing with insufficient capital.

Early this morning I composed a limerick on that infernal and un-vanquishable bore, Mrs. Miller, whose room is next to Eden's.

> There was an old woman named Miller
> Whose acquaintances wanted to kill her.
> When they put her in ice
> She sniggered, "How nice!"
> For nothing could possibly chill her.

And sent it in to Eden by special messenger.

Monday, February 8th.

I walked yesterday morning into Italy, and got a few good ideas for the novel, and was rather impressed by all the pomp of the boundary business between France and Italy. The views from the road are wonderful. In the afternoon we had tea at the huge, showy, smart, and not bad Winter Palace Hotel.

But I am now unsettled here and want to return to Paris, as some of the party is getting on my nerves.

Eden and I were discussing the *Spectator's* notice of *My Devon Year* and its remarks on his style, and I formulated the theory that the faults (admitted) that the *Spectator* found in his style were due to the too small proportion of verbs in his sentences compared to nouns and adjectives.

On testing, I found that in the quoted passages there were 420 nouns and adjectives to every 100 verbs. In a famous passage towards the close of *Hydriotaphia*[1] I found there were only 183 nouns and adjectives to every 100 verbs. We both thought this line of enquiry might be pursued further with advantage.

He said he had, long ago, met an American woman who had aspired to be a poet and had submitted her verse to Longfellow in his old age, and called on him and received his advice. She was young then and very pretty. "How can I thank you, Mr. Longfellow?" she cried earnestly. "You can give me a kiss," said Longfellow. She said to Eden, "I was so taken aback and startled that I just kissed him and ran straight out of the house."

Thursday, February 11th.

Battle of flowers yesterday. Rather feeble, but perhaps as good as could be expected at Mentone.

---

[1] Sir Thomas Browne's *Hydriotaphia, Urn-Buriall.*

Saturday, February 13th.

I left Mentone last evening at 8.15, and arrived in Paris at 7.40 this morning, absolutely promptly. It must have rained much in the night, but the sun shines now and there is a faint indication of spring in the air. I was very keen on getting news of the war,[1] but there seems none to be obtained. The only real English newspaper in Paris, the *N.Y. Herald,* is certainly siding strongly with Russia. It is when one wants authentic *news* that the defects of a country's press begin plainly to appear—especially news which is difficult to obtain and easy to imitate.

Monday, February 15th.

I was influenza-ish all day yesterday and on Saturday evening—until last night, when it passed off. We dined on Saturday and yesterday at Sylvain's, and last night went into the Casino de Paris for an hour or so.

I heard again the story of the life, death, and burial of the mysterious pretty Englishwoman from Liverpool who gave lessons in English to a constant stream of *monsieurs chics,* and expired alone at 7 Rue Bréda after being robbed by a Spanish male friend. The arrival of the English relatives and all that! It seemed to me I might use up a lot of the stuff in *The History of Two Old Women,*[2] which it seems more and more likely will be my next serious book.

I transcribe some notes which I made some weeks ago of conversations with a spinster aged perhaps 41. She said: "Sometimes I never speak to a man (except tradesmen) for six months together. I see my brothers in the holidays for two months. My three brothers-in-law are all charming and kind to me. But I do not understand men." (She harped continually on this.) "I am not at ease with them. I do not know how they think. Still, when I talk to them I enjoy talking to them. Often when I get the chance of talking to them I don't do so, because I can't talk about their things, books, sport, and so on. Moreover, I am independent of men. I can manage without them. Many women simply can't. And I hate to think that I am depriving a woman of a man when she needs him more than I do. When you have got a man you can always see some woman who is hating you for having him. There are so many more women than

---

[1] War between Russia and Japan was declared February 10 of this year.
[2] *The Old Wives' Tale.*

ever—not nearly enough men to go round." (When I explained to her how slight the excess of women over men really was, she showed extreme surprise, and seemed scarcely inclined to believe me.)

She said later: "The busiest people are the happiest. To have an object in life . . . ! When you have no object in life, when you feel you are useless, not wanted, no good in the world, then I see no good in living. To have some gift, to be clever—that is the thing." (Presumably she was speaking generally, but whatever she said I felt that she had herself always in mind.) Again: "I know my brain is weak; it lacks certain convolutions. I can lose my head immediately. I can't concentrate my thoughts. And I have no sense of locality. . . . But I can talk to children; I know how they think. I can remember my own childhood, my infancy, and it seems as if I could remember little else afterwards. I can remember being sung to sleep, and how amazed I was because they changed the tune. Can't you remember that? Can't you remember how disturbing and vexing it was to have the tune changed? Yes, I suppose that *is* a gift, to understand children. I ought to have been a nurse."

On the whole a curious mixture of pride (vanity) and self-depreciation, the former instinctive, the latter due to intellectual processes. A haughty, arrogant mien, the sort of mien that, in English people, naturally maddens foreigners.

I went last night to see *Siegfried* at the Opéra, and came away in a mood to swear that nothing should ever induce me to go to the Opéra again in search of my own artistic pleasure. A tame performance without any distinction of any kind. The orchestra was rotten—and you could see even from the parterre that the gestures of the conductor proclaimed him a silly old fool, wrong-headed, dry, academic, and bereft of enthusiasm. All the ugly grotesquerie of the first and second acts was insisted on instead of being ameliorated. *Siegfried* is an opera which needs the greatest tact in production. I can easily understand, now, how at first Wagner's works were merely laughed at. If they were produced new today they would be laughed at. They are so different from anything else, and their beauty seems to exist side by side with their Teutonic gawkiness—in a sort of fourth dimension which only the trained eye can perceive at all. . . . A crowded and talkative audience; in fact everything possible against Wagner. (Nevertheless 5 of his operas are now in the regular repertoire of the Opéra.) Some moments I enjoyed extremely despite all the drawbacks: still, the Opéra is a European scandal. It ought to be at Bucharest or Cairo.

I went out this afternoon (Mardi gras) towards the *grands boulevards*. The crowd got thicker and thicker and confetti more and more plentiful. I left the Rue Montmartre for the *passages,* and became blocked in the Passage Jouffroy and so returned. The carnival was nothing but an excuse for stupidity and horseplay. It began to rain, and soon rained heavily, and kept on till 8.30. I was morosely glad to see the carnival thus ruined. It may break out again tonight, though I had promised myself a concert of old music tonight, but after trudging in the wet to the hall in the Rue d'Athénès, I found the place shut up. I must have mistaken the night.

So I spent an hour at the Moulin Rouge, picking up trifles and boring myself.

Wednesday, February 17th.

I really enjoyed working on my novel today, and this although I had a headache most of the time.

Saturday, February 20th.

Last night at 11 I finished another section of *A Great Man*, having written 8,300 words in 4 days.

Weather still bad; rainy and windy.

Sunday, February 21st.

Last night *Nana,* drama in 5 acts drawn by William Busnach from Zola's novel, at the Ambigu. . . . A thoroughly rotten and crude melo-drama, interspersed with "comic relief" of the most footling sort. Yet it made one think of the book. And my admiration of the book leapt out again into a flame. It is not one of the greatest books, but it is super-latively *done,* a tremendous achievement of colossal and distinguished labour. How must Zola have felt when he wrote the last lines!

I drank some tea at midnight. And reaching home found a telegram from Harrison of the Haymarket, saying that Lewis Waller [1] wanted a play, and might he see *The Chancellor?* The tea and the telegram pre-vented me from sleeping.

This afternoon, Lamoureux concert, to hear, chiefly, Richard Strauss's

---

[1] The actor-manager.

Life of a Hero. It came at the end of an exhausting programme, but I was much impressed by its beauty. I heard it under difficulties, for the audience grew restive, talked, and protested. One old man insisted on going out. There is a rule about not entering or leaving during a piece, but this old man cried so loud and shook the doors so that the *pompiers* were obliged to let him through. Applause and hisses at the end, from a full audience. One more exhibition of the *bêtise* of an audience when confronted by something fresh, extravagant, and powerful. It would be absurd to condemn this or any other particular audience, for all audiences are alike. The sarcastic and bitter opposition must be taken as a tribute to the power of the art. Was not *Tannhäuser* simply laughed off the stage at the first performance? I liked the piece better than I thought I should —a great deal. The first thing of Richard Strauss that I have heard.

Twelve thousand five hundred words written this week.

Wednesday, February 24th.

I walked about Paris most of yesterday, and bought a few reproductions and engravings of pictures. Towards evening I had collected my ideas. I began to write at 9.15 P.M., and finished a short chapter before 12.30.

Just now, as negotiations about two of my plays are pending, I am in a great state of secret excitement and have postponed going to see friends and asking them to see me and generally organizing a social campaign, until something has been decided one way or the other. I had another letter from Louis Calvert this morning as to *The Wayward Duchess.*

Thursday, February 25th.

I worked nearly all day yesterday, till 11 P.M. This singular industry is becoming monotonous.

Reading *Notes sur Angleterre* last night—a wonderful book—I was amused by Taine's noting young Englishmen sleeping with open windows in winter as a sign of primitivism, a sort of healthy reversion to original type. His remarks on *Punch* are extremely clever and ingenious, in the way of finding the very roots of our national character in that periodical. *Punch* will always be able to say that Taine gave 3 pages to praising it.

Sunday, February 28th.

I finished another section of *A Great Man* yesterday at 3.30 P.M., having written nearly 10,000 words in a week. I ought easily to complete the book by March 20. It seems amusing enough, and very good in places. But if I treated this as a draft, and really thought out types and made the book fuller, I could make it much better. However, I have a mania for producing a lot just now. And further, this sort of book, though I can do it, is scarcely my natural *genre*. I do not take quite the same terrific interest in it as I take in a serious book, nor do I get quite the same satisfaction out of a passage which I know to be well done. And often I have the greatest difficulty in starting my day's work. I am all right when I have started. But the starting is *pénible*.

Monday, February 29th.

Last night seemed to be one of the bitterest we have had in the present cold spell; yet I noticed a number of people sitting out quite unconcernedly on the *terrasses* of the cafés on the *grands boulevards*. Some cafés had thick mats spread over the *terrasse*, and one had a coke brazier red and smoky, set among the tables.

When a youngish horse is just starting out fresh from the stable in the morning, up a hill, with a light trap behind him, he brings his nose down under his neck, so that the line of the head is parallel with the fore-leg before it takes a step; his hind feet slip a little perhaps on the stones, and he pulls bravely. That is a beautiful sight. It was the first thing I saw, going out yesterday morning.

Tuesday, March 1st.

I bought a new copy of *La Grande Encyclopédie,* bound in cloth, 31 vols., for 290 francs, yesterday morning. Schwob, on whom I called yesterday afternoon, praised it highly. He mentioned specially such articles as *Aristotle* by Boutroux, as being the very finest of their kind. I looked up this, and it certainly impressed me. Brunetière's article on *Style* is admirable; also Remy de Gourmont's on *Aretino*. Schwob was in bed, and had been there for a month. We discussed the war, and Dickens. He stood up for Dickens, and said that, for style, the opening of *Hard Times* is one of the finest things in English. Of course I disagreed. He said that Dickens's ghost story, *The Signalman,* was "plagiarized" from something in Defoe's essay on apparitions, but much improved. He told me about the dinner to Edmund Gosse. Said Gosse was charming, but pedantic.

Wednesday, March 2nd.

I walked a good deal yesterday: extremely cold. I called in at the Petit Palais and saw some good things that I had not noticed before. I was in search of ideas for the Continental part of *A Great Man*. But I could not keep my mind off the serious novel which is to make a third to *Anna* and *Leonora*. I thought of a fine name for the title: *Carlotta*. About 6 o'clock, after useless efforts all day, I got the leading idea which I wanted for *A Great Man*. In the evening, concert. Quartets of Brahms and Beethoven, and songs by Brahms, Schumann, and Schubert. Full house. The affair was most inspiriting. Again I could not keep my thoughts off *Carlotta* (as I shall now call it [1]), and it seems that after all I may do this book before I do *The History of Two Old Women*. . . . This morning, snow.

Monday, March 7th.

The Davrays dined with me last night at the Hippodrome, and afterwards we went to the Grand Café. He gave me sundry particulars about the French dinner to Edmund Gosse, and said that Gosse's speech (which he, Davray, translated into French for him) was simply admirable and was continually interrupted, at every sentence, by applause. Schwob's speech in English was also very good, he said.

Gosse received the offer of his appointment to the Librarianship of the House of Lords on the very morning of the banquet. He was asked, privately, to accept the offer at once, as the King (it was known) had a candidate, and the House of Lords people wished to be able to say, when the King came forward, that the appointment was already filled. So, Davray said, Gosse told him. Davray saw the letter offering the appointment, from Sir Henry Lowndes Graham,[2] and said it was extraordinarily flattering.

Davray gave me a new instance of politeness. At some English house a foreigner called (nationality obscure, I forget, something small), wear-

---

[1] Subsequently christened *Sacred and Profane Love*, but published in America as *The Book of Carlotta*.

[2] Clerk of Parliaments 1885–1917.

ing what looked like an overcoat. The hostess urged him to take it off; said it was the custom etc. He took it off, and appeared in his shirt-sleeves. Consternation of the hostess, especially as other guests were expected. Presently Laurence Housman came in and was advised privately of the situation. Housman took off his own coat, and sat down also in his shirt-sleeves; then complained of the cold, and demanded from his hostess permission to resume his coat; the foreigner followed his example.

"C'était très fin," commented Davray. After this I was surprised to learn that Housman spoke no French at all. It seemed to me, somehow, that a man capable of that ought to be a perfect French scholar.

I had great ideas this last day or two of a chart of English literature, chronological; divided in coloured sections showing different groups such as poetry-history, drama, etc. . . . and showing the "contemporaneousness" of authors and works exactly. Thus the years, from "Summer is y-cumen in" down to H. G. Wells, would be marked perpendicularly and the "contemporaneousness" shown horizontally. It would be possible to see at a glance what poetry, history, theology, etc., was being produced at the date, say, of *Tom Jones;* and how *Tom Jones* stood with *Clarissa,* or *Hamlet* with *The Broken Heart;* and also the ages of the authors at the dates of their various works would be automatically perceptible.

Such a chart would be extremely useful. A month's work, with nothing but Chambers's *Encyclopædia* of English literature and the *Dictionary of National Biography,* would suffice for it. I would try to include all the authors dealt with in the former. I seem to see myself doing it, for fun, after an illness, or when I was thoroughly exhausted with creative work.

Wednesday, March 9th.

I finished *Le Crépuscule des Dieux* yesterday, and was very much disappointed in the book. When we were discussing it on Sunday night Davray admitted that it "lacked life." It also lacks construction. The author thought the theme was big, and it isn't. It is only royal. The meant-to-be-big scenes, such as the attempt to poison the Duc, are absolute failures. Further, the symbolism of the title, borrowed from Wagner, and the use made of Wagner's opera at the beginning and at the end— these things are too facile. A really great artist would not have employed them. Davray said that Bourgès's style was such that it was a pleasure to read it. Perhaps so. Nevertheless I do not attach any importance to Elemir Bourgès. I can see he is one of the "idols" of a group of enthusiasts—such as we have now and again in England.

Concert of the Nouvelle Société Philharmonique last night. Beethoven's 32 variations the principal item, and a lovely violin sonata by Corelli. In Liszt's Hungarian Rhapsody No. 11, I seemed once, for a few seconds, to get a hint of the joy which many people find in these compositions.

Two curious things I have noticed lately. The Société Protectrice des Animaux keeps spare tip-horses all day at the foot of the principal inclines in Paris (e.g. Rue Notre Dame de Lorette), and car men can employ them for the ascent for one penny. Another thing is that, just about now, there is an eruption of women in the street selling all sorts of veils. They carry their light gauzy stock in an open umbrella held downwards.

Thursday, March 10th.

I wrote all day yesterday at *A Great Man*, 3,400 words. And I can now see the end of it. With luck I shall finish it on Monday.

I can see at once that *Les Liaisons Dangereuses* [1] is a great work. It has the classic truthfulness and sobriety on every page. Letter XVII in which Cécile describes the covert love scene between herself and the Chevalier Danceny is a most perfect and marvellous rendering of a young girl's feelings. It seemed to me to be one of the most beautiful things of the kind I had ever read.

Sunday, March 13th.

I finished *A Great Man* at 11.30 this morning, having written about 10,000 words in the last 5 days. I am more satisfied with it than I thought I should be. I began it with an intention merely humorous, but the thing has developed into a rather profound satire. I began the book about the 10th December; during 2 weeks of the time between then and now (Christmas) I put it aside, and during 3 other weeks I put it aside in order to write the play with Eden. So that I have been engaged on it

[1] By Choderlos de Laclos (1741–1803).

9 weeks altogether. It is 60,000 words in length, and my eighth novel of one sort or another.

On Friday and Saturday I had an extremely severe cold in the head, but nothing could prevent me from finishing that novel. I was in the exact mood for writing, and had all the ideas arranged in my head.

Monday, March 14th.

This morning I read through as much as was necessary of *A Great Man*, and at half past 2 took it away to the post office. I had sealed it up, and they made me unseal it, because it was for a foreign country. I am now haunted by a slight fear of its being lost in the post, and by a grave fear of its being dull and not funny after all.

Wednesday, March 16th.

I meant to go and see *L'Etrangère* [1] at the Français on Monday night, but was too unwell—a mysterious lassitude. So I bought *La Petite Roque* of Maupassant instead, and came home. Yesterday I bought Taine's *Graindorge*. This book brought to a head the ideas which I have had for writing "impressions" of Paris. I find I must write something. I can't lie quite fallow. Moreover I have now been in Paris exactly a year, and my ideas are becoming defined. So this morning I started a book of impressions, with an account of, and reflections upon, the opening of the Concerts Berlioz, which I went to last night. It is probable that this book, if I continue with it, will reduce my journal to a naked record. I am worried with an idea for placing the impressions serially in various papers.

Friday, March 18th.

Yesterday morning I received a letter from Whitten asking me to discontinue my *Log-Book* in *T.P's Weekly* in 6 weeks' time from now. This rather depressed me. I enjoy doing these articles, and I shall have to make up the £165 a year by other work—probably fiction. So all my work will be fiction.

Wednesday, March 23rd.

On Friday night last *Le Dédale*, play in 5 acts, by Paul Hervieu. I

---

[1] By Dumas *fils*.

thought this one of the greatest modern plays I have ever seen, especially as to the 3 middle acts. Constant spiritual action of the piece, and constant drama, conflict of emotions, etc., rising at times to great heights. The famous catastrophe of the precipice in the fifth act did not convince me; nor was I convinced of the necessity for any such fatal tragedy at all. On the other hand the catastrophe may have seemed ineffective because I demanded a scenic effect which the stage-manager could not realize, or had failed to realize: the sense of a dizzy height etc. . . . When one has been extremely pleased with a work one always tries to reason away what one fears may be faults.

On Saturday morning I went down to Les Sablons to stay with the Davrays. We went for a walk in the forest of Fontainebleau in the afternoon. I noticed on entering this vast forest, intersected with glorious roads, a characteristically French signboard: "General instructions for reading the signposts in the forest." The system of signposts seemed to me to be absolutely complete. I found the forest quite up to my expectation, but bigger.

We proceeded to Nemours, a delicious old town with a castle, ramparts, moats, and the Loing; full of wonderful views. Madame and I went to buy cakes and we all had tea on the pavement in front of an inn; while the landlady and another woman sat and sewed near by. Seeking the *garçon,* to pay the bill, I got into a vast kitchen full of all kinds of curious domestics and copper pans. Passing along the street we saw a tailor, old, in black, white hair, and a strangely shaped head, standing at the door of his shop. Davray and I both exclaimed at once: "Balzacian." *Ursule Mirouet* is laid in Nemours, and the extraordinary veracity of Balzac's descriptions strikes one everywhere. His descriptions were not exaggerated. I was enchanted with Nemours. We came back to Les Sablons on the great Paris-Antibes road, passing from that to the great Paris-Marseilles road, stupendous highways both, straight, interminable, with double rows of trees on either side.

At night music, and that freedom of speech which is one of the joys of France.

On Monday Dr. Vallée[1] took Madame and I to Fontainebleau. The Napoleonic suites of rooms and all the others impressed me much. Napoleon's bedroom with the cradle of the Roi de Rome and its gold

---

[1] A Paris physician, and friend of Arnold Bennett.

guardian angel (much like the angel on the top of Burslem Town Hall) remains in my mind. In the vast hall of Henri II we saw a mouse run across the floor.

Thursday, March 24th.

I have already received more than 100 pages of proofs of *A Great Man,* and expect to get the rest by the end of the week. Yesterday I did nothing but write letters and correct various proofs, and do another sketch for my *Notes on Paris.*

Friday, March 25th.

I spent a lot of yesterday afternoon in the Louvre picture galleries trying to get into a frame of mind sufficiently large and expansive for the creation of the central idea for my sensational romance. The chief result was a bad nervous headache, which did not, however, prevent me from eating well. I went to bed at 10, and had the idea for the "scene" of the book in the middle of the night.

Wednesday, March 30th.

Complete proofs of *A Great Man* corrected for press returned to Chatto and Windus today.

Just now I am spending several days in the utmost tranquillity. I have gradually seen that my sensational yarn must be something remarkably out of the common, and that therefore I must take the greatest care over the conception. I found that ideas for it did not come easily. I did not, however, force them. Then I had the idea for the "scene" of the book. Then I thought I would buy and read Gaboriau's *Le Crime d'Orcival,* of which I have heard so much, and see whether that would conduce to a "flow" in me, as Balzac always does. It did, at once. It is, I think, the best elaborate long detective story that I have read. It contains much solid and serious stuff, is extremely ingenious and well planned, and has real imagination. I have been reading this during the day, and correcting proofs at night. My sensational work does not and would not in the least resemble Gaboriau's, and yet Gaboriau has filled me with big, epic ideas for fundamental plot—exactly what I wanted. The central theme must be big, and it will be; all the rest is mere ingenuity, wit, and skill. I have not yet finished reading the Gaboriau book. I read it, and think of nothing, not asking notions to come; but they come, and I am obliged to note them down. The weather being extremely uncertain I have been unable to go out much, and so my existence has been quite extraordinarily placid. I go to bed one night, and then the next night, and there seems scarcely 5 minutes in between.

Monday, April 4th.

Unable to write my journal at all these last few days. All ideas of writing were put out of my head, and so I suffered obscurely from that uncomfortable feeling which a person who lives in a groove has when he is shifted out of his groove. Godfrey arrived on Thursday morning to spend Easter with me. The presence of another man always in the flat disturbed me, especially at times of dressing and undressing. He has slept badly on the sofa bed. Friday afternoon, while I was resting and Godfrey out, there was a ring at the door and Webster appeared. He was over in Paris to meet a girl named Lavard. He and she came to tea on Friday and again on Sunday; they left this morning. We lunched with them at the Hôtel Monsigny on Saturday.

I finished *Le Crime d'Orcival* on Thursday, and it leaves me with a high respect for Gaboriau.

Wednesday, April 6th.

"At home" at Mrs. Ullman's yesterday afternoon. Various people there: nephew of Whistler, looking rather like Whistler, very decent. Also Alfred Sutro [1] and his wife. But I had a very long talk with a disappointed young American actress, very much disgusted with the world, and another very long talk with the wife, or widow, of a scientist. Everybody was American except me. Several of the women were pretty with an American prettiness, but none of them could be called really intelligent except the hostess.

Thursday, April 7th.

Thinking about my new serial today, and got one or two ideas after several hours; but I had a cold all over me, and the weather was too wet to walk much.

Moréno sent me an urgent note to go and dine with them. Schwob

---

The English playwright and translator of Maeterlinck.

dined in his bed and we dined at a table at the foot thereof, while the Chinaman waited. Herz, the impresario, had asked Moréno and Coquelin *cadet* [1] to do a season in London together, but he wanted a short play, half in French and half in English, to begin the bill, and he wanted it written specially for her and C.C. She asked me whether I would write it if Herz arranged terms with me. I said I would. Both Moréno and Schwob, with their curious sanguine temperaments, seemed to regard the affair as an absolute certainty, but I think it is far from that. Herz hasn't even got a theatre in London yet. However, I drove with her to her theatre, and left her there, and at that moment she seemed certain that all was smooth. She was to telephone to Herz this morning, and Herz was to see me, and I was to write the play, and they were to play it, and it was to make a great splash, and the season was to be an enormous success, and much money was to flow into all pockets.

Saturday, April 9th.

I went to Schwob's yesterday, and then took Moréno and her precious *griffon belge,* Flip, in a cab to the Gaîté Theatre, where we saw Henri Herz, and discussed the proposed play for Coquelin *cadet's* and Moréno's proposed English season. The matter seemed to be arranged subject to Herz getting a London theatre. Herz and Moréno were evidently old friends. It was all *tu* and *toi*. She called him *mon petit chéri,* and he called her *ma belle créature*. Very theatrical. I liked him. She told me I should. He seemed straight, and rather English in affairs of business. The two united to curse Maurice Bernhardt, for whom they couldn't find adjectives sufficiently bad. It seems he takes all his mother's money, with the result that the underlings at her theatre are not paid. Moréno gave me a very funny account of how Sarah fooled, and amused herself with, an American female versifier whom we both knew, who wanted to read to Sarah a drama in verse on the subject of Delilah. Sarah took her into her *loge,* and kissed her, and induced her to believe that they were thoroughly intimate, and then kept her on toast for week after week, never allowing her actually to read the play.

Monday, April 11th.

On Sunday morning at 9.30 Whitten turned up unexpectedly. I

---

[1] Ernest Coquelin (1848–1909), younger brother of the more famous Benoît Coquelin (1841–1909).

lunched and dined with him, and amid acres of interesting talk discovered that *T.P.* was dispensing with my services in order to economize.

Wednesday, April 13th.

A heavy thunderstorm broke over Paris yesterday and lasted from 4 to 10 P.M. I was in the Parc Monceau when it began with a slight shower only.

It is extraordinary the terrific upset made by a shower of rain in a placid park peopled by nursemaids, children, mothers, and old people. Great excitement over perambulators, mothers searching for cabs and driving off with the kid, leaving the poor nurse to trudge home in the rain with the empty perambulator; crowding under inadequate shelters, and so on. "Maternal solicitude" is all over the place.

Davray called in the afternoon. I did nothing but moon over my next book.

Friday, April 15th.

I dined at the Schwobs'. She expressed her entire satisfaction with the scenario of the play. He was talking a lot about his voyage in the South Seas, on Captain Crawshay's steamer. He said Crawshay was a terrific swearer, with very conventional and proper ideas, and he could only read one author—Washington Irving. He could not understand the craze for R. L. Stevenson. He admitted Stevenson was a man of parts, but stated that his books were impossible.

I spent the afternoon in the Bois, searching for ideas for the book, and I really did find some, which contented me. It was beautifully warm, indeed hot; but close and oppressive towards evening. Paris is at its best on these oppressive evenings, when all the cafés are full of crowded languor. I thoroughly enjoyed the journey by bus and steamer to Schwob's. The voyage from the Quai Voltaire to the Ile Saint-Louis, just before 7 o'clock, was extremely impressive. It seemed to me as good as the Thames at its best.

Saturday, April 16th.

In Claudius Clear's [1] letter in *British Weekly* yesterday, I read as an actual fact of a case in which a man had substituted a wax figure for a real person in a coffin. It was just this device that I invented myself and

---

[1] The pseudonym of Sir W. Robertson Nicoll, editor of the paper.

meant to use in my new serial. And I shall use it anyhow. It was an immense coincidence that I should have read it in *British Weekly* yesterday, when I was fully engaged on the plot. I got the first instalment into order yesterday.

Tuesday, April 19th.

I went to the Concert-Berlioz on Sunday morning. I was struck by the wonderful cleverness of Saint-Saëns. It was the Algerian Suite, which I knew thoroughly, and yet it seemed to appear to me in a new light. I don't think it is first-class music by any means, but it is wonderful music. I also heard Beethoven's "Eroica."

Yesterday afternoon I went to the Salon (Société Nationale), and though I was exhausted afterwards, I thoroughly enjoyed it. The Salon seems to give a perspective of French life every year. I once thought it was on the average no better than the R.A.; but it is—a great deal. There is a good deal of English work in it, very distinguished. The virginal simplicity of Lavery's English girls strikes a curious note there, so different from anything else. I wanted to write my full impressions (not artistic, but human), but I saw I could not find time and energy just now when I am beginning a new book. Some time I will cease all creative work for 6 months, and keep a journal in detail of all my impressions.

Wednesday, April 20th.

Yesterday I started my new romantic book, *Hugo,*[1] with great fervour, and much enjoyed the day's work. I have announced to Pinker that it will be infinitely better than the *Grand Babylon Hotel;* so it will have to be.

Thursday, April 21st.

I continued to work well yesterday on *Hugo,* in the afternoon and again late in the evening till 11.30. I went down to Montparnasse and had tea with Mrs. Stapley, who had hunted up an Empire *secrétaire* for me, in fact several. Afterwards we went to view them. The best one had a mirror at the back, above the small drawers. I said to the shopwoman that I objected to a mirror. "Ah!" she said. "But when Madame

---

[1] *Hugo, A Fantasia on Modern Themes,* was published by Chatto and Windus in 1906.

leans over your shoulder while you are writing——!" I bought the *secrétaire* and also a clock for 140 francs.

Tuesday, April 26th.

In response to a telegram I went to lunch with Aleister Crowley[1] and his wife (Kelly's[2] sister) today at Paillard's. He had been made a "Khan" in the East, and was wearing a heavily jewelled red waistcoat and the largest ring I ever saw on a human hand. I rather liked him. He said some brain specialist had told him that what made a great brain was not the number of facts or ideas known, but the number of facts or ideas co-ordinated and correlated. I said, "Of course." Talking about Beardsley, when I said that people had said they had met him and seen him in the flesh after his death, he said he knew a man who had met Oscar Wilde in the Pyrenees while Oscar was in prison.

Wednesday, April 27th.

Yesterday when I was in Paillard's, it occurred to me that the difference between the most excessively *chic* restaurant and an ordinary good one is very slight. Paillard's has the reputation of being the best, or one of the 3 best, in Paris, and therefore in the world. Yet it is small, and not in the least luxurious, and the waiting is no better than it is elsewhere. The *monde* has no special appearance of smartness. The food was very good, and so was the wine. But scarcely appreciably better than at Sylvain's, Maire's, or Noel and Peter's. And the prices were about 25 per cent. dearer than at those other places—not more. In the evening, at a Boulant, I had for 6d. a *bifteck* and soufflé potatoes better than which could not possibly be obtained anywhere, at no matter what price. When you have thoroughly good, well-flavoured, tender meat, perfectly cooked —you cannot surpass that.

Today I finished the final form of the first instalment of *Hugo*. It seems good. But my mind has not been at all gay. I think I should be gayer if all my friends didn't live so far off. Ile Saint-Louis, Montparnasse, Champs-Elysées, Quai Voltaire—they are all too distant for chance visits. Every visit must be arranged beforehand; a nuisance.

---

[1] Author of *The Diary of a Drug Fiend,* etc., and the centre of many literary legends. He was also a post-war figure in New York's "sophisticated" literary set.

[2] Gerald F. Kelly, the painter.

Friday, April 29th.

I spent the whole of yesterday on the play, *Christina*. Constructionally, I don't think Eden has improved it. It is possible he may have spoilt the last act through too much cleverness. But he has certainly developed the whole thing considerably, and made Barbellion into a new "stage type."

With my *Log-Book* finished, and the play out of hand, I ought to be able to give myself up almost entirely to *Hugo*.

Thursday, May 5th.

Yesterday afternoon I went to the exhibition of *primitifs français* at the Pavillon Marsan in the Louvre. I was not overstruck by the exhibition; what impressed me was the colossal interiors of the pavillon, which after all is only a mere incident in the Rivoli façade of the Louvre. I also saw one of the best-dressed women that I ever did see. She was tall and, I think, American. She was wearing a fortune, and in perfect taste, too. She set for me a new standard in frocks.

Just now I am reading the Letters of Horace Walpole and re-reading *La Cousine Bette,* both with great joy.

Friday, May 6th.

Miss Thomasson gave me a dinner at the notorious Bohemian Restaurant Garnier in the Boulevard Raspail last night. Crowded, chiefly with Americans. We dined out in the street, fenced about by trees in tubs; and I was introduced to about a million girls. The food was mediocre —not so villainous as I had heard; the wine was bad, and this morning I had a headache. Afterwards at Miss Thomasson's studio I met Hubert Bland and his Liberty-clad young daughter Rosamund. Mrs. Bland [1] was too indisposed to come. I also met Sep's friend and champion, Berta Ruck,[2] and some other people. Late, an artist named K—— came in; a loud, gross man. He had been dining with "Johnny Lavery," and he was full of Johnny Lavery's wonderful new German model whose portrait is in this year's Salon. Told us how she was aged 19, and the rage of Berlin, asked to lunch at the Embassies, received 5 proposals in 3 months; how Lavery looked after her, sent her to bed at 9.30 every night; how she refused to sit for any one but Lavery, and would only sit even for him

---

[1] Well known as a novelist and children's writer under the name of E. Nesbit.
[2] Author of many serials and wife of Oliver Onions, the novelist.

2 hours a day, and he had to hire a woman to play to her or talk to her the while.

Today I wandered about searching for the final complications of instalment 2 of *Hugo*. I got most of them by 7 P.M.

Monday, May 9th.

I dined with Hind, who had 3 hours in Paris on his way to Genoa. He told me that Max Beerbohm lived on the £5 a week he got from the *Saturday Review*. Strange, if true. After a great deal of talk about journalism I felt an inclination to go in more for journalism. But, as I told Hind, I had contracted an almost invincible *dis*inclination either to asking for work or to do any work that was not directly commissioned beforehand.

Tuesday, May 10th.

There was a phrase in the newspaper yesterday about the "great and continual accumulation of unemployed capital in Paris." Here is an instance, which I know of, of how some people can save even in a city where wages are generally low and living is generally dear. A widow aged 56 lives alone in a single large room in Montrouge, for which she pays 200 francs a year. She is a sempstress, and goes out by the day. She is fully employed and has often to "refuse" days. Her wages are 3 francs or 3½ francs and *all* food. If she does not take dinner in the house she gets an extra half franc. In order to net this extra half franc she often dines with one of her grown-up daughters. All her clothes she manages to "make" out of the sempstress "perks," lawful or unlawful. She has therefore an income of about 100 francs a month (for she works Sundays), and practically no expenses. I am told she is always buying City of Paris stock etc. The thing is typically French. One of her daughters, a *lorette* in quite a small way, has saved 8,000 francs in 3 years. A son, a picture-restorer, is also continually saving money. On the other hand the eldest daughter, a dressmaker, with a staff under her, is spendthrift, and so is the youngest son, just finishing his military term. There must be many families like that in Paris, quietly and really prosperous.

Miss —— came to dine with me. We walked up to Sacré Cœur, and then dined at the Hippodrome. Then we had coffee at the Café Riche, and I drove her home at 12.30. I got to bed at 1.30. I talked to her nearly all the time about the relations of the sexes, and having once embarked on the enterprise of making this virgin of 30 or so see that she knew nothing really of what constitutes life, I duly finished it.

Wednesday, May 11th.

Mrs. D. telegraphed me to go and dine with her. She has got still another butler, a bigger fool even than all the others. She has been ill with fever, but looks as beautiful as ever. After we had exchanged notes on everything, we began as usual talking about happiness, unhappiness, and the relations of the sexes. She said her life was miserable. I said of course mine was.

Yesterday I sketched out instalment 3 of *Hugo*.

There are often signs that the Paris edition of the *N.Y. Herald* is edited by a man who has a most peculiar and futile sense of the grotesque. This morning there was a really extraordinary sign. *Apropos* of Stanley's death, the leading article was neither more nor less than a brief medical treatise on the complaint of which he died. A general treatise, not at all with special reference to Stanley! It gave detailed instructions about quantities of medicine etc. Yet the news of Stanley's death [1] was known early yesterday morning. Even in the news columns the subject had not been tackled—merely borrowings from the *Telegraph*. Either the editor had shirked the thing, and in pure idiocy had dug up something out of a medical dictionary, or he had dug up something out of a medical dictionary from a sheer desire to be grotesque and to flout his public. Considering that the *N.Y. Herald* was the first newspaper to employ Stanley, the thing may be regarded as peculiar in the highest degree.

Thursday, May 12th.

I walked a good deal about Paris yesterday, arranging instalment 4 of *Hugo*. I got down, via the quays, as far as the Luxembourg, and saw the temporary exhibition there of Manet's, Monet's, and that school. Manet's *Nana* was the chief thing. I thought how much more it had aged than the book. As a matter of fact I think Manet's conception of Nana rather narrow—the idea of a man who had not "knocked about" enough. The picture would be masterly had he not entitled it *Nana*.

---

[1] Sir H. M. Stanley, the African explorer, had died the previous day.

Then I had tea, and bad tea, on the Boulevard Saint-Michel and came home on the omnibus, having bought a reproduction of a fine sketch by some artist unknown to me for 5 sous.

At 10 P.M. I strolled down to the Folies Marigny. There is certainly only one tolerable music-hall in Paris, and this is it. The performance was rotten, of course, but the audience! Crammed, stylish; many women —some extremely beautiful; many toilettes. I only stayed an hour and walked home.

Today I write out the sketch of instalment 4.

Saturday, May *14th*.

I may now be said to be in the thick of *Hugo*. I worked at him an hour in the morning yesterday, an hour in the afternoon, and 2 hours at night, finishing at 12.30. And he has the air of being very good. The rest of the time I chiefly wasted, but I read a lot of Balzac and Walpole, and contemplated my future.

The noises of Paris become more and more exasperating as summer approaches. A chair-mender who cries every morning at 10.30, I should like to destroy; also the parrot who exists on a window-sill on the first floor of the next house. The rattle of cabs I have grown quite accustomed to.

Sunday, May *15th*.

Mrs. S—— came for tea and a literary consultation in the afternoon. This woman, who has certainly seen the world and men, really thinks that she can earn a living by writing short stories—and without much delay. Yet she has done practically nothing whatever in literature. She arrived here in a highly nervous state, owing to a street accident or something, and then she had the imprudence to have a heart spasm and a small crisis of illness. But I walked her off safely at 6.45, and then I dined on the terrace of Sylvain's and much enjoyed it. The evening was magnificent, and I had a strong desire to write a poem. However, I wrote letters till 11.30.

Monday, May *16th*.

The weather continues simply glorious, and all the cage-birds in the windows of the *maison meublée* next door conspire to make concerted music.

I finished the second instalment of *Hugo* yesterday afternoon, after lunching with C.L. It exhausted me. Then I went to view Paris from the top of Montmartre and found all Paris there doing the same thing. I went down on to the Boulevard after dinner, and began to compose a poem at the Napolitan. But it got on my nerves so that I was obliged to leave it and come home and write letters.

Tuesday, May 17th.

Being disappointed in a rendezvous by women, and having finished work for the day, I went down to the Salon des Artistes Français and found it theatrical, depressing, and often repulsive. But there were a number of beautiful things there. Afterwards I voyaged on the Seine to Bercy and back, the boats crowded with interesting artisans, and the weather sublime. Miss Thomasson, who came up to dine with me, said she considered there were as many good things in the old as in the new Salon. After dinner she did a night sketch from the terrace of the Café Abbaye Thélème in the Place Pigalle.

Wednesday, May 18th.

Yesterday was really hot. I had to work in my shirt-sleeves. I did so much that in the evening I was exhausted and had to go to bed.

I finished *La Cousine Bette* again this morning. It is magnificent, but there is a wild creative rush about it that is rather too wild. The trick of leaving out is pushed to its farthest, perhaps too far, and though the book is long it contains nothing but fundamental stuff. Often, it seems to me, Balzac has not given sufficient care to the manufacture of convincing detail. He must have been decidedly in a very frenzy of creative impulse when he wrote it. The scene which remains most clearly in my memory is that in which old Hulot comes to Josepha for shelter and aid; her part in that has a tremendous *brio*. *Brio* is the word for the entire book.

Thursday, May 19th.

Today *A Great Man* is published, my sixth published novel, and my eighth written novel. My copies of it arrived yesterday. I read through most of it in the evening. I thought one or two parts were too technical in detail; but on the whole it amused me well enough. I was struck by the ease and virtuosity of the writing (on that plane of writing) and by the sound construction. I don't fancy holes can be picked in these aspects of the book. But humour is often a matter of opinion.

Whit-Monday, May 23rd.

I have suffered heavily from liver for 4 days. The attack went off last night, suddenly, as all such attacks do. I continued to work on *Hugo* except on Friday, when I could do nothing. I finished Part I of him last night about 11 P.M. I heard disturbingly from Pinker on Friday night that Chatto wanted after all to publish *Teresa* and *Love and Life,* and had bought the illustrations for the former.[1] For about an hour I was nearly telegraphing to Wells that I would go over on Saturday to consult him. I couldn't think of any one else whose opinion in a matter so involved between business and art I really cared twopence for. However, I decided to wait till the next morning. And by the next morning I had thought of a compromise which satisfied me and ought to satisfy Chatto. This compromise would involve the re-writing of *Love and Life,* and I rather think I should enjoy doing that, because the fundamental plot of it is so good.

On Saturday, the *Pilot* ceased publication, to my real regret.

Tuesday, May 24th.

Mrs. Devereux and Mrs. Laye lunched with me at Sylvain's yesterday. "So you've started your carriage again?" I said to Mrs. Devereux. "Yes," she said, "I couldn't do without it. Hang expense." They had both had the good taste to have read my new book and to enjoy it thoroughly. They really have a profound sympathy with each other, these sisters. And I like to have them side by side and to sit opposite to them.

Mrs. Devereux said she was at a dinner party the other night at which were also W. S. Gilbert and Douglas Straight.[2] Straight was talking about peculiarities of memory, loss of it, etc. He said he could remember incidents when he was in Naples at the age of 2. But if he was asked where he dined last week he couldn't remember. "No," said Gilbert. "And if you could, probably you wouldn't be able to tell us."

Mrs. Laye maintained (not *apropos* of the above) that men didn't like

---

[1] *Teresa of Watling Street* was published in October, 1904.
[2] Sir Douglas Straight, editor of the *Pall Mall Gazette.*

being made fun of whereas women didn't mind; she said she had been astonished at some men. She told a good thing of a very old man on his dying bed giving advice to a youngster: "I've had a long life, and it's been a merry one. Take my advice. Make love to every pretty woman you meet. And remember, if you get 5 per cent. on your outlay it's a good return."

Afterwards we went to the Exposition des Primitifs. I enjoyed it much more than I did the first time, partly because it really *is* good, and partly because Mrs. Devereux, who is fearfully keen on primitivism, pointed out qualities to me.

When they left me I went down to my Empire furniture shop in the Boulevard Raspail, and bought a bookcase, a fire screen, a *suspensoir*, and two chairs, which I am eagerly expecting tomorrow.

Thursday, May 26th.

Wells, Whitten, and Marriott think that *A Great Man* is my best book. And Phillpotts is enchanted with it.

Friday, May 27th.

Today I am 37. I have lived longer than I shall live. My new series begins to appear today in the *Windsor*. My name is not on the cover. Anthony Hope's stands there alone. And I am 37. Comment is needless.

I have now warned both the Mater and Tertia that I shall get married before I am 40.

Tuesday, May 31st.

I went down to Moret on Saturday morning and nearly missed the train owing to my servant. I was astonished how, during the journey on the Métro, the apprehension of missing the train at the Gare de Lyon got on my nerves, though it was a matter of no importance, as there are plenty of trains. My nerves were all raw when I arrived at the Gare, and I was physically exhausted through urging the Métro train to accelerate its movements. When I reached Moret, I found that Davray had mis-read my letter and had engaged a house for me under the impression that I was coming for my promised sojourn of a month. So that had to be undone.

In the afternoon I saw the ceremony of the annual *revision des chevaux* which takes place all over France about this time, every horse in France, except certain mares, being at the call of the Government for military purposes. It occurred under a tree in the open space between the Mairie, the church, and Davray's garden. A captain was seated at a small table, and by his side the mayor's secretary (the schoolmaster—exactly like all village schoolmasters, whether in England or France), and a soldier. A military vet., another soldier, two gendarmes, and two men that looked like *gardes champêtres* were also in the show; also a dog that lay under the table. The vet. and another man could have done the whole thing easily. Quantities of sheets of paper, minutely ruled with millions of lines for statistics, filled the table. As each horse of the commune was brought up, the vet. looked it over and described it very briefly for the captain to write down, and the captain asked questions as to ownership etc. At the last moment a young man galloped up on a black draught horse, and in answer to some query replied as he slipped off the horse, *"C'est un étalon, comme moi."*

The vet. seemed a nice quiet dutiful man, younger than his grey hair; he looked as though he had discovered gradually that life must be a compromise, after all. He was sad. The captain, aged 50 or so, had the narrow, roughly gay, and intensely narrow-minded face of an elderly officer who has failed to rise. The whole affair was eminently French and picturesque too.

Later, Davray and I walked down to the banks of the Seine, which to my astonishment was close to. A beautiful stream, broad, and surrounded by fine scenery, and not a pleasure-boat in sight. Everywhere, the most superb acacia trees with their aphrodisiac smell. Then we went for a walk in the forest.

On Sunday we messed about, and in the afternoon went to a river restaurant (called, of course, "Robinson") where the *amoureux* of the district forgather and amuse themselves on swings. A *partie carrée* of 2 brothers and 2 sisters diverted and interested me much: they were so human, and so French, and so naïve; and the fleeting charm of the girls (neither of them pretty) was so soon to fade, and the men were so soon to become mature and *bête*.

We then walked along the canal and inspected the life of the canal people. The hovels on the banks, where they live when they are in the district, were disgusting. The general landscape, viewed at large, and ignoring many small blots, was simply superb.

An English couple (a Liverpool merchant aged 32 and his pretty wife aged 24, on their honeymoon) were arrested on Saturday for having, or attempting to have, sexual intercourse in the Place de l'Archevêché. This struck me as one of the funniest examples of crass "Englishness" and contempt for foreigners that I have ever come across—*the* funniest.

Wednesday, June 1st.

Yesterday my *femme de ménage* told me that her husband had re-turned to her, and that they were both going to their native district of Auvergne. This origin of the *femme de ménage,* I am told, explains her singular and astonishing stupidity. Yesterday she achieved a miracle of stupidity in the way of trying to keep milk cool under a jug of cold water—no doubt to crown her career. It would have been an excellent idea for milk-cooling if the water had not got into the milk.

I had to prospect after another *femme de ménage.* There is no doubt that women are tremendously pleased with themselves when men pre-tend to be absolute fools and ignoramuses in domestic matters, and to rely on *their* superior sagacity and experience. I do it, partly because it pleases them so, and partly because it amuses me a little.

Thursday, June 2nd.

Neither yesterday nor today have I been quite sufficiently bursting with health to think seriously of the details of the plot of the second part of *Hugo.* However, I have got the plan and the "feel" of it, and also one or two detached episodic notions. The weather has been thor-oughly wet and rotten.

I walked down to the Louvre in it yesterday, and had a desire to com-mission copies of the Botticelli frescoes on the Daru staircase—in water-colours. It was a great day for copyists. I saw scores. One old man, who was copying a Raphael head, struck me particularly. He had leaned back against the rail to rest for a few minutes. He was old and poor, shabby, rather dirty, with shaggy thin grey hair. And he seemed absolutely dis-gusted, hopeless, and feebly bitter. I could not help feeling shocked by the sight, for of course this man had started out in life with the idea that he was going to succeed as a painter.

Afterwards I went on to my Empire shop and bought 2 occasional tables, a candlestick, and a flower-glass, all strictly Empire. I have now done buying furniture. I only want bibelots and things.

I bade good-bye to my stupid *femme de ménage* this morning. She has been here 8 months and we have never exchanged "general ideas"— not once.

Friday, June 3rd.

Some time ago a man named Martin had relations, *comme maquereau,* with a courtesan. She found a rich protector, and told Martin frankly that she could only see him on the quiet in future, as the rich protector would be jealous. Martin got into her apartment, stood behind the door, and struck her dead with one blow of a knife in the heart as she entered one night. She was only a *fille,* and the affair was considered as a *crime passionel,* and Martin was acquitted (*doux pays!*). I was told yesterday that Martin, handsome and well dressed, frequents the Folies-Bergère and other places, and has relations with other women. There are a number of women who are proud to shake hands with, to drink with, and to be the mistress of an assassin. "He killed a woman at one stroke!" In certain circles Martin is the vogue! This is one of the most curious, and yet natural, things I have heard about Paris.

Sunday, June 5th.

I did collect a few more ideas yesterday afternoon. Then Miss Thomasson came to paint a still-life of some corner of this room, for me to give to the Mater. She talked more than painted, but made a good start.

After dinner, we took coffee in the Place Blanche, and talked there till just 11 o'clock, me getting worse and worse. However, I talked all the time, explaining at great length my ideas on women, sometimes making her laugh at what she considered my naïve absurdities and then making her suspect that perhaps my absurdities were not so absurd after all.

Wednesday, June 8th.

I got one or two really admirable ideas for *Hugo* yesterday, just as I was recovering from another attack of liver. Miss Thomasson came in the afternoon to paint again, and by arrangement I left her here alone for a couple of hours. I went into the Parc Monceau to write, and was much preoccupied by the spectacle of two English governesses (or nursery-governesses) with two small French children, who were both doing everything that ought not to be done in the management of a child. Still, I expect most children of that class have to struggle through the same stupidities and lack of imagination. It is chiefly lack of imagination that makes governesses worse than futile.

Afterwards Miss Thomasson and I went to drive in the Bois, and then we dined at Lavenue's, Montparnasse. A mediocre good restaurant. At her studio, later, two Americans came in, waistcoatless, and talking very Americanish, "bully time" and so on. I thought, "What terrible people these young American painters are!" Yet afterwards, when I was alone with one of them, I found him full of most excellent sane views about women, amateurs, work, life, and things of that kind. It is a pity that the American accent is *absolutely* ugly, and not merely strange to our ears.

Thursday, June 9th.

I continued slowly to gather ideas yesterday. In the evening Rickards arrived. We had a tremendous deal to say to each other, but we could scarcely begin last night. At first I felt rather depressed, as I often do when a long-expected visitor comes. There must be some simple explanation of this, but I don't know what it is.

Monday, June 13th.

Lunched with R——*chez* C. She had taken pains to have a lunch more than usually nice. If any one had told her that she was nervous before this young man whom she regards as an absolute infant in all really interesting matters, she would have laughed. But she was. She had bought a large new hat, and it was nothing but nervousness that made her suddenly try it on me as I sat balanced on the edge of a couch. After discussing the really interesting matters for 2 hours, R—— left to get shaved, or to get a second shave or something.

We went down to Miss Thomasson's for tea, and sundry most interesting persons came in. However, in about an hour R—— had arranged to spend the following day with Miss Thomasson in a river excursion. We were late for dinner because the dullest of the visitors failed to perceive, until he was told, that he ought to go.

Tuesday, June 14th.

I wrote to Sir Douglas Straight the other day to complain of a review of *A Great Man* in the *Pall Mall Gazette*. It had grossly misrepresented the plot, and so I explained my conception of the negative duties of a reviewer who did not read a book.

Straight's answer is to review the book again, very favourably, under the title *Second Impressions*. At the end of the review he says, after stating that he has read it twice, "We say this the more readily because in first acknowledging the book, we recorded what was, after all, a superficial impression, and in making amends now we have said no more than any fair-minded reader will admit it deserves." This is decidedly handsome. But many people will think I am a friend of Straight's and that the first review slipped in without his knowledge.

I finished Walpole's Letters yesterday. To follow the whole of a man's long life like this (the letters stretch over 60 years) is quite affecting. After the middle period the letters fall off in interest, but towards the end there is a decided renaissance both of wit and wisdom. In many letters his character appears as really noble and distinguished. On the whole the correspondence has come up to my expectations.

Thursday, June 16th.

Tonight I received a bundle of press-cuttings of American reviews of *Anna,* more than a year old. I was surprised to find how very favourable they were. Some of the names of the papers were funny, as e.g. the *Omaha Daily Bee*. The *Bee* was not too flattering, but gorgeously condescending.

Sunday, June 19th.

I was thinking the other day, while reading a very sensual love-scene in *Le Lys Rouge,* that a novelist never describes the *déshabillé* of the male in such scenes [1]; I can't remember an instance where he even hints at it. This shows how incomplete "realism" is. I see no reason why the appearance of the male should not be described in a manner to assist the charm of the scene. But tradition is decidedly against the practice.

I drafted the 7th instalment of *Hugo* yesterday.

---

[1] By Anatole France. Such a scene Bennett afterwards described in *The Pretty Lady*.

The Ullmans and Rickards dined with me; Rickards ¾ hour late. Ullman brought out a theory that Wagner, though a great man, was essentially vulgar. He characterized as vulgar all the stage settings on which Wagner set so much store. I would agree as to the *Ring,* but not as to the other operas. *Tannhäuser* may be, and is, lovely. So is *Tristan.* He said that with the same talent Wagner would have been a much finer artist had he been English or French; he was influenced by the fundamental German vulgarity. I could see what Ullman meant, but I thought he was chiefly wrong. However, he argued very well.

Later Rickards and I went to the Moulin de la Galette and saw some good dancing. He leaves this afternoon for London. Reading *Le Lys Rouge* tonight. The love-scene (Chapter 23) in which Thérèse tries to rid Decharte of his *idées noires* concerning her absolute fidelity to him is extremely fine in its sensual way. It is just the sort of thing that A. France can do, and it atones for much of the "invertebrate" quality of the book. If I can accomplish anything as good in *Carlotta* I ought to be satisfied.

I had *idées noires* myself tonight. There are certainly times when the fact that existence is a choice of evils presents itself too clearly.

Monday, June 20th.

I worked from 10 to 6.30 and then dined on the boulevard, and went to see *Cyrano* with Moréno as Roxane. It is a highly elaborate exercise in the obvious, but the verbal and structural adroitness of the whole thing is tremendous. It amused me; I must say that for Rostand. Moréno was coldly distinguished. Her diction and her gestures were exquisite. And she had a sore throat and a cough.

Wednesday, June 22nd.

After working all day yesterday I went down to Montparnasse for dinner, and came across Mrs. Stapley at the Chat Blanc. At least she came across me. She told me how from her window she had seen workmen emptying vast quantities of bones out of a ditch in the Montparnasse Cemetery, morning after morning. She said it must have been either a "potter's field," or some part of the Cemetery allotted to paupers, whose "remains" are only given 3 years. She described the finding of one solitary coffin, and how the bottom fell out and a skeleton came to view with a few rags of clothes. Her version of these sinister sights, as seen at early dawn, was rather effective. Then afterwards I went with her to the Café des Lilas for coffee. And later I came across Kelly and others at the Café de Versailles, and stayed talking some time. The evening outdoor life of Montparnasse, in its circles so exclusively English and American, makes no appeal to me at all. It seems obviously "insular," the contented ignorance of these people concerning the real life of the city in which they live.

Today I wrote *Hugo* from 10 A.M. till 7.15 P.M. and then wrote letters from 9.15 P.M. to midnight. It is a long time since I wrote so many words in a day. I have done 10,000 words of *Hugo* in 3 days.

Friday, June 24th.

Last night I had a long and very real dream of a great French novelist of the nineteenth century named Valentin Chéri. He was something in the style of Beyle, but wrote between 1860 and 1870. I can no longer remember the names of his best books, but I did know them in the dream. And I was astounded to find that in all my surveys of French fiction I had invariably forgotten Chéri. I wondered how soon some one would point out the extraordinary and repeated omission and prove that I had no business to write about French fiction. Even after I was wakened Chéri continued to be real to me and to cause me uneasiness on the score of my carelessness and ignorance. And it was not till I had got up and begun to drink my tea that the mists cleared away and I perceived that the whole thing was nothing but a dream. I have seldom had a dream more real and fuller of circumstantial detail.

I called on Mrs. Le Gallienne this afternoon, and found sundry women there that I knew. She has a nice womanish flat, once part of a convent; with a little daughter [1] and a tremendously English old nurse.

Monday, June 27th.

Hind, returned from his European tour, dined with me last night at the Hippodrome. He said he had not talked to any one since he saw me last, and that when the tour was about two-thirds through he felt very stale. He had stopped in 18 towns, and was much struck with Buda Pesth, as I expected.

---

[1] Miss Eva Le Gallienne, the actress, was five years old at that time.

Afterwards we went to the Moulin de la Galette, and made observations to each other about Youth, Desire, and so on. Nearly all Hind's ideas are sentimental and wrong, and his judgments on literature are quite impossible nearly every time; but he has a charm. Perhaps it is his naïveté—a rare enough quality.

I see at the beginning of this volume I noted an instance of the *sans gêne* of Montmartre.[1] Here is another. On Thursday last, at the Restaurant Boulant, a young *cocotte* came in with two young men and her *bonne à tout faire*. The *bonne* was not neat or clean, and was in her working dress. They dined all together and laughed and talked much. Perhaps it was because the domestic cuisine had gone wrong. But more probably the *cocotte* had only just arrived at the dignity of a *bonne* and was bound to show her off.

Monday, June 27th. Paris.

I had a letter from M. Berquand asking me to go and see him at the Hôtel Terminus.[2] His room was No. 465. I found it with the aid of a boy. M. Berquand is getting old. He struck me as a man of sincere character, and trustworthy. He said he had been mute till the age of 8, and thence till the age of 26 had stammered so badly that he was practically incapable of speech, and entirely incapable of earning a living. He had to be kept by his family. He then studied all the systems, maintained a strict silence for 6 months, and cured himself in a year. He has travelled all over Europe on tours of curing, and has "orders" from most European sovereigns. I arranged to go to Aberdeen on 1st August. He asked me a lot of questions, and said he was quite certain of success in a month or 5 weeks. In spite of the interview with him I felt rather depressed than otherwise.

Tuesday, June 28th.

I went down to Kelly's studio, a very large one, and he showed me a lot of his work which interested me very much. He made some good remarks about the present condition of painting. He said painters were afraid of making mistakes, afraid of being vulgar, and that they never

---

[1] See page 115.
[2] This was Bennett's second attempt to have his stammering cured.

used their eyes in search of material. They all painted the same things. He said some artist had said to him, "We paint like governesses." I certainly thought Kelly was doing good and original work, both in landscape and portraiture. Afterwards he took me to dine at the Chat Blanc. Stanlaws, the "creator" of the "Stanlaws girl," was there, an American, and also a girl I had previously seen at Kelly's. The girl and Stanlaws and the man who was the girl's host threw bread at each other, and sang American songs very loudly. It was terrible at times. I could not stand such manners and customs for long. It is these things that spoil Montparnasse. We finished up at the Café de Versailles.

Thursday, June 30th.

I went down last night after dinner to see Mrs. Le Gallienne, and found she had just been dining with Hind and a Miss Macdonald, a beautiful girl whose father and brother are Paris correspondents of English papers. We all went out to the Boulevard Saint-Michel and had coffee at the Café Harcourt. An enormous crowd of students and *bourgeois,* with the orchestra in the centre, and *cocottes* wandering continuously around the circumference: a warm night. Mrs. Le Gallienne talked to me with much freedom about her husband. She said she had found she could do nothing more for him, and, as they differed as to the desirability of life in New York, she had left him, and they corresponded, and so on. She described how charming he was when he *was* charming, and how diverting it was to live with such a wayward artistic temperament. There was one thing she could say—he had never bored her. However, she had had enough of the artistic temperament.

Today I finished the second part of *Hugo.*

Wednesday, July 6th.

The other evening Mrs. D. said some man had said to her that for a first-class man there could be nothing between a *cocotte* and a *grande dame;* it must be either the one or the other. I had heard the saying before. I should say it is very true. The only question is whether, for a man ferociously egoist, the advantages and disadvantages of the *cocotte* and of the *grande dame* respectively are not about equal. I think they are. I know that when we were dining last night at Marguéry's and talking purely personal gossip, I had a feeling of content which I should like to have a bit oftener.

Thursday, July 7th.

I took a turn through the Parc Monceau to the Etoile and back through the Champs-Elysées last night between 9.30 and 11 in order to clear off a headache. Honest lovemaking in the Parc Monceau. In the Champs-Elysées I saw 4 girls, aged 14 or less—one didn't seem more than 11 or 12—being taken about by older women for the excitement of senile appetites. Some day soon there will be a tremendous outcry concerning this procuring of children. The police will become suddenly active in arrests—and then things will settle down again.

There were many pretty and well-dressed women in the Champs-Elysées sitting patiently on chairs under the trees awaiting some masculine advance. I was astonished how distinguished some of them were. It was a lovely night, warm and starlit. Paris at its most Parisian. The lights of the al fresco music-halls, and the occasional bursts of music and applause that came from them, produced an extraordinary effect.

Friday, July 8th.

I went down to Montparnasse for dinner last night. There was also present young P., a youth of 23 or so, rosy, healthy, reserved, mannered, with the University twang; tremendously English; a little shy and nervous, but underneath that a happy and proud conviction that Cambridge stood for all that was highest in human civilization; he had just been made a fellow of his college. About 11 P.M. I went with P. and B. to the Bal Bullier. The Bal and the garden were crowded on this hot summer night and the whole scene was beautiful, charming, and entirely wonderful. P. thought the general effect was "pretty." But on the whole neither he nor B. saw much to admire. The spirit of the place, the singular "Latin" charm, escaped them. They looked on it as a haunt of "vice," and dull at that. I told them what I thought of it. I said that when they grew older they too might possibly admire what they did not admire now. They admitted the possibility, and deplored it. "You mustn't think," I said, "that I despise your ideas." "Oh, don't trouble about that," said P., with that cruel affectation of humility which youth puts on; "I'm quite used to having my ideas despised." I could see he was incapable of imaginatively realizing that at the present moment he might be blind to certain forms and aspects of beauty which later would reveal themselves to him. They both thought all the women ugly and graceless. We had a drink in the garden. "How do the men arrange for women at Oxford and Cambridge?" I asked P. bluntly. I meant to startle him. He was startled. However, I got him to talk after a bit. He said that up to 60 years ago (he thought) colleges had their special stews. But these were now done away with. There were *cocottes* at both places for undergraduates etc. But men found it pleasanter to run up to town. I said, "I'm not talking about undergraduates; I'm talking about dons, fellows, etc.—the mature men who are not married." He assured me that the vast majority were chaste, and that unmarried male public opinion— the public opinion of smoking-parties and late evenings—was honestly and sincerely against irregular intercourse. I said that I was astounded. I said I had never heard tell of such a class of men before. They were surprised that I was astounded—P. and B. were. I could see that they regarded me with mild, impartial, and dignified curiosity as a strange sort of person with ill-regulated ideas. P. thought that human nature was becoming more "moral"—that there was a "change for the better" in the last century. He talked neatly, and I think sincerely. He believed in greater freedom for sexual unions of a permanent kind—he knew two couples who were not married and who were nevertheless received everywhere. But (he continued) this increased freedom could only go "hand in hand with" a decrease in prostitution. I listened. I respected him. He could not help being slightly priggish. I did not express my views, but I purposely kept recurring to my amazement at the existence of a body of unmarried men, not priests, in whom chastity was the rule. And they thought more and more what a naïve creature I was. But of course I must have inspired them with doubts as to their own position. "Don't you think women are the most interesting thing in the world?" I asked. P. considered judicially. "One of the most interesting!" he said. I gathered that both these men were virgin. And I am sure that they looked on the "initiation" as a mere formality to be gone through. They neither of them thought, honestly, that they had anything to learn. They were tolerant, from their heights, towards the pathetic spectacle of humanity. Always B. was the least priggish and convinced. But I liked them both. Essentially, they were rather girlish.

As I drove home, I thought the whole episode was really rather funny. I don't suppose that P. is likely to change much. He is too deeply impregnated, by heredity and tradition and upbringing, with "English culture"—he is incapable of seeing the "Latin" side of things in general. He is the sort of man that has "made England what it is." He stands for all that is best, and all that is worst and most exasperating, in the English character.

Saturday, July 9th.

I went to the Bois yesterday afternoon and had tea at the Pavillon Royal. I was finding ideas for *Hugo,* but a party of women came to the next table and ordered tea—well dressed, mature, *rusées*—and stopped me. It is extraordinary how much more critical such women are than men. The *garçon* was *agaçant* (I had not found him so); the tea was bad, the cakes were bad. But the women, by dint of not sparing the *garçon,* got the best that was to be got out of the place. And they gossiped all the time in their cold, pretty, rapid, hard tones. When I left the place was beginning to be full of such parties, with a few men here and there. Middle-aged women, well dressed, had appointments to meet each other there. The day was torrid and superb. The lake glistened, and the park-men were watering everywhere, so that there was constantly the sight and sound of spirted water. A few motors dashing about, and many carriages. Everything characteristic of July and the end of the season. I walked slowly all the way home, stopping now and then to make notes of my ideas as they occurred to me. Before I went to bed I had finished *Hugo* in my head.

Wednesday, July 13th.

I have written 12,500 words of *Hugo* in 3 days. On Monday I utterly exhausted myself in writing between 3 and 4,000. Yesterday between 10 A.M. and 12.30 P.M. I wrote over 6,000 without much exhaustion.

The secret is to take a little "recess" every 2 hours at most. Today I wrote 2,500 words between lunch and dinner, and am tired. I felt I owed myself a prize for all this virtue; so I went out and bought 7 volumes of fiction—d'Aurevilly, Balzac, Maupassant. I have long wanted *Les Diaboliques*.[1]

---

[1] By Barbey d'Aurevilly.

The July Fair has been in full swing since Sunday, and I have examined it in detail. Last night I saw a gingerbread stall take fire. I was within a yard of it, but I watched other people put out the flames. The woman in charge behaved very well until the thing was quite finished, and then she nearly fainted while waiting for a glass of *eau-de-vie*. A stout, heavy, clumsy, and not-easily-moved woman, shabby—not in the least Parisian. The entire fair might have been burnt down. But of course one gets used to carrying one's life in one's hand—especially in Paris.

Thursday morning, July 14th.

Although I rested well last night, I heard the music of the *fête* each time I wakened; so at 4 A.M. I persuaded myself to get up and take a look at it. There was one roundabout going in the Place Blanche. Everything else was closed. A bright, hot morning. All the great *restaurants de nuit* were shut; but one café, the Coquet, next to the Cyrano, was open and had tables in the street. The stout lady in the cash-desk seemed just as usual. The "place" was thick with *serpentins*. A few cabs waiting about, and a few idlers like myself. The women on the roundabout screamed just as they always do. They did not look very tired. There were 4 on one pig.

I then went down towards the Opéra. I saw that the footpaths were swept by women in blue—with magnificent carriage and figures. I suppose that is due to the magnificent gesture of the broom. On the Boulevard des Italiens, 3 of them abreast were sweeping the broad *trottoir*. It was a fine sight. At the Opéra a large crowd for the *matinée gratuite* had already gathered—some hundreds; policemen to keep order.

This was the *real* people—dirty, stinking, brutal, importunate; the scum! Nearly all men, but just a few women. Some persons were lying asleep on the pavement. I noticed many other early-morning items, and fête-day items: such as omnibuses passing, full of policemen in spotless white trousers; a cavalry officer in full splendour walking to his rendezvous; many people beginning the day's enjoyment on their way to railway stations etc., the women dozing in the newspaper kiosks awaiting the morning papers; a youth walking along the middle of the road smoking a pipe a yard long; a drunken man trying to get up a fight with a barman concerning a small tricolor which he carried. Many bars were open. I returned home at 5.05 and wrote this at once.

Sunday, July 17th.

Yesterday at 7 P.M., after a week of slogging, I finished *Hugo,* which I think is my eighth novel. I have got that off my mind and now this morning I lose a front tooth, just to be supplied with a new worry.

Thursday, July 21st.

Last night Dr. Mackenzie brought Robert Barr to the Chat Blanc. I had not seen him for several years.

Barr has known most people, including Mark Twain. He said Mark told him that his average expenditure was $35,000 a year, and that once when they got short he and his wife went through all the accounts and found the only things on which they could economize were *Harper's Magazine* and a cheaper closet-paper. He told me he knew of Mark having offers of $50,000 for a series of lectures from Pond, and $52,000 for 52 weekly articles from Hearst of the *N. Y. Journal.*

Barr gave a lot of his own experiences as a journalist in America, which would have been very interesting and amusing if Barr's mind had any actual distinction.

Monday, July 25th.

I have read 3 stories out of the 6 in d'Aurevilly's *Les Diaboliques.* They are extremely fine: proud, lofty, Spanish. *La Vengeance d'une Femme* has the best Balzacian romantic quality in it. It reminds one of *El Verdugo* or *Les Maranas* or *Les Mémoires de Deux Jeunes Mariées.* These *Diaboliques* really are *osés;* one can understand why on their original publication public opinion should have insisted on their being softened down. As a matter of fact only a great artist can be extremely and revoltingly improper. The achievement of the obscene is never the reward of mere perverse audacity. D'Aurevilly was a great artist, and he decidedly wrote a book compared to which the average pornographic production is a devotional exercise. He is always tremendously distinguished. Certainly *Le Rideau Cramoisi* and *Le Plus Bel Amour de Don Juan* are among the most perfect and most powerful of short stories.

Saturday, July 30th. Sandgate.

I came here to Sandgate by the 4 express from Paris on Friday. Wells and I walked the whole of today out in the country and lunched off bread and cheese at the second highest inn in Kent. We talked shop and women most of the day. He told me he had written a little humorous novel on the lines of *The Wheels of Chance,* and had been trying to persuade Halkett to take it for the *Pall Mall Magazine.* Halkett protested he was delighted with it personally, but as to his public—well, the "range of the story was rather narrow." Wells defended it, and instanced Jacobs [1] as a proof that the public did not object to narrow range. "Yes," said Halkett solemnly, "but Jacobs is a humourist." Wells was evidently very dissatisfied with his position. He talked seriously of gambling with 6 months of his time in order to try to do a couple or so of plays that would possibly bring in a fortune. He said he wanted £20,000 as a capital basis.

I wrote my story *A Dog in the Five Towns* for *T.P's Weekly* Christmas number; finished it Thursday afternoon.

Sunday, July 31st.

I had a lot of curious sensations on returning to England after an absence of 7 months—especially on wakening up in an English house— shaking off France, and readjusting my perspective of England and finding how fine England was and how I was full of sympathy for it, and all that sort of thing. But I was too tired and too idle and too busy with Wells to bother about putting them down. Nearly all Wells's conversation would make good table-talk and one has a notion that it ought not to be wasted; it is so full of ideas and of intellectual radicalism. It seems a pity that it should not be gathered up. But after all there is a constant supply of it. You might as well be afraid of wasting the water from a brook. I read the proofs of *The Food of the Gods* these last two days, and gave him my views on it. He was very keen and restless and nervous to hear them.

Talking of education, he said there was a particular time in human growth when each particular thing should be taught—before which it would be too soon and after which it would be too late.

The Rationalist Press Association would have liked to issue a 6d. edition of *Anticipations*. However, Watts broke it gently to Wells that "God" was mentioned several times in the book and their subscribers

---

[1] W. W. Jacobs, author of humorous sea stories.

would not like it. "Of course," said Watts, "I know you only use the word figuratively." "Not so figuratively as all that," said Wells.

Mr. and Mrs. Wells gave me between them a history of Gissing's[1] tragedies. Gissing lived connubially with a French woman. Wells gave me a full account of how he went over to Saint-Jean de Luz when Gissing was dying, full of queer details. Gissing's mouth had to be wiped out with lemon water, and his body sponged over with absolute alcohol. Wells did this. The woman was incompetent and stupid. The alcohol gave out, and he had to use methylated spirits. There was only one towel. One corner had to be used for the mouth-washing, another for the methylated spirits business. The corners got mixed up. Gissing, delirious, resisted. Then Wells had to *insist,* the woman objecting, on handkerchiefs being used; she said the handkerchiefs would get dirty at once—etc. etc., similar incredible stupidities.

Sunday, September 25th. Paris.

Ever since I left Paris I have wanted to come back. I came back on Friday and I am satisfied. I think I have never enjoyed the return to any place so much before. I could not keep my journal in England; there was no calm. And I was too busy with the Berquand treatment, which has yet to prove whether it will ultimately be a success.

Monday, September 26th.

My absence has had the effect of showing me how well I am established in Paris. Wherever I go, in restaurants and shops, I am recognized and greeted with the warmest cordiality. In 3 places today I have been the subject of an ovation. You would not get the same treatment in London under any circumstances. My books and my pictures (a few of each) have safely arrived, and I have bought a new bookcase and some other things, and I feel much more at home in Paris than ever.

Wednesday, October 5th.

My flat is repapered, my books shelved and pictures hung, and today I resumed my normal daily existence. I wrote about 3,000 words of the second story in the comic *Jack Stout* series. I am just getting over influ-

---

[1] George Gissing (1857-1903), whose books, *The Private Papers of Henry Ryecroft,* etc., were neglected during his lifetime and became the subject of a "cult" after his death.

enza and colds. Today also I received my fox-terrier pup Fly, and took it to the restaurant for dinner.

I am now certainly settled down in Paris. I was reading in the first two volumes of my journal tonight, and found to my astonishment that I began it 8 years ago. Some of it is very "young." But it was all enormously interesting, and some of it remarkably good.

I continue with *L'Assommoir*. It is not on the level of *Nana*. It seems all very earnest and meticulous. Yet in the scene where Gervaise is brought to bed of Nana, described with the fullest detail, no mention is made of the presence of Gervaise's elder child. But the presence of that child in such a small *appartement* must surely have been a considerable item in the affair. Also the scene in which Coupeau falls off the roof is distressingly forced and clumsy, with its artificial "preparation."

My hand trembles as I write; it has trembled all day. And I seem to remember noticing the same tremor very frequently this last few weeks. I certainly cannot write my old fine "hand."

Friday, October 7th.

In chastising my little dog, I find it is quite easy to lose control of myself momentarily and to treat the little brute cruelly. I did this once this afternoon and was so disgusted at myself that my hand trembled afterwards so that I could scarcely write my letter to the Mater.

Sunday, October 9th.

Tonight I revised all the stuff for my book of stories, *Tales of the Five Towns,* to be published in January. In reading over *A Letter Home,* which I must have written about 1893,[1] I was a little surprised at the technical skill of it, seeing that it was the first story of any real decency that I ever wrote, and I was not in the least surprised to find it sentimental and conventional here and there. However, I only altered one word in it.

Wednesday, October 12th.

I wrote the third *Jack Stout* story in 2 days, finishing it last night. It is a bad story well done.

---

[1] Published in the *Yellow Book* of 1895. See p. 8.

Tuesday, October 18th.

Just recovering from a very bad cold.

I can easily understand the violent prejudices and the wish to be deceived in peoples when altercations are in progress. I want Japan to win in the war, and because I want Japan to win I find myself, in spite of myself, minimizing every shred of Russian success and magnifying every success of Japan. I know that my attitude in reading the news is prejudiced, and yet I cannot alter it. All I can do is to admit that it is prejudiced.

Wednesday, November 2nd.

I got so busy finishing *The Adventures of Jack Stout* before F. and F.'s arrival that I couldn't trouble to make even the smallest notes in a journal. Then Frank and Florrie [1] came, and they left on Saturday morning. On the Monday of their arrival (24th) I lost my little dog Fly. I went down to Moret on Saturday afternoon and returned yesterday afternoon. I liked the country so much that I determined to go there a great deal more, and I arranged to have a little first-floor suite in the house of a gardener named Lebert at the rate of 2 fr. a day whenever I wanted it. The forest was magnificently tawny.

Friday, November 4th.

Today I came down to my new lodgings at Les Sablons. The bed-sitting-room is large with a bare polished floor and a portrait of Melanchthon (in a fur coat) on the walls. Antoine Lebert and his wife, the householders, have lived in Paris 31 years, and are retired here. They keep a large garden and grow grapes on long walls. Bunches still remain on certain vines which are covered with a kind of coarse muslin.

The rooms face south and the weather is cold and lovely. I went for a walk in the forest, which was magnificent, but I felt suddenly tired and came back and fell asleep over Butler's *The Way of All Flesh* in an armchair which at first I had thought to be extremely comfortable.

The Way of All Flesh is exceedingly good in parts. Whenever the author is satirical he is excellent. And now and then he gets a sudden sharp effect of pathos. He is very careless in details of construction, writes without dignity, and has a tendency to moralize at length. But I read

---

[1] His brother and sister.

the book with real zest, which is rare. There is a vast amount of naked truth in the book.

Saturday, November 5th.

I am very well fixed here. The old couple are so decent, such *braves gens;* they exhale such an atmosphere of a life's effort nearly accomplished. They may be narrow, but they have worked honestly and lived sanely. They like being praised, as all right-minded people do. And they are so simple. Imagine taking to a garden after 31 years of railway work in Paris!

I walked into the forest this morning. There was a foggy mist everywhere, and on all sides could be heard the dropping of water from the drenched trees. And looking into the depths of the forest one could conjure up the magic of *As You Like It* and *Midsummer Night's Dream.* At intervals cavalry trotted past towards Fontainebleau. One officer read a newspaper as he trotted along. For the second time in 8 days the Government was in danger of falling yesterday.

I was thinking this morning that the United States republic has substituted an aristocracy of commercial cleverness for the old forms of aristocracy. It is said that every man has an equal chance in the U.S., and he has. But commercial aptitude, with as little honesty as possible, is the only thing that will be of use to him. And everything is so arranged that the "risen" can trample on those who have not risen.

Tuesday, November 8th.

Davray read a lot of poetry on Saturday and Sunday nights, and reintroduced me to Verhaeren and Mallarmé. I am now reading Verhaeren with avidity, and getting ideas from him. I finished *Vathek* [1] yesterday. Superb imagination, and superb irony, and superb style. The style often amazed me.

I went out with Dr. Vallée in his little motor car yesterday afternoon. He visited sundry patients of the peasant class. He told me how inexpressibly dirty some of the interiors were which he had to visit. Then we went on to Montereau, a little industrial town where sugar and pottery are manufactured. The sole charm of this terribly provincial little town is the rivers Yonne and Seine which pass through it.

---

[1] By William Beckford (1760–1844).

It was night when we arrived. He put me down at the principal café. I put my head inside; the interior was full of citizens playing cards and billiards, and of dogs and of smoke. I ordered tea on the *terrasse*. Then I walked with him through the town: dark, petty, sludgy, typically provincial; one could feel that there were no ideas moving in this town. He had lived there once for some months and he told me how there was nothing there, no movement, no anything. But there existed an extraordinary number of pretty girls who worked in the pottery: this cheered me somewhat. He said that on Sundays the people put on their best clothes and merely walked about the streets. Then we crossed the Yonne, an impassively broad stream, mysterious in the night. A few steps further and we crossed the Seine, much smaller than the Yonne and running parallel to it, or nearly so.

Friday, November 11th.

Davray told me a curious history about Héran the artist. When the latter first came to Paris from Germany he could not speak much French and was incapable of inventing the legends for his drawings. He did a drawing of a woman and two niggers (something he had seen in a café) for a small comic weekly, and the editor added a legend which led to a prosecution for indecency. Héran, the editor, and the proprietor were collectively fined 2,000 francs. That is, each was liable for the whole sum. Héran was told that it would be all right and that of course the paper would pay.

Between 2 and 3 years afterwards, Héran was summoned out of bed one morning by two police officers and taken to prison. The hour was 7 A.M. He had had no warning of any sort. The fine had not been paid. He wired for Davray. Davray went to see the "Receiver of Fines," who was sympathetic but said he could do nothing. At length he said he would order Héran's release on payment of 666 fr. 66 c., and that Héran must then petition the President of the Republic to be freed, personally, from the remainder of the liability. Davray spent several days in collecting the money by means of subscriptions from his own friends. He told me how when he went to Anatole France, Anatole France, after hearing that an artist was in prison, would wait to hear no more, but immediately gave him some money and sent him off to the next place. At length, after very great difficulty, the money was collected, and Héran set free.

Afterwards, the necessary petition was signed by Anatole France, Hérédia, Berthelot,[1] etc., and instantly granted.

I went for another ride, this time exclusively in the Forest, with Vallée yesterday afternoon, returning in darkness. I leave here today. I have been almost happy, and have worked well. Quite half of the work on *An Angel Unawares* we have now accomplished. The first act stands complete. I must have written 8 or 9,000 words in the week. Further I have got quite an insight into modern French poetry.

Monday, November 14th. Paris.

I spent the whole of yesterday *en ville*. I went to Ullman's Sunday morning reception at his studio, and found some magnificent pictures, and much praise of my books.

At 6 o'clock, I went to the Café D'Orsay, and had a *vermouth-cassis,* and then I walked all the way by the Seine to Schwob's. He was alone, and the Chinese servant had been ill and looked sickly. Moréno was away on tour. We were intensely glad to see each other and shook hands with both right and left hands. He was much better, and his interest in books had revived. Books were all over the place and he had got a lot of new ones. Ting watched over us while we dined, and Schwob gave me the history of his transactions as to plays with David Belasco. Then he asked if I cared to go out, as the carriage was at his disposal. The carriage proved to be a magnificent Dion cab, and I suppose it belongs to Moréno. We whirled off to La Scala. It was hot and crowded.

Schwob said he enjoyed music-halls and frequented them, and he certainly enjoyed this. Some of the items were very good. He has the habit, which one finds in all sorts of people, of mildly but constantly insisting that a thing is good, as if to convince himself. If I began by saying that a thing was not good, he at once agreed. His taste, though extremely fine, is capricious; it is at the mercy of his feelings.

He whirled me home in about two minutes. I tremendously enjoyed the evening. He was absolutely charming, and his English is so good and sure, and he looked so plaintive and in need of moral support, with his small figure and his pale face, and his loose clothes, and his hat that is always too large for him. Yet I don't know any one who could be more

---

[1] Philippe Berthelot (see p. 198) later became Clemenceau's trusted adviser during the World War.

independent and pugnacious, morally, than Schwob. I have never seen him so, but I know that he would be so if occasion arose.

Wednesday, November 16th.

I went with the Davrays to the "Mardi" of the *Mercure de France* yesterday, and became acquainted with a lot of people, including Stuart Merrill,[1] and Philippe Berthelot and his wife. Merrill is a stout heavy man with irregular teeth and the look of an Englishman. He is obviously very good-natured, but it seems as if in him a nature originally extremely alert had been stupefied a little by habit. He talks English with a slight foreign accent.

Berthelot, just returned from China, was absolutely charming; a man about 33 or so, decorated, with a frank face and perfect manners, as becomes a man in the Foreign Office. His wife is a woman of decidedly remarkable personality; older than he, thin, tall, with a worn but attractive face, and strange tired eyes. Georgette Leblanc [2] was at the reception: a big, florid, and extremely intelligent woman.

Saturday, November 19th.

On Friday night Mrs. Devereux told me a fine retort of a pressing lover to a refusing mistress. "Bah!" she said. "With people like you, love only means one thing." "No," he replied. "It means twenty things, but it doesn't mean nineteen."

Tuesday, November 22nd.

Yesterday I finished the second act of *An Angel Unawares*. The third will be very easy to do. So today I began to plan out in detail the first part of *Sacred and Profane Love*. I walked all about Moret this morning, and got somewhat lost in the forest this afternoon. Then I read Swinburne.

The first part of *Sacred and Profane Love* is going to be entirely magnificent. I outlined the plot to Davray. I don't think he was very struck by it, and he asked whether the British public would stand it. However, from a crude outline he had nothing upon which to judge.

---

[1] The French Parnassian poet of American origin.
[2] The actress, known for her twenty-year association with Maurice Maeterlinck, which she tells about in her *Souvenirs* (1931).

Wednesday, November 23rd.

I noticed in the forest yesterday afternoon that the noise of the wind in the branches was indeed like the noise of the sea; but always distant— the noise never seemed to be near me. I got lost once, and took one path after another aimlessly until it occurred to me to steer by the sun. The moonrise was magnificent and the weather became frosty. After leaving Davray's at 10 o'clock I went as far as the forest, but the diverging avenues of trees did not produce the effect I had hoped for; there was too much gloom.

Today I began a sort of *S. and P. Love* draft, chiefly because I was too nervous to begin the actual writing, though I had finally settled on the opening phrase.

Monday, November 28th.

I went to tea at Cornillier's yesterday and met, *inter alios,* Mrs. Le Gallienne and Mrs. James Welch.[1] So I asked these two to dinner. We dined at the Place Blanche and then went to the Bal du Moulin de la Galette, which was certainly more wonderful than ever as a manifestation of the French spirit. The fair was proceeding on the boulevard. When we went up to the Moulin the music of the hobby-horses was deafening. But when we came down the legal hour for music had passed, and we were all three struck by the ghostly feeling of these merry-go-rounds revolving, brilliantly lighted, but quite silent.

I tried to find a leading idea for the concert scene in *Sacred and Profane Love,* but could not. I read late, and dreamed about the scene all night, and got it all mixed up, and generally wasted a vast amount of energy with no result at all.

Tuesday, November 29th.

Dinner at Mrs. Devereux's last night, Schwob there. We talked a good deal about Meredith, and Schwob showed an extraordinary knowledge of the byways of English literature. He said Meredith was certainly the son of a tailor, and quoted a passage from *Peter Simple* [2] where two characters go to "Meredith the tailor," and he said this was George's father. It appears that Meredith now talks in a loud voice, but continually in-

---

[1] Herself a well-known actress as Audrey Ford.
[2] By Capt. Marryat.

terrupts the conversation by talking to himself, mere senility of course. He has "ataxy" or something of one leg and limps and always tells any visitor that he had the misfortune to hurt his ankle that very morning. Schwob heard this from Oscar Wilde and didn't believe it. However, when Schwob called on Meredith, sure enough, he had hurt his leg that very morning. Schwob's enthusiasm for Meredith's last book was magnificent. He looked ill, but he was in his best form, and speaking beautiful English.

Mrs. Devereux had been to hear the trial of a *crime passionel*. A man had cut his wife's throat with a razor from ear to ear, but, through some fortunate movement of the woman, had only severed the skin. "A close shave!" said Schwob at once. I could see he was extremely pleased with this really admirable comment. He beamed after he had said it.

I searched after that idea for the concert chapter of *S. and P. L.* all day with no success. I stayed late at Mrs. Devereux's, and then read a lot afterwards, and I didn't go to bed till nearly 2. I dreamed of the chapter all night and woke up at 6.30, after which I didn't go to sleep again. To-day, I received the "Fantasia" of Chopin from Tertia. This is the *clou* of the chapter, if only I can make it so.

Wednesday, November 30th.

I met Emile Martin [1] by appointment at the Palais de Glace yesterday. A large circular place: curiously ghostly effect of the electric light on the powdery surface of the ice. This is evidently the resort of high-class *cocottes, rastas,* and rich wastrels. Some of the women were excessively *chic*.

I spent another day yesterday in searching for the idea for my next chapter, and I found it towards evening.

Thursday, December 1st.

I worked yesterday.

In the evening *L'Escalade* by Maurice Donnay, at the Renaissance. This is quite a minor piece, with insufficient material, and what material there is, not too well arranged. It is surprising to me how a man like Donnay

---

[1] An intimate personal friend of Arnold Bennett, who introduced him to many aspects of life in Paris and helped him to settle there.

could let such a work go out of the manufactory. Guitry and Brandès were magnificent, full of distinction; Guitry's son had also his father's distinction.

Saturday, December 3rd.

I dined at the Ullmans' and played Beethoven, Schubert, and Grieg with him. And got up this morning with a peculiar sort of a headache. I finished the concert chapter yesterday.

Sunday, December 4th.

Mme. Cornillier took me to see Mme. Debraux yesterday, right at the other end of Paris. Immediately she began to talk I saw again how wonderful she was. There was a young poet there who was pessimistic and disillusioned to the point of being rude, but a good fellow fundamentally. Mme. Debraux wiped the floor with him in argument.

I remember that Schwob said at Mrs. Devereux's: "You English care about the end of a play. I mean your cultivated opinion. It may end sadly or happily, but the end must be good, logical, and strong, if the play is to satisfy you. We French are not particular about that. A weak close does not annoy us if there has been sufficient good stuff in the play." I recognize the truth of this. But how strange that the French, so preoccupied with form, should be like that!

Wednesday, December 7th.

I came down to Les Sablons yesterday. A magnificent tempest began about noon and is just now dying. When I went out this morning in my big overcoat into the rain and wind, I felt how splendid it was to be in the country. Last night was absolutely black. I went to have tea with Mrs. Spear and found all her three daughters there. The two eldest, aged about 18 and 19, are charming. There are, I suppose, no such French girls. The French girl is sacrificed to the French woman—and no doubt the French woman is worth the price. I had an extraordinarily rich tea of home-made jams and cakes. I was very facetious, I don't know why, and I made them laugh continually. It is very satisfying and contenting to make young girls laugh by simple means. I stayed two hours.

I went on pretty well with *S. and P. Love* today.

Saturday, December 10th.

X—— described the general sensations of being well drunk as magnificent, splendid. "But," he says, "you mustn't set out to get drunk. It must take you unawares." He told me that when sober he frequently lost umbrellas, but when drunk never. He made a special point of retaining his umbrella then in his hand; it became his chief concern in life. Once he got badly drunk at Maxim's. He just had sense enough to take a cab to the rooms of a mistress he had then. She received him and undressed him and put him to bed. But he would not "leave go" of his umbrella during the process. He passed it from hand to hand as she divested him of his coat, waistcoat, and shirt, and he took it to bed. And he said, "She became very angry with that umbrella."

I was extremely pleased with what I did yesterday of *S. and P. L.,* but when I read part of it this morning my enthusiasm was a little damped.

Wednesday, December 14th.

I worked at *S. and P. Love* till 11.30 Monday night; beginning at 3.30 in the afternoon, and I recommenced early on Tuesday and had got to the end of the first part by midday. I slept a long time after lunch and woke up with the first headache I have had for months. I went down to Rachilde's [1] reception at the *Mercure de France* to meet Davray. He took me to an old bookseller's named Lehec, in the Rue Saint-André des Arts. We could scarcely get into the shop for books. Lehec told us he had a hundred thousand; the place smelt of damp paper. He was an oldish thin man, wearing a hat and a black smock like a French child's pinafore.

I wanted a good edition of *The Memoirs of Fanny Hill.* [2] He had a copy upstairs in his flat. He took us up, in the dark, to the third story, and having opened the door made us enter quickly lest his cat should escape. When he had struck a light we saw the cat—a superb Persian. A curiously arranged flat, small, very clean, and bourgeois. It reminded me of what Sister Glegg's might have been—in *The Mill on the Floss.* Here again all was books. He at last, after searching through several

---

[1] Mme. Alfred Valette, author of many novels and plays, among which *Dans le Puits* is very well known.

[2] A famous pornographic work by John Cleland. It appeared in 1750 and the author made the great sum of £10,000 from its sales.

portmanteaus full of bawdy English books, found a fine edition of *Fanny Hill* in two volumes. I have since read this work. It is certainly a master-piece of pornographic *literature*.

Davray and I went back to the *Mercure* and met the usual crowd. But Henri de Regnier,[1] tall, thin, grey, severe, and looking quite the Norman aristocrat that he is, was there—talking to Georgette Leblanc. The latter is decidedly very beautiful. Davray told me that to have Regnier dangling his legs from the corner of a table and talking obscenities in his calm exquisitely polished way was a delightful experience. Rachilde gave me some madeira which did not arrange my deranged stomach. Davray was depressed, so I asked him to come and dine with me and Emile Martin. We met Martin at the Café Riche, where I had an absinthe. I could not judge whether or not it did me good.

Afterwards we didn't quite know what to do, and Martin suggested that we should go down to the Port Maillot and see the cafés frequented by chauffeurs and their mistresses. *Ca nous changera un peu.* We went, wandering down through the Palais Royal and then taking the Métro. We got a good café but it was empty, and we saw only one chauffeur and *he* hadn't a mistress.

Thursday, December 15th.

I dined at Schwob's. Moréno had returned. She was dressed in black with gold jewellery, and was more captivating than ever. I immediately forgot her capriciousness and my small grievances against her. She still remains without any pose; and she still constantly says things of the most extraordinary penetration and delicacy. Raphael,[2] the Paris correspondent of the *Referee* and the *Sketch,* was invited to meet me. A pronouncedly Jewish face. Very polite and pleasant.

Sunday, December 18th.

I finished the last act of *An Angel Unawares* this morning. Tea at Mrs. Devereux's on Friday to go on to a concert with Mesdames Debraux and Cornillier. The former looked more beautiful than ever I have seen her. It was a concert given by a music mistress in a *rez-de-chausée;* full of women and girls; too hot, with a *salamandre* in full blast. Not bad as

---

[1] Parnassian poet and author of many novels and plays.
[2] J. N. Raphael, journalist and playwright.

a concert, but too long. I asked Mme. Debraux to dine with us on Sunday night, but she had another engagement. However, she said she would try to break that. I called on her yesterday afternoon to know what she would do, and after we had talked half an hour on books and music, she said, *"Eh bien, je vous donnerai la réponse: Oui."* I should have been desolated if she had said No. I went to Lapérouse on Friday night and dined there and ordered the dinner for Sunday.

On Friday, Raphael came to lunch with me. He did the reporting of the Dreyfus case at Rennes for the *Daily Mail,* while G. W. Steevens [1] did the descriptive stuff. He astounded me by saying that Steevens, after arriving at Rennes with a perfectly open mind, came at length firmly to believe that Dreyfus was guilty.

Monday, December 19th.

I sent off the last act of *An Angel Unawares* yesterday morning. In the afternoon I went to have tea with Miss Thomasson; I was slanging Harris as typical of all that was most repugnant to me in the Quarter, and a moment afterwards he and his wife called in, and outstayed me. I thought that Harris, though insufferable, was perhaps less so than I had imagined.

December 30th.

I left Paris last Wednesday week, and stayed two nights with Wells. I read the typescript of the first part of his new novel, *The Comet.* [2] He said that his financial position was becoming more and more secure. I came to Burslem on Friday. I ought to have gone to Phillpotts's today, but was stopped by a wire yesterday.

Walking through the town yesterday I saw two child's funerals exactly of the same kind; a procession of 5 or 6 pairs of women in black with white trimmings; two pairs carried the small oak coffin which was covered with wreaths and which they held by white cords over their shoulders. Immediately behind the coffin, the chief mourners, in one case a man and a woman. The coffin occurred about the middle of the procession. These little forlorn smug processions ambling towards the cemetery were very curious.

---

[1] Gifted journalist and war correspondent (1869–1900).
[2] *In the Days of the Comet* was published in 1906.

1905

Monday, January 2nd. England.

Last year I wrote 282,100 words, exclusive of re-writing. This comprises 2 plays with Eden Phillpotts, *Christina* and *An Angel Unawares,* the greater part of *A Great Man,* the whole of *Hugo,* and one-third of *Sacred and Profane Love;* also a series of facetious short stories entitled *The Adventures of Jack Stout* and one other short story. I don't think I ever did anything like so much creative work in one year. I made no particular advance commercially. I had several grave disappointments including the result of my visit to Scotland,[1] and the result of *Christina,* the loss of a dog and a pocket-book, and the commercial failure of *A Great Man.* On the other hand the artistic success of *A Great Man* was a genuine surprise to me. I firmly decided to marry.

I came down to Torquay last Friday. Eden and I have worked on *An Angel Unawares,* and tomorrow it will be completely finished.

Tuesday, January 3rd.

Today we put the last touches to the play. I am frankly rather optimistic about it. Eden is too, but not frankly. It is the most saleable thing I have ever done, either alone or in collaboration.

Thursday, January 5th.

I went with Mrs. Phillpotts to tea at the Findlaters'. A spinsterish house. A mother aged over 80, rather fine, keen on liberal politics and the

---

[1] To be cured of stammering.

Scottish church crisis. I liked her. Then the three daughters. Mora the oldest is the housekeeper, non-literary, aged about 43; a sort of Cinderella, certainly made use of and squashed by the other two. The other two are Jane Helen and Mary, aged from 36 to 40, better dressed than Mora, positive in their opinions, quiet, refined, and above all things canny. A nice Scotch tea with good old silver spoons and admirable scones; literature discussed rather from the business side. Jane Helen told me one interesting thing. She met Kipling just after his great illness.[1] He told her that he felt that artistically he was done for, that his old vitality was gone and would never return. Time has proved this so far.

Wednesday, January 11th.

Today I recommenced the actual writing of my novel.

On Wells's recommendation I have been reading Henry James's *The Ambassadors*. I have read 150 pages out of 450, and I have given it up. It certainly does contain, as Wells said, some wonderful little pictures of Paris and the Anglo-Saxon colonies there. The writing, though difficult, is amazingly adequate. It is merely perfect. But I found the plot clumsily managed, and a very considerable absence of passionate feeling. I came to the conclusion that the book was not *quite* worth the great trouble of reading it.

Friday, January 27th.

I have recovered from a bad attack of influenza—three days in bed. All my work upset. I find I can't recommence writing without a change and I am going to London a week earlier than I meant. I have read a great deal in Mark Twain's *Life on the Mississippi*, a fine, amusing, interesting work quite new to me. Also Balzac's *Rivalités* with much gusto.

Monday, February 6th. Paris.

I am now settled down in Paris again. I had 5 days in Putney and London and practically negotiated the sale of plays to Harrison and to

---

[1] Rudyard Kipling was in New York when stricken with this illness. The newspapers showed proper gratitude for the copy thus afforded by working the town up to a high state of excitement. The front pages dripped with sick-room news, bulletins from the medical men and stories about the crowds that stood watch before the patient's hotel, the Grenoble, at Seventh Avenue and 56th Street. Later Kipling is said to have said that the American people never forgave him for not dying in New York.

Legge, had one talkative evening with several men at the flat, and came over here on Friday. The first thing I noticed on landing in France was the thin and exiguous "feel" of the folded French newspaper compared to the English. I went down to see Mme. Debraux on Saturday evening and found her if anything rather more fine than before; then I dined at the Chat Blanc with the Montparnasse crowd. I lunched with Kelly on Sunday in his new studio up in the heavens; had tea at the Cornilliers'.

Tuesday, February 7th.

I went to see R. after dinner last night. His *petite amie*, Aimée, was there; they had just finished dinner. We began to talk about dogs, and then about a dog of Moréno's which I said had *mœurs extraordinaires*. Immediate interest was aroused, and we were soon discussing sexual peculiarities in general. Aimée said I was the first Englishman she had ever met who had "large ideas" about love-making and who could discuss the subject naturally.

Saturday, February 11th.

Schwob told me when he ardently wanted a book his voice always went hoarse in asking the price of the bookseller. A bookseller sufficiently acquainted with human nature, he said, could take advantage of such a symptom; and some did. He instanced Rahir of the Passage des Panoramas, whom he called one of the three greatest booksellers, if not the greatest, in Europe. The other two would be Rosenthal of Munich, and Quaritch. He said that he was dining with M. L. of the Français the other night. She has a wealthy lover and keeps a considerable state. Though very ignorant of literature, she has just "taken to" collecting books, and she described to him her feelings when looking at a fine book. They were the same as those of a woman tempted by lace, jewels, or a man. The desire was imperious and must be satisfied. . . . And this in an ignorant woman!

Sunday, February 12th

I went to the Bal Bullier. Driving home, I happened to overtake C.; so I got out and walked up the street with her. Some one had told her that my portrait of her in *A Great Man* was very cold and unsympathetic. I merely said, *"C'est un malin qui t'a dit ça."* I don't think I ever met any woman with a prouder independence of spirit than that girl has.

Monday night, February 13th.

Today I really recommenced work, and I worked all day. Idleness is a very bad thing indeed for me in every way.

Tuesday, February 14th.

I went to the new Bal Tabarin last night. I think it is the only ball in Paris that is open every night. I saw the famous "La Goulue" there perched on a high chair at the bar; a round, vulgar, rather merry face, looking more like a *bonne* than a dancer and a *dompteuse des lions*. With an expenditure of 7 francs on drinks with another ex-dancer, I learned something about the life of the paid dancers in public balls. They get 4 francs a night, *et elles peuvent trouver de bons amis,* said the ex-dancer, whose younger sister, a fine big girl with a clear complexion, was dancing the *quadrille réaliste* on the floor. This sister, I was told, made 5,000 francs besides her pay as a dancer during the short season at the Jardin de Paris last year.

Thursday, February 16th.

Tristan and Isolde at the Opéra last night with Mrs. Devereux. Everybody and everything thoroughly bad, except Alvarez, and even he frequently sang through his nose.

When I told Mrs. D. how surprised I was to learn from the newspaper that A. B. Walkley [1] was married, she said that his marriage was one of the cardinal facts of his life.

Mrs. D. said that perhaps I should not at first care very much for Walkley; that he united a very broad mind with a good deal of superficial conventionality, was prim, precise, very difficult to please, and ferociously ironic, etc.

Tuesday, February 28th.

While I was lying in bed yesterday morning I read in the *Figaro* that Marcel Schwob had died on Sunday. He dined with me on the 16th and

---

[1] Dramatic critic of *The Times.*

seemed vivacious enough. Since then I had heard nothing. I lunched with the Davrays yesterday, and Davray cried in talking about it. He had just been to the house and seen Maurice Schwob. In the evening I received from Maurice Schwob, via Philippe Champion, a request that I should communicate with Marcel's English friends. Moréno is only supposed to arrive in Paris this morning.

I had some excellent ideas for *S. and P. Love* yesterday and Sunday.

Thursday, March 2nd.

I went with Raphael to Schwob's house yesterday morning. We arrived late and the *cortège* had gone; so we signed our names and departed. The *concierge*, moved, told us that Moréno was excessively fatigued and that her brother was "in the article of death." This phrase on the lips of a *concierge* was striking.

I dined with Raphael at the Café Zimmer in the building of the Châtelet.

Raphael told me a good story about Tree. Tree came to Paris and went down to the Français to demand free tickets. He was knocked about from one official to another till he found the right one. "*A quel titre, monsieur?*" asked the official.

"*Je suis M. Tree,*" said Tree.

"*Mais à quel titre demandez-vous des billets?*"

"*Je suis M. Tree, l'acteur de Londres.*"

"*Ah, vous savez, si nous donnions des billets à tous les acteurs de Londres . . . !*"

Friday, March 3rd.

Somerset Maugham came up for tea. He has a very calm, almost lethargic demeanour. He took two cups of tea with pleasure and absolutely refused a third; one knew instantly from his tone that nothing would induce him to take a third. He ate biscuits and *gaufrettes* very quickly, almost greedily, one after the other, without a pause, and then suddenly stopped. He smoked two cigarettes furiously, in less time than I smoked one, and solidly declined a third. I liked him. He said he had sold a play to Liebler through Fred Kerr,[1] on the terms of £300 down, and £100 every quarter until they produced it—in advance of royalties. I asked him

---

[1] Frederick Kerr, actor and at one time manager of the Court Theatre.

if he liked the Quartier Montparnasse and he said, "Yes; the atmosphere of it is rather like Oxford." He said that as soon as he could he should spend 3 years in travel.

Saturday, March 4th.

Raphael and Company dined with me at the Place Blanche and then we went to the Alhambra, and I was introduced to the manager, a young and extremely English man who could scarcely speak any French. Houdini (an American), the "handcuff king," was the principal attraction. It appears that this man really *has* a gift for getting out of handcuffs and picking locks. He certainly did some extraordinary things last night —including one in which Raphael's overcoat took a share. Raphael told me that Houdini "had got out of all the principal prisons in the world." In Germany he challenged the police to put him in a cell that he couldn't escape from. They took the challenge and he won. But they denied that he had won (from motives of policy). He brought an action against them which lasted 3 years (costs £1,000), and ultimately gained the day.

Thursday, March 9th.

I dined at the Chat Blanc. Aleister Crowley was there with dirty hands, immense rings, presumably dyed hair, a fancy waistcoat, a fur coat, and tennis shoes. Stanlaws was saying that the indecency of the Moulin Rouge etc. "wasn't 30 cents" by the side of Coney Island. I had heard this before. He described the rag-dance, which used to be danced everywhere but was lately forbidden by the police. It appears to be a combination of a waltz and the *danse du ventre*. He described a number of other Coney Island contrivances for the exhibition of women's legs and underclothes.

Monday, March 13th.

I brought Kelly down to Les Sablons on Friday. Davray told him, in talking about Meredith, that Meredith had told *him* that the preface to *The Egoist* is merely a series of imitations of various authors that Meredith knew, one after the other. Meredith read aloud this preface to Davray, vocally imitating each author, and Davray said the effect was astounding.

Thursday, March 16th.

Yesterday I finished the second part of *Sacred and Profane Love*. The book so far is over 6,000 words longer than I had anticipated, and I think the second part is rather better on the whole than I expected it would be when I started it.

I have read Oscar Wilde's *Intentions,* and found it really very good, better than *De Profundis*. I read also in *The Importance of Being Earnest,* and found that admirably witty.

The French are a "stuffy" nation; but they *do* hang their bedding out of the windows in the morning to air. This is more than can be said of the English.

I go to Paris tomorrow, with some regret. I could easily become a countryman completely.

Saturday, March 18th.

Kelly gave me a notion for a dramatic situation the other day; two people married who find themselves brother and sister. I saw I could turn it into a good unprintable short story. While I was talking to Davray on Thursday at tea, the thing suddenly presented itself to me as a play for the Grand Guignol, and changing the conversation abruptly, I told him I had a subject for a play for the Grand Guignol. I saw the whole play, in two acts, like a flash, and I described it to him. He said, "We ought to do that together." At 6.30 I began to write the first act. I had to meet Vallée at dinner at 7.30. I worked from 10.30 to 11.30 P.M., and yesterday for 25 minutes, and I had finished a full draft of the first act. I read it to Davray last night at the Nouvelle Athènes in the Place Pigalle, and he was much struck by it. I propose to write the second act today. Davray will re-write it in French. I have written it part in French and part in English.

Sunday, March 19th.

I finished the play, *Que Faire?* yesterday afternoon. At night I went with Raphael to see *Thérèse Raquin,* with Aimée Tessandier as the mother. She was certainly very fine. Most of the rest of the performance was ignoble. Raphael, who lives in the same house as she does, told me that she started life in Bordeaux. The play is a good play spoilt by clumsiness. I didn't go to bed till 2 o'clock, and then had to read *The Times*.

Tuesday, March 21st.

I went to see Dr. L. yesterday. He has a flat on the entresol in the Rue Marbœuf, *en plein quartier chic.* The door was opened by a rather agreeable, but not *excessivement chic,* girl, who politely picked up a pencil which I dropped. She showed me into a fairly spacious waiting-room, horribly and characteristically furnished. A crimson plushy carpet all over the floor, a set of chairs and a sofa all in their *housses;* a modern Louis XVI table richly gilt and fairly well made, bearing old copies of *L'Illustration* and *La Vie en Plein Air.* A huge lamp standard in a corner; a piano with draped back; a column surmounted by a specimen of *art nouveau* statuary; to wit, a withered tree, with a huge rock near it, the rock cut in the form of a face, as big as the tree—this in bronze. Two pairs of double doors heavily draped. Odd statuettes and signed photographs of men.

The doctor surprised me by appearing through doors where I had not expected him. A man about 30, *hérissé,* hair and beard sticking out; slightly stiff in manner, but improving later. Beyond muttering the word "Vallée" he made no reference to the extremely *empressé* introduction which I had to him. He evidently sprang from the lower middle class and was unable to rely on his manners.

He took me into his consulting-room, a room more frankly and awfully *art nouveau* than the waiting-room, but less distressing, because it was all in one scheme and showed some sense of design. I soon found that he knew his business; but with that he proved to be somewhat vain and self-important. He wrote out his *ordonnance* at excessive length, with *premièrement, deuxièmement, troisièmement,* and so on. He drew me the design of a *canule,* and he couldn't help referring to that design twice afterwards, as it were fishing for praise of his ability to draw at all. However, he was extremely practical. I should say he would be a brute in a hospital, and a brute with women. He looked a brute. But in some ways I did not dislike him. He is an *arriviste,* and quite young.

Friday, March 24th.

Yesterday I had the idea of translating Verlaine. I did the *Chanson des Ingonnes*—rather well, I thought. Anyhow it got so into my head that I was quite unable to proceed with the excogitation of my sensational plot for Tillotson's serial.

I also began to write, or rather sketch out, some "maxims."

Monday, March 27th.

I dined at Mrs. Devereux's last night. Numerous people there, including a Roumanian, Vaschide, who is an official specialist here in Paris on experimental psychology. He told me he was 30. He looked like a free *garçon* of a pronounced type, and I was astounded to hear that he was a married man with a family. He seemed rather mad himself, but very interesting.

As I came home I called at Graff's for a milk, and Raphael was there, with Lonergan of the *Daily Telegraph*.

All last week I devoted myself to the sensational serial and succeeded fairly well in planning it out.

Friday, March 31st.

I went around with Vallée last night to see some of his patients. One was at Champagne—what is called a Cité Jardin, built for the employés of the Creusot Steel Company. The population must certainly be over 1,000; and is probably much more. We arrived when it was nearly dark. Vast blocks of houses 4 or 5 stories high, of dark stone, and fearfully ugly and forbidding. A "place" here and there, and plenty of vacant plots. It was extraordinary how a 4- or 5-storied block struck one as being out of place in the country, where land is plentiful. The houses were a cheap imitation of Parisian houses. No lights on the stairs, no lights in the streets, but windows lighted here and there, giving hints of mean interiors. He stopped in a narrow street (why narrow I cannot imagine), quite short, containing, however, 3 cafés—all pitchpine and zinc and a too cheap simplicity. It was Mi-Carême and the air was full of the sounds of uncouth instruments. A little troupe of masquers arrived from the outskirts, where the large residences of the Creusot managers are, and passed into a café. The whole impression was terribly forlorn, ugly, and dispiriting. It was a beautiful evening, with a warm, caressing wind, and flashes of lightning.

Saturday, April 8th.

I saw Miss Le Quesne yesterday at the Ullmans'. I had not seen her for about 10 years. I should not have known her. She did not know me. In fact she did not even remember meeting me. When we went together afterwards to call on Mrs. Le Gallienne, and Mrs. Le Gallienne was away in London, I was surprised how eagerly Miss Le Quesne played with the Le Gallienne infant, arranging with her to go into the Luxembourg gardens the next day and so on. She committed the usual feminine indiscretion of saying in the child's presence that the little thing looked pale, etc.

At night Mrs. Devereux dined with me at Noel and Peter's. For the first time in the history of our acquaintance she was prompt. At least not prompt, but in front of time. Women are never exact. I was exact, and so she had to wait.

I have been "driven" this week, and have not been able either to practise the piano much or to keep this journal. On Tuesday I got all my ideas together for the third instalment of the serial. But I dined with Misses Thomasson and Hergersheimer in the evening, and Miss Thomasson spent an hour from 7.45 to 8.45 in her studio, lighted by a single small lamp, in making a mayonnaise. Consequently the dinner was 75 minutes late, though excellent. The mayonnaise succeeded admirably. I ate too much of it, and what with this and the dinner being late, I had a bilious attack the next day, the first for about a year.

I have had our French play typewritten. The typist brought it herself this morning. She told me, incidentally, that French theatrical managers were very conservative and had a prejudice against typewriting. As a matter of fact they are not in the least conservative. They are *routinier,* which is not the same thing.

Sunday, April 9th.

Cornillier called yesterday morning, and I was telling him about a good early picture by Tissot [1] that Ullman had bought for 200 francs. He said that a long time ago Tissot had a mistress, with whom he had continued relations for a considerable period. He decided to break the *liaison,* and he wrote one letter to his mistress, giving her the gentlest possible hint that the affair must ultimately come to an end, and another letter to an intimate friend, a man, saying brutally that he was sick of the thing and wanted to marry. He mixed the letters up, and the mistress received the wrong one. She committed suicide. Tissot was deeply af-

---

[1] S. J. S. Tissot, the genre painter. He died in 1902.

fected, regarded himself as her murderer, and became *dévot.* This was really the origin of his journeys to Palestine and the ruin of his art.

In the evening I went with Ullman to Antoine, and saw *Les Avariés,* which is an extremely good sermon and an extremely bad play, and *La Parisienne.* I was more enthusiastic than ever about the latter. I can recall no portrait of a woman which is at once so true and so brilliant. But what a storm it would raise in England! I enjoyed myself. And as I walked home, I thought how fine Paris was, and that in old age, or even earlier, if I quitted it, I should look back on these days and perceive that I had been happy.

Wednesday, April 12th.

I received Wells's book, *A Modern Utopia,* and I called in at the Café de la Paix and read 50 pages of it to the sound of music.

Tuesday, April 18th.

Yesterday I came down to Les Sablons, extremely depressed. I felt as if I wanted to reform the whole scheme of my existence. Mme. Davray said that it was indigestion, and asked me to dinner.

It is extraordinary how enthusiastic and graphic Davray always becomes when he talks of Oscar Wilde. This afternoon he finished an article on him, and at tea began to talk. He recounted lots of things. Here is one. After coming out of prison Oscar became friendly with Esterhazy,[1] very friendly. Davray protested, and said Esterhazy was a *crapule* and all sorts of things. Oscar agreed. "But," he said, "I must make my society of thieves and assassins now." (This is a translation of the French phrase.) "If Esterhazy had been innocent I should have had nothing to do with him."

Good Friday, April 21st.

Vallée dined with me last night. Afterwards the doctor and I motored to Fontainebleau. Moonlight in the forest. We visited the two *cafés chantants* of the town, which were like *cafés chantants* everywhere; yet rather surprising to find them in the midst of the forest. What interested

---

[1] The villain in the conspiracy against Captain Dreyfus.

me much more than the singing *cocottes* was the old, old, ugly women who played the piano at each place. Finished women! They looked as though they never could have been young and gay.

Adolphe Ratté, poet, came in, wearing corduroy and carrying an outlandish dagger-cane. He has grey hair and a seamed face. He showed me his last book of stories, which was sticking out of his pocket. He has actually written some 10 volumes! He recited Verlaine and Baudelaire admirably. Vallée said he knew by heart over 10,000 lines of Hugo.

Thursday, April 27th.

I couldn't concentrate my ideas yesterday. I met Miss Thomasson at the Salon in the afternoon, and dined with the Raphaels at night. It is about a fortnight ago that I began to keep a notebook of observations upon women and the relations of the sexes, and this notebook is and will be apt to take things away from this journal.

Saturday, April 29th.

Morrice came and dined with me last night. He is an old *habitué* of the quarter. And though he had not been here for years, the old waiter at the Jouanne tripe shop, where we dined excellently, remembered him and how he liked his tripe. Morrice plays the flute charmingly. He performed Bach, etc. At 11 o'clock he said he must go. But he stayed till 1 o'clock.

I found him a most distinguished person, full of right and beautiful ideas about nearly everything. He said a number of brief things that were like knocking holes into the receptacle of his philosophy and giving glimpses of the treasure within.

Monday, May 1st.

On Saturday I dined with Martin at the Restaurant Italien, and then we went to Buffalo Bill. Most lugubrious, for besides bad weather there was bad lighting, and little to see. We left almost at once and went to the Bal Tabarin in "the ball of the models of the two salons."

Towards midnight there was a colossal crowd. Indeed I have never seen such a sight at a ball. A group of middle-aged married men on the loose like boys were near to us, and also a group of American girls in charge of a man. When the *défilé* began it was impossible to move on the ground floor; the air was full of *serpentins,* and the band was deafening. The *cocottes* were perhaps not worthy of the occasion.

I left Martin there at 1.30, after having drunk more champagne than was absolutely necessary to sustain life.

Saturday, May 13th.

The Marriotts left yesterday morning, after an uneventful visit. I finished the second part of the *City of Pleasure* on Thursday. Though I have dined out every night I have found nothing of special human interest, except about women, which I record elsewhere. I was telling Martin on Wednesday night at the Folies Marigny how depressed I was on Sunday and how, to cap all, I suffered horribly from jealousy in the evening, and he said: *"Mais qu'est-ce que vous voulez? Ca, c'est la vie! Mieux ça qu'une vide? Moi, je n'ai jamais été plus heureux que quand je me trouvais malheureux!"* This somewhat profound observation, exactly agreeing with what I have been preaching for 20 years past, coming from the son of a pork butcher, surprised me, though I had always known that Martin is a delicate observer of himself and of others. I complimented him on it several times during the evening.

Monday, May 15th.

I dined with Ullman. Talking about the standard of living, I agreed with him that except for food it was decidedly low in Paris. He is much struck by the primitiveness of things here just now, because there is no place in the whole of the house where he lives to store a perambulator. Some people who live opposite to him and pay 3,000 francs rent are obliged to store their perambulator at a coal dealer's round the corner. He described the luxuries and conveniences of the finest flats in New York. Rent $15,000. With that, a ballroom (I mean a private ballroom for each flat), and a completely fitted hospital (also for each flat). Facilities for posting letters in the flat itself. Also soundproof walls.

Tuesday, May 16th.

Morrice dined with me and stayed till 1 A.M. He has the joy of life in a high degree, and he likes living alone. "I enjoy everything," he said. "I got up this morning, and I saw an old woman walking along, and she was the finest old woman I ever did see. She was a magnificent old woman, and I was obliged to make a sketch of her. Then there was the *marchand de quatre saisons*. His cry is so beautiful. I began to enjoy myself immediately I got out of bed. It is a privilege to be alive." And so on.

Thursday, May 18th.

Miss Thomasson said last night one of those picturesque things that only Americans do say. Of a Frenchman whom we know: "He learnt to dance much more slowly than you do. He's nervous. If you look at him he fancies you are counting his legs, and I'm sure he thinks he's got about six."

I finished (and began) the twelfth instalment of the *City of Pleasure* yesterday.

Friday, May 26th.

At Hélène Berthelot's yesterday. A perfect museum of Chinese art. I saw some stereoscopic photos of Chinese tortures. They made me feel queer. Mme. Berthelot told me a curious thing about them. When he took them the young photographer was so occupied with his work that he thought nothing of the scenes he was witnessing. But when he developed the negatives and printed them and saw what he had witnessed, he fainted.

Friday, June 2nd.

I finished *The City of Pleasure* on Tuesday morning, being heartily sick of it. Everybody is in Paris now, and I have dined with friends every night for weeks past.

It was with intense pleasure that I turned back to *Sacred and Profane Love* after *The City of Pleasure*.

Wednesday, June 21st.

Last night I dined in the Bois with Ochs,[1] the financier, and Mrs. and Blanche Devereux. A lovely evening. I found Ochs an extremely agreeable and rather intelligent man—a little nervous under his worldliness. I went to his rooms at the Hôtel du Rhin afterwards, and he promised to come up here.

---

[1] Adolph Simon Ochs, owner of *The New York Times*.

Monday, July 17th.

I came down to spend the summer at Les Sablons. I still had 5,000 words of *Sacred and Profane Love* to write, and I finished the book yesterday morning before lunch. I wrote the third part with less verve than the other two parts, and was doubtful of it several times, but when the thing was quite done it seemed to me all right. During the last week or two I was unable to think seriously about anything else, and I couldn't make notes or keep journals or anything of that kind, though I had to worry myself during two days over a suggested alteration of the comedy *An Angel Unawares*. Now that the novel is done I hope to return to journalizing.

Saturday, July 29th.

Dined last night with Barnard,[1] the American sculptor, down on the banks of the Loing at Moret. He is doing the sculpture for the façade of the Capitol of Pennsylvania—a building 1,000 feet long and 450 feet high. Chiefly two enormous groups containing 33 heroic figures, feeble in sentiment and academic in design. What interested me was the intense absorption of the man in his work, and his energy. He is a little man with staring black eyes (one queer) and the deep strong voice of a very strong man. He has a huge old stone building by the river, rather like a church, but not one; and it was curious to see this statuary for an American State being quietly produced here.

Tuesday, September 19th.

I resumed work last Saturday, after the longest holiday I have had since I can remember. Except a few hours' work on a play, I had done no work for over two months. On Saturday, Sunday, and yesterday I wrote a story called *The Murder of the Mandarin,* and I posted it at once to the typist. In the evening I rode over to Marlotte and dined alone with Mrs. ——.

Mrs. —— told me about Frank Harris. She said he was 43 when she first met him in 1895.[2] He then had a fixed idea that he should die at 44. She said no man had ever influenced her so much, though there was no question either of love or even affection between them. All London

---

[1] George Gray Barnard.
[2] He was then 39. He died in 1931, aged 75.

believed he was her lover, and all London had ample cause for believing so; but as a fact he was not in the list of her lovers. He did what he liked with her. Over and over again she had waited hours for him. He had a marvellous voice. Lamperti offered him 5 years' tuition if he would only study, free, and said he would be the greatest bass that ever had been. His eloquence was astounding. He made a political speech, and was adopted as Conservative candidate for one of the Ridings. No dinner party was complete without him. Carlyle had thought very highly of him, and this opinion was echoed by a later generation. Lord R. Churchill thought him the greatest man he had ever met. John Walter of *The Times* believed in him long after most others had ceased to do so.

He bought the *Saturday Review* for £5,000 and sold it for £30,000. He had no moral sense. He treated everybody shamefully. But he was never mean. He was the sort of man who would stab a person in the back and rob him of all he possessed, and then give the entire proceeds to another person. He was easily influenced, and easily intoxicated by his own eloquence. During the Boer War, he was at a luncheon party, and began to talk about the sufferings of the Boers in such a manner that the entire party, including a general returned from South Africa, and anti-Boers to a man, was literally reduced to tears. Finally he burst into tears himself, jumped up, and left the house.

Wilde offered him the leading idea of *Mr. and Mrs. Daventry,*[1] and he bought it for £100 and afterwards gave Wilde two further sums of £50. Harris wrote the play, got it produced, and made £4,000 out of it.

Wednesday, September 20th.

I have been re-reading Kipling, and thought *Without Benefit of Clergy* fine, and yet perhaps not great. Other things pretty good, but certainly not great. Also William Watson, as to whom I am obliged to revise my estimate. If he isn't sometimes a great poet, he comes near to being one. And now I am re-reading *Wilhelm Meister* after about 20 years.

Wednesday, September 27th.

I finished another short story today, *The Long-Lost Uncle,* and sent it off to the typist's. I went to Paris on Monday and returned yesterday, and again felt very strongly that a few months of Paris would suit me. I read

---

[1] Produced by Mrs. Patrick Campbell, at the Royalty Theatre, October 25, 1900.

Phillpotts's new book of stories, *Knock at a Venture,* and wrote to him about it today, and today I received a long letter from him about my book. His praise is very simple and detailed and notable, but on the whole I am inclined to think he doesn't like the book as well as *Leonora.* Altogether I must have written 4,000 words today.

Friday, October 13th.

During the last week I have thought persistently over *Whom God Hath Joined,* and have had very good luck in finding ideas. So much so that on Tuesday night even, I was able to relate the whole plot to Mme. Jane. Since then I have begun to sketch an outline of the first 30,000 words.

Saturday, October 21st.

I wrote the fourth of a series of Five Towns short stories complete on Wednesday; nearly 5,000 words. With the result that I had a violent colic after dinner, and a bilious attack yesterday.

Sunday, October 22nd.

I dined with Raphael and Madame last night. Went to bed ill and got up ill. This morning I went to Mrs. Devereux's by appointment and was told we had to lunch with Ochs at Chevillard's at the Rond Point. Ochs was waiting for us. Francis de Croisset [1] came in, kissed Mrs. Devereux's hand twice in about 3 minutes, and left: a young dandy, very young, and not quite quietly dressed. We then, after lunch, went to the Autumn Salon just for a quarter of an hour, to look at the Rodins. It was the first time in my life that Rodin's work has appealed to me. Then to the Colonne [2] concert, which was crowded and bad. But the Brahms Symphony No. 2 pleased me very much. After the concert Ochs and I went for a walk along the quays, and then he came up here to have tea with me.

Tuesday, October 31st.

On the previous Friday, after the first performance of *Der Freischütz* at the Opéra, I met Maugham in the street with Violet Hunt [3] and an-

---

[1] Author of plays and travel-books, among them *Nous avons fait un bon voyage,* etc.

[2] Edouard Colonne was for many years a pillar of musical life in Paris. At the invitation of the Philharmonic Society he once visited New York to conduct a few concerts.

[3] The author of many sprightly novels and of a *chronique scandaleuse* entitled *The Flurried Years* (American edition: *I Have This to Say*).

other and much younger girl named Ripley, very pretty. I went to Constan's with them. The two women came and had tea on Saturday. Although Mrs. Devereux said the worst things of Violet Hunt on Sunday, so much so that Mme. Cornillier wanted to meet her, I found her pretty all right. She said she had read all Casanova at the age of 16: sufficiently startling.

Thursday, November 2nd.

Yesterday was All Saints' Day, and I walked in the Montmartre Cemetery. It *was* rather like a City of the Dead. Certainly as much a relic of barbarism as anything one is likely to see in Paris, with its tons of flowers and ugly wreaths ornamenting the most deplorable monuments and houses of corpses. Vast crowds of people, many in black, but not all; many, if not most, out for an airing: moonstruck crowds before certain monstrous mementoes of surpassing vulgarity. A very few women here and there with moist eyes. A file of soldiers (seasoned) at the gates, made to supply the absence of an iron railing to separate incoming from outgoing crowds—and naturally looking stupid. Also policemen and officials. In the street flower shops and stalls, and wreath shops and stalls and quantities of cabs.

At night I went to Calvocoressi's,[1] and met Vignès[2] the pianist, an extraordinary enthusiast for Russian music and an exceedingly fine player. The two first played a duet, and then Vignès had the piano to himself. What struck me was the fine pure quality of the pleasure we obtained, all of us, the simplicity of the enthusiasm; and yet what years of cultivation had gone to provide it, in all of us. Calvocoressi's mother sat upright, on an ordinary cane chair, half blind with cataract, and encouraged our enthusiasm. I expressed my pleasure. *"Mais croyez-vous que nous ne sommes pas heureux comme tout, tous les quatre!"* said Calvocoressi, his face beaming.

Vignès, having played a piece, would usually turn back the pages to find some particular passage and would end by playing the whole thing again. When explaining the beauties of passages while he played them he became quite incomprehensible to me, what with his bad accent and

---

[1] Cipa Calvocoressi, music critic and lecturer. The Calvocoressis became great friends of Bennett.

[2] Ricardo Vignès.

his rapidity. Yes, what struck me as I came away was the singular "purity" of it all, the absence of sex, of anything in the nature of an after-taste. It reminded me of fine musical evenings in London.

Sunday, November 5th.

I finished the seventh and last of my short stories yesterday, and have now the prospect of nothing to do but my novel during the next 4 or 5 months. In that time I ought to be able to finish it.

I dined with Martin last night, and at dinner we suddenly had the idea of going to hear Risler [1] play five Beethoven sonatas at the Salle Pleyel. It worked out excellently, much better than a theatre. Then we went down to the Café Viennois for drinks, on a muddy night, and saw the most awful *viveurs* and women at the café. Awful! Bald-headed, foul persons!

Tuesday, November 7th.

I have just finished reading *L'Œuvre*. It has taken me a long time, because I left it in the middle to read Wells's *Kipps*. What a colossal affair it seems by the side of *Kipps,* so serious, tremendous, and imposing. The middle parts seem rather carelessly done, the detail piled up without sufficient attention to the form. But the final scene between Claude and Christine—the fight between love and art—is simply magnificent; it moved me; it is one of the finest things in Zola. It is overdone, it goes further than the truth; but purposely; Zola has stepped into the heroic in this scene, as he does now and then. All the close of the book is most affecting.

Thursday, November 9th.

Yesterday I formally began to write *Whom God Hath Joined,* and at 11 P.M. tonight I had written 1,000 words.

Thursday, November 16th.

I finished the first chapter of *Whom God Hath Joined* yesterday at 7 P.M. Ten thousand words odd. And it seemed to me rather original and rather good, and quite unlike anything I had done before.

La Rafale, by Bernstein, in 3 acts, at the Gymnase. I had heard a good

---

[1] Edouard Risler, popular piano virtuoso.

deal of the play, which is a success, and of Simone Le Bargy in it. Crowded house on Tuesday. The play was clever but factitious, very showy in treatment. Simone was better than the play, but not a great deal better. She is much above the average "leading lady"; there is not, however, a great deal of truth to life in her performance. Her talent seems more imitative than original. On the whole my opinion of the Paris stage is certainly declining. The number of things really first class is excessively small, and the success of such a show as *La Rafale* does not make for righteousness, either artistic or moral. Deceit and swindling and gaming are the three things held up to one's sympathy in it. A house full of fine frocks, and much sniffling in lace handkerchiefs during the scenes held to be poignant. A wretched, uncomfortable, dangerous theatre, like all the rest.

1906

I left Paris on December 8 and spent two nights with H. G. Wells. I then went on to London, and stayed there till the 21st December. On the twentieth I dined with Violet Hunt, at her club, the Victorian; she gave me bad champagne. Afterwards we went to the Alhambra, and talked all the time.

On the twenty-first I went down to Burslem, and stopped with the Mater till January 1. The last Sunday afternoon of the year I spent with Absalom Wood, going about Burslem and Tunstall, seeing his architecture and his laying out of the Tunstall Park. I had an important idea for a novel or a series of novels entitled *The Town,* or *The Borough of Bursley,* in which the development of the organism of the town under modern influences should be the chief theme. The conversion of the town refuse (160 tons a week) into electric light at Bursley impressed me; it is one of those slightly sentimental, morally spectacular aspects of municipal life that *do* impress.

I went down to Torquay on January 1 and stayed till the ninth with Phillpotts, and we talked over various schemes, including the projected serial, which, however, is not yet definitely commissioned. He read aloud *Hugo* to his wife, accomplishing it in 3 nights, and the success of the book was brilliant. He sent the book to Curtis Brown [1] for me, with a view to its being placed in America, and I went to see Brown in London on the tenth, on my return to London. He seemed hopeful.

The same evening I took the Mater and Tertia and William to see *Peter Pan.* We all thought it a work of sheer genius. I regarded it as

---

[1] An American whose Publishing Bureau has offices in New York and London.

the finest modern work for the English stage, despite the fact that I had an awful nervous headache.

I came to Paris on the twelfth. I had left Paris with regret and melancholy, and although I enjoyed much of my time in England, and my impressions of England after nearly a year's absence were vivid and very interesting, I was glad to be back again in Paris.

During 1905 I published 3 books. *Tales of the Five Towns, The Loot of Cities,* and *Sacred and Profane Love.* The latter went slowly into a second edition and was also published by Tauchnitz. It appeared serially in *To-day,* and the second serial rights were bought by Tillotsons.

I wrote:

1. The second and third parts of *Sacred and Profane Love.*
2. *The City of Pleasure,* a 60,000 serial for Tillotsons.
3. The first 30,000 words of *Whom God Hath Joined.*
4. Eight or 10 short stories, all about the Five Towns.
5. A new series of *Savoir Vivre* articles for *T.P.'s Weekly,* which began on December 1. Also some articles for the *New Tribune.*
6. A little French play in 2 acts, translated by Davray. Title: *Que Faire?*

My total of words was slightly over 200,000, much less than usual, but then I took two months' clear holiday in the summer. On the whole not a satisfactory year. Genuine success seemed, as usual, to delay and postpone itself. But I find that I am much less interested in money than Phillpotts and Wells.

Thursday, January 18th.

Today a contract was definitely fixed up with *T.P.'s Weekly* for a serial by Phillpotts and me at the price of £450. The first 3 instalments to be delivered by 20th February.

I bought 3 books this afternoon, having gone out in very bad weather to get theatre seats, and it seemed as if I had begun book-collecting again. I certainly wanted to have some books bound, and the idea of fine simple severe bindings seized hold of me. But one cannot buy bookcases, and bibelots, and sterilized plants, and cigars, and jewellery, as I have been doing lately—and indulge in bookbinding too.

Friday, January 19th.

Having no engagement, I went down to dine at the Chat Blanc. Only

O'Connor and Stanlaws were in the private room. They had not left Paris for Christmas, and they seemed rather sad and bored and deserted. Some general talk about the English elections,[1] but they didn't know enough to make it sufficiently interesting for me, so I turned the chatter on to the transport of part of my library from London to Paris. Stanlaws related his theatrical experiences, and I related mine, which were very similar. And then we began to talk about whether pictures that were really first class could be got for 500 francs, and the opinion seemed to be that they could. We kept on chatting till after 10, when the restaurant was deserted, and then we drifted out into the cold squally night. The other two went on to the Café de Versailles I expect, and I took the electric car and the Métro, home, reading *Le Temps* all the way, though I had *King John* in my pocket.

Saturday, January 20th.

After having dined with Raphael on Thursday night, I called at the Bureau de Tabac opposite the Opéra under the Grand Hôtel to buy cigars and cigarettes. The *patronne,* a stoutish powdered agreeable woman of 50 or so, was in charge, with a young girl apparently her daughter. There is also a *patron;* quite a family affair. *"J'aime beaucoup mes clients,"* said the *patronne,* and one could see that she *did* love not only her regular clients but the whole business. I told her that I called in nearly every night to buy a Mexican cigar, and yet she had not recognized me. "That's because I'm not here at the time you call," she said, which was true. "But I'll come down earlier to see you. I shall know you in future." There was a charming air of intimateness about the whole place, despite its extremely central position and fluctuating cosmopolitan *clientèle,* and this air I noticed for the first time. I also noticed for the first time the immense variety of stock which the French Government offers to its customers. It appeared that the manufacture of the flat Jupiter matches had recommenced, and I bought some for my flat matchbox. "We have ordered 10,000," said the *patronne.*

Sunday, January 28th.

Late tonight I finished the first instalment of *The Sinews of War,* as

---

[1] The General Election that returned Campbell-Bannerman and the Liberals with a sweeping majority.

the *T.P.'s Weekly* serial is to be called, and thought it very good. It took me 2 days' hard work. George Ullman and I dined together at Boivin's, and had a quite exceptionally fine dinner. Then he came here, and I began to play the piano, and to my surprise roused him to enthusiasm. He thanked me again and again. He left at 11.15, when I wrote the last paragraphs of the instalment.

Monday, January 29th.

After having written my *T.P.'s W.* article today I went out for a stroll through Paris, meaning to reach a bookshop on the Quai des Grands Augustins. I went down the Rue Notre Dame de Lorette, which I think is the street that pleases me most in Paris—and I bought Arsène Houssaye's *Souvenirs de Jeunesse,* which I have been reading tonight. In the Passage Jouffray, where I frequently find a book, I found nothing, and when I got to the Grands Augustins the *étalage* of the shop was already taken inside, it being 6.30.

I do enjoy these slow walks through Paris on fine winter afternoons: crowded pavements, little curiosity shops, and the continual interest of women. I walked back to the Châtelet station of the Métro and went to the Concorde and thence walked to the Place de l'Opéra, stopping at the Trois Quartiers shop, where there are some very nice things. Then I went to the *Standard* office, and Raphael came out and dined with me. I got home at 10. I have had several days of regular unhurried work lately, interspersed with such strolls. I have come to the conclusion that this is as near a regular happiness as I am ever likely to get.

Tuesday, January 30th.

I went down, partly on foot and partly by omnibus, to the Quai des Grands Augustins. It was a perfect morning. I had the itch to buy a book or two, and I gave way to it.

I collected my ideas for the second instalment of the serial, and between 3.30 and 4.30 I wrote 500 words of it.

Friday, February 2nd.

I went with the two Ullmans to *Fidelio* at the Opéra Comique last night. The usual slightly hurried dinner and general excitement in order to get seats. And, the seats being got, the usual exit before the performance to have a cup of coffee in a neighbouring bar. The usual disgraceful physical conditions of the seat—bad air, talkative neighbours, and a very imperfect view of the stage. I was inclined to change my opinion of the libretto, and to give Beethoven credit for having chosen it not so badly after all. There are situations in it that are heroic, but which less fine music might have rendered footling. The constant grand beauty of the music is what chiefly affects one in memory after the performance. It was a wet and very muddy night. But we walked home because we had such need of fresh air after the poison of the theatre.

Thursday, February 8th.

I half expected O'Connor tonight—kept the evening free for him—but he did not come. So after some hesitation I determined to spend it by myself, just to see how I got through with it. The restaurant was too full, and the service slow, and I didn't enjoy my dinner, and I ate too much, and read the *Tribune* all through. I came home at 9.30, and read a little of Voltaire's *Candide*—I bought a nice edition of his *Contes* yesterday, half bound, for 2 francs, and enjoyed it very much.

Then I meditated on the serial and got one or two notions. I was very gloomy at first, but got cheerful about 11. I think I could accustom myself to reading in longer spells, and to spending evenings alone fairly comfortably if I tried.

I am reading George Moore's *The Lake*. It is so smoothly written and so calm and beautiful that I can enjoy reading it without even taking in the sense. Frequently I have read half a page without grasping the meaning at all, or trying to grasp it. It is a most curious novel, perhaps not really good, but certainly distinguished in a Yeats-y way.

Monday, February 12th.

I called at a *bureau de tabac* this morning to buy a box of Mexican cigars, and was told that the State was out of stock of them, and would not have any more ready till next month. A good example of State management. The same thing happened with Jupiter matches a few months ago.

I have been having difficulties with the tenants overhead, through the medium of the *concierge, apropos* of pattering about in boots on uncarpeted floors. I asked what the monsieur was by profession, and was told that he was manager of a large business office, and that he sang at the Opéra (presumably in the chorus) 3 times a week. This seemed to me very Parisian.

Tuesday, February 20th.

Opéra masked ball on Saturday night. The Atkinses[1] supped with me at the Place Blanche. We got to the restaurant too soon, and found all the waiters asleep in odd corners, and the room darkened. It was like going into an enchanted palace. We woke it up, and lighted it up, in an instant. By the time we left, 12.30, there was a noisy band playing, and a crowd of guests.

We got to the ball at 12.45. Already an enormous crowd. Great cohorts of men in silk hats. I should say the men outnumbered the women by 5 to 1. The people who looked really well were the chorus girls etc. from the Opéra who were thoroughly used to fancy dress and knew how to walk and how to dine. Outside these, and a few professional men, there was almost no fancy dress; but plenty of dominoes. The *coup d'œil* in the *salle* was superb, and the orchestras (3) fine and deafening, as they ought to be.

There was, relatively, very little dancing. Not a single well-bred Frenchwoman there, so far as I could see, and very few *toilettes* worth a damn. But the general effect was dazzlingly immense. And the cohorts of men, all on the look-out for something nice, seemed to lurch from time to time in one direction or another, as crowds do, bodily, and sometimes even to stampede. There was something undignified in these masses of masculinity. The waiters and *ouvreuses* seemed politer and gayer than usual. We left at 3.15. Many people had preceded us.

I was a wreck on Sunday, and the noises of people overhead got on my nerves. However, I wrote a brief account of the ball for the *Standard*, rather sardonic, and took it down to the office.

Thursday, March 1st.

Today I finished one half of the serial *The Sinews of War*, and to-morrow it begins to run in *T.P.'s Weekly*. I have kept my contract with myself, and the stuff is good of its kind; but I am slightly overworking. I sleep badly and digest not well.

---

[1] J. B. Atkins, at that time Paris correspondent of the London *Standard*, was later for many years editor of the *Spectator*.

Wednesday, March 28th.

I finished the seventeenth instalment of *The Sinews of War* today, which leaves 3 to do, and this evening, on my return to Paris from Moret, I received in a letter from Phillpotts an adumbration of the plot for our next serial in collaboration.

Lately, besides having the influenza, I have been occupied in putting my Moret flat into an artistically habitable condition. Yesterday morning in a second-hand shop in Moret I found a Louis XV commode in carved oak in excellent condition, and bought it for 45 francs without bargaining. I also bought a rather worn Empire bookcase for 20 francs. Impossible to keep my journal while I am so preoccupied with the serial and with questions of cretonnes, carpets, and the arrangement of old furniture and purchasing of fresh.

Sunday, April 1st.

Reception at Mrs. Devereux's last Thursday. She told a story about young H——, whose father left all his money to build churches in uninhabited districts, instead of to his relatives. Speaking to a professing Christian, the son said, "I wish I had your sure belief in hell." On being asked why, he replied, "Because I should be certain that my father was there."

Last night I was with Martin at the Opéra Comique—the third performance of Erlanger's *Aphrodite*—a rotten thing; but Mary Garden was good as the chief strumpet. Miss Green [1] told me today that there was a regular tariff for singers who wanted to make a start at the Opéra Comique. It cost 30,000 francs to appear as Carmen; only 10,000 francs to appear in *Lakmé*. Calvé paid 30,000 francs. She explained how some of the greatest artists were absolute frosts at the beginning. Jean de Reszke was hissed off the stage etc. From this she drew hope for her own career, as she quite expected to fail at the start. She said that Mary Garden was a great success from the first night. The soprano of Charpentier's *Louise* broke down suddenly one night (in health, I think), and Mary Garden was among the audience. She presented herself for the rôle. Carré asked her if she had ever sung with an orchestra. She said she had, but it was a lie. Certainly when I saw her again last night I was much struck by her ease of manner on the stage. She seemed born to it.

[1] See p. 236.

Thursday, April 12th.

I finished the writing of *The Sinews of War* on Saturday last, and afterwards Eleanora Green dined with me at the Place Blanche, and I took her to the Grand Guignol. I began this book on the 26th January, and it contains 85,000 words.

I came down here to Les Sablons yesterday. Mrs. Le Gallienne was already at the hotel, and she dined with me. Talking of village scandals, and of the circumstances which had made S. M. drink worse than ever, she said that there was more drinking in Denmark than even in England. Entertainments are gayer there (she said)—in fact hospitality is not the same thing as in England or France—and people do not consider they are enjoying themselves till they are a little drunk. This applies to the best society.

Today at lunch she said that she "came out" at 13. She went to balls 2 or 3 times a week. Stayed up till 3 or 4 A.M., and was at her studio, painting, at 9, had a little sleep again after dinner, and then to another party. And so on. And she never felt tired. "But one *does* pay for it, all the same!" she said. Her father let her read everything as a child. Gave her the free run of his library. "What have you been reading today?" he asked her. "A book called *Cousine Bette,*" she replied, "and it's very interesting." She was then aged 11. She said she should do the same to her own daughter.

Thursday, May 3rd.

A week last Friday night I went to England, reached Waterloo on Saturday morning and Burslem on Saturday afternoon.

Impossible to make notes.

I went to have tea with Mrs. Green. She said that there were things in *Sacred and Profane Love* that she thought no man could possibly have known. She asked me how I knew these things, and whether women had told me. I said that women had not told me *those* things, and that I merely felt that those things must be so.

I left the mater's on Thursday in a snowstorm and went to London. I hurried off to the St. James's Theatre to see *His House in Order,*[1] and found a theatre organized and worked with the perfection of a battle-

---

[1] By Sir Arthur Wing Pinero.

ship. An air of solidity, richness, cleanliness, decorum; punctuality, short entr'actes; general care for the public. Such a difference from Parisian theatres. The only things that were bad at the St. James's were the play and the acting. The play, which is a great success, and has been seen 3 times and written about 3 times by William Archer,[1] and praised by Walkley and Joe Knight, is most certainly a thoroughly pretentious, sentimental, and dull play. It never convinces. It is badly conceived in its very essence, and in execution the skilfulness is only episodic. Some trifling passages of dialogue are absolutely true to life, startlingly so. And I can only account for them by the supposition that Pinero has overheard them and dragged them bodily into the play. Five-sixths of the acting was mediocre and worse. And I was struck by the funeral gait at which English plays are "taken."

However, I enjoyed the whole evening because it was so English and I was observing so interestedly the whole time. I walked home.

I left London for Paris on Monday night. I said I would be in Paris for the May Day troubles, and I found nothing but a Sunday calm.

Saturday, May 5th.

Tonight, at Antoine's, *The Wild Duck.* An interesting experience, to see how one's ideas have developed! There was something, after all, in the old cry against Ibsen that he was parochial. The play still seems clever; it is sometimes brilliant. But it never strikes one as beautiful. And it *does* seem fearfully Norwegian. The symbolism is simply deplorable, even in its ingenuity. If any one had hinted such ideas to me about Ibsen 15 years ago, I should have accused him disdainfully of an inability to appreciate masterpieces. Yet now I am pretty well convinced that Ibsen is not a writer of masterpieces. And he is stagy! He who was supposed to have rejuvenated the entire technique of the stage has become stagy in 15 years! I was several times bored by the play, but nevertheless, a most interesting evening of historical retrospect.

This afternoon I went to the Musée Guimet with Mrs. Farley, and saw the mummies of Serapion and Thais. These mummies drew all

---

[1] The dramatic critic; his versatility included the translating of Ibsen's plays, the writing of biographies and of an original play, *The Green Goddess,* in which George Arliss had a great success.

Paris a few years ago. And I can understand. The ascetic iron contrivances of the desert anchorite, still attached to his body, were very
convincing, and there is still *quelque chose de chic* about Thais. As Mrs.
Farley said, "They beat Paul and Virginia, don't they?"

Sunday, May 6th.

And yet I was thinking this morning in bed that perhaps I was too
hard on Ibsen last night. We owe him a great deal after all. He made
one of those steps towards realism which alone constitute the progress
of art. He is very able; he is in no sense an amateur, but a thorough
expert; and if he doesn't find actually much beauty, he shows us where
to find it.

At the Cornilliers' today some talk of Rodin. Henri Havet stated definitely that he was going mad, was in fact mad. Of erotomania. He said
also that he did pieces of sculpture and then deliberately broke them.

Some one remarked that an artist had the right after all to break up
a piece that did not please him.

"Yes," Havet explained, "but not to send it broken to an exhibition,
in imitation of the Venus de Milo etc." A Mme. Nock (?), a very pretty
woman, who knew Rodin personally, gave a curious experience of his
peculiarities. He is in the habit of showing little erotic pieces to lady
visitors. He took her to one such, a woman seated or bending down in
the middle of a plate. *"Le sujet était assez clair,"* she indicated.

He asked her what she would call that, by way of a title for it. She
said politely, *"La source de volupté."* "Splendid!" said Rodin, and
scratched the title on the plate. The very next day her sister was at the
studio, and was shown the same piece. "What would you call that?"
Rodin asked her. "The water fairy," suggested the sister. "Splendid!"
said Rodin, and wrote the title on the other side of the plate. Some one
said that he got his titles like that, by asking every one and then choosing
the best.

Cornillier said he once sat next to Rodin at lunch, and happened to
say that a certain woman was not pretty. "What!" cried Rodin solemnly.
"It has happened to you sometimes to meet a woman who was not
beautiful? I have never met a woman who was not beautiful."

I remembered, then, Rodin's dictum, published somewhere, that everything on earth is beautiful. With this, in a way, I agree.

Thursday, May 10th.

On Monday night, when I was at *L'Enfant Chérie,* by Romain Coolus, with Miss Green, I had most distinctly the sensation of being shocked. It was in the last act. An old man has been abandoned by his mistress, who has found another lover. The old man's daughter tries to get the mistress back for her father, as he is mortally struck by grief. There is a scene between the two women, in which the daughter urges her father's mistress to return to him. "Look here," she says, in effect, "even if you can't go to him altogether, you could surely see him one or two afternoons a week." I suddenly felt myself shocked; other people were in the same case. I can't at the moment remember ever having been shocked before. The experience gave me an idea of how pious Philistines must often feel, and was therefore useful. My being shocked was absurd. At the same time the scene was clumsy and bad artistically. Had it been good, should I have been shocked?

Kreisler [1] concert tonight with Martin. The enthusiasm was not overpowering. It was Kreisler's tone that pleased me most.

Sunday, May 13th.

A month ago the French inland postage was altered from 1½ to 1d. I happened to see the notice of the change received as instructions to the postmistress at the local post office at Les Sablons. I don't know how many post offices there are in France, but there must be 50,000 at least. This notice was not printed. It had been written in violet ink in rather cramped irregular calligraphy, and then multiplied on one of the old-fashioned "hektograph" machines, as we used to call them. At the same time as the change of postage, a new *carte-lettre* at 1d. was introduced. I asked for one of these *cartes-lettres* yesterday at Les Sablons, but none had yet been received.

I came down to Les Sablons yesterday. It is summer. The garden full of sun and flowers, the roads humming with insects. The chestnuts in front of the house "snowing" all the time. Bright blue sky, with a border of "capricious towering" white clouds. I walked up to the "grand entrance" to the forest this morning, and it was so beautiful and so imposing that even Henry Ward Beecher's silly remark about a tree being

---

[1] Fritz Kreisler, the Austrian violinist.

finer than a cathedral seemed for the moment to be not so idiotic and meaningless after all.

Thursday, May 24th.

I finished another section (of 10,000 words) of the divorce novel on Monday night, having written it in 8 days.

I spent this afternoon with Eleanora Green. She told me a saying of her little brother who was taken by his mother to see the central meat markets: *"Maman, il doit y avoir pas mal d'accidents ici."* As an unconsciously horrible remark of a child's, it wants beating.

We went to the exhibition of Gustave Moreau's paintings. An artist, but not a great painter. Magnificent conceptions of literary subjects, well but not adequately treated. His preoccupation with the story of Salome is singular. We noticed one small painting where Salome was holding the head on a charger high up out of the way of a little dog who was yapping and leaping after it. Plenty of people in the large stuffy room. Then we drove to the Bois to have tea at Armenonville. Vast holiday crowds (this being Ascension Day), much dust and movement. We walked about the fortifications.

Friday, June 15th.

At 5 P.M. on this day in the forest of Fontainebleau I became engaged to marry Eleanora.

Friday, August 3rd.

At 11 A.M. on this day, at Caniel, my engagement to Eleanora was broken off.

In the meantime I had, with the utmost difficulty, finished my novel, *Whom God Hath Joined.*

NOTE BY D. C. B.

[Arnold Bennett's fiancée referred to above was a young American girl belonging to one of America's most distinguished Southern families, who had settled and made their home in Paris. Although not endowed with wealth, the family was gifted with taste and intelligence and Miss Eleanora Green possessed uncommon beauty. Her young brother, Julian Green, has of late years achieved distinction and fame for his powerful and original books (written in the French language) and he ranks among the most important and arresting of younger writers—especially in France. Another sister, Anne Green, has also successfully published two novels and Arnold Bennett's fiancée has written a study of her family's life in Paris in which she brings in the episode of her engagement to Arnold Bennett and a study of him at the time. "She was remarkably beautiful, having green eyes and red hair. Her mind and spirit were quite unusual, and equal to her physical beauty," writes her most intimate friend at the time.

Young and inexperienced, Miss Green was, however, unwilling to be drawn so soon into marriage and its ties. She had a definite "Melisande" quality.

These facts, and their implications, are important to those who would understand what was behind the reserved yet ornamented façade which Arnold Bennett presented to the world. Readers without the clue to his passion for essential, pure, beauty of mind and spirit, no less than of outward perfection, have not the key to a quality, and to a passion which underlies the whole of his work, however different its mood.

For his work contained this paradox—as did his personal taste and temperament. While it was definitely robust and, with gusto for detail and for material effect, the inner spirit of the author, directed always towards beauty and a kind of perfecting of material existence, was intensely shy and averse to the profanation—the "vulgarization"—of unreserved expression. There was in his mind a holy of holies, a presence to be inferred but never exposed.

The breaking of this engagement was a hurt that he bore marks of to the end of his life.

For some time he threatened Miss Green that he would write a *rosse* novel which would stingingly reveal this bitter experience. Instead, he drew from a different source of inspiration his great novel of life's tragic-comedy with its theme of the melancholy healing passage of time, *The Old Wives' Tale*.]

[Eleven months passed before Arnold Bennett resumed his diary, the next entry being dated July 19, 1907. He was married to Marguerite Soulié at Paris on July 4, 1907.—EDITOR.]

1907

Friday, July 19th. Les Sablons.

I only noticed yesterday that the mark of the aged female peasant in this village is a cap (I suppose it would be called a mob-cap—but I don't know what a mob-cap is at all), which is drawn very tightly over the head, very tightly indeed. It is apparently formed out of a cotton handkerchief, for there are the ends of bows to be seen at the top-back of the head and also below. These aged creatures are almost without exception deformed, chiefly by vast deposits of fat. They wear very short skirts (always some shade of blue much washed out); and, like the majority of peasant women of no matter what age in this district, they have exceedingly unpleasant voices.

But an even more extraordinary specimen of the sex passed along the high road last night while we were dining. This was an old woman harnessed to a small cart containing merchandise that I could not distinguish. On either side of the old woman was harnessed a dog about as big as a pointer. An old man stalked majestically behind at a distance of several yards, carrying a very long staff, and uttering at regular intervals a mournful cry of a few syllables which doubtless referred to his wares. The woman was, in the accepted phrase, "little more than a brute," and there was no doubt about, no concealment of it. They did not belong to the district. Probably they toured like that through a whole department, or several departments, and as Mme. Bergeret suggested, might be in easy circumstances.

Talking about eating, Mme. Bergeret said that in the Midi (neighbourhood of Toulouse specially) there used to be men who prided themselves on enormous powers of eating. They did not usually eat a great deal, but on occasions, when put to it, they would perform terrible feats such as consuming a whole turkey. The result sometimes was that they were very ill. The method of curing them was to dig a hole in the muck-heap, strip the sufferer naked, put him in the hole, and pack him tightly with manure up to his neck. The people who did this did it with gusto, telling the sufferer what an odious glutton he was. The heat generated promoted digestion in a manner almost miraculous, and next day the sufferer was perfectly restored.

Saturday, July 20th.

There was a repercussion on me last night of the Lever *v.* Associated Press libel case. After all, even in an ultraplutocratic newspaper office like Harmsworth's a verdict of £50,000 damages must cause some friction, and probably a good deal of moral suffering on the part of the personnel.[1] The spectacle of Lord Northcliffe in a rage is quite human and touching. In my present series of articles for the *Evening News* on buying a library, there were two articles praising and blaming in detail various cheap reprints. The first was printed without the least comment. Then (the next day) came the Lever verdict against the *Daily Mail* and the *Evening News,* and last night I received a very apologetic letter giving every reason but the right one why the second article should be shortened and modified. One phrase in the letter (which was impeccably polite and in good taste) struck me as very naïve and funny: "It is almost impossible for one who is outside a newspaper office at the moment quite to judge the relative position of affairs." *Je te crois!* I wrote at once and gave them a free hand.

Yesterday and the day before, in two walks in the forest and by the Seine, I constructed completely the first 3 acts (4 scenes) of the play which I am taking from *Anna* for the Stage Society.

Monday, July 22nd.

On Saturday morning I walked for two hours in the forest, and completely finished the construction of the Five Towns play. I saw a big,

---

[1] On July 17, 1907, Lever Brothers were awarded this unprecedented sum of damages. Bennett was apparently in error; it was not the Associated Press but the Associated Newspapers, Ltd., the Northcliffe organization. They had accused Lever Brothers (soap manufacturers) of establishing a soap trust and engaging in devious monopolistic activities.

strong deer that crashed fiercely through thick bushes like a stag out of Sir Walter Scott, stood watching me some time, and then crashed and crackled off again. Once I sat down to rest on a felled tree, and a squirrel appeared. It bounded to within a few yards of me, then sprang up a tree, hung to the bark like a fly for several seconds, and finally ran higher very rapidly, at the same time taking to the side opposite to me so that I could not see it. The tree was not a large one nor had it either many branches nor much foliage, but I could not find the squirrel, though I walked round and round it and searched most carefully.

One might well call it a solitude, the forest! Yet at the end of a very long avenue one suddenly sees a puff of vapour arise and slowly disappear. It is the dust of an automobile flying down the Route Nationale, which cuts through the centre of the forest.

In pursuance of my new invention of Sunday, I did no work of any kind yesterday. I trifled with the art of illumination, and read the greater portion of Jeanne Marni's *Pierre Tisserand*—chiefly to please Mme. B., who is aunt of the author. Some of the dialogue in it is truly admirable. But all these novels of sexual sentimentality are altogether too narrow in outlook: they lack nobility: they do not arouse a single really fine emotion. This is what there has got to be in *The Old Wives' Tale*—a lofty nobility. I got it now and then in *Whom God Hath Joined*, but in the next book I must immensely increase the dose.

During the last day or two both Marguerite and I have definitely decided that we prefer living in the country. I had settled that we wanted a small *château*, in this district if possible, where there is forest and river and heaps of other scenery. And we were to have an auto and a small yacht on the river, and to give up the Paris flat: this change was to occur in about two years' time when my lease of No. 3 Rue d'Aumale would expire. Before dinner we went for a walk to Saint-Mammès, where the water was busy with great barges. And I had suddenly the great idea of abandoning my deep ambition for a sea-going yacht, and having a barge as big as their barges, fitted up as a luxurious houseboat, with a small motor attached. This would serve as a complete moving home in summer, and we could go all over France in it. (We should keep the flat.) Indeed we could go all over Europe in it. This scheme took hold of me so strongly that I thought of nothing else all the evening, and became quite moody.

July 23rd.

I began to see yesterday how my "fine writing" and illuminating must develop. I saw that I could only advance with any hope of continuing by uniting utility with beauty; that I must not therefore make fine manuscripts for the sake of making them, but rather in connection with my own work; also that I must form a natural hand that could be written quickly. These principles having been arrived at, I began to practise a little.

M. and I went for a short walk in the forest last night. The moon was nearly full and very bright. But the effect was disappointing. I have noticed this before. To be at its best moonlight wants to be seen over a large flat landscape or on water. There is very little in the tree-tracery business—silhouetted against the moon, etc.

Yesterday I walked along by the Seine again in the morning, and constructed the short story which is ordered for delivery by the end of the month. In the afternoon I seemed to do nothing but oddments of high unimportance.

Wednesday, July 24th.

Mme. Bergeret was telling us at dinner about Armand Sylvestre,[1] who knew her dead sister very well: what a *bon garçon* he was, and how he continued up to his death to pay allowances to all the mistresses he had ever had. By the way, he was never content with one at a time. She said that he talked with the same free wit as was found in his stories, especially his earlier stories.

Mme. Bergeret gave us also a history about a pig with a green tail, which she said happened to Sylvestre himself and was used up in one of his early stories. I have noted this in my plot-book. I see no reason why I shouldn't use it in some form myself.

Rappacini's Daughter in *Mosses from an Old Manse* is a good story, in the Poe manner, quite equal to Poe. I must find out which learnt from the other. Yesterday evening I began to read Carlyle on Goethe. Much of the stuff was wordy and too vaguely ecstatic, but his enthusiasm for Goethe inspired me to read Goethe. Curiously, I had already ordered the Eckermann *Conversations.*

Last night I received a note from Davray to say that my French piece,

---

[1] Pen name of Paul-Armand Silvestre, author of novels and plays, including *Arlette.*

Que Faire?, would probably be played during the winter, and asking me if I could supply a *pièce gaie,* or the materials for one. It never rains but it pours. Two plays are now decidedly on the carpet in London, and two others are approaching the carpet; and if there is any certainty in the theatrical world at all (which there is not) my Five Towns play is assured of production. And yet I do not seem to have any real faith in the production of any of these pieces.

Thursday, July 25th.

I finished Carlyle on Goethe. Not really good. A tiresome style, and not enough form, and very little clear thought, and practically no detailed information. Noble mouthings—but mouthings!

Sunday, July 28th.

The Marriotts came on Friday night. I found I was so excited that at dinner I could not eat slowly, and I was indisposed afterwards. Marriott and I went for a ride yesterday morning, and he was most enthusiastic about the countryside.

I began a poem on Thursday morning.

Calvocoressi came down for the day yesterday. He had just been to London. He said what struck him about England, and especially London, was its extraordinary *convenience.* The same thing strikes me about Paris. He gave reasons. I gave reasons. But his were better than mine.

Monday, July 29th.

I spent an hour and a half yesterday morning in writing 4 lines of verse, and another three-quarters of an hour in sketching out 4 more lines. At this rate according to my present spare time, I should accomplish one short poem in about 6 weeks.

Marriott said it was the hottest day he ever remembered. To me it was merely hot. I did "illumination" all afternoon.

After dinner we walked by the Seine and then up the escarpment to Ezy, where there was a *fête;* at 9.10 there was nobody there, certainly not more than 10 onlookers in the whole field. Hobby-horses, shooting-galleries, spice-stalls, all stood as if enchanted under their oil-lamps, on the grass. The dancing tent was being lighted up. The small bandstand in the centre of the tent was empty, and a card bearing the word

"Mazurka" hung from one of the 30 brass chandeliers. The manager of the tent and his wife were putting the lamps slowly into the chandeliers, she seemed extremely gloomy. A waiter with a napkin round his neck, and a boy-waiter, stood talking to some friends at a trestle table in the part of the tent reserved for drinking. I spoke to them. The waiter turned, glanced at us, and then resumed his talk with his friends. We sat down at a table just outside the tent and after a time the boy came and served us. Two or three more wanderers came and peeped at the tent and departed. Then a whole family, including a little boy of 5 or 6, came and sat down in the drinking part of the tent. Two young girls with bows in their hair ran along to the tent from the shooting-gallery, skipping and leaping, and then back to their business.

A few more people arrived and made remarks about the emptiness and deadness of the tent. Most went again, but some stayed. Then the music of the hobby-horses, which we could not see from our table, began. We left, crossing the field. The hobby-horses were moving, scarcely any one on them. Half concealed in the centre, a white horse was dragging the machine round. A man standing on the revolving platform held the horse's bridle with his left hand and turned an organ with his right. A number of very young men had just arrived. One said to another: *"Si tu"* —I forget what—*"je te passerai ma main quelquepart."*

We left the *fête*. It was a magnificent night. The courtyards and front rooms of Ezy seemed to be all occupied by families drinking wine at tables on which were oil lamps. But the streets of the village were lighted, at intervals, by electricity. We passed out of the village, by the outskirts of the forest, over the railways, where signals were burning, waiting for distant trains. The moon rose, exactly like a tremendous, and tremendously yellow, Chinese lantern.

All the time I had my wife on my arm; she had just got over an attack of neuralgia and was limp, and only not fatigued because she was happy. She seemed to exhale a sentiment. And Marriott and I were exchanging jokes in the antique Chelsea manner, and precisely in that flavour, occasionally making a very good one. When we got home he sang songs. I thought the words of "Come into the garden, Maud" were really very magical for Tennyson. I regretted that Marriott, among a lot of "moderate to fair" songs, had not one of great style. All his favourites were less than first-rate.

Tuesday, July 30th.

Mrs. Marriott told us a curious thing about Marriott, which I did not know. In reading a novel, if towards the end it threatened to become very sad, he would not finish it. Nor would he allow any one to tell him what the end actually was.

M. had her first lesson on the bicycle yesterday evening. I ran after her for about a quarter of an hour only, and was bathed in sweat and also exhausted.

Wednesday, July 31st.

I seemed suddenly yesterday afternoon to wake up from the industrious calm of my honeymoon. The need came over me all of a sudden to leave my desk and go out for a walk. Although I had not really been working very hard, the top of my head felt as it feels when I *have* been working too hard at a serious book. M. came with me. We walked to the other end of Moret. Gradually I began to feel better. I said that I must have an excursion, a movement right out of Les Sablons. She said she perfectly understood that it would do me good to get away from her for a bit. So we at once arranged with the Marriotts that the males should cycle to Nemours and the women go there by train for the day, today. At night I read to the Marriotts 4 of my poems.

Thursday, August 1st.

Marriott and I rode to Nemours yesterday through the forest. A magnificent lunch on the terrace of the Ecu de France, one of those provincial French inns with a personnel apparently very numerous, including one or two wenches of neat and agreeable manners. Then our wives arrived, and we climbed to the roof of the donjon and tasted and savoured the famous view of town and country from the top, the country running right up to the town as Hardy describes it at "Casterbridge." Then we got separated, and Marguerite and I went to look at canals and buy cakes, and we had glimpses of the Marriotts now and then across the square going into a church or something. Lastly we had tea (our own) at the Ecu, and the women went back to the station, and Marriott and I rode home through Episy and Ecuelles, one of the most beautiful pieces of simple highway scenery that I know. And not a motor car! Then we came into Moret, and to the Paris-Marseilles Route Nationale, and were immediately enveloped in the dust and fumes of cars.

At night Marriott was talking of the greed of certain famous painters. He said that at a pension *table d'hôte* on the Continent, when the fish came round, F—— would help himself to two whole soles, of course quite regardless of the rest of the company. Similar tales of B——,[1] who must be an inconceivable boor. When the round did not begin with B—— and he saw the dish travelling from person to person, he would cry out aloud his fears that not sufficient would be left for himself. On the other hand when the round began with him he would take so much that the waiters, perceiving his greed, would next time begin so as to serve him last. Marriott has also told (and Mrs. M. too) numerous almost incredible stories of B——'s tyranny over his wife—under the guise of being utterly devoted to her. That is to say, he passes his life in forbidding her to do, to eat, to enjoy, things that he considers dangerous for her. The attitude has become a mania; it springs of course from a purely selfish fear of losing her. Without knowing B——, I have acquired quite a violent distaste for him; and each fresh tale that I hear of his monstrous egoism gives me a sort of morbid pleasure. I thought I might use him up as the husband of the stay-at-home sister in *The Old Wives' Tale*.

Friday, August 2nd.

I went out for a walk yesterday afternoon and stayed out two hours and a half. It rained about half the time. I meant to try to finish my poem *A Love Affair*, and by good luck I finished it. Nearly all the time I was walking very slowly in the forest. I was so tired in the evening that I could scarcely keep awake. Marguerite also was tired, through the strain of listening all day to English as it is mumbled by the English. Afterwards I wakened up, when I wanted to go to sleep, and explained to Marguerite the inadvisability of being jealous of my verse.

A LOVE AFFAIR

Down flew the shaft of the god,
Barbed with miraculous change.
Struck—and a woman emerged from a clod.
This was strange.

---

[1] A member of the Royal Academy.

Eyes and a mouth it had owned,
Movable head that would nod,
Waist and a bosom agreeably zoned—
But a clod.

Now when her eyes met the male's,
Flame from them wrapped him in fire;
Breath of that bosom o'erwhelmed him in gales
Of desire.

Stung by the flattering wave,
Proudly his manhood he spent.
Rare was the gift of her soul—for she gave,
But he lent.

Wit she had none to amuse,
Knew not the trade of a wife,
Heard not the voice of the muse. Now the muse
Was his life.

Weary, he called on his God:
"Quench me this woman I've kissed!"
Lo! In due time she returned to the clod.
She was missed.

Saturday, August 3rd.

Yesterday I finished the full draft of the second act of the play, being thus one day in advance of my programme. I have not yet spent on it, in any one morning, more than an hour and a half. The fact is that all the imaginative work in it seemed to be, and really was, done before I started.

Last night I had a letter from Pinker enclosing for signature a most unsatisfactory contract for *The Statue*. I flatter myself that this almost certain loss of money, at a time when I particularly want it, did not disturb me for more than a few minutes. Thanks partially to my diligence in daily absorbing Epictetus.

Tuesday, August 6th.

It was really hot and heavy yesterday. After dinner we sat a longish time under Chinese lanterns in the garden, and after the women had gone to bed I began to try to explain to Marriott the philosophy of the Stoics, the inferiority of ambition as a motive and of glory as an end, etc. But I doubt if he understood what I meant by control of the mind and its consequences. "Well," he said, "let's continue this conversation another night. I'm going to bed." I was specially interested in philosophy, as understood by Marcus Aurelius and Epictetus, because during part of the day I had been trying, without much success, to put it into practice in my relations with Mme. L.

Thursday, August 8th.

By giving half an hour a day to it, I am slowly getting through d'Annunzio's *Il Piacere*. I could read it without a dictionary quite as well as I read *Fromont jeune et Risler aîné* [1] without a dictionary 17 or 18 years ago; but I am learning Italian more conscientiously than I learnt French. What strikes me in the novel itself is the extraordinary narrowness of the "observing outlook"; the thinness of the texture; and the obvious fact that the larger part of it is nothing but slightly poetized autobiography. Occasionally a description is good, but the whole affair seems to me to be much too facile and slender.

Saturday, August 10th.

At last I think I have got into a fairly "formed" formal hand for "fine writing," and for the writing of my next novel in particular. I wrote a letter in it yesterday and gave it to Marriott to criticize. He found no fault with it at all. Indeed he was very enthusiastic about it and sent his wife up to look at it. He said it would puzzle Johnston,[2] the author of the textbook on writing and illuminating, to produce anything as good in the way of ordinary quick calligraphy. Also that if I wrote a whole book keeping up to the standard, it would be unique in the world. When I lamented that one could not get a really *black* ink that would run through a fountain-pen, he said he preferred the slightly greyish tint of common ink. He dissuaded me from doing the novel in double columns.

Yesterday I seemed to pass an entirely satisfactory day: Italian, piano,

---

[1] By Alphonse Daudet.
[2] Edward Johnston, author of *Writing and Illuminating*.

my play, writing finely, excursion with my wife, good meals, and reading my own stories at night in the garden to the Marriotts, who laughed continually as people ought to laugh at such stories. I also had news of the sale of *The Ghost*[1] in Germany—not that the sale of *that* book gave me much pleasure.

Tuesday, August 13th.

It was a near thing yesterday afternoon whether I should idle away the time in dalliance, or make a start with my new poem, *Town and Country*. However, as M. was employed in miracles with a cycling skirt, I went off down to the banks of the Seine and composed 10 lines, while men caught fish from punts and women crossed in the ferry, their coloured blouses reflected in the water, and fish jumped, and a tug struggled upwards with 5 barges—until the clock at Champagne struck 6, when I strolled home in the still strong sunshine, vainly attempting to find a rhyme to "faith" other than "wraith."

Wednesday, August 14th.

After two days' work on the final writing of the play[2] I now perceive that it will be a great strain to finish it at the rate of two acts a week. I gave nearly 4 hours of concentrated desk-work to it yesterday, and over 3 hours today, rising today before 6 o'clock. Some months ago, at intervals, I seemed to detect a very slight temporary deterioration of my eyesight. Then I noticed nothing. Today I was conscious of a certain uneasiness in the organs. Several times there was a mist before my eyes, as there is now—a mist which I can dispel by a strong effort of the will, but which returns. I wonder whether this is the end of my hitherto magnificent eyesight, or whether it is merely due to my having got up too early this morning.

Friday, August 16th.

We rode this afternoon to Fontainebleau, to partake with Martin of an iced drink called *galerne*, special to the town. This, with cakes, on the pavement, at two little tables. The usual *monde* of comfortable idlers, and continual passage of small autos, carriages, cyclists, and tradesmen's

---

[1] This had been published in England in January, 1907.
[2] *Cupid and Common Sense*, produced by the Stage Society, February 2, 1908.

carts. An old beggarwoman, who stank horribly, came and begged. Martin grumbled at her, and almost pushed her away, and then called the shopwoman and remonstrated with her for allowing her customers to be so bothered. He laughingly said that she ought to keep a boy on the pavement with a whip. One felt the instinctive antagonism of the bourgeois for the ne'er-do-well, which neither the beggar's age nor her sex could disarm. And the face of the shopwoman took on the hard expression of her class, usually worn by that class when engaged in defending the rights of its patrons against the mob.

August 20th, 21st and 22nd.

On Sunday morning I had an idea for writing a book about the village, to be called *In a French Village*. So I may as well begin it at once. Here is the opening:

People who pass, at various rates of speed, along the high road that runs through this village, imagine that it is one of your "one-street" villages. They are wrong. The houses and gardens which border the high road are not even characteristic of the village. They have suffered contact with the world and so lost some of their local qualities, like a native who has travelled. The villagers living on the high road have become sophisticated. Even the sight of a flying automobile whose driver is quite unaware that the rear portion of his vehicle has caught fire and is a mass of roaring, leaping flame, does not move them to a shout. They calmly watch it go by, and, when it has disappeared into the forest, smile, and chatter in an ordinary tone.

The real village lies back from the road, in the form of a rectangle to the north and of a semicircle to the south. Some 1,200 persons live in and about this rectangle and this semicircle. The semicircle, though superficially smaller, is the more important and the more densely populated. And the curving street which bounds the semicircle (the high road being the chord) is the genuine village street. You turn into it from the high road, and never seeing more than a few yards in front of you bear consistently to one hand, until with surprise you discover yourself in the high road again. No automobile penetrates into this nameless street except the automobile of the doctor (driven by the doctor), and the little noisy fussy automobile of the "Venerable" of the Germinal Lodge of Freemasons (driven by the fat white-coated Venerable who has friends in the street). It is a street of white cottages, large and small, some with forecourts, some with gardens carefully half hidden behind walls and railings. At one spot the close line of property defence is broken to let forth a narrow lane that leads to a corner of the forest. At another the street bulbs out into a wide space which ought to be styled the Grande Place (but is not). From this space another street escapes, parallel to the high road. Here are a grocer's shop and a café whose very names are unknown to lethargic persons who live on the high road.

As we approach the high road again, the shops increase. There is a baker's, a saddler's, a carpenter's. There are also two large-ish houses facing each other. One is occupied by the ex-postmaster. Occasionally, by luck, the great doors are open and one has a glimpse of a vast, vague, Versailles kind of staircase (the adjectives have a relative value only). At the corner of the curving street and the high road is the ex-post-office, where *sabots,* chocolate, literature, cheese, ink, plasters, and Chinese lanterns are sold. Here is the Piccadilly Circus of the village. The curving street, having skipped over the high road, straightens itself and begins its business of bounding the rectangle. Here is the chief hotel (telephone, private dining-rooms, banqueting-hall—for the Freemasons), another hotel, a café, the fruiterer's, the chief baker's, and the barber's; the butcher is near, but to have the cobbler and the new post-office and tobacco shop you must descend the high road into the residential portion of the village.

The chief impression of Semicircle Street (it must be christened) is one of white walls, immense iron gates painted a slate-grey, and large patches of green on the walls. The size and solidity of the gates would indicate behind them winding drives terminating in palaces. But in many instances, supposing that you blew a trumpet 7 times and the gates fell backward, they would, lying flat, about cover the demesnes they protect. Opened wide, they would admit the passage of traction engines and caravans; however, they are never opened wide; they grudgingly swing a few inches, and a woman or a child slips in or out, and they swing back. They are provided with automatic clarion bells, so that as the villagers pass upon their ways the air is full of brazen melodies.

The patches of green have usually a curious effect of defying nature.

You see vine leaves, which have arranged themselves in impeccable oblongs or squares on the walls, flourishing richly from no stem. You must look more closely to detect where the stem comes through the wall from the secret garden behind. But many other vines spring openly and without fear from unprotected strips of ground that in a town would be footpaths. They rise leafless for several feet—perhaps 6—the bare stems being covered with a rough lattice work, and then burst suddenly into a rich fury of foliage. Hundreds of such vines tempt the dishonest in September; yet, to such a point has public opinion been educated, the dishonest never yield. Here in this village we are on the edge of the district which produces the finest table grapes in France. We are near immense villages which exist in, for, and by grapes, where a peculiar quality of grape-nourishing soil is so precious that vines are planted in it everywhere, even to both sides of every street. I have been told, and I do not hesitate to believe, that in those regions land may be worth over £1,000 an acre. Naturally, there one may steal anything except a grape, just as in certain [of the] United States one may steal anything except a horse. And the public opinion of those villages has extended to us.

When one has accustomed one's self to this sight of desirable and lusty vines in public thoroughfares, one may notice in Semicircle Street the high rose-trees, where roses spy on attic windows in December, the wooden perches which sundry inhabitants fasten to their front walls for the convenience of wild birds, and the beautiful shapes of the ironwork of pump-handles and cellar gratings.

Thursday, August 22nd.

In the night the temperature fell to 15° Cent. [59° Fahr.], in my bedroom. I went out for a walk at 9 A.M. It seemed like autumn, with a mild cloudiness, and damp, clasping cold. And everything seemed very beautiful and strange. I thought what a pity it would be if I could not spend the autumn in the country. I walked by the little field-paths about the village "allotments," where one or two men and women were working and a dog pointing. I went far enough to see the view of Moret, and then returned, calling at the barber's. *"Fait froid,"* said the barber, rubbing his hands.

Play progressing well. I said today that my health had become so disconcertingly good that I felt as if I ought to go and see a doctor about it.

Sunday, August 25th.

The village is now "full" for the season. And in the morning, out of the windows of cottages comes the sound of women singing to cheap pianos. Bad songs, false sentiments, false notes, out of tune. It has a "shocking" effect on the ear in the midst of a beautiful landscape. All the painful, artificial, idle, vicious mediocrity of Paris seems to surge out of the windows.

I had the idea today of introducing a French public execution scene into the second part of *The Old Wives' Tale.*

August 26th.

We bicycled yesterday through Montigny, Grez, Villiers-sous-Grez, Larchant, and Nemours. And I exhausted myself in pushing Marguerite about 10 miles altogether against a head wind. We had tea at Villiers, just a straggling village without any attraction except that of its own life. During our meal the drone of a steam-thresher was heard rising and falling continually.

Tea in the street; they brought out and pitched for us a table, also vast thick basins, which we got changed for small coffee-cups. But we could not prevent the fat neat clean landlady from serving the milk in a 2-quart jug which would have filled about a million coffee-cups. We sat in the wind on yellow iron chairs, and we had bread and perhaps a pound of butter, and a plate of sweet biscuits which drew scores of flies. Over the houses we could just see the very high weather-cock of the church. Everything was beaten by wind and sunshine. From the inside of the little inn came hoarse argumentative voices. Curious to see in this extremely unsophisticated village a Parisian *cocotte* of the lower ranks. She was apparently staying at the inn. With her dog, and her dyed hair (too well arranged), and her short skirt, and her *matinée* (at 4.30 P.M.), and her hard eyes, she could not keep from exhibiting herself in the road. The instinct of "exposition" was too strong in her to be resisted. She found fifty excuses for popping into the house and out again.

Then we rode through woods 5 kilometres to Larchant. You know that the cathedral at Larchant is a show-place because the post cards are 2 sous each. Then the 8 kilometres of straight but atrocious road to Nemours, whence, having deposited our wives at the station, Marriott and I rode home at 12½ miles an hour.

Wednesday, August 28th.

I went yesterday for a day's cycling with Marriott. I chose a circular route that avoided the big main roads and we only met one auto all day, and that was as we crossed the Paris-Marseilles road at Villeneuve-la-Guyarde. If you stick to one clearly-defined main road, you must travel a long way before you escape from the circle of influence of the familiarity of home. The road itself is a thread which ties you. But if you choose cross-country routes you are in the unfamiliar, the strange (which you desire) at once almost.

The chief thing that interested me, visually, was the sight of a flock of sheep on a distant road. They were so far off that their movement forward was scarcely more perceptible than that of a star, yet the air was so clear in the sun that the separate forms of the animals could be distinguished. A great cloud of dust rose from them, spreading out like a balloon of which the flock was the car. It was exactly as if the sheep were on fire. This ought to be described in a novel.

I am so tired today as to be depressed.

On Monday I finished my poem *Town and Country*.

TOWN AND COUNTRY

> God made the country and man made the town
> And so man made the doctor, God the down.
> God made the mountain, and the ants their hill,
> Where grinding servitudes each day fulfil.
> God doubtless made the flowers, while in the hive
> Unnatural bees against their passions strive.
> God made the jackass and the bounding flea;
> I render thanks to God that man made me.
>
> Let those who recognize God's shaping power
> Here but not there, in tree but not in tower,
> In lane and field, but not in street and square,
> And in man's work see nothing that is fair—

Bestir their feeble fancy to the odd
Conception of a "country" ruled by God;
Where birds perceive the wickedness of strife
Against the winds, and lead the simple life
Nestless on God's own twigs; and squirrels free
From carking care, exist through February
On nuts that God has stored. Pray let them give
The fields to God's kind hand for just a year,
And then of God's own harvest make good cheer.

This cant of God and man would turn me sick,
Did I not deeply know the age was quick
With large conception of a prouder creed
Whereon we shall not feel the craven need
To count ourselves less noble than a weed.

For me a rural pond is not more pure
Nor more spontaneous than my city sewer.

Friday, August 30th.

Before tea yesterday I finished the play, and called it *Cupid and Common Sense*. It seems to me to be one of the best things I have ever done; quite as good as most of my novels. The title is merely *ad captandum*.

Sunday, September 1st.

Every night now the tree-toads (if they *are* tree-toads) sing from dusk till some unascertained hour in the middle of the night. One of them near this garden, or in it, makes a noise of absolute regularity—a long note and a very short pause—for hours and hours.

I notice that in building here—there is a house going up in the main street—when the workmen finish a chimney they do as is done in England, they stick a flag on it—the tricolour.

Yesterday morning at 6.30 when I looked out of the window the forest was half hidden in mist. In a few minutes the mist had rolled over the village, and in another few minutes all was clear. The day developed into heat.

I finished the play, definitely, giving all the stage directions etc., and then we rode over to Fontainebleau to lunch with the Martins.

Monday, September 2nd.

Yesterday I recopied certain scribbled pages of the play, and did the title page, and packed up the whole thing for England. This manuscript is certainly by a long way the most ambitious and beautiful I have ever done.

Tuesday, September 3rd.

Charny. We left home this morning on a short cycling tour—Marguerite's first. We got to Chéroy at 11.30, and had lunch at the Ecu de France, as I had last week with Marriott. It was practically the same lunch. Exactly the same 6 market people had lunch at the same table as last week. The market, however, seemed to have less animation.

Immediately after lunch we went on to Courtenay, 20 kilometres, largely through woods. A delightful old town on the side of a steep hill, approached by a semicircle of road. We had tea on the terrace of a nice hotel, and bought postcards and sent them off. As Marguerite did not feel tired we left Courtenay at 4.15, and cycled on to Charny, 19½ kilometres. This was the best part of the ride. A perfect road, as far as Douchy, across what I took to be a high tableland of large easy contours. The character of the country had now completely changed. It was a cider country. Immense pear trees dotted the plain, as far as we could see, and apple and pear trees lined the roadside. Great farmhouses a mile or so apart, with long, low expanses of roof. Ploughing in progress everywhere. The colour of the earth was a light grey—lovely with the grey-greens of the trees. We then descended into the valley where Charny lies. It rained a little before, and very smartly after, our arrival in an apparently inhospitable hotel with a difficult landlady. Marguerite had severe indigestion. I washed her feet—a unique experience for me. I felt like Mary Magdalen. I soon got on good terms with the landlady—a *brave femme* and a wonderful cook. She gave me one of the most perfectly cooked dinners I have ever eaten. *Soup au lait, cervelle de bœuf matelotte, haricots verts, veau rôti, omelette au rhum,* and a peach; excellent light wine. What would a meal in a similar hotel in a similar townlet in England have been? Then a cigar and a London paper. Expenses today, for us two: Lunch 5.50. Tea 60 centimes. Sundries 1 franc. These figures, which include tips, will be very interesting 20 years hence.

Yesterday I wrote a short story, asked for for the Christmas number of the *Sketch,* entitled *The Widow of the Balcony*—another Vera story, 3,000 words; and I began to think seriously about my novel.

Wednesday, September 4th.

This morning, having paid a bill for 7 francs 20 centimes for the two of us, we left Charny at 7.20. Cold; misty; a morning breeze ahead; cattle and sheep passing; road for miles covered with dung. The route to Toucy lies through a valley, and skirts the railway and a small stream; many poplars; also hedges everywhere; but the leading feature of the landscape certainly poplars. Marguerite's knees gave way at Villiers Saint-Benoît, a little town; so we stopped for tea; it was 9 o'clock. We had done 16 kilometres. We could not get good butter, butter coming into the town only once a week. I saw a magnificent team of four white oxen pulling a wagon.

We stopped at Leugny for lunch and tea, Madame's knees having given way completely. An untidy village, with a broom left lying in the middle of the road near the church. Curious signs over the inns etc., of soldiers cut out in thin wood, designed with noticeable skill. We stopped at a good inn. Good food, as everywhere. I went up to a bedroom to rest, and found a series of old coloured engravings depicting the life of a French sailor,[1] who achieved promotion by distributing "objets d'art" (a hand mirror) to the natives of the Marquesas Islands and thus establishing the *"domination française,"* and ended by marrying a rich girl whom I rescued from pirates. I walked round the village. At the back of most of the living-rooms, in a curtained alcove, was a bed. We then cycled slowly, over magnificent roads with a glorious gradual descent at the end, to Courson. Complete change in weather (which became splendid) and in character of country. No hedges, immense spaces. We reached the town at 6 P.M. and cows were entering it from all directions; they are stabled. A picturesque, poor little town; no railway; we met the aged, rotten and dirty diligence (2 services a day). The remains of a *fête* in the town; one merry-go-round, making its own electric light; rest of town in darkness save for stars. We sleep here. The best hotels in this district seem to be all named "Cheval Blanc."

---

[1] Probably Captain Marchand who visited the South Seas in 1842.

Friday, September 6th.

Vezelay. We reached this celebrated village yesterday afternoon, after two very considerable hills. The character of the country changed again after Courson, becoming bleak, very undulating, and stern. We passed through a forest and through a rainstorm, sheltering at a farm under a shed which showed the results of the peasant's habit of never destroying anything. We soon arrived at Coulanges sur Yonne, where a newly married couple were parading the streets after the first night shaking hands with their friends. The bride did not at all look as if she had been recently startled. We had two large bowls of hot milk for sixpence. Then we went on to Clamecy. After we had crossed the ridge the country became much prettier in quality and more picturesque. The Boule d'Or at Clamecy is chiefly made out of an old church. You dine in a chapel while grocers talk grocery at the *table d'hôte* (2 francs 50.). Then we came on to Vezelay, up enormous hills on good roads. Scenery quite equal to its reputation. Vezelay also. The largest church that I remember seeing. M. being unwell, we only did 43 kilometres yesterday, upon which she went to bed. Vezelay in situation and character strikingly resembles the villages in the Apennines; but it is much more civilized, and yet, although frequented by autos, it is not very spoiled.

Vermenton. We got here at 6 o'clock, having done 48 kilometres during the day. We left Vezelay at 10 A.M. having viewed the church again. The scenery grew more and more picturesque. All day we have followed the valley of the Cure. At Sermicelles we joined the great Paris-Vintimille highroad. No. 6., and went south by it to Avallon, genuinely old and beautiful, with renowned views from its renowned ramparts. Then we retraced our steps to Sermicelles, and came along northwards by No. 6. This part of the route, as far as Vermenton, is the "show" part. It is more than merely picturesque. Arcis-sur-Cure is the star village. Vermenton is the nicest small town (2,000 or so people) we have met with. In front of the hotel is the church, with a singular tower. At the barber's, I learnt that the town has been lighted by electricity for 12 years. The current is turned off at 11 P.M. You can have light either by meter, or at the rate of 3 francs per month per lamp. The electricity is a private enterprise, financially successful, and every one seems to be very discontented with it. The inconvenience of having no electric light after

11 P.M. on *fête* days was much insisted upon. Today, being on a great roadway, we were annoyed by autos. We were in the valleys today, and the character of the people, as exemplified by manners at inns and hotels, seemed softer than we have met with during the previous two days.

In every town, notices of *fêtes* and other forgatherings of various societies, showing a vast collective life.

Before starting this morning I made an excursion on my own to the church of St. Père sous Vezelay; a superb monument, in a mean village covered with cowdung. I did 7 kilometres—half like going down the side of a house, and half like going up the side of a house.

Saturday, September 7th.

St. Julien. We kept to the great main road as far as Auxerre. Picturesque enough. For a city of its importance (2 daily papers—16,800 inhabitants) Auxerre does not make enough show. Not a single fine thoroughfare, nor square, nor a single big shop. In the cathedral, which is fine, I was particularly struck by the large quantity of magnificent old stained glass. A little after Auxerre we left the high road and struck off to the left. We had tea at Guercy. Then Marguerite, who had been a corpse in the morning, suddenly felt strong, and instead of stopping at Joigny we came on here, never once touching the high road. We arrived at nightfall. Hôtel des Bons Enfants. Much business going on, and the landlady preoccupied and brusque. For this she apologized afterwards. In an hour and a quarter after arriving, we had eaten a perfect dinner of seven courses. We passed through, all day, an extremely busy agricultural country, populated and active everywhere.

Monday, September 9th.

Yesterday we rode home from Saint-Julien. It was very hot, and once we were misdirected. Also the first part of the journey was very heavy. We arrived at 5.30, after about 70 kilometres. I drank 2 glasses of soda and milk, then 4 cups of tea, then 2 more glasses of soda and milk; then nearly a bottle of white wine and half a siphon; then 2 cups of hot camomile. By this time it was 9 o'clock and I had got the better of my thirst.

We did a little over 300 kilometres in our 6 days; and the total expenses were 119 fr. 70 c. Deduct from this a minimum of 65 fr. which we should have spent had we remained at home, and the cost of the holiday comes out at 54 fr. for two people.

Wednesday, September 11th.

We were both of us still tired yesterday, and I was still thirsty. I began to work at once. I wrote letters all morning, and in the afternoon I read through Phillpotts's draft of *The Sole Survivors,* and was much more pleased with it than I had expected to be. Before dinner I had reconstructed such parts of it as seemed to need reconstructing, and was ready to begin the final writing today. When I think that this is positively the last piece of dramatic work I shall ever touch, unless and until I have something produced, I feel immensely relieved.

Friday, September 13th.

Three days' attack of influenza, or chill, by which I was incapacitated from any reasonable work.

I recovered today, and resumed *The Sole Survivors,* with hatred of it. I also went out into the forest and found some pretty good ideas for my novel.

I finished the fourth volume of Taine's letters. I have now changed my opinion about Taine being prejudiced. But the only dignified reason I can discover for his pessimism is his state of health. He was undoubtedly a great and an austere man, with very high principles. He thought only of his work, which was the ascertainment of historical truth. Not a single reference in all this volume to his money affairs, and scarcely a reference to physical comforts.

The portrait of the man gradually grew clear to me, and inspired me with ideals similar to his own: the doing simply of the work which one believes to be best, and the neglect of all gross and vain considerations. Why should I worry after fame and money, knowing as I do that these will not increase my happiness?

As I could not write I had leisure to think about myself. I saw that even now my life was not fully planned out; that I was not giving even an hour a day to scientific reading, to genuine systematic education; and that the central inspiration of my novel was not fine enough.

Today I began to rectify this, resuming my Spencer. I came across something good in Spencer, in the essay on *Progress:* "the profoundest of all infidelity—the fear lest the truth be bad." Even such acquaintance as I have with Spencer has enabled me to perceive the inconceivability of at least two newspaper interpretations of the new theory of matter in Gustave Le Bon's new book [1]; viz., that matter is quickness, a form of movement. In my pre-Spencer days I might have been capable of accepting such rot as at any rate suggestive. (I don't know if Le Bon is as silly as his critics.)

I bought Taine's *Voyage en Italie,* and was once again fired to make fuller notes of the impressions of the moment, of *choses vues.* Several good books by him consist of nothing else. I must surely by this time be a trained philosophic observer—fairly exact, and controlled by scientific principles. At the time one can scarcely judge what may be valuable later on. At the present moment I wish, for instance, that some school-mistress had written down simply her impression of her years of training; I want them for my novel. The whole of life ought to be covered thus by "impressionists," and a vast mass of new material of facts and sensations collected for use by historians, sociologists, and novelists. I really must try to do my share of it more completely than I do.

Saturday, September 14th.

I worked from 6 to 7.45. Then after breakfast I read Epictetus and Spencer, did my Italian and my piano. After lunch I read Conrad's new book, *The Secret Agent,* then went out and collected ideas for my novel. After tea I wrote letters and took a stroll with my wife. After dinner more piano, and French poetry; then this journal. In short, a damned virtuous, high-minded day.

Monday, September 16th.

We went out in the morning with a bottle of wine and a pasty etc. attached to our bicycles and lunched 10 miles off in the woods of Champagne, on the roadside, near to a large-ish property, preserved for game but arranged with a lack of taste and of dignity impossible in England. A ridiculous ornamental water, of irregular shape, in front of the house. This water passed by a tunnel under the road and terminated in a pool of disgusting filth. In the centre of the water was an island rockery, and on this rockery a large vase, about 3 feet high, gilded all over, with

---

[1] *L'Evolution de la Matière.*

a plant on the top of it bearing pink flowers. The effect was lacerating.

Lunching modestly thus by the roadside, shut in by two estates of wealthy people, it was impossible to crush altogether the snobbish feeling that one ought to despise one's self for the crime of being simple and unwealthy. I certainly have a liking for domestic display and largeness for their own sake.

I have almost decided to take this house from the Leberts, and there is no doubt that it is quite adequate to our needs. Yet because it makes no display, because it is obviously not the conventional residence of a man of means and manners, I think I am making a mistake. Nevertheless I realize most clearly that the problem of domestic menial service must become more and more acute, and that the utmost diminution of such service is not only right but expedient.

I could not sleep well last night, nor the night before; and not all Epictetus and Marcus Aurelius could ensure cheerfulness and perfect equanimity. However, I worked as much as usual, and now after tea, as I write this in the garden, with my feet chilled and the first breath of Autumn blowing on me, I am recovering command of the forces.

Thursday, September 19th.

I recovered this morning from a mysterious malady which resembled influenza in the intestines. It did not prevent me from working every day. In reading Smollett's *Travels* it has occurred to me that I go about very blind, wrapped up in myself.

This morning in the meadows down by the river I saw an affair arranged for twisting rope. The rope stretched over 2 or 300 yards. The strands of it were twisted by means of a simple apparatus with a large wheel, at one end. It was curious to see the rope rapidly twisting at the other end, right out of sight of the wheel. The mechanism is doubtless an outdoor adjunct of a ropery at Saint-Mammès which I discovered yesterday only. Smollett would have known all about that ropery and that alcohol extractor; he would also have acquainted himself with the commercial, social, and political economy of the entire district, as with its archæology and geography in detail.

Today I finished the construction of the first part of *The Old Wives' Tale*. I also conducted a sort of preliminary treaty with the Leberts and their architect for getting this house altered and taking it on a lease.

Monday, September 23rd.

Young men marched about the village yesterday to the accompaniment of one grotesquely-sounding brass instrument—difficult to imagine anything uglier or less dignified than this music, to which even portly, grave firemen in uniform will consent to parade themselves. I asked the barber what the noise was about, and he explained that it was the young conscripts who had on the previous day received their marching orders (*feuilles de route*) and were being merry (no doubt factitiously) previous to their departure a fortnight hence. Immediately afterwards entered another customer, a middle-aged man, who put the same question as I had put. *"C'est qu'ils ont reçu leurs feuilles,"* replied the barber; these were his exact words, I think. The enquirer's eyes questioned for a second or so, and then he understood. Several middle-aged men began talking about the shortness of service nowadays. They were all agreed: *"Deux ans—c'est rien."*

Lately I have several times seen grown men and women holding cows on a rope in a field while the cows pastured. This morning I saw a man and a woman and a boy entirely occupied with 5 grazing cows. Economically justified, this means, must mean, that any device for tethering the cows (granted the absence of hedges and of trees suitably placed for tethering) would cost more than the value of the labour of these 3 persons. Smollett would enquire as to this. On the opposite side of the road were several cows tethered in an orchard. The absence of hedges in France has certain inconveniences.

Wednesday, September 25th.

A certain amount of reading has been done lately. Conrad's *The Secret Agent.* A sort of sensationalism sternly treated on the plane of realistic psychology. A short story written out to the length of a novel. Nothing but a single episode told to the last drop. The Embassy scenes did not appear to me to be quite genuine, but rather a sincere effort to imagine events for which the author had nothing but psychological data of a general order. But the domestic existence of the spy, and the character of his wife—the "feel" of their relations, very masterly indeed, also the invention of the idiot brother-in-law for the doing of the crime. On the other hand, the contrivance of the mother-in-law's departure, though the departure in itself was excellent, seemed clumsy; and the final scenes between the wife and the anarchist after her husband's death rather missed fire in their wildness; they fail, not in the conception but in execution. On the whole, coming after *Nostromo,* the book gives a disappointing effect of slightness.

Smollett's *Travels in France and Italy.* A fine *splenetic* book, thoroughly interesting. The kind of book that a few men might, and probably do, cherish as a masterpiece too special in its flavour to please the crowd. It gives the impression of a sound, sincere personality, not very cultured in the arts, but immensely well informed, and breathing a hard, comfortable common sense at every pore. A doctor's personality, and yet still more the personality of a police magistrate; slightly less *doux,* and more downright, than that of Fielding. One leaves this book in thankfulness that one is not an eighteenth-century traveller.

Spencer's *Genesis of Science.* A long essay, superb example of his power of building a solid superstructure on the basis of a single axiom. Continuous reading of this kind is like a series of physical exercises and cold baths—invigorating.

Having no more philosophy at hand, I turned to Lessing's *Laocoön* to taste for a change the philosophy of art.

Ullman came. We went for a walk by the rivers. A pinkish-mauve flower was in bloom everywhere. It is called the *fleur d'hiver,* is said to be very poisonous and to herald the colder weather of autumn.

Thursday, September 26th.

All day the drone of a threshing machine near by, rising and falling, with an occasional high shriek of a whistle to signal a stopping or a starting. A hot heavy day, with undecided hints of a storm. For several days the fine weather has shown a disposition to be capricious. Yesterday afternoon there was a boisterous wind, with a few drops of rain to threaten my beautiful white hat. Night fell to its howling. But later it died away, and this morning the sky was as pure as ever. It grew hotter, and I had to change, first into a white waistcoat, and then into a different suit. The temperature in my room was 22°. Then cloud came, full and dark and ragged, only to disappear completely and leave the sky without a mark.

After lunch I stood at my open window and watched two bees visit every flower on a bush, entering completely hidden into each blossom and emerging after a few seconds. I was surprised at the certainty, rapidity, and thoroughness with which they exhausted the bush of perhaps a hundred flowers. Then I sat down and wrote the first of 12 articles for the *Evening News*—1,000 words in 1¼ hours. M. was asleep all the time.

Friday, September 27th.

The threshing machine was this day established exactly in front of this house, and the wheat to feed it was thrown down from a first-floor garner next door. Thirteen men, including the farmer, were employed from 6 A.M. to 11 A.M., two throwing down the sheaves, two passing them up to the machine, two placing them in the machine, two receiving the straw from the machine, two binding the straw in sheaves, two carrying it away, and the engineman. So far as I could see, the total result was about 7 sacks of grain. I haven't yet ascertained the selling value of the sacks, but in any case the net profit must be very small. Mme. Lebert said that at this season the farmers helped one another, and thus there were probably little extra wages to pay, but it was the custom to feed the helpers. What struck me was the abrupt, breathless finish to the process of agriculture. An expanse of land ploughed and sown and acted on grandiosely by sun and weather during months and months, the plants with infinite slowness taking matter from the soil and from the air. Then the reaping, which is comparatively slow, and the carriage to the garner. Up to this stage the product of the year is still large and imposing. Then it is thrown to this ruthless machine, and in a moment, amid a puffing and a whirr of wheels, grains of wheat begin to trickle out of the side of the machine into a sack. And before the day is half over a few sacks leaning against a tree-trunk represent all that is really valuable of the result of the year. The chaff makes a huge pile and the sheaves of straw a pile much huger. But the real "end" of the business is in those insignificant sacks.

Saturday, September 28th.

Today I finished the second act of *The Sole Survivors* and wrote the second of my *Evening News* articles. It rained definitely, and in the rain I went for a walk in the forest. Summer is now over. Yet all day the temperature in my room has been at 20° [Cent.]. In a conversation with

Lebert I seemed to gather that they had finally decided to alter the house in order to retain me as a tenant.

Tuesday, October 1st.

Yesterday I schemed out Act III of the play, and wrote the third article of the *Evening News* series, and my Italian, etc.

After working from 5.45 A.M. to 4 P.M. I went out for a walk in the rain. It cleared up at once, and I did about 10 miles by the Seine as far as Effondré, and home again by untried paths through the forest at 6.30. During most of this time I elaborated the opening of my new novel. I was tired in every way.

Mme. Lebert has ascertained for me that a threshing machine, with 12 men, will thresh 60 sacks of wheat in a day at 30 frs. the sack; that the men get 5 frs. each and their food, and that the machine costs 50 frs.; that altogether the work runs to 2 frs. a sack.

Saturday, October 5th.

Curious example of wit in Wordsworth; I should imagine it to be rather rare: The description of the old pack of cards in the first book of *The Prelude,* pp. 17–18 of the Temple Classics edition. I am now reading *The Prelude* with intense pleasure. I have abandoned several other books in order to read it.—*Travels of Wilhelm Meister,* Taine's *Voyage en Italie,* and Lessing's *Laocoön.* I have just read half of Proctor's *Primer of Astronomy,* and now for the first time understand how not only the varying lengths of days, but the seasons, are caused by the plane of the equator not being the same as the plane of the ecliptic. Simple enough! Perhaps one day I may comprehend the precession of the equinoxes.

I had a headache for 3 days, but I did my daily portion of *The Sole Survivors* and finished the thing, which I have damned a hundred times, yesterday morning. This is the last play I will ever touch until I have a play produced.

On Tuesday I begin my novel.

Recently I have taken to long walks in the forest. On Wednesday I discovered the Malmontagne, with wide views of the forest. In nature it is large spaces, bleak, with simple outlines and little noticeable detail, that appeal to me most strongly. I am more "sympathetic" to Dartmoor than to any other spot on earth. Next to that, the sea. Here, what chiefly appeals to me is the forest seen in the mass from a height, and the long smooth stretches of the Seine between Saint-Mammès and Montereau. With such things I class in my memory the panorama of the Apennines, spotted with hill towns as seen from the first range behind San Remo.

On Thursday it rained nearly all day and I walked two hours in the rain. The horse chestnuts in the road are dropping their fruit like heavy ammunition, and people are gathering it for cattle food.

Lee Matthews [1] wrote me yesterday that Professor Gilbert Murray,[2] one of the reading committee of the Stage Society, was delighted with *Cupid and Common Sense*. This gave me much pleasure. It now begins to look as if this play would really be produced.

Tuesday, October 8th. Paris.

I went to Paris yesterday morning at 7 o'clock. Bad weather. It being Monday morning, the train was crowded. I got to the Rue d'Aumale on foot and by omnibus. And in the omnibus I noticed that 2 of the 3 horses had sore feet.

Lunch at the Davrays' in their luminous new flat in the narrow Rue Servandoni. Victor Tissot was of the party. Editor of Hachette's *Almanac,* of *Mon Dimanche,* etc. What I call a typical Frenchman. Grey, aged between 50 and 60. In neat mourning. Low voice, with an air of quiet, resigned, amused, ironic philosophy. Talked well. Talked apparently on a system. He would go from subject to subject, and was careful to "play fair" between your subjects and his. Travelled a good bit. Spoke of the most awful hotels as mere regrettable incidents in travel, but not worth making a fuss about. The queerest thing he told us was about a hotel at Pau, where, he being a *monsieur seul,* he had been refused a room on the ground that the hotel was a *hotel des familles* and *messieurs seuls* were dangerous. He naturally told the landlady that if that was all he could easily find a woman and return with her in a short time.

When I left it was fine. I walked along the Rue de Rivoli, and saw my books on sale, then took the Métro to the Rue Hamelin for tea. Roy Devereux, just returned from Italy, was unwell and gloomy but resigned. She gave me Elinor Glyn's *Three Weeks* to read, as she

---

[1] An intimate personal friend, member of the Stage Society and closely connected with the theatrical world.

[2] The famous translator of Euripides, and writer on the Greek drama.

wanted my opinion. She said it was vulgar, but she liked it. I read it in the train back. Naïve and worthless, utterly. Its naughtiness, which has caused such extraordinary protests in England, is merely childish in its imitative conventionality of viciousness. A réchauffé of Ouida.

Wednesday, October 9th.

I have often thought, during the last year, upon the uselessness of trying to describe faces in literature. No vision is raised by particularization in words. I now find this minutely explained in Lessing's *Laocoön*, which is certainly a most useful and illuminating treatise for the writer. Homer, it seems, never described Helen. He merely said she was beautiful, and kept insisting on the fact and showing the influence of her beauty—as on the elders. This is the way to follow. Lessing's theory of the propriety of describing ugliness is ingenious, and perhaps good. The choice in subjects of a painter like Delacroix will not justify itself under Lessing's philosophy, and Lessing is undoubtedly right. Delacroix was great in spite of his choice of subjects. *Laocoön* has clarified and confirmed my ideas very much.

Yesterday I began *The Old Wives' Tale*. I wrote 350 words yesterday afternoon and 900 this morning. I felt less self-conscious than I usually do in beginning a novel. In order to find a clear 3 hours for it every morning I have had to make a time-table, getting out of bed earlier and lunching later. This morning I calculated that I could just walk to the Croix de Montmorin and back in an hour. I nearly did it this morning without trying, in heavy rain. Tomorrow I may do it. A landscape of soaked leaves and thick clouds and rain—nothing else. But I like it.

Thursday, October 10th.

A magnificent October day. I walked 4 miles between 8.30 and 9.30, and then wrote 1,000 words of the novel. This afternoon we penetrated into the forest with our bicycles and without a map! Had to walk miles, got lost gloriously, and at last reached home after 2 hours 40 minutes of labour. Far off, in an unfrequented path, we came across 3 old women sitting in the hedge and discussing mushrooms.

Monday, October 14th.

A young man named F—— came to spend the week-end with us. I

found him very enthusiastic about poetry, music, clothes, furniture, and architecture. He had a number of tales to tell of the stage in London. He confirmed my notion that Granville Barker [1] was very conceited. He said that the Court Theatre had really made a lot of money, but that at one time everybody believed it to be Shaw's own venture, that is to say, financially. He said that the best pieces had been the greatest failures, e.g. *Pan and the Young Shepherd*,[2] and a piece of Hauptmann's, which played altogether to £13. He said that the season at the Adelphi of Hall Caine's plays was Hall Caine's own, that the profits on *The Bondman* averaged £75 a week, and the losses on *The Prodigal Son* £75 a night.

Wednesday, October 16th.

This morning I had news of the death of N. Vaschide, head of the Paris Psycho-Pathological Laboratory, aged 33, who leaves without a *sou* his young and beautiful wife and a baby. Roy Devereux writes me condemning the social order on the strength of this. But he died of tuberculosis in the ganglions and of deliberate overwork. When I saw him at the opera in June, I almost foretold his death. He was a worker, a madman, and obscure both in thinking and writing, a wild enthusiast who would have made a mess of his life even in a Utopia, and withal a very lovable person of no real importance.

I have now written 7,000 words of the first chapter of the novel, and am still far from the end of it. Regarding it objectively, I do not see that it is very good, but from the pleasure I take in doing it, it must be.

Nothing but rain. I walked 4 miles in 59 minutes this morning in the rain. And this afternoon I went with Marguerite to Moret in pouring rain. A promenade on a thoroughly bad day in autumn is the next best thing to a promenade on a fine late spring morning. I enjoy it immensely. I enjoy splashing waterproof boots into deep puddles. Now it is dark, and I write this by my desk-lamp (after only 1½ pages my eyes feel fatigue) and it is still raining on the window.

Friday, October 18th.

Calvocoressi said that you can call a man anything in Marseilles ex-

---

[1] Playwright, actor, and producer. Among his best-known works are *Waste* and *Madras House*. Granville Barker produced many plays by Shaw, Galsworthy, etc., at the Court Theatre.

[2] By Maurice Hewlett, produced in March, 1905.

cept *mobile*. Call a coachman a *mobile* and he will get down from his box and try to kill you. The majority of the Marseillais have of course no notion why they object to being called *mobile*. The explanation is that during the Franco-German war Marseilles enrolled a regiment to go to the rescue of Paris. This *garde mobile* got as far as Avignon, where, some one shouting "Prussians," it threw down its arms and ran back home. Calvocoressi is a native of Marseilles.

Sunday, October 20th.

A curious instance of avarice from Calvocoressi. An old lady living in a 9,000 fr. apartment in the Avenue de la Grande Armée, who pays two servants 150 fr. per month each in order to induce them to stand her avaricious ways. There is a story in this. If a piece of mutton was bought that was too much for one day and not enough for two, she would say to the servant, "Supposing I don't eat any today, will there be enough for tomorrow?" "Yes, Madame!" And she would starve. If her son was reading the paper in the evening she would say, "Anything interesting in the paper?" "No, nothing special." "Then let us turn off the light and sit in the dark and talk." When alone in the evening, in order to save the electric light, she would spend her time in promenading on the staircase.[1]

Monday, October 21st.

Today I finished the second chapter of my novel. I seem to be rather uneasy as to its excellence. The date of the first part worries me, as my own recollections don't begin till 10 years later than 1862. However, the effect of the novel will be a cumulative one.

Lately I have been overworking, in spite of all resolutions to the contrary. I rise at 6.30 or so, and after reading Italian, one hour's walking, etc., I begin on the novel at 9.30 and work till 12.30. Then my afternoons are often taken up with articles. I had meant to keep my afternoons quite free of composition. Nevertheless, my health, thanks to walking 4 miles in an hour each morning, is simply admirable, and I sleep well. But my eyesight is weakening.

---

[1] This information was used by Arnold Bennett 10 years later, when writing *Riceyman Steps*.

Wednesday, October 23rd.

In reading Stendhal's unpublished journal in the *Mercure de France,* it seemed to me that in *my* journal I wasted a great deal of time in the proper construction of sentences. Quite unnecessary to do this in recording impressions.

Still much rain. A perfect baptism of damp this morning in the forest, though not actually raining. The forest all yellow and brown. Leaves falling continuously. Horse-chestnuts quite yellow. Sound of water occasionally dislodged from the trees by wind.

I have written over 2,000 words of third chapter yesterday and today. I planned the chapter perfectly yesterday morning in the forest.

Saturday, October 26th.

The forest is now, for me, at nearly its most beautiful. Another fortnight and the spectacle will be complete. But it is really too close to our doors for us to appreciate it properly. If we had to walk 5 miles instead of 500 yards in order to get into one of these marvellously picturesque glades, we should think we were exceedingly lucky in being only 5 miles off and not 50. On the whole a very wet month, with, on days free from rain, heavy persistent fogs lasting till afternoon. The sound of voices is very clear in the forest in this mushroom weather. I have learnt a little about mushrooms. I have tremendously enjoyed my morning exercise in the mist or rain. But mushrooming only interests me when the sport is good.

In general, slightly too much work. 18,000 words of *Old Wives' Tale* in 2 weeks 4 days.

Much tempted to throw up my Italian and my piano, on account of stress of work, but I still stick to both of them.

Monday, October 28th.

I began work on the scenario of an operatic libretto from *Antony and Cleopatra* yesterday afternoon, and I finished the whole thing this morning before lunch—complete in all details. I ripped to pieces two copies of Hunter's school and student's edition of the play, in order to save myself the trouble of copying. I have never done as much work before in the time.

Autumn in the forest. The colours get richer and richer; and one's fingers colder. Many parts are now quite covered with new red leaves. Fogs every morning. In my morning exercise I have timed myself and find I can walk uphill at the rate of 7 kilometres an hour for at least a quarter of a mile. I could no doubt do several miles at this speed.

I have just finished reading Norman Lockyer's *Primer of Astronomy* and I now understand sundry things I didn't understand before.

Thursday, October 31st.

This day I finished the longish article on *Mental Stocktaking* for *T.P.'s W.*, Christmas number. And I also finished correcting the proofs of *The Statue*.

Apropos of the agitation for abolishing the censor in England, it occurred to me that not even the advocates of freedom seek to justify the free treatment of sexual matters in any other than a high moral-pointing vein. The notion that sexual themes might allowably be treated in the mere aim of amusement does not seem to have occurred to anybody at all.

First day of St. Martin's summer today apparently. As soft and treacherous as a day of spring. In 4 days I have written probably about 10,000 words.

Monday, November 4th.

Calvocoressi came down on Friday. Stayed 30 hours. We went through my scenario of *Antony and Cleopatra,* and he was entirely delighted with it. *"J'en bave,"* he exclaimed to M.

F—— came on Saturday. I got him on to theatrical gossip. He regarded Waller as a mere irresponsible boy, always shirking business, always losing money to his backers. As an instance of business methods of running a theatre: dress rehearsal of some "Waller play" was simply awful. Waller stopped it and drove off to Comedy Theatre to get hold of Louis Calvert. L.C. wouldn't come. L.W. begged and prayed, and at last L.C. yielded, giving orders that the waiting company should go out and eat or rest, and be back sharp at midnight. He began sharp at midnight, made the company first of all play the piece through as it stood, and refused to allow even Waller to comment on it. This took 6 hours. Then 1 hour's rest. Then he started over again, and began to cut heavily.

People complained that he had left out all the first half of the first act, that every one was lost, etc., but he carried through the autocratic rôle, got the parts re-typewritten etc., and finished about 11 A.M. There was no other rehearsal. F—— said L.C. ought to get £100 for the work.

He said Beerbohm Tree was quite mad, and that the theatre only went on at all because a certain number of plain stupid people in it just went along and ignored him. Tree was now always in a "dither." His silly practical jokes (such as taking a girl super's hand and gazing long at her and saying: "I love you. What is your name?" and turning his back to the audience and making horrible faces so that the other players should have to laugh) were on the increase.

I finished first half of first part of *Old Wives' Tale*. 8.30 to 11, walk by Seine and in forest. Thinking about next chapter of *Old Wives' Tale*.

Sunday, November 17th.

We went to Paris on Friday for a dinner at Roy Devereux's, I bought Octave Mirbeau's *La 628-E8*, and read it with immense gusto. It reinforced the impression that has been growing on me for some time that I waste a vast lot of ideas and impressions because I have not *quite* got the trick of throwing them into form instantly and of intensifying them to a degree sufficiently poetical. If I forced myself to exert the necessary energy and skill for a short time I should arrive at it.

Both Taine's various travels and this book of Mirbeau's are nothing but impressions simply *pitched* together; and much of their charm and verity lies in that. I made the experiment on returning from Paris yesterday of writing my sensations of the morning. I did about 1,000 words of *heightened* stuff in about 40 minutes, and thought it pretty good. But it must be dashed down, written with the utmost possible rapidity. Therefore I fear I should have to abandon this format of page and this handwriting for something larger and more cursive. And this I should regret.

November 19th.

The Leberts in the little shut-off room in kitchen. Just room for 3. Fire burning in corner. Lebert with newspaper that he glanced at mechanically, with his cap on. Mme. half seated on corner of something. Cat.

I ask them details of siege of Paris.

It seems to have left no particular mark on their minds. They thought more of accident just before, and they had a lot of potatoes. They had 3 children (went to school as usual). At first meal 125 grammes each per day (but only 30 grammes later). Had 3 *bons de pains* every other day (1 lb. each person per day). As employé of railway, he was requisitioned for ambulance work when necessary. On field of battle when a horse fell the man leapt on it, and cut it up and carried it off. He was in Garde Nationale (1 fr. 50 per day). Exercise every day. The different companies of G.N. usually traversed Paris with their *musique*.

Personne ne travaillait.

The cold. The waiting on the greens.

Rice requisitioned specially for soldiers.

Convinced that Government did tricks with food towards the end, so as to induce the people to acquiesce in capitulation. Description, *exprès,* of food.

When capitulation announced, Garde Nationale (300,000) *faisait des potins.* Government accused of treachery.

Black bread, horse-chestnuts and *avoine.* During 10 or 15 days this bread quite uneatable. It destroyed stomach unless cooked over fire.

He bought wood at 5 fr. the 100 kilos.

When the Germans entered by Champs Elysées, only Bonapartists and Royalists (among Frenchmen) were there. Republicans kept away. Cafés closed. One alone was kept open, and was afterwards sacked by the mob.

Prussians confined to Champs Elysées, Cour la Reine, and Place de la Concorde. Those who tried to *forcer la consigne* were roughly handled. One killed. This pride of Parisians in keeping away during 24 hours of German occupation seemed to strike the Leberts more than anything else. Otherwise they seemed only to attach importance to the siege because I did. Like inhabitants of picturesque town or curious village.

During the commune they lived in a cellar for a fortnight. Baker next door, and they got bread over wall. When this (for some reason) could not longer be done, they called out to passers-by to order bread for them, or something of that kind. Their cool tone in saying, "Yes, we slept in cellar and kept shutters closed because there were always shooting bands in the streets."

Wednesday, November 20th.

I have had several days of hesitation about the format of this, the eighth volume of my journal. I thought, and still think, it too small for really fast writing, and I can only arrive at getting down my impressions of things in full by writing fast—pell-mell, without regard to sentence construction. Mirbeau's book *628–E8* has shown me, again, what a lot of stuff, perhaps as valuable as his, I lose by not writing it down. I have made, in the last 3 days, three full-ish sketches that I may use later, and that certainly would have been lost if I had not seized them and held them.

I still hanker to write a book (and publish it) of personal impressions. Had several ideas lately for articles. One: *The Individualism of Socialism;* dealing with what socialists such as I ought to do in the way of personal living, and dealing also with the fact that all political questions, such as those which agitate socialists, are simply questions of machinery—and do not directly touch the question of living (interiorly).

Mme. Lebert withdrew from her offer to let this house (Les Sablons) with vegetables and fruit for 1,000 fr. a year. She shied at the vegetables and fruit. I would not give way; so we most amicably and affectionately agreed to part. I find myself, on the eve of going to England, without a programme, which is rather disconcerting. However, we are free to live where we like: by the sea, e.g. I feel I want to live by the sea, in Holland, at Fontainebleau, and on the south coast of England, all at once.

I am getting rather tired of the confinement of this little flat; but one day I shall go back to the evenings here, in the room where I work and sleep, with M. sewing or trying things on her *mannequin,* and the constant preoccupation of the fire and the temperature and my cold— with regret, as a perfect time.

Regularly I have been doing 2,000 words a day at least. 12 to 1,500 words of my novel in the morning, and pieces of articles in the afternoon. I am now almost sure to do 365,000 words in the year.

Friday, November 22nd.

Idea for *rosserie* in my newly designed book, *Things as They Are:* M. Barrès's discourse at the Academy on prizes for virtue. 300 fr. to parents of 20 children, etc.

Tuesday, November 26th.

Yesterday I walked to Fontainebleau in the pouring rain, and walked in and about the town for over 2 hours with a house agent, looking at possible houses. I saw one small one, surrounded by a walled garden, that might suit. Distinct pleasure in examining these houses. I fell in love with the one I liked, and at once, in my mind, arranged it as it ought to be. I lunched at the Cygne, had coffee at a café, and walked all the way home—and it never stopped raining! Then after tea I wrote 1,300 words of the novel. This morning, while the whole place was being upset with preparations for our departure, I wrote 2 to 300 words more of the novel, and this afternoon I packed my large trunk and arranged my papers. That I should have worked so easily at my novel in all this mess shows how it has got hold of me, or I of it.

Tuesday, December 3rd.

Idea for a funny story about a cat. The Devereux's cat. Each of the 3 women swears it belongs to her. Two of them have written to thank me for looking after her cat. In the story, some man might draw a great advantage by flattering 3 different owners of the same cat.

Another idea, very vague, from an article by Lenôtre (*Vieilles Maisons, Vieux Papiers*) in tonight's *Temps,* showing how the *ménage* Tison [1] gradually turned right round and ended by favouring the royal family in the Temple, and how Tison came even to risking his life in order to create a few illusive hopes for Marie Antoinette. I ought really to keep the article. I will. The whole thing, transferred on to another plane, might be made very moving. But some historical novelist ought to treat it exactly as it is.

Mrs. Belloc Lowndes [2] told me that the prices paid to novelists in London were still going up; and, as a positive fact, that Hewlett got £3,000 down for *The Stooping Lady* in U. S. A.

I finished the first part of *The Old Wives' Tale* here in Paris on Friday afternoon.

---

[1] The Tisons, husband and wife, were sent by Pétion de Villeneuve to act as servants to the Royal Family when in the Temple prison.

[2] Sister of Hilaire Belloc, and wife of Frederick Lowndes (of *The Times*) is the author of several novels including *The Chink in the Armour,* etc.

Wednesday, December 4th.

Came to England. Impressed again by the extraordinary self-consciousness of travellers. On the platform at the Nord, another man and I tramping up and down the platform got half-smothered in a cloud of malodorous steam. He could not help turning to me as we emerged, to share his sensations with me by means of a gesture. Had he not been on a journey he would have ignored my existence. The English side of the journey has improved. Better carriages: electric light, contrasted with oil in French train. (Strangely mediæval—oil lighting, requiring men, ladders, and very heavy lamps.) Permanent way much better in England than in France. Carriages quieter. Porters better and more agreeably man-like.

Thursday, December 5th.

Called on Farrar.[1] He said: "The health of London has been simply appalling this year. The death rate has dropped to 11 per 1,000. During one week in November I had no one to call on at all. Other doctors were in the same fix." He could not explain it at all. The only phrase he could use was "a sort of wave of good health passing over." He said he had been typing an article on Dickens for Theodore Watts[2]: how the old man, his young wife, his secretary, and his assistant secretary all helped in it, and that for some time there were 1, 2, and 3 calls every day at the house *apropos* of the typing of some fraction of the article. The old man often came himself to see how a fragment of 50 words or so looked when typewritten, so that he could judge better of the effect. In brief, the whole enterprise (of 5,000 words only) was a terrific business.

Friday, December 6th.

Dinner to Pinker last night. I sat between W. W. Jacobs and H. C. Marillier.[3]

Pett Ridge[4] told one good story about the little boy who said there were only 9 Commandments, and when his father said that at any

---

[1] Formerly his medical man.

[2] Theodore Watts Dunton was at that time 75 years of age. He died in 1914.

[3] Art critic and author.

[4] William Pett Ridge includes among his novels *Mord Emily, The Wickhamses,* etc.

rate when he went away there had been 10, replied, "Yes, but mother broke one last week." Jacobs said it was disgusting getting older, and that he hated that young men should raise their hats to him out of respect for his superior age.

Daily Despatch offered me 6 guineas a column for articles, 50 per cent. above my previous highest price. I had the idea of doing a series of impressions of the new London for them. A little in the G. W. Steevens style. One notion for an article was the underground foreign population of waiters in London.

Monday, December 9th.

On Friday I went all down Fleet Street to find the offices of *Manchester Daily Despatch*. Couldn't find them; had to go back to Pinker's to get address. The house ultimately proved to be a large building with gold signs all across it; only I was looking for something small. Sutherland, the London editor, a very quiet self-contained man. His coldness startled me at first, as I was boiling over with articles. However, I liked him. I suggested subjects for 6 articles. I got back to Putney at 6.30, and we all dined at Sharpe's; a musical evening, of which the features were Sharpe's interpretations of Ravel, and Cedric's imitation on his 'cello of a motor bus starting in Putney High Street.

Tuesday, December 10th.

We went looking at private hotels today. Quite horrified by a decent one in Queen's Gate. Pail on stairs. Yet comfortable. But too horribly ugly and boarding-house-y: I had begun by putting cost at £40 a month. I then dropped it to £25, under M.'s influence. It must now go up to £30 or £35. Lunched at Harrods Stores, crammed; had to wait a minute for a table. Home in petrole-ous omnibus. This morning I walked 5 or 6 miles through Roehampton and Barnes. Impressed by the cleanliness, order, and sober luxury of all the dwellings I saw. I found most of the plot for a humorous novel; I hope to find the remaining part of the plot tomorrow.

Sharpes and Chapman [1] here last night. I asked C. what Lane would

---

[1] Frederic Chapman, literary adviser to the publishing firm of John Lane.

say if I asked him to publish a book of poems. He instantly said, "He would say, 'Give me your next 3 novels and I'll publish your poems.'"

Saturday, December 14th.

Yesterday morning I went for a walk along Chelsea Embankment. Magnificent architecture and landscape. Nothing to equal it in Paris for luxury, richness, sobriety, and atmosphere. I then wrote the first of a new series of articles for the *Despatch*.

On Thursday we lunched at Mrs. Laye's. Lee Mathews was full to bursting of my play. Mrs. Laye wanted to become a member of the Fabian Society.

Sunday, December 15th.

Last night, reception and musical evening given in our honour here at Marriotts'. The things that struck me: general aging, sadness of Tora Hwass, impossibility of E.A.R., genius of Hazell's songs. Why "The Devout Lover," a conventional, rotten song, became utterly conventionalized and as hard as a pebble, a thing now accepted without examination.

I walked along Lots Road this morning. River fine, but a horrible neighbourhood. There is one row of houses with a most extraordinary mask of a man with Dundreary moustaches on the keystone of the arch of every front door. Awful colour, the buildings. Smashed panes, mended with paper. I came across the huge generating station of the Electric Tubes, and saw in it my article on London. Singular clinging constructions of wood at either end. Whole thing enormous. Continuous roaring sound. Cheerful for neighbouring houses.

Scores of seagulls sitting in orderly rows on the railings of an unused pier; and one on the top of a lantern.

Tuesday, December 17th.

Yesterday, lunch with the Lowndes's at the Sesame Club. I liked the club till I re-visited the Garrick Club in the evening. Walked about London in the afternoon alone, had tea at the Cabin in the Strand; music, young women, and dalliance, and the Strand pavements overhead. I saw articles in it. I decided to offer a whole month's impressions to the *Tribune*,[1] and I sent them a note this morning. During the afternoon I called on Drinkwater [2] (Secretary of the Stage Society), Pinker, and Curtis Brown.

Dined with Pett Ridge at the Garrick. Pett Ridge said Arthur Morrison [3] had sold his Japanese pictures to the British Museum for £4,000, and bought a motor car. Also that B. Pain had bought a car off W. S. Gilbert and sold it again. We finished about 10. I had a fairly clear idea of P. Ridge's bachelor life. I liked much of his taste, and all his quiet "fundamental decency." Witty enough. Tales about old Hy. Kemble,[4] e.g. speaking to young Bancroft [5] (aged, kind, trembling voice): "Your mother was a beautiful actress, a most delightful actress, but as for your poor bloody old father—well, there it is—it's no use talking."

Sunday, December 22nd.

We came down to the Potteries yesterday afternoon. Seemed to have better ideas as to the scientific causes of provincialism.

I went for a walk this morning up Sneyd Green.[6] Untidiness; things left at loose ends. Broken walls, deserted entrances to what had been spacious gardens. Everything very misty. Curious enclosed "ash-court" place, with an iron device in the middle. Pit shafts—one only fenced in, another with a wall 12 or 15 feet high and a low wooden door in it. Men in bright neckties sallying forth, rather suspicious, defiant, meanly shrewd look. Mean stunted boy crouching along smoking a pipe which he hid in his hand while holding it in his mouth. Complete waste of Sunday: deserted goal posts in gloomy mist. Mild wind. Cold, chilling, clammy. Idea: public baths never bring in great profits to relief of rates, like gas. . . . I was forgetting to note the sound of hymns from chapels and schools. People going into Catholic chapel. Kids waiting outside school-room door (Sneyd Green), evidently while first prayer was being said.

---

[1] Liberal daily paper that started in 1906 but was discontinued in 1908.
[2] John Drinkwater, the poet and dramatist.
[3] Best known for his *Tales of Mean Streets* and his detective stories, *Martin Hewitt, Investigator,* etc.
[4] Henry Kemble (1848-1907) was a member of the famous English family of actors.
[5] Sir Squire and Lady (Effie Marie Wilton) Bancroft were very popular actors of the London theatre.
[6] Sneyd Green appears as Toft End in the Five Towns stories.

Tuesday, December 31st.

I spent just over 23,000 fr. this year, and earned about 32,000 fr. I wrote *The Statue* (with E.P.) and *Sole Survivors* (with E.P.); *Love and Riches, Death of Simon Fuge,* 5 other short stories. First part of *The Old Wives' Tale.* About 46 newspaper articles. And my journal. Also my play, *Cupid and Common Sense,* and scenario of a new humorous novel, *The Case of Leek.*[1] Grand total: 375,000 words. This constitutes a record year.

---

[1] Subsequently entitled *Buried Alive.*

1908

Thursday, January 2nd.

The most horrible east wind, which incapacitates me from arranging my thoughts in the streets. I began *The Case of Leek* yesterday, according to programme, and continued it today. But yesterday I was cold and today I had a headache. 1,600 words in 2 days. Chief observation in London: that it is a city of very rich and very poor. The vastness of this rich quarter is astonishing. In Bond Street this morning the main thing to be seen was the well-groomed, physically fit male animal: a sort of physical arrogance with it.

January 4th.

I continue to walk about and to have the richness of London forced into my head. It is almost disconcerting to think that all this vast idle class has to "go" one day. The idlers in this hotel make an imposing array. Offensive, many of them.

Curious example tonight of unconscious and honest sexuality by a decent woman. A Scotchwoman (age about 45) sitting by the fire in the lounge describing to another woman her sensations on seeing a regiment of Highlanders (with music) pass along Princes Street, Edinburgh. "I couldn't bear to look at them—made me cry—my heart was so full. Nothing moves me so much as a regiment of Highlanders. Their costume . . . and so tall . . . such fine men . . . such white skins. . . . But I shouldn't like to be in the same room with them. I shouldn't like to know them." She was quite unaware that phrase after phrase which she used was an expression of sexual feeling.

281

Finished first chapter of *Case of Leek,* and must write it again, damn it.

January 5th.

One must never, when in a country, say that a certain phenomenon could not be in another. Often in Paris I have said, on seeing the backs of houses, "English building laws would never allow that cramping of space and lack of light." And also, on being forced to go out of my way by a cab whose driver had chosen to draw up exactly on a crossing, "London police would never allow that." Both these things I have seen today. The back parts of this very hotel are probably as dark as anything I have met within Paris.

Every day's experience shows the folly of mutually exclusive generalizations concerning two countries.

Frost and fog today. Curious romantic scenes around the Round Pond, its centre lost in fog, and exotic birds wheeling in and out of the unseen, and slipping on the ice when grabbing at food thrown to them. Sparrows hopping amongst them. Chatted with a policeman at the corner this morning. Evidently very young. So young and fresh that the only really policemanish thing about him was his uniform. A sort of man dressed up as a policeman. I have noticed this before in young policemen, but have never defined it so well.

Friday, January 10th.

I finished the first chapter of *The Case of Leek* on Wednesday— 5,400 words in 3 days—despite worry. But it was a sort of second writing, as I had to begin it all again on Monday.

Today I went to a rehearsal of *Cupid and Common Sense.* Not *quite* so depressing as I had anticipated. But bad enough. I was struck by the immensity and the wearisomeness of the producer's task.

January 17th.

Another rehearsal yesterday at Terry's Theatre. I saw all the play. It exhausted and depressed me very much. Nothing seemed to get over the footlights. The players now played too quickly instead of too slowly. Local accent all wrong, and certainly incurable. But the other people seemed to be quite cheerful and optimistic. All the surroundings—the

manufactory of amusement repelled me. Women cleaning and whispering, etc. Cold. Oil lamps to warm. Smallness of theatre.

Proceeding regularly with *The Case of Leek*. Today I re-wrote what
I wrote yesterday. Tomorrow I shall have finished a quarter of the
whole. I am deliberately losing sight of the serial, and writing it solely
as a book.

I do this just a little under the influence of Pinker, with whom we
lunched at the Gaiety on Wednesday. He was quietly pessimistic as to
serial markets; and advised writing for book-form, and then seeing
afterwards if a serial can be carved out of the book.

Sunday, January 19th.

Mist yesterday morning; fog this morning. Both days I noticed "the
gigantic ghosts of omnibuses" in the gloom. It is a phrase to use.

I called and saw Vedrenne [1] at the Queen's Theatre yesterday afternoon. Seemed a decent sort of chap, more sincere than the run of them;
also he kept his appointment to the minute. He said that in the theatre
he thought that "the author was everything." I of course agreed. Said
he had been paying G. B. Shaw £4,000 a year for 4 years past. And
that he took £1,300 in Dublin in a week with a Shaw play. Also said,
speaking generally, that he lost a lot of money last year. Said he had
taken on Waller for 5 years, and had bought a "morality" play by Conan
Doyle.

My reading is unsatisfactory. I read a bit of the *Prelude* today. I don't
seem to get *into* either Acton or Greevey. But I stick to Marcus Aurelius.

Thursday, January 23rd.

I had tea with Lena Ashwell [2] on Tuesday; her elder sister was there.
Beautiful old house, arranged with taste. Flashes of common sense and
of insight, but a little embittered. This would doubtless pass as intimacy
was gained. She told me how Frohman [3] had refused *Leah Kleschna*. [4]
Reason: because he thought the public would not be interested in a

---

[1] J. E. Vedrenne was associated with Granville Barker in the management of the Court
Theatre.
[2] English actress.
[3] Charles Frohman, prominent New York manager, who was drowned when the
Lusitania sank.
[4] By C. M. S. McLellan. Produced at the New Theatre in 1905.

thief. When it had succeeded he paid a premium of £1,000 to get control of it, and then went about buying every play that had a thief in it. This anecdote has the same elements as nearly all the other anecdotes she related.

On the previous night we saw the piece, *Irene Wycherley*,[1] about which every one is talking as the best piece in London. Lena mentioned its author and me as signs of a renascence of the drama. A curious mixture of ancient convention and bits of novelty. Exceedingly amateurish, and mostly bad, but pervaded at times by a very distinct feeling for the dramatic.

Rehearsals of *Cupid and Common Sense* now going much better. I began yesterday to get quite enthusiastic.

Friday, January 24th.

Lunch at G. B. Shaw's yesterday. Mrs. Shaw a very agreeable, sympathetic and earnest woman. She looked just like the mother of a large family. Shaw came in just as lunch was served. Naturally self-conscious and egotistic; but he evidently made a decent effort against this. Talked most of the time during lunch; has a marked accent, and a habit of rubbing his hands constantly while talking. He related a tale about Estelle Burney and the Shelley Society much as a practised talker in literary circles might have related it. St. John Hankin,[2] who was there, would have related it much better.

Saturday, February 1st.

Dress rehearsal of *Cupid and Common Sense* began at 12.45 on Friday the twenty-fourth, and finished about 4 o'clock. This was the copyright performance. A bill outside announced that admission was 1 guinea. Performance extremely depressing. Lucy Wilson was got up more like a Spanish dancer than anything else. There was a sort of half rehearsal on Saturday. The first performance on Sunday night was much better. It held the audience. Lee Matthews said I must respond to the call, and I did; besides, I wanted to.

The performance on Monday afternoon was better, and though there

---

[1] By A. P. Wharton, produced at the Kingsway Theatre, October, 1907.
[2] Humorous author, playwright, and contributor to *Punch*, etc. Died in 1909 at the age of 39.

was less applause, I think the play had a greater success. Wells was delighted, impressed rather deeply, I thought. Some of the newspaper notices disgusted me. Especially *The Times* and the *Manchester Guardian*. But as they begin to come in, now, I perceive that on the whole they are favourable, and that the public is getting ripe for such a play as I wrote. I was ready to begin work on Thursday, but was stopped by a headache. Yesterday I wrote 2,700 words of the novel.

I made up our accounts tonight for the first month of the year, and found that we had exceeded our allotted sum of £50 per month for everything, by £8 17s. 7d. or £2 a week. This did not surprise me, but it disquieted me. The sum includes the monthly share of all rents, etc. I do not think we can live here at this hotel on £50 inclusive of everything; but we shall certainly do February on less; for one thing it is 3 days shorter.

Today I finished one third of *The Case of Leek*.

February 6th.

We went to see Hornung's *Stingaree* on Monday, and I arranged with Vedrenne to compress it into a good shape and give it guts, with a view to turning from a failure into a success, subject to Hornung's consent—for £100. However, on Tuesday afternoon Vedrenne telegraphed me that Hornung refused his consent.

Friday, February 14th.

We have seen two plays by G. B. Shaw: *Arms and the Man* and *Captain Brassbound's Conversion*. I have been impressed by the moral power of both of them. The latter is frequently dull, but *good* except in its melodramatic skeleton, which is unblushingly absurd. On the whole, my opinion of Shaw is going up. The most surprising thing about his plays is that they should find a public at all. They must have immensely educated the public.

Yesterday I finished two-thirds of *The Case of Leek,* writing 4,800 words in the day. Difficult to live properly here. I seem to have no time and yet I waste time. I am reading nothing but Francis Newman's [1] *Phases of Faith*. It is amazing in its ridiculous seriousness about dog-

---

[1] Brother of Cardinal Newman.

matic questions, for instance as to the relations between Christ and God, but it is thoroughly sincere and well done and therefore interesting.

Saturday, February 29th.

I finished the humorous novel, *Buried Alive,* on Thursday morning. Except one chapter, which I thought would be the best in the book, it is all pretty good. I handed the complete MS. over to Pinker yesterday.

We have certainly been living at a great pace; at least I have. Out almost every night. Yesterday I went over the *Evening News* Office, and much wanted to use it up for a story. Whitten came to lunch on Tuesday, and ordered 16 articles. Pett Ridge came on Wednesday for lunch, and told us a funny story about a page at a ladies' club who made an income by cutting politenesses out of telegrams which he was entrusted with for despatch.

We have been to the Exhibition of Fair Women at the New Gallery. The *clous* of the show were 3 Sargents, all of which I should have greatly admired 6 years ago—and now I did not care for them at all. Ugly colouring and much mannerism. And I used to think he was a great man! We went to the British Museum. Elgin marbles the greatest sensation I have had for a long time. I used to think them cold. Now I see how passionately they were done. The illuminated MSS. also made an entirely new appeal to me. And I was more than ever determined to do some decent illumination.

Thursday, March 5th.

Orage, editor and proprietor of the *New Age,* came on Monday night, and I sold him *How to Live on Twenty-four Hours a Day* for his new series, and promised to give him an article on Wells, or an interview if Wells would agree. Went down to Wells on Tuesday, dine and sleep. He wouldn't agree. Said interviews must "occur," with which I agreed.

Found him harder, yet politer and more reasonable in argument and posture than ever before. Seemed discontented about money, while admitting that he was making £3,000 out of *War in the Air,* which he wrote easily in 4 months. We had not enough time really to come to grips about things. He was extremely witty and fine about the attitude of Keir Hardie [1] and so on (but not sufficiently sympathetic). He told a

---

[1] James Keir Hardie, a miner, one of the earliest and one of the best-known Labour members of Parliament.

really astounding tale of a dinner given by Cust [1] to about 20 men, including Balfour and himself, when the house got on fire over their heads. Talk so interesting that dinner went on, though Cust was obliged to absent himself once for a few minutes. Perfection of menservants who offered bath-towels with the port to protect from firemen's water coming through ceiling. Talk to accompaniment of engine throbs, swishing, tramping, etc. Guests obliged to move table further up room out of puddles. Dinner lasted till midnight in dining-room, when they went to drawing-room to view the place gutted. One of the finest social recitals I have ever heard.

Saturday, March 7th. Les Sablons.

Je me plais infiniment dans ce pays. A walk yesterday afternoon, 5 miles in the rain in the forest, after a day spent in writing a feeble-forcible article on Wells's *New Worlds for Old* for the *New Age*. A superb book this.

Six miles this morning in the forest, in fitful sunshine. When I looked about me in the forest I wondered that I could have endured 3 months in a city. Large spaces of sky. River rapid, and in flood, isolating many trees. Excellent food; attentive simple-minded cook. Grocer's wife had a baby. Local youths drawing their conscription numbers. News of a Freemasons' banquet, and of failure of a girls' school. Such are the events. I have time to think of writing another poem—subject in my head for just a year. I resume the piano, read newspapers more leisurely, and get excited about posts and about the sins of omission of local tradesmen.

Monday, March 9th.

Calvocoressi, upon my saying that *La Terre Qui Meurt,* though mediocre, was sincere, replied that Bazin had not struck him as a sincere man but rather as a *sinistre fumiste.* He instanced that at Rodaconache's when the hostess said to him, *"Prenez donc ce fauteuil,"* he had responded, *"Non—merci, j'en ai un ailleurs."* A trifle, but it does seem rather bad.

Today I began to prepare for taking up again *The Old Wives' Tale.* It seemed to come quite easily. Two hours at it in the forest.

---

[1] H. J. C. Cust, member of Parliament and editor of the *Pall Mall Gazette.*

Thursday, March 12th.

I have tried for two days to find rhythms for two poems that I found ideas for—one elegiac and the other Aristophanic, and can't.

I have read through first part of *Old Wives' Tale,* and am deeply persuaded of its excellence. *Aussi ai-je pris mes dispositions pour commencer la deuxième partie samedi.* The ideas have come quite easily.

Today I had a notion for a more or less regular column of literary notes—title, *Books and Persons*—for the *New Age,* and I wrote and sent off the first column at once. I began to work this morning in bed at 6 A.M.

Yesterday I cycled in showers and through mud to Fontainebleau to meet the architect at the new house. Found it damp, but the work more advanced than I expected.

Been reading Lord Acton. I am driven to the conclusion that his essays are too learned in their allusiveness for a plain man. I should say that for a man who specialized in the history of the world during the last 2,500 years they would make quite first-class reading.

Wednesday, March 18th.

In two hours of working this morning (1,600 words) I absolutely exhausted myself, so that after lunch I was so *fichu* that I scarcely knew what to do. In 3 days 4,000 words of *Old Wives' Tale,* 2 articles, some verse, and general scheme of long article on London theatrical situation. Also ideas for a big play about journalism for the Stage Society, designed to thrill London. Marguerite came back last night from two days in Paris, and brought two books—new, French, fresh as fruit. Astonishing the pleasure of merely contemplating them as they lay on the table. I must really, once settled in Fontainebleau, resume the good habit of buying a book a day.

Worried about the finances of Fontainebleau lately. Still, I kept myself in hand very well until the moment arrived last night for me to receive a crucial letter from Pinker. It was handed to me in the dark street. I had some difficulty in not stopping to read it under a gas lamp. I read it at the station. All right. No mistake, the constant practice of M. Aurelius and Epictetus has had its gradual effect on me. Have never worked better than these last days. Lovely weather, but chilly. Chilblains on hands. Immense pleasure, pretty nearly ecstatic sometimes, in looking at the country, in being *in* it, particularly by the Seine and in the forest. I said to myself the other morning that the early savage used to prowl about from his cave like that, and that I might almost meet one in that forest; whereupon it occurred to me that I was exactly the early savage over again, prowling round his cave, with the same sniffing sensations of instinctive joy in nature. Very curious, this getting down to the bedrock.

Reading continues to be unsatisfactory. No work of *longue haleine* to read. Can't begin till we are installed in Fontainebleau. Also I can't stick to the piano: not enough music here; nothing but Chopin's mazurkas and preludes, and Mozart's sonatas. Quite possible to play these till they give an effect of tedious beauty. Thus, though enormously productive, I have time on my hands, even with journeys to Fontainebleau and reading 6 newspapers a day.

Last week I began a column of book gossip for the *New Age*. Pleasure in making it *rosse*. Writing under a pseudonym, I seemed to think that as a matter of fact it must be *rosse*. Strange! This week's was better than last.

Thursday, March 19th.

I thought this evening that if only I was installed definitely at Fontainebleau I should be perfectly happy. Difficult to realize that even there something (undiscoverable) would still be lacking, and that I cannot ever be happier than I am now and here—in perfect working order and in good health and with my wits.

I have never been in better creative form than I am today. A complete scene of the novel (1,700 words) this morning in 2½ hours, and 1,000 words of an article on the theatre before dinner. Beautiful cold weather. Four miles in the forest this morning; two miles' stroll this afternoon. I want more books here, not to read, but merely to see them around me. I read an extract from Brunetière's criticism in the *Deux Mondes* of *Une Vie*—cold, unappreciative, very niggard in even modified praise. This made me more content with some of the reviews of my "big" books. I suppose that some day a collected edition of *my* novels will be issued—similar to that of Maupassant's now appearing. I hope that when it does I shall be neither dead nor in a madhouse.

Monday, March 23rd.

Been reading *Une Vie,* after I suppose about 10 or 12 years at least. Rather disappointed, though it held me. I don't think, e.g. that Tante Lison is very good, and the avarice of Julien is not managed with much originality. Also a general air *terne,* as though lacking in liveliness, as though the book were rather self-conscious. However, I am only halfway through it. I don't like *L'Humble Vérité* on the title page. Seems a bit affected. This never struck me before.

Much more pleased than I was with Lord Acton. The two essays on the history of freedom were not good specimens. He has a pretty wit in biographical stuff, and does Buckle to death with fine youthful ferocious cruelty. His learned allusiveness is assuredly sometimes *voulu.* If it isn't it shows a strange lack of imagination. Altogether, jolly good. It is a pleasure to be in such company, though often one is unable to keep up with the allusiveness. As a display of learning—dazzling. Even in science and philosophy he is terrific.

Change of weather last night. Today, first day of spring. Twelve kilometres in forest. Through too much work I slept badly for several nights, which upset my digestion. Still my output is enormous. Pleasure in being in the country increases. Yet a certain dissatisfaction, an expectancy, behind the content. Probably this will always be there, wherever I am and whatever I am doing.

Tuesday, March 24th.

Arrival of 4 books today, ordered from the *Mercure de France,* nicely half-bound. Astonishing, how much simple and perfect joy can be bought for 15fr. 60c.! I don't buy half enough books. Fine walks in the forest. Sunshine. Warmth. Cutting new books. A good patch of my novel. Great fun in reading the account of the 200-million-franc *krach* by a financial swindler in all the papers today. Another slice of my article on London stage. Embroidery design for M. Thus my day.

Wednesday, March 25th.

The news of the triumph of beer in the Peckham election this morning really did depress me. I understood, momentarily, the feelings of the men who give up politics in disgust; and I also understood the immense obstinate faith of those who fight for Liberalism all their lives. It is the insincerity and the deliberate lying of the other side that staggers me. I read in the *Daily Mail* this morning that when the news of the triumph of beer got into the music-halls last night there were scenes of wild enthusiasm, and perfect strangers shook hands with one another.

However, I worked well all day.

Friday, March 27th.

I walked to Fontainebleau, and back, this morning, to see the house. Depressed to find no workmen in the house, but delighted by the effect of 3 days' gardening on the garden. As to depression, I was struck, on reading M. Aurelius this morning, at my childishness in being depressed and angry about the Peckham election. It takes years to learn to practise by instinct a principle which you intellectually realize. You simply forget it at the critical moment. Same with M. this evening, in discussing house-keeping. I was continually ignoring principles.

Saturday, March 28th.

Finished *Une Vie*. Disappointed. No novel affected me as much as this did when I first read it about 10 or 12 years ago. It made me sad for days. Now I find it *bâclé* in parts. Too much left out—and not left out on one guiding principle but on several. The stuff not sufficiently gathered up into dramatic groupings. Recital often too ambling. Rosalie at the close rather conventional; overdrawn into a *deus ex machina*. The book too short. Sometimes too full, sometimes too hasty. But of course good. The best thing in it is the sea excursion of Baron, Julien, and Jeanne before her marriage. Paul's letters home are invariably admirably done.

Received today copies of *The Statue*. I hope I have now done with sensational work.

Monday, March 30th.

Curious affair in the village yesterday. Owners of land bordering the forest have the right to catch such deer as they find on their land. Now is the season when deer stray, in search of young shoot. They stray about dawn. Villagers organize a sort of surprise for the deer. They arise before dawn and lie in wait. Yesterday morning 60 people caught 6 deer. The deer were killed in an open yard close to this house, and blood ran in gallons into and down the road. The 60 people drew lots for the best cuts, and one hears the monotonous calling of the numbers. One-tenth of a deer for each person. This morning I saw 4 *biches* and 3 *cerfs* slowly cross the road in the forest, about 100 yards behind me.

Yesterday I finished the 5,000-word supplementary instalment for *Helen with the High Hand*,[1] begun on Saturday afternoon, and I posted it to Pinker this morning. Very proud of my extraordinary industry and efficiency at the present moment. Over 100,000 good words written in the first quarter of this year.

I tried yesterday and today to comprehend a résumé of the metaphysics of Professor Bergson in the current *Mercure de France,* and simply couldn't. Not the first time I have failed to interest myself in metaphysics. History and general philosophy much more in my line.

Wednesday, April 1st.

Decided that I really must confine reading newspapers to odd moments, and read every day some part of a serious work of instruction, and also some verse. So yesterday and today I swallowed the whole of Hayes's *Secret of Herbart.* Now I understand what Herbartianism is. Hayes too dithyrambic and formless. Nevertheless he communicates his enthusiasm.

Acton improves the more I read. I *enjoy* that learned company. It is like the *Athenaeum en grande tenue.* Stendhal interests me the most. What an example of a man *qui se fout du style littéraire!* Why trouble to write well?

Yesterday and today I drafted the whole of the play *The Snake-Charmer,* 1 act.

Eyesight troubling me again—due to careful (not small) writing of my novel.

I expect I am as happy now as I can be. I have learnt a lot, and am learning.

Friday, April 3rd.

Easily influenced! In reading Léautaud's Preface to the *Plus Belles Pages de Stendhal,* I found him defending Stendhal's hastinesses of style; never going back etc., "getting the stuff down" (as I say) without affectations or pose; reading a few pages of the Code to get himself into the

---

[1] Published in March, 1910.

"tone" of plain straightforward writing. Now I could quite see the weakness of the argument, and I knew the clumsiness of Paul Léautaud's own style. Yet so influenced by what he says that I at once began to do my novel more *currente calamo!* Sentences without verbs, etc. See chapters in Part II, birth of baby and kids' party, etc. Yesterday I wrote 1,700 words in 2½ hours. Stendhal attracts me more and more.

Today received Tauchnitz Swinburne. I came across *England: an Ode.* I would not write a thing called *England: an Ode.* This patriotism seems so cheap and conceited. I would as soon write *Burslem: an Ode* or *The Bennetts: an Ode.* I would treat such a theme ironically, or realistically. But loud, sounding praise, ecstasy—no.

Every morning just now I say to myself: *Today,* not tomorrow, is the day you have to live, to be happy in. Just as complete materials for being happy today as you ever will have. Live as though this day your last of joy. "How obvious, if thought about"—yet it is just what we forget. Sheer M. Aurelius, of course.

Each day, thrice, I expect romantically interesting, fate-making letters. Always disappointed. Astonishing how I have kept this up for years.

Eyesight going wrong again. Ought to go to an optician at once. But can't put myself out to go to Paris, hate the idea of explaining to an optician, etc. Yet I know I run risks. Yesterday I decided to go, and felt easier; today my eyes are better and I put it off.

Sunday, April 5th.

I finished this morning at 8.30 A.M. the *Snake Charmer,* melodrama in one act.[1] I have no real expectation of its ever being played. I make £25 out of it, down, and that is all I am sure of.

Habit of work is growing on me. I could get into the way of going to my desk as a man goes to whiskey, or rather to chloral. Now that I have finished all my odd jobs and have nothing to do but 10,000 words of novel a week and two articles a week, I feel quite lost, and at once begin to think, without effort, of ideas for a new novel. My instinct is to multiply books and articles and plays. I constantly gloat over the number of words I have written in a given period.

All I want now is about 5,000 francs extra to fix us in the Fontainebleau house.

---

[1] Intended for a music-hall sketch.

Monday, April 6th.

In the Victorian *History of Staffs,* the political section, by W. H. R. Curtter, which I have read all through, struck me as very much lacking in distinction. The chief things that I gathered from it were (1) the primitiveness of politics up to the Revolution, (2) the immense power of big families, (3) the fact that politics were chiefly a game between them and the King, (4) that the origin of the Staffordshire knot seems to be unknown. I shall now read the economic section.

Finished another sub-section of *Old Wives' Tale* this morning.

Seine like a sea.

April 7th.

Reading Leonard Merrick's *The Actor-Manager.* Decidedly good. Very good. Merrick is at his best in scenes between men and women. The relations between Blanche and Oliphant are perfect. On the other hand her parents (especially the father) are purely conventional figures, and the father is handled with brutality. A Dickensy feeling here and there which makes you feel uneasy. He tries too hard to avoid sentimentality, and doesn't always succeed.

Forest. Roar of wind in branches above while uncannily calm in shelter below.

Thursday, April 9th.

Finished *The Actor-Manager* in 24 hours. This is praise of it. The interest keeps up, but the book ends abruptly, and unreasonably, long before the story is finished. A good book, but rather monotonous in colour and movement, and practically no backgrounds in it at all. As for scenic effects, whether of town or country—scarcely an attempt. It is excellent so far as it goes; but it lacks. It lacks the romantic feeling or summat.

A great spring day today. Also yesterday. I walked to F'bleau and back yesterday morning; and wrote 2,000 words of novel in the afternoon. This afternoon we had tea in the garden—first reflection of the year outside.

Sunday, April 12th.

Ill Friday and Saturday. Migraine. Recovering today, and this evening began to think of Part III of Book II of *Old Wives' Tale.* Last night I had news of settlement of all questions which might lead to financial worry. Therefore quite free in mind as to this for a long time to come. I *felt* free.

Yet today, somewhat depressed, entirely without cause, save physical fatigue after indisposition. This shows how "the state of mild worry" is a habit, even with professed philosophers.

Good Friday, April 17th.

On Wednesday we went to Paris to prepare for the removing. Yesterday I went twice to the Foire du Jambon, and bought a few frames and two tiny coloured panels. Returned home in crowded 5.15 exhausted. Particularly M. Perhaps for the first time she felt that the country was better than the town. This morning I went over to the house, on foot. M. came by train and had her first sight of the house. Ordeal passed off very well, as everything was in order. This afternoon I wrote a *T.P.W.* article. No mistake, my control over my brain steadily increases.

Wednesday, April 29th.

On Thursday last, the twenty-third, we moved into our new house, Villa des Néfliers, Avon. By Monday morning we were sufficiently straight for me to resume my novel.

Ullman came down yesterday, fresh from U.S.A. I said: "What is your general impression? Is the U.S. a good place to get away from?" He said: "On the whole, yes. But for a visit, I am sure it would interest you enormously." He said that I could form no idea of the amount of drinking that went on there. I said I could, as I had already heard a good deal about it. He said, "No, you can't." He stuck to it, though I tried to treat the statement as an exaggeration, that in the principal clubs everybody got fuddled every night.

Noticed in myself: A distinct feeling of jealousy on reading yesterday and today accounts of another very successful production of a play by Somerset Maugham—the third now running.[1] Also, in reading an enthusiastic account of a new novelist in the *Daily News* today, I looked eagerly for any sign to show that he was not after all a really first-class artist. It relieved me to find that his principal character was somewhat conventional, etc. Curious!

---

[1] *Jack Straw*, Vaudeville; *Mrs. Dot*, Comedy; *Lady Frederick*, Court.

Saturday, May 2nd.

Today I finished the death of Samuel Povey in *The Old Wives' Tale.* Thought it perhaps a shade too stiff, too severe, as a narrative; no little dodges to divert the reader on his way. The fact is: I have been influenced by Beyle's scorn of ornament and device.

I haven't yet arranged my days here. I am doing no reading, no fine writing, no disciplinary thought of any kind. It is true that I still spend about two hours a day in working at the arrangement of the house, but then I get up at 6.30, and before 8 I have had my tea and read newspapers and correspondence. I am still hoping to keep this journal more fully; but I shall never do it in this format, which is too small. I dream of a folio double-column page, and I will realize that as soon as I have finished the present volume, if I can find a good paper that is not too opaque. That is the sole difficulty.

We both enjoy ourselves tremendously here. I take a pleasure that may be positively called "keen" in walking across the park, getting a shave in a picturesque talkative barber's shop, and then strolling about the town. Our surroundings are certainly almost ideal; and the weather now is ditto. The fruit trees are in blossom. Lilac and peonies are coming. I startled a lizard yesterday in the forest. And there is a general cloak of thin green on the branches. We have tea in the kiosk, and eat our other meals with the door open. Today I had to close the *persiennes* of my study against sun and heat. And this month I shall be 41!

Monday, May 4th.

These are the things that give me the liveliest pleasure among the little things of weekly life; opening and glancing through the *Athenæum* and the *Nation* on Monday mornings, especially the advertisements of new books; walking in the park and in the town in the morning when everything is fresh; eating my lunch; drinking tea; and reading after I am in bed. The mischief as regards the last is that I always get sleepy too soon. I finished my *T.P.* article at 9 A.M. this morning, and then strolled about town and forest, finding and arranging ideas for next chapter of *Old Wives' Tale.* But I also found a most charming *brocanteur,* with lovely Empire *guéridons,* for sale at a reasonable price.

This afternoon I received a letter from a girl, *apropos* of *T.P.* articles, chiefly recounting how she had tried and failed to commit suicide, and analyzing her feelings towards a stronger individuality with whom she lived, and asking me, *inter alia,* to write an article on free love. Quite a document, which may be useful.

Monday, May 11th.

Since Tuesday last I have written an average of over 2,000 words a day, including 12,500 words of novel. I finished the second part this afternoon at 6.15, and was *assez ému.* This makes half of the book, exactly 100,000 words done. I had a subdued bilious attack practically all the time since Tuesday, but just managed to keep it within bounds. With all this I naturally shirked journalizing. I must not forget that I also corrected, in this time, more than 250 printed pages of proofs. I had 3 books to correct at once: *Buried Alive, How to Live on Twenty-four Hours a Day,* and *Helen with the High Hand.*

Thursday, May 14th. Paris.

We went to Paris on Tuesday morn. I couldn't get used to the town. Felt as if I had been dragged out of my groove and resented it. But of course the weather was awful. Yesterday morning had *petit déjeuner* at the Café de la Régence, as 10 years ago when I first came to Paris. And I enjoyed it just as much, perhaps more, except the newspapers, which had lost their old romance. I should think so indeed, seeing what I know of them!

I took measures, getting addresses etc., to recommence, modestly, my career as a book collector. I bought *L'Intermédiare* and got catalogues, which gave me a keen pleasure. Today I meant to plan out my average day as I mean to live it here; but I have not done so. For I am now "settled down" definitely, and must arrange my life. One of my notions is to study French more methodically; my knowledge of it does not improve fast enough; not even as fast as my accent—and that is not saying much.

Sunday, May 17th.

At last I have begun to receive catalogues from second-hand book-sellers in Paris. I ordered 3 cheap books this afternoon, to make a commencement. This afternoon M., Emily, and I went for a walk in the forest. Many people. A too sophisticated air. At the Caverne Augas a man

with candles, on the make. Beautiful paths and glimpses and set panoramas, but unpleasing because part of a set show. Then sudden arrival
on the Route Nationale 5 bis. Autos struggling up it, noisily, all the time,
in a faint cloud of dust. Bicyclists, chiefly walking. General Sundayish.
Something that rouses always the exclusive aristocrat in one. M. getting
tired, and more tired, and assuring herself by questions that I am taking
the nearest way home. Then the arrival, amidst forced cheerfulness, and
a realization that one's feet ache. I ran upstairs to read catalogues. The
first languors of summer sunsets. House overrun with ants. Slight dis-
quiet on account of this plague of ants. New carpets arrived this morning,
re-arousing our pride in our toy house. I forewent my afternoon sleep
in order finally to arrange the second spare bedroom.

Monday, May 18th.

Lately I haven't been reading Marcus Aurelius, or anything in that
line, nor thinking about that sort of thing. No meditation. But I have
written week by week articles that have made a stir in *T.P.'s W.*, explaining just how people ought to live.

For some weeks I have been occupied with the proofs of 3 books:
Helen with the High Hand (*The Miser's Niece*), *How to Live on
Twenty-four Hours a Day,* and *Buried Alive.* Tonight I finished the last
of these damnable nuisances. Today I began seriously to construct Part
III—Paris—of *The Old Wives' Tale,* and got on pretty well, in spite of a
headache.

Wednesday, May 20th.

I wrote a complete short story, *The Tight Hand,* 2,300 words. A good
idea, rather spoilt; funny, really humorous, but not enough construction
to it, and the effect rather anticipated. But I couldn't do it again. With
me, the rough has to go with the smooth. I know I have been right in
always refusing to do anything twice over, or to alter anything once done.
M. was in Paris. I had finished at 3 P.M.

After tea I sought out all the books I have acquired during the year,
and ranged them apart. At the end of the year I shall visually know
what I have done in the way of book-getting. I then had to decide what
I should read, of heavy stuff, and I settled on Lewes's *History of Philosophy.* Mme. B—— came. Speaking of her cat, she said: "I give him

everything except liberty. I can't give him that because I haven't got it."

Friday, May 22nd.

Learnt this afternoon that we are cut off from telegraphic communication with Paris; yesterday's storm blew down 2 kilometres of telegraph poles on the other side of Melun. Not a word about these disasters in the Continental *Daily Mail,* of course. It was full of its third anniversary and of the horrible agonies of a man in U.S.A. who died slowly of hydrophobia.

Saturday, May 23rd.

Today I seemed to get a little nearer the state of mind and the mode of life that I have aimed at. I finished the story *The Glimpse* for the Christmas number of *Black and White* (much too good, too spiritual). It gave me a headache. In the afternoon I continued reading Lewes's *History of Philosophy,* which I have undertaken in all its bigness.

While reading it I was seized again with the idea of learning Latin decently; it was so strong that I could scarcely keep my attention on the book. Another example of the undiscipline of the brain.

Yet I have gradually got my brain far better under control than most people. Always haunted by dissatisfaction at the discrepancy between reason and conduct! No reason why conduct should not conform to the ideas of reason, except inefficient control of the brain. This that I am always preaching, and with a success of popular interest too, I cannot perfectly practise. It is the clumsiness of my living that disgusts me. The rough carpentry instead of fine cabinetry. The unnecessary friction. The constant slight inattention to my own rules. I could be a marvel to others and to myself if only I practised more sincerely. Half an hour in the morning in complete concentration on the living-through of the day, and I should work wonders! But this all-important concentration is continually interrupted—interruptions which weaken it; sometimes deliberately abandoned for concentration on matters of admittedly inferior importance! Strange! One can only stick to it.

It is humiliating that I cannot get through one single day without wounding or lightly abrading the sensibility of others, without wasting time and brain-power on thoughts that I do not desire to think, without yielding to appetites that I despise! I am so wrapped up in myself that I, if any one, ought to succeed in a relative self-perfection. I aim at as much, from love of perfection and scorn of inefficiency as for my own happiness. I honestly think I care quite as much for other people's happiness as for my own; and that is not saying much for my love of my own happiness. Love of justice, more than outraged sensibility at the spectacle of suffering and cruelty, prompts me to support social reforms. I can and do look at suffering with scientific (artistic) coldness. I do not care. I am above it. But I want to hasten justice, for its own sake. I think this is fairly sincere; perhaps not quite. I don't think I scorn people; I have none of that scorn of inferior people (i.e. of the vast majority of people) which is seen in many great men. I think my view is greater than theirs. Clumsiness in living is what I scorn: systems, not people. And even systems I can excuse and justify to myelf. No, my leading sentiment is my own real superiority, not the inferiority of others. It depends on how you look at it.

Monday, May 25th.

It occurred to me, for the first time I do believe, that women, when very intimate, have coolnesses and difficulties just as men do and perhaps more. I had always unthinkingly assumed that women, on such terms, always understood each other and held together perfectly. I can see the origin of my error, dimly; it has something to do with the idea of women's solidifying themselves together in a little group as distinguished from the whole male sex, of their understanding each other so much better than any man could understand them that they understand and sympathize with each other to absolute perfection. Curious misconception, but natural.

I see that at bottom, I have an intellectual scorn, or the scorn of an intellectual man, for all sexual-physical manifestations. They seem childish to me, unnecessary symptoms and symbols of a spiritual phenomenon. (Yet few Englishmen could be more perversely curious and adventurous than I am in just those manifestations.) I can feel myself despising them at the very moment of deriving satisfaction from them, as if I were playing at being a child. And even as regards spiritual affection, I do not like to think that I am dependent spiritually, to even a slight degree, on any one. I do not like to think that I am not absolutely complete and sufficient in myself to myself. I could not ask for a caress, except as a matter of form, and to save the *amour-propre* of her who I knew was anxious to confer it.

Two hours' walk in the rain in the forest this after-tea, when ideas for my play, my novel, and a story, *The Cat and Cupid,* simply bubbled up out of me.

Tuesday, May 26th.

It must be very difficult, I think, to be really generous, i.e. to give something which you need. I doubt whether in this strict sense I have ever been really generous in all my life. I felt it this afternoon, in talking with E., when it was a question of giving £20 before I had heard definitely from my architect that the landlord at Paris had undertaken to refund my deposit. I might really want that £20, and though I decided at once to give it, I gave it not from a spontaneous instinct of generosity, but unwillingly (within myself), and in obedience to my ideas of rightness and propriety. Something forced me to give it. This is not generosity.

As at meals I sat between E., in tears and full of disasters, and Mme. Bergeret, an old woman, untidy, *radoteuse, maniaque,* though witty sometimes, and M. away in Paris, the unpleasant, empty, unsatisfying greyness of existence weighed on me. I *en voulait* against E. for being unfortunate, and against Mme. B. for being old and *maniaque,* and I wanted to be surrounded by youth, beauty, and worldly success. Yet only 4 hours previously I had been preaching to myself that it was my Reason's business to manufacture my happiness out of the raw material of no matter what environment I found myself in.

I have now added to my daily affairs a little systematic study of French, a little miscellaneous reading, and a little odd writing work, which for the moment is to take the shape of translating Verlaine. So, after being here over a month, I have at last got into my desired routine, completely.

This morning I read through Part I of novel, and thought it was devilish good. Tomorrow I begin Part III.

May 27th.

My birthday. 41. I read some of the memoirs of Boston [1] today. Of

---

[1] *A General Account of My Life.* Thomas Boston (1677–1732) was a Scottish divine and theological writer. His book was republished in 1908.

course morbidly religious, but very well written. I can conceive that the average of writing at the end of the seventeenth century was higher than it is today.

Friday, May 29th.

Just to note what the Bal des Quat'z Arts was in 1908. Calvocoressi went to this year's ball, being officially invited as a director of the Russian opera. He said that there were a large number of women there absolutely naked, and many men who wore nothing better than a ceinture of bones which concealed nothing. Calvo said that on leaving at 4 A.M., he saw a naked woman calmly standing outside in the street, smoking a cigarette, surrounded by a crowd of about 200 people. He said he had heard that afterwards a procession of nudities was formed and went down the Champs Elysées. The ball was held at the "Bowling Palace" (or some such hall) at Neuilly, so as to be "out of bounds" of the City.

He took me yesterday afternoon to make the acquaintance of the Godebskis,[1] at Valvin. Husband, wife, 2 small kids. Poles. Among the most charming people I have ever met. Purely artistic. Godebski once owned and edited a little review. Looks like a Jew but is not one. I saw on a table a copy of Mallarmé's *Divagations,* with the *envoi* from the author *A son vieil ami, Godebski.* Not interested in anything but artistic manifestations. I said I had gas and they hadn't. Godebski said he didn't like gas lamps. I said, "For cooking." "Yes," he said, carelessly, "but with alcohol and oil they can manage." Didn't care a damn about inconveniences. A whole crowd of artistic youth there; various French accents. A picturesque, inconvenient house, full of good and bad furniture in various styles. A large attic, with rafters, formed the salon; a good grand piano in it. Déodat de Séverac played his new suite. He seemed a very simple sincere person, especially in his ingenuous explanations of his music: *"J'ai voulu évoquer. J'ai voulu évoquer,"* again and again. Curious: everybody was enthusiastic about the inventive fancy shown in knockabout turns on English music-halls. By chance this was all they found on this occasion to praise about England. But Mme. Godebski said to me, "I love the English language and everything English."

I worked well at *Old Wives' Tale* yesterday, but indifferently today.

---

[1] Cepa Godebski became an intimate friend of Arnold Bennett. He is a painter of considerable repute in Paris.

I lack male society. A monotonous effect. Also the gardener spent too much money on stocking the garden. So that tonight I felt as if I wanted a change rather acutely.

Tuesday, June 2nd.

Gradually got involved in one of my periodic crises of work, from which I emerged last night, having written the first chapter of Part III of *Old Wives' Tale*, a 4,300-word story (*Cat and Cupid*), and 2 articles. Considerable inconvenience from sleeplessness.

Wednesday, June 3rd.

Paris yesterday, upon Calvo's invitation, to see *Boris Godounoff* at the opera. Very fine. Especially chorus and general completeness of production. Impression left of the barbaric quality of Russia; and its intense earnestness in art also. As to the composition, assuredly great. No close construction in it, its construction must certainly have been a matter of haphazard—I don't care what any one says to the contrary; made one feel the unimportance of great skill in construction. Look at the haphazard way in which all Goethe's things were constructed. Uncanny effect of seeing suddenly a masterpiece of which one had scarcely heard and of which one knew nothing, and yet which was written in 1874 or published then.

I went "behind" afterwards with Calvo. After all, the romance of the organization of these affairs interests me quite as much as the art work. Vast stage. Not well *agencé*. I went to see the *foyer de la danse;* got it lighted up specially for me. Most disappointing. Quite small, with the end wall one vast mirror. Piffling, compared to its traditions. I should say not more than 30 feet long. Sloping floor: curious, the effect of the rail put in front of the seats, against the walls. Of course it is for the *danseuses* to hold on to while they practise their postures. But it seems as if it was to keep the *abonné* admirers from touching the girls' flesh. Similar effect to that of the *grilles* behind which sit Arab whores in Algeria. Eminently suitable to the character of the room.

Chaliapine [1] was great and profound. Calvo introduced us afterwards, on the stage. I hate these introductions, but I was glad to go through the

---

[1] Fedor Chaliapine, the basso, first sang in Paris in 1907.

tedium of this one. A very tall man, with a noble bearing and a fine face. He is undoubtedly a sublime artist.

Much wandering about behind scenes after the performance. Inexpressibly tedious. The Calvos and we had drinks on the *terrasse* of Julien's. I was too exhausted to be intelligent. Bedroom in the hotel where every noise could be heard. Impossible to sleep. When I heard an alarm-clock go off in the midst of these multitudinous sounds, that struck me as that rare thing, a really *humorous phenomenon.*

I was out at 8 A.M. today. Certainly what interests me is organization. Outside the Magasins du Louvre, the despatch of thousands of parcels in dozens of vans was in full swing. A great effect. When I returned, in less than an hour, everything had gone. At 8.25 the interior of the shop was in going order, and well sprinkled with customers. The employés had a strange *un*-tired air.

I had the good luck to get a first ed. of Becque's *Les Corbeaux* at Stock's for 4 fr. Tresse was the original publisher. They said it was their last copy. It ought to be fairly rare.

I also bought, what I had been wanting for some weeks, Forel's *La Question Sexuelle*. Also an album of modes, 1830–1870, *extrêmement intéressant,* and most useful at this exact moment for *Old Wives' Tale.*

Wednesday, June 10th.

I have now begun upon a modest but regular course of book-buying, and have worked up quite a pleasure in reading catalogues. I read through Gougy's catalogue of more than 100 pages on Sunday. Also I have got into the way of expecting books to arrive; when I have ordered a book I am impatient till it comes, and decidedly disappointed if it doesn't come.

Further I am making a visitation of my books, and making discoveries of good things that I had absolutely forgotten. Thus today, having a bad headache, I found Mérimée's *Portraits* and read the account of Beyle.[1] Good. Also Freeman's primer of the history of Europe,[2] which I have possessed for years, and often meant to open, but never have done till today. I found I had a good Elzevir Livy: it must be one of the smallest folios ever printed. Cause of headache mysterious. Probably a slight touch

---

[1] *Portraits Historiques et Littéraires* contains an essay on "Henri Beyle (Stendhal)."
[2] *A General Sketch of European History,* 1872.

of sun. I walked in the sun yesterday afternoon, and I climbed into cherry-trees to gather cherries in the sun. No work this morning.

Bought a fine fourth edition of *Clarissa Harlow,* and a most respectable *édition très estimée* of Pascal.

Godebski and his wife and Maurice Ravel [1] and a nameless boy of about 20 came yesterday, very late, for tea. My previous very agreeable impression of the Godebskis was confirmed. Also I reflected that I liked the company of boys of 20, and that I ought to cultivate it.

Sunday, June 14th.

Have had two books published lately—*Buried Alive,* Wednesday, June 3, and *How to Live on Twenty-four Hours a Day.* I don't know the date on which this was published officially, but within the last day or two.

I gave Chapman and Hall a great idea for advertising *Buried Alive:* namely, to place a sandwichman outside Mudie's. The man was there at 9 A.M. on the third. At 10.30 Mudie's had sent down a message to C. and H. to say that if the man was not withdrawn they would send back what copies of the book they had already bought and ban the book entirely. So Waugh [2] made the man promenade up and down Oxford Street instead. Autocratic.

June 26th.

In my fifteenth "human machine" article in *T.P.'s Weekly,* I wrote: "Meat may go up in price—it has done—but books won't. Admission to picture galleries and concerts and so forth will remain quite low. The views from Richmond Hill or Hindhead, or along Pall Mall at sunset, the smell of the earth, the taste of fruit and of kisses—these things are unaffected by the machinations of trusts and the hysteria of Stock Exchanges." The *Westminster Gazette* quoted this, and more, but it left out the words *"and of kisses."* Characteristic of the English newspaper!

Seriously disturbed by my novel. It is an immensely complicated undertaking. I took a day off yesterday and went to Paris with W.W.K., chiefly for the Gaston La Touche exhibition. Rotten. He is always occupied with the feeblest symbolistic satire upon sensualism. Apes for men.

---

[1] The composer.
[2] Arthur Waugh, managing director of Chapman and Hall for many years. His sons are the writers Alec and Evelyn Waugh.

Women dreaming of satyrs etc. But you see he really enjoys and admires the sensual spectacle. I could use up this show ironically in some descriptive passage very well. Regular life entirely upset by my novel.

Sunday, July 19th.

I don't know when I wrote the last entry.

I finished the third part of *The Old Wives' Tale* on Tuesday last. Everything else gave way before it, and I simply did nothing but that book. It meant the utter defeat of all other plans. I spent Wednesday in reading through the second part.

Tomorrow I shall begin to think about the fourth part of the novel. Reviews of *Buried Alive* and *Twenty-four Hours a Day* have been simply excellent. But I have heard nothing encouraging about the sales of either book.

Thursday, July 23rd.

We returned today from a 3 days' bicycling tour. Tuesday: Pithiviers, via Chapelle-la-Reine and Puiseaux. Yesterday: Château-Landon, via Beaumont. Today home, via Nemours. Total expenses 49 fr. 15 c. I made a lot of notes. I also made 5 sketches, which I am now trying to sell as illustrations for an article. We were immensely impressed by Château-Landon. On returning home it is always a damned nuisance to look through accumulated newspapers—especially reviews of novels, and to read summaries of the publishing season which make no reference to one's self.

Sunday, August 30th.

Finished *The Old Wives' Tale* at 11.30 A.M. today. 200,000 words. Now I can begin to keep this journal again.

Tuesday, October 6th.

At 2 A.M. on Thursday the first we arrived in Paris from Italy. We had 2½ days of fever in Paris. Though we did almost nothing I was excessively fatigued. I went to the Galeries Lafayette with Marguerite and had a few large, synthetic impressions about that. I was more than ever convinced of the unhappiness of the vast majority of the inhabitants of a large town—owing to overwork, too long work, and too little pay and leisure. I had more than ever the notion of a vast mass of stupidity and incompetence being exploited by a very small mass of cleverness, unjustly exploited. The glimpses of the advanced and mad luxury floating on that uneasy sea of dissatisfied labour grew more and more significant to me. I could have become obsessed by the essential wrongness of everything, had I not determined not to be so. These phenomena must be regarded in a scientific spirit, they must be regarded comparatively, or a complete dislocation of the mind might ensue.

We reached home on Saturday at 5.30, I in an advanced state of exhaustion, and depressed by fatigue (also by the defection of a servant—not that that caused me any inconvenience). I went out into the forest on Sunday morning to find ideas for an article, and except that the odour was much finer, it was just like the height of summer. Crowds of people, some movement of pleasure traffic, burning sunshine. This morning I walked for two hours in the park in search of my play, and I found a fairly complete scheme for the whole of it. Title to be, provisionally: *What the Public Wants: A Tragedy in Five Acts* [1]—really, of course, a satiric farce. I think I can now go ahead with it.

Monday, December 14th.

We left Fontainebleau and arrived at Dijon for dinner. Hôtel de Bourgogne. Excellent steam-heated room 7 francs. Otherwise hotel not too well kept. It rained from the time of our advent till nearly 9 A.M. the next morning. I walked out at night, and saw a chemist make me a *cachet* of pyramidon. Mystery of *cachets,* for me, is now for ever gone. Genuine effect, in the main street, of a town consisting chiefly of confectioners and gingerbread makers. Trams floating about rumblingly and ramblingly all the time. Witnessed an encounter between a young and attractive *grue* and a young man. They knew each other. After standing for a time under the glass marquise of the principal drapery shop, she shut up her own umbrella, and they went off together under his. I got as far as the portals of an "Alcazar" music-hall—all placards, and then came back to the hotel, and tried to read Huxley in bed. Couldn't.

It is only at night, when there is little of it, comparatively, that you appreciate how much light there is when there is supposed to be none.

---

[1] Produced at the Aldwych Theatre on May 2, 1909, and transferred to the Royalty three weeks later.

At 3 A.M. you can discover traces of it everywhere, and it has a very beautiful quality.

All very well to say that only a really strong nature can say "I was wrong," and that the inability to say it is a proof of weakness. Most people who say it say it impulsively, and are undoubtedly not only weak but capricious also in their judgments. It has got to be said very rarely, and with complete absence of theatricality.

Our train for Switzerland was the Paris-Simplon day express. Very English. Chiefly Englishwomen. Their lack of charm was astounding, absolutely astounding. And their aristocratic, self-absorbed voices made me laugh. The English consciousness of superiority is sublime in its profound instructiveness.

In the Jura it rained heavily all the time, and there was a lot of snow on the ground. Seventeen minutes' wait at Pontarlier. A town lost in the hills, and carpeted with sodden snow. A waiter came through the train, very briskly, taking orders for tea. After a few minutes he said he couldn't serve any more, as there would not be time. I heard two Englishwomen complaining to each other that one man was ridiculously insufficient to attend to all the train. Having no imagination, it did not occur to them to imagine that the presence of even one man, and a smart man, to serve tea in that hole for a few minutes each day was sufficient of a miracle. They would have liked a whole population to await there, ready to start into life and serve them when they happened to pass. The train went on. They still calmly deplored that they had been unable to get tea. Very wild scenery. An old castle on a crag. As fantastic as Doré and Walter Scott and close to the frontier. They never noticed it, but continued vaguely about tea. I now learnt that one of them had traipsed through the snow to the buffet and had found "quite a large restaurant," but nobody there, not even the unique man. This in a tone more calmly resigned than ever to the idiocy of foreigners. I can make an article out of this for the Manchester *Despatch*. Soon after the castle, we skirted the tiniest mountain village, all lit up with electric light. Observations to be made as to this, in defence of absence of electric light in England.

Vevey (quite dry—rain everywhere else). A different climate. Mild, *sec*. I bought a Swiss cigar, and we got into a tiny Swiss tram. Had the Swiss feeling. Feeling much intensified when, in the waiting-room of the funicular, we found a vast musical box, which I caused to play for 10 centimes. Really rather a good device, especially when you have 45 minutes to wait.

I was so anxious to see the panorama this morning (*Wednesday, 16 December*) that I slept badly. I thought it wonderful, but I was disappointed because it seemed so small. I had expected something much bigger. Well, it has been "growing on" me all day. I thought the highest mountains on the opposite side of the lake were about 3,000 or 4,000 feet high. I found the Dent du Midi was about 10,000 feet high. I thought this Dent was 8 or 10 miles off. I found it was 24 miles off (38 kilometres). My opinion of the panorama is going up every minute. I can understand that it is one of the finest in *Suisse*. Sloppy snow everywhere under foot. Not cold enough, they say. Below us, cloud effects on lake continually changing. Really the scene is enchantingly beautiful. We see Vevey as though from a balloon. At night its lights are fairy-like—I wish there was another word. Can't find one instantly.

Thursday, December 17th.

In the basement of this hotel, very dark with windows that look on a wall that supports the earth, is the laundry, where human beings work all day at washing linen. We live on the top of all that, admiring fine literature and the marvellous scenery. And today the cloud scenery, floating above the lake and below us, was especially marvellous.

The library I brought away with me consisted of 3 volumes of *Les Origines de la France Contemporaine, Notes sur Angleterre, Graindorge* [all by Taine], 2 volumes of Huxley's *Essays,* Andrew Lang's *Origins of Religion,* Lyall's *Asiatic Studies, The Ancient Wisdom, The Prelude* [Wordsworth], *Les Jeux Rustiques et Divins, La Vie de Henri Brulard* [Stendhal], Davies's *Nature Poems,* Moréas's *Paysages et Sentiments, Ainsi parla Zarathoustra* [Nietzsche], a volume of Plutarch, a volume of Montaigne, *L'Ile des Pingouins* [Anatole France], a volume of *Mémoires d'Outre-Tombe* [Chateaubriand], *King Lear, Le Hasard du Coin du Feu* [Crébillon *fils*], *Confessions of St. Augustine,* Baedeker's *Switzerland,* Pennell's *Normandy* (to imitate the sketches), Whitaker's *Almanack,* Roget's *Thesaurus,* Bellows's French-English dictionary, *La Guenille* by Charles Derennes, Tauchnitz selections from Swinburne,

Renée Mauperin [Goncourts], *Inferno, Maxims of La Rochefoucauld,* Michelin Guide, British Museum *Guide to Manuscripts.* Thirty-five volumes.

But the only books that I really do *mean* to read are *Les Origines, Confessions of St. Augustine,* and *Le Hasard du Coin du Feu.* The rest are simply brought in case I might want something. It is the surest way to avoid reading. And I should like to avoid reading for about a month. Today I began a story.

A youngish Englishman with his wife, and a boy of about 10. I saw a large red book on their table at dinner, and this intrigued me. I talked to the man after dinner. Indian civil service (anyhow, something in India). A brick-coloured face. Monotonous voice. Tall and thin. Takes *The Times.* Very cautious in his statements. Talking about India, he said the hotels were pretty bad, but not dear, and that travelling was not at all impossible. As to administration, he said that "we had been treating them too kindly, and they didn't understand it." Exactly, to a word, the phrase one hears and reads in novels etc. Still, when I said that we had no moral right in India at all, that it was simple cheek on our part, he quite agreed.

Monday, December 21st.

We *luged* today for the first time. It was pointed out to me that hat-pins were dangerous. A young Scotch girl offered to take me in tow after I had made one or two excursions myself. So I got behind her. "I'll take your legs," she said. And took them. No accidents.

Christmas Eve.

The Anglo-Indian recently described is a major in the army. I only learnt this tonight. It probably accounts for his excellent stupidity which inspires respect. His wife, at first very *rébarbative,* grows more likeable every day. Some of them began talking about suffragettes last night after I had said to the major, seeing him reading *The Times,* "So Christabel is out, it seems." [1] A Yorkshire young woman asked Mrs. Major if she was a sympathizer. "On the contrary," said Mrs. Major, "I am very much

---

[1] There had been an attempt on October 13 to "rush" the House of Commons, and a serious disturbance took place in Parliament Square. Mrs. Pankhurst and her daughter Christabel were arrested and sent to prison.

ashamed of them." The usual rot was talked. However, Mrs. Major said that she thought women ought to be on certain committees. The young Yorkshire lass said she thought woman's place was the home. (It is incredible how people still talk.) I then burst out, impatiently: "Yes, and what about the millions of them that have to leave home every day to earn a living? What about the mill girls, and the typists?" This quite unsettled them. They then agreed that unmarried women ought to have the vote. But their whole talk and all the phrases they used were too marvellously stupid.

There is something very offensive to me in the English temperament abroad. Conceit, primness, a profound unconscious consciousness of being superior and in the right. The major's female cousin and her two little children and a pretty governess came today, so that there were 7 at his table. The party had a frightfully English look. All 3 women pretty, though the mothers are getting on, and badly dressed. Yes, very antipathetic. Yet you must respect them. Mrs. Major irreproachable, and so splendid with the children afterwards. Marguerite said, of Englishwomen in the mass, abroad, "*Ça suinte l'ennui.*" It is so.

Xmas Day.

Xmas dinner. 40 people. Lights turned out for entry of blue-burning Xmas pudding. Admirable dinner.

December 31st.

Dance. Games. "God save the Queen," and varied songs at the hotel. "God save the Queen" (or King) in various languages. Servants watching eagerly at nothing from behind a curtained window.

I have never worked so hard as this year, and I have not earned less for several years. But I have done fewer silly things than usual.

I wrote *Buried Alive,* ¾ of *The Old Wives' Tale, What the Public Wants, The Human Machine, Literary Taste: How to Form It;* about half a dozen short stories, including *A Matador in the Five Towns;* over 60 newspaper articles.

Total words, 423,500.

1909

Friday, January 8th.

I wrote the first chapter of new humorous novel [1] (5,200 words) on Sunday and Monday. Spent Tuesday and Wednesday in bed with a consequent migraine. Was very feeble on Thursday, and managed to write a *New Age* article and a lot of correspondence, and to do a drawing for an illustrated article today.

After my row with "Claudius Clear" I find in today's *British Weekly* an apology from him, and a signed review by Professor John Adams [2] of *The Human Machine*—I think the first regular review of a book of mine that has ever appeared in the *B.W.* C.C. once based an article on *Fame and Fiction,* but it was not a review. It was merely an insolence.

Miss Sains told me that she had known Rhoda Broughton,[3] who had had sisters who didn't treat her properly, and that the ill-used sister in her early books was herself. Miss Sains had also met Mrs. Humphrey Ward.[4] "A charming woman. So nice. Always took two years over a novel. So particular. Always began by making a *lot* of extracts from other books, which she used in her own books. Her own books were *largely* made up of ideas collected from other books." In short the usual clumsy crude account of a writer by a person ignorant of composition, and yet giving a rough notion of the truth, unconsciously.

---

[1] *The Card,* called in America *Denry the Audacious.*
[2] Professor of Education at the University of London.
[3] A prolific novelist, author of *Not Wisely But Too Well,* etc.
[4] Gladstone praised her *Robert Elsmere* (on a postcard, a favourite means of correspondence with him), and its subsequent incredible success is often ascribed to that occurrence.

Saturday, January 9th.

Maiden, aged about 30. Self-conscious. Big nose and eyes, and big features generally. Badly dressed. What is characteristic about her is her pose in an arm-chair at night, needle-working. One arm always on chair arm. Looks intently at her work, with virginal expression, while others are talking. Then at intervals looks up suddenly; you can't see her eyes for the white gleam of her spectacles, and she seems to embrace the whole room, or perhaps the talker alone, in a wide, candid, ingenuous glance as of surprise, as if saying slowly, "What the hell *are* you talking about?"

A honeymoon pair came the other night. Across the dining-room they looked immensely distinguished. He might have been a brother of Rostand. Marked waist. Fine nose. White hands. She seemed mysterious in a da Vinci way. I made sure he was some sort of an artist. No. He proved to be in business. When we saw them close to in the little reading-room— intense vulgarity of gesture, movement, etc. He seemed more like a barber's assistant and she a *vendeuse mal élevée*. Long time since I have been so taken in. Interesting to watch how gestures effective at a distance (theatrical) grew vulgar close at hand.

I did 4 sketches and 1 water-colour today, and found all sorts of ideas for novel, easily.

Sunday, January 10th.

Miss Sains related stories of a young woman well known to her who had charge of a crêche of 30 infants, and amused herself one day by changing all their clothes so that at night they could not be identified, "and many of them never *were* identified," said Miss Sains. "I knew all her brothers and sisters too. She wanted to go into a sisterhood, and she did, for a month. The only thing she did there was one day she went into the laundry and taught all the laundry-maids to polka. She was *such* a merry girl," said Miss Sains simply.

Monday, January 11th.

Mme. Posfay was in the courtyard of the palace at the time of the murder of the King and Queen of Serbia, but knew nothing. "What are they throwing bolsters out of the windows for?" she asked. It was the bodies.

Thursday, January 14th.

A lake fish for dinner last night called *ombre*. It smelt bad, and I did not taste it; the smell was too much. M. said it tasted a little bad. I seemed to taste it in all the food afterwards. It smelt all over the dining-room, and I could distinctly feel the smell of it in my stomach this morning. I taxed the head waiter with it this morning, and by dint of assurances, he being an honest man, he convinced me that it was quite fresh. It is by some people considered a delicacy, and it costs 4 francs a kilo. But he said it scarcely ever suited English people, and he had formerly told the landlady that it was a mistake to serve. What we regarded as tainted is its natural fresh taste. The flesh is very soft. He said the fishermen caught it too young, would not give the fish a chance to mature.

A man about 50, thin-chested, with a bad cough low down in the chest. Face like the typically middle-aged English gentleman face in Du Maurier's *Punch* drawings. Big nose, wide melancholy eyes, and enormous drooping moustaches. He watched M. and me playing billiards for some time. Then began to smile sympathetically when we smiled. Then we asked him to play. He refused, in a thin, weak voice. Said it was a great pleasure to him to watch us play, and that we played much better than he did. (Spoke French well, with a German or Swiss-German accent.) Then he agreed to play. When he took up a cue I at once accused him, from his gestures, of being a good player. He said, no, positively. He only knew *la théorie*, a little, and could not play. We were much better. Certainly (he said) I was much *plus fort;* I could see better. He soon outplayed us easily. After he had made a *série:* "*Vous avez eu la bonté de marquer pour moi, monsieur?*" An exaggerated timid politeness, funny from his ferocious and vast moustache. He gave hints to M. with the same ritualistic deference. In the end he won handsomely, and thanked us handsomely, saying it was a *hasard, seulement,* and that he only knew a little of the *théorie*. I left the room. He said good night. Immediately afterwards he left the room to go to bed, and seeing me at a distance, from the foot of the stairs, called out again, "*Bon soir, monsieur.*" Quite abnormally timid and shy. It will be interesting to see what there is underneath this *couche*.

Monday, January 18th.

Miss Blenkinsop on American sleeping-cars: "A lot of student girls were in the same car with me. They all got into their beds about 8 P.M., wearing fancy jackets, and they sat up and ate candy. I was walking up and down, and every time I passed they implored me to have some candy, and they implored each other to try to persuade me. They were mostly named 'Sadie.' At 1 P.M. they ordered drinks round. They had been eating candy all the time. I was obliged to have a drink with them. At 5 the next morning they were all sitting up again and eating candy."

Magnificent weather since Saturday.

Sunday, January 24th.

Thursday—goose. Friday evening bilious attack. But it did not stop me from working. Yesterday I finished the first third of *Denry the Audacious*. And ideas still coming freely! Today it occurred to me to utilize my Jacob Tonson [1] column in the *New Age* for the material of a book on the subject of the modern novel, its future, its moral, etc. After arranging all my ideas for next chapter this morning, I arranged ideas for first chapter of this book on the novel this afternoon.

Arranged with Tauchnitz to abridge the *Old Wives' Tale* so that he can get it into two volumes. A damned nuisance, yet I secretly consider myself fortunate to get it in. I had begun to think the thing was off.

Letter from Waugh today to say that the book is still selling, and their own traveller anxious that no new book should appear till this has run its course. All very healthy. A fourth edition is now quite possible. I had not in the least hoped for this success. It alters the value of all my future books. Yet I was depressed all afternoon because I could not make a sketch. Another proof that public success is no guarantee whatever of happiness or even content. I think it makes no difference.

In becoming acquainted with people you uncover layer after layer. Using the word in my sense, one person may be the most *distinguished* of a crowd on the first layer, another on the second, and so on. Until after uncovering several layers, you may ultimately come to a person who, down below, is the most distinguished of all—on *that layer*. The

---

[1] Bennett borrowed the famous 17th century publisher's name as a pseudonym for some of his own writings.

final result may be quite unexpected. I suppose that the inmost layer is the most important, but each has its importance.

Wednesday, January 27th.

Finished today the fifth "deed" of *Denry the Audacious.* It is pretty good. Probably too good for a serial. Also received a copy of the third edition of *The Old Wives' Tale,* and began to cut passages of it so as to make it short enough for Tauchnitz. Not so difficult as I expected it to be, but nevertheless a desolating and unsatisfactory business. Arthur Waugh wrote me that it was "a sacrilege."

Although I now do more work, more regularly than ever I did, I feel tired more definitely and more consciously than I did 4 or 5 years ago. I remember when I was writing *Leonora* at the Hôtel du Quai Voltaire, I used to go out into the Rue de Rivoli (towards the end of the book) with a sensation as if the top of my head would come off. But I did not recognize it as fatigue, simply as the result of worry, a nuisance. I can now work hard all morning and I feel tired, and I know that if I kept on after lunch I should probably be ill. But by consciously refusing to think of my work, by vegetating, I can be sure that by tea-time I shall be restored, and can work again for a bit without letting myself in for a bilious attack. But I have to *ménager* myself.

On Monday and yesterday afternoons I wrote the first chapter of a book about novel-writing and the fiction-reading public, which will appear in pieces over Jacob Tonson's name. I was most enthusiastic over it. I calculate that in 20 weeks it will be done, and a striking book ready to be published. This is an extra. The notion probably came to me from my instinctive hatred of wasting newspaper articles. I hate to think that anything I write is bad enough, or fragmentary enough, to be lost for ever in the files of a paper.

I am writing a pretty good lot, but I am not doing much else. Not yet at the end of the second volume of *Les Origines*—in two months. No other reading, except newspapers as usual, and bits of Poe. Rather startled by the first-classness of some of Poe's lyrics, such as the *Haunted Palace.*

In weather, the season continues bad. Two days of fog or mist, then one day of splendid sunshine. And so on. No snow on the south face of the mountain. *In* the mountain, in the protected folds, large quantities of snow. I go walks there, and follow tracks made by an animal alone—I don't know what animal. When there is the least danger of slipping, I think, "If I fell and sprained my ankle it would probably mean my death." This is quite exciting, half pleasant, half unpleasant. When venturing up a steep slope to find a possible path, I think, "I ought not to do this." The great danger is certainly that of exposure after an accident.

I am always meaning to write character sketches of people in the hotel—as exercise—but I never do. The fact is that to write a 65,000-word book, full of novel incident, in two months, and a showy *travaillée* article once a week, leaves one with not much energy. The time-table has to be followed with exactitude, and it is *assez juste*.

A middle-aged Dutchman instructs me in billiards most evenings.

February 8th.

R——, a man fresh from Cambridge (Queen's College), said that religion was very strong there. Prayer-meetings etc. A group of 6 had prayed for him because he played poker. He said also that socialism was very strong in Cambridge, and referred to the *New Age* as something notoriously brilliant and powerful.

A neurasthenic in the hotel. Very tall, thin, aged about 24, rather elegant. I saw him on the morning after his arrival. He came down early to breakfast in pumps—a fairly mad thing to do. Then he was not seen again. Red-haired. *Fils de famille de Paris.* Wanted to bring the valet with him, but his parents wouldn't let him. Arrived here, couldn't bear to be alone in his room. Then imagined himself ill and had a professional nurse in. His mother was telegraphed for. She came last night, and was very cross. Said it was always the same when her son travelled alone. She was very angry about his having a nurse.

The *maître d'hotel* began telling me stories of neurasthenics. He said there was one at another hotel here who imagined that he could not bear any one on either side of him or above him or below him. So that he had to pay for 5 rooms.[1]

Tuesday, February 9th.

Keen frost and bright sunshine. I went to toboggan down a steep

---

[1] This is said to have been precisely Marcel Proust's invariable custom.

slope, but when it came to the point I was afraid and started halfway down, and rolled over. Afterwards I would not try from the top, though twice I climbed to the top meaning to do it. Curious. No danger, as snow is thick. But I had the *trac*.

Thursday, February 11th.

Books acquired: *Tono Bungay,* H.G.W.; *The Kiss,* Anton Chekhov; *The Black Monk,* Anton Chekhov.

Finished today the shortening of *The Old Wives' Tale* for Tauchnitz. I have cut out 30,000 words, or two-thirteenths. There was scarcely a line which I did not regret.

Snow. When it snows the temperature rises. Yet the women generally put on an extra shawl in the hotel, because the aspect outside is white. No arguing with them.

Friday, February 12th.

Girl with voluptuous laugh, short and frequent. Half Scotch, half English. Age 24. Very energetic, obstinate, and "slow in the uptake." Red cheeks. Good-looking. Athletic. Shy—or rather coy. Always the voluptuous laugh being heard, all over the hotel. A wanton laugh, most curious. Her voice also has a strange voluptuous quality. They say the Scotch women are *femmes de tempérament.* This one must be, extremely so. And her athleticism must be an instinctive *remède contre l'amour.* Manners and deportment quite irreproachable, save for this eternal, rippling, startling laugh. It becomes more and more an obsession. One waits to hear it.

Tuesday, February 16th.

Up in the woods. Long snow path. Greenish-brown-black colour of wood cut and uncut coming often in the distance, or rather flaming out with a spark or spot of ochreish raw wood—the end of a fresh-cut log. Immense amount of wood-cutting on the mountain-side. All the upward paths lead up to and stop at either a farm or a wood-cutting place. The paths seldom join each other. They are nearly all blind. But this morning in a snowstorm I found a path that led clear over the top of the mountain to the southern slope; a long way. It stopped at a wood-cutting, or diminished rather to a track of a dog's feet, which went under a hedge and reappeared on the other side. But the slope was too steep for me to follow. I could see Attalens. So I had to turn back. Clouds broke, and strong sunshine.

Yesterday I finished three-quarters of *Denry the Audacious*. I think that in book form I shall call it *The Card*. Good honest everyday work, vitiated by my constant thought of a magazine public.

Saturday, February 20th.

I was responding to Pauline Smith's [1] curiosity about the personalities of authors when Mrs. Smith began to talk about Kipling. She said he was greatly disliked in South Africa. Regarded as conceited and unapproachable. The officers of the Union Castle ships dreaded him, and prayed not to find themselves on the same ship as him. It seems that on one ship he had got all the information possible out of the officers, and had then, at the end of the voyage, reported them at headquarters for flirting with passengers—all except the chief engineer, an old Scotchman with whom he had been friendly. With this exception they were all called up to headquarters and reprimanded, and now they would have nothing to do with passengers. I dare say there is some "feeling" and some exaggeration in this, but Mrs. Smith was sure of the facts.

I got from the *New Age* new novels by John Galsworthy, Barry Pain, R. Le Gallienne, and Mrs. Nesbit. [2] Reminded me of reviewing days. Tedious. Disappointing, except the Barry Pain, which I could read. I couldn't *stick* the Galsworthy. I won't do any more of this quasi-reviewing.

I had a letter from Lee Matthews saying he could positively sell *What the Public Wants* to Hawtrey, [3] and possibly to Lena Ashwell; but that he had read it to Tree and supped with Tree, and that Tree could not see anything in it at all. My thoughts are now disturbed by theatrical matters.

Thursday, February 25th.

I went out yesterday afternoon. Strong northeast wind and very hard

---

[1] Arnold Bennett subsequently wrote a preface to her novel, *The Little Karoo.*
[2] Respectively: *Fraternity, The Gifted Family, Little Dinners with the Sphinx,* and *Daphne in Fitzroy Square.*
[3] He played Sir Charles Wogan on the production of the play at the Royalty Theatre, May, 1909.

frost. I had my face wrapped up, but after a mile I could not stand it any longer, and had to come home. It was a terrifying and very painful cold: the keenest I have been in.

Friday, February 26th.

Marguerite and Pauline Smith came back from Vevey today with particulars of a *maniaque* shop there, where, when you had bought an article, it was taken from you and a number given in exchange. You then, after purchasing all you wanted, paid at the desk, and then went to another part of the shop, where were a number of pigeon-holes numbered. Your articles were then taken out of the pigeon-holes corresponding to your numbers and wrapped up. The wrapping up could not begin till you had paid. At the wrapping-up place were a number of little brown paper bags containing pieces of string. Each bag had a different length of string. The packer chose a suitable length from the bag containing pieces only of that length. One can imagine the fussiness, indeed mania, of the proprietor, and hell of a time that the girls employed in it must have.

I found quite early this morning all the ideas for last chapter of novel. This afternoon I reviewed Barry Pain, Galsworthy, Le Gallienne, and Mrs. Nesbit for the *New Age*. Quite like old times. I fell at once in my old quiet habits of reviewing; but the stuff written was, I think, much better—certainly had more *souplesse*.

More and more struck by Chekhov, and more and more inclined to write a lot of very short stories in the same technique. As a fact, *The Death of Simon Fuge,* written long before I had read Chekhov, is in the same technique, and about as good. Though to say anything is as good as *Ward No. 6* in *The Black Monk* wants a bit of nerve.

Tuesday, March 2nd.

I finished *Denry* or *The Card* yesterday at 11 A.M. Began it on January 1, I think. 64,000 words. Stodgy, no real distinction of any sort, but well invented, and done up to the knocker, technically, right through.

Today we leave, at 2.19, from Vevey.

Monday, March 8th.

Paris. *Le Juif Polonais.*[1] Enormously *naïf* and simple. Quite interest-

---

[1] By Erckmann-Chatrian.

ing, as primitivism. There must be some quality in it, or it could not have lived so long. Guitry showing all his customary restraint and fineness. Quite different from Irving. But my impression remains that Irving's ecstasies of fright and remorse were pretty good too. Curious, on Friday, how Mme. M. talked enthusiastically about Guitry. But she always does, whenever he is mentioned. I mean curious that a *tout à fait petite bourgeoise* should so often have such right perceptions about art.

Dined with the D——s on Thursday. D. had had some business with the *commissaire de police du quartier,* with whom he is on very good terms, and in the well-furnished bureau of the *commissaire* he saw a picture by Harpignies.[1] "A gift," said the *commissaire.* "The old man and I had a little business together not long since. . . . *Il avait houspillé une petite fille.*" And the old man is about 80. Thus these things can be arranged in Paris.

Exposition de la Société des Aquarellistes Français at Georges Petit's. I went to pick up hints about technique. General level very low. Coming out, I met procession of autos depositing elegant women at the door. I doubt if the auto has yet been properly done from the elegant and the purely romantic qualities it has. Then, similar thought to that caused by the Debussy singer at Ullman's—all those painters having painted for a year to give, ostensibly, momentary pleasure to a few elegant ununderstanding persons. Something fine about the notion somewhere. I thought I could work it up for *The Glimpse.*

England.

We left Paris on Saturday, March 6, at 8.25. Traversing hundreds of miles of snow.

Gestures and style of people walking down to work past the Mater's window in the morning ought to be noticed. There are young men who seem so absorbed in a pipe as to be smoking it with their whole bodies. General deliberation and heaviness.

Thursday, March 11th.

Went to meeting of Tunstall Town Council in the afternoon (of which notes elsewhere). On the way there, down Scotia Road, I saw a

---

[1] Henri Harpignies, the landscape painter (1819–1916). He had an exhibition in London when he was 94.

knot of girls here and there who had obviously left their work on a bank to come out and watch. Heads wrapped up in cotton against powdery workshops. Standing still in raw cold, very ill clad. They were waiting for a funeral to pass. I saw this funeral just starting from a cottage lower down. The hearse just moving from the side of the road to the middle, and the procession hopping over snow heaps to join in. Two women, noses in handkerchiefs, immediately behind hearse. They seemed to place their handkerchiefs in position and to begin to cry just as procession started. About 15 or 20 men behind. Quite half without overcoats. You thought of the waiting hatless at the grave etc. Extremely foul and muddy road, and a raw day. Crowd blocking the pavement in front of the house. Burly Podmore elbowing his way through it to get in. As I forced my way past, smell, and sound of crying came from the house.

Sunday, March 14th.

Hawtrey, after accepting *What the Public Wants* on his own—that is, so far as he was concerned—found himself obliged to refuse it because his syndicate funked it. He said he thought he could ultimately have persuaded them, but we would not give him time. This is yet another instance of the way in which plays are chosen. This was on Thursday. On Friday, Trench[1] wrote me definitely commissioning a play, subject to seeing a scenario.

Thursday, 18th. Dinner with Lee Matthews, and went with him to see Waller in the *Musketeers.* A humiliating spectacle. *Tuesday, 16th.* Saw Pinker: and Whitten lunched with me at Gatti's and invited me to Omar Khayyam Club dinner.

Lunched with Herbert Trench at United Universities Club and heard about his rather airy plans for a high-class theatre.

Friday, 19th. Lunch at Frank Harris's, and met Newbould, Crawley, and John Tweed.[2]

Thursday, 25th. Lunch at Ritz with Newbould, Harrises being there. New Gallery. Conder pictures. Tea at Carlton.

Friday, 26th. "Fraternity" dinner offered to me. It is to be noted that I spoke for 35 minutes.

---

[1] Herbert Trench, director of the Haymarket Theatre.
[2] The sculptor.

Saturday. Dinner at Goolds. Notable drive through Maida Vale regions, especially Blomfield road and its canals.

Sunday, 28th. Sharpes here for the evening. *Papa et fils* played Borodine.

Monday, March 29th.

No time nor inclination to keep journals. Last week I wrote two articles for *New Age* and a short story for Tillotsons.

Thursday, April 1st.

Wednesday night. Omar Khayyam Club. Centenary dinner to celebrate birth of Fitzgerald. 90 diners. I made a speech to M.P.'s, ambassadors, magistrates, Academicians, publishers, poets, and scientists. Frascati's restaurant. Effect of crowded restaurant. Various dinners (8, I think) going on at once.

Sunday, April 4th.

Friday. Lunch with Wells at Reform Club. I wanted to belong to this club. Went to N.L.C. and got proposed as temporary member. Tea with Carl Leyel at Savage Club. Bozmans and Chapman here in the evening.
Saturday. Enfeebled. Boat race.

Tuesday, April 6th.

Expected first rehearsal of *What the Public Wants* yesterday, but of course it was postponed.

Wednesday, April 7th.

Dinner at Ford Madox Hueffer's.[1] John Galsworthy and wife there. Slight *gêne* on my part on first encounter with Galsworthy, seeing my recent articles on him. However, we did well together, and he asked me to dinner. Hueffer said that Henry James dictated so slowly that he insisted on his amanuensis having a novel open before her to read while he dictated. He said that Conrad was still as late as ever with his copy.

Good Friday, April 9th.

All these days magnificent weather, east wind having gradually died

---

[1] Ford Madox Hueffer, who did not change his name to Ford Madox Ford until 1919, was at this time editor of the *English Review*.

down. Putney Bridge and High Street at 11 A.M. Talk about road to Delhi. "I met a hundred men on the road to Portsmouth and they were all my brothers" (Indian proverb).

Sunday, April 11th.

Yesterday, visit to Kew Gardens, preceded by death of Swinburne. Seventh day of cloudless sky.

Monday, April 19th.

Rehearsals of *What the Public Wants* began on Tuesday.[1] Thursday, met Whelen, Tree's private secretary, at Lee Matthews's Club, and gave him ideas for a *Don Juan* for Tree. Friday, went down in motor with Frank Harris and wife and Marguerite. Met A. G. Hales, war correspondent, there. He gave us his experiences of spiritualism, and an address in Peckham Rye. So we said we would go. We had a great lunch at the Royal York Hotel, kept by one Preston,[2] with the manners of a little duke. At night M. and I dined with the Galsworthys. Saturday, another rehearsal. I then went to the Club and slept.

Thursday, April 29th.

On Wednesday the twenty-first we went to spend the night at H. G. Wells's. After that I got more and more absorbed in rehearsals. Couldn't think of anything else. Tuesday I had lunch with Chapman to meet S. Reynolds,[3] at the Mont Blanc. W. H. Hudson and Edward Garnett[4] also present. Ravel, Schmitt, and Delage came to have tea with me at the N.L.C. on Wednesday.

Whelen had tea with me on Thursday. He said Tree was coming to the performance on Sunday, and that he would provide *W.T.P.W.* an afternoon theatre if no one took it for an evening bill. I also promised to do him a translation of *La Parisienne,* which he promised to produce, somewhere.

---

[1] At the Aldwych Theatre, where it was produced by the Stage Society, May 2.

[2] Mr. Harry Preston, the well-known sportsman.

[3] Stephen Reynolds was then assistant editor of the *English Review.* He published several novels before his death in 1914.

[4] The author of *Green Mansions* was one of several famous writers who owed much to the early help of Edward Garnett, at that time literary adviser to the publishing firm of Duckworth & Co.; he had previously served T. Fisher Unwin and William Heinemann in the same capacity, and now fulfills this role for Jonathan Cape and The Viking Press.

I saw Pinker on Tuesday, who had got an offer from Methuen [1] of £300, £350, and £400, on account of next 3 books.

Wednesday, May 5th.

First performance of *What the Public Wants* at Aldwych, May 2, 1909. Second performance Monday afternoon, May 3.

Thursday, May 13th.

Curious difference between the evident enjoyment of the critics both on Sunday and on Monday and the cold, carping tone of most of their articles. There were only a few really enthusiastic notices. Particularly good ones in the *D. Chronicle*, the *Saturday Review*, and the *Westminster Gazette*. But all the others, however cussed, recognized that they had something striking to deal with.

Lunched with Frank Vernon, Wednesday the fifth. He had produced *Cupid and Common Sense* in Glasgow on the previous Thursday and told me of its striking success on the first night. I heard later that it played to £188 during the week. This seemed to me small, but the theatre people regarded it as very good.

Thursday, *What Every Woman Knows*, J. M. Barrie. A despicable piece. He surely must have known what putridity he was turning out. Some very good farcical or light comedy work in first act.

Sunday night. Annual Dinner of Stage Society. M. and I on either side of chairman. It was nearly 11 when I was called on to speak; so the speech I could have made was not delivered. Moreover, audience tired.

On Monday terms were definitely arranged with Hawtrey's Syndicate, headed by Tom B. Davis, for production of *What the Public Wants* at Royalty. I was at theatre and Hawtrey presented to me various members of the cast he had engaged, including a young woman named Cleaver for principal part, who impressed me.

On Tuesday the contract was signed and Tom B. Davis paid over a cheque for £100. No sooner was this done than I met Hawtrey by chance in the street, and he was very angry with Davis, who would not agree to estimate for scenery etc. Hawtrey had cancelled rehearsal for that afternoon, for (as he said) diplomatic reasons—so as to force the hand of the Syndicate by making them think he would chuck it all up if he could not

---

[1] The publishing house of Methuen published Bennett's *Clayhanger*, and most of his books immediately following it.

have his way. He said Syndicate were hard up. This worried me. I was glad to be leaving London the next day, with a postal strike in France.

We arrived at Fontainebleau at 9.30 Wednesday night, the twelfth, having been absent 5 months. Now my ordinary life is to recommence.

Sunday, September 12th.

Prince Kropotkin's memoirs.[1] No translator's name on title page. I wonder if he wrote them in English himself. Many awkward turns of phrase, and errors, such as "griefs" for "grievances." The book is different from what I expected but quite as fine.

He really is very reticent about himself. For instance, he doesn't relate his marriage, so far as I remember, though towards the end of the memoirs his wife figures frequently. He does give a new and dramatic impression of the persecuting attitude of all governments towards genuinely "advanced" thought and propaganda, and of the injustice they will do to attain their ends. Even Switzerland. He was least persecuted in England. But he speaks of England as a living tomb one year that he was obliged to spend in London about 1880, before Burns, Morris, etc. No socialist society there. Hyndman[2] was the sole advanced worker. Tremendous change since then. He seems to be very careful in his statements; yet he says that *all* governments maintain spies and *agents provocateurs*. A very simple and straightforward character. Discusses very simply everything that comes in his way. Extremely philosophical in his acceptance of "the fortunes of war." Never seeks to "dress his window." The picture of his childhood is the most picturesque, the most effective. But he never seeks an effect. Evidently he and his friends were of a morality far higher than even the average highly moral. On the whole I should say his life was a happy one. He is naturally dead against prisons, as I suppose all intellectually honest people must be. He lays stress on the cruelty to a prisoner's dependents caused by imprisoning. I had not so clearly pictured this before. At first I was surprised, but not on reflection, by his statement that French prisons are more humane than English, and less degrading also to the dignity.

---

[1] *Memoirs of a Revolutionist* appeared in 1900. Kropotkin wrote it in English.

[2] Henry M. Hyndman founded the Social Democratic Federation and the periodical *Justice*. He was a noted agitator at the close of the nineteenth century.

Monday, September 13th.

Finished *Memoirs of a Revolutionist.* This book leaves a fine impression. Strange *naïf* turns of phrase here and there; but this may be the result either of writing in a foreign language or of translation.

I wrote the first of a series of 6 *chroniques* this morning for the *Reader's Review.* Preceded by a walk to the Point de Vue de Calvaire, as usual quite unusually marvellous. Never will I live in a big town again, I think. I couldn't deprive myself of country walks before my work. But I never learn any more about the "country," habits of trees and birds etc., nor even nomenclature. I have no desire that way.

This afternoon I went down to the Seine and did an aquarelle of *Les Platreries.* 2½ hours. Then we had tea at the Godebskis', in their little dining-room.

Chilly, but a beautiful grey September day. 15½° all day. Beautiful evening for a family-chilly dinner in the Kiosque. Thirty pages of *Magic Flute,* duet, after dinner. I am going to read *A Sportsman's Sketches*[1] again.

Tuesday, September 14th.

Parot, the carpenter, came today, for a job. I once shook hands with him in a burst of fellowship, and always since he makes a point of this ceremony. He shook hands today. I left him with Marguerite. I was standing at the top of the garden when I heard him coming downstairs to depart. I walked hurriedly round behind the kiosk so that he should not see me and I should not have to shake hands with him. I did this almost before I thought what I was doing. Why? A decent, independent chap, vigorous and energetic. Young. What is at the back of my mind is probably that I resent his insisting on the "privilege" which I once granted him. Funny.

Tonight I began to read again *When I Was a Child,*[2] with a view to my next novel, which I think must contain, near the beginning, a grimmish detailed sketch of industrial child-life in 1840, about.

Sunday, September 19th.

Thomas Seccombe took three meals with us on Wednesday and Thurs-

---

[1] By Turgenev.
[2] *When I Was a Child, By an Old Potter,* published in 1903.

day. He and I talked "shop" most of the time and walked a great deal in the forest. I discovered that he was chiefly a professor of history [1] and "Prior" of the Johnson Club. Yet even he was fairly convinced that Germany would try to take South Africa from us, and that if they couldn't put their heel on the population, having taken possession of the Colony, they would exterminate the population. He offered this view quite seriously. Very reasonable and *doux* in argument. He gave me some curious proofs of the popularity of *How to Live on Twenty-four Hours a Day*. For instance, he was in a hotel one day and a motor party came in for lunch, and after lunch a young man of the party picked up the book, said its title was funny, began to read it, and couldn't be got away therefrom into the motor. Seccombe left on Thursday afternoon, having impressed me very favourably as a cultivated, open-minded, courteous, and subtle brain.

Olive and Gabrielle left on Friday morning and M. went with them to Paris. The Godebskis came for dinner.

I read a lot of Professor X. and E. Y. In a letter to Frank Harris I described their Shakespearean criticism as "undistinguished and laborious muck." He fastened on the phrase with delight. It is violent but pretty true. All these professional critics utterly fail to comprehend the creative processes. How should they? They sentimentalize them. I ought to write about this somewhere.

Monday, September 20th.

Bazar de l'hôtel de ville, Fontainebleau.

I wonder how a description of this shop, the largest in the town, would sound 50 years hence. You go through a rather narrow vestibule, where soap, note-paper, and pins, studs, etc., are displayed, into a large hall, height of two stories, a wide staircase at back, wide galleries round, and a roof of which the middle square is glazed. Cheap goods everywhere. Drapery, silks, ribbons, nails, ironmongery, glass and earthenware, leather goods, stationery on the ground floor; arranged on stalls and counters, in between which are spaces for walking. In the basement, *articles de ménage.* The staircase lined at either rail with lighter articles of furniture. In the galleries, chiefly light furniture; extended on the walls, showy carpets, flowered etc., at such prices as 49 fr. We went to buy a screen.

---

[1] He was lecturer at East London College.

They had only one, four-fold, and we wanted three-fold. Ranged below it were several toy screens. The price of the sole screen was 19 fr. Near by were about a dozen cheap marble-top washstands. Wicker chairs and flimsy tables about. Still, you *could* buy there nearly everything (non-edible) that goes to the making of an ordinary house. The frontage of the shop is of course an ordinary house frontage. The shop itself must be a courtyard roofed over. It is in charge mainly of women. Sitting high at the cash desk near the entrance are two controlling women—one sharp and imperative in manner; with the table of electric switches at their right hand. They look up from books to direct entering customers, and when they know what customers want they call out a warning to the assistants within. Very smiling, with a mechanical saccharine smile.

The bulk of the assistants are youngish girls; some pretty, all dressed in black, with black aprons, scissors, etc., and blackish hands. They do not seem keen, but rather bored. Certainly the wages must be low. Hours about 12 or 13 per day—that is to say, hours during which shop is open. Besides these, there are a few men, who wear blue smocks, and attend to furniture, ironmongery, and similar departments. One of these, with one girl, is always at the *étalage* at the front, where trinkets and souvenirs and post cards are exposed. Men seem even more discontented than the girls. I never saw any one there who looked like a proprietor or supreme boss. The whole shop is modelled on the big general shops in Paris. There are similar shops now in most provincial towns. In Toulouse there were half a dozen splendid ones.

In all, the conditions of labour are disgusting to the social conscience, though probably better than in *ateliers*. There is a feeling of cutting down expenditure, especially wages, in order to sell cheaply, while making a good profit. A feeling that everybody concerned is secretly at the beginning of a revolt, and that the organizers of the whole organism are keeping out of the way. Yes, there is certainly this feeling! I am always uneasy when in such shops, as if I too were guilty for what is wrong in them. Of course nearly all shops are on the same basis of sweating, but in some it is masked in magnificence, so that one has to search for it.

A handful of customers always in, and a continuous movement near the entrance.

At closing time the *étalage* has to be carried in, and there is left a prodigious litter of bits of paper which has to be swept up. Then early in the morning (less than 12 hours after the closing) there is the refixing and arrangement of the *étalage,* and the gradual recommencement of the day.

Some of the women have a certain *coquetterie.* But not the young ones; the controlling women of 40 or so. These have the air of being always equal to the situation, but they are not. I remember once half the staff (it seemed) was worsted in an attempt to make a bicycle pump work that I had bought. They all conspired to convince me that it was quite in order, but I beat them, and they had to take the pump back. One of the controlling women began on a note of expert omniscient condescension to me, but she gradually lost her assurance, and fled. A man would not so easily have done that.

I went on preparing Act I of *The Honeymoon*[1] this morning, and had some success.

Friday, September 24th.

Lee Matthews came on Wednesday night. Thursday morning Lee M. and I walked in the forest. He said that he had got Tree to come to his flat, and his wife read to Tree the scenario of my *Don Juan,* and Tree said he was afraid he hadn't enough dash to carry it off. He took the MS. away with him, and Lee M. has heard nothing since.

In the afternoon he and I went to Moret by train, and walked down to Saint-Mammès and up the Loing to Moret town. Beautiful hot day, with sailing architectural clouds. A great population of barges. We saw a Flemish barge, with white sculpture work on the doors of its cabin, all painted very nattily, with little imitations of the deck of a ship; very clean; a few plants in pots, including a peach tree in full fruit, loaded, in fact; also embroidered lace curtains at the little cabin windows. A delightful object. You never see a French barge like this.

On getting home I found a letter saying that Pinker had sold *What the Public Wants* as a serial to *McClure's* for £100. The U.S.A. is certainly a very strange market indeed.

Yesterday I finished a story, *The Heroism of Thomas Chadwick.* This makes the third in about a fortnight. One of them, *Hot Potatoes,* is just twice too long for the amount of material in it.

---

[1] This was produced at the Royalty Theatre, October 6, 1911, under the direction of Dion Boucicault.

Saturday, September 25th.

Finished this morning the arrangement of first act of *The Honeymoon.* I went to Moret again this afternoon with the others. I searched all the river from Saint-Mammès to Moret for a subject, and couldn't settle on a good one. Then I began to sketch an old man in a punt fishing, but I was taken away from it and made to go and have tea at "Robinson." Blackish brown rats (not very big) kept coming up out of the bank to drag away at a large crust of bread that some one had tied by a string to a chain. Half tame. Not being able to carry off the bread, they would nibble and eat off it *in situ.* We saw a wedding procession, preceded by 3 musicians—a fiddler, a silver instrument, and another. Working people. Men in silk hats and short semi-frock-coats. The men had obviously drunk about as much as they could manage. Only one or two girls in white—the bride and another. Perhaps 30 people altogether, including quite young ones, aged 15 or so. Bride about 25 or 26, certainly not a virgin. Procession came up from Saint-Mammès, crossed the Loing Canal, and disappeared towards Moret. As it approached the town the musicians began to play, and some of the people danced along. One couple stayed lingering behind; the man ran behind a tree while his girl waited for him; then he rejoined her, and they walked on slowly after the procession. Nearly all the people had a brutish and very stupid look. In towns only as big as Fontainebleau, these marriage processions have ceased to occur, but they continue in villages. Our cook Maria had two days off not long since for her brother's wedding. The festivities lasted two whole days.

Our late servant Jeanne, who had only been with *commerçants,* was much exercised by our finicking and ritualistic methods of eating—spoons laid to right and at back, forks differently, certain particular plates, etc. She must have thought it all very ridiculous, but of course she said nothing. One day Marguerite was offering some food to the dog, who refused it, and as he was ill she tried to put it down him with a spoon. Jeanne said: *"Il fait des manières, lui aussi!"*

Sunday, September 26th.

I nearly continued my ordinary work today (contrary to firm resolution) but refrained at the last moment. The excuse was that if I did work I might finish the series of articles for *The Reader's Review* before we go to Paris on Thursday. I determined to find a subject for verse, and I found a whole series—about the castle of Fontainebleau. I settled on the detail of the first poem. This satisfied me for the day, and I did no more. I shall have to look up Taine before I write it. . . .

Monday, September 27th.

Wrote draft of first act of *The Honeymoon.* Shirked it all the time. Read the papers, mended the stove pipe, practised the overture to *Preciosa,* read more papers, upset a 4-lb. jar of jam; but I finished it by 11.30. About 3,000 words.

This afternoon I elaborated somewhat the first poem about Fontainebleau, and looked up the necessary references in Taine. But I could not work at it. I was too exhausted to do anything.

Book bought. *Trees and Tree-drawing.* I read all the interesting part at once, and got quite a shilling's worth of wrinkles.

Tuesday, September 28th.

I wrote this morning the third article (*Fiction*) in the series for the Home Reading Union. And then my *New Age* article, dealing with Chesterton's and E. V. Lucas's essays.[1] Continuing Taine's *Origines,* I thought how absurd I was that I had not before read a similar work on English origins. But I could not think of any similar work.

After dinner I reached down the first volume of A. W. Benn's *Modern England,* which I have had for about a year, and found that it was dedicated to Bernhard Berenson,[2] which made me favourable to it. That a historian and publicist should be sufficiently intimate with, or an admirer of, a first-class art critic to wish to dedicate a book to him, is certainly a proof of the former's breadth of sympathy. I read the first chapter. Good; but very inferior after Taine. Still a work of genuine culture, and marked by liberal principles; perhaps he shows too much emotion when his feelings are outraged, as by the ill treatment, industrially, of children. A historian has no business with righteous indignation. He ought to be above that. Cruelty to children is not worse than a lot of other cruelties. I admired the book; well written, though perhaps a shade turgid. But I doubt if I shall finish it. I want something more masterful and of genius.

Reflecting on my poem about Fontainebleau, I settled on the general

---

[1] Respectively *Tremendous Trifles* and *One Day and Another.*
[2] The authority on Renaissance art.

form and metre, and composed the first line. I can now go on with it any time.

Wednesday, September 29th.

We went to the Godebskis' for tea. As soon as we got there it began to pour with rain and it kept on. Frank and Ida Godebski playing Borodine, and the rest of us at the wide open window, with the landscape of Verlaine behind a mist of rain; and the regular noise of the rain on tens of thousands of leaves. The young Jean worrying the dog. Marguerite and Mimi, damp, came scurrying in dishevelled from the forest with whole bags of mushrooms. Then tea below. Opening the window for air, down there. Then more Borodine upstairs. The perfectly exquisite attitudes and gestures of Mimi playing with the dog. Steady rain. Afraid of the journey home, I order a carriage on the understanding that it is a closed carriage. The doctor comes, and frightens Marguerite in spite of her assurance about the mushrooms. Still Borodine. Darker. One candle is found for the piano, and the music goes on in a little sphere of radiance (yellow) in the growing dusk. The surface of the river looks like the sea in shallows. Then the carriage comes, and it is open, with a hood. Marguerite's bicycle, damaged, has to be piled on to the driver's knees. M., Florence, and I crowd under the hood, and Frank sits opposite in his new overcoat. I keep rain off our knees with an umbrella. Cold, slow drive. The tram car, flashing, passes us. Its platforms are piled up with cycles. We eat some of the mushrooms for dinner. Then preparations for our departure tomorrow.

Today I wrote the fourth article for *The Reader's Review,* on *How to Use a Public Library.* I did nothing at my poem. I read Taine, A. W. Benn, Nietzsche, and Turgenev.

Thursday, September 30th.

After much rain, an exquisite morning. The views of the Seine as I came up to Paris were exceedingly romantic. I came without sketchbook, and my first desire was to sketch. So I had to buy a book. M. and I then went to the Aviation Exposition at the Grand Palais. Startled by the completeness of the trade organization of aviation; even to suits, for aviators, and rolls of stuffs for planes. We first remarked the Farman aeroplane. Vast, and as beautiful as a yacht. Same kind of beauty. Yet a new creation of form, a new "style"; that is newly stylistic. I had been reading Wilbur Wright's accounts of his earlier experiments as I came up in the train, and I wanted to write a story of an aviator, giving the sensations of flight. I left M. and went to the Salon d'Automne. But I found it was the *vernissage* and so I didn't enter. Crowds entering.

My first vague impression was here at last defined, of Paris. Namely, the perversity and corruption of the faces. The numbers of women more or less chic also impressed me. A few, marvellous. It was ideal Paris weather. I saw what a beautiful city it is, again. The beauty of this city existence and its environment appealed to me strongly. Yet the journey from the Gare de Lyon on the Métro had seemed horrible. Also, I had waited outside the *bureau de location* of the Français for it to open, and had watched the faces there, which made me melancholy. Particularly a woman of 60 or so, and her virgin daughter 30 or 33. The latter with a complexion spoilt, and a tremendously bored expression, which changed into a mannered, infantile, school-girlish, self-conscious, uneasy smile, when a punctilious old gentleman came up and saluted and chatted. The fading girl's gums all showed. She was a sad sight. I would have preferred to see her initiated and corrupt. She was being worn out by time, not by experience. The ritual and sterility and futility of her life had devitalized her. The mother was making a great fuss about changing some tickets. This ticket-changing had a most genuine importance for her. The oldish girl, mutely listening, kept her mouth at the mannered smile for long periods. But I think she was not essentially a fool.

Friday, October 1st.

We dined at the Bœuf à la Mode. Americans, Americans everywhere. A dull, good, nice restaurant. I gave the waiter my usual 10 per cent., which happened to be 70 centimes. He was apparently not content, but politely thanked me. As he carried the plate out with the change on it, he held it the least bit in the world at arm's length, exposing it with scorn to the inspection of the *chasseur* as he passed him. It was a fine, subtle gesture, and pleased me as much as it annoyed me.

Sunday, October 3rd.

Row with the landlady of the Hôtel de Liège about price of room. When she had no other resource of argument left she said: *"Vous êtes plus riche que moi. Je travaille du matin jusqu'au soir,"* etc. It seemed curious to hear this kind of thing in a hotel in the middle of Paris. In her anger she also accused me of sleeping all day in my bedroom, doubtless because I retired there to rest at intervals. It is simply astounding how I can get tired when in Paris or London on a holiday. A nervous fatigue that is positively acute. Half an hour's rest will drive it away for a time. But it will begin quite early in the morning. Salon d'Automne yesterday afternoon. I enjoyed it greatly. It was certainly an education to me, far more interesting than the Spring Salons. Except in a few wilful jokes, you could see a real idea in everything if you searched for it. I got several more notions for *natures mortes*. Also I got my eyes opened a little wider.

Monday, October 4th.

I have now read *L'Echéance, La Sérénade,* and *Le Maître* of Jean Jullien. What is the matter with these plays is that they are *too* direct, too summary. I think they lack artifice. They are just pretty fair stories told dramatically with vigour and with a certain truth of characterization. Certainly always with a desire to be truthful. The bottom of my objection to them is that they aren't complicated enough. But they are very much on the right lines. Further, I don't think he knows his *milieux* sufficiently well. You can't take a *milieu* at random because you think it is a *milieu* that ought to be "done," and then work it up by swotting.

This morning I walked out in the forest for two hours and definitely arranged the opening scene of *The Honeymoon,* which I shall write tomorrow. Then, having time to spare, I wrote part of a *Books and Persons.* I began painting my water-colour this afternoon. After tea we went for a walk as far as the canal. The stove which I had ordered for the hall came today, and was much too large; it would heat a church.

Tuesday, October 5th.

At 8 o'clock this morning I began to write the first scene of *The Honeymoon.* I worked at it at full tension till 10.30, and then stopped. I don't think I am quite satisfied with it. I doubt if I have got the right tone. I may begin it again.

The finally corrected proofs of Harris's book on Shakespeare [1] reached

---

[1] *The Man Shakespeare and his Tragic Life Story,* by Frank Harris.

me. I have read a quarter of the book since dinner. My previous impression of it is deepened. The thing is masterful and masterly.

After lunch I was certainly a little depressed about my play. I painted from 1.15 to 3, not very well. Then read an exceedingly fine leader in the *Nation* on the situation in Spain. Then tea. After tea I went for a walk in the forest, beyond the railway. It rained as I started. A close autumn day, with a wild sky and the forest streaming. The sun set in a sea of gold light. Crimson lay about, both in East and West. Ivory clouds showing beyond the ragged edges of grey or sepia clouds. I was out for 1½ hours, and while walking, with constant interruptions for controlling the dog, I wrote 14 lines of my poem on Fontainebleau.

Wednesday, October 6th.

Not quite satisfied with the "key" of the opening of *The Honeymoon,* I decided to begin it again. But I had a headache and a creative malaise this morning, and couldn't work easily. I sat down, and then at once got up and went out for a walk to the Point de Vue de Calvaire. Exquisitely brilliant morning. I thought I would exchange morning with afternoon. So I read my Taine finishing the third volume of the *Revolution.* And I carried a water-colour a stage further. But I couldn't begin to work after lunch either. I said I would have tea early and work after tea.

Then there came an extremely enthusiastic letter from George H. Doran,[1] the American publisher of *The Old Wives' Tale,* expressing deep admiration etc. and asking the "honour" etc. of publishing other books. He said he had sold two editions of 1,000 each and was now ordering plates (of his own, I suppose) for another edition. This produced a disturbance in me. I had to answer it, and send it, with a copy of my answer, to Pinker. At 4.15 I did at last begin on the play. I re-wrote the first scene and made it much better. Then the dog was lost, and I went out to find him, and found and castigated him. After dinner I read another 100 pages of Frank Harris's *The Man Shakespeare* and was indeed deeply impressed by it. It is the *only* book on Shakespeare. I always

---

[1] George H. Doran & Co., and later Doubleday, Doran & Co., published practically all of Arnold Bennett's books in the United States from 1909, onward, and republished several of the earlier books. The chief exceptions were the three novels published by Dutton's (see p. 342).

thought so, ever since I read the opening chapters in their first form a year ago.

Thursday, October 7th.

Received this last day or two the following books: Frank Harris's *The Man Shakespeare,* in proof sheets stitched together, but with the margins very well arranged.

A Russian translation of *The Grand Babylon Hotel,* published at Moscow last year.

American edition of *The O.W.T.* in an awful vermilion and gilt binding.

The Glimpse, which was published yesterday. My thirtieth published book, not counting the Phillpotts collaborations.

I worked fairly satisfactorily on the play this morning. After lunch I went out for a walk to get the necessary ideas for the beginning of the new series of articles in *T.P.'s Weekly.* I got them.

Friday, October 8th.

Mistake yesterday. *The Glimpse* was published today and not on Wednesday. I received today a highly enthusiastic letter from Waugh about it. He does not think it will sell. I have a wild idea that it will.

A wild wet morning, and it was very fine in the rain on the hill at 8.15. I came home and wrote the first of new series of articles for *T.P.'s Weekly* on English family life. Rather pleased with it.

After lunch I painted. Then had tea here, and went down to Godebski's for tea afterwards. Wonderful colours on the Godebskis' house and trees. Showers and wind. After dinner I finished Harris's *Shakespeare,* amid enthusiasm. I telegraphed him that it surpassed my most sanguine expectations and was glorious. It is. But I wish I hadn't got to write an article on it.

Monday, October 11th.

Last night I began talking to Pauline Smith about her work, though I had some difficulty in getting *her* to talk. She gave me a notion of a half-formed scheme for a novel—nothing really but a dim idea. I enlarged it and straightened it out for her, and by my enthusiasm lighted hers a little, indeed much. I poured practical advice into her for an hour, such as I don't think she could have got from any other living man, and such as I would have given my head for 15 years ago. I told her exactly what to think about today and it was arranged that she should report to me tonight how far she had proceeded and that we should go further with the plot. After dinner tonight she began to read. It is true it was one of my books. I gave her a chance and waited for her to put the book down. Then after about half an hour I said: "I shan't let Pauline read any more of my books. She doesn't do anything else." She smiled, and murmured, "Just let me finish this." I then played a sonata, and then ostentatiously waited. No sign. She kept on reading till 9.30, and then went straight to bed. I now feel that the next word spoken between us as to her novel will have to come from her.

I wrote the Swiss waiter scene in *The Honeymoon* today, and part of my article on Frank Harris's *Shakespeare* book this afternoon. The Godebskis and Boucher came for tea. I received *Ann Veronica*[1] today with the inscription "The Young Mistresses' Tale, to Arnold B. with love from his nephew H.G."

Wednesday, October 13th.

A letter from Waugh yesterday, rather more cheerful about the prospects of *The Glimpse,* because his wife had read it and was as enthusiastic about it as he was. In the evening I got Pauline Smith to talk about her novel, but I think I mentioned it first. Sheer magnanimity and obstinacy mingled.

Thursday, October 14th.

Headache, began yesterday. The camel's back-breaking straw was probably a Dutch cigar that Godebski gave me. I nearly cured the headache twice today and then brought it on again by working.

Godebski's for tea yesterday.

I finished *Ann Veronica* yesterday. The last 30 pages are the best. But still, a minor work. Seems to me much too short; incidents not described in sufficient detail. Mere writing impudently careless of dissonant effects, and full of extreme colloquialisms.

I did another 600 words of the play yesterday.

---

[1] By H. G. Wells.

Saturday, October 16th.

Another magnificent review of *The O.W.T.*, in the Chicago *Dial*, sent to me by the literary editor of the Boston *Transcript*, who says that the *Dial* is the only distinctively literary journal in America.[1] *Per contra*, an entirely unappreciative review of *The Glimpse* in *The Times*.

Tuesday, October 19th.

This morning I had that excessive consciousness of one's self which comes from being a little over-tired, or (I have been told) after a "drink," and which is favourable to creative work. I finished my first act easily. I may enlarge it a bit. This afternoon, we went to the Rocher d'Avon.

Wednesday, October 20th.

I seemed to spend most of last night in reading a back number of *Blackwood's* which happened to be by the bed. From the memories of a General Russell,[2] I learnt that conscienceless as governments are now to some of their younger servants, they used to be even worse. He was asked to go on a secret mission, and told that if he was "caught out" the government would disown him. He accomplished the mission, was not caught out, and sent home a lot of useful and authentic information. But the government declined to pay a penny of his travelling expenses. What a damned young fool he was not to get them before he started! Not only that; but his information being distasteful to the supreme chiefs he was in disfavour, and was refused a berth in the Intelligence Department which he wanted to enter. However, after about a year he was "forgiven."

The most interesting aspect of his souvenirs is that which shows that he accepted all this as a matter of course. The turpitude of governments appears to be axiomatic in the minds of the "services." There is something

---

[1] Founded (in 1880) and edited uninterruptedly by Francis F. Browne, the *Dial* (a semi-monthly) remained for many years the only exclusively literary periodical in America. Its standards (not excluding the typographical) were dignified, and its contributors—often professors in colleges throughout the country—were men of parts. The *Dial* was something for Chicago to be proud of. In 1916, after Mr. Browne's death, his sons relinquished the paper to new owners, who shifted the emphasis to the social sciences with Thorstein Veblen as the star contributor. Later the *Dial* changed hands again, to become a stimulating and provocative monthly of progressive tendencies in all the arts. It died in July, 1929.

[2] Major-General Frank S. Russell described his experiences in the Turkish war and Near East, in *Blackwood's Magazine*, August, 1909.

fine about the calm fatalism of such patriotism. He doesn't seem to have been ashamed of his country as represented by the government.

I got up exhausted. Misty. I was drawn towards the Place d'Armes instead of the forest, in order to see the dismantling of the circus. I saw it, half down: all the male performers were working as skilled labourers. This afternoon the trucks were loaded for entrainment at the station.

Then I went on up the Rue de France—a highly typical provincial residential street—to the Fourche, where a lot of soldiers were being drilled in squads of 16, 8, 6, 4, and even 1. I saw one man spend at least a quarter of an hour drilling a single awkward recruit, giving him the most minute instructions how to stop, start, and turn, with repetitions endless. He would say, *"Non, la patte droite est trop tournée,"* mingling such phrases with stiff, shouted, conventional martial commands. Here one got down to the very unit of French army manoeuvres. I don't know what they teach privates inside barracks, but outside they teach them nothing except to be machines capable of executing only the most rudimentary tricks: scarcely even the beginning of even the A B C of military skill. One sees nothing but drilling, and hears nothing but the monotonous practice of drum-beating and crude brass instruments. All brutalizing. All the men were in fatigue whitish cotton or linen, except two officers in red trousers. The general tone was kindly, even friendly. All this in a pale autumn mist.

I got on slowly this morning, but I was alone all afternoon, and by 5.15 I had broken the back of the construction of Act II of *The Honeymoon.* Later I wrote my *New Age* article.

Thursday, October 21st.

I find that if I am to begin my new novel[1] on 1 January, 1910, I must make a series of small preliminary enquiries. I do this perhaps at the rate of half an hour or an hour a day. I have read *When I Was a Child,* and all I need of Shaw's *North Staffordshire Potteries,*[2] and tonight I re-read the social and industrial section of the Victorian history, which contains a few juicy items that I can use. I work on the plot itself about once a week when I have an hour and feel like it.

Nothing at all occurred today, except that I began the actual transcrip-

---

[1] *Clayhanger.*
[2] By Stebbing Shaw.

tion for my projected dictionary of the literary ideas of W. S. Landor. I found this rather amusing and not in the least fatiguing. It is the sort of thing one could do while recovering from influenza.

Friday, October 22nd.

Letters from Frank Harris and Wells and his friend about *The Glimpse.* But really I have had very few letters about it.

Extraordinarily beautiful morning in the forest, and ideas for the second act arrived one after the other in a manner very creditable to them.

Monday, October 25th.

After two days' dyspepsia; I began at a quarter to 8 this morning, and at 11 o'clock I had been out for a walk in the rain and read the newspapers and written a complete draft of Act II. I hated doing it. This afternoon, after painting I walked to Les Platreries and arranged the whole scheme, and most of the characters, of my next novel—the first of the trilogy. Assuredly a great day. After that I did a bit at my Landor dictionary, and then it was dinner time.

I read the first story in *Actions and Reactions* [Kipling], and then, tonight, in order to compare, I read *On Greenhow Hill* and *The Man Who Was,* and I saw an article, rather respectful to Kipling in his decadence. He was never great; but the stories of 20 years ago are touching, if boyish. The new stories are feeble, but he has always been a highly conscientious craftsman. *Ceres Runaway:* Alice Meynell writes exactly the same now as she always did.

Weather colder; but still mainly bright. Magnificent moonlight night. What I am always wanting to do is a few landscape sketches, in words, just as material for use. And I never seem to have the energy or the power to concentrate sufficiently for useful observation. But yesterday and Saturday, in my dyspeptic idleness, I had several ideas for new books.

Wednesday, October 27th.

I came to the conclusion yesterday afternoon that I had been shirking the play somewhat. And so I determined that this morning I would do 3 hours' genuine hard labour on it—no messing about and wasting time. Which I did, rising up to that intent, fortunately in good form, 7.45 to 9.30, and 10.15 to noon. I wrote a good 1,000 words and was exhausted.

Yesterday evening I read, very badly, the first act to Pauline Smith and Marguerite, and with Pauline, who alone could follow it, it certainly had a *succès très vif*. I was quite hoarse after reading it. I saw a few things in it to modify. I have never read a play aloud before. It is a very severe and excellent test, especially when the reading is inefficient.

Today I heard from Pinker that Dutton's had offered £250 down and a good royalty on each of my 3 next novels for U.S.A.[1] This shows how enormously one's prospects can change there in a year. A year ago no American publisher would publish my work on any terms, and the copyright of *The Old Wives' Tale* was lost there from this cause. I am now sure of at least £600 each on my next 3 novels. By the afternoon post I had another letter from Pinker indicative of still further offers and hesitating about accepting Dutton's.

Sunday, October 31st.

Last night we went to see *Le Roi* in the cinematograph *salle* of the town. Full house. "*Quel monde province!*" My little doctor—I forget his name—sat behind me, and was anxious for us to walk in the forest together in the evening. Unhappily he seems entirely uninteresting. My plumber, my house painter, my bicycle dealer, and my house agent, were there with their wives. This seemed to be practically the only "world"— that of *commerçants*. But Marguerite saw a general's wife whom she knew (without the general). It seemed much more *province* than Burslem, for instance. It is from such an audience that one may see how small Fontainebleau is. Doubtless the society which considered itself *haute* kept away. And the theatre is in their minds designated as for the tradesmen. A plain interior, with a too low-arched roof, ugly with pitchpine, green hangings, and very badly disposed electric lights. Hard seats, with an appearance of chic. Very hard seats, after two hours.

This afternoon and tonight I read *Suzette* of Brieux, which is now a *demi-four* at the Vaudeville. Very workmanlike and good first act. The other two acts no good at all. It is simply astounding that a man so imperfectly endowed as Brieux can make such a deuce of a reputation among intelligent people.

---

[1] E. P. Dutton & Co. published Arnold Bennett's *Clayhanger, Denry the Audacious,* and *Hilda Lessways.*

Wednesday, November 3rd.

Goodish progress yesterday and today with play. I got on to the big scene of the second act today and found one or two rare jokes for it.

Tonight I transcribed from the Victorian *History of Staffs* all the notes I want for my next novel.

Friday, November 5th.

Last night, *Le Foyer,* by Mirbeau and Natanson. Fairly bright and well contrived, with a crude, cruel half-lighted satire. The time passed quickly. The suggestions of immorality were pleasingly outrageous. But immediately I got outside, the whole structure fell to pieces in my mind, and I began to cover it with scorn, to Marguerite, who said I was always too severe and that she had never heard me unreservedly praise any modern French play except *La Parisienne.* But really this play is quite untrue to life (it only resembles life in a journalistic way), and the basic idea of it (a woman getting money from an *ex-amant* to save a husband who ends by being *complaisant*) is quite banal. Loosely constructed. While pretending to realism, grossly caricatural. It is astonishing how tenth-rate stuff will cause a stir if it is only journalistically violent enough.

Went to bed at 1.15, dead. A freezing cold night. I arose at 6.20 as usual. I was tired but fresh. Magnificent morning, but I forgot to look at the sunrise. I wrote my fifth *T.P.* article on *The Revolt of Youth,* and my *New Age* article. I spent a lot of time reading the Steinheil trial, [1] which began on Wednesday, with a vague notion of using it some day for French stuff in a novel.

Saturday, November 6th.

I received copies of the U.S.A. edition of *The Glimpse.* Horrible binding. In glancing through it I noticed several misprints. The American spelling of course one accepts.

I had a superb walk in the forest. At 9.30 I began, very unwillingly, the last day on my second act. I was rather pleased with it at lunch time. After repose, I threw my painting over and finished the act. I then fiddled

---

[1] Mme. Steinheil was accused of murdering her husband and her mother-in-law. After a sensational trial lasting 10 days she was acquitted.

about with tea and Max Beerbohm [1] and the *procès* Steinheil until 4, when I was obliged by my conscience to go to the barber's.

Happily it is a stately barber's, where hair-cutting and friction are treated with adequate solemnity. In the half-light, with its mirrors and rococo woodwork and complicated apparatus, it had *du style,* tradition behind it. A little framed notice was hung up, as always on hunt days: *Rendezvous de chasse. Croix de Toulouse.* All this kind of thing will belong to a past generation, probably, before I'm dead. I shall recount it as something antique, quaint, and scarcely conceivable. The entire atmosphere was old-world.

I came home when there was a star in a field of blue green above pink, above purple grey that mingled with the smoke and the roofs of the houses. A simplified tableau seen from the lower corner of the Rue Bernard Palissy. Then I came in and read my dose of Taine.

Tuesday, November 9th.

Today I rose in excellent health, began my last act, and at 5.30 had written one-third of it. I received a complete bound set of my Tauchnitz works from the Baron. Though ugly, the format was not too ugly to please me. I put the row of 12 volumes in Marguerite's *secrétaire.* Pauline seized *A Great Man* out of the lot, and has been reading it at every spare moment and smiling to herself the whole time. Not to be outdone, I began to read *Buried Alive,* and also smiled the whole time. I don't think I have ever read a funnier book than this.

Friday, November 12th.

Taine's long essay (over 100 pages) on Balzac, is really very good reading, especially when he comes to describe the big characters, such as Joseph Bridau, Grandet, and the Baron Hulot. Lying awake last night, after a fearful crash caused by the faience suspension falling out of the ceiling in the hall, I had a desire to do likewise for one or two English novelists. It is Taine's method that appeals to me, and the intoxicating effect of a vast number of short sentences or clauses hurled down one after another.

---

[1] Reading his *Yet Again,* which elsewhere Arnold Bennett described as "an absolute masterpiece."

Sunday, November 14th.

I finished *The Honeymoon* at noon yesterday. I read the last act after dinner. It was a considerable success with Pauline Smith, but not with Marguerite, as she could not follow it.

Mme. Steinheil acquitted last night. I have kept the newspapers giving a full account of the whole process, as I had a sort of idea I might do something with it sometime. I could certainly contrive something very striking out of the description in tonight's *Temps* of the scene outside the Palais de Justice while the verdict was being awaited.

The dog woke me up last night after I had had 3 hours' sleep. After that my nerves were too tightened for me to try even to sleep (as I had just finished my play). I lay awake and listened, rather frightened, to the various noises, all very faint, that I could hear. (I had quietened the dog with a slipper.) Marguerite, the clocks, another noise, regular, that I couldn't and don't understand, and still others beneath these. About 5 I went on with Taine on Balzac, and came across some magnificent pages of generalizations about the art of observation.

Monday, November 15th.

A grand, wet, gloomy, foggy day. I went out at 4.30 for a walk for an hour and a half, and it rained nearly all the time. It was dark when I re-entered the town from the Carrefour de l'Obélisque, and got from under the dripping trees. I was damp, but I stood, chilling, to look at bookshops. During this promenade I cleared my ideas considerably for the novel—of which I still lack the title.

This morning I received a copy of the third American edition (the first printed in America) of *The Old Wives' Tale*. Very ugly, and they have had the damned cheek to put "A novel of life" on the title-page.

Wednesday, November 17th.

News yesterday from Pinker that Nelson's were ready to buy *Buried Alive* for their sevenpenny library. Extraordinary how a really honest book won't die. I've noticed it again and again. I'm always noticing it. And I really had *not* given up hope for *Buried Alive*.

Been correcting, and adding stage directions to *The Honeymoon*. I was charmed with the second act this afternoon. I shall do the third act after

I have written a short story, *Why the Clock Stopped,* for which I got the plot yesterday.

Last night Pauline Smith read me the second chapter of her South African novel, and it was excellent.

On Monday night Devic [1] talked for two hours. All I retained was that in some French Alpine villages when a person dies in winter, his body is put away in an attic till spring. Natural refrigeration, of course, and the ground is undiggable!

Friday, November 19th.

Yesterday I finished making a list of all social, political, and artistic events which I thought possibly useful for my novel, between 1872 and 1882. Tedious bore, for a trifling ultimate result in the book. But necessary. Today in the forest I practically arranged most of the construction of the first part of the novel. Still lacking a title for it. If I thought an ironic title would do, I would call it *A Thoughtful Young Man.* But the public is so damned slow in the uptake.

I am now getting to the end of my year's work. In a week, I shall have nothing to do except collection of information on the spot for the novel.

Today I finished and mounted another water-colour, of Arbonne—one of my least rotten.

Tuesday, November 23rd.

I have now written for rooms to hotels in Paris and London. First preparations beginning for our departure on Saturday. I am completely sick of all literary work, and could not possibly find energy to keep a journal *convenablement.* Very cold weather also. I began a chill yesterday, and today, as I was walking down from the Point de Vue de Calvaire, I had a stab of lumbago, and had to stand still for a few seconds in order to collect myself sufficiently to go on. But I have had worse lumbago than that in my time.

Friday, November 26th.

Exhausted. Especially with putting away books, dismantling the house, selecting all the necessary literary apparatus for our absence, packing it and my clothes, and smoking too much. After tea I went up into the

---

[1] A chemist friend.

town, to see the Foire de Sainte-Catherine. Too idle and bored to note features. Except these: Men singing songs—in set fashion—in order to sell the music. One man sang and accompanied himself on a sort of little organ. Another—an oldish man—had an orchestra of two behind him: rather an elaborate apparatus for so small a *commerce*. Secondly, a female quack, in mourning, stumping it from the box-seat of a large, gaudily painted and gilded chariot. She spoke well and clearly in a quiet, carrying voice. Just as I paused in front of her for a moment, she said, holding up a bottle: *"Nous avons ici un ver solitaire sorti d'un homme de 42 ans, qui a 15 mètres de longueur."*

H. W. Massingham [1] wrote me yesterday inviting me to contribute to the *Nation*. No editorial invitation has ever flattered me as much as this. He said he considered *The Old Wives' Tale* to be one of the one or two really great novels of the last 30 years.

Wednesday, December 1st. England.

Arrived at Burslem last night. Noted, for third novel in trilogy, scene in train, and Shields' dentist scene, in special notebook. Wild weather. Glass lower than it has been all this year, I think.

Friday, December 3rd.

Barometer lower this morning than I ever remember seeing it. Howling wind all night, and sleet driving about when I drew up the blinds.

Yesterday morning I began to get information out of Dawson [2] for *Clayhanger*.

Saturday, December 4th.

Yesterday morning I came to Manchester (where I write this, before leaving it again). Midland Hotel. Large Bible in the room.

I was entertained to lunch by Haslam Mills and G. H. Mair.[3] The second, Scotch, educated at Edinburgh, Oxford, Grenoble, and Paris. Evidently considered to be one of the stars of the future.[4] Slight, delicate

---

[1] Under whose editorship the *Nation* rose to its commanding position in British journalism.
[2] Mr. Joseph Dawson owned a shop at Burslem and was registrar.
[3] Of the *Manchester Guardian*.
[4] G. H. Mair was subsequently assistant editor of the *Daily Chronicle*. He died in 1925.

man, with a face retreating at the bottom. Scotch accent. The renowned
C. E. Montague was present; also A. N. Monkhouse. [1] Montague, though
a Londoner born and bred, looks the typical provincial—rather like an
intelligent S.S. superintendent; quite grey hair, low collar and queer
necktie. A rather tight, prim way of speaking; when he disagrees or is
not convinced, he is sometimes silent, with a slight working of the
muscles of the face; probably due to sloth. They told me afterwards that
he lived in a shell; but yesterday he came out, and people were surprised.
Monkhouse a large grave man, slow-speaking, with an extraordinary
sedate and sincere charm.

The lunch was very agreeable indeed. Mills has a good manner, which
he has conventionalized and hardened, of telling yarns. All the talk was
"shop." Lunch lasted till 4. I then went with Mair and Mills to the file-
room of the *Guardian*. And when I had done there I was told that a tea-
fight was awaiting me. We came back to the Midland. A man named
Agate [2] (not quite on the staff) and another man now joined us. Younger
and less brilliant than the others, but still very fine. Even the satellites on
the *Guardian* have their precise notions about Goncourt. We took tea
till 6.15, when I went to the Gaiety Theatre to meet Iden Payne. [3] He
took me out to dine at the Brazenose Club, where the food was excellent.
He looks like a little original wild member of the Fabian Society. Cape
instead of overcoat, held on by bands crossing the chest. Mair said he had
seen him in sandals in his office. Highly intelligent. Self-centred. Insignificant to look at. He then took me to the dress-circle. Performance of
Every Man in His Humour. We missed most of the first act, so I didn't
follow it, and found a lot of it confusing. But I thought the performance
extremely artistic, and it provided me with a whole series of new sensations. I came to the hotel for half an hour and wrote to M. Then I went
back to the *Guardian* office and was introduced by Mair to another series
of *Guardian* men, and I stayed till 1 A.M. to see the first edition printed
and despatched. I read a copy of it, and J. S. Mill, till 2 A.M., and woke up
at 10 A.M. with a headache caused by too strong cigars. Yesterday was
one of the most agreeable days I have ever spent in my life. (I wish I

---

[1] Montague was chief leader writer of the *Manchester Guardian;* A. N. Monkhouse, on
the editorial staff.

[2] James Agate, at that time dramatic critic of the *Manchester Guardian*.

[3] Director and producer of Miss Horniman's Manchester company, and similarly active
in the United States for a time.

was not too idle to write it all up.) The fact is that *this* sort of thing is the real reward for having written a few decent books.

Sunday, December 5th.

I happened to see Conrad and Hueffer's *Romance* at Frank's at lunch today, and I took it to read. I read about 20 pages after lunch, before the gas stove in the bedroom, but I doubt if I shall get much further in it. Also I doubt if I shall read much more of J. S. Mill's *Autobiography* here. I cannot read in Burslem. All I can do is to go about and take notes. My mind is in a whirl all the time. I have only been here 5 days, and yet all Paris and Avon seems years off; I scarcely ever even think of these places and my life there. Sometimes by accident I speak to myself or to one of the children in French.

Yesterday I got back from Manchester for lunch. Then a long yarn at Dawson's, recounting the glories of the *Manchester Guardian*. Maud came, and talked opera rehearsals from the point of view of a minor principal. Then I sent for Russell and he came at 9.30. Frank and his crowd called at 11.30, and we all went to Frank's. I came home at 12.50 and slept very dreamlessly till 7. The Sanatogen [1] cure, which I began on Wednesday, is already working.

Tuesday, December 7th.

Dawson's yesterday morning, acquiring stuff for *Clayhanger* until Edmund Leigh called, and he orated for an hour with such persuasive effect that in the end I volunteered to write a political manifesto for the district; for which afterwards I was of course both sorry and glad.

Wednesday, December 8th.

Dawson and dentist yesterday morning. I made real progress in getting information from Dawson. After dinner I went to the Grand Theatre, 9.15 P.M. I was profoundly struck by all sorts of things. In particular by the significance of clog-dancing, which had never occurred to me before. I saw a "short study" for *The Nation* in this. Towards the end I came across Warwick Savage and walked home with him. This was a pity because I had got into an extraordinary vein of "second sight." I perceived whole chapters. Of all the stuff I made sufficient notes.

---

[1] Once a widely advertised German nostrum.

Thursday, December 9th.

Enthusiastic letter from Lee Matthews about the play. Yesterday morning I sat with Dawson and Cartledge on the magistrates' bench. I made some notes. One hopeless case, showing the criminality of the criminal system. A woman who had been in and out of prison since 1876, and she got another month.

Saturday, December 11th.

Yesterday morning I read my political manifesto to Dawson and Edmund Leigh with great effect. The printing of it was put in hand instantly. I went to meet Marguerite at Stoke, 3.35. Appalling weather. I slept part of the time on the sofa. Having been occupied with politics more or less for two days, I quite forgot to take current notes. I pulled myself together and began again this morning.

Wednesday, December 15th.

M. less than convalescent, but we went to the Opera Society's *Mikado*. Chiefly noted the impossibility of getting anything really striking out of such material. But the organization and *ensemble* were admirable. After that, and adventures in and out of cabs and cars, we supped at Russell's, M. being nearly dead.

Thursday, December 16th.

Yesterday morning I did part of the walk that Clayhanger must do as he comes finally home from school in the first chapter of *Clayhanger*.

I was urged to go to London tomorrow to meet G. H. Doran at the Savoy, but I telegraphed refusing today.

Slight signs last night on the part of the wire-pullers to soften down my manifesto, but I refused to do so. It went to press today.

Friday, December 17th.

After failing to stick to any novels, I have read *The Study of Sociology* [1] all week.

Tea at Florence's, with about 12.

S.B. came to the Mater's after supper, and I slanged him for his attitude

---

[1] By Herbert Spencer.

towards honest musical criticism, and for other things. Then Edward came. Then Florence. Then R., fairly full of etchings and whiskey.

M. better. I have kept up very well so far, but I could not stand much more of this life.

Sunday, December 19th.

We reached London prompt at 4 P.M. and found the Strand Palace Hotel very well organized, and strangely cheap. What makes this hotel unique among English hotels is such things as hot and cold water lavatory in every room, free baths, no tips, second serving of any dish without extra charge. I think there is no other hotel that offers these things. I would stay in it, were it only for the lavatory and the bath. The difference to the comfort of the client is tremendous. Odd that in 1910 such elementary conveniences and common senses should be unique. You can live completely and keep yourself clean in the Strand Palace for

Room, bath, breakfast	6	0
Lunch	1	6
Tea	0	6
Dinner	2	6
Per day, absolutely inclusive	10	6

Tuesday, December 21st.

Dined at Wells's; Lowes Dickinson,[1] the Rothensteins[2] and T. Seccombe. The first-named *était tout de suite extrêmement sympathique*. Before he went he asked me to go and stay a week-end with him at Cambridge. Rothenstein a good, elaborate talker: some talking for the sake of talking, the kind of thing that is like dust in my particular mouth. Mrs. Rothenstein never reads or goes to the theatre, but keeps herself mentally alive out of her children and out of Hampstead Heath. They said she was a ballet dancer. Anyhow when asked to dance while H.G. played the pianola for certain couples, she refused totally. Richard Whiteing,[3] Mrs.

---

[1] G. Lowes Dickinson, classical scholar, critic, and psychologist, is best known for his *Greek View of Life* and *A Modern Symposium*.

[2] William Rothenstein's portrait drawings include the most important literary and artistic people of the day.

[3] The journalist and novelist among whose works the best known is *No. 5 John Street*.

Nevinson, and a whole family of Radfords came in after. The whole family was exceedingly typical. The worn, bright mother, the pure, downright, clever daughters, all young, and the elegantish young son. Also a doctor who could do excellent cockney imitations. Mrs. Nevinson was agreeably disagreeable of demeanour at first; I soon broke down her barriers by talking about H.W.N.'s [1] *Neighbours of Ours*. Richard Whiting was old, deafish, a good quiet talker, and he had a sort of startled enthusiasm for *The O.W.T.* He was halfway through it, and it appeared to have knocked him over quite. But Lowes Dickinson was my man.

I came back down the Tube with Seccombe, who had to go to Acton. My first visit to Hampstead, except once to the Heath, by train.

Thursday, December 23rd.

Tuesday night Rickards dined with me, we went to *The Blue Bird* [2] at the Haymarket, and then to Gambrinus, where he ate an enormous sandwich and drank stout. He talked about himself the whole time, except when the curtain was up, from 6.40 to 12.15. Of course this exasperated egoism was painful as a disease to witness, but his talk was exceedingly good and original. Artistically and intellectually I don't think he has gone off.

To lunch at Wells's. He and I talked his scandal from 12.15 to lunch time. Robert Ross,[3] the Sidney Lows,[4] Mrs. Garnett,[5] Archer, and the young Nesbit girl who was mad on the stage. I liked Ross at once. I got on fairly well with Archer. He bluntly asked me why I had said in print that he and Walkley were the upas-trees of the modern drama. So I told him, less bluntly. I consider that he has no real original ideas of his own. I mean to cultivate Ross.

Friday, December 24th.

After tea I went to see Palmer,[6] who wanted to republish *The Truth*

---

[1] Henry W. Nevinson, then war correspondent in Morocco; journalist, novelist, philosopher, fine flower of English culture. His latest book is *Goethe, Man and Poet* (1931).

[2] By Maurice Maeterlinck.

[3] The executor of Oscar Wilde's literary estate was a journalist and author of books on art.

[4] Sidney Low was editor of the *St. James's Gazette* until 1897 and the author of *The Governance of England* and *The Vision of India*.

[5] Constance Garnett, the wife of Edward Garnett, is known for her translations of the great Russian novels.

[6] Frank Palmer, the publisher. *The Truth about an Author* was originally published anonymously by Constable.

about an Author. He said he would pay £25 down in advance of royalties. I agreed to this.

He told me all sorts of tales about Harris.[1] As e.g. that Elder Dempsters offered him and his wife a free passage and a month in one of their hotels somewhere for something, and he asked for two months, which they refused, whereupon he was perfectly furious. He told Lord Grimthorpe, who cried: "The scoundrels! Have my villa." And this is why Harris and his wife are now living free in Grimthorpe's villa.

Palmer's tales about Harris's proof corrections were fantastic. He showed me a copy of the ordinary edition, finally finished, with most complicated alterations which Harris wanted in the limited edition. Palmer said it couldn't be done; whereupon Harris said, "I have no further interest in the limited edition," and went off in disgust.

Tuesday, December 28th.

Yesterday morning I went over the Wesleyan Westminster building with Rickards.[2] He is now gradually getting hold of me again as a great artist. With regard to the building—cornices, showing horizontally through scaffolding. Huge upright girder halfway through a doorway. Huge tripod of derricks going up through reinforced concrete floors, and so on. Iron tufted bars for reinforced concrete. Pools of water. Going up and down ladders. Cement-y dirt and mud. Sticky feeling on hands afterwards. Vibration of talking in crypt-like basement. Sound of people in street talking as if in building. Sounds of water and mysterious sounds actually in building. Whole structure penetrated by ventilation flues— looked like Oriental places for chucking down women into underground rivers. Contractors' and architects' offices on entering. Clothes and boot brushes. Effect of grand staircases sketched out in stone and brick. The centre of the building was only a vast emptiness, with a long iron girder poised on either side—supporting, ultimately, the galleries. Blue light, distinctly blue, coming down into basement through holes.

Wednesday, December 29th.

Bournemouth yesterday. I shall never forget the appalling sensation of turmoil and jolly, rough manners I had during lunch at the Hydro.

---

[1] Frank Harris.

[2] The firm of Lanchester and Rickards, subsequently Lanchester and Lodge, were architects of the Central Hall, Westminster.

A huge place. Crammed dining-room. Strident orchestra (women), rushing waiters of both sexes. Heaps of food but no service. *Patron et patronne* very good-natured. The whole crowd out for a lark, and enjoying the infernal vulgar din. A grand fancy dress ball the night before. What must it have been like? After seeing this and the town I decided absolutely against Bournemouth. It was symbolic that I couldn't even get China tea there. Six hours in train. I got back to the hotel at 7.30. I had spent a day and a pound in discovering that Bournemouth was impossible.

Thursday, December 30th.

Lunch with Pinker yesterday. In the grill room at dinner we met Hamilton Fyfe [1] and his wife. He told me that of all the *Daily Mail* sixpenny novels, Charles Garvice's [2] sold the best. He also said that while in Canada with Kennedy Jones, [3] he gave the latter *Hugo* to read. He had enjoyed it himself, but K.J. was furious that it had been foisted upon him. He had no use for it at all. It angered him. When Fyfe said that he had entirely missed the point, he swore he hadn't, but that the point was all rot. Yet Fyfe said that he had never known K.J. so enthusiastic about a book as about *The O.W. Tale.* He was tremendously struck by it, and gave instructions that I should be approached about a serial for the *Daily Mail! !* As a fact, I was, in Switzerland last year.

Friday, December 31st.

Hueffer came to lunch. He was genuinely pessimistic about commercial chances of the artistic novelist. He said that Conrad was in indigence. He gave a lot of interesting particulars about Conrad.

Another lesson last night about free seats at theatres. Criterion had telephoned last week I could have seats. I called at box office yesterday afternoon and was told by a man in it that I could have two seats for last night. When we reached there in the evening two other men were in the box office. They seemed inimical. I gave my card, as they knew nothing. One of them said, "This conveys nothing to me." He then tried to be polite. So did I. I told him not to trouble, whereupon the other

---

[1] Special correspondent, was at this time dramatic critic of the London *World,* and the author of a play.

[2] Author of a great many works of extremely popular fiction including *A Coronet of Shame, Where Love Leads,* etc.

[3] Manager of the London *Daily Mirror,* the *Daily Mail* and other newspapers.

man handed me two tickets, in silence. A little of this kind of thing goes a long way.

When I saw the acting and *mise en scène* of *Don*,[1] I positively shrank from the prospect of the fight which I must necessarily have for years and years, if I am to get any sort of a decent production with such intractable material. It seemed to be all hopelessly wrong and conventional. But it wasn't. The play contained a fine central comic idea, clumsily and inadequately handled, nevertheless with fine moments.

Trench is supposed to be the artistic manager. Still, on first page of programme, his own name and Wyndham's name, and name of piece, but no name of author!

---

[1] By Rudolf Besier, produced at the Haymarket, October 12, 1909.

Sunday, January 2nd.

On Friday night, our last night in London, we went to the Tivoli. There were no seats except in the pit; so we went in the pit. Little Tich was very good, and George Formby, the Lancashire comedian, was perhaps even better. Gus Elen I did not care for. And I couldn't see the legendary cleverness of the vulgarity of Marie Lloyd. She was very young and spry for a grandmother. All her songs were variations on the same theme of sexual naughtiness. No censor would ever pass them, and especially he wouldn't pass her winks and her silences. To be noted also was the singular *naïveté* of the cinematograph explanation of what a vampire was and is, for the vampire dance. The stoutest and biggest attendants laughed at Little Tich and G. Formby. Fearful draughts half the time down exit staircases from the street. Fearful noise from the bar behind, made chiefly by officials. The bar-girls and their friends simply ignored the performance and the public. Public opinion keeps the seats of those who go to the bar at the interval for a drink.

Going home, stopped by procession of full carriages entering the Savoy and empty carriages coming out of it.

We came down to Brighton by the 1.55 on Saturday, to the Royal York. In the afternoon I called at the Exeter to learn the terms there, as Farrar had recommended it. When I gave the landlord my card, he started back, let his hands fall, and said, "My God! Is it you?" This was the first landlord of my acquaintance who had ever read anything, much less a book of mine. He seemed to know me pretty thoroughly. I gave him my card at the end of the interview, and then the interview had to begin all over again.

However, we didn't go to the Exeter, as when it came to the point, the celebrated Harry Preston of this celebrated hotel would not let me go. He agreed to my terms.

Our first stroll along the front impressed me very favourably, yesterday afternoon. But I am obsessed by the thought that all this comfort, luxury, ostentation, snobbishness, and correctness, is founded on a vast injustice to the artisan class. I can never get away from this. The furs, autos, fine food, attendance, and diamond rings of this hotel only impress it on me more.

This morning I worked genuinely for an hour on the construction of the first part of my novel.

Monday, January 3rd.

I have read about a third of Edith Wharton's *The House of Mirth.* Not fine, but capable. No connection with literature; a certain fairly agreeable bitterness of satire now and then. It can just be read. Probably a somewhat superior Mrs. Humphrey Ward. I stopped reading it in favour of Marcus Clarke's *For the Term of His Natural Life,* which I picked up here at Brighton in a sixpenny edition. I am enjoying this, though in form and plot it is very *naïf.* I could drop it without tears.

Today I wrote a *New Age* article, arranged the outline of an article for the *Nation,* and schemed out the first 9 chapters of *Clayhanger,* which I hope to begin to write on Wednesday. This afternoon we moved into our new room on the fourth floor, and I arranged everything for my work. We walked on the pier, and I saw subjects for water-colours and pastels.

The one advance which I made last year in worldliness was having a play put on at a West End Theatre for a run. That it failed is a detail. I bet it won't fail ultimately.

I wrote last year: *The Card,* novel; *The Glimpse,* novel; *The Honeymoon,* 3-act comedy; scenario for a play on the subject of *Don Juan; The Revolver,* short story; *The Tiger and the Baby; Under the Clock; Hot Potatoes; The Heroism of Thomas Chadwick; Why the Clock Stopped; The Boy, the Girl, and the Blue Suit;* 70 odd articles; my journal. Total 312,100 words. Much less than the year before.

Tuesday, January 4th.

When I came downstairs this morning, full to the brim with the first chapters of *Clayhanger,* I found a letter from Herbert Trench asking me to alter tremendously the third act of *The Honeymoon.* My soul revolted, but of course I gradually gave way and then wrote him that I would.

I was occupied with letters till 11, and then I went out to recover myself for *Clayhanger,* and I did do so. I worked till 1 o'clock, and again after lunch, and again after dinner. So that now I have got the opening of the book pretty ripe.

This afternoon we went to have tea with the Sidney Lows at the Metropole. Low told me how he discovered Kipling, and how his superiors on the Indian daily didn't think anything of him at all, but Low insisted on getting hold of his stuff. It seems he was very shy and young at the start. Low also insisted on Hall Caine's powers as a *raconteur,* as proved at Cairo, when he kept a dinner party of casual strangers interested for 1½ hours by a full account of the secret history of the Druce case, which secret history he admitted afterwards was a sheer novelist's invention.

When H.C. was with S.L. in Egypt he saw everything as a background to *The White Prophet,* which was originally meant as a play for Tree. When S.L. showed him the famous staircases in the Ghezireh Palace he said, "I can get three different entrances underneath that." And when he saw the Pyramids, he said, "Tree can do simply anything with those," etc. The S. Lows said he was the kindest nicest sort of man in private life (but S.L. told me behind his hand that he was apt to be tedious on the subject of himself, and *naïf*). Present also, *inter alia,* the wife of T. H. S. Escott,[1] who lives at Brighton, but is paralysed. He still works and produces, however, and has a new book just coming out.

Wednesday, January 5th.

This morning at 9.45 I began to write *Clayhanger.* I felt less nervous and self-conscious than usual in beginning a book. And never before have I made one-quarter so many preliminary notes and investigations. I

---

[1] Political and historical writer. He succeeded Morley as editor of the *Fortnightly Review.*

went out for a little recess, and at 1.30 I had done 1,000 words, which was very good for a first day.

We went to the Aquarium after tea, and heard mediocre music, and saw first-rate fishes etc., living long under highly artificial conditions. The seals and alligators seemed to be intensely bored and sick of life, but perhaps they weren't. Then I came back and wrote half an article for the *Nation* about the Hanley music-hall.

Earlier in the afternoon I went out and viewed the shore, and the launching of fishing boats. All kinds of activity in progress, spoiling to be described. But now that I am on my novel I am tied up again for six months from anything really swagger in the way of description.

Weather misty. No visible round trace of the sun. The hotel is haunted by barrel organs. In fact in various ways Brighton seems to be what London was. Its architecture is old Belgravia and Tyburnian. There is "Ye Olde Bunn Shoppe" just close by here, and a general "feel" of Bloomsbury and muffins.

Sunday, January 9th.

Last week I wrote 4,500 words of *Clayhanger* and two articles. So that it was a good beginning. Rickards came on Friday night. Up till then the only dissipation we had was a visit to the Aquarium. His conversation remains what it was, the most human and genuinely poetic in texture of any that I have ever enjoyed. But he must be allowed to talk only of his own experiences. Every now and then he constructs a very fine and original general idea. Last night we went to the Hippodrome, a vast circular human sight. And he made a good caricature of Seymour Hicks [1] who was in a stage box. Hicks is staying here. He wore a flannel shirt all day and all evening, but dined upstairs, probably to hide it. Drove off to the Hippodrome at 9, and there rolled about with laughter at the comic turns in the sight of all. I liked him for his frank coarse enjoyment of the most mediocre things. He had a fine rich voice, and his unavailing but well-meant efforts to appear natural and non-celebrated are our joy.

Letter from the new editor of the *English Review* [2] asking me to contribute.

---

[1] Proprietor of the Aldwych and Hicks Theatres.
[2] Ford Madox Hueffer.

Tuesday, January 11th.

Too excitingly busy just now to keep this journal every day. Hueffer telephoned me on Sunday at lunch time asking me to do him a 3,000-word political article on the crisis [1] for the twentieth. In pursuance of my policy of never declining work that I am practically challenged to do, I accepted without a moment's reflection, though I knew that 12 guineas will be far from repaying me for my nervous expense on it. On Monday morning the *Sunday Chronicle* telegraphed accepting my price of 10 guineas for an 1,800-word article. I posted the article to them tonight. And in the last two days I have also written 2,700 words of my novel. In fact, terrific productiveness!

Grand rolling weather. Foamy sea, boisterous wind, sun, pageant of clouds, and Brighton full of wealthy imperative persons dashing about in furs and cars. I walked with joy to and fro on this unequalled promenade. And yet, at this election time, when all wealth and all snobbery is leagued together against the poor, I could spit in the face of arrogant and unmerciful Brighton, sporting its damned Tory colours.

I heard the door-keeper of this hotel politely expostulating with a guest: "Surely, Mr. ———, you don't mean to say you're anything but a Conservative!" Miserable parrot. After reading some pessimistic forecasts of the election I was really quite depressed at tea time. But I went upstairs and worked like a brilliant nigger, and counted nearly 5,000 words done in two days, and I forgot my depression.

Certainly this morning as I looked at all the splendid solidity of Brighton, symbol of a system that is built on the grinding of the faces of the poor, I had to admit that it would take a lot of demolishing, that I couldn't expect to overset it with a single manifesto and a single election, or with 50. So that even if the elections are lost, or are not won, I don't care. Besides, things never turn out as badly as our fears. It is only when one does not fear that they go so surprisingly and bafflingly wrong, as with the Socialists at the last German general election.

Tuesday, January 18th.

Une espèce de financier, M.D., staying here indefinitely and going up to London every day, said the other night during a political discussion

---

[1] The Budget had been thrown out by the Lords in November, Parliament had been dissolved, and a General Election was to be held on January 14.

that there were "40 chaps" in his office, and that he believed there were 40 radicals amongst them. This cheered me somewhat. Reminiscing about Barney Barnato with another old Tory here, he said that though B.B. was utterly uneducated and showed it in ordinary conversation, yet he could make a speech perfectly correctly; also that he could and did recite from memory whole acts of Shakespeare without a single false pronunciation or emphasis.

Since Saturday night, when I stood out in the rain and wind 2¾ hours to see the election returns on the *Daily News* lantern screen in the Old Steine, I have been perfectly obsessed by politics, perhaps to my harm artistically. Today I finished my 3,000-word article on *The Forces behind the Elections* for the next issue of the *English Review*. I don't think very much of it. It has a certain elegant quality—but is too vague. It lacks personality. The fact was I hadn't anything particular to say and anyhow wasn't in a state to say even what I had to say.

Hueffer came down for the day on Sunday. Of all the interesting things he said all I remember at the moment is that he was staying lately with Lord Pauncefote for a few days' shooting and that Lord P. drank champagne himself and gave whiskey and soda to his guests. It seems Mond [1] has bought the *English Review*.

Frightful weather; wind, rain, and gloom. And perhaps the chief origin of my existing dissatisfaction with things in general is that on Friday I had to consult an oculist, as I could only explain my headaches by the theory of a strain on my eyes. Yesterday I began to wear glasses. It is no light thing to begin suddenly to see the novel you have started with the naked eye, through a pair of eye-glasses.

Friday, January 21st.

I am gradually showing most of the symptoms of the average crass Tory. Merely to hear the opposite side discussing politics and agreeing with one another makes me furious and also coldly self-contemptuous. No doubt the elections are genuinely on my nerves. Depressed about them; preoccupied by them. After all, even allowing for Tory intimidation in villages, the nation will broadly get what it wants, anyhow. And

---

[1] Sir Alfred Mond, the financier associated with the world's chemical markets, was created a baronet in 1910. He is said to have served as model for H. G. Wells's industrialist in *The World of William Clissold*.

I suppose that no politics, however idiotic, can make a great difference to the situation of middling, comfortable persons like me. Yet I continue to worry because the fools won't vote right, and I lie awake at night thinking about their foolishness. We went in the motor bus to Shoreham this afternoon, in superb freezing weather. The intervening villages between here and Shoreham are fairly ugly and industrial, but the shipping was agreeable after the complete absence of it in Brighton, and Shoreham had points. The choleric little man who speaks French so glibly and is so damned silly on politics proved quite nervously agreeable on the motor bus, and was most touching on the subject of sleepless nights.

I began a new chapter of *Clayhanger* at 5.15 today, after teasing the ideas for it since 7 this morning. I am trying to lift the whole thing up to a great height, but I feel sure that up to now it is nothing more than interesting in a nice quiet way.

Monday, January 24th.

I got so absorbed in my novel that the elections ceased to excite and disgust me. On Friday, Saturday, and today, I must have written 6,000 words of it, and not bad.

I was just going to bed after dinner when the fierce little Tory Mister came and sat down for a prolonged conversation about hotels in Switzerland. Since our conversation in the Worthing motor bus the other day he had suddenly discovered my identity. He soon began talking about books, and fetched his wife, who is "a great reader" and of whom he is very proud. They have been married over 30 years, childless, and get on splendidly together. She is half French—French father—of the Polignac and d'Alhémas families, proud, quiet, distinguished. Certain books she couldn't read because they are on the Index. We talked for about two hours. I could have got on with that man very well in spite of his Toryism (and certainly I could have got on with the woman) because he is so nervously alive, even when tedious. But they went today, "hoping to meet you again" etc.

Curious the *naïveté* of stock-brokers. M.D. asked me if I knew "the real truth"—namely that Carnegie had given a million to the Liberal funds for the elections, "not of course for philanthropy's sake, but because he knew he could get his money back quick enough if Tariff

Reform could be stopped." He really believed this. He is a nice honest simple man, but his *naïveté* is remarkable. So is the *naïveté* of most other people here, I find.

I ought to do a brief account of my own psychological state during the elections. In some ways it had the faults shown by the Tory mentality.

Sleety and awful weather tonight. Chilblains on hands, etc.

Wednesday, January 26th.

I have done 2,000 words each day this week of *Clayhanger*, the stuff getting better, I think, each day.

Last night Orage sent me the first novel (I think) censored by the Libraries under their new scheme. I read 100 pages of it.

Perfect weather today. Hard frost. Chilblains on all my extremities. Still reading *Le Rouge et le Noir* with humility.

Thursday, January 27th.

Searched off and on, from 7 A.M. till 8 P.M., for a motive bit of plot to carry along the material of my next chapter. Found it during dinner. But these delays are rather depressing, and even now I am not sure if it is first class.

Monday, January 31st.

Tertia and family and the Mater came down on Friday. I began *Clayhanger* on January 5 and up to today have written 33,200 words of it. Total of over 45,000 words for the month. I had a letter from Hueffer this morning, in reference to my eulogy of the *English Review* in the *New Age* saying I was the only one who had not tried to thwart him etc. A characteristic letter.

Suggestion that I should do a weekly article for the *Daily Chronicle*. I said I would do it if I was free to be genuine and not merely bright, etc. I wrote to Tillotsons yesterday in reply to a demand for stuff, refusing to work any more at the old price.

Thursday, February 3rd.

On Tuesday we went in a taxicab to lunch with the Lucases [1] at Kings-

---

[1] E. V. Lucas is the author of more than fifty works including books of essays, novels, and children's verse.

ton Manor. *Un petit pays perdu.* I found Lucas slightly more Lucas than ever, and liked him more. His wife is like a nice Ibsen heroine. House slightly bare; a good staircase; plenty of colour; and some good little pictures.

The other morning I watched the seagulls helping the scavenger to scavenge the remains of the daily fish market on the beach. Rain. Strong wind. They could not alight. They had a lot of balancing and steering to do. They dived again and again for the same bit of offal, missing it, till they got it. Then each prize-winner sailed off against wind with difficulty towards Palace Pier, and out of my sight somewhere; but some seemed to swallow the piece *en route.* I was watching them alight in the water the other day; all did exactly the same; a planing descent, then, close on water, 2 or 3 half-flaps, a raising of the head, and they were afloat.

A steady 2,000 or more words per day of *Clayhanger* (except Tuesday of course). I read a lot of it on Tuesday, and found it more "coloured" and variegated than I had expected.

Wednesday, February 9th.

On Monday morning, in the bedroom and in the drawing-room, I finished the first part of *Clayhanger,* 42,000 words instead of 40,000. I wrote 2,000 words and was nearly going mad at lunch time, but Webster and M. humoured me.

This morning I walked out and ordered a pair of spectacles, and began to get my ideas in order for the second part of *Clayhanger* and did get them in order, rather well. On Monday I received a belated request from the *Manchester Guardian* to do a special telegraphic criticism of *Chantecler* [1] for them. Of course I was here instead of in France, and it was too late. Nevertheless, even had everything been favourable, I doubt if I should have faced the unusualness and the worry of the task.

Hubert Bland, having based his article in *Sunday Chronicle* of 30 January on statement that *The Glimpse* and other books were banned by the Libraries, I wrote to Smith's, Mudie's, and *The Times* Book Club to ask if this was so, and if so why? They all replied that it was absolutely

---

[1] By Edmond Rostand.

untrue. Smith's said they had 500 copies of *The Glimpse* in circulation at that moment.

Friday, February 11th.

Dinner at Chelsea Arts Club. Room long, low. Billiard room. Rules and cues still hanging on walls. Some men in elegant evening dress; some in fair ditto, some in smoking jackets, some in morning coats, some in lounge suits. Frampton[1] in the last, with rough hair. Shannon,[2] in chair, *très élégant.*

New ventilation put in roof for this banquet. Ventilation bad. Dinner sound. Service mediocre. Man on my right who grumbled at most things.

Caricatures, drawings, and paintings round walls. Whitish walls. No elegance of furniture. The whole place rather like a studio.

Shannon's speech good. When replies began, *il commençait de se dégager* an atmosphere of brotherly love (which I found afterwards to be quite false). You might have thought that success in an artistic career depended chiefly on help from fellow artists. It grew almost maudlin. Enormous log-rolling, not principally as great artists, but as true friends, etc. Notoriously untrue, of course.

Note that the points of my speech that raised laughs were that I had bought pictures by members, that Orpen[3] was a child, and that each member of the Club who was made A.R.A. was a hatchet buried in the ribs of the enemy.

Enormous applause of younger A.R.A.'s, Derwent Wood, and Orpen. When I mentioned Foster (Club organizer) in my speech, they called for a speech from him afterwards. A very strong man. He went out. Several tried to drag him into the room but could not. They say the Club owes everything to him.

After regular speeches, comic speech read by Cavaliere Formili, interrupted by an arranged suffragette invasion. Coarse jokes here. Political opinions of majority seen at once. Invaders in costume, also policeman. One put his legs down hole in roof. This rather *naïf,* rather feeble. Then continuation of Formili. The professional humorist, Walter Emanuel,

---

[1] Sir George Frampton, the sculptor.
[2] James J. Shannon, the Anglo-American artist.
[3] Sir William Orpen.

read out sham telegrams from people who couldn't come. One or two pretty good. The rest idiotic, in the conventional *Punch* manner. (He is "Charivaria" of *Punch*.)

I had to go out here, as the chill caused by opening windows for invasion got into my guts. All fires let out in other rooms. I stayed near bar, talking to various people. Konody,[1] Conrad, Hardy, Turner, Cillick. We got colder and colder. I peeped into the big room sometimes. Ventriloquism, songs, piano, etc. Not quite full now. The distinguished Shannon still sitting there bravely enjoying, with his monocle.

Sunday, February 13th.

Today I tackled the question of notes.

I also finished correcting the proofs of *Helen with the High Hand*. Mr. and Mrs. Granville Barker and Dr. and Mrs. Wheeler came for tea. They were very indignant against Herbert Trench for having abandoned the repertory, short interrupted run scheme at the Haymarket —Barker particularly—and I think they were right.

I wrote an indictment of Brieux this morning for the *New Age,* knowing that he is well loved by the Barkers and the Stage Society generally. I saw Zangwill [2] for the first time. He and Tree and Sutro dined together at the hotel.

Monday, February 14th.

Today I began to get my second part of *Clayhanger* in order. I finished reading the first part and found the penultimate chapter a bit dull, the last good and solid.

Tonight I finished *Le Rouge et le Noir* for the second time. Nothing to beat it for solid truth anywhere, and nothing outside Russia to beat it as a special novel in the grand manner.

Thursday, February 17th.

Yesterday appeared the first of my series of articles in the *Chronicle*. In discussing the opinion of the young man of 1960 about *Chantecler* I said *"the young man of 1960, whose mother's parents probably met the*

---

[1] Paul G. Konody was then art critic of the *Daily Mail*.
[2] Israel Zangwill, best known for *Children of the Ghetto*.

night before last and were rather taken with each other"! The editor cut this phrase out.

I began to write the second part of *Clayhanger* on Tuesday. I did 2,000 words, and a *New Age* article, and a lot of letters at night, and a description of *Clayhanger* for the publishers' Catalogue. I was very exhausted.

£12 odd is my share of result of nine performances of *What the Public Wants* at Glasgow recently.

I wrote to Trench on Tuesday, telling him definitely I wouldn't alter the last act of *The Honeymoon*.

Two thousand words of *Clayhanger* today, and an evening of heavy correspondence. And I walked twice to Hove, and once to Black Rock, and once to the end of the Pier. We had tea with Mrs. Granville Barker (Lillah McCarthy), who asked me to write a monologue for her. I said I thought I would.

M. finished copying her first short story, *Les Chouettes,* today. And I read it. I was quietly astonished by the excellence of its construction, its little fine *aperçus*, and its general stylishness and genuine interestingness.

February 20th.

All secure in the hotel. But terrific wind beating on south windows and general shaking. Go out. You then see hotels from outside. Blocks of stone and yellow light, immensely secure. Very brilliant in lower stages. Aquarium a cluster of lights with its little absurd tower. Moon in cloudy sky. Little crowds at two points near pier. Vast sea of foam for about 200 yards out. Rows of little people in half-distance silhouetted like a long-toothed saw against this. I find the general look of these groups of people perhaps the most interesting. So small. Waves breaking over jetty and over Marine Drive. Waves coming between jetty and pier, running along wall of jetty in a line like the curves of a long rope shaken to imitate waves. Noise of naked shingles. Plenty of suffused light about. Sheet lightning from time to time.

There was a wonderful sunset the night before, salmon (and a salmon sea) in south, pink to east, and sapphire to west. In 15 minutes it was all grey. But while it lasted the sky was a composition in itself.

Monday, February 21st.

Mr. and Mrs. Lowndes came down on Friday before lunch and left yesterday morning before lunch. And we talked vast quantities of real "shop." I took a walk on Saturday with Lowndes and he made one very good joke, which I shall certainly divert to my own purposes. I wrote 2,600 of novel on Friday, and about the same on Saturday. On Sunday morning I carried Mrs. Granville Barker's hot-water bottle on to the pier for her. I called on them in the evening and had a bit of yarn. Barker told me some plots of plays he had produced. He said A. Schnitzler [1] was the best writer of one-act plays, and recounted the plot of *In a Hospital*. I then had a great desire to write a big one-act play. The plot of *In a Hospital* as recounted by Barker was very striking.

Received from Chatto and Windus's the 1s. edition of *Sacred and Profane Love*, on which I am to get £5 per thousand. Finished proofs of *Helen with the High Hand*, and received the first proofs of *What the Public Wants*.

Wednesday, February 23rd.

Yesterday Mrs. Granville Barker, nurse, and a Miss Ponsonby, came for tea. The last had come down from London to recount triumph of Galsworthy's *Justice* to the wife of its producer. She is an *au courant de tout* woman, and when talking to an author about criticizing a work of art says, "Oh, but you great men can see the technical side and all that," etc., in quite a serious tone.

M. and I went to see *The Merry Widow*.[2] I felt I *had* to see it, in order to be *calé* on such things when it came to writing about London.

Same thing over again. Indeed I could notice no difference. Music even much less charming or superficially and temporarily attractive than I had expected. Troupe of about 40. Elaborate costumes, scenery, and appointments. Sylvia May, Kate May, and the other principals, all chosen for their looks. Not one could avoid the most elementary false emphasis. Thus Sylvia May looking at a man asleep on a sofa: "But *he* may wake up" (when there was no question of another man asleep) instead of "He may wake *up*." This sort of thing all the time. Also such things as "recog*nize*." Three chief males much better. All about drinking and

---

[1] Barker adapted and produced *Anatol* and other plays by the Viennese dramatist.
[2] The operetta, composed by Franz Lehar.

whoring and money. All popular operetta airs. Simply nothing else in the play at all, save references to patriotism. Names of tarts on the lips of characters all the time. Dances lascivious, especially one.

I couldn't stand more than two acts. Too appallingly bored.

Friday, February 25th.

Yesterday I signed contracts with Dutton's of N.Y. for £1,000. Not much; but the most I have yet signed for in a day.

I wrote 2,300 words yesterday, and began feeling a wreck last night. Feeling complete this morning. Couldn't work, I walked about Brighton in cold showers till 12.30 and managed to get my first love scene into something like order.

Monday, February 28th.

This morning, I received C. E. Montague's novel, *A Hind Let Loose,* which I am to review for the *Guardian.* A destructive unrealistic thing; it put me off my work, but I wrote 3,400 words of *Clayhanger* nevertheless, and a lot of letters etc.

Friday, March 4th.

Going along the Strand on Wednesday afternoon I met Alphonse Courlander.[1] Just the same. Wanting to know what kind of book the "book of the future" would be, so that he might write in that style. Very disappointed because, at the age of 28, he had not made a name. "The worst of me is I'm so imitative," he said. "Every good writer I read strongly influences me." Pathetic, wistful figure. He never *will* make a name.

Tea at Rumpelmayer's. Mrs. Lowndes. Met a young novelist named Walpole.[2] Stayed there fighting against the band of music till 6.15. Then dressed. Dined with Webster, Dolly Smith, and poet Wayle at Treviglio's. Both Dolly and I had forgotten tickets; so we had to drive to Golden Cross Hotel, and to Bayswater to get them. Reached Albert Hall and costume ball of the Chelsea Arts Club at 11.15. Left at 4.15. Got into bed at 5 and was up at 8.30. No China tea at Golden Cross Hotel.

[1] Journalist and novelist, author of *Mightier than the Sword.* He died October 23, 1914, aged 34.
[2] At this time Hugh Walpole was 26 years old and had published *The Wooden Horse.*

Sunday, March 6th.

I got to work again yesterday, and wrote 2,000 words of *Clayhanger,* which words I thought pretty good; but I am not very hopeful about the absolutely first-class quality of the whole book. In the afternoon we went out to the cliffs, beyond Black Rock, and I made a sketch. Marvellous fine weather, with east wind. In the evening the hotel was full of fair women and brave men.

Lately I have been reading Stephen Crane's *Bowery Tales,* which was quite readable, and excellent even, in parts. Also Sturge Moore's *Art and Life* (about Flaubert and Blake) which in spite of its careful second-rate quality, I found enormously stimulating, if only on account of the extracts from Flaubert's correspondence and from French criticism. It certainly bucked up my novel quite appreciably. Also a bit of F. M. Hueffer's *A Call.* Slick work, but not, I fear, really interesting. He doesn't get down to the real stuff.

Tuesday, March 8th.

Last evening at 7.30 I received a letter from Trench, accepting *The Honeymoon* definitely. (And today I heard from Lee Matthews, who had received the second £100.) I had a great fit of triumph, as I thought about all that this Haymarket play *might* mean. But it soon passed. I had been looking for this Haymarket acceptance for weeks as a sort of goal, but it meant nothing to me, really. In fact this morning I soon found a new source of worry, as my *Chronicle* article did not appear as it ought to have done.

I wrote 1,200 words yesterday, though not making a start till nearly 5 o'clock. And 2,300 words today. But it will take me all my time to finish the second part of *Clayhanger* by next Thursday. Yesterday morning, being not fit enough for work, I walked to Rottingdean and back along the cliffs. The sight of sea and downs did me a sort of vague spiritual good.

Man bearing a card: blind, through boy throwing mortar. Discharged by 4 hospitals. Incurable.

He evidently had been a street beggar for a long time. He had the continual stamping movement of such beggars. What a tragedy! It wouldn't bear much thinking about.

Thursday, March 10th.

Neuralgia all these days. Still averaging over 2,000 words a day of novel. Neuralgia only in gums etc. Probably due to cold.

Sunday, March 13th.

For several days much bored with neuralgia and indigestion. Still, I stick to it. But on Saturday I began to feel that I shouldn't finish the second part here. I collected ideas well on Saturday. M. went to London on Friday, and I worked so much after a bad night that I was painfully tired and kept showing it nervously to myself when I went for a walk at 6.30. On Saturday morning I wrote *New Age* article and *Chronicle* article this morning.

Thursday, March 17th.

Impossible to finish the second part of *Clayhanger*. If I had finished it I should have spoilt it. I got up to within a few hundred words of 80,000, but the second part will exceed the advertised length by 5 or 6,000. Moreover I was frightened by a lot of extraordinary praise of *The Old Wives' Tale* that I have recently had. I was afraid *Clayhanger* was miles inferior to it, and that by going on blindly I might lose a chance of bucking it up in Switzerland. . . . Neuralgia gradually getting better. Tomorrow we go to Paris via Newhaven. Our stay here on the whole has been a very great success. We have both enjoyed it. I have written over 100,000 words, and Marguerite 3 short stories. But I doubt if the climate suits us now that it has duly braced us up. Certainly I need less sleep; but smoking seems to affect me more and I have had neuralgia and headaches, largely of course due to my book. But I have a feeling now against the climate.

Tuesday, March 22nd. Switzerland.

We left Brighton on Friday morning. We stayed 3 nights at the Hotel Terminus. I went for a voyage up the Seine to Charenton and back. I then went to the Exposition des Indépendents, and there met O'Connor and Root. One or two charming indecencies in the show. Tea at Weber's in the Rue Royale. Dined at Godebski's. Afterwards Ravel, Calvocoressi, Delage, Simon, and l'Abbé Petit came in. On Sunday morning I wandered about and looked into Notre Dame (Rameaux). I bought a good edition of Stendhal's *L'Amour* on the quays and at once took ideas from it for *Clayhanger*. We left the hotel at 7.10 next day A.M. and arrived at the Hôtel Belvédère, Mont-Pélerin, at 9 P.M. after a perfect journey in fine weather.

The novel seems to be looking up slightly. Anyhow it is being done honestly.

The reviews of *Helen with the High Hand* are exceedingly polite and kind, but they do not gloss over the slightness of the thing.

Among recent American reviews of *The Old Wives' Tale* is one which says that the book would have been better if it had only a little sense of humour, the verdict being that it is tedious and unenlivened by either humour or observation.

One of the most marvellous sunsets I ever saw tonight. The peaks of the Dent du Midi sticking alone out of cloud high up in the sky, like rosy teeth.

Good Friday, March 25th.

Six days of perfect weather, with a north and northwest wind and nothing visible all day in the strong sunshine. I was able to begin the final chapters of the second part of *Clayhanger* without much difficulty on Tuesday, and I have averaged over 2,000 words a day of it. I finish tomorrow. The second part will be 50,000 instead of the estimated 40,000 words.

It is surprising that, a fortnight ago at Brighton, I could have thought it possible to finish the second part there. I had only allowed 2,000 words for the most important series of scenes—love scenes—in that part. On the whole I think it is fair. Anyhow it is honest and conscientious. I wrote 3,200 words yesterday, and pretty nearly killed myself, and was accordingly very depressed at night. This morning I went a long walk and wrote 1,000 words in an hour this afternoon.

Reviews of *Helen with the High Hand* strangely kind.

Saturday, April 2nd. Milan.

We left the Hôtel Belvédère on Easter Tuesday. The company there was more interesting than last year. There was also an American, the adopted son of an old American-German woman (both of them came down to breakfast very early, earlier than we sometimes), and he was exceedingly cultivated if not highly intelligent. When he got on to the subject of Charlemagne I had to shut up. They were queer mysterious people. They were very friendly with a young Egyptian nationalist, with whom they constantly went walking. Whenever we came across them basking during one of these walks, there was always a pair of hair brushes lying near. We never understood these hair brushes. Then there was a Mrs. P. and her daughter, who had apparently met Marguerite at the Ullmans'. I had two long talks with the mother, who is tall and thin, and desired embonpoint "comeliness," to be matronly, as she called it. I told her it wasn't a sincere desire, and that she was only searching for compliments. A well-meaning but hasty and silly woman, redeemed by a genuine anxiety to bring up her English vicaragey daughter in the best way. The little Krafft girl, aged 15 or 16, had said to her that she would like to go on the stage, but she couldn't, because it would be necessary for her not to be an honest woman, and she wished to be an honest woman. Mrs. P. pretended to be horrified by this candour, and said how glad she was that her daughter had not been there to hear it. We had a long yarn about this, and I told her she was bringing up her daughter entirely wrong, with all this "innocence" convention, which I said was merely Oriental. She vehemently dissented. But I kept repeating she was wrong, and at last she said reflectively, "I wonder whether I am!" Not that I have any hope of having changed her heart; she would fly back to her old notion as soon as I had left her.

I wrote 3 articles and 11,000 words of my novel during our 7 clear days in Switzerland.

We found the Rhône Valley less tedious than we had expected, and the Simplon shorter, and the Customs quite harmless. It was very hot as soon as we got fairly into Italy, really hot. The views of the Italian lakes came up to our hopes. The Hotel Bellini is a good *hôtel de passage,* dominated by Germans, not agreeable fellow travellers, and it's no use pretending they are. There was also a school of *jeunes filles* in the hotel, chiefly Germans seeing cities during the Easter holidays. Their laughter heard occasionally from the interior of bedrooms was very agreeable. The hotel was full and remained full.

After tea M. and I went into the town. Took a tram. Quite an adventure taking a tram in an absolutely strange town where you can't speak the language. We came to the Duomo by the Victor Emmanuel (rather disappointing, this). The cathedral impressive, though you can see at once that it is meretricious in many respects. We saw it in a grand afternoon light that really did "flood" it. And its mere size was prodigious to us. And it seemed to be on fire with orange yellow rays of light. We couldn't see any chairs. The whole floor space looked empty. Then, after a time, we saw a squad of about 500 or 1,000 chairs. We had missed them in the vast area. The Victor Emmanuel Gallery and arcade also pleased us. M. was ravished, enchanted by everything; said all the women were pretty etc., all this because the atmosphere reminded her of her *midi*. We walked about till she was dead nearly.

Auguste Foa, my translator, came to see me after dinner. Young man, 32, dark, slim, hat on one side, very sympathetic and agreeable. He told me some depressing things about Italian literature. He said all his literary articles brought him in £40 a year. I shall put some of his facts into the *New Age*.

Sunday, April 3rd. Florence.

Lunch yesterday with F. Grierson at Pension Paoli. He still looked astoundingly young.[1] His wig was curiously long, his moustache of course dyed. But he had not the skin, wrinkles, nor above all the gestures of a very old man. He can't be far off 70. He may be more than 70. He said he seldom went out now, and would not dress for dinner under any circumstances. Therefore ate in his room in the hotel. Ate little. He had very good ideas about food and general management of the physical machine. Mysterious person. When I asked him if the *New Age* paid him for his articles he said no, "somebody else pays me." He said he could not work for nothing now, and vaguely that he had lost his money.

Tuesday, April 5th.

Reading Stendhal's *Rome, Naples, et Florence*. . . . Impossible to study Italian. Simply can't be done. Between the town, my novel, articles, and sketching, I haven't a moment.

---

[1] Francis Grierson was at that time 62 years of age. He had made his début in Paris as a musical prodigy but had abandoned music for literature in 1875. His books of essays he wrote in French as well as English.

Wednesday, May 25th.

We returned home yesterday after 3 exhaustingly impressionful days in Paris. We unpacked all our trunks yesterday before dinner. Dined on the *terrasse* of Brunet's, and found the price of meals had gone up from 2 fr. 75 to 3 fr. Now they give coffee, worth about 1 *sou*.

Our waiter, who was in rather a hurry to dine himself, was cheerfully cynical about the continual rise of prices in Fontainebleau. When I said I couldn't drink the wine that was *compris,* and that I knew restaurants where they would give you mineral water instead, he said, with a singular intonation, "Not in Fontainebleau, anyhow!" He said he had had 15 years of Fontainebleau, and implied that he had nothing to learn about the methods of the tradesmen here. I saw him dining afterwards. He was one of those waiters who have learned a whole philosophy in the practice of their vocation. Secretly scornful of human nature, yet indulgent. Impassive, and supremely capable of keeping his end up.

M., after engaging a servant today, told me of the reply of the mother's, made to her on several occasions by different mothers when asked if the daughter could cook: "*Je crois bien qu'elle sait faire la cuisine. Quand je ne suis pas là elle fait la soupe. Et elle sait faire cuire un morceau de veau à la casserole.*" This seems to be the last word of cooking in that class. It throws light, the phrase does, on their habits.

I had all sorts of straightening up to do today; task loathsome. Through messing about it took me 2 hours to dress, and when I had done a thousand things of no importance I went out for an hour into *my* forest, and began to arrange ideas for the last part of *Clayhanger*. They came fairly well. I bought papers at station on way home and put on my eye-glasses to read them as I walked along. Then I thought, "M. Porrier may be in the Avenue des Carrosses and would see me in my eye-glasses for the first time." I didn't want him to see me in my eye-glasses for the first time. Although I laughed at myself, I had somehow taken the glasses off before I arrived at Avenue des Carrosses.

Thursday, May 26th.

Not much success in ideas for *Clayhanger*.

Saturday, May 28th.

I was 43 yesterday.

Last week at the Gaiety, Manchester, *Cupid and Common Sense* played to £202 11s. It was the week of the King's funeral,[1] and there were 5 evening performances and a matinée.

Yesterday I had more success in finding ideas for the last part of *Clayhanger,* but I had no success in drawing. I seemed to spend all afternoon in merely arranging still-life subjects, and I couldn't decide on any of them. But on Thursday night I did a pretty fair study of Marguerite. I couldn't read anything, except newspapers. I couldn't answer any arrears of correspondence. And after doing nothing all day I was so tired I had to go to bed at 9.15.

Monday, May 30th.

Yesterday morning I had written a 1,700-word holiday article (200 words too long) for Tillotson's before 7.30 A.M. At 10 o'clock I began to do a *nature morte,* and with intervals for food and nap, I worked at it till a quarter to 6. This is the first entire day I have ever spent at painting. The best picture I have ever done. I shall finish it today. Marguerite went to Paris after lunch to see her father and family generally, and came back with fine tales; so that most of the time I was alone with the dog, who was most gloomy. When I had done painting, I began to read *Whom God Hath Joined* and couldn't leave it. I read about 70 pages of it. This is the sort of book that insists on being read.

Am just reading *A Man of Property* bit by bit. There is a boyish quality in it sometimes, a capriciousness and a wilful acerbity and exaggeration, that I like. Certainly I should say that the erotic parts— and there are plenty of them—were done under the influence of George Moore. If Galsworthy had never read and admired George Moore, the similarity is extremely remarkable.

Thursday, June 2nd.

I was in bed all day on Tuesday with a *migraine;* it sounds nicer than bilious attack. All due to eating a *fricot* on Monday night. This almost made me resolve to take nothing but bread and milk in the evenings. I should mind these disturbances less if the resulting headache did not make it practically impossible for me to read. I awoke at 2 A.M. and after then scarcely dozed. I just passed my time in disgust, waiting for

---

[1] Edward VII died May 6, 1910, and the funeral took place May 20.

the posts in the hope that something interesting might arrive by one of them. Nothing did. 6.30, 9.15, and 2.30. But I got up at 5.30 and made some tea.

Up till noon I still hoped, in spite of millions of experiences, that I might be able to work in the afternoon. I glanced through all the newspapers, and made my head worse just as it was easing. I took nothing but milkless tea till the evening, and then a morsel of arrowroot. To starve and to lie flat—this is the only treatment. By 7 P.M. I could read a little without making myself worse, and I began my new Stendhal, *L'Abbesse de Castro*. It opens slowly and finely. The intrigue is exactly the same, in essence, as that of the *Chartreuse* and of *Le Rouge et le Noir*. Did he ever think of anything else except capturing the affection of women under the most difficult conceivable circumstances?

I began to work after tea yesterday, and wrote 1,400 words of the first chapter of the last book of the eternal *Clayhanger*. This morning (after supper of bread and milk) I arose in fine health at 5.30. I made tea and read a lot of my manual of tree-drawing that I bought a year ago and had scarcely looked at. And then I finished the first chapter of *Clayhanger* at 8.45, having written about 1,600 words in 2¾ hours. My day's work was thus done before breakfast.

Friday, June 3rd.

3,000 words done of last part of *Clayhanger*. There is no doubt that when I finish my work at 8.30 or 8.45 A.M. I have a considerable leisure before me. At least it seems so. But then I haven't finished it then. After 10 I go out to arrange ideas for next day. That takes an hour. I may make a sketch *en route*. Anyhow I do nothing else but that and a letter or so before lunch. I must doze after lunch, and then read over my morning's work and occupy myself with the afternoon's post. Tea time. Then I have 3 hours. Part of it must go in a walk. Yesterday I painted for 1½ hours of it. Then there is a lot of time after dinner (which for me now consists of a basin of bread and milk).

Last night I read André Chénier after playing the piano. Some of him amused me. I wish I could read miscellaneously like that every night. The *pharmacien* came in, late. I wanted him in my heart to leave at 10. He didn't leave till 10.30. I had so violently wanted him to go that when he did go, I couldn't sleep at first, and I had been thinking over my work at 4.30 that morning. *This* morning I got up tired at 5.45 and decided to put off my work till after 9 o'clock breakfast. I read Tennyson's *Palace of Art*. Some exceedingly brilliant suggestive impressionist landscapes in it, and pretty clever phrasing here and there. But the real basis of the poem seemed to me to be entirely banal, the notion of a fairly thoughtful clerk.

Saturday, June 4th.

Ravel and his mother came for tea yesterday; only both of them preferred water to tea.

Yesterday I finished *A Man of Property*. A really distinguished, passionate, truly romantic universal book. Many small faults, but the only large fault is that the end is not an end. The situation between Soames Forsyte and Irene his wife is not solved. But it is an impressive book, no mistake.

This morning I finished the second chapter of last part of *Clayhanger*.

Monday, June 6th.

On being asked by Marguerite today whether she had *fait une promenade* yesterday afternoon during her Sunday *congé*, Martha, our new maid, said, "*Non, Madame, ma mère ne sort jamais.*" But had she no *petites camarades* with whom she could have gone out? Vaguely: no. "*Mais je connais bien la fille de l'épicier. Alors je suis allée chez elle, et nous avons causé.*"

This was her holiday. On Sundays, after she has washed up after lunch, she is free till it is time to come in and prepare dinner. At all other times she is at our disposal. She rises at 6—I hear her—and comes down at 7. She goes to bed about 9. Never reads. I doubt if she ever has a bath. She enjoys going out on errands, even to the post. Age 18. Plain. *Mal ficelée*. Can't get her apron right. Very quiet. Doesn't seem to want pleasure. Cow-like, and contented to work mildly all the time. When I say she ought to go out more, Marguerite gets excited and says that she has nowhere to go to, and that it would spoil her; that it is against the custom of the country. She is just an ignorant passive slave, earning 35 fr. a month and her keep and her bed. In 2 months' time she is to have 40 fr. She is not a fool, and learns her work pretty quickly, and having learnt it, does not forget it. Her mother comes twice a week to do rough work; a horrible-looking creature, very ugly, coarse, and without any remains of charm of any kind. There is a little hunchback brother *toscalgique* or *tuberculeux,* who for months could do nothing but sit by the fire and shiver. He has been sent to Bercke and is now a little better. The father is a carman with his own cart and either 1 or 2 horses.

Today I finished 7,000 words of the fourth part of *Clayhanger.* It is gradually beating *aquarelle* in the competition for my attention.

Continuous heavy thunderous weather. Steady temperature of 20° in the house. I ventured into a white waistcoat today. The weather is more like a Turkish bath than anything else. Not that I have ever had a Turkish bath.

At Mme. R.'s I met Brunet Huart, the painter, aged 84. He wore light striped trousers, a waistcoat of black velvet, a rather large tie, rather large and striking gloves, and generally was dandiacal.

He remembered Florence in 1858, and the anecdotes of King Victor Emmanuel's circus-like appearances in the *casini.* He liked Kipling, also Wells; but he thought Wells didn't explain enough. He remembered the fighting in the auditorium of the Théâtre des Variétés on account of a play which made fun of shop assistants. The theatre was full of shop assistants and their sympathizers. When the noise grew unbearable, an actor came forward and thumped furiously on a table. Everybody was so staggered by this impudence of an actor to his public that silence ensued and the actor said: "No! Never shall a counter-jumper bring this curtain down." The old gentleman was afraid of motor cars, and in particular of his young cousin's driving. He had just returned from a round of family visits, ending at Bourges. Then he curved off into a long story of an adventure in the Palazzo Orsini in Rome (when paper money as small as 5d. was issued—current in the city only), where he got enormous attention from a *concierge* by two payments of a franc each. "The *concierge* would have given me a bed in the palace, I think," said he. He had a curious and unusual knowledge of the relative sizes of things from St. Peter's downwards. He was certain that a revolution would occur within 6 months, precipitated by losses due to inundations and bad harvests, and consequent labour unrest. He said that he had painted all his life, but had entered the studio of a celebrated master only at the age of 25. He now got his military friends, colonels and so on, to send him down a soldier with a horse for 2 or 3 hours daily. Here he explained in detail how he taught the soldier to lift up the horse's leg so that he could see how the light fell on the legs of a galloping horse. Even recently he had painted in the rain, enjoying the "pretty colours," *teints* of barley, oats, etc. He kindly offered to criticize my drawings. He was full of various energy, and affirmed that he had not begun to feel old until he was 70. His chief subject was undoubtedly the Palais Royal.

"And, of course," he said. "The Palais Royal was in all its splendour in those days, and the plays given there were *really* witty." (1850 to 1860.) But the samples which he offered of Palais Royal wit in those great days were feeble and flashy. He seemed to be able to remember in detail all the Palais Royal burlesques of popular tragedy, and he quoted miles of tirades in verse. He talked well, if too much.

Wednesday, June 8th.

Last night there was a concert in the Place Danecourt. We walked there, having missed a car, through the most beautifully coloured streets in Europe. Wonderful salmon tints in the sky, also an extraordinary calm. We arrived late. The *terrasse* of the *grand café* was bulged out nearly to the newspaper kiosk, and crammed. Three or 4 waiters rushing about and sweating. We went into the café, of which the glazing had been removed for the summer. Many officers of the 15th Regiment playing cards—chiefly bridge. I got two chairs and placed them close to the entrance, and stood waiting for M., who had disappeared. A young officer came forward to take one of them. I stopped him. As he persisted, I insisted. *"C'est à vous?"* *"Oui,"* I said (no ceremonious titles). *"Vous l'avez prise?"*

He asked me in such a tone suggesting that I had not, that in my excitement I replied *"Si"* instead of *"Oui."* We glared at each other for an instant. I could have killed him. *"Eh bien, gardez la,"* he said roughly, and went off to get another chair. All the blustering *poltroonery* of the man came out in a flash. Afterwards I heard him saying something to another officer about *"ce bonhomme-là,"* pointing to me. I thought about this for a long time, forgetting the music, and constructed all sorts of versions of what would have happened if we had had a row. Colonels seemed to be thick upon the ground. I thought of all the wonderful apt, polished, polite cutting things I might have said.

After a time M. and I discovered that we had both of us absolutely forgotten the dog. He was lost. I went out to search for him in the crowd: no success. The band was playing in a ring of electric light and the scene was quite picturesque. We walked all the way home, as there was again no car. The sky, a wonderful dark transparent green, with church towers and things silhouetted against it. Before we got home we heard the dog barking in the garden. Marguerite had said he would be there.

Since I began to limit my dinner to a basin of bread and milk, I have ceased to suffer from indigestion.

One thousand words of last part of *Clayhanger* now written.

Saturday, June 11th.

I began *Le Crime et le Châtiment,* which I have been wanting to read again for about a fortnight. The scene in the café and Marmeladoff's confession seems even finer than it did when I read it at Hockliffe. It is certainly one of the very greatest things in fiction. Absolutely full of the most perfect detail. It really disgusted and depressed me about my own work, which seemed artificial and forced by the side of it. I expect that in most of my work there is too much forcing of the effect, an inability to do a thing and leave it alone. I wrote nearly 4,000 words of *Clayhanger* yesterday and Thursday.

Yesterday, walking in the forest, I thought of all the life in it, humming, flying, crawling, jumping, etc., the tiniest insects that you can scarcely see, the ants, all sorts of flies, worms, beetles, bees, snails, lizards, *and the gigantic birds.* As for the rabbits, squirrels, and deer, they are simply monstrously gigantic compared to the mass of the life in the forest.

I didn't seem to be getting near to the personality of Hilda in my novel. You scarcely ever do get near a personality. There is a tremendous lot to do in fiction that no one has yet done. When M. comes downstairs from the attic, in the midst of some house arrangement, and asks me if such and such a thing will do and runs up again excited—why? And the mood of the servant as, first thing in the morning, she goes placidly round the house opening the shutters! The fact is, the novelist seldom really *penetrates*.

Sunday, June 12th.

There is certainly a *rosse* pleasure to be got from reading a thoroughly mediocre thing by a writer generally esteemed great but whom you don't happen to admire. I am reading a portion of Tennyson every morning just now, and I have got to the play, *The Promise of May*. It is a masterpiece of tedious conventionality—of no value whatever. I should say it shows every side of Tennyson at its worst. No realism of any kind. All the old tags and notions; and what notions of philosophy as shown in the hero! I really enjoy reading this exquisitely rotten work.

Yesterday, wrote complete chapter of *Clayhanger*, 2,400 words. But I had to work at the thing practically all day. I finished about 5.30, after 12 hours off and on. I really doubt whether, as a whole, this book is good. It assuredly isn't within 10 miles of Dostoievsky.

Continuous bad weather.

Tuesday, June 14.

I seem to be doing an average of 2,000 words a day now of my novel. Only 13,000 words remain to be done. But they are very much on my mind. When I am not working here, I am walking in the forest and worrying over the invention, 5 to 7 miles a day. I rise at 5.45 and go to bed about 9.30.

Wednesday, June 15th.

Juliette said the other night: "*Ça fait du bien de manger les asperges. Ça lave la vessie.*" She and Marguerite had a great banquet of snails yesterday. They and the servant ate 150. Marguerite said: "It's horribly cruel. I couldn't do it as Mother does. She puts them alive into cold water, and lets them boil up slowly, *à petit feu*. It's horribly cruel." And she went on eating them. Last night they were again collecting snails in the garden, and Marguerite came across one of the other sort of snails, *limaces,* big things without shells. It had two tiny little ones with it. "I can't bring myself to kill them," she said, "but they do a lot of harm. I wish you'd kill them." I instantly put my foot on the three. She squirmed with horror and went off.

2,400 words of *Clayhanger* today.

Friday, June 17th.

Ballet Russe at Opera. *Scheherezade* was the *clou*. Never saw anything *si belle*, i.e. *si barbare, si luxurieuse à la fois*. I had from it all sorts of ideas for my Paris impressions. I was much struck by the feminine grace of Nijinsky, Diaghilev's favourite. Pale yellow hair, an intensely perverse look, and enormous art as a dancer. I understood a little for the first time the possibility of a man charming a man sexually. This was really interesting.

Sunday, June 19th.

Henriette S—— and daughter R. came down yesterday for lunch and stayed till this morning. To be plunged into this perfectly non-artistic society was very bad for my novel.

Thursday, June 23rd.

I have just (3 P.M.) finished *Clayhanger,* one week in advance of time. 160,800 words. For the last few days it has monopolized me. But quite contrary to my general practice towards the end of a novel, I have kept in magnificent health.

Tuesday, June 28th.

The journal will now be left till about the middle of August. I am finishing up odd articles this week, and shall begin a proper holiday on July 1, as sworn.

260,000 words written this half year.

Sunday July 10th.

I have been reading Andreyev's *Le Gouvernement*. Pretty good, but too long; also sentimental in places, and to my mind influenced by *The Death of Ivan Ilyitch*. A fairly good third-rate serious artist.

This was the first full day of my seaside holiday. It takes some time to get used to the great central fact that you have nothing to do that must be done.

Monday, July 11th.

It seems that the *curés* in Brittany forbid dancing, except at wedding feasts. Nevertheless, in this village there is dancing in the very shadow of the church every Sunday afternoon after vespers. We saw it yesterday afternoon. About 10 couples. The *charcutière* danced with another girl. Heavy girls. One couple obviously in love. A drum and a brass instrument.

We cycled this morning to the ferry on the way to Saint-Pol. Beautiful country. There is only one road in and out of this village, and no turning out of it for 5 or 6 kilometres. This afternoon I was too idle to paint, so I did a pastel of the panorama towards Saint-Pol.

Of the 3 men here, one is a *passementier,* and another, a commercial traveller, and the third a *fabricant* of something. They sit at a table and sing together. The luggage of one married pair arrived tonight, 36 hours late. The wife is of the odalisque sort, and she put on some more striking clothes at once. She lolls at her bedroom window for 30 to 60 minutes each morning. A beautiful young woman. *Elle se cambre tout le temps.* She would have made a good *courtisane.* Alcock says that she leaves a table at which an intellectual conversation is proceeding—about war or feminism, for instance—with a gesture which says, "What has all this got to do with IT?"

Tuesday, July 12th.

We discovered another bay this morning, in the estuary of the Morlaix River, and a fine yacht lying in it. Also the château on the shore, and some racing boats and a boat-builder's.

I began a water-colour in the afternoon, and M. and F. A. went out and discovered the real high road to Morlaix, for some strange reason not marked on my maps.

Alcock said that Werge had been playing a lot in *Electra,* and considered Strauss [1] to be more of a mathematician than a musical composer. When rehearsing, if the players tried to put any musical feeling into their playing, Strauss stopped them and said: "No, not like that. You are not musicians, you are wild beasts." This is the most illuminating thing about Strauss's genius that I have heard.

---

[1] Richard Strauss conducted a performance of *Electra* at Covent Garden in the spring of 1910.

Friday, July 15th.

Fête yesterday. Alcock left at 5 P.M. in a most ancient wagonette, and we drove with him to the top of the village. Although there were 3 windows open in the wagonette it was hotter inside than outside—stuffy. Horse collars of straw, harness chiefly of rope. In speaking of the horses Alcock again called them "cat's meat." In the morning we went sailing for 1½ hours—5 fr. We were carried into a small boat, and then rowed to the smack, which was in charge of two men.

After dinner I walked about a mile up the estuary of the Penzé on the sands, and back, and then up the village. Chinese lanterns, band, dancing, silhouette of large church, silhouettes of figures, Bengal fires, very noisy fireworks. Hotel du Kelem very bright with lanterns. Parading about in adjacent lanes, the Parisians and other visitors, arms entwined sometimes, women in white wool loose jackets, as in Switzerland in winter. Moon through clouds. Not quite dark. I came home at 9.50 quite recovered, and read *Eugénie Grandet*.

We were wakened up in the night by a very heavy thunderstorm. The thunder really was dramatic; quite as good as Drury Lane.

Monday, July 18th.

Tertia said that the Mater said, on seeing *Carmen* at Hanley Theatre, "I don't like that woman at all."

It rained all day yesterday, and was raining heavily when we went to bed. Rain appalling. The *employés du* Louvre discovered the gramophone at night and danced to it.

By the way, the chief point about the gramophone performance was the intense and simple pleasure of the people in it. The two men bent over the instrument, smiling as they might have done to a baby that was crooning.

Sunday, July 24th.

Ile Callot yesterday morning. Strong smell of seaweed spread over the fields for manure. Just a few groups of cottages or hovels collected round the church. A church there since the sixth century. Primitive. Probably barbaric. The men working barefoot in the seaweed did not even look up as we passed. At night we saw from dining-room windows the islanders going home in their carts. A girl waiting to be taken up in a cart. Sun already set. Silhouette dark blue-black of horse, cart, and people —no details in side outline.

Monday, July 25th.

Characteristic gesture of an old fisherman. He took off his cap, held it upside down under his mouth, dropped his plug (of tobacco) into it, and whipped it on his head again, all in the twinkling of an eye.

Godebski said that C. L. Philippe [1] never saw the sea till 2 years before his death. Fargue [2] took him to Havre. On meeting the sea, he lay down in a sort of ecstasy or hysteria, on his stomach, and lapped at each wave as it came in, as if determined to make up for lost time by the violence of his sensations.

Thursday, July 28th.

Excursion to Roscoff yesterday. Left at 9.15. Sea choppy, but it calmed down. The fishermen *ont levé des casiers en route.* So that we soon saw what a complicated process has to be gone through before a lobster, for example, is put on the table. *Vielles* as bait for *araignées,* and then *araignées* as bait for lobsters. Cutting of nerves to prevent them eating each other. Taking bearings as *casiers* are thrown down again into the sea. We reached Roscoff about 11.30. Tide out. The damned tide was out all day.

Lillah McCarthy wrote me, suggesting subject for a one-act play which she wanted to do at Palace next month.

Friday, July 29th.

Heavy storms of rain and wind yesterday afternoon and evening. The barometer just now seems to have no effect whatever on the weather.

Julien Savignac by Ferdinand Fabre. This is quite a readable book. Old-fashioned and sententious sometimes, but strong in the places where it ought to be strong. I have read about half of it. I don't suppose I shall read any more, as I have other things, but I would read it sooner than read nothing on a desert island.

---

[1] Charles-Louis Philippe, novelist, best known for his *Bubu de Montparnasse.*
[2] Léon-Paul Fargue, the poet.

Monday, August 1st.

Too short of sleep and sardonic to write anything yesterday. Baptism of a new pleasure boat, the *Blanche,* yesterday. Three *curés* and 3 choir-boys with instruments, and a bottle of champagne to do it. Nearly upset in going out in dinghy.

Tuesday, August 2nd.

Women minding cows. Fat, old, in many skirts. They just stand, moving slightly from time to time. Towards 5 or 6, they pull the cows home by rope, but on approaching stable the cow trots on in front. A sign of barbarism, this. Very queer that even an old woman's time is not worth more than that of a cow, that she can't earn enough to keep a cow.

Monday, August 15th.

I have now taken, what nearly everybody said I was incapable of taking and never would take, a long holiday. From July 2 to yesterday I did nothing whatever in the way of work except 3 short articles for the *New Age,* which I was obliged to do. Of course I had to attend to my correspondence; but I kept that as short as possible. I wrote an illustrated journal at Carantec, and I also did a number of paintings and sketches.

We came definitely home on Friday night, and found everything in order. Today I resume my literary business. The 3 things that occupy me are: a good short story for *T.P.'s Magazine,* my *Life in Paris* for the *English Review,* and a play founded on *Buried Alive.*[1]

I have done no regular sustained reading now for something like 10 months. So I shall resume Taine. I propose to do as I did in May and June here. Get up at 5.30, and begin creative writing at 6, and finish that on most days before breakfast at 9 A.M. I have now satisfied myself that it is my best time for working, particularly now that by means of milk dinners I have cured my biliousness. It is 3 months since I had a headache due to indigestion. After breakfast I can do my oddments and correspondence etc., and arrange my ideas for the next day, and thus have the whole of my work finished at noon. Afternoons for reading

---

[1] This was *The Great Adventure.* See page 399.

and painting and crass idleness. I have openly sworn—openly, in order to make it impossible for me to forswear myself decently—never again to work as hard as I have done in the past.

August 16th.

I decided yesterday that though I was still lacking the first 220 pages of proofs of *Clayhanger* I had better get on with what I had. I corrected the whole of the third part, and was very pleased with it indeed. In fact it so held me that it distressed me, and afterwards I couldn't think of the story *Mimi,* which, however, I began to write at 6.30 this morning for *T.P.'s Magazine.* I seemed to be correcting proofs most of yesterday. I couldn't draw, nor read.

Already at 9 this morning I was tired of work. I went to the market at 10. Was struck by the confused murmur of tongues in the covered market—seemed to be the beginning of some new and closer perception of this organism.

I *did* read last night the Comte d'Haussonville on Melchior de Vogüé. Perhaps the latter was not quite the mandarin I have publicly charged him with being.

Friday, August 19th.

All proofs of *Clayhanger* came on Wednesday morning, so that after 9 o'clock in the morning I did nothing on Wednesday and Thursday except correct them. 575 pages. I finished them on Thursday afternoon. Errors in the typescript made them very amazing. A great deal of it is as good as anything I've done. I noticed the far too frequent use of the word "extraordinary," but I hadn't sufficient interest to suppress it occasionally in correcting. I loathe altering a work once it is done—no mistake about that.

Monday, August 22nd.

Finished *Mimi* yesterday morning, and this morning I sent off the ink copy for U.S.A. and a wretched illegible carbon copy to *T.P.'s Magazine,* the original commissioner. I began to read Edward Gibbon's *Memoirs.* I had tried before. I found now that all they want is proper skipping at the start. You soon come to the interesting parts.

Friday, August 26th.

Nothing done this week. I began to write my *Seeing Life in Paris* for the *English Review* on Wednesday morning, but only did a bit. Owing to too much smoking I was indisposed yesterday and did nothing except a *New Age* article. But I got up at 5.45 this morning, and stuck to *Life in Paris* for 90 minutes. After breakfast, owing to Turkish-bath weather and neuralgia, I did nothing.

Reading Gibbon's *Memoirs*. Yes, it is worthy of its reputation. But I am reading nothing else.

Cupid and Common Sense revived at Gaiety, Manchester, on Monday last for 6 nights.

Friday, September 2nd.

I did no work since Monday. On Tuesday I went to Paris. Lunch at Martin's (his cousin Eugène was there). I met Lee Matthews at Hotel St. James at 6.10. We discussed plays and his projects till 7.20. Caught 7.55 home, for bread and milk at 9 P.M. I bought nothing. Couldn't work next day nor yesterday. But I resumed *Seeing Life in Paris* this morning, and did 1,200 words. Yesterday afternoon I just did a *New Age* article. By first post I received news that Pinker could sell serial use of *The Honeymoon* to *McClure's Magazine* for £200. I cabled to accept, provided dramatic rights not jeopardized.

On Tuesday I received two rather racy letters from editors of American magazines asking for help.

Monday, September 5th.

Finished yesterday the first 8,000 words of *Seeing Life in Paris*. I shall now leave it for a time. We cycled down to see Mme. Bourgès on Saturday, but naturally she had gone to Paris days ago. Afterwards I went to bed with influenza, but found that I hadn't got it.

Wednesday, September 7th.

Being unable to get rid of influenza-ish inquietudes of the stomach, and having had several very bad nights *de suite,* I stayed in bed today, and therein read and wrote. Yesterday I finished the third or the fourth perusal of *A Mummer's Wife.*[1] This book really is original and fine and

---

[1] By George Moore.

beautiful. The Islington scenes are superb. You have squalor and sordid-
ness turned into poetry. And the painter-like effects of visualization are
splendid throughout. Language a bit clumsy and coarse occasionally.
"Booze" and "boozed" are amazing words. There are others. But what
an original and powerful work!

Last night I began Spencer's *Autobiography,* and this morning, by dint
of much wakefulness, I had arrived at page 224. I found it very interesting and jolly well done. It is much better done and much more artistic
than J. S. Mill's autobiography. Nevertheless Spencer's little attempts at
narrative in the manner of a novelist—beginning, for example, with a
fragment of conversation, or with such a phrase as "If on such a day
any one had been looking at such a spot they might have been surprised
to see," etc., are funnier than he intended.

Friday, September 9th.

After a series of disastrous experiments in *aquarelle,* I began a flower
piece today which promised rather better.

This morning I began to write the preface to Agnes Farley's *The Belmont Book.*[1] It seems as if it will take me from 4 to 6 mornings from
6 A.M. to 8 A.M. This is what you may call friendship. Frank Harris now
wants me to write a 5,000-word article on his *Women of Shakespeare.*
But if I do it some one will have to pay me for that. It will be worth
at the very least £30 in U.S.A., whither it is destined.

Each morning this week, except Wednesday, when I spent the day
in bed, I have walked in the forest between 10 and noon, constructing
Buried Alive. Today I have got as far as the end of the fifth scene; that
is, the first scene of Act III. I do a scene a day. But I perceive a deadlock
for either tomorrow or Sunday.

I shall soon have finished the first volume of Spencer's *Autobiography.*
And I have read 100 pages of *Les Origines* in 3 days. Beyond this nothing.

Tuesday, September 13th.

My old Gaveau piano went on Saturday. I sold it for 250 fr., the money
to be spent on hiring. I got a Pleyel grand instead. I had to spend Friday
night in altering the arrangement of the whole room for the reception

---

[1] This appeared in March, 1911, under the pseudonym of Vados.

of the grand. Naturally when it came I had to spend a great deal of time in playing.

On Sunday morning arrived the first copies of *Clayhanger*. It is the best produced of all my novels, I think; but I could have spared the girl's portrait on the cover. I read a lot of it, and thought it pretty good. A few misprints. On reflection I think it does contain more sociology than *The O.W.T.* I had promised this in the prospectus of it, but I was afraid I had not fulfilled the promise. It was only when Marguerite began to read the book that I realized—without her asking any questions—how full of difficulties it must be for a stranger, and how unlike the ordinary good novel. On Sunday I at last finished a water-colour, of a flower bowl, that was not absolutely putrid.

Yesterday we went to Paris, M. and Gabrielle at 7.24 and I at 8.56. I went straight to my coiffeurs, but owing to *affluence de monde* I had to be coiffed by the *patron,* who is not as good as either of the *garçons,* though good. Hence I was disappointed of my expected perfection.

Wednesday, September 14th.

I finished the rough construction of the *Buried Alive* play yesterday, and decided to change the title and the names of the characters. The new names I searched out this morning.

Beautiful promenades in the forest yesterday. In the morning I was astonished by the grandeur and multitude of the spider's webs. I broke two to see what they would do, but they did nothing—just hung loose in the breeze.

Thursday, September 15th.

At page 172 of Vol. VIII of *Les Origines de la France Comtemporaine,* in a figurative description of modern France, I at last came across a clear instance of Taine's bias against *la France contemporaine.* He is always very convincing, but I always suspected the existence of this bias —shown as much in his later letters as anywhere—and here is a good example of it.

This morning I began the *brouillon* of the play, and wrote the first tableau.

Clayhanger published in England today. In U.S.A. publication is delayed about a fortnight.

Says Herbert Spencer, speaking of Thackeray's insignificance at dinner (*Autobiography*, II, 91): "I have heard that he could be a lively companion; but it seems possible that usually when in company he was occupied in observing traits of character and manner. A painter of human nature as variously manifested must ordinarily be more a listener than a talker." Yes, perhaps. But unconsciously occupied. The painter of human nature is not consciously engaged in the act of observation.

The chapter of the *Autobiography* dealing with the finishing and publication of *First Principles* is unimposing, and disappointingly deficient in emotion. (Compare Gibbon in the finishing of *his* big work.) Nothing of real interest is recorded about the undertaking. This is a pity. But everywhere Spencer's narrative skill is very clumsy, and his little attempts to be dramatic are extraordinarily feeble. I am struck in reading by the stolid indifference with which his biggest books were received. It was appalling; it desolates. Yet this kind of reception is quite common. I am also struck throughout by a whole series of odd remarks—almost asides—which give you the disconcerting feeling that nearly all common valuations are relatively quite wrong. That is, that nearly everything— gifts, acquirements, possessions, achievements—is either under-valued or over-valued.

When I think how *First Principles,* by filling me up with the sense of causation everywhere, has altered my whole view of life, and undoubtedly immensely improved it, I am confirmed in my opinion of that book. You can see *First Principles* in nearly every line I write.

Monday, September 19th.

This time I will make notes on the newspaper criticisms of my novel. On day of publication, two. *Times* very good; well written. But a half-hidden unwillingness of admiration and of subjection. This sentence is well meant but quite wrong: "Its aim, not to exalt, or essentialize or satirize, but to present, life." A review nothing like as good as that of *The O.W.T.* but still jolly good (9 inches). The other one on day of publication was in *Evening Standard,* entitled *Under the Microscope.* A review full of clumsy but not malignant malice. On the whole a damn silly review (10 inches).

Day after publication. R. A. Scott James in the *Daily News. Mr. Bennett and the Ages.* Very sympathetic and appreciative. "A work that will surely be memorable." But the review was badly done, perhaps from haste. Well meant, but what damned rot and untruth. (1 col. 5 ins.)

I finished the draft of half of my play yesterday morning at 7.15 A.M. I worked off and on during most of the rest of the day in arranging the third act, but did not succeed very well. I had a bad cold. Every morning now for about a fortnight I have walked for 2 hours in the forest. Still immersed in Spencer's *Autobiography*. His description of the other boarders at the boarding-house where he stayed so many years is agreeably ironic.

Wednesday, September 21st.

Yesterday while reading, in bed, a biographical account of me in the N.Y. *Bookman*, M. began to cry. She had the delusion that she was reading my obituary.

I certainly pay much more attention now to the oncoming of autumn than I used to.

Reviews of *Clayhanger:*

Perfect review in *Glasgow Herald* on day of publication. Nothing could be more appreciative nor show more insight than this (12 ins.).

Daily Mail and *Observer* (9 ins. and 15 ins.). Usual rot about total absence of plot, and about cinematograph, and photograph, and that book might end anywhere or nowhere. "It is unsatisfying because life is," etc. And yet in all this a note of genuine appreciation.

Tomorrow I expect to finish draft of play. Today I signed contract with Doran for republication of old books in U.S.A., 12 or 13 of them, I think. Pinker wrote me that Macrae (Dutton's London manager) had told him that *Clayhanger* was in his opinion the "biggest proposition" that he had met with for a long time.

Thursday, September 22nd.

Finished draft of play.

Day of mild unpleasantnesses. The review of *Clayhanger* in *Manchester Guardian,* though good, was not as good as I expected. I expected the eager sympathy of G. H. Mair and Co.! The review was signed by strange initials ending in Y. Moreover it was placed after a review of M. Hewlett [1] by Dixon Scott. Now if they had given my book to Dixon

---

[1] Maurice Hewlett's *Rest Harrow* was published that year.

Scott! Further, the Johnny deprived me almost utterly of the sense of humour and of the sense of beauty—especially in comparison with De Morgan and Wells.

En voilà une affaire!

A couple of years ago I said enthusiastically that if *Cupid and Common Sense* was produced in Hanley it would play to £500 in a week. Today I got the figures for the 3 performances in Hanley. Total £75 13s. 10d. Even allowing for a certain amount of cheating such as is charged against that theatre. . . .

Also I made a mess of another water-colour. Hence depression, though my affairs are prospering as they never prospered before. Which shows how little content has to do with prosperity.

Sunday, September 25th.

A lot of reviews this morning, all satisfactory; that is to say, free from fatuity in carping.

Two in *Glasgow News* (1 col.) and *Birmingham Express* (6 ins.) really very fine. The rest all very appreciative and sympathetic.

Morning Leader (5 ins.).
Christian World (6 ins.).
Scotsman (5 ins.).
Onlooker (5 ins.).
Daily Chronicle (M. P. Willcocks, 11 ins.).

Devic called last night, and related how he had forced a bailiff to leave by the window instead of by the door.

Monday, September 26th.

A. and J. S—— came yesterday for the day. Drive in the forest. It is in this sort of encounter that one feels the immense gulf between an artist and people who have simply no traffic with art at all. One can, however, find something in common in the discussion of relatives and in the contemplation of nature. With J., who spent her youth in a baker's shop, and is the widow of one artisan and the wife of another, sitting opposite me in the carriage, and smiling at jokes which she only half understood but *did* half understand, and admiring trees and vistas and things, I had a most distinct feeling of sympathy and a perception of a faint charm that emanated from her.

This morning I did begin, after much hesitation and fooling about, the final writing of the play. I rather enjoyed it, once started, and took pleasure in the exercise of skill in arranging the last details of movement. This afternoon, after water-colouring, I began the ninth volume of *Les Origines*.

Wednesday, September 28th.

Paris yesterday. We went for a drive at 6, till 6.45. I took the opportunity to see the Place des Vosges. Immense noise and movement of kids playing in central enclosure—enclosure full of trees and various *baraques*. Enormous accumulation of traffic at junction of Place du Châtelet and Bridge. Twilight Paris etc. Very agreeable and romantic, but not really beautiful. We met M. under the Odéon arcades. She and I dined at Voltaire's. Like a *province* in Paris. I had my usual milk. Then the Odéon. *Cavalleria Rusticana*, played melodramatically. I suppose no other way. Not so bad. Then, what I had partly gone to Paris for, *Les Corbeaux*.[1] This piece soon began to get hold of you. Clumsy sometimes, in construction. Also some asides too long, especially at end of last act. And yet the final scene, though at first it seems to come after the real close, and though it is long, is tremendously effective in the result and brings the tired house down. The naturalness and truth of the piece must have been astounding when first produced, and are still very remarkable.

Friday, September 30th.

I also had an idea of keeping, from January 1, 1911, a book showing dates of appearance of all articles, books, plays, etc., and of books read, and of books acquired. In fact a chronological chart of all my literary activities.

Today I finished Spencer's vast *Autobiography*. The first volume is perhaps superior to the second, but I read it all with interest, and especially the reflections of old age at the end. Its fault is lack of emotional quality, and of elevation in the style. You get from it no sense of a mighty work accomplished—no sense of mightiness at all.

I was put into a strange state yesterday by reading Methuen's advertisement in the *Westminster Gazette*. My novel, having now been pub-

---

[1] By Henri Becque.

lished a fortnight, had taken its place lower down their list—was indeed only one of a very mixed lot of novels. Lucas's *Mr. Ingleside,* being their last published, was head of the list. They have just invented a new and striking dodge of indicating the number of editions printed of a work by putting a small elevated numeral after it (as if indicating a raised "power"). Thus Lucas's was *Mr. Ingleside,*[3] and it has only been out a week. No number after *Clayhanger.* A [2] after many of the other novels.

I began to foresee a comparative failure for *Clayhanger* in England, and then also in America. Useless for one to argue that my contracts in England and America assure me a reasonable income for 3 years, whether the publishers lose or not! Useless for me to argue that it is absurd for me to *expect* even a good circulation for books like *Clayhanger,* which arouse enthusiasm in just a few beings! I was most markedly depressed by that small [3] after *Mr. Ingleside.* I had a sense of injury too. This in spite of the fact that I cannot make less than £1,500 next year, and may make £2,000 or over—and this by doing only the work that pleases me —my very best work. I was still gloomy this morning. I hated to go on with my play. But I did go on with it. After a restless night, I got up at 6.30 and worked till noon. I shall finish the first tableau tomorrow.

It is now almost certain that *A Man from the North* will be reprinted.

I notice that a Bath paper, announcing *Cupid and Common Sense* for next week there, thinks fit to explain that the author, "A.B.," is a novelist of repute. This at the age of 43, after having written what I have written.

Sunday, October 2nd.

Yesterday I had a goodish large notion for the Hilda book—of portraying the droves of the whole sex, instead of whole masculine droves. I think I can do something with this, showing the multitudinous activities of the whole sex, the point of view of the whole sex, against a mere background of masculinity. I had a sudden vision of it. It has never been done.

Finished Gibbon's Autobiography. It is a distinguished book, but my feelings about the author are mixed.

Monday, October 3rd.

Disturbed yesterday by M.'s slight indisposition, I had, naturally, a new flow of ideas, as always when disturbed. I kept thinking of a sort of "annual" of Bennett's gossip on literature and life. It could easily be done every year, if I got into the habit. A notion for a paper worried me—on Flaubert. And so I wrote it this afternoon. 1,000 words.

Friday, October 7th.

Yesterday I had a letter from A. M. S. Methuen congratulating me on *Clayhanger* and saying he "hoped and believed it would do well." In the afternoon I saw announcement in *Westminster Gazette* that it is in its second edition. Naturally my one desire is that it should reach a third.

On Wednesday I had a long and generally enthusiastic letter from Doran, who had just read *The Truth About an Author,* etc. The same night I sent him new matter to add to *The Reasonable Life,* and corrected sheets of *How to Live on Twenty-four Hours a Day*—all done between 4.30 and 7.15 P.M.

Thursday, October 13th.

Weather still very mild. But today, owing to heavy rains, we had to lunch indoors. This is our first indoor autumn lunch.

Railway strike since Monday night, but we are not affected. Each evening I have gone to the station to get *Le Temps,* and each evening the crowd and the anxiety of the crowd waiting for papers have increased. Yesterday evening, as the news was disquieting, I went again to the station after dinner to post a letter to Cook's, asking for banknotes. An omnibus slowly overtook me on its way to the station. Even on this line the strike had been announced to begin at 8 P.M. last night. There were a few dim figures in the fearfully badly lighted omnibus that went very slowly along—decrepit horses etc. A mediaeval vehicle even at best, and the impression last night was of the saddest and most wistful vehicle that ever lumbered along. The *voyageurs* seemed wrapped up in sadness. Where were they going? Would they ever arrive? Where would they spend the night? The worst of these awful omnibuses is the lamp and the deafening rattle of the windows as the thing jolts along. . . .

However, there has yet been no strike on this line.

The play goes on steadily. I ought to finish the second act on Saturday.

Although there are 4 acts, this means that at least two-thirds of the actual work is done.

Tuesday, October 18th.

Letter from Doran yesterday expressing much enthusiasm for *Sacred and Profane Love*. So I read the first third of it last night before going to bed. I found it very young. It seemed to contain some good stuff, but also a proportion of cleverly arranged effects—effects of which the real difficulties had not been met. Still it interested me.

Thursday, October 20th.

Now I am reading Sainte-Beuve almost for the first time. Except for a few of the *Causeries de Lundi*—and that a long time ago—I have read nothing of him. I read the essay on Mme. de Sévigné last night (and ordered a volume of her letters this afternoon). I read the essay on Bayle this afternoon (and read Bayle's preface to his *Dictionnaire* tonight). There is no doubt that Sainte-Beuve is excessively *agréable à lire*. He flatters you into believing that your taste is as cultivated as his own. And, in the essay on Bayle, his remarks on the *esprit critique* are full of nutriment brilliantly served. It has seemed to me that these days I am living, as distinguished from preparing to live. In autumn weather; plenty of heavy continuous rain, which is pleasant to hear when you are safe in the house and busy in the house, and the ground floor and the bedroom floor are both warmed. Work in the morning, on the play, which goes pretty easily. Sleep and reading after lunch. Thirty pages of Taine per day, *comme devoir*. New books coming in every day. Grand piano. Discovery of playable Schubert. *Clayhanger* in its third English edition. Agreeable tension of anxiety of waiting for news of this book's reception in America. Journey to Paris now and then. Miscellaneous browsy reading in the evening. Good appetite. The drawbacks to this idyll are—no progress in drawing, fairly bad sleeping, and some neuralgia. But then it must never be forgotten that since the end of May last, thanks to evening bread and milk, I have never had more than one hour's continuous stomachic headache. . . . It cannot be long before some infernal nuisance supervenes. Such a state of content will not be allowed by destiny to last much longer.

Friday, October 28th.

M. went to Paris yesterday to look for a furnished flat, and among many impossible ones discovered one that *may* do. Her report was that the majority of the furnished flats to let in the centre were most obviously *cocotteries*.

Today I finished Act IV of play, which will be called *The Great Adventure*.[1] Although never working very long at it together, I haven't thought about much else.

Neil Munro[2] in a letter yesterday pointed out to me that Aylmer Maude's *Biography of Tolstoy* (Vol. II) contains Tolstoy's admission of the justice of my criticism of *The Death of Ivan Ilyitch* in the *New Age*. The criticism was really Farrar's, and I gave it as that of a doctor.

I had my first American review of *Clayhanger* on Tuesday, signed Howard Fitzalan (*N. Y. Morning Telegraph*). He said the trilogy would make a "million-word novel" (this was the title of the article); he plumed himself on having "boosted Arnold" for 6 years, and was very flattering in general, but said the novel would not sell.

November 6th.

On Saturday, October 29, M. and I went to Paris to look at furnished flats, and we took one at 39 Rue de Grenelle at 225 fr. per month. I should have made some notes on the hunting if I could have made them a week ago.

I had a fearful headache the next morning. It was the beginning of a slight influenza, from which I have not yet entirely recovered. The Davrays came for tea on the Sunday afternoon, and he told some good stories about General Galliffet.[3]

On Monday, Tuesday, Wednesday, and Thursday I was unfit for work. I tried to begin Act 4 of *The Great Adventure* on Wednesday, and simply wrote rot. On Thursday I decided to leave the play and write the next *Paris Night* for the *English Review,* which I did on Friday and yesterday, doing altogether 5,000 words in the 2 days.

---

[1] Produced at the Kingsway Theatre, March 25, 1913.
[2] Journalist and novelist, author of *Ayrshire Idylls*, etc.
[3] He distinguished himself at Sedan, in command of the Chasseurs d'Afrique. He was Minister of War in 1901.

Friday, November 11th.

Still unwell all week. Nevertheless I finished *The Great Adventure* this afternoon at 4.30 P.M., 4 days in advance of time. Actual dialogue 20,300 words. I shall doubtless cut it to less than 20,000. There are now 2 complete plays of mine—this, and *The Honeymoon,* renounced by Trench—for sale.

The two American reviews of *Clayhanger* to which I looked forward with the most interest, *Boston Evening Transcript* and *Chicago Evening Post,* are both absolutely satisfactory in their enthusiasm. Doran wrote me, in response to my query, that he had sold about 12,000 of *Old Wives' Tale* to date, and that the demand seemed like continuing indefinitely. About the same day I got a cutting from U.S.A. saying that at end of October on the New York street cars *The Old Wives' Tale* had been advertised as one of the "best sellers."

Friday, November 18th.

We came to Paris last Monday. On Thursday, having at last got the stove fixed in the bedroom, I began to do a little work. We went to tea at the Ullmans', specially, as I gathered, so that Mills of Duffield's, New York publishers, would meet me. Frightful weather yesterday. Much journeying and changing on underground. Snow and rain this morning; but it cleared up at 10 A.M. I have now begun to go through *Sacred and Profane Love* to consider ideas for the preface to it, to get my next *Paris Night* into order, and generally to re-find myself.

Sunday, November 20th.

On Friday Dr. Otto (of Tauchnitz) came for tea, and stayed for about 2 hours, and produced a most favourable impression on both of us. Also he was exceedingly flattering in a very discreet way. Talking of relations between publishers and authors, he said that Macmillan's had published for Rhoda Broughton for 45 years, but she had never seen any member of the firm; apparently didn't want to.

Thursday, December 8th.

I have been working daily at construction of *Hilda Lessways.* As it was pouring with rain this afternoon, I went to the Gare d'Orsay, and had tea on the platform *terrasse* of the café, and walked about for 2¾ hours, and really worked excellently at the first book, and was moreover all the time amused and diverted by the phenomena of the terminus. This is a most excellent dodge for wet days.

Monday, December 12th.

Sunday night we called on Ella D'Arcy,[1] and I made her promise to bring me the novel she had written some years ago and then left in a drawer because one publisher, John Murray, had refused it.

On Saturday appeared in the *Nation* the most striking article on me that has yet been written.

Continuous progress with the construction of the first book of *Hilda Lessways.*

Saturday, December 17th.

Full day today. Perpending on *Hilda Lessways* all morning. Sketch in Luxembourg gardens after lunch. *New Age* article after tea. Odéon Theatre (*Les Trois Sultanes* and *Les Fourberies de Scapin*)[2] tonight. I had to read through *Les Trois Sultanes.* I went into Saint-Sulpice again this morning to look at Delacroix, and came across a great ordination service. Dozens of young priests in parti-coloured capes etc. drinking the sacred wine with elaborate ceremonies, music, etc. They were all, or nearly all, tonsured. A startling mummery, right in the middle of Paris. Crowds of women.

Tuesday, December 27th.

Doran came Saturday night for dinner. We went on to Nisia Edwards's *Réveillon* and got home at 4 A.M. I fed Doran at restaurants. I arranged with him for publication of one of Tertia's books, and also for a Christmas booklet of my own. Discussion also about syndicating "Jacob Tonson" in the States. I left Doran last night at his hotel. He departed for London this morning. Exceeding politeness is one of his qualities. Weather rotten. Too much occupied to write down the things I have heard from and observed in Doran.

---

[1] She had published two novels in 1898.
[2] By Favart and Molière, respectively.

Friday, December 30th.

This morning I got a letter from Pinker saying that he and Doran thought they could get me £1,000 for the serial rights of *Hilda Lessways* from the Philadelphia *Saturday Evening Post*.

December 31st.

This year I have written 355,900 words, including *Clayhanger, The Great Adventure, Paris Nights, Night and Morning in Florence,* and probably about 80 other articles. I think only one short story, *Mimi*.

The last excellent item of the year was the letter referred to in the previous entry.

1911

Friday, January 6th. Paris.

After several days' delay owing to indisposition, I began to write *Hilda Lessways* yesterday afternoon; only 400 words. Today, 1100 words. It seems to be a goodish beginning.

On Wednesday the Godebskis [1] came for dinner, and Simon, Châteaubriant, and Fargue came afterwards. I got from the last all details necessary for my preface to the English translation of *Marie-Claire*.

The *Chronicle* asked me to resume my articles at 5 guineas a col. I asked for six.

Thursday, January 12th.

I went to see Lee Matthews [2] and B. de Zoete at Hotel St. James Sunday afternoon. Discussion of play prospects.

Monday.

B. de Zoete and Violet Hunt came for lunch. Calvo [3] for dinner. F. M. Hueffer [4] and V. Hunt came after dinner, and stayed till 12.15. He smoked 4 of my cigars and took away another 2 to smoke at his hotel. He

---

[1] Cepa Godebski, a painter of considerable repute in Paris, was an intimate friend of Arnold Bennett.

[2] An intimate friend, member of the Stage Society.

[3] Cipa Calvocoressi, music critic and lecturer, and a close friend of Arnold Bennett.

[4] Ford Madox Hueffer, who did not change his name to Ford Madox Ford until 1919. Violet Hunt, the novelist and author of racy memoirs, collaborated in 1915 with Mr. Hueffer to write *Zeppelin Nights*.

told us Conrad had first idea of writing through seeing a "Pseudonym" at the bookstall at Vevey Station. He chose English in preference to French because, whereas there were plenty of stylists in French, there were none in English.

Wednesday.

Today I received cable from Brentano's saying that *Buried Alive* was "going strong," and asking permission to reprint in U.S.A. instead of buying Tauchnitz sheets.

I finished third chapter of *Hilda Lessways*. Usual doubts as to whether the thing is any good.

Friday, January 20th.

Impossible to keep this journal while I am beginning *Hilda Lessways*, and either going out or receiving, every night and Sunday afternoons. The stuff is slowly improving. I had not been able to even read, until I received H. G. Wells's *The New Machiavelli*. This book makes a deep impression on me, and even causes me to examine my own career, and to wonder whether I have not arrived at a parting of the ways therein, and what I ought to decide to do after the book—after *Hilda* is finished. London or Paris?

Sunday, January 22nd.

Friday night, visit with Châteaubriant to Romain Rolland. Found him in a holland-covered room, disguised bed in one corner. Tea at 9.45. Sister, spinster aged 35. Bright, slightly masculine. Mother, an aged body, proud of children, shrewd, came in later. Romain Rolland, arm in sling; large face, pale, calm, kindly, thoughtful, rather taciturn. Giving a marked impression of an absolutely honest artist, and a fine soul. Considerable resemblance to Marcel Schwob [1]; but bigger and more blond. No particular talk. But an impression of rightness, respectability in every sense, conscientiousness, and protestantism (intellectually).

---

[1] Marcel Schwob (pseudonym: Loyson-Bridet), general writer and bibliographer, had been an intimate friend of Arnold Bennett until his death in February 1905.

January 31st.

I went to see the historic Durand Ruel collection. The furniture of the abode was startlingly different, in quality and taste, from the pictures. All the furniture might have been bought at the Bon Marché. The table in the dining-room was covered with the chequered cloth so prevalent in small French households. (In this room was a still life of Monet.) The doors, however, were all beautifully painted in panels. Aged and young domestics moved about. There was a peculiar close smell—no, not peculiar, because it permeates thousands of Paris homes.

From the front windows was seen a fine view of St.-Lazare Station, with whiffs of steam transpiring from the vast edifice. The visitors while I was there included two Englishmen; one very well dressed, though his socks were behind the times and he had rouged his nostrils; some Americans, and four doll-like Japanese. Certainly the chief languages spoken were American and Japanese. The "great" Renoir (the man and woman in the H box of a theatre) hung in the study. It was rather thrilling to see this illustrious work for the first time, as it were, in the flesh. There were Monets of all periods, and the latest period was not the best. A magnificent Cézanne landscape and a few other Cézannes; Manet, Dégas, Sisley, Boudin—all notable. Yes, a collection very limited in scope, but fully worthy of its reputation. Only it wants hanging. It simply hasn't a chance where it is. The place is far too small, and the contrast between the pictures and the furniture altogether too disconcerting. Still, the pictures exist, and they are proof that a man can possess marvellous taste in a fine art, while remaining quite insensitive in an applied art.

Afterwards I called in on a painter in Montmartre, and learned to my astonishment that it was precisely he who had painted Durand Ruel's doors. 70 doors had been ordered.

The painter told me how Durand Ruel had bought Renoirs for 20 years without selling. The "great" Renoir had been sold at Angers for 400 francs, after a commissioning amateur had refused to give Renoir 1500 francs for it. The amateur had said, "Yes, it's very good, of course, but it isn't what I expected from you." (They always talk like that—these commissioning amateurs.) Then Durand Ruel bought it. And now he has refused 125,000 francs for it. In my friend's studio I was told how dealers who specialize in modern pictures really make their money. A "lord" wants to dispose of, say, a Rubens on the quiet. It comes mysteriously to the dealer, who puts it in a private room and shows it only to a very few favoured young painters, who pronounce upon it. Soon afterwards it disappears for an unknown destination. The dealer is vastly enriched, and he goes on specializing in modern pictures.

Wednesday, February 15th.

I got as far as the death of Mrs. Lessways in *Hilda Lessways* on Sunday afternoon, and sent off the stuff as a specimen to Pinker yesterday. 33,000 words. During this time I haven't had sufficient courage to keep a journal. I suspect that I have been working too hard for 5 weeks regularly. I feel it like an uncomfortable physical sensation all over the top of my head. A very quick sweating walk of half an hour will clear it off, but this may lead, and does lead, to the neuralgia of fatigue and insomnia and so on, and I have to build myself up again with foods.

Yesterday I signed the contract with Vedrenne and Eadie for *The Honeymoon* at the Royalty Theatre.[1]

Sunday, February 26th.

Reviews of *The Card*[2] much too kind on the whole. 6 on the first day, 6 or 8 on the second. Dixon Scott's in *Manchester Guardian* one of the best I ever had, and no effusiveness either.

I did practically no work between Monday and Saturday, but 3500 words on these 2 days. In between, I was mysteriously ill. I hope to finish the second part of *Hilda* a week today. But *tant pis* if I can't. News of edition of *Sacred and Profane Love*[3] with my water-colour cover arrived from United States on Wednesday, together with figures showing that Doran had sold about 35,000 copies of my various books (in about 8

---

[1] J. E. Vedrenne and Dennis Eadie managed the Royalty Theatre together in 1911.
[2] Just published in London. Its American title was *Denry the Audacious*.
[3] *Sacred and Profane Love* was published in England in 1905. The American edition was called *The Book of Carlotta,* Bennett's original title for it.

months, I think). This does not include Dutton's books nor Brentano's editions of *Buried Alive.*

Wednesday, March 1st.

Dinner last night at Maurice Ravel's. He played us extracts from the proofs of his new ballet, *Daphnis et Chloë,* and I was much pleased.

This morning I found that W. D. Howells had devoted the whole of the "Easy Chair" in March *Harper's Magazine* to me; very friendly. So I sat down and wrote to W. D. Howells.

Tuesday, March 7th.

Last week appeared March *Bookman,* being an "Arnold Bennett number," with a pretty good article by F. G. Bellamy. I got six different letters about different businesses from Doran yesterday.

Monday, April 10th.

We left Paris on Friday morning. On Wednesday night I saw Copeau's adaptation of *Les Frères Karamazov* at the Théâtre des Arts, and it was very good. It finished at 12.55 A.M.

April 21st.

London. Palace Theatre. Pavlova dancing the dying swan. Feather falls off her dress. Two silent Englishmen. One says, "Moulting." That is all they say.

We got to London at 4 P.M. Friday, and I came straight down to Burslem.[1] On previous visits I have never made adequate notes, but this time I am doing a little better.

Sunday, April 23rd.

I lost my note-book of the Potteries, and only began a new one 2 or 3 days before I left. On Tuesday the 11th I went to Manchester to stay with Mair till Thursday. I met the usual fine crowd, and also Stanley Hough-

---

[1] The town in Staffordshire where the Bennett family lived. It was the Bursley of the *Five Towns* stories.

ton,[1] who impressed me; and Irene Rooke,[2] whom I liked; and, in particular, a certain Hughes, of Sherratt & Hughes, the largest booksellers in Manchester, who told me he had sold 950 copies of *Clayhanger,* and over 400 of the cheap edition of *The Old Wives' Tale* in 3 weeks (I think).

M.[3] came to the Potteries on Thursday. On Saturday we went down Sneyd deep pit, and on Monday to Rode Heath. We came to London on Tuesday, and Marguerite went direct to Pinner. I came to 2 Whitehall Court, and what with the Authors' Club, and the N.L.C.[4] next door, and a fine bedroom on the 7th story, I ought to be comfortable. I took up *Hilda Lessways* again on Thursday afternoon, and shall finish reading what I have written this morning. Better than I expected. At the Authors' Club, I have met Morley Roberts, Charles Marriott, and Charles Garvice.[5] Some of the men seem to waste 3 hours in gossip every afternoon.

Saturday, April 29th.

Lunch with Massingham at Devonshire Club. Afterwards Shorter [6] and Robertson Nicoll [7] joined us, and then Lewis Hind.[8] When Shorter said he would willingly tell me the name of a young artist of genius whom he had found, only for the moment he could not recall it, everybody laughed, and Nicoll said to me, "There's much more in Shorter than you think!" Roars of laughter. It was a good *rosserie* for Shorter. They stayed till nearly four, and then Massingham and I made an arrangement for articles for the *Nation.*

M. and I dined at Romano's and then went to the Tivoli. Harry Lauder was, as I expected, very common and under the mark.

---

[1] A playwright of the Manchester school, who died in 1913.

[2] At that time playing in Miss Horniman's company at the Gaiety Theatre, Manchester.

[3] The first Mrs. Arnold Bennett, *née* Marguerite Soulié. She is referred to by this initial almost always in the Journals.

[4] The National Liberal Club.

[5] Three veteran novelists. Roberts was then 53 years old and had already published nearly fifty books. Marriott, born in 1869, published *The Romance of the Rhine* in 1911. Garvice's romances, including such works as *A Coronet of Shame* and *Where Love Leads,* enjoyed tremendous popularity in England and America.

[6] Clement Shorter, the eminent authority on the Brontë sisters, published that year an edition of *The Complete Poems of Emily Brontë.*

[7] Sir W. Robertson Nicoll edited the *British Weekly* and wrote for it under the pseudonym of "Claudius Clear."

[8] C. Lewis Hind published his work on *The Post Impressionists* in 1911.

Thursday, May 4th.

Worked all right in the morning. Josiah Wedgwood [1] lunched with me at Authors' Club. I saw Vedrenne at 5 P.M. (also Eadie), and learnt that *The Honeymoon* probably could not be produced owing to impossibility of getting either Irene Vanbrugh [2] or Alex. Carlisle in London, and uncertainty of Doris Keane in New York. However, they had cabled to the latter.

Wednesday, May 10th.

Wells came in to take me out to lunch at N.L.C. I didn't go. Mrs. Wells was lunching with Marguerite on ground floor. We dined alone at Grand Hotel Grill, and afterwards I went to N.L.C. Nothing there except food for thought. Yesterday Mrs. Belloc Lowndes [3] lunch at Sesame —Mrs. Aria, James Douglas, Seccombe, etc. An American came to tea. Dinner at the Gourmets with Waring. Lord Howard de Walden also came. A nice intelligent boy, very well used to things and people. We all went to *Fanny's First Play* (poor) and then saw Lillah McCarthy [4] afterwards, and I finished up with Waring at Authors' Club.

Friday, May 12th.

Scott-James [5] for lunch yesterday. He seemed to be a severer and better critic than I had thought. Granville-Barker came in while I was writing for *M'chester S. Chronicle*. He said he had never made any money out of his plays except as books.

Monday, May 15th.

Saturday night Rickards [6] dined with us at Café Royal. Afterwards we saw George Moore, and later, at the M——, a fine selection of *souteneurs*.

---

[1] England's most notable exponent of the single tax, and author of *Essays and Adventures of a Labour M.P.*
[2] The actress, wife of Dion Boucicault.
[3] Wife of Frederick Lowndes of *The Times* and sister of Hilaire Belloc. She is the author of several novels.
[4] The actress, then wife of H. Granville-Barker.
[5] R. A. Scott-James, at that time literary editor of the *Daily News*.
[6] Edwin Rickards, of the architectural firm of Lanchester and Rickards, was one of Bennett's oldest friends.

Lowndes came for lunch today, and Austin Harrison for tea. Then Authors' Club banquet to Tree, Courtney in chair. The most appalling orgy of insincere sentimentality. I left at ten, utterly disgusted and exhausted.

Monday, May 22nd.

A long day of work in the Club library yesterday. At 7.15 I walked up to Pagani's. Dined with Austin Harrison there; other guest, May Sinclair, and the Howard Joneses. Mrs. Jones extremely beautiful. An American with no accent. Jones from Potteries. After midnight Harrison, May S., and I went off in a taxi. I dropped Harrison at Davies St. and took May S. to her studio in Edwards Sq. I rather liked this prim virgin. Great sense. She said she lived absolutely alone—not even a servant.

Wednesday, May 24th.

I finished the 5th part of *Hilda* yesterday morning. Yesterday, lunch with Mrs. Lowndes at Sesame. Maurice Hewlett, just like a boy, impulsive and exaggerated and quite grey. I liked him at once.

Thursday, May 25th.

Mozart, Strauss concert. 3 P.M. Old man with St. Vitus next to us. He stood some time at door with young girl in charge, waiting for first piece to finish. She armed him with difficulty to seat. F.C.B. helped him to sit down. Long thin legs. Knees that stuck out to next seat. Both hands trembling violently nearly all the time. Kept his head down. Took him about a minute to lift up one hand to his face to move his specs. Peculiarly smooth reddish skin of hands. The girl put programme in his hands. He could read it, in spite of shaking. Handkerchief stuck in waistcoat. She wiped his moustache for him. She took his gloves off, and afterwards put them on. He never looked up the whole time. Once, not being comfortable, he had to be lifted and re-sat, and at intervals he stood up, holding on the front seat. All his movements very slow and trembling. Once when hand on knee it did not tremble. Lips, and especially upper lip with moustache, trembling all the time. We left her arranging him for departure.

Saturday, May 27th.

44 today. Yesterday for a change we lunched alone and dined alone. Dined at Savoy Grill Room. The only good service I have come across this time in London, outside clubs. Performance of *Nan* at Little Theatre in the afternoon. Splendid.

Monday, May 29th.

Dined with Larbaud at the Cecil, and the rest of the evening at White-hall Court. We met Wheeler by accident at Appenrodt's, and he told us all about his difficulties with the production of Reinhardt's *Œdipus,* and how Lafayette, who had promised to find all the money, was burned to death the day before the contracts were to be signed.

Tuesday, June 6th.

Week-end, Friday to Tuesday, with Atkins at Brightlingsea. One of the times of my life. Perfect weather; a most pleasant house, brains, and two days of yachting.

Thursday, June 8th.

Tuesday, Florence [1] and Rickards to dinner. R. and M. and I went to *Playboy of the Western World*. Splendid, but I was too tired to appreciate it properly. Yesterday, Irving Brock of *N. Y. Times* came to see me; an argumentative person, but I rather liked him. Dinner at Albemarle Club as guests of May Sinclair.

Friday, June 9th.

Lunch with T. B. Wells, one of the editors of *Harper's,* and Pinker. Vague talk of his buying my American impressions. Pinker had sold my next humorous serial to the Hearst combination for £2000, all serial

---

[1] Arnold Bennett's sister.

rights. This means at least £3000 for the novel, or 1s. a word. I was justly elated.

Knoblock dined with me at the Club, and we settled the main outlines of our play.[1] Today I wrote him putting our terms in writing.

Saturday, June 10th.

I wrote the last chapter but one of *Hilda* yesterday. Contract with *Harper's* laid down for serial rights of 6 articles on the United States for £800.

Sunday, June 11th.

Reflections at Piccadilly Circus upon my article thereon for the *Nation*. Rideing, editor-in-chief of *Youth's Companion*, came for lunch, and told me with a grin the funniest things about its editorial policy. Sexual love is banned. At most, at the end of a story, it may appear that a girl is beginning to care slightly for a lad.

Wednesday, June 14th.

On Tuesday morning I finished *Hilda Lessways*, which is exactly 100,000 words—a curiously good forecast. Yesterday afternoon, tea at Lady Ottoline Morrell's. I re-read *Hilda* and put in chapter headings after dinner.

Saturday, July 1st. Fontainebleau.

I finished *Just at a Venture*, story for *The Odd Volume*, on Thursday; and last of *Life in London* series for the *Nation* today. Frank Vernon came to see me yesterday afternoon. He said Marie Tempest wanted to play in *Honeymoon*, in co-operation with Vedrenne, and wanted her first entrance made much later in the first act. I declined to alter the play. He said I was right. At best, even if the thing comes off the date of production will be changed.

---

[1] This was *Milestones*, by Arnold Bennett and Edward Knoblock, not produced until March 5, 1912, at the Royalty Theatre.

Saturday, July 8th.

I began to write my little book on Xmas,[1] on Wednesday last. On Thursday I went to see the Wellses[2] at Pont de l'Arche. I came back yesterday, and found myself in a railway accident at Mantes, 6 wounded.

There had already been a breakdown in a tunnel. Officials said that a *rotule* of an *attaché* had got broken. It was repaired, and we jolted onwards at, I should say, about 30 or 35 kilometres an hour. Then just after we passed Mantes station there was a really terrific jolting. I knew after four or five jolts that one coach at any rate had left the metals.

I was in a sort of large Pullmanesque compartment at the back of a first-class coach, two or three coaches from the engine. The windows broke. The corridor door sailed into the compartment. My stick flew out of the rack. The table smashed itself. I clung hard to the arms of my seat, and fell against an arm-chair in front of me. There was a noise of splintering, and there were various other noises. An old woman lay on the floor crying. I wondered, "Shall I remain unharmed until the thing stops?" Immense tension of waiting for the final stoppage. Equilibrium at last, and I was unhurt.

I couldn't get out at first. Then some one opened the door. I soothed the old woman. I took my eyeglasses off and put them in their case. I found my hat (under some débris) and my stick. My bag had remained in the rack. I left the train with my belongings, but I had forgotten all about the book I was reading, *L'Ève Future*. This book was all that I lost. Two wounded women were ahead, lying out on the grass at the side of the track.

Up above, from street bordering the cutting, crowds of people were gazing curiously, as at a show. One woman asked if she could do anything, and some one said, "A doctor." I walked round to the other side of train, and a minor official asked me and others to go back. *"Ce n'est pas pour vous commander, mais . . ."* We obeyed. Two coaches lay on their side. One of them was unwheeled, and partly sticking in ground.

---

[1] *The Feast of St. Friend,* published in October 1911.
[2] Mr. and Mrs. H. G. Wells.

No sound came from an overturned 2nd-class coach, though there were people in it.

Presently some men began lifting helpless passengers on to cushions which had been laid on the ground. I had no desire of any sort to help. I argued incompassionately that it was the incompetent railway company's affair. I held my bag and stick and I looked around. I didn't want to see any more wounded nor to be any more *impressionné* than I could help. My recollection of appearances quickly became vague. I remember the face of one wounded woman was all over coal dust. We had shaved a short goods train standing on the next line, and the tender of the train was against our coach. A young American said that it was sticking into our coach, but I don't think it was. He said that the front part of our coach was entirely telescoped, but it wasn't entirely telescoped. It was, however, all smashed up. My chief impression is of a total wreck brought about in a few seconds.

I walked off up line towards station and met various groups of employees running towards train. At last two came with a stretcher or ambulance. I passed out of the station into the *place,* and a collector feebly asked me for my ticket, which I didn't give. I went straight to a garage and demanded an auto for Paris. But all autos had been taken off to the scene of the accident. Having been promised one in due course, I waited some time and then had a wash and took tea. I couldn't help eating and drinking quickly. Then I was told that two Americans wanted an auto. I said that they might share the one promised to me. Agreed. At last my auto came. The price was 100 francs. A Frenchman came up who wanted to get to Paris quickly (he had not been in the accident), I gave him a place for 20 frs. making a mistake in thus dividing 100 by 4. This detail shows I really was upset under my superficial calmness. We went off at 5.50.

Friday, July 21st.

Everything neglected in the way of notes, while writing *The Feast of St. Friend*. I did it in 12 working days, and finished on Wednesday.

The Honeymoon arranged for with Marie Tempest and Lillah McCarthy anxious to buy *The Great Adventure*.

Monday, July 31st.

The Dorans came on Wednesday last and left this morning. *Séjour agréable pour tout le monde.* Doran showed great optimism about future sale of my books, and was quite ready to offer £1500 on account of a new novel to be written in 1914.

Sunday, August 13th.

I began to write *The Family* (tentative title of play in collaboration with Edward Knoblock) on August 1st. I had finished the first act on August 6th. He revised it (but slightly) and on Friday the 11th he read it in our kiosk to the Mairs, Alice Kauser, and her brother, Ed. Sheldon, and me.

I read the draft of what I had done of the 2nd Act. *Succès très vif.* I shall finish the 2nd Act on Wednesday, and count to have the whole play finished on the 29th. I write a scene of the play each morning, and Knoblock comes in most afternoons for tea, to go through what I have done.

I didn't alter at all his construction of the 1st Act, but I have immensely improved his construction of the 2nd, and I shall entirely reconstruct the 3rd. His revision consists chiefly of rearranging the dialogue here and there, and shortening. Whenever he adds a phrase of his own it is heavy and uncolloquial, and has to be altered. Still, he knows the stage, and his help is valuable. Also the original idea of the play was his, and the skeleton his. Nevertheless I do not in the least regret the collaboration. It will have occupied me less than a month.

Saturday, August 19th.

Finished 2nd Act of *The Family* on Wednesday, and I began to write the third this morning. I have found two good titles for this play: *The Man with the Scythe,* and *The Milestones,* or *Milestones.* The latter will probably be used.

I have been reading *Tom Jones* for about a year. I finished it the other night. It is equal to its reputation; consistently interesting. There is no dull chapter. But he makes the hero too good. He seems to think that so long as Tom goes in for a little miscellaneous fornication he will be saved from priggishness. I doubt if this is so, especially at the end, where Tom's angelicalness upon the misfortunes of Blifil is really a bit thick.

Wednesday, August 30th.

On Thursday, 24th, I finished the play, which we finally decided to call *Milestones* (my title). Knoblock finished the revision of the last act on either Friday or Saturday, and it was sent to the typewriters on Monday.

I leave for London tomorrow morning, and do not mean to live at Avon any more.

October 7th. Lusitania.

The Honeymoon produced at the Royalty last night. Lukewarm. Supper at Marie Tempest's afterwards. Home at 2 A.M. I had finished packing at 10 A.M. Left at 11.15 for Euston.

My fatigue had been slowly increasing for a fortnight, and this morning, after about 3 hours' sleep only, I was just at the end of my tether.

2nd class crowd afar off.

Much waiting and crying for them.

None for us.

We left at 5.40, landing-stage; then anchored in river to wait for tide. Hire of 4s. for deck chair. Must be some remnant of an ancient custom.

Gent at dining-table: "I wonder how many souls we have on board." Strong also on the indecency of the Russian ballets, which, however, he much admired.

Curious recurrent moaning sound at night, apparently of wind in ventilators, or something.

Sunday, October 8th. At sea.

Strange noises through the night. Tappings. Waiting for the dawn to come, forgetting that there could be no dawn. The dawn was the turning on of the electric lights in the corridor.

Barbers. An American shave 1s. Very elaborate, and I felt I was in

America. Tipping downwards of chair, putting you at his mercy. A very clean shave. Dropping a bit of powder on towel, and then rubbing it in. Then hot damp towel, and very elaborate rubbing dry. He then wanted to do my hair, but I told him it was not my style to have my hair too rough.

Walk on navigating deck, where all the ventilators were secretly whirring, and two engineers arguing about a valve. Steering places hidden off. Top steering place deserted, so that it seemed as if the ship was steering herself. I look down a shaft like a coalpit (into depths of ship), which is lighted at stages by electricity, and there is a great draught *up* it. What it was for I didn't know. Enormous amount of covered-in machinery on top deck, but I could actually *see* one fan whirring.

Lovely morning. Rippled sea as we leave Ireland. Dining-saloon for breakfast. Size of it shown by sudden perceptions that features of people in opposite corner were blurred by distance. But the great sensation of this part of the ship is that of waiters and parlourmaid persons walking rather quickly long distances in straight lines, bearing plates often. They must walk very many miles in a day. A blue and white nurse-looking person approaches out of the distance, and gets clearer, and as she passes you see two rampant lions on her breast—*the sign of the Cunard*.

Humility of people waiting till they are served. It would want some pluck to make a row in this place, the stewards are so self-respecting.

Going out on to starboard deck (on this floor), I am startled to see it crowded. Steerage passengers. This is their playground. I walked round the forward part of the ship and saw their dining-rooms, kitchens, and broad staircases leading to different sections of berths. I had a glimpse of one berth; it seemed all right. All along deck here and there were entrances to paradises forbidden to them. Netting hung down from deck above gave sense of being cooped up. Certainly they were very close together. A certain natural brazenness about some of them—girls, who would not give and take to me in passing.

I discovered vast parts of the ship whose existence I had not imaginatively preconceived.

Monday, October 9th.

7 A.M.

Ragged sky. Black water all round horizon. Nothing in sight. Moon not set. Full moon.

Again, sense of unsuspected populations. This sense helped by a mysterious ringing of a bell in distant part of ship, calling some unknown population to its meal.

Inspection of ship with Mr. A——, Chief Steward.

3rd Class. Inoculation for smallpox. Fares £7.

Men watching girls, and girls then watching men. "Having their sweet revenge," said A. Another of his great phrases was "No time like the present."

1st Class. Kitchens. All this steerage was another world mysteriously opened. We went back into a still unknown part of our world.

Roasting ovens. Intense heat. Revolving spits.

Special orders primed on a board with hours marked; then I heard a man call out, "Baked potatoes for 4 at 8 o'clock. Extra order."

Fire. In 1st class kitchens, a table of posts for every man. I noticed a list of about 30 or 40 stewards "to control passengers."

52 cooks for 1st and 2nd class.

The baking goes on day and night, never stops.

Dough-mixing by electricity.

Potato-peeling machine.

Egg-boiling machine. 1 minute, 2, 3, etc. Automatically lifted out when done.

Firemen's kitchen.

Special menu for leading firemen. 12 leading firemen. Meal served every 4 hours (goes down by lift) night and day. 110 firemen on each watch.

Every member of crew has a bunk.

In each store dept. (wine, grocery, etc.) in the depths of it, a quiet, generally nervous man, keeping accounts on a green cloth.

The second class was like 1st class on a small scale. Less space. Had we not been in 1st class it would have seemed spacious and magnificent. Many obviously well-to-do men in smoke-room. Fine view over stern of ship.

Purser at dinner.

He said he knew practically the whole of the professional gamblers. Once 2 got on unawares. At night when smoking-room full, he got carpenter in, who prominently took down all warning notices of gamblers and prominently put up new ones underlined with red ink. Still, they won 40 dollars off a man, who, however, refused to pay.

Forbes-Robertson, Knoblock, Burton, and me in lounge after dinner. Got talking of theft of "Mona Lisa," and then each told tales of thefts— marble mantelpieces out of Russell Square, etc. Italy; pictures rotting from damp through neglect in Venetian churches, and so on, until one had the idea that the whole art world was undermined and everything going or gone.

Bit of wind at 11 P.M. Looking through porthole of hall of E deck. Waves swishing by. Hopeless position of any one overboard. Suddenly a wave bangs up against porthole with a smash, and you draw your face away startled.

Visiting ship with Chief Officer.

Chart Room. "Holy of Holies." Brass and mahogany effect. Dodge for detecting and putting out fires in inaccessible holes. Fan to draw out smoke, and steam attachment to drown it. All same pipes. 4 or 500 feet of piping at least.

Sounding tubes (?) wire draws out water from a tube. Even the wire so drawn in by an electric motor. It can be done at full speed.

Bridge. 75 ft. above sea. The house was carried away and wheel carried away once by a wave—one wave. One dent, made by glass, left in wood, to commemorate the day.

Telegraphs. Telephones. Private telephone for chart room that does not go through Exchange.

Subterranean signalling. A bell sounds through it like tapping a pencil on wood. Nantucket bell heard *16 miles off.*

Down below, forward of steerage, capstan gear.

The cables will each break only at 265 tons. That is, they could hold in suspension 26 10-ton trucks of coal. The capstan gear is so strong that it will break the cable if it is overwound.

Imagine 265 tons of M.P.'s dropped into the sea.

Well may all this powerful machinery be encaged, just like wild beasts in a menagerie.

7 different steering gears. The last by a hand wheel almost direct. Auxiliary engines, etc. We went down 2 or 3 stories from lowest passenger deck and saw the tremendous gear actually at work, slowly and apparently capriciously moving to and fro at intervals in obedience to sailor on bridge 5 or 600 feet away and 70 feet higher up.

Up and down steel ladders. Climbing over moving chain (like a bike chain) of steering-gear, through stray jets of steam, in a forest of greasy machinery, guarded by steel rails, grease on floor: all apparently working alone under electric lights, but here and there a man in brown doing nothing in particular. Dials everywhere showing pressures, etc.

Up a flight to dynamo room.

Machines revolving 1200 to the minute.

Then to stokehold. Vast. Terrible. 190 colossal furnaces, opened and fed every 10 minutes, and coal flung in. Mouths of furnaces seemed to me very high for coal to be flung into them. This effect was like that of a coal mine with the addition of hell.

This was the most impressive part of this ship. It stretched away with occasional electric lights into infinite distance. 1000 tons of coal a day. Finest coal. Very hot. An inferno, theatrical. Above, confectioners making *petits fours,* and the lifts going for 1st-class passengers.

Invited into Captain's room. He showed us his photograph after being invested C.B. by King.

Talk of Royal Family. The Englishman's reverence for his old institutions, of all kinds, and his secret sentimentality (according to F.R. the

King was fine fellow, and the Queen a woman of really unusual brain-power) comes out all over the ship the whole time.

Marvellous after-sunset exactly ahead, as we came out. Sea like slightly uneasy oil.

Previously, at dinner, the purser on his Airedale terrier, Paddy. So comprehending that when his wife and he wanted to say something they did not want the dog to understand, they had to spell out the important word, instead of pronouncing it.

Dr. Hutchinson introduced himself to me in smoke-room, as being a great admirer. He began to talk about his biological researches and travels and theories, and kept on—very interestingly, and never referred to my work at all.

He said that the progress of sanitation in Naples (where up to a few years ago there were no privies at all) was very much hindered by the fact that a company paid the corporation 300,000 francs a year for the right to remove human excrement. Another company pays 100,000 for right to remove dog excrement. (Same thing in Constantinople, Aleppo, etc.) Dog excrement sent to U.S.A. for preparing of kid gloves, etc. Nothing like it for that.

Wednesday, October 11th.

Impossible to round the forward part of the boat deck without a struggle. The variations of temp. and the differences between temp. of sea and air are quite remarkable.

At 2.30 we passed the *Baltic;* which left L'pool on Thursday, 2 days before us. When I looked again at 3.30 she was out of sight.

Thursday, October 12th.

Up at 5.35. Entire ship's company seemed to be at work. I asked for tea, and got it at once, with apologies for it being Ceylon instead of China, as the storekeeper was not up.

L.W., the little, well-dressed wealthy traveller (with valet and house-keeper) who gave us a most appetizing account of Yucatan, with the most beautiful women in the world.

Subdued excitement as to hour of landing tonight, and conflicting prophecies. Turning up of people never seen before.

At 5 P.M. ship supposed to dock at 9 P.M. Continued appearances of people never seen before. Also, although 4 hours yet to pass, men in hats and town overcoats, instead of caps, etc., women in large hats, which seem extraordinarily large and grotesque. General excitement.

Montague Glass introduced himself.

Friday, October 13th.

Last night. Taking pilot and (?) health officers aboard. But perhaps they were ship's officers. First we saw some coloured lights which we took for something on land. It proved to be a ship, and then it proved of course to be the pilot-boat. We had been burning flares.

Doran and two press men came into saloon off revenue cutter. Only I didn't know they had come off revenue cutter, and I didn't know Doran had done a great feat in getting there. I was interviewed by 2 journalists apparently on behalf of the crowd. This was while ship was manœuvring into dock. And at last we went on shore, after I had been interviewed by 3 other people. Irvin Cobb was part of our group.

Called at 2 hotels (free lunch-counter, etc.) and had time at the N.Y. Central to go to Hotel Belmont, which was our second hotel. I had had views of Broadway, 14th Street, 5th Avenue, etc. Lots of sky signs. Roads up. Not very many people, but a sensation of grandness, immensity, lights, heights. Streets full of holes. The Elevated, on a forest of pillars. Cable cars long and noisy, but fewer at that time of night.

We got into a long train, smoker—rather shabby, and exactly at 11.19 left the station. I had a lot of evening papers, a wilderness to me. We crossed the Harlem, saw the old ship canal, and then skirted the Hudson. Very blue arc-lights. Through the town a regular succession of lightning glimpses of long streets at right angles to the track.

Cobb said you could see N.Y. and get a good idea of it. I said, "But what about the home life of people to learn?" He said, "There is none. It's a half-way house. Constant coming and going, and changing of centres and so on. Only one man in 3 is American born." He indicated a whole vast quarter as we passed—probably several miles—which he described as nothing but apartment houses and bedrooms. . . . Arrival at Yonkers. Station being reconstructed. All wood stairs, etc. A buggy, on remarkably thin wheels, and 2 horses, brown and white, ill-groomed, waited for us. And we seemed to drive a very long way. Through an Italian quarter. We passed through a district full of remains of decorations of Christopher Columbus Day, which was yesterday. At last, after sundry hills and dales, into an obviously residential quarter. Here roads all interminably winding curves. Then the house.

Today, walk down to Yonkers with Mrs. D.

Young men and maids coming from high school.

Station wagons—thin wheels.

Ice wagon—"Danger."

One or two old Colonial houses.

A "tinder" boarding-house, all wood, rather nice.

Outdoor boot-blacking stands.

Roast chestnuts.

Beautiful Hudson, gasometer, and sugar refinery.

Strangeness of hearing *English* in this strange place.

Badness of tram lines at intersections.

Saturday, October 14th.

Going down change at 155th on to Elevated.

No crush. First view of baseball ground.

The effect of millions of staircased windows of apartment houses, with glimpses every now and then of complicated lines of washing.

Street after street, dirty streets, untidy, littered.

Baseball game. Giants v. Athletics, N.Y. v. Phila.

Again cigarettes, chewing-gum, programmes.

Cheers for kid practising, sharp sort of cheers.

Advertisements round arena.

Drive through Central Park, and then past Carnegie etc. houses.

Pitcher lifting left leg high. Tip on right toe.

Applause for a run. First red man near to me in joy.

Members of audience being turned out.

The catching seemed to be quite certain,

As rare as a woman in a ball match.

As difficult as to make a first base.

The eagles on top of stand.

The yellow ushers against the dark mass.

The blue men against a red-bordered mat, N.Y. police.

The blue purple shadow gradually creeping up to the sign,

"The 3-dollar hat with the 5-dollar look."

A 2-base hit is the height of applause, real applause.

Chewing-gum.

Combined movements of jaws.

Obstinacy of chewing gum at *end*.

The pitcher is the idol of the affair, as may be seen when he comes in to strike.

The hunchback mascot of Philadelphia.

I was told afterwards that the real 1st-class stroke of the game was a player jumping instead of *sliding* on to a base. Had he slid he would have been touched. Welter of autos and torn paper afterwards.

Sunday, October 15th.

The friendships between American men seem to be more charming than between English. They call each other more by their Xtian names, and are softer to each other. "A very dear friend of mine" is a frequently heard phrase. (Messmore Kendall & J.H.D.) They are more caressing with their voices.

One of the greatest sights in America: Irvin Cobb like an Indian god sitting at the shinery opposite Park Hill Station having his shoes shined. And they *were* very well shined, too.

The flexibility of arrangements for business and social affairs. Ingenuity expended in getting things to fit in for comfort, etc.

Sunday morning. Auto trip into N.Y.

The sheer Italian beauty of vista of Fifth Avenue.

Gigantic fine cornices, etc.

All N.Y. packed in. 2 steps from Wall Street is Syria and Greece. In and out of Chinatown in a moment.

My *intense* fatigue afterwards.

Interminability of Broadway.

Tuesday, October 17th.

Doran and I took 3.34 Congressional Limited from Pennsylvania Station to Washington. This station is very impressive. Silence. Not crowded.

Trains a mere incident in it, hidden away like a secret shame. Tunnel under Hudson. Very neat, regular, and well lighted: seen from observation car. Noise from steel. Jolting of smoking-car. General jolting when brakes put on.

Electric sign sticking up high as we passed through Baltimore in the dark: "Baltimore, the electric city."

Arrival at fine station at Washington.

Apparently a long drive to Shoreham Hotel, across avenue after avenue. Still, all the air of a provincial town. Had to get out of bed to extinguish final light, otherwise good hotel.

Congress chamber.

Old Congress chamber is a sort of rule-chamber. Its astounding collection of ugly statues. Whispering point, where Adams fell. I was exhausted after this. Declined to visit Library of Congress. Saw Washington monument. Phallic. Appalling. A national catastrophe—only equalled by Albert Memorial. Tiny doll-like people waiting to go into it.

Sub-guide said, pointing to a portrait in oils: "Henry Clay—quite a good statesman," in a bland, unconsciously patronizing way. Guide also said of picture, "Although painted in 1865, notice the flesh tints are quite fresh."

General effect of Washington. A plantation of public edifices amid a rather unkempt undergrowth of streets. Pennsylvania Avenue the great street. Cheapness of its buildings (old private houses turned into business) as the thoroughfare approaches the Capitol.

The White House very nice architecture. Rather small. Distinguished. Overflow of Capitol into huge buildings at either side rather to front of Capitol. Dome too big for sub-structure. The wings rather fine.

Badness of saddle of mutton at bkfst. Finger bowls after every damn snack.

Wednesday, October 18th.

Met Macrae in big hall. We had bkfst. in station restaurant. Open 6 A.M. to midnight. Kids in certain parties. High chairs for kids. One party, husband (who had probably come to meet after their absence from home), wife, and 2 children. Youngest kid slept. Other, boy about 5, sat up in chair. Great calm gaiety, a delightful scene—mother particularly.

Heavy rain.

Thursday, October 19th.

Lunch at Harper's, with chief members of staff including Major Lee,[1] under presidency of Colonel George Harvey.[2] I liked Harvey. Quiet, ruminative, accustomed to power, and so on. Good laugh. Good story. But a sinister-looking person, rather. T. B. Wells had come to fetch me in taxi. Very heavy rain. We called at Brevoort-Lafayette for Frank Craig, who is to illustrate my articles, and for whom Wells had an inordinate admiration. I thought he said, "Clean, wholesome," which is just what Craig is. The clean young governing-class Englishman to perfection. I liked him much, but I doubt his views in art.

Lunch was at Lawyers' Club, in a private room thereof. Rex Beach, one of the best sellers, there. Nice athletic youngish man. Then I was taken to Harper's office—two Elevateds—and shown over it. Old-style building for America.[3]

---

[1] Albert Lee had been editor of *Harper's Round Table* in 1895-9 and editor of *Harper's Weekly* in 1901-2, but at this time he was managing editor of *Collier's Weekly*.

[2] He was president of Harper & Bros., 1900-15. In 1921-3 he was Ambassador Extraordinary and Plenipotentiary to Great Britain.

[3] The Harper's offices were then in Franklin Square. They were not moved to their present location on East 33rd Street until about ten years later.

Humorous serial sold for £2000 to Phillips.

Then to Waldorf, where a room had been obtained, and to bed for ¾ hours after a bath. Considering I had had only one hour's sleep at most in night on train, I was doing pretty well.

Still heavy rain off and on. We drove to Republic Theatre (Belasco) to see *The Woman* by William C. De Mille. Telephone girl play. Melodrama plot. Essentially childish. Nevertheless, in spite of too much talk in 1st act, I was not really bored. It appealed to the child in me.

Guggenheim pointed out to me at theatre.

Looked like a little grocer.

Pirie MacDonald, 10 A.M.

Photographer of men.

Electric blue light.

Shirt and belt.

Gesture of triumph with bulb at end of tube.

Squeezing tube harder and harder as he makes the exposure. Boyish gestures.

"Not *at* my eyes. *Into* my eyes. That's it. Just a little more challenge. A *little* more. That's it. Don't wink. We'll try again. I'll just play *round that spot*.

"D'ye know, I feel kind of guilty." Then history of yarn. English path. Late. "I was thinking of that this morning. I got up thinking about that, instead of about A.B." Then, as I was going: "Don't expect anything mighty grand. What I've been trying to do this morning is A.B. as I've seen him in his books. I may be wrong in my interpretation, just as you may be in your interpretation of a person."

P.M.: "I want you to dash your head round."

Me: "I was afraid of moving my head too far."

P.M.: "Don't be afraid. This place is yours. If you want to spew on the floor we've got people who'll clean it up.

"I've made money so that I can take *you* this morning and tell a 100-dollar client to go to the devil; that's what I've made money for.

"Joy isn't a contortion. It's something right deep down. Put your back against the chair. Get your back right against it—like an Englishman, that's it."

He told Doran, on bringing proofs, that if he hadn't read my pocket philosophies he couldn't have got such a good portrait.

Friday, October 20th.

Lunch, with Paul Reynolds and Whyham (*Metropolitan Mag.*) at Players' Club. Pictures and playbills at Club. General frank air of good fellowship at principal central table. Interviews, including 2 good ones from *Tribune*.

Then Doran took me to *New York Times* Building, where almost 1st person I met in editorial office was Brock, who had come to see me in London. We were shot up to top, about 27 stories altogether. View of New York. Yellow and blue lights. View of bridges. Feeling on top of being on top of a great cathedral (about 350 feet high, I suppose); solidity of parapets. But Metropolitan tower looked much higher. Steamers moving about on river. Fine wet wind.

Then down to see George Buchanan Fyfe on 16th floor. Curious three-cornered room. "City" editor. Stopped his leader to talk to us for 15 minutes. Sharp "Williamson" sort of man. Feeling of him being in an eyrie. All rest of staff without coat or waistcoat—belted. Then down 4 stories below ground to see machine room. Blue corpse light, as outside Paris opera. Rolls of paper being arranged on their steel angles. (Cf. Brock writing story of aviator's fatal fall, 20 stories above.)

Then to low dancing hall—an old man, really old, probably official of house, dancing with a young girl. 35 cents entrance. Mineral water. Small band. Rather shabby Montmartre. Doran didn't know how it was arranged with police. All the women were tarts. We stayed 10 minutes. Bed at 1.10.

Miss Gurney and Mrs. Doran for tea. Then I went to Altman's store and McCreery's store with Mrs. D. Marvellous white effect of former. Shop girls not so prosperous-looking and rather sloppy, but a few were pretty, and one had the mien of Marie Tempest with a waist too thin. . . .

Miss Gurney said women were not as well turned out here as in London.

Saturday, October 21st.

The Dorans dined with me last night at Louis Martin's. Café de l'Opéra, the place where only morning dress was allowed and it failed. Pruger used to have it. It is now an ordinary restaurant. Very glittering, with scenery painted on some walls, and the wall opposite street all mirror. Friezes of bulls (Egyptian character of decoration) and other animals. Strange statuary.

Then to Astor Theatre, where Henry B. Harris presents *The Arab,* a play of the Orient, by Edgar Selwyn.

Afterwards Mr. and Mrs. Edgar Selwyn (Margaret Mayo) invited us and Mr. and Mrs. Crosby Gaige to supper at Knickerbocker. Another lofty large restaurant. Food quite good. Both Selwyn and wife agreeable. She a smiling little thing, with a cute eye. She told me she had 4 companies playing *Baby Mine* in America, and that each of them brought in more than London. Gaige put in that one week's royalties at San Francisco brought in more than 8 in London, where play was a success. Selwyn said American theatres held more. His held 1800 dollars per performance and it was a smallish one. They played to 16,000 or 15,000 dollars a week on road, and in N.Y. Actors got more. He played in *Arizona* in London, and one American actor had to leave. They got an English one at 1/6th his screw.

Journeyed by Elevated (change at 155th) and N.Y. and Putnam R.R. to Yonkers. Talk about the sadness and raggedness of this. Occasional ship. Brokendown wooden houses. Sloppy planks. One house had drifted out into Hudson River and sunk. Mrs. D. said that really terrible crimes were committed here. Sight of 2 or 3 pleasant young children on stoop of a wooden house. Sloppy ends of cars.

All this in fine driving rain.

Monday, October 23rd.

Walked up 5th Avenue in bright warm sunshine at 12.45. The skyscraper coming at fairly regular intervals (apparently) seems to divide length of street and so aid perspective. But buildings are so big that they deceive you as to their nearness. Fine blue sky and general feel. Cornices of architecture again. Otherwise nothing very special. This walk, though hurried, was very pleasant.

Lunch with Mrs. Ullman [1] at Arts Club. Mr. and Mrs. May Wilson Preston, Mr. and Mrs. Day, Mr. and Mrs. Doran, and me. May W. P. was in great form. When Alice said something cutting about George, May said, "Now you're making a noise like a wife." She was one of the liveliest and wittiest women, if not the most so, I have met in N.Y.

Tuesday, October 24th.

It is only 17 days since I left London, and it feels more like 17 weeks.

Dinner with Mr. and Mrs. James Clark and Mrs. Adelaide Ames and the Dorans at Rector's. During dinner a pianist played a ballade of Chopin's. Never heard such a thing in a restaurant before.

To the Playhouse, managed by Wm. A. Brady. *Bought and Paid For,* a play in 4 acts by George Broadhurst. This is the best new Anglo-Saxon play I've seen for a long time. Perfectly simple story of a poor telephone girl marrying a wealthy man who turns to drink: with her comic sister and extremely comic brother-in-law. These were the only necessary characters. The rest were servants, including a fine Japanese servant. The brother-in-law was colossal. Splendidly drawn comic character. Whenever the author might have excusably gone wrong, whenever the thing was really difficult, he came out well. The reconciliation at the end was excellent. The drunken scene in second half of 2nd act, with its clear suggestion—both there and at beginning of 3rd act—that the husband outraged the wife sexually while drunk—was very excellently unpleasant. In short, I really enjoyed this play. The story was interesting and the sense of character very strong indeed.

Upton Sinclair. A brief chat. Not a bad sort of chap, I thought.

---

[1] The former Alice Woods. She and her husband, George Ullman, were great Paris friends of Arnold Bennett.

For the doorman, the Waldorf is simply a place where the doors revolve 18 hours a day or more.

Wednesday, October 25th.

Last night. Rhodes,[1] dramatist, came in with Knoblock for tea. Mrs. Adelaide Ames and her friend (heralded as beautiful, Gibsonish). Mrs. Glaesner came for tea, too. Knoblock dined with me and Rhodes (societyish dramatist) at Café Martin, and then I took them to Wallach's to see George Arliss in Louis N. Parker's *Disraeli*. Doran joined us. An awfully tedious play. English players. Just the Louis Parker artificial drivel. We left after 1st act. We came to the Waldorf bar. Went to bed before 12. Rhodes wanted to take me on to the Guinnesses in Washington Square; I wouldn't go.

Bad night.

I had breakfast in bed. Very well served on table brought in. Soft-boiled eggs. Difficulty of breaking them into glass. Appointment with Björkman [2] at 11 and with Arthur Hooley [3] at 11.30. Björkman too talkative. An analytic and probably uncreative brain, but very decent.

I said, "A good book is interesting. A book that isn't interesting isn't good."

Arthur Hooley said instantly, "Could you say that of a man?"

At 2.30, Lingley called in his auto to take me to Columbia University. 20 minutes' drive.

Classes chiefly closed at 3 when we got there. We were met on steps by Dean Keppel. Proved himself more and more pleasant as interview and inspection went on. Showed me the leaf in looseleaf book of information about each student.

Took us to modern history laboratory, where I saw a Chinese tabulating history of world day by day.

---

[1] Harrison Rhodes's *Ruggles of Red Gap* was produced in 1915.

[2] Edwin Björkman's book *Gleams* appeared in 1911. He is best known for his translations from the Scandinavian, including the plays of Strindberg.

[3] Before 1908, when Hooley came to America, he had collaborated with Bennett in writing plays which were never produced. Hooley wrote under the pseudonym of Charles Vale.

Then to political laboratory. Same kind of thing, but not yet quite in working order. All vast rooms; well equipped. Then to see 2 chambers. 3 dollars a week. Simple, quite large enough. Photographs on shelves, etc. Sofa bed. Very nice in adolescent way. Met hunchback contributor [1] to *Atlantic Monthly*. This man had to pay his way—got 25 dollars a month from Keppel for certain editorial work.

Loyalty of men together who join in a certain year. They will club up years afterwards for a contribution to University. Such as a flagstaff, or marble seat.

Then to the gymnasium, basket-ball and baths (naked) under that.

Then to Horace Mann school. Grey-haired ladies knocking about corridors. Started originally as school for teachers to learn to teach in.

Tea at Faculty Club. Talk with young Professor (Walker?) [2] of English who taught Shakespeare, chiefly by making youths read the plays. He said they read them for story.

Also visit to Thorndike, head of English department in University. Grey-haired young-looking jolly man, who made us sit down and gave us cigarettes.

I came away pretty nearly dead. Impressions. Size. Groupings of buildings. Richness where richness advisable, as in libraries and chapel. Manual work of kids of 10 in model houses, and reinforced concrete. Ferns, etc., in Horace Mann School.

Drive home by Riverside Drive. 1st U.S.A. warships with patent wirework masts that are said to be indestructible.

Drive back to Waldorf. Wait at top of 5th Avenue (Plaza corner) and watch crowd going home. Richness. Tiffany's by night. A dazzling and lovely building.

University Club, glorious buildings.

Traffic. Policemen with coating of dust on blue coats.

Impression of youth and hope and inspiringness.

---

[1] Randolph Bourne. He was also on the staff of the *New Republic* from its inception.
[2] Possibly Professor Charles William Wallace, noted Shakespeare authority.

Thursday, October 26th.

New York (or Yonkers). Young people coming out of school or college. Confident. Defiant. Phrase: "These *invaders* of *our* time, *our* earth."

October 27th. Boston.

Blotting-paper in U.S.A. is darker and thicker. Blue and green, till you aren't sure what it is.

Corrigan came for breakfast. Went out with him to see booksellers.

Jordan Marsh the principal. Pitman, head of book department. Largest booksellers in town. Young Jordan (a grandson) absolutely English—manner, accent; rather aristocratic. Complete counter given to my works.

Visited 7 other stores. Lauriat—bluffer, nice assistants. De Wolfe. Narrow, noisy, curly streets. Business character of England. So much so that nothing struck me as queer or curious the whole morning—except the size of everything. Jordan Marsh's probably bigger than Harrod's.

Excursion to Cambridge, and Harvard with Basil King,[1] who came to fetch us and insisted on us taking tram. King said every one did it and we must do it. Remember underground tram station and gradual emergence, *very uncomfortable.* View across from Charles River. Strange idea of building an island and putting cathedral on it. Town of Cambridge, rather slatternly. Then we came to residential part.

House of Lowell. *First thrill.*

House of Longfellow. Kids of town had bought plot of ground in front so as to assure him from being built in.

Long walk with stalwart Basil King. Ex-parson. He said major vices did not exist in this community of professors, writers, and professional men.

A.B.: "No adultery?"

B.K.: "None.

"Extraordinary state of intimacy we live in," he said. "But we live for social service—for each other."

---

[1] His *The Street Called Straight* was published in 1912.

Then Professor Schofield took us in charge in a fine motor car. Brief visit to University. Saying: "You can always tell a Harvard man, but you can't tell him much."

October 28th. Boston.

Library. The Puvis de Chavannes (blue going so well with marble) are the most beautiful things in America.

Yesterday. Pre-revolutionary homes still occupied by same families at Cambridge.

Auto drive—continuation after Public Library. Parks. Fenlike park. Skirting Brookline—richest per capita. Mrs. Jack Gardner's[1] house with a screen to cut off school.

Women chauffeurs.

Pleasure roads only.

Yacht clubhouse overlooking old harbour. 4-masted schooner.

Boston is a circular city, repeated ad infinitum.

Harbour, 6-masters.

Then vast wool warehouses.

"Coffee and spices."

Then circular streets. Elevated. Tram cars.

Fearful racket.

To Boston Yacht Club; in an old warehouse.

Low ceilings—great beams.

Extreme and splendid nauticality of this club.

Wheel of *Spray* in which the regretted Slocum wafted himself round the world.

Huge square porthole (faced with arm-chairs with great wide arms), across which ships are continually passing.

"Best thing about Boston is 5 o'clock train to New York." (Thomson.)

I had no glimpse of real Bostonians, "old Back Bay folks" who gravitate between Beacon St. and State St. and Somerset Club and never go beyond. Confusing New England with the created universe.

---

[1] Mrs. John L. Gardner was the owner of one of the finest private art galleries in the world.

Navy Yard. *Constitution,* built 1799.

Roomy, much metal.

Then into Italian quarter, curving tram-liney streets, cobbled; Italian signs up and down, and so gradually into business quarter, which I saw yesterday with Corrigan (all previous part of morning so different from this).

Legend of Paul Revere floating like a mist through Italian streets.

Paul Revere's signal church spire, by Wren. (Closed [?] because only 6 in congregation.)

Old State House. Beautiful building. Massacre close by. Lion and unicorn on roof.

Boston is finished, complete.

Sunday, October 29th.

Lunch with Rideings at Brandon Hall on way to Brookline or at Brookline. He came to fetch me. Fine morning. He grumbled at everything.

"This is the most snobbish place in the world. There is no real democracy. First thing people do is to show you their family tree and prove that they came over in the *Mayflower.* Very dear. . . . I would accept 1/3rd less salary to live in England," etc.

Tuesday, October 31st.

Dinner at Margaretta Deland's[1] on Sunday night. Mrs. Deland was extremely sympathetic. Note her hands, strong and decided.

We left Boston by 9 A.M. train. Invited by telephone to lunch at George Day's, treasurer of Yale (at New Haven). Horrible railway station at New Haven. Drove up in a sort of funeral carriage. Nice wooden quaint house. G. Day a very quiet and patriotic sort of man (had chucked banking to do this). Tales told of his saying at football of a member of opposing team in game he was watching, "Kill him, I can't stand his red stockings coming up the field." President Hadley and his wife came to lunch. President Hadley a remarkable man. Extremely nervous laugh

---

[1] Her novel, *The Iron Woman,* was published that year.

(very like Lanchester). Greatest authority in America on railway eco-
nomics. Speaks Latin. Lectures in German at Berlin. Tells funny stories
and remembers all sorts of punning rhymes. His wife excellent. I didn't
see university, except drive round, and yet here I got the best idea I
have had of university spirit, fine.

Character of American men in lips more than in anything else. Sticking out and holes beneath. Strange outlines formed by lips.

New York. The incapacity of Americans to deal with street traffic is
shown in everything—from elevated to absence of refuges even in main
thoroughfares.

Wednesday, November 1st.

To dinner last night at Waldorf: Doran, Knoblock, E. Sheldon, and
Hopwood, a dramatist (author of *Nobody's Widow*). This was Hal-
lowe'en. Kid's parties, etc., and general appearance of festivities in
hotels.

Then to Hippodrome, where Hopwood had obtained a box. A vast,
ingenious, striking and impressive, and grossly inartistic spectacle, *Around
the World,* "conceived" by Arthur Voeglin. We just missed the *clou*—
the sandstorm in the desert. But we saw the forest fire, and noted particularly the realism of the clouds in the yacht scene in Honolulu harbour. The Irish scene was prodigiously idiotic. The final tableau: waterfall, electric bulbs all over it, and girls behind that in bowers of light, a
great tank in front, out of which came a golden barge, swans, and real
people. Nobody knew how it was done. Hero the "eccentric millionaire,"
of course.

Thursday, November 2nd.

Lunch at Harvard Club. 15 men. Sisson and Lingley hosts.

The Return of Peter Grimm, by David Belasco, in 3 acts, at Belasco
Theatre, 44th Street.

I should soon get tired of Belasco's productions. Can see same style
in this as in *The Woman.* Nice, agreeable, ingenious. Fundamentally

impossible and unconvincing. All the ghost business infinitely too solid. Still, a great cleverness about the whole thing.

Theatre only built 5 years, but very fussy, dim, old-fashioned architecture. A fashionable audience. Only you couldn't see it. Place full.

Dinner at Delmonico's. Nothing particular. A rather swagger crowd.

We called afterwards at the Lambs Club to find Tarkington. Wasn't in. The Lambs was like what one would have expected the Lambs to be. We then went to the Princeton Club, and found Tark. Rather round-shouldered and ripe.

Friday, November 3rd.

Messmore Kendall's lunch.

Judge Gary (steel trust president) on my right. Slow to talk. Rather dull. But very wise and upright. Said he was making 75,000 dollars a year as a lawyer when he chucked law. Said up to 6 years ago J. P. Morgan had never spoken in public—that after, for 1st time, he had said just 6 words in public, he told Gary that he had been obliged to hold on to a chair.

Advanced and good, fair, honest views on women's suffrage.

Kendall on my left, and then Dan Guggenheim, eldest (?) of 6 or 9 brothers—anyhow chief of them. They never took same steamer or train. A short, merry man. I liked him very much. Very frank. He was U.S. envoy to coronation of George V. President of Smelting and Refining Company. Head of Alaska and Yukon explorations.

R. W. Chambers.

Colonel Braden, the great copper man.

Very agreeable lunch.

I forgot to put down Mr. Cahan, editor of the Yiddish *Forward,* Socialist. A Russian Jew, very enthusiastic for literature, and for any work. Urged me to go and dine with him one night. This man seemed to know as much about art as anybody I've met. And he assured me, what I'd previously heard, that my stuff and art generally was better understood on the East Side than anywhere in N.Y.

Saturday, November 4th. Waldorf.

7.45. Business men—the humanity beneath. A man said, "I'm just going to get a bromo-seltzer."

Thus giving the whole show away.

Postal Telegraph. Girl coming behind her counter in hat and cloak, and turning on her counter lights and opening up her shop.

Luggage men sitting in a group under stairs and discussing their affairs.

Princeton.

Man conducting the "official yell."

Quarterback calling numbers.

Adams said there was a Glee Club concert last night that was delightful. Contortions of enthusiasts. Artistic amenity in contrast to this bloody barbarity.

Reserve men waiting in pairs under red rugs. Whole crowd rising up and sitting down at points of play.

Nassau Club. Confusion.

Princeton Inn. Confusion.

After freshman game met Booth Tarkington at Nassau Club. Drink in dining-room. He said he had been drinking beer with undergraduates late, and then couldn't sleep owing to men singing Chinese songs all night in corridor.

Auto back to club and then to field.

Coloured effect of hats on stands, heaps of violet colour.

Harvard opposite to us.

Cheer-leaders with megaphones.

Standing up and sitting down. At high moments standing on seats.

Accident at start. Man led off amid cheers.

Several minor accidents.

Naïve and barbaric! Merely an outlet for enthusiasm.

Touch and goal scored.

Left at half time.

Sunday, November 5th. New York.

Cobb on interviews:

You gather that an extremely brilliant young man or woman has been interviewed by a very commonplace stranger. Confused in her presence. She picks him up on an absurdity, with a brilliant inspiration. Then another "brilliant inspiration" and so on.

If interviewers had achieved the excellence of American oysters, American journalism would be better than it is. They don't come with prepared questions and are ignorant. No one knew less of my books than they did. They want you to write their interviews for them. Women so infernally badly dressed.

"It is so pitifully easy to be flippant."

Tuesday, November 7th.

Dinner last night given by the Dutch Treat Club at Keen's Chop House. Over 100. Wallace Irwin gave a good skit on "How to Live in New York on 48 Hours a Day."

In a few words I said I would thank him in print.

I walked down to 34th Street to waterside offices of Italian lines; saw *Duca degli Abruzzi* half ready to go. A lot of people on board and a line of 3rd-class passengers waiting outside shed for admittance. Nothing but Italian spoken all round me. This swift transition from 5th Avenue is very picturesque.

Declension of streets sets in immediately after Broadway. 6th Avenue is atrociously paved.

After 7th the declension is frank.

10th and 11th are appalling, atrocious, and some of the sidewalks staggering—unworthy of the suburbs of a small provincial town.

Trains allowed to shunt over 10th and 11th Avenues. Extraordinary.

This was election day. I saw the sinister but genial fellows bearing openly the insignia of Tammany. Don't, please, think that Tammany is a disease that happens to have attacked N.Y. It is as much an expression of N.Y. character as the barber's (remember my shave this morning at Waldorf), the pavements, the fineness, the interest in education, etc., etc.

Thorough badness of barbers.

Dinner at Sherry's. Robert H. Davies, Franklin Adams, Doran, and I. Davies told how he interviewed Li Hung Chang for W. R. Hearst. Hearst, on it being pointed out to him that bribery would be necessary to get round the whole crowd of Dutch waiters at Waldorf (where he had a suite), said he would give 1000 dollars for the expenses of the interview. Davies went straight to the head underling and gave him 500 dollars in cash, simply to say whenever asked, "Who is the greatest journalist in N.Y.?" that Davies was the greatest journalist in N.Y. Said Davies to underling, "When you've been asked this question and fallen down in a fit, rise up and breathe the sacred name, and keep on breathing it." Ultimately, after a week, Chang sent for Davies. And Davies entered his suite, "with my shoes in my hand." He interviewed him through an interpreter. At the end Davies said: "I asked his Excellency if he spoke English; he answered in English, 'No.' Asked if he was rich, he said, '600,000,000 dollars today; nothing tomorrow. All I have is at the mercy of the State.'" He was very curious about rich men in America. Later he sent for Davies as a private man and spoke to him in English. He asked if Davies was married, and Davies said he wasn't because he couldn't afford to be. He then said: "Get money. Get a wife. Get a home. Get children."

Wednesday, November 8th.

C. called. Talked very interestingly. X., who I said had seemed to me, positively, an honest man. He denied it. Told me, what he said was notorious, X. had committed adultery with a girl and had two children by her. Then his wife had died, and he had thrown her over for the "large florid creature" now his wife. Girl had only got her rights through a lawyer. Still he admitted that X. was honester, and had the new sense of right and wrong to a greater extent, than any of his rivals. But he had done all the usual bad things. He said there were two people in each big trust man—the head of the vast corporation, and the private individual. He said X., like others, by the force of his character and his autocratic spirit, had killed really efficient co-operation round about him, and that the other best men had left, because no room for them.

Lunch at Aldine Club, given by Phillips of *American*. Miss Marbury, Miss Anne Morgan, Miss Ida Tarbell.

These three women all extremely interesting; all different, yet intimate, calling each other by Christian names, coming together on a purely personal basis just like men.

Elisabeth Marbury. A very business woman. Fat. Human. Kindly. Shrewd. Very shrewd, and downright in her remarks.

Anne Morgan. Handsome, complexion going. Apparently doing nothing, but interested in everything. Art, for instance, (and art dealing) and reform. Knew France and Germany well. Spoke firmly and efficiently. Showed us her beautiful new enamel cigarette case, with her monogram worked regularly into all the crossing lines of it. A peculiar accent. Evidently an energetic woman. Again, efficient. Good judge of human qualities, and wide in interests. At 10 to 3, I said, "It's 10 to 3; I must go." "Yes," she said quietly, "I must be going soon. We're going down to Washington by the 3.30."

Ida M. Tarbell. The most wistful and inviting of these 3 spinsters. A very nice kind face, of a woman aged by hard work, by various sympathies, and by human experiences. A sort of appealing face, and yet firm and wise. When asked to go down to Washington with Anne and Bessie, she said, "I've only just come back (where from ?), and I haven't been at my desk for 4 or 5 days." Just like a man. One imagined her desk.

Miss Hale's report on immorality of Boston. Her visit unawares to house of assignation.

Saturday, November 11th.

Last night. Dinner at Mrs. Edgar Selwyn's. Then Geo. M. Cohan's theatre.

The Little Millionaire, written, largely composed, and produced by G.M.C., who takes the principal part and who built the theatre. He has in particular a voice, but he is a good dancer. Man about 35 probably, slim, and looks on stage what he probably is—a mixture of shrewdness and good nature.

Brings his family into show. Both his father and mother have principal parts, and he is ingenious enough to make them marry at the end. The last curtain is he and his father doing a *pas de deux*.

A N.Y. institution, apparently beloved.

Plot of piece quite clear. In 3 acts. "The Action of Act II will not be interrupted by musical numbers." The second act is beautifully constructed, and dramatically effective, and full of invention of all kinds. No salacity in the piece at all.

Sunday, November 12th.

Yesterday. Abraham Cahan came to fetch me for lunch. Mr. Cahan at Café Boulevard (2nd Ave.), "Art Nouveau" in dining-halls. Mrs. Cahan a little, fatigued-voiced, Russian woman. Unable any more to go to Russia owing to warrant being out for her spouse (owing to spy's revelations). Long talk on literature. Home by surface car. Cahan said: "Russians talk a great deal more than English. They like talking, and I'm going to talk." He did.

Why is not N.Y. the real America? It seems real enough. Is it more material than, say, Paris, or Hamburg or London? What's up with it, anyhow?

Why are the few artistic people in America so internecine?

Art will come unconsciously, and it will be jeered at.

Monday, November 13th. Twentieth Century Limited.

Telephone, typist, library, papers. All this is typical.

Began by running fairly smoothly.

Along the Hudson. Ugly general effect.

Stop in the mysterious electric-signed city of Albany. Crossing Hudson. River steamer with several stories.

Watched changing of enormous engines.

Before Syracuse 10 P.M. night train running through night. Mysterious habitations, stations, and hints of strange life.

Authority of train men compared to English guards. More like naval officers.

"Syracuse bids you welcome." Electric sign on probably town hall.

Tuesday, November 14th.

Night a series of short dozes.

Rang for tea at 7.45 (N.Y. time) and attendant said no dining-car till Elkhart, 1½ hours off, and that engine had broken down at Cleveland, and train was 2 hours late. I got up 1½ hours later and went out of compartment and asked one of head-men and was informed train 2 h. 10 m. late. Train full of hungry passengers. I had felt our car chilly. Found observation car damn chilly, and everybody complaining, and attendants excusing.

Before all this, fine steamy view of Toledo, at about 7 A.M., with river and chimneys various shades of grey and black.

Line quite straight for innumerable miles. Slight coating of snow. Flat.

2 dining-cars for breakfast. Nevertheless a queue, women and men waiting 20 minutes at door.

Arrived Chicago. 10.45 (1 h. 50 ms. late.)

Blackstone Hotel. Taylor (Frank Adams of Chicago *Tribune*) for lunch.

Opening of Art Institute.

Mobbed by women.

Woman: "I'm a regular Bennett fan."

Autograph hunter who followed me round and was always staring right in front of me.

Reporter who on being refused an interview at once said, "Well, can I follow you round, and take down any observations you make?"

Female reporter afterwards who called me "my dear man."

Met Thomas Nelson Page and his wife.

Scene from my window. Morning. Michigan Boulevard. Sound of

trains puffing. Skyscrapers with ledges of snow. All roads chiefly snow-covered. Frost. Procession of autos. Many snow-covered flat roofs of lower buildings. Illinois Central Station apparently in front. Grey, dirty bituminous region. Can't keep hands or linen clean.

Barometer lower than it has been during my stay in U.S.A.

Wednesday, November 15th.

Rottenness of female interview in Hearst paper *Chicago Examiner*. Next reporter told me the Hearst paper had mercilessly guyed all best men in Chicago.

Man who telephoned to Doran, "Tell Mr. Bennett he stinks." This would probably happen in no other city in the world. I might say, "Chicago is the city in which this happened to me." But I won't.

Lunch Chicago Press Club. I applied for foreign membership. Douglas Mallock in chair (editor of *The Lumberman*). Two members made speeches as "Mr. B. would have spoken if he had spoken."

Number of doctors. Two said that my books, *Human Machine* and *How to Live on 24 Hours a Day,* were regularly prescribed to patients. One said that they had "changed his whole life." Number of autograph hunters.

On the way, in cab in which they fetched me, Goble and another member expressed sorrow and disgust of club at interview with me in *Examiner* today.

Chicago city of superlatives.

Biggest store, bookshop, press club, post.

Reynolds Club (students).

Commons (replica of Oxford).

Fine twilight effect on magnificent boulevards.

Then reception at Mrs. Judson's.[1] She looked after me grandly. Tea. Told girls not to talk till I had had tea.

Then stood in corner of drawing-room, and procession of faculty and wives filed past me, and I joked with each.

Nice, unassuming large house.

---

[1] Wife of Harry Pratt Judson, then President of the University of Chicago.

Drive home with Hutchinson to Blackstone.

Half an hour to prepare to go in Ross's auto to dine at his house in Evanston.

Drive out to Evanston. Long gas-lit roads. Very smooth and straight on the whole, but with half-made bumpy intervals.

Entire company interested in children.

Talking of kids, I must not forget 2 stories of Cobb's. Elizabeth Cobb, when her parents began to spell: "Too damn much education here for me." And of another girl, when her parents began to whisper: "What's the good of being educated, anyway? When I've learnt to spell, you whisper."

November 16th.

Floyd Dell, successor to Francis Hackett, of *Chicago Evening Post* (literary), called to see me.

Hamlin Garland came to take me to lunch at the Cliff Dwellers.

Charles Hutchinson, the banker, and originator of Art Institute and all sorts of municipal stuff, had found time to come during morning and arrange flowers; on principal table. Many handshakers and autographs. Talks with architects and musicians. Then Garland, with his two brothers-in-law, Taft [1] (sculptor) and Browne [1] (painter), and Jensen (a Dane, head of parks section), took me in auto to make circuit of boulevards round city.

Fine internal "landscape" gardening. Enormous completeness of everything, and fine upkeep of everything on boulevards.

River. They turned its course towards Mississippi, so as to get rid of sewage. This is most remarkable thing I have come across, spectacularly.

Smell of stockyards.

Taft's studio. Colony created by him after 20 years' dreaming. A dreamy timid man. Several young sculptors and sculptresses said to have great talent, at work on vast municipal sculptures (such as groups and bridge near University). Sense of enormous protracted detailed labour in these undertakings.

---

[1] Hamlin Garland and Charles Francis Browne had each married a sister of Lorado Taft.

Dinner at C. L. Hutchinson's.

Ayer and wife (collector, etc., aged 70), Burnham (architect), Miss Monroe,[1] Mr. and Mrs. Ryerson. President and Mrs. Judson.

Some good and many bad pictures.

A crowd of younger ones came in afterwards.

General impression of shallowness left after seeing all these people. As if one had come to the end of them at once.

Yet Hutchinson's idea of hospitality, and of how to look after a sought-for visitor and how to leave him alone, is unequalled by any one else's in U.S.A. so far.

Spectacular effect of their municipal spirit (born in '71). Curious wistful quality in their constantly expressed inspiration after "The City Beautiful."

Letter (probably falsely) signed "Jack London" of abuse about interview with me in the *Examiner*.

Home at 11.30.

Wet street view of Michigan Boulevard with flood of yellow reflections and the 2 long lines of lights, punctuated by red globes showing crossings.

Chicago is full of public spirit.

Friday, November 17th.

Maurice Browne called 9.20.

Prim little professional Englishman. Very nice. Gloomy about art in States.

Went to Sears Roebuck & Co. in their auto. Got on very well with Murkland, head of book and China dept.

8 million dollars business last month.

Over 7000 employees. Over 4000 women. 5½ millions of large catalogues sold. Big bill-typing room. 600 clickers.

Gradually on to car-yard, where cars being filled up. This yard of cars sent out full every day.

But most interesting thing was glimpses of real life of these outlying communities everywhere, as seen in ugly common simple stuff they

---

[1] Miss Monroe's magazine, *Poetry*, did not begin to be published until October 1912.

ordered. Thousands of cheap violins. In one basket ready for packing, all sorts of little cooking utensils and two mugs (fearfully ugly) labelled "Father" and "Mother." 4-cent curling-iron. Most startling realistic glimpses of home life. All the life (cheap music, chairs, etc.) of these communities and separate farms could be deduced from this establishment.

Concert of Thomas orchestra in Mrs. Hutchinson's box. Good. Piano (bad) coming up through floor. Bauer pianist.

Then to Little Room in a studio in Fine Arts Building.

Met Jane Addams at Little Room. A middle-aged benevolent creature.

Dinner given by Herbert Kaufman. Very nice table in handsome private room.

Mr. and Mrs. Medill McCormick. She daughter of Mark Hanna.

Mrs. Cobb, daughter of Governor of Ohio.

John McCutcheon, who does a cartoon every day for *Tribune*.

McCormick (young man retired on account of nervous breakdown) is a good radical and well up in English politics.

"Ruth," he said suddenly to his wife, in tone of commanding suggestion. And they went and the party broke up at once. 10.10. I was glad. I was just going to break it up myself.

Saturday, November 18th. Indianapolis.

Set out for Indianapolis this morning at 9.47.

Sort of accommodation train.

Chiefly flattish country (with welcome breaks), yellow stubble land. Occasionally a dark muddy river. Single track (after once clear out of industrial Chicago, which seemed to be one vast shunting yard). Stopped at little towns. At very little ones. A group of men and a woman. Man holding gun and shot rabbits, and dog leaping up at it. Wooden houses with concrete narrow walks and grass on either side. Fat little German girl (daughter of house) cleaning windows.

Arrived Indianapolis 3 (12 minutes late, about). Maple trees in all streets. Monuments to sailors and soldiers. Dome of State House.

State fair ground outside town. Said to be same in all State capitals.

Dinner. Tark,[1] Doran, Craig, me.

Reception at night. About 40 people. Meredith Nicholson.[2] Senator and Mrs. Beveridge (very beautiful, with a soft, and probably Washingtonian, voice); also wife of ex-President Harrison. Numerous provincially dressed girls and women. One débutante almost the only person who wasn't shy. She had made her début yesterday evening and gone to bed at 2 o'clock. Said she slept very well.

Punch in study made by 2 Japanese boys from University Club.

Sunday, November 19th.

Lunch of ten people at Tark's, including Meredith Nicholson and Tark's father.

Afterwards in auto to pay several calls, including one on James Whitcomb Riley. Fine old man, recovering from paralysis. Red face, yellow teeth, right hand affected, sitting in corner in easy chair. Fire. Mid-Victorian feel. An old friend near him. Talk about a picture of a literary star of good order. Here it was, and in a literary town. Why say there is no American literature? Riley has infectious laugh. Told funny tales of his tragic adventures in lecturing tours, and how he slept on two boxes, one a little higher than the other, covered with papers. Inquired about Lucas. "Tell me about Lucas." Then talked about my books. "I didn't mean to talk about them, to talk 'shop,' but I couldn't help it." Women talking in another room.

Monday, November 20th.

Indianapolis just beginning to spend money. Malaria is gone. Just beginning to be sure that Indians aren't coming and that there'll be plenty of wood. Even now it's rather daring to buy a picture. Formerly you could spend money only on a house, because that was solid and could be sold. And of course you had to have wallpapers and stove.

And now gradually to Art Institute with loan collections, and ripping aquarelles by Winslow Homer.

---

[1] Booth Tarkington.
[2] His *A Hoosier Chronicle* appeared the next year.

Wednesday, November 22nd. Philadelphia.

Took train for Philadelphia Monday at 7.05 P.M. and arrived at Phil. promptly at 3.30, about. Had a drawing-room to myself, but slept little. Row in other part of carriage between conductor and a passenger in middle of night.

Geo. Hellman looked me up in Bellevue Stratford Hotel, and took me to a bookseller (Dr. Rosenbach) where there were some 1-class MSS., Caxtons, and W. de Lourdes. Also old English MS.

Dinner: Corrigan, Craig, Hellman, and me. Last night opera. *La Gioconda.* Caruso.

Malignant ugliness of house. If any spark of artistic feeling in Philadelphia, the place would have been ripped to pieces.

Enormous place. Crammed. But very wealthy and a few very fine dresses.

In train, Corrigan's criticism that *à la carte* service in American trains much better than *table d'hôte* service on European trains.

Bad service at breakfast. "Right away." This is one of the most deceitful phrases in the U.S. language.

Visit to Wanamaker's. Largest organ. Wireless between N.Y. and Philadelphia establishments. Mrs. Hall, book-buyer, said that *How to Live* had eminently stimulated sales for all books mentioned in it—for example, Krehbiel's *How to Listen to Music.*

Lunch at Bellevue Stratford given by G. H. Lorimer of *Saturday Evening Post.* Sam Blythe and Irvin Cobb principal talkers. Racy tales and slang, politics, and murders.

Crossed ferry to 23rd Street. Wonderful view of N.Y. as if on a hill, topped by tower. Mrs. Schiff's auto, with English servant, waiting. She took me to Waldorf, where I soon found Doran. Dined with him and Mrs. Doran. Then I went to elder Mrs. Schiff's box at opera, where were elder Mrs. Schiff, Mr. and Mrs. Mortimer Schiff, the Hellmans, and a Schiff cousin from Frankfort.

Faust, with Geraldine Farrar and unknowns. A lifeless performance. Fine house. Plenty of pearls. I was in the "horseshoe" (W. C. Whitney's box next door).

The open boxes at Metropolitan Opera give the women's dresses a better chance than in London. There is apparently less talking than in London.

Thursday, November 30th..

The Dorans, T. B. Wells, Inglish, John Macrae, Davies, and May Preston came to see me off; not to mention several reporters and photographers. The *Lusitania* left at 9.30 A.M., having been delayed half an hour waiting for the mails. I met the Forbeses on board about 11, and Edgar Selwyn at lunch. Mrs. Selwyn much later. These two had gone to bed at 2.15. Either they or the Forbeses had received a lot of fruit and flowers, and Forbes had installed a supply of champagne at the foot of the table, in ice. I helped to consume everything except the flowers. I had, nevertheless, previously sworn neither to drink nor smoke on board. But having drunk, I thought I might as well buy the best cigar and the oldest brandy on the ship; which I did, and stood liqueurs round. This was after dinner.

I was overcome by sleepiness both before and after lunch and also before dinner; the air gave me a headache. I was very gloomy, spent all afternoon alone and had tea alone, and wondered what the hell was the matter with life anyway. I was all right after I had tasted champagne again.

We spent the whole evening in talking shop, Edgar Selwyn being the quietest. Boat rolled, always. In the middle of the night she rolled so much that she overthrew my red clock. Also fiddles on the tables, last night at dinner. Quite unnecessary, but it is probably a dodge to convince passengers that they are good sailors. No fiddles on at breakfast this morning, when they were necessary and crockery was rattling and crashing about all over the place. The Selwyns and the Forbeses had parting gifts which they displayed, but I also had a parting gift, which I did not display. It was an article for desk use, in silver, heavy and elaborate, engraved with my name, and the card on it bore the following words: "Thank you for all the delightful things you have written and are going to write during the coming year." George [1] will think he can guess the woman it came from at first guess. He couldn't. But he might guess it in three, perhaps. And I had five letters from other ladies, chiefly hating *Hilda Lessways,* but nevertheless all rustling with flattery.

Friday, December 1st.

A general feeling of cold on the ship—no doubt the contrast with N.Y. hotels and houses. But the *Lusitania* is an English ship, and you know it. However, the head dining-room steward is apparently a Frenchman. We had a Thanksgiving dinner last night, and the Frenchman had menus specially printed for our table. Thus, although dyspeptic, I had to eat something of all his dinner, though it irked me to do so.

First gleams of sunshine this morning, after snow and rain. Not caring to read any books that I had, I got *L'Anneau d'Améthyste* out of the library.

Saturday, December 2nd.

Following gale, overtaking us. I began to construct a 1-act play for ship use, and this put me off going to sleep last night, and then I was kept awake by rolling and noises connected therewith. Hence, bad night. Read a lot of *Sanine.* Insincere, voluptuous stuff.

Went out at 10.30. High seas. Whole surface of sea white with long marmoreal lines of foam. Through the mistiness the waves on the horizon looked as high as mountains; or high as a distant range of hills. Curious that distant waves should seem so much higher than those close to. Ship rolling enormously, and her prow yawing about. Yet forward, sheltered by deck-houses from following gale, one had no sensation that the boat was moving forward. Walking backward, from stem to stern, the following gale struck one sharply in the face, though one was running away from it at about 30 miles an hour.

Big squall gradually overtook us. All sunshine clouded out for 15 minutes and snow came down almost horizontally, and much faster than

---

[1] George Doran.

the ship in the same direction. The wind blew spray fiercely off the water in clouds. The screws half raced from time to time.

From newspaper: Annual Meeting of Children's Aid Society. "Bad food, excitement, noise have favoured development of St. Vitus's dance among young children. Poor food, little sleep, and long hours of confining work, have had effect on older children.

"In 3 months during summer over 1000 boys taken up for rowdyism in public places and conveyances.

"During year 8125 homeless boys sought shelter in our homes—a record!"

While waiting in barber's shop, read Jane Addams on *A New Conscience and an Ancient Evil*. Dept.-store girls spending their whole evening in *bathing their feet* and going with men because they were just "sick."

15,000 dept.-store girls in Chicago downtown.

Sunday, December 3rd.

Still rough sea and following gale, and creaking and noises all night. Not yet one good night's rest on this steamer.

Mr. and Mrs. Compton Mackenzie had tea with me. She is a beautiful young woman.

Concert in aid of Seamen's charities last night. Half of it done by Harry Lauder.

I read most of Artzibashev's *Sanine*, skipping. Mostly clever, *naïf*, and dull. Some of the salacious parts are pretty good. But how infantile, these Russians!

Monday, December 4th.

Following gale all yesterday, and the ship yawing about before it. This morning, moderation, and wind from the south. Supposed to get to Fishguard at 8.30 tonight, and Liverpool 8 A.M. tomorrow. I gave my dinner-party last night. Each of the others—the Forbeses, Mr. and Mrs. Selwyn—had given a dinner. I had a chill again. But last night I slept well for the first time on this voyage. These big ships, it seems, are difficult to steer, hence the yawing, and hence the comparatively slow runs.

Friday, December 8th.

Arrived Fishguard 9.30 P.M. Monday. *Standard* man came off to interview me. I gave him all he wanted. Arrived L'pool Monday 8.15. Got to Burslem for lunch. Saw Mater.

Arrived in Paris Thursday at 6.30 P.M., nearly 2 hours late. Very seasick indeed. *Descendu avec M. au Meurice.*

Total expenses of American tour to this morning £252 5s. 8d.

1912

January 6th. Cannes, Hôtel Californie.

Georges d'Espagnat came for lunch yesterday; we drove to Maugin's— he with us—and we deposited him at station at 4.15. He had come from Renoir's villa at Cagnes. He reported how Renoir's pictures 15 years ago were admitted by dealers to be unsaleable. Now the slightest sketch fetches 4 or 5000 frcs. And pictures which formerly had a theoretical price of 5000 frs. sell for 70 or 80,000. Dealers came down from Paris while D'Espagnat was at Renoir's, and bought and paid for everything that Renoir would let them take away. He has been a terrific worker, and in spite of very large sales, still has 2 or 300 pictures to be disposed of. He now lives luxuriously. Formerly *dans la dèche,* D'Espagnat had known him rent splendid houses in which he could not put furniture. He is 71, and scarcely able to move a limb. Cannot rise without help. Has to be carried about. Yet manages to paint, even large canvases. He said to D'Espagnat that were it not for ill health, old age would be a very happy time, as it has all sorts of pleasures special to itself. Although so old, he has a son aged only about ten. This child came as a surprise, and Renoir was furious.

I finished the first three of my *Harper's* articles on U.S.A. yesterday.

Hundredth performance of *The Honeymoon* last night.

Accounts for provincial performances of *W.T.P.W.* and *C. & C.*[1] show

---

[1] Respectively *What the Public Wants* and *Cupid and Common Sense.*

that those plays are playing to better money now in provinces than ever they did.

Thursday, January 18th.

Yesterday I finished the fifth article of the *Harper's* series. And today I turned towards the construction of the sequel to *The Card* [1] for the *American Magazine*. It is only between two spells of work that I can find time for unimportant correspondence, notes, etc. My days are always absolutely full; without counting that I have had three abscesses, two together, as a result of a chill in December. The last one is not yet gone, quite.

I am now in the full swing of my ordinary day; writing, reading a lot of newspapers and several books at once. I bought Whymper's *Scrambles among the Alps* and Stendhal's *Vie de Napoléon* and began reading them together, and immediately felt that I had got hold of two rattling good things. These, with a more or less daily instalment of Sorel's *L'Europe et la Révolution Française,* keep me busy.

Tuesday, January 23rd.

The other day a *vendeuse* and an *essayeuse* came up from the Maison de Blanc, with a *robe d'intérieur* for M. and another for Mrs. Selwyn. A porter of the Maison de Blanc carried the box. The general tableau—the two *employées,* young and agreeable, but certainly not *vierges,* with soft, liquid, persuasive voices, speaking chiefly English; the frothy garments lying all about on chairs and in the box, Selwyn, Alcock, and me lounging on chairs, and M. and Mrs. S. playing the mannequin, and the porter waiting outside in the dark corridor—this tableau produced a great effect on me. Expensive garments rather—and I felt that for my own personal tastes, I would as soon earn money in order to have such a tableau at my disposition, as for a lot of other seemingly more important and amusing purposes. A fine sensuality about it. There was something in the spectacle of the two *employées* waiting passive and silent for a few moments from time to time while we talked.

---

[1] The American edition was called *Denry the Audacious.* The sequel was *The Regent,* published in 1913.

Weather still very bad indeed. Heavy rain stopped a projected drive this afternoon. We did, however, yesterday make our auto-*canot* excursion to Les Îles Lérins without getting wet. Seaward tower on Île Saint-Honorat, quite striking. On grass by this was an old shepherd tending brown sheep. One of these sheep had 3 tufts of old wool left on the back, making her look like a kind of miniature triple dromedary. Marguerite asked the shepherd what it was for. He replied: *"Oh, madame, c'est seulement un peu de vanité."* He was quite simple, and answered simply, but he was evidently a bit of a character.

Saturday, January 27th.

Yesterday we went to Monte Carlo. Tables more tedious than ever. We came home by the Corniche. It began to rain. Brakes got hot and we had to stop. At Nice it was raining well. Twice or three times the driver lost his way.

I began my sixth American article for *Harper's* on Thursday. The two letters that T. B. Wells had written me show that *Harper's* do not at all appreciate these articles. But they probably will do when they have appeared in book form and people have begun to talk about them.

Read in a gulp *He Who Passed*,[1] sent to me by J. B. Pinker. Second- or third-rate; and a very poor end; but nevertheless containing a goodish picture of theatrical life in U.S.A.

On Saturday we drove to Napoule. And the colour was more wonderful than I ever remember seeing it anywhere, even at Fenayrols-les-Bains. The fields were all pools, and all the pools were full of sky and cloud. The view of Grasse was enchanting.

Tuesday, February 6th.

On January 31st I began an attack of *gastro-entérite*. Very decidedly ill on Wednesday afternoon. Full development of attack on Thursday. Doctor on Thursday and Friday. I got up for a few minutes yesterday morning and more in the afternoon. Not yet achieved complete disappearance of symptoms. While ill, I read Dostoievsky's *Le Sous-Sol*, which is great.

---

[1] It had just appeared anonymously.

Larbaud, who calls to see me nearly every day, prefers it to anything else of Dostoievsky's. Also Dostoievsky's unfinished *Le Crocodile*. Good.

Last night I listened to first act of Selwyn's new play, and the criticism on it was united—good beginning, and imperfect end. I ought to have begun my humorous novel on Thursday last, and I have not yet begun it. But on Sunday night I decided on the title *The Regent*. I read a lot of *The Oxford Book of English Verse*, just bought, with great satisfaction.

Sunday, February 11th.

Pinker came Thursday night. Friday we did little, but drove out. Saturday we went out in auto for the day, to Grasse, Gourdon, Gorges du Loup, Tourette, Vence, Antibes. On Thursday, by chance, we saw hydro-aeroplane in action at Juan les Pins. Very agreeable to see. I get better every day but do not propose to begin work again till Wednesday.

Friday, February 16th.

On Monday we all went and deposited Pinker with the Williamsons [1] at Monte Carlo. We lunched with them at Ciro's. On Tuesday, M. and I motored over to Grasse to have tea with the Galsworthys, and the interview was very agreeable.

On Wednesday morning at 7 A.M. as programmed a week ago, I began *The Regent*. By noon this morning I had written 4500 words of it.

Yesterday afternoon Mrs. Julia Frankau (Frank Danby) called to make my acquaintance, and produced a very agreeable impression indeed on us and on the Selwyns. A thorough London type; very chic, extremely capable and alert, of wide ideas, and of a sympathetic nature. She must have a full life, with a large family and her literary work, of which latter, by the way, she said about twenty times—really—that she was ashamed.

Tuesday, February 20th.

Yesterday the Frank Harrises called and took us to Saint-Raphael for lunch. He said: "God when he was young had a liking for the Jews. But when he was old he had a senile weakness for the English."

---

[1] C. N. and A. M. Williamson are known chiefly for their detective stories.

Thursday, February 29th.

This morning I had passed the 20,000-word mark of *The Regent*. It is going along with great ease. Pinker returned from Monte Carlo here on Tuesday, and the Williamsons came yesterday, when Selwyn and I gave a most admirable luncheon at the Casino restaurant. In the evening the whole band of us dined with Mrs. Frankau.

Monday, March 4th.

Coal strike began last Friday.[1]

Said Mrs. Frankau, who with Sydney Pawling came for tea yesterday: "Of course I'm feudal. I'd batten them down. I'd make them work. They *should* work. I'd force them down."

A man stopped me on the stairs the other noon, and asked me my opinion about Kipling's neologisms. He had been reading an article in *The Times*. I referred him to Wordsworth. He understood. Staggering, to find any Englishman in a cosmopolitan grand hotel with even a faint curiosity about the processes of literature. Such a thing never happened to me before.

Wednesday, March 6th.

Milestones by me and Knoblock produced at Royalty last night. I had four telegrams today, all agreed as to its immense success, if only the coal strike won't upset it.

Battle of Flowers yesterday. The most interesting people were the flower-venders. 3 frs. the *panier,* without the *panier!* Quarrelling and grumbling about ticket-holders all the time: "*Vous avez le No. 1. Eh bien, le No. 1 est pris. Vous pouvez vous mettre là. Qu'est-ce que ça fait?*"

Five sisters (secretly bored) in carriage, all dressed alike. American imitation of a rowboat. Mother as a sailor. Habit of thinly dressed women standing up in carriages all the time and exposing themselves. Rapacity of two young shop girls or something who placed themselves in the wrong

---

[1] The general coal strike of 1912 actually began on February 26 and lasted until April 6.

seats in front of us and snatched in the most shameless manner at all the bouquets that were thrown our way. They worried us to death. Astonishing the joy one took in a really pretty woman in white, when there happened to be one.

Larbaud brought André Gide in at 5.30. And we kept them to dinner and had a great evening that finished at 10 P.M.

I wasn't so well today.

Saturday, March 23rd.

I finished the first part of *The Regent* on Tuesday and wrote *Clay in the Hands of the Potter* for *Youth's Companion* (Boston) on Wednesday, and sent it off on Thursday. The Selwyns came over for lunch on Thursday. On Friday we went to Monte Carlo, and had lunch with them —Mary Moore, Charles Wyndham,[1] and H. B. Harris (N.Y. theatrical manager) being of the party. At the Hermitage. Food not so startlingly good as rumour says. Beautiful view of the harbour and yachts from the Selwyns' bedroom. Selwyn was still worrying me to write a play on *The Card*. We went and came home by train.

Coming up to hotel in omnibus, an oldish sea-captainish sort of man said to a youngish red-haired woman that miners had refused the terms of the Minimum Wages Bill. "But of course they refuse everything!" said she scornfully. I must have a strike in my continental novel. It is very funny that all the English inhabitants of grand hotels should be furious because miners insist on a minimum of 5*s*. per day for men and 2*s*. per day for boys.

Good Friday, April 5th.

Knoblock and sister came last Saturday. On Wednesday we excursioned to Monte Carlo, and lost about 500 frs. between us, I having played to amuse Gertrude Knoblock. I was ill yesterday through too much smoking (immediately) and did nothing, and very little today. Two chapters of *The Regent* remain to be done.

---

[1] Mary Moore and Sir Charles Wyndham were the joint proprietors of the Wyndham Theatre. They were married in 1916.

Thursday, April 11th.

Today at 3.30 I finished *The Regent*, 78,200 words, written in two months less three days. So far this year, I have written:

Four articles of *Your American States* (two last year, 10,000) for

Harper's	22,000
Clay in the Hands of the Potter for *Youth's Companion* .	2,200
The Regent	78,200

102,400

This morning the Knoblocks departed in an auto for Paris. They picked up Walpole and Anderson at the station.

By the way, at the Princess's Restaurant, I saw Lord X. He looked a vulgar and damned scoundrel. Not his fault, of course.

I have read Walpole's new novel, *The Prelude to Adventure;* satisfactory—and am to try to arrange a contract for him with Doran.

Wednesday, April 17th. Paris.

We left Hôtel Californie, Cannes, at 7.50 on Monday morning and got to the Hôtel du Rhin, Paris, at 11.45 at night. Flat in this hotel, 2 bedrooms, servant's bedroom, bathroom, sitting-room, and *débarras,* for 50 frs. a day, all included (*troisième*), but no central heating.

Saturday, April 20th.

Wednesday night *Le Petit Café* by Tristan Bernard at Palais Royal. Excellent, and well played. Yesterday the Selwyns and Calvo came to lunch. Only their anxiety to meet us here and hear the rest of my comic novel prevented them from going home with the H. B. Harrises on the *Titanic.*[1]

Tuesday, April 23rd.

Sunday at Fontainebleau, packing up books.

I told Selwyn I would turn *The Murder of the Mandarin* into a one-act play.

[1] The White Star liner *Titanic* had gone down with 1513 souls on board, April 15.

Finished reading *Quentin Durward* last night. A few goodish scenes, but on the whole mediocre and careless. I made a few notes as to it at the back of the *édition* Nelson.

Monday, April 29th.

Left Paris and got to Newhaven yesterday. Drove car for the first time this morning round about Newhaven.

Went over to Brighton to see the Sharpes.[1] Newspaper man in street talking to Oswald Sheppard (Bonnot [2] killed yesterday): "I wish I'd been in Paris yesterday. I could have made a bit o' money. When Crippen did it, I made £3 before 5 o'clock. Nobody got no change that day. . . . Now they mucked up this *Titanic* disaster for us. They put on the bills '*Titanic* sunk.' That was no use to us. They ought to have put 'Hundreds drowned.' Then we should have made a bit."

Sunday, May 5th. London.

I came from Newhaven to London yesterday morning in the car, and drove it myself as far as Putney Hill, 62 miles, in under 4 hours.

May 29th.

John Burns, National Liberal Club.

He did not smoke. The first thing he said was, "We must talk about Federation"; then he immediately changed the subject to the strike. He talked most of the time leaning back in a chair and looking round sharply if he thought any other person in the smoking-room was observing him. Often he left out his "h's" on purpose. When he had told me that he had read all that I had written, obviously a lie, and I said that I could not understand how the busy public men had the time to do all they appeared to do, he said that public men soon began to cultivate a special faculty.

He said, socially speaking, England is the laboratory of the world. At the present time all the new movements are initiated here; untrue! He

---

[1] A family of musicians, old friends of Bennett.
[2] A notorious Paris bandit who was killed after the siege of his house by the police.

said, "I get more letters about my town planning and housing scheme from the United States than I do from England." He then, after quickly asking me about New York and Chicago, went on to describe his own adventures in New York, Chicago, and Denver. He explained how the editor of the *Chicago Record & Herald* came out thirty miles from Chicago to obtain his impressions of the city before he had arrived, and when he declined, became angry. Afterwards he saw this man in Chicago and made his celebrated epigram that Chicago was "a pocket edition of Hell," or, if the newspaperman preferred it, "Hell was a pocket edition of Chicago." This man worked up such an agitation against Burns that when the time came for him to speak on "The Duties of Citizenship" at a very large meeting in Chicago, not a single member of his committee dared to appear on the platform. However, he came on alone and little by little won the enthusiastic sympathy of the audience. As he did so he said that he could hear the members of the committee coming, one by one, behind him on to the platform. All this made a very good story, but he must have told it a great number of times, and have gradually arranged the details for his own glory. He said that his little epigram about Chicago had been appropriated by Choate, and that Choate had stolen more of his things than any other man in the world.

He then described how in the strike at the docks, either last year or the year before, he was sent down by the Prime Minister to try to persuade the men to obey the leaders. He took a lot of matches out of the match stand and arranged them in two squares. He said:

"Well, there were 5000 military in this square and 15,000 workmen in the square next door. And there was only a gravel path of about twenty feet between the two. The Socialists were walking round the outskirts of the crowd, pointing to the soldiers, who could plainly be seen, and the guns, and things looked very threatening indeed. I regard this as the greatest crisis that I have ever been through. I remembered my old cry, and in a voice of thunder I shouted out, 'A gangway, lads,' and they made enough room for me to go into the centre and stand on the cart. I talked to them and called for three cheers for the leaders, and so on, and so on, and I could see their old-time affection for me returning," etc., etc. These were the exact phrases he used. He was not exactly conceited, but vain in a rather ingenuous way. He spoke freely of the conceit of other people.

As we walked home, passing through Downing Street, a young boyish-faced man in evening dress, carrying a bag, came out of the Prime Minister's house. Burns called across the road and then went to meet him in the middle of the road and spoke to him for a minute or two. Practically all the illumination came from a small gas lamp over the Prime Minister's door. This was Mr. Asquith's secretary. He seemed to be to me an exceedingly ordinary and good-natured young man.

As we passed along the front of Wellington Barracks, Burns began to explain how the moral conditions of the soldier had improved during the last twenty or twenty-five years. He said, "There, in spite of all their faults, are 8000 of the very finest infantry in the world."

As one soldier after another came walking along in the gloom, he seemed to be able to tell at a glance from the medal strips, even in the dark, what campaigns they had been through. He remarked how they were all walking perfectly straight and how twenty-five years ago not one of them would have been able to walk straight, or, perhaps, even to walk at all. This is a specimen of his picturesque way of stating things.

Tuesday, October 1st.

Hospital for Incurables. West Hill.

What must be feelings of patient as he drives into entrance of this Hospital and sees the big sign, "Hospital for Incurables"?

Thursday, October 3rd.

Granville-Barker's *A Winter's Tale* at Savoy. Quite half the words incomprehensible. Esmé Beringer alone was clear. No music. Impossibility of seeing whole of stage from front row of dress circle, near middle, without leaning on the balustrade. Scarcely ever possible to distinguish blank verse. Revels in last act agreeable. Very little good acting—except Whitby's Autolycus and Esmé's Paulina. Lillah [1] fairish in last scene,

---

[1] Lillah McCarthy played Hermione.

when she could be statuesque. The text was given almost integrally, and one perceived portions of dullness which might have been cut with advantage. General impression of a simple, good, impossible plot with lofty emotion in it—delectable enough after *Bunty*. But the beauty of detail nearly all lost. From such a performance no one could divine that this is a late play of Shakespeare. Wilkinson's setting unimportant. Many of Rothenstein's wild-cat costumes were merely idiotic. A few, imitative, might pass.

October 6th.

Boer War.

Mrs. S.'s story, gathered in S. Africa, of Kitchener suddenly appearing in ball-room of Mt. Nelson Hotel, where officers sent down by Roberts as worse than useless were dancing with prostitutes, etc.: "Gentlemen, your train leaves in ¾ hour. You will be there. So shall I." Some of them had to turn up in dress clothes. K.'s idea was that they should at any rate do *some* kind of work, so he drove them out of there. . . . She said that of one cargo of 319 nurses that went out, 300 were dead in 2½ months, owing to idiotic hygienic arrangements and general stupidity. I doubt the figures.

October 7th.

Beecham at rehearsal. A player said, "You said you'd beat 4 in that bar, sir, but you're only beating two." Beecham: "You're thinking of another bar." A voice: "Four ale bar." Roars of laughter.

When Henry Wood conducts, he changes three times a day. Perspiration. It drops out of the back of his flannel jacket, having penetrated it. Always takes his waistcoat off. Cedric[1] spoke very highly of his extraordinary energy. Often stays up till 2 or 3 or all night, reading scores. On a Wednesday, in midst of Birmingham Festival rehearsals, he said: "Energy! You shall see next Monday—I shall have some sleep on Sunday night. Wait and see me on Monday."

---

[1] Cedric Sharpe, the well-known 'cellist.

October 8th.

2nd Post-Impressionist Exhibition. Self-satisfied smiles of most people as they entered. One large woman of ruling classes with a large voice and *face-à-mains,* in front of a mediocre picture: "Now no one will ever persuade me that the man who painted that was serious. He was just pulling our legs." Self-satisfied smiles all over the place all the time. One reason of the popularity of these shows is that they give the grossly inartistic leisured class an opportunity to feel artistically superior. A slight undercurrent of appreciation here and there. A woman to whom a young man pointed out a pencil drawing by Matisse said, "That's what I call beautiful." (It was.)

I met Frank Harris. He was prepared on principle to admire everything, though there was a large proportion of absolutely uninteresting work. When I said I had seen much better Picassos than there were there he hardened at once. "I find it all interesting," he said grimly. The photograph room, where photos of Gauguin, Van Gogh, etc. were supposed to be on sale, was in charge of an ignorant young ass who had all the worst qualities, from the languishing drawl to the *non possumus* attitude, of the English salesman.

October 10th.

Dinner. Talking about women's suffrage, some one said that it would come when the majority wanted it, and George Moore said: "The majority never *wants* anything. I don't think the majority even want to breathe." He talked in this pseudo-effective strain nearly all the night—probably nervousness as usual. About half a dozen times he repeated that for *The Winter's Tale* Barker had made the stage "look like a public lavatory." He said he liked farces and preferred *Charley's Aunt* to Barker's *Winter's Tale.* And he thought *Lady Windermere's Fan* was "a charming and fine comedy." Which it is not. Not until somebody said that *The Importance of Being Earnest* is the finest farce of modern times (which it is) did he think at all of Wilde's only good play. He liked Becque, and he thought Ibsen's dialogue unequalled and that it would probably not be beaten by anybody hereafter. But he regarded the theatre generally as a clumsy and infantile art, in which he was quite right. "You've made a very great deal of money," he said to me politely. I told him that that wasn't my fault, and I couldn't help it. Whereupon he emerged from his *gaffe* with a certain grace by saying with a serious air that he wished *he* could do it.

Pawling came and interrupted us with a tale about the Luard murder, explaining that only one ring had been taken from Mrs. Luard, and that that ring contained a stone taken from an Indian idol, that old Luard received many letters accusing him of having killed his wife, and that he then committed suicide; and now that Luard *fils* had telegraphed to England from India that the jewel was mysteriously back on the idol in the temple! ! ! "Strange, isn't it," he said, "that there was an Indian exhibition that year?" I asked if this remarkable story was in the papers. He said enigmatically that it would not be "allowed" to get into the papers for several days yet, and that the Government had ordered an inquiry. He thoroughly believed the tale; he hugged it and loved it. He always has some such tale to tell. And yet if one told him he was ingenuous he would be astounded.

October 12th.

Tate Gallery. Crowds. A class of girls. Many couples, who simply used the place as they would a park in summer. One couple stood right up against Steer's "Music Room" (which I went specially to see) for about a minute, and then retired saying it looked queer. This picture still seems as good as I first thought it was. What's the difference between a lot of Post-Impressionism and Turner's "Interior at Petworth," a picture I never remarked before, but one of the finest pieces of rich colour in the world? Very little difference in method of seeing and treatment. Note the dinginess and dirtiness of Turner's paint-box in a glass case. Inconceivable almost that those pictures came out of it.

Tuesday, October 15th.

Today I began a new novel—the serial for *Harper's*. Since April I have

written naught but 4 articles—two for *Harper's* and two for the *Strand*.
I did practically nothing in London and in Brighton. We shall probably
be here until we go to our new-old house—Comarques. Thorpe-le-Soken [1]
—at the end of next January. In the meantime I have made a lot of
notes which are being typewritten daily by a succession of secretaries. I
began secretaries again in May, and am already at my third.

October 21st.

Romano's. This restaurant is quite different at lunch from dinner.
Groups of theatrical people entering; mutually known, a few actresses,
pretty and vapid. On the whole the most ingenuous crowd of people
to be seen in any restaurant in London. Waiting bad. Tables too close
together as usual.

F.H. told me more fully than ever before the story of Oscar and *Mr.
and Mrs. Daventry*.[2] He said he gave Oscar £50 for the screen scene
and £50 for the whole scenario. He never got the scenario, though he
paid for it. Oscar was to have written the first act. Mrs. Pat [3] insisted on
F.H.'s writing the first act. F.H. refused as it had been allotted to Oscar.
Then Oscar refused. So F.H. did it. F.H. then found out that Oscar
had sold the screen scene and the scenario to Leonard Smithers, and the
latter showed him the whole MS. of scenario signed by Oscar. F.H., after
saying to Smithers that he didn't want the scenario and that in any case
he owed him nothing, promised £50 in any case and £100 if play succeeded well. He said he hadn't a cent at that time. Smithers got the
money from F.H. in tens and twenties. F.H. gradually found out that
Oscar had sold the screen scene and scenario to eleven different people.
When taxed with this by F.H., Oscar didn't deny it. He merely said,
"The fact is, Frank, by writing this play and getting it produced you're
taking away one of my sources of income!" Later Oscar asked for another £150. He badgered F.H. till he got it. He then said: "Frank, you've

---

[1] A Georgian mansion in Essex bought by Bennett. It was named after a Huguenot
family who settled there.
[2] Frank Harris's *Mr. and Mrs. Daventry* was produced at the Royalty Theatre in
October 1900.
[3] Mrs. Patrick Campbell, the actress.

paid me £250 for the screen scene from *The School for Scandal;* and you're a very poor man of business." Thus F. H.'s version.

F.H. said that Oscar was most brilliant as a talker during his last days in Paris. He had listened to him for five or six hours together, saying nothing but "Go on, Oscar. Go on."

F.H. stuck me out that *Lady Windermere's Fan* was good. Indeed, he said it was one of the six best comedies in English!

October 28th.

Politics at Reform Club. Lunch with Methuen, Spender, and Mac-Kinnon Wood.[1] Latter got into Cabinet within 5 years of entering Parliament. Scotch. Broad, heavy; no perceptible Scotch accent. Same agreeable self-satisfaction as other prominent Liberal politicians in the marked inequality between two Front Benches. He said: "What sort of a show do you think they'd have (with Balfour absent) if they introduced Tariff Reform Bill? *We* should have the time of our lives." Also like other Liberal politicians, he expressed the most absolute confidence in Asquith's efficiency. Nobody seemed to think that Tariff Reform Bill ever would be introduced. MacKinnon Wood regularly said nothing when he had nothing to say. The unwillingness of everybody to discuss the details of the Balkan War[2] was astonishing to me.

Wednesday, November 6th.

Day before yesterday, after having written about 6000 words of new novel, I decided to begin it again, in a somewhat different key, but with exactly the same construction. And I did begin it again, and at once felt easier in my mind. I also decided that I would not make a fine MS. of it. The regularity of the lines and handwriting does not seem to accord with style in which this novel is to be written. A freer style than before— a little more capricious and swinging.

I had to interrupt the work last week but one to do an article of reminiscences for the *Metropolitan* and the *Strand,* and again on Sunday to

---

[1] M.P. for St. Rollox Division, and Secretary for Scotland in the Asquith Cabinet.
[2] The First Balkan War had broken out on October 15.

review Allan Monkhouse's new novel, *Dying Fires,* for the *Manchester Guardian.* This last is a good book.

Also I have begun to order a new library of music, through Sharpe, and the first noble batch of stuff came today. More in a few days.

Tuesday, November 19th.

Last week appeared in *La Grande Revue* the opening instalment of Maurice Lanoire's translation of *Sacred and Profane Love.* This is the first of my serious novels to appear in French. The first serious story was *The Matador* in *La Nouvelle Revue Française* in August.

Today I heard from Pinker that he had bought back from Constable's their rights in *The Truth about an Author* for £40. It was issued about ten years ago, and the financial result of the English publication to me is thus, so far, a loss of at least £30.

Walford Davies's Phrases in Conducting a Rehearsal

Must be all dubious.

I want a savage staccato.

Nice and limpid.

Nice and stormy.

Nice and gusty.

Nice and manifold.

Weep, Mr. Parker, weep. (Mr. Parker weeps.) That's jolly.

Press that "A" home.

Don't handicap the crescendo.

It's not a bee's wedding, it's something elemental.

Gentlemen of the first fiddles.

Try it slurred, a sort of dot and carry two.

Not a wind you can cut with a knife, you must come and die.

This echo is so teasing.

Sorry to tease you.

An intimate 'cello solo.

Sixth desk forward, please. (Somebody in the orchestra, "Sign please.")

Sigh and die.

Can we court that better?

Now, side-drum, assert yourself.

Everybody must be shadowy together.

I want it mostly music.

That regular rum-tum which you do so ideally.

Let the pizzicato act as a sort of springboard to the passage.

A freshness inside the piano.

A sudden exquisite hush.

December 31st.

A material year. Largely occupied with intestinal failure and worldly success. By Chetham Strode's direct treatment of massage and vibration I am now almost cured of intestinal caprices, but I shall ever be feeble in that quarter.

All my five later plays have been performed this year. About 1155 pfces altogether. I received (less agents' commissions) about £16,000 during the year, which may be called success by any worldly-minded author. It is apparently about as much as I had earned during all the previous part of my life. And I bought a car and a yacht, and arranged to buy a house.

We came to Paris to finish the year, after I had written one quarter of my serial story for *Harper's*.[1] This gave me the chance to heighten the plane of the rest of the novel. We stay at the Hôtel du Rhin, and pay 50 frs. a day for a fine ground-floor flat. Most exhausting holiday, in spite of the extreme excellence of the food in this hotel.

Gold scarce in Paris, on account of Balkan War and on account of fear of a big war in the spring. Nearly all change given in silver.

I wrote comparatively few words during the year. About as follows: *The Regent,* 80,000. *Those United States,*[2] 35,000. *Harper's* serial, 25,000. Articles, 20,000. Total, 160,000, without counting Yacht Log, Journal, and a fair quantity of notes. Possibly 200,000 in all. But then between April 1st and October 1st I did practically nothing.

---

[1] *The Price of Love,* published in book form in 1914.
[2] Published in America as *Your United States.*

1913

January 6th.

Henry James at Pinker's. Very slow talker. Beautiful French. Expressed stupefaction when I said I knew nothing about the middle class, and said the next time he saw me he would have recovered from the stupefaction, and the discussion might proceed. Said there was too much to say about everything—and that was the thing most felt by one such as he, not entirely without—er—er—er—er—perceptions. When I said I lay awake at nights sometimes thinking of the things I had left out of my novels, he said that all my stuff was crammed, and that when the stuff was crammed nothing more could be put in, and so it was all right. He spoke with feeling about his recent illness. "I have been very ill." Said he was now settled down in Cheyne Walk, and had one or two faithful dependable servants, and so on. An old man, waning, but with the persistent youthfulness that all old bachelors have.

January 28th.

Political debate between G. B. Shaw and Hilaire Belloc as to connection between private property and servitude. At Queen's Hall.

Went with Vaughan. Crammed, at concert prices. Not a seat unsold. Shaw very pale with white hair, and straight. His wife beside him. Effect too conjugal for a man at work. Sidney and Beatrice Webb next to them. Effect also too conjugal here. Maurice Baring supporting Belloc, both very shabby. Maurice with loose brown boots and creased socks.

They spoke thus: Belloc 30 mins., Shaw 30, Belloc 20, Shaw 20, Belloc 10, Shaw 10. Time was kept to three minutes. Belloc's first was pretty good. Shaw's first was a first-class performance, couldn't have been better; the perfection of public speaking (not oratory); not a word wrong. But then afterwards the impression that it was a gladiatorial show or circus performance gained on one, and at the end was a sense of disappointment, as the affair degenerated into a mere rivalry in scoring. Still I have never seen Shaw emotional before, as he was then. Curious trick of audience, as of all audiences, of applauding sentiments with which they were already familiar, and receiving anything relatively new in silence.

January 29th.

First production of *Rosenkavalier* in England.

Covent Garden. Began at 8.20 (20 minutes late) and finished at midnight, with many cuts. Then 30 minutes' wait nearly, for motor in procession of motors. The thing was certainly not understood by stalls and grand circle. What its reception was in the amphitheatre and gallery I was too far to judge. First act received quite coldly. Ovation as usual at end—and an explosive sort of shout when Thomas Beecham came to bow. The beauty and symmetry of the book came out even more clearly than on reading it. An entirely false idea of this opera so far in England. Not sensual, nor perverse, nor depraved. It is simply the story of a young man providing a tragedy for an ageing woman by ceasing to love her, and an ecstatic joy for a young woman by beginning to love her. All the main theme is treated with gravity and beauty. The horse-play, and the character of Ochs, and the 18th-century colour is incidental. It seemed to Rickards, F. Lanchester, Walpole, and me to be a work of the first order.

January 30th.

Courting.[1] Tonight sheets of rain, strong wind. I put on overshoes and

---

[1] This incident made an impression on Arnold Bennett; he frequently mentioned it subsequently and worked it into the courting of Elsie and Jo in *Riceyman Steps.*

mackintosh to go to the corner of the street to the post. Several times lately about 10 P.M. I have noticed a couple that stand under the big tree at the corner next to the pillar-box, shielded by the tree-trunk from the lamplight. They stand motionless, with hands nearly meeting round each other's backs, tightly clasped. They were there tonight. The man was holding an umbrella over them. Can't see what sort of people they are. In the first place I don't like to intrude and in the second place the shade is so dark.

Tuesday, April 1st.

On Tuesday, February 25th, I came to live at Comarques, Thorpe-le-Soken. Marguerite came on the previous day. But the last carpet was only put down (on the stairs) on Saturday last. Even now fenders and fire-irons are not complete. And we find that we could do with many more small pieces of ornamental furniture to finish off the appearance of the rooms. However, the house is done.

On Monday, March 3rd, we went to London (Berkeley Hotel) for the dinner to celebrate Mrs. Atkins's [1] recovery, and for the anniversary of *Milestones,* and for rehearsals of *The Great Adventure.* After being very lively at the Atkins dinner at the Café Royal on Monday, Marguerite fell ill. No sleep. No sleep for two nights. I had Farrar,[2] and then two nurses. One of them, an Irishwoman, lively, who broke most things she touched, came up with us to Comarques on Monday, March 10th, and stayed about a week. The *Milestones* anniversary supper was a great success except for the absence of Marguerite.

Great Adventure produced at Kingsway on Tuesday, March 25th. M. said it was the most successful 1st night of mine she had been at. But she's been to so few. It finished at 11.40 and thus made the critics cross.

Knoblock told me about a fortnight ago that in discussing terms of French contract for *Milestones* with Lucien Guitry he said, to shelter himself behind me as regards certain conditions, *"M. Bennett est très*

---

[1] Muriel Atkins, wife of J. B. Atkins, editor of the *Spectator.*
[2] Bennett's doctor and life-long friend.

autoritaire," whereupon Guitry said, *"Quelle belle chose, l'autorité: mais —pourtant . . . !"*

We went to London on Saturday last, and I saw my first public performance of *The Great Adventure*. House held £125. Barrie with an adopted son on either side was there and he never laughed. C. K. Shorter in a box opposite roared nearly all the time. Wish Wynne a genius. I formed the opinion that there was a goodish run in the play.

Thursday, April 3rd.

Hugh de Sélincourt came in the afternoon, and left yesterday afternoon. His face is getting more and more strikingly bizarre in its line, and his hair much greyer. He said Coleridge's *Ode to Dejection* was one of the supreme things. He was convinced that both Lord and Lady Northcliffe were "dead keen" on his work, and that satellites in the *Mail* office were up against him. Anyhow he had received two autograph letters from Northcliffe, and Lady Northcliffe, in response to a long telegram from its parents, had been to see the baby Bridget. At present De S. gets £100 down and 15 per cent royalty, and he has published seven books. These details will be precious in 50 years.

Unable to resume my novel yet, though I am now on the very edge of doing so.

Friday, April 4th.

Yesterday morning I wrote a complete 1500-word article, *Phenomena at Covent Garden,* for the *New Statesman*—a gift to the Webbs, due to the skilful fascinations of Beatrice Webb. I was tired after it. I read Coleridge's *Ode to Dejection,* and liked it, but didn't think it one of the supreme things in the language. . . . Another of an intermittent series of bad nights, so that I couldn't resume novel this morning as I meant to do.

Receipts of *Great Adventure* at Kingsway mounting up. Which inspirited me somewhat.

Monday, April 7th.

Last week, being in need of an inspirational bucking-up, I dropped *War and Peace* and read Balzac's *Curé de Tours* and *Pierrette*. Latter better than Saintsbury says it is. Balzac was an ignorant and a crude man, often childish in his philosophizing. But if he had been properly educated and influenced he would have been a great social philosopher. His *aperçus* are often astounding. And his vitality is terrific. He made *War and Peace* seem very tame. He is full of inspiring and agreeable ornament. Nothing of the kind in Tolstoy. All a flat recital. Often dull, unless you give yourself to it. But if you do, he is never dull. Some of Tolstoy's long descriptions (such as of the wolf-hunt on Count Ilza's estate) are extremely beautiful. Natasha is the most beautiful character— anyhow up to p. 700 or so, where I now am.

Monday, April 14th.

Advance of age. I now sit down to brush my hair and put my collar and tie on. I also take a decided pleasure in forming habits, and re-forming old ones connected with the furniture from Fontainebleau, whose little peculiarities of locks and knobs, etc., I recognize again with positive satisfaction. The pleasure of doing a thing in the same way at the same time every day, and savouring it, should be noted.

I am now at close on p. 1000 of *War and Peace*. Curious, the episode of Lavrushka the valet, and Napoleon, in which he takes a historical incident, and feigns that as recounted in history it is all wrong, and gives you what he alleges to be the real truth. Even in this early book his theory of war is already fairly complete and obvious.

Wednesday, April 16th.

Fourteen hundred words yesterday. And passed p. 1100 of *War and Peace*. The description of Borodino is excellent. And as for the French entry into Moscow, it is interesting to compare the account by a French sergeant (I forget the name) published last year or so—2 years ago perhaps.

Monday, April 21st.

We went to London on Thursday, I for dinner of Omar Khayyam Club. Interview with Pinker, who lunched with me, and told me privately of his scheme for increasing dramatist's royalties according to length of run. This at Reform Club.

Exhibition of Max Beerbohm's cartoons at Leicester Galleries. Crowd. I was at once recognized—with a certain lack of politeness—by two men. I was ill all day. Probably liver—anyhow pains in back—very mysterious and disconcerting. Bad night. Same illness on Friday complicated by dyspepsia. I went to Leicester Galleries and bought my caricature. Then to Agnew Galleries to see alleged finest collection of water-colours by Turner ever got together. I thought both the Blue and the Red Righi rather overpraised, and I preferred the "Scarborough" picture—marvellous microscope figures of women in foreground. A few loud-voiced English upper classes patronizingly present. This show superb, but still I left it with slight disappointment—a flat feeling, a suspicion of prettiness and academicism. Lunch alone at Reform. Ill.

Thursday, April 24th.

Finished *War and Peace* on Tuesday. The last part of the Epilogue is full of good ideas the Johnny can't work out, and of course, in the phrase of critics, would have been better left out. So it would; only Tolstoy couldn't leave it out. It was what he wrote the book for. The first part of the Epilogue is as good as anything. All that domesticity is superbly rendered, with a natural and yet ruthless veracity. The battle of Borodino is fine. The Rostov family is fine. And many of the "set" descriptions of Russian life—such as the wolf-hunting on the Rostov estate. Terrific book. I wanted to write one of the same dimensions. And the final thrills of it *did* inspire me to a good basic scheme for the foundations of the third *Clayhanger*.[1]

I am just finishing instalment three of the *Harper's* serial (out of 8). It is sound, but not brilliant. Returns of *Great Adventure* at Kingsway going up. Over £150 a night now. Could scarcely be better.

---

[1] *These Twain*, not published until 1916.

The *Velsa* [1] arrived at Brightlingsea from Ostend yesterday. We drove to Harwich yesterday afternoon and saw the Gothenburg steamer. I wanted to go on it but wasn't sure what country Gothenburg is in.

Began to read correspondence of Flaubert yesterday. Letters at age of 9 and 10 are remarkable.

Finished Sitwell's *Cannibals of Finance* yesterday. A naïve and rather impressive book, confirming one's view of the autocracy that rules U.S.A.

Finished also the Webbs' book on highways. [2] This is an absolutely efficient work.

Friday, April 25th.

Yesterday we went over to see the *Velsa* in Brightlingsea creek. Lovely weather, but bar. falling quickly and wind S.E. She looked superb in every way, except inside the engine case. Entirely Dutch crew, of whom two cannot speak any English at all. I liked the aspect of the cook, but it was impossible to communicate any ideas to him direct. We got home at six o'clock; we forgot the dog on the land, absolutely; but he was collected by the harbour-master and saved for us.

Dreadful worry over third instalment of *Harper's* serial. It is an infernal nuisance writing scenes which you know all through are only sound instead of being fine. Health imperfect.

I now notice one or two devoted heads among critics who lose no opportunity of going for me both tooth and nail. And it is astonishing how this small minority of criticism, convinced though one may be that it is obviously wrong-headed, and perhaps malicious or prejudiced, has a capacity for annoying the successful person surfeited with money and laudation.

Tuesday, April 29th.

Ill for last 3 days. Perfectly laid aside by a sort of chill effect yesterday. Began to read Flaubert's correspondence all through the other day.

---

[1] A Dutch yacht, lying anchored in the Thames off Richmond when Bennett bought her. She had an auxiliary engine and could navigate by sea or canal.
[2] *Bibliography of Road-Making and Roads in the United Kingdom.*

Much of it is as depressing as the rest is inspiring. The letters to Madame X are the most terrible, and must have been terrible to receive. This sentence (Vol. I, p. 107) shows the *maladif* quality of Flaubert very well: *"Un amour normal, régulier, nourri et solide, me sortirait trop hors de moi, me troublerait, je rentrerais dans la vie active, dans la vérité physique, dans le sens commun enfin, et c'est ce que m'a été nuisible toutes les fois que j'ai voulu le tenter."* Also his declared habit of cutting himself off absolutely from the world in order to have peace! What a mad scheme for a novelist! It is this kind of thing in Flaubert that stopped him from being in the first rank.

Friday, May 2nd. On board Velsa *in Harwich Harbour.*

The W.'s with infant and nurse came on Tuesday. Almost at once, in my study, W. began to tell me a dramatic story of a shindy with his wife over her Uncle Joe. The latter wrote to W. as to his mistress; W. left the letter lying about, and Dorothy picked it up, and learnt that Uncle Joe had a mistress. Horror! Hysteria even! She would not listen to anything. She would not admit his right to have a mistress, nor that it was no business of hers. She wrote a long letter to Uncle Joe belabouring him, and ultimately W. allowed this letter to be posted. And U.J. committed the folly of replying to it in an apologetic tone. It seems she has still not got over it. She told W. she would have preferred to be deceived. She has naturally much changed since becoming a mother. She is the young mother and nothing else, and her outlook on everything is deeply influenced by the relation of everything to the infant. She has a somewhat worn expression, anxious, and even slightly hysterical. Her outlines have all changed; and her face is thinner. She is yet full of the shock of being a mother.

Saturday, May 31st.

J.C. came yesterday to make an oil sketch of me. When I went into the drawing-room he said, "I knew you couldn't like me to make all that journey alone." He had brought his chief model with him. Damned cheek, I thought it. But a beautiful girl—especially lips and main lines of body. In C. all that I didn't like physically was his sloping shoulders. But then Swinburne had them. But a very little of this kind of young man goes a long way with me. His ignorance of everything except just his work is too trying. Can't dress; can't dress his hair, can't even look dignified except in the face, which he keeps clean-shaven. Has read practically nothing, and has seen very little. Comes into a 1700 A.D. house and asks you whether you have built it! And so on. Fastened on to a tiny reproduction of a nude by Cranach, and said it was the most beautiful thing "in your house." He wants taking seriously in hand by an expert for about 5 years and merely educating. He seemed a strong man, and did a good sketch of me.

Wednesday, June 4th.

Still unable to do my work. *Une espèce de rechute.* Very bad headache on Monday. But I have amused myself with D'Aurevilly's *Une Vieille Maîtresse*—admirable romanticism. The Granville-Barkers came for the week-end, and made one or two efforts to get my new play. We went to Flatford Mill on Sunday afternoon. Very luscious and English. The finest of the sort.

Saturday, June 21st.

Vedrenne and Eadie came up to lunch yesterday, in order to angle for my next play. However, they were agreeable, and did not angle too much.

Today I began the last of the nine articles for the *Metropolitan Magazine* and wrote 1800 words before one o'clock. Quite unable to work yesterday, through being wakened up again, in the middle of the night (2.38) by a banging door.

Knoblock comes today for the week-end.

Friday, June 27th.

Went to London on Tuesday for Cedric's concert and returned yesterday. At the concert I seemed to see every one I had ever known up to the age of thirty. Vast air of a family party about it. Simultaneous carrying of two similar bouquets by two attendants up the two aisles to Evelyn Jennings after her first group of songs. Probably most of the friends were nervous.

In the afternoon, just after our arrival, we saw the King and President Poincaré pass,[1] two lonely men, one red and gold, the other black and white and bald, along the empty road, with soldiers and policemen dividing them from a thin crowd.

Wednesday morning, David Rice accosted me in Bond St. Hadn't seen him for at least 15 years. He cursed the British tradesmen. So did I. On Thursday morning I went into a swagger West End hosier's to buy a necktie. I said "Good morning" on entering. *Vendeur* was a man of 50 at least. Through sheer social clumsiness and heaviness he made no response, didn't even smile. It was not that he meant to be impolite. He thawed before I had bought two neckties, and gloomily saluted me as I went out. Many of the shops in this district are being cleaned and garnished at 10 A.M.

At lunch on Thursday, 3 Amazons in silk toppers in grill-room, with two men. Very quiet and nice. Contrast to bevies of American girls on previous day, couldn't even use knives and forks properly. But well dressed—good hats.

Saturday, June 28th.

I went to launch of *Velsa* at 5, but she was already gone. So I put off in a rowboat and waited for her to return. The new engine was pulling her along at a fine speed. Good sensation in boarding her, in Brightlingsea reach. Guest and two other fitters on board. The cockpit in a fearful mess.

E. V. Lucas came, and after dinner went to bed with a cold.

Wednesday, July 2nd.

Lucas left on Monday night. We drove him to Colchester. Progress made with three of his plays.

I read through first half of *Harper's* novel yesterday and found it *très*

---

[1] The newly-elected President of the French Republic, paying an official visit to England.

convenable. Some things in it jolly good. But now I want to write an entirely different sort of novel—as regards construction and manner and material.

Friday, July 25th.

Returned from yacht Monday afternoon. I wrote over 5000 words of *Harper's* novel in 3 days up to last night. Health about 95 out of a possible 100. Yacht waiting at Harwich for a favourable wind to go to Denmark. N.E. again this morning. I went out for a walk, and at Landermere I asked a bargeman on a barge in what direction wind was. He said due E. and stuck to it, though he must have known it was N.E. "Due east according to our flag. It may have northered out a bit since this morning, but not much." He gazed idly up at our flag. "I wish it wasn't, I want to get out o' here. How long do I think it'll last? I think it'll last for 2 or 3 days. I hope it won't. If it keeps on I shall get my rigging down and poke her out—over these pleasant flats." A nice humorous card. But still I don't understand why he should stick to his error about wind.

Wednesday, July 30th.

H. G. Wells and wife and Mrs. Byng (future neighbour) [1] came yesterday for lunch and tea. I beat H.G. at tennis; he played in bare feet.

Friday, August 29th.

Yesterday I returned from my cruise in the Baltic round about Denmark. I kept the log, but made no general observations in it. What strikes me now most as regards Denmark is the charm, beauty, and independence of the women. They go about freely, sit in cafés together, smoke without self-consciousness. They seem decidedly more independent than Englishwomen. The men have charm of manner, especially of voice and tone. The race is evidently receptive, and it must be beneficially influenced by the attractiveness of its women. On the other hand, Den-

---

[1] Wife of General Julian Byng, created first Baron of Vimy in 1919. Mrs. Byng, *née* Marie Evelyn Mareton, was at this time engaged on her first novel, *Barriers.*

mark struck both Rickards and me as being an unimportant and dull little country. Its villages were simply naught. They had nothing, except a material sufficiency—no beauty, no evidence of ancient traditions. The landscape also was practically everywhere negligible.

Admirable voyage home, though we *did* have to sleep in the saloon. Fine food on the *J. C. La Cour* (2000 tons). Smooth sea. Sunshine. Heat. Favourable wind. But about 20 miles or so of fog after we left Eshey on Wednesday evening. The boat *empesté* by a gang of English girls— probably clerks in some large establishment—doubtless quite decent in their own line. But terribly *gauche,* ungraceful, and unfeminine and *mal ficelées* by comparison with the Danish.

Today I began the reading of Lavisse and Rambaud's *Histoire Générale*,[1] an enterprise less enormous than the writing of it, but still enormous.

Sunday, August 31st.

Read through the third quarter of the *Harper's* serial this morning. It seemed goodish. But there is no doubt in my mind now that I want to change to another sort of novel—much more autobiographical than I have yet written. The first and third part of *The Glimpse* contained a lot of essentially autobiographical stuff, and *Clayhanger* something of me as a boy. But I want to write more immediately autobiographical work. The third *Clayhanger* must be quite different from *Clayhanger* and *Hilda*. I think I am now beginning to be anxious to write the 3rd *Clayhanger,* but there is a play, also two stories, to come in front of it.

A Reverend Falconer called yesterday and tapped Marguerite for a sub-scription for his orphanage. He showed a list of subscriptions from people in neighbourhood, and there was no subscription on it of less than £1. So Marguerite gave £1. Naturally. The psychology of charity be-comes clear. It is fairly certain that the Rev. F. does get and accept sub-scriptions of less than £1, but he keeps them out of his show-list. That there might be disadvantages in an orphanage directed by a Church of

---

[1] *L'Histoire Générale du IVe Siècle jusqu'à nos Jours* by Ernest Lavisse and Alfred Rambaud.

England parson had not occurred to M. She saw that people in the neighbourhood had given, and none less than £1; so she gave £1. This afternoon a band passes along the road, with several collectors. Quick! Sixpence for the band! (Gabrielle says, *"On demande des sous."* That is enough.) What the band is, what the subscription is for, nobody has the least idea.

Friday, September 5th.

Richard Pryce came on Wednesday and before night he had read to us his play founded on *Helen with the High Hand,*[1] which was all right in essentials. He worked on a few minor alterations yesterday.

By yesterday evening I had written 3400 words of *Harper's* novel in three days. By means of sharp exercise and perspiration I about cured my liver in 6 days, despite a N.E. wind.

Sunday, September 7th.

The extreme inventiveness of some dreams is remarkable. I dreamt last night that I had to rush every few minutes to see Russian trains come into a tube station, as I was expecting a friend from Russia, I think. Between two trains, I strolled off the platform on to a bridge over a canal, on which were ships whose immense and very ornate bowsprits came up as high as the bridge. Turning another way, I saw a very muddy road, and in this road a little acrobat (one of a troupe) was performing. He was 8 or 9 years of age. The greasy road was a very difficult take-off, but he had to do a double somersault with such a take-off, and he did it, two complete revolutions, with only a slight slip on his back on alighting. He then lay on his back in the mud to do another trick, and I then noticed that he was smoking a thick strong cigar, puffing away at it all the time. He was forced by his brutal persecutors to smoke this awful cigar all the time, and to keep puffing at it continuously. A tremendous refinement of cruelty. Even as I write my gorge rises at the memory of the cigar in his small mouth. He clenched his small hands to prepare for the spring from his back. He did this several times, and then I woke

---

[1] This appeared in 1914 under the same title.

up. I can't imagine what led to this dream, unless it was my physical exercises daily and a fairly strong cigar at night.

Tuesday, September 9th.

Yesterday was a proper sort of day for my trade. 400 words before breakfast. After breakfast, newspapers, cigar. Then 800 words. Then dictation of letters. A few Muller exercises. A quarter of an hour in garden. A section of Lavisse's *Histoire Générale*. Lunch. Flaubert's correspondence. Sleep. Early tea. In car with Marriott[1] to Landermere to make a watercolour—4 to 6 o'clock. Car came back to fetch our things. We walked home. Over 2 miles, mostly uphill and over rough ground, in 29 minutes. Profuse perspiration. Change. Bath. Dinner. Champagne. Cigar. Coffee. Bed at 10 P.M. and a very fairish night. Absolutely no time at all cut to waste between 7 A.M. and 7.30 P.M., when we dine. I can always do more work when I have many other things on hand, and when I am following a programme that is rather a tight fit for the day.

Wednesday, September 10th.

W. W. Ellsworth, president of the Century Company, came to lunch yesterday. Man of 60. Deaf. Carrying an apparatus like a camera with him for hearing. Liked A. C. Benson, and so on. It was understood he took 6 yachting articles for £1000, and engaged Rickards to illustrate. The most interesting thing he said was after he had looked round the grounds, and I questioned him as to his own home. "Yes. I have a very beautiful country home. I can only go down to it for week-ends, but the rest of the time I spend in my N.Y. flat and I'm quite comfortable. Every member of my family has a particular and tender regard for our home. We've had it for forty years. There's one place in the gardens enclosed by four trees, and plenty of other trees round about. We've had three weddings there and four funerals." I rather liked this. It would be impossible in England. I also liked his attitude to Minetta[2] when I

---

[1] Frederick Marriott, the artist, was an early friend of Bennett's.
[2] Child of the Marriotts, who were guests in the house at this time.

held her to him to say good-bye before she went to bed after lunch. First he kissed her hand, and when she was told to kiss him he said, evidently moved, "May I really?" He must be somewhat sentimental in business where money is not concerned. Very pleased with his new editor, Yard. He told one or two mildly bawdy stories, including one of a studious farmer who announced to a lady (Ellsworth's sister-in-law) that he always gave names to his animals from books, and that the bull she had just bought from him was called Sir Galahad. He said that Jack London had gone into the ranch business, had a payroll of 2000 dollars a month, and had bought a stallion for 2500 dollars and expected the Century Company to pay increased advances to pay for all this, and sent them abusive telegrams when they didn't.

Sunday, September 28th.

To Marguerite's golf club yesterday. We went there through a street of villas, with tennis-lawns rather close fitted, etc. Excellent imitation of suburbs of London, and cleaner. Golf club. House the most miserable architecture, with no proper place for autos to drive up to, though plenty of autos, and so far as I knew, no accommodation for chauffeurs. Whole place too small. Men's rooms (lords at ease therein). Common tea room (devilish cold in winter) and women's quarters. Course beautiful. Shut off from sea by a natural sea wall. Some gestures of men in playing a ball superb in ease, laxity, and strength. Women following a couple of men about who were playing. Doubtless wives or lovers, etc. Immense sense of space. Also great sense of a vast organization. But no artistic sense. The architecture, I repeat, miserable, piffling, mean. And a rotten little 3-cornered flag flying "F.G.C." instead of a superb standard floating in the breeze. The women in white or gay colours were not unattractive in the mass, and some were beautiful, and quite a few pretty. Certain matrons also very agreeable.

Thursday, October 2nd.

Finished *Harper's* serial, *The Price of Love*, at 12.15 on Monday last, in a state of some exhaustion.

Thursday, October 16th. Antwerp.

Last night we drove to Harwich, took G.E.R. steamer *Vienna,* and arrived at Antwerp at 8.15 A.M. today. Grand Hotel. Room and bathroom, both large. 20 frs. Old-fashioned and ugly; but seemingly good. Dreadful ride in hotel omnibus over cobbled roads from quay to hotel. We drove out at 10 A.M. in closed cab, round boulevards to Musée Plantin, where I searched for a particular room whose details I thought I had remembered for 16 years, and couldn't find—indeed was about convinced that such a room had never existed.

Friday, October 17th.

Last night in lounge of Grand Hotel Antwerp. Old-fashioned decoration. Old-fashioned lettering over door (Fumoir, Restaurant), once considered, no doubt, the latest fashionable form of lettering. Plush ornamented doors with glass doorknobs. There is something poignantly pathetic about such decoration, still dignified, but pitied, where once it inspired perhaps almost awe.

This morning absolutely perfect October weather. Musée Royal. Very fine old masters. Modern side rotten. Market place. Endless time on chimes from 11.30 to 11.41. We went into cathedral—and the carillon started again for 11.45. Big pictures in cathedral veiled in green. *Loucheness* of ecclesiastical attendants. Market afoot in market place.

After lunch we visited port. Finest thing in Antwerp. We were first struck by little *brasseries* along good main street, each with a little *grue,* aproned and *nu-tête,* sitting outside sewing, to attract; they must be extraordinarily attractive to sailors. Scores of these places. Glimpses of streets *encore plus louches.* Immense impression of *travail.* 30 miles of quays. New basins still being constructed. Bridge from one road to another opened for passage of steamer. Much traffic held up on both sides. By the time it is closed again, hundreds of workmen collected, and dozens of heavy wagons. Some men chewing monstrous lumps of bread. Red Star liner *Lapland* had arrived from U.S.A. Long processions of returned emigrants therefrom; some stupid, some full of character. One procession solely men (with a long *camion* in middle full of their handbags), another both of men and women; all had little round discs on breast.

I saw one steamer move out (scraping her side all the way) and a larger one come into a basin with 4 tugs. Immense area of port. Superb view of Antwerp with spires from one spot, over blue water. Magnificent sunset; all masts and derricks gradually became black and silhouetted. Drove back to town, passing through 2 streets full of *cafés concerts*. Same effect of silhouette against superb red and orange. Port full of grain and wood.

Sunday, October 19th. Brussels.

We came to Brussels yesterday. Journey 28 min. M. indisposed. At Gare du Nord scarcity of porters, and very bad and unwilling work because tips are put into a common fund. It takes one man's time to watch what the men receive. A non-porter said to me, *"Les porteurs sont trop fainéants pour venir ici"* (i.e., to the far end of the platform when the train stopped).

I walked out alone, and was astonished at the liveliness and richness of this small town. I dined alone at Restaurant du Helder, and it made much the same impression on me as 17 years ago. Good, but not good enough. Too dear. Still, a discreet place, with good service. A fat middle-aged man came in with a *grue*. *Grue* very vulgar. She turned her head away from the *grosse* brute most of the time, and sneered a lot. The efforts of the man to be gay and natural were rather good. She was just another of those who are content to take money which they are too careless to earn.

While here we had news of the production of *The Great Adventure* in New York on Thursday last—ten days late. It does not seem to have been a very *éclatant* success.

Wednesday, October 22nd.

Drove about. Admirable lunch at Restaurant Étoile. Then Musée Royal, old masters. Satisfactory. Then Palais de Glace. Tearoom *gratuit*. Many *gentilles petites femmes*. Ideas for *Don Juan*. Dined in hotel at night. Not good. Then Donnay's *Les Éclaireuses* at Théâtre du Parc. First two acts *passablement amusants*. Third feeble. Fourth rotten. False throughout, with too many idiotic *jeux de mots,* but impression of first two acts agreeable though mediocre. This suffragette play is supposed to be very advanced. *C'est déjà vieux jeu.* Oldish couple behind us who told a friend that they had not brought their daughter, who was just about to be married, as they feared it might unsettle her. Brussels public very stolid and uncomprehending.

Thursday, October 23rd. Paris.

Arrived in Paris at 5.15 yesterday afternoon. Some delay at *douane.* Cepa here (Hôtel du Rhin) at the same time as us; *et puis Ida.* We dined quickly and unpacked and dressed with marvellous haste, and were at the Théâtre du Vieux Colombier at 8.30 for dress rehearsal of *Une Femme Tuée par la Douceur,* and *L'Amour Médecin,*[1] with Copeau in charge. Crowded with first-night public, and literary public. Many women trying to look young and only succeeding at a distance, with worn-out skins. Many very cheaply dressed. In fact nearly all the literary public had the air of beng *dans la dèche.* Extraordinary muddle at *vestiaire.* A slight feeling of preciosity. But play well and sincerely done. A *naïf* thing, getting fairly strong towards the end.

Sunday, October 26th.

Thursday afternoon Calvo took us to Salle des Fêtes du *Journal* to see a Russian *danseuse nue—séance particulière.* She was not *nue,* but with a "diaphony" that was better. About 20 people, including the most serious, such as Kostilev, the Russian. The offices of *Journal* vast. *Salle* overdecorated and without originality; still, in a recognizable style. Nothing in the slightest degree *troublant* in the dancing. Middle-aged *dame* at piano. A well-known little sculptor explained. . . .

Friday, October 31st.

Yesterday afternoon I went with Cepa to Hessel, 26 Rue La Boétie,

---

[1] *A Woman Killed with Kindness* by Thomas Heywood; *L'Amour Médecin* by Molière.

and bought a small Vuillard for £100. Tea alone. Then with M. to view
Rue du Faubourg St.-Honoré. Just dark. Nothing like this in London
for luxurious shoppiness. Bought books.

Monday, November 3rd.

Lunch at Martin's.[1] Tea at Cornillier's, where Janvier, Roy Devereux,
Esther Swanson. Dined at Henri's, and then with Mme. Edwards to
Le Secret by Bernstein—Bouffes Parisiens. The rottenest piece by Bernstein, and almost by any one, that I ever saw. I had to go twice to see
Simone[2] in her *loge*. (Electric light in quantities, both at top and at
bottom of her *psyché,* burning all the time.) Dark eyelids. She said she
liked *Le Secret* very much and thought *Le Vieil Homme* idiotic. However, I gave my view. I said, *"Vous êtes magnifique, mais sans vous la
pièce ne serait rien du tout."* She swallowed it with ease. She spoke English very well indeed, but with an accent.

Wednesday, November 5th.

Yesterday afternoon, Ravel, Mme. Andrée, the Godebskis, and Calvo
came for tea. The Bions dined with us at Ciro's, and then to the revue
at La Cigale—which might have been worse. Indigestion yesterday and
today. The strangest phenomenon in Paris is the interest excited among
sane people such as the Godebskis by the appointment of a new director
of the Opéra.

Thursday, November 20th. England.

I meant to begin writing of my play *Don Juan* on Saturday the 15th,
but was somewhat indisposed. I began it on Monday 17th. . . . Fred and
Stanley Alcock[3] came last Thursday (13). Stan. left on Saturday and
Fred on Sunday, in his car. Marguerite and I went to London yesterday
for the first Sharpe concert. Lunched at Carlton. Lack of *chic* among

---

[1] Emile Martin was an intimate friend who had introduced Bennett to the life in Paris
and had helped him to settle there when he first came.
[2] Mme. Simone had appeared in *Le Secret* at the New Theatre, London, in June of
this year.
[3] Early friends of Bennett.

women there. As Nisia Edwards said of Savoy—*vieux chameaux*. I then went to Reform and conversed with Methuen. Last week (motor-show week) was the finest *The Great Adventure* has had. On Saturday we all went over to a special Red Cross matinée of *The G. A.* at Colchester, with Shiel Davy and Athene Seyler in principal parts. It was an admirable performance. I went and saw Athene and Shiel in their retreats.

Friday, November 21st.

Walking last night for exercise along the Station Road (6.30 P.M.), I saw the light of Clacton (not the lights—the light) and of Frinton, over the brows; a reflection in the sky. . . . Idea of a desolate coast (relatively) with the human settlements rather precariously here and there upon it. Darkness everywhere and just those lights on the clouds from below. Sense of the adventure of living on the earth at all; and of the essential similarity of all human existences. Idiocy of loathing or scorning a different kind of existence from your own; e.g. my attitude towards the primness of Frinton and its golf club.

I am putting rather more work into draft of *Don Juan* than usually in my drafts of plays. The realistic idea has gone nearly altogether in this play. In its ignoring of realistic detail in order to get an effect required, it is rather impressionistic. This is the first time I have realized the possibility of a similarity between literature and art in impressionism. I expect that in looking for a parallelism to art in literature I had been looking for the wrong thing, while the right thing was under my nose all the time.

Monday, November 24th.

I finished the draft of the first act of *Don Juan* this morning. It is not a good draft, but it is perhaps a better one than any draft of any previous play of mine.

As I was reading history this afternoon, I thought: "I am 46. On the decline. Why fill my head with knowledge?" An absurd reflection, but it passed several times through my mind.

Friday, November 28th.

Deranged slightly all week with a chill on the colon. B. came yesterday for the day to discuss wills and leases. He told me with perfect seriousness a story of a commercial enterprise in which he was interested —a search for the Ark of the Covenant, Urim and Thummim, plate of the Temple, etc.—based on a cipher discovered by a Finnish scholar in an early copy of the book of Ezekiel at St. Petersburg. Over £3000 already spent on the excavations, stopped by Turkish authorities, who have now given permission again; but the affair is in suspense at present, as the principal contributor of funds (who has already given £20,000 alone) is in a lunatic asylum. The singular irony of this did not seem to strike B.

Thursday, December 4th.

On Tuesday Arthur L. Humphreys[1] came up to lunch, and to inspect my books with a view to a catalogue. He told us how he had walked from London to Land's End, and from London to Edinburgh, at 37 miles a day. We took him to Landermere, Kirby-le-Soken, Walton, and Frinton. He seemed determined to find out about the history of Co-marques. Often in France, but incapable of speaking French with any fluency. He said that he thought novels of today immensely superior to those of 20 years ago. He said that at Xmas, numbers of people made up their minds to buy "*Whitaker*[2] and one other book." The other book might be a volume of devotional verse. He said that novels more and more dominated the book market.

Monday, December 8th.

J. C. Squire came on Saturday. Long hair; Jaegerishly dressed. But sound, competent, honest in argument. He was highly in favour of the Webbs etc. and said the *New Statesman* was going on excellently, as to finance. He could not appreciate Tailhade's verse. Left this morning, very Jaegerish.

---

[1] Partner in the firm of Hatchards, booksellers.
[2] *Whitaker's Almanack.*

Monday, December 15th.

Excursion to Ipswich, Saturday. Shops closed at 1 P.M.—at least all good ones except antiquaries. We went into three and bought a number of things. Ravel [1] also. Walpole came in the afternoon—6.40.

I began the actual writing of *Don Juan* on Friday afternoon, and it seemed to go fairly well. I read *Bubu de Montparnasse* lately. A little book; good. *Dans les Rues,* of Rosny aîné, which describes the making of an *apache.* This is a less absorbing book, by a greater man than C. L. Philippe. Some of the scenes in it are magnificent. It did not enchant me as did some of *Bubu,* but it held me.

Saturday, December 27th.

Rickards came on Christmas Eve. Doran came on Sunday morning. Hysterical cook of 40-odd left on Tuesday, and we did without. Doran left this morning, to spend week-end with Ernest Hodder Williams. He said that while he was there he didn't have to go to chapel, and Ernest didn't go either. Wednesday, Thursday, and yesterday I wrote 4500 words of a short story, in spite of guests and eating.

Sunday, December 28th.

Sketch, "Buttercup-Night," by Galsworthy, in yesterday's *Nation.* He calls buttercups "those little bright pieces of flower china out of the Great Pottery." Another phrase: "Man playing his little, not unworthy, part in the great game of Perfection." I object to this kind of thing. Much of the sketch is very good.

I am now re-reading *The Way of All Flesh.* It stands it. There is very little wrong with this book, even technically. But the trick of reading a piece of the narrative to the hero himself and then writing down what the hero's comment on it was is a mistake—especially when it is repeated.

Wednesday, December 31st.

I finished *The Way of All Flesh* yesterday. All this book is good. I even suspect it may be better than I think it is.

---

[1] Maurice Ravel, the composer, was then Bennett's guest at Comarques.

I finished the first act of *Don Juan* yesterday. It seems *assez bien*.

According to Miss Nerney's[1] calculations there have been over 2700 performances of my plays during this year. I have published *The Regent, Paris Nights, The Plain Man and His Wife* and *The Great Adventure*. I have written most of *The Price of Love,* the whole of *The Story Teller's Craft,*[2] sundry articles, 2 short stories, and one act of my new play. I did no work for over a month when we moved into Comarques; I took the whole of August for a holiday in the Baltic, and 3 weeks in Belgium, and Paris in October and November.

Added later.

Net earnings received during 1913: Books, £6924 18s. 1d. Plays, £8524 19s. 0d. Total, 15,449 17s. 1d. The gross sum (before paying agents' fees) was £17,166 10s. 1d. In addition, interest on investments, £405 11s. 3d. All this handsomely beats last year's record.

---

[1] Miss W. Nerney, Arnold Bennett's secretary.
[2] Published in America in 1914 as *The Author's Craft.*

1914

Thursday, January 1st.

I read J. H. Rosny's *Les Xipéhuz*. It is like early Wells. Good, but entirely arid, as it has no individual human interest, or scarcely any. Also it is short. Also there is no explanation, or theory given of the "Farms." Thus a question is raised without being settled, and legitimate curiosity unsatisfied. Nevertheless it has interest. Evidently the book has reached some permanency of fame despite its extreme shortness, as mine is the *édition définitive*.

I met Dr. Hare on road this morning and again as I was coming into the house. In the meantime he had been to a labourer's cottage. Mother of 15 kids, youngest 4 months old and fed on Nestlé's. Father earned 15*s*. a week. Two boys helped to support. Eldest boy not son of husband; a bastard of somebody else, accepted as a matter of course. No trouble. Said woman: "I'm washing. It's a lot o' work—washing for ten people." Cottage absolutely clean and tidy. One son down with influenza. Several children still living at home.

Hard snow on ground, bluish tinted (I suppose from sky) with blue shadows. Birds seem to be a little less shy just now.

January 3rd.

The Spences came over to dinner on Thursday night from the Grand Hotel, Frinton. Spence said that Mrs. Maybrick was understood to be guilty,[1] and that she had confessed to wardresses immediately after sentence. It was said that she had arsenic in pocket of her *peignoir* and administered it by means of a handkerchief pressed to Maybrick's mouth when he complained of dry lips or something of that kind. But Spence did not explain how Charles Russell remained always persuaded of her innocence.

Monday, January 5th.

Finished *Marie Donadieu* in the night. On the whole it is not as good as *Bubu,* but it contains fine scenes. But they nearly all talk too much. And they nearly all talk as Jean alone (and the author himself) would really have talked. It is wonderful talking *per se.* Some of the love scenes are perhaps more vivid than any great novelist could have written (e.g. Dostoievsky and Turgenev), and yet the book is not great. It has no large architectonic quality. Some of it is dull, also; but this may happen in almost any book.

I walked all yesterday morning, and worked all the afternoon. I did over 3 mortal hours on *Don Juan* this morning. It exhausted me. I had meant to go on with it this afternoon, but by the time I had done a lot of damnable correspondence about other people's affairs, I had nothing left in me except the desire for exercise.

Referring to Vedrenne's habitual phrase in negotiational bluffings—"I'll throw all my cards on the table"—I was told that Marie Tempest and Graham Browne, at Pall Mall Restaurant, crowded, saw Vedrenne come in and look round, and Marie said, "What's Vedrenne looking for?" whereupon Browne replied, "He must be looking for a table to throw his cards on."

I finished big love scene in Act II this morning.

No work yesterday as I had almost no sleep the night before (and very little the night before that).

Monday, January 12th.

This morning I finished the second act of *Don Juan.*

---

[1] Of poisoning her husband. She was tried in 1889.

More information as to the L.C. holiday in August. A specimen of the co-operative holiday of the middle class, where under the strain of idleness and new conditions most of the manners (mediocre at best) of the middle class go all to pieces at one moment or another. The secret provincialism of the whole crowd (except the younger generation) came out clearly. A set that frequents only itself.

Sunday, January 18th.

Barber's yesterday at Frinton. Read[1] said he had been there and that it was smart and clean, but lacked things. Behind tobacco shop. Long white curtains over window (clean) to hide back yard. Very small room. Very small fire. 3 marble basins with fitments.

No antiseptic arrangements so far as I could see. Room cold. Sturdy small boy who opened door for me, knickers, apron (not clean). "Shall you operate on me?" "No, sir," with a grin. Man doing shaving. No greetings from barber. Dirty apron and coat hanging up on wall. Array of mugs with sponges. I stood with back to fire and looked at *Daily Mirror*. Had not to wait long. Place looked clean but wasn't. Thick dust on gas shades and many cobwebs. Chair too high, a modern chair, which required footstool. I commented on height. Barber said: "It's not high enough for me as it is. I always have to stoop." I suggested footstool. He said, "They do have them in some places." I asked if business was good. "No, very short season." A nice mild man, tall, badly shaven; baggy, worn knees. But decent. No energy. Had to go out in middle to talk to a customer about mending a pipe—"Excuse me, sir." Parted my hair on wrong side and badly. Shoved his sleeve in my eye. Didn't show me the back of my head. Doubtful towels. India-rubber sponge. Price 10*d*. Still, a decent chap. (If I write an article out of this, I might describe Paris barbers, and insist on inferiority of English barbers, with general reference to slackness and inefficiency.)

I finished 3rd act *Don Juan* on Friday night, after fairly huge labours. Read nearly all of Tristan Bernard's *Amants et Voleurs*. The first tale (long), "Sabre et Casque," is admirable. The rest are merely brief *fait-divers*.

---

[1] Bennett's chauffeur.

Also in John Mitchel's *Jail Journal*.[1] This is a good browsing book. Much of the self-analysis or self-description is tedious. It could be cut down and made manageable.

Lastly, Conrad's *Chance* came yesterday. Read 150 pp. This is a discouraging book for a writer, because he damn well knows he can't write as well as this. The episode of the arrival of the news of De Barral's bankruptcy at his house in Hove where his daughter and her superb friend of a governess are living is simply sublime. I know nothing better than this, and precious little as good. I happened to read it in the night.

Saturday, January 24th.

Touching the alleged fact that a name scarely counts with a theatrical manager in choosing a play, Nancy Price offered Pryce's version of *Helen with the High Hand* to Frohman, who offered to do it only on the condition that I would sign it. As I had always declined to do this, of course the thing was off.

I finished Conrad's *Chance* in the middle of the night. It is very fine. The best chapters are "The Governess" and the last one. The tea party chapter and "On the Pavement" chapter are too long. The indirect narrative is successfully managed on the whole, even to fourth-hand narrative, but here and there recounted dialogue and gesture is so minute as to be unconvincing.

In P. G. Hamerton's *Round My House* (p. 160) he says that rise in prices during "last ten years" in France had been so great as to induce some French people to dispense with servants. No date on this book. No clue to its date. But I should put it in the seventies. I suppose this rise-of-price business recurs at intervals, and always makes the same upset and then adjusts itself.

All this week I have taken a long walk in the mornings and worked on *Don Juan* in the afternoons, with some success. I am now on the last scene of the last act.

---

[1] John Mitchel, the Irish Nationalist, was sentenced to 14 years' penal servitude for inciting to rebellion. After some years he escaped from the penal settlement in Tasmania and settled in the United States. His *Jail Journal, or Five Years in British Prisons* appeared in 1854. It has been re-issued many times.

Saturday, January 31st. London.

I finished *Don Juan* on Sunday night, rather to my surprise. Got to Berkeley Hotel at noon on Wednesday. I lunched with Mrs. Lee Matthews. Scott-James came at 5 to beat me down in price of an article for his new paper.[1] Sharpe concert at night. Acute neuralgia. Little sleep. Thursday—Pinker in morning. Bob Davis and wife to lunch. Much pleased with them. Lucas to tea, Atkins and Rickards to dinner—then to Olympia. Not bad. Friday, McKinnel, Wheeler, and Pryce here at 11. Then to Vaudeville Theatre. Welch ill. Rosher and Methuen to lunch at Reform. Henry James joined us afterwards and reminisced excellently. Hy. James said of Reform: "This is for me now a club of ghosts. There were special corners and chairs. It is fuller, too, now than it used to be." He also said that the club was built before clubs were fully understood, and he objected to largeness of atrium or *cortile,* making all rooms round it seem small. He described in full James Payn's[2] daily life: drove down from Maida Vale or somewhere to Smith Elder's, and left there before 1 in order to be at club at 1. Numberless friends. Amusing companion. Played whist, etc., every afternoon and got home (driving) about 7. Never walked. Never wanted other interests. No intellectual curiosity. Large family, but was not interested in it. I asked when he did his work. James said he certainly never worked either afternoon or night. He was continually politely sarcastic about Payn. He now lives on river at Chelsea. He likes pavements, shopfronts, and the convenient taxi. He said, "If I was rich, instead of being in grovelling poverty—" He made as if to go once; then asked if he might stay a little longer, and did so.

Monday, February 9th.

Thursday last we went to London by car and ran into a coal cart at 11.10 A.M. in Lee Bridge Road. Much excitement and crowd. It gave me a headache, which grew capriciously and lasted. Marguerite absolutely calm throughout. Back axle bent and much damage to coachwork. Still, we finished journey in car.

---

[1] R. A. Scott-James started the *New Weekly.*
[2] Editor of the *Cornhill Magazine.*

Afternoon, 5 P.M., *Parsifal* at Covent Garden. Putrid performance. Bodanzky commonplace conductor. Poor orchestra. Appalling scenery, costumes, and scenic effects. Ugly. Kundry, good singer. Rotten female chorus, amazingly ugly and ill-dressed. Also long stretches of dull music. I never saw uglier scenery. I went to sleep in middle of each act. Over after 11. Great deal of music fine; better than I expected. Friday, Pinker to lunch at Berkeley. Vernon came. Details settled for production of *A Good Woman*[1] ("Be sure your sins will find you out") at Palace Theatre on Monday 16th. At night, first night of *A Midsummer Night's Dream* at Savoy. Stylistic quality of much of this play is marvellous. But the two love stories and the love-philtre-ing tedious. Scenery not really good, but exquisite after Covent Garden.

Saturday, February 14th.

I finished the third of the *Velsa* articles for the *Century* on Thursday morning, and finished reading and correcting typescript of *Don Juan* on Thursday afternoon. Also I finished reading Jules Romains's *Mort de Quelqu'un*. This short novel, though often amateurish and indeed sometimes puerile in technique, is a really original work. The collective feeling of groups of men, and the influence of thought on thought, are remarkably done. It could properly be called "psychic."

Yesterday morning we came to London. Lunch at hotel. Then rehearsal of *Helen with the High Hand* at the Vaudeville. Dined at hotel. Then Zangwill's *Melting Pot* at Queen's Theatre. A dreadfully bad piece. We left after the 3rd act. All *vieux jeu;* hollow, reverberating with clumsy echoes of old-style eloquence. No human nature in it, except a bit regarding home life of Jews.

Monday, February 16th.

Schmitt for lunch, ½ hour late. Drank a lot of stout, and thoroughly enjoyed eating and drinking. Upstairs in sitting-room he objected to having a small table by his side for coffee, as it morally prevented him from getting up and walking about at will. We took him (Rickards also,

---

[1] *Rivals for Rosamund.*

who came to lunch) to Wallace Collection. I noted a fine "Music Lesson" of Steer, and a small picture by Léopold Robert. We left Schmitt and his Baedeker in street to find his way to Russell Sq. alone. Then all of us to South Place Institute for concert. Quartet of Ravel, and Quintet of Schmitt.

Wednesday, February 18th.

Rivals for Rosamund received with amiable indifference at Palace Theatre on Monday night. Last night I went to see it myself with J. Atkins. The first half was quite well received; the last half coldly. This was right. It is no real good, and if I had realized this earlier I would not have let it be done. Production and acting goodish.

Characteristic of theatrical methods. My name was misspelt on the painted notice in front of the Vaudeville Theatre, and the title of the short play was given wrongly in the illuminated sign in front of the Palace Theatre.

Dress rehearsal of *H. with High Hand* on Monday night was good. The original end had been restored, with my chief emendation preserved.

Thursday, February 19th.

Returned home yesterday afternoon. I bought *Autobiography of Mark Rutherford* and *Mark Rutherford's Deliverance* in 7d. editions at station. And in the night I had finished reading the latter. Very impressive and original. Fine style; no scheme of construction. As a continuous narrative, extraordinarily amateurish. The man had no notion of fiction. But a work not easily forgotten. Full of wisdom and high things.

Middle-aged couple in our compartment yesterday. Well and quietly dressed. Upper class. Restrained. Extremely good natural and trained manners. The woman (35) especially was charming in her admirable breeding. Evidently wealthy. They talked in such a low tone that, although the articulation was perfectly clear, one did not hear unless one listened. After about an hour the woman, reading *Daily Mail,* said, "What is a tympani solo?" The man made a gesture of non-comprehension. She passed him the paper. He read the passage and made a scarcely perceptible sign of ignorance. "Don't you know?" she asked quietly. He repeated the sign—would not speak (as they were not alone). Her glance seemed to say to him, "Pardon me asking you such an outlandish impossible thing." She took back the *Daily Mail*.

Saturday, February 21st.

Pianoforte recital by F.M. at Frinton Hall last night in aid of Tendring parish funds. Hall centrally heated, but draughty. Uncomfortable chairs. Rush-bottomed chair (cost about 3s.) for pianist. Old Broadwood baby grand. Pedal creaked. Rotten tone. Ladies of Frinton and of Tendring parishes in evening dress. Two parsons, who felt they must speechify afterwards. Pianist a man about 40; agreeable, slightly curt smile. Ferocious look when he was playing, often. Beethoven, Rameau, Chopin, Scarlatti, Debussy, Liszt, etc. Piano impossible. Intense, almost tragic sadness of provincial musical affairs, second-rate or tenth-rate under bad conditions. A gentle snobbishness (artistically) among the women. One man (friend of pianist) called out 2 or 3 times after a piece, amid the applause, " 'Core, 'core," very loudly and staccato. And he had his encore. Audience determined to appreciate high-class music, and applauding the noisiest and most showy. Crass inertia and stupidity of sundry women around me, determined to understand and to enjoy nothing.

Saturday, March 14th. On board Velsa.

I finished the last of the 6 articles *From the Log of the* Velsa on Monday March 2nd and was exhausted. Tuesday I packed and arranged, and on Wednesday March 4th we came to London. Dined with Rickards and Pryce at Pall Mall Restaurant and then to see *Helen with High Hand* at Vaudeville. The audience were very pleased by the play.

On Friday we came to Paris. Roughish crossing. On Saturday, March 7th, Théâtre du Vieux Colombier. *Le Testament du Père Leleu* (Martin du Gard), *La Jalousie de Barbouillé,* and *La Navette.*[1] Excellent. Quite a good audience. Met Morrell and Lady Ottoline M. Previously to this we

---

[1] *La Jalousie* was by Alexandre, after Molière. *La Navette* is by Henri Becque. Jacques Copeau was the director of all three.

had been to a *conférence* on "Musical Geography" by Calvo. Dined at Cepa's. Bions called before dinner. Fargue, Vignès, Sert, and Aubry came in afterwards.

Wednesday, March 11th, we came to Hyères. We joined the yacht on Friday morning.

Tuesday, April 21st. Orvieto.

Left the yacht yesterday.[1] *Histoire avec octroi.* The head thereof said our baggage ought to be examined by customs. At last, after much worrying of himself, he told us to go. Fine weather. Rather windy. Dusty. Splendid skyscapes. The Campagna full of purples and bright greens. Turned off high road to Viterbo in order to see Capricola and palace thereof. Lunch at Viterbo after a sharp descent from chilly hills. Old waiter at hotel said he had always been honest. Thus he was a Roman, and did not like to say that Viterbo water was better even than Roman water, but it was, though it was against the interest of the hotel trade in mineral water to say so. I drank it. Curious medieval (S. Pellegrino) quarter at Viterbo.

Then to Montefiascone. Great view of purple and bright greens. Hundreds of sq. miles. Then descent to Lake of Bolsena and Bolsena town and then rise to hills, and sudden view of Orvieto in midst of amphitheatre of hills. Unsurpassed. Like a slow mushroom grown there. Serrated outline of towers. We were met by hotel boy at gate of town. Hotel dei Belli Arti. Dear. Fairish. Slept in a longish room of a palace with large paintings of Judith and Holofernes, etc. Marble floor. Plenty of pre-Renaissance architecture in this town. I walked to bottom end of Corso Cavour last night (clear—after rain) and heard voices and saw groups and lights behind blinds. Everything was alive up the dark courts, lighted by one electric lamp. At 9, groups of well-dressed families began to emerge from courts to see last performance of a Fregoli imitator named Marbis, who was doing *Zaza* all by himself.

---

[1] The *Velsa* had been sent by canal through France to Marseilles, where Arnold Bennett boarded her, and coasted along the Riviera and Italy. His wife went by car. The *Velsa* was lent to the Admiralty during the War and was afterwards sold.

Wednesday, April 22nd. Siena.

Too ill most of yesterday to sit up in the car and be intelligent. Before leaving Orvieto we went into cathedral. A fiendishly noisy office going on between 3 or 4 old priests with awful voices. No audience. Chapels good. Well pleased. Then round town. Went to find very early church, S. Giovanni, *très* primitive. After we had entered it and gone away, it occurred to me that we had not seen it at all, but another quite ordinary church. So much for one's artistic education. *On gobe tout.* Gorgeous and glorious drive over mountains from Orvieto. At first we couldn't see Orvieto Cathedral; then we saw its peaks, and then we couldn't see anything else; it was the one thing that stood out on Orvieto's hill. Lunch at Montepulciano. I couldn't see it, but I walked about a bit, after taking a room at Albergo Marzocco to sleep in. Fine palaces. A great deal of Garibaldi.

Then to Pienza, where the piazza is small but fine. At S. Quirico, Read wouldn't stop, and we had a lovely glimpse of a primitive carved church. Had I known the name of the place I should have stopped the car, but I didn't. As it is, the glimpse remains exquisitely in the memory. This is a good way of seeing things occasionally.

Arrived at Siena at 3.50. Surprised at liveliness and beauty of this town. Drove to Duomo, 7.15. Office going on. Crowds entering, large crowds. Priests at a large desk transacting business with the faithful in front of a large box marked *oblazioni*. Then a monk in a brown robe appeared in a high pulpit and began to preach. We had to leave.

Thursday, April 23rd.

Yesterday spent chiefly in following Baedeker up and down Siena, with good results. The most memorable single thing we saw was a picture by Sano di Pietro (with a woman in it) on the ground floor of the Palazzo Communale. The charm of the cathedral is extreme. Fine Renaissance altars and things in various small churches. Casa di S. Caterina. Very little of it left. A bit of alleged old floor, carefully boarded, with hinges here and there. The place chiefly a series of very ugly chapels. In charge of a young agreeable priest.

On piazza of S. Agostino I essayed a drawing, with bad results. I managed to convey to the *cocher* that I wanted some picturesque scene to draw. He tumbled instantly. He found 3 all good, but only one in the least suitable for me.

Friday, April 24th. Pisa.

San Gimignano and Volterra, both visited yesterday *en route* from Siena to Pisa. In each place we had a man who described himself as *le seule guide de la ville* and who was intelligent. Both places=reputation. Etruscan Museum at Volterra *très bien arrangé.* At lunch there we saw a man whom I took for an English archæologist, but he was an American alabaster merchant. San Gimignano the most complete place we have seen. Roads excellent up to halfway from Volterra to Pisa. Then baddish. Two tire bursts, and a kid with handcart ran into us. Pisa very sad. *Tristesse* of Piazza del Duomo. Leaning Tower just as idiotic as I thought.

Saturday, April 25th. Albenga.

Yesterday, Pisa to Massa, Spezia and Genova. Vile, dusty, busy road to Massa and beyond. Flat. Marmoreal environs of Carrara. Over hills for a few miles into Spezia good. Fine hill road (1700 ft.) to Sestri di Levanti. With snow peaks in very far distance. This was truly sublime. From Sestri to Rapallo, road follows coast. Got Max's[1] address at post office and went to Villino Chiaso for tea. Max in whites, no waistcoat, and a calico sort of jacket. Fine tiled terrace. He was engaged in altering a portrait of George Moore in *Century* in order to tease Moore. Fine tea. Good servant. Picked a lemon off tree for tea. Arrived at Genoa 7.55. Left there this morning at 9.30 and reached Albenga at 1.25. Level crossings rather lucky, but up to Savona progress very slow.

Sunday, April 26th. Menton.

Quite decent roads all the way yesterday. Read ran out of essence near San Remo. Also pump went wrong and tire flat. Sundry delays. It began to rain. Arrived at Menton 6.40 (French time).

---

[1] Max Beerbohm.

Monday, April 27th. Aix-en-Provence.

Pneu troubles up to Cannes and delay there. Left Cannes at 2.30. Slow through the Esterel, but after Fréjus a tremendous pace. We reached here (152 k. from Cannes) at 6.20. General elections; everywhere streets full of outbursts of chairs and tables from cafés. Fête. After I was in bed, silly asinine cheering of crowds swindled by astute politicians. Such fragments of election literature as I saw were just as absurd as in England, but not more so.

Tuesday, April 28th. Carcassonne.

Row with Jewish landlady at Aix yesterday. Lunch at Avignon. Now, all the way yesterday and today, vineyards for hundreds of miles, and men with tanks on their backs syringing them with sulphurous stuff. Sunny, breezy; roads good only in parts. Cathedral good.

Went on in afternoon to Nîmes-Arènes, then on to Montpellier. A great noisy city. Scarcely any sleep. Large theatre. Really very many large cafés round about it. This morn. we came straight through Béziers to Carcassonne, 146 k. in 3¾ hours over very indifferent but straight roads. I had quite a wrong idea of Carcassonne. I thought the town itself (30,000 inhabitants) was a monument. However, the *cité* as restored by Viollet-le-Duc is highly curious. Also church therein. Guide thereat (*né dans la cité*) who said, apropos of *embrassement général* after annual Comédie Française show, that *"le forum de Rome et le Kremlin de Moscou ne sont rrrrien à côté de cela."*

Thursday, April 30th. Toulouse.

Rain last night, the first appreciable for about a month or more. Drove aimlessly about in the afternoon. Lift boy in this hotel, aged 13, works from 6.30 to 11 P.M. or later every day. He has been here a month and looks aged. He is very nicely and smartly dressed, and very small, and he spoils the hotel for "thinking people." The young man aged 17 or 18 who served our *petits déjeuners* this morning excused his delay with *"Je suis seul."* Certainly overworked. Last night in the rain, paper-sellers and tram-conductors in felt sandals that would sop up water like a sponge.

Friday, May 1st. Tulle (Corrèze).

Left Toulouse at 8.50 A.M. Not a *ville sympathique*. Population brusque and rude and *vie dure pour les pauvres*. Rain stopped us from going to S. Sernin yesterday afternoon, but the antique church of St. Étienne was close by, so we went to that. The valley of the Corrèze between Brive and Tulle is lovely. The Corrèze runs rapidly through the length of this town. An important place for only 15,000 inhabitants.

Sunday, May 3rd. Bourges.

250 kil. yesterday. Generally over 1st-class roads. Up to Gueret mountainous. Afterwards for the most part long, straight roads. Arrived at Bourges at 4.45. Very windy. A good deal of praying in churches just now. Many women, but not one man in cathedral. Some young girls doing the stations of the cross while taking an unfeigned interest in me.

Monday, May 4th. Paris.

We reached Fontainebleau at 12.20 yesterday. Have done about 150 k. in 3 hours on the way. Long, straight, pretty good roads. We left F'bleau at 1.30. All right to Villeneuve St.-Georges. Then the *entrée dans Paris était fantastique. Gare à Vincennes,* etc., etc. Arrived at hotel at 3.45 P.M., having motored from Rome without killing even a fowl. Sole incident—a boy and handcart ran into us near Pisa.

Monday, May 11th. London.

Dined at Godebski's last Wednesday, and lunched with Martins. I came to London Thursday. On boat long talk with Pullman agent, once coachman to British Embassy. Atkins dined with me at Reform Club, and Maurice Baring joined us afterwards. Visits to his flat and to Atkins. Friday, lunch with Pinker and son at Arts Club.

Wednesday, May 20th. Comarques.

Two watercolours with Rickards. Too much tennis. Bad nights. I resumed *Universal History* [1] reading yesterday, and also began to write an article for the *New Weekly* and *Harper's Weekly* on *The Barber*. I finished it this morning. This is the first writing work I have done since early in March. All last week I planned the first part of *Clayhanger III*, but I seemed to get little inspirational force for it. I turned to Turgenev, which caused my blood to flow. But the mere reviews of Mrs. Parnell's *Life of Parnell* [2] (publ. yesterday) inspired me much more than Turgenev—gave me the heroic mood. For Clayhanger also is irremediably in love.

Tuesday, May 26th.

Two aquarelles on Sunday.

Yesterday at 5.55 A.M. I began to write the third *Clayhanger* and did 1200 words in the morning.

Thursday, May 28th.

47 yesterday. Very sleepless night. Many annoyances in the morning; chief, a summons to Chelmsford jury for June 11th, the week I have made all arrangements for being in London. Fatigue, and this, put me right off the novel. M. returned home, uncured of her special complaint, but otherwise well. I finished *A House of Gentlefolk*. [3] Somewhat disappointed with the latter half. But it was a book after Mrs. O'Shea's *Life of Parnell*. Some of the latter is *really* interesting, but most of it dull, and all of it marked by a character fundamentally vulgar. But she was a beautiful woman.

Tuesday, June 2nd.

On Sunday before breakfast I wrote a play, *The Alarm*, in one act, for the Actors' Orphanage Garden Party on June 23. Intended to play 5 minutes.

Read Ransome's *Oscar Wilde*. Well-meant stuff. Curious that a man

---

[1] *L'Histoire Générale du IVe Siècle jusqu'à nos Jours.*

[2] Mrs. Parnell was the former Mrs. O'Shea, whose relations with Charles Stewart Parnell, the Irish political leader, had caused a celebrated scandal contributing to his downfall.

[3] By Turgenev, also translated as *A Nest of Nobles.*

with such decent notions on style should have none. After reading Dostoievsky's *Les Précoces* it suddenly occurred to me, a few pages from the end, that it was merely an episode lifted from *Les Frères Karamazov*. The name Karamazov does not occur in the first part of the book, and when it does occur the translators somehow transmogrify it into Chestamazov.

Sunday, June 7th.

Vernon came for lunch Tuesday, and had no progress to report.

The Edgar Selwyns came for lunch and tea Friday. Edgar told us about Al. Woods, once a cheap-theatre manager, thence out of that by cinemas, and now one of the chief N.Y. producers. It was he who said after 1st Act of *Milestones,* "Who is this guy Bennett?"—after second, "No, you couldn't give it to me!" and after 3rd: "He's got me. It'll never *stop* running in N.Y." He says he *smells* a good or a bad play. Showing MS. of an accepted play to Edgar, he said: "Smell that. Smell it. Doesn't it smell good?" Once when listening to an idea for a play, he sniffed all the time—sniff, sniff, sniff—and at the end said, "No, that don't seem to me to smell very good." Once Michael Morton intruded on him; he refused to listen, but Michael made him. Michael said: "My idea is for a little Russian girl who wants to study, and she can't get away unless she takes the prostitute's ticket—the yellow ticket as it is called. That's what they have to do, you know." Said Woods, startled: "It *is?* It *is?* I'll buy your play." Morton said it wasn't finished. "Never mind. I'll buy." And he bought it on the spot. He always thus makes up his mind at once and won't wait. The legend is that he never makes a mistake. But it can't be so.

Walpole came yesterday for the week-end, without collars or toilet things. Great croquet this afternoon.

Yesterday I finished 1st chapter of *These Twain,* 5900 words, and I think it fairly good.

Sunday, June 14th.

Went to London by car last Wednesday morn. Two tire breakdowns. Acute liver attack on previous day, and not recovered.

We dined at Ritz, with Robert Loraine and Mimi Godebski, as guests of Edgar Selwyn and wife. I took them all, and the Retingers, to 500th performance of *Great Adventure*. After that with M. to Granville-Barker's supper and dance at Connaught Rooms. Lillah was my partner, but Asquith came uninvited, and she had to look after him. He took Ainley's place on her left. When I bet Ainley a quid that play would not be running on September 1st, Asquith took the stakes. He was in great spirits. He drank a little, but more mineral water than champagne. We left at 2.15. Met Meyerfeld, translator of *Milestones* into German. Went home at 2.15 A.M.

Thursday morning Pinker came to breakfast. May Wilson Preston and Dr. Carl Otto came for tea. Friday, Ellen Glasgow and Mrs. Westmore Willcox to tea. The former deaf, but pretty, plump, intelligent, and extremely well read.

Friday, June 26th.

Sculpture in garden to be finished tomorrow. Sundry watercolours. Nevertheless I have never in my life worked better than this week, despite liver on Tuesday. I have now written over 20,000 words of *Clayhanger III* and got to the end of the party which opens the book and the quarrel after it. Seems all right. Written with ease on the whole. I was up most mornings at 6.

Monday, July 13th.

I returned from yacht last Monday. Much interested now in question of getting a new yacht. 150-ton schooner, crew of 8, speed 8 knots, draft 7 ft. This is what I want.

I went to London on Friday. Collins came on Saturday morning and read his Grand Babylon Hotel play to me. I joined yacht, with Swinnerton, at Westminster Bridge at 3 P.M. I returned home at 9.35 A.M. today by yacht.

Tuesday, July 21st.

Marguerite went to Paris to be operated on. She returned home cured on

Saturday the 18th. I did no work whatever on my novel all last week, and have not yet resumed.

Thursday, July 30th.

Between the last entry and Wednesday week I did no work at all. Felt queer and couldn't collect ideas. I think it was a chill in the head. But thenceforward I worked well and did an average of over 1000 words a day for ten days. I finished a long chapter yesterday. Last week-end on Broads in yacht; did 2500 words in the two days. I go on board the yacht tonight for an excursion to Cowes, timed to leave tomorrow morning at 6 A.M.

WAR JOURNALS

1914-1918

1914

Thursday, August 6th. Thorpe-le-Soken.

On arriving at Brightlingsea on Monday afternoon, I was told that petrol could not be got in the district, that it was fetching up to 10s. a tin at Clacton, and that Baggaley, the regular hirer of motor cars at B'sea, had gone forth in an attempt to get petrol. At Clacton yesterday the price was 2s. 3d. or 2s. 4d. a gallon. I have 60 gallons in stock.

A great crowd of holiday makers at Clacton in the showers yesterday. No difficulty about getting change for a £10 note in gold and silver. At the fish shop, slight increases of price in poultry and eggs. The man said there was no chance for him to make money (in response to a friendly jibe of M.'s). He said he expected to get no more fish after that day.

Yesterday we heard noise of explosions destroying inconvenient houses at Harwich. The sensations of Harwich people must be poignant. Nevertheless the G.E.R., in yesterday evening's paper, was advertising its Hook of Holland service (with restaurant cars, etc.) exactly as usual, and I believe the boat left last night. We also heard thunder, and the children affirm that they distinctly heard the noise of firing—not explosions. (Report of action in North Sea in evening papers.) I saw one warship in the offing at Clacton, but an ordinary steamer coming to the pier, and a barge sailing northwards.

An officer came yesterday to complain of a fox terrier (? ours) which flew at dispatch-riders on motor bicycles. He said it would be shot if found loose. These dispatch-riders are the most picturesque feature of the war, here. They rush through the village at speeds estimated up to 50 miles an hour. I am willing to concede 40.

I agree that Russia is the real enemy, and not Germany; and that a *rapprochement* between England and Germany is a certainty. But I doubt whether it is wise, in the actual conduct of affairs, to try to see so far ahead. I think that the belligerency of England is a mistake—for England. Yet if I had had to choose, I believe my instinct would have forced me to make war.

Sir Edward Grey's astounding mistake, in his big speech, was the assertion that the making of war would not much increase our suffering. It will enormously increase it. The hope for us is in the honesty and efficiency of our administration. The fear for France springs from the fact that the majority of French politicians are notoriously rascals, out for plunder. The corruption of Russian administration is probably even worse. The seriousness of the average French private will atone for a lot, but it will not—for instance—create boots for him. The hope for France is that the German army, arrogant in its traditions, etc., may be lower than its reputation.

After reading the diplomatic papers leading up to the rupture between England and Germany, this morning, one has to admit that Sir E. Grey did everything he could, once he had stated his position. The war is a mistake on our part, but other things leading to it were a mistake, and, these things approved or condoned, the war must be admitted to be inevitable. Judged by any current standard, Sir E. Grey is a man of high common sense. He has not yet grasped the movement of social evolution, but then very few people have. And you cannot properly or fairly try to govern a country on a plane of common sense *too* high above its own general plane.

Apart from Germany two countries are pre-eminently suffering at the beginning of the war—France and Belgium. Both are quite innocent, Belgium touchingly so. I can imagine the Germans among them if they get the upper hand. The Germans are evidently quite ruthless and brutal and savage in war. This is logical, but a large part of their conduct is due to the arrogant military tradition, which will one day be smashed. If Germany is smashed in this war, the man most imperilled will be the German Emperor. If she is not smashed, the man most imperilled may be the Tsar.

I am told, convincingly, that a firm at Clacton is making an extra £50 a week out of bread, through increased charges for which there is no justification. It appears that the farmers all round have raised the price of butter 3d. a lb.

Miss Osborne and a girl friend came round yesterday afternoon to ask for linen or subscriptions for the local branch of the Red Cross Society. Mrs. Byng is ready to lend Thorpe Hall for a hospital. These young ladies have no orders or permission yet from the War Office, but they wish to be in readiness. This instinct to do something on the part of idle young women, or half idle, is satisfactory to behold. All about this district and all about many other country districts are many middle-class young women, and scarcely any young men for them to consort with—I mean even in ordinary times. Now, there will be fewer young men than ever.

On the day after the war the boys [1] wanted a tent. They had one, beyond the pond. It cost one day's labour of a carpenter. This tent is used by everybody except me nearly all the time. The whole household seems to live in it. Today the boys are making wooden swords. Yesterday a village boy gave me a military salute.

Edith Johnston recounts how her father is laying in ammunition against the time when the populace will raid the countryside demanding provisions; he, being a farmer, is to be called on early in the proceedings, and he is determined to give out his stores evenly and not to the strongest. Each morning he summons all his men and explains to them the course of the war, so that they shall not be misled by rumours. Edith thinks that a war is necessary and advisable, as the population is too thick.

Friday, August 7th.

The news of the sinking of the *Amphion,* by striking a mine, and of

---

[1] Nephews, who were staying at Comarques when war was declared.

the weakening of the defence of Liège made a silent breakfast table. Nevertheless, these things are preliminary trifles of infinitesimal importance. My Central News service of war telegrams began at 6 P.M. tonight with an unofficial (Raffles) statement that the Germans before Liège had asked for a day's armistice, having lost 20,000 men. This uncertain news animated me much. The postmaster himself brought the telegram. I asked him if he would like to put it in the post-office window. He said he should. In reply to a question he said he had been having very little sleep lately (P.O. being open continuously night and day), but that he had had a good night last night; he had the telephone by his bed, but no call.

Rumour through M. this morning that Read might have to join forces as ex-Territorial, and that Lockyer as captain of rifle club might also have to go, made me think, startled, "We should have no electricity and should have to use candles." This seemed dreadful at first, but by the afternoon I was reconciled to the idea of no electricity and also to the idea of the garden being neglected.

Lockyer told me that it was suspected that 8 or 9000 Colchester men had already been shipped to Belgium, leaving last Friday, long before war was declared. Certainly the silence of the newspapers as to the Expeditionary Force is superb. He said that miniature rifle clubs had been in existence and full practice for six years now and that the members had been told that the object was to repel a German invasion. He suggested that the captains of clubs should be called together with a view to preparing some definite general organization to offer to the Govt. in case of need (not for an invasion, but for anything) and that I should write to J. Parkes, secretary to Clacton district. This I did. He was quite ready to serve himself, and Cook also is ready to go (as ex-Reserve man); both have families. I asked Read if he thought of offering himself as an ex-Territorial. He said he had no thought of going unless it was compulsory.

Saturday, August 8th.

Miss Nerney told me that while people were reading the copy of the telegram to me, shown in the post-office window yesterday afternoon, one man asked, "Who is Arnold Bennett?" The reply was, "He's the War minister." Then, in correction: "Oh, no, he isn't. He's the actor chap that lives down the road."

Rumour that a miller at W., settled there some years with his family and often suspected of being a German spy, is now proved to be a German officer, and plans of Harwich, etc., have been found at his place; and that he and 2 others are now imprisoned at the hotel.

Today I got postal orders as currency.

The boats were still running to Flushing.

We received the Paris *Journal* for Wednesday. It consisted of one sheet, 2 pages, and gave chiefly the news of Germany's declaration of war on England and a report of the *séance* in the Chamber. M., in her pleasure at a French paper, pinned it to the hall curtains for all to see and read, long after all had read it.

Sunday, August 9th.

Yesterday Johnson, ex-tobacco merchant, called on me in a state of some excitement. Tall, thin, nervous man. He began by saying, "I am a great patriot." He said superiorly: "I know the Germans. They are traitors. I have seen this coming for years. I have £3000 in cash. I am prepared to use it for the country." His scheme was that the Government should give authority to take over the small mills (why only small?) of the district, and that he should manage them without profit, so as to prevent the exploitation of small people now going on. He had already got promises of produce of 4000 acres at rather less than market price. The extreme improbability of such a scheme's ever being sanctioned, the absurdity of it, the rights on which it trampled, the excessive difficulty of it—these things seemed not to have occurred to him at all. It was all simple and patriotic to him. He wanted me to guarantee £1000 and to give the support of my name (this was what he came for), and he had got Syme to guarantee £1000. On this he was prepared to start.

To soothe him I said I would write to some one high up as a preliminary, and I wrote to Spender,[1] without, however, concealing my view from Spender. Johnson was soon launched on his camping experiences in Turkey, where he went to buy tobacco. He is a very decent, agreeable, well-intentioned oldish man, speaking fairly correctly except that he adds *r* to the end of too many words. He farms his own land.

Then the Mathewses came. The Rev. M.,[2] a very nice chap indeed, had suddenly discovered that Redmond was a good man; but he learnt from me for the first time at 5 P.M., 8th Augt 1914, that Ulster is not all Protestant. He was staggered to learn that quite 50 per cent of Ulster is Roman Catholic. Although he had to make an announcement about it in the pulpit tomorrow, he had not yet understood the object of the Prince of Wales's Relief Fund. I explained it to him. By the way, I have no desire whatever to contribute to this spectacular affair. I have taken measures to be told of any bad cases in the village (none at present), and I have authorized Pinker to use £100 privately among really necessitous authors. I have the same feeling against funds as I have against committees.

Referring to my permission to postmaster to exhibit my war telegrams at the post office, I read the following on a telegraph form outside the P.O. yesterday: "British Gold Coast Forces Take German Togoland. No resistance by permission of Arnold Bennett Esquire."

Monday, August 10th.

The alleged spy (ex-Austrian officer) is perhaps not a spy. But he has to report himself to the authorities every twelve hours.

The only important rise in price is in butter, 3*d*. a lb. The rise in bread is not the same everywhere.

Daking came to see me yesterday about taking the farm. He is in charge of the National Service League in this district. He asked me if he could hold a committee meeting here. I said he could. He said he had spent £25 himself on the League. He was quite prepared to go on

---

[1] J. A. Spender, editor of the *Westminster Gazette*.
[2] Rev. H. G. S. Mathews, rector of Beaumont with Moze, Essex, the Bennetts' neighbour.

with the preparations for taking the farm, but he said, "I shall look nice if the Germans come and take it from me." At the back of the mind of every one is a demi-semi fear lest the Germans should after all, by some *coup,* contrive an invasion. And that is the only fear. The fear of revolution or serious social uproar after the War does not trouble anybody. Few even think of it.

When one sees young men idling in the lanes on Sunday, one thinks, "Why are they not at the war?" All one's pacific ideas have been rudely disturbed. One is becoming militarist. And the usefulness of certain organizations upon which one looked with disdainful tolerance is now proved by events.

The alleged spy has to report himself only once a day at noon. Nothing incriminating has been found in his house.

The family went to Clacton this morning. They said it was practically emptied of visitors and sundry of the big shops closed until 6 P.M., being out of supplies. Nevertheless, in a four-mile walk round about here this afternoon, I met a quite unusually large number of motors and other vehicles, many of them obviously pleasure and tripper parties.

Mrs. and Miss W. have taken the pictures down in their house and otherwise dismantled it and sent the silver to the bank. But why they have done this neither they nor anybody else seems to know. I suppose it is the mere result of a vague fear.

Wednesday, August 12th.

No definite news yesterday, and probably there will be none today. I am in *full* work, and only a defeat of the Allies will put me off work.

Thursday, August 13th.

Tennis meeting at Mathews's, Beaumont, yesterday. The universal tale of ladies was that they were going to begin Red Cross shirt-making, etc. Our house alone had actually bought its materials and begun. It was said that a band of ladies had collected and gone to —— Hall to scrub, and when they got there found they had not one scrubbing-brush. The idea of certain ladies was to cut out the garments and then send them to cottage women to sew, without payment. Butter only, among provisions, is definitely higher, by 3*d*. a lb. Best sugar between 4*d*. and 4½*d*. I am paying 1*d*. extra per gallon of petrol; that is, the same price as before the reduction a few weeks ago.

I have now had the following hits:

Serial publication of *The Price of Love* suspended in *Daily News,* ostensibly on account of paper famine.

Book publication of ditto indefinitely postponed.

Other autumn books probably ditto.

Vedrenne announced today that autumn tours of *Milestones,* if railways permitted them to go out at all, would be a heavy loss, and would I forgo my fees? I declined. Knoblock, he said, had agreed.

Receipts of *The Great Adventure* at the Kingsway showed a fall of about £500 on the previous week.

No definite news again today, except formal declaration of war last night by England against Austria.

Monday, August 17th.

In the midst of this war I wrote over 7000 words in six days, ending Friday.

No war news till last night, when Japan's ultimatum to Germany reached me by wire after I had gone to bed and to sleep. The dog, hearing the telegraph messenger, woke me.

Yesterday, a request from the *Daily News* to write on the War. Today, ditto from *Everybody's Mag.* Yesterday, inspired somewhat by *D.N.'s* request, I wrote an article on *What the German Conscript Thinks,* this in addition to 2 hours' revision work on novel.

Friday, August 21st.

Davray [1] wrote me the other day from Paris, stating without any hint of scepticism (1) that the menu of the dinner which the Kaiser was to eat in Paris on August 12th had been prepared in advance. And (2) that

---

[1] Henry D. Davray had translated Bennett's novels into French.

in the cellars of the Hôtel du Rhin a garlanded bust of the Emperor had been found ready to expose in the Place Vendôme when the Kaiser should pass through.

Great spectacular depressing fact of the surrender of Brussels to the Germans this morning. But by the afternoon I had got quite used to it and was convinced that it was part of the Allies' preconceived plan and that all was well. But before getting this reassuring conviction I had gone upstairs and written 1200 words in 2 hours.

Sunday, August 23rd.

A tale yesterday that eighty men had been engaged all day in searching for a spy who had not been found (in this neighborhood, that is)!

Sullivan [1] said that he had an enormous belief in the British Expeditionary Force and that he thought it would "cause consternation"! Nevertheless he was sure that the Germans would get to Paris, and he bet me a present worth £5 that they would.

Tuesday, August 25th.

Yesterday's rumours. Mathews (who came with wife and daughter to play tennis) said that a friend of his had a friend who with others had been sent out to Belgium, a fortnight before the declaration of war, with British guns for the Liège forts and to instruct the Belgians in the use of the said guns. This friend's friend had not returned. The theory held by the friend was that the Germans were taken by surprise by the range of the Liège guns. This reminds me that, though we had constant news that the Liège forts were holding out, we have only had indirect news that they have fallen. Clemenceau is right in demanding full news of defeats.

Psychological consequence of fall of Namur: We were all discussing last night what we in this house ought to do if Germans came. The general result was: nothing.

---

[1] The late Herbert Sullivan. He collaborated with Newman Flower in publishing the life of the composer, Sir Arthur Sullivan.

Thursday, August 27th.

Talk with old farmer down Golden Lane this morning. Said he was 78 ("but I'm done for") and had farmed there for 50 years. He said he had often been to Brussels as cattle dealer. What surprised him there was that people kept pigs in cellars under their houses. He said he didn't know my opinion, but he thought Germany was short of money and couldn't last. Then he said, "Now tell me, Mr. Bennett, is it true they're a-killing women and children?" He said the harvest was very good, and that at Laudermere Farm they had got 20 sacks of wheat to the acre. Many farms, he said, got only 3, 4, or 5. One of his larger fields was being used for cavalry (or perhaps field-artillery) manœuvres. I asked him whether he charged the Government anything for the field. He said: "No. They've got enough to pay for." Lastly he suggested to me "a matter of business." "I know you're a business man, Mr. Bennett; I can see it in yer face." To wit, that I should have my mare covered by a piebald pony that he knew. He said I could work her up to the day she foaled and begin again a week afterwards.

Saturday, August 29th.

It is now reported that Dr. H. (who nevertheless knows colonial and frontier quasi-military and military life), as well as Mr. Johnston, can do nothing but read the papers, and think, think, think, and mourn because English youths will not enlist. It was given forth that while at Tendring and Weeley and other villages the response to the call was excellent, the response in Thorpe was miserable—indeed, it was said, only one man. No doubt every village is saying the same. In any case the alleged state of affairs would be explicable by the fact there is a camp at Tendring and another at Weeley and youths are thereby fired.

However, on inquiry from other sources I found that Thorpe was doing excellently. Lockyer, a grim and very serious patriot and the chief pillar of the Rifle Club, said that 5 men had gone from his club alone. Cook, second gardener, who belongs already to the National Reserve, put down his name again, and was told that for the present he was not wanted. Few young men, eligible for recruiting and able to go, remain.

Miss Nerney said the same. It was she who told me that Mrs. Wood (parson's [1] wife) had said to a young man who offered certain sorts of help: "You can only help in one way. You can enlist." As parson's wife and familiar with the village, she knew or ought to have known that the young man had a widowed mother depending on him. Mrs. Wood is a very decent woman, and that she should have said such a thing shows how far the feeling of the middle classes will carry them.

Yesterday morning I wrote an article telling some incontrovertible truths about this recruiting question. Mrs. Sharpe "agreed with every word of it" but did not think it ought to be published. Marguerite did not like it at all. Both were afraid of it. I should not be at all surprised if the *Daily News* is not also afraid of it. In that case I shall probably send it to the *New Statesman*.

Monday, August 31st.

Rickards and I met H. in the street. Jaunty but gloomy. He said there was only one thing "to save this country"—vastly increased recruiting. When I said that soldiers could be had quite easily if we would pay fairly for them, he at once said: "Bounty? Yes, the U.S.A. paid a bounty of £20." The usual charitable idea, not a proper salary. He said it was the middle classes that shirked, not the lower and not the upper. It did not seem to occur to him that the whole organization of the army was such as to keep the middle classes out of it—save as privates.

Our young women and M. paid another visit to another camp yesterday. Officers wire appointments here, etc. They call here in motors to make appointments. Good news yesterday, as to moving of German troops from western frontier. The bill came for the British stand, between 5000 and 6000 losses, but the news that they were thoroughly reinforced was good. The girls came home with a positive statement from the camp that 160,000 Russians were being landed in Britain, to be taken to France. The Colonel had brought the news from Colchester.

The statement was so positive that at first I almost believed it. But after about an hour I grew quite sceptical. Only the Archangel route

---

[1] Rev. A. R. Wood, vicar of Thorpe-le-Soken.

could have been used. Think of the number of ships and the amount of convoying necessary. In the end I dismissed it and yet could not help hoping. . . . Rumours in village as to it also. Debarkation said variously to take place at Harwich and in Scotland, etc. Numbers went up to 400,000. The most curious embroidery on this rumour was from Mrs. A.W., who told Mrs. W. that the Russians were coming via us to France, where they would turn treacherous to France and join Germans in taking Paris. "We could not trust the Russians." This rumour I think took the cake. Yet Mrs. Sharpe asked me seriously whether there was any fear of such a thing.

Wednesday, September 2nd.

Yesterday I received an official invitation to go to London to meet Masterman [1] as to the war.

The agent for Mrs. Cowley came and rounded up six men for recruits on Monday night. Cook, second gardener, left this morning. Lockyer says that practically all available men in village have gone or belong to some reserve or other.

Thursday, September 3rd.

London absolutely as usual in summer, except the "call to arms" on the taxis. Atkins lunched with me at Reform. Atkins believed in Russian troops story, but had not much inside news. Belloc said it was a question whether Germans would break through Allies' line yesterday or today. Spender told me a lot of useful stuff for articles. He also said that Kitch. had 150,000 recruits before he would admit 100,000, and that he now actually had over 200,000 while still advertising for them. Recruiting organization had broken down, and the recruiting campaign was off.

Conference at Wellington House of "eminent authors," Hall Caine, Zangwill, Parker, among them. Masterman in chair. Zangwill talked a great deal too much. The sense was talked by Wells and Chesterton. Rather disappointed in Gilbert Murray, but I liked the look of little

---

[1] Rt. Hon. C. F. G. Masterman, Chancellor of the Duchy of Lancaster.

R. H. Benson.[1] Masterman directed pretty well, and Claud Schuster and the Foreign Office representative were not bad. Thomas Hardy was all right. Barrie introduced himself to me; Scotch accent, sardonic canniness. Afterwards I went with Wells to his flat; all alone there. A young Vowles came in with his own recruiting story, which I arranged to turn into an article. I was much pleased with the serious, confident, and kind demeanour of every one. But Spender told me that the military clubs were full of old officers in a panic. I had such a fearful headache after the conference that I had to dine alone at the club. I bought *The Riddle of the Sands*—very annoying style.

Saturday, September 5th.

Joseph Retinger came yesterday for the night. He had taken 3 weeks from the Russian-Polish frontier to London—six days in prison at Vienna and six days in prison at Paris. He said that there were no uniforms for 800,000 French reservists, and that for three days no reply had been given to a patriotic offer of 200 combined tailors to set to work on the uniforms, materials being plentiful. He also said that Messinez (ex-Ministre de Guerre) was a *cas pathologique,* often fainted at Cabinet meetings, etc. He said that such men as Berthelot (now practically in charge of French foreign politics) were very sanguine as to the result of the War. He had plans for Poland but did not strike me as having lost any of his impracticalness, nor did he inspire any confidence. He was fairly wrong in his estimate of U.S.A. opinion.

Monday, September 14th.

Nothing much happens. I wrote *Liberty* last week for the *Saturday Evening Post,* and *Daily News* article last Sunday but one and yesterday. Pinker came up on Friday for week-end. He confirmed a tale of Miss Nerney's (from France) that the lack of support to British army in early stages was due to a general forgetting a dispatch in his pocket for two days and that this general was shot.

---

[1] Monsignor Benson died this same year. He was the author of several works on Catholic subjects, and the brother of two other distinguished writers, A. C. and E. F. Benson.

The theatrical business varies with the war news, I think. Week ending Friday 4th it was more than £100 less than previous week. I am expecting that for last week, with German army in retreat most of the time, it will be up again considerably.

No certainty yet as to the alleged Russian army in France. Military officers up to yesterday have always believed the tale, and indeed positively asserted it, here. But yesterday Miss Hatchett found a colonel who said it was false and who could explain how the rumour first arose.

Sunday, September 20th.

Yachts, dinghies, and other small boats were moved inland from Brightlingsea creek last week, as part of a plan for defending Brightlingsea and the Colne in case of a German invasion. The notion seemed to be that the G.'s might use them as pontoons. I said to old Capt. Brand that it was only done because a number of people had a desire to do something, and this strange proceeding could not do any harm. He said the same thought had occurred to him. We met a lot of these boats in military carts. Sullivan told me there were about 200 of them.

No news last week.

Constant flow of one or two military officers in and through this house, on account of Mimi [1] and Miss Hatchett. The latest move—a night excursion in car to see searchlights playing on the sea off Frinton.

Tuesday, September 22nd.

News of sinking of *Aboukir, Hogue,* and *Cressy* (12,000 tons each), by submarine or submarines, startled me in the middle of my work this afternoon. I thought: Suppose all our fleet sank in this way? But then I thought: We have twice as many submarines as Germany, and the trick ought to work both ways. Nothing in the war yet has affected me like this news, of which no details to hand. Thursday I contemplated an article about terms of peace to be imposed on Germany.

Monday, September 28th.

Cook came to see me last Sunday but one. He was happy in camp at

---

[1] Mimi Godebski.

Dovercourt. He said that inoculation was being practised against enteric and that it was useless. I contradicted him firmly, but probably without effect. He said that tattooing was a better preventive of enteric. He is extensively tattooed. I think he was tattooed in India. His chief argument in favour of the excellence of tattooing as a preventive was that "they put gold in it" where he was tattooed.

I met Dr. H. yesterday morning. He had been having a pow-wow with an old friend not seen for 20 years, Col. Robertson, in command of new battalion at Colchester—a great maker of soldiers, keen, etc., etc. He had come back with the usual fine crop of rumours that flourish in camps and in naval ports. Serious misunderstandings between French and English commanders. French short of ammunition. Serious leakage at the Admiralty in the very highest quarters. Our 3 cruisers were given away, etc., etc. A French general shot by court-martial, etc. I disposed at once of the last tale, and sniffed at all the others, and I especially protested against the implication, every time the word "German" was used, that the Germans were superhuman. His wife in the afternoon said that I had quite changed him. But I bet he is the same as ever today. I learnt from Mrs. H. that there is a serious undercurrent of fear of a German raid in the village.

Friday, October 9th.

Last week I learnt that, owing to the glut of English authors' "distinguished 'copy'" in U.S.A. offered practically for nothing either in order to get it published quickly, or because American copyright had been sacrificed to instant publication in England, there was no longer any market for such copy in U.S.A., American editors, with characteristic foolishness, setting down as valueless that which they could get cheap. I was told that they now adopted a patronizing smile towards all English war-"copy" other than news. Thus our literary patriotism has cost us authors money and done no good. Personally, a contract for 10 articles for £1000 was practically arranged for me and then called off. This was for American use of *Daily News* article; so it was a clear net loss.

Today I acted on notice to reduce lights, on account of Zeppelins.

Monday, October 12th.

Lunch at Mrs. Hausberg's. I met a really intelligent officer—the first —Captain Montagu Browne, brigade-major or something at Colchester. He, of course, did not believe in the possibility of an invasion. But others did, and were ready to bet on it. With him a Colonel D., retired for many years, but now at work again administratively. Amiable and decent, superficially smart, but politically a fool. Said (quite nicely) that since the Boer War there had been nobody interested in British Empire. "Party" was the chief concern, and how longest to remain in power. When I asked, "Who *has* been looking after the British Empire, then?" he made no answer. Afterwards he took me aside and said how interesting it was to meet me, and praised my books, and even showed knowledge of them. He had a Rolls-Royce car, which he looks after entirely himself, except washing it. Said, even then he couldn't afford it.

German bomb dropped on roof of Notre Dame yesterday.

Sunday, October 25th.

No news except newspaper news, and no time to write it down even if there was any. I spend 1½ days a week on war articles. Village lamps not used for a time. Now they have been blacked halfway down the sides. A useless precaution. Our house is now heavily curtained everywhere except on top floor, where curtains are most needed. I only do what I can there, servants being incurable. I saw a regiment moving on Friday. Wretchedly badly made, cheap-looking uniforms. A red coat here and there. Marguerite had a letter from Auguste this morning from Marseilles to say that his regiment was starting in the direction of Belfort on the 20th.

Charles Wyndham and F. Harrison both opened their theatres every afternoon last week and gave only two performances in the evenings. Most other theatres begin their evening performances earlier. From tomorrow *The Great Adventure* begins at 7 P.M. and finishes at 9.45.

Wednesday, October 28th.

F. W. Wile (*Chicago Tribune*) came to interview me yesterday, and

I gave him a scheme for a court of Belgian inquiry to be held at The Hague under ægis of U.S.A. during the war—not to affect the course of the war or to attempt to stop the war.

He told me that T. P. O'Connor told him that the authorities made recruiting in Ireland as difficult as they possibly could. Also that Kitchener, as usual, said the war would last 3 years.

Wounded announced to arrive in a day or two at our hospital, Thorpe Hall.

Wile said that Northcliffe presided every night at the nightly editorial council of *Daily Mail*.

Also that *Chicago Tribune's* first correspondents at the war were collared by German staff and spoilt and became pro-German, and were deeply impressed because they had never seen a big army before. *Tribune* continued pro-German, as 25 per cent of its readers at least were Germans. Took Wile's first impartial article with fear, but it had a great success. *Tribune* had rather forgotten its 75 per cent. Attitude changed.

Friday, October 30th.

On Wednesday I finished the second part of *These Twain*.

This afternoon I wrote my contribution to *King Albert's Book*—Hall Caine's scheme.[1]

Wednesday, November 4th.

Came to London yesterday morning. The Atkinses arrived on Saturday and left on Monday. An impression of off-season half-emptiness throughout West End. Girls driving motor cars. If one thinks about recruiting one soon gets obsessed by number of young men about the streets. Lunch with Pinker at Arts Club. *Price of Love* had sold 6700 in England and 3500 colonial. Season good, at shops; but libraries "obstructive," as Pinker said.

---

[1] *King Albert's Book* was published as "A Tribute to the Belgian King and People from Representative Men and Women throughout the World," and was sold for the benefit of the *Daily Telegraph* Belgian Fund. Arnold Bennett's contribution was *The Return*, an account of his first visit to Belgium and an anticipation of the feelings of expatriated Belgians on their return after the War.

He had seen Conrad that morning, just returned from Austrian Poland. C. had no opinion of Russian army and had come to England to influence public opinion to get good terms for Austria! As if he could. Pinker had also seen Henry James, who often goes to see Page, American Ambassador, in afternoons. They have long quiet talks together. First time H.J. opened his heart to Page, he stopped and said, "But I oughtn't to talk like this to you, a neutral." Said Page, "My dear man, if you knew how it does me good to hear it!" Hy. James is strongly pro-English and comes to weeping-point sometimes.

Then tea at A.B.C. shop opposite Charing Cross. Down into smoking-room. A few gloomy and rather nice men. One couple of men deliberately attacking dish of hot tea-cakes. Terrible. Familiar smell of hot tea. A.B.C. shops are still, for me, one of the most characteristic things in London. *Milestones* on buses again. Same servants at hotels and clubs.

After tea to N.L.C., but I saw nobody I knew. Then, through latest dusk, to Reform, where Rickards and I dined. London not so dark as I expected, owing to lamps in centre of roads throwing down a volume of light in the shape of a lamp-shade (they are blackened at top). After dinner, Ponting's Antarctic cinema,[1] followed by poor war pictures. Provincial-seeming audience. Woman behind me continually exclaimed under her breath, with a sharp, low intake of breath, "Oh," "Oh."

Two nice old Johnnies at Reform Club, phlegmy-voiced, one fat, one thin, quoting Latin to each other over their reading. One said he had a music professor from Liège coming to stay with him—seemed rather naïvely proud of it. Many old men at Reform. Their humanness, almost boyishness, comes out. Lying placards on evening papers. *P.M.G.:* "Great German retreat," on strength of a phrase in Belgian *communiqué* affecting one small part of battle line only.

Thursday, November 5th.

Morning. Print Room, Brit. Museum, to see watercolours by Cotman, Bonington, and Girtin. Several Cotmans were inspiring. The finest thing

---

[1] Herbert G. Ponting accompanied the Scott South Pole Expedition, in charge of the photographic department, 1901–13, and was in 1914 lecturing in London on the Scott Expedition and its findings.

seen was a small sketch by Bonington. These in new gallery of B.M. Very bad direct light. New galleries very ugly and crude.

Then to see Humphreys at Hatchards, where I bought a Baskerville Congreve in 3 vols. There Lucas telephoned me. He came here for tea. Said he had written his *Swollen-Headed William* [1] in 3 hours and that 42,000 had been sold up to yesterday. He is doing a revue for Hippodrome; a cheap production, Harry Tate the only expensive item. He told me about the war visit of Barrie and Mason to U.S.A. It was decided without consulting Spring-Rice (Ambass. at Washington), and Masterman forgot even to tell him of the visit until visitors were within 36 hours of New York. Spring-Rice didn't want anything said by English visitors just then—and rightly. He had the steamer met, and he stopped all talking by Barrie and Mason. Mason returned home at once, and Barrie remained in concealment with Frohman for three weeks.

Then to see Vedrenne (and Berman) at Royalty. Returns of *Milestones* revival bad. Vedrenne said if he couldn't take £400 a week he should close the theatre.

Sunday, November 8th.

The Great Adventure finished its London run last night (673 performances).

I came home on Thursday.

Yesterday sale and show at Frinton, organized by Marguerite for Belgian refugees. Total gross receipts, £82 6s. 7d. and about £3 more to come. Expenses under £5, I think. Opened by Marguerite, who during her speech kept jabbing a pair of scissors into green cloth of table. Hall full of exhibits, plants, flowers, jam, vegetables, and sundries; and of visitors.

I walked out to sea. Lovely afternoon. I went home for tea and wrote most of a war article and returned at 8 P.M. for auction of things left. This auction, worked with difficulty by a good auctioneer, fetched over £8. Young housewives hesitated to buy astounding bargains in fruit, etc. The affair as a whole was a very striking success.

---

[1] E. V. Lucas's *Swollen-Headed William* was published with drawings by G. Morrow.

Tuesday, November 10th.

Alcock came yesterday. He told us a lot about transport work. He said Newhaven port had a huge sealed envelope of orders to be executed on receipt of code telegrams. When the first telegram came, the orders proved to be dated 1911. This was rather good. The orders, as I heard them, seemed excellent.

Telegram that cruiser *Emden* destroyed.[1]

Friday, November 13th.

Last Saturday Miss Nerney began her services at the hospital (Thorpe Hall). She was to work from 7.30 to 3.30 and from 7.30 to 6.30, alternate days. This was adhered to for two days, but afterwards she was kept till 8 each night. She says there is no rest all day. Nevertheless there must be women in the village who could do this work in part. Every other week she has free. As the arrangement of 7.30 to 8.30 every day brought her work for me to a standstill, I gave notice that it would have to be altered.

More wounded came at the beginning of this week, 14 English. There were already over 20 Belgians.

Knowledge of soldiers: a grenadier at Thorpe Hall, wounded, told Alcock on Wednesday that the Germans had a gun with a range of 22 miles!

Monday, November 16th.

Yesterday I received a letter from Maj.-Gen. Heath (commanding South Midland Div.), asking if I would be military representative on Thorpe Division Emergency Committee (for preparations against invasion). I answered I would, but that as I was regularly criticizing the War Office in the press, and might continue to do so, perhaps he would not care to have me. This morning he wired me to meet him at 1.45 at Crown Hotel here. As I was going there two cars full of him and his

---

[1] This German cruiser had done much damage in the East and had kept nearly the whole of Admiral Jerram's fleet in search of her, when she was finally run down by H.M.S. *Sydney* at Cocos Island.

staff passed me. I can't distinguish ranks by uniforms, but most of these men had red round their hats, and I knew that that meant importance. Ryder (landlord) took my card into the room where the officers were. A middle-aged officer came out: "Are you General Heath?" I asked. "Oh, no," he said, rather alarmed.

General Heath then came out, and took me into the room. A man about 55, tallish and thin, with a good grey moustache. He had just begun to smoke a briar. He said at once that my journalism needn't affect the situation at all. He asked me whether I was in favour of civilians sniping at soldiers—"murdering" them. I said emphatically I was not, and that I thought the idea absurd. (Evidently he had read Wells's letter to *The Times* advocating this, and had heard it discussed.) He said he was glad to hear my view, which was his own. Speaking with slight feeling, he said that if he caught any civilian "over there" doing it, he should deal with him. I suppose he meant after the Britons had reached German territory. He then said, laughing, that Sullivan (who was in the room, and on his staff as interpreter!) believed in sniping by civilians. He said one of my duties would be to get intelligence. He introduced me to his representative, Captain Chesney, and thanked me very much, and I said: "Not at all. Not at all. Only too glad," and I departed, after ten minutes.

Later, Bertie Sullivan came here. He said he was doing the same sort of thing at Brightlingsea. He told me of astonishing "coincidences" at B'sea. How on the same day the customs officer's telephone wouldn't work, signalling was thought to be seen from the second martello tower (belonging to a suspicious family) on Beacon Hill, and a man had seen bubbles (indicative of a submarine) in B'sea Reach, and two other coincidences which I forget. Next day the Blackwater was "swept" by the new apparatus for a submarine, also the Colne, but naught found; and in fact there was nothing in the whole thing.

He told me that the Wallet was being closed by a boom. The War Office theory was that if an invasion was attempted it would be within the next fortnight. He said there was absolutely no co-ordination of effort against invasion, and in particular no co-ordination between Navy and Army. Yet almost in same breath he gave me two instances of the Admiralty's informing War Office of certain facts. He said B'sea had between 8 and 9 per cent of its population in the forces. As sergeant of special constables his difficulty was the utter stupidity of people. Men kept writing week after week that B'sea water works ought to be guarded etc. and at last demanded a military guard for it. In the end I think they got it, but I am not sure. Sullivan agreed with me that the chance of an invasion was nil. Also he couldn't see the use of more new armies beyond what we have in training, as we wouldn't arm them etc., etc. He said Kitchener didn't believe in invasion.

Friday, November 20th.

It is said that 40 troop trains went from the South, Cromer-way, to supply troops against a feared invasion last Monday. All I know is that the traffic was considerably upset by troop trains, and newspapers were 3 hours late.

An Emergency Committee meeting for Thorpe Petty Sessional Division called at Colchester for tomorrow, but I received a letter this morning from Capt. Chesney, S.M. Division, to say that it had been found that such divisions were too big and that they would be split up, and would I act as military representative on the Tendring (Thorpe) Police Division. Now I don't know if I am to attend the Colchester meeting tomorrow.

On Wednesday afternoon I went to Burslem to see Mater, reported to be past hope. I saw her at 8 P.M. and remained alone with her for about half an hour. She looked very small, especially her head in the hollow of the pillows. The outlines of her face very sharp; hectic cheeks; breathed with her mouth open, and much rumour of breath in her body; her nose was more hooked, had in fact become hooked. Scanty hair. She had a very weak, self-pitying voice, but with sudden outbursts of strong voice, imperative, and flinging out of arms. She still had a great deal of strength. She forgot most times in the middle of a sentence, and it took her a long time to recall.

She was very glad to see me and held my hand all the time under bedclothes. She spoke of the most trifling things as if tremendously important—as e.g. decisions as if they were momentous and dictated by profound sagacity. She was seldom fully conscious, and often dozed and woke up with a start. "What do you say?" rather loud. She had no pain, but often muttered in anguish: "What am I to do? What am I to do?" Amid tossed bedclothes you could see numbers on corners of blankets. On medicine table siphon, saucer, spoon, large soap-dish, brass flower-bowl (empty). The gas (very bad burner) screened by a contraption of Family Bible, some wooden thing, and a newspaper. It wasn't level. She had it altered. She said it annoyed her terribly. Gas stove burning. Temperature barely 60°. Damp chill, penetrating my legs. The clock had a very light, delicate striking sound. Trams and buses did not disturb her, though sometimes they made talking difficult.

Round-topped panels of wardrobe. She wanted to be satisfied that her purse was on a particular tray of the wardrobe. The Mater has arterial sclerosis and patchy congestion of the lungs. Her condition was very distressing (though less so than the Pater's), and it seemed strange that this should necessarily be the end of a life, that a life couldn't always end more easily. I went in again at 11.45 P.M. She was asleep, breathing noisily. Nurse, in black, installed for night. The Mater had a frequent very bright smile, but it would go in an instant. She asked for her false teeth, and she wanted her ears syringed again, so that she could hear better. This morning she was easier, after a good night, but certainly weaker. Mouth closed and eyes shut tight today. Lifting of chin right up to get head in line with body for breathing. A bad sign.

Monday, November 23rd.

Sisters Campion dined here Saturday. They explained that there were only 60 soldiers at Frinton and that they had a tremendous lot done for them in the way of entertainment and comforts. They said, however, that after quitting the social club at night—cocoa etc.—the men could go to their canteen and get drunk, and did so. These sisters run a Badminton Club, a choral society, the Women's Liberal Association branch, and other things, yet play a round of golf every day. Wesleyans. Father a great Wesleyan. Orphans, with a trustee; live in a little house with one servant, are very active, and seem to have a jolly fine time. Almost laid up with a liver attack this week-end.

Tuesday, November 24th.

The Mater died, unconscious, yesterday at noon. The telegram awaited us when we came back from tea at Mrs. Tollinton's at Tendring yesterday. Cold upstairs room, with bedroom grate—a bedroom used as a secondary drawing-room. Three great windows. I got near the morsel of fire. Mrs. Tollinton *mère* a widow with cap. The wife's sister in black, with a nervous habit of shrugging her shoulders as if in amiable protest or agreement with a protest or a humorous comment.

Friday, November 27th.

M. and I went down to Burslem for the Mater's funeral on Tuesday afternoon.

The Mater died about 1 P.M. on Monday.

I learnt from Jennings that the "last journey" had to be "the longest," i.e. corpse must always go longest way to cemetery. I asked why. He sniggered, "So as to prolong the agony, I suppose." Real reason nowadays and for long past must be ostentation. We naturally altered this.

Walk downtown. Some bricks dry before others. Prominent yellow painted stone-facings of Macintyre's. Abolition of most crossings in Waterloo Road, to disgust of residents. I saw new Coliseum Theatre. New window in Mr. Povey's side-room at top of Church St. Church St. was cleaner and better kept.

Funeral. Too soon. Orange light through blinds in front of room. Coffin in centre on 2 chairs. Covered with flowers. Bad reading, and stumbling of parson. Clichés and halting prayer. Small thin book out of which parson read. In dim light, cheap new carving on oak of coffin seemed like fine oak carving. Sham brass handles on coffin. Horrible lettering. Had to wait after service for hearse to arrive. Men hung their hats on spikes of hearse before coming in. No trouble in carrying coffin. I kept Uncle J.L.'s arm most of the time, as he is nearly blind. He told me he still managed 700 accounts. Long walk from cemetery gates to region of chapel. By the way, the lodge at gates is rented as an ordinary house to a schoolmaster. John Ford's vault next to Longson, with records of his young wives ("The flower fadeth," etc.). This could be exaggerated into a fine story. No sign of any other coffins, of course, in Longson vault.

Curious jacket and apron of first gravedigger. Second stood apart. Both with hats off. Parson put on a skull-cap. On return, carriages trotted down slope from cemetery, but walked as we got to houses near Cobridge station. "Nest Egg Factory" en route. 2 cottages turned into works.

Saturday, November 28th.

I met Colonel Tabor (of Cyclists) in the road yesterday. He said that the War Office was apparently taking quite seriously the danger of a raid. He said that many officers were now having a few days' leave and that one had breakfasted in the trenches and dined in his club in London.

The Colchester road is being mined just east of the point where the Tendring road branches off. Four or six soldiers digging holes on either side of the road (4 in all), about 4 feet cube. The bridge next to the railway station is also being mined. Twelve engineers in the village, and more to come. B. told us that an officer on Submarine E9, which sank the *Hela,* had told him that E9 only rose to surface by chance, because some one wanted to excrete, and W.C. can only be used when at surface.

Commander refused at first; told man to wait ½ hour. Man couldn't. Boat therefore rose. *Hela* was seen and torpedoed. Such was the tale. It seemed to me odd that defecation on board a submarine could only take place when she was at surface.

Tuesday, December 1st.

On Saturday ended the run of the first revival of *Milestones*. For nearly three years I had had a performance, and frequently two, every night without intermission in the West End of London.

Two officers of the North Devon Hussars came for tea on Sunday, Money-Coutts and Solomon. Both very intelligent. The first writes. The second paints; I showed him all my pictures. They told us of a subaltern of engineers who had charge of a squad of sappers at work mining in the village and that he was billeted in a cottage here and very lonely. I went with them to find him; Michaelis, Australian, and obviously a Jew. Very intelligent and with a sense of humour. He came to dinner on Sunday, and today he installed himself here entirely. He is of the 2nd Field Company (Territorials). Aged only 18. A boy. Yet he is in command here.

Friday, December 4th.

Patriotic concert last night in village schoolroom. Full. All the toffs of the village were there. Rev. Mathews and family dined with us before it. Most of the programme was given by soldiers, except one pro. It was far more amusing than one could have expected. Corporal Snell, with a really superb bass voice, sang two very patriotic, sentimental songs, sound in sentiment but extremely bad in expression. They would have been excruciating in an ordinary voice but he was thrilling in them. Our Lieutenant Michaelis was there, after mining the roads, together with a number of his men. The great joke which appealed to parsons and every one was of a fat lady sitting on a man's hat in a bus. "Madam, do you know what you're sitting on?" "I ought to. I've been sitting on it for 54 years."

This morning, with an endorsement by G.B.S. himself, I received a suggestion from Mark Judge [1] that I should edit Shaw's manifesto for volume publication.

Gales blowing for days.

Sunday, December 6th.

Major Danielsen asked me on Tuesday to write to the press about behaviour of civilians in case of a raid. I did so, and sent the letter to, *inter alia, The Times,* where it made a great effect. Major-General Heath, G.O.C. South Midland Division, wrote me on Friday, saying that he agreed with every word of the letter, but that I ought not to have written it in my capacity of military representative or to have mentioned him as

---

[1] The Chairman of the Committee on War Damage. He published *The War and the Neutral Powers—International Law* in 1914.

my authority. This is very characteristic of the official fear of responsibility. The military are really *very* anxious for their views to prevail, but they don't want anybody to know!

Meeting yesterday of Emergency Committee at Colchester. Representative of police there—an awful, beefy, decent piece of stupidity. I paid for maps for parish councils. Badges for special constables simply cannot be got.

Returning to Emergency Committee, we haven't yet been able to get out of headquarters what roads they will want if there is a raid nor to settle with police what the signal is to be.

I am now fairly *in* the last part of the third *Clayhanger*.

Wednesday, December 9th.

Sub-committee meeting yesterday with H. Sullivan here as to signalling order to evacuate. I found he knew more about handling populace than any one I had yet met. He said, "I ought to have been chairman of the committee." He was right.

Today I communicate with banks as to what they will do.

Saturday, December 12th.

I heard of some documented account of work in trenches, so awful that it could not be printed. Maj.-General Heath, however, said he should send it to some people. Colonel Phipps, who had just left a man who had just arrived from the front, said that in some places trenches of English and Germans were only 5 and 7 yards apart. Heath told me he had got into a row with 3rd Army about my letter to *The Times*. But it was now all "purged." To make conversation, or perhaps because he thought it was the proper friendly thing to do, he began talking about books—*The Crock of Gold*, etc. He had no use *at all* for Wells. I caught 5.41 home. Very wet.

Tuesday, December 15th.

London yesterday. Visit to L. G. Brock, secy. of National Relief Fund, at 3 Queen Anne's Gate. Formerly house of Sir E. Grey.

I then went to inspect establishment of Women's Emergency Corps at Old Bedford College, Baker St. Miss Ashwell in charge. Vast effect of femininity. A general exhilarating effect. The young women badged as messengers, standing in two lines in outer entrance hall, earnest, eager, braced, made a specially characteristic feminine effect. One stopped me at once as I entered and asked me if she could do anything for me and then if I was A.B. I returned by 5.30 train.

Wednesday, December 16th.

Concert in aid of National Fund by Frinton Choral Society last night at Frinton Exhibition Hall. Very bad music, especially the ballads—all appallingly dull. A madrigal by Beale, fine, badly sung. Also in a pot-pourri of national airs, the air *The Minstrel Boy* seemed a masterpiece. It is. Orchestral suite rotten. Two apparently professional female singers sang with some skill the most putrid things; their gestures and facial movements comic, but of course they are too close to the audience in these small halls. The ordeal is too much. Audience asked for a lot of encores, especially of the worst things, that were freely given. The only fun in these affairs is comic remarks to your friends and the examination of all these ingenuous English faces that are nevertheless so difficult to decipher. I imagine all the people in their homes, in natural poses. A few tolerably dressed women in the audience. But for the most part a fright-fully inartistic audience, showing their lack of taste in everything except their reserved demeanour.

Saturday, December 19th.

Major Danielsen and Lieut. Goodhart called on me this afternoon. Danielsen told me that their intelligence department was extraordinarily good and that they had news of the visit of German ships this week at 5 o'clock on the evening before they arrived. I did not, however, under-stand why sufficient big English ships could not arrive in time to deal with them.

From Thursday in last week to last Thursday I did nothing on my novel. I was fairly free to go on with it on Wednesday, but I had neuralgia. I wrote 2500 words of it yesterday.

Monday, December 21st.

Gen. Heath, Col. Ryley and a sub called to see me yesterday morning. Heath, still greatly preoccupied with the question of civilian behaviour in an invasion, showed me a proclamation which he was having printed about sniping etc. He also showed me a draft proclamation to coastal population about bombardment. It was clumsy. I offered, with proper diffidence, to re-draft it. He consented. The others seemed slightly staggered. I posted him the new draft last night.

Two naval officers, Lieut. Hogg and Assistant Paymaster Simmons, on motor bikes for tea. Hogg told me tale of a soldier (cavalry) wounded in a charge, who lay on field with the spear of a lance sticking in him. Another English soldier came along and was asked to remove spear. Just as he started to do so he was shot through the brain. Then a group of Germans came along and began to loot. Without troubling as to the spear, they took the wrist-watch off the cavalryman's wrist, but just then a shell burst among them, killing or disabling all of them, but leaving the cavalryman untouched. He was ultimately saved.

Tuesday, December 22nd.

Major Danielsen came over again to see me yesterday afternoon, with a letter from G.O.C. saying that my amended form of his proclamation about bombardment was much better than his. They have accepted our suggestions for dispensing with the police as a means of transmitting the emergency order. This must have been a great step for Heath to take. Danielsen gave me the secret word with which any emergency order will begin.

Today I heard firing at sea which seemed to be like a battle and not like firing-practice. The first time I have had this impression since the war began, though we have heard firing scores of times.

This is the most gruesome item I have seen in any newspaper. It is from an account of life in Brussels in *Daily Telegraph*, December 15th:

"Since the fatal attacks on Ypres and the Yser a new recreation has been created for the Bruxellois, namely the trains of the dead. These pass through the suburb of Laeken, and go by way of Louvain and Liège to Germany, to be burnt in the blast furnaces. The dead are stripped, tied together like bunches of asparagus, and stacked upright on their feet, sometimes bound together with cords, but for the most part with iron wire. Two to three thousand pass with each train, sometimes in closed meat-trucks, sometimes in open trucks, just as it happens. The mighty organization will not suffer a truck to go back empty; a dead man has no further interest for them."

Referring to the firing, Brig.-General Hoare called on me yesterday afternoon, and, after doing business, asked me if I had heard the rumour that Yarmouth had been bombarded. He had heard the rumour and (characteristically) had started out to trace it and curse the originator. He traced it to the stationmaster at Thorpe, who said he had had it from a Clacton journalist who passed through in the train. Apparently it was quite untrue.

I forgot to say earlier that Maj.-Gen. Heath told me he thought of having a proclamation printed in German for the benefit of invading Germans, warning them that if they did certain things certain punishments would without fail ultimately follow. Rather good.

Wednesday, December 30th.

Great storm on Monday night. We lost 5 trees. A large elm blew across the road, broke telegraph wires, and broke through the vicarage fence, and blocked the road all night. While I was out at 10.30 P.M. inspecting I heard another tree crashing and fled. Old oak fell into the pond.

Thursday, December 31st.

Mr. F., maltster, with £200,000 worth of buildings and stock at Mistley, called with the secretary of his company as to order for destruction of the whole thing in case of emergency. He, of course, wanted a proper guarantee of compensation. His best argument, however, was that a fire would block both the railway and the highroad to Harwich. Speaking of military measures, he told me he had been to the Home Office and that there had actually been drawn up an order to prevent certain things' being imported in this part of the world, lest advantage might accrue to invading enemy. The order was never promulgated.

1915

Thursday, January 7th.

Dr. H. called this afternoon in a great state of excitement: "I've called about a most unpleasant thing. But I thought I ought to tell you," etc. His news was that the village was seething with the news that R. was a pro-German, and taking advantage of his position as chauffeur to the military representative to transmit secret information as to English plans through his sweetheart, a German girl, to the German authorities. H. believed it, or half believed it.

Friday, January 8th.

I wrote to the police inspector last night and he called to see me today. He said he was constantly having complaints about signalling etc., all absurd. I told him that R. was engaged to an English girl and that the whole thing was idiotic. He said he had received a letter about it (signed) and had to make a few inquiries, but expected, of course, no result. A very decent sort.

Tuesday, January 12th.

Captain Bath and Lieut. Way of Ammunition Column of W. Somersets billeted here yesterday. 40 horses in Daking's yard. Bath told me a tale of a party of German officers who spent some time in his town, Glastonbury—I think last year—with a fleet of cars in which they went out every night. They had a field and pretended to be perfecting a process for getting petrol from peat. They showed some petrol stated to be so obtained. Then they departed suddenly and mysteriously. I asked: Why all this? He said it was to reconnoitre the country. I asked why they should reconnoitre the country at night when they were free to do it in the daytime, but he had no answer. Anyhow, he was fully persuaded that it was a great case of "intelligence."

Danielsen came to see me yesterday as to the case of the postmaster at X., an alleged spy. The contents of a military telegram of no importance had been divulged. I knew that this had happened to civil telegrams up there in the past. I sent for the postmaster here and questioned him, but fruitlessly. Speaking yesterday of the difficulty of dealing with spies, Maj. Danielsen said: "It's this damned vote-catching government. They're out to get the vote of the alien." He is a quite honest man and seemed to believe this. That the spy business was the exclusive affair of the War Office and that he was arraigning the beloved K. of K.[1] did not seem to occur to him.

Saturday, January 16th.

London, to see work of Queen's Fund. I took Mary and Richard to London, and Tertia[2] met us at L'pool St. Train late. I have never known the 10.07 not late. Lunch at Mrs. McKenna's.[3] Largish house in Smith Sq., designed by Lutyens. Very bare and lacking in furniture. But there was some good furniture. Present: Masterman, full of good humour; Brock, secretary of National Relief Fund; and Mary MacArthur,[4] stoutish matron, with a marked Scotch accent. I met her on doorstep and introduced myself. I liked her. Mrs. MacArthur had prepared a timed programme of our pilgrimage, with times in it for leaving, like 2.48. We kept to it fairly well.

Sunday, January 24th.

In pursuance of rumour that 30,000 Germans were to land at once,

---

[1] Kitchener of Khartum.
[2] Tertia was Arnold Bennett's sister, and Richard and Mary were his nephew and niece.
[3] Rt. Hon. Reginald McKenna was Chancellor of the Exchequer in 1915.
[4] Mary MacArthur was also secretary of the Women's Trade Union League and of the National Federation of Women Workers.

S—— of Tendring made all his household sleep in clothes on ground floor.

Monday, February 1st.

Meeting of T.E. committee at Colchester on Saturday.

Richmond came on Saturday for week-end to give me all particulars of slacking by members of the Amalg. Soc. of Engineers in war contracts. His firm is making shells, mines, and submarine engines. He said there was not a great deal of money in it, and that the contracts supervision dept. of War Office was saving enormous sums.

Richmond told me that a submarine had attacked Barrow. This must have been the same vessel that sank several steamers in the Irish Sea on Saturday. But nothing as to the attack has appeared in the papers.

Went down to see trenches made by Michaelis's men today.

Thursday, February 4th.

A wealthy maltster called to tell me all he knew about spies and suspects at Mistley. He said there was nothing of the sort, and all he could speak of was one or two people afflicted with "cussedness"—people who *would* argue that the English were no good and that the Germans must win, etc. He saw this cussedness in various forms all over the country. I agreed. But he said that it was all due to the abolition of flogging. He brought ingenious old arguments in support of flogging. The chief was that if you fined or imprisoned a man you punished his wife and children; whereas if you flogged him you punished *him,* and the thing was over at once. He got quite excited on this subject and could scarcely leave. A quiet, nervous man—public school etc.

Saturday, February 6th.

Yesterday Brig.-Gen. Hoare (called the Brig) came to inspect ammunition column's horses. He asked W. full details of every horse. W. only knew about 20. He invented the rest. He says you must never say "I don't know" in the Army. Hoare asked him if horses were getting chaff. He said they were (it was true). When asked how, he was floored and ultimately said he bought the chaff himself. A lie! "I must speak to you about that later." Later Hoare took him on one side and said: "It's very kind of you to pay for that chaff out of your own pocket. Don't do it in future. The proper thing to do is to exchange spare horse-rations with farmers for chaff."

Saturday, March 6th.

I finished *These Twain* yesterday. Doran came for week-end.

Monday, February 22nd.

Friday, Saturday, and Sunday I corrected *These Twain* and cut it from 128,000 to 100,000 words.

Saturday, March 6th.

Marguerite went to London on Monday, and I (in the car, and taking Michaelis) went Tuesday. Michaelis had to go to Braintree for an "explosives course," and *un nommé* Rogers came here to take his place. Miss Weeley as usual came to stay in the house during our absence.

Committee meeting of Allies Wounded as usual on Tuesday afternoon. Before that, lunch with Eve at R. Thames Yacht Club. Good club, with good bedrooms to be had. Met there an infernal bore, red-faced, middle-aged man, owner of a fair-sized and smart cutter at Brightlingsea. He said a vast number of silly things. "When I trust a person, and that person breaks his faith—especially if he belongs to the working classes—then I'm death on him. Now the son of my steward—my steward that I had for 25 years and who venerated me; he kissed my hand when I went to see him when he was ill in bed etc.—now the son of that steward," etc., etc.

Dinner with Atkinses as guests, at Treviglio's. Then to Coliseum, but there wasn't a seat. Then to Alhambra, which was almost empty. A ghastly show. Wet night. Wednesday, National Gallery. Rickards. He and M. lunched at Appenrodt's. I lunched alone. Afternoon, tea at Cedric's. Betty and M. went to theatre together. I dined alone at Reform, and listened to some amazingly dull talk by 3 old jossers at table next to mine. Cedric came to see me there. Thursday, I had Masterman, L. G. Brock, and Lanchester to lunch, and the last explained admirably his scheme for finding work for prof. classes by making surveys of towns. Afterwards when Masterman and I were alone, I expressed to him my notion of the way he had been treated, and he seemed rather touched. He told me that Kitchener was no great shakes. Obstinate, not open to new ideas; no great brain power. But he had the quality of acknowledging that he was wrong, after an interval. Tea at Rickards's. M. and I dined at C. P. Trevelyan's.[1] F. W. Hirst, editor of *Economist;* Noel Buxton, with a new and beautiful wife. Norman Angell[2] later. In the end I should like Trevelyan. My *D. News* article was really appreciated. Norman Angell was markedly affected by the war. When I said that worrying was useless, he became even graver and said, "It's very serious, very serious." He is a good man.

Nothing much Friday morning, except drilling and physical exercising of troops in Hyde Park. Very varied. Echoing of commands over Kensington Water and so on. Drove home in the afternoon.

Saturday, March 13th.

Went to London Tuesday morning. Pinker called at the hotel after lunch. Harmsworths[3] starting a new weekly (he didn't know what—afterwards disclosed as the *Sunday Pictorial*) and they wanted some star contributions—1500 words. They came to him for advice and help. Their idea was Corelli and Haggard! He suggested me at £100 and said I was the greatest and most expensive star. They at once accepted. I wrote the article on Wednesday and it was advertised on Thursday. Pinker offered H. G. Wells, but when approached, Wells said he had already written on the subject suggested, and moreover he was very busy with his novel. In the end the *Sunday Pictorial's* star trio was me, Horatio Bottomley, and Austin Harrison!

---

[1] Charles Philips Trevelyan resigned from the Government in protest at the policies that involved England in the War. He was the eldest son of Sir George Trevelyan, the biographer of Garibaldi.

[2] The present editor of *Foreign Affairs* was knighted in 1931. His most widely read book is *The Great Illusion.*

[3] The family name of Lords Northcliffe and Rothermere.

Lunch every day at hotel. Wednesday night, Bach's *Passion* at St. James's Church. Much material in this assemblage. Performance mediocre, with vast cuts. We dined at A.B.C. restaurant for 1*s*. 9*d*. the two, because I had written a £100 article that day. Thursday, Pauline came to lunch. Night: *The Man Who Stayed at Home* at Royalty. Very mediocre. Very well acted. Returned home yesterday.

Sunday, March 21st.

We went to London on Tuesday. Auction sale of pictures etc. on behalf of Wounded Allies' Relief Committee at Hotel Victoria in the afternoon. Spent over £12. Evening, M. went to Kennerleys.[1] Sydney Harrison came to talk at Reform Club after dinner. Very polite and amiable, but a perfect infant in literature. Wednesday, the Morrells to lunch. Evening, *The Man Who Stayed at Home,* with Emily at Royalty. Thursday, Hirst and Lowndes lunched with me at Reform. Afterwards, I had a long talk with Clutton-Brock—a first-class man. Dinner at Websters'. Tremendous Englishness of their house. Came home Friday afternoon. I wrote half an article at Reform Club Library. Knoblock came on Saturday for week-end. On Saturday a new cook arrived, drunk.

Tuesday, March 23rd.

We brought Knoblock to town yesterday morning in the car. Previously I had got rid of temporary cook, a drunkard. Lunch at Reform, where I met G. W. S. Russell and Clutton-Brock. I stayed in all afternoon reading Hueffer's *When Blood Is Their Argument,* which is not good. Dined in grill-room. Then to *première* of Barrie's *Rosy Rapture.* Met Vedrenne, Algar Thorold,[2] Spencer, and Charlton, editor of *Sunday Pictorial,* who said he was, and really seemed to be, very pleased with my article last week. He said that circulation of their second number was a million and a half. *Lever de rideau, The New Word,* quite good in a small way.

---

[1] W. W. Kennerley (brother of Mitchell Kennerley of New York) was born in Burslem and was an intimate of the Bennetts from childhood. He married Bennett's sister Tertia, and is the "W.W.K." to whom *The Old Wives' Tale* is dedicated.
[2] He was then on the editorial staff of *The Truth,* and the author of a few biographies. In 1917 he joined the Foreign Office and served in Italy on a Mission of Propaganda.

Rosy Rapture good here and there, but on the whole very tedious, and mostly conventional. Tons of flowers for Gaby Deslys at the end. On entering I was greeted by cries of my name in the pit. I think this never before happened to me. Much difficulty in getting car at the end of the show. Wet night.

Wednesday, March 24th.

Mair [1] and Sullivan came to lunch. As usual, Mair was full of authentic information on things. Meeting of W.A.R.C., 4–5. Then I went to see Sharp and Squire [2] at *New Statesman* office. Rumours as to its imminent death untrue. They asked me to qualify as a director. I said I would.

Webster dined with me at the Reform.

Thursday, March 25th.

Lunch at Knoblock's. A Marquis de Rosalis, Italian, speaking French and English fairly well, and emitting platitudes on the situation throughout.

Mrs. Lowndes gave dinner at Sesame Club. Mrs. Reg. McKenna, Lockwood (an American Rhodes scholar), us, and Sir George Riddell, who came very late. He said the Press Bureau had sent out a notice to newspapers, asking them to stop being optimistic. On the top of this came the interview (Havas Agency) with Sir J. French, predicting a short war.

Friday, March 26th.

E. V. Lucas and wife to lunch. We went to picture show, "London Group" at Goupil. Cubists idiotic. Some nice things, but all imitative. Dinner at Morrells': Lowes Dickinson, Bertrand Russell, Whitehouse.[3] All these very much upset by the war, convinced that the war and government both wrong etc. Afterwards, an immense reunion of art students,

---

[1] G. H. Mair, formerly on the editorial staff of the *Manchester Guardian,* and later of the *Daily Chronicle,* had resigned from the latter position to work for the Foreign Office. He was appointed to the League of Nations Secretariat in 1919.

[2] Clifford Sharp, editor of the *New Statesman* since its foundation in 1913. J. C. Squire, the present editor of *The London Mercury,* was then a leading contributor.

[3] Lady Ottoline Morrell's house was at this time the centre of a group that included D. H. Lawrence as well as Bertrand Russell and which looked upon the War as a moral crime.

painters, and queer people. Girls in fancy male costume, queer dancing, etc. A Japanese dancer. We left at 12.15. Pianola. Fine pictures. Glorious drawings by Picasso. Excellent impression of host and hostess.

Saturday, March 27th.

Lunch with Clutton-Brock at Reform. Natl. Portrait Society in morning and Natl. Gallery in the afternoon. Dinner with G. H. Mair at Carlton. He is in the secret service, and told us a lot of really interesting things about the war—wireless, submarines, press campaigns in Europe, British spies, etc., etc. He was quite as optimistic as I am.

Sunday, March 28th.

Rickards dined with me at Reform. Then music—Mina Parkes—at his place. F.L. came in, fat, intellectual, and inartistic, and began explaining how Brahms ought to be sung, and rather mucked up the show. I played accompaniments. This morning, R. and Miss Parkes and I were at Westminster Cathedral at 9.45 for the blessing of palms by Cardinal Archbp., and High mass, with an old St. Matthew Passion sung. All this cathedral scene ought to be described in detail. We met Webster. Then to St. Paul's Cathedral, which seemed very English and narrow. I had not been inside St. Paul's for about 20 years. It seemed small, very Italian, and splendid.

Wednesday, March 31st.

I dined with Knoblock at the Garrick and then to Nat. Sporting Club. Digger Stanley *v.* Berry Barnards. Eagerness of seconds. Four seconds for the swell boxers. I met James Pryde and Arthur Morrison, the latter small and shrewd.

Yesterday Swinnerton, with a new brown beard, lunched with me at Reform.

At 6.45 I was at St. Paul's Cathedral to meet Webster for Bach *St. Matthew Passion.* The scene from the stall was superb, with the aged white-haired figure of the conductor (surpliced) at the west end of the choir. Choir boys seated on benches in corners to help in singing.

Thursday, April 1st.

I returned home yesterday afternoon. Lunched with Pinker at the Arts Club and discussed project of me going to the front.

Superb weather.

Good Friday, April 2nd.

Having cleared up all my correspondence and found room for all accumulations of new books, I decided yesterday to get ideas into order and begin my new novel, *The Lion's Share*, today. I was rather disturbed by the prospect of going to the front with G. H. Mair.

Saturday, April 10th.

I finished the first instalment of *The Lion's Share*, 12,500 words, today, having begun it on Good Friday and written an article as well.

The novel is light and of intent not deeply imagined, but it seems to me to be fairly good and interesting.

Thursday, April 15th.

The Ammunition Col. of the Somerset Battery (Capt. Bath and Lieut. Way, officers) left here this morning to go into huts with the Battery at Great Bentley. Last night we went to Marguerite's Soldiers' Club, but very little was going on there, except a gramophone actuated by a young woman who sat between two soldiers. It seemed that many of the soldiers had asked for passes to go out to supper. There must have been many farewells. The woman in charge of the refreshments had the same monotonous faint smile that she always has. Her husband is at the front.

We went and came in the car and met officers with a lamp on their rounds. I walked round by the sea wall, and as I came home old Carter told me that there was a deserter from the Battery and that 8 or 10 cyclists were out after him. He was a young man who hated being in the Army. Still, being a Territorial, he chose it early.

Saturday, April 17th.

Frank Swinnerton came last night. He and I dined together while

Marguerite and Edith Johnston went to dine with Hope at the Grand Hotel, Clacton. Swinnerton told me that all the publishers were in an appalling funk at the beginning of the war, and that H—— sacked half his men and reduced the other half to half salaries. The ghastly vileness of this proceeding ought to be dwelt on. It must have been very common. He said publishers were doing well, and that his firm, Chatto & Windus, were calmly proceeding with their autumn list. Collins's edition of Keats was selling jolly well.

Report in *Chronicle* yesterday that a Zeppelin had dropped bombs on Clacton, on its way to Harwich, in the middle of previous night. Untrue. Miss Nerney, however, coming home from some kick-up at 12.45 A.M., said that she and her friends heard the airship and that it was very loud indeed. They could not see it. I was asleep.

Monday, April 19th.

Owing to alleged existence of a German spy in British officer's clothing and in a car, in this district, order that no officer shall be out at night in a car unless on duty and with the password of the day. Personally, I don't see what good this will do. Highly inconvenient for officers. One officer coming through Chelmsford got stopped on his way to this district. He did not know of order and had no password. He telephoned for help. A dispatch cyclist was sent from Great Bentley to give him the password. This cyclist, although on General Hoare's orders, was not allowed to go through Colchester, and in the end the officer had to get home by train.

Rickards and Pinker came on Saturday. Yesterday, R., P., Swinnerton, and I went for a walk to Laudermere and had drinks at the pub. Pinker told me he had arranged to sell my "front" articles (if I go) to the *New York Times* for £100 each, for America. He also told me that Hy. James had intimately conversed with two men sent on missions by Wilson through Germany. One, unofficial (the "King of Texas," great friend of Wilson's),[1] to ascertain state of Germany (? and Austria); the other, official, to try to arrange something as to complex social relations (Ger-

---

[1] Colonel Edward M. House.

mans with American wives etc.). These two men only met at the end of their work, and in London. They agreed in their observations.

1. German Government had no hope whatever of a victory.

2. German Government was in a "state of *terror*" as to the British Navy, feeling themselves like men in a room from which the air was being slowly withdrawn.

3. Food question likely to be very troublesome before harvest.

4. No first-class leader in Germany.

Wednesday, April 28th.

I finished the 3rd instalment of *The Lion's Share* on Sunday, wrote an article on Monday, and went to London yesterday for Wounded Allies' Committee meeting, at which I was in the chair.

After lunch I had a talk with Spender, who told me that Italy had "signed on" definitely in the Quadruple Alliance. He gave the war another 18 months. I asked him if he kept a diary. He said no. He said that at the beginning of his intimate friendship with Rosebery, Rosebery asked him if he kept a diary. "I'm glad," said Rosebery when he had the answer; "now I can be free with you."

Saturday, May 8th.

Lusitania sunk at 2.30 near Cork Harbour. It was on the posters at 5.45. At first I did not believe it. It made almost no impression on me. Then I went back to buy a paper.

Pinker told me some good new small things about the conduct of the war. He gets most of his information through Henry James.

Wednesday, May 12th.

We came to London yesterday, bringing Pauline Smith.[1]

Shopping all afternoon with Marguerite. Two dresses bought at Selfridge's by Marguerite. Crowds of women in Oxford Street and Regent Street just as usual, and shops just as usual.

The *chic* of the women in Piccadilly collecting for Russian wounded

---

[1] Bennett had written a preface for her novel, *The Little Karoo*.

was quite remarkable, and the total improvement of Englishwomen in this respect in recent years is astounding.

Festival of British music at Queen's Hall last night, alone.

I met Ernest Newman, who was very canny and very himself.

Thursday, May 13th.

Lunch yesterday with Wells and Gardiner at Automobile Club. Wells said he knew that French (Sir J.) believed the war would be over in June. Afterwards with H.G. to Royal Academy. I had no use for Sargents, Orpens, or Clausens. A fairish crowd there. Then to tea with him at Carlyle Club. First time I had been in this club. Furnished in a horrible manner. The tea, however, was good.

Then to meeting of executive committee of Wounded Allies at Sardinia House. It lasted from 5 to 7.35, and Lord Swaythling kept relighting *one* cigar the whole time.

Dined with M. at hotel. Then to reception at Charles Trevelyan's to meet the managing committee of the Union of Democratic Control. But the only member that I found there was Arthur Ponsonby; a pale, light, large-foreheaded man. Seemed surprised when I said that Germans would be beaten and that Government would stand. All these chaps have twisted ideas.

Monday, May 17th.

Saturday, I re-wrote the London-to-Paris chapter of *The Lion's Share*. I added an amusing incident, but did not treat it very marvellously.

I saw coming up Whitehall the Cadet Corps, with many shrill bands, a long snake curving through the Mall into the gardens of Buckingham Palace, where they were to be received by the King. Nearly all were in uniform, and all had rifles. They marched excellently, putting all their brain into marching and marking time. Command from time to time to change shoulders with rifle. Also *left*—right, *left*—right. Also lowering of big drum by white-leather-aproned drummer, sometimes with aid of a companion, to his side after end of a *morceau*.

May and Emily came to dinner. Then Coliseum, which was excessively dull. But we had a good box for 10s. 6d., and the sight of the immense crammed house was very good. Everything in this place is so damned ugly. Genée danced old-fashionedly well, amid rotten scenery. Great difficulty in getting taxis nowadays at night. On three evenings (1) we took motor bus, (2) we took four-wheeler, (3) we took motor bus.

Yesterday I wrote my *Daily News* article, *The Pogrom*, at the Reform Club, lunched there, and slept there afterwards. Very agreeable.

Tuesday, May 18th.

Sir George Riddell sent a man and a car to conduct me to St. Dunstan's, Regent's Park, where Arthur Pearson has established a home for blinded soldiers. Very large place; belongs to an American financier named Kahn. 15-acre garden etc.

Pearson very natty, and a constant and rapid talker. Practically *quite* blind. He may have vague sensations of dark and light. His wife came. He kissed her hand when she left. I liked her. Two blind officers, a secretary of Blind Institute, Pearson's secretary, the matron, a wounded soldier, and the Bishop of London for lunch. The last is certainly clever—for the *mot* particularly. He is, perhaps excusably, deeply impressed by the fact that he is Bishop of London, but he turns it off always into a joke. Thus: "When I get into a car it always breaks down. People say the Bishop of London is a Jonah," etc. "A strange thing for the Bishop of London." Small, thin, sharp face, with small trembling eyes. Ordinary Tory ideas. He told us that every general had told him to impress upon the country that the Army was very short of ammunition, and one general told him he was only allowed 2 rounds a day! He spoke agreeably, with simple wellworn forms of jokes, to the men after lunch about his experiences at the front.

Wednesday, May 19th.

Wells, Archer, and Sep[1] lunched with me at the Reform. Archer, Wells, and I arranged a scheme for an organized protest against yellow pressism concerning aliens etc.

---

[1] Arnold Bennett's youngest brother.

Friday, May 21st.

Yesterday I lunched and dined at the McKennas' and learnt a lot about the crisis. Runciman fine. McKenna and Asquith and others extremely hurt and pained by the crisis. Kitchener not very good. Crisis made by Repington's article in *The Times*. Churchill with French at same time as Repington. Rep's article "arranged." Excellent War Office defence against charge of lack of shells; namely that French, knowing circumstances, demanded a certain quantity, and that this quantity was not only supplied but doubled. Fault therefore with leaders at front. French not now liked by Army, who want Robertson. Battle of Aubervilliers of Saturday, 8th, bloodiest of war. Not a defeat, because men could not be shifted, but we lost 28,000 men. Operation undertaken against advice of other generals.

In evening, after dinner, Hobhouse, Postmaster-General, came in to learn from McKenna his fate, who, however, couldn't tell him. As I had been attacking Hobhouse fiercely in *Daily News*, McKenna saw him alone in the drawing-room. I just caught a glimpse of him.

Saturday, May 29th.

London yesterday for the day. New English Art Club. Very interesting water-colours of Steer etc.

Lunch with Mair at Garrick Club. Mair said that *Princess Irene* blew up with 300 mines on board. He said that whereas Fisher went to bed at 10 and rose at 5, Churchill stayed up later and would come to Admiralty after dinner and alter disposition of ships while Fisher was asleep. Churchill sent in a telegram to be approved by Fisher; Fisher declined to approve it. On the intermediary's suggesting that instead of sending a blank refusal he should draft a new telegram, he did so.

Mair said that Simon was going to be much more strict with the censorship and that it was intended to prosecute *The Times*. He also said that Fisher, on being appointed, ordered 300 craft of various sorts. One firm alone made 24 light cruisers. There are special craft for going up the Danube and special monitors for running over mine fields to attack Cuxhaven.

Thursday, June 3rd.

Dance last night in aid of blinded soldiers and sailors. About 40 people paid, and something over 30 came. Receipts about £11. Curious method of sitting out. Couples went to sit out in the motor cars waiting in the stable yard. Coldish night. The earnest air of young couples, especially the girls, and the short-statured girls sitting about in my study, my bedroom, and M.'s rooms, also on the top stairs, was just as comic to me as ever it was. It is the small girls who seem to take the dalliance so seriously. I danced with six women—a record.

Monday, June 7th.

Now that Zeppelin fatalities are no longer fully reported in the papers, it may be noted (from Miss Nerney's brother, who is in an anti-aircraft train and knows) that eighty houses were destroyed at Sittingbourne the other day and not one life lost.

Official telegram today that 5 killed and 40 injured in raid on east coast last night.

Sunday, June 13th.

The *Strand Magazine* objected to my novel *The Lion's Share* on the ground that it contained suffragette scenes. They held a meeting of directors and solemnly decided that the *Strand* could not print a suffragette serial. However, I think that I have reassured them.

Wednesday, June 16th.

Still waiting for a telegram permitting me to go to the French front.

I was told positively on Monday that Dardanelles were forced. Last night Asquith said that there was no truth whatever in the rumour. This rumour has been very strong.

Sunday, June 20th.

London on Friday. I paid three visits to Godfrey, Mair's secretary, to get my passport for France and police pass, and in the end the police pass was wrongly filled up. The passport had been marked Havre instead of

Boulogne, although no passengers are allowed to land at Havre. Godfrey's calm under these provocations was remarkable.

I leave for London and France tonight.

[Arnold Bennett went to the western front, June 21st, 1915, and was there until July 13th, 1915.—EDITOR.]

Monday, June 21st.

Victoria Station 7.45. Given a form to fill up. Couldn't get a big bag through without registering. People coming off train. Shabby, respectable girls etc. Hot summer's morning. Soldiers, officers. Staff officers on train.

A general: crossed sword and baton with star: "What I should really like to know is how they relieve those trenches at night."

Fine voyage.

My police pass saved me a great deal of trouble of waiting at Folkestone, more at Boulogne. Channel covered with shipping. Boom for several miles outside Folkestone, buoyed at about every 100 yards.

Impression at Boulogne of men of military age not engaged, similar to that at Folkestone.

Arrival of bevy of nurses, white starched muslin blue- and red-edged in car at "Stationary Hospital." Arrival of Army Postal Van, with legends about Y.M.C.A. and Kaiser written with a finger in the white dust on the sides.

Étaples. Hospitals and camp. As English as England. Hay in some places made and laid in cocks. Arrived Abbéville 4.15, having taken 3 hours to do 80 or 90 kil. The whole line, station and scene, makes an impression like perpetual Sunday, except for soldiers and camps.

Amiens. Very old man in a new long blue blouse and swagger check trousers showing beneath, acting as porter and shoving a truck along. Probably had retired and been brought back again.

Paris. I had at first a rather false impression about streets; in big streets over half the shops were closed. Then I recollected that the hour was after 7. A peculiar feeling, certainly, all over Paris. No auto buses, but trams. Few taxis. I saw the horse bus, Madeleine-Bastille, with a woman in charge, bareheaded, and with a great black bag over her abdomen. About 40; on easy terms with the passengers.

Mair and I went to Godebski's after dinner. Godebski would not believe 33 submarines sunk. Very harsh on Italy. Paris even darker than London. Same impression in Paris as in London of young men not in uniform. Plenty of young men in streets.

Wednesday, June 23rd. Paris.

I learnt yesterday that it was impossible to leave yesterday for the front. Gide, Godebski, and Mair came to lunch. Gide intellectually more than ever like an orchid.

General Sketch of Impression of Paris.

View from hotel. Destruction of gardens and architecture; St.-Clotilde. Station. Trees. Young man and woman playing silly ball game in dust. Shops. No buses. Concierges sitting out at night on pavements. Very close and hot, and as it were expectant. Number of young men for various reasons left. Lack of chicory and salt. Sound of guns at St.-Mair-Georges. Variety of uniforms. Bad puttees. Women's heavy mourning.

Thursday, June 24th. Paris.

Dinner last night at Mme. Edwards's. An astounding flat. Ph. Berthelot, Gide, Mair, the Godebskis, and Legrix (young novelist). Berthelot was as mysterious as ever. When I flattered him about *Le Livre Jaune*, he told me that he had to leave documents out. One an absolute prophecy of the course of the outbreak of war, from a Pole, received a month in advance. It was too true for any one to believe that it wasn't a fake. The other a quite authentic statement of the war plans of the Germans, as to aeroplanes, shells, trenches, strategy etc. This was received a year before the war. It couldn't be published because the French War Office had taken no action on the strength of it, though they knew it was authentic. It was tremendous accusation of the French War Office. Only a summary was given in *Le Livre Jaune*.

June 24th. Meaux.

House by roadside, roof damaged, contents taken away by G.'s. Why? What they couldn't take they destroyed.

Trenches. Character of country: rolling upwards. Farms. Wheat, oats, *poppies*. Heavily wooded in places. High horizon of tree-lined roads. Tombs here and there.

Thence to Chambry. Many tombs in wheat and hidden by wheat. Barbed wire on four stout posts (a bird on post), white wooden cross. Always a small white flag. Not always a name. On every side in these fields the gleam of cross or flag, as far as you can see. Scores and scores. Dark green-purple of distant wooded hills against high green of fields.

Cemetery used for firing from. Holes in wall.

Wheat absolutely growing out of a German.

The battlefield is between Barcy and Chambry. Barcy is high; Chambry is low, like Meaux. Round through battlefield German Army was going southeast, and chiefly east.

General impression: How little is left. How cultivation and civilization have covered the disaster over!

June 25th. Paris.

Mair and I dined at Meaux. Lord Esher came in, wearing a fancy military costume—perhaps that of constable of Windsor Castle. A star was depending from his neck. As soon as he saw my eye on it he tucked it inside his double-breasted khaki coat.

We are to go to Rheims on Saturday.

June 26th. Rheims.

Château Pommary.

Trenches at 80 metres apart. German first-line trenches like a road. Champagne proprietor who didn't want me to drink water.

Low, short sound of firing. A little smoke and dust.

Crowded roads. 80,000 men entrenched in front of us. Desolation. Days when 3000 *obus* fell. Shrapnel last week—no good except to break windows.

June 28th. Château-Thierry.

Arrived here last night at 7.20. We took drinks at headquarters of a commandant of whom I didn't catch the name. This drink (lemon and water and sugar) restored me more than any drink I ever had. We did a great deal of rough walking yesterday—estimated 20 miles. I put it at 12.

June 28th. Merval.

German prisoners collecting muck in a courtyard under a guard. When told of possible exchange of prisoners they said, "No."

Ambulance de premier ligne. Tent operating-hospital. Ether smell. This is the first hospital after the *poste de secours* near trenches (30 yards). Some cases operated on here in an hour after wound.

In one case at Tirlemont an ambulance (field hospital) with 200 *blessés* departed in 60 minutes.

June 30th. Paris.

Ravel came to lunch. He is a *second* in autos. He wanted to be in aviation, but his friends would not help him on account of danger.

July 8th. Near Ablain.

Young prisoner, 21, just caught. Trousers and coat pierced by bullet. Consumptive, enfeebled. Called up in Dec. 1914. Examined by officer, then went off with a soldier. Had work in paper factory. Infinitely pathetic. Scared little consumptive. Why military ambition?

Ablain, seen from here, is merely rafters.

Passage of wounded.

After car came to Road 2 Souchez, Germans began to fire on Road 78, high explosives. Searching road at 50 yards' distance or 100 up and down each shot. Almost every 2 minutes, and 1 minute sometimes. Tremendous waste of ammunition. The thing burst before sound of sizzling had finished reaching your ears.

Nearest shot 100 yards.

Friday, July 9th. Doullens.

405 and 407th Reg. passed through in auto buses, chiefly Berliet. Many roofed in, others with canvas tops, and window holes either empty or mica-ed. Young and jolly.

1200 lb. meat in wire safe per day.

26,000 meals a week.

July 12th. Ypres.

Market place full of people, up to April 22. Acacia trees still flourishing. St. Martin's stands, but irreparable. Only walls left, and tower skeleton. Organ stands. Apse blown out. Vast heaps of bricks in meeting of transept and nave etc. All yellowed by picric acid.

Big guns. Wireless report of shot reaches Germans before sound of explosion.

Boches shelling towns by sections.

Behind cathedral 50-ft. hole by 17-inch gun into graveyard; bones all over hole.

Grande Place—except for one white building (convent) all the rest jagged needles of walls.

Sat in a shell-hole to do sketch in front of convent. Aeroplanes overhead.

High wind. English guns booming. Fitments in houses creaking and rattling and cracking.

Houses full of disordered belongings.

On ramparts, dug-outs, birds lustily enjoying odour of gas from shell. *We never saw a Boche aeroplane.*

Friday, July 16th. England.

I returned home from the front yesterday, after 2 nights in London at the Savoy. By the evening I had dealt with all arrears.

The *Strand* people are obstinate in their objection to *The Lion's Share.* On the other hand, the *Metropolitan* (New York) are delighted with the work, and openly say so.

Considerable movement of troops round about here. Towns apparently being fortified etc. General coming down from London to confabulate with Brig.-Gen. Hoare on the spot. A current belief that the War Office expects a raid from the German fleet. I don't think the War Office does. If it does, why does it let the Somersets go a whole year without firing a single shot of any kind in practice?

Thursday, July 22nd.

Mysteriously and intestinally ill for a week. Unable to work. Convalescent this morning only. Miss Weeley told me yesterday at dinner that all the bees had died in this district, and that the reason was they had not been "told" about the war.

It appears that bees should always be "told" about deaths in the family and other important happenings; otherwise they will die. She met a woman in the road with a lot of honey and asked her how it was that she almost alone had succeeded with her bees. The woman said: "Ah! But as soon as the war broke out I went and told my bees all about it." Miss Weeley believed in this superstition. Edith Johnston said that her parents had lost 7 hives out of 9.

Monday, August 9th.

After my return home I was ill with colitis until the end of July and in bed for 9 days. I did not resume my visits to London until August 6th, when I had a long talk with Spender and Masterman, who agreed that not only was the Russian administration corrupt, but the War Office was thoroughly Germanized until after the beginning of the war. Even Witte was pro-German until Turkey came in. Spender said Russia had 7 million men trained but not armed yet.

Renewed activity up this coast about preparations for invasion. Generals came down from town, and I had communications with Lieut.-General Sir A. R. Martin, K.C.B.

Saturday, August 14th.

London. Masterman lunched with me at Reform.

W.A.R. Committee. George Whale [1] joined it. Tea with Pinker after it. Then long talk with Dr. Brend afterwards. He had brought over wounded from Ostend in October and was very impressive about official incompetence. A positive man; rather agreeable.

I dined with Clifford Sharp at Romano's. He told me that Brooks had told him Brooks was in Northcliffe's room when N. himself dictated the *Daily Mail* article about Kitchener, and that it was very much stronger then than in print. It seems Northcliffe, having no sons, is very keen on his nephews. He has already lost two in the war, if not three, and he regards them as having been murdered by Lord K. When remonstrated with about his attitude to Lord K., he burst out, "But he's murdered my nephews!"

Saturday, August 21st.

It now appears from my official correspondence with headquarters that in case of invasion the military people have not yet got their transport into order; they admit that it will not be in order for 2 months, and they are still "going to" indent. They want to indent from this coastal division, where transport is already inadequate and any evacuation would be very sudden. I am trying to stop them.

Also, without any corresponding change in the arrangements for evacuation, the direction of the evacuation has been taken out of the hands of the committees which organized it and put into the hands of the police, who know nothing about the arrangements.

Pinker told me that British Army now held 160 miles of French front; that new horizontally effective bombs were now perfect. War Office had said that no bombs could be effective at 50 yards away on the level. Inventors said it could. Bomb made and tried. An officer was to let it off electrically at 70 yards. War Office protested that he could not be in danger. He was killed—hit in the breast by a bit of projectile.

Also great muddle in landing at Suvla, Dardanelles. Troops 24 hours late. Otherwise they might have got right across peninsula. Fearful row.

---

[1] Solicitor, ex-mayor of Woolwich, and one of the founders of the Omar Khayyam and Pepys Clubs.

2 Generals sent home. I talked somewhat with a Russian in N.L.C. (in French). He had great blame for his countrymen's administrators—*"ces voleurs."*

Thursday, August 26th.

An oldish woman was carrying a pail of water past the nearest cottage of the row of cottages on the left of the Harwich road; at Thorpe Green.

"It don't get no nearer," said another woman within the cottage.

She was referring to the well in the field, two or three hundred yards away, which supplies these cottages with water.

"No, and it don't get no lighter," said the water-carrier.

"It's too far," they agreed.

So it is. There is a water-main runs down the road or very close to it; and yet these cottagers have to carry water a ridiculous distance in pails. It is astonishing that they don't contrive a water-cart on wheels, easy to push. To get enough water for a bath would take a woman several hours by the present system.

The chaplain to this brigade told me yesterday at tea in the garden that he was very friendly with Y.Z., the composer, and that Y.Z. would ultimately rank with Wagner. He was arranging for the performance of one of Y.Z.'s works with due solemnity when somebody told him that this composer's alleged wife was not his real wife, who still lived. The chaplain had to retire from direction of arrangements, but he was not acutely disturbed. He said to Y.Z., "Don't you think you could make a clean breast of it and explain things fully to people?" And Y.Z. did so to the organizers. He explained how he could not work when living with his real wife, whereas now, with No. 2, he had composed so-and-so and so-and-so. Further, No. 2's money was necessary to his material existence. Whereupon somebody in the room offered to give an income to Y.Z. so that he could quit No. 2! The thing had not been settled when the chaplain last heard. I asked if Y.Z. was a communicant. He said: "No, he doesn't quite know where he is. He's trying to find himself. I tell him to take his time."

Yesterday I finished sixth and last article on the front.

Saturday, August 28th.

The other day, when I reminded an officer concerned with emergency arrangements here that a secret word had been given without which no order to evacuate was to be considered genuine, he replied that he had never heard of such a word, but would look into it. This is a good example of official negligence. Had I not brought up the matter, the whole emergency scheme might have been vitiated if an invasion had suddenly taken place.

To Harwich yesterday. I took a map in the car. I asked sentry at entrance to search the car. He declined. Nothing said as to maps. No printed notice as to maps. On leaving, I was stopped and sent back with a soldier to headquarters. Maps were not allowed. The A.P.M. himself had seen me looking at the map. The attitude of the A.P.M. and another official, who both interviewed me, was grotesque, and I have written formally to wake them up.

Wednesday, September 1st.

After over a week's delay I received my first article on the British front back from the censor at G.H.Q. With the exception of about three words the whole of the censoring struck me as entirely futile. I keep the censored copy as a curiosity.

Thursday, September 9th.

Yesterday I finished a supplementary article (hospital) on the front. I am now quit of all this, except that I may write a preface for the book form. I can now turn to the last half of *The Lion's Share*. Besides this I have my next (London) novel in my mind, and my war play, which will advance every time I think about it for an hour.

I read a year or two of De Goncourt's journal recently. Very good. In fact it had the finest effect on me when I was exceedingly annoyed.

Saturday, September 11th.

Tea with Pinker at A.B.C. He told me about a new and marvellous brand of British mines that would float into German harbours, but wouldn't float out again.

During the day, from Davray, Waller, and Rickards, I got information as to Zeppelin raid on Wednesday night.[1] Davray on roof of the Waldorf. He said Zeppelin was fairly low over roof. Searchlights on it. Star-lights. Fairy-like. Shots at it. Then it rose and went northwards. Spectacle agreed to be superb. Noise of bombs agreed to be absolutely intimidating. And noise of our guns merely noise of popguns. One bomb in garden of Queen's Sq. had smashed windows and indented walls and smashed window frames on three sides. Two hospitals here. A lot of the glazing had already been repaired. Much damage at Wood Street, Cheapside. I didn't see it. Two motor buses demolished with passengers. Rickards, who went out at 11.15 (visitation at 10.50—he was in bed and went to cellar), said it was very strange to see motor buses going along just as usual, and a man selling fruit just as usual at a corner. People spoke to each other in the streets. Waller said streets near bomb in City were two inches deep in glass etc. I didn't see damage in Theobald's Road. It appears there had been a raid over New Cross on Tuesday night. Queen's Square was rather like the front—Arras, for example.

Mrs. T. to lunch. Her father, a bishop, has just lost his wife. A grand-nephew was told to write condolences to him. The boy, aged 11, wrote first: "Dear Grandad: I am very sorry Grannie is dead, but we must make the best of these things." Told that this wouldn't do, he tried again: "I am very sorry Grannie is dead. But you may be sure she is far happier where she is." This also being condemned, he wrote a conventional letter about Grannie having always been kind to them all, etc.

Wednesday, September 15th.

Zeppelin excitements nightly. It was said in the village that a Zeppelin hung over the village church for an hour on Monday night, but I did not believe this. A station porter, however, told me that they could see a Zeppelin on Sunday night, as it passed. He said that another Zeppelin or

---

[1] On the evening of September 8 a number of Zeppelins raided London and the suburbs. Considerable damage was done, 20 killed and 86 injured.

some Zeppelins had been signalled for that night (Monday). It was dark when I talked to him on the dark platform. (They had had instructions as to lights by telegraph.) The only lights were the reds of the signals, high up. I asked him as to Marguerite's train. He said that the train had "asked" for the line and would arrive soon. This mysteriousness of un-seen things known to be coming—such as Zeppelins and trains—was rather impressive. Then suddenly a red light changes to green in the air. Two engines attached to each other rumble through the station. Then M.'s train. And after a long delay Marguerite's silhouette very darkly far down the platform.

Monday, September 27th.

Capt. B. called late last night. He said he had heard that the *Mauretania* had been sunk with 6000 soldiers on board, but did not believe it. He liked telling it. He said that a friend of his, commander of a T.P.D., had told him that 21 German transports had recently been within a compara-tively short distance of the English coast. "They got away again 'by a miracle,' " said the commander. "I can't give you particulars, but it was a miracle." The commander told him that in the affair he had been re-sponsible for sinking 10 German submarines and that 11 were sunk alto-gether. All had double crews. I said to Captain B., "Did the commander tell you this with his own lips?" He replied: "He did. He is a friend of mine." B. said he believed the transports were empty.

B. also related how a man who had gone to the Dardanelles had prom-ised to send a bit of blue ribbon in an envelope as soon as they were forced. No word. Just the blue ribbon. Thus no trouble with censor. Well, the ribbon arrived on Friday, and the man who had received it (in police force) had himself told B. yesterday of the incident.

Saturday, October 2nd.

London yesterday. Tailor's. Then to McKenna's for lunch. Reggie came in late and left early. There were also Marguerite, John Burns, and a young doctor whose name I missed. McKenna was very strong against conscription. He said it would lose the war. He said the army was already too large for our resources, that the demands of the Allies were always growing, and that the financial strain was very great. John Burns was in great form and less vain than usual; in fact, scarcely at all vain. He gave most amusing and convincing pictures of artisan family life, etc. He said that when he had been buying a book too many he would leave it at the club and then take it home last thing at night, after his wife was in bed, and hide it.

Then to National Liberal Club to meet Percy Alden, M.P., who interviewed me for a syndicate of papers. He said there were only two things he could do really well, sail a small yacht and control a meeting. Driving with him to Liverpool St. Station afterwards, I heard of his speechifying tour round the world. He said that in Japan he saw a factory where between 2000 and 3000 girls were employed. Girls gathered from country districts with dreams of town life, flower festivals, etc. These girls worked in two 12-hour shifts, night and day, Sundays included. They slept in huge dormitories. The sight of them, dirty, dishevelled, crowded, asleep in the dormitories—and the Japanese by predilection such a clean and neat people—was awful. It was absolutely forbidden to leave the factory at all. They were bound for three years (sort of apprenticeship), and they earned $2\frac{1}{2}d.$ a day, of which $2d.$ was deducted for food. Food chiefly consisted of soup with fish-tails and heads therein, bodies of fish being reserved for managers etc. When he talked to a big Japanese statesman about industrial conditions, statesman (I forget his name) said that there was no need for trades unions in Japan as all Japanese loved each other so much that abuses would be impossible. Alden said things had slightly improved.

Home by restaurant train.

Monday, October 4th.

Mrs. Green today said that she had been talking to a young sub at Queen Alexandra's Hospital, Millbank, wounded in Dardanelles. He told her that one day they had to put up wire entanglements and there were no posts. A number of stiff corpses of Turks were lying about. They upended them and stuck them into the ground like posts, and fastened the wire to their heads. Mrs. Green said to us, "What will the youths of 19 be like afterwards, who have been through this kind of thing and got used to it?"

I should say that in most respects, and to all appearance, they will be like others who have not been through it.

Started 6th instalment of *The Lion's Share* today.

Saturday, October 9th.

Left home at 10 A.M. and drove over slippery roads in a Scotch mist to Little Easton. I walked with Wells in the park at dusk. Stag rutting season. All the bucks were roaring like lions, and we were somewhat intimidated. Two of them made a show of fighting, but funked it. Before this, original ball games in the arranged barn, in front of which a farmyard and cesspool had been turned into a very sightly sunk garden with bathing tank in the middle.

Immense park, belonging to Lady Warwick, and practically wasted for useful purposes. And there must be hundreds such.

"It ought to be taxed out," said H.G.

Tuesday, October 12th.

I returned from Wells's yesterday morning and wrote my article in the afternoon. I had a great time there. There were about 18 people to hockey on Sunday afternoon. Newman Flower, of Cassell's, came on Sunday for the night, and Clarkson, chairman of National Steam Car, and others, came for supper on Sunday night. It is Wells's tremendous energy that makes the place so entertaining. If there is no real talking, then he must instantly play at some game. I played at Badminton, hockey, his own patball, etc. He has turned a barn and a farmyard into something very nice, and a great "escape" from the house. He works in his bedroom at a very small table and has a primus stove to make tea there. He sometimes gets up and works in the night. The house is partly steam-heated and is fairly comfortable and very bright, but some of it is badly planned and arranged. It is like a large cottage made comfortable by people rich but capricious. H.G. drives a car very indifferent bad, but he enjoys driving.

Saturday, October 16th.

London yesterday. Show of French drawings about war at Leicester Galleries. I bought a Hermann Paul for 8 guineas. The Forains were very fine indeed. 50 guineas each.

Monday, October 18th.

Capt. K. and Capt. B., stationed here, recounted the Zeppelin attack on their camp in Epping Forest. It was apparently brought on by a light in the officers' mess. It seems that the Zeppelin hung over the camp. It dropped several (4 or 5) explosive bombs right in the camp, a few feet (under 20) away from where K. actually was. None of these bombs exploded. They buried themselves 10 feet in the earth. They were excavated without accident. K. said the soldiers used pick and shovel in digging them out, with perfect indifference to the danger. The Zeppelin also dropped a number of incendiary bombs which the soldiers put out as they fell. It seems to me that the fact that incendiary bombs were dropped shows that the Zepp did not know that it was over a tented camp. The object of setting fire to tents is not clear at all, as the men could easily get away and the damage would be inconsiderable. The explosive bombs weighed one hundredweight each, and the incendiary bombs about 15 lbs. each. K. said he could not assert that he actually saw the Zeppelin. He said the men saw whole fleets of Zeppelins. Apropos, Rickards related last night that Webster came across a crowd in the centre of which was a man pointing to the sky and raging excitedly: "There she is! She's hit! She's hit!" Webster said, "You think that's a Zepp, but it's the moon." The crowd dissolved.

Tuesday, October 26th.

Mr. and Mrs. H. G. Wells came for tea yesterday and left after lunch today. He told me he regarded E. Carson as the really sinister and dangerous figure in politics today. Immediately after it was established that he would not compromise on Home Rule the Austrian note was sent to Serbia. Germany thought she was safe so far as concerned England.

Last week Gardiner kicked against my article showing the financial danger of recruiting. But he printed it in the end, unfortunately cutting out the very part in which I saved myself by blessing the present recruiting campaign and expressing the hope that only at the end of the 6 weeks' trial would recruiting be stopped.

Friday, November 5th.

Chrysanthemum show here yesterday for the Red Cross. Only our own plants. About 60-odd people. A singer who came from London for her expenses, £1 1s. 0d. Of course far more women than men, but still a few men (and officers). It was a success, £23 net. But it is a strange, though ingenious, way of getting money. The people could afford more by paying directly, like income tax; but they prefer to pay more indirectly; that is, to indulge themselves in amusement while "helping the cause." There is something to be said for it.

On Wednesday night my new bookshelves in Miss Nerney's room were inaugurated.

Monday, November 8th.

Lieut. E. came to dinner last night. He had had eight months at front at Armentières and Ypres. Only about 2 officers left out of his original lot. He said they spent 12 days in trenches and 6 out, but frequently 14 or 16 in and 4 or 2 out. They had to walk about 10 miles to and from trenches with 90 pounds on their backs; on arriving in trenches they were so tired that they didn't care whether they were under fire or not. But the return journey was worse, as they had had no exercise for nearly a fortnight, being in trenches. In rest huts, no beds. They had to sleep on wooden floors, so that they hated these rest-huts and preferred the dugouts. He had been out over six months (I think) before he got leave at all. He then could not go to sleep in bed until about 4 A.M. and was strongly tempted to lie on floor, but refrained. Also, being in a room put him off sleep. He said food was fairly good. But Tommies used to put the bully beef on parapet of trenches. The supply of it, of course, could not be stopped. Everybody liked "Maconochie" rations, veg. and meat, which could be taken hot or cold. A certain amount of looting. He took a clock valued by a Harrod's furniture expert out there at 80 guineas. But he left it. He also had a camera. His company commander made him send his camera home so that he could report no cameras. But this C.C. fell ill, and his substitute never asked about cameras; so E. sent for his again. He has a lot of photos. He was particularly calm, simple, measured, and *posé* in his demeanour; he gave very good descriptions, and exaggerated nothing.

Friday, November 12th.

On Wednesday at tea Mrs. M. described the luxury and liveliness of life in the European colony of Shanghai but afterwards admitted that its scourges were typhoid and abscess on the liver. Most of her best friends she had lost through typhoid (males, that is). Later she gave me her views on men and women. She was bringing up her little sons with the idea that they must be nice and helpful and protective to all women. They thoroughly understand that at the earliest moment they must buy a motor car for their mother. She is afraid of scandals, being a young and attractive widow, but gives cocktails to her assembled friends every Sunday morning in a place like Frinton! She said there were three things any man could give to any woman without fear of being misunderstood —flowers, chocolate, music. She was great on what women could expect from men. Doubtless owing to her widowhood. She lamented that labour was so dear in England. "It was because the working classes lived too well." I expect she has all the usual colonial social political ideas. In the end she displayed a pleasant conception of life—limited to her own class, of course. The general impression of her ideal was very agreeable.

Wednesday, November 17th.

Yesterday morning, barber's. Reform. Directors' meeting, at noon, of *New Statesman,* Shaw, Webb, Simon (large employer at Manchester), and Clifford Sharp. Shaw said we ought to attack Asquith. Said we ought to make Haldane P.M. Shaw had no conception of public opinion at all. Afterwards, in the street, he told me he had talked like that as a "hygienic operation" and that it was necessary to exaggerate in such hygiene; he wanted to stir Sharp up. He said he went to Torquay sometimes for a holiday and worked harder than ever. The fundamental decency and kindliness of Shaw were evident throughout.

Sunday, November 28th.

London on Thursday. Drummond Fraser, managing director of Manchester & Liverpool District Bank, told me positively that America had quite failed to take advantage of chance of becoming the world's financial centre and that after the war everything would revert to England as before.

Saturday, December 4th.

London, Thursday. Slept at R.T.Y.C.[1] Very good. I finished *The Lion's Share* on Wednesday night and slept very ill and was really too fatigued for London, but I took a tonic, which did me good. Max Beerbohm lunched with me at Reform, and I urged him to start on some cartoons.

Tuesday, December 7th.

Came to Manchester by Midland 4.30. On arrival at Central Station a young officer who had slept and in between had made much litter in the train was met by his family, one by one. First father. "Hello, Dad," etc. Dad was a tall, thin, grey man; they kissed. Then little sister running along; then big sister, more reserved, but very welcoming, with a touch of sisterly superiority. All this was a very agreeable sight on the worn wooden platform, strangely out of date, of the Central Station.

Thursday, December 30th.

I wrote 272,200 words this year, not counting journals. I had the best book and serial year I have ever had (though I didn't issue a single new novel), and by far the worst theatrical year since before *The Honeymoon,* I think.

I finished re-reading *Esther Waters* last night, after a bad bilious attack. It still vigorously lives.

---

[1] The Royal Thames Yacht Club.

1916

Saturday, January 1st. Comarques.

Masterman had lunch with me, and R. Ross [1] joined us. Masterman said that in the still existing crisis, McKenna and Runciman had both actually resigned, as they could not get a guarantee that the army should not be allowed to exceed a given total, they being convinced that we could not financially carry on unless a strict limit was set. Asquith then implored etc., wrote letters etc., and the subject was reopened.

Wednesday, January 5th.

After an immense day's work on Monday I came to London with M. yesterday. The Italian *maître d'hôtel* of the restaurant spoke with amazement and respect of the British. "They spend as much as ever. We are doing more business than in peacetime. They do not look at their bills. They do not inquire about prices. They pay. They have money. They can afford to wait and make Germany wait. They never give in. They always win. They are prodigious!"

At night my second visit to *Romance* with Doris Keane in it. She played even better than before. She has a most powerful personality. Yet afterwards in her loge, embracing and stroking Marguerite, whom she had never seen before, she told us that she thought she had played rottenly. After 9 performances the previous week she had got gastritis and

---

[1] Robert Ross, journalist and art critic, was the executor of Oscar Wilde's literary estate.

had taken practically nothing but hot water for 4 days. She is a very attractive woman.

Saturday, January 15th.

I went to London Wednesday and returned Friday and was ill nearly all the time with dyspepsia. Edward Garnett lunched with me on Wednesday. He said he had an important matter to discuss. It was a project for a weekly penny political paper to tell the truth about politics. He wanted me to give up everything and edit it, also to start it and organize it. He had the title and a plan of contents, including chiefly a series of "Fables for Liberals." He had written the first fable himself. When I asked him what he would do, he said he only meant to contribute, himself. He was quite sincere and had not begun to suspect that the scheme originated in his idea for a fable about Liberals who had lost their trousers.

From the Reform I went to the *Statesman* to discuss with Sharp the notion of some plainer writing about political facts. I had previously seen McKenna's brother, who told me that Reginald was still quite determined to leave the Cabinet if it tried to outrun the constable. He indicated that the financial situation was exceedingly grave.

At night I dined with Atkins, who told us he had met an old friend that day, an American journalist named Marshall whom he had known in the Cuban War and who had been shot in the spine in a very interesting way, so much so that it ought to have been impossible for him to live, and two medical books had been written about him. He walks with a stick or sticks. This man was coming to Europe journalistically, and Bernstorff had him in at the Waldorf-Astoria and said to him, "You can have £50,000, not dollars, before you leave this hotel, if you will go to Europe in German interests." Marshall refused. Bernstorff then went further and told him he could have the biggest journalistic scoop that any journalist ever had; namely, he should be taken from Belgium to Berlin in a Zeppelin and there have an interview with the Kaiser and be brought back. Marshall refused. Atkins said he knew Marshall very well and vouched for his honesty. The Zeppelin excursion was afterwards accepted by another American journalist, whose name I forget, but he died in the Zeppelin on the way. Atkins also told us that Lord Cromer had told him that an English officer out in Russia on military contracts business found himself absolutely unable to do the business without baksheesh to officials, which he refused to give. He then managed to see the Tsar, who affected great surprise and went over the heads of the officials—but how long the Tsar's arrangement "worked" Atkins couldn't say.

Tuesday, January 18th.

Came to London yesterday with M. Lunched at Reform and saw Spender and his new contributor, whose *noms-de-plume* are Action Front and Boyd Cable. He writes descriptive stuff very well. I should say a good soldier, very earnest and obstinate and lacking in humour. He said that the Flanders campaign had done good to the Indian soldiers because it had shown them what western fighting was and how little chance a mutiny could have.

This was *en route* to Assault-at-Arms at National Sporting Club in aid of W.A.R.C. The place not full. Very few ladies, though a ladies' night. Two British and one Russian nurse. The former jealous of latter, who had to stand on platform while her postcards were being sold for £5 and £10 the set. Bookmakers and similar people bought, and allowed to be sold again, a Shetland pony, dogs, a stamp collection. A music-hall star, in an evening dress with a red tie and worn-out boots, was auctioneer part of the time.

Saturday, January 22nd.

Too ill in London to write any notes. I even forget what I did. We dined at the Carlton with Dorziat[1] and Knoblock. She is a little worn physically. Very intelligent and amusing and natural. Then to an absolutely dreadful Scotch play at Royalty, *Bauldy*. As bad as *Bunty* and longer. We saw Eadie, Vedrenne, Vernon, Eaton, and others. Wednesday I lunched with Doran and Messmore Kendal and Wells at Savoy. H.G.

---

[1] Gabrielle Dorziat, the French actress, appeared several times in England and also played in English.

held forth on the future of N. and S. America. Eaton came to tea at Berkeley and explained his triumphant progress. At night (M. having returned to Thorpe in order to go to the Colchester Hippodrome) J. R. Richmond dined with me at the Yacht Club, and we went to *Il Trovatore* at Shaftesbury. Very old-fashioned, with a few good things. Horribly conventional plot and acting. I walked to hotel in thick rain. Thursday, Doris Keane came to lunch. I learnt a lot about her and got some general ideas as to how to write a play to suit her. She said she was very fond of women—and also of men too.

On Friday after a third sleepless night I lunched with Methuen at the Reform. He told me *These Twain* had sold 13,350 in the first week. Some rotten reviews. Apart from other things, the book is too jolly true for some people. They say it lacks the ideal, and mean that it refuses to be untruthful. Several of the best critics have noted this with satisfaction and laudation.

Monday, January 31st.

I only found out last night that Swinnerton was really interested in music. Vernon came up on Saturday. Very military. Yesterday morning I drove him and M. and Swinnerton to Frinton. In the afternoon Corfield persuaded me to go out for a ride with the officers and Vernon. First time across a horse since end of 1902. We went to Frinton. Very fatiguing for me. I did some work before dinner. In the evening piano and discovery of Swinnerton's interest in music.

Friday, February 4th.

I went to 47 Bedford Sq. yesterday morning to see Roscoe, secretary of Teachers' Registration Council. A downright Midlander, with traces of accent. He gave me information for articles on education. The whole feel of 47 is now changed—for the better. Clearer and brighter everywhere.

Lunch at the Reform. I saw Methuen, who said that the Publishers' Association had unanimously decided to issue novels at net prices and at prices varying according to length—from 4s. 6d. net to 7s. 6d. net. I don't think it will work, at 7s. 6d. net anyhow.

Two committee meetings at W.A.R.C. Lady Paget came over half an hour late. She is a master-woman, and well accustomed to command. Every one says she is an unrivalled "beggar." She enunciated her principles of begging, ruthlessly. They were excellent. She is now starting out to collect a million for blind soldiers. If she gets £5000 from our Caledonian Market Show I shall be far more than satisfied.

Monday, February 7th.

On Saturday night great excitement about two men who, challenged by sentry of the ammunition park near the station at 7.15 P.M., had run away. Ammunition of all the district is kept there, including 300,000 rounds of rifle, etc., etc. The marauders vanished, though pursued. Clacton was called up by telephone and kept up most of the night. Officers were called from dinner. The missing men were supposed to correspond with 2 escaped Germans interned from Dorset. The one best seen had a rope and walked noiselessly—hence rubber shoes! Why? Etc., etc. No capture yesterday either. The funniest thing is that one of the guard, or perhaps it was the sentry himself, says that the marauder must be a German, because when he challenged, the fellow distinctly called out "Von."

Way and a Dr. G. of R.A.M.C. came for the day yesterday. The latter bald, thin, big nose, self-assured, goodish talker, but too interested in his own doings. He had not been to Dardanelles, but recounted tales of champagne luncheons, together with rude lack of hospitality to visiting officers, of the administrative staff (seventy-odd) stationed permanently in a ship at either Mudros or Imbros. They had very bad reputation. Soldiers could not get fresh potatoes, though vast stores of potatoes were rotting not far off, because lighters were plied by staff for their sporting excursions. And so on.

Thursday, February 10th.

Came to London yesterday. First good, clear frost of the winter. Very sharp. Lunch at the Reform. Pinker came. Methuen joined us about alleged coming "revolution" in price of novels. It seems that of the council of the Publishers' Assoc., who had suggested it, only four published novels at all, and none published novels on any scale. Characteristic. We told him that the scheme of different prices would never work and coached him as to what he should say at the grand meeting on Monday.

Then to W.A.R.C. offices. Difficulty with Lord X. as to my having put name of Queen Alex. on posters for concert. I flatly disagreed with him, whereupon he said I was logically right, and I drafted a letter for him to write to the Queen.

Friday, February 11th.

E. McKenna gave me an idea for a novel. I pointed out the defects of it, and he was going to think it over further. I met Atkins coming out of the Travellers' Club. He said *These Twain* had kept him from his proper amount of sleep and that every episode in it was true of every husband and every wife. Then 3¾ hours of Wounded Allies' Relief Committee. Rush to Treviglio's at 6.50, where M. and Webster dined with me. Thence to Stanford's new opera, *The Critic.* Thoroughly rotten. The only fun is in the clowning, and this to the accompaniment of music without a spark of humour. One or two primitive musical jokes. Scarcely an original air in the thing, but when he borrows an air from an old song, how fine it sounds!

Monday, February 21st.

Haymarket concert in aid of W.A.R.C. at night. This went off without a hitch, and I was very glad when it was over. I had no particular trouble, but I will never organize another. The theatrical element, Ainley and Nelson Keys, [1] had a much greater success than the musical element. The latter was naturally jealous, but could not help peeping and hugely enjoying the former. One is more struck than ever by the forced cordiality of all greetings and all praise in this *monde.* Miss Ada Crossley, the oldest singer there, has very great charm, and she got the first encore. After Ainley, people began to go, and after Nelson Keys a lot went.

---

[1] Nelson Keys became known to the American public through the very popular first *Charlot's Revue.*

These two had each more than one encore and occupied a great deal of time, so that the concert was not over till 10.25.

Sunday, February 27th.

Went to London on Wednesday afternoon last without this volume. Snow. Dined at Lord Swaythling's. About 12 diners. I sat between Viscountess Camperdown and Lady Asquith. Bad music. Lord Chancellor [1] came late, and informally, straight from House of Lords. He came up to talk to me—said he had often seen me at the Reform. He gave me the best praise of *The O.W. Tale* I ever had *viva voce*. He said he knew Asquith liked my late appreciation of Asquith. I said I didn't always praise ministers, referring to my slanging of himself as head of Press Bureau. He seemed to catch this and smiled. He is a captivating man.

Walker came at noon to discuss Shaw's idiotic proposal for a coalition of intelligentsia. W.A.R.C. meetings all afternoon till 7, after a lunch with Masterman about an article I was to write for him in U.S.A.

At home we learnt that small German raids expected. All local garrisons doubled. Two batteries in the village, etc. Great excitement. I had heard nothing of this in London.

Tuesday, February 29th.

As regards the great invasion scare. The two batteries "stood by" yesterday morning from 4 A.M. till sunrise and today from 5.30 A.M. till sunrise, all ready to move off—except that bits weren't in harness. The assistance which came in a hurry from Colchester here consists of convalescent wounded gunners from the front, appointed only to light duty and to extreme emergency duty. In the fatigue of yesterday's field day (which was utterly useless) the wounds of two of the gunners were reopened. It is considered that the early morning standing by is connected with high water and that some attempt at a landing is feared. Only the Ammunition Column remains in Thorpe. The two batteries have taken with them 100 rounds per gun. The rest is stored in our outbuildings.

---

[1] Lord Buckmaster.

Saturday, March 4th.

Went to London Wednesday. Lunch and sleep at Marriotts'. Then national "economy" meeting at Guildhall, where I sat next but one to Barrie. McKenna spoke well but too slowly. Kitchener read badly a speech which had been prepared for him. Balfour was pleasing.

Then a meeting of the new Art and Industries Association, at Art Workers' Guild. Some of the Labour people were funny. The representative of gold and silver workers drank too much. A successful working bookbinder slanged trades unions. Turner of Shop Assistants was good. A working man got up at the end, and having evidently screwed himself up to the point, said angrily that nobody had asked him to speak, a plain workman, and that most awful bosh had been talked and that nobody there understood working men.·

Saturday, March 11th.

Birthday dinner at Mrs. McKenna's. Short dinner, but 3 man-servants. Birrell, very boyish, with much grey hair and short of a front tooth; decided, gay, wary. Edwin Montagu[1] and wife, both very Jewish. Diana Manners in a low-necked short frock, with no shoes and stockings. Nothing seemed to be known about future of war, and McKenna didn't seem to believe in a smashing of Germany; but Montagu did. Montagu rather diffident and quiet. It was stated that nobody *could* be worse at the War Office than Kitchener. He wasn't even a brute.

Friday, March 17th.

To Grafton Gallery, where the most mixed show (Allied Artists' Assocn.) you ever saw. Good modern things and cubism, and the rottenest amateurishness of the worst old-fashioned kind. For instance, a cat sitting on a polished floor, and necklace thereon, with the title "Reflections." No Strand picture dealer would have dared to put it in his window. The place was ready for a reception to Pachmann. I don't know how we managed to be let in. All the snobs began to arrive. We

---

[1] Second son of Lord Swaythling and financial secretary to the Treasury.

left then. Tea at Hatchett's. Then to Westminster Cathedral for evensong. Beautiful darkening empty building, very sad, and a sing-song by six priests and their leader. I dined at the Reform, alone, and alone to the Alhambra. Very empty. *Les grues* allowed to sit in back row of dress-circle. London very wet and dark and many *grues* mysteriously looming out at you in Coventry Street. Impossible to see their faces at all.

I slept at R.T.Y.C. Thursday morning, long séance at barber's. Then to W. Nicholson's. He was in a black leather jacket, covered with paint. He gave me the portrait of Wish Wynne that was used in the production of *The Great Adventure*. He showed me some most ingenious still lifes and Eric Kennington's biggish war picture—very striking.

Monday, March 20th.

The Ammunition Column received the order to depart on Friday night at 10.30—to leave on Saturday. The actual departure, which we witnessed between 5.30 and 6.30 P.M. on Saturday, was a striking proof of the vast inferiority of horse and mule traction to motor traction.

One mule wagon had to be unloaded twice, as the mules wouldn't or couldn't draw it. General mix-up and dinting of gate-posts. Part of confusion may be the fact that the O.C. had lost both his subalterns and had to do everything himself. However, he had an excellent sergeant-major. On one wagon was perched his servant, holding his dog under one arm and a parcel of a large photo under the other. The departure had the air of a circus departure badly managed. Then, of course, on arrival at Weeley (2 miles) they had to take everything to pieces again.

Meantime new units were coming in, and it was getting dusk, and an officers' mess was being fixed up roughly at Culver House. The melancholy of evening over it all, but it was a warm evening. Few drops of rain. Then in darkening village you saw groups of men with piles of kit-bags lying in front of them, waiting to get, or trying to get, into Workmen's Club, where a lot of them billeted.

Lovely night. Bright moon. Trot of a horse occasionally till late.

Wednesday, March 22nd.

According to the Swedish betting, this is the day, at least, on which the German fleet ought to come out.

I received a letter from General Martin, chief military representative for Essex Emergency Committee in case of invasion, this morning, asking me to give him a few more copies of the Tendring Division Instructions, drawn up by me, to be used as a guide for other divisions. This shows that instructions have not yet been issued in some divisions. I thought ours were very late, seeing that the W.O. instructions were revised over six months ago. Also it seems strange that the W.O. should depend on the chance of the instructions in one division being competently drawn up, for the example of other divisions. You would have thought that the Central Emergency Committee would have drawn up a model set of instructions. However, the incident shows that literary merit is appreciated, even in military circles.

Friday, March 24th.

On Wednesday night a Welsh vet officer came here to sleep. 60. Very provincial and polite and talkative. All about Lloyd George [1] and Wales and Stanley Weyman. Just like middle-class provincials in Potteries, except for accent. Speaking of billeting in Manningtree, he said that billetees had to cook for soldiers, while not finding the food. *"Now, many of them didn't like it,"* he said with sympathy and conviction, as middle class speaking of and understanding middle class. It was absolute Five Towns. No member of upper middle class would have said it like that. A member of upper middle class might have laughed, or said it indulgently, or said it comprehendingly, but not with the same unconscious sympathy.

Saturday, April 1st.

Today I began on construction of *Carlotta* play for Doris Keane.

Last night about 8.45 we heard a rattling of windows. denoting distant explosions. We at once thought of Zeppelins.

---

[1] Became Secretary of State for War in 1916.

This morning the post was 80 minutes late, and at 11.45 the newspapers due at 9 A.M. had not come. No sound of a train yet heard. Rumour of a raid with 18 Zeppelins. Magnificent spring morning.

Friday, April 7th.

The end of winter was very sudden last week. On Tuesday last week was the worst blizzard for 50 years (in which our car got smashed up against a tree that had fallen across the Colchester road); snow, slush, etc. And on Saturday the sun was very hot and the roads full of flying dust. Just like summer, even to the E. and the N.E. wind.

I really "got on to" first scene of *Carlotta* play on Wednesday.

Friday, April 14th.

London yesterday. Interview (with Mrs. Scott) with Selfridge[1] in his office. He is very proud of his Information Bureau. He wanted the Christian name of the superintendent of Islington Cattle Market. He got it from his Information Bureau in about 3 minutes. There was a small closed roll-top desk in his room. It is his son's, aged 16. Boy now home for holidays from Winchester. He was upstairs learning accountancy. He takes a boxing lesson every day at 12.30. His father showed us photos of him at his desk in various attitudes, including the attitude of dictating to a girl clerk. I continue to like Selfridge.

Wednesday, April 19th.

Dr. Slimon reports to me that at the meeting of chairmen of Emergency Committees and military representatives at Chelmsford on Friday, which I could not attend, under the chairmanship of General Paget, Paget insisted on the strong probability of an invasion between Harwich and Maldon in July or August.

The naval opinion at Harwich, I hear, is that the Harwich flotilla could not deal with the covering ships of an invading force and that, so far as the Navy was concerned, the force would land and the convoy

---

[1] H. Gordon Selfridge, the American-born owner of one of London's great department stores.

be taken in the rear. It is also said that the German submarines are trying to mine the course of the proposed expedition and that we are sweeping their mines and mining *contra*.

Pauline Smith came on Saturday, having lost her luggage on the way. Voice perhaps feebler than ever. She is highly intelligent.

Wednesday, April 26th.

In addition to marking the opening of the water-colour season, yesterday had some importance in the war. About midnight (previous) an orderly came on a motor bike and looked in the front garden. I challenged from the window. He had an order for Lieut. Myers to report at once at the Orderly Office. Myers was up all night. Then in the morning's papers was the news of the capture of Sir Roger Casement in an attempt at gun-running in Ireland. Then Myers came in with the news (which he had overheard on the telephone) that a German fleet had been within five miles of Lowestoft between 4 and 5 A.M., and also that Zeppelins had been over. Then General Y. and 2 of his staff called to see me. This was in the middle of breakfast. Y. wanted information about the emergency scheme for the civil population. He said he had nearly ordered the evacuation of Frinton, Walton, and Clacton, in the night. I gave him some documents and also wrote him later in the day. One of the dangers in this district is that some one like Y. may try to order an evacuation, either when it isn't necessary or in a manner contrary to the military authorities' own instructions. It was characteristic of the Army that *I* gave him his first copy of the instructions ordered and approved by the Army!

Then came telegram with official news of a short naval action off Lowestoft. Then came telegram that Betty Sharpe had had a daughter. Then came the daily French telegram. Then came telegrams of riots and seizure of the post office at Dublin. Then came telegram as to Zeppelins. To continue the tale, this morning I had a letter from A. G. Gardiner practically putting an end to my connection with the *Daily News*.

By the way, the cyclist who called up Myers, going immediately after-

wards to Frinton without any lights (as ordered), ran into a car and
broke both his legs and fractured his skull. He is supposed to be recovering.

Friday, April 28th.

London yesterday. Very warm.

At the barber's, while I was being pedicured in the inner room, a
young voice came in and asked whether it could cash a cheque for £1.
Yes. Well, pay the cabman and have the luggage brought inside, and
send down to ——'s and ask for the box of cigarettes that was ordered
by Mr. A. The voice, rather high, kept on all the time. Its hands were
being manicured. Then it was called to the telephone. A Mr. Barlow.
It sprang with enthusiasm to the telephone. It trembled while it greeted
"dear old boy." It explained that it was going down to Windsor by the
1.15 to play golf and would return that day but didn't know whether
it was expected to play after lunch or after tea. It would "love," "love,"
"love" to do something with Barlow in the evening. Time passed. It
was 12.45, and anxiety for the train began. A friend came in, evidently
to join the Windsor excursion. Certain shopping had to be done on the
way to Paddington, but evidently this was given up. A taxi was ordered,
and it was ordered to be turned in the direction of Piccadilly, and
luggage was to be put in. Then one cigarette was to be taken out of
the cigarette box and the box put in a certain bag. At last the voice left.
What change remained out of the sovereign, or how the voice would
get to Windsor, I don't know. By the way, to save time, the cheque was
filled up by a member of the staff so that the voice should only have
to sign it.

Went to see Lady Paget at 35 Belgrave Square. House in holland
covers except one room, in which she saw me. Open door answered by
chauffeur, who raised his hat and came into the house to do it. Decent
woman; not much humour, but commanding. We got on excellently.
She slanged the idleness of society helpers and believed most in American
women for charity. She is one.

I came home by 6.38 and had three beef sandwiches at one end of the journey and some cold bread and butter pudding at the other. I walked into Red Cross concert at Vicarage Hall and was instantly called on to sing a comic song, which I did.

Tuesday, May 2nd.

The MS. of *Helen with the High Hand* sold for £27 at the Red Cross sale at Christie's on Friday. This was the last day of the sale. Bookseller Beaumont bought it. Galsworthy's MS. of *The Freelands* sold for £26.

Friday, May 5th.

London yesterday. Mair mysteriously telegraphed me to go to an "important" luncheon at the Garrick to meet a Swedish author. During morning he telephoned that it would be at the Savoy. The author was Brunius. Also present George Alexander, H. B. Irving, W. L. Courtney, another Swede living in England, named Valentin, I think, and Mair's colleague, Carnegie. I had to sit next to Brunius. He seemed a very nice, sound, provincial chap, with pretty bad English. But what the luncheon was for, and why such a strange gathering, I haven't the least idea. It was a Government luncheon, in a private room at the Savoy. Brunius specializes in Shakespeare, and he had come over for the celebrations. Alexander is very well preserved and behaved with great restraint (especially for an actor or any sort of *artiste*); quiet voice. Tells a story lengthily and without a spark of originality, but with effect. I had to leave at 2.50 for meetings.

Invasion alarm getting more acute on this coast.

Monday, May 8th.

Reading Marcel Dupont's *La Campagne* last night and night before. There is no genius in it. 40th edition. But it gives a plain notion of what war is, and some things are moving. Curious sensation lying in bed reading this, nightingale singing violently across the road, and horses and motors passing at intervals, and the thought that exactly similar scenes might be occurring here at any time, and that *this* house might be a ruined château and that *our* furniture might be defiled by German officers. At any rate according to the theory of the War Office. A period of extreme vigilance now on. It is a pity here that at new moon high water is at midnight. If high water was at 6 A.M. at new moon the periods of vigilance would be fewer if there were any at all. One night out of three our lieutenants have to spend at the telephone in the orderly room—8 P.M. to 8. A.M. The defensive works are being increased all along the coast.

Friday, May 12th.

London yesterday. Lunch with the brothers Buxton.[1] The elder told me the younger (my opponent as to pacificism in the *Daily News*) had ruined his sight in reading up land facts for Lloyd George's Land Valuation. He cannot read at all and can write very little. He looks much younger in every way than the bearded M.P. I like both of them very much. The younger thought the Reform Club "uneconomic"—especially the hall—evidently he has very little æsthetic sense.

On the way to Sardinia House a man overtook and accosted me. It was Coveney, once articled clerk at Le Brasseur & Oakley's. I had not seen him for 23 years at least. I knew him at once, and he me. It is true that he had written to me about a year ago asking if I was the A.B. he knew. He told me that Sparks, whom I put into *A Man from the North* as Albert Jenkins, was now a middle-aged man and apparently very able.

Mrs. Selfridge and Olga Nethersole at the W.A.R.C. sub-committee. Olga fat and oldish, with lightish hair, puffy face. She spoke well and sensibly. Mrs. Scott said she had a beautiful house and evidently plenty of money—I don't know where from.

Saturday, May 20th.

I slept at Reform Club. "Kemp! chamberlain!" Kemp is an ageing little man; very precise. "Did you know Mr. Henry James, sir?" Well, this was his room (next to mine) for fifteen years. Of course he had it beautifully furnished. In the morning Kemp came in and brought tea

---

[1] Noel and Charles Roden Buxton. They were both sent on a mission to secure Bulgaria's adherence to the Allied cause in 1914–1915, and they collaborated in a work on the Balkan situation.

and arranged everything in the small room (it really *was* small), and then walked to door, turned round at door, and said formally, "Your room is quite ready, sir," as if you didn't know. He is very careful lest he should give you anything to do, or too much to do. He doesn't say, "If you'll ring, sir, I'll do so and so." He says, "If you'll *just touch* the bell sir," etc., etc.

Friday, May 26th.

Some weeks ago Davray, official press agent of French Government, asked me to write an article on conscription in England. He laid down the lines, which he had taken from previous articles of mine in the *Daily News.* I wrote the article exactly on these lines and he was most enthusiastic about it. It was for *Le Temps,* which the Government now controls. The French censor turned it down entirely, and Davray in a letter to me this week gives the censor's actual words. He says the figures were not official (which they were) and might give rise to polemics; moreover, that conscription was now accomplished and there was no more to be said. But he had kept the article since before the final conscription bill was brought into Parliament. The censor's reason for refusing the article was, of course, purely political. This article gave the arguments on both sides; it stated that conscription—certain to come—would not greatly increase the army—and spoke of the necessity of trade, munitions, etc. The censor didn't like that.

The article would have cleared up misunderstandings into which the French public have fallen. The censor didn't like that, either.

Another curious example of rumour: that passports to soldiers on leave were now endorsed with the words that if the war ended before the leave ended the soldier must report at such and such a place, etc. This rumour, on reflection, is transparently idiotic for lots of reasons; yet many people believed it. I half believed it. Pinker believed yesterday that peace negotiations were on the way.

Monday, May 29th.

Talking with Captain ——, brigade major, last night, apparently an intelligent man, I mentioned the corruption of the Russian administration. He said, "Well, we aren't much better ourselves." I then learnt that he believed that Essen was not attacked by our aeroplanes because Asquith holds shares in Krupps! And yet one is expected to discuss politics seriously with such intelligences.

Thursday, June 1st.

Lieut. Myers told me yesterday that the gas officer came down yesterday to inspect gas-helmet efficiency of troops down here. Asked what would be the effect of gas on horses, he said he didn't know. And he an alleged expert. He afterwards found out from a man in the A.S.C. who had been at the front what the effect was. Myers pointed out that the whole A.S.C. here had only 25 helmets. The gas officer said that that would be all right and that as soon as an alarm was given the necessary helmets would be forwarded! I seem to see it!

Sergeant Humberstone had his son down here yesterday. Humberstone has been all his life in the Army—Coldstreams etc.—and is called "Dad" by all the other non-com. officers.

His son received a commission on the field for gallantry. When he came home, considerably knocked about, and met his father, his father saluted him, whereupon the son threw his arms round his father's neck and kissed him. During his visit here, father has introduced him with restrained pride to Myers and others. Humberstone is a very nice old man.

Monday, June 5th.

A brigade staff captain, speaking of invasion last night, said the Germans were expected to try for it in August and not before. He said they were waiting for a chance all last year. 3 Army corps had been practised in landings for a very long time. The finest troops. But lately, one corps, or part of it, had been taken for Verdun. Asked how he knew all these things, he said, "Intelligence." He spoke of a marvellous intelligence man named ——, now at Harwich, with whom he had talked, and who had recently penetrated the German lines, disguised as a woman, etc. He said the German plan was to land 40,000 men in one mile of coast. Lighters,

containing 1000 men each, to be towed over by destroyers. Gas shells.
Monitors with 15-in. guns to destroy our coast positions first. He said
we had done an enormous lot within the last few months, but that six
months ago there was nothing and the original British plan had been to
let the Germans penetrate 20 miles or so before tackling them. Now the
plan was to stop them from landing, and he thought we should do it.
He said they would probably try two places at once—here, and near
Newcastle-on-Tyne. Nothing he said altered my view that they couldn't
reach the coast at all. I told him this, and he said he was glad, but that
all precautions had to be taken.

The Captain said the district was full of spies, which I thought exaggerated. He said tennis lawns were inspected as gun positions prepared,
but they had never yet, in digging up a lawn, found any trace of preparation. I should imagine not. The buried gun and the prepared emplace-
ment stories show the inability of staffs to distinguish between rumours
probable and rumours grotesque.

Thursday, June 8th.

Came to London Tuesday morning for the Wounded Allies' "War
Fair" at the Caledonian Market. Heavy shower. Great success. I sold
books at M.'s stall. After 5.30, crowds of young women came to look at
books and some to buy. One well-dressed man had never heard of Balzac.
Demand for Kipling, Chesterton, Conrad, and me. Difficulty of selling
autographs. Enthusiasm for Jepson's *Pollyooly*. Met Pett Ridge, and he
looked just like an actor. Various estimates of profits of 2 days, but you
can see that the men keep estimates lower than their hopes. Thus Mr.
Henry—£8,000 to £15,000. Selfridge estimated attendance first day at
from 25 to 30,000. I agree. Yet one man in charge of a gate said that
through that gate alone he estimated that 30,000 people had passed. And
so on. There were not enough goods, nor stalls. The place looked nearly
empty when I arrived, and remained so. It was too big. I did a very good
trade in books, but I brought down prices at the end considerably, and
autographed favourites were going for 3s. and even 2s. 6d. Habit of
women of squealing out in ecstasy over name of a book and then refusing

even to consider the purchase of it. Perhaps they were so startled to find that they recognized a title.

News of Kitchener's drowning came at noon on first day. His sister Mrs. Parker was at M.'s stall, but she had left before it came. The rumour in the afternoon that Kitchener was saved roused cheers, again and again. . . . The Fair did not agree very well with my advertised descriptions of it, but it went excellently despite weather, and refreshments were fairly well managed. Bank took £800 of silver alone in car to bank on first night, and 4 or 5 men were counting hard all day.

Monday, June 12th.

Brig.-Gen. Y. dined here last night. He has been a soldier all over the Empire. He said: "I wonder whether they'll give votes to soldiers after the war. . . . The men who do the bulk of the work of the Empire never get a vote because they're always away. Kitchener, Curzon, Milner, never could exercise their votes before they were lords," etc. This was quietly said, but meant. It certainly gave a point of view. It showed a feeling. Of course Y. is in favour of all fit men of military age joining, and thinks tribunals ridiculous. But he is very quiet over it. Equally of course, he sees only the military argument. He has no imagination, no prophetic view, no wish for a better England, except militarily. But he must have done a certain amount of work in his time.

Friday, June 16th.

London yesterday. Spender told us some funny stories of his personal relations with the Kaiser. He said that in a talk about theology, the K. insisted that Boyd Carpenter was our greatest theologian.

In the railway carriages of the G.E.R., after 22½ months of war, they have at last got notices warning about spies and overheard conversations.

Tuesday, June 27th.

C. G., poet and friend of Larbaud, came to see us on Sunday morning. He ought to have arrived on Saturday, but had difficulties with police. He said that a prominent lady of Lyons (his native town) had urged that it was essential that the Croix Rouge should keep its character *mondain*. That in the *midi* most ladies went in for a little mild *croix rouge par pur snobbisme,* and then only in the mornings; afternoons for amusements. He said that the arrangements for wounded were still bad and had been appalling. He gave dreadful first-hand descriptions of wounded journey-ings. He said all French officers were in the first place dandies and in the second place afraid of the *jalon supérieur,* etc. Jealous, and careless of their men's lives; and that thousands (tens of) men's lives had been use-lessly lost simply because C.O.'s did not like to risk the reproach of inactivity. His indictment was terrific and almost wholesale. In brief— men splendid, officers rotten, system bad and corrupt. At the same time he said that the defence of Verdun was one of the very finest things of the war—sublime, etc., etc. But he apparently saw no contradiction be-tween these two attitudes or points of view of his. Much truth, or some truth in all he said, but no perspective, no realization of the good side.

Thursday, July 6th.

Not very optimistic about the big push,[1] which began last Saturday. Was told that minister's secretary had seen a telegram, and told him, to the effect that troops had once more overrun the points at which they had been ordered to stop. I didn't hear at what point or points this occurred.

Friday, July 14th.

London yesterday. Selfridge was extraordinarily eloquent and sane on the matter of the relations between employer and employed. But he was very jealous on politics. He said whenever politics came near their store they trembled. Asked by me what he considered the sphere of politics, he said politics was to govern. Apparently the immense difficulty of defining politics had not occurred to him. He has no trades unions to deal with. He said he gave a lecture at Leeds University and that the atmosphere was clearly hostile to employers. There can be little doubt that the condition of affairs in his store is just about ideal.

---

[1] The great British offensive along the Somme front.

Monday, July 17th.

I finished the *Carlotta* play yesterday morning.

On Thursday last I had a dictaphone installed here.

Saturday, July 22nd.

London, Thursday. Lunched with Pinker at the Arts Club. Club pretty empty. But before this, I walked through the City to Pinker's via Gracechurch St., Monument, etc. Places I had scarcely seen before. Very interesting and material for next novel. Tremendous impression of wealth and of common sense.

I sent *Carlotta* play to Doris Keane last night.

Friday, August 11th.

A fortnight ago last Wednesday we began my first holiday since the war. Slept at St. Pancras Hotel, which is rather like a church inside, with the longest corridor I ever saw.

Next day: Glasgow via Midland because it alone has kept restaurant carriages on its trains—I mean the three Scottish routes. St. Enoch Hotel. Fine suite for 25s. Richmond took us to the Alhambra, at the instigation of Marguerite. I was unwell through sleeplessness next day, so instead of visiting shell works we motored to Loch Lomond and so on. Very successful. Weir dined with us, also Richmond. Next day, Marguerite did shell works in morning. We lunched at W. Weir's, and in the afternoon went with Richmond to his new house at Blanefield, Kirkoswald, Ayrshire.

We stayed at Blanefield from the Saturday evening till Thursday morning. I soon got an effect of the county of Ayrshire, with its own character and industries. It is proud of its agriculture, especially potatoes. Ayr is a granite town, rich, with a good bookshop—out-of-the-way water-colours therein. Turnberry golf course, with big hotel, said by some to be the finest golf links in the world, is about 4 miles off Blanefield, on coast. Diversion from domesticity is to dress up and go there for dinner. I played a few holes (averaging 12) with parson of Kirkoswald.

Parsons have evidently more prestige in Scotland than in England. This one, though a mediocrity, had a lot, and "carried" it well. Absolutely old-fashioned in his ideas, I was told, but he has travelled. His greatest fault was the small joke. Beautiful church by brothers Adam, but when I said it was beautiful he seemed quite surprised, though of course agreeing.

Burns lived in Kirkoswald for 6 months "to complete his education"; so it has fame, and the churchyard draws people—I forget why.[1] Parson's house full of agreeable old things. Many books, but not a good collection.

We also went to Culzean Castle (Marquis of Ailsa). Superbly situated, right on the edge of the sea. Large. Built by Adam. Magnificent, and splendid rooms. But several generations of owners had done nothing to furnish it worthily, and the modern side stairs were terrible in every way. The main stair and the oval well are lovely. I did one or two water-colours at Blanefield, mostly very bad.

Thursday to Airemore, in Strathspey, right in the Highlands. A panorama of Cairngorm mountains in front of hotel. Very fine.

We left for Edinburgh on Monday and were much pleased with Edinburgh. An old driver, a shade drunk, drove us over all the town, and was most informing and useful. Great contrast between the fineness of Edinburgh and the dowdiness of Edinburgh and the dirtiness of its shops and cafés. Its site has really been *très bien compris,* and its natural advantages, scenically, are terrific.

On Wednesday we went to York, and had a very taciturn driver. I got some ideas for my next novel. At Edinburgh and York we stayed at railway hotels. In railway hotels as regards food the thing to do is to stick to the grill and the sideboard, which railway companies understand, for lunch and dinner.

Thursday, August 17th.

Yesterday I cycled to Frinton to see the shooting of the R.F.A. The target was the Frinton lifeboat, about 300 yards out. The guns were at

---

[1] Douglas Graham (Tam O'Shanter) and John Davidson (Souter Johnnie) are buried there.

Coldharbour, north of Frinton, range of about 2500 yards. L. seems to know nothing about artillery (yet he was in H.A.C.), and he was made observation officer so as to save him from having to shoot. He could not observe. He had no notion of observing, beyond marking a plus or a minus. The R.G.A. subs explained things to us, and were useful, at any rate to me. Half the shooting being over, a policeman was clearing people off the beach because of the danger. Last night at dinner I had the account of the shooting itself from one who had had to do some of it. He said the observation officer was supposed always to be a first-class gunner, as everything depended on him, but that an observation officer was not really necessary in this case (direct fire etc.). The generals were kidded accordingly. There were three generals. One of them knew nothing or little about gunnery. He made a great noise, and wanted a great noise made—explosions, and to see shells dropping in the sea. He told the gunners to fire quickly, and to remember that this was not manœuvres but war (which happily it was not). He constantly deranged Gen. Y.X., but Gen. Y.X., being a thorough expert, and not to be ruffled, went ahead and gave quiet orders to the gunners, ignoring Gen. Z.'s notions. Z. wanted rapid firing. Y.X. said, "What is the use of your firing the next shot until you know exactly what was wrong with the last and why?" Y.X. was evidently the bright spot in the proceedings.

What strikes me is the inability of all these generals to control themselves. They behave like kids with autocratic power. People like French merely dashed round, stayed 2 minutes and said, "Excellent, excellent." The whole body of subs is against the plan of defence, and calls it silly.

Speaking with Mason as to this, I said that it seemed improbable that the staff should be all wrong and the subs and captains right (though I agreed with the latter), and Mason said it was not improbable because the subs had had experience and the others hadn't. I think I have forgotten to mention that the observing officer was not informed that the lifeboat was not the target and that the target was an imaginary point beyond it.

Tuesday, August 22nd.

Invasion alarm Saturday night. Warnings to local units in the morning that there was Zepp activity. Second warning, instituting P.O.V. (Period of Vigilance) in the afternoon. At 11.30, after men in bed, orders came to R.G.A. (heavy guns) to take up positions at Frinton. In 45 minutes they had departed. This was good. Their guns were in position at 2.30 A.M. Nothing doing. They still regard the whole scheme of defence here as grotesque. At 3 P.M. Sunday P.O.V. was called off. In the meantime German fleet had definitely retired and we had lost 2 light cruisers.

Sunday, August 27th.

London last Thursday. At 4 P.M. S. S. McClure came by appointment and had a talk. He was very laudatory about England. Frankly considered himself one of the world's greatest experts on public opinion. Said law was respected in England and not in America. Said he had seen a customs official very roughly manhandled on quay at New York before an admiring audience of sailors etc. who thoroughly appreciated it.

Our own anti-aircraft shrapnel fell at Laudermere quay on Thursday night. Getting closer. At first it was thought to be a bomb, but it wasn't.

Saturday, September 2nd.

London Thursday. In the afternoon we saw the films of the Somme offensive. Very instructive and salutary. Dined with Mr. and Mrs. Gilbert Miller, who took us to see *Daddy-Long-Legs* at the Duke of York's, which Miller is at present controlling for America. An absolutely putrid play, with a new actress, Renée Kelly.

Sunday, September 10th.

London Thursday to Saturday. Dorziat lunched with us at Berkeley on Thursday. 2 committee meetings of W.A.R.C. As there was nothing for publicity committee to do we adjourned for a month. The general view among the W.A.R.C. was that the French authorities no longer wanted English hospitals. Wounded were now being treated chiefly just behind the front.

In view of recent round-ups, and my youthful appearance, I am now carrying about my birth certificate and registration card.

Thursday, September 28th.

Corfe Castle. I came down here on Tuesday to join John Wright in half a week of water-colouring. The New Forest was in its best form. All the scenery of the Isle of Purbeck very fine. Corfe Castle is spectacular. It was very wet yesterday. I did a water-colour through the rainy window in the morning, and part of an interior in the afternoon. Wright knows every one in village. He told me how at the beginning of the war there were women here also who carefully explained to their inferiors how they were to behave when the Germans came.

Friday, September 29th.

The butcher's daughter practises the piano close to the hotel very well and brilliantly. Her Chopin is understood to be remarkable. Today it is raining all day, very heavily. Nevertheless, this morning, under an outhouse shed at Wright's, I did one of my best water-colours. Unfortunately I heated the sketching frame to dry it, and it stuck to the varnish and is now torn.

Weather is in fact horrible. Landlord full of theories about Zepps and moon, because once in the Navy. I don't know how it follows, but it does. Last evening I did a water-colour in blacksmith's garden. He related to us how a "picture" hawker had tried to sell him a pair of pictures. "Look here," said blacksmith, "if you can show me a place to hang 'em in my parlour, I'll buy 'em." Hawker entered and looked. "Nay, guv'nor, you've done me. There's no room." And there wasn't, for portraits of Kitchener, French, etc., etc.

Saturday, October 7th.

I went to London on Thursday. Lunched at Lady Paget's. She was late—her doctor being late—and she sent word down to Mrs. Lewis

Harcourt and me that we were to begin. The business was the appeal I had written for the American Women's Hospital. I liked Mrs. Harcourt. Youngish. Quiet. Self-possessed. She said that they asked her not to take a maid when she went to the continent, but she met on the journey an American woman with two maids. Lady Paget came down when our lunch was nearly over.

She told us private information about the way Zepps are caught. Two aeroplanes go up with a long wire between them. When they have got this wire against the Zepp they electrify it and it sets fire to the Zepp. Also they entangle the Zepp in the wire and thus drag the Zepp along. She seemed to believe all this. Some people will swallow anything.

Yesterday, lunch at McKenna's. Runciman (looking ill again). Lord Fisher, Duchess of Rutland, and Mr., Mrs., and Miss Davison. Davison is a partner in Pierpont Morgan and is arranging loans. Before lunch Mrs. —— took me aside and explained that I had to be polite to Davison, as if people weren't polite to him he wouldn't let us have any money. She was quite serious. The whole family had been to the front as far as Rheims. I liked the look of Davison.

I sat between Fisher and the girl. In two minutes he had referred to "bloody experts." Touching Falkland battle and Cradock's defeat, he said that a tortoise had been sent to catch a hare, and then two tortoises. He ordered the two fastest ships there were to go off at once. People protested. An admiral came up from Portsmouth and said that really they ought to be overhauled before leaving. "Not at all," said Fisher, "they must leave tonight." And he said to me: "They only arrived ten minutes too soon. The only real victory we've had at sea yet. It doesn't want an expert to see that a tortoise can't catch a hare, and that a hare has never yet been wounded by a tortoise and won't be." Then the phrase about bloody experts. He was evidently still feeling his shunt from the Admiralty. He said: "I was the only one who objected to the Dardanelles expedition. Kitchener was in favour of it. He's dead. Won't say anything about him. He got the Order of the Garter. I got the order of the boot."

He said that in October 1914, having *carte blanche* from Lloyd George, he ordered 612 new vessels for the Navy. He didn't think the German line would be broken in the west, and was in favour of an invasion of Pomerania, only 82 miles from Berlin. He said that this possibility was the only thing that had ever made Frederick the Great afraid. He seemed to have developed this scheme. He told some excellent stories with strong language. They say he is like a boy. He absolutely is. He said: "I'm told I shall live till I'm 110. So I've plenty of time yet." He gave me his favourite quotation:

> Not heaven itself upon the past has power,
> What has been has been, and I have had my hour.

They also say that he smacks more of the forecastle than of the bridge. There is something in this, too.

Monday, October 9th.

Clegg brought a Capt. B. (of his Battery) to lunch. Had been out at Ypres ten months and then wounded in the head, in front of right ear. He carries a good scar. He talked well, and said he should like to write if he could. I told him he could.

He said the newspaper correspondents' descriptions of men eager to go up over the parapet made him laugh. They never were eager. He related how he had seen a whole company of men extremely pale with apprehension and shaking so that they could scarcely load their rifles. Then he said that men who nevertheless *did* go over in that state were really brave. He told us how his battery saw hundreds, thousands, of grey figures coming along only 1000 yards off, and every man thought he would be a prisoner in ten minutes, when suddenly thousands of Canadians appeared from nowhere, and the Boches fled. The cheering was delirious. He told this very dramatically, but without any effort to be effective. He said he really wanted to be back with the battery. For a long time the fellows wrote to him regularly once a fortnight, and every letter ended with "When are you coming back?" He said they had had glorious times now and then, glorious. He said that to sit on a factory chimney and see the Boches going over was better than big-game shooting. He said the Boches had any amount of pluck and grit. And Clegg said that even in hospital they would stand things that an Englishman probably wouldn't. Both Clegg and B. facetiously contrasted the rough, anyhow, bumping treatment the wounded get on their way from the firing line (when they really *are* ill) with the hushed, tender, worshipping treatment they get on arriving in London when many of them are doing pretty well.

Wednesday, October 25th.

On Friday I went to Nottingham under charge of Captain Lloyd, R.N., to inspect a national projectile factory. Article written on this for munitions ministry propaganda.

On Sunday in a dreadful east wind we went to Peldon to see the Zepp. It was worth seeing. Was told, *inter alia,* that Air Department had refused offer of 100 engines a week eight months ago. They said they had placed sufficient orders, and would not believe that some of the firms who had accepted orders would never be able to deliver. Now they want more engines. They also need larger planes to go to Essen. They have refused and still do refuse the only size of plane that will satisfactorily bomb Essen, on the plea that it is "aerodynamically" wrong.

Thursday, October 26th.

Came to London. Lunched with Clutton-Brock and Judge Evans. The latter a collector. Then old Rawlinson came to the same table, also a collector. Their talk was rather refreshing and reassuring. It showed how painters materially live.

Worked on my novel (after a sleep) all afternoon till 5 P.M. I dined alone and went alone to Aldwych in the dark in a creeping taxi to see *Il Seraglio.* In time for second act. Long, tedious waits. A few too-well-dressed women in boxes, attended by their courts. Lovely tunes in opera. But otherwise nearly as ridiculous as musical comedy.

I got some cigarettes yesterday with a card of astronomical information about Mars. Some boys may grow up with cigarette cards their sole education.

Friday, November 3rd.

I came to London on Wednesday and took possession of apartment C at the R. Thames Y.C. which I have rented. Rather like celibate life in Paris again. I dined at the Club and read Macready's diary; extraordinary sensation of having resumed a closed chapter of existence.

Thursday, dined with M. at Elysée Restaurant. Dancing by two nice professional girls at intervals. Young nut who came in at 9.31 and asked whether it was just before or just after drink-closing time. He crossed legs and leaned on stick before beginning to ask waiter.

Caledonian Market this morning. I got there too soon and saw trucks and hand-carts and carts being wheeled up by all sorts of people— many foreigners. Type of pale puffed skin, or pinched and full red lips. I went back to tailor's to try on, and went to market again at noon, when it was in full swing. I bought an eastern bowl.

Thursday, November 9th.

At night I went to Lord Mayor's banquet with Regge of Frinton. I asked usher if I *had* to be received. He said I could please myself; so I wasn't, and joined Pett Ridge and another acquaintance whose name I couldn't recall behind a barrier at the entrance. Fisher got loudest cheers. Funny to see Asquith followed by his wife and daughter. Reception, in library, took at least an hour. Names called from usher to usher, and ushers walked continually up and down the length of the library with guests. In great hall, about 1500 guests. Beef carvers at foot of big sculptures, with rags and knives in sheaths, stood on high platforms carving barons of beef. At the end, a policeman lifted one old carver down. Procession inwards of nobs. Maids of Honour with pink bouquets for Lady Mayoress. Trumpeters. Inauguration march by solicitor, X.Y., awful tosh. Soup tepid. Fish cold. Pheasant good. Cold meat good. No veg. Sweets excellent. Fruit good. Wines good. Box of

2 cigars and 2 cigarettes to each male guest, but no smoking in hall. Awful dowdiness of women, including nobs. After dinner, Maids of Honour appeared in a row in balcony in front of Lord Mayor, and arranged their pink streamers to hang over balcony. Reporters had seats near nobs. Took about 5-minute turns, and handed a watch to each other. Trumpeting before L.M.'s chaplain's grace (short and inaudible) before and after meal. Trumpeting (2 pairs of trumpets, one echoing the other, very good; trumpeters covered with gold braid and with black velvet jockey caps) before each toast. Comic toastmaster who had a huge rosette and scarf, and looked up to skies in announcing toasts. . . . Loving cup never reached us. . . . General effect, old stonework, carving, sculptures, 2 galleries (top: musicians), to left of L.M. wooden beams, gilded roof. Dependent flags. Stone inscriptions round roof. Old flags at one side. City costumes, gilded. Black velvet and lace costumes. Levée costumes. Military ditto. Foreign ditto. Vast epaulettes of Ministers. Lord Mayor leaning back with false ease in his great gilded chair. Many City officials behind him. Look of tradition, city-ness, grooviness, in ugly and yet often decent faces of men.

Councillors had to wear their mazarine (?) costumes (trimmed with fitch fur) at reception, but some took them off for dinner (£12 each). Electric chandeliers. Flowers on tables. Rows of heads. . . . Blackened windows. Policemen at every door. Draught on my head. Ben Davies sang *God Save the King* very well. The name of Venizelos aroused easily the most cheering. Herbert Samuel spoke without conviction. Balfour was resentful, defensive, and then over-confident (as to ability to prevent future Channel raiders from getting back). He said "the service which I for the moment represent." French Ambassador quite inaudible after first few sentences. Lord French perky and sure—kept looking down at MS. Asquith was the best. Diction uneven but phrasing absolutely perfect throughout. He was grim but not boastful.

After Asquith, I left.

Tuesday, November 14th.

I came home from town on Friday afternoon, with Swinnerton and

Marguerite. Swinnerton was walking out on Sunday evening (dark) in the village looking for me, and not finding me, he asked a little boy whether he had seen a gentleman, Mr. Bennett, with 4 dogs. The boy mumbled a negative. Swinnerton then proceeded to describe me, etc., and the boy said, "I seen Mr. Bennett with *one* dog."

Yesterday Miss Nerney calculated that I had written 16,000 words of my new novel.[1]

Thursday, November 16th.

I came to town yesterday morning with Mrs. Lowndes, who had come to us on Monday afternoon for two nights. Two nights of excellent gossip and scandal. She was very nice about servants, war economy, etc. She said she had A1 knowledge that German supplies would run seriously out at the end of February.

Thursday, November 23rd.

In the afternoon, after some work, I found I had a chill on the stomach. I went with precautions to the Aldwych Theatre and got the last remaining circle seat for the first performance of *Aïda*. Theatre full. Goodish performance but offensive scenery that tried to be original and was only imitative and ridiculous. Oh! Russian ballet, what horrible sins you have caused.

Friday, November 24th.

I went to tea with H. G. [Wells] at St. James's Court. He told me his scheme for a whole series of new books, some being novels. He wants monarchy destroyed, of course, and to have a new religion (that there is one God—and apparently he can be what you like) without priests or churches. He thought very little of British high command at the front, had had difficulties with censor about his articles on the front, and meant to say what he thought in a book to be issued in January.

I was still suffering yesterday from my stomach chill, but I wrote 1000 words.

---

[1] This was *The Roll Call*, published in 1918.

I went up to the Omega workshops by appointment to see Roger Fry. Arrived as arranged at 2.30. I was told he was out. Then that he was at his studio, down Fitzroy Street. I went there and rang. He opened door. "Come and have lunch," he said. "I've had lunch, it's 2.30," I said. "How strange!" he said. "I thought it was only 1.15." Then as he went upstairs he cried out to a girl above: "Blank (her Xtian name), it's 2.30," as a great item of news. Fry expounded his theories. He said there was no original industrial art in England till he started, i.e. untraditional. He said lots of goodish things and was very persuasive and reasonable. Then he took me to the showrooms in Fitzroy Square, and I bought a few little things. I did not buy a fine still life by Duncan Grant. But I may, later. I gradually got to like a number of the things, especially the stuffs. He said manufacturing (English) firms roared with laughter at his suggestion that they should do business together. One firm quoted an impossible price when he asked them to make rugs to his design at his risk. But when a eulogistic article appeared in *The Times* they quoted a lower price, a reasonable one. He said that both French and German firms would take his stuff. I began to get more and more pleased with the stuff, and then I left with two parcels.

This morning I went to Carfax Gallery and bought a Sickert, "Coster Girl." Had some talk with the proprietor, who was highly intelligent, and stuck to it that Claude Phillips, though he couldn't write, had real taste. The boss thought Sickert the greatest artist of the age.

Saturday, November 25th.

The manager of the Carfax Gallery told me yesterday that some people were very antagonistic. One old gentleman in white spats said he had read in *Morning Post* a good account of Sargent drawings and he had come to see them. When he saw them he said that he regarded the show as a swindle—that it was robbery to charge 1s. for such an affair. Clifton gave him his 1s. back.

Thursday, November 30th.

It was only last week that I received a copy of the entirely new and revolutionary Instructions to Emergency Committees, which were issued on the 16th August last. Even then I only got one copy. I asked for half a dozen more and got one more.

Thus for three months the whole scheme has been changed and I, in charge of a district including several towns and 30 parishes, was entirely ignorant of it. So were the civilians concerned. I protested, but I got no explanation.

Sunday, December 3rd.

Central military representative for Essex has no copy of Scheme K, which is the present emergency scheme. He lent me his only copy. When he has to consider it in order to advise me on doubtful points I have to return it to him. It is printed. I have been able to get only one other copy. So the preparation of instructions for this division drags on. The matter is supposed to be urgent.

Thursday, December 7th.

Tuesday afternoon I read through what I have written of my new novel. Not so bad. Undoubtedly I have been refreshed and invigorated by reading Dreiser's *The Financier*, which absolutely held me. *The Titan*, which I am now reading, is not so good.

I came to London yesterday with M. Rebecca West, Gladys Wheeler, and H. G. Wells lunched with me at Romano's. Wells called my fob "gastric jewellery"! He offered to bet 2 to 1 that the war would be over by August next.

Friday, December 8th.

Dined at Thatched House with F. Rosher, Swinnerton, and Sir James Dunlop Smith, political secretary to the India Office. Among a number of interesting stories he told how he had found the largest ruby in the world (rather larger than the bowl of an ordinary liqueur glass), a historical stone, lost for 70 years, in a necklace of the Queen's.

Wednesday, December 13th.

Lieut. R., of a mobile Anti-Aircraft unit stationed at Thorpe, came for tea. He said he carried £15,000 worth of stores. He said that after big raid at Hull, end of last year about, when Mayor of Hull had been assured that Hull was one of the most heavily defended places, and a Zepp dropped 15 bombs in the town, the population afterwards mobbed officers, and A.A. officers coming into the town had to put on Tommies' clothes. Also that Naval Unit was telegraphed for and that when it came with full authorized special lights, the population, angry at the lights, assaulted it with stones and bottles and put half of it in hospital, and had ultimately to be kept off by the military. He outlined complex administrative system of unit, and showed how utterly and needlessly idiotic it was. He told me how he had been sent to some golf links with a big mobile gun, and had put gun into a good spot where it interfered with play on first hole, the officially indicated position being a bad one. The affair was urgent, as a raid was expected that night. He successfully repulsed various complainants from golf club; but next morning an infantry officer came specially down from War Office, with instructions (positive orders) that gun must be moved. R. gave reasons against. Infantry officer: "I don't know anything about artillery but that gun has got to be moved. It is my order to you." In order to fix gun in inferior official position, R. indented for railway sleepers to the tune of £127, and got them. Meanwhile the golf club professional had told him that it would be quite easy to modify the course.

Thursday, December 21st.

Ill ever since last entry.

I got up for lunch Tuesday and also yesterday. Today I was up for breakfast and have read through last finished chapter of new novel. But I can't yet write, except articles (for *Statesman*). During illness I have had excellent ideas for novel.

On Tuesday we had cable that Marguerite's sister, Gabrielle, had died at Pau.

Sunday, December 31st.

I finished the first part of my London novel this afternoon, 35,000 words. I wrote only 127,600 during the year. The totals of later years, however, cannot be compared fairly with totals of earlier years, as latterly I have not counted my journal.

We had 10 to Xmas dinner. I read *The Old Wives' Tale,* the first time I have read it through since I corrected the proofs 8 or 9 years ago, I think.

1917

Thursday, January 4th. London.

Came to town yesterday. Lunched with Wells and his two boys and Ross at the Reform. Ross told me, as regards inaccuracies in *Dict. National Biog.*, that he offered to look through the proofs of Wilde's biography, but proofs were never sent to him. He found 18 mistakes of fact in the biography.

Gardiner, editor *Daily News,* suggested that I should resume writing for *D.N.* I said I would resume only on similar conditions as before; namely that I had a regular commission for articles, to appear at regular intervals—I didn't mind what the intervals were.

After the immense public row between Lloyd George and Gardiner, the following lately occurred. T. P. O'Connor came up to Gardiner and said: "You may be interested in a piece of information which I have. It is not second-hand. I myself heard the words spoken. The other day Ll. George spoke of you in very friendly terms. He said you were not like the rest. Your difference of opinion was honest and he respected it. Yes, he spoke in the kindliest terms of you." A few days later another henchman of Ll. G. came up to Gardiner at the N.L. Club and said, "You may be interested to know that I heard Ll. George speak of you in the very friendliest terms the other day." And so on, as before. Thus is it sought to work the oracle.

Vedrenne wrote me, giving way and agreeing to pay £200 down on

611

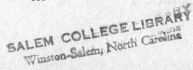

receipt of MS. of a play for Eadie, for option on it. He had said to Pinker, "I never have paid and I never will pay to read a play."

Friday, January 5th.

Wounded Allies' Committee in afternoon.

I read *Le Mystère de la Chambre Jaune* again. Not bad.

Evening I went to M.'s flat, and we dined at the Ristorante del Commercio, or some such name, in Frith St., very well. One of those family restaurants. Papa, stern, in charge, mamma pleasant, also in charge, a nice girl to help. Glimpse of kitchen with chef and a woman and a girl. Three children of papa and mamma messing about most of the time: girls of 7 or 8, in white silk with gilt and silvered diadems, and a smaller boy. This place was very agreeable.

This morning I called first on M. Then to see Lanchester, who described to me his scheme for tabulating information for Neville Chamberlain and Man-Service Board in the form of maps and charts. Very interesting. He also showed me a set of competition plans for use in my novel. Then to Carfax Gallery to pay a bill for a Sickert. Clifton said that Conder[1] was very casual. He would be out with Clifton towards evening and would say, "I've got no silk and I'd like to do a fan tonight," and he would go into any little draper's in a side street, the big shops being already closed, and buy a yard of silk of no matter what quality. He nearly always worked by candlelight.

Monday, January 8th. Comarques.

I came home on Friday afternoon, with Swinnerton. Walpole came the next day, and we had two uproarious evenings, too long and too smoky. Walpole insisted on my finding for him all Jacob Tonson's articles in *New Age*.[2] He spent all Sunday afternoon in reading them, and said that a selection from them ought to be published in volume. Swinnerton said that Chatto & Windus would be delighted to publish

---

[1] Charles Conder (1868-1909), the artist whose exquisite painting on fans gave him a particular vogue.

[2] "Jacob Tonson" was the pseudonym under which Bennett wrote his early articles for this periodical.

the volume, and I practically offered him the volume. Both of them left on Monday morning.

Saturday, January 13th. Comarques.

Wednesday evening I went into Westminster Cathedral and saw how to use it again in my novel. Very cold day. Nice warm cathedral. Ugly chapels, detail invisible. A non-R.C. parson or two squinting about. Noise of a charwoman washing floor. Exceedingly few people. Then at 10.10, either prime or tierce. A few performers came in, after a bell had rung, took their seats, and then the intoning begins, scarcely audible for a second or less. It "steals out." Words utterly incomprehensible. Outside, front of shop devoted to rosaries, crucifixes, etc.

Friday, January 19th. London.

Lunch at Reform today. Informed positively that Nivelle was to include all British Army in his command. It was said that he said of Haig: *"Il n'est pas assez souple. Il est trop orgueilleux."* This statement absolutely contradicted by Press Bureau tonight. Tonight in Piccadilly an immense red flare in sky, followed by a great explosion. Piccadilly rather excited. Mair informed on telephone at 10.30 that chemical works at Blackwall exploded and set fire to South Metropolitan Gasworks. "Thousands of wounded in hospital." We shall see if this is the fact.[1]

Mair and Willie Weir and George Whale dined with me tonight at Yacht Club. Very interesting. Mair said there was nothing in alarm of German invasion of Switzerland and that it had been deliberately got up by French authorities (who said Foch was at Besançon and actually began to dig trenches) in order to get Swiss securities out of Switzerland into France for purpose of helping to regulate exchange.

Mair promised to take me over London in airship.

Wednesday, January 24th. London, Yacht Club.

I came to London yesterday morning. Hard frost and cold travelling.

---

[1] This was the disastrous explosion at Silvertown when many workers were killed and injured.

Lunch with Pinker at Arts Club today about the whole question of cinematograph rights, which I regard as a swindle on the author. Constant fine snow showers.

Sunday, January 28th. Comarques.

On Thursday Wells and I dined at Reform. Tossed for bill and he lost. Then we went to Petit Riche basement restaurant and saw the Hayneses, the Lynds, and Rebecca West.

I came home on Friday morning. I am in unusually good form for work. In spite of radiators and fires, it is very difficult to keep the house warm. N.E. wind and frost.

Saturday, February 3rd. London, Yacht Club.

Went to London on Wednesday morning.

Wells and I lunched together again at Reform. He and Gardiner were in favour of communal feeding in case of starvation, as most efficient, beginning in schools. But Wells took submarine menace, like me, very calmly. On the other hand, Donald[1] and R. McKenna were much upset by it and gave dramatic figures. Afterwards I took Wells to Burlington Fine Arts Club to see English aquarelles, and he took me to call on Mrs. De Boer, and we took her to Roger Fry's at Omega workshops.

Monday, February 5th. Thorpe-le-Soken.

The announcement that U.S.A. had severed diplomatic relations with Germany caused really very little discussion here. It was discussed a little at lunch. Already the intensely misunderstanding and unjust attitude of M. and officers (some of them) to U.S.A. is changing. At tea, when Lieut. and Mrs. Tracy[2] came, it was discussed a little, and Mrs. Tracy well formulated for me the advantages of an "American peace," that is, an unbiased peace, which was received with silence not altogether hostile. Afterwards Clegg agreed with me as to the advantages of the

---

[1] Now Sir Robert Donald, editor of the *Daily Chronicle*, 1902–18.
[2] Louis Tracy, the author and journalist, had recently returned from America, where he had lectured extensively on the War.

"American peace." During the remainder of the evening nothing was said as to America.

Thursday, February 8th. London, Yacht Club.

Dined at Mme. Van der Velde's and sat at a spiritualistic séance with a clairvoyant named Peters, who brought his son, a youth in R.A.M.C., home for a few hours on leave. This son said there were 500 professed spiritualist soldiers at Aldershot. Theosophist. Peters (*père*), man of 45 or so. Short. Good forehead. Bald on top, dark hair at sides. Quick and nervous. Son of a barge owner. Present: Yeats, Mr. and Mrs. Jowett (barrister—she very beautiful), Roger Fry, hostess, and me. Peters handled objects brought by each of us. His greatest success, quite startling, was with the glass stopper of a bottle brought by Jowett. He described a man throwing himself *out* of something, down, with machinery behind him, and a big hotel or big building behind him. Something to do with water, across water. He kept repeating these phrases with variations. The stopper had belonged to the baronet (I forget his name) who threw himself off a launch, in response to a challenge from X., at 3 A.M. into the Thames, after a debauched party up river. All the passengers were more or less drunk. He was drowned.

He succeeded, with my toothpick, in getting me to the Potteries and into the office of the Staffordshire *Knot* or *Sentinel,* and described a man that might be either Goold or the editor of the *Sentinel,* and said that known or unknown to me, this man had greatly influenced me. He insisted on the word "Zola." "Zola." He said there was a message to tell me. I hadn't done my best work. I am morally sure he hadn't the least idea who I was. And even if he had, he didn't know the tooth-pick belonged to me, even if he knew it was I who had brought it, which he might conceivably have done as it was the last thing he picked up off the tray. I made full notes.

Friday, February 9th.

I wrote 1200 words of London novel.

Today George Moore and W. Sickert came to lunch. Sickert had swum that morning and skated. He had his skates with him—no over-coat. I said little. They talked. Moore was the man of letters. He said, of a Landor dialogue between Horne Tooke and Johnson, that it would not interest ordinary people, but that a man of letters might read it under his lamp at night with great amusement.

Sickert said that he cooked his own food and cooked it very well. Formerly he used to read between spells of painting during the day. Now he cooked. He would go over to the stove and say, "*Ça mijotte.*" They both used a lot of French and spoke it very well. Moore recited a French ballad which he had written about a *maquereau*, which I thought rather good. Then he recited Villon. Moore evidently wants to get into the theatre again. Unfortunately I had no encouragement for him. He has an idea for dramatizing *The Brook Kerith*. He is naïvely and harmlessly vain, and very agreeable. I enjoyed these men very much. 1500 words.

Saturday, February 10th. London, Yacht Club.

Continuing Moore and Sickert from yesterday. Moore seemed to have detached himself almost completely from the war. He said he didn't read newspapers now, as they only made him feel depressed and did him no good. He said several entirely foolish things, such as that he could not understand (very much emphasized) how any one could read a *war book*. To read about new war devices he could under-stand, but how any one could read a war book he could *not* understand. Sickert was much more reserved—he is much more normal.

Wednesday, February 14th. London, Yacht Club.

I met Dr. Shufflebotham (Stoke) and went with him to the Palladium (where the entertainment was awful). He told me one of the principal poison-gas factories was in Burslem. He said they had gradually learnt the effects of the gases on the Germans by the effect of the gases on their own workpeople, over *half* of whom had been on compensation during the past year. He told a funny tale of how in the early days there was a massed band Sunday fête (semi-religious) in Burslem Park, to which all the children in white came after Sunday school. Children began to cry. People said it was symptom of whooping cough. Then to cough. Further symptoms. Then adults began to cry and cough. Word went round at once, gas escaping from a factory. Every one fled from the park. Bandsmen dropped their instruments. Two of them met at gates. "Bill, where's thy bloody drum?" "It's where thy bloody cornet is, lad."

Tuesday, February 27th. London, Yacht Club.

We came to London yesterday morning. Stage Society in the afternoon. *Good Friday* by Masefield. A terribly dull and portentous thing in rhyme. I was most acutely bored. I found that all the élite said they liked the damned thing.

Shaw and Lee Matthews and I had tea together. I shifted Shaw a little in the end.

Last week I finished reading the Balzac vol. containing *La Recherche de l'Absolu* and *La Peau de Chagrin*. Both these are very fine indeed. The short stories, *Le Chef d'Œuvre, Inconnu,* and *Melinoth Reconcilé,* are good, the last the best. *Jesus Christ in Flanders* is negligible. On the whole a terrific volume.

Thursday, March 1st. London, Yacht Club.

Sharpe lunched with me at Reform Club. I seemed to be wandering about all day in search of ideas for novel. R.C. Cathedral. Lanchester's Bond St. shop, clubs. By about 6.30 I had got them all. A Lieut. Bayne (Gordon Highlanders, lost his left arm) dined with me and Shufflebotham at Café Royal—very well.

Shuff told me that when he went into factory for lachrymatory shells at Walthamstow the water poured out of his eyes and filled a jug.

Friday, March 2nd. London, Yacht Club.

I wrote about 1500 words of novel yesterday.

After dining alone at the Reform I went up to Roger Fry's newly constituted Omega Club in Fitzroy Square. Only about 2 chairs. The remainder of the seats are flattish canvas bags cast on floor near walls and specially made for this. An exhibition of kids' drawings round the walls. Strange crowd, including Mme. Van der Velde, Lytton Strachey, the other Strachey,[1] Yeats, Borenius, etc. They all seemed very intelligent.

Wednesday, March 7th. London, Yacht Club.

I returned home from London on Friday last, wrote large quantities of my London novel each day, wrote my Sardonyx article in odd moments, and came back to London again yesterday.

Lunched with Wells. The Webbs said that the new "business men" officials had upset all Whitehall. New ministers' habit of writing letters from home and getting answers at home and thus springing surprises on departments is also much resented.

I worked all afternoon at Y.C. Massingham, Ross, and I dined together. I was thus between two pacifists.

Massingham told a good story of an Australian who was asked his opinion as to the end of the war. The Australian said, "I think what my friend Fritz thinks. Fritz was my German prisoner—a very decent sort of chap. Fritz said, 'You'll win, but you'll all come home on one steamer.'"

This of course expressed Massingham's view beautifully, also Ross's.

Thursday, March 15th. London, Yacht Club.

H. L. Rothband,[2] the Manchester manufacturer, lunched with me yesterday at Reform, about his scheme for employment of disabled soldiers. Curious mixture of ingenuousness and acuteness. I missed the beginnings of a shindy between Spender and Massingham. Masterman brought this safely to an end by leaving the smoking-room with Massingham and sitting in the gallery. Spender was with Buckmaster.

I wrote another 1100 words of novel yesterday after another very bad night, and I was so exhausted in the afternoon that I could scarcely even walk.

---

[1] John St. Loe Strachey, editor of the *Spectator*.
[2] Sir Henry Lesser Rothband was originator of the scheme for the King's National Roll for Finding Employment for Disabled Sailors and Soldiers.

Penry Williams told me on Monday that he had his beagles with him at Bournemouth. They raided a butcher's shop. The dog-master asked butcher what the damage was. The butcher said £6. The dog-master said, "I'll toss you for it." They tossed and the butcher lost. This is a good sporting-military story.

Friday, March 16th. London, Yacht Club.

Another 1400 words yesterday morning of novel. Mair lunched with me at Reform and Davray joined us.

Mair said that Nivelle, in London this week, had been made C.-in-C. of all armies (French and English) on the western front, but that the appointment would of course not be published.

Afterwards we went to the Omega Club, and saw dancing by an alleged marvellous boy dancer. He did seem pretty fair for a kid. I asked if he was Russian and learnt that he had been discovered in Brondesbury and was entirely English.

Thursday, March 22nd. London, Yacht Club.

I had neuralgia a lot yesterday. Went to see M. in the morning. I curiously enjoyed going to A.B.C. in Piccadilly at noon for hot milk and a sandwich. Tonight, though, I have bought a first edition of an evening paper in order to read the morning's news over again. This is almost indispensable to a morning visit to an A.B.C.

I bought the new Conrad, *The Shadow-Line*. Good.

Friday, March 23rd. London, Yacht Club.

Today I began to find ideas for second part of my London novel, while spending most of the morning at barber's and in meditation in library of Reform Club. Much good political and military converse with Wells, Gardiner, and Massingham after lunch at Reform, and a solitary afternoon here.

I finished Conrad's *The Shadow-Line* last night. A short story disguised as a novel. Very good, but a certain anti-climax where the climax ought to be.

Saturday, March 24th. London, Yacht Club.

Dined with Sir W. Weir (Director of Air Supply), Major Weir (Flying Staff, W.O.) and Richmond, at Savoy, after spending ½ hour in the Angelica Kauffmann room at Weir's flat.

They began to try to startle me right off. Weir and Richmond said that the labour situation was acutely bad. Tyne strike not better. Men out at Barrow, and men out at 3 or 4 small factories that worked for Weir. The strikes were not officially countenanced by trades unions, the organization alien (U.S.A.) working through shop stewards, etc.

The Barrow men were stopped by men they knew a long way from their shops, and they obeyed the order to strike. The orders were mainly transmitted not by post but by motor bicycle. The Government knew all about it, as the trades unions had told them everything as fast as they learnt it.

After very long faces, both Weir and Richmond said that though it might be very awkward, it couldn't be permanently serious, as the men generally being honest and patriotic would not stand for it. Also that to catch hold of a few leaders (who were simply seditious) would do a lot to stop it. Then I was told of a new invention of a Rumanian, Constantinesco, for the transmission of power by means of an elastic fluid. This device is now actually in use in the machine guns of aeroplanes, but he said its applications were endless, and that it would revolutionize machinery. The Government will not at present let anything be published about it at all.

Weir—and all these Weirs are real experts—said Constantinesco was one of the great men, in his own line, of a century. Then they began on submarine question. Very serious. Weir said that if things went on as at present transport would be *vitally* affected in less than four months. Still, he believed in our victory in the field.

Talking about the labour question, they all greed that the margin of labour was sufficient; that is, that the Government could draw all the men it needed for the Army out of essential occupations and that the men left in the essential occupations could do all the work, provided they would *produce their maximum output,* which they don't and won't. All three were enthusiastic about the effort of France. W. Weir said that as regards aeroplane supply, the Germans got the best designs they could, and made a lot of it, telling the manufacturer meanwhile to use the field experience of his machines in thinking out a new and better design, but sticking to the execution of the original order. We were always trying after improvements, and Weir said that you can't "force" technical progress advantageously beyond a certain speed. The result was that while we always had easily the best machine in existence we never had enough. He intended that this should be remedied in May.

Monday, March 26th. Comarques.

Strange rumours on Saturday night. As that Ireland had revolted again and reserve batteries were being sent from Woolwich to Ireland by special trains. (Apparently quite untrue.) Also that five German cruisers were lying off Harwich. What the British fleet was doing meanwhile was not explained. Many troops were undoubtedly drafted into this district, and on Sunday morning Liverpool Street was a pandemonium of returning officers summoned by wire, necessitating special trains.

Friday, March 30th. London, Yacht Club.

I was wondering yesterday whether I ought not to keep a list of prophecies made to me.

Donald said that the Russians would make no offensive this year and that had it not been for the Revolution they would have made peace.

W.A.R.C. meeting, with funny written descriptions of rows between doctor and administrator and nurses at our Balkans Hospital.

Dined with M. at flat. Then to Ambassadors, but were too late for the ballet *Pomme d'Or*. Vansittart's French Revolution play, *Class,* was a pretty good idea spoilt by lack of invention and uncertain handling. Anatole France's *Man Who Married a Dumb Wife* served very well. Pierre Veber's *Gonzague* (with Morton), a common farce of intrigue, was a most ingeniously constructed affair. There is nobody in England (whether or not as bereft of genius as Veber is) who could construct a little farce so well. Nothing to it, but very agreeable to witness. Excellently produced and excellently played. This was the best evening I have had at the theatre for I don't know how long—perhaps during the war.

R. Donald said that he was getting some men to write messages to Russia for cabling, but he had to obtain Lloyd George's approval first. During the afternoon he sent me up a note to say he had obtained the approval and would I send in a 500-word message quickly.

Saturday, March 31st. Thorpe-le-Soken.

I came home yesterday morning. Beautiful day. Snowfall and a lot of rain this morning. As soon as the rain ceased at noon, the whole landscape began to steam, even before the sun had got fairly out.

Notice outside shop in the village this morning: "*A few potatoes. 2 lbs. each customer. No bags found.*"

Wednesday, April 11th. London, Yacht Club.

Last week I had an immense burst of work. I did not go to London. I wrote about 5000 words of my novel (including 2500 in one day), and finished penultimate chapter of it. On Monday I wrote *Daily News* article and more *Statesman* stuff. I slept badly the whole time, but a dinner at the Greys' on Saturday, where we met the ultra-blonde Danish dancer Karina and her husband Captain Janssen, did me good. Karina ran over Janssen in her auto and broke both his legs, and then married him. He looks after Karina so completely that he even cuts out leather for her shoes. She is very pretty and agreeable. I sat next to her and enjoyed it. Hard frost driving home.

Thursday, April 12th. London, Yacht Club.

Lunched with Davray and a Canadian officer (name forgotten) who knew 14 languages. He had been through the Russian Revolution and told me he didn't trust any of the parties.

T. Seccombe was to have lunched with me next Wednesday, but he made a mistake and came yesterday. He therefore joined us. He said that the pupils at the Royal Military College were now the most extraordinary crowd. Poets and novelists pullulated among them. He thought there might be 1 or 2 geniuses. He instanced Arthur Waugh's son, aged 18, who had written a remarkably realistic novel of school life (Sherborne).[1]

Webster and Swinnerton dined with me at Reform. Swinnerton showed me a letter from Walpole describing Russian Rev.; Walpole has written the official account of the Rev. Deaths 5000.

Thursday, April 19th. London, Yacht Club.

I dined with Sir W. and Lady Weir at Savoy. She was very agreeably dressed. Weir told me that sometimes delays in supplies of air machines were difficult to explain to public. He had ball bearings for aeroplanes on 3 ships from Norway. He asked for these to be convoyed. They were not convoyed. The Germans sank all of them. He had been to an Imperial War Conference and spoke very highly of Colonials, especially Smuts. I said Smuts's first speech on arriving was fine. It was about aeroplanes. He said that after 21 months' delay, housing for work people at Farnborough was at last being put up. Weir told me he had established the first regular commercial air service in the world (he thought) just lately: a daily service for his own use between London and Paris, 3 hours. 6 machines employed.

Friday, April 20th. London, Yacht Club.

Yesterday I began to think that the *tone* of the end of my novel wouldn't do. So I spent the day, exhausted, partly in dozing and reading, and 1½ hours at barber's, and generally thinking over the climax, which I ultimately got right. I dined with Wells at Reform. He had worked all day, and arrived only at 8.40. We had champagne. We tossed for the bill— he lost. This is the second time lately he has lost to me.

Tuesday, April 24th. London, Yacht Club.

Great creative week-end. I wrote over 3000 words of novel on Saturday and Sunday. This novel is to be called *The Roll Call*.

---

[1] This was *The Loom of Youth*, by Alec Waugh, published in 1917, with a preface by T. Seccombe.

I came to town this morning and lunched with Webbs. Webb told me that Lloyd George, contrary to the usual habit of ministers, would not deal with papers. He preferred to be talked to. Webb said that most ministers were followed about by dispatch boxes full of papers which they had to approve and initial. Sometimes hundreds of papers. He said there were several grades of keys; the highest would open all dispatch boxes. When he was at the Colonial Office he had a second-grade key, which would open some dispatch boxes but not all.

He said that ministers were still unable to get anything done as Ll. G. would not face the labour of deciding and giving authority. Mrs. Webb, who had just returned from a meeting of Reconstruction Committee, said that at one meeting recently at 4 P.M., just before the meeting started, the Marquess of Salisbury went to the mantelpiece and prayed aloud. She was talking to somebody else and could not hear what he said, but he was certainly praying aloud.

Webb told me that Russian sailors, fleet enclosed in ice, had put a lot of their officers through the ice, and the ships were therefore useless. Germans knew this and were preparing expedition accordingly. Talk of British and French naval officers going over to take charge, but these officers said they would prefer to take their own crews.

Wednesday, April 25th. London, Yacht Club.

I walked down past Buckingham Palace this morning. Two naval petty officers outside in full fig, and their women. A police superintendent (?) and a policeman at gates. Former said to latter, "We'd better be getting 'em in," and then to the sailors: "You decorations? Come on. Come along. Come on," curtly, as if they had done some deed suspicious, and not valorous. The sailors talked with their women for a few moments and then went obediently within the precincts. They were two roughish, short, thick-set chaps.

Called at Reform Club, where I spent 40 minutes with Wells and an American journalist-lecturer-professor named MacDonald, over here for the New York *Nation*. Wells was talking about the after-war exacerbationary reaction on nerves, which would cause rows, quarrels, etc. unless it was consciously kept well in hand, and MacDonald said that a year or so after the San Francisco earthquake prominent S.F. men would disappear; they were in sanatoria etc. Also lifelong friends, such as business partners, would quarrel over some trifle, each go to his solicitor, and never speak to one another again. He said that Gilbert Murray would not be a good Ambassador for U.S.A., as university influence was now over, there, and that the sources of opinion were the large and small towns of the Middle West. It was there that German and other pacifists worked with most success.

Monday, April 30th. Comarques.

Today, in accordance with time-table, I finished my novel *The Roll Call* at 4 P.M.

Friday, May 4th. London, Yacht Club.

I came to town on Tuesday meaning to take a few days' holiday after I had written my *Statesman* stuff. But Pinker had arranged for me to do the official War Savings article in 3 days for the *Strand* so that it could appear in their July number. So that I had to begin at once. And I had so much neuralgia yesterday that I couldn't do anything at all.

On Wednesday at the Reform I met the poet, Siegfried Sassoon, and considerably liked him.

Sunday, May 6th. Thorpe-le-Soken.

Returned here on Friday and met Bertie Sullivan in the train. Carrying F.O. mails over to Holland in the *Copenhagen,* he had been torpedoed by a submarine. He said 6 subms. waited for the boat, in 3 pairs. He was shaving. He seems to have kept pretty calm, but he said he couldn't get his boots on. "I was flurried," he said. Of 17 bags, he saved 16 and sank one. Result, after several days, a sort of lack of feeling in fingers. (It was March and he was not in rowboat for long.)

Yesterday, for the first time, and at my suggestion, we had no bread on the table at dinner. People who want it must ask for it from the side-board. Wells gave me this tip. The value of these dodges is chiefly disciplinary. If the whole of the well-to-do classes practised them, the wheat problem would be trifling.

Wednesday, May 9th. London, Yacht Club.

On Sunday I had an idea for a short novel about an episode in the life of a French *cocotte*.[1] I thought I could tell practically everything about her existence without shocking the B.P. On Monday afternoon after doing my *Daily News* article I did my first water-colour of the season. In the garden. Rather goodish.

I came to London Tuesday. Lunched at Webbs'. Apropos of Squire's poem in current issue of *Statesman* the Webbs were both very funny, Mrs. Webb especially. She said: "Poetry means nothing to me. It confuses me. I always want to translate it back into prose."

Two quartets and a quintet before dinner at 8.45. Good male dinner, with champagne. During and after dinner, we had from Norton the finest exhibition of story-telling I ever heard. I was exhausted with laughing.

Later, W. Alcock[2] gave several parody treatments of *Three Blind Mice* according to Haydn, Chopin, Mendelssohn, and Grieg. Admirable. Werge and Hill played solos. I got to the Club at 1 A.M., and a half-dressed, half-asleep waiter let me in. This was one of the finest evenings I ever spent in my life.

Today Squire, Siegfried Sassoon lunched with me. Squire revealed himself more and more as being prim. He said he didn't like indecent jokes; didn't care for eating, either. Happily he likes drinking. Sassoon is a highly promising boy.

Friday, May 11th. London, Yacht Club.

Kindersley and Gardiner lunched with me at Reform, as K. wanted to meet G. K. talked very well. I shall tell him he ought to go into Parliament. I wrote part of another *Cosmopolitan* article in the morning.

---

[1] This was the origin of *The Pretty Lady*.
[2] Dr. Walter G. Alcock, the organist, and his wife Naomi were very old friends of Bennett.

After lunch it was funny to see H. G. Wells talking with an Indian ruler (I didn't catch his name) whom he was entertaining to lunch. He brought him to us. The ruler talked very sensibly, with a slight accent but extremely correctly. His burden was: "England cannot now throw us over by abandoning the monarchy. We need it."

Russian Exhibition and Tolstoy play with Marguerite at 5.30. I met George Moore on the way there, and he said that he had never made money out of his books worth talking about. £1500 or so out of *Esther Waters*, £1000 out of his latest, and so on. It seems that before I asked them to lunch he and Sickert had had a frightful row, which began by a newspaper scrap and ended by Sickert's inviting himself to dinner at George's and getting practically turned out. This was George's version. They had not met since till my luncheon. At that affair they were charming to each other.

Sunday, May 13th. Comarques, Thorpe-le-Soken.

Robert Ross gave a lunch at Automobile. Mr. and Mrs. Edmund Gosse, Eliz. Asquith, Mrs. Colefax, Captain Miller, and Dr. Borenius. I sat between Eliz. A. and Mrs. Colefax. Eliz. A. looks quite young. She seemed decent and hard, and socially extremely experienced. A tendency to phrase-making. Much deep ignorance of literature and even superficial ignorance, e.g. she didn't know that the French translations of Dostoievsky are incomplete and the English ones are complete, and read D. in French. She thought it easier to write a novel than a short story. She said she would send me a play of hers to read. It arrived today. I liked old Gosse again. He is anyhow educated.

Saturday, May 19th. London, Yacht Club.

I was looking out of the drawing-room window at M.'s flat yesterday morning when I saw two buses go along and then two more. And then, after about 5 minutes, 2 more. I said, "The bus strike is over!" It was. It had begun on Sunday.

Lunch at Reform. Wells came up here for tea. It was while talking to him that I had the idea of transferring the scene of my French *cocotte* novel from Paris to London, a vastly better idea, full of possibilities. H.G. certainly liked the idea.

Friday, May 25th. London, Yacht Club.

I returned to London Tuesday. Squire and Desmond MacCarthy[1] lunched with me at the Reform. At night after writing the Sardonyx article I went to Russian concert at Russian Exhibition, and it was very good. The pianissimos of the balalaika orchestra were marvellous, especially with music like Borodin's. On the other hand I had little use for Tchaikovsky's *Grand Trio* (A minor). Place pretty full.

But the chief thing yesterday was that I began on my novel about the French *cocotte,* with gusto.

Friday, June 1st. Thorpe-le-Soken.

Last Sunday my 50th birthday. Twelve people to dinner.

I went to London on Wednesday. Eliz. Asquith and J. C. Squire lunched with me at Ristorante del Commercio, Frith St. She certainly does amuse, but she is too professional over it, and she is a bad listener. Very neat.

She said that George V. really loved Mary and liked her much even while she was engaged to his brother. An absolutely conscientious monarch. She said that he had an immense regard and affection for her father, and that when it was a question of Asquith resigning, the King said, "If my Prime Minister resigns, I shall resign." Lately they were at Windsor and the King said, "I am so glad to have my Prime Minister back again with me."

Thursday, went to Philharmonic Hall to see the *Intolerance* film. A stupendous affair—I mean the Babylonian scenes. They were indeed staggering. But the modern story, though it contained some good rough satire on women social reformers, was very crude—even to an auto racing a train! A most fatiguing 3-hour affair.

Today lunch given by Davray to M. Helmer, an *avocat* of Colmar, in England to give lectures about Alsace-Lorraine. T. P. O'Connor, Massing-

---

[1] The present editor of *Life and Letters.*

ham, Gardiner, Spender, and 4 Frenchmen. T.P. began to Gardiner and me about his early youth. He evidently has a fancy for this sort of reminiscence. He said he had been the most trustful and easily deceived man imaginable. It was all very well, he said, but the connections of a simple man with women were apt to have "pecuniary endings."

Friday, June 8th. London, Yacht Club.

Walking about these streets about 10 to 10.30 when dusk is nearly over is a notable sensation; especially through Soho, with little cafés and co-op clubs and women and girls at shop doors. It is the heat that makes these things fine.

Afternoon, idea-finding for final section of first part of my *cocotte* novel.

Saturday, June 9th. Comarques.

Siegfried Sassoon lunched with me at the Reform yesterday. He expected some decoration for admittedly fine bombing work. Colonel had applied for it three times, but was finally told that as that particular push was a failure it could not be granted. Sassoon was uncertain about accepting a home billet if he got the offer of one. I advised him to accept it. He is evidently one of the reckless ones. He said his pals said he always gave the Germans every chance to pot him. He said he would like to go out once more and give them another chance to get him, and come home unscathed. He seemed jealous for the military reputation of poets. He said most of war was a tedious nuisance, but there were great moments, and he would like them again.

Thursday, June 14th. London, Yacht Club.

I came to London Tuesday, unwell. Lunch at Webb's. I spent the afternoon in writing *Observations*. Dined at the Reform with Clutton-Brock, who said that Wells was very rude to him about his very polite review of *God the Invisible King* in *Times Literary Supplement*.

Then I went slowly to Drury Lane to *Tristan* and arrived before the end of the 1st Act. I went to meet Turner, the *New Statesman* critic. Too much light on the stage at the crises, and horrible competition between the band and the singers; ugly costumes and scenery; and Rosina Buckman and Mullings both leviathans. A terrible sight. The second act was better, darker, and quieter. When King Mark began his monologue I departed. I thought the music was surviving pretty well.

On getting to Yacht Club from Richmond at 1.30 I had a telephone message from Marguerite to say that she and Anna were in the air raid[1] at Liverpool Street and unhurt. Today I found out that though the end of their train (11.38) was bombed, M. knew nothing of it, and Anna was only sure that she saw smoke "by the side of the train" behind her. Neither heard cries of wounded, nor broken glass or anything. M. heard 4 bombs or 5. Anna said she heard a noise and thought it was guns; then she saw a girl porter running and heard her cry "Oh" and thought it was an accident. When she realized that it was bombs she remembered nothing more till she "found herself" near underground lavatory, where people were taking refuge, with M. They were in different carriages and had lost each other. She saw people "crouching down" (near base of girders, apparently).

This morning I saw remains of a German aeroplane being motored up Piccadilly.

Thursday, June 21st. London, Yacht Club.

Atkins and Ross lunched with me yesterday here; and a very good lunch. I was startled to find Ross believing in the legend that the Germans had been cooking all their mortality figures since 1870. This shows how far a good brain can be deteriorated by a fixed idea. Whenever Ross talks about the war his whole face changes.

Friday, June 29th. London, Yacht Club.

No work yesterday. Lunched with Atkins at Reform and stayed there till 4.30. Afterwards I slept and read Dent's book on Mozart's operas, with profit. Dined with Marguerite at the Desmond MacCarthys', Wellington

---

[1] In the aeroplane raid on London of June 13, there were 157 killed and 432 injured. One of the planes was brought down.

Sq., but got to the Square too soon and idled round 2nd-hand shops and also listened to a Salvation Army street-corner show, which I think was the worst I ever did see. Four or five women and two men were the performers. It was ghastly in its melancholy, stupid, and perverse ugliness. One relatively pretty woman about 26, with the marks of pietistic obstinacy in her, sang a solo hymn in the most ridiculous way. Total audience, one boy.

Went to bed soon after 11, to read, for the first time, *Wuthering Heights*.

Friday, July 6th. Ludlow, Charlton Arms.

I came to Ludlow today. Fat female aristocratic in train. Dust cloak. Flower outside it. Jewel to fasten it. Many rings. Manicured. *Queen, Tatler*. Ethel M. Dell's latest novel. 3 cushions in a decided leather "envelope." Elaborate lunch-basket. Greedy. When ticket collectors came, she referred them, with an apprehensive gesture, to her maid, lest she might be bothered. Two of them knew of her maid. The third said roughly, "I suppose your maid has *your* ticket?" Her fear about being worried about anything was obvious. At Shrewsbury she held "envelope" while maid put cushions in it. Maid got her out of train and transferred her to Ludlow train. There was another and older and worse woman with an aged maid, in the same compartment. Very hard. She was met by a companion sort of girl at Birmingham.

Thursday, July 19th. London, Yacht Club.

I dined alone and Frank Shufflebotham, who had not been able to dine, came along here shortly after 10 P.M. He said that up to now £100,000,000 had been spent on gas, of which a large portion has been spent on experiments on animals such as guinea-pigs. He said that a certain firm had made £42,000 in 6 months clear profit on their gas factory with a capital of £1000. The Government put up the stills etc., which at the end of the war are to revert to the firm, and provided the whole of the raw material. This raw material for this one factory, in the shape of chemicals, has cost 2 millions in the last twelve months. I gathered that such factories exist up and down the country.

Friday, July 20th. London, Yacht Club.

Barrie came to lunch with me at Reform. 25 minutes late. He was very agreeable. He talked several times of "my boys." One is at the front.

Marguerite and I dined at a new restaurant, the Ivy, opposite Ambassador's Theatre. Very good. Then Brieux's *Les 3 Filles de M. Dupont.* It was much worse than I expected. Extremely crude throughout, and so false sometimes that I could not look at the stage. However, a great tract for those who need such things. Ethel Irving was very good, but she seemed to me to tear the big scene to pieces. She screamed hoarsely throughout it.

Wednesday, July 25th. London, Yacht Club.

Great raid over Felixstowe and Harwich on Sunday morning about 8.15. Heavier bombardment than we have ever heard before. For the first time the females fled to the cellar, and the temporary cook (who had been in a previous raid at Felixstowe) almost had hysterics. I was just beginning to shave, and so I did shave, but the row was disturbing. It ceased in a few minutes (during which over 40 people had been killed or injured). No firing nearer than 7 miles from us. The "air-raid warning" came through from the comic War Office about ½ an hour after the raid was over.

I came to London yesterday; lunched at Webb's, where was Glynne Williams, the new editor of the *Statesman.* Company *très sympathique.* Wrote my article in the afternoon, and went to dine at Barrie's with Thomas Hardy and wife. Barrie has an ugly little manservant and the finest view of London I ever saw. Mrs. Hardy a very nice woman, with a vibrating attractive voice. Hardy was very lively; talked like anything. Apropos of Chekhov he started a theory that some of Chekhov's tales were not justifiable because they told nothing unusual. He said a tale must be unusual and the people interesting. Of course he soon got involved in the meshes of applications and instances, but he kept his head and showed elasticity and common sense and came out on the whole well. He has all his faculties, unimpaired. Quite modest and without the slightest pose.

They both had very good and accurate appraisements of such different people as Shorter and Phillpotts.

Later in the evening Barrie brought along both Shaw and the Wellses by 'phone. Barrie was consistently very quiet, but told a few A1 stories. At dusk we viewed the view and the searchlights. Hardy, standing outside one of the windows, had to put a handkerchief on his head. I sneezed. Soon after Shaw and the Wellses came Hardy seemed to curl up. He had travelled to town that day and was evidently fatigued. He became quite silent. I then departed and told Barrie that Hardy ought to go to bed. He agreed. The spectacle of Wells and G.B.S. talking firmly and strongly about the war, in their comparative youth, in front of this aged, fatigued, and silent man—incomparably their superior as a creative artist—was very striking.

Thursday, July 26th. London, Yacht Club.

Headache yesterday after Hardy and cigarettes. Shufflebotham lunched with me at Reform, and then we had a Turkish bath, which with me last nearly 3 hours. Dined at the Reform with Massingham, who, like me, was going to the opera. He likes eating and drinking. Not much, but well. We had caviare, and we shared a trifle of champagne. Opera. I met Ernest Newman, very estimable and sound as usual. We agreed in our estimate of Beecham. He astonished me by saying that he liked a great deal in *Louise*. Apropos of Ravel he said, "No great man is ever idle"; which is very true. Apropos of Newman's liking *Louise,* Hardy said that he liked Lytton and that *Pelham* was a very able book. Both Hardy and Barrie expressed great admiration for Trollope, but they both expressed perhaps a little too much.

Friday, July 27th. London, Yacht Club.

American article yesterday morning.

Dined at flat and then with M. to *Marriage of Figaro.* Dramatically the last act is very poor in both scenes. Musically it is as good as the rest. Shaw grumbled much at the performance. The sentimental interest, as

Newman said to me, is the best part of the opera, and the Figaro music is not very surpassing. The sentimental songs were celestial.

Saturday, September 1st. Comarques.

I took a month's holiday, ending yesterday. We went to spend 2 days at the Schusters' during it, and I saw the first batch of the American Army from the windows of the Yacht Club during it.

Health not very good during it, but a distinct benefit as regards the outlook on work actually in progress. I made some advance in water-colours, and more still in monotypes. I didn't read a lot. Hardy's *Pair of Blue Eyes*, full of fine things and immensely sardonic. Murray on Euripides—formless, but gradually getting at something. Reminiscences of Tagore—good. *Duchesse de Langeais*, quite a major work, which thoroughly held me.

Friday, September 14th. Thorpe-le-Soken.

On Wednesday Shufflebotham carefully examined me at the club and decided that I must be X-rayed. He guaranteed that I had had appendicitis several times without knowing it. He also insisted on a new visit to the oculist. All these things added to my gloom due to the sudden and long attack of neuralgia.

Thursday, September 20th. London, Yacht Club.

I began to write at 6:30 A.M. yesterday, and I had written a chapter by 12.15. Then X-ray séance at Harley Street (all the large front waiting-rooms of Harley St. with people reading old weeklies in them while waiting).

I lunched with Shufflebotham afterwards at Pagani's and had another séance, to watch the progress of the bismuth, at 5 P.M. Rain most of day, and I was walking about most of the day in the rain. Only spent 2d. on transport.

Friday, September 21st. London, Yacht Club.

Radiographed for the 3rd time yesterday, and nothing found wrong, except the common slight slowness of the work in the colon. Lunched with Davray and Weil (ex-member of the Reichstag). He was dining with Jaurés when Jaurés was killed in the restaurant.[1]

Monday, September 24th. London, Yacht Club.

Marguerite came to town this afternoon. I worked till 3.30 P.M., and then, seeing I could do more writing and could reflect just as well in train, I came up to town so as to save half a day tomorrow. I was unwell and without energy all day. Nevertheless I worked satisfactorily in the train. Then air raid.

I had a great subject for a water-colour on Saturday. I put my *enceinte* French Renaissance virgin (white) and the black *juju* that Molly Green brought from Nigeria for Marguerite, side by side, and called the picture "The Gods." A fine composition and a real subject. I started the sketch but couldn't finish it in the time. However, the subject will keep.

Wednesday, September 26th. London, Yacht Club.

A raid began precisely at the moment I left the Yacht Club. The buses seemed to quicken, the streets appreciably emptied. Most people hurried; I did; but a few strolled along. I was glad when I got to the Albany. Firing when there nearer, and everything was faintly lit up with flashes. I found that the Albany alley had been covered with thick glass thrown over from an explosion or a hit on the Academy on the previous night.[2]

Thursday, September 27th. London, Yacht Club.

Dined with M. at Waldorf. To get there, strange journeys in Tube. Very wet. Very poor women and children sitting on stairs (fear of raid). Also travelling in lift and liftman grumbling at them because no fear of raid, and they answering him back, and middle-class women

---

[1] The great French Socialist leader was assassinated on the eve of the outbreak of war, July 31, 1914.
[2] For about a week there were almost daily air raids over London. From September 24 to October 1 there were nearly 50 people killed.

saying to each other that if the poor couldn't keep to the regulations they ought to be forbidden the Tube as a shelter from raid.

S. said he had seen dreadful sights of very poor with babies in Tube on Monday. One young woman was in labour. He asked her if she was and she said that she was, and she had got up because she was told to go with the rest. He got her taken on a stretcher to a hospital. Proprietor of a restaurant where I lunched today with Swinnerton said that although his place was always full at night, he only had four people on Monday night and *not a single customer* on Tuesday night (fear of raids). He said also that at fish and vegetable markets he couldn't get what he wanted because supplies were not there, and that wholesalers had not taken supplies because they couldn't dispose of them, and that stuff was rotting. A raid was feared tonight, but evidently the German machines were turned back before reaching London.

Wednesday, October 10th. London, Yacht Club.

Dined with George Whale at the N.L.C. and in his great ugly sitting-room took what I wanted from his large collection of notes on war superstitions for my novel. His notes were extremely interesting.

Wells came in and slanged the Webbs as usual, and incidentally said: "My boom is over. I've had my boom. I'm yesterday." He said that in air raids he was afraid of going to pieces altogether; so if there was a balcony he stood on it. He had been through several raids at Southend. He said, "I get huffy and cross just as if——" but I can't remember his comparison.

Thursday, October 11th. London, Yacht Club.

Met Crane yesterday with Wells at Reform. He wouldn't talk at first, but afterwards talked excellently, till nearly 4 o'clock. He has spent several months in Russia every year for either 20 or 30 years. Also travelled through Asia sundry times and been U.S.A. Ambassador to China. Calm quiet man about 60. Very modest and yet knowing himself.

Rather sentimental about friendships and family relations, but very wise and balanced. He was pessimistic about Russia. Said Kerensky was a good young lawyer and nothing else. Related how K. had ordered a good place for the sister of his mistress in Imperial Theatre, and it was refused, and he had to give in.

He gave a very good account of the Rasputin régime and showed how complex the situation was and how a Rasputin could not be understood by Westerns. About the East, he showed how the boycott of Japan in China (unordered but complete and irresistible) had put a pause to Japan's scheme of conquest in China.

Friday, October 12th. London, Yacht Club.

Granville-Barker (2nd Lieut.) lunched with me here yesterday. He said he had to do with *liaisons* between British and U.S.A. Governments, and the latter said that they want, in addition to the official views, the views of the Independent Left. So he came to get mine. He had got Wells's and 2 or 3 other people's.

He said that the U.S.A. people were not greatly impressed by anonymous opinions. It was useless to say, "It is thought—" But if you said, "So-and-so thinks—" the thing carried weight.

Tuesday, October 16th. Comarques.

Went through all first two books of *cocotte* novel, and fairly well pleased with everything except last chapter or so. Today I tabulated all my information and ideas afresh.

Wednesday, October 24th. London, Yacht Club.

I finished a chapter of my novel this morn, and did packing. To-morrow I go to Ireland at the request of G.O.C. Ireland, Intelligence Department.

Tuesday, November 6th. London, Yacht Club.

I returned from Dublin on Saturday exhausted; neuralgia. I spent

Sunday all alone between this and the Reform Clubs, and wrote my first Irish article complete.

In the evening I read a lot of Alec Waugh's *Loom of Youth* with great interest.

Sunday, November 18th. Thorpe.

I made the acquaintance of Lord Beaverbrook Thursday week. He and Ross lunched with me on Friday. At this second meeting he asked me to take him to Leicester Gallery, where I had mentioned there was a good etching of Rops. I did so, with Ross. He asked which was the etching, bought it (20 guineas), and gave it me on the spot.

This was at only our 2nd meeting. *Un peu brusqué.*

Wednesday, November 28th. London, Yacht Club.

I finished *Gulliver's Travels* on Sunday. The final episode is the best, and is indeed very fine; but all the difficulties of detail in describing horse life are evaded. The thing could have been done much more convincingly. On the other hand the comments of the horses on human character and manners are superb.

Sunday, December 9th. Comarques.

Better arrangements must be made for keeping this damned journal. On Thursday last I made my début at the Other Club,[1] to which I was elected without my knowledge. I sat next to F. E. Smith,[2] who is a live companion, inclined to recount his achievements, but interesting and informed. Duke of Marlborough in the chair—merely to propose the Royal health.

Sir Mark Sykes seemed the most interesting man there. He did a very original caricature of F. E. Smith and me. I heard he was the best amateur actor in England. He certainly has brains, and political brains. Lutyens amiably played the amusing fool. I greatly enjoyed the affair.

Turkish baths and a little dissipation have lately improved my health, and greatly improved my capacity for finding ideas and working.

---

[1] Carlton Club.
[2] Barrister, diplomat, later Earl of Birkenhead.

Tuesday, December 11th. London, Yacht Club.

Wrote an article yesterday for *Daily News* showing advisability of preparing peace terms and insisting—what few people seem to understand—that this can go on with ardent prosecution of war.

Wednesday, December 12th. London, Yacht Club.

Poetry recital at Mrs. Colefax's. Tea first; the usual crowds; but Spender and Garvin were there. Drawing-room nearly full. Miss McLeod, a woman with straight, thin, ruthless lips, read admirably 2 poems of Sassoon's. The best thing for me was "Hippopotamus" by T. S. Eliot. Had I been the house, this would have brought the house down. One of Miss McLeod's poems was pretty goodish too. Gosse, except for his opening speech—a bit long—made an excellent chairman. On the whole the affair was by no means so bad as I had feared. The Sitwell family was much in evidence, *tres cultivée.*

Thursday, December 13th. London, Yacht Club.

I was told the following at dinner last night. Two working men were in the Tube and began arguing whether a certain peculiarly dressed person in the same carriage was or was not the Archbishop of Canterbury. They bet. To settle it one of them went up to the person and said, "Please, sir, are you the Archbishop of Canterbury?" The reply was, "What the bloody hell has that got to do with you?" The workman went back to his mate and said: "No good, mate. The old cow won't give me a straight answer either way."

Friday, December 14th. London, Yacht Club.

During the evening F. E. Smith, Attorney-General, rang me up— how he got hold of me God knows—and said, "Will you go to the United States with me on Saturday morning?" He then spoke, low, some confidential remarks about his mission. I didn't catch them all and didn't get him to repeat them as I hadn't the slightest intention of going —especially for 2 months. He said, "Nominally you'll be my secretary, but only nominally, of course."

Although I like him as a companion I didn't see myself going to U.S.A. as F.E.'s secretary and boon companion. Still, he has considerable points.

Fog and mist, and a most damnable romantic London. I walked from Oxford Street to Piccadilly. Scarcely one of my "pretty ladies" about.

Saturday, December 15th. London, Yacht Club.

Dined with Benchers of Gray's Inn in hall, to meet Lloyd George and heads of Air Service. F. E. Smith in chair. A very "short," very ordinary dinner, and plenty of wine. I think Lord Halsbury made the greatest impression (aged 96–7) by his forceful way of saying that a man who made a bargain and didn't keep it was "a dirty scoundrel." Tim Healy and Garvin both quoted a good deal from all sorts of things. Ll. G. spoke for over an hour, too long, and said all sorts of platitudes for public consumption. His "set" effects were failures. But he had some great similes. Winston Churchill, after the principal speech, made an amiable tour of the tables. He wore all his military medals dangling on the lapel of his dress coat. (I suppose this is all right, but I had never seen it before except on the dress coat of the hall porter of this club.)

Sunday, December 16th. London, Yacht Club.

Dined at flat with M. and Richard [1] (who came home yesterday) and then to Barrie's *Dear Brutus,* where we had seats in the back row of the dress circle. A great success, and deserved. For a fanciful play the idea is A1, and it is worked out with much invention. As soon as I saw the scheme of the play I feared for the last act. However, the last act was very good. I enjoyed the play nearly throughout.

On coming away, vast jostling crowds in the streets, and the feel of a tremendous city in the dark.

Monday, December 17th. London, Yacht Club.

To Stage Society performance, where, owing to a misapprehension, we arrived an hour late.

---

[1] Richard Bennett, the nephew whom Arnold Bennett adopted, was at this time at school at Oundle.

Part of a ballet we partly saw from the upper circle, and it seemed very English and stiff and *voulu* and poor; but the old music was fine. Then I got the committee to take us into their box, and we saw Granville-Barker's play, *Vote by Ballot.* It contained any amount of witty and true dialogue, but it was not what I call a play. Theatre packed. All the usual crowd. Wives and mistresses of the same men all mixed up and friendly together.

Got to club at 9.40. Cut a lot of Chaucer pages, but I didn't read any because the glossary is all at the end.

Cut a lot of Rabelais pages. Read some of that and found it good. Also same in middle of night. Also Butler in middle of night. Rotten neuralgic night, but I feel a certain liveliness *ce matin.*

Tuesday, December 18th. London, Yacht Club.

To lunch at the Reform Club, where I joined Robert Ross, who had two young poets, Robert Graves and Philip —— (I forget his name and am not even sure if he is a poet). I was very pleased with both these youths. Lately I am more and more struck by the certainty, strength, and unconscious self-confidence of young men, so different from my middle-aged uncertainty and also my lack of physical confidence in my own body. In the afternoon 2¾ hours hard, in which I wrote 1200 words of *The Pretty Lady.*

Wednesday, December 19th. London, Yacht Club.

I was wakened out of my after-bath sleep by news of impending air raid. This news merely made me feel gloomy. I didn't mind missing dinner at flat, or anything—I was merely gloomy. As soon as I got out into Northumberland Avenue I heard guns. Motors and people rushing. Then guns very close. I began to run. I headed for Reform Club and abandoned idea of reaching the flat. Everybody ran. Girls ran.

However, I found that after the Turkish bath I couldn't run much in a heavy overcoat. So I walked. It seemed a long way. Guns momentarily ceased. So I didn't hurry, and felt relieved. But still prodigiously gloomy. I reached the club. Hall in darkness. No girls in coffee room.

The manservants manfully tackled the few diners. Nothing could be had out of kitchen, as kitchen under glass and deserted.

All clear at about 9.30.[1]

Thursday, December 20th. London, Yacht Club.

Swinnerton came to Yacht Club for tea, and stayed 80 minutes. He said that *Books and Persons* had sold 3400 and was still going steadily on.[2] He told me about his new novel of Barnet society and said he had consulted *Clayhanger* to see how I got over certain difficulties, but couldn't find out. I certainly couldn't tell him.

Saturday, December 22nd. Comarques.

Wells came for tea to Club on Thursday and talked about his very long novel, which he stated to be terrific indictment of the present state of England.

Sunday, December 23rd. Comarques.

Captain Hill and wife came last night. He related how after a long period (several weeks) of "special vigilance" he was sleeping in a blanket on the floor of the gardener's cottage at Thorpe Hall when a dispatch rider burst in just like a stage dispatch rider, at 3 A.M. The dispatch contained one word, which for Hill had no meaning. The rider couldn't tell him anything and only insisted on a signature in receipt, which of course Hill gave. Hill then got up and went to see another C.O. near. This C.O. had received the same message and also had not the least idea what it meant. Other C.O.'s were afterwards found to be in the same case.

Hill asked another C.O. to ring up the staff. C.O. said he daren't. So Hill did himself. He asked the telephone clerk what the message meant. The clerk replied that he knew but he daren't tell. Hill then told him to summon the brigade major. Clerk said he positively dare not. Hill

---

[1] Five aeroplanes bombed London, causing the death of 10 persons. There were over 70 injured.
[2] A collection of the Jacob Tonson articles.

insisted and took responsibility on himself. Brigade major came to telephone, using terrible language. It then appeared that the incomprehensible word was a code word signifying that the period of vigilance was over. Only no C.O. of unit had been previously informed of the significance of the word. The whole episode, with its middle-of-the-night business, absurd secrecy, etc., was thoroughly characteristic.

Tuesday, December 25th. Comarques.

War. Only about half a pint of methylated spirits left in the house. Marguerite decided to keep this in stock for an emergency of illness etc. Wise. So I can no longer make my own perfect tea at what hour I like in the morning. And this morning I had poor servant-made tea. However, there is a hope of my getting some other heating apparatus.

Je me suis recueilli somewhat yesterday for my novel, with difficulty. I re-read some of it in typescript and thought part was dullish and part interesting. Reading *Georgian Poetry 1916–1917* seemed to buck me up to raise the damn thing to a higher plane than it has yet reached save in odd places here and there.

Wednesday, December 26th. Comarques.

Only seven sat down to dinner last night, owing to difficulties of transport and engagements of officers for mess dinners. This is the smallest Xmas dinner we have had in this house. Soldiers were noisy outside during the day. Mason came for lunch and stayed till after nightfall. He rode off in falling snow, having made Richard a present of all the chemical reagents which he had ordered for him.

I read a lot, all I shall read, of Saintsbury's *History of the French Novel*. Very prolix, and bursting with subordinate sentences and clauses, but containing plenty of useful information; also it shows that he does understand something of the craft of novel-writing. His tracing of the development of the technique of the novel in the 17th cent. is interesting and, to me, quite new. The amount of this old man's reading is staggering.

Much bad music after dinner.

Thursday, December 27th. Comarques.

Dinner last night at 2/1st London R.G.A. at Bentley Huts. Caffery came and fetched us in a Ford car. About 30 people. Goodish dinner. I did nothing all the evening except sit in front of the stove. Solo whist and bridge partners, and much noisy dancing. After midnight the Ford car could not be started, and it never was started, though 6 men spent pretty nearly 2 hours on it, with blowpipes and things. M. and Olive slept at Steel and Caffery's lodgings. I came home in a G.S. wagon with 2 horses and 2 men, easy chair in wagon, rugs, eiderdown, and a rug like an extinguisher all over my head and face. Freezing hard, but I was quite warm. This journey took about 1½ hours. I made the two men happy and then had a hot bath and must have gone to sleep about 4.40. I slept till 8. I was thoroughly bored until it was discovered that the car wouldn't start. Thenceforward I was quite cheerful.

1918

Tuesday, January 1st. Comarques.

Much work on the novel these last two days. I wrote 2600 words yesterday. Last year I wrote 255,000 words. Not bad, considering the circumstances.

Wednesday, January 2nd. London, Yacht Club.

Came to London yesterday. George Paish's food-question lunch, arranged for yesterday, had been put off without warning me. So I lunched with Ross at Reform. Afterwards, Turkish bath with Masterman, who said that the shine of the present Honours List would be nothing to that of the List when Ll. George quitted the premiership. He would have everything to wipe up, then.

On reaching the club I read the Book of Esther in the Eversley Bible, which I have newly bought. A good Eastern story, exceedingly ingenuous, all based on copulation.

Thursday, January 3rd. London, Yacht Club.

Lane told me a British bomb had descended through the roof of his house and wrecked his library, but the damage was only £46. More Bible reading here this evening. I Kings makes excellent reading. But the way David ordered executions before he died, and Solomon upon his ascension, is rather startling.

Monday, January 7th. Comarques.

Sundry officers, including Saunders Jacob and Cummings, dined on Saturday night, and the delight of these two in singing more or less at sight good and bad songs from the *Scottish Students' Song Book,* to my bad accompaniment, was most extraordinary. Last night Richard was talking about being set to learn 40 lines of *L'Allegro* in 45 minutes prep and to write essays in ten minutes. What a fool of a master! It appears that this master once said in class, "Your Hall Caines, Arnold Bennetts, and H. G. Wellses will pass away and be forgotten. Classics will remain." I couldn't find my Milton, but on my offering a reward of 6*d.* Richard found it. I re-read some of *Paradise Lost* and thought it very fine and interesting. The remarks of Adam and the angel about the relations of man and wife have not yet been beaten for sense.

Tuesday, January 8th. Comarques.

Another chapter of *The Pretty Lady* yesterday. Too much smoking, ostensibly to provide Richard with tobacco ash for chemical experiments.

I have read 100 pages or so of the Hammonds' *Town Labourer.* There is undoubtedly a pleasure in reading recitals of horrible injustice and tyranny.

Wednesday, January 9th. Comarques.

I didn't like reading the child-labour chapter in the Hammonds' *Town Labourer.* It exceeded the limits in its physicalness. I wish I had read it before I wrote the child chapter in *Clayhanger* to which the Hammonds refer. I could have made that chapter even more appalling than it is. But at that date probably all the materials had not been collected, as the Hammonds have since collected them.

Friday, January 11th. Comarques.

Marguerite bought a pig at the end of the year. It was a small one, but we have been eating this damned animal ever since, in all forms except ham, which has not yet arrived. Brawn every morning for break- fast. Yesterday I struck at pig's feet for lunch and had mutton instead;

they are neither satisfying nor digestible, and one of the biggest frauds that ever came out of kitchens. All this is a war measure, and justifiable. I now no longer care whether I have sugar in my tea or not. We each have our receptacle containing the week's sugar, and use it how we like. It follows us about, wherever we happen to be taking anything that is likely to need sugar. My natural prudence makes me more sparing of mine than I need be. Another effect of war is that there is a difficulty in getting stamped envelopes at the P.O. The other day the postmaster, by a great effort and as a proof of his goodwill, got me £1 worth, which won't go far.

It occurred to me how the war must affect men of 70, who have nothing to look forward to. The war has ruined their end, and they cannot have much hope.

Sunday, January 13th. Comarques.

I outlined in the bath this morning an idea of a play about a man being offered a title and his wife insisting on his accepting it against his will.[1] Spender told me that such a man had once asked him for advice in just such a problem, and he had advised the man to suppress his scruples and accept the title. Ross said that this would be a good idea for a play, and it is.

Tuesday, January 15th. London, Yacht Club.

We came to London this morning, dog, Richard, cook, M., and me. Lunch at Webb's. Then I hurried back to Reform Club to join after lunch the Writers' Group. A peace campaign on foot—i.e. peace with German people. Spender, as usual, had the most information to give, and it seemed very well founded. After dinner to *Sleeping Partners* at St. Martin's. Adapted from Sacha Guitry. Slow at first, but very adroit and amusing indeed as it progressed. Seymour Hicks had all the jam and was marvellously good. We all really enjoyed it. I met Lucas in the entr'acte and he took me round to see Hicks, whom I instantly liked and decided to ask to lunch.

---

[1] This was *The Title*, produced at the Royalty Theatre, July 20, 1918.

Sunday, January 20th. Comarques.

I went to the Leicester to see the Dyson war-drawings and ended by buying a Brabazon gouache. I was hoping the sight of pictures would stimulate my novel-cerebration, but it did not. However, yesterday, after a sleeping draught, I was in form again and wrote over 2000 words, a complete chapter.

Heard at the Reform on Thursday afternoon on very good authority that a telegram recalling Haig and appointing Allenby in his place had been drafted and was to have been sent on Wednesday, but was withheld for further discussion on Thursday.

Monday, January 21st. Comarques.

M. has now joined a Y.M.C.A. canteen for soldiers coming home on leave, near Waterloo Station. The hours were from 10.30 to 3 P.M., no interval for lunch. She came home and said that "any fool could do the work" and that it was "easy and interesting." She was going to undertake 4 hours on Tuesdays, Thursdays, and Saturdays, going to town on Monday afternoons, thus leaving only Sundays for Comarques. However, I stopped this. She really began as a formal helper on Saturday. She was put on to washing-up. She had a nice girl of 15 as colleague, very smart. It seems they had to work at really top speed all the time, in order to cope with the demand. This was for 3½ hours—11 to 2.30 or so. No interval of any kind for lunch, even a sandwich, not 5 minutes. A cup of coffee brought to them, from which they snatched sips. (No breakfast before starting. No dinner in the evening, owing to concert.) Standing all the time. There is no doubt that she and all the other women think this rather fine, but still she admitted that it was thoroughly bad organization. Women do like this exhausting kind of work. It wears them out and then they think they have done something grand.

Tuesday, January 22nd. Comarques.

Miss Nerney found I had written already 75,000 words of my novel, which was to be its total length. And there are probably 5000 more words to write.

I read Balzac's *Une Double Famille*. Very good, but the plot by no means clear at the end. In fact, though I have now read the thing probably 3 times, I don't really know what happened in the interval before the epilogue. Still, his leaving out is very fine and effective as a rule.

London, Yacht Club.

Came to London this morn. Great outcry at the Reform about a new rule against having guests to lunch. I was asked to draft a protest and I did so. Just as I was going away Gardiner introduced me to Col. Repington, now celebrated for having thrown up his *Times* job as a protest against attacks on the General Staff. He has very large eyes and must be a strange old man. He said, when I said that the matter with the war cabinet was that it was not *English,* "Yes, did you ever know a Celt to win a war?"

Thursday, January 24th. London, Yacht Club.

Rumours from two sources of food riots, either in Camden Town or in Highgate, or both; quelled by the military. I gravely doubt the last detail.

Monday, January 28th. Comarques.

Today at lunch-time I finished my novel *The Pretty Lady*—about 80,000 words. The close seemed to me to be rather ingenious, well executed, and effective. But for years past I have ceased to try to judge the value of a novel until it has been published for a year or two—I mean one of my own. I thought *The Old Wives' Tale* was dull when I had finished it.

Wednesday, January 30th. London, Yacht Club.

I came to London yesterday morning. No posts and no newspapers at either Thorpe or Colchester, so that my first news was obtained in London of the "great" air-raid. Lunched with Runciman and Buckmaster in order to get particulars of any Liberal party programme there might be. Runciman talked very well, and with firmness. He complained of the Liberal press. His programme had evidently not been put together; and he admitted that any anti-government concerted action by Liberals (such as he himself directed) was done without either the approval or the help of Asquith. Yet he would insist that Asquith was the actual, veritable leader of the Liberal party!

Then Turkish bath with Masterman and Walpole. Walpole very young, strong, happy, and optimistic. He said he enjoyed himself all the time. Masterman very gloomy and cynical, and prophesying the most terrible things. He said he hadn't had a happy day for 19–20 years, and that the only thing that really bucked him up was winning an election. In fact he was a sad spectacle. The Galsworthys and a Mrs. Bainbridge came to dinner at the flat.

Air-raid maroon warning at about 10 P.M. We went down into the bank basement, which is well heated, and stayed till 12.30 A.M. Marguerite and the cook knitting. I noticed that John [Galsworthy] was just as chivalrous to the cook as to any of the other women. He even gave her a chocolate. The time passed quickly, even on hard chairs. From time to time I went out. The red warning with "Take cover" on it shone steadily at the intersection of Oxford St. and Tottenham Court Rd. But people were walking about. Infrequent guns. Then the G.'s ventured to depart.

Thursday, January 31st. London, Yacht Club.

Collecting ideas for my article on the future of the Liberal party. Then to show of the Senefelder Club at the Leicester Galleries. There was a lithograph of Forain, "Conseil Juridique," which put everything else in the show clean off the map. I couldn't think of anything that I had ever seen more perfect. 28 guineas; so I didn't buy it. A loud-voiced old man in very sporting costume, and deaf, came in with a fairly young woman, who called him alternately Claudie and Sir Claude. It was Claude de Crespigny, the sportsman. Many of these chaps have very loud voices. He said 2*s.* 6*d.* was too high a price for entrance, had never known entrance to a gallery to be more than 1*s.* He was mollified when he learnt that 2*s.* 6*d.* paid for two. He had come to see a painting by Laura Knight of a prize-fighter. As soon as he saw it he shouted: "I think they ought to give you your money back. It's not like —— at all. He hasn't got those muscles on him—never had. And look at his legs. And look at the size of the ring. It's not 8 feet square." However, the woman soothed him, and in the end he seemed to be quite a decent sort of chap.

Lunch at Marlborough Club. The first I saw at the Marlborough was the Duke of Marlborough. I like this chap—also he said he was very interested in my articles and agreed with them. I liked him the first time I saw him. Ex-King Manoel was there, lunching like nobody at all with two military officers. Then to Reform Club to meet Wells, who was very angry with the insular commercial machinations of the aeroplane m'facturers, who, he says, are greatly over-represented on the Civil Air Transport Committee, of which he is a member. He told me the latest theory is that the first floor of a well-built house is safer than the basement in an air-raid, owing to the new heavy delayed-action bombs which go through everything and burst only when they can't travel any further.

Wednesday, February 6th. London, Yacht Club.

Gardiner and Massingham at club in afternoon were extremely gloomy, but Spender preserved his even temper as usual. So did E. M'Kenna keep cheerful. I heard various interesting things, but can't remember them, except that U.S.A. has 400,000 men in France now, but frankly admitted its present inability or absence of military genius to organize a *fighting machine* at present. It is to be hoped that it will improve. It seems as if Ll. George had got his way as to a united command in west.

Friday, February 8th. London, Yacht Club.

I seemed to do nothing yesterday morning except call on M. and write letters and just reflect for a few minutes on the first article of my 2nd series for the *Cosmopolitan*. Lunch at the Reform with Ross and Chalmers Mitchell. Mitchell, aged 53, with his grey hairs, stuck to it that he had found a sound definition of poetry. I forget what it was. I told him he ought to know better at his age than to imagine that poetry could be defined. Hedley LeBas told me that my amateur article outlining a policy for the Liberal party had made a deep impression on Gulland, the chief whip, who said it was the best article on the subject he had seen for years, and he "should show it to Asquith." Majestic and impressive phrase. "Show it to Asquith."

Saturday, February 9th. London, Yacht Club.

I heard that all merchant vessels leaving Egypt were agog as they left to know whether they would be escorted by Japanese or British men-of-war. If by Japanese they were happy, as the Japanese had never lost a ship. If by British, they became very gloomy.

Buckmaster told me that Lady Buchanan [1] told him last night at dinner more and more astounding stories of Petrograd. After a debauch, heaps of dead, wounded and drunken lying together—literally in heaps. In order to get some people out of a mixed lot in a cellar, the cellar was flooded. No result, except that the water froze, and will remain frozen till the spring. Two regiments of women and one of young men alone defended the Winter Palace. When it was taken the women were captured, tortured, and raped. Some killed themselves; some escaped to tell. Massingham said that a friend of his had seen men burnt alive in kerosene tubs on the Nevsky Prospect.

Monday, February 11th. London, Yacht Club.

I came up a day earlier in order to meet Grey [2] at Spender's, as one of the "Writers' Group." The "Writers' Group" now consists of George Paish, A. G. Gardiner, J. A. Spender, J. A. Hobson, Graham Wallas, Lowes Dickinson, Gilbert Murray, Hartley Withers, Leonard Hobhouse and myself. We lunched first at Café Royal, the name of which had rather startled Gardiner & Co., at the start. At Spender's there were

---

[1] Wife of Sir George Buchanan, British Ambassador at Petrograd.
[2] Viscount Grey of Fallodon.

also invited M'Kenna, Runciman and Buckmaster. Webb and Henderson had been invited to lunch with us. They came also.

Grey looked younger than I had expected. Hair scarcely grey. Trousers too wide. He played with a pencil-case half the time. He looked well, and spoke easily, clearly and well. We all sat in chairs in Spender's study in Sloane Street, surrounded by Spender's water-colours, some of which were very good. Grey said that both Italy and Rumania had not been asked to come in. They suggested coming in, and gave their terms, which in the main we had to agree to, in order to prevent them being inimically neutral, or, as regards Rumania, going over to the other side. He said that agreement with Russia, as regards giving her Constantinople, was result of Turkey, after promising to be neutral, wantonly attacking her ports. He explained why none of the principal Governments *dared* make peace—they could offer nothing to their peoples to show for the war.

Paish made it absolutely clear that unless men could go back to field *this* autumn there would be famine in 1920—spring. There seemed to be no light at all until M'Kenna, who came late, said that the only hope was a new attempt at an international labour conference. He said he was quite sure international labour could agree on something reasonable, and that if they did, the hands of Governments would be forced. M'Kenna was valuable in insisting that the idea of us trying to make peace now on the assumption that we had won was idiotic. He said that if we held out till 1920 we could have everything we wanted. He showed how tenacious Germany had always been in all her wars and that even the labour terms of peace gave no help to pacifist Germans. All were agreed that this government must be overthrown.

Wednesday, February 20th. London, Yacht Club.

We now ask nearly every one whom we ask to dinner to bring some food. On Saturday I finished off the proofs of *The Pretty Lady*. I can now see things that I have left out of that novel. Nevertheless the story held me well as I read it again—a good test.

Thursday, February 21st. London, Yacht Club.

I lunched with Rosher to meet Kennedy Jones at Thatched House Club. He is a Glasgow man, aged 52, with pale eyes, and when talking he screws them up a little and looks far away as if cogitating on the most difficult and interesting aspects of what he is discussing. During the lunch he said that *he* was really the parent of the new journalism, because he was the journalist—and it was he who had gone to Northcliffe with the idea of buying the *Evening News*. This I fairly believed. He also drew out of his pocket a cutting from a Bristol newspaper about 7 ins. long of a speech of his. He said this showed what attention his remarks had in the press. He spoke humorously but was serious behind the humour, or he would not have pulled the thing out of his pocket at all. I laughed and said it proved nothing, because he could do what he liked with any newspaper. He laughed and said I was cynical.

He related stories of how American newspaper owners stole men from each other and how Hearst had stolen X. from Pulitzer, and Northcliffe had stolen him from Hearst, in each case after being specially requested not to do so. He said Northcliffe had taken on Wells for the *Mail* because he felt that "new ideas" were coming and he wanted to be able to say when they did come that he had favoured them etc.

K.J. struck me as a powerful and ruthless man, but I wouldn't have any of his ruthlessness. When he was firm, I was firmer. In spite of the superior knowledge of which he boasts he has already lost 2 bets to Rosher about the war. I wouldn't like to be one of his men, but he was interesting enough to meet.

Wednesday, March 13th. London, Yacht Club.

The Writers' Group entertained Asquith at the Reform last night, and there was a very good dinner and plenty of various wines. Twelve people. Asquith looked very well. He came in a smoking jacket and a good soft silk shirt, but his overcoat and soft hat were ridiculous. Only Spender, of the hosts, was in evening dress. Asquith ate and drank and laughed well. He has a good "contained" laugh at implications. He showed no signs of decay. He was surrounded by first-class men, some

very first class, but easily held his place as chief man. He did not talk
a lot in the discussion, but he talked well and showed a complete grasp
of the subject, which was the respective virtues of a conscription of
wealth and a heavier income-tax to meet after-war budget. It was admirably carried on by George Paish, Sidney Webb, Hartley Withers,
Graham Wallas, and J. A. Hobson. Withers (anti-conscription) was
beaten, indeed yielded at the end. The conclusion was that super-tax
should be *much* more steeply graded and that as much of national debt
should be paid off by conscription of wealth as would enable income-
tax to stay at 5*s.* in the £.

Apropos of taxation Spender told a funny story. He said a Frenchman
(official) in England had recently asked him for details of our income-
and super-tax. Spender gave them, but the Frenchman would not believe them. He could not credit the high rates, and demanded documentary proofs. When he got them and was convinced he exclaimed,
"Mais c'est l'anarchie!" which incidentally shows how anarchy can be
confused with its most striking opposite.

Friday, March 15th. London, Yacht Club.

Rumours all day of peace offers. Clemenceau and the whole Versailles
conference in London for pow-wow, and so on.

Monday, March 18th. London, Yacht Club.

On Saturday we went to Oundle to stay with the Sandersons [1] for
the week-end, and I greatly enjoyed it—especially Sanderson's company.
He is a great modernist, with a fruity sense of humour and much personal power. Food excellent, Mrs. Sanderson being a *maîtresse-femme.*
On Saturday night we attended a school debate on the subject, "Is
enough as good as a feast?" Not brilliant, but one or two boys had a
pretty turn for sarcasm. On Sunday, the first morning Church of England service I ever (I think) attended in my life. In the afternoon two
masters gave us the *Kreutzer Sonata*—just that. The piano part was
played by Brewster, the mathematical master, very well. Applause not

---

[1] F. W. Sanderson, headmaster of Oundle School.

allowed. Then S. and I and Chadwick (apparently running the library etc.) went to the library and art rooms, and I aroused the sympathy of S. by inveighing against there being reproductions of only old masters on view. He knows nothing about painting, but he was at once very anxious for me to send him a list of very modern painters. I also objected to the prominence given on the walls to mere large photos of cathedrals. Chadwick agreed. This will be altered. I looked at my watch. 8.10! "I shall catch it," said S. He hurried off to the waiting supper. I liked Sanderson very much indeed.

Sunday, March 24th. Comarques.

The great German offensive began on Thursday and yesterday. After various delays due to exhaustion and neuralgia I began my new play. I wrote the first scene from 5 to 7 P.M. The most magnificent weather of late that the English mind can imagine.

Tuesday, March 26th.

Brothers McKenna at Reform Club on bad war news. They came in together. I said, "The brothers," and they sat down with me, and asked if I'd been to any newspaper offices to get news. "My God! It's awful," said Ernest, in a quiet, disgusted, intensely pessimistic tone. I referred to Spender's 2 articles that day. Ernest said Spender was a good man, kept his nerve—but Reginald looked at the first article, saw one line, and said: "Now I need read nothing but that. The man who will say that——" etc. Ernest said: "There's only one thing to do. Call Parliament together at once and get more men." Reginald repeated this after him. They had evidently been long talking together and had exactly the same ideas on everything. "Robertson was right. Jellicoe was right," said Reggie oracularly. "Robertson is on the beach. Jellicoe is on the beach. In order to be on the beach you only have to be absolutely right."

Wednesday, March 27th. London, Yacht Club.

Lunch at Webb's. Webb said his wife couldn't sleep on account of the war news, and he had to exaggerate his usual tranquil optimism in order to keep the household together. It was one of the rare human touches I have noticed in the said household. However, they were soon off on to the misdeeds of the Reconstruction Committee. I was told that the whole of the staff on the Department of Information had resigned when Beaverbrook was appointed minister over them, refusing to serve under "that ignorant man." They won and were transferred to the Foreign Office—one more instance of the hand-to-mouthism of Ll. George. Went to Reform Club to see papers. Massingham was so gloomy he could scarcely speak. The brothers McKenna came in, intensely pessimistic. I was rather ashamed of them. Spender's two articles in the *Westminster* were A1 for fortitude and wisdom. I think more and more highly of this man. Then to flat to dine. Electricity not working there. Gloom of candles. M. very gloomy about the war. This sort of thing always makes me cheerful.

Sibyl Colefax gave a very good description of the "all clear" signal in a few words at dinner. She said she was walking with her husband in the streets towards the end of a raid. Everything was quite silent. Then the searchlights began winking the "all clear" all about the sky. Then the sound of the "all clear" bugles was heard. Then the footsteps of a man. Then the footsteps of ten people, of twenty, of a hundred. The town was alive again.

April 4th.

Lloyd George's introduction of Man Power Bill, for conscripting Ireland and raising military age etc. Policeman looks at card outside. Then you go up on a lift. Through an outer room with one or two journalists, hat pegs, etc. Then an inner room, with two Morse instruments tapping, and then into Gallery, at entrance of which your ticket is looked at again by an official (very friendly with all reporters, and doing their little errands etc.) in evening dress with large insignia on his breast.

Two rows of seats with narrow desk all round. A few standing at either corner, including Spender, Gardiner, and me. Reporters passing in and out all the time, crushing past; a horrible lack of space. No light in House of Commons except through glass roof. No repose in Press

Gallery. Sharp corner of elaborate wood-carving against which you knock your head if you sit or lean in corners. Glimpse of Ladies' Gallery above, with glimpse of a smart woman, past first youth, with complexion *soigné* but going. Looking from left, I could just see Ll. G., Churchill, Bonar Law, Cecil, Balfour, etc., on right. House full. 12 or so standing, between cross benches. (Gallery opposite full. Side galleries half full.) Two M.P.'s wearing hats. As the M.P.'s left, they bowed awkwardly to Speaker in getting up if in front rows or on reaching central space if not; and on coming in they bowed either on rising or on reaching open space. Speaker under a canopy. Cheap effects of Ll. G. looking round as if challenging; trick of dropping his voice for last, rather important word of sentence. Unpleasant Nonconformist voice.

He did not know his case, and having made a muddle, deliberately left the muddle. Truisms about values and will-to-win cheered. Proposal to conscript Ireland cheered loudly a long time by Tories. No applause as he sat down. The whole thing a vast make-believe, with an audience of which a large part was obviously quite unintelligent and content with the usual hollow rot. Ll. G.'s oratorical effects very poor—like a Lyceum melodrama. Asquith with long hair very dignified, at home, and persuasive.

Wednesday, April 10th. London, Yacht Club.

Too much occupied and preoccupied with the British defeats, the Government proposals for increasing the army, the publication of *The Pretty Lady,* political journalism, the gardening and household difficulties, chill on the entrails, neuralgia, insomnia, Marguerite's illness, the nightly rehearsals in the small drawing-room of a play for a Red Cross performance at Clacton, and my new play—to be bothered with this journal or with notes of any kind. However, I did at last, in spite of all distractions, get my play going, and it *is* going.

Meeting of British War Memorial Committee this afternoon. Beaverbrook arrived. He told me that he liked *The Pretty Lady* better than any other book of mine, and better than any other modern book. As regards sales I hear that it is "doing very nicely."

Maurice Baring and F. Swinnerton dined with me tonight at Yacht
Club. After F.S. had gone, Maurice grew communicative about the war.
Knows Haig. Thinks him a real personality, with decision, grit, and
power of command. Never rattled. A good soldier, but not a genius.
Henry Wilson a wind-bag. He spoke in the *highest* terms of Trenchard,
chief of Air Service; also very highly of Cox, chief of Intelligence. He
said that Gough and others protested against having to take over extra
front, as ordered by war cabinet. Gough's front was under-manned and
under-gunned. No reserves in France. Depots empty. Ll. G. always refused to look at facts, but liked ideas, grandiose etc., for new stunt.
Gave particulars of how Northcliffe had announced months ago that
Robertson would be attacked and have to go; ditto in regard to
Spring-Rice. Cabinet did not believe in German offensive. Soldiers
did.

Haig told cabinet long ago facts as to inferiority in man-power and
expected them to be frightened out of their lives. They were not, as
they did not believe in offensive. He expected an attack on Haig next.
He didn't think we should lose war—we could hold on and Germans
would crack. He said that Haig had no desire to conceal the facts as to
lack of troops and spoke freely of them and permitted others to do so.
Unfortunately, of course, one can't print the facts, although the Germans probably knew them pretty well.

Thursday, April 11th. London, Yacht Club.

I went to see Beaverbrook this morning to ascertain, in view of the
fact that I am to write for *Lloyd's Weekly News,* whether he was going to buy the paper, and if so whether he meant to change the politics.
He said he wasn't going to buy it. Before this Beaverbrook asked me
to accept the directorship of British propaganda in France. After objecting, I said I would think it over and let him know. He said no one
could know French psychology better than I do—this conclusion he
drew from reading *The Pretty Lady!* Rothermere was in the room before we began business, walking about, sitting down, standing up. He
wanted a holiday. I told him it would pay him to take one. He said

he couldn't. "Here's this great united Air Force of 170,000 men just come into existence. I can't leave the baby."

Tuesday, April 16th. Comarques.

On Sunday I wrote to Beaverbrook agreeing to his request that I should enter Ministry of Information in order to direct British propaganda in France.

Friday, April 19th. London, Yacht Club.

Lunch at Reform, where Spender was exceedingly good and Davray exceedingly emotional. In the afternoon I wrote a preface for the catalogue of Paul Nash's exhibition. I dined with the Nicholsons at the Café Royal grill. Lutyens and Mrs. Stuart-Wortley were there, the latter nervous and quiet, the former full of puns and tiny jokes, but agreeable and ready to stand being teased. Then I saw Nicholson privately as to his proposed work for Memorial Committee and his situation in the army. Before going to bed I wrote a report on this for the committee. A day! Last night the new Military Service Act became law, and I am now legally, at nearly 51 years, in the Army Reserve. I saw Dennis Eadie yesterday going from his rehearsal at the Haymarket to his lunch at the Carlton and had a few words with him. The matter was not mentioned, but he was evidently preoccupied by his impending military obligations.

Friday, April 26th. London, Yacht Club.

On Wednesday night I had Professor Henry S. Canby (English literature) of Yale after dinner at the Reform. Wells joined in. A young man, probably about 30. He made one or two shrewd remarks and liked *Candide*.

Sunday, April 28th. Comarques.

Today I finished the second act of my new *Honours* play,[1] after two sleepless nights. I read a lot of *A Dreary Story* of Chekhov in the night.

---

[1] *The Title.*

I had read it once or twice before. It now seems to me quite fresh, full of new powers and beauties, and one of the finest things I ever did read.

Mair told me about painted girls in the Registry department. I had myself noticed some others, with studiously considered gait, in the corridors. Mair said that one of the Registry girls met him in tube train. She smiled. He acknowledged. Then taking out her meat card, she leaned over and showed it to him, exclaiming, "What about that for a meat card?" The idea was that he should thus learn her name. Mair said that he advised her to use her coupons with care and handed the card back.

Wednesday, May 1st. London, Yacht Club.

I came to London yesterday and interviewed Beaverbrook and Roderick Jones [1] at Ministry of Information and arranged that I should begin as head of British propaganda in France next week.

Thursday, May 2nd. London, Yacht Club.

Cravath said, apropos of an Englishman named Broughton who had lived 25 years in the U.S.A. without losing his spots, that Cravath's youngest daughter, on seeing Broughton on board a British ship on voyage to England, said to her father, "Poppa, I always used to think that Mr. Broughton was affected, but now I see he's only an Englishman."

Yesterday I had lunch with Ross and a flying officer friend of his, Beverly Robinson, who had escaped from Germany after 2½ years' imprisonment. Robinson's account of the escape was not exciting. His account of prison insolence by the brothers Niemeyer *was*: ordering officers to kneel after stripping them in the presence of soldiers etc. He told me he'd got most of the books he wanted and had formed a library of 500 books. But he could not get *Books and Persons*. It was stopped by the censor. I couldn't think why until he reminded me that it contained a couple of pages about German colonies. This is a really remark-

---

[1] Sir Roderick Jones, chairman of Reuter's and in 1918 appointed director of propaganda.

able instance of German thoroughness. He tried to get them to tear out the two pages and then give him the book, but they wouldn't. He said they were intensely easy to deceive. He would hear *nothing* of their starving. He said he had got an excellent meal at a railway buffet for 4 marks.

Friday, May 10th. London, Yacht Club.

I finished my play *The Title* on Wednesday, but in order to do so I had to knock myself up and also to inform people with whom I had appointments in London that I was laid aside with a chill. I wrote the last act in four days' actual work.

Then yesterday I came to London to take up my duties as head of the French section of the propaganda department of the Ministry of Information. On the whole the first day was rather a lark. It began with a lunch to Allied journalists, where I sat between *Le Journal* and *Le Petit Parisien* and had the *Débats* opposite. I didn't like my room, nor my staff being on different floors from me.

Night: Dinner of the Other Club. I made the acquaintance of Smuts. He has a peculiar accent (foreign) and puts his hand on your knee constantly while talking to you. A man of principles, and a fine man; but I doubt if he is the great man some of us thought. He was quite serene about the approaching end of the war.

Saturday, May 11th. London, Yacht Club.

Dined at F. E. Smith's. An enormous house, considering it isn't a special house, but only at the corner of a row (32, Grosvenor Gardens). The library is even equal to his boastings about it, but he would continually refer to prices. What astonished me was that he does not keep even really valuable books (from £100 to £2000 apiece) under glass. He was greatly amusing over incidents of his American trip and especially as to how he and his brother Harold, in one of the dryest States, Nebraska, made the professor of rhetoric at some university drunk— although this professor was the origin of the dryness. They drank to the great orators and then to the stars of American literature. At the end the professor said, of F.E., "The most brilliant man I ever met," and later, to friends, he said of F.E., "He is a *whale.*"

Tuesday, May 14th. London, Yacht Club.

Did 4 hours' hard work at the Ministry. People kept coming into my room on various excuses, but just to look at me. Miss Nerney began to work there yesterday. I have now abandoned literature until I am chucked out of the job, or the job ends, or I am called to a better one. But I do journalism, and a damned nuisance it is. Two articles this week. Three next week.

Friday, May 31st. London, Yacht Club.

Other Club dinner last night. Justice Darling came after his day in court over the Billing-Maude Allen case. He has poor literary views. Kept insisting that *Salome* was nasty etc. *I* said it was only poor. A thin little man, rather clever and agreeable. He has a hell of a job on and knows it. Beaverbrook made £85 in bets over the distance of Château-Thierry from Paris. Smuts presided. I sat next to him.

Tuesday, June 4th. London, Yacht Club.

In arranging for the King to attend Westminster Abbey on France's Day I thought I had set in motion a great thing to my credit. It was not so. I was misled. I took things for granted, made mistakes on them, and the whole affair had to be cancelled. Religion was at the bottom of the trouble. Hence the trouble. At the last moment I was asked to write the British contribution to the first daily joint wireless messages sent out to the world by Britain, France, and Italy together. I wrote it between 6 and 7.

Wednesday, June 12th. London, Yacht Club.

Usual hour home Saturday afternoon, and usual early train back here on Monday morning. I have now somewhat lessened the strain of writing articles and doing other extra-office odd work by the discovery that a lot of the extra-office can be done at odd times intra-office.

Last night, dinner inaugurating the Groupe Inter-Universitaire Franco-Anglais, at Pagani's. A big gathering—in the chair Guéritte, with his hearing-apparatus. A most charming man, though he did call on me for a speech after I'd signed to him that I wouldn't speak. All the speeches in English. Several Frenchmen spoke English very well. This organization is based on a smaller organization of which the rules were: no subscriptions; no chairman; no toasts; no speeches—the idea being simply the interchange colloquially of opinions. On the whole I thought last night's affair wasn't so bad—for sense. I met Denison Ross (now Sir), head of the School of Oriental Languages. A wild, very interesting person.

Friday, June 14th. London, Yacht Club.

Wednesday night. Dinner of the Writers' Group. Gilbert Murray read his draft of a Liberal manifesto for us to sign. It was a superb piece of really sound and elegant writing and was generally approved.

Tuesday, July 2nd. London, Yacht Club.

Last Friday, for Ministry, I saw Generals Macdonogh and Macready (first visit to War Office) and Albert Thomas.[1] I finished up at William Weir's and saw Richmond and two brothers and two wives. Saturday I learnt at home that Lockyer was called up for medical exam. Last night I dined with Beaverbrook, the Edwin Montagus and Diana Manners being of the party at the Savoy. Dinner arranged for 9 P.M. At 9.15, Montagu and I, having waited, began. The rest arrived at 9.20. When the conversation turned on Diana being the original of Queen in *The Pretty Lady* my attitude was apparently so harsh that Beaverbrook changed the subject. We afterwards went 5 in a taxi to B.'s rooms at Hyde Park Hotel. After a time Diana and I sat on window-sill of B.'s bedroom, looking at the really superb night view over the park. One small light burning in the bedroom. B.'s pyjamas second-rate. Some miscellaneous talk about life and women. After they had all gone but

---

[1] The French Socialist politician.

me B. asked me what I thought of Diana. I told him I thought she was unhappy, through idleness. He said he liked her greatly.

Friday, July 5th. London, Yacht Club.

11th anniversary of our wedding yesterday. We dined at the Café Royal. Raymond Needham [1] came and lunched with me at Yacht Club and told me much about Lord Beaverbrook and much as to his own private affairs. On Wednesday night Eadie came to the flat and read two acts of *The Title* very well. The first act, though I thought consistently good, seemed a hell of a length.

I lost my food card.

Tuesday, July 16th. London, Yacht Club.

Far too busy with ministerial work, articles, or official dinners and rehearsals of *The Title* to be able to keep up any diarizing at all. I went to the dinner to the Canadian journalists at the Savoy on Friday last, Beaverbrook the host. Lloyd George sat at the end of one table and Borden, the P.M. of Canada, at the end of another, and I heard of smaller P.M.'s of various territories in Canada.

Yesterday Beaverbrook asked me to take control of another department at the ministry in addition to my own. I temporized.

Dinner to American professors last night.

Thursday, July 18th. London, Yacht Club.

Minute from war cabinet yesterday censuring me for my most successful pro-France article in the *Observer* on Sunday. It had been used on Monday by *Daily Mail* as an axe to hit the Government with about "baleful secrecy." Lord B. was furious and asked me to write a pungent letter in reply, which he signed. By evening Ll. G. had apologized and promised to have a new minute of the cabinet prepared.

---

[1] Raymond Needham, K.C., was at that time private secretary to the Ministry of Information.

Tuesday, July 23rd. London, Yacht Club.

I went home on Saturday afternoon, after witnessing dress rehearsal of *The Title* on Friday night at the Royalty. On Sunday morning I received five telegrams, from which I gathered that the play had quite succeeded with the first-night audience. I came to town yesterday and found that the first-night success had been really immense. Eadie asked me to go and see the 3rd act last night. M. and I went, and he and his wife were there. He admitted that the Sampson Straight scene went better last night than on the first night. There is really nothing wrong with it except that, like anything else, it could be improved. So I agreed to improve it for him.

Friday, July 26th. London, Yacht Club.

Major David Davies asked Massingham, Gardiner, Gooch, J. Douglas, and McCardy to lunch yesterday at the Carlton, about his League of Nations Association. Coal-owner. Said to be worth £3,000,000. Very simple-minded. Spoke of "some one named Mrs. Humphrey Ward," "some one who is called 'Q.'," etc. But he has faith.

At night I went with Needham to *Le Coq d'Or*. We were too close to the trombones. The only music of Rimsky's that I ever liked. I thought the tale rotten and the spectacle 2nd-rate. Still, I enjoyed the whole.

Tuesday, July 30th. London, Yacht Club.

Back home Saturday afternoon. Thoroughly unwell. I went to bed after dinner and arose for lunch on Sunday. Some tennis. Some spelling-game. 200 pages of George Moore's indecency, *A Story-Teller's Holiday*— very good.

Friday, October 4th. London, Yacht Club.

This journal broke down through pressure of work and neuralgia. I have lost priceless things by this slackness.

The French section at the Ministry of Information began to buck up in July and August. I got a special grant of £100,000 out of the Treasury and the appointment of Lord Lytton as British commissioner of propaganda in Paris. Roderick Jones recommended this man strongly, and I accepted him blindly on the importance of his name to French society. He left yesterday on his mission.

M. and I and Richard went for a holiday to Cleveden on Sept. 10th. Richard stayed 7 days, and we 16, we being held up by the railway strike. In the end I got a car down from London. On my return I found myself appointed at the M. of I. to the post of director of propaganda (vice Sir R. Jones), together with general supervision and co-ordination of all departments of the ministry, i.e. deputy minister. This is the most marvellous, disconcerting, and romantic thing that ever happened to me. At any rate, whatever happens, I, an artist, shall have had the experience. It would be enormous fun except for the responsibility and the 3 A.M. worryings.

Tuesday, October 8th. London, Yacht Club.

At night, having been reproached about not visiting the artistes at the Royalty, I went there, and saw bits of the play and all the artistes except Joan Carey. They seemed very well pleased with everything. A poor house. Nigel Playfair told me he was trying to get the Lyric Opera House at Hammersmith for what is wrongly called a repertory theatre. He had got the rent promised, but one of the London ring of managers had made a bid over his head without even having seen the theatre, just in order to keep the ring closed. Playfair didn't know whether he would get the place after all. I told him if he did I might collect £2000 for him.[1]

Thursday, October 10th. London, Yacht Club.

At the Ministry yesterday I found out that the meetings of the Turkish committee were being held at the offices of the British-American Tobacco Co. I at once wrote to the minister and told him that I meant to revoke his order to that effect.

---

[1] When the plan was further matured Arnold Bennett became one of the directors of the Lyric Theatre, Hammersmith.

Saturday, October 12th. London, Yacht Club.

Dinner of Writers' Group last night at Reform, at which it was decided to drop our 3-months-debated manifesto entirely as being quite absurd in present circumstances. A wise decision, my God! Spender spoke about the poverty of Germany and of a great struggle between inhabitants of 2-room tenements in poorer quarters and the police. The police laid down that it was unsanitary for people to sleep in a room where cooking was done. This, of course, would have put the whole family into one room to sleep. They could not enforce the decree practically. Then they had kitchens constructed in new tenements in such a manner, so full of corners, that beds could not be put into them! He also spoke of seeing a highly-respectable-looking long row of tenements in Munich, as to which a guide friend said to him: "You see those houses. There isn't a w.c. in the whole row. When the tenants want a w.c. they go to that beer-hall there and have a drink in order to use a w.c." Ellery Sedgwick, of the *Atlantic Monthly,* was at the dinner. I talked privately to him afterwards and walked with him back to the Ritz and gave him my ideas on most of the big political personages. I was just in the humour for being highly indiscreet, and I was indiscreet. He said seriously to me at the end, "You may like to know that I accept your judgment absolutely." Every now and then in the rain he would stand still in order to put an important question.

Tuesday, October 15th. London, Yacht Club.

Reflection upon the German answer to Wilson's reply to their request for an armistice made me think the end of the war was getting very near and that the whole policy of the M. of Information would have to be swung round. I drafted a minute before catching train; Mair added to it a little, and when I showed it to Beaverbrook in the evening he said he would use it as a minute to the cabinet. For me there was already an air of unreality in the work of the ministry and especially about our scheme for re-organizing it.

Saturday, October 19th. London, Yacht Club.

I heard through Mair from Buchan, who was in the F.O., that Germany had capitulated to all Wilson's terms and that the Kaiser had abdicated. This was the F.O. information. Strange. It proved not to be true. A day later, Milner was being interviewed in the *Evening Standard* (or was it the *P.M.G.?*) to the effect that all Germany was not militaristic—in a word, to the effect that some mercy ought to be shown, lest Bolshevism should appear in Germany and spread everywhere. It was a move to save the Kaiser, instigated by cold feet in the F.O., the cabinet, and elsewhere. And afterwards Mair told me that the F.O. had intimated to Wilson that his terms would not quite do.

Beaverbrook away from Ministry all this week. Rothermere gave a dinner in my honour at the Marlborough Club last night. He chose his company in the most extraordinary way. Australian Hughes, a good talker, sheer brass, but a good slashing talker; very deaf, with an apparatus looking like a rather large kodak closed, on the table, and a flex from it to his ear. Henry Dalziel, a bluff person, not without a certain attractiveness. Hulton, Andrew Caird, manager of the *Daily Mail,* bluff and decent and crude, but clever. He told me everything I already knew about propaganda after dinner. Churchill, Blumenfeld, somewhat quiet. F. E. Smith came very late and said little. Churchill talked the best. I like Rothermere. He told me he wanted to sell all his papers except the *Sunday Pictorial.* He said he had worked hard since he was 14, and if a man had succeeded and chose to slave as hard as ever after 50, it merely proved that that man didn't understand life. He was turned 50.

This morning Major Holt came to me from Beaverbrook and said that B.'s doctor has advised him to resign, but he hadn't yet taken his decision. Of course this meant that he *had* taken his decision. B. is certainly unwell with glands, but equally certainly ill health is not his full reason for resigning. I propose now to write to him and say that I shall resign.

Wednesday and Thursday nights I slept at the flat.

Wednesday, October 23rd. London, Yacht Club.

When Northcliffe returned from America and was appointed head of enemy propaganda, he kept the title of the organization he had controlled in the U.S.A., namely British War Mission, and he still uses this for his Crewe House organization.

Some time ago he approached the Ministry of Information and the War Aims Committee to form a committee to co-ordinate policy in regard to propaganda. An excellent idea. This committee, however, was called the Policy Committee of the British War Mission, which in itself was a bit thick, seeing that the M. of I. is a far more important organization than the enemy propaganda show. When the Germans began to be defeated, Northcliffe called the committee together to draw up peace terms to be used as groundwork of propaganda. Mysteriously, all the govt. departments began to be represented in this committee, including Reggie Hall, a very great man in his secret service business for the Admiralty, but, I should have thought, unsuited to draw up peace terms. Including also a number of absolute duds.

This committee drew up its Allied peace terms and submitted them to the war cabinet. The war cabinet said it was very busy and couldn't consider them and turned them over to Balfour to pass. Balfour passed them. Reggie Hall then suggested a serious alteration, namely that the non-return of the German colonies to Germany should be removed from the "negotiable" to the "absolute" group of conditions. (Quite right!) These terms of peace will form the basis of all our propaganda. This is a really good story and shows Northcliffe's lust for power very well, for of course he lords it over the committee.

I have slept at the flat since end of last week. Very exciting and rather uncomfortable, with a mad servant aged 70 in the place. Saturday night: *As You Were* at the Pavilion. A few fair jokes (verbal). As a whole, terribly mediocre. Every scene turned on adultery, or mere copulation. Even in the primeval forest scene, an adultery among gorillas was shown. This revue is the greatest success in London at present and is taking about £3000 a week. In bed all day Sunday with neuralgia. Poured with rain all day. It now appears that Beaverbrook, more and more ill, will resign. Confabs daily between me, Snagge, Mair, A. J. Bennett, and Needham. Reconstruction within the ministry going steadily on.

Thursday, October 24th. London, Yacht Club.

I had to lunch at Savoy yesterday with Davray to meet Painlevé, Steeg, and another French politician and Wickham Steed. Painlevé came only for a quarter of an hour, as he had to lunch with Ll. G. Steeg, *rébarbatif,* and as I knew his connection with Malery, I at once didn't like him. Davray, however, said afterwards that he was quite all right and *extrêmement constructif.* He looked rather like a fairly strong Nonconformist preacher. Steed did not impress me as a strong or a first-class man. He talked a great deal too much about foreign politics and really didn't say much that we don't all know without saying. He may be a nervous man. Tall, very thin, silly beard. He certainly didn't appear as an original thinker at all. Around this cascade of words, the fearful din of the restaurant. I did manage to get Painlevé off politics and on to personal, concrete things such as his impression of Ll. George. The usual awful ignorance of the Irish situation.

Sunday, October 27. London, Yacht Club.

Interview with Masterman on Friday apropos of his "Literature and Art" department at ministry being broken up. He had a bad cold and was gloomy. He resented the provisional arrangements having been made through his 2nd in command and not through him—though he had been greatly away, ill. Still, at the bottom of his heart he wasn't really worrying, because his own place and salary were secured, and this, of course, was bound to affect him. Considering that he had been a cabinet minister early in the war and that I, politically a nobody, was now his superior, he behaved excellently in an extremely trying situation. So did I.

The sensual appeal is now really very marked everywhere, in both speech and action, on the stage. Adultery everywhere pictured as desirable, and copulation generally ditto. Actresses play courtesan parts (small ones, often without words but with gestures) with gusto.

Tuesday, October 29th. London, Yacht Club.

News of Austrian separate demand for armistice yesterday afternoon. I heard a newsman in Oxford Street cry: "*Evenin' News*. Last edition. All abaht it. Tonight's and tomorrow night's too. Only one German left."

Meeting of Nationals in the morning, at which I preside. About 30 present. Masterman insisted on the dangerousness of our handling and spreading documentary peace terms which the government had approved but would not publicly approve and certainly would not publish. Suppose these came out. He called them trinitrotoluol. He didn't seem to see that this was one of the essential, primary risks that a Ministry of Information must take.

Wednesday, October 30th. London, Yacht Club.

I was summoned to Beaverbrook yesterday. He was in bed, bandaged, depressed, having been told by the doctor in the morning that he had septic poisoning. When Lady B. and Needham had left the room, he began to smoke and to talk intimately, and said: "You know, Arnold, my life has been all crises. I was worth 5 millions when I was 27. And now this is a new crisis, and it's the worst." However, he cheered up. Bonar Law came in and was very courteous and cautious to me. He said his sister had been a very great and constant admirer of mine, but since *The Pretty Lady* she had done with me.

Beaverbrook's resignation in the papers. I got instructions to carry on.

Thursday, October 31st. London, Yacht Club.

Beaverbrook was as bright as anything yesterday. He was up, laughing, and had had news of a quack doctor who had cured some one with the same disease as he has. (Nobody, however, knew what the disease was.)

Dined with M. at Barrie's and saw his Lutyens room. Good, short dinner. He told me that he didn't smoke till 23 and that he wrote *My Lady Nicotine* before he had ever smoked. He said when he first came to London, he dined on 2*d*. a day (four halfpenny buns or scones) for a year, eating them in the street, and ate little else. He wrote about two articles a day and sold about one in six. He found at the end of the year that he needn't have been so economical, but he was afraid of the rainy day. He said it took a long time for him to see that there was any material in Scotland. He wrote *An Auld Licht Wedding* and sold it and thought he had exhausted Scotland. Next few articles he didn't sell, and then an editor said, "We liked your Scotch stuff." So he wrote *An Auld Licht Funeral*. And so on.

He told us that he had had Asquith and Birrell to dinner the other night and had arranged with Asquith's daughter-in-law and another female friend that they should dress up as housemaids and serve the dinner. They did so. The daughter-in-law wore a black wig. Neither Birrell nor Asquith recognized the women. But after dinner, in the drawing-room, Asquith said, "One of those maids is extraordinarily like my daughter-in-law." Barrie told this practical joke with great restraint and humour.

Wednesday, November 6th. London, Yacht Club.

On Monday at lunch at the Reform I learnt the details of the secret history of Northcliffe's encyclical to the newspapers of the world about the proper peace terms with Germany. According to C.M. the idea of the letter was not N.'s at all, but C.M. got Campbell Stuart to persuade him to do it. Stuart took N. out to lunch for that purpose. The thing was written by C.M., but the style being too good, it was re-written down to some resemblance of Northcliffe's supposed style. Northcliffe then signed it and immediately went off to Paris (where, as Beaverbrook told me last night at dinner, Lloyd George took good care not to see him at all), to be near the scene of the armistice negotiations.

Monday night dined alone with M. at flat and came home to club in pouring rain, because M. said Fifi wouldn't sleep anywhere but in the bedroom, and I said I could not sleep with the dog there.

Thursday, November 7th. London, Yacht Club.

Yesterday afternoon I arranged with Alistair Tayler that he should join the Board (Playfair and I being the others) of the Hammersmith Lyric Theatre enterprise, and that I should be the chairman.

Friday, November 8th. London, Yacht Club.

Yesterday afternoon my secretary was twice rung up by officials at the War Office to know if the war was over—that is, if the armistice was signed. The rumours were immense and numerous.

Yesterday Lillah McCarthy made a determined effort to get my play *Instinct* out of me, after a refusal. But I put her on to Pinker, and she failed. By 10.15 she had already rung me up three times.

Tuesday, November 12th. London, Yacht Club.

In Sunday's papers we saw the abdication of the Kaiser. Returned to town yesterday morning. In Lower Regent Street first news that armistice was signed—a paper boy calling out in a subdued tone. 10.45. Maroons went off at 11, and excited the populace.

A large portion of the ministry staff got very excited. Buchan came in to shake hands. Girls very excited. I had to calm them. Lunch at Wellington Club. We had driven through large crowds part way up the Mall and were then turned off from Buckingham Palace.

Raining now. An excellent thing to damp hysteria and Bolshevism. Great struggling to cross Piccadilly Circus twice. No buses. (It was rumoured that tubes stopped. I believe they were stopped for a time.) It stopped raining. Then cold mire in streets. Vehicles passed, festooned with shouting human beings. Others, dark, with only one or two occupants. Much light in Piccadilly up to Ritz corner, and in Piccadilly Circus. It seemed most brilliant. Some theatres had lights on their façades too. The enterprising Trocadero had hung a row of temporary lights under one of its porticoes. Shouting. But nothing terrible or memorable. Yet this morning Brayley, my valet, said to me the usual phrases: "You wondered where the people came from. You could walk on their heads at Charing Cross, and you couldn't cross Picc. Circus at all." When he came in with my tea I said, "Well, Brayley, it's all over." He smiled and said something. That was all our conversation about the end of the war. Characteristic.

Last night I thought of lonely soldiers in that crowd. No one to talk to. But fear of death lifted from them.

Thursday, November 14th. London, Yacht Club.

I dined at flat on Tuesday night (Pinker there) and slept there; so I didn't see anything of the "doings." But there was a bonfire in Piccadilly Circus, kept alive by theatre boards and boards off motor-buses. Girls are still very prominent in the "doings." Swinnerton told me that the staidest girl they had suddenly put on a soldier's hat and overcoat and went promenading in them.

Was told that the scene at the Carlton on Monday night was remarkable. Any quantity of broken glasses, tables overturned, and people standing on tables, and fashionable females with their hair down. On Tuesday night I noticed that all the principal restaurants had commissionaires in front of doors scrutinizing people who wished to enter and keeping out (apparently) all who had not reserved tables. Last night a cabby told me he would go westwards but not towards Piccadilly Circus, as he did not know what would happen to him.

The feature of last night was girls with bunches of streamers which they flicked in your face as you passed.

Friday, November 15th. London, Yacht Club.

My resignation from ministry took effect yesterday. Buchan, the liquidator, came down to see me and was very explanatory and apologetic. The behaviour of the Cabinet to me was, of course, scandalous. But they have treated many others similarly; so I was not surprised. The only notice I got was a Roneo'd [mimeographed] copy of the war cabinet minute. I was never consulted in any way.

Luncheon to Robert Donald at Connaught Rooms. 400 there to honour him because he had not sold himself to the new proprietors of the *Chronicle.* The toastmaster in a red coat was the cream of the show. He had a terrifically bland manner, especially with his supplicating hands. And having prayed silence for toast of King he rushed madly right round the room and played "God save the K." on the piano.

At night, dinner to American editors of trade journals at Savoy. Smuts in the chair. Nothing special except that Smuts claimed some German colonies for British dependencies.

Afterwards, Snagge and Kindersley and I went to ball-room. Packed with dancers. Coon band. A few couples sitting on stairs. A few drinks. Some women in a great state of sexual excitement. Others not. The dancing custom of pressing the abdomens of the partners together is really very remarkable indeed and shows an immense change in manners if not in customs. The whole affair was a fine incitement to fornication.

Tuesday, November 19th. London, Yacht Club.

I went to Wells's alone for the week-end. Second time I have gone away alone because M. could not leave her dogs. Five guests at the Wellses'.

Thursday, November 21st. London, Yacht Club.

Attending ministry about an hour a day, and yet I seem to have no time to think out plays. I had tea with Max [1] yesterday. He wanted to compare my desire to express myself and make money with the political desire to get titles, but he failed.

Saturday, November 23rd. London, Yacht Club.

My article in the *D.N.* which ended by blaming Liberal leadership, on Thursday, must have caused some commotion, seeing that Asquith himself wrote me a polite letter of self-justification. Most Liberals are delighted with the article, and Asquith said he was in general agreement with it.

Tuesday, November 26th. London, Yacht Club.

Week-end at Beaverbrook's, Cherkley Court. Good, except not enough food, B. not being interested in food.

I read B.'s printed account of the conspiracy that overthrew Asquith in Dec. 1916. It was exceedingly well written and showed great judgment of men and some sense of historical values. In fact it was remarkable and heightened my originally high opinion of Beaverbrook. The War Office and Ll. G. both came badly out of the account, especially the former. B.'s

---

[1] Lord Beaverbrook.

own share in the affair is kept very modestly in the background. He seemed almost inclined to publish it in the *Daily Express*. I advised him against this.

Tuesday, December 10th. London, Yacht Club.

Week-end at Dr. F. Keeble's at Weybridge. Lillah McCarthy also there.[1] In spite of my neuralgia we had a great week-end, full of good and not too serious conversation. I promised to write her a play on the subject of Judith, if a firm contract was made at once.[2] In fact I constructed the play on the spot, after having read Judith myself and having heard it read by Keeble. (Some difficulty in getting an Apocrypha.)

Saturday, December 14th. London, Yacht Club.

Interview with Lillah McCarthy and Drinkwater at Adelphi Terrace at 12.45. I promised to write *Judith* by the end of January, and they promised to produce *Don Juan* also. In the afternoon Captain Basil Dean came to see me about his London theatrical scheme. He said he could get and control £20,000. I definitely promised to write a play for *him*, too. This, with Goodall's, Vedrenne's, and Lillah's, makes 4 plays!

We dined at the Galsworthys', Grove Lodge, Hampstead, and the Masefields were there. Mrs. M. and I got on excellently. Masefield gloomyish, and very precise in diction. Fine voice. Diction of a public speaker. Galsworthy very nice. Ada Galsworthy adorable.

Sunday, December 15th. London, Yacht Club.

I began the scheming of my play *Judith* yesterday. At his request I went and had tea with Weir yesterday. He wanted me to put a speech into order for him which he is going to deliver at Manchester on Friday and in which he will define the proper British air policy for the future. He told me some interesting things. He said that the great difficulty in long-distance flying now was not mechanical but navigational. A big machine had started for India from London on Friday and, coming into

---

[1] Lillah McCarthy was divorced from Granville-Barker in 1918. She married Professor Keeble in 1920.

[2] *Judith* was produced at the Kingsway Theatre, April 30, 1919.

a storm, had come down in France. He said that the commander, a general, was a first-class pilot etc., but if he had been a really 1st-class expert in navigation, such as they did possess, he would never have come down. Weir said that he had been up in a "flying boat" weighing 17½ tons, carrying 9 passengers and a ton of goods, that travelled at 118 miles an hour and carried petrol for 1000 miles. He said that the flight to the United States would occur between March 15th and April 15th. On politics he was extremely grave and bitter.

Thursday, December 19th. London, Yacht Club.

I met a Captain Griffin (from Walsall) at Reform yesterday, with Shufflebotham. He had been wounded 9 times, I think; prisoner in Germany. Was reported dead. After he returned to life, his solicitor, among other bills, forwarded the following: "To memorial service (fully choral), 3 guineas."

Friday, December 20th. London, Yacht Club.

Welcome to Sir Douglas Haig and 4 carriages full of generals yesterday. Vast crowds in front of Reform Club. Girls at windows opposite covered their shoulders in the cold with national flags. Reform full of women, boys, and kids. In ground-floor room, east, grave members standing on tableclothed tables in front of windows (me too) and in front a dame covering the throats of two small boys. All front windows of club occupied by women. Roadway kept by very few police. Roadway sprinkled with gravel. Cheering in distance. Handkerchiefs taken out. One or two mounted policemen on fine horses. Then a sort of herald in a long hat. Handkerchief-waving; cheering, louder and louder. Then the four carriages, 3 in 1st carriage and 4 each in the other 3. Generals wore no overcoats. One or two bowed and smiled. Gone in a moment, and we all jumped down and turned away. Such was the welcome to Haig and Co.

THE JOURNAL

1919-1928

1919

Saturday, January 11th. Comarques.

Having given up all the work except *Observations* for the *New States-man* I came to Comarques on Saturday last, 4th inst., with the intention of writing *Judith,* the play for Lillah McCarthy, and finishing it before 7th February. I began it on Sunday, 5th inst., and tonight, 11th, I finished the first act.

Last year, in spite of the fact that I was engaged officially at the M. of nformation for 7 or 8 months, I wrote 165,700 words of my own stuff.

Tuesday, January 28th. Comarques.

I finished *Judith* yesterday at 7.30, having written it in twenty-three days. I had several very slight headaches, but no dyspepsia worth a damn. Nervous dyspepsia did give indications of attacking me, but the mysterious and expensive tablets which I got kept me in excellent order.

Saturday, February 8th. Comarques.

Judith was delivered yesterday week. On Tuesday Marguerite met Lillah McCarthy, who nearly fell on my neck in the street, from enthusiasm about the play. Eaton also wrote to me that he was "violently enthusiastic" about it.

These two and old Drinkwater came to dinner at the new flat on Tuesday last. Drinkwater said nothing good or bad as to the play until late in the evening, when I asked him.

He then said indifferently that he liked it, but didn't care much for the last act, or words to that effect.

Sunday, February 16th. Comarques.

I am chiefly occupied with the stage. I give a considerable amount of time to the Lyric, Hammersmith, where money has been lost in my absence, owing to the lavish expenditure. And I am also being drawn into the production part of *Judith*. Lillah McC., Drinkwater, Eaton, and I had a séance of nearly three hours on Tuesday about the cast.

I finished Professor Arthur Keith's *The Human Body* (Home University Library). A thoroughly sound little book, rottenly written, even to bad syntax. It is strange that these experts, such as Keith and Sidney Webb, do not take the trouble to be efficient in their first business, the vehicle of expression

Monday, March 3rd. Comarques.

On the 1st I began my book on women,[1] but I only wrote about 100 words. I meant to go on with it yesterday, but couldn't. After muddling about nearly all day I began at 5 P.M. and wrote 600 good words before dinner. The book is now really begun.

Wednesday, March 5th. London, Yacht Club.

We came to London yesterday. M. went to Newcastle to stay with the Shufflebothams. Swinnerton, Playfair, and A. E. W. Mason dined with me at the Garrick. Mason told us some of his secret service adventures in Mexico. He was very good as a *raconteur,* and evidently has a great gift for secret service, though he said he began as an amateur.

Mason said that practically all the German spies and many of the Zeppelin men carried a packet of obscene photographs on their persons. I fully expected he would laugh at the reputation of the German Secret Service for efficiency, and he did. I felt sure the German temperament is not a good secret service temperament. Too gullible and talkative. Mason

[1] *Our Women: Chapters in the Sex Discord,* published in 1920.

said their secret service was merely expensive. Money chucked away idiotically.

Saturday, March 15th. Comarques.

I went to London on Tuesday after a solitary week-end here in which I earned £300 in two days, by hard work.

Tuesday night M. and I attended the first rehearsal of *Judith*. It was in Eaton's room at the Royalty. The Royalty was in process of reparation, and there was an almost continuous slapping noise of whitewashers in the room above.

Later rehearsals were held in the Ampthill Room at the Connaught Rooms. Happily, the leading lady, Lillah, is easy to deal with. Eaton knows immensely more about producing than I do, but I was able to convince him that his plans for the murder in the second act were all wrong and that my original plans were all right. I also changed Lillah's conception of her acting of it. In fact the murder scene will be the author's own.

March 27th. 17 Berkeley St., London.

The 285th and last performance of *The Title* occurred on Saturday last at the Royalty. A good house. The provincial tour which began some weeks ago was a failure for the first fortnight.

While I was being shaved at the Reform on Tuesday, Henry Norman came in and waited. He read me a letter from his wife, who is inspecting the fronts to make a record for the Imperial War Museum. He told me other things not in the letter as that Englishwomen are still looking after French *permissionaires* at the railway stations and that Frenchwomen do nothing in this line and even try to prevent the Englishwomen from getting lodgings in the towns. I regard Englishwomen as silly for doing it. It seems that the French soldier is very rough when drunk or half drunk. One woman had coffee thrown in her face three times. Another was stabbed and killed. The English psychology is very queer in these things.

Friday, April 11th. Comarques.

Richard, M., and I went to Eastbourne last Saturday for the first production of *Judith* (Devonshire Park Theatre).

Lillah McCarthy behaved well, considering her double anxiety of manager and star—both as it were making a fresh start in life. Lillah had there Dr. Keeble (her fiancé), her mother, her sister, and a niece and nephew, offspring of another sister (or brother). All these were all over the theatre all the time. She protested that all the creative producing work had been done by me, M., and her. I had to put this right.

Evidently Lillah is used to authors who will stand no damned nonsense. She got rather excited after both 2nd and 1st performances, because Bagoas's rushing forth and killing a spying woman detracted from her kissing Holofernes, and she had to be soothed. Her tent costume frightened one of the lessees of the theatre. Above a line drawn about ½ inch or 1 inch above the *mont de Vénus* she wore nothing except a 4-in. band of black velvet round the body hiding the breasts and a similar perpendicular band of velvet starting from between the breasts and going down to the skirt and so hiding the navel. Two thin shoulder straps held this contrivance in position. Bracelets and rings, of course. The skirt was slit everywhere and showed the legs up to the top of the thigh when she laid down there at Holofernes's feet. She looked a magnificent picture thus, but a police prosecution would not have surprised me at all. She gave an exceedingly fine performance—as good as could be wished for. The house was very full for the first night. (Capacity about 115–120.)

I refused the persistent calls for author and sat with Lillah's maid in Lillah's dressing-room until the calls had finished. Terrible silly mishaps occurred with the sack containing Holofernes's head in the 3rd act, despite the most precise instructions to the crowd. Further instructions to the crowd and similar mishaps on the 2nd night.

I took supper 3 nights running, and survived it.

Sunday, May 4th. Comarques.

I never before took so much interest in the production of a play of mine. *Judith* was produced at the Kingsway Theatre, London, last Wednesday, 30th April. It certainly bewildered people. Numerous comic touches were quite lost in the 1st act. In the 2nd act Lillah McCarthy had put down her dress as low as it was at the first night at Eastbourne (after raising it for later performances at Eastbourne and for dress rehearsals in London). The end of Act II might have been spoilt by an untimely descent of the curtain 10 seconds too soon. The performance as a whole was excellent. The disinterested applause was fair. The interested friendly applause was too insistent. House held over £150, the highest first night the Kingsway ever had, I think. The ordinary first-night public was *dérouté*. Common people seemed thoroughly interested and well pleased.

The press criticisms next day were without exception unfavourable. The Sunday criticisms that I have seen were not bad, though there was much exception taken to Lillah's nudity in Act II. In general the press quite failed to comprehend the play and said the most ridiculous things about it, showing immense stupidity.

Thursday, May 8th. London, Yacht Club.

Came to London on Tuesday after a week-end in which I did nothing but get up to date with my things. Saw *Judith* on Tuesday night. The news that Hardy was enthusiastic about the play gave me more satisfaction than anything that has happened to me for a long time.

Wednesday, May 14th. London, Yacht Club.

Constant insomnia. Doing nothing except the series of articles about women, which I shall be immensely relieved to finish. Then a year of plays. Seeing Rickards weekly.

The receipts of *Judith* were just under £900 last week, the first complete week. Marguerite began to be less sure about its success. I know that there is too much psychological realism in the play to please a large section of the public. On Monday night the receipts fell to £56. This was a bombshell, especially for Marguerite. We knew after this that the play must be regarded as a failure.

Friday, May 30th. London, Yacht Club.

A political dinner having been put off, I found myself aimless, but I also found Siegfried Sassoon, Osbert Sitwell, and Robert Nichols, and went with them to the Russian ballet. Promenade.

H.G.'s *The Undying Fire* came along. The machinery of it is bad and unconvincing, but the stuff is good. I hope to finish my damnable, pedestrian, fair-minded, sagacious woman book on Monday.

Monday, June 2nd. Comarques.

Today at 4.30 I finished my book about women. I haven't yet come to any conclusion as to its value. I now have 3 plays to write in the next nine months, all commissioned; and fortunately I have nothing else.

Thursday, June 5th. London, Yacht Club.

Dined at Osbert Sitwell's. A pert parlourmaid and a good-looking young male servant. Good dinner. Fish before soup. Present, W. H. Davies, Lytton Strachey, Woolf, Nichols, S. Sassoon, Aldous Huxley, Atkin (a very young caricaturist), W. J. Turner, and Herbert Read (a very young poet). The faces of Woolf, Atkin, and Read were particularly charming in their ingenuousness. Davies I liked. He had walked all the way from Tottenham Court Road to Swan Walk. A house with much better pictures and bric-à-brac than furniture. In fact there was scarcely any of what I call furniture. But lots of very modern pictures, of which I liked a number. Bright walls and bright cloths and bright glass everywhere. A fine Rowlandson drawing. Osbert is young. He is already a very good host. I enjoyed this evening, though I knew I should have indigestion after the creamy sweet, and I have got it.

I dined with Garvin tonight at the Café Royal. Knoblock also there. Garvin said: "I said to Ll. George, 'The 19th century was the century of the vote. The 20th century will be the century of profit.' He was rather struck by that. I'd given him something portable."

Wednesday, June 18th. London, Yacht Club.

Basil Dean and Alec Rea [1] came to tea here, and I was very pleased with

---

[1] The backer and chairman of the Liverpool Repertory Theatre.

them and their general attitude. They proposed to try out *Sacred and Profane Love* at Liverpool on September 15th and to open at Aldwych about October 1st.

Basil Dean told a good rehearsal story. He said that they rehearsed Shaw's *Pygmalion* for 9 weeks at His Majesty's and that in the middle Mrs. Pat Campbell went away for two weeks on her honeymoon. When she returned she merely said by way of explanation, "George (her new husband)[1] is a golden man." There was some trouble about her rendering. When she had altered it she said to Shaw, "Is that better?" Shaw said, "No, it isn't. I don't want any of your flamboyant creatures, I want a simple human ordinary creation such as I have drawn." He was getting shirty. Mrs. P. C. was taken aback. She replied, however, "You are a terrible man, Mr. Shaw. One day you'll eat a beefsteak, and then God help all women." It is said that Shaw blushed.

Thursday, June 19th. London, Yacht Club.

Masterman and I got Barrie to lunch at Reform Club. He remained very quiet for nearly 2 hours and then began to talk about the cricket team that he used to organize. For about 10 minutes he was brilliant.

Tuesday, July 1st. George St., Hanover Sq.

Peace with Germany was signed on Saturday.

Wednesday, July 9th. George St., Hanover Sq.

Official religious celebrations took place last Sunday. Official pagan celebrations will take place on Saturday, 19th, but the chief interest of an enlightened public has been the lawn tennis championships and the transatlantic voyage of R34. My chief interest has been my new play, of which I started the actual writing on Thursday; and the process of getting fixed in this flat—interminable. However, the play is so interesting that I don't mind sleepless hours in the night, as I can think about it and see part of it.

Tuesday, July 22nd. Comarques.

Marguerite came home yesterday from the peace celebrations on Satur-

---

[1] George F. M. Cornwallis-West.

day. She said, *"Tu n'as pas idée.* The air was positively *warm* with the *frénésie* of the reception of the procession." The only thing that happened at Thorpe was that the village mob threw an adulterer into the mill pond because he'd attacked the woman's husband. They would have lowered him into a well, but they couldn't find a rope.

Massingham and Masterman came for the week-end. Leslie Green was the fourth. Much fine wine. Much tennis on Saturday. Masterman showed great gifts at tennis and didn't use them. He was beaten. Characteristic. He said he had an article to write urgently. He didn't write a line. But he was a perfectly delightful companion. And when Massingham read the first act of my play aloud, Masterman grasped all the points and difficulties with astounding quickness.

Massingham worked hard and wrote an article on prohibition in America. He showed an all-round highly sensitive appreciation in all the arts. Masterman left on Sunday night, and Massingham yesterday.

Wednesday, July 23rd. Comarques.

Adding to her descriptions of peace procession last Saturday, Marguerite said that many women cried during the clapping and cheering. On the other hand the emotion of some women (better classes) in windows seemed forced and unnatural, or hysterical.

Way gave reminiscences of marching in Palestine and Asia Minor. Horses without drink for 3 days. One well 50 to 70 feet deep, one canvas bucket only could be lowered at a time, ½ of water spilled at each raising. Each horse required about 8 buckets; they were simply mad for water. They had no camels, when camels would have made things much easier. A camel can go without water for 5 days. They averaged 12 miles a day for 37 days in one march.

Friday, August 1st. Comarques.

I spent an evening with Walpole last week and we went to the Russian ballet, *Three-Cornered Hat.* After the hysterical laudation of *The Times* I feared for this ballet, and I didn't, in fact, care so much for it. Monotonous and noisy. But I might like it much better later on. This has occurred more than once before. I remember when I found *Carnival* tedious. Hughie introduced me to one Bruce, a tall diplomat, young and agreeable.

He suggested we should go and see Karsavina afterwards. I said I was too ill, and I was. But I might have been warned by Hughie that Bruce was Karsavina's husband.

Last Saturday with Leslie Green to the finals of the Frinton lawn tennis tournament. I had a longish talk with Mrs. Lambert Chambers, who in her talk, herself, and her play, fulfilled my hopes of the truly classic player. I liked her.

August 15th–20th.

Motor tour with Beaverbrook to Aberdeen.

I only saw Max afraid or out of feather once, and that was when we landed in a poor hotel at Perth on Sunday afternoon for the night. He could not stick it. We went on to Aberdeen.

We travelled up to the rate of 75 m.p.h. Passed a racing Mercedes at 69½ and somewhere near Forfar on the way to Sterling, killed 3 partridges on the wind-screen out of a covey that was picking in the middle of the road and failed to get up quick enough.

Max's interest in the Border—chieftain robbers and their keeps and methods—was very noticeable. He returned to the subject again and again.

He told me that some one said of him: "He began at   [1] and   wasn't big enough. He left Montreal because Montreal wasn't big enough. He went to London and London wasn't big enough, and when he gets to hell he'll be too big for hell."

At Perth, dining, we met Lord Dewar. Excessively rich, but won't spend money. He said sorrowfully that he would have to spend 7 hours in the train the next day in order to get to Harrogate. The idea of having a car had not apparently occurred to him.

Max gave me the history of the last 15 years of his father's life, beginning with the old man's phrase when he retired from the pastorate at the age of 70, "The evening mists are gathering"—meaning that doubts had come to him about the reliability of the doctrines he had been preaching.

---

[1] So in Bennett's manuscript. Probably the place is Halifax.

He died at 85, and in his last years he spent 55,000 dollars of Max's money. It is a great subject for a novel.

August 26th. Dublin.

At 7.30 the bookstalls were opening at Euston. The girls thereof all read either the *Mirror* or the *Sketch* at once, in their spare intervals. The *Daily Express* was sold out at 7.45 A.M.

Nothing special on journey. I thought of 14 titles for Edyth Goodall play. On the steamer an Irishman from New Zealand, who hadn't been home for 21 years, told me at great length how his luggage had not reached the boat. He simply, however, had not looked after it. When I left him he seized on to another man and treated him the same as me, but at greater length still. A feckless fool. Had wasted his passage over. In N.Z. he had caught enteric through letting an enteric patient drink cough-medicine out of the bottle, his bottle.

We arrived at 6 P.M.

August 27th. Dublin.

Horse Show. Lady jumpers who jumped better than the men. Irish faces of nearly all the girls in the Grand Stand. A certain chic. Many good-looking men. Motor-car enclosure full of cars all higgledy-piggledy. *God Save the King* when H.E. (French) came and left, and very feeble cheering of the same. The women won the jumping competitions easily. It seems a few of them go round and round Ireland, jumping; but this is the first time they have been allowed to jump at Dublin Show.

August 29th. Dublin.

Hired a taxi for 3 hours and went with O'Connor and Bodkin [1] to search quays in pouring cold rain. I bought four pictures, two lacquer tables, and 3 fine Victorian vases. I went to bed at 5 P.M. and got up at 7 to go to Bodkin's. Good dinner. Goodish talking. Especially from old Miss Purser [2] who had known Marie Bashkirtsev intimately and now, at

[1] Sir James O'Connor, the prominent Irish lawyer; and Dr. Thomas Bodkin, writer on art, and in 1927 appointed Director of National Gallery of Ireland.
[2] Olive Purser was the first woman student to obtain a scholarship after the admission of women to Dublin University.

75, owns a stained-glass factory in Dublin and bosses it herself. Bodkin is acquiring fine pictures for songs. Fancy getting a Diaz in Belfast for a song. He has a magnificent Bloemaert, and Domenico Feti. And he knows a deuce of a lot. He saved me from buying an alleged oil painting in the style of Poussin by suspecting that it was merely painted on an engraving. The dealer, who was quite honest, took the backing to pieces and we all examined it, and it *was* painted on an engraving. Last night's was a mixed dinner—I really believe the first I have been to in Dublin.

August 30th. Dublin.

Yesterday I went to see George Russell (Æ.) in the morning at Plunkett House—3rd floor, editorial offices of *The Homestead*. Susan Mitchell there as sub-editor. Russell very untidy. Longish beard. Gleaming glasses. He said he could not stand the dullness of the walls. So he had given 4 afternoons to painting the whole of them with figures and landscapes.

Russell said he had said to Yeats that Moore's *Hail and Farewell* was the finest biography Yeats would ever have.

Later, to the Phœnix Park races. Very Parisian in general looks, this meeting. I spent most of the time with the wife of Boss Croker. About 44. The most beautiful woman at the meeting. Of Cherokee descent, and very proud of it and full of interest in Cherokee music and history. Her tips, however, were no good. Boss Croker moved about, indifferently benevolent.

August 31st. Dublin.

Yesterday morning with O'Connor and Bodkin to National Gallery, where James Stephens is registrar. A little thin man, untidy, strange accent, with a continuous flow of ideas and fancies. He said *The O.W. Tale* was "it," but *The Pretty Lady* was "itter," and he put it at the top of all modern fiction. (On the other hand, a society journalist at the races in the afternoon said to some one, who told me, that Elinor Glyn would have given the story "a more human touch.") Stephens seemed to me to be a stronger man than I had thought. He said that anybody who re-wrote Doyle's detective stories from the standpoint of psycho-analysis would make a vast fortune. He gave me further tips about plots in Irish literature. Then we saw a few pictures in the Gallery, and then off somewhere else to see young Clarke's stained glass. Then lunch at Dolphin, and O'C. and I joined X. and wife and friend for Phœnix Park. X. is a solicitor, with 7 children, goes racing, lives very well, keeps his mother, and hires autos on contract. O'Connor said he made £1600 a year. The mystery of how Irish people cut the dash they do is very deep. They must be improvident. Racing a gay sight. Vast crowds. Much money lost, as the starting prices are an organized swindle. In one race there were two horses at even money. However, nobody cares. Got home at 6 and slept. *Soirée tranquille.*

September 2nd. Midland Adelphi Hotel, Liverpool.

Came here from Dublin yesterday. Pouring rain. Packed steamer. Couldn't move on it except with greatest difficulty. People placidly getting soaked through while being ill. I felt sure my luggage would reach Liverpool with me. It didn't. Great melancholy. Fruitless expeditions by hotel people to lost luggage office. At 9 P.M. I strolled up there myself, and the trunk came in at that identical moment. It was like a miracle.

On Sunday we drove over Wicklow mountains and things to Glendalough; ancient ecclesiastic city. Much of the scenery was superb. I drank 1½ bott. of stout, which gravely incommoded me. Yesterday I sat in wet boots after leaving the boat, 12.30 A.M. to 9.30 P.M. No alternative. Yet did not catch cold.

September 4th. Liverpool.

At 6 I went down to the pier head and witnessed the departure of a liner, the *Canada*. Boats of all sorts, rafts. Passengers all packed on starboard rails. Crowsnest. Going and coming over gangway seemed as if it would never cease. Absurd tiny fluttering of handkerchiefs. Then drawing in of hawsers. Bell ringing. Band: *Auld Lang Syne*. She slipped away. No perceptible movement of propellers, but the helm moved. She just grazed floating outposts of landing-stage. A tug joined her and closed her. Many other steamers made much smoke, obscuring her and the distance. She seemed to stop in mid-stream a few hundred yards down, the tug hugging her starboard bow. People said she would wait there till midnight. It was a moving sight.

September 6th. Liverpool.

W. G. Fay came to dine with me last night. He entered the hotel and then the restaurant with almost as much modesty and diffidence as if he had never had any experience at all. He said he was not interested in money and had kept all his simple habits. He told me how he and his brother had started a theatre in Liverpool with £5 capital each which they previously had to work for and save. They took a hall and made the seating themselves. He said his father was a civil servant and he was to have been one, but he failed at the prelim. and hated it. During his first theatrical enterprise he worked as an electrician in Dublin from 8 to 6. Then worked on his theatre from 8 to 11, and then would go and talk to Yeats or Martin or Russell till 2 or 3 A.M. He said the opposition to the *Playboy* was indirectly due to the opposition to *The Well of the Saints.* The opposition to the latter made Synge say, "I'll write something that *will* make 'em sit up." He wrote the *Playboy* and it *did* make 'em sit up. He said that at the first night not a word could be heard after the first three minutes. All had to be in dumb show. Later he had policemen to chuck out the worst rowdies. Then the theatre was empty. But he kept open, playing to £2 or £3 a week. He stopped all newspaper advertisements and hoarding advts. and kept on. He used to invite the audience to collect in the first row of the stalls. He lost many of his friends and has never got some of them back. After 6 months the newspapers asked for seats. He said they must pay. They said they wanted his advts. back. He said they would have the advts. on condition that they didn't say in the paper that his theatre was empty. He would let them slang his plays and his players, but not say that his theatre was empty. Then the hoarding people came and made peace. He won out. It seems that Yeats, Lady G.,[1] and Synge were directors at this time.

---

[1] Lady Augusta Gregory, writer of poems, plays, and stories and one of the active movers in the Irish literary revival.

This man was a hero and never shows. He is full of creative ideas about the theatre. Afterwards we went down to the theatre, and later we went with Olive Brook (lead in *Over Sunday*) and Clift (business manager), and I saw these people eat supper at their hotel, the Stork, where you could get drink afterwards.

This morning I went with Iris to choose a *jeune fille* costume for the first act.

Friday, September 19th. Comarques.

Sacred and Profane Love was produced at the Playhouse, Liverpool, last Monday 15th, at 7.30. The audience laughed when Iris Hoey called out "I cannot bear it" as the hero was playing the piano. True, the playing was appallingly bad. This ruined the first act, Sc. 1. Act 1 Sc. 2 went perfectly. The hold of the play on the audience gradually increased, and at the close an emphatic success was undeniable. I took a call because I had to. Then I had to take a second call. A thing I never did before.

1920

January 6th.

At Garrick last night Mair told us that he was absolutely sure that Shaw had not been an ascetic. Also he said that, in reply to an American criticism to the effect that when talking about love G.B.S. did not know what he was talking about, G.B.S. wrote to the paper to say that few people could possess greater practical experience as amorists than he possessed. This found us very startled and Anthony Hope incredulous, but Mair reiterated that he was quite sure.

As to Shaw's amorism. It occurs to me that only a practical man would have written the 1st act of *Man and Superman*.

January 11th.

Symphony concert yesterday at Queen's Hall with Sassoon and E. M. Forster. Henry Wood having a chill, Frank Bridge conducted in his place at a few hours' notice. After Schubert C major symphony, much applause at such good conducting at such short notice. Members of the orchestra applauded their conductor, and there was general mutual applause. Sassoon said: "I often wish when all these mutual compliments are going on they'd give the composer a show. Instead of pointing to the orchestra, why doesn't the conductor hold up the score and show it to the audience?"

At night Olympia, Victory Circus, with M. and the two Sitwells. Circus part, fair. Performing seal the best. Why can all performing seals do balancing feats infinitely better than Cinquevalli himself could ever have done?

March 9th. London.

I went with Swinnerton on a month's holiday to Portugal on Jan. 29 and returned last Wednesday, March 3rd. While I was away, *Sacred and Profane Love* finished its London run at the Aldwych of just over a hundred performances. Still, I made quite a lot of money out of that play. On Feby. 2nd, *Sacred and Profane Love* started its American career under Frohman & Co. with Elsie Ferguson as "attraction" in Pennsylvania and went on to Baltimore for 2nd week, and the receipts for first fortnight were 25,000 dollars. On the same day, Feby. 2nd, a spring provincial tour (21 weeks) of *Milestones* started at Oxford.

W. R. Hearst newspapers asked me if I would go to Russia to interview leaders and examine Soviet system for them. I said I would go for 2000 dollars a week, plus all expenses, and a journalist-courier with me to see to all formalities. They said this was prohibitive and offered alternative to send me in tow of the Allied Commission going out to Petrograd at £200 a week to include expenses. I refused.

I also got the idea for my next novel (on the old age of Max's [1] father, as related to me by Max himself) fairly complete, and I read *Le Curé de Campagne* for the death-bed scene at the end. I shall have a great death-bed scene at the end of my novel, and I want to stage it with the utmost magnificence. I got a tip or two from Balzac, but he is not at his best in this book and can be bettered.

Lately we have seen 3 revivals. *Arms and the Man* seemed better than it did 25 years ago. Very fine. Shaw's title to be the modern Molière not so rocky as I had thought. On the other hand *Pygmalion* is on the whole poor. Most of the characterization is quite rotten, and wilfully made so for the sake of art and eloquence. The last act is foozled. Mrs. Campbell was superb. There is still nobody else to touch her. Last night *The Admirable Crichton*. Excellent. I liked it better than when I first saw it, much better.

---

[1] Lord Beaverbrook.

Wednesday, March 10th. London.

In search of ideas for island play, I spent yesterday morning in walking about and went to the stores and bought things in 4 departments. A wonderful and delightful way of spending time and money. Better than most theatres. It is surprising that rich or fairly rich people don't consciously practise. "Let's go and spend £100 somewhere." Or even only £10 or £5. I think this sort of activity does stimulate creative ideas.

Philippe and Hélène Berthelot came for dinner last night. Also Massingham and Legros. Berthelot said that he read from 11 to midnight. Then worked from 12 to 3, writing out his telegrams, and got up at 7.30. He had done this for six years—I think he said without a break. He talked exceedingly well, indeed perfectly, rather in the manner of Cambon. All his judgments seemed to be quite detached and fair. But you could see he was the official, crafty, urbane, and also good-natured. He told several funny stories, two pathetic ones, quoted *mots,* quoted poetry; and poured my best champagne into a tumbler of water; didn't smoke; and left at 10.30, having given us a most finished entertainment.

On the other hand, he never once showed the slightest curiosity about anything whatever outside his own sphere of action—not the slightest. He had a great notion of Ll. George's agility of mind and quickness to grasp new ideas. He said that among the big men at the Conference, Clemenceau was the only one who thought only of his country. (True, I imagine. But I wish he had thought of it differently.) He was politely fierce against Hoover, while recognizing his value. Of Wilson he said that during the war he had all his immense correspondence from persons unknown to him classified regionally etc., and got local people to report on the senders, and thus arrived at a notion of what public opinion was in each district, and suited his political arguments to that district, and thus in the end managed to bring the U.S.A. into the war. I thought this rather good, but Berthelot despised it, and implied that a truly great man would convert the state of public opinion by means within his own mind, not employing machinery.

As a fact, Berthelot has little use for public opinion. He said, *"On peut toujours s'asseoir dessus."* He said that Wilson had got on by failing at everything: the bar, university, New Jersey, etc.; and that some people *did* get on like that: which is true. His judgment on the man's double quality—idealistic, and yet ruthless in affairs—was excellent. But he didn't seem to realize that this judgment doesn't dispose of the Americans and of their future predominance. You can understand the secret disdain of such a highly-cultured, broad-minded, efficient, conscientious, and industrious man, descendant of a great father and the finest civilization, for the crudeness and mental slovenliness of representatives of the U.S.A. and even of England. And he gave us a great show.

Saturday, March 13th, 1920.

   Players and Authors.

   I saw on a bus an advertisement of a play called *Come Out of the Kitchen*. Above the title was the name in very prominent characters of Miss Gertrude Elliott. Below the title was a line in characters so tiny that I could not decipher them. However, the bus stopped. I went close, and read the name of Alice Duer Miller. It may be, and on the other hand it may not, that Miss Alice Duer Miller has a clause in her play contracts, as I have in mine, obliging the theatrical manager producing the play to print the name of the author in all advertising matter. In either case, the appearance of Miss Alice Duer Miller's name on that particular advertisement was as nearly perfectly futile as makes no matter, for not one person in a thousand would read it or perhaps notice it at all. There can be no doubt that in Great Britain the name of Miss Gertrude Elliott has incomparably more advertising value than that of Miss Alice Duer Miller. But even so the disproportion between the types of the two names was excessive.

   I am not, however, among those playwrights who kick angrily against the great importance given to players in theatrical advertising. Theatrical advertising is mainly under the control of players, who are human. If it were under the control of authors, players would not have much of a show, authors being equally human. And there is a good reason for the players' advantage; the public is more interested in players than in authors. It sees players; it likes them, loves them, worships them. Players feast the eye. Authors are seldom seen; discreet authors never. And when authors are seen they amount to nothing at all as a spectacle. I once lately "appeared" against my will, after a first performance. Some said maliciously that the unwillingness was unreal. This was nothing. But one reporter stated that I was wearing a blue shirt—naughty fabrication which I felt compelled to contradict. Nevertheless, although I fully admit the superior advertising value of players' names—Barrie himself has never got more than even with his interpreters in size of type—I do not think that players are more important than authors to the success of a play.

A good play may and sometimes does triumph over bad players; but the greatest player cannot make the public go to see a play that it doesn't want to see—at any rate in sufficient numbers to put money into the purse of the manager. Some managers are, if possible, more human than either actors or authors. They print their own names larger than anybody else's. Nay, they sometimes entirely suppress all other names. This is not business; for the public assuredly has no whit of interest in theatrical managers. It is merely megalomania. I have thought of inserting a clause in my contracts to the effect that my name shall be printed at least half as large as that of any player. This would coincide fairly well with my idea of a good subtle joke.

Monday, March 15th, 1920.

Women's Education in 1920.

The daughter of a rich friend of mine came to see us yesterday. Her age is sixteen, and she is at a French "finishing school" in Mayfair. This school, which moved over here from Paris during the war and will shortly move back again, counts among the most fashionable establishments of the kind, and is I suppose an example of the best and costliest that the rich have managed to get organized for the education of their daughters in the medieval year of 1920. It has twenty-eight pupils. Miranda told us that there were no rules. I discovered, however, that there was at any rate one. Namely, that pupils, out alone, may not acknowledge salutes from male acquaintances in the street. I asked Miranda whether, if I met her, she would cut me. She replied that she would not. Mistresses and pupils rise at about 8.30 A.M., but Miranda rises an hour earlier in order to practise the piano, of which she is very fond. She "learns" nothing but music and French. Nothing. She shares a bedroom with three other girls. All the pupils are English; but only French may be spoken in the presence of mistresses, who nevertheless are beloved. I should say that such a school would "finish" any girl, unless she happened to have a very powerful and unfinishable personality. The Renaissance seems nearly due.

Tuesday, March 16th, 1920.

Style.

"The King and Queen were present at a first night in a London theatre last evening for the initial time in their reign." I take this from the dramatic criticism, *not* of a provincial but of a London daily. It is quite a first-rate example of bad English. The culprit, whose name is well known to myself and other members of the London literary police force, evidently thought that it would be inelegant to use the same word twice in two lines; so he substituted "initial" for "first" in the second line. The affair must have cost him considerable cerebration, and no doubt he was rather pleased with the elegance of the result. Perhaps he had never reflected that words express ideas, and that, therefore, if a precise idea recurs, the precise word for that idea ought to recur. The idea expressed by the word "first" is precise enough, and no other English word means what "first" means. Certainly "initial" does not mean "first." Still, the man meant well. His misfortune was that, having picked up a good notion without examining it, he imagined that repetition was inelegant in itself. Repetition is only wrong when it is unintentional, and, when, being horrid to the ear, it is reasonably and honestly avoidable. On the other hand, repetition, used with tact and courage, may achieve not merely elegance but positive brilliance. What a phrase, "the initial time"!

Thursday, March 18th. London.

Saturday. Knoblock's play *Mumsee*, Little Theatre. After the first night he cut off the last (fourth) act entirely. Which leaves the play ending in a raw stump. It is astounding how people can do these things, with apparently no sense of the fact that they are butchers.

Yesterday I had my first dancing lesson.

Today I lunched with Newman Flower. He knew Hardy's mother. His mother lived in the original thatched cottage. She said to Flower that she couldn't understand how Americans would give her as much as £1 for a straw pulled from the roof-thatch.

Friday, March 19th. London.

Yesterday morning, after careering in the park after play ideas and catching them, I went to Neville Lewis's show and bought a small picture of a woman suckling a child (portrait of Madame Litvinov) for 15 guineas. Clifton, with whom I had a talk, told me of the times when a Johns could be bought for 10 guineas—and damned few buyers. He said he had once sold a very large pastel of Johns's for 10 guineas to a woman and had never heard of it since.

I heard yesterday that the first week's receipts of *Sacred and Profane Love* in New York were over 16,700 dollars. This easily bangs *Milestones* and all my other records. My royalties on that week exceed £350. My faith in the theatre as a means of artistic expression was, of course, instantly re-established. It would be.

Sunday, March 21st. London.

Yesterday morning I wrote the first scene of 2nd act of the play which for the present I am calling *Caspo*.[1] It turned out more vivacious than I had expected, but then I took the precaution of inspiring myself with the spirit of Italian comedy *dell' arte,* and I used one or two more of its jokes. The success (apparent, anyhow) of *S. & P. Love* in New York gives me hopes of one of my other plays being soon produced there. I find the elation caused by a 16,000-dollar week in New York wears off in about 24 hours, but it faintly reappears at intervals.

At night to Coliseum to see Barrie's *The Truth about the Russian*

---

[1] It was subsequently rechristened *The Bright Island*, produced in 1921.

Dancers. I bought the last two stalls on Wednesday. The stalls only filled up towards 9.30—proof absolute of what made those particular people buy those seats. Much of the piece is very amusing and well imagined. But Karsavina has no atmosphere in which really to exist.

Thursday, March 25th. London.

I went down to see E. last night about her affairs and especially about the efforts being made by the landlady to turn her out of her house. I had a strong impression of the acute misery caused to people by the shortage of houses. It seems that agents have notices fixed on their doors: "No unfurnished houses or flats of any description to let under £160 a year." I also had a strong impression of the misery among demobilized girls, many of whom can get neither work to do nor rooms to sleep in. City people, it appears, instantly turn down any application from a W.A.A.C. or W.R.E.N. etc. City people are always very imitative. I went and came back in a bus, between 8.30 and 11. I suppose that few of the people in the buses thought that their lives were hard, but I thought so.

Wednesday, March 31st. Comarques.

On Sunday, performance by the Stage Society at Hammersmith of Ashley Dukes's translation of Georg Kaiser's *From Morn to Midnight.* This play, though mostly ineffective and very mad, improved as it went on. It had ideas. It showed how all English and French dramatists are in a rut. Its last scene, saving of souls at a Salvation Army meeting, was strikingly good.

Monday, Gilbert Miller and Stanley Bell lunched with me. I wanted to talk about Miller's projected block of flats; but they wanted to talk and did talk about a dramatization of *The Card* and *The Regent,* for which they guaranteed me as many lightning changes of scene as I might demand.

Sunday, April 11th. Comarques.

P. J. came on Friday for a week-end of painting with me. But the weather has gravely interfered with it. He was in heavy artillery during the war. He said the staff orders of the British Army so far as he knew them were uniformly bad—always full of errors and negligences which had to be corrected on the telephone so far as possible, though any attempt to correct from below was always much resented (and often revenged) from above. He instanced a celebrated international footballer who was a staff captain and hopelessly stupid throughout. His indictment was most calm but most sweeping. On the other hand, he highly praised the staff work of both the Australian and the Canadian armies, which he always found efficient, correct, and as simple as possible. He said these staffs went solely for essentials and had a horror of filling up the useless forms which ravaged the British armies. He said, e.g. the heavies in which he was never had any horses or mules, but nevertheless had to fill up forms 3 times a day (among countless other forms) giving a return of horses and mules.

I read the *Mémoires d'une Chanteuse,* attributed to Wilhelmine Schröder-Devrient (in French). I don't think it is hers, but it has very powerful passages, is informed by a comprehensible philosophy and wisdom of life, and must have been written by an individual with some individuality. But, except at the close, it is obviously "composed" in general form, so as to lead on from one outrageous scene to a scene still more outrageous. It is a masterpiece in its way, but very *cru,* as a German work ought to be. The French translation is funny in places. The word *aphrodisiaque* is constantly used as if it meant a contraceptive device.

Wednesday, April 14th. Comarques.

I went to London today. Stores and other things before lunch. At the Reform I saw Spender for the first time since his return from Egypt. He goes to my (and the King's) tailors, and if his attire was not always the perfection of quietude, he would have to be called a dandy. When you see him in a tight corner in debate, and ultimately flooring everybody— which I have never known him fail to do—you perceive that he is a man capable of passion—though always restrained passion. I lunched with Swinnerton and Wells. I told H. G. that he ought to spend some of the profits of *The Outline of History* on new clothes. He said *The Outline of History* was ruining him—in income tax.

I had no tea, but read Emerson's essays instead. The essay on History is very noble.

Monday, April 19th. Comarques.

Frank Swinnerton came for the week-end, and I got endless gossip literary. Among other things he told me that Robert Nichols seriously advanced the proposition that his new sonnets were better than Shakespeare's. On Saturday we went to Bertie Sullivan's for tea, and went down among the yachts again. Sullivan told me that I could get a 100-ton trading ketch all transformed and well finished into a yacht for £3500, and that it would cost less than £1000 a year to run. Considering that I could make more than £1000 a year out of it in articles, and that also I could do all my ordinary writing on board, I determined to have it. Robert Nichols gave me Henry James's copy of the Fowler translation of Lucian in 4 vols. Looking through these volumes in bed last night, I found that the only part of which the leaves were cut was the Dialogues of Courtesans. Swinnerton and I agreed this morning that it was a very pretty problem whether these leaves were cut by Henry James or by Robert. Swinnerton left this morning in lovely weather.

Tuesday, April 20th. Comarques.

Yesterday I wrote the explanatory matter for the play *Caspo*, and today I almost decided to call it *The Bright Island*. Also I reflected and decided upon the theme and general plot of my next play (for Eadie). Tonight, drawn thereto by a reference to Rossetti's sonnet, *The Last Days of My Life*, in Blunt's diaries,[1] I read the same. Exceeding fine. Also a number of other sonnets in *The House of Life*. Also some Francis Thompson, chiefly about girls' love. These things gave me the idea that I might conclude my next play with something very fine about love.

---

[1] *My Diaries, 1888–1914*, by Wilfred Scawen Blunt.

Thursday, April 29th. London.

I came to London on Tuesday and went to the dentist, who threatened me with wholesale extractions, as several teeth were exuding pus.

Wednesday morning I had 90 minutes' business with Pinker and Eric at their office, after Pinker's return from America. He enlarged on the importance of the film business in the U.S.A. He said that all the big theatrical people were in the film business. Further that my play would not have been produced if the film had not been bought, and that it was very difficult to get any play produced without the concurrence of the film people, who regarded the play production as an advertisement for the film. They gave big prices when circumstances were favourable.

Wednesday, May 5th. London.

I went for week-end to Beaverbrook's on Saturday and returned on Monday. Max has now two crazes—playing tennis all day and sleeping at night in the garden. He gave me the full history of his relations with his father as material for my next "big" novel. (But I'm afraid I shall have to write a little one first.) He also promised to tell me stories of "deals" as material for short stories. Especially Strathcona's [1] life in England.

He had a series of Mutt and Jeff cartoons in which Ll. G. and Bonar Law were Mutt and Jeff, and Ll. G. was always playing tricks on B. Law. He said that in the end Law asked him to stop this and he stopped it. Ll. G. expressed earnest curiosity to see these things, and so Max asked him and Mrs. Ll. G. to come to Cherkley with several other ministers to see them on his private screen, and Max got an orchestra, which cost him £25. Ll. G. saw the whole lot. Max said it was an ordeal for him (Ll. G.) and that Mrs. Ll. G. was very subdued during the rest of the evening. Practically the whole Bonar Law family came down in batches while I was there. All perfectly delightful,—papa, 2 girls, and 2 boys.

Monday night: *Mary Rose,* Barrie's new play at the Haymarket. Tedious. The papers for the most part hailed this work as a great masterpiece.

---

[1] Baron Strathcona, the former Donald A. Smith, was, like Lord Beaverbrook, a Canadian.

Last night, *The Skin Game,* Galsworthy's new play at the St. Martin's. This play may be a melodrama, but it is a very good one indeed and it holds you absolutely. It is very well acted. It is a tale, an incident, whose effect depends on a coincidence, and it has no general significance. The writing and the observation are excellent. After this show we went to Lillah and Fred Keeble's reception after their marriage. Lillah most beautiful. Lady Wyndham was there; aged. I thought, "Lillah will be like that one day." But perhaps she never will be like that. The usual crowd.

Monday, May 10th. Comarques.

I spent the week-end in doing gratis work for other people. Alterations and additions to *The Beggar's Opera* for Hammersmith, a prospectus for the *New Statesman,* and a descriptive sketch of H. G. Wells for W. Rothenstein's new book of drawings. I also finished the proofs of *Body and Soul.*

I read Atkins' and Ionides' *A Floating Home* all through. It is a very good book indeed. Some of my illustrations to it are fair and some are merely awful. I read most of Aldous Huxley's *Leda.* The first poem in it is the best modern poem I have read for years. This last week I have read Ernest Newman's book on Gluck.[1] It is a youthful work, published 25 years ago, and written in style very much less sure than his present style, but it is the goods.

Saturday, May 15th. Comarques.

Wednesday I went down to Bournemouth to see Rickards, and I returned on Thursday. Glimpses, through Rickards, into a vast world of sickness and tragedy—a whole world complete in itself and looking on angrily and resentfully and longingly at our world. The fact is that Rickards has stood very admirably this trial of being all of a sudden cut off from our world and all that he so extremely *savoured* (rather than *enjoyed*) therein. So has Mina Rickards. He grumbles terribly, but he has stood it, and his judgment has remained sane. On Thursday night we

---

[1] *Gluck and the Opera,* by Ernest Newman, published in 1895.

took Richmond to see Sacha Guitry and wife in *La Prise de Berg-op-Zoom*. Episodically very amusing. But nothing whatever in the play. Sacha is really a better actor than an author. He is really very good. Yvonne Printemps young and fairish. It was rather pathetic to see the once young and worshipped Suzanne d'Avril playing the small and purely farcical part of the *ouvreuse* in the 2nd act. *L'assistance était très snob.* I took pleasure in pointing out to sundry acquaintances in the foyer that what we were seeing was really nothing in particular and that the whole season, artistically, depended on Lucien Guitry's interpretation of his son's clever 2nd-rate boulevard plays. The acting generally, however, and the production, were without question superior to English ditto.

I got some books on St. Paul and began to read them.

Saturday, May 29th. Comarques.

Thursday was my 53rd birthday, and I had rheumatism all day.

James Douglas was in the strangers' room of the Garrick lunching a boy. Afterwards he introduced me to this boy, who proved to be the celebrated Colonel Lawrence.

Saturday, June 19th. Comarques.

I came here for the summer yesterday evening. A fortnight yesterday Basil Dean refused *The Bright Island* and forfeited his £200 "caution money." Yesterday it was accepted with enthusiasm by the Lyric, Hammersmith, which theatre had refused *Sacred and Profane Love,* which Dean subsequently accepted with enthusiasm.

Saturday, July 3rd. Comarques.

In spite of queer health and much loss of time, a period of hard work is setting in. I have got more into the habit of getting up about 5.30. This is a great advantage. I wrote the opening scene of my new play on Thursday.

Yesterday I went to London and, with Lasky and Pinker at lunch, made a contract with Lasky for a film. Lasky asked me to go and stay with him in the cinema city in California and offered to pay my fare both ways. I have to deliver this film in 6 months. I have to deliver a 100,000-word novel in about 7 months, and a series of, say, six short stories before the end of April anyhow.

Monday, July 5th. Comarques.

Edgar Selwyn here for the week-end. Edgar gave me some good tips about screen writing. He said: You haven't got to write for London, you have to write for Thorpe. I added to this and said: You have to write for a Thorpe man who can't hear and who can only read simple words. I see that any projected revolution in the film can only be done gradually.

Edgar told me that the rents of N.Y. theatres ran from 40 to 70 thousand dollars p.a., and that the Morosco was 45,000. I already knew how much the Morosco holds. It held 16,000 dollars a week for *Sacred and Profane Love*. Edgar read 2 acts of *The Bright Island* while he was here, and I doubt if he saw anything in it at all. He said that political plays always failed in the U.S.A. and that you could not interest the U.S.A. people even in politics themselves, to say nothing of plays about politics. I don't believe either of these statements.

Speaking of the labour question in the U.S.A., Edgar said that for the big labour meetings the streets were always choked with cars—and not Fords either. It is obvious, of course, that if there are 12 million cars in use in the U.S.A. a vast number of working men must possess cars. It means one to less than every nine of the total population, men, women, and children.

Monday, July 12th. Comarques.

I finished the second act of Eadie's play [1] yesterday afternoon at 7, having written 1500 words of dialogue in 3½ hours. This is work. I was extremely exhausted. I took my Sunday today. Drove to Clacton this morning, but had no interest in it. Weather full of heavy thundershowers with

---

[1] *The Love Match*, produced in 1922.

hurriedly hot interludes of tropical sunshine—reminding one of Conrad's equatorial landscapes. Beneath all my work and occupations, I have been getting information as to yacht for sale. This is really interesting. I must have a yacht rather bigger than I ought to have. This will give me the new interest and anxiety which I want.

Monday, July 19th. Comarques.

I finished Conrad's *The Rescue* yesterday. It is better than some of his recent things, but it has dull passages. Also the motivation, especially of the Malay minds, is obscure. But some of the situations are fine. The opening reads so stiffly that it might have been written a long time ago, when Conrad was learning to write. I at last got *Flatland* the other day, price 30s. It is quite up to its reputation. The author only fails towards the end, when he tries to do sustained conversations. He can't do convincing dialogue. He is fine at exposition, irony, and genuine creative imagination; but he cannot do the picturesque; he can't "reconstitute" a scene as a whole.

Monday, August 2nd. Comarques.

Having begun my play, now called *The Love Match,* on 1st July, I finished it on 31st ditto. The stuff in it is all right, I think. But I should not be at all surprised if Eadie declines to take up the option for which he has paid £200.

Yesterday evening I finished *La Chartreuse de Parme* and immediately began *Le Rouge et le Noir,* of which I have already read over fifty pages (8 A.M.). The *Chartreuse* is very great. It is only in reading such parts as the escape from prison that one sees that the technique of the novel has advanced. This part is not fully imagined; it is very well imagined up to a point, and very well invented; but the physical acts of escape are not as well rendered as Stendhal probably intended them to be. However, the wit, the power, the variety, the grace, the naturalness, and the continuous distinction of this book will want some beating. In reading Conrad lately, I sometimes had a sense of effort. Not so with this, which

I have now read three times. The opening of *Le Rouge et le Noir* has the air of being *très ingénue,* but after 20 pages you see *avec qui vous avez à faire.*

Friday, August 6th. S. W. Hotel, Southampton.

I came down here on Wednesday with Bertie Sullivan in a hired Rolls-Royce from London to buy a yacht. Bad weather. We lunched at Alton on Wednesday, and then went on and inspected the much-vaunted *Julia* schooner. £5000 odd. No good. Ruled right out. (All yacht yards are closed this week up to Thursday, in spite of the fact that it is Cowes week and any racer might want repairs in a hurry.) Yesterday morning we tried to see the *Hinemoa,* but couldn't, in spite of appointment. At 11 A.M. we went to Cowes and I saw *The Wanderer,* ketch, 88 tons, and decided to buy her if I could get her at my price, £2500, including a motor launch and two dinghies. By 9 P.M. I had got her at my price subject to inventory and survey. I reckoned she will cost £1500 to put right below.

Saturday, August 7th. Royal York Hotel, Brighton.

On Thursday I saw two of the finest yachts afloat. *Iolanda,* which I have often admired at Cannes. The other yacht was the Duke of Westminster's *Belem,* lying in the Medina near to *The Wanderer.* A converted French merchantman. Fantastic luxury, but real taste. I got some ideas from it for *The Wanderer.* A lovely ship. Allen said the Duke had spent well over £100,000 on her and that £35,000 would buy her; which probably meant £25,000. The wages bill must be £700 a month. She appears to be used for only about a week or so a year. This is a social crime.

I think I should fancy more than any of these boats the *Shenandoah,* a 3-masted schooner, with a big beam; she floated on the water like a duck and looked superb. When we went out from the Supermarine Yard in a launch to inspect the motor launch that goes with *The Wanderer,* we went close by the *Shenandoah,* and it was sickening to think she wasn't mine.

Friday, August 27th. Comarques.

Yesterday afternoon I received the second and final part of the survey of *The Wanderer,* and it was thoroughly unsatisfactory, so that I was obliged to refuse the yacht. The first part had been pretty good, especially for a 60-year-old boat.

I read *Erewhon* again. The nature descriptions are as good as anything. The best *Erewhon* parts are the criminality of ill health and the musical banks. The "machines" part is not nearly so good. The form of the book is very clumsy, and the philosophic theories ought to have been worked more ingeniously into a narrative of picturesque events. It is much inferior to *Gulliver* as a whole, but the finest parts seem to make it a classic.

During the last two or three weeks I seem to have done nothing, but still I have done something. Idled with Swinnerton at Clacton and Frinton. Finished my sketch of Rickards for the Rickards book. Got into final order all the matter for the first annual volume of *Things That Have Interested Me* and evolved the idea and structure of my film. Also I have played a lot of tennis and can now play four sets in an afternoon without dropping down dead. Croquet has also improved. But still no water-colours at all since Portugal. I expect I shan't do any now this season.

Friday, September 3rd. River Black Water, on board the Yacht Zoraida.[1]

On Sunday morning I had a telegram from Pauline Smith that Rickards had died at Bournemouth early that morning. Tubercular meningitis.

Gilbert Miller was at Comarques for the week-end. I made some progress in intimacy with him. He left on Monday morning, and André Gide and nephew came in the afternoon for one night. I had great book talks with Gide. I had to leave at 8 A.M. Tuesday to go to R.'s funeral.

---

[1] Lent to Arnold Bennett by Herbert Sullivan.

Wednesday, September 8th. Brightlingsea, on board the Zoraida.

We left Harwich about 9.30 yesterday, but there was no wind till after lunch, so that instead of going to Burnham as intended, we came in here. Flat calm this morning at 7 A.M. Ronald, mate, slept ashore, and came aboard in a fisherman's boat. The 3 men in the boat went to a small smack close by, pumped her, and then went somewhere else, two of them rowing face to stern and standing up. Smacks' sails everywhere being set, rattle of running rigging and anchor chains; small boats moving everywhere; riding lights extinguished etc., etc. A yacht towed out by a Gvt. steamer.

Sunday, September 26th. Glasgow.

We drove in Richmond's open car yesterday up W. side of Loch Lomond and past Lochearnhead and home by Stirling. About 135 miles. Driving rain and mist nearly all day, so that we saw Scotland in a characteristic aspect. After dinner at the hotel 10 P.M. we went out to view the streets. Renfield Street and Sauchiehall Street crowded with people, largely young. Many picture palaces. In quiet side streets off Renfield Street and Sauchiehall Street I noticed large knots of men. It took me some time to find out what they were doing. The largest group was a thick ring, in the middle a man about 32 was quickly selling tracts. His speech was finished. He had some scrap with a man in the crowd, but apologized and said he had no intention of being discourteous. At last I discovered that he was an advocate of birth-control. He must have been doing pretty well out of it.

In a smaller group a man was advocating something about franchise. He argued with his little audience, whose nearest faces were within a foot of his own. A few others craned their necks to listen. The social tone of the argument was admirable. These street phenomena seemed to show how Scotchmen like argument. Not one woman in these little crowds. Presently two pairs of tall policemen from different directions converged on the two groups and very quietly and persuasively broke them up.

Waiter in coffee-room at hotel didn't know that *riz de veau* meant sweetbread, in fact asserted that it didn't. It often happens that waiters don't know at all what they are selling and don't care. They ought to be told in detail every day.

Saturday, October 2nd. Durham.

Left Edinburgh yesterday at 10.20 and missed the fast connection at Newcastle for Durham. Newcastle is a vast, dirty, and dishevelled station. It doesn't seem to belong to anybody in particular. Enormous *ennui* of the casual local train to Durham. A few "first seasons" (I thought) in our compartment: men well accustomed to the boredom of travelling in slow trains. I went to sleep and only awoke as we were entering Durham. At station the stationmaster asked me if I was the Earl of Darnley. Presently the Earl of Darnley arrived with wife. He is in fact rather like me but older and bigger. We stuck our luggage on a cart for the hotel and went direct to the cathedral.

This cathedral comes up to expectations. It is not a homogeneous whole, but many of the parts are magnificent. The verger who guided us was dignified and very funny at times without knowing it. Still, he told us a lot. It is a gigantic affair, this cathedral, and I regret that the view from the north side shows up so acutely the disparity of the towers. The view from the river is all that Turner & Co. made it out to be.

Thursday, October 7th. London.

Monday night, *The Romantic Young Lady,* from the Spanish, Royalty Theatre. A pretty fancy, but feeble and lacking consistent invention. Tuesday, Shufflebotham came to dinner and told me his troubles. Swinnerton was also here with his troubles. Still, much gaiety. Last night, *The Whiteheaded Boy,* at the Ambassadors with Maire O'Neill, Sarah Allgood, and Arthur Sinclair. On the whole a very good thing, superlatively well acted by the principals. Maire O'Neill and Sinclair together were most richly humorous.

Saturday, October 9th. London.

Yesterday afternoon I went down to Cambridge to stay a night with Rivers [1] and see to Richard's induction into Clare College. Train full of undergrads and relatives. Tea at Rivers's. Then by "backs" to Clare where I saw Richard's rooms.

I dined with Rivers in St. John's hall. A "short" dinner, too short, and professors etc. rather dull. Too cautious; too pedagogic. Another professor there, agriculture. I forget his name. His chief interest seemed to be the history of the barley plant. Went on with him to Rivers's, where there was another psychologist (psycho-analyst) who had just been on a visit to Freud. Freud speaks English perfectly. Talks little. Gets the "patient" to analyse himself. Was told afterwards that a good psycho-analyst would charge 300 guineas for a case, which might employ one hundred hours. I went to bed hungry, and woke up so hungry at 3.15 that at about 5 I got up and searched for cake and found it. Three undergrads to breakfast, besides Richard. But among them only Davison (poet) talked. He *did* talk well. Rivers's delightful personality! Richard's work seems to be arranged so that he has no afternoons for sport. Laboratory every afternoon, including Saturday. Cambridge was most beautiful. We went into King's College Chapel and heard choir practice.

Thursday, October 14th. London.

Yesterday afternoon while I was correcting proofs Robert Nichols burst in, much disturbed about his own gloominess. After tea he began telling me about ragging at Winchester in his time—presumably about a dozen years ago. He said that he and two other kids were often put up side by side against a wall, and the game was to throw boots between their heads. He was thus frequently hit in the face. Another dodge was to fill a canister with ordinary gas, and light it at a little hole in the top, put it under a cane chair, and put the boy with his behind naked on the chair. The heat was not unbearable, but the affair always finished with an explosion, and waiting for this expected explosion *was*

---

[1] W. H. R. Rivers, noted psychologist and anthropologist, author of the classic work on *The Todas.*

nearly unbearable. And so on. And so on. He said that there had been several attempts at suicide and one suicide.

Monday, October 18th. London.

Coal strike began today, but accepted with a notable calm. I worked every day on my novel last week.[1] Beaverbrook and Masterman came for lunch on Friday. Max in great conversational form and histrionically effusive about inner history of the cabinet.

Tuesday, October 19th. London.

At Siegfried Sassoon's suggestion we went last night to Flonzaley Quartet's chamber concert. Haydn, Beethoven, Schumann. I made notes of it for a chapter in my new novel. Seemed thin, and too small for the hall. Anyhow I was bored. Ottoline Morrell was there. Distinguished features. In fact a personality. She left with us after the Beethoven. Siegfried, delighted with the music, would not leave till the end.

Thursday, October 21st. London.

Rivers came to lunch at the Reform on Tuesday. He and Shufflebotham were talking about miners' eye-diseases etc., and Rivers said that the danger factor on the nervous system had never been taken properly into account. Shufflebotham said that he had been preaching it for years. Shuff said that you could always distinguish miners from potters on their way to early morning work. Miners had an apprehensive look. Potters would whistle on the way to work, miners never. It appears that some one has just pointed out in *The Times* that if you put the mines in order of frequency of accidents and also in order of majorities for strikes, the two lists coincide! All this, of course, so far as the miners are concerned, is chiefly subconscious. Shuff said that of course boys voted for strikes. They had not had time to become accustomed to the danger, and the instinctive reactions were very strong.

I got frightened about the opening of my novel, *Mr. Prohack*, yesterday. But on reading it through I thought it wasn't so bad.

---

[1] *Mr. Prohack*, published in 1922.

Saturday, October 23rd. London.

George Sampson came to lunch at Reform on Thursday. Sassoon, with Jascha Heifetz, violinist, and his pianist. Something distinguished about Heifetz. Very young. A gold collar-pin and a pearl scarf-pin. I went with those three to a concert of Josef Hofmann at 3 P.M. They said he was the finest pianist in the world and that there was no good second. This is his reputation in America. (They are both—Heifetz and his accompanist—markedly Americanized.) Hofmann certainly played magnificently, but the programme was not a good one. I thought of asking the three to come along for tea, but decided not to, in view of my interest in my novel.

Yesterday M. and I lunched with F. Swinnerton at Café Royal to meet the St. John Ervines. This was quite excellent. I dined with Reeves Smith at the Savoy to meet Sharper Knowlson, and Dr. S. Knowlson decidedly better than his writing.

Sunday, October 24th. London.

Reading Repington's diary (*The First World War*). It is an inexcusable violation of confidences, but emphatically it is "the goods."

Four orators in Hyde Park. One: a sort of imitation working man, old, on political themes. Good crowd. Extremely dull. Two: an oriental preaching Islamism in fluent English with exaggerated r's. Extremely dull. Three: a young man preaching I don't know what, though I listened several times. Monotonous gestures. Extremely dull. Four: an evangelistic scene. A little man with a big nose, and a group of attendants including 5 or 6 dull women. Bad singing of bad hymns. Extremely dull. Still, he did say: "When I lived in the country and worked on my farm the girl came out and shouted (very loud), '*Mr. Way!*' '*What?*' '*Dinner.*' Ah! That was a good moment. But God's dinner is better than that. On the farm I wanted a fresh dinner every day. God's dinner lasts for ever," etc.

Wednesday, October 27th. London.

I finished the fifth chapter of *Mr. Prohack* yesterday morning and corrected all the proofs of the E. A. Rickards book in the afternoon—and they wanted a lot of correcting. When they were done I suddenly realized that I was exhausted and that the top of my head was coming off. Jascha Heifetz concert at Queen's Hall. M.'s one idea as soon as the concert had begun was to depart again. I thought Heifetz was a marvellous performer, with a lovely tone, but his interpretation of César Franck's sonata did not excite me.

Friday, October 29th. London.

Haidée Wright, Vernon, and the Alec Reas for dinner. Haidée very like the 3rd act of *Milestones* and exactly like the 2nd act. Depressed and captious about the world generally, though much pleased with an alleged *renaissance* which she has observed in English acting. A strong, "vibrant" (as they say) personality, always interesting. You can see all the time why Haidée Wright is a great actress. Something is always oozing out of her. She is very shy and nervous and diffident, yet well aware, somewhere within herself, that she is a person of considerable importance in the artistic world.

Sunday, October 31st. London.

Friday night, Olive, Marguerite, Legros, and I went to the Hammersmith Palais de Dance. It was the first time I had ever danced in public. However, there was no ordeal about it. I even danced with M., who knows less about dancing than I do. Intense respectability of the whole place. The instructresses had a certain *chic*.

Yesterday I went with M. to Dickens & Jones' new shop, just opposite in Regent St., and was much pleased with the ribbon department. I was as usual struck by the felinity of the women customers with the *vendeuses*. These latter, I suppose, get into a habit of diplomacy and forbearance. They need it, by God! One phrase that girls must have been taught is, "Are you having attention, Madam?" The dress department head (a decent, worn, diplomatic sort) showed enormous tact, after we had put her to a certain amount of trouble about a dress which we had not the slightest intention of buying, by saying, "Perhaps you would like to call and see it again on Monday."

Tuesday, November 2nd. London.

I concocted a film plot yesterday evening in the streets between 5.15 and 7.15, after spending most of the day in worrying about the proposals and cast for a revival of *Milestones*. I first heard of this affair on Wednesday last from Eric Pinker on the phone. He had just heard of it, but negotiations had previously been going on between Eadie and Bright (on behalf of Knoblock). I refused to agree to Eadie's being the producer and wanted to cable to Knoblock. Miss Nerney, however, learnt on the phone from Bright that Knoblock had left no address and that Bright had a power of attorney and that Bright agreed to Eadie's being the producer. So I agreed.

On Friday evening Eaton came to see me and assured me that Eadie would produce it all right, which I much doubted. He also showed me a copy of his letter to Eadie, in which he indicated that there would be no trouble about the casting and that I should only have to be formally consulted. On Monday I learnt from the Pinkers, on going to see them, that Bright and Vaughan had fully discussed the cast on Friday. Why they didn't ask me to join in I don't know. I then got Eric Pinker to send to Vaughan for the cast, and he brought it up to me here yesterday at 3 P.M. The only "name" in it was Eadie's, with possibly Harben's. I told him to say that I insisted on Haidée Wright for Gertrude. I said that a failure of this revival would damage the play for ten years, that the bulk of the players were unused to London, and that everything centred round the star, whereas there never has been a star in *Milestones;* and I wanted some balance to the star in the shape of a first-rate actress in the most important woman's part. I said that Haidée W. had a good figure and could make up for the first act at least as young as Eadie, and that she was perfect for the other acts.

The *Star* rang me up yesterday and asked me to review Mrs. Asquith's book for Friday. I wondered about the reason of this move till I saw the *Evening News* with an enormous announcement that Churchill was going to review it for the *Daily Mail*. Evidently the papers are going to make a tremendous feature of it. I refused.

Wednesday, November 3rd. London.

Macbeth last night at the Aldwych with the American actor Hackett and Mrs. Patrick Campbell. He has good diction. Mediocre as a whole and largely bad. Mrs. Pat inaudible. Witches appalling. Music ditto, besides being much too slow and besides being played in darkness.

November 8th. London.

Difference between London and provinces. I have several times noticed in provincial theatres and music-halls that the men in the audience do not stand still when the national anthem is played. They do not even take off their hats (or caps). In West End theatres the observance of the protocol is still absolutely strict.

Thursday, November 11th. London.

Last night Bertie Sullivan and I gave a dinner to Harry Preston. Tom Marlowe (*Daily Mail*), Seymour Hicks, and Reeves Smith (Savoy Hotel) also present. Hicks told a number of fine stories, and a few really great; but Tom Marlowe told the best one. Harry Preston was very flattered and quiet. Hicks is a great wit. His flashes are almost continuous. When we were talking about black puddings and the constituents thereof and then got on to chitterlings, lights, etc., he said, "All this ought to be in the Christmas number of *The Lancet*."

Wednesday, November 17th. London.

On Monday, MacAlarney of Famous Players called to discuss my project for a film. On the whole he warmly approved it. He showed excellent understanding of the characterization and the psychological implications thereof (no—it was not Monday, but one day last week). I was to have proceeded with the film yesterday, but could do little owing to lassitude and engagements. I did a bit, and this morning in a very brilliant hour in the streets I did a whole chunk. In fact all the first part.

Sunday, November 21st. London.

Dress rehearsals of *Milestones* on Thursday–Friday. The first performance last night. I took Bertie Sullivan and Legros. Much real enthusiasm. But by last night I had got tired of the play and went home gloomy. I introduced Legros to English clubs yesterday, and he was immensely struck. *"Quelle vie charmante!"* he said at the Garrick, where all the members chaff each other.

Wednesday, November 24th. London.

At work on film all morning. Lunched with Pinker and Swinnerton at Reform, and then I got information from Shufflebotham about the nursing home for my film. Barrie, Elgar, Massingham, Hy. Head, and Sassoon to dinner, and Rivers came afterwards. Massingham had forgotten the date, had to be rung up, and arrived 45 minutes late. Large quantities of interesting things were said at this dinner. Some of the fellows stopped till 12.25. I smoked too much. But I have survived it all right. Barrie said he never went out at all except to dine with me once a year. Elgar is fine, though in fact they all were.

Tuesday, November 30th. London.

Friday I went to Brightlingsea to see the yacht again, and I made further arrangements for changes therein.

I read Lawrence's new novel, *The Lost Girl*. It would be absolutely great if it had a clear central theme and comprehensible construction. It doesn't end; it stops. But it is very fine indeed, the work of a genius. It held me. I read it in less than 24 hours.

Saturday, December 4th. London.

Today I began to work on the film and other things, though short of sleep. I took M. this afternoon to see the Japanese prints at the B.M.[1] and was more impressed than the first time even. Of course the mummies held M. on her way through their rooms. She is obsessed when she

---

[1] The British Museum.

sees them by the fact that they once lived, loved, etc. To be just, she showed just as much interest in the Greek sculpture. We were struck anew by the immense size and grandioseness of the B.M. It is a very efficient affair. Crowds of people, especially girls, most of them uncomprehending. Experts giving popular lectures.

Wednesday, December 8th. London.

Last night reception at Edith Sitwell's and Helen Rootham's. Two small rooms very full of smoke and people. But not dull. I have never been bored there.

Yesterday at the Reform I was told that Shaw said that he had received a film offer of £10,000 per original film, he to furnish two films a year. I gathered that he was going to accept it.

Friday, December 10th. London.

Wednesday night, first performance of the Swedish ballet at the Palace. This affair was very good. Particularly the *El Greco,* the *Nuit de Saint Jean,* and the *Vierges Folles.* Yet a number of idiots in the press yesterday morning treated it with cold condescension and said that Russian ballet had spoilt us for anything third-rate! The *El Greco* was a wonderful reconstitution and thoroughly well done.

Saturday, December 11th. London.

Yesterday lunch with Thomas Vaughan, partner in God knows how many theatres, M., and Gilbert Miller also. This lunch must have cost Tommy £10. The beefsteak was a failure.

Last night a dinner, organized by Albert Rutherston, to Nigel Playfair, to mark his departure to the U.S.A. to produce *The Beggar's Opera* there. Milne was in the chair and made a brilliant sort of speech full of jokes, proposing Nigel's health. The speeches were too few and too short, and after them there was an anticlimax.

This morning at 12.30 I finished the writing of my first film. I have temporarily called it *The Wedding Dress.* It has taken 25 days, out of which I was ill on 7 days and did nothing whatever. I should estimate that the MS. is about 10,000 words.

Sunday, December 19th. London.

The last few days, having delivered the film, I have read through the first instalment of the novel, *Mr. Prohack,* and been inspiring myself for the next instalment. I read George Moore's play which he sent me in the edition de luxe, *The Coming of Gabrielle.* The idea is very ancient and the plot very clumsy, but there are very bright distinguished things in the dialogue, which is highly readable without being at all fireworky.

I gave permission to the Everyman Theatre to do *The Honeymoon.* They did not consult me in any way about casting, scenery, production. The first word I had from the theatre was 2 tickets for the first night. I returned them. In the first place I had a curious absence of all desire to go, and in the second place I thought it was like their darned cheek to ignore me entirely until the first night. The thing has been played in Manchester and Harrogate before the London production tomorrow. I only knew of this from the papers.

Tuesday, December 21st. London.

Last night, Helen Rootham's friend, the Serbian, Milrénovic, came to see me. He arrived at 9.40 and left at 11.40. Previously M. and I dined alone. He said he had lived in London six years without knowing any one, and had thought, within himself, about religion. He seemed rather profound: full of fine ideas of which perhaps about the hundredth part will be realized in about a century. I told him practically how to begin to realize his dreams.

On Sunday night Legros dined here, and then he and I went to the Stage Society show at Hammersmith. H. O. Meredith's *The Forerunner* was one of the feeblest things I ever saw on the stage. Then Franklin Dyall introduced me to the author. I said to him, "You have written a highly curious play." Later I said, "You have written a damned curious play." This was the best I could do.

Christmas Day, 1920. London.

Two thoroughly bad nights, full of the church clock. Still I wrote over 4000 words of my novel in 3 days, with lots of preoccupations.

This afternoon I finished *L'Immoraliste*. It is a better novel than I had thought, full of emotion wherever the wife comes in. No such novel could be published in English. It is philosophical, realistic, and even homosexual. Construction a bit confused, but it is a book. I now want something else to read.

Sunday, December 26th. London.

I gave my Xmas dinner last night at Claridge's. M., Legros, and Lorna Lewis, who told me she was 20½ and Welsh. A vast crowd; the two lounges added to the restaurant. Many family parties. Impossible not to contrast this show with the financial crisis now existing. A crude contrast, of course. But interesting to think of the apprehensions in the minds of many hosts there. Crackers, paper caps, and much throwing of paper missiles.

Thursday, December 30th. London.

In spite of much fatigue after Xmas night I did some work on my novel in the afternoon. Yesterday I lunched (alone) and dined at home and wrote 2100 words, also of my novel. After dinner I went out to be polite to the members of the *Milestones* company. Eadie was very gloomy. Stella Jesse, Ada Barton, and 2 others were the gayest. Stella asked me whether I could tell her what old gentlemen with long beards did with their beards when they took a bath.

The front-of-the-house manager displayed the usual illogical optimism in face of a poor house. The night was awful and the audience thin and chilly (according to Eadie). Perhaps that accounted for the atmosphere of the dressing-rooms. I think that Harben was the only realist in the assembly.

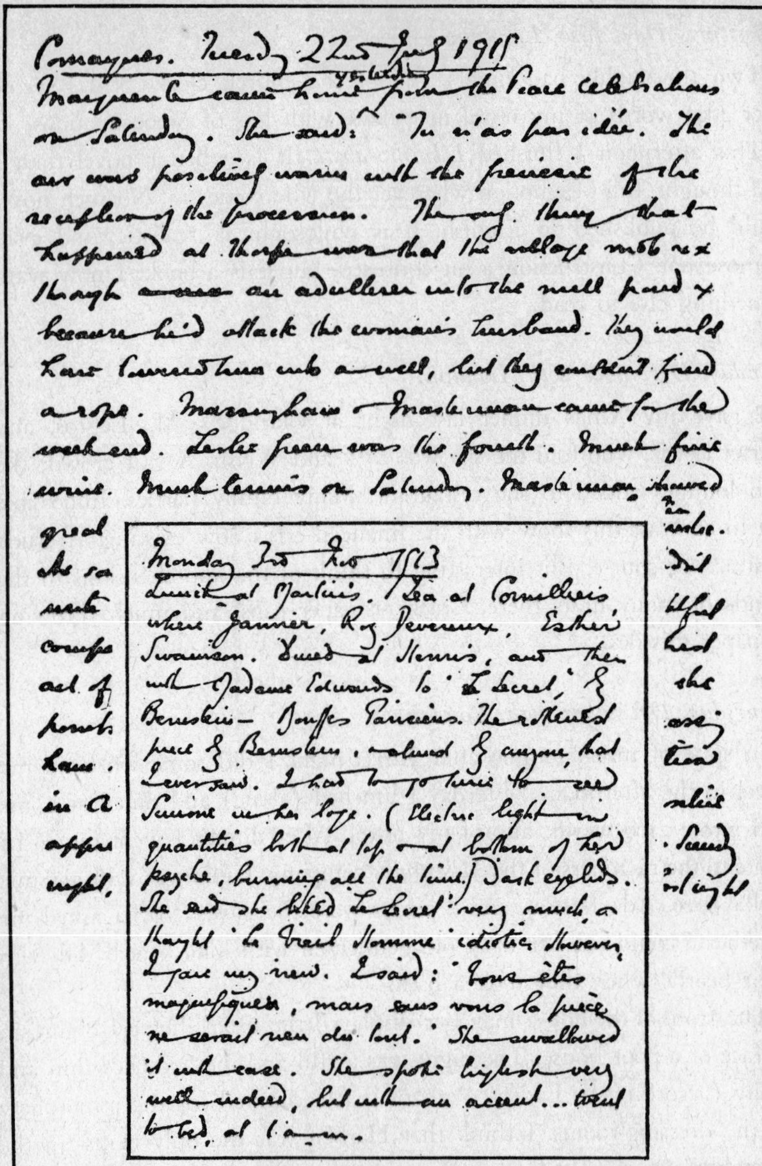

Comarques. Tuesday 22nd July 1919

Marguerite came home yesterday from the Peace Celebrations on Saturday. She said: "Tu n'as pas idée. The air was positively warm with the ferocity of the reception of the procession. The only thing that happened at Thorpe was that the village mob threw an adulterer into the mill pond & because he'd attack the woman's husband. They would have carried him into a well, but they couldn't find a rope. Marguerite & Maslemann came for the weekend. Lasting peace was the fourth. Much fine wine. Much tennis on Saturday. Maslemann showed great

Monday 3rd Nov 1913

Lunch at Martin's. Tea at Cornillier's where Jannier, Roy Devereux, Esther Swainson. Dined at Henri's, and then with Madame Edwards to "Le Secret," by Bernstein — Bouffes Parisiens. The rottenest piece by Bernstein, almost by anyone, that I ever saw. I had to go twice to see Simone in her loge. (Electric light in quantities both at top and at bottom of her psyche, burning all the time.) Dark eyelids. She said she liked "Le Secret" very much, and thought "Le Vieil Homme" idiotic. However, I gave my view. I said: "Vous êtes magnifique, mais sans vous la pièce ne serait rien du tout." She swallowed it with ease. She spoke English very well indeed, but with an accent... Went to bed at 1 a.m.

FACSIMILE PAGES FROM THE JOURNAL AT DIFFERENT PERIODS

1921

Saturday, January 1st. London.

Thursday, Friday, and today, as M.[1] was lunching out, I lunched at the Reform, twice with Swinnerton. Thursday night W. W. K.[2] came to dinner to discuss Tertia's investments; but most of the time was occupied by Marguerite in discussing her recital work. Last night: New Year's Eve dinner at the Savoy. I made some notes on this for my novel. It was a vast, well-dressed, vulgar rag, and cost me about £27. We invited Olive, Esmond Hogg, Vernon, and Miss Tennyson Jesse.

I did over 5000 words of my novel[3] on Tuesday, Wednesday, and Thursday; but owing to shortness of sleep none of it yesterday or today. Last year, I published *The Log of the* Velsa and *Our Women. Sacred and Profane Love* was produced in America and India.[4]

I wrote 145,100 words.

I had over 600 and probably at least 630 theatrical performances during the year. The returns for the colonies and the provinces have not yet all come in; and the amateur performances are not counted in this total.

Monday, January 10th.

Today I lunched with George Moore at 121 Ebury St. Nice London

---

[1] Bennett's wife, *née* Marguerite Soulié, is thus referred to throughout his Journals.

[2] W. W. Kennerley, a boyhood friend, had married Bennett's sister Tertia. *The Old Wives' Tale* is dedicated to him.

[3] *Mr. Prohack* was published in 1922.

[4] *From the Log of the* Velsa first appeared as newspaper articles in 1914. The play *Sacred and Profane Love* (based on the novel of the same title published in 1905) was first produced in 1919.

house, with fine pictures. A marvellous Claude Monet and ditto Constable. I said: "So you have two Manets." He said: "I am the only man in London who has two Manets." The house was very neat and well kept; but, in the nicely furnished embrasure on the half-landing, I saw a collection of hat boxes, etc. hidden in a corner.

Moore said that even *I* used French words sometimes in writing, and that he objected to it. I said I never did. He cited the word *"flair."* I told him it had become English. He wouldn't have that. He was curious about the financial side of letters. Like other people, he could not believe that I can't get my plays produced.

He said that when Bernstein had a play on the stocks he went to a manager and said to the manager: "The play will be finished on such a date. You will pay me so much. I shall have so much for scenery, etc. I shall be allowed to engage *artistes* up to so much weekly. I shall conduct the rehearsals. *You* will be permitted to come to the last 3 rehearsals." He assured me this was true, and that the manager would (at any rate officially) know nothing about the play till the end. Moore has no use for Hardy or Conrad. He spoke of "Hardy the Villager, Conrad the Sailor, and James the Eunuch"; and said that Hardy was one of George Eliot's miscarriages.

Thursday, January 27th.

A desolating night on Monday at the New Theatre, to see Matheson Lang in Thurston's *The Wandering Jew*. Terribly old-fashioned and ugly, but his acting very good. Lang wanted to buy *Don Juan*[1]; but he insisted on doing his own scenery and producing. Also he would only pay me half my demanded terms. So I told Eric Pinker to call it all off.

On Tuesday we took Jean Godebski to the Aladdin panto at the Hippodrome. Goodish. I met Harry Preston there. In 2 minutes he had given me a cigar, invited me to a dinner, and invited me to a boxing match.

Wednesday, Norman Mackinnel came here for tea and bought *The*

---

[1] Bennett wrote *Don Juan de Marana* in 1914.

Love Match on my terms. He asked me to try to get Gladys Cooper for the principal woman. I wrote to her at once.

Sunday, January 30th.

I bought another complete Chekhov for this flat yesterday. Couldn't do without it any longer.

Monday, February 14th.

Thoroughly indisposed for a week. But immediately I began to feel better I began also to feel that I could finish up that damned novel in no time.

Tuesday, March 8th.

I went to Cambridge on Saturday to see the Greek play, and felt obliged to write an article about it for the *New Statesman* on Sunday instead of taking a holiday.

On Sunday night we went to a very good party at Mrs. Ralph Hammersley's, where 2 good playlets were performed, the food was good, and there was dancing afterwards. All was for the best at this party.[1] Last night Heinemanns gave a dinner to introduce their new partner, Page, to British authors. There were about 35 people. I sat between Pinero and Sir Francis Fuller. Hall Caine made a prodigiously idiotic speech, in which incidentally he proved that he was responsible for the choice of Page's father as U.S. ambassador to England. Page made an excellent speech. Lately, thanks to yeast, I have been sleeping immensely better.

Tuesday, March 22nd.

Too much society and theatres. Castlerosse's dinner last Wednesday at Ritz, to which M. and I were invited to impress Valentine's prospective father-in-law, Baron de Forest. Max[2] gave a dinner at his tennis house

---

[1] It was at this party that Arnold Bennett first saw Dorothy Cheston (afterwards Bennett). She was acting in one of the playlets.
[2] William Maxwell Aitken, Baron Beaverbrook.

on Thursday. M. and I, the Aga Khan, Scatters Wilson, and Venetia Montagu. A film afterwards in the dining-room. Film rotten. Everything else very good. Last night we dined at Swaythlings' to meet French Ambassador, 22 people. I was much less bored here than I feared, and the cigars came up to expectations. M. goes to France tomorrow.

Sunday, April 17th.

I was too much worried with *The Wedding Dress*[1] film to write anything here. I finished the entirely new version of the film today, 27,400 words, and feel relieved.

During M.'s absence in France and Italy I have been doing a lot of dancing—3 dances a week, and going to bed late, and with results on the whole good.

Tuesday, April 19th.

I finished Strachey's *Queen Victoria* this afternoon. It is only a sketch, and the part dealing with the widowhood (40 years) is really too outliny. The style seems artificial often, and the brilliance sometimes fails. Still the thing is on the whole very brilliant and very readable. It has real imagination throughout, and is generally judicious. The restraint of the continual irony is extremely effective. In brief, this book is truly a great lark.

Thursday, April 21st.

Yesterday afternoon. Clark's second concert, at Aeolian Hall. The place was practically full. I was bored by the Scarlatti *Pastoral Cantata* and by Mozart's *Haffner Serenade,* which to my mind were not well conducted. Of the modern music Bliss and Vaughan Williams knocked the French composers, Tailleferre, Poulenc, and Milhaud, all to bits. The Bliss conversations were amusing. Milhaud's jazz overture or symphony was a lark, but too long for a lark. I did not work afterwards, though I rushed away from the concert in order to work.

---

[1] A film Bennett was writing for Lasky.

Reading Chekhov's *Notebooks*. Gorky's reminiscences of him are very good indeed.

Saturday, April 23rd.

I read through the first four instalments of *Mr. Prohack* and to my surprise I was really pleased with it. The hero seemed to me to be a new sort of character, and the story made me laugh again and again. The St. John Ervines and Swinnerton came to dinner. At 10.45 Mrs. St. J. Ervine and I went to the Grafton to dance. We returned at 12.55 and the other two were still gossiping. I lent St. J. E. the first 3 scenes of *The Love Match* to read. He gave me to understand today that he was considerably impressed by them.

Wednesday, April 27th.

By the last post last night I received the proofs of the first instalment in *The Delineator,* of *Mr. Prohack.* To my intense disgust I saw at once that they had cut it. Considering that the number of instalments and the precise length had been agreed by me in accordance with the editor's own suggestion, this absolutely disgusted me, and I have written to Pinker that I don't want to correct any more proofs.

In the night I finished the tenth volume (just out) of Chekhov. Apart from "Ward No. 6," the only long story, I think the best thing in it is "The Frost." It struck me on re-reading "Ward No. 6" (for the 3rd time) that this tale is not at all like any other tale in the volume, and that there are very few Chekhovs like it in manner in any volume. In places it seems to have been written under English influences. It is a most terrible story, and one of the most violent instances of Chekhov's pre-occupation with Russian slackness, inefficiency, and corruption. M. and I spent yesterday evening at home, me being wrapped up in a dressing-gown to save electric radiators.

Thursday, April 28th.

Lord Justice O'Connor came for lunch yesterday. He is still paying visits to London to negotiate a settlement. He didn't seem too hopeful, and the difficulty was to get either side to put anything in writing. Previous to this I had written 1100 words and was perfectly exhausted and *énervé*. In the evening I joined Beverley Baxter, Helen Drury, and X. (Gaiety actress) at Queen's Hall dinner-dance. After midnight the place got rowdy with rattles, trumpets, balloons, etc., etc. Left at 12.30. I greatly enjoyed this evening, but was not absolutely raving about X., who was stiff, and said she had a sense of humour, which is always a sure untruth when anybody utters it.

Tuesday, May 3rd.

I am still reading Moore's *Héloïse and Abélard,* very slowly. Some of it is fine, but on the whole it is *délayé.*

Saturday, May 7th.

Futile reflection about *Mr. Prohack* most of yesterday; but I got the ideas at night. I arose early this morn and had written another 600 words before 8.15 and 1000 before 10.30. Today we go to Thorpe,[1] and on Monday I go to the yacht.

Friday, May 20th.

Yesterday was what can be lawfully called a full day. After a late night dancing I made my tea at 7 a.m. and worked. Correspondence and advising M. about her Anglo-French Poetry Society, and receiving Robert Bion (who arrived on Wednesday from Paris) took me till 10.45. I went out for an idea-collecting walk and returned before 11.30. I wrote only 300 words by 12.30. M. and I had to leave at 12.45 to lunch at the Lovat Frasers' and meet Bruce and Karsavina[2] at 1. Karsavina has a perfectly marvellous charm. She is shy and rather reserved. Dressed in nice colours. This lunch was quite all right. No nonsense about it. And I liked Bruce.

We had to go to the Eric Pinker wedding reception at Claridge's after-

---

[1] Thorpe-le-Soken in Essex, where was the Bennetts' country place, Comarques.
[2] Tamara Karsavina, the Russian dancer, and the wife of H. J. Bruce, British diplomat.

wards; we got there at 3.20. Eric and his brother of excellent demeanour and form. The bride, a young widow, pretty and very reserved, which I liked. Orchestra and a dance. I saw Mrs. Perrin and Archibald Marshall, and made the acquaintance of Phillips Oppenheim, a jolly middle-aged grey man (who danced with his daughter and with M.) with probably no artistic perceptions, but an excellent sort.

Sunday, May 22nd.

George Moore for lunch. He is very prejudiced, especially on the old subjects of James, Conrad, and Hardy, but extremely interesting, though long-winded. He said he much wished our acquaintance to continue. He said that Christine [1] was the finest *cocotte* in literature, and that I must have lived with her, and actually witnessed the Sunday afternoon kitchen scenes, etc. I don't think he believed my denial of this and my statement that it was all invented, including Christine. I didn't tell him that when I was hunting about for a physique for Christine I saw Madame R. accompanying her husband at a concert, and immediately fastened on her physique for Christine—sadness, puckering of the brows, etc. Moore told me he was writing five short stories about celibates. He gave me a rather full account of one story, which seemed very good and Moorish. He left at 3.30. . . . Fiddled about all afternoon. No ideas. I went to the Burlington Club. *Personne!* Then to the Reform—*Personne!* But at the Reform I read Conrad's essay on de Maupassant and then I read the first part of *Yvette,* and this did me good.

Monday, May 23rd.

After dinner, M. and I walked in Hyde Park for an hour, and saw the rhododendrons, the amorous couples, the avenues, the *grues,* and heard the band. It was a very beautiful and amusing evening.

Friday, June 3rd.

1900 words yesterday of *Mr. Prohack,* and no feeling of fatigue. I was in first-rate health. I am beginning to doubt now, have been for some

[1] In *The Pretty Lady.*

time doubting, whether there is any validity in the theory that writers work best when they are just a little bit off colour.

Today I go to the yacht.

Wednesday, June 15th.

I began to write the last chapter of *Mr. Prohack* at 3.57 yesterday and wrote 1200 words by 6.30, being then perfectly exhausted, though I had written easily. My health was all wrong, as it generally is when I'm finishing a book. Alistair Tayler came to dinner, and we (including Marguerite) went to Harriet Cohen's concert. Very good playing. The modern music came out pretty well, but there was nothing first-class. I was never really "held" for more than a moment at a time. I ought to have been at the Eng. concert at Queen's Hall hearing Gustav Holst's *Planets*. All this because I liked Harriet Cohen's physical style and her playing.

Friday, June 17th.

I finished *Mr. Prohack* at 3.57 yesterday afternoon. Last night Cochran dined with me, and at 10 p.m. we went to see *Petrouchka*. The dinner was to discuss the idea of me writing a revue with Lucas for him.

Sunday, October 30th.

I left the yacht on Oct. 1st, and came here. I had kept the log regularly. But here, owing to conjugal worries, I could not possibly keep this journal. On Tuesday 18th inst. I consulted Braby [1] as to the marital situation. I determined that nothing should be done until after M.'s recital at Lady Swaythling's on 19th inst. This was the last evening I spent with her. Braby sent for her on the Thursday. She wrote him on Thursday night confirming her desire for a separation. Yet on Friday she asked me to take her to a concert! I told Braby about this, and he wrote suggesting that she should go and live somewhere else.

On Saturday morning 22nd inst. I went to the Tate Gallery so as to be

---

[1] His lawyer.

out of the house. When I returned she had gone, but I did not know this until the next day!

Wednesday, November 23rd.

On this day the two parts of the deed of separation between my wife and myself were formally exchanged by our solicitors and the matter is complete.

* * *

Saturday, December 3rd. Yacht Amaryllis, *Nice.*

I arrived here on Wednesday morn 11.1 to join Bertie S.[1] on his yacht. Magnificent morning. Cloudy afternoon. Continuous rain on Thursday and Friday. Gradually clearing today with some sunshine, and rather warmer.

La Tosca last night. Theatre, very ugly, full of provincial people and Americans. The bulk of the French women fat and plain. Also the same for the chorus in the opera. The story of *La Tosca* childish and made more childish by the "production." Excessive ugliness of the 1st act *décor,* church scene. Also of last act, top of tower, with the ridiculous sky border and side pieces. 2nd Act (Palazzo Farnese) not much better. Crucifix on back wall, placed there *à propos des bottes,* but you knew that it would be used before the end of the act, and it was, to put by body of murdered Scarpia. The childishness of the thing positively revolting. The 3 principal parts well sung. Scarpia (Vigneau), Floria Tosca (Brunlet) and Cavaradossi (Lapelleterie). The last a preposterous figure as a painter in 1st act. His painting of the picture very funny. Music very and consistently clever, and some parts of it beautiful. Full theatre. Casino on a vast scale. Few *cocottes* and those poor. The *"dancing"* (the French phrase now) *très triste.* Few couples, and dowdy. But everything very well managed. The provinciality of audience the most striking thing.

This afternoon we went into the Jetée Promenade. Another casino on

---

[1] Herbert Sullivan, nephew of the composer, Sir Arthur Sullivan.

a vast scale. Dancing there was better; but no *chic*. True, the season has barely commenced. Views of town as we drove after lunch in search of cigars very imposing and fine. I was really impressed in the warm evening air. Double rows of trees in electric light, etc.

Sunday, December 4th.

I began to write *Lilian* at 3.30 this afternoon, having walked about most of the morning. Sea-front, Jardin Public, food at the Café of the Casino Municipal, home exhausted—collecting and arranging ideas. The Riviera is not a place that I can walk in without fatigue. The others drove over to Beaulieu. I wrote partly in saloon and partly in my cabin, and had done 1200 words as the clock struck 7.

Lovely sunshine this morning. Cloud and some rain this afternoon. At 9 p.m. stroll round into Jetée Promenade with Biron and home by Place Masséna. A warm night.

This morning I found that while the new town was very Sunday, commerce seemed to be proceeding very busily in the old town. At Jetée tonight a lower middle-class crowd, not too full. Immense blaze of electricity. The Casino Municipal was brilliantly lighted and doubtless a packed crowd within; but deserted without. Not a soul sitting on the *terrasse* of the great café.

Tuesday, December 6th.

3300 words of *Lilian* in 3 days.

In the portico of an imposing building on the quay today I saw a notice to tenants of which the following were some of the items:—not to empty dust-pans out of the windows; not to strike matches on the walls; not to put obstructive matter down the w.c.'s. As a fact nearly all buildings are imposing. At a little distance this one looks like swagger flats. It was of course inhabited by poor tenants. Some of them perhaps one or two roomers.

There has been a renaming of streets and Squares in Nice. Avenue de la Gare is now de la Victoire. There is a Roi Albert Ier and a Guynemer, etc., etc.

Wednesday, December 7th.

Last night at the opera *Les Huguenots,* with Gramer (tenor—not bad) and Gellay (soprano—bad)—the worst operatic performance I think I ever saw. It showed up the marvellous absurdity of the operatic convention. Female hags, really and visibly old, in chorus; also men nearly as ugly and equally wooden. The ballet comic in its puerility and ugliness. Many principals in the cast of course. Tenor good, but a putrid actor and a *fat* of the worst description in his self-complacency. Groupings idiotic. Orchestra bad. Intonation 75% bad. The thing left the audience very indifferent except for a few high notes.

It is wonderful how in these performances some individual will be found to cry "Bravo" at any imitation, however feeble, of a showy thing. This happened at the end of a *pas seul* of the most mediocre sort. When a song pleases at all, the *pleased* at Nice will begin to applaud before it is over. The theatre itself, showy in an old-fashioned conventional sense. 3 tiers of boxes, or apparently boxes, with the royal box occupying 2 tiers in the centre—like the Costanzi at Rome. Usual decorations. Heaps of room for orchestra. The auditorium and audience were like the performers and the performance. Seen 1000 miles off they would look like the real thing.

Provinciality of Nice at this season passes description. I couldn't make out a single well-dressed woman, and very very few either young or pretty. The dowdiness in general was dreadful. We left after Act 3 and walked home. It was a pleasant change today to go to Monte Carlo. By motor bus, very luxurious. 8 francs inside and 6 out. 50 minutes lovely ride. Marvellous weather. Few on the terrace before lunch. One or two ogling *grues,* and a few really well-dressed women. Marvellous sunset for 30 minutes. Then dark. A very agreeable day. 600 words before starting.

Thursday, December 8th.

1400 words today.

The clock of the church opposite our stern strikes the hours twice, the second time about 2 minutes after the first. I suppose the people have to be reminded that the hour actually *has* struck and that time is not standing still. Detail characteristic of the regional failings.

Tuesday, December 13th.

I finished 10,200 words (the first part of the novel—there are to be 4 parts) on Sunday at 6.30 p.m. having written them in one week and 3 hours, I wrote 2400 words on Sunday.

I dined Martin (Bertie's Spanish friend) at Maxim's last night. We then went to see Polaire in Nozière's *Marie Gazelle* at the Trianon Casino (usually a cinema, I think, but originally a theatre). A mediocre play, but magnificent acting by Polaire, really exceptional. The house was full, or nearly. In spite of beginning at 8.45 instead of 8.30 and of very long *entr'actes* to enable the *boule* and the baccarat to function, the thing was over at 11.40. We had meant to paint the town red, but as we could not begin this job till 1 a.m. at the earliest and there was nothing to do in the meantime, we decided to go home.

In this town, which is not large, there are 4 theatres that give opera or operette (the 2 municipal theatres, the Jetée, and the Renaissance). There is the theatre we went to last night. There are several music-halls, including the vast and dingy Eldorado, which must hold quite 4000 people, and, I think, 13 cinemas. The bulk of these places are supported by the population and not by visitors. You see visitors only at the Municipal theatre and the Jetée. Sundry, if not most of them, have large gaming-rooms. The population is certainly fond of pleasure. The architecture is good, dignified, in a good tradition—even the newest buildings. There are book shops.

At the same time, as I was walking home the other night from *Carmen,* I passed a big house in the Rue Cassini where the *vidangeurs* were at work. Several huge cylindrical carts. No *hose* and *pump;* the excreta was carried in pails from the fosse through the courtyard, and the men mounted to the tops of the cart-cylinders by a movable staircase. The floor of the courtyard was splashed with excreta. *I* thought that the performance of *Carmen* was not at all bad (certainly the best operatic performance I had seen here). Bourgeois as Carmen was too old, but she was slim and acted excellently. Nevertheless, the show was hissed several times, and on Monday morning the *Petit Niçois* gave it and Bourgeois a brutal notice. Till then I had thought that the papers praised everything local.

Thursday, December 15th. Amaryllis, *Cannes.*

We left Nice at 9.40 and reached here at 3.30 on Tuesday. Cold and rough. Housekeeper and steward both ill. Lunch at 3.45. But the boat behaved well. I had a headache yesterday. No work. Work resumed today. Much Casino yesterday. Learnt a little about chemin de fer. Last night at Casino, dancing only during *entr'actes* of theatre. Great dowdy theatrical crowd watching a few of us dancing. The melancholy of the great hall at 3 p.m. before the afternoon concert starts is terrific. They keep *boule* going all day whether anyone is playing or not.

Friday, December 16th.

I began 2nd part of *Lilian* yesterday afternoon. I played chemin de fer after dinner under Bertie's tuition and lost 200 francs. At the table there were more women than men. Two lovely women came in later to another table. The status of some of these women is mysterious. They do nothing but play, and if they are *cocottes* they must do their business very slowly. If not *cocottes* they must be *femmes entretenues,* or very near it. But a number of them are too old to be *femmes entretenues,* though perhaps not too old to be *cocottes.* Gamblers are very ingenuous. They believe in such things as the effectiveness of a *faux tirage* of *cartes, fait exprès* to change the luck. They constantly talk of how near they were to winning a large sum—if only the bank had won one more time; etc. As if they were not always very near to making a large sum, and that the nearness of the big win was not the very essence of the charm of gambling.

Sunday, December 18th.

I am still writing over 1000 words a day of my novel. I worked all day, and stayed at the Casino till 11 p.m. and actually took 10 francs off the *boule* tables. Lovely weather. Yesterday, white flannels for the first time. Also flower in buttonhole. There are millions of carnations. It is singular the number of people with a strong instinct to pretend to think that what they have or do is really done. They will deceive themselves for days, and they thirst for laudation in secret which they do not accept at its face value. Then, in a few days they suddenly declare the truth. Strange that last night at the tables there was scarcely a *cocotte*. The band seemed to have withdrawn altogether for a night.

Tuesday, December 20th.

I wrote nearly 2000 words on Sunday and was so exhausted that yesterday I did nothing except correspondence. No reflection.

Monday, December 26th.

On Saturday I finished the second part of *Lilian*, having written nearly 23,000 words in less than 3 weeks. A good performance, having regard to the amount of gaiety accomplished at the same time. I danced every day, sometimes twice a day. *Denise* on Friday with Miss Aitken. Very old-fashioned and very dull, with a few very good scenes of *raisonnement*. The sentimentality of the last act brought the house down several times; it must be this that keeps the play alive. For Réveillon we dined with the Patrick Warrens at the Beau Site—a really charming free-and-easy family. I danced at the hotel all the evening; then gave a supper including two of the Warrens at the Casino.

Bertie lunched us at the Réserve on Christmas Day. Ideal. He also dined us at the Casino, a rather showy dinner. He gave us the Pol Roger Goût Américain 1911 that Warren had introduced me to the previous evening, and of which we had 4 bottles at my supper. Rather sweet, but a marvellous wine. Warren said he drank it every night. Fine dancing after the dinner by the pros and semi-pros and *cocottes*. One of the officials of the Casino, if not two, sat at the same table as three *cocottes*. Tale of a *cocotte* who got into debt of 700,000 francs at the Casino, went off for a few days, and returned with the money. How? The band that plays on the Croisette is the most *petit bourgeois* thing you ever saw. Chiefly middle-aged and old men. Townsmen. No string instruments. Dirty old music of the French al-fresco concert variety—and never straying out of the accepted convention. Round about the Casino through various windows in the morning you can see rehearsals of various things to be done. Opera. Choruses. Band, etc.

Joel's yacht *Eileen* came in the other day and left this morning for Naples with the family on board. His display of deck electricity is very showy, as at Deauville; but it is a great yacht. The *Lorna* came and left. *Finlandia, La Résolue,* and *Sita* (a very old Rothschild yacht) are now here, and next to them—us. Splendid weather most of the time; but damned cold sometimes in the morning. Still, no overcoat required to go across to the Casino on Xmas night. Still reading, slowly, *The Brothers Karamazov.*

Tuesday, December 27th. Amaryllis, *Monte Carlo.*

Yesterday lunched with Sholto Johnstone Douglas and wife at Hôtel Bristol, Cannes, to meet Jean de Reszke and wife. De R. is 71, fat, but looks decidedly younger. When he came in he said: *"Ah! Vous voilà enfin. Ma femme ne parle que de vous. Elle vous lit toujours,"* etc., in a teasing tone. He acts and relates and makes jokes the whole time. Full of life. Delightful with children. Pleasantly *rosse.* His wife, Breton, aged nearly 60, slim as a girl, beautifully dressed in black. Full of *chic.* Very beautiful even now. *Rêveuse, sentimentale, pessimiste* (through having lost her son in the war, I think). Quite enchanting. Her admiration for my novels made her nervous and shy. Ditto me. But we got on excellently. Afternoon, tea party given by old Mrs. Aitken (Max's mother) at Casino. Me the only guest. Dined on yacht. Then a dance at the Hotel Bristol given by Mrs. Douglas, Elinor Glyn, and a Mrs. Robertson. Room too small, dancers too numerous. A lot of us left early in consequence. But a few stuck and had a good time in diminished company till 2 a.m. Finished at Casino and saw a lot of people and some high play. We left Cannes this morning at 9 sharp. A perfect day except no wind. Engineer proved himself finally and eternally a hopeless fool. He messed up both the starboard and the port engines in the end. We sailed an hour or two, and entered the harbour here under one engine at about 4 p.m. having taken 7 hours for about 20 miles.

Thursday, December 29th. Amaryllis, *Monaco*.

The Casino and the private rooms both dingier than ever, and the crowd also looks dingier. The Sporting Club is much smarter and its crowd smarter. Its decoration is horrible but costly. Bar-Restaurant. In the afternoon I took "dancing tea" alone at the Café de Paris. Great crowd; tiny square for dancing in the middle. Fearful jostling. One professional turn. The bartender had told me that the *femmes* were *gentilles,* but they *ne me disait absolument rien.*

Friday, December 30th.

Monaco *ville* yesterday morning. I walked through most of the old narrow streets, some completely arched over—all with dark stone stairways—some marble. The place built for summer, not winter. Some streets can get no sun whatever.

Dinner with Hyde Kennard at the Sporting Club. I got my ticket and paid 50 frs. for it. Then to the play-rooms. Scarcely any young women; but a certain air of social distinction about all the groups. The whole lot very ingenuous. Roulette, baccarat, chemin de fer, and trente quarante were played.

Saturday, December 31st.

Lunched with Biron at the Sporting Club. I began Part III of *Lilian* in the afternoon and wrote 800 words. Then to the International Sporting Club, where there was more gambling. Lady S. believed that there existed a small number of people who played regularly, daily, very carefully, for small sums, and regularly won small profits—sufficient to pay their hotel bills. They left off when they had made "quite a little." She told of a friend who *always* made, every year, at least £60 out of the Casino. But the champion tale was Mrs. Pilcer's, about the Germans. Before the war the Germans gambled here, but not like the French in the true gambling spirit. They left the tables when they had won—not when they had lost. They all did this. Of course it was very German and marvellous of them. Matters got to such a point that the Casino authorities said that if the Germans continued to come, and to play in that way, the Casino would have to shut down. Mrs. Pilcer apparently quite believed all this story. As it is the sort of thing that leaves you speechless, I said nothing but "How interesting!" Which indeed it was. Mistralish wind, but sunshiny.

1922

Sunday, January 1st. Amaryllis, *Monaco.*

Worked yesterday morning, and strolled about the town with Biron. Night, ballets at the Casino Theatre. More gold on the interior of this theatre than I ever saw in any other theatre. Two ballets: *L'Idole aux yeux verts,* by I forget whom. Utterly 10th-rate in design, scenery, choreography, music, dancing, and everything. The second, *Hamlet, divertissement* by A. Thomas, had some goodish tunes in it, and a more classical feel, and the *première,* though a 2nd-rate dancer, had grace and charm. So it went down well. All the attendants at the theatre wear steel chains round their necks. Afterwards Bertie and Mme. Raquet played in the rooms and both lost. We took Madame R. on board and went to the Sporting Club, where Winston Churchill was playing chemin de fer and losing. Afterwards he played baccarat at a table at which Vagliano the Greek shipowner offered open bank.

Monday, January 2nd. Amaryllis, *Monte Carlo.*

Great sunshine. Too tired to work, I went on to the Terrace to think, and the first person I met was the Mrs. B. with whom I had arranged to dance this afternoon. Shortish, slim, pretty, *bien habillée.* She had a dog. She said her husband went to early service while she took care of the dog, and she went later while he took care of the dog. This vaguely disturbed me. I rashly said in talk that I never went to church. Did I believe in a Supreme Being? Yes. Did I believe in the divinity of Christ? No. Did I believe in the Bible? Parts of it. How could I only believe in parts of the Bible? And so on, showing the most dreadful crudities of thought, accompanied of course by absolute certainty of being right. She was soon telling me that once one believed that the English were the Ten Lost Tribes then the whole Bible became perfectly clear, and one could see that all its prophecies had been or were being fulfilled. Further, that the second coming of our Lord was expected about 1935, and then the Jews had better look out for themselves, and there would be a thousand years of peace. Thirdly, that all the great historic dates of the world had been engraved long in advance in a secret place beneath the Great Pyramid, and they were all correct. They could be seen by anyone who understood how to read them. . . . She tried to get me to church with her (room at Grand Hotel). However, I shall dance with her.

Sunday, January 8th.

At night, I was invited by Mrs. X. to dine at Ciro's. A good nicely decorated, *chic* restaurant and food good, but the dinner was awful. The hostesses, Lady Y., Lady Z., and Mrs. X. All covered with jewels, chiefly pearls. In addition, a niece of Lady Z.'s, a Miss S., younger and more stylish, with whom I danced. The men I didn't know, except Ian Macpherson and a youngster named Shaughnessy. The whole company acutely dull, conventional, and ignorant. We broke up at 9.30 for gambling, but Ian and I went to Oreste's. This was one of my outstandingly "hellish dinners." I couldn't get anything out of anyone except Ian. They couldn't see jokes, and knew nothing real of either politics or the arts. Still, Ciro's is a good place. The Grande Duchesse X. came in after dinner with her maid-of-honour. Apparently notorious. Tall, slim, straight (damnably ugly), dressed in white, and a good dancer. Aged about 60, I should say. Danced with her godson (really her son) who had come in with two *cocottes,* and other young men. Maid in black, sat alone. After we had been at Oreste's about half an hour the maid came in and took a table and sat gloomy and solitary, and then the Grande Duchesse came in, quite bright and agreeable to the maid, and danced with more young men. The maid, a nice-looking mournful girl of about 30, did not dance—did nothing. The

Grande Duchesse seemed to me to have bits of a Romanov face. Her being in these places reminded me of Princess Philippe de Bourbon at Cannes frequenting hotel dances. *Quel changement.*

Monday, January 9th.

No novel yesterday. Saturday night I had danced so much and heard so much jazz band—the tunes ran through my head in bed and I danced in bed—simple fatigue.

Tuesday, January 10th.

After fiddling about fruitlessly in search of little bits of mechanics, I wrote the whole scene in the afternoon, about 1400 words, in spite of a headache due to too much exercise in the morning. Grande Duchesse, with maid, was there again, and I was much relieved to see the maid, dressed in black, and sad to match, dance twice. I was told also that on the Sunday night the Grande Duchesse stood half-bottles of champagne to the professional *danseuses.* The resort is run on exactly the right lines. There is freedom combined with *tenue,* and the manners of the *danseuses* are perfect of their kind.

Wednesday, January 11th.

No luck with engineers on this yacht. The new young one from England was returned as hopelessly incompetent on Tuesday. He was seasick in harbour and knew nothing of the engines or the dynamo. He was put ashore on Monday night. Although ill up to the time of going there, as soon as he knew he was to sleep ashore, he bucked up, shaved, and made himself spruce. He did not turn up to report yesterday morning. The skipper went to fetch him. Said the skipper afterwards: "There he was, having his lunch, among ladies with furs, and him with a knife and fork *and a serviette.* I soon pulled him out of that." It was the serviette that upset the skipper. Relating the thing to me, after he had told Bertie, the skipper added: "Now if it had been *me* it would have been different."

1500 words yesterday. I called on Baroness Orczy according to promise, and found a villa stuffed up with furniture, and her husband's pictures. But all of them very decent agreeable people. I stopped an hour—nothing notable in the talk.

Friday, January 13th. Amaryllis, Nice.

Wednesday morning last dancing lesson from Pauline. I gave a dance tea at the Park Palace, having written 1000 words. Yesterday we left Monaco harbour at 9.30. In about an hour the new engineer was seasick and the engines had to be stopped. Scarcely any wind. We made Nice, instead of Cannes, at 2.30, the engineer having recovered sufficiently to bring us to our berth. That done, he left, saying he had had enough of the sea, and we are now stranded again.

Sunday, January 15th. Amaryllis, Cannes.

Friday night, *dîner de gala* at the Negresco. Bertie, Mme. Raquet, Miss Foster, and me. The room rather good. The mayor of Nice, who was also a *senateur,* died on Thursday morning, and there was no music at the Casino in the afternoon. Madame Raquet gave her opinion that there would continue to be no music so long as the mayor was *"lying down."* This is about the best piece of Anglo-French I ever heard.

This morning I finished Part III of *Lilian* though distracted from my ideas by the news (1) that Olive Valentine was engaged, and (2) Dunlop shares were to fall still lower.

Wednesday, January 18th.

I finished the third part of *Lilian* on Sunday morning. This leaves me less than 6000 words to write. On Monday I did no work and yesterday I did little but reflect upon the novel. I got a Frenchman whom I knew in London, and whose name I have perfectly forgotten, to introduce me to Marjorie Moss and her partner Georges Fontana. I made a rendezvous with her for lunch on my yacht at Deauville in the summer, as she said that she loved yachting. I finished Matthew's life of Christ on Monday morning. It was worth reading. I was specially struck by the cumulative force of the Sermon on the Mount.

Saturday, January 21st.

I began the 4th and last part of *Lilian* yesterday and wrote 1600 words. Old Cecil Quinton, the yacht-racer and original owner of the *Cicely* (now *Lamorna*), came to lunch with his wife. He said that the *Cicely* once did 17 knots with 2 patent logs—"and *they* didn't help her much." He also told tales of an old illiterate captain whom he took ashore to watch over a flat in Buckingham St. and who in a storm would "stow" all the crockery, etc., affirming that the house was rolling. Also he sat in his room with only a small blue jet of gas-light. Asked why he didn't have it higher, he said because he had noticed that when he blew out the gas at full there was much more smell than when he blew it out from a little point. He had been blowing out the gas nightly for weeks. Old Quinton is 70 odd and was racing in the eighteen seventies.

On Wednesday night and last night Laura Aitken came down to dance with me. Last night Bonar Law came and joined us for a few minutes, showing all his usual extraordinary charm. He said that for 12 months he had been perfectly happy to be idle, but during the last month idleness had begun to bore him.

Friday, January 27th.

I finished writing *Lilian* on Tuesday last at 10 a.m. Since then, as usual after these feats, I have been ill, chiefly in bed.

Saturday, February 4th.

Since I finished *Lilian, rien.* Persistent chill and cough, which practically disappeared yesterday. Very wet weather, followed by high W. and N.W. winds. Nothing much doing. I took my ticket today for London for Tuesday next. My play *The Love Match* produced at Folkestone last Monday. I did half a water-colour on Wednesday but couldn't finish on account of fatigue and approaching sunset.

Read H. G. Wells's *Bealby*. Amusing, but I don't yet (50 pp. from the end) see the moral basis of it.

Tuesday, February 7th.

I calculated the other night that the big table (50 *louis départ*) took 2900 frs. every ten minutes, and therefore that it must make about £140,000 in the season. Some other people told us that the Casino calculated to make an average of 30 louis per day out of each person who played. A bank manager here told us that a number of rich men (including Guggenheim) started to play at 2 a.m. with total resources of probably about 5,000,000 frs. They played till 7 a.m. when each person announced that he had practically no money left beyond a few thousand francs. It had all gone into the *cagnotte*. And of course if you play long enough all the money must eventually reach the *cagnotte*. The percentage is probably much bigger than at roulette or 30–40. This is the last day of my holiday. I leave by the 2.16 p.m. de luxe.

Saturday, September 29th. Ciro's Club.

A waiter brought me a card. It was Mrs. H. P.'s. I went over to her.
She said she had beautiful musical evenings. I said I hated musical evenings. She said they weren't really musical evenings but general affairs,
with dancing, but fine music. She knows a lot of people, including Austin
Clarke, an Irish poet, who she said had annoyed all Ireland by his truthfulness (I think). She quoted from him: "O Irish girls, are you as dirty
as the holy water you dip your fingers in?" "Or something like that," she
added. Also an officer on *The Quest* expedition[1] I objected to high-
brows. She said there were now no highbrows in Chelsea. I said the
King's Road was a solid mass of them. She asked me to ask her to dance
and I did so. During the dance, she asked me if she looked well (before
this she had asked me to pay her compliments. "We women always want
them"), and referred to her sojourn in a sanatorium (lungs). She said
she was now practically cured. She said: "Do you know what I live on
now?"

"Eggs and milk?"

"No."

"Stout, perhaps?"

"No. Love." At this point she put her cheek on my breast and
"snuggled." She said she was happiest when men were in love with her,
several at a time. As three men were at that moment, I said: "But can

---

[1] Sir Ernest Shackleton's last Antarctic expedition.

you love them all at once?" "Oh!" she said. "My love isn't like theirs. Mine's mental love." I said: "What about H.?" (Her husband.) "Does he make love to you?" She said that H. never did and that H. said that husbands and wives never did that now. (Quite serious in her recital of all this.) An outrageous woman.—"You must come and see me," she said. "I shall be delighted to," I said.

Savoy Dinner, given by the Savoy to a few journalists and Sassoon and me, to introduce (privately) the new "Savoy Orpheans" the wonder-band. Temple in chair (as publicity manager) and Blumenfeld[1] on his left. Talking about Hannen Swaffer, Blum. said he was very clever and had been in Blum.'s employ on the *Express* about twenty years ago; but Blum. had sacked him because he wore blue undershirts. He sat down to the table to write and exposed his blue undershirt to the wrists, and Blum. stood it as long as he could and then sacked him. Probably quite untrue, but Blum. told it very well. The Orpheans are about twelve in number and for the most part play strange instruments all looking like silver and gold. The piano has two manuals with a harpsi-chord attachment. Black trumpets—conductor a Britisher. (No doubt to smooth things over with the Ministry of Labour who always object to importations of labour.) They played bad music well. "You see the man the second from the right?" said Temple. "That's Count G., the finest saxophone player in the world. Nine out of ten people won't know he isn't an ordinary fine player, but the tenth will, and the tenth will make the fortune of our band, which has been collected from all over the world. You see that thing under Count G.'s chair? It's a bird-cage. There's a canary in it. He left the bird in New York. It fretted. He cabled for it. It is the only canary that has crossed the Atlantic alone. Count G. gets £83 a week. The band costs between £430 and £460 a week." (I had guessed £200 a week.)

Sunday, September 30th.

William Hale White, "Mark Rutherford."

When Fisher Unwin sent me the new uniform edition of Mark Ruth-

---

[1] R. D. Blumenfeld, editor of the *Daily Express.*

erford (uniform only in size and binding) the other day, I began to read the volumes and kept on, beginning a new one straight on after the previous one, like Anthony Trollope wrote his novels. I said some years ago that his prose was almost the finest modern prose.

I still think his prose is generally very fine, but it is rather untutored: he is not safe from bad grammar, or from indefensible phrasing. Also he makes his characters talk wonderful prose, even the lower middle-class characters. His characters are chiefly lower-middle class, and upper labouring or artisan class, with a sprinkling of professionals. They are chiefly dissenters and atheists. The atheists are the sheep, and the dissenters the goats. His places are small towns or large villages in the Eastern midlands, and sometimes the inner lower-class suburbs of London—Clerkenwell, Brondesbury, etc. His interests as a novelist are chiefly spiritual and intellectual, that is, strictly religious and philosophical. He explains his characters' "views" usually before anything else. And they argue with each other at length. The sisters Hopgood argue with astounding skill in beautiful sentences, using a vast vocabulary. He simply cannot construct. *The Revolution in Tanner's Lane* is the worst example of this (perhaps his best novel). It is really two separate novels, joined by a mere accident of relationship between a girl in one and a girl in the other. There is no sign of the revolution in Tanner's Lane until nearly the end of the novel. I think that he must have constructed as he went along. Clara Hopgood is not about Clara Hopgood at all, but about her sister Madge Hopgood, and Clara is only dragged in at the end. Throughout Madge is the principal character. (Cf. *Rhoda Fleming,* which is really a novel about Dahlia Fleming.)

He is fond of sudden deaths, generally caused by chills following on getting wet through. Also he seems to get tired of a story and compresses the important part towards the end into a page or two. He can be slyly amusing. Thus (beginning of *Catharine Furze*): The Bell Inn's "handsome balcony on the 1st floor, from which Tory county candidates, during election times, addressed free and independent electors and cattle." (He had referred to the cattle pens, a permanent feature of the marketplace and high street.) Also (same place) about "half a dozen old skulls" found in a gravel pit. "As it was impossible to be sure if they were Christian, they could not be put in consecrated ground; they were therefore included in an auction of dead and live stock, and were bought by the doctor." There is quite a lot of this kind of thing imbedded in the sombre narratives. He is always getting new, original wisdom, observations on life, character, manners. The love interest is always there, but seldom the chief interest. He deeply understands and knows small dissenting provincial communities, and such things as free-thought political clubs.

He always moves his plot on by means of pure accidents—often by flood and field, sometimes by people forgetting something and turning back; also by death or narrow escape from death. In fact his incident-invention is childish—and hasty. There are two deaths from consumption in *Catharine Furze,* one of his best books if not his best. Also he is too hard on his unsympathetic characters. The conversion of Orkid Joe in *Furze* is comic in its wording. Some of his wordings seem to show that he does after all believe in orthodox Christianity, despite his gibes at professing Christians and his sympathy for atheists.

His best contributions to literature are his spiritual stimulation, and his singular wisdom about the conduct of life. All his books are full of both.

Lunch to Mrs. W. Randolph Hearst. (Really given by Mrs. W. R. H. and arranged by Ray Long, editor of the Hearst monthlies.) I was the star guest. On the left of the hostess-guest was A. S. M. Hutchinson, and G. K. Chesterton was at the other end of the table, at right hand of Mrs. Young, a travelling friend of Mrs. Hearst's. This arrangement irked me, but the lunch was a great lark, and I enjoyed it. Mrs. Hearst very pretty, even beautiful and well preserved. She had a "down" on film-stars. She wanted me to go and stay on their ranch and said they had 30 miles of Pacific coast of their own. Among those present were W. L. George, Rebecca West, Michael Arlen, Edmund Dulac, Phillips Oppenheim, and C. G. Norris (brother of Frank Norris), wondrously shirted and necktied, and his wife Kathleen who sat next to me, and carried on with me a spirited flirtatious conversation.

Saturday, October 6th. Alhambra.

Richard [1] and I went to see Rastelli, juggler, Italian. Very good. But a shade monotonous in invention. He did some of the Cinquevalli tricks, with a soft ball, not a hard. One of his best was juggling with two balls by his head alone. His finest thing was juggling with eight disks (not for long) while doing something with his head—I forget what.

Griffiths Brothers with a horse now, not a donkey, were side-splitting. So was Potter, a "comedian."

Apathy of audience to all the good things. Applause, but not enough. Slow motion film of Carpentier *vs.* Beckett. Very impressive. Like doom. Sort of inevitability. Beckett slowly falling. The towel floating into the ring, etc.

Gloominess of Alhambra and stodginess of audience compared to my recollection of 1889. Yet probably no real difference.

When one gets intimate with a woman she generally makes assertions about herself to show that she is not like other women. A man seldom tries to show that he is not like other men.

Friday, October 12th.

Tania said, discussing her new repertoire: "The Chopin Mazurkas are patriotic. The Polonaises are political. I shall play them in a political manner."

Newman Flower told me that C. K. Shorter went down to see Hardy and asked to inspect his manuscripts, which were stacked in boxes in an attic. Having inspected them C. K. S. said: "I'll have the lot bound for you." Hardy agreed. The manuscripts were bound but very cheaply and badly indeed. Before sending them back C. K. S. wrote: "I think you said you'd give me two manuscripts." Hardy kicked at this but agreed to give him one—*The Return of the Native.*

---

[1] Richard Bennett, Arnold Bennett's nephew.

Thursday, December 27th.

Kingsway Theatre. *Twelfth Night.* When I took my friends into box, there was not a soul in the stalls; two people came in half-way through 1st act. Handfuls of people in other parts of the house. The first effect was pathetic. The comic actors had a tendency to hurry. This went off. Excellent performance. Audience very appreciative. I enjoyed it more than the other two performances which I had seen. Then we went behind to Dorothy Cheston's [1] room, and heard about things. At first they said: "We'll just run through it." But D. said: "A. B.'s in the house." "That's *someone* to play to anyhow," said Viola Tree. At one point Viola Tree slipped into her part in *Midsummer Night's Dream,* but slipped out again. The whole performance was very good. The thing was caused through the most amateurish advertising. The troupe *had* to laugh. Dorothy Cheston went off quite merrily with Pat Warren and Richard to the Savoy for a bite of supper. I came home with Claude Warren and put her and her bag into a taxi for Paddington. She would arrive at Henley 1.17. *Quelle vie!* Curious that D. C. seemed to see nothing queer in the statement that the company decided to play up because *I* was there.

---

[1] This is the first reference in Arnold Bennett's Journals to Miss Dorothy Cheston, who was to be so closely associated with him during the remaining years of his life. He went to Liverpool to see his play *Body and Soul* performed by the Liverpool Repertory Company, which included Miss Viola Lyell and Miss Dorothy Cheston, who played the leading parts. Their friendship strengthened as time passed, and later they came together. Although he was unable to get his freedom in order to marry her, their relationship was generally and openly accepted, and their domestic and social life differed in no respect from what it would have done had a legal ceremony been possible. In 1926 she became the mother of his daughter Virginia Mary, before whose birth she had changed her name by deed-poll to Dorothy Bennett. She was alone with him when he died, and through his last illness.

1924

Tuesday, January 1st.

Chelsea Arts Club Fancy Dress Ball last night with Dorothy. Seemed to be fairly well organized on the whole, though it was impossible to get supper without standing in a crush on stairs for a very long time. The supper was free. The light refreshments downstairs were not free. Still, one got them. All boxes occupied. 3 or 4 thousand people I should think. Beauty of building. Commonness and poverty of most of the costumes. I was disappointed too in the female beauty. Orchestra goodish. Processions and stunts rather poor. Fantastic noises. Some drunks. I saw few friends or acquaintances. On the whole a mediocre show, I was glad to get away (1.20 a.m.). My chauffeur seemed to me to be a much superior person to most of the revellers. In fact it struck me as being somewhat under-civilized, below the standard set by ordinary standard conventions of style, and rather studio-ish.

Wednesday, January 2nd.

Yesterday New Year's Day. Begun in alleged gaiety till nearly 2 a.m. A bad night. No work—exhaustion. Listlessness. A few New Year resolutions lying about in odd corners of mind. Perhaps only two. To read more and to "go out" less: i.e., to possess oneself more.

A somewhat *mondain* lunch given by Willie Maxwell and wife at Garrick Club. I sat between Mrs. W. B. M. and a Mrs. Gladstone; she went in her car to conduct a crèche at Stepney daily. Husband apparently in India. No atmosphere of New Year resolutions there, but I enjoyed it. Some sleep, continually disturbed by servants and secretary coming into the drawing-room. George Doran came and we talked satisfactory business. He left before 6 and I reposed still more.

Dined at Ethel and Nan's; goodish dinner. Not a trace of New Year's resolutions. Raymond Mortimer and *les précieux,* but with an active and vigorous mind. George Moore came in after dinner, and sat on Mortimer considerably about French novels.

Friday, January 4th.

Yesterday, highbrow tea at Ethel's. Logan Pearsall Smith and L. H. Myers (the author of *The Orissers*) and young Marjorie Madan and me the guests. Myers is a thin dark man, *silencieux, un peu précieux,* but apparently of a benevolent mind. Certainly a highbrow; L. P. Smith also. L. P. S. started the affair by saying that he had been asked by a publisher to make a list of 23 books of *permanent* value published in the 20th century. He read us the list, and several times amiably altered it according to our criticisms. He had no use for Hardy, and I had little for H. James. Then we went on to make a similar list of French books, and it was not nearly so good. This tea was a real success.

I was the first to leave at 7.5. I hurried home and went on to a dinner at Sinclair Lewis's timed for 8 o'clock. It began at 8.30 long after the 4 guests had arrived. I did not get enough to eat. Present a young quiet English sort-of-journalist named Belgion and Sir George Maclaren-Browne (British representative of the C.P.R.) and Lady D. K. These two were fine. The talk at the end of the dinner went to old C.P.R. days, and the careers of the famous Van Horne and Jim Hill. Lewis thought of it as an idea for a novel: what I should say it was. Lewis has a habit of breaking into a discussion with long pieces of imaginary conversation between imaginary or real people of the place and period under discussion. Goodish, but too long, with accents, manner, and all complete. He will do this in any discussion; he will drag in a performance, usually full of oaths and blasphemy. A most striking contrast between the dinner and the tea. The latter all bookishness and what is called, I believe, culture.

The former all life and scarcely any bookishness or culture at all.

Lewis soon began to call me "Arnold," and, once begun, he called me "Arnold" about 100 times. He has things to learn, but I like him. He showed me the first typescript of his new novel—all blue and red with millions of alterations—a terrible sight.[1]

Saturday, January 5th.

Last night, *Peter Pan,* Adelphi. One kid said (I was told): "Oh mother, Peter Pan's grown up." This play wears excellently well. But it isn't about P. P. and not growing up, it's all about the mother-theme, with which Barrie must have been greatly preoccupied when he wrote it. The real mother dominates the first and last acts (in particular, last scene but two and last scene but one). In the other acts Wendy plays at being a mother and P. P. at being a father. Everyone wants to be mothered—even Smee —except the braves and some of the pirates. The play is simply all mothering. Even the dog is a mother-nurse. It is full of the most charming fancy and invention, and often very true to life.

Wednesday, January 9th.

A snowstorm, with howling wind, last night and through the night. I walked home from D.'s. Feeling of exhilaration, despite conditions. I looked out once or twice during the night. Snow falling. This morning same. Scraping of spades of cleaners of pavements rather exhilarating. I suppose this exhilaration may be due partly to the increased light due to the snow. But one has the same exhilaration from a very thick fog, especially if one has to go out in it. Sensation of difficulties to be conquered, no doubt. Snow is now (10.30 a.m.) beginning again, and I have to get to Cheapside. Will exhilaration continue?

The Bone families (James and Muirhead) asked me to lunch with them at the "Fish Ordinary" at Simpson's in Cheapside. While we were chatting before the meal a waiter came along and protested: "You've missed Grace." We had. An old gentleman was in the chair, and he had risen and said grace. (He said grace at the end, and we listened respect-

---

[1] *Arrowsmith* was published in 1925.

fully then.) The point of this Fish Ordinary (which is said to take place four times a week) is that at the end a big Cheshire cheese is brought on, and served round (by the Chairman) and after he has done this, the company, each member of it, guesses the height, girth, and weight of the cheese. If anyone succeeds in all three, champagne and cigars are served all around, the winner gets a printed certificate of winning, and "his name is put in the papers." No one guessed either 1, 2, or 3 today. I was miles out. As far as I could learn the cheese had only been fully guessed, in 100 years, about 15 times; but 3 times in the last 10 years. Waiters very nice, but firm withal. They told us that cheesemongers came especially to guess, but were never anywhere near right in all three.

James Bone said that he took Don Marquis, the American writer, there and introduced him to the real chairman (now ill) as an American from New York, whereupon the Chairman said he was particularly glad to meet him as in his opinion America was our finest colony. Bone related this for a fact, implying that the Chairman had not yet heard of the Independence of U.S.A.

Bone and wife had been staying with Joseph Conrad. They said that he said about *Riceyman Steps:* "It has always been Bennett militant; but this is Bennett victorious."

Tuesday, January 15th.

Yesterday afternoon I suddenly decided that I couldn't proceed with my story about Elsie until I had been up to Clerkenwell again. So at 4.50 I got a taxi and went up Myddleton Square. Just before turning to the left into this Square I saw a blaze of light with the sacred name of Lyons at the top in fire, far higher than anything else; also a cinema sign, etc. making a glaring centre of pleasure. I said, surely that can't be the Angel, Islington, and I hoped that it might be some centre that I had never heard of or didn't know of. Certainly its sudden appearance over roofs was very dramatic. However, the old chauffeur said of course it was Islington. Rather a disappointment.

Myddleton Sq. with its Norman windows of its 4-story houses, and church nearly in middle, with clock damnably striking the quarters, was very romantic. I had to correct several of my memories of the architecture. I walked round the Square gazing, and going up to front-doors and examining door plates and making notes under gas lamps (very damp and chilly) while the taxi followed me slowly in the mud. Then I drove up to the Angel and saw that it had truly been conquered and annexed by the Lyons ideals. Still, it was doing good up in Islington, much good. Compare its brightness and space to the old Angel's dark stuffiness. Then I drove to Dr. Griffin's to get information about the organization of the life of panel doctors. I got home at 6.30 and I had been in other worlds, though less than two hours away in all.

Wednesday, January 16th.

Lunched yesterday at Thesiger's to meet Princess Marie Louise (daughter of Princess Christian). She married a Prince Albert of Anhalt, lived in Germany nine years, then got a separation. A woman of 51, dressed in mourning for her mother. Everyone called her "ma'am" or "madam" in every sentence, except me, and the women curtsied to her, and Thesiger said the only thing insisted on was that he should meet her at the door when she came.

Her lady-in-waiting, Miss Hawkes, was there, too. Marie Louise kissed her heartily when they met. Seemed a fairly sensible woman and pretty wise. Said nothing in particular but said it neatly, used of course to deference, which she received in plenty, though Thesiger teased her the whole time. Still, I was glad I had not been effusive when she wrote to me about the Queen's Doll House twice, as I might have got dragged into St. James's Palace, which I should have hated, I know.

Friday, January 18th.

Emerging last night with Duff Tayler from Garrick. A very damp and chilly night—"struck through you." Stopped by a fairly well-dressed man of fifty or so. A woman with him walked on. She was very soberly dressed. Too dark to see properly. "Excuse me speaking to you, but are you a member of the Garrick?" "I am," etc. (Duff left the talk to me.) "I hope you won't be angry," etc. "Needless to say that if you're a mem-

ber of the Garrick, you're a gentleman. You won't be angry. You're looking very serious."

"I am a serious man."

"You're an author or something."

"No, I'm just a man."

"But all you Garrick fellows are celebrities of some sort . . . ? Now that
lady there is my wife. She *is* my wife. We're in a deuce of a hole. Really
in a hole. I'm a friend of W. B. Maxwell. You know him? Now if he was
in this club, it would be all right. But he isn't. I'm a gentleman. Public
school man. My brother is a general at Cardiff, that is to say, he's really a
brigadier general. Willie Maxwell will tell you. I must introduce her to
you" (making a move, which I discouraged). Many more prefatory remarks, and me getting colder and colder, and Duff putting in a word
or two now and then. "Now if you could oblige me with a little—just
until the Bank opens tomorrow morning. Give me your name and I'll
leave the money for you in an envelope tomorrow. I'm a gentleman. You
can trust me . . . ? Otherwise my wife and I are in for a night out."

"I'm afraid I can't do that," said I. He didn't seem very disappointed.
Strange how these people can hope for success in cadging. He probably haunted the entrance to the Garrick all the evening. Duff said that
his object in wanting to introduce his wife to me was to get hold of my
name. The man had a weather-worn face. Spoke quite well, and was
undoubtedly what is known as a gentleman. It was a hell of a nasty
night, though not actually raining at the moment. The wife was waiting
about 100 yards up the street. I could see she was dressed in brown. A
most deplorable case, the case of this man.

Saturday, January 19th.

Talking to Harry Higgins [1] Thursday night about the possible rent of
the Vienna opera. He said that *he* was quite willing to let them have
Covent Garden, and that the difficulty would be with the permits from
the Labour Ministry. He said that in old days the orchestral players were
utterly unscrupulous about sending deputies to rehearsals, and that he had

---

[1] Chairman of the Grand Opera Syndicates.

to keep a special man to stop players from signing the attendance book and then rushing off somewhere else to another engagement. That Augustus Harris used to have as many as twenty absentees for one rehearsal. He said that Harris was robbed probably more than any other theatrical manager.

Harris used to be in the silk trade. Men would bring him silks to look at, and he would examine with a glass, very professionally and say: "Finest quality," etc. and buy. But when the silks were wanted for costumes, etc. they could never be found. Higgins said that these thieves would have a van waiting at the other side of the theatre to take away what Harris had bought. Doubtless some poetical licence. Duff Taylor said: "But *did* Harris *really* know anything about silk." "Oh yes, he knew about silks, but he didn't know how to keep them when he'd got them."

Saturday, February 2nd.

Yesterday, lunch at Savoy with Reeves Smith, Rupert Carte, Thornewill, and Temple. Afterwards they showed me over the hotel.

The waiters' tips are put in a *tronc,* and divided each week into *parts* (French word). Some men get a little over 1 *part,* and some as low as ⅛th of a *part.* A *part* may mean £8 or £10 a week. It appears that if any waiter is cheating he can usually be detected, by the law of averages. The waiters have their own clerical work done; but it is checked by the hotel, "to see fair play." The *maître d'hôtel* takes no share in the tips. In the credit department, I found that all mistakes on the wrong side, in bills, if waiters' fault, have to be paid by the waiters.

Chambermaids keep their own tips individually. Ditto valets. Valets do a business in clothes-pressing, etc. The charges for these go on the hotel bills, but the money goes to the valets. Door-porters pool their tips.

Tale of the head of the cloak-room; been there for ages; remembers people's faces, often without troubling as to their names. He took an overcoat from an old gentleman, and gave it back to him at the end without a word.

Guest: How did you know that this is mine?

Employee: I don't know, sir.

Guest: Then why do you give it to me?

Employee: Because you gave it to me, sir.

Kitchen. Head chef under thirty. Worked his way up. Wore a natty little white cravat without collar. Stores. Fish in tanks. The man who calls out the orders as they come down is called the *aboyeur.* I didn't see a great deal of special interest in the kitchens, except the patent washer-up.

Power station. Artesian wells. Geared turbines. Power for carpet-sweepers, pumping, etc., etc. The power station looked like the stoke-hold rather, of the *Lusitania.* Run by oil now. Ventilated by vast draughts of cold air through trumpet-like things. Water heaters for both.

Graph Office (Capt. Jack). Graphs for various receipts. In summer receipts for rooms go up, and restaurant receipts go down. Londoners away in summer. Hence there are two publics. The travelling, and the home publics—very distinct.

Audit Dept. Every bill separately checked—but afterwards. Every query on them has to be cleared up.

Printing Office. All menus, cards, programmes, and large bills. In their spare time they do the hotel's commercial printing (such as order forms).

Repairs Department. I didn't see this. But they plan all their big carpets there. However, I saw through a window in the side-street the room where 10 to 12 women repair the hotel linen every day.

Laundry. Clapham. I didn't see it. An American expert said it was undoubtedly the finest equipped laundry in the world.

Bedroom and suites. 6 guineas a day for double bed and sitting-room, bath, etc. 9 guineas for two bedrooms and sitting-room. It pleases visitors best that the rooms should be if anything too warm when shown. Thornewill had given orders previous night that one suite should not be let, so that I might see it at my ease.

Sunday, February 3rd.

On Friday Denison Ross produced a theory that all art sprang from the contemplation of the veining of marble. He spoke also of pictures in fires and in clouds and said how much these were superior to human early effort (he knew this last was rot). He referred to the celebrated ugly marble in grill room of Holborn Restaurant, called the "Gorgonzola." He said he had seen in this a great battle, and he was sure it represented the great battle in which the Gorgons overthrew the Zola system.

Monday, February 4th.

Yesterday, walking on Thames Embankment near Grosvenor Road, met Sidney Webb and wife. Beautiful morning. They were quite happy strolling along. Of course I stopped them. I said to Sidney: "Well, how do you like things?" (meaning the first Labour Government, being in the Cabinet, etc.). He said: "Oh, I think it's a jolly lark." Then they asked me rather anxiously what I thought of the Cabinet—that was their first question—and my answer pleased them. Discussed various individuals. Told me how people were impressed by the really business-like qualities of the new ministers. I said: "Evidently they are business-like—the praise is quite justified." "Well," said Mrs. Webb as they left, "they *do* work. You see they've no silly pleasures." I said: "I hope they have; I hope they have!" She wouldn't have it. And as they walked off Sidney said, about "silly pleasures": "And here she is taking me out for a constitutional." Evidently he didn't like that. Clearly these two are never tired of their job. And they have no pleasures except their job, and no distractions except perhaps reading novels.

Tuesday, February 5th.

I finished *Lucien Leuwen* on Sunday. Two pictures of society, at Nancy, and in Paris. At Nancy, military, social, political, passional. At Paris, political social, flirtatious. It develops really into a political novel, and Lucien's excursion to Caen and another place to influence elections on behalf of a minister makes the Paris half provincial again. It must be one of the best and truest political novels. And as regards the local aspects of national politics (intrigues of prefect, etc. and those for or against him) it must be about as true today as it was in 1830. The whole thing is almost savagely ironic. All very fine. This is Jean de Mitty's edition (1901) *"reconstitué sur les manuscrits originaux."* Highly serious that one chapter, and that one of the most important—(Lucien's return to Nancy to see his worshipped Bathilde de Chasteller, whom he thinks has had a child) —is entirely indecipherable in MS. and is therefore omitted. I should have thought some expert could have made out the more than usually change-ful cipher or cryptogrammic form in which Mitty says the book is written and this chapter particularly.

Wednesday, February 6th.

Audrey Lucas, E. V.'s sole child, invited herself to tea yesterday. Audrey was quite changed. More self-confidence, breadth of range, and courage. She has been four months in N.Y. assisting in a children's book-shop on 53rd Street. She lived by herself on 12th Street. I asked her about lonely evenings. She said, well she had to write letters and see to her clothes and go early to bed, but still some evenings, especially at the start, were lonely. Afterwards she knew more people. Now back in England permanently. I was very pleased with Audrey this time. I liked her as a child. Then later she left me cold, and now I like her again.

Friday, February 8th.

Last night, 1st performance of *The Way of the World* at Lyric, Hammersmith. I have seen two rehearsals and the performance of this play, and still do not know what the plot is, nor have I met anyone who does know. Further, the balance of the play is astoundingly neglected. There is a very long (and good) scene in first act preparing the entrance of Petulant, and of course preparing an audience to believe that Petulant is the chief character, whereas Petulant does nothing whatever in the play, and might, so far as the plot is concerned, be left out. The two chief characters in 1st act are not as they ought to be Mirabell and Fainall, but Petulant and Tony, the character played by Playfair (I forget his name —Sir Wilfull's half-brother). And so on.

The play suffers through the proper names abounding in the short "i" vowel sound and other shorts. Mirabell, Millamant Witwoud, Wishfort, Wilfull. One gets confused.

The last act drags terribly, and is enough to kill any play. It seems to me that Congreve had something of the superior and really snobbish artistic negligence of Wilde and Byron. Anyhow his play suffers. It is celebrated; but it cannot hold the stage because of its crude and inexcusable faults of construction. Were it well constructed, it would easily rival Sheridan and Goldsmith.

What liberty was allowed to unmarried girls in that period. If Millamant was not a widow—and I never understood that she was (same for Marwood), they must have had a great deal of licence.

The performance, and production last night were admirable. The play will fail, but it must add to the prestige of the theatre. Edith Evans as Millamant gave the finest comedy performance I have ever seen on the stage. I went behind afterwards, told her so. "How exciting!" she said.

Saturday, February 9th.

Last night I told Walter Roch we would go home by bus instead of taxi because it was more interesting. He agreed. We had to wait 5 minutes in Piccadilly for a 19 or 22 bus. (I took a chill here, which much impaired my night's rest.) While waiting a very little oldish, spinsterish, thin, misshapen, stooping woman came slowly along, carrying two large neat parcels, strapped together, with a string handle. She was neatly dressed, polished shoes, but misshapen and queer—probably about 45. She could walk with great difficulty a few yards only, using all her might to lift the bulky double package, and then stop and rest and start again. She seemed so exhausted that I went up to her and asked her if she wanted a bus. She said: "No," but I didn't think she meant it. She then said she had to get to Holborn and that 44 bus went there. I said: "You're on the wrong side of the road," and I almost picked up the package to carry it across Piccadilly for her. She said she didn't want a bus, hadn't any money. She seemed to me to be too neat and self-important and obstinate for me to offer her the fare.

Then in the bus we saw a respectable man kiss a little girl. She got out and left him.

So that we were rewarded for our bus ride.

Monday, February 11th.

Last night, Fellowship of Players performance of *Macbeth* at Strand Theatre with Beatrice Wilson and Edmund Willard as principals. Arthur Bourchier was asked to speak a few words "to begin with." Speech called for at the end. Ernest Milton [the producer] made it. It ended thus: "Whatever in the production is good in the production is the players', whatever is bad is the producers'." "No, no!" protests from stage, etc. More applause. Why will stage people do these things? God knoweth. It was all so characteristic, and so childish, and so "stagy."

Wednesday, February 13th.

Last night, performances by students (actors, actresses, orchestra and conductor all students) of two one-act operatic things at Royal College of Music. I was given a seat right at back of long, low "Parry Opera Theatre," next to the Director's chair, which remained empty for some time. Then Sir Hugh Allen bustled up in the dark. Light tweed suit and a vigorous, active air. I rather liked him. You could see he was on his own dunghill. He showed me the stage. The scenery was appalling in its infantile ugliness, and ought not to have been permitted. We were too far off to hear and see the first opera (a scene from *Martin Chuzzlewit,* awfully good), and for Armstrong Gibbs's and A. P. Herbert's *Blue Peter* we got seats in the front row and too near. But even then the words could not be well heard owing to bad elocution. Aveling, the registrar, clutched on to me; he began on highbrows. He said the students were all perfectly mad on (what he called) highbrow music. Never talked about anything else. Evidently he resented it. I suppose he meant all the post-Brahms composers. I must say the Dickens opera was stuffed with cleverness (D. Martin Wood, composer), not modern but damned ingenious and graceful. It really held both Duff and myself.

Saturday, February 16th.

J. B. Priestley's article on me in *London Mercury* for February. After quoting from *The Author's Craft:*

"With the single exception of Turgenev, the great novelists of the world according to my standards have either ignored technique or have failed to understand it. What an error to suppose that the finest foreign novels show a better sense of form than the finest English novels!"

He goes on himself:

"What an error indeed! The fact is, of course, that the art of fiction as practised by the great novelists *is* technique, and any other 'technique' is either some inferior method or a mere catch-phrase of the pontifical critic."

This is a bit thick. It is easy to show where very many of the great novels fail in technique (*Anna Karenina,* e.g.) and where they could have been improved if the author had had the advantages of Flaubert, de Maupassant, or even Chekhov. They are great in *spite* of carelessness, and their carelessness is often notorious. I thank heaven I have always gone in for technique. And *The Pretty Lady* and *Riceyman Steps* are both, in my opinion, jolly well constructed and *done* books.

Monday, February 18th.

At Harold Snagge's yesterday and day before. Basil Lubbock (author of *Round the Horn before the Mast*) told various of his adventures in two wars and in Klondike and as a seaman. He said, and repeated, that he had met only one or two British cowards. Practically everybody was brave in danger. He excepted shell-shock, and also "panic" affecting a number of people together.

Either he or Snagge told of some of the methods at Ford works. When the employees come in and hang up their street things, the hook is whisked up high in the air, and does not come down again till shutting-off time, so that nobody can prepare to go in advance. Also a man had been employed for some time and thought he was doing quite all right, when the manager sent for him and told him he could leave as they didn't want men like him. He asked why. "Look at these photographs," said the manager. One snapshot showed the man stooping to speak to a fellow-workman as he was passing from one spot to another. The other showed him looking into a doorway which was forbidden. I should want very high wages for work in these conditions, I think.

Tuesday, February 19th.

D. and I to first night of first playing of *Back to Methuselah* last night at Court Theatre. "House full" boards outside before the performance. I had asked for and offered to pay for seats, in order to please D., but I received an apologetic letter from the manager to say that they were *really* all gone. Afterwards a box was returned and Barry Jackson himself gave it to me; which, I thought, was rather graceful. The affair was a *solennité*. But not quite the usual kind of 1st night. Walls of box dead black and of stone. We could see the empty orchestra, and the nakedness of Adam and Eve. Curtain going up announced by a sort of clash of a cymbal. I was very bored by the play, I could see nothing in it; neither action nor character nor a sermon nor wit. The game of finding new words played by the characters seemed silly. It was too far round to go to smoke in the interval, so we stayed in our tomb. In the second act I went to sleep and had to be wakened for fear a snore might be heard on the stage. Audience indifferent but very polite. Many calls. Play began at 8.37 and ended at about 10.15. Barry Jackson said author in house but wouldn't appear till the last night. Shaw had box over us. His programme fell down at the end and was wafted into our box. D. took it away as being historical. A most depressing night.

Friday, February 22nd.

Yesterday, lunch with Burton Chadwick, M.P. I happened to say that creative writing was in my opinion the hardest work there is. He tried to believe me, but was genuinely startled. He said quite sincerely: "Well, you do surprise me. I always thought it was quite spontaneous—the author sat down and wrote what came into his head. . . . Well, yes. I suppose he *must* think it out a bit."

Saturday, February 23rd.

Last night. Goethe's *Faust*, Old Vic. Translated by Graham and Tristran Rawson. Nearly in full; only a few scenes shortened. 25 scenes. Elaborate. Rough. Orchestra of about 25, choruses off, etc. From the start you had an impression of grandeur in the "spring-for-flight" of the work.

It got a bit tedious in the middle, but was going very strong when I left at 11 p.m. Theatre people came into our box with visitors' book for me to sign. We had box 8. Box 7 can only be entered through box 8. The underground lavatory down ruined steps between ancient walls very picturesque and primitive. Reminiscent of primitive continental lavatories. In fact comic. Large-ish audience. Very quick to laugh at the right points, and not to giggle, which ridiculous and childishly exaggerated sense of the ridiculous is the curse of West End audiences.

Tuesday, February 26th.

First night of *Kate* (or Love will find out the way—Good God!) at Kingsway last night. It fell flat in the audience. The applause exclusively friendly applause. The thing was killed by a perfectly rotten book. The plot was unfollowable and the words terribly dull. No one that I saw in the audience thought other than that the thing was a frost. We went behind to M. Gordon's dressing-room. Full of flowers and bonbons (costly) and 2½ bottles of champagne which I was asked to open. I opened one. Completely different atmosphere. Marjorie after her great effort, needing praise and optimism, and getting them from half a dozen people. Difficult to know whether these artists really believe in a success, when any grain of common sense should tell them that the thing was bad and failed to please. A woman saying: "I'm *sure* the stalls liked it." Me saying: "Delightful, you were splendid, Marjorie." (Well, she was, but had nothing to do.) "Beautiful production," and so on. All praise. No criticism. Not a hint as to badness of book. We go. On stairs I meet Donald Calthrop. Well, he asks me my view. I tell him I like the production (I don't—yet we are very intimate), music, performances (yes, true) I give a slight hint as to badness of book. He likes it all right. But supposing I told him book was bad enough to bust up any show. We drove homewards, Dorothy and I, and say again and again that the thing is hopeless. And in scores of cabs and autos radiating from the theatre to all points of the compass people are saying the same thing. But the artists and the aged authors of the book are trying (not successfully) to convince themselves that the thing is a success. This is a 1st night sample of many 1st nights.

Saturday, March 1st.

Max Beaverbrook lunched with me yesterday. Asked "What about the Tory party?" he said: "A. is an idiot, B. has sciatica, C. is whoremongering, and D. is taking dancing lessons."

He said he had been cured of his illnesses (whatever they were) by cutting of all fleshmeat and all wine, and that he felt perfectly well. At lunch he had nothing but an omelette *fines herbes,* boiled potatoes, and carrots, and stewed fruits, and very little even of those. He kept his jacket buttoned all the time, and it was not very well cut. At 2.45 he went off to the dentist. He was extremely interesting all the time. He slyly acknowledged defeat when he came in. I had distinctly told him I wouldn't go to his place till he had been to mine again. He tried several times to worm out of it, and he told Helen Fitzgerald that he should beat me. However, in the end he yielded. It was a new experience for him.

Monday, March 3rd.

At Ciro's last night. D. seemed to have caught a chill and she complained that the hot room was very cold. "It's very draughty," said she. "I can't feel any draught at all," said I. She said: *"It's when the waiters pass."*

Tuesday, March 4th.

Feeling well and idle yesterday morning I went out for a walk and got into the Victoria and Albert Museum. In the galleries I met Eric Maclagan, Keeper of the Sculpture, and he said: "You must come and see the finest Chinese sculpture in England." So I went with him into a closed gallery and saw it. 7th century (Tang). A Buddha. I said: "There is no Western art." He entirely disagreed. He said that he thought Western painting much finer than Eastern, and the same for sculpture—but I forget his comparisons. He said we got into the way of comparing primitive Chinese with Renaissance and later European, and of course we didn't see in the latter what we saw in the former.

Quantities of rotten pictures at South Kensington and many good ones. The place is close to my house and I hadn't been seriously into it for years. I went ostensibly to think about a story, but thought very little.

Wednesday, March 5th.

Yesterday afternoon Thomas Bodkin [1] called to see me. He has purchased a fine old Flemish primitive for £1000 from a clergyman who believes it to be a Perugino. He showed me a bad photo of it—very fine. His business in London was to arrange to re-sell it, and he explained the grave difficulties attendant upon the enterprise—not being done in the eye. He had determined to give the job to Tancred Borenius to do. The picture is passed with 1st-class honours by various great experts. He said: "The man who can sell that picture properly is almost as clever as the man who painted it." He told us a number of stories about his own smaller finds (some of them of thrilling interest), and how people owning pictures who asked for his help were too stupid and too set in their own ideas to be helped.

Thursday, March 6th.

German film last night at Polytechnic Cinema. One has the idea that all films are crowded. The balcony here was not 15 per cent full. A gloomy place, with gloomy audience. No style or grace in them. All lower middle class or nearly so. The hall tricked out with a silly sort of an ikon, illuminated, of Death, to advertise or recall or illustrate the film. The orchestra most mediocre. Played all the time, and three performances a day! Hell for the players I should think. Also the horrid habit of illustrating certain points musically, or noisily. The clock must strike, etc. And a special *noise* as a sort of *leit motif* for death. Lastly three small common Oriental mats (probably made in England) laid in front of the screen on the stage to indicate that much of the story was Oriental. The captions etc. were appalling, and even misspelt, such as "extention," "Soloman,"

---

[1] Trustee, subsequently Director, of the National Gallery of Ireland.

etc. The phrasing! Good God. "The City of Yesteryear" meant, I believe, the cemetery.

The film was, compared to every other serious story film I have seen, very good. Much of it absurd and filmily conventional; but it held you. It had an idea and it refrained very well from sentimentality. The acting was good, and quiet. The thing made me see how I loathe American films and film actors and actresses. The men particularly and most of the women. Perhaps on the whole I prefer even English films to the crass conditions of the American.

Tuesday, March 11th.

I lunched with Donald Calthrop yesterday. I knew the Kingsway *Kate* was a failure. He showed me the figures. He had been away for the week-end. Motoring up yesterday morning he had had an idea for a revue. He had seen that it would be better for his backer (who had written him decisively that he would finish up in three weeks) to close the theatre at once and spend what he would have lost in producing a cheap revue (no scenery).

His notion was to produce this revue in less than three weeks. True, it is not yet written. He asked me if I would edit it. So I said I would, but on the understanding that he took a month to do it in. We went through all the items he might get at once, and the authors whom he could approach at once. The revue was to be called *Pass the Port, Please,* and the nature of it was that some people are dining together and instead of going out they amuse themselves, and then call up the servants to help them in amusing themselves. The servants are headed by Sidney Fairbrother, whom the backer had engaged for another three months yet at £50 a week. I said the backer hadn't yet agreed. In fact he knew nothing about it. Well, D. C. said he would see the backer that afternoon and phone me at 7 p.m. I stayed two hours nearly with him. He phoned me at 7.25 saying that the backer was very interested, and could he see me today. He is to lunch with me today, and that is how theatrical business is done.

Wednesday, March 12th.

Phillpotts's rustic comedy *The Farmer's Wife* at Court Theatre last night. This play is, really, far less naïve than the vast majority of West End society plays. Far less. The cynical wisdom of the "hind," "Churdles Ash," is much better than that of Pinero's "Cayley Drummles." The plot is neither more nor less conventional than West End plots, while the characterization is immensely superior. I liked most of the play. So did Dorothy. The love scene in the last act between the farmer and his servant was really beautiful. Yet I asked Hubert Griffith (*Observer*): "Do you like this play?"

"No." He certainly did not. He could see nothing in it.

I asked George Mair (*Evening Standard*): "Do you like this play?"

"No." He could see nothing in it.

These people could see nothing in *The Farmer's Wife* because it was rustic, and dealt with a life of which they knew nothing and for which they cared nothing. Eden has put a lot of careful observation of manners into this play.

No place, taken in a certain way—in its weak spots—is more provincial than the West End.

Thursday, March 13th.

Mrs. D. K. came to see me, recommended by Richmond. Twenty years ago she toured in musical comedy for 4 years. Sick of the life, she "really" married to get out of it. Thought she had made a "good" marriage. Fred her husband on a tour. He in business. Now has children 18, 17, and 15. Business absolutely failed. They have come to London; daughter is learning singing (generosity of Richmond) and Daisy is attempting to get back on stage again, after 20 years. Nice little slim thing, very neat, doesn't look the mother of a girl of 18. Well spoken, vivacious. She stammers sometimes, but never on stage. Has all the old theories about stammering being due to carelessness, and curable by beating the hand, etc.[1] Her father stammered. Her family make fun of her stammering, which she hardly likes. Talking about reading, she said all she wanted

---

[1] Bennett himself stammered and had attempted several cures without success.

was peace—peace to read, which she preferred to anything. But she couldn't get peace. Why not? Was there never to be any peace? etc. She reads in bed. She said she had met my wife in Glasgow. I said: "She's left me." She didn't know, and apologized for mentioning the matter. I said: "Why not?" She said marriage was a great strain, and how anybody could live with anybody else for even a year was a mystery to her. Evidently she felt the strain of marriage rather severely. A temperamental woman, with charm: vivacious and cheerful most of the time, but with frequent revelations of her secret deep dissatisfactions. A niece of the late Amy Roselle, who was murdered. Half ashamed and half proud of this connexion. I rather liked her, and was no doubt influenced by her evidently genuine admiration for some of my books.

Friday, March 14th.

Yesterday, Reform lunch. Talking about gambling. It was defended by James Currie and even by Lord Buckmaster. Stated to be the one distraction of the people. There is, however, fornication. Lord R. said that 40 years ago, walking up St. James's Street he used to be accosted by 6 or 7 prostitutes, and by 2 at once. Certainly the change on the streets is tremendous. I said there was, however, just as much fornication as ever, and must be, and I think this is so. Nevertheless, I agree sometimes with R. D.'s old assertion that copulation is largely a matter of habit. She ought to know. She described herself to me in a letter as a *"grande amoureuse."* R. said there were far more "amateur *cocottes.*" Probably true. Gardiner told of what a girl in the East End had told his daughter who had been staying at Toynbes settlement. This girl, educated, some sort of a clerical or administrative or inspectional post in some quasi-charitable affair in East End, said that she gambled every day, and that everyone she knew gambled. She said she often lost (I bet she did), but she wouldn't do without gambling for anything. It was always exciting and provided a new sensation every day. . . .

Apropos of all this, when I was coming home from Hammersmith in the Tube yesterday evening, two workmen got in, one about 35 and the other 18 or 20. They carried paint pots and "turps" pots wrapped in paper and covered at top (paint pots, i.e.) with paper with a hole for brush handle to poke through. Dirty. Shabby. Dirty hands. Dirty caps, with big peaks. The young one wore black leggings. They pushed the cans as far as possible under seats. The young man was smoking a cigarette. As soon as they sat down each of them pulled a new packet of chewing-gum from his pocket, stripped off the paper, broke the packet in half and put one half into his mouth. I didn't notice any actual jaw-motion of chewing. The young man kept on smoking. The chewing-gum business was evidently a regular thing, and much looked forward to. Obvious satisfaction on their faces as they opened the packets. After a few minutes the young man pulled a novelette from his pocket and went on reading it. (The elder had nothing to read.) Minor distractions of the people: cigarettes, chewing gum, novelettes. I forgot to mention that the young man carried a coil of rope within his buttoned jacket. It stuck up towards his neck.

Wednesday, March 19th.

The Gondoliers at Prince's last night. I thought this was better than it proved to be. There are at least half a dozen magnificent tunes in it, and beyond those—nothing. Immense *longueurs* in the action, especially towards the end of each act, and the "climaxic" explanation on the other hand is much too hurried. The fun is merely childish. Also it is "healthy" fun. The one joke of the gondolier about taking off his cap or anything else in reason "seemed quite shocking." It was all far too respectable. The packed audience was also stodgy and ugly. In fact you wondered where the people came from—so dull were they. However, the applause was much less than it used to be. The whole affair dull, save for the magnif. tunes. I don't want to see any more G. & S. Fundamentally the thing is dead.

Friday, March 21st.

At Ethel Sands at tea yesterday—Leslie, brother of Shane Leslie, sat next to me on the sofa, and after a time said: "Are you interested in Russia at all?" After my reply he went on to say that he had been there last autumn, and I must say that he replied very intelligently and carefully

to all my questions. But what struck me was the crudity of his gambit.
He was full of Russia and he opened in that way.

He left, and Cynthia Noble took his place; a very fashionable young
woman, probably only about 20–21, with a perfectly *maquillée,* etc. face.
I almost immediately began with her on my subject of late hours, drugs
(aspirin chiefly), cocktails, liqueurs, and salts; all of which I cursed. I
was glad to find that she was prepared to talk about salts. She agreed
with me as to cocktails, but not in much else. However, what struck me
a long time afterwards was that I had opened on my subject just as
young Leslie had opened on his.

Monday, March 24th.

At the Aldwych Theatre last night Gilbert Frankau suddenly said to
me: "I wish I was always calm like you. I mean every day in the small
things. Oh, I'm all right in a crisis. Give me a crisis, and I'm equal to it.
But in the small daily things, no. I wish I was like you." What he meant
I don't know, nor apropos of what he was speaking.

Tuesday, March 25th.

Last night at the Colefax's Ethel Sands said that on Sunday night she
was in bed at 9.30 and slept without a break till 8 o'clock. Arthur Colefax
said that he would sleep fourteen hours without a break if he was not
called. He was called every morning. He liked a little snooze before
dinner. Now last night *I* had what I call a goodish night for me. 12.30
a.m. to about 2.55 a.m. Then about 3.15 a.m. to 5.45 a.m. Then a few short
snoozes, totalling perhaps 40 minutes at the very most. In all 5½ hours.
I don't think I have ever had to be called, certainly not for 20 or 30 years,
even for the most urgent or early occasions. I can always be sure of being
awake for anything in reason.

Friday, March 28th.

Edith Sitwell last night told me of the feuds in the verse world. Osbert
is always planning some literary practical joke against someone. Siegfried
Sassoon won't speak to Osbert now because (he says) Osbert will never

leave him alone. He won't speak to Edith, because Edith will not stop Osbert doing his tricks. "But what can I do?" said Edith. In revenge, Sacheverell Sitwell swears he will never speak to Siegfried again. It appears also that either Siegfried won't speak to Robert Graves or vice-versa.

Monday, March 31st.

I met George Moore last night at a Phœnix performance. He said he wanted me to go and dine with him and that he would tell me about *Riceyman Steps*—a lot of things that I don't know (he said). Then he told me. He said it was the only really objective novel ever written, and very original. (I knew from others that he thought very highly of it.) He said: "It has no form whatever, *no* form. It is not very carefully written —it is adequately written. It has no romantic quality. Yet it holds you. A bookseller crosses the road to get married—that's all. It is disturbing to think that hundreds (he should have said millions) lead their lives just like that. The book is the FACT (he emphasized the word several times) and that's all." Then he repeated about great originality, lack of form etc. . . . Considering that in my opinion it is very well constructed . . . !

Thursday, April 3rd.

Beaverbrook on the phone the other day, after seeing Shaw's *St. Joan*. "Arnold, what do you think of *St. Joan?* I haven't seen many plays; my experience is limited, but it is the greatest play I ever saw. . . . Arnold, I've come to the conclusion that there's a technique for playwriting. There's a trick in it—a technique, and I've thought it all out. My theory may be wrong, but it deserves consideration because I've thought it all out very carefully."

Here was a perfect example of the working of that masterly and yet often crude brain. He didn't see the ridiculous side of suggesting that a dramatic technique existed. But I have no doubt that his own independent theory of dramatic technique will be very interesting and well worth listening to.

I remember he once told me that he wanted to write some narrative (I think it was the life of Christ) in the form of a novel. But he found he couldn't do the dialogue. So he read in *The Old Wives' Tale* to "see how it was done." But even then he couldn't do dialogue. So he gave it up. He told me all this quite simply and naturally, without noticing the comical ingenuousness of it.

Friday, May 9th.

Last Saturday we went to the Ba-ta-Clan, Paris, to see *La Danse des Libellules,* which I had been told was rather good and very gay, and which I had also heard was the most undressed "revue" in Paris. Paid about 9*s.* 6*d.* a seat. House full, though theatre a long way off. I soon saw it wasn't a revue, but a musical comedy. Then things in it seemed to remind me of other things. Then we looked at the programme and saw the name of Franz Lehar. It proved to be the French version of what is called in England *The Three Graces,* a perfectly terrible piece of inane dullness of which we saw the first night at the Empire some months ago. It was not gay. It was not particularly undressed. However, it was perhaps less boring than *The Three Graces,* no doubt because the resounding acoustics of the old-fashioned renovated *salle* made some of the hearing difficult. A *petit bourgeois* audience. A few people in evening dress and one woman fairly striking. A long interval for the *journal lumineux* and for the loud incessant hawking of constables. The usual terrible hags as *ouvreuses* and programme sellers. The usual narrow passages. The *contrôle,* usually so smart with the evening suits, was very shabby. At the end of Act II we got a taxi to the Quai d'Orsay Hôtel, and the taxi and the driver were both apparently in the last stages of poverty.

Saturday, May 10th.

I saw Sir Edward Elgar at Garrick the other day. I said I was working hard. He at once said: "Ah, you work because it pleases you; we poor men work because we have to." He seldom talks to me without mentioning his poverty and my riches. I suppose this is natural, and I expect I should do it in his place. *I* have a grievance, and it is that I sleep badly, and I am always mentioning it. "Do you sleep well?" I asked him. He said he, did, generally. He said that for thirty years he had had "a tea-machine" in his bedroom, and if by chance he woke up and didn't think he should go to sleep again easily, he at once got up and made tea and did one or two hours' work. I said I couldn't work in the middle of the night. "Not original work," he said, "but there is generally other work waiting to be done."

Tuesday, May 13th.

Yesterday after lunch I went with L. Faber to Haymarket to meet Hilda Trevelyan, etc. at rehearsal of *Great Adventure*. Faber gave his coat and hat to stage-doorkeeper to look after. Therefore so did I. I've never seen this done before. Enclosed stage, curtain down, etc. Very, very small after Drury Lane. I was introduced to La Trobe, the quiet stage manager with a great reputation, and to Hilda Trevelyan. Nothing but banalities said between us. Seeing D. standing by herself meekly in the wings, I called her out and introduced her to Hilda T. Then rehearsal began. Old Horace Watson appeared for a moment and nodded to me and vanished again. It only wanted Harrison to appear similarly. This theatre seems to be a sort of enclosed ring, which no one can enter save by permission. Old courtesy is preserved there, and cleanliness reigns. At the stage entrance is a card, and written on it (ought to have been printed): "Please wipe your boots." I have never seen this before at a stage-door.

It took me one hour to get from Piccadilly Circus to my house. Arrival of King and Queen of Rumania at Victoria and their drive to Buckingham Palace. A wild disarray of ordinary traffic. Everything seemed to be diverted. Even Sloane St. was full of wrongly numbered buses. Opposite Hyde Park Corner, very long waits. At last, seeing myself alone inside the bus, I went up the stairs. "No room on top, sir," said the conductor, standing at the top. I continued my way up the stairs. "No room here, sir," he insisted very firmly. "All right," I said *pettishly*. "I'm not coming up." And I stayed on the top step to look. I saw flashes of squadrons of trotting household cavalry in breastplates and helmets, and so on; all picturesque and survival-ish, and highly comic when thought of as real soldiers. Vast crowds of people. No glimpse of sovereigns. Possibly about 100,000 or 200,000 persons inconvenienced by this show. (Still it had to be done.) Later the conductor came inside and said most politely: "There's room on top now, sir." I thanked him with equal politeness. These conductors are the right stuff, wonderfully trained.

Wednesday, May 14th.

Day before yesterday morning I saw, rather too late to judge it, a bus advertisement of *London Life*.[1] Believe me that thenceforward I looked for nothing else in the streets but that bus advertisement. I didn't see one during the remainder of the day. Nor yesterday until about 7.45, when just as I was reflecting about something and had forgotten the advertisement, I saw one out of the "tail of my eye." Too late. It had gone. I am now thoroughly preoccupied with that advertisement in the streets, and shall be till I get used to it. Few street things or advertisement things give me so much satisfaction and interest as my things on the buses. Just like Georgie Dream in *London Life*.

Thursday, May 15th.

Tailor, Collins, came to try on yesterday. Of the overcoat he said: "It's a beautiful back on you, sir." And of another coat: "It's a lovely run, sir." Also of the same coat: "This is a *young* coat, sir," meaning it made me look young. He also said, when I said I liked the pattern of the new suit: "One mustn't always wear dark clothes, sir. Makes you morbid. This plum colour is a pleasant change."

Friday, May 16th.

Max told the following last night. He had bought the story from a divorce detective for £50 but dare not use it. A woman consulted a divorce detective about her husband's apparent infidelity, and the 'tec said that before doing anything she had better cease to live with him, as, if she lived in the same house, she might "condone" his offence and so endanger a divorce. She said she didn't want a divorce, she was very much

---

[1] His play, then being produced.

in love with her husband, and she only wanted to know who the other woman was.

The 'tec at first refused the case, then took it on. The woman then told the 'tec that her husband was in the habit of going away for week-ends, never saying in advance that he was going to stay away, but always telegraphing that he was detained. One night while he was asleep (after return from a week-end) she went through his pockets and found a letter from a house agent by the seaside to say that he could have possession of a certain house; also a cloak-room ticket, Victoria Station. The ticket was for a smallish bag. The 'tec and the lady went together to Victoria, and got the bag, which was locked. The 'tec pulled apart one side of it, and bloodstained stuff was disclosed. They left the bag at the cloakroom. "What can this be?" the 'tec in effect asked. "Nothing," said the lady. "My husband goes fishing and he's probably put a wounded fish into an old shirt or something." And she went on: "Now, you're in *my* service? You're in nobody else's?" The 'tec agreed and she reiterated the fact and he positively agreed.

Sometime later she rang up the 'tec and said: "My husband had just left for Victoria in a taxi. You had better watch him there and if necessary follow him." The 'tec replied: "Something grave has occurred, and I must ask you to come here to my office at once, and bring a woman friend with you. Most important." He insisted. She arrived at his office at 6.30. The 'tec said: "I'm sorry to inform you that your husband was arrested for murder at 5.55 at Victoria." The lady said: "You villain. You scoundrel. It is you who have sold him to the police. Yet you swore you were in my service only." The husband was ―――― now of course in prison.

I was in the Park yesterday thinking about a short story, and saw a woman on horseback with an old man who had a striking resemblance to Cunninghame Graham. The woman stopped her horse and spoke to me. She said I shouldn't remember her name and I didn't. She then introduced me to Cunninghame Graham. C. G. didn't hear. "Who are you?" he asked. "Ah," he said, "I didn't recognize Mr. B. in a hat. The photos of him――" I took off my hat and showed my hair, and said: "Is it true to the photos?" I complimented him and asked how he was. He said: "As well as possible under the reign of MacChadband." Prejudice against Labour showed itself instantly, and you could see that the Labour regime was very much on his mind, since it leaped out at the first opportunity.[1] I stuck up for Ramsay MacDonald. He said that the Clydesiders and especially Kirkwood, always called him MacChadband (because he preached so much). I said he was a very decent fellow. "So was Judas— a very decent fellow!" said C. G. and went on a bit about Judas, larkishly.

"Who told you that, C. G., about Judas?" I asked. He hesitated and said: "I—I got it out of the Talmud." I said: "I see, I withdraw. You have the better of me." He stretched out his hand to say good-bye. A sporting sort of cuss.

Saturday, May 17th.

Lilian Braithwaite lunched with me yesterday at Kettner's. She told me that when her daughter Joyce received a certain play to read, with a view to playing a part, she said to her mother: "Well, I don't see how they *can* ever produce such a thing. It's too awful, absurd" (or something like that). Lilian also read the play and came also to the conclusion that the play would never be produced because it simply couldn't (not that I attach too much importance to the views of actors on plays and parts). How- ever, the play was somehow produced, and it was a most dreadful frost. The curious thing is that the libraries made a *deal before the first night* (Why? Why couldn't they wait a day?) on the strength of Marie Tem- pest and Marie Lohr being in the cast. As if any names ever saved a hopeless play or even a very bad play. Producing may save a pretty bad play, but acting never. So I think. The Library Committee (supposed to consist of the greatest experts in public stage-taste in London) must have seen a rehearsal or so, or at any rate read the play.

Last night to Lena Ashwell's "Once a week players" performance of Shaw's *The Devil's Disciple* at the Century Theatre, Archer Street, North Kensington, produced by Beatrice Wilson.

Beatrice said she had had to produce the play in ten days, and they always did plays in this period. They dispensed practically with props and

---

[1] The First Labour Government was then in power.

scenery. Just a few tables, chairs, window-frames, door-frames and curtain. Same furniture throughout, whether for a general's headquarters or a widow's modest home. Three soldiers stood for a "square" of soldiers at the execution, etc. Everything very poor and cheap; but nicely done—not overstepping the modesty of nature—and the play held you, except the last 5 minutes which were very poor. A fellow named Henry Oscar played the lead. Evidently of much experience. Handsome. He did very well. Has done Shakespeare tours. The dialogue is exquisitely written—better than Shaw is writing now, I think. Less glittering, but as pure and fine as Congreve.

I contrasted all this poverty with the great costliness of our Drury Lane production, with its lavish advertising, etc. Dean is producing *London Life* with the most notable skill. You would say he knew everything about plays and producing. Yet the taste of people generally fails somewhere. He wanted me to introduce into the part of the Prime Minister Holyoke (played by Henry Vibart and supposed to be a mixture of Asquith and Balfour with a touch of Rosebery) the words: "Wait and see." I refused absolutely at once. Imagine the cheap roar which would follow such a despicable sally.

Monday, May 19th.

Interesting, and indicating woman's lack of the sense of proportion—all women's nearly—I have noticed that they will always give more importance to the welfare of flowers than to the welfare of people. I have noticed this over and over again.

Tuesday, May 20th.

All day yesterday rehearsing *The Great Adventure* with Leslie Faber at the Haymarket. He was very good in explaining to the usual incompetent young actors how to do a "hesitating" scene in a "clean" way. Also in explaining that the proper sequence in acting was "thought, movement, speech." These young people apparently knew nothing and have to be shown the least things, the most obvious things. At the same time Faber, the star, was doing comic business with hot milk while Honoria made her great speech descriptive of the Abbey—a monstrous thing which would have absolutely ruined the speech. Of course I stopped him. He then said he thought *I* should! [1] Good God! He also made even Hilda Trevelyan deliver 40 or 50 words straight up stage only because he wanted to be ranging to and fro at the back of the stage. I stopped that too.

Friday, May 23rd.

Rehearsal. X. complained much the other day about the producer's harsh attitude. "He never gives us any praise. I can't sleep. If it hadn't been for my kind author, I should have walked out before this." This is a woman of 45-50, thoroughly experienced, ought to know life, married, etc. Yet she behaves very much like a child. All stage artists more or less the same. This producer is rude to young beginners and he ought not to be; but he is never more than hard or harsh to the others. He did spring on to the stage after a scene the other day and say: "This is appalling." But so it was appalling. It appeared that many of the company had been antagonized by him. I explained to this actress all the weight of worries and hard work on his shoulders—immense; far greater than hers, etc. She began to perceive things. The next morning I spoke briefly, but with a solemn, beginning, to the producer: "You'd better give them some praise today." He said: "I give H. lots of praise in private." "The women," I said. He said, with significance: "Thank you." On the following day everything was all smiles, and X. radiant, positively. "How *did* you do it?" she said.

What a world!

Saturday, May 24th.

Yesterday at rehearsal of Act IV, Sc. 1 of *Great Adventure,* Faber asked another actor what his feelings were—what it meant to him, when Carve showed his two moles. This actor hesitated some time, and then said: "It means I'm ruined." On being informed that the case was precisely the

---

[1] *i.e.* he thought that A. B. would do comic business with hot milk while Honoria spoke if Ilam Carve were really A. B.

reverse he said: "The play as a whole has never been shown to me, and I don't know the story." He had rehearsed the scene several times; the scene explains itself; yet he had never understood its point. He had just gone on playing it with an entirely wrong set of simulated emotions within him. Even at the worst one would have thought that he might have bought a copy of the play for 3s. 6d. and read it. I admit that in my opinion the play ought to be read in its entirety to the Company.

A man at the Haymarket told me yesterday that he had just seen in Piccadilly an old lady, parading with a board: "I am the widow of Bennet Burleigh,[1] the famous war correspondent, and I am forced to this method——" I forget the rest. Anyhow, she must be an old lady of some character.

Monday, May 26th.

I was told that the organist of Westminster Abbey got a salary of £350 a year, plus a house. How he was to keep up the house on the £350 was not explained. The theory was that his position enabled him to do profitable business, such as teaching, for himself. In the meantime four canons receive £1000 a year each for three months' work, and hold livings besides. This matter ought to be gone into.

Tuesday, June 10th.

I went to the *Great Adventure* at the Haymarket on Saturday night for the 2nd act only, in order to see what Ilam Carve was doing during Honoria's long speech in Sc. 2 describing the funeral. I found that the star was playing the fool and getting laughs the whole time, drawing the attention of the audience away from the speech and preventing it from getting over. So I wrote to him to try to stop this. He was, like many stars, flagrantly breaking a rule which he would lay down for every other member of the cast.

---

[1] Bennet Burleigh died June 17, 1914. He had been for thirty years war correspondent for the *Daily Telegraph*, during which period he had gone on every campaign and war of any note.

Wednesday, June 11th.

Robert Bion told me yesterday that he had had considerable difficulty in getting into England. He had no difficulty in getting to Dover, but there he was stopped, and the people in charge told him he must go back, he could not be permitted to enter:—unemployment problem—law that no foreigner must be allowed to take a job that an Englishman could do. Robert, who is no fool, pointed out that no system of warning people was in force, that he would have all his expenses for nothing, that Wembley was being advertised and pushed abroad and people were being urged to come to see it, but apparently when they reached England they were turned back. The underling in charge listened, and was decent in manner and attitude, and then said he would ask his chief. The chief came and heard, and then said laconically: "Let him in." And that is how things are done. No official reason for "letting him in."

Tuesday, June 17th.

Elsa Lanchester and Harold Scott came to lunch yesterday. She had a most charming dress, homemade. She said she had made it out of dusters, and I believe she had. Very young. A lovely complexion, wonderful shock of copper hair; a rather queerly blunted nose. Harold staggered her and D. by arriving in a hat. He never wears hats, but had apparently decided to learn to dress. Both deeply interested in their cabaret schemes. Discussing it among themselves and with Dorothy. Largely ignoring me, though with no conscious rudeness. Youthful severity on older people. I offered to pay for some chairs and tables for their cabaret, but they were not at all keen on them, apparently preferring the audience to sit on the floor. However, they took them. I should say that these people are bound to do something good. They are full of *original* inventiveness and of distinction.

Monday, September 8th.

Alex Erskine's consulting-room. Neurologist. He has told me wonderful stories, which I believe, of trance states, etc. He had a youngish subject to go to sleep in my presence. After I had gone, he said to the subject: "Did you see into that man's (my) mind? What did you see?" (This was while the subject was awake.) The subject said: "His mind is like this. If you want to stop his stammering, tell him to stammer like hell and insist on his stammering." I thought this was rather good. I have always noticed that when I practised Coué-ism on myself, the impediment got worse.

Nevertheless, under Erskine's daily suggestion, and reading many times and saying many times daily to myself: "I have *perfect* confidence in myself. I am *never* nervous. I have *complete* control over my speech," the impediment gets less. In seven séances Erskine has failed to put me to sleep. But I have gone off once or twice for a few seconds; only the slightest noise or movement or touch wakes me up.

Wednesday, September 10th.

T. S. Eliot came to see me at the Reform Club last night, between two of my engagements. He wanted to interest me in Virginia Woolf's reply in his *Criterion* (2nd reply it really was) to a few remarks of mine about character drawing in fiction about a year ago in *Cassell's Weekly*. He wanted a contribution on the subject. I said I would do one, probably in the form of fragmentary notes, but that I wouldn't give a date for delivery and I would make it a reply to her. Pale, quiet, well assured. He works at Lloyd's Bank, in a department of his own, "digesting" foreign financial and economic journals. Interesting work, he said, but he would prefer to be doing something else. He edits the *Criterion,* and writes, in the evenings. I said to him: "I want to ask you a question. It isn't an insult. Were the notes to *The Waste Land* a lark or serious? I thought they were a skit." He said that they were serious, and not more of a skit than some things in the poem itself. I understood him. I said I couldn't see the point of the poem. He said he didn't mind what I said as he had definitely given up that form of writing, and was now centred on dramatic writing. He wanted to write a drama of modern life (furnished flat sort of people) in a rhythmic prose "perhaps with certain things in it accentuated by drum-beats." And he wanted my advice. We arranged that he should do the scenario and some sample pages of dialogue. I found him extremely sound in taste. He had excellent views about the "Virginia" school of fiction. He had discovered Pauline Smith's stuff in the *Adelphi* for himself, etc. I liked him much more than ever before.

Thursday, September 11th.

I was thinking about what T. S. Eliot and I had said about character in fiction. A character has to be conventionalized. It must somehow form part of the pattern, or lay the design of the book. Hence it must be conventionalized. You can't put the whole of a character into a book, unless the book were of inordinate length and the reader of inordinate patience. You must select traits. You must take many traits for granted, and refer to them, as you do and must refer to them in a way to show that they are conventionalized. If you wanted to get at total truth you'd only get a confused picture. Question: Does a novelist want his characters to remain in the mind of the reader? Some novelists don't. But I do, for one. Dickens's characters remain in the mind. They may perhaps be too conventionalized, too simplified. Same for Thackeray—Dobbin and Amelia. But they remain in the mind. No novelist can always be creating absolutely new, or fresh, characters. Balzac used the same frame of conventionalization over and over again. His titled amorous dames many of them of the same pattern. So did Shakespeare. So did Scott. This implies a form of conventionalization. Then half-critics say, when they observe the necessary conventionalization, that there is no character-drawing at all. The thing is to produce an impression on the reader—the best you can, the truest you can: but some impression. The newest despisers of form and conventionalization produce no impression at all.

Friday, September 12th.

I walked forth and visited second-hand shops (and bought one Staffs figure group 25*s.*) yesterday morning, and searched for and found a lot more really useful ideas for my new play *The Dance Club*. This notion of combining second-hand shops with creative cerebration is a very good one. But I walked too far, and after my afternoon sleep had neuralgia, which lasted throughout the night. I went to Ciro's to meet D. and while waiting for her met Rothermere. He was saying: "What?" "What?" louder and more gun-like than ever. He said: "I particularly want to have a talk with you." So I asked him to lunch. He merely said: "I'll come, I'll come," in a tone as though announcing something surprising.

Monday, September 15th.

Yesterday D. and I drove up to Jack Straw's Castle, via Golders Green, in a taxi and had a good view of the garden cities or suburbs north of London. Enormous 12.30 crowds on road-terrace in front of Jack Straw's Castle. I very much doubt if I had ever been up there before. Fine views of London, and Primrose Hill (?) in between. A very clear and rather windy day, and yet some mist over London, showing, comparatively, what sort of a hole we live in. I was afraid of Jack Straw's Castle at first. But upstairs the dining-room was all right. Nice cornice. Nice old, broken over-mantel, and not a bad wall paper. 2 or 3 waiters, with perhaps third-hand dress coats. But decent waiters. "The beef's English, sir," etc., with assurance. Curious clientele. A fat man and his fat wife. The man wore his hat all the time, and had his napkin under his chin. A big grey moustache. Evidently a powerful character. They both silently gave all their attention and energy to the business of eating. After lunch the terrace-road practically empty. We went and sat in the sun below. Day full of colour. It ought to have rained but didn't.

At night. Lanchester & Scott's "select evenings." Opening of season. About 50 people there; mostly young; mostly in morning dress. A beautiful Canadian girl whose pink dress I nearly set on fire with a dropped cigarette and to whom I gave a card of introduction to Basil Dean. Of course she wanted only the "tiniest part" in any of my plays. Room too dark for my taste, and floor too dark—too darkly stained. The play performed was Tristan Bernard's *Sylvie,* one act. Full of soliloquies and old-fashioned dodges but it was full of life still. Translated and produced by Dorothy. "Stage" much too dark. No farcical comedy could get its full effect in such a gloom. That is certain. Still it went well.

About "Uncle Spencer." This is the first book of Aldous Huxley's that I have really liked.[1] Character drawing in it, for the first time in his books. Uncle Spencer is *drawn,* emphatically. But technically the story is clumsy. The story nearly ends artistically. Aldous doesn't finish; he ceases. But another perfect page and the end would have been good. He shirks the final difficulty and so there is no end. Same with the next best story "Little Mexican." No end to it. But the character drawing of the N. Count is good. "Fard" is a Chekhov story. But the feelings of the maid when mistress tells her to rouge herself to hide her tiredness are shirked.

More about novel writing and character drawing. You couldn't fill in a whole character except in a book of enormous length. The young ones don't seem to me to "select." They shove in pell-mell whatever happens to strike them. They don't construct even a character. Then they think they are truer to life: but they aren't. Description of faces is futile. Waste of time. Give the reader something to hold on to, and then let him fill in for himself.

Tuesday, September 16th.

Constance Duchess of Westminster's furniture being sold up today at Cadogan Square. I went to look at it yesterday morning. There is no reason why the furniture of a Duchess should not be showy, or ugly, or dull, yet it shocks one to find it so. I was surprised at the smallness of the house, too. A policeman in the hall. Dealers and go-betweens in the porch. One of them asked me if he could do anything for me. I said I'd see; but I saw nothing I wanted. When I came out he gave me his card and he told me he could get me anything I wanted anywhere at any time. He said he knew my face, but not my name; he said: "We never forget a face—except those who owe us money."

Erskine told me yesterday that on Friday a young gardener came to him. He stammered terribly—terribly. But he was a "lovely subject." He got him to sleep at once. And when he came out he scarcely stam-

---

[1] *Little Mexican and Other Stories,* published in America as *Young Archimedes and Other Sketches.*

mered at all. The man was dazed. He couldn't believe it. He said: "My wife won't know me." He was to return on Saturday morning to be finished off. He never came. Nor did Erskine hear from him. Why didn't he come? Was he scared of a second experience? Or does he think that he is sufficiently cured for practical purposes?

I went into the Oratory yesterday morning to think out characterization of *The Dance Club* play. Men were tuning the organ and calling out to one another monotonously. Cleaners sweeping and dusting (11.30 a.m.). I chose what I thought was a quiet place in the nave. A cleaner came up behind me and said: "You're getting the dust here, sir. *But I'll be as quiet as I can.*" Very polite. I then noticed that the air was full of dust. He had somehow crept up behind me without me noticing it. So I went off into a transept.

Tuesday, September 23rd.

Aldous Huxley came yesterday afternoon to do what he had called on the telephone "pay his homage." He looked older and more distinguished. His clothes seemed to be Italian and in material if not in fit very nice. Altogether he looked better and talked more easily. We agreed on nearly all literary questions except the value of his *Antic Hay*. He likes that book, thinks it has a point to it. He seemed to agree with my few criticisms of "Uncle Spencer." He said his wife had driven him in a Citroën from Florence to Ostend, over the Alps, etc. Said she was mad about driving, and a bit inclined to be a speed-merchant. He told me some funny tales about Fascism. One friend of Mussolini's made 40 million lire in 2 years. He had four very big motor cars of the —— Company. It was found out that in exchange for these cars he had let the company off taxation for two years—had promised to do so and *had* done so. The consideration for this great act seems rather trifling to me. I told Aldous there was bound to be a big rumpus in Italy soon. He thought there was too, but he couldn't see quite what was to be done against 400,000 well-armed Fascists, the only power in the country. I asked Aldous to come early and he came early. After 1½ hours I had to tell him I had to go out. So he left. Very agreeable meeting, this was.

Friday, September 26th.

Lord Dewar made a speech at the anniversary of the Savoy Orpheans Jazz Orchestra on Wednesday night. It had a lot of wit. He said, e.g.: "It is fortunate that our jazz bands only use blank cartridges."

Max Beaverbrook rang me up last night and said: "Arnold, I want to tell you. The *Daily Express* has been offered a biography of you written by Mrs. A. B. They wanted to make it a condition that we should treat the offer as confidential, secret; but I absolutely refused to do any such thing. So I'm telling you. Our man has read it all through and likes it. Says he wouldn't mind anyone saying of him in his lifetime what is said of you in the book. If you have any objection I won't buy it: but if you haven't, I'd like to." I reasoned that if the *Express* or any other paper refused it, M. would put the refusal down to me and would be accordingly resentful. She would never understand the awful bad taste of the whole thing, whether accurate or inaccurate, praising or blaming, etc. It is bound to be published somewhere; it is bound to make people think that I am partner in the bad taste. But if it is to be published I would sooner it be published by someone who is very friendly and who will take care that nothing offensive appears in it.

Saturday, September 27th.

Max rang me up again yesterday about M.'s life of me. He said he had now read it all through, and it was unadulterated praise. The parts describing me at work were good and interesting: the literary criticism dull. He said he would certainly put a prefatory note at the beginning, to say that she had been separated from me for some years.

Without that (said he) the thing would be "intolerable," as anyone not in the know would think I had been conspiring with her to make some advertisement for myself.

Yesterday, after some hesitations, I began the final writing of the 1st act of *The Dance Club*. I went to Brompton Oratory in the morning to get some colour for the opening. I sat there about 15 minutes and got one idea, and suddenly saw that I could start. So I came back home and from

12 to 1 wrote my reminiscence from my 1907 journal, so that I should be quite free in the afternoon. After lunch I went to bed, and began to work at 3.30 only. I did the two opening scenes, up to the opening of the 1st big scene between Lucien and Flora, so I was very content, because I worked very conscientiously.

Monday, September 29th.

Miss E. B. used to be my secretary about 30 years ago on *Woman*. I never saw her from that day till Saturday. She had called without an appointment and I wasn't in, and then had written, and I saw her on Saturday at 3—only she was 25 minutes late. She was quite blind, except that on good days she can see the red of a pillar box, etc. She looked much the same and spoke in the same rather positive cheerful way. She was now living in a basement room and was well looked after and happy. She had a roll of MS. music. She wanted to help Mr. R. who had done so much for her. Mr. R. had written a song which he thought would unite the warring sects of the Irish nation if only it could be made widely known. I examined the song. It was impossible for me honestly to give any sort of encouragement. She then showed me two MS. poems, short and not much below the level of the popular ballad. I said they might do for ballad music. I said the only thing for R. to do was to go and see a publisher. I strongly urged that he should not publish at his own cost. I then went down and fetched Mr. R. Mr. R. was reading the *Daily News*—absorbed in it, he seemed. As soon as I spoke he gave a jump, dropped his eyeglasses and sprang up. He had lots of schemes. One was for a weekly magazine of poetry. Another was for penny volumes of verse; one of his own for instance, entitled "perhaps" *A Bunch of Roses*. "Get Smiths interested in it; people would see it everywhere on the bookstalls, they would pick it up as they went home, and it would have an enormous sale." This was his second string if he failed to unite Ireland ("help to cement the bonds of brotherhood") with his song. I could see that he meant, whatever I said, to print that song at his own expense after all. He had simply got to see it in print.

Tuesday, September 30th.

On Sunday night when I came home from the theatre F. W. B. was just leaving. He stopped (and kept me up) to tell me about Marguerite. She had been to Putney to see Tertia and William who were out. So she went to F. W. B.'s hotel (with Robert Bion) unannounced, and found Frank. She asked him to identify a photograph of the Newcastle Middle School. He did so. She told him that she had written 15,000 words of articles on me (evidently she is proud of the number of words), which were to be published in the *Express*. She said that she meant to write two or three other works about me. This was only the first one.

All deplore her bad taste.

Wednesday, October 1st.

I took Sissie last night to *Fata Morgana* at Ambassadors. Jeanne de Casalis, Tom Douglas (American boy—very good), Reg. Bach and others. A fine ensemble of acting, and a good production. House full. The play did not seem to be anything very important. Rather shop-girlish. Untrue. Sentimental. Still, the woman was well and harshly drawn, and there were touches throughout that were "continental" in the sense of "free" handling of situations. I thought, contrary to general opinion, that Acts II and III were quite as good as Act I.

We sat in the front row of the dress-circle. What a dowdy—and untidy-haired set of women. Very few people in dress circle in evening dress. Provincial. A bit stupid. No style. This seems to me to be a considerable change from pre-war.

The Great Adventure played to £1610 last week—its best week. But it is coming off on Oct. 18 because the receipts fell for two weeks earlier (in the run) to less than £1200 a week. Harrison had the right to give me notice to terminate the run. And he did so, not believing in the chances of the play. He was justified though to my mind a little panicky. He made contracts with McKinnel and others for Galsworthy's play *Old English,* and he must keep them, or it pays him better to keep them, or he thinks it pays him better to keep them.

Thursday, October 2nd.

Osbert Sitwell lunched with me yesterday at Reform Club. By arrangement, Swinnerton joined us. Before lunch S. Sassoon came up and said: "Can I lunch at your table today?" (In pursuance of my reproaches that he would keep by himself in the club) I said: "Certainly. You must. Osbert is coming." Sort of silly feud between him and Osbert. S. S. drew back but I made him come. A little occasional acerbity in S. S.'s tone at times, but it was quite all right. At the end I made S. S. see Osbert out of the Club.

Saturday, October 4th.

I finished the final (2nd) writing of the 1st act of *The Dance Club* yesterday at 6.45 p.m. This act seems to me to have more emotion in it than anything dramatic that I have written for a long time. Some of it I rather enjoyed writing and looked forward to the labour of writing.

Tania and Evelyn Forster dined here last night and Arnold Bax and Mr. and Mrs. D. F. came in afterwards. D. F. seems more decent than I had thought. But he is really very simple and provincial. He is a member of the Dail and apt to refer to that and to address you as if *you* were the Dail. He forms his sentences too elaborately for conversation. He told some good stories—not too well. *Mrs.* D. F. told a good story. About some semi-swell who was at a village party. A girl who had come from a village a mile or two off cottoned on to him and at the end said: "Will I lay with you tonight, sir." "Certainly not," said the visitor. "But I'll walk home with you." Long dark walk. Cold night. The girls hated it. A neighbour said: "Sure and that was what she wanted but she didn't like to ask for it."

Wednesday, October 8th.

Walking in Fulham Road yesterday morning I saw in a slatternly chemist's shop a section of window given to "Yeast is life. Vitamines mean health. X—— Yeast Tablets. . . . A lightning pick-me-up" guaranteed (or money back) to aid headaches, etc. in 5 minutes, flatulence, etc.

in 5 to 10, stomach trouble in 10 to 15, flu, cold in 24 hours. I went in
and bought some—probably because I used to take yeast and it may have
done me a certain amount of good. I didn't know what was in the
tablets (beyond yeast). I knew that for many years I had tried all sorts
of remedies, and that not one of them had succeeded with me. Yet,
as usual, I had hope again. I believed again, etc., etc. I took stuff blind
again. This indestructible (though often destroyed) faith in quack
medicine advertisements is a very interesting and perhaps almost universal trait. I took a tablet. Felt nothing. But about tea time I felt a
rather wonderful change in my organism. After tea I took two more
tablets—or was it before tea? Anyhow I felt very much better. I took
two on going to bed, and I have had the best night for many weeks. In
fact I slept 5¾ hours, of which 3¼ at a stretch. I felt I could do with
more sleep; but I couldn't get it. However, I have much more energy
and optimism today.

In the afternoon I went up to Charing Cross Road to look at bookshops. Plenty of people looking at them. What struck me was that about
half of the books outside the shop are so displayed—generally so low
down—that you can't see the titles without physical feats. They are not
attractively displayed either. They are, as a general rule, stacked anyhow
on the shelves and without order.

Thursday, October 9th.

Friendships made between young women on the telephone—solely. I
have come across more than one instance of this. They like the tones
of each other's voices and the things they say. And the friendship grows.
Then comes an invitation to tea or another meal. "Do come." "I should
love to," etc. I wonder what the results are. But I never hear. This
method of companionship (sightless) is very queer.

One sees very frequently young women and girls together in the street
(lower middle class and a bit above) giggling with much vigour. Whenever I have heard them talking in these giggles, the matter has been
utterly trifling. They will giggle "consumedly" if crossing a road and in
danger of death from a bus; or at some peculiar sight. They will cling

on to each other while they giggle. In the male sex this phenomenon is practically non-existent.

Friday, October 10th.

I dined at Knoblock's last night. The Cochrans were there. Also the Gerald Kellys. They were just off to America—portrait painting. Cochran told at some length the story of how he got Trini from Seville to London—negotiations with parents. She was seventeen. She insisted that she should be taken to a bull fight, and that a carriage of a certain sort with coachmen and footmen dressed in a certain way should call for her. She lived in a foul street, which Cochran's Spanish friend forbade him to enter. So he waited for her at the bull-ring. She didn't come. Then they went to find out. Trini and her mother were in bed. Father had taken all their clothes and sold them for drink and had also sold the two bull-ring tickets which Cochran, according to contract, had bought for them near the box in which he was to sit with Trini. However, she went the next Sunday. The contract included Britain and America. There was a devil of a business about California being in U.S.A. Trini couldn't be permitted to go to California where there were brigands, cowboys, and all sorts of horrors. So the contract was altered. "The United States of America, except California."

Kelly told me of two poetical sayings to him of an old woman who lived all alone. "My visitors are the night and the day." And "I am as lonely as an asparagus." (The wild asparagus, which grows high and thin on one stalk here and there on the plains, and out of which a lovely something is cooked—I forget what.)

Saturday, October 11th.

White Cargo last night by Leon Gordon. Playhouse. This is not a good play, but it is the ground plan of a good play. It has form, and it has a great deal of truth here and there. Most of the dialogue is wooden, conventional, etc. Most of the acting is conventional and even bad. But Horace Hodges as a dipsomaniac doctor, with a charming disposition, was admirable. Nobody else earned my praise. What is enheartening about this play is that it does try to be realistic, and there is no concession to sentimentality in it, even at the end, and no love story with a dawn, and what there is ends ruthlessly—and yet the play is a success, and was obviously liked. Indeed I have seldom heard more applause in a theatre on an ordinary night. And at the end the people did not want to go. Audiences, however, are terrible. In the 3rd act, at perhaps the most tragic moment of the play, a character has to say of another: "Poor bloody fool." Roars of laughter. Why? The censor has only just begun to allow the word "bloody" on the stage.

Monday, October 13th.

On Saturday night I dined with T. and his fiancée, an American widow with 2 children and some money. She had that American feminine way of implicitly or explicitly expecting a sort of homage from men, and of putting them gently in their place at intervals. She did this to T. several times. When I said: "Do you know what are the two best things in America?" she said: "I should like to know what *you think* are the two best things in America." She was impressed by London, but apparently had little use for Englishmen. Seeing a big foot under a table, with a not well-shaped shoe on it, she murmured to T. that that was an Englishman's foot. At another part of the conversation, I said that Englishmen had points, and she said: "Oh! I am sure they must have." American women are metallic. They may tinkle sweetly or harshly, but they are metallic.

Thursday, October 16th.

I noticed last night for the first time that the lamps in the Square at this date are lighted by lamplighters.

Dinner party at Wells's last night. This party was apparently got up to meet Margaret Sanger. G. B. S. left silently immediately after dinner. Mrs. Shaw stayed on. E. W. MacBride, zoologist, is a very jolly, boyish, comic-looking clever old man.

This morning, two black nuns, heavily draped, begging in Ovington Street. They walked up the narrow front steps exactly side by side. The senior held the book, morocco bound. The junior rang the bell and then they stood side by side, the junior with crossed arms. While waiting they faced right angles to the door. At one house they were evidently refused at once. They descended the steps side by side. At the next house they stayed a minute or two and probably got something. *Même jeu.* I saw them mount the steps of a third house.

The day before yesterday I was passing down towards King's Road, when a shabby young man with three medals on his coat held out a bag to me. I am always inveighing against the sin of charity in the street; but there was something painfully silly and futile in the aspect of this young man, and I stopped, and said: "Look here, I object to this sort of thing. However . . ." And I threw 6*d*. into his bag. "Good luck to you, sir," he said foolishly. I then noticed another young man with a barrel organ in the gutter, and the organ started disgustingly playing. A rotten lapse on my part.

Saturday, October 18th.

Last night I had a letter from a solicitor and notary at Ayr telling me that Professor Grierson of Edinburgh University had awarded me the Tait Black Novel Prize for 1923 for *Riceyman Steps*. Money: £141, and asking me if I would accept it! I replied that I would. This is the first prize for a book I ever had.

Monday, October 20th.

Collins the tailor, trying on new trousers on Saturday, asked me whether I wanted a "break" at the foot. As I hesitated he said, "Just a shiver." I said yes. Shiver is a lovely word for this effect.

Tuesday, October 21st.

Lawrence Langner came to see me yesterday. He said positively that the American taste was against drawing-room plays and decidedly in favour of what he called *genre* plays, i.e. plays of character strongly developed, middle class or lower middle class. He urged me to write a Five Towns play, even if I did it specially for U.S.A.

Wednesday, October 22nd.

First night of Galsworthy's *Old English* at Haymarket. Generally speaking untrue. Still the principal character, fine old English man of business, had a coherence of its own and was well played on old-fashioned lines by McKinnel. Sissie liked the whole of the play except the end, when the old gent dies of over-drinking. She simply disliked this because she is so strongly teetotal. Similarly she disliked the old man's pious daughter, because she objected to the bad qualities of the character. Apparently in Sissie's mind there is a complete confusion between moral and artistic perceptions. I have noticed this before in her at the theatre. And she is 54 or 55, of wide experience in affairs, a magistrate, a public speaker, and no fool.

Wednesday, October 29th.

Last night with Lucas to *Charlot's Revue* at Prince of Wales Theatre. Largish theatre and very full. Revue chiefly idiotic. Maisie Gay and Phyllis Monkman both admirable. Monkman acted an emotional part in a Chink tragedy marvellously well. Audience quite undiscriminating, enjoyed almost hysterically the most silly infantile things.

Saturday, November 22nd.

Depression, because I saw no prospect of finishing *Dance Club* play today or tomorrow, as I had hoped. I gave up all notion of finishing and couldn't think of any of the ideas necessary for the final scene between Flora and Clair. When I got home from the Empire I was, as a consequence of neuralgia pains, a bit sick. This sickness in turn at once relieved the pain. Instantly I felt better and instantly the hope of finishing the play miraculously returned, and ideas for the last scene came into my head and I became actively creative again. I have noticed this before: return of creativeness immediately upon surcease from pain.

Sunday, January 18th.

I got home on Thursday night in a thick fog after a calendar month of almost continuous sunshine in Genoa, Naples, and Pisa. Owing partly to the soft influences of the climate and to a self-determination to do absolutely nothing for a month, I did not keep a journal. This was a great mistake. And the self-determination was not kept, for I did begin to write an article for Tom Eliot's *Criterion* and failed to finish it.

Chiropodist yesterday. He congratulated me on my toenails. Said they were strong—a sure sign of a good constitution. He said in a sort of ecstasy: "It's a grand thing, a nail is!"

Tuesday, January 20th.

One of the main things, at my age, is to avoid strain—"pushing forward" (as you do when you are in a taxi and are getting late for an appointment). Nearly all my life I have been keeping to a time-programme, and I have been doing it until quite recently, and have carried programmes through in spite of neuralgia and such obstacles. I think that now this method results in less instead of more work. On Sunday afternoon, after two hours' work with Knoblock on *Mr. Prohack* in the morning (with neuralgia) I gave up the bit of re-writing that I had meant to do in the afternoon, and stayed in bed all afternoon, and of course felt much stronger. In fact towards six I was really inclined to

clear off some small oddments, including a 300-word of appreciation of
Thomas Hardy for *Harper's*, which I did, all right.

Yesterday morning my scheme was to re-write the end of Act II of
Prohack in the morning. However, I had a sense of rush and strain
even before breakfast, and so I became placid and gave myself all day
to finish Act II, and telephoned to Knoblock suggesting that he should
put off our appointment to proceed with Act III from 3 p.m. yesterday
to 11 a.m. today. He agreed. I finished the Act easily at 7 p.m. and in
the meantime had read the whole of Johnson's little book on me.[1] (Not
bad.) The sense of strain had gone, and though I had neuralgia all day,
I felt better, and had quite a fair night and began to do letters and oddments at 8 a.m. in good form.

Wednesday, January 21st.

Anthony Hope told me last night at Lady Russell's[2] dinner party
that on every first night Henry Irving gave an immense champagne
supper to about 300 people—journalists and friends. Also that all sorts
of people had free entry to the theatre on any night—and if no seats they
stood. You only had to know Irving or Bram Stoker or Loveday[3] in
order to be let in, without any trouble. Hope had the *entrée*. Irving also
had a heavy permanent salary list. Hope said that his sister-in-law
Suzanne Sheldon was engaged by Irving by the year, but never played
for more than 3 or 4 months in the year. Hope said humorously that all
subscription lists were opened by Irving as a matter of course by "Henry
Irving, £105." And so on. I asked how Irving could live. Hope said he
thought he did not make anything out of the Lyceum, but made large
sums on tour and in America. There must have been a chronic state of
hard-up-ness. Hope said that towards the end Irving had the beginnings
of a great success with *Richard II*, and then fell down and hurt his leg,
and couldn't play. They tried Herman Vezin, etc.,[4] but nothing would

---

[1] *Arnold Bennett*, by L. G. Johnson.
[2] Countess Russell, the well-known author of *Elizabeth and Her German Garden*, etc.
[3] The author of *Dracula* joined Irving in 1878 when he took over the Lyceum Theatre;
H. J. Loveday was stage-manager for many years. He died in 1911.
[4] A great Shakespearian actor, had played with Phelps. He died in 1910.

work. However Irving left £10,000, which surprised Hope, who expected only a schedule of debts. He said that Irving would never pay a royalty to an author, because he would never give to anyone even the theoretical right to inspect his books. His attitude towards the author was the old one: "Send for the fellow and we'll tell him what we want him to do." He would pay as much as £1000, but not more—without difficulty. Hope said that Bram Stoker came to him, Hope, more than once, suggesting that he should write a play, but Hope wouldn't write without a royalty and Irving wouldn't pay a royalty.

I met Ian Hamilton [1] last night at Lady Russell's, and he is a very nice and artistic sort of an old man. I like him much. I praised his writing highly (which it deserves—what I've read of it, and I've thought so for years) whereat he was clearly much pleased. "I feel several inches taller," said he on leaving, using a terrible *cliché,* as even artists will. He said he couldn't work much because he had so much to do—travelling and speechifying—in connexion with ex-service men's organizations.

Last night I had more distressing instances of my failure to recognize people whom I know. Three. Lord and Lady G., whom I had met at a luncheon some weeks ago, and Mrs. Cazalet, whom I surely ought to know quite well. I hadn't the least idea who any of them were, and each of them had to make the first move, while I groped after the identity. Coming home from Pisa last week I met, at different parts of the journey, four people whom I knew and hadn't, again, the slightest notion who they were.

Still reading Stendhal's *Mémoires d'un Touriste,* slowly. Second time. Why? I suppose because of the fellow's mind, also because of slackness in starting something else. Yesterday I at last bought *A Passage to India,* [2] and Lady Jones's pseudonymous *Serena Blandish,* [3] which is greatly praised. I began the latter at once, and doubt if I shall praise it myself. Seems to me to be too pastiche, mannered. I also bought Legouis and

---

[1] General Sir Ian Hamilton. His dispatches from Gallipoli and *Gallipoli Diary* were literary masterpieces.

[2] By E. M. Forster.

[3] *Serena Blandish, or the Difficulty of Getting Married,* by a Lady of Quality.

Cazamian's *Histoire de la Littérature Anglaise,* chiefly in order to read the pages on myself. In the way of negative criticism I thought them good; but less so in the way of positive appreciation. However, they show some insight and a desire to be judicial: which is something.

Thursday, January 22nd.

I read a fair lot of Enid Jones's *Serena Blandish* early this morning, and liked it more. It is a pastiche, and the writing is therefore mannered, and sometimes she slips, constructionally or grammatically, in her elaborations. But there is stuff in the book—ideas, and some nice turns of plot and idea. I am getting to like the book; which shows that until you are quite sure that a book isn't and cannot be good, you may profitably proceed with it.

Friday, January 23rd.

Last night Y. told me about Lord X. Son of a successful grocer. Went to Cambridge and became a wrangler. Nonconformist. Like many Nonconformists had a passion for politics. Entered Parliament, stayed there for over 20 years, and was always foiled by Lloyd George. Not even a Chairmanship of Committee, nothing. Retired then, and went in for business. Formed coal-combine of mines, or helped to. Put in charge of the Miners' Association for buying timber for pit-props, and bought timber himself against the Association. Great row, which Y. helped to settle. Later he got a peerage.

He was not a really good business man, and he was never really rich (half a million or so). Then Ll. G. called him in to be director of ——. He did nothing himself, but employed others, and spent his time with the Press. He was always very keen on the Press. Had become very friendly with Northcliffe, who helped him a lot. Before this he had already become a "business" figure in the world. His great belief was that the chief thing was to be renowned. It didn't matter what you did so long as you were renowned. He got this more and more in his high Government position. He became a national figure (quite wrongly). He had a slight "Puck-like" humour, which enabled him (with a few intimates, such as Y.) to laugh at the swindle of his own success and illustriousness.

His great difficulty was always that he could not express himself in the spoken word. Hopeless as a speaker. Even at meetings presided over by him he made hopeless failures. Then he caught pneumonia, pleurisy, and died, just as he was looking forward to a really very great future. (I must have a very great death scene in my novel on him.[1]) His death was his greatest splash. His wife and house were untidy (meals late or no meals), hostess coming in from hunting at all hours, etc. He had no comfort there. (He had married much above himself.) All this the background of the mysterious woman whom nobody knew—the woman whose suicide really gave me the first idea for a novel. When he was ill once, X. sent for Y. and gave him £25,000 bonds which he was to hand over to the bankers of the unknown if X. died. X. merely said that this woman had been his companion, his only companion. Y. was not at all sure if she had been his mistress. Later when X. was about dying, his wife sent for Y. and said X. was very keen to see him. X. then told Y. that there was no further need for the £25,000 bonds, as the lady was dead—had committed suicide (some time before?). (Here is the kernel of the novel.) Y. returned the bonds.

Tuesday, January 27th.

I finished Forster's *A Passage to India* this morning at about 5 a.m. The central part of this book (the trial, etc. of innocent Aziz for an attempt on Adela Quested in a cave) is a magnificent piece of work. I should call it strictly first-class. The herd instinct among the British section of Chandrapore is perfectly done. There are also many other very fine, and even first-class things in the book. It is all very good indeed. The writing here and there slips up over phrasing—is a bit too clever, or a bit too pert or colloquial; but on the whole the style is excellent.

Yet the book left me with a sense of disappointment. I think the reason is that I don't know quite what it is about. Aziz, the Moslem doctor, is

---

[1] *Lord Raingo*, published in 1926.

the chief character, and he is lifelike. So are all the Indian characters. So
are most of the British characters. He gets into a mess with the British
Raj through the hysteria of Adela Quested, and gets out of it again
through Adela's honesty. You are made to see that there are two sides
to the Indian question, with considerable impartiality. But as soon as
Aziz is acquitted, the story seems to curve away towards Aziz as himself,
scarcely related to the British Raj problem. Some chapters, then, are a
bit feeble because his psychology, and that of others, is merely described,
instead of being exemplified in incident. Then the story pulls itself together, and Aziz goes to a Hindu native State as doctor. All the life there,
especially the religious, is beautifully done; but it doesn't seem to relate
itself directly to the problem of the previous part of the book. All details
are good; but the ensemble is fuzzy, or wuzzy. Although I only finished
the book three hours ago, I don't recall now what the purport of the end
of the book is.

Lee Matthews brought Komisarzhevsky to dinner last night to discuss
The Bright Island, which K. is to produce for the Stage Society. He
doesn't look above forty. A nearly bald head. Nervous. Shy. Melancholy.
But he soon warmed up under treatment, and I found he could laugh
like anything, especially at the amusingness of his own ideas for producing the play. I liked him.

He said he worked under the Soviet for some years. The work was
interesting, but the conditions appalling. He had to produce two or
three purely propagandist plays each season as a condition of being allowed to work at all. All his household possessions were taken from him.
His valuable library was taken and given to some public library. When
he got to Western Europe he hadn't a cent or any possession. They
talked (he and Lee M.) about some boy actors that they had seen in
London (some Church Guild affair) and how good they were, showing
that the Elizabethan stage needn't have lost much by having boy actors.
Lee M. said that play-producing by church boys had brought him back
into the Church of England, and he now officiated at services—very well
indeed. He would.

I was at a private show of Ernest Thesiger's own water-colours at Holy

Trinity Rectory yesterday. He is selling them to get money to help the son of a coachman to be a singer. He said: "I heard that man (now twenty-five) sing in the choir yesterday, and I thought how fine it was to be able to help such a voice (baritone) to be brought to perfection and heard by all the world." Well, it is a fine thing, and shows a curious side of Ernest's very complex character.

Wednesday, January 28th.

Last night B. and Y. at the Yacht Club told me more about the story of X. for my projected novel.[1] One curious part of the tragedy of course was that X. was lifted to office by Lloyd George, the man whom he hated and who hated him. Ll. G. wanted a Liberal badly and so put him into office. X. said of Ll. G.: "That man will do three things: bring consols down to less than 50, ruin the Liberal Party, and ruin the British Empire." He has done two.

X. was Puck-like, loved to make mischief, loved chicane. Had a pretty sense of humour of his own. There was a discrepancy between Y.'s testimony at the Reform (23rd inst.) and at the Yacht Club. Last night he said that X. had a first-class head for business. Not really interested in money. He wanted the reputation for money rather than the money. He was always searching for a doctor who would sound his heart and "give him ten years" of life. He never got any doctor to go beyond five years.

X. had no social gifts, but once they gave a ball at their charming old Queen Anne house, which was such a horror of untidiness inside. X. went to bed at 11 p.m. His bedroom had been used as a cloak-room for ladies; but this did not deter him. He merely thought that his wife had been undressing in his bedroom.

M. B. said he heard X. make a pitiable exhibition of himself in some self-defence in the House of Lords. You thought: "Well, if the Empire at war is in charge of men like that . . ." etc. X. persuaded himself that Ll. G. gave him office because of his merits, because he could not ignore his merits. As regards his illness, he knew he was done for, and he told

---

[1] *Lord Raingo.*

Y. so. The legend grew. As B. said, he was a front-page story for days. Eminent doctors begged to be allowed to go and help. Secretly a Welsh witch was brought in and the doctor found a charm under the pillow one day! His passion for publicity continued till the end. And while he was preparing to enter Heaven special messengers were still bringing press-notices to him. At last he died.

Owing to his lack of conversation he was in the end taken for a strong silent man. He kept shorthorns, and would go in frock coat, etc., full fig, to see them at local shows, and would turn up his trousers and wade through masses of muck and mud very bravely.

Saturday, January 31st.

Last night with Duff Tayler to *Jitta's Atonement*, adapted (nominally "translated") by Shaw from the play by Trebitsch. Fulham Grand. This play made a very deep impression on both of us. Shaw has taken an obviously conventional and machine-made play of Trebitsch's, left the first act in all its conventional competence, "situation," and dullness, and then in the 2nd and 3rd Act treated the development of the theme realistically and wittily. The effect is simply electrical. The play wakes up, the artists wake up, and the audience wakes up. Enthusiasm obtains.

The mere idea of starting on a purely conventional 1st Act and then guying it with realism and fun, shows genius. In the other Acts there is some of the most brilliant work, some tender, some brutal, and lots of the most side-splitting fun that Shaw ever did—and he is now approaching seventy, I suppose. The "hysterics" scene of laughter between the widow and the mistress of the dead man is startlingly original. The confession scene between the mistress and the daughter of the dead man is really beautiful. The fault of Shaw's changes is that the husband of the dead man's mistress, a shallow person in the 2nd Act, quite suddenly in the 3rd Act becomes a wit and a practical social philosopher of the very first order—a Shaw at his finest. There was a very good audience, and any quantity of appreciation and delight. And this in spite of very, very little good acting and a great deal of very bad acting. Nancy Price was the best of them. Frith better than anybody could have hoped for. But then they had something to do, something that *made* them come to life. At this moment Shaw is packing the big Regent Theatre with *St. Joan.* And a repertory theatre begins a series of twelve of his plays at the Chelsea Palace next week. At this rate Shaw will soon be nearly as popular in London as he is in Berlin and Vienna.

Monday, February 2nd.

Nolan [1] at lunch yesterday told me, apropos of Burma and the big industrial companies there, that at the end of the war when young ex-officers went over to take posts in, e.g., one of the oil companies, some returned almost immediately, dissatisfied. Nolan said their attitude was: "We won the war; we want good money and we aren't going to work for it." Nolan seemed to have a slight sub-conscious prejudice against the young who "won the war." He gave instances of dissatisfaction. One was that one of the companies had a rule that newcomers could not join the gymkhana club until they had passed the language test—or at the end of a year, whichever came first. This rule was strongly resented by ex-officers, and I can easily believe it. I should have resented it myself. One said: "I'm not a child. I've led men over the top, etc., etc., and I won't be treated as a child." And he went home by the same boat as he had come in. Others left in two or three months.

It is all very well for the companies to say that an incentive is needed to make the men pass the language test; but this does not seem to me to be the right kind of incentive. Drunkenness is, or was, the great trouble with the young men. Nolan said that the civilians, even if Scotch, thought of nothing but making money, and dismissed all intellectual activities even in the evenings. In the evening they talked business also. He said, and Mrs. Nolan also, that the Burmans were very artistic, naturally so, and you perceived it in everything immediately you entered the country. They used costly "worked" articles (such as lacquered stuff of high quality) for daily use. Nolan said that the Eurasian problem was growing. They now had to be called (officially) Anglo-Indians. A mis-

---

[1] J. J. Nolan, an old friend of Bennett's, had edited the *Rangoon Times,* 1915–20.

nomer, for they were the fruit of all sorts of mixtures, such as, e.g., Portuguese and Chinese.

Wednesday, February 4th.

The Vortex, by Noel Coward, Royalty Theatre. As Pauline Smith was ill, I took Evelyn Forster instead. This play has made a great stir. First Act played 43 minutes, and the first half-hour, and more, was spent in merely creating an atmosphere. Talk whose direction you couldn't follow. No fair hint of plot till nearly the end—and hardly even then. Five unforeseen entrances of important characters. One might have been excused. In 2nd Act, some tiny glimpses of dramatic talent and ingenuities. The end of this Act, where the son plays the piano louder and louder while his mother makes love to a young man, is rather effective, original, and harrowing. The atmosphere of a country-house week-end party is fairly well got. Technique marred by important characters coming in unperceived and overhearing remarks. The 3rd Act contains the whole of the play, and is in effect a duologue between mother and son. Coward plays the son well, and Lilian Braithwaite gets through the mother as a sort of *tour de force*, but she never gives a convincing picture of an abandoned woman. The end is certainly harrowing to a high degree. But not much effect of beauty. Some smartness in the play, and certainly the germs of an effective dramatic skill; but really I saw nothing that was *true* except in minor details. I dozed off once in the last Act and Evelyn had to waken me.

At Harry Preston's lunch at the Embassy yesterday, Tom Marlowe, editor of the *Daily Mail*, repeated with still more conviction that newspapers had no influence on public opinion.

Friday, February 6th.

I asked Miss Nerney,[1] who has just typed the 1st Act of my new play, *The Dance Club*, if she liked it. She said: "Yes—fairly." She can always be relied upon to say what she thinks about my work. Evidently she did

---

[1] Arnold Bennett's secretary.

not much care for it. She said: "I don't like it half as much as *Mr. Prohack*. There's a lot more in *Mr. Prohack* than in *The Dance Club*." What puzzles me is whether she is put off by the subject (as I believe she is), or whether this is a true artistic judgment according to her standards. This puzzle I shall never solve; she could not solve it herself.

Saturday, February 7th.

I dined at Theodore McKenna's last night. Some time ago, he went to lie down under the light of his violet-ray lamp (equivalent of sunlight or some such thing) over his bed, and went to sleep and stayed under it 1½ hours. Now the longest time you ought to stay under it is 20 minutes. One or two skins were burnt off. He could scarcely talk, or eat. His tongue shrivelled and hard. He was all black. Even the ear which was pressed on the pillow was burnt; the sweet influences of Pleiades had gone right through his head. He went to the office for three days—no pain for a day—but then had to go to bed and didn't get out of the house for a month. (He then had to go to America on business, and afterwards to Smyrna.) Said to be a unique case; in the *Lancet* this week or next.

Monday, February 9th.

Met Lord Haldane again Sunday night at Colefax's. He seemed to be in a continual state of bland amusement—mildly diverted by everything. He gave a long account of passages between Gorchakov, Bismarck, and Beaconsfield, at the Berlin Conference when Dizzy ordered a special train for home, and this so frightened Gorchakov, as a kind of ultimatum, that G. arranged to get a special order from his Imperial master countermanding first order (for a port in the Aegean for the enlarged Bulgaria). Haldane said this account had never been printed and differed from the accepted account. But I can't help thinking I had read it before. Yet he seems to be an accurate man. He was very agreeable. Rather apt to go into a bit too much detail in his accounts of things.

Performance of *Henry IV, Part II*, by Fellowship Players last night at the Regent Theatre. This was very good indeed on the whole. The performance of Hay Petrie in the small part of Silena was simply amazing.

I never saw anything better. There is hope for acting. (Also Shakespeare is just about as good as his reputation.)

Thursday, February 12th.

Tayler and I went into *Mother Goose* pantomime at the Hippodrome last night. A melancholy interior, not giving any effect of gaiety. Everything poor and second-rate, except the grace of Isobel Elsom perhaps. Tedious! Tedious! Ugly! Yet I suppose this is just the sort of thing we used to admire at Drury Lane in the far past. But the worst part of the affair is the drab, dull, or silly, or stupid audience—comprising many provincials. How they laughed at the feeblest jokes, and broke into uncontrollable applause before the end of the most ordinary stunts.

Tuesday, February 24th.

I had *une espèce de grippe* all last week and wrote nothing whatever. Dorothy returned from Italy. The first (of two) performances of *The Bright Island* took place at the Aldwych Theatre on Sunday, 15th. The play was coldly received on both Sunday and Monday. The points were not seen by that portion of the audience which applauds. Yet the play had succeeded at rehearsals. Many people thought it amusing and true. I think that for one thing the audience was bewildered at the start by the strangeness of the scene, the "Commedia dell' arte" names of the characters, and the political quality of the plot. Also by the even-handed rigour dealt out to both political parties. The Press, with the sole exception of *Truth*, who liked it and praised it and said it ought to be revived before a "more intelligent audience," slanged it like anything. Not partially, but wholly. Some said that I ought to be stopped from writing such plays, a great mistake, deplorable, and so on. It was the worst Press any play of mine ever had.

Fjellsted [1] told me on Saturday a story of how trouble may be caused by indiscretion. The story was told to him by a patient, a Justice of the Peace, and it happened to two of the J.P.'s friends. One of these two had a splendid car, and the two went out for a drive. They overtook two

---

[1] The masseur who attended Arnold Bennett.

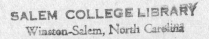

nurses from a nursing home, and offered them a lift, which was accepted. They came to London (I think). The four met again in the evening. Later one of the nurses found herself pregnant. She did not even know the name of her lover; but he had told her that a well-known surgeon had performed a rather peculiar operation on him. She went to the surgeon and actually got the man's name and address. She then wrote to her lover, and mentioned the other man and the other girl sufficiently for people who knew the circle to identify them, and told him of her condition. The letter to the lover was opened by the lover's daughter (one of those careless go-as-you-please households where everybody casually opens everybody else's letters). The daughter showed the letter to her mother. The mother identified the friend and went and told the friend's wife. Finally she went to the nursing home and denounced the second girl, who was dismissed. Only it happened that she denounced the wrong girl, and the wrong girl brought an action for damages, and damages had to be paid. Also of course the lover had to pay for his illegitimate child—£1 a week. To say nothing of the horrid mess in the two homes. The moral is, don't pick up girls when you are motoring, and, if you are a girl, don't be picked up. Also if you let a man seduce you, get at any rate his name and address. But chiefly, have an absolute rule in your home that your letters are to be opened by nobody but yourself.

Monday, March 9th.

The embracing qualities of revue seem to be more and more in evidence. I saw Ernest Thesiger last night at Hubert Griffith's war play *Tunnel Trench*. I knew he was to play in a revue (of Cochran's, Noel Coward's, etc.). What surprised me was that he should pass about six weeks in the country playing it before London—he who never plays out of London. He has left the Dauphin in *St. Joan* to go and play in revue. At the *Tunnel Trench* party afterwards on the stage of Prince's Theatre I saw Margaret Halstan, who was the original Emily in *What the Public Wants*. Hadn't seen her for years. The next moment I was talking to Haidée Wright, said to be our greatest tragic actress, and the real star of

Milestones. She said *she* had been asked to play in revue. She had in-quired what she would have to do in the revue and the reply was that she would have to be an old woman in rags and try to ride a bicycle and fall off it, and that was all. So she refused revue.

Tuesday, March 10th.

Sloane Street up from Pont Street to the bottom; a shade under half a mile I suppose. Curious fact; they are laying a pipe, or rather six pipes, earthenware, all in one, and I have never had enough curiosity to ask what this pipe is, and why it should be in six divisions. I think it must be water, as I often see an official "Turncock" strolling about. But the incuriosity is the interesting thing. The street is being repaired (wood) very rapidly and very well and very noisily. The noise of about a dozen drills (for boring out and breaking up the concrete) is awful. Men live in it all day, and those who use the drills have their hands vibrated all day. The whole thing is a "perfect hive," and a wonderful scene. Part of the street was totally up and repaved about two years ago, or less. Why this so soon duplication of work? Another instance of the amateurish-ness and "loose-limbedness" of London government.

Wednesday, March 11th.

Spring Cleaning at St. Martin's Theatre, by Fred Lonsdale, last night, as guest of Castlerosse, with D. House full. House full every night. There is a lot of wit in this play, and the opening scene, wherein a lot of decadents and homo-sexuals, etc., come in to the hero's house for cock-tails is very ingenious and well managed. Afterwards there is nothing that seems real, save an odd remark. The "great" scene in the 2nd Act where the hero introduces a prostitute to his wife's dinner party is not in the least convincing, and the prostitute (well played by Cathleen Nesbit) is like no prostitute that ever was. All the 2nd Act is absurd. The 3rd Act, scenes between husband and lover chiefly, is equally false, but it is saved, partly, by some fine lines and by Ronald Squire's acting as the lover. This Act owes everything to Squire. On the whole perhaps not a totally wasted evening. But I don't know. If the play runs for a long time, I shall be surprised. I should think it would peter out un-expectedly. My theory is that a play which pretends to be serious and is not will not run for very long though it may make a great splash at the start. A spurious play may run if it is dull and all alike. However, the whole subject is very complicated.

Thursday, March 12th.

The head of the little dancing school, where I am daily being taught to dance, came in to watch me being taught yesterday. He said to me: "What you want is courage, decision. Don't be afraid of 'em (women). Remember they have to do what you want. You've *got* 'em. And it's the only time you *have* got 'em."

Friday, March 13th.

Swinnerton told with more detail yesterday the story of his birth. He said: "I was born in the drawing-room, and only my mother and I were present." The nurse came in later, and said: "Oh, of course he's dead." His mother questioned if he was dead. The nurse repeated: "Yes, he's dead. He must be dead." He also told how he was at the funeral of Victor Hugo. He was carried there, at the age of 1 year, in the arms of his mother, or someone.

Monday, March 16th.

A 6½-hour night last night after a week or so of bad nights. Well, I was in a high state of nerves yesterday. Barrie and Eliz. Lucas were dining at Savoy Café last night, and afterwards he took D. and me with Eliz. back to his flat. He said an extraordinary thing had happened to him. A man who had never written a play before sent him a 1-act play, which he, Barrie, passed on with a strong letter of recommendation to a management, which management accepted it the next day, and is to produce it next month. I showed Barrie my praise of the last act of *Dear Brutus* in yesterday's *Observer*. He agreed with my remarks on the easy-ness of 1st Acts. He said a play of his of which only the 1st Act was good was *What Every Woman Knows*. He said he wrote that Act in two days. The 2nd Act took weeks, and the 3rd Act took months.

Saturday, March 21st.

We were at Lady Colefax's supper to meet John Barrymore on Thursday night. There were no Asquiths there. Asquiths seemed to occupy all the boxes on the 1st night of Barrymore's *Hamlet* at the Haymarket. Also they were photographed in their boxes. Barrymore, at the supper (where he arrived after 1 a.m.) seemed to be partly exhausted. He looked distinguished but didn't talk distinguished. During songs he closed his eyes and seemed to sleep. Then he exclaimed: "Oh, for some Cointreau!" very urgently, and it was brought quickly to him. He is very shrewd and perspicacious.

Well, we left the Colefaxes' supper party at 2.40. S. C. told me she went to bed at 5. She was called up at 8 on the 'phone by Irene Curzon who told her that Lord Curzon had died at 5 a.m. and could S. come to her at once. S. went.

S. said that one of the shocks of her life occurred when, at the supper party given by Lord and Lady Oxford on the first night of Elizabeth Bibesco's play, *The Painted Swan*, photographers were brought in to photograph! Private house. The host said that Elizabeth's health and the health of her play must be proposed. But nobody would propose it (no doubt shyness). Finally papa proposed it. S. recounted a very characteristic saying of Lady Oxford's on seeing an attractive hat: "That's a hat to go to a concert half an hour late in." Asquithian all over.

Monday, March 23th.

T. Bodkin came to lunch on Saturday. As to the language question in Ireland he said that the language law would entail a lot of extra work on schoolchildren, who already of course had more subjects than they could cope with. He said that the official language for Parliamentary Bills was Gaelic, and that they were issued with an English translation; but the amendments were proposed and passed only in English. Also that there are three varieties of Gaelic spoken by three different small, mutually distant groups of people—as widely different (he said) as Normand from Provençal; and that which variety should be used had not yet been officially decided. Also that the Gaelic vocabulary was absurdly inadequate for modern needs, and that many words had to be invented.

Bodkin said that his wife, being an ardent Catholic, went into a retreat for a few days every year. The last time the spiritual adviser enjoined her on leaving to get and read three books, (1) some work (I forget) of St. Benedict, (2) Thomas à Kempis, and (3) *How to Live on 24 Hours a Day*. Bodkin understood that one reason for including the latter was that I advocated a time set apart for reflection.

Tuesday, March 24th.

No! No! Nanette at the Palace Theatre last night. This is supposed to be the most popular musical comedy of modern time. Edgar Selwyn saw it in Chicago, and praised it very highly. It contains three or four extremely catchy jazz tunes. Also Binnie Hale—who is young, has style, charm, and is a very good dancer—for a star. It also contains Joseph Coyne, who is simply admirable, and Geo. Grossmith, who is good. These two together on the stage do admirably funny scenes. It also contains some women who are competent or a bit more. The music is "catchy." It is perhaps the best musical comedy I ever saw.

Thursday, March 26th.

I was walking in Selfridge's basement yesterday afternoon, idling between two appointments, when I met Selfridge in rather old morning suit and silk hat. He at once seized hold of me and showed me over a lot of the new part of his store. Cold-storage for furs—finest in the world. Basement hall 550 feet long. Sub-basement with a very cheap restaurant where they serve 3000 to 4000 customers a day. He introduced me to the head of his baby-linen department saying: "Here is a gentleman wants things for three of his children, one is three months, another ten months, and another a year old." Then up his own private lift to the offices and his room, where I had to scratch my name with a diamond on the window—with lots of others. He showed me a lot of accounting. Then downstairs to book department. Fine bindings, etc. His first remark was, taking up a book: "Human skin." I had to hurry away. He kept on insisting that it was wonderfully interesting. And it *was*.

Saturday, April 4th.

Yesterday afternoon, after parting with Edgar Selwyn and promising to write a play with him in the summer, I went to the special matinée of the Academy of Dramatic Art at the New Theatre. The judges for the Gold Medal were in two boxes: Bancroft,[1] du Maurier, and Gladys Cooper, etc. Pinero, Loraine, Matheson Lang—a frightening array for the students. What struck me most was the badness of the *producing* of the playlets given. It was all bad and much of it very bad.

Monday, April 6th.

Some weeks ago Mrs. S. M. recommended to me some anti-fat pills made and sold by a chemist at Nice. The course was six boxes. I got the six boxes from Nice and began. Mrs. S. M. positively assured me that they were quite harmless and very effective. After I had taken a little more than two boxes, I began to notice that I perspired very freely and also was short-winded after any exertion. Also that my heart made a too loud noise and was rather irregular. So much so that I could not sleep on my left side on account of the thumping row. Fjellsted, my masseur, told me my heart had been affected by something—he thought it was due to veronal, of which I had taken one dose for insomnia. (By the way my sleep grew heavier but much more broken, and no better as regards total quantity.) I hadn't and haven't told him about the anti-fat pills as his feeling against all pills is so strong.

I then sent for Dr. Griffin. He examined me and said my heart was organically quite all right, but that it had been upset by the pills and that I must at once cease to take them. He came a second time on Sunday, and said that the improvement, though noticeable, was very slight. I still have to walk upstairs very slowly and to avoid any physical strain. Dr. Griffin had the pills analysed. The analysis on the box (in accordance with French law) says: "Iodothyrine," "Hypophyse," "Surrénales," and "Génésiques." He said that the quantity of thyroid (cheap) was

---

[1] Sir Squire Bancroft, President of the Royal Academy of Dramatic Art, actor-manager, and writer of memoirs, was the husband of Marie Effie Wilton, the famous actress, who died in 1921.

larger than in the formula, while the other things (more expensive) were less than in the formula on the box. He said that I oughtn't to take medicines without consulting him. And of course he is quite right. It is perfectly staggering the idiotic things even a wise man will do.

Tuesday, April 7th.

Max Beerbohm, with others, dined here last night. I hadn't seen him for ten years (at the Reform Club). He was more delightful than ever. His mind is sound right through; and he is often witty. Some people have told me that he would dine out and say nothing but the most ordinary things. Last night he said scarcely anything ordinary. He was unaffected, modest, and thoroughly wise, and made a great impression on everybody. After the Maughams and the Parsonses had gone, he expanded even more to Kathleen Long, Dorothy, and me. I asked him what kind of cigarette he preferred, Eastern or Western. He said it didn't matter. He just took whatever came. He didn't care about many things, and as soon as he owned something that he had wanted it ceased to please him.

His age proved to be 52, whereas mine was 58 in May next. He said he *wanted* to be 58—every year was a conquest. He did *not* envy young people; in fact he felt sorry for them. Their lives also were precarious. They might die any day, and if they did die—what a suck-in for them! How much they would have missed—without knowing it. He said he had no feeling for London. He liked to visit it, but only on the condition that he could leave it and return to Rapallo. He said that he couldn't possibly have the romantic feeling for London that I have, because he was born in it. "The smuts fell on his bassinette." Whereas *I* could never lose the feeling of the romanticalness of London. He told me that I was in his new series of "Old Celebrities Meeting Their Younger Selves", shortly to be seen at the Leicester Galleries. The legend under the drawing of me was:

> *Old A. B.* Everything worked out according to plan.
> *Young A. B. My* plan.

What a depth and width of criticism of me in this!

Good Friday, April 10th.

On Wednesday John Barrymore came to lunch with S. C. and Dorothy. He was Bohemianly and shabbily dressed. He remarked at once on my pictures, was much struck with the dining-room, picked out the interesting things in it at once, and when we went upstairs he said it was the most beautiful house he'd been in in London. He liked the odd little stairway leading to nothing on the first floor. This I suppose was characteristic of him. He looked tired and plain, but talked with the full beauty of his voice, was very masculine and powerful, and very friendly and responsive. Of course he is used to talking. He talked admirably, full of ideas which he expresses very picturesquely. He has read a lot.

What was interesting was the way in which he regarded all plays from the acting or actor's point of view. This seemed quite natural and proper. He wants plays in the grand manner of romance and emotion. I could see what he wanted, and had a desire to write it. Dorothy mentioned *Don Juan*. He said he was glad that that had been brought up, and that he would now like to play it. He refused it last year because he had been playing showy womanizing parts too much and wanted a change into something classical or more austere. He several times said he was too tired to do anything, but he seemed very well and strong, apart from that. The next day the Haymarket Theatre had to be closed, and he was laid aside with a bad throat.

Barrymore said that the German people who wanted him to go to Berlin told him that his company would not be good enough for Berlin, and he would have to change it. He rather agreed with this verdict on them. Said they were all too gentlemanly and afraid of being not-gentlemanly. He said that the U.S.A. was the worst place to live in in the whole world, and that he liked to play in England better than anywhere. He inquired whether it would be possible for him to make a living in England.

Tuesday, April 14th.

D. and I dined at the Café Royal (in the café) on Easter Sunday night. I hadn't dined in that room for years. It seems to have come through all the changes and rebuildings of architectures and times with scarcely a change. The whole atmosphere was almost, you'd think, just as when Henri Rochefort [1] was there daily. Fine wine. Cigars at A1 condition. I saw a very arty or studio-ish figure there and couldn't think who it was. Tall, thin, bearded; brown clothes, black tie, red handkerchief. As soon as I shook hands with him, I remembered. Darrell Figgis.[2] He was cheerful, with a background of melancholy. He comes over on journalistic business, stays at the R.A. Club in order to have a swim in the morning, and generally eats at the Café Royal. There he was all alone on Easter Sunday evening, reading an American collection of short stories by post-war Russian authors. All very characteristic.

I asked him to come to our table later. He did. He talked merely at intervals, but is rather provincial in his method of referring to himself and what he has done and what he has said. Dublin is very provincial. He agreed with my harsh verdict on Æ., etc. He was wearing fine rings. Perhaps two of them were his wife's.

Thursday, April 16th.

Temple introduced yesterday, at Reform Club, a young fellow named Scripps. Father is proprietor of a "chain" of thirty evening newspapers from the Atlantic to the Pacific. He said that the aims of Ku-Klux Klan were different in different States. In some they were anti-Catholic merely, e.g., others were anti-nigger. All Scripps papers were anti-Klan. He had received threatening letters from Klansmen but nothing had ever happened to him. In some Southern States bullets had been fired through windows, but nobody hit and nobody took any notice. In one town, a strike of their street boys had been engineered through the boys' parents, and it had halved their circulation for a time, especially as the boys' "route-books" (with names and addresses where papers had to be delivered) had been nefariously burnt.

Scripps explained how the Southern block of States simply had to vote Democrat because of course they couldn't vote Republican. Hence if a

---

[1] Victor Henri, Marquis de Rochefort-Luçay, the French journalist and political leader, died in 1913.
[2] Irish author and politician.

Democrat candidate got only five more States in addition to the Southern, he had a fair chance of winning. The Scripps papers had run
La Follette for the Presidency at the last show. Very great opposition to
him, but it had not cost them anything in circulation. Scripps seemed a
decent family sort of a young man, belonging to a "house" of some sort
—in this case a newspaper house—with traditions behind him. He
showed sense when I asked him how K. K. Klan was to be put out of
existence and he answered: "Oh, I expect it will just die out."

Saturday, April 18th.

Lees-Smith [1] lunched with Glynn Williams [2] and me at the Reform
yesterday. He told me a lot of things about the Labour Party. He said
that Wheatley was no good, had no mind, and would probably do no
more. I had thought he had no mind. I asked him about the causes of
the fall of Ramsay MacDonald. [3] He said he was very able, industrious,
educated, travelled, and could make a good speech at an hour's notice
on anything. He was cautious rather than sagacious. He said one of his
chief faults was that he could not delegate anything. He must do everything himself, even to telephoning.

Lees-Smith was at Chequers on the first day of R. M.'s office as P.M.
and he said that on that day R. M. always answered the telephone himself. Another fault was that he in practice looked on all jobs as equally
important, could not differentiate between them. He said that at the
beginning of the week when R. M. fell (the critical debate was on a
Wednesday, I think) R. M. had not decided his policy. Owing to Trade
Union Congress and things he had only the Monday morning in which
to think out his policy; and he spent the whole of that morning in a
second meeting of a Committee about the Dawes Plan, which Lees-
Smith himself thought it scarcely worth while to attend. He said that
R. M. had four times the energy of an ordinary man and that his looks
had helped him a great deal.

---

[1] Subsequently minister in the Labour Government, 1929–31.
[2] Editor of the *New Statesman.*
[3] The First Labour Government had been defeated in November, 1924, after a few months
in power.

Thursday, April 23rd.

Three first nights this week.

The Torch Bearers by George Kelly (U.S.A.)

Fallen Angels by Noel Coward.

Ariadne by A. A. Milne.

These plays played about two hours each; the first rather less than two hours. All were light, artificial, conventional, not true to any kind of life, and fundamentally old-fashioned. Marie Tempest was astoundingly fine and finished in the first. As for the second, I had been saying for weeks that Tallulah Bankhead couldn't act, and she gave a superb comedy performance. (She would not have been much good in Maugham's *Rain*.) I usually hate Fay Compton on the stage. Yet she was admirable in Milne's play. On each night I was in the main bored—perhaps least at the first play. Asked to describe Coward's play by Mrs. Theodore McKenna, I said: "It is a piece of damned cheek." So it is. She fully agreed. Still, I rather like him putting 2 drunken young women on the stage. It prepares the way for a more serious realism, and it helps to tear off the tulle rags of chivalry, etc., which is all to the good.

Saturday, April 25th.

Talking of sleeping, at the Embassy Club last night Lord Ashfield said that his habit was to go to bed at 11, be *in* bed by 11.30, and to read till 1 o'clock. He slept four hours; then was awakened by asthma and had to treat it, and then slept for another 3 hours. He had to be ready to meet his heads of departments at 9 a.m. He said he had never been able to find a cure for asthma. Going out, we met Luigi, who was saying to someone that the entrance fee to his club was £21 and the annual sub. £8 8s. I said I never paid for my night clubs. He said: "But you shall be an honorary member. I shall be delighted." He said the same to Ashfield, and gave us forms. It was funny to see a survival on these forms "Name of Regiment." Good God!

Monday, April 27th.

The tickets for the first performance of Cochran's revue *On with the*

Dance are priced at 27s. This arose through a mistake in reading hand-writing. The price was really 24s. The tickets were printed and many of them were sold, and nobody in authority noticed the mistake. Then Cochran decided that the higher price should remain. Many had paid 27s. by error. The rest should pay the same. How characteristically theatrical this mistake, the negligence, the ultimate solution.

Tuesday, April 28th.

I went to Chinatown last night with Beaverbrook and Ashfield. Penny-fields is the name of the chief street, Limehouse. We went to the Lime-house Police Station first. It took us exactly fifteen minutes to drive there from Ciro's. Great change in a short time. We saw some "curios" (as the Chief Inspector called them) first. Explanation of "Fantan" and "Pluck Pigeons." The first seems a purely childish game in which the bank pays 2 to 1 winnings on a 4 to 1 chance.

Then out with the Inspector to Pennyfields. No gambling after 8 o'clock, he said, usually not later than 7. We entered two Chinese restaurants (11 p.m.) where lots of people were drinking tea. Humble people. All very clean and tidy indeed, and the people looked decent. A few nice-looking prostitutes—chiefly Jewesses. Nearly all houses closed. Some windows, said the Chief Inspector, were always shuttered. "They don't like the light." Glimpses of curtained bedrooms higher up. We went into a Chinese Music Club, where four men were playing Mah Jong and one strumming a sort of Chinese guitar, with very large string-pegs. Their singing nights were Wednesday and Saturday. A suggestion that they should sing was not well received. They were very polite but didn't want us. We were to have seen the Chinese Chapel, where the religion of Confucius is practised; but it was locked up.

Then we went into a pub (closed) and found one or two old topers (friends of proprietor's) drinking stout after hours. We were taken upstairs and there saw a wonderful collection of Chinese carving of all sorts—chiefly picked up from sailors. Lastly, return to police station. No prisoners. Cells marvellously clean and sanitary. Steam heating. Temp. must be 63 at least. Plank bed, white as a yacht's forecastle, but a pretty comfortable pillow: one rug. On the whole a rather flat night. Still we saw the facts. We saw no vice whatever. Inspector gave the Chinese an exceedingly good character.

Wednesday, April 29th.

Noel Coward lunched with me yesterday and answered all my arguments in criticism of *Fallen Angels*. He said that he wrote it in five days, and *The Vortex* in four days (or three). When he once began, he worked straight through. He showed much intelligence. He said he meant to write a *really* good play, and a *really* good novel. He has a little house in Majorca, where he is going with his mother. And in the autumn to play in *The Vortex* in New York. I was pleased with him.

Thursday, April 30th.

B. N. Opera Co. last night at Golders Green Hippodrome. Drove there in taxi. It was like arriving in the centre of a big town. Flat performance of *At the Boar's Head* by Holst, and *Gianni Schicchi*. Much of the music of the former lovely. But the whole conception wrong. Wells said to me: "The idea of it is fundamentally stupid. The dialogue was complete before Holst began even to touch it." It was ridiculous to set it to music. Much of the acting rotten. Dame Quickly particularly. Wrong notion of character. Doll Tearsheet a bit better, but too'plain and dull for a stage-whore, though she corresponded with the reality of lots of whores. *Gianni Schicchi* rather better, but the hero was played dully. When we came out, not a taxi. Buses flying off packed. We got on to a bus (top) and waited five minutes before it started. Then changed to a taxi near Marlborough Road. Home here soon after 11. Everything was interesting except the performances.

Monday, May 11th.

On Friday, at lunch at the Vineyard, I had my first long serious detailed talk with Max Beaver [1] about political material for my novel *Lord Raingo*. It lasted just 1½ hours. He was marvellously effective and

---

[1] Lord Beaverbrook.

efficient. He didn't need to be told what sort of stuff I wanted. And he gave way at once when he was on the wrong tack—for me. He has exactly the right sort of imagination, and a very powerful and accurate one. He can invent pieces of plot to fit certain incidents, and is just as interested and as effectual in the matter of women as in the matter of politics. I got an immense amount of stuff. So that was all right.

Yesterday afternoon I taxi-ed up to see Barnsbury, so well spoken of as a curiosity by W. Whitten. It is a curiosity. The Sphinxes and little Cleopatra needles in front of the porticoes of a long row of houses in Richmond Rd. are too marvellous. There is quite a lot of other Empire ornament round about here. Barnsbury Square is very good. And so is Malvern Terrace. The taxi and D. and I attracted attention, and while we were strolling around a nice polite (and no doubt curious) boy (Jewish) came up and asked me if I wanted "Miss Galway's house." It never occurred to me to ask who Miss Galway was. I should have liked to know.

Tuesday, May 12th.

Opening of the "most magnificent dance club in the world," the Kitcat, last night. I took D. and we met Donald Calthrop and Miss Adair, Harry Preston, John Leigh, etc., etc. For an opening night (it had, however, been opened to the Press the night before) it went very smoothly. Packed with people who had dined there. Floor and balconies all crowded, and people standing all round the balconies trying to see down into the ball-room and not succeeding. To see this space crammed with dancers who could only sway to and fro, to hear the row of the Vincent Lopez £1100 a week band from New York, and the other lower noises—gave you the impression that the bottom had fallen out of civilization.

Friday, May 15th.

Dinner of "The Other Club"[1] last night in Pinafore Room, Savoy. Birkenhead got across the subject of Marie Stopes, and said that he called *Married Love* disgusting, etc. He referred to Lord Chief Justice Hewart.

---

[1] The Carlton Club.

He said you couldn't go on Circuit for years without acquiring a certain breadth of mind and that Hewart had that mind. If you wanted to talk about the amours of a goatherd and his charge, Hewart would talk with you, but equally he would talk about anything else. Birkenhead kept on about Marie Stopes. He had no reasonable arguments, and everything (nearly) he said on the subject was either specious or silly; but he phrased his matter well. He never gave in.

Later I was talking to Lutyens who was in one of his fantastic veins. He took up the subject of whales. He said whales were nice respectable animals, warm blooded, had breasts and things and loved their young deeply, and that they could certainly be tamed—they would do anything for food—and used as draught animals. He drew marvellous pictures of the King and Queen being drawn down the Thames in the Royal barge by a team of whales who had been fed on tomatoes or something, to make them spout red. He said we had wasted whales, and the species was being extinguished. He was really very inventive, imaginative, and funny over this fantasy.

Sunday, May 31st.

Lack of entries during the past fortnight is due to visits to Oxford to the Keebles [1] (week-end) and to Torquay to Phillpotts's (three days; to work on libretto of a comic opera with him), and to simultaneity of beginning a new novel *Lord Raingo* and the beginning of the German Opera season at Covent Garden. The novel began with great vim on May 13th and went well. But the change of habits due to opera, and sundry odd articles that I had to do gradually sapped the vim.

I went to the opera three times, *Rosenkavalier, Tristan,* and *Valkyries.* In each case the damned thing begins at 7–7.15 and ends at 11.20 or 11.25. You can only have high tea first, and then you must go out to supper afterwards. Natural fatigue of 4¼ hours' great music, plus *dérangement* of habits, causing indigestion causing insomnia—and there you are.

I liked the three operas much better than ever, and stand more im-

---

[1] Sir Frederick and Lady Keeble (Lillah McCarthy) were old friends of Arnold Bennett's.

pressed than ever by the bigness of Wagner. I used to be overawed by the mere achievement, apart from its creative force. Now I am not. After all, creatively, these operas are very simple, and the artist is tied by scarcely anything in them. He is in an ideal world. He hasn't got to think of half so many things as a novelist in a long realistic novel. The hardest mere "work" is the scoring, and many composers could and do score with far more complexity than Wagner. Still, the power and the beauty of Wagner are staggering. There was great singing.

The yachting season. Everyone has been predicting a fine summer on the strength of a warm May. The *Marie Marguerite* [1] was to have left the Colne to meet me at Southampton, last Wednesday. It began to blow a S.W. half-gale—gale on Wednesday morning, and it has been blowing the same ever since. She had not left the Colne last night.

Tuesday, June 2nd.

Yesterday I began on the political part of *Lord Raingo*, and had to go cautiously. But I did 1200 words, with increasing confidence. A heavy day's work anyhow. Olga Lynn brought Rudolf Kommer, Reinhardt's right hand, for tea. He wanted to see me. He told me some things I didn't know or had forgotten. He said that *The Great Adventure* had been produced in Vienna and failed—owing to production. Also published in book form in Berlin.

Wednesday, June 3rd.

Rudolf Kommer said on Monday that, though the actors were better in Germany and Austria than in England, nobody there could play "the English gentleman" as quietly as it ought to be played, and that I should find all performances of my plays "noisy." He spoke of "English gentlemen" with great admiration and respect, as of something unattainable. He also said that *The Pretty Lady* was on a plane by itself, the finest war novel—"with nothing of the war spirit in it." "A wonderful idea seeing London life in war through the eyes of a French *cocotte*."

---

[1] Arnold Bennett's yacht.

Monday, June 22nd.

On Saturday I returned from 17 days' yachting. Not two minutes' rain in the whole time.

Tonight *The Cherry Orchard* is transferred from the Lyric, Hammersmith, to the Royalty. This I think marks a definite turn in public taste toward true plays. I have been remarking this turn for some years, but managers seem to be quite blind to it.

When Fagan produced *The Cherry Orchard* for us at the Lyric, we thought it ought to be done but did not believe in it. The first performance was splendidly received. But we did not believe in it. On the Thursday after the first performance (Monday) none of us believed in it, and Fagan met the directors and agreed without argument that the thing was a failure. But a few days later he was believing in it (by reason of the enthusiasm of small audiences), but the returns were still awful, and the loss heavy. Then the returns enormously improved. Loss became a profit, and tonight this most disconcerting and original play is going in a sort of triumph to the West End, where no manager would have looked at it a month ago. All this is owing to N. Playfair having seen it done at Oxford, and being firmly backed by me in his desire to have it done at the Lyric.

Wednesday, June 24th.

When I saw the above play again at the Royalty on Monday, in a by no means full and rather apathetic and not at all first-night audience, I was struck still more by the power and beauty of the play. I remember Jacques Copeau coming to me during the Stage Society performance of *The Brothers Karamazov* in a state of nervous gloom and exclaiming: *"Ces malheureux artistes!"* and asking me why I hadn't warned him or done something; whereas I didn't know anything about the performance.

The revival of *The Beggar's Opera* last night at the Lyric, Hammersmith, was an affair of *prodigious enthusiasm*, and well done in some ways. Here is an absolutely English thing, understood by English artists, and done by them excellently well so far as the limitations of their gifts would allow. The music is lovely, heavenly sometimes, and the dialogue always brilliant. Also it is daring and bawdy, with robust ideas about life. This is in my opinion one of the most wonderful entertainments I have ever seen.

Thursday, July 9th. Salzburg.

As soon as we had got into Germany [1] (Kehl, I think, about 4.30 a.m. yesterday) the country began to be German, quite conventionally. There is no doubt you can get a more intimate and romantic view of a strange country early in the morning. You then know when people actually get up, and what they look like when they are up. Putting bedclothes out at windows. Pensive girls at windows. Men and boys loitering in lanes, and waiting to begin to work. A curious softness and humanness over everything. Sudden increase in Germany of official uniforms. The railways seemed to have got back to decency and efficiency. Munich. Great lakes and mountains east of Munich. Wonderful to regard; and, with thin tapering spires of churches, quite conventionally German. The German of opera scenery. Sunday when we got into Salzburg—Tyrolean hats and garments. It seemed comic—nature imitating art.

Saturday, July 11th.

I have not seen a well-dressed person in this lovely town. Day before yesterday we went up a lift to the "Café-Wein" Restaurant on a mound of the Mönchberg. It is just opposite my window on the other side of the river but about 300 yards further down. The lift takes about a minute and in that minute a marvellous change has taken place. You see the entire town at your feet, and the surrounding country gets itself into proper proportion. The centre of the town is a mass of domes and towers, which I have certainly not yet unravelled. We dined at the said Café-Wein Restaurant, but indoors because it began to rain, and rained heavily and kept on raining with one short surcease, which we used to get down again in. I reckon the current of the river is doing 4 knots all the time. In flood it must do a lot more. A few punts are tied up to the banks here and there, doubtless for transport, but how they are

---

[1] Late in June Bennett started on a yacht cruise in Northern Europe.

manœuvred I can't guess. Much of the baroque architecture is fine. The Mozart House is a lovely building. Something in the nature of an artistic manifestation is always going on. Concerts daily, somewhere. *Die Fledermaus* last night. The "Don Cossack" choir tonight. A Mozart evening (up at another hill café) on Thursday night. Also a circus at times. There seems not to be a single decent drapery shop in the town. I mean of the women's kind. The dresses of the women attest this. It is really a very remarkable fact.

Wednesday, July 15th.

The scenery around is wonderful. There must be about a dozen 10,000 ft. mountains in the region. But we soon tired of this imposing, picturesque scenery. It is as if it was done on purpose—some *tour de force* of a creator. Sunday was a fête day here. The fête of the fire brigades. They came from all around, including adjacent Germany. The café-restaurants were full of firemen, in poor ill-fitting uniforms, at lunch. Procession very long. Full of engines and ladders, and one very old engine, and banners and bands. One brigade was headed by a girl in white; at least she seemed to be a girl; but she might have been the wife of the huge framed glittering man who was walking by her side. The affair had a certain medieval or Renaissance quality, but lacked both vitality and efficiency. After it we drove in a little victoria to see the castle (Lustschloss) at Hellbrun, a few miles off, along a monotonous road chiefly quite straight. This castle has lovely gardens; but the "practical joke" quality of the fountain-work (designed to soak the king's guests by surprise) and the childishness of the working, water-driven models in the gardens, gave you a sinister insight into the mind of a foolish king.

Much work in mornings. I am reading Hamsun's *Segelfoss Town*. It is not his best work, but contains very fine things indeed, and is never sentimental. I read some of Robert Bridges's poems again, including the one containing the line "The horses of the strong south west," which has remained in my mind for many years. It is a superb short poem. Yesterday was what I call a full day, after a rotten night. I didn't get up till 8 o'clock; then breakfast; by 11.15 I had written 950 words of the novel. I then dressed and went out to recover, to reflect, and to find a new restaurant. We lunched at the new restaurant. Back to hotel to sleep, read, and tea. Then by the giant lift to the Café-Wein Restaurant on the Mönchberg; walked on the said berg for a long time (acutely picturesque). Then descended by the lift and to St. Peter's Keller for dinner; place crowded. Then to hotel for tickets for theatre, and to *The Blue Bird* (Russian troupe as in London) at Stadtheater. Some of it very good; a little of it magnificent.

Thursday, July 16th.

Walked up to the top of the Kapuzinerberg yesterday afternoon. The entrance begins only about three minutes from this hotel (Oesterreichischerhof), and the distance of climbing is only about a mile, I should think. But it is very stiff work indeed. The path is stepped and tended and signposted with great Teutonic care and thoroughness. Some English say it is too well done. How absurd! (In the war we copied everything but German thoroughness—I mean in the press.) These signposts indicating distances in time are most useful. At the top (it took me an hour with frequent rests) a café, *tout arrangé*, for tourists, with "fine" views of Alps. These *Aussichts* of Alpine stuff leave me definitely rather cold. Visited the Kurhaus on the way back to the hotel. Vast and gloomy— especially the restaurant where an "Alpine evening" was to take place last night. Feared it and avoided it, and dined at the Mirabell Garden Restaurant where also I had lunched. At lunch, Jerskny, director of the Blue Bird troupe had a table, with several of his artists; they were extremely jolly and giggled like anything. At night: music. Waltzes and operatic selections. Electric light; hence theatrical trees; dogs playing with each other; outsiders staring; girls carrying beer all the time; a girl wheeling round and round a thing like a perambulator containing all sorts of confectionery; she did this for 2 hours and was still doing it when I left. I finished Hamsun's *Segelfoss Town* last night. It does not hold together very well, and is inferior to his best work; the interest is allowed to shift too much from character to character. The characters are apt to appear and then fade. But it contains four really splendid things, and some fine humour and ditto wit. There is a tirade against actors and actresses which is devastatingly funny and true. The translation is very good indeed.

Friday, July 17th.

I did no actual writing of my novel, and damned little thinking about it. I just lay about and read Francis Hackett's *That Nice Young Couple,* which after 100 pp. seems to begin to have some theme to it. I went out and bought some cigars. About 4.30 went up to Hoher Salzburg. A very Margate-ish crowd; indeed the same sort of crowds everywhere. They stream into the town daily. Coming home, I met Kommer; or rather he stopped me and offered me a piece of paper. For a second I didn't know him. He had inquired at all the hotels for me (including this one) without success. He had then gone to the police, who informed him at once that *E.A.B.* was staying at the Oesterreichischer, and gave him a bit of paper to that effect; this was the paper he was exhibiting to me in the street. Kommer told us that when he was producing *The Miracle* in Cleveland (staggering success), he could never get any eatable food there. He said that when he and Diana Cooper dined at the house of the richest millionaire in Cleveland, the ices are actually bought at a store —not made in the house. He said that the modesty of Asquith's country house "The Wharfe" was one of the things that struck him most. Said it couldn't happen anywhere else. Asquith had been P.M. for eight years. He said that in any other country a man who had been P.M. for eight months would retire rich. He said he was now working on the German version of *The Great Adventure* and that Reinhardt would do it in both Berlin and Vienna. Probably some delay as there was great row between German managers and German stars. The managers had decided that no star should get more than £15 a night and the stars had struck. He said that the actor who took Ilam Carve made as much as £100 a night because he took 25 per cent of the receipts. When I told him the plot of my *Flora,* he said it was a sign of a wholesome public that such a plot, so simple, should be certain to arouse protest. He said that in Berlin, if you wanted to make a scandal in a theatre, you had to have a mother committing incest with *two* sons; one wasn't enough.

Saturday, July 18th.

Last night we went to dine with Kommer at Max Reinhardt's *Schloss*, Leopoldskron, about ten minutes' drive from the town. It is a really huge house, with magnificent views of Alps on one side, and the Hoher Salzburg fortress on the other. So fine as to be scarcely credible. The house was built by an archbishop-prince about 1700 or 1680. Vast. Vast rooms. I mean really vast. We dined in a tiny dining-room that you could scarcely see, only it was larger than my ditto at home. The real banqueting-room would have held 12 or 20 such rooms. Reinhardt's private suite—study, bedroom, bathroom, and dressing-room is simply colossal—like a dream. The dressing-room would occupy twice the space of my drawing-rooms together. The finest rooms are the chapel and the big reception-room over it. I should say that each of them is 30 or 35 feet high at least. Not a single room was really finished off complete, except the big reception-room.

Kommer said that Reinhardt has a mania for building and transforming. He has no use for a finished place. We saw a lovely music-room, nearly finished, upon which a Salzburg artificer had been at work for ten years. Reinhardt is seldom there. In theory he is there for 4 months in the year; but in practice he is generally away from it. At the moment he is in Venice. He spends all his money on it. The profits of the Denver *Miracle* built an enormous semi-circular wall round two-thirds of the estate. It is a good wall.

He is incurably lazy about everything except producing itself. Kommer said he had known him for twelve years and worked closely with him for four years, and had never received a letter from him or seen his writing. No intensity of urgency could make Reinhardt write a letter, or (it seems) even dictate one. Telegrams were his method of communication. He said R. was a very quiet, very modest, very shy man, with no knowledge except of his own subject; but *full of sense*. He never had known him to say anything foolish. Also he was never a bore.

Yesterday I wrote 1100 words of the novel. I am still wondering whether they are good or evil.

Wednesday, July 22nd.

Great heat. No waistcoat even in the evening. Went to a performance of Leo Fall's *Madame Pompadour* at the Stadttheater last night—this piece was recently a failure in London, I think. Pompadour is a great part, but it is certain that Evelyn Laye couldn't play it. Last night the part was played by an ageing actress, who would however still "pass." She had some good notes left, and sang with style. All the spoken parts were rotten. The comedian part was nicely played, with restraint. The chorus was the worst chorus I ever heard. The finale of the 2nd Act made you wonder how the manager had the damned cheek to present such a thing at all. Leo Fall seems to me to be the best of these Viennese operetta composers. Certainly much better than Franz Lehar. It seems that all the fashionable operetta composers congregate at Ischl, in the Saltzkammergut (and near here), and that such composition is a regular industry there.

Friday, July 24th.

Today I finished a long chapter of *Raingo* . . . 32,000 words in all up to date. Great heat these last few days. Finally getting rid of my neuralgia, I stayed in my room till evening yesterday, and wrote in pyjamas and was still much too hot. But for me, heat favours work. I wrote 1500 words today. Salzburg is now filling up more and more. And a few smartly dressed people are to be seen about and the restaurants are even fuller than before.

Saturday, July 25th.

The Austrians are a cheerful, polite people, apparently thoughtful for animals and other helpless beings. The work in the countryside seemed at this season to be chiefly carrying hay (on long horse or ox wagons) and transporting tree-trunks. Also sawed wood was stacked at roadsides waiting to be moved.

The Austrian cuisine is certainly rich. Always thick sauces. And rich cakes for sweets. Stewed fruits. Fish is mainly trout.

Sunday, July 26th.

At night Kommer went with us to dine at Hôtel de l'Europe near station. Biggest and most fashionable hotel in Salzburg. Large numbers of people. Much American accent, including that of the editor of the N.Y. *World*. Some fair frocks. A bad band. I had thought there was no dancing in Salzburg.

Kommer suggested that I should re-write the book of *Orphée aux Enfers* for production by Max Reinhardt in New York. I did not refuse. He told me that the big theatrical people in New York had no interest in or knowledge of the theatre as such; but were just speculators and adventurers. Much the same in London. I thought a great deal about my novel yesterday, but wrote nothing.

Monday, July 27th.

It cleared up yesterday afternoon, and after I had written 1000 words of *Raingo*, I went for a walk up stream on right bank. Many people, including the ticket taker at the theatre: great hat-raisings and exchanges of politeness. At night, before dinner, Kommer took us to *Orphée aux Enfers* at Stadttheater. It began at 7.30. I had never seen this before. The music is delicious. So is the plot. The production was terrible, and I don't see how it could have been better in the circumstances. I calculated that the stalls, full, held about £20 only. To which Kommer retorted that the actors didn't get more than 3 million kr. a month (which is about £9 sterling)—at most. I asked: "Is it worth while doing things when they have to be done so badly?" He said: "Why, of course! For instance here; they do everything. In May last I saw even Galsworthy's *Windows* here." He then recounted what the theatre meant to him in his native town (Cernowitz, Eastern Austria), when he was a schoolboy. He said it coloured his whole life. They did everything, very badly, and he saw everything. He said: "I couldn't *walk* to that theatre. I had to run there."

Cernowitz is a small town, but it had a municipal Academy of Music, and the director of the Academy wrote a serious opera. Nobody outside Cernowitz wanted to produce it; but Cernowitz wanted to produce it, and did. After the first performance (or the 2nd or 3rd) the Burgomaster came on the stage amid terrific applause and presented to the composer 1000 gold ducats in the name of the town. Fancy such a thing in England! Kommer said that all these small theatres (about 400 in Germany or in Germany and Austria) are the origin of talent. Reinhardt started at Salzburg. Some actors look on a place such as Salzburg as the final goal of ambition, after having played much in inns and similar fit-up places.

Tuesday, July 28th.

Kommer came at 6.45 and we were to have gone to a rehearsal of *The Miracle,* but there was to be no choir that night, he found, so we didn't go. I was determined to dine one night at the Horn Hotel with the golden sign, and we went there last night. The food was excellent and cheap and the wine excellent. We talked about the organization of the people's pleasure. Kommer quoted Chesterton as saying that since Dickens no one in England had cared for the people's pleasure because the Tories hated the people and the Liberals hated pleasure. Kommer pointed out how in Continental cities a young man could get decent civilized pleasure for almost nothing, especially in Berlin, Paris, and also in the smaller cities such as Salzburg. But not in London. When he was young in London there was nothing. Everything closed earlier (it closes earlier now) and there are only the night clubs even now, and they are not for the poor. We have the loveliest river, and it is not organized. The restaurants and cafés are rotten, and not *accueillants,* no choice of food and the food bad, little music, and it is so difficult to get to the places—you have to change and do all sorts of things. In places like Vienna, Berlin, and Paris, all such places are easy to get to (especially in Teutonic countries) and the entire population goes out to them on Sundays.

As regards the stage Kommer said that young actors were not supposed to live on their salaries. Parents tried to stop their children from going on the stage, because of the hazardous nature of the career; but once the children were there they helped them to make a start. The profession had a good social standing. He said that German (not Austrian) actors were impossible creatures to live and work with. Outrageous. He said they had twelve German actors in *The Miracle* at New York, and they caused far more trouble than all the rest of the 350 to 400 in the company put together.

I wrote another 1000 words of *Lord Raingo* yesterday morning.

Friday, July 31st.

Wednesday morning, collecting ideas, I went for a walk down stream on left bank and up stream on right bank. Plenty of life going on on these banks; dogs playing in shallows; a dog being caught in current and carried down at a great pace and ultimately getting across. Boys playing in shallows. Fishermen. Old people on benches chatting and making fat poodles sit up too long. Poor women sewing and knitting. Fairly well-to-do young mothers with perambulators, and occupying a whole bench with piles of sewing work and spending a large proportion of time staring admiringly at the baby. Young girls in converse. Water cart (motor) rushing along and creating at first a prodigious dust. I got ideas for my next section; but returned home with the beginning of neuralgia. I worked in afternoon, but my neuralgia got worse and worse, and I stopped after 800 words.

Sunday, August 2nd.

Through Hallern to Golling, a large village full of medium hotels. Lunch at the Alte Post, whose proprietor, Steinach, told me that the hotel had been in the hands of his family for 111 years. Began lunch with the largest trout I have ever seen—caught 2 hours earlier. Golling and other villages near have a character of their own. The gables of the houses face the streets; wide eaves, sometimes a balcony under the eaves with a tiled roof of its own. Brightly painted window frames and shutters, and plenty of flowers on the sills. Plenty of visitors. At the Alte Post were four rooms fairly full of lunchers; we lunched on the *terrasse*. After lunch took a

2-horse carriage to see the waterfalls. The car couldn't go, because the bridge over the Salzach is forbidden to cars. About 10 minutes' drive, and then about 50 minutes to climb steps and things in order to see the 3 waterfalls, one above another. The waterfalls were fully up to descriptions thereof and really most impressive. I have never seen anything to beat this drive for grandeur of scenery. At Werfel we stopped at 4 p.m. for coffee at an outwardly unassuming hotel and had superb coffee and cakes, very well served by a smart, slim, sparkling waitress. Within I saw the kitchen and a chef in a chef's white cap making pastry. It was strange to see this perfection in a village lost in the mountains.

On the way home, between Hallern and Salzburg we came upon a motor accident, collision; the road was unnecessarily blocked for a long time during palavers between the respective owners and drivers and the gendarme. The chief words repeated 1000 times, were *"mein lieber Herr."* Everybody nervously excited but very polite and restrained. After dinner Kommer came along to the hotel with Rosamond Pinchot and 2 German journalists. He introduced Rosamond. A day or two ago he had told me the astounding story of how Reinhardt had seen this society girl on the tender, going to America, and had instantly said: "Here is the girl who can play the nun" (*The Miracle*), and had ultimately engaged her, though she had had no experience whatever of the stage, nor any longing to go on the stage.

I finished *The Kellys and the O'Kellys* yesterday morning: Trollope's 2nd novel, written at the age of 34. This novel is consistently excellent, and Algar Thorold's introduction to it is absurdly trifling and inadequate. The characterization is admirable, strong, true, and sober.

Monday, August 3rd.

Yesterday afternoon I began to read *Anna Karenina* again. And it did me much good, providing the inspiration I needed for my own work.

Tuesday, August 4th.

Bad weather again yesterday. I went out in the morning to get ideas, and got cold instead. The river raged downwards; all shingle banks had disappeared, and the torrent stretched clear from bank to bank. Umbrellas the chief sight in the town.

Wednesday, August 5th.

Another 1000 words of *Lord Raingo* yesterday afternoon, between 5.15 and 7.15, after a bad night. Kommer joined us late at lunch in the Mirabell Garden, among the wasps. After dinner we went to the Café Corso, to hear the Hungarian musicians—Zigeuner Kapelle. These Austrians are gayer than the English. They laugh easily and have pleasant faces and eyes, though grace is not always one of their qualities—except of manner. The men generally have a little thing like a small feather duster stuck, brush up, at the back of their hats. Pants are more and more often embroidered. I saw two country well-off lads on Sunday with a string of silver coins round their waists. The bow-neckties are rather good—bright and with nice patterns, and small. Knapsack carrying, and also by girls, is very common, and pretty heavy knapsacks too. The passers-by are now much less dowdy than a month ago, and one sees that fashion binds after all the whole female sex of Western Europe together—when the money will run to it.

Thursday, August 6th.

At night, with Kommer, to a rehearsal by Reinhardt of *The Miracle*, at the Residenz. I saw a little insignificant man in the gloom which covers the floor, but not the upper spaces, of the vast room; and it was Reinhardt. For an instant he seemed *quite* insignificant. Then at once you saw he was not. He stood well on his feet, had fire and authority, and yet was always quiet and smiling. I was much impressed by him. I also liked much of the acting. This rehearsal was an experience. It lasted till 11 p.m. A dreadful night to drive about the streets in a fiacre behind a very old white horse and a very old driver.

Friday, August 7th.

Yesterday lunch with Max Reinhardt at the Schloss Leopoldskron. The house looked much more in order and "finished" than when I was there last—except the chapel, which was still a lumber room. Reinhardt has great authority—with all his quietness and shyness. Linguistic ignorance separated us, but we got on very well indeed. Kommer says that he still has no idea of time—or rather of what is possible and not possible to do or get done in any given time. What he is doing just now (*inter alia*, rehearsing two plays at once) seems prodigious. The invitation was for 2 o'clock but Kommer said 2.30 would do. Reinhardt arrived at about 2.40; then took some of the guests for a stroll in the garden, and I should say that lunch began about 2.55. He arises at 10 when working, and goes to bed about 4. When idle he gets up for lunch.

Saturday, August 8th.

Kommer was to have come with us to S. Wolfgang; but Franz Molnar and Lili Darvas (star Hungarian actress [1]) had arrived from Munich and were going to S. Wolfgang in the afternoon, and we were asked to join them. But I wouldn't.

We got to the Villa Frida at 3.45, the hour at which Kommer had sworn he would have Molnar there. They came at 4.30. Lili Darvas a languishing nice dark woman of about 30—said by the other women to be surpassingly beautiful. The others kissed her quite passionately. Molnar is a well-set-up *militarisch* man of 50 or more, with near white hair and a monocle. Both were alleged to be able to speak French. They said a few phrases to me, but evidently could not understand very clearly what was said to them. This became tedious; still it was a pleasant tea party. Lili Darvas had a good emerald ring, much admired. She showed ear-rings to match, bought in Venice; and all the women envied her her beauty, her talents, her fame, and the admiration and generosity of the well-set-up, famous, gifted Molnar. It is a very agreeable milieu for a time. But I always wonder what is going in the end to happen to such people.

Monday, August 10th.

I only had 3¾ hours' sleep on Saturday night, and yet wrote 2300 words

---

[1] Molnar's wife.

on Sunday. Kommer gave a lunch, at which we met Hugo von Hofmannsthal and wife. He is a very jolly fellow, about 45 I should say, and looking
younger. 3 children practically grown up, I understood. Just bought his
first car, of which he was most naïvely and charmingly proud. He said
that of course I, being a novelist chiefly, wrote all the year round and
that he, being a dramatist, *worked only in the autumn.* I was delighted
with H. von H.; also with his wife.

Leave tomorrow, by the Orient Express. I shall have been here 33 full
days, and I estimate I have written over 35,000 words despite chronic and
acute neuralgia.

Tuesday, August 11th.

Mrs. Pinchot came to dinner last night. Then we went to a concert of
new composers at the "Big Hall" of the Mozarthaus. Bad for sound.
Then to rehearsal of *The Miracle* in the new Fest-Spiel Theatre. It
seemed absolutely impossible that the theatre should be finished for
Wednesday. It seemed about half done. The organ was working. The
rehearsal very rough. Kommer told me that von Hofmannsthal was about
52; had made a great name by two poems at the age of about 18-20. A
rich man, but after the war without a cent.

This morning I went to a rehearsal of von Hofmannsthal's *The Great
World Theatre* in the still far-from-finished Salzburg Festtheater. I asked
him when he wrote the play. He said in his funny clipped English: "I
wrote it in 1920 (or 21?). There was Bolshevism in Munich and Bolshevism in Buda-Pesth. We Austrians were between the two. I said:
'Shall we turn Bolshevik?' and I said: 'No, I think we shall not.' Partly
because we have a certain natural common sense, and partly because we
have been living happily for hundreds of years. So I wrote the play." The
little speech was rather touching and very charming. All the acting at
this rehearsal was admirable.

The Orient Express came into Salzburg punctual to the minute, and
left ditto. It took us a full 45 minutes to get baggage through the Customs
and to pay for registration, and get passports passed. I got one passport
from an official after final inspection just as the train was leaving. A

tremendous thunderstorm as the train passed through Bavaria. It was scarcely over when we reached Munich at 8.15.

Friday, September 4th. 75 Cadogan Square.

The big new French clock was on the floor in the box-room. She said: "I put it away there because it stuck out on the mantelpiece, and all the curves of the ornament, leaves and twigs and things, seemed to be the same as the curves of my nausea. So I put it away till the nausea has gone."

She saw two nice-looking little boys in the restaurant at Harvey Nichols, and kept on referring to the extraordinary niceness of the face of one of them. At last she said: "I should like my boy to have a face like that." The secret was out.

Friday, September 11th.

She said: "I've never enjoyed things so much. The sky. The mind. He is a happy creature (note "he is" not "he will be"—less than two months gone). This does not mean that I'm happy. But he is. Also he is adventurous. I have a much stronger feeling of the adventure of life than ever I had before. (But she always had it.) When I take a taxi, I'm apt to think of the danger in the traffic, to him and to me. But when I think it over I say: 'This is life. This is adventure.' . . . Of course if it's a girl I shall have to adjust my ideas, but she'll be the same, really. I don't think the name 'Delphine' will suit her." (My random suggestion.)

Sunday, September 13th.

A great fertile spurt of writing lately. Finishing today. I wrote two short stories: "One of These Quarrels" and "The Cornet Player" (for the *Strand Magazine*—10,000 words in all) in nine days. I found the plot of the second one the morning after I finished the first one, and began to write it the same afternoon.

D. said, while we were eating fried roes on toast at dinner last night: "We're eating 'young'!"

Tuesday, September 15th.

Talked to W. J. Locke last night at Garrick. He said he had practically a life contract with Hearsts for serials, going on till 1932. I said if I offered a story for a serial they always wanted it altered. He said with him, never. Once he had his hero try to commit suicide. Hearsts said that they had a strong Baptist connexion, and that readers might object to the hero having a tendency to suicide, and would Locke turn it into an accident (motor car, it was). He did so. On another occasion they wanted the end of a story altered. He said: "If you can get one of the clever young men in your office to alter it I shall have no objection." This certainly was a masterpiece of a reply, and made Duff Tayler and me roar. Of course Hearsts left the thing alone. On another occasion they wanted a tale altered. He replied by cable: "Wife won't let me." He said he worked between 10 p.m. and 2 a.m. and never at any other time. His first story (a short story £2 10. 0.) appeared in *London Society* in 1882, in the same number as an instalment of Wilkie Collins's "I Say No." This is what they call a "link."

Monday, September 28th.

D. said: "I've taken him to a concert and a picture gallery, and a Charles Chaplin film." D. Massingham replied: "He won't want any educating by the time he's born."

Tuesday, October 6th.

Yesterday, the funniest sequel to the great publicity I had over my scrap with the Bishops in the *Daily Express*. Someone starting a new *advertising agency* where the advertising was to be "strictly scientific," wrote offering me the post of "head" of it—managing director. I had no capital to find and was to have a high remuneration from the start. I was so tickled and touched by this that I told nearly everyone, and I recounted it in 3 personal letters yesterday morning.

Wednesday, October 14th.

D. having been much disturbed by revelations of character during a visit to Brighton with me on Monday, could not go to sleep. She told me that her infant had been subjected for the first time to evil influence and was unhappy and uncomfortable; also that he turned over about 1 a.m. However, this experience somehow made her see the relations of good and evil, and how good could creep in when evil had been cast out, etc. Although the whole experience was perhaps an illusion, it was so real to her that it excited her very much, and her account of it was very interesting—especially with all the detail which she always gives.

Friday, October 16th.

This morning I made my will leaving everything to Dorothy except what I have earmarked to give to Marguerite.

Wednesday, November 11th.

I finished Part I (including all the political stuff) of *Lord Raingo* on Monday afternoon, to my great relief. While doing this I could not be bothered to write journals or do anything that I was not absolutely compelled to do. 83,000 words of the novel are now done. Beaverbrook has read all but the last 4 (short) chapters, to vet. it for political correctness, and he is enthusiastic about it, thrilled by it. He only found one small slip in it (about the time at which it would be possible for *Raingo* to leave the House of Commons after hearing a debate). He found another slip; but it wasn't one. He made 2 suggestions, one for altering the wording of a telegram, and the other in a form of address. It is *marvellous* to me that I have been able to do all these complicated politics without once getting off the rails. I can scarcely believe it.

Beaverbrook said he would guarantee the rightness of the politics. He said it was the finest thing he had read for years. Miss Nerney also describes it as "a very fine book." So I am rather reassured. I shall leave it now for ten days while I write an article and work up the libretto of the *Bandits* which Phillpotts and I are doing for music by Austin.

Yesterday I corrected the typescript of a short story "The Cornet Player," which I think is the most original story I have ever written.

1926

Friday, January 1st. Hôtel de Russie, Rome.

Three Madonna churches in Piazza del Popolo. I went into two this morning at 11 a.m. At S. Maria del Popolo, fine church with two good chapels, lovely design, and some good baroque, mammoth music and choir. Quite a congregation. All the high altar lit up by electricity like a booth at a wakes. At S. Maria del Monte Santo, two altars were being served at once. More gorgeous priests. Congregation spread over the floor on chairs, anyhow, as at a drawing-room meeting. Collection being made by a dwarf in a short white thing over black; dirty face; very dark. 80 Santa Maria churches in Rome.

Later I went into the same church (S. M. del Popolo) again with D. Another Mass afoot, but the electric illuminations of the high altar had been extinguished. Why? A larger congregation. We made out the paintings by Pinturicchio, Raphael, etc., and sculpture by Mino da Fiesole. This church ought to be seen again and again. It shall be. We drove up to the top of the Janiculum Hill, for the view of Rome at sunset. It was marvellous, rose-tinted; then the sun disappeared, and the show was suddenly over. Crowds of people up there. Crowds everywhere, for New Year's Day holiday. Then we came home from Janiculum and I wrote 1000 words of *Raingo* in 90 minutes.

One of the chief curses of Roman street life is the hooting of the motors. Incessant and peculiarly strident. If it isn't altered, the population will develop some nervous disease.

Saturday, January 2nd.

Called at American Express Co. Grumbling American woman, repeating grumbles, about not being served quickly at the tellers' desk. If things don't go smoothly American women usually frown and change their sweet tone for a sour. They have the air of wanting to call in the police at once, D. said.

I finished Baring's *Cat's Cradle* at 5.45 p.m. 720 big pages. Its curious fault is that it reads as if it really had happened: a report of actual events. It has taken me 14 days, about, to read.

Going out to dinner, passing a barber's shop. Vision of the barber standing quite away from the half-shaved customer and flourishing his razor in argument.

Friday, January 8th.

After siesta we went for a drive up the Janiculum Hill, and saw Rome. On the way up the driver stopped suddenly and despite protests got out. He said in Italian, pointing: "House of Torquato Tasso, author of *Jerusalem Delivered*. He enjoyed the sun, meditated, and then wrote." I thought this wonderful; it was so naïve and so direct, with a smile. Then we descended to the Tiber, and saw the outlet of the Cloaca Maxima, and the Temple of Vesta and Fortune, and home along the left bank of the Tiber. I then wrote 1200 words (good) of *Raingo* in 2¼ hours. Dined at hotel.

Monday, January 11th.

The Queen Margherita funeral took place this morning. The *maître d'hôtel* had seen it and he described it to us. The electric street lamps on the route were draped in crêpe and lighted. A good scheme, that London would never have thought of. The walls of the streets have been covered with large black appeals to members of various societies to honour the mourning for the Queen. This afternoon, crowds in the streets. Shop-shutters lowered, but the majority of the shops open—with a gloomy, holiday air. But no sign of gloom in the demeanour of the thousands of saunterers.

Tuesday, January 12th.

I began to revise recently written bits of *Raingo* at 7 a.m.

I went alone to St. Peter's. In the past I have been painfully wrong about this church. It has grandeur, homogeneity, and form. Some of the architecture is superb. But the paintings are terribly mediocre. On the whole I was far more impressed than ever. I liked even the façade. The dome seems nothing at all close to. I drove there in a taxi and home in a fiacre. The Romans are worse than the Florentines for strolling casually in the roadway quite heedless of traffic.

Home at 4.10, had tea, and had written 1000 words of *Raingo* before 6.30—although I was rather depressed about the general "feel" of the end of the book. I fear people (discerning persons) may ask: "What is the book *about?*" and I mayn't be able to answer them. I don't know, articulately, what the "idea" of the book is.

Thursday, January 14th.

Neuralgia all night. I finished Gerhardi's *The Polyglots* in the night. This work is too long, lacks shape, and has a few short passages of merely silly jocosity, but as a whole it is individual, original, comical, touching, and full of flavour. In the night I also read a lot of *Candide*. The most amusing novel ever written.

Sunday, January 17th.

A holiday. We did the Forum for an hour and a half before lunch, and as usual I saw lots of fine water-colour subjects. The marble of the portico pillars of the temple to Antoninus and Faustina, in the midst of which temple the Papacy had the damned cheek to build a church. But what a water-colour! We only tackled one small corner of the Forum, and only tackled the surface of that. The interest is prodigious.

There may be a lot of gambling (lotteries) in Rome, but there must be little on racing or games, and not a trace of that newspaper service of gambling which is one of the most striking things in London streets.

Tuesday, January 19th.

Lunch at the hotel. Tea at Frank Schuster's apartment in the Palazzo Cini. Afterwards he and we went to a concert in a drawing-room in a palazzo in the Piazza Paganica. We got there at the stated hour 5.30 precisely, and the concert had begun. It was to boom Mark Raphael, a young East End Jew, with a nice voice and no distinction. The concert party consisted of Raphael, Roger Quilter, and Maude Valerie White. The last accompanied several of her own songs sung by Raphael. She is a very old woman, but plays with immense *brio* and decision. Her eyes flashed, and she sometimes said or sang the words to herself, with her witch-like fallen-in mouth closed. Also she would look full at the singer sometimes, as if to admire or to inspire him. She became extraordinarily young, fiery, and humorous while playing, and made a fine sight. Quilter seemed quite a *sympathique* person.

Friday, January 22nd.

I re-read *Candide,* and was rather disappointed in it. Even on its own plane it is very far-fetched. No construction, and not much material coherence. The hero is a perfect fool, an incredible fool, throughout. The same may be said of *Zadig,* which also I am now reading. Zadig is an idiot. But both tales "read themselves," and are studded with great larks. Everywhere the misfortunes of the virtuous are grossly overdone.

Saturday, January 23rd.

I didn't begin to work till 6 p.m. Lunch at the hotel. Then we went for a drive. Right down right bank of Tiber to the place where I moored the *Velsa* before the war. Much interested to see this again. It was a good spot. Then we drove around seeing Jewry, including the Marcello Theatre, with little shops in its ground-floor arches, odd dwellings above, and apparently large flats in the superimposed modern part—by modern I mean three or four hundred years old. Then to varied odd remains, and we came to an enclosed place where "excavation" was actually in process of being done. This was thrilling.

Since the 1st Jan. the street, traffic-controlling police, newly initiated by

Mussolini, have been very proud of their new uniforms and mackintoshes. In the Corso the horn-hooting seems to be less. But I must inspect this after my novel is done.

Tuesday, January 26th.

I finished *Lord Raingo* at 5.30 today, having written 2000 words in the day. Total length: 130,200 words. I liked the last chapter. Very tired.

Friday, January 29th.

I read *in* the first number of the *New Criterion*, in which are some weird things, including one by Gertrude Stein, out of which I could make nothing; and not much out of T. S. Eliot's essay on what a review ought to be. Aldous Huxley's story "The Monocle" was good in detail, but had absolutely no plot, and is really only a sketch. Perhaps he meant it for a sketch; only I think he meant it for a short story and failed to bring it off.

Saturday, January 30th.

Better night. Six hours in all. I did my exercises at 2 a.m. Then went back to bed and woke up at 5.45. What relief! It was good sleep. Then woke up again. It was 6.40. What relief! I saw the whole world differently.

We went with Martin Wilson to St. Peter's. I was determined to go up to the roof, if not to the cupola. It was very easy to go to the roof—by the lift: which we did. 5 lire apiece. Size of the Cyclopean statues in the top of the façade. Ugliness of them also. Plenty of room to walk about, though much space is roped off. There are dwellings on the roof, and one post-card, etc. shop. Fine views of Rome, campagna, hills, sea-lined. Much of the leadwork very finely finished. But the roof of the nave seems to be tiled. Views of the Vatican and its gardens, etc. Then to the cupola. As far as the Whispering Gallery it is quite easy. Excellent stone steps. The view of the interior of the church from this gallery is very fine and restful. Human dots on the floor crawling about. Letters 6 ft. high. Altar as high as Farnese Palace. Dome as big as Panthéon. Cupola 55 ft. high, as high as a hotel. Ball holds 16 people. But the queerest thing about deceptive size is that the *panes* of the glass windows at back, which seem about 8 ft. high in all, must be each 4 or 5 ft. high and there are at least eight of them one above another. A little world of *guardiani* at the various stages; all very polite. The next stage, to the west gallery (top of the "drum" before the "spring" of the dome begins) is also easy. Floor of church still further away of course. Beauty and fineness of all the mosaic work, with which the dome and drum are entirely covered; the labour of it. I learnt that all the pictures (Raphael, Domenichino, etc.) in the church are mosaic. Only two oil pictures (small) in all church. Climb to cupola fairly easy; but through much of it you have to walk, bent sideways. View from cupola. The whole business is very impressive indeed. The church is a lovely thing.

Sunday, January 31st.

Yesterday I bought a set of tortoiseshell brushes and things for D. We spent a lot of the morning in the Villa Borghese which was surprisingly full of fine and half-fine things. The celebrated Titian, "Sacred and Profane Love," improved as one looked at it. Fine Correggio, and Cranach, Raphael, etc., etc. And curious, interesting minor things. Also fine sculpture, including Houdon's "John the Baptist," in glass. Marvellous. Also "the most richly decorated room in Rome." Perhaps it was.

Miss Baskerville,[1] who seems a very sound, sensible woman, told D. on Saturday night that Mussolini was suffering from some such disease as abscess in the bowels. That no surgeon would operate on him because every surgeon feared the consequences to himself if Mussolini should die under his hands. She said he was really ill, and that many men would simply retire from work in his condition, whereas he carried on three departments of state. There will be a nice mess when Mussolini does die, as he probably will soon.

Wednesday, February 3rd.

After tea I went into S. Maria of the Miracles in the Porto del Popolo, because it was open, and I was too feeble to walk. All at once in a different world (with the lounge of the Hôtel de Russie just across the

---

[1] Rome correspondent for the New York *World*.

street). Church scarcely lit. A few people, chiefly old and poor. A choir boy or acolyte moves about, bowing to altar every time he passes in front of it, lighting a bit of electric light. Then a bigger acolyte, a tall man, appears, and climbs up and does things to the altar. People come in, like the others chiefly old and poor and mainly women, but a few aged men. The priest comes with hands together, and kneels at altar, and begins to chant, and the congregation gives the responses. I should say quite twenty minutes this goes on. It is wonderful how the congregation remembers the responses. Meanwhile the boy, having left bell-ringing to priest, begins to light tall altar candles by a light on the end of a long stick. He has difficulty with some of them. Somebody hidden behind the altar helps with a still longer stick—uncanny effect of this longer stick moving about without hands. At last all lighted. An older priest, only in black—no ornaments—has come and sat at a desk within the choir. Church now lit. Very effective. Then an organ (?American) in a gallery strikes up. It is awful. Also a small hidden choir, equally awful. A tremendously long and monotonous choral business. I left before it was over. I had been in the church 50 minutes at least.

Thursday, February 4th.

Night moderately bad. Finished *Fathers and Sons* article for *Sunday Pictorial* at 6 p.m. At 11.20, D. and Martin Wilson and I went to Palatine Hill, and saw (chiefly) the views therefrom—and especially the dome of St. Peter's, like a pearl (really, in the soft light). It was a wonderful humid day for colour, and of course it rained before we reached Ranieri's for lunch. Livia's house. Tiberius's palace, etc. It seems that in the garden on the top, the State grows all the old Roman plants. I began to get tired *immediately* I began to walk about seeing sights. After lunch I ached in every limb, and I still ache, and I have neuralgia. It is always the same. Before returning to the hotel for siesta we called at a jeweller's to buy a Roman pearl for me.

Friday, February 5th.

I spent a lot of the morning at the top of the hotel garden, which I have never discovered before, after having been here over seven weeks. Marvellous view over Rome, of which I made a sketch. I thought about my new novel,[1] had quite a lot of excellent ideas concerning it. After siesta we took a taxi and drove along dusty and dull and very bad roads to Tre Fontane—the place where Paul's head or Peter's head jumped three times after being cut off, at each place producing a fountain. There are three churches, and if they locate the fountains, Paul's or Peter's head must have very considerably bounded. Two churches were open, both very poor and odd and neglected. In fact—no interest at all—yet it is a place one is supposed to go to!

Saturday, February 6th.

I did a little bit of reflection on my new novel in the church of S. Maria del Popolo. Then at 11.40 we drove to the Lateran museum, and saw the sculpture. The mosaic "unswept floor of a dining-room" is very amusing, and throws a light on Roman table-manners, etc. "Sophocles" equal to its reputation.— Nothing else that *really* remained in the memory, though there are lots of very fine things. We found no pictures at all. Some damaged frescoes. The Christian museum we wouldn't look at. Somehow Rome makes one notably anti-Christian. What chiefly struck me was the desire of the *custodiani* for human society. Of course one may say that all they are after is a tip. But long after he perceived clearly that I had no tip for him, one of them followed me about. I have noticed the same thing at Naples museums. I finished Mrs. Millin's *God's Step-Children*. It is decidedly a good book. We dined with the Sullivans at the Grand Hotel. The atmosphere of the Grand Hotel is as if it is always Sunday there. At another table there was a solitary old woman, fat and ugly and distinguished. I cried aloud at the sight of her entrance—she was so queer, and so impressive. Afterwards in the lounge she had five men, not all old, in tow. She dominated them, talked like a man and laughed loudly also like a man. We learned she was from Naples, and an author. I didn't catch the name clearly. Anyhow I had never heard it before. Not often do you see such an impressive personality.

---

[1] *The Vanguard.*

I returned to reading Chekhov's letters to his wife Olga. They are good, if monotonous. Olga is always setting herself right in footnotes against his false accusations against her of negligence in the matter of writing to him. She is right to do so, but it is funny.

Sunday, February 7th.

As I passed across the end of the hotel lounge tonight the noise of the American accent everywhere was simply awful. The American tourists will overrun Europe like the Goths soon. It is positively frightening.

Monday, February 8th.

After waking about once an hour from midnight to 5 p.m. I arose at 6 and wrote the first scene of a new sensational, comical, moralistic larkish novel, and have been completely exhausted during the rest of the day.

I have gone back to reading Stendhal on Rome. A relief. This book is always interesting.

Wednesday, February 10th.

I found out that an instrument which I had often heard in the hotel jazz band and thought was an ocarina was really a common steel saw, about 20 inches long. The player holds the handle between his knees, and the thin end in his left hand, and strikes or strokes it with a drumstick. Bending the saw raises the note. He can thus, within a very limited register, produce a sort of a tune. It is a wonderful piece of completely idiotic ingenuity.

Sunday, February 14th.

A lovely day and D. *would* go out for a drive along the Via Appia Antica. I told her it would tire and upset her, but she wanted to go, and the advantages of seeing the Campagna on such a day were obvious. The views were marvellous, especially the skies and the other distances.

D. wanted to see it for "the last time." Lots of people take a keen pleasure in the supposed sadness of seeing a thing for the last time. D.

repeated the phrase again and again, probably about twenty times during the afternoon.

Monday, February 15th. Hotel Nettuno, Pisa.

I find that this year I have written more words than I have spent lire, and as a lire is worth 2*d.* and my words ought to be worth nearly 2*s.* each, I should be all right on balance.

We left Rome easily and comfortably for the 11.55 *lusso* to Paris, and got off the train at Pisa punctually at 5.25. A marvellous, cloudless, sunshiny day, with ditto scenery the whole way and smooth travelling.

Tuesday, February 16th.

At 8.30 a.m. I received a note from C. K. Scott Moncrieff asking to see me and offering to show me things in the town. He came at 11.30. Lame, quick, fussy. Very talkative (smartishly) and rather nervous at first but not later. He said that Lucca was only twelve miles off. This was on our way to the cathedral. I wanted to turn back at once and get a car for Lucca, which had always been romantical to me on account of a chapter in Heine's *Reisebilder*. We couldn't get a car in the town. All had gone or were going to Viareggio for the Carnival. However, after an early lunch we did get a car.

At Lucca we got a *carrozza,* and went through the town at walking pace, and saw cathedrals and churches. Very fine and distinctive, and Moncrieff a good guide. A rich town, prosperous, clean, self-contained, and self-sufficient. More so than Pisa. The oil business and farming must be money-making. But I asked for the Bagni di Lucca, made fascinating to me by Heine—and they were twenty miles off. So I was baulked there. At San Frediano, Lucca, it was interesting to see the altar where Francia's "Entombment" once was. Who pinched it and put it in the National Gallery I don't know.

Wednesday, February 17th. Hotel Miramar, Genoa.

Pisa Duomo in morning. As Ash Wednesday, service going on. Large audience of choir boys and *écoliers* and a few schoolgirls and old people.

Many guests of various ranks. The parson began to preach, got up full speed in about twenty seconds, and then never paused or even hesitated for a word for half an hour. Then he sat down and wiped his face, and then, still sitting, talked to the congregation about a collection. When you were close by he was perfectly audible. Twenty yards off you distinctly heard two voices, and still further off you heard three or four voices, a babel of voices, all furiously arguing or wrangling. It was a most curious echo effect.

Arrived at Genoa at 6, on time, soon after a stormy sunset. Hotel here far fuller than we had ever seen it before. I finished Macaulay on the "Wars of the Spanish Succession," and began *Pilgrim's Progress,* which promises well.

Thursday, February 18th.

We didn't go out at all until 3.30 p.m., but I had done a lot of thinking about my new novel. I think I shall call it *The Vanguard.* We drove along the sea front, and then back into the town by the Via XX Settembre. By this time I was dying to write Chapter III, so I continued to drive home while D. walked. I began to write at 5 p.m. and at 7.30 had written the chapter—1200 words. All my chapters are going to be short in future.

I am not very keen on *Pilgrim's Progress.* So far it is too full of minute "similitudes," which are tedious. I doubt whether I shall finish. The question is: Do children read it all? Or do they skip the morality and theology for the more active parts? I doubt whether the book is holding its own in the public esteem today.

Friday, February 19th. Hôtel Winter Palace, Menton.

I wrote 700 words of the novel (*Vanguard*) before leaving Genoa for Menton. A beautiful day, hot. The atmosphere of the Winter Palace is mainly English. The dinner scene in the large restaurant was markedly English. I haven't yet heard an American accent; which is very odd after Rome. The clients neatly dressed if without distinction, and everyone behaving quietly and correctly.

Sunday, February 21st.

An overcast day. As D. wanted to rush off instantly to Monte Carlo, I hired a car (only 150 fr.) and at 11.50 we did rush off. Lunched at Hôtel de Paris, as being the best place (180 fr. with tip). The only person I knew there was T. P. O'Connor, looking very definitely old. Then across the road to the Casino Theatre: *Boris Godounoff.* I had forgotten what this *salle* looked like. Built by Farmer about 1878. The richest, ornatest, gildedest thing in Europe I should think. Full of nudities and semi-nudities, in colours, gold or white. Two of the boxes, very large, look directly away from the stage into the auditorium. The sloping ground floor is well arranged, and 900 people can see very excellently. We were in the back row (87 fr. for 2 seats—not dear). A mediocre but not entirely odious performance. This opera wears very well.

There were some decent people—a few—at lunch at the Hôtel de Paris; but on the faces of most, the consciousness of being correctly at the Hôtel de Paris. We got back to the more agreeable Kensingtonianism of the Winter Palace, Menton, at 6.15, and I went to bed for an hour. We dined late, and the big restaurant was nearly empty.

I finished Macaulay on "Pitt." He is always very instructive, and he has caused me to desert Stendhal, Bunyan, Chekhov, etc. I expect I shall stick to him till I have finished the volume.

Monday, February 22nd.

Fearfully noisy band to tea in the afternoon, and a terrific racket of conversation in the lounges after dinner but happily music in the evening only twice a week. The amount of Puccini played in Italy appals the conception. It is dreadfully vulgar stuff. *Tosca, Bohème, Butterfly, Tosca, Bohème, Butterfly.* Luscious, obvious, easily graspable stuff, all commonplace, with bits of something at rare intervals that is not so bad as the rest.

I read Huxley's Indian diary in the American *Bookman.* Admirably done, but very short. A good example of honesty making the *best* use of trifles. I suppose that Aldous will waste nothing of these Indian experiences. He will use up every bit of it. He certainly throws one or two new lights on India.

My *Things That Have Interested Me* (3rd series) was published on or about the 15th. The reviews I have had so far are quite favourable, some of them very favourable. But the critics are all wrong. They say that this is the best of the three volumes. I think it is the worst.

Tuesday, February 23rd.

Beaverbrook arrived, with Morris Woods, from Nice. Max talked with us for about an hour, and then dashed off again, to Cannes, to meet his mother and Gladys. He said his heart gave an extra beat now and then; but he wouldn't have a big (or a little) doctor for the disease. He had bought James Mackenzie's book on the subject,[1] and stood by that. He said that he was a sure mark for any big and strong-willed doctor, and feared to enter on the career of an invalid. I suggested that he should visit a doctor anonymously; he agreed that that might do. He was play-ing golf daily. Freddie Lonsdale was with him. Max was going on an Eastern Mediterranean tour in the *Mauretania* on Saturday night, from Villefranche. He had taken five cabins and hadn't yet invited any of his guests. He meant to invite them tonight.

Saturday, February 27th.

Reflected in garden for forty minutes after I was dressed. I sat in the sun without moving and yet perspired. This was before 11.30. At noon we started to drive over to La Turbie to lunch with Max and Gladys B. Magnificent drive along the Grande Corniche. The party consisted of the two B.'s, William Gerhardi, and a fellow named Mayhew (with a most singular overcoat)—staff of *Chicago Tribune*. A good luncheon party in strong sunshine, with a tang in the air. Max restless, Gladys delightful, Gerhardi in better form than usual. Gerhardi had met Rothermere last night at dinner for the first time. Asked by Max what he thought of him, Gerhardi sides-splittingly replied: "I think he has a sweet nature." Max roared himself red in the face. Max asked me how much I would take for film rights of *The Pretty Lady*. I said I had got £2000 for *Sacred and Profane Love*. He said he would pay this if he produced the film.

---

[1] *Diseases of the Heart*, by Sir James Mackenzie.

Monday, March 1st.

A lovely and marvellous day of spring weather. We now have "chocolate milk shakes" for tea, from the American bar. They suit me perfectly, and cost 6 fr. each. I finished the volume of Macaulay's Essays yesterday, and began to read it again today. Rather wonderful thing! I can't remember that it ever happened to me with a book before.

Tuesday, March 2nd.

Harriet Cohen came for lunch at 12.45, exactly on time. She had walked up from the station. She said she never spent a penny she could save. She looked older and better. She was just the same as of yore, except that her stories had got more and more dramatic and perhaps violent. When I took her back to the station at 6 p.m. she said that she loved all the attentions she had received at the welcome back, and that she felt she belonged to the public. "We do, you know," she said. Yet she seemed about three-quarters sincere.

Saturday, March 6th.

I returned to reading Stendhal's *Promenades dans Rome.* Then I sat in garden, and thought out next chapter of my novel. We just got back to the hotel at 1 p.m. for lunch. Neuralgia. I slept fifteen minutes, and woke acutely nervous and still neuralgic. I went in to D. and said: "I can't sleep, and I can't work either." She said: "Perhaps you can begin packing my valise." She was sewing. I made no reply, but returned to my room and began to write. I wrote 1100 words—a complete chapter—in seventy-five minutes, and then felt better.

Monday, March 8th. Hôtel de Noailles, Marseilles.

I walked by myself to the Vieux Port; returned and took D. to the same and we walked around. Lunched at Rest. Bristol (under Hôtel ditto). Admirable restaurant. Superb *bouillabaisse.* Then at 4.30 to film *Knocke.* This film, despite serious faults and *longueurs,* was decidedly interesting. Came out into darkness at 6.40. The Rues Cannebière and

Noailles (one street) broad with broad footpaths full of jostling crowds and traffic. For movement and bigness and life it had nothing to learn from the Grand Boulevard. In fact a great scene like a capital.

Wednesday, March 10th. Dominion Hôtel, Avignon.

Today for the first time I knew what the *mistral* can be. It blew strongly, a harsh, cold-warm, dry wind that dries you up and discomforts the skin. Also the town is full of dust. I thought of a longish article on hotels this morning, and I wrote 1000 words of it before dinner, upset though I was by the *mistral*. I think it must be the *mistral* which unfavourably affects the temper and manner of employees here. The *mistral* is *agaçant*.

We drove in clouds of dust to the Cathedral. Closed, but the post-card seller took us by a side door. It is a very remarkable piece of architecture, and not much like anything else. Then we saw the "point of view." Fine. It disclosed the strange interest of all the district around about. A district for centuries "not France." "France lies over there."

After lunch and siesta I went alone to the Palais des Papes. The Palais has little or no æsthetic interest. Its interest is archæological and social. Only one open staircase. All the many others, together with endless narrow corridors, are cut in the thick walls (8 or 10 ft. thick), as it were secretly. And everywhere are little holes, through which everyone could be spied on by somebody else. An impression unpleasant, mean, and particularly medieval.

Wednesday, March 17th. Bristol Hôtel, Paris.

We drove to André Maurois's house at Neuilly. Nice ground-floor flat with garden and two children (boys 4 and 5), the daughter aged 12 had gone to her *"cours."* Portrait of the dead mother on table in drawing-room. She was beautiful. Something tragic about this. Maurois, slim, slight, Jewish; charming; with an open mind; interested, admirably urbane. Agreeable talking. It was all very nice. We left at 3.50, and Maurois drove us to the Faubourg St. Honoré in his car. I dozed. At 6.30

I went out to sample the Champs-Élysées in the half-light, and began to like Paris again. Dined at the hotel. Good. Then to Théâtre Fémina for Bourdet's *La Prisonnière*. Crowded. Heated. People came in half an hour late, noisily. Play began 17 minutes late. Ended 11.45. The first act terribly Bernsteinish and old-fashioned. Nothing to it. But in 2nd act, when it appears that Irene's *frison* is a Lesbian attachment, things begin to look up a bit. But the play was always wooden and antique in treatment; especially in dialogue. It was admirably acted by three women. Mme. Sylvie as the heroine, Irene, was very fine indeed. I had sandwiches at the hotel. Muriel Foster came along, and talked a bit. Alfred Sutro and wife had come along at dinner time.

Thursday, March 18th.

To Théâtre de l'Atelier (Dullin's theater and formerly the Théâtre Montmartre). We arrived after the curtain had gone up on *Il faut qu'une porte soit ouverte ou fermée*. Not a bad little trifle, but it is wonderful how this trifle does survive. It was badly played. Then Marcel Achard's new play *Je ne vous aime pas*. We expected much from this and were disappointed. Nothing *to* it. No idea behind it. Just larking about. The first scene was good. We stuck out two acts (out of 3) and then came home. Alfred Sutro came in with Mrs. Arthur Symons. Mrs. Symons astounded me by her certainty that Walter Sickert was over seventy years of age,[1] and the same age as George Moore. He doesn't look it.

I have now read most of the juice in Becque's *Souvenirs*. Fine things in it. But it isn't really souvenirs. It's a collection of articles. Becque seemed to be interested in all aspects of the theatre—the economic quite as much as the artistic. He has fine plain style for plain articles. There ought to be a full life of the fellow.

Sunday, March 21st. Hôtel Métropole, Calais.

Left Paris by the noon train. Very full. Three *voitures supplémentaires*. At Calais it was blowing very hard, and the sea was covered with white. Of course we decided not to go on.

---

[1] Walter Sickert was, in 1926, 66 years of age. George Moore was 73.

Monday, March 22nd. Hôtel Terminus, Calais.

We walked after breakfast to the Gare Maritime and gradually came to the conclusion that it would be impossible safely to cross today. So, for a change, we engaged rooms at the Hôtel Terminus, which is very Victorian. Good rooms; no w.p. baskets. Then we walked all the way back to the Métropole, quite a mile over rough surfaces—2 miles in all, and lunched and paid the bill and finished packing and got to the Terminus Hôtel at 2.10 p.m. in time to see the steamer come in. No one seemed very ill or distressed. Sleep; much needed. Tea. I wrote a little sketch of *La Prisonnière* at the Théâtre Fémina. We had tea in the station buffet, and ordered our dinner there. Before dinner we strolled on the long platforms to see the evening boat come in. It was twelve minutes late. Terribly cold, windy, and the wind full of coal dust from train engines. Saw the boat, and the people go through the customs, and into the trains for Paris, Rhineland, and Warsaw. Goodish dinner in the buffet. Went to bed early in the Victorian hotel, which demanded that an article should be written on it. I might write the article.

Tuesday, March 23rd.

Another very windy day. I walked out to the sea, and the weather was very bad. I walked quite 4½ miles in high wind and I felt exhausted. But after a rest in a damnable uneasy chair, I began to work in the bedroom and wrote 1400 words of a sketch of Calais in about an hour and a half. Then I went out and saw steamer arrive and three big trains depart. All the trains—Hazebrouk, Brussels, and Warsaw; Wiesbaden; and Paris—were late, and all very sparsely occupied. Station full of black smoke. The bookstall girl shutting up her shop, bending down, her skirts moving in the wind. But the wind was steadily decreasing and it was less cold.

Friday, March 26th. Claridge's Hotel, London.

London shops have a display far inferior to Paris shops. No style in setting out goods. There is simply no comparison between London and Paris in this respect. An article ought to be written about it, but no paper publishing drapers' advertisements would publish such an article.

Sunday, March 28th.

I wrote 1400 words of *The Vanguard*. Or rather I re-wrote them. Still it was a good morning's work. Lunch at hotel. A man's face at the next table puzzled me through lunch; it was Esher's. After lunch Marie Tempest and spouse [1] came and talked to me in the restaurant. She said that before her son was born she drank a pint of champagne at lunch and another at dinner—every day.

After tea we went to the film *The Sea Beast* at the New Gallery; the idea being taken and slaughtered from *Moby Dick*. A filthy and preposterous thing and humiliating to watch. John Barrymore the chief interpreter. A dreadful Hollywood girl as the heroine; obviously chosen for her looks, which were dreadful. This film really did annoy me. We didn't see it all. The immense hall was by no means full; especially the dearest seats were nearly empty when the Barrymore film started (it was a continuous performance). The films of the Boat Race and the Grand National were not bad. The Grand National seemed to be all falls. It seemed most brutal, and I was minded to write an article about it. Also about the Boat Race, which ruins the hearts of so many youths. No. 5 in the Oxford crew this year collapsed before the end, and I expect that his heart will never be the same again. Of course he is branded, with pity, in the papers. He even has headlines. He must have had quite an agreeable week-end.

Thursday, April 1st.

I went out to buy an opera hat, and some flowers for D. Then I worked for an hour and a quarter. We dined at 7.15 in order to go to *A Cuckoo in the Nest* (with Ralph Lynn therein) at Aldwych Theatre. The plot is utterly conventional, and so are most of the jokes. What makes the play worth seeing is the clowning of Ralph Lynn, trying to sleep under the washstand in the bedroom of a lady not his wife. This is very fine

---

[1] She married W. Graham Browne in 1921.

indeed; it is a sort of genius; but then I always liked Ralph Lynn. The acting of Yvonne Arnaud is very excellent. She makes a living person out of the dead lines of Ben Travers. Same for Tom Walls (one of the owners of the enterprise); he gave a most finished performance.

Friday, April 2nd.

To Good Friday *Parsifal* concert at Queen's Hall. Moderate audience, but both circles very full. Moderately bad listless performance. My view of *Parsifal* was confirmed. It has good bits in it. It is spoiled by a silly magical elaboration of a good story; it is pompous, self-conscious, and too long. Still, great things in it. Walked home amid the Sunday crowds. Knoblock and Duff Tayler came to dinner, and it was a very lively evening, in which everyone complained that the others wouldn't give him a chance to talk. Knoblock told one of his best invented stories. He said he was in Greece at a hotel at Easter when an Englishman who knew classical Greek said it was quite easy to speak modern Greek if you knew classical. He said to a servant in classical Greek: "Christ is risen." The man bowed, went out, and came back with the scholar's shaving water.

Saturday, April 3rd.

I am now getting into de Burgh's *Legacy of the Ancient World*. It is not very clearly written, and not easy to read; the man has apparently not a broad mind: but it is packed with the stuff, and though the fellow's writing is a bit ordinary his ideas and generalizations are pretty good and sometimes rather distinguished. In the morning, early, I went into Selfridge's, which ought not to have been open, and bought a pencil that writes in four colours and a combination magnifying-glass, inch rule, and letter-opener. All very attractive, indeed irresistible.

Wednesday, April 7th.

Lionel Barton, one of the founders of the new Theatre Arts Club, came to see me at 12.20 about the proposed production of *Don Juan* at the club theatre in the autumn. He seemed intelligent and was quiet. We discussed producers and I settled on Komisarzhevsky. We discussed the casting of *Don Juan,* and settled on nobody.

Thursday, April 8th.

I finished Christopher Morley's book *Thunder on the Left* yesterday. Much boomed. 70,000 copies very quickly. He even says that it will "literally" make your hair stand on end. Why, I don't know. Some clever bits in it. But it's obscure, ill-combined, and unevenly written, and it bored me.

Sunday, April 11th.

I went up to the Maternity Home at 10 o'c. and we went back to the hotel for lunch and repose. D. and I dined at the Hanover Restaurant. Then we drove back to Welbeck Street, where I stayed till 10.30. I heard D.'s views of the psychology of nurses, and learnt a few things about the atmosphere of a Maternity Home. The doctor also threw light on the mentality of nurses. He said: "Of course you *must* see the humour of nurses." The nurses were admittedly very nice young women, the night nurse particularly.

Monday, April 12. 75 Cadogan Square.

At 9 a.m. received news that D. had slept 4¾ hrs. at 27 Welbeck Street. I cleared up correspondence, and arrived at Welbeck St. at 11.50. Took D. out for a short walk. At 1 I went to lunch given by International Magazine Company to Ray Long. At 3.15 I left the Ritz and went straight up to Welbeck St. I left just after 12.30 and drove home. I met Siegfried Sassoon at the Reform. I was most dramatically struck when I saw the bassinette or cradle full of clothes lying all ready outside D.'s door.

Tuesday, April 13th.

I went up to Welbeck St. at 9.30 and saw the child at 10 a.m., two hours old. She weighed 8 lb. 1 oz. and had a big head.

Wednesday, April 14th.

I arose and did oddments from 7 a.m. I cleared up oddments and answered letters till 11.30 and then drove up to 27 Welbeck St. to see Dorothy. She was in good form.

I began to work again on novel at 3.30, after a lot of fiddling about due to disturbed afternoon sleep, and worked till 5.55, writing nearly 1200 words besides revising a lot more. Then I went up to see Dorothy again.

A few days ago Wells advised me to read *Nature* or to try to read it. This was after I had enlarged on my ignorance of all sciences. He said: "Be patient with it. Give it a chance. After a time you'll suddenly find yourself understanding some article that you've read." So I began this work. It is rather interesting.

Thursday, April 15th.

Breakfasted early, and had a lot of letters about Virginia Mary.[1] Drove to 27 Welbeck Street and arrived there five minutes after my advertised time. 10.15. I stayed till 5 to 11 o'clock. D. was getting on, but not very much.

A great sense of rush all day. I sat in the small drawing-room after dinner, and smoked a cigar, but could not read. I could scarcely look at a paper even.

Friday, April 16th.

These days, going to bed early, I arise at 6.30 or 6.45, or even earlier, and do an hour's work or so before breakfast, and in addition am dressed for breakfast. I didn't dress for breakfast for years, because the *masseur* came after breakfast. I don't have him at present, as my health is so much better (owing to him). Much of my time now, while D. is in the maternity home, is taken up with her and with arranging things for her. I wrote 700 words of novel *Vanguard* in the morning and 800 in the afternoon. I was at the Home by 12 o'clock, and stayed till after 1 o'clock. Then at 2 I drove home—(these days I have to drive everywhere to save

---

[1] The names Arnold and Dorothy Bennett had given to their daughter.

time; if I manage to walk to the top of Sloane Street, it is all I can do)
—and slept and went on with my novel till 4.30. Then I had chores to do.

The baby has to take the air as from Tuesday next, and there is nobody
to take her out, and no perambulator for her to go in. The infant still
squints a bit. Otherwise she is improving daily in appearance. It is astonishing how the nurse can be genuinely fond of the kid. She must be
genuinely fond of dozens of kids every year. She is a very nice woman.

Monday, April 19th.

I arose at 5.45 and began the day. I went out after breakfast and after
fiddling about, and took bus to Victoria and then explored Vauxhall
Bridge Road, Tachbrook Street, etc., while searching for ideas for the
continuation of the *Vanguard*. I found one or two skeletons of ideas for
the novel, and came back fairly satisfied with the morning, but chilly.

Beverley Nichols came in to see me by appointment. I am the subject
of one of the essays in his new book, and he had written to say that he
wanted to look at me again, and get a proper picture into his head. So
I gave him a look and two cigarettes. He left shortly after 4, and then
I went up to Welbeck St. I stayed with D. till 8.10.

Tuesday, April 20th.

I reached the Nursing Home at 12.15. I was very tired, through walking in the Park. But I had got one gleam of an idea for my next chapter.

I dined at Reform with two fellows, and afterwards found Gardiner,
Tudor Walters, Chalmers Mitchell, and a man named Wilson who I
think is Chairman of G.W.R. Walters was extraordinarily informative
and interesting on the subject of the coal situation.

When I came out of the Reform, it was pouring with cold rain. I drove
home and the chauffeur said that 65 was the highest number in Cadogan
Square. I assured him I lived at 75.

Wednesday, April 21st.

I have begun to read *Rhoda Fleming*. Goodish. But he *will* make all
his characters talk smart or epigrammatically, and every now and then

he foolishly tries to justify this smartness by some psychological explanation. Some of the dialogues are very tedious and untrue. Still, there is stuff in the book. Last night I received the English translation of Gogol's *Evenings on a Farm*. I shall read that now.

Thursday, April 22nd.

Headache all day, chiefly owing, I think, to the 1½ glasses of Pommery and Greno 1906 champagne that Beaverbrook gave me. At first I thought I could think (novel), but I couldn't. I meant to go out for an aimless walk, and then I saw that it was the Private View of the Seurat pictures at the Lefèbre Galleries, so I went there. The Seurat pictures want a lot of seeing to appreciate. In the big picture "Poseuses," one thing that strikes you is the loving patience of the execution—equalling Memling's, e.g., the pictures were badly framed, but according to Seurat's own ideas. Then I walked down Piccadilly, criticizing new architecture, to the Yacht Club, where Eric Pinker lunched with me, and gave me news about myself and my market. He had hopes of a play or so being sold.

Then I went to the New Gallery to see the new Jannings film, *Vaudeville*.[1] It is very fine, despite a simple and rather crude story. All the pictures make "designed pictures." I should say the prisoners' exercise was inspired by Van Gogh. Even the empty interiors are like Cézanne. The close-ups are wonderful in design. This is where Charlie Chaplin is utterly beaten by the German film. Jannings is an exceedingly fine actor, too, and puts Jack Barrymore right under. The film lasted 90 minutes without break. I should have liked a break.

Friday, April 23rd.

To Garrick to dine with Duff Tayler at 7. John Drinkwater came in. Chudleigh[2] came in from Squire Bancroft's funeral, and told funny stories of Bancroft's own humorous behaviour at funerals. B. loved going to funerals. While amusing and amused, Chudleigh was both touched and a bit frightened by Bancroft's death. Then Tayler and I

---

[1] Produced in America as *Variety*.
[2] The late Arthur Chudleigh, well-known London theatre lessee.

went to inspect a performance of *Riverside Nights* at Hammersmith. House packed.

Saturday, April 24th.

Reading *Evenings on a Farm* (Gogol) sent to me by Chatto's. Jolly stuff. Classical stuff; now getting a bit *démodé*. I wrote 1100 words of *The Vanguard* at intervals during the day. I lunched at home, after going for a two-mile walk in the King's Road. I went up to the Home about 4.45, and was nursing the baby when Knoblock came into the room and was much taken aback at the spectacle.

Tuesday, April 27th.

I drove to the Sitwell Concert, *Façade*. Crowds of people, snobs, high-brows, low-brows, critics and artists and decent folk. I enjoyed this show greatly. The verses are distinguished; the music (Walton) equally so.

The "scene" (flat) by Frank Dobson was admirable.

Wednesday, April 28th.

The Herberts were taking me to Barnes Theatre to the first night of Komisarzhevsky's production of *The Inspector-General*. Komy produced this as a broad farce—I think rightly. Some said that some of the effects were absurd and wouldn't be understood by a Russian peasant. But I think they were traditional.

Thursday, April 29th.

I went out fairly early, and arrived at Welbeck St. just on 12 to meet the Deputy Registrar of the Parish of All Souls (Marylebone), who brought his official book to Dorothy's bedroom, and filled it up there and we both signed it, and I gave him a £1 in an envelope, and off he went. He had very dirty finger-nails, and was a very untidy specimen of an official. Yet he was a "deputy Registrar." Then I walked down to the Reform and at last got the ideas I wanted for the end of my current chapter.

Friday, April 30th.

Weather still rotten. I went out to find ideas and to go to the private view at about 10.15 after having done chores. I got to the Royal Academy shortly after 11, having walked all the way, not feeling tired. I soon came across Lillah McCarthy. She was with Lady Simon, who left us. Then we began to meet lots of people, from Lady Oxford and daughter Bibesco upwards or downwards. Margot was strangely polite. Alfred Sutro sent his love to Dorothy. Henry Ainley came up, and in a hard clear voice said: "Arnold, how is your daughter?" I said: "I needn't tell you she's the finest kid ever born." He said: "Yes, I've got several of them myself." Robert Hudson and Lady Northcliffe his wife. Mrs. Charles Masterman, I didn't recognize her, she looked so young and simple. I left with great difficulty at 12.15, after meeting lots more people; I was home before 1 for lunch, and hadn't got a single idea for my next chapter. After sleep I stayed in my study till after 5 struggling for ideas, without any success. Then I went up to Welbeck Street.

Saturday, May 1st.

Started on the correction of the 2nd part of *Lord Raingo*. Two hours or so of this, and then I went up by bus to Welbeck St. The miners' strike was on, and the posters said that the Trades Union Council had ordered a general strike in sympathy at midnight on Monday. Great gloom, especially as I had been sure of, and had prophesied, a settlement of the coal trouble.

Immense crowds of labour people in Hyde Park, and long lines of lorries, char-à-bancs, and carts, etc. in the road parallel with Park Lane. All this of course was an ordinary May Day demonstration, but it looked as if it was a consequence of the miners' strike (as it is called).

Sunday, May 2nd.

F. Marriott[1] called to see me. I had written him telling him about my daughter Virginia. He was very kind and agreeable, and told me a lot about Marguerite, but I told him more about Marguerite—including

---

[1] Frederick Marriott, the artist, was a very old friend of Bennett's.

various things that startled him somewhat. I started again on the correcting of the last part of *Lord Raingo* and I finished it before 4 o'clock.

Tuesday, May 4th.

Today was the first day of the general strike. Many more motors about. I walked round to Victoria, which was shut up (both stations), one small entrance guarded by policemen. I heard someone say that a train had gone somewhere during the morning. Yet in the vast empty stations Smith's bookstalls were open. So were (outside) the cafés. The populace excited and cheery, on this 1st day of the strike. No evening paper. News from the wireless at very short intervals, half-hour intervals at night up to midnight. I should think that nearly all theatres would soon be closed. Already today there has been a noticeable increasing gravity in the general demeanour.

Wednesday, May 5th.

No post this morning; no newspaper. Some rain, which will make a lot of difference to workers who have to walk to business. I hear of people walking 12 miles each way; but I doubt it. I saw girls of the Times Book Club staff being sent home in 2 cars tonight at 6 p.m.

Lunch at Reform at 1.30. Upstairs, Gardiner, Tudor Walters, Hedges, Jim Currie, Sassoon, and Lord Devonport. Most people gloomy, but all uncompromising. General opinion that the fight would be short but violent. Bloodshed anticipated next week. Plenty of wireless messages, futile. Typescript printed *Times* and *Financial News*.

Thursday, May 6th.

Another N.N.E. wind. Not a taxi on the streets that I saw. It is now over a week since I did anything on the novel—the last day being Thursday, 29th April. I went for a walk to Brompton Rd. to spy out the land. Eleven buses passed the top of Sloane St. in five minutes at 4.30. Only two of them were "Generals," and both of them had a window smashed. I saw more in the evening. A policeman and a special constable on every

"General." I drove up to see Griffin about *Lord Raingo,* which he had medically vetted for me. He was very pleased with the book.

Dined at the Yacht Club, after some trouble about me not being in evening dress (a new rule I had never heard of). However, I insisted on dining there, and did. Imagine enforced evening dress in the middle of a General Strike!

Friday, May 7th.

To offices of the *New Statesman* at 2.30 for director's meeting. The *New York Herald Tribune* wired me for a strike article to be cabled to New York, 1000 words.

Saturday, May 8th.

I began to write my *Herald Tribune* article at 10.5 a.m. and finished it at 12.30 (1000 words). Lunch here alone. Then to the masseur's, and back at 4.15 to correct my article. Dr. Griffin came at 4.50 to go through with me his criticisms and suggestions as to the medical part of *Lord Raingo.* I was much relieved to find that they amounted to nothing at all. The only *real* one occurred where I had made a temperature go up when it ought to have gone down. This novel is now finished, thank God! It has cost me a lot of hard labour, one way or another.

I've been reading *Le Lys dans la Vallée* lately. I've read about 140 close pages, and I don't think I shall read any more. A few pages here and there are really good. And the story is designed, organized, constructed. But the book is ruined by sentimentalism and *sensiblerie* and eloquence. There are no chapter divisions and many of the paragraphs are far too long. I wouldn't mind the dialogue being stilted, but I object to its awful eloquence. Never was there a woman, really, as angelic as Henriette, and if there was she ought to have been abandoned to a brutal and licentious soldiery. Yet when I first read this novel, perhaps thirty years ago (in a rotten English translation published by Dents) I enjoyed it immensely and thought it was a masterpiece. I fear Balzac is going to pieces. The last time I read *Le Curé de Tours* even that seemed to be rather thin and tedious in parts. Ditto *Le Père Goriot*. I suppose I must try to read *Splendeurs et Misères* again. If that won't pass, I'll try *Cousine Bette*, which I think is the finest Balzac, and if that won't pass I shall denounce Balzac as a back number, to my extreme regret.

Sunday, May 9th.

At 2.35 I was back at Welbeck Street for the final departure and I came away with Dorothy, kid, and much miscellaneous baggage, and was duly received in state here by the servants.

The Messmore Kendalls came for dinner. Owing to strike they are leaving for New York months earlier than they intended. Kendall showed the intelligent American's usual admiration for England's demeanour in a crisis.

During afternoon Osbert Sitwell rang up to know if he could call. He came a few minutes later, with Richmond Temple, and they had tea. Osbert was wound up in a scheme with Lady Wimborne and Lord Reading for ending the strike. Fruit of a luncheon at which Thomas was present. It appeared that Reading had tried to get at Baldwin but had been stopped by Churchill and F. E. The notion of a man of Reading's eminence being "stopped" on his way to see Baldwin struck me as comic. They then both agreed that the thing sounded very improbable. I said that Reading might have reasons for saying he hadn't been able to get at Baldwin personally. I also asked if Thomas could deliver the goods.

Monday, May 10th.

Desperate efforts to resume work of *The Vanguard*, which I have not touched since April 28th. I walked off to the Victoria and Albert Museum just after 10, determined to find ideas for my next chapter. Very few people in the Museum. I sat among the Constable sketches and *did* get one or two notions. My barber said he was going that night to try to get a job on the Underground. He said that in his opinion "Everybody ought to help." This phrase is now a terrible cliché. His opinion was that after this strike is broken strikes ought to be forbidden by law. Needless to say he is very fond of wireless.

Tuesday, May 11th.

I am still sticking to my point with everyone that the calling of the general strike is a political crime that must be paid for. Also that the general strike is revolutionary, that is, aimed at the authority of the Government. How this can be denied when the Unions Council has the infernal cheek to issue permits to goods and vehicles to use the roads and railways, I cannot understand. As if anybody could possibly need permission to use roads except in a revolution.

Desmond MacCarthy rang me up at 7.20 to ask me to sign a letter reinforcing that of the Archbishop of Canterbury and others 2-3 days ago suggesting terms of peace. The essence of the proposal was that the general strike should be called off and the mine-owners' lock-out notices withdrawn *simultaneously*. This didn't seem to me to be right. Then after some argument, especially after I heard that Sharp had signed it, I agreed to sign my name. But my conscience was, and still is, against the idea. However, I think Sharp's judgment is better than mine, and moreover I can always comfort myself with thoughts about the great traditional British policy of compromise.

At 5 o'clock today George Doran startlingly called. He had come by the *Aquitania,* which had arrived a day earlier than he had told me, and had driven up from Southampton. Driving through London he happened to see "Cadogan Square" on a wall and called in. Shows what Americans can do!

Wednesday, May 12th.

The general strike now seems pitiful, foolish—a pathetic attempt of underdogs who hadn't a chance when the over-dogs really set themselves to win. Everybody, nearly, among the over-dogs seems to have joined in with grim enthusiasm to beat the strike. The Doctor called yesterday morning, and even he had been working at "criminal investigations" for the Government. (He spoke of deaths resulting from East End rioting.) Willie Maugham was working at Scotland Yard till 8.30 of a night—I don't know what at. Special constables abounded. I anticipate that the Tory press and the speeches of reactionary politicians will now be terrible.

Thursday, May 13th.

Everyone is still preoccupied with the strike, or rather with what is called "the new strike." Duff Tayler told great stories of his adventurous journeys on the Tube trains driven by swagger youths in yellow gloves who nevertheless now and then overran the platform with their trains, or pulled up too short. Also of University porters with gold cigarette cases and an incredible politeness and fatherliness towards you for your safety. Maugham was what he called a "sleuth" at Scotland Yard. A police car was sent for him always. The first night he worked all night from 11 p.m. to 8.30 a.m. He said the last few hours, after the dawn, were simply terrible, and he couldn't see how he would ever be able to get through them. I don't know what a "sleuth" is.

Saturday, May 15th.

To *Lady, Be Good!* musical comedy at the Empire, Fred and Adele Astaire being the stars. These two fill the theatre, even during a general strike. And they deserve to do so. Also they do it on the strength of having performed in London in only one musical comedy previously—and a perfectly silly musical comedy *Stop Flirting. Lady, Be Good!* is not anything like as bad as *Stop Flirting,* nor is it even as bad as the critics and others said it was. It is bad, like all musical comedies, but it is one of the least bad musical comedies I have seen for a very long time. The Astaires did not please me as much as they did in *Stop Flirting;* but they are very fine.

Saturday, May 22nd. Amberley.

Lovely weather. I walked up on to the Downs in the middle of the morning. Sun. Prospects. Three teams of horses rolling a field. Hawthorn everywhere, a little red, all the rest white. The most insistent phenomenon, however, is the song of birds. You hear that everywhere and practically all the time. I hoped there was going to be a cricket match in the village field close by this house; but there wasn't. Nothing except a few children using the swings.

I finished *Cousine Bette*. It holds you throughout, but it is very high-flown and sentimental, and the good women are far too good, and the bad a little too bad. It becomes melodramatic in the end. The "Brazilian" is used in a manner very effectively dramatic towards the end and at the end. I then began Dreiser's *An American Tragedy,* a book of immense length—2 vols. 900 pages or more. Written in a very slatternly way; in fact dreadfully written. Seems ordinary at first, and in the main is ordinary; but after 40 pages it does begin to hold you. The fellow has a large sense of form, and an eye for things that count with the imagination.

Sunday, May 23rd.

I wrote 1100 words of *The Vanguard* in the dining-room during the morning, after various short strolls. I meant to write another 900 words but somehow couldn't begin.

Dreiser's *An American Tragedy*. I have already read 150 pp. of this novel. The mere writing is simply bloody-careless, clumsy, terrible. But there is power, and he holds you, because his big construction is good. The book quite woke me up last night, just as I was going off to sleep.

Monday, May 24th.

Before tea and after tea I watched the cricket match on the village green between Amberley and a boys' school team from Worthing. It was a good, poor match. Much of the village was present, including our charwoman, in a flame-coloured frock. Children swinging on swings in the corner of the field all afternoon; boys playing a little cricket of their own behind the pavilion.

I read a lot of Jules Lemaître's *Impressions du Théâtre*. Full of plots. I got a notion for a play-plot from his account of a play by Brieux. I also read a bit of Dreiser's *An American Tragedy,* which is still holding me. Also more poems by Christina Rossetti, disfigured by mannerized and dull drawings by her great brother.

Dorothy loves this life, and I don't entirely hate it. But the house is a bit small for a writer and a baby. When I came in this morning to work, Virginia was crying loudly and perseveringly, and the little lawn was being mowed. Fearful row. But I worked.

Tuesday, May 25th.

I heard definitely from Marguerite this morning that she would not agree to a divorce. Couldn't work. I went out for a short walk, past the castle and through fields. The spectacle grew more and more lovely. Suddenly I came to the river Arun and no bridge. A ferry which is not available during·the day, but a man happened to be on the spot, and he ferried me over. At Bury church I learnt that it was three miles to Amberley, unless I went back by the ferry. I wouldn't go back by the ferry. I therefore walked the three miles, and got back at 11.45, tired but in much better health. Also I had picked up some ideas for my novel *en route.*

Saturday, May 29th.

I have now finished the 1st vol. of Dreiser's *An American Tragedy*, and it is certainly in its main features exceedingly good, and true. The psychology again and again strikes you by its fineness and also by its originality.

Monday, May 31st.

I went for a walk at 10.10 along the straight Storrington Rd., and sat on stiles while thinking out my next chapter. I was reading about Scott's methods in the *Times Lit. Suppl.* on Sunday, and it seems he wrote the last chapters of *Woodstock* at the rate of one chapter, or about thirty printed pages a day, consecutively. Well, it is almost miraculous. It must have been 5 or 6000 words a day. And once written the stuff was not re-read or looked at, at all, until the proofs came in. If I could write anything like that I should only work six months in the year. I suppose it's true.

I nursed Virginia for 20 minutes, while D. played a Bach-Tausig Fugue etc. It is very interesting nursing the baby for a short time; but the narrowness of the baby's interests must make it tedious quite soon. I kept the creature very "good."

Tuesday, June 1st.

Tremendous morning's work. In the afternoon we drove out in a Napier car with good springs and bad engine from the Norfolk Arms, Arundel. We stopped a long time at Arundel, while Dorothy shopped. Then to Climping, past Climping church (Norman 13th Cent.) Then via Rustington and Angmering, to Littlehampton. Littlehampton scarcely coincided at all with my memories of it—about thirty years ago. The Sharpes and F. Alcock and I slept there one night, and heard a Norwegian crew singing some songs. Most romantic. And I remembered the softness of the ebb tide, and craft coming down it swirling, and being kept straight by all hands and then dropping a stern anchor on which they could swing themselves straight; then the anchor hiked up again.[1]

Wednesday, June 2nd.

I wrote 1100 words before lunch, and never went out except into the garden for 30 seconds at a time. After lunch I finished *An American Tragedy* by Dreiser. This book must be 250, or 300,000 words long. Taken as a whole it is very fine and impressive. He has held it together everywhere magnificently. It has no humour, and lots and lots of original, true psychological observations. This must be one of the very finest American novels.

I had ordered the complete works of Herman Melville on Monday. They arrived yesterday in three large parcels, of which I only opened two, because I didn't want to begin reading *Pierre* (which was in the third parcel) immediately—not until I had assimilated *An American Tragedy* a bit. So I went on with Macaulay's "Essay on Frederick the Great," which is very good reading.

Saturday, June 5th.

While I was working here in my bedroom, I saw a funeral come up,

---

[1] In 1897.

four men carrying a coffin on their shoulders, and some nice flowers on the coffin, and a few black-clothed villagers of both sexes behind. I wrote a few words, as it seemed, and I looked out again, and the people were coming back, minus the coffin, much disburdened, and feeling easy and free. The burden had been put down in the grave in a very short time.

Monday, June 7th.

I had a most marvellous walk on the Downs south of here this morning. The weather was warm, sunshiny, and dappled with sky-changes of large light clouds. The landscapes astounding. The turf very easy to walk on. I was out just under 2 hours, and saw 3 people, and 2 dogs and lots of sheep. After afternoon snooze I wrote 1500 of novel straight off, before tea. After tea I thought it prudent to do no more.

Tuesday, June 8th.

This day the hatching took place in several of the four nests of house-martens under the south eave of this house. Today I saw in the June number of *La Nouvelle Revue Française* an advertisement of *Le Spectre,* by Arnold Bennett. I expect I wrote this about 27 years ago.[1] Nobody thought anything of it, and I didn't. And yet the very high-brow *N.R.F.* chooses it to begin its campaign for "imposing me on the French public"; (according to the words of Gaston Gallimard, who has now written to me twice). All of which is very strange. I have sent to London for a copy of *The Ghost,* so that I can see what it really *is* like. I know the basic idea is all right.

Wednesday, June 9th.

After a little hesitation, I set to work on a new chapter of *The Vanguard* and wrote 1800 words in just three hours (3 o'c. to 6 o'c.). It meant ten words a minute throughout, and really more than that, because at 4.15 I made my own tea (or rather my own verveine) and partook of the same in a leisurely manner with brown bread and butter. And all

---

[1] *The Ghost* was published in 1907.

this after a rotten bad night. Pride! Vainglory! In the evening (when it rained tremendously) we paddled down to Mrs. Glenister's bungalow. At the end of the evening, she turned on the loud-speaker wireless, *Valkyries* in the room. I don't seem to be able to get over the amazing magic of this wireless device. The music seems to come to you from nowhere, and you wonder where it has been hiding while waiting for you to want it.

Thursday, June 10th.

I have now worked myself into a spell (which may prove short) of mass-production in *The Vanguard*. I wrote 1100 words before tea today in less than 90 minutes, and another 500 words after tea in about 30 minutes. All this, for me, is very quick work, though Trollope beat it practically the whole time, and so did Scott. Before my writing today I went for a walk to Northstoke in rotten, very windy weather, and got caught in only one shower, from which I protected myself under a hedge. About four miles, I suppose. Then after work I went out with Dorothy up to the Downs, and I reckon by the large scale map that we walked at least four miles and a half. It was all very splendid, with skies full of disasters and great distance-effects. This makes the longest walking I have done in a day for years.

I read about half *The Ghost* yesterday. It begins brilliantly, but is not so good later on. But it is all fairly good and an excellent performance for a first book (as I believe it was). I am still puzzled by the *N.R.F.* beginning their publication of my novels with this book, but I am less puzzled than I was before. *The Vanguard* is better than *The Ghost* in truth to nature and in skill of handling material, but that it is fundamentally better in creativeness and verve, I doubt. Neither of them is more than a fantastic lark, nor pretends to be more.

Friday, June 11th.

The novel may be good or it may be bad—but I am doing it easily, and at a great rate. It is not invention that lacks, but rather imagination. John

Cowper Powys walked over the downs from Burpham today, and arrived before noon and stayed till after 5.30. He was delighted beyond measure when I spoke very highly of Dreiser's *An American Tragedy*. He said Dreiser was very susceptible to praise. He said that Dreiser had sold the film rights of the novel for $50,000. Powys is a very sentimental man in many ways. He was rather in favour of the general strike, but gave in instantly to my argument that it was right to squash it; but I expect he is in favour of it again by this time. He has very fine literary taste, except when it is misled by his few prejudices. I asked him about his days (not evenings) in provincial cities in America. He said he did nothing except walk about. He wanted to work, i.e. write, but couldn't work in a hotel bedroom; at least had not seriously tried to. I told him I had written lots and lots in hotel bedrooms and he said that he should try. An untidy fellow, of very great charm.

Friday, June 18th.

I walked out at 9.50 to get ideas, but didn't get just what I wanted, so I came in and instead of trying to write the unkneaded I corrected about 15,000 words of *Lord Raingo* proof. Then I went out for another walk, and got my ideas a bit clearer for *The Vanguard*. I wrote 1800 words of them in the afternoon.

I have begun to read *Two or Three Graces* because Aldous Huxley is coming on Sunday for the night, and I must know something about his new book.

As regards my novel, I now write it straight off without re-reading what I have done or what I am doing. I don't re-read it until a few weeks after it is completed. This will both save trouble and give the thing a better chance in a final revision. But it means keeping your head pretty level while planning and writing the chapters.

Yesterday Ralph Pinker wrote to ask if I would do an article on "Marriage 100 Years Hence" for the *Daily News* at 2s. 6d. a word. I said I would. This is my highest price for journalism up to now. What footling subjects these editors choose! Only the other day I wrote on "What Is the Right Age to Marry" for the *Daily Express!*

Sunday, June 20th.

Dorothy and I went by the meadows towards the Arun, for a bit of a stroll towards noon. After lunch we waited about for Aldous Huxley, who had said he would come soon after lunch. In the meantime a strange man came up to me in the garden—I don't know how he got there, he was merely there—and said he wanted to photograph me. I dealt with him as I do always with these fellows—said we were brother journalists and I didn't *want* to be photo'd and I was sure he would understand. He did: he gave in at once, but asked me to go out and speak to his "art-director" who was outside. So I went out, and we had a most cheery triangular chat for 15 minutes in the middle of the road. Both the men were very agreeable and decent. We parted great friends. Aldous Huxley, driven by Julian Huxley and wife, arrived about 4.45. I didn't recognize Julian. We all went for the "meadows" walk.

Tuesday, June 22nd.

We went in a car to Arundel at 2.45 to shop. I spent the half hour at Arundel in seeing the two principal churches there. The parish church has been the subject of a row between a Duke of Norfolk and the Church of England. After a law case, the Duke got the chancel, and the Church of England got the nave and a solid wall was built to separate them. This reminded me of the soldiers keeping the peace between rival Christians in the big church at Jerusalem.

Wednesday, June 23rd.

My ideas were not sufficiently creative for me to go on with the next chapter of *The Vanguard;* so I went on correcting the last 30 odd galley proofs of *Lord Raingo.* I finished these immediately after lunch. Some portions of part 2 I think are dull, and lacking in drama, being merely descriptive if taken separately. I may, however, be wrong, as I was very tired while correcting them, I was tired physically as well as a bit mentally.

Virginia is visibly growing up daily. She has learnt how to make noises and likes to make them.

Friday, June 25th.

I walked in the morning along my now-fixed Storrington Road, which suits me very well for thinking because it is not distracting, and then I began to write.

Hearing a *Twilight of the Gods* record on Thursday night, I had a mood for really lifting up the love scene between Harriet and Luke today in *The Vanguard:* but I doubt if actually I did lift it up very much.

Sunday, June 27th.

I finished reading *Pierre.* This novel is not equal to *Moby Dick;* but it is full of very fine things, and a most remarkable book. Melville's idea was the grand romantic manner, and when he succeeded in it, he *did* succeed. His humour too is very rich. I think he must have been influenced by Rabelais, though there is nothing Rabelaisian in the book. The pity is he gets so many incidents improbable, when with a little more invention and trouble he might have made them quite probable. Nevertheless, I think it is entitled to be called a great book—even if *manqué* here and there.

Saturday, July 3rd.

We drove over to Tertia's house which she has rented for three months at Aldwick, near Bognor, after lunch. Pauline Smith was there. Very silent. But with more secret fire in her than any of them.

Wednesday, July 7th.

On the whole I think *Buddenbrooks* is a very fine work. But the end seems to tail off. In fact it is definitely unsatisfactory, and is unprepared, and feeble. An accidental death for Hanne, the last of the book's heroes, is not good enough. His mother, Gerda, is kept too much out of the foreground all through the book. She is labelled enigmatic, or mysterious, but the effect of enigma is not achieved by silence. Nearly all the other characters are superbly drawn. The family scenes are admirable. The feeling of the passage of time is achieved. Withal, a certain lack of fundamental emotional power, I think. Anyhow, there might have been more with advantage. It is a book to have read, and I enjoyed it very much.

Thursday, July 8th.

I finished *The Vanguard* today at 4.15, having written 5500 words of it in two days. I began the work on 8th February in Rome; it was very seriously interrupted by the birth of Virginia, and I wrote the 10 or 12,000 words of it all over afresh, and I'm glad I did it. I wrote the last two-thirds of it here at Amberley in 44 days. I have never worked more easily than during the last six weeks.

Friday, July 9th.

Yesterday while waiting at Amberley station for Dorothy's train I was told by the porter that in alternate weeks he started work (now I forget whether it was) 4.45 or 5.15, but I think the latter. He said he belonged to a "band." I found that his band consisted of six, and he played the fiddle. They played for dancing at house-parties, etc., and got a fair amount of jobs in the winter and a few in summer. He said that one night not long since he finished off at 3 a.m. or later, and had to be at work at 5.15 (or 4.45). I asked him if he practised daily. He said no—practice was more necessary when you were learning than later! I said: "But of course it's always an advisable thing, isn't it?" He agreed.

Saturday, July 10th.

Y. came at 6.55 leaving a bag marked in large letters "Foreign Office." In some talk after dinner I found that he had strangely unscientific ideas. Some pamphlet of Haldane's [1] had actually persuaded him there was a prospect in the future of making synthetic babies, and he really believed that some very low form of animal life had actually been made by synthesis. He stuck to it. It had not occurred to him that any such feat would have made an absolutely unique stir in the world, and make such a step in knowledge as no other step could be compared to. He began to argue like this: "But nobody thirty years ago would have believed about wireless." He hadn't seen that the two things were not comparable, wireless

---

[1] Probably *Dædalus*, by J. B. S. Haldane, published in 1924.

being purely a mechanical affair. In short I was shocked by his attitude. Later, he gave in.

Thursday, July 15th. 75 Cadogan Square.

At 8.10 I dashed off to the Savoy for the dinner of the Other Club. This was a very agreeable evening. I sat between Anthony Hope and Archie Sinclair. A. S. told me a lot about religion in Scotland and his own views. Mason was fine on Morocco and Lyautey, etc. Quite a lot of champagne was drunk, and the laughter was most uproarious during the latter part of the evening. Neither Birkenhead nor Churchill could come (being in the House) and Lloyd George had a chill. I stayed till the end, 11.20 or so, and then drove home.

Friday, July 16th.

The other day Philip Nichols was urging that it was undignified for me to write for Sunday papers, etc. But I argued him out of it. I have rather a passion for a big public and plain subjects.

Dorothy and I dined as guests of T. Bodkin at Kettner's; and then Dorothy and I went on to Colefax's for supper, and Bodkin walked home hatless by himself. Berners, A. E. Mason, Christabel Maclaren, Spring-Rice (nephew), Geoffrey Scott, Ernest Thesiger, the Denison Rosses, the McClintics (she is Katharine Cornell, the American actress) and Elinor Wylie (author of *The Venetian Glass Nephew*). I liked the McClintics. *He* is a producer, and had good ideas about plays.

Monday, July 19th.

Dorothy and I had to go to a lunch of Canadian teachers and wives given by Lady Beaverbrook at Stornaway House. Max has brought the whole lot over at his own expense and pays everything. The lunch was well done. Jack Seely, on account of his Canadian political and military connexions, was the chief guest. They were a very decent lot indeed, and I liked them. By the way, they call citizens of the United States "Americans." Max was shy as usual; he gave me a great cynical wink now and then. He even hid himself sometimes.

Tuesday, July 20th.

Eric Pinker and Carl Brandt, his American agent, came to lunch. I got on well with Brandt, and he encouraged me by definite statements that certain publications really *wanted* my work.

Wednesday, July 21st.

We went to the Ruth Draper matinée. A packed and putrid matinée audience at the Garrick, nearly all women. Laughing in all the wrong places—giggling, whispering. Tea-drinking. Ruth is very clever. She is a wonderful imitator, but not much of a creator. Some things, however, such as the Englishwoman showing her garden were splendidly cruel. Others feeble and formless. The observation seems to be exact but superficial. She is highly skilled, and looks nice.

I am still reading *Sous le Soleil de Satan*. It is definitely not good, but I mean with God's help to finish it.

Thursday, July 22nd.

This day Dorothy came "definitely" to live here, and slept in her own bedroom next to mine. Most of her furniture was also moved in.

Tomlinson told me that he was getting on with his novel [1]: but it is very slow—the hardest work, and very difficult. But he seemed fairly satisfied with result. He was in a rather grim and even savage mood at lunch, and quite as deaf as usual.

Friday, July 23rd.

We have a new temporary cook, rather aged. I had ordered a water-ice for dinner. She announced to Fred: "I have poured the water on the ice for the water-ice!"

Saturday, July 24th.

I walked after breakfast to the Tate Gallery, and heard a lot of a very good lecture in the French room on 19th Cent. French painters.

I feel much relieved now that I chucked that blasted book *Sous le*

---

[1] *Gallions Reach.*

Soleil de Satan, which has made such a stir in France—no doubt because the devil is one of the characters in it. It is not a good book; in fact it is a dull book. I am now reading Trevelyan's new *History of England;* which will be a biggish task to finish. Miss Nerney stayed here all afternoon typing out *The Vanguard.* What a factory! I shall have to correct the whole of that in the next few days. It is impossible for me to read as much as I think I ought to read.

Monday, July 26th.

Wakened by a *History of England* falling on the floor at 3.25. I should have had a good night if that damned book hadn't fallen. By strict attention to business, I wrote 1100 words of my *nouvelle,* with which I was not ill-pleased.

Friday, July 30th.

The day began with a heavy shower followed by drizzle, which prevented me from walking and so getting my ideas. So I drove to the Tate Gallery and got my ideas; I also saw for the first time the basement galleries containing many dreadful Sargent water-colours and a whole collection of modern French small pictures, including Braque. I also heard one of the Tate lecturers, not so good as the one I listened to the other day. This was a younger man, and much more of a finicking highbrow. He was talking of Romney, and rather severely. He said that "Romney was often vulgar—that explained why he was so fond of Emma" (Hamilton). True, perhaps, but this young man's style was far too condescending. I wrote 1000 words of my *nouvelle.* I drive it on by force somehow. I really ought to have gone out for a walk afterwards, but I was too tired.

I continue to read Trevelyan's history, but I don't read enough at a time.

Saturday, July 31st.

I walked to Victoria after breakfast, just to see the sight, which was worth seeing. The Bank Holiday crowd was about the size I expected. Long, thick queues in various places of the station, both inside and outside. But all quite orderly. And the sight of the 3rd-class Pullman was satisfactory. Although far more people travel now than 40 years ago, they travel far more comfortably and with more dignity. I saw no crushing and crowding. Nevertheless, it must be quite an enterprise to take a family away, with all baggage, on the Saturday before Bank Holiday. In the late afternoon, when I walked down King's Road as far as The World's End, there was proof that most of London had stayed in London. The side streets of King's Road are at least as interesting as the main road itself. I suppose painters don't paint them more because they can't get a calm "sitting."

I began to go through my books with a small-tooth comb, as I have no more room and there are hundreds lying about, and therefore hundreds must be sold. I hope to finish this job tomorrow. Before dinner and after dinner I read in *Pausanias's Description of Greece*. It is really a tourist's guide-book. Stuffed with guide information, but rather curt. Some of it is very interesting and all of it must have been interesting to people of his own time. I shan't read any more of it, because it is all more or less the same, and because the thousands of proper names are very confusing, and little if anything remains in the memory.

Sunday, August 1st.

In the afternoon I walked up to Hyde Park and the first thing I heard was a military band playing the *Meistersinger* overture. It sounded very odd indeed, all transmogrified, and it was not at all well played. Very few people in the 2½d. reserved seats, but plenty of applause. The Sunday afternoon crowd in the Park was decidedly less than usual. A girl or so sitting by herself bored. Ditto a young man or so. Sad spectacles on a holiday.

I read 60 or 70 pp. of *Gentlemen Prefer Blondes* at last. It is very good in its way, and shows good observation. But it is also very monotonous. I shan't read any more of it.

Monday, August 2nd.

I strolled off in the morning heat to South Kensington Museum to find ideas for the next chapter of the *nouvelle,* and after a time I did find them. As I was sitting in the large front hall to right of entrance making notes, a middle-aged man accosted me uncertainly and asked if I was A. B. I was very amazed and said curtly: "Yes. Who are you?" He said: "Oh, no one. A very humble admirer. I've never seen you before, but I recognize you," etc. etc. He wouldn't go. A shabby man, who spoke English with a marked accent. He might have been some Indian mixture—I don't know. He interrupted my work by a piece of damned cheek, but it is somehow flattering.

In the morning I received a cable from Doran about *Lord Raingo,* in which he said that competent readers "acclaim *L. R.* as the peer of the *O. W. T.*—praise indeed." This was after he had written me not very optimistically about the reception of the book by the critics (on account of its English politics and its war atmosphere).

Tuesday, August 3rd.

I went to the Tate Gallery in the morning, and soon got all the ideas I wanted for my *nouvelle*: I also saw several pictures I hadn't noted before, including Daumier's "The Good Samaritan." This picture ought to be upstairs, and not hidden away.

Wednesday, August 4th.

I had lunch at the Yacht Club. This has now become a regular fixture with me. It will cease soon, and I shall vanish from the club restaurant as mysteriously as I came. I read the first two chapters of *A Pair of Blue Eyes* yesterday afternoon, because my Trevelyan's *History of England* was upstairs and I was too idle to fetch it down and all my Hardys were in my study at hand. I liked these chapters. They were better than I should have expected in an early book. At least I think it is an early book. I had never read it before (I think) and yet it seemed familiar.

Friday, August 6th.

Walked up Regent Street to the Ambassadors Club in Conduit Street to a lunch given by Vernon Mackenzie, the London editor of the *Inter-*

national Magazine company, to meet Anita Loos, author of *Gentlemen Prefer Blondes*. A long narrow table. I was put opposite to Anita. She was all right. We could talk easily across the plank called a table. She is *very* short and slight, and dark. She said she had spent nearly all her life in the movies, writing scenarios. As regards literature, she had given up imitating others (such as Flaubert) because she found she couldn't get her effects with a large vocabulary, but only with a small and very simple one. And so on. Showing that she *had* some artistic interest in the business. She had read philosophy, but had given it up, because she had found it didn't get her anywhere. This is just my attitude. She has large dark tired eyes, and is very much a brunette. Slight tired drawl.

Saturday, August 7th.

This afternoon I finished all except the last big scene of my *nouvelle*. The most difficult part is the one I have just done, and it is not so bad as I feared. I found a new way of getting to the Tate Gallery, via Victoria and thence by tram. It has taken me some years to think of this, but I have thought of it. With luck fifteen minutes will cover the whole thing. I heard part of a good but too detailed lecture on Hogarth as a story-teller, and then devoted myself to the Blake drawings, which I have always avoided here hitherto. What terrific stuff. These in their largeness and simplifications are quite as good on inspection as any for the novelist who is trying to move on a high plane.

Tania Cohen came after dinner. Full of Switzerland and young men and jewellery and noctambulism and discoveries in French literature and herself. She said that to most men women had always to pretend that they had no brains. Of course this is a commonplace of talk, and I have often doubted it. But Tania seemed quite serious. She said she was tired of pretending she had no brains. She said she was very much better—cured, but not yet "immunized" from attack in the future. Very excitable, lively, sympathetic, self-conscious, and also histrionic.

Sunday, August 8th.

I lunched with D. here; and then felt that I must have some adventure.

It was a very nice afternoon, with threatening clouds. I hurried out and taxied to St. Paul's, which is still half closed and no doubt will be for years.[1] Still it is neatly and tidily half closed. Immense flock of tame pigeons on the piazza, being fed. A congregation (sparse) assembling inside for a service. I then took a bus for Hackney Wick. I thought that would do as well as anywhere. But before I got to the Wick I saw buses going in the opposite direction to Blackwall Tunnel, which I had never seen. So I got off, and took one of these latter, and went all down the Burdett Road into East India Docks Road to Poplar, and I saw big steamers and even a fine 3-master, and a huge home or hostel for sailors. Incidentally the top of the slope leading to the tunnel. The thoroughfares are superb in width and very clean, and I noted lots of very interesting things. The East End keeps on till you get to Aldgate when it stops all of a sudden, and you begin to see Theatre Ticket Agencies. I should have been late for tea if I had not taken a taxi at St. Paul's again. But all the round trip to and from St. Paul's—I should think about 10 miles—I did in buses.

Thursday, August 12th.

I had a great desire to go and see what the other side of the river was like opposite the Tate Gallery, and so by tram and bus, I went. What a quick change there is immediately you cross. Stone setts instead of wood or asphalt. *Many* more horses than the N. side. Much more noise, more dirt. More physical labour. There are various big factories just close to Vauxhall Bridge, not to mention the railways. A great press of road traffic. Semi-slums. I walked up several semi-slummy streets, such as "Italian Walk." Then I went back over the bridge—at once calmness, quiet, and no horses. Very dramatic. The whole escapade only took me a little over an hour.

Saturday, August 14th.

I soon began to think about my new short story this morning, and I

---

[1] The choir of St. Paul's was closed for repairs on the dome, April 1, 1925, and was opened again by the King on June 25, 1930.

wrote 500 words of it this afternoon. But I was very tired in the afternoon. I walked up to the Wallace Collection, across the park, in the morning, and had a look at some fine pictures.

Today was the first day of the last Test Match, and the weather was all right for it. It is strange how I can keep up my interest in big cricket, seeing that I haven't been to a first-class match for very many years, and have only watched village cricket—and even that only very spasmodically.

Monday, August 16th.

At 11 a.m. I suddenly went off to the Oval to see an hour of the 5th and last Test Match. Crowd very quick to take up every point. Every maiden-over cheered, for instance. Women fainting here and there. Attendants to look after them. Cricket cautious and very slow. Great roar when Woodfull's wicket fell. Met the Sword brothers, the elder of whom accosted me. Short talk with them. Heat of the crowd. Great difficulty of seeing anything at all, even by tiptoeing and craning.

I read several stories in *Stories of Crime and Detection*. Poe is the best. Austin Freeman next. Conan Doyle poor. Bramah far-fetched and unimpressive. These people have an idea and seem to be without the imagination or the skill to use the idea. Of the new people I think Austin Freeman is certainly the star.

Tuesday, August 17th.

In spite of interruptions I wrote 1300 words of my new short story before lunch. A hot day. Later in the day I decided on the title of my *nouvelle,* to wit *The Woman Who Stole Everything*.

Viola Tree was bidden to lunch for 1 p.m. She was very good, strange, bizarre, vague, and original as usual. She has a most marked and often very sympathetic individuality. She hated the Lido, where we are supposed to be going.

Saturday, August 21st. Royal Albion Hotel, Brighton.

We came down to the above hotel by the 3.5 train. Dennis and May Eadie were in the train. Dennis excessively gloomy about the theatre. Yet he is a charming and an honest man, and we like him.

Harry Preston came to see us in the restaurant, and began his proceedings by giving me three very good Corona cigars. At least the one I smoked was very good. I gave him a cigar—the first thing I have ever given him.

Sunday, August 22nd.

At 4.35 we hired a car and went to take tea at the Lewises, The Grange, Rottingdean. About 10 or 12 people there. Sir George Lewis had ridden two hours on the Downs, had bathed, and had played tennis. Both Sir G. and Lady Lewis curiously and naïvely house-proud and garden-proud. The garden is fine, with various lawns and good trees and fruit. Lewis explained how he had bought a hill on the Downs in order to preserve a view unspoilt. He has 71 acres of his own. He is very agreeable as an Oriental is agreeable. Lady Lewis also was most agreeable; she kissed Dorothy like anything at parting, yet had scarcely known her before. They were extremely hospitable. I had quite a chat with Sir G. and Lady in the former's little room where he works—for he always works. They were most insistent on me arranging for German translation of my books.

Monday, August 23rd.

A misty morning. Yesterday at dinner a man walked across the dining-room and thanked me for writing my books. He then wrote a note and sent it to me by the *maître d'hôtel,* apologizing for his bad form. In this note he excused himself by saying that he had just parted from a son— gone to Singapore for five years. I think he had had too much to drink.

Elizabeth Lewis came for lunch, and Harry Preston had a special grouse cooked for us. Harry, wife, and child drove us to his country house, beyond Burgess Hill, for tea, and we had to have eggs for tea. It is a small house, with large grounds. The kennels are his pride—bull-terriers. He was very "down" on Alsatians, which he said were the rage but were very treacherous and soon reverted to the wolf.

I have been reading *A l'Ombre des Jeunes Filles en Fleurs,* and I still maintain that it is a bit on the dry side, though very good. It doesn't impassion *me*. I shouldn't care much if I didn't read any more of it. It lacks juice. It has almost no concern with anything except analysis of views and feelings—especially snobbishness. No landscapes, no furniture, no corporate life. No general "feel" of things. This sort of business satisfies Walkley, but it could never satisfy me, in a novelist.

Tuesday, August 24th.

Very little reading today. Idleness is the death of reading. So is industry.

Thursday, August 26th. 75 Cadogan Square.

At 11 a.m. I bused and walked up to Charing Cross Road and bought *Lamiel*, a novel by Stendhal that I had never seen, and couldn't remember ever having heard of; also Vollard's little book on Cézanne, which is very interesting; also a selection of the writings of Charles Maurras; also an Ital.-Engl. Engl.-Ital. Dictionary. Then I came home again, somewhat sated, and had lunch with Dorothy. Then I bused and walked to Hammersmith for the Lyric Board meeting, where I was told that the author of "Tommy Make Room for Your Uncle," composed in 1876, had come into the theatre to hear his own song sung, and was pleased with the performance thereof. Such is life.

Noel Coward and Molly Seton Kerr came to dinner. I was once again very pleased with Coward. I think he will come through in one way or another. He is a serious young man, with a sense of humour. He would have nothing to drink at all, except water. And he left early—10.35— because he had an early rehearsal tomorrow. Imagine it!

Sunday, August 29th.

I was determined to write another impression, and did so, though it took me some time to get a subject. I walked down to Albert Bridge to get it, and I got it, and came back and wrote it.

I seemed to spend a great deal of time reading Wells's *William Clissold,* of which I nearly finished the first vol. I also nearly finished Stendhal's *Lamiel.*

At about 5.15 Dorothy and I went out for a City excursion. We drove to St. Paul's Cathedral first, of which the front was in the usual Sunday mess; a fearful litter of paper, and kids feeding the birds, and hawkers: all extremely untidy, slatternly, etc. Even offensive. The inside was as it was the last time; but I saw the dreadful Watts's pictures. Also "The Light of the World." It is all pretty dreadful, and I suppose it will remain so for years—until the repairs are at last finished. Something ought to be done about the front space on Sunday afternoons.

Then we walked on to Southwark Bridge and on to London Bridge (both very empty) and had a good look at Adelaide House (by London Bridge); this is a rather remarkable office building, done under strong American influence. It is very interesting. We saw also a number of alleys and lanes. Then from London Bridge approach we took a bus to the Bank, and at the Bank another bus to Sloane Square.

We then dressed and went to the Savoy Café for dinner. Hadn't been there since last December. Saw Golding Bright and wife. The latter started immediately to talk of the baby and thence jumped to her own baby (killed in the war, I think). "He'd have been thirty today, if he'd lived." She was absorbed in babies. She's 65, and thinks always of her son.

Monday, August 30th.

I finished reading *The World of William Clissold,* vol. 1, and I thoroughly enjoyed it; it held me; I read it with gusto. So in the evening I wrote to Wells and told him so.

I finished the *Lamiel* of Stendhal during the night, I also read a lot more of Vollard's *Cézanne.* This book gets better as it goes on. I leave it behind me with regret. I read the opening of *The Regent,* and was so struck by its solid and amusing excellence that I had another copy found for my own use, and I am taking it away with me.

Tuesday, August 31st. In Simplon-Orient Express (between Paris and Brigue).

I left with Dorothy at 10.50 a.m. The journey went very smoothly. No delays. The sea quite smooth, and lovely weather throughout. We drove across Paris to the Gare de Lyon.

The nights on these trains are still barbaric in their arrangements. *Why* should one be awakened at 5 a.m. because one is entering Switzerland. We only go through Switzerland, etc., etc. Sleep is exceedingly difficult. Still, I got some and Dorothy got more. Dorothy read a lot of Galsworthy. I read some of *The Regent*. Parts of it are very good. But there are dull parts in it, too.

Wednesday, September 1st. Hotel Commercio, Venice.

After a long journey (beginning as regards this day with a heavenly breakfast at 7 a.m. in the train and brightened by the sharp self-consciousness which one has after a bad night, and proceeding by Lake Maggiore and Garda) we arrived at Venice at 5.21, only six minutes late. We plunged straight into a gondola. We liked the Hotel Commercio because it is not in the least the *genre* Palace. The scene on the Piazza, and in the small square (giving on the Canal) where the big band was playing, were simply marvellous at night. Unique.

Friday, September 3rd.

At Florian's we met the Lee Matthewses and many more, a Miss Beauclerk, who wrote the *Green Pavilion* (or some such title—I forget). And I went and sat for a bit at Dulac's table, where I was to meet and did meet, Dulac.[1] He assured me that he had promised Puccini some old Chinese tunes for *Turandot*. He forgot the matter, and Puccini wrote and reminded him. Dulac then composed some Chinese tunes himself, and sent them, and Puccini used some of them. Then to *terrasse* of Florian again. Lots of acquaintances. Band playing Wagner on a marvellous temporary bandstand in centre of Piazza. Sudden shower of rain. *Terrasses* emptied in a moment, and colonnades crammed. The band seemed to have been magically dissolved away by the rain. It was all very wonderful.

---

[1] Edmund Dulac, the Franco-English artist and illustrator, is also a musician and a maker of bamboo flutes. The title of Miss Beauclerk's book is *The Green Lacquer Pavilion*.

I heard that a film company is paying the city a million lire for the right to use the city as a background.

Saturday, September 4th.

I had an appointment with Alf Mason[1] at Florian's at 11.30. Previously I had seen Dulac and Miss Beauclerk, etc. Alfred and I went off in his gondola to see the Accademia. A fine gondola all black and gold with the funny extra furniture of a chair to match. Very comfortable. I was rather disappointed with my first view of the Accademia. The pictures seemed to be too exclusively Venetian, and I could not see Titian's "Assunta." We stayed there till exhaustion set in, and then went by small canals to Ristorante Bonvecchiato for lunch. Picturesque and good. Then we walked and got lost, until suddenly I saw a street I knew, close to this hotel. But I could not have found my way back to Bonvecchiato though it could not be more than a third of a mile off.

Saw Mrs. Lindsay in the Florian colonnade and she re-introduced me to Lady C., who wanted me to exert myself to get the O.M. [Order of Merit] for George Moore. She said that Balfour was favourable but would never actually do anything to help anyone.

Sunday, September 5th.

We hired a gondola this morning and went to Church of St. John and St. Paul and then to the small Church of Something dei Miracoli, very grand and quiet, but not thrilling. Then on to Grand Canal, which we came down, seeing all the flags and carpets exposed to decorate houses for the Regatta this afternoon. It was certainly a most wonderful and lovely scene. We also inspected two hotels, the Europa and the Britannia, with a view to moving from the Commercio. We liked both of these hotels, and at the Britannia were offered the apartment where Verdi had composed *Rigoletto* (a bad opera) at 450 lire a day. We could decide on nothing, as nothing (except the Verdi) was free.

---

[1] A. E. W. Mason, the novelist and playwright.

Thursday, September 9th. Hotel Britannia, Venice.

A heavy day. After buying sandwiches, etc. we went off in a launch to Torcello, calling on the way home at Burano. Torcello church is exceedingly fine as to the interior, and the adjoining church interesting as an exterior. There are some low reliefs of animals in the former which are lovely, but, as they were not mentioned in the guidebook, of course we could not guess the period with any accuracy. Tourists would be most uncomfortably helpless without guidebooks.

Burano is the lace place. The women work in the doorways of the houses, over coloured paper upon which the pattern is printed or carboned. We saw one old hag with her hair hanging down; she was doing nothing. Portraits of *il Duce* on all the walls. The launch had a deckhouse with flowers and hand mirror, and was quite nice. Two hands, both very charming. We dismissed the launch at the Lido, and saw Mason, and had tea there, and we then came home with him. Both of us completely exhausted by a long day out, we got home broken at 11. No sooner was I in bed than my mosquito canopy fell down and the wooden frame gave me a good crack on the head.

Saturday, September 11th.

We went to the Scuola di San Rocca to see Tintoretto and Titian. It is, however, impossible to see these pictures owing to them being very dark and hung between great windows which dazzle the eye and darken the pictures. So we couldn't appreciate them. Two great thrills today. The Bellini altar piece (tri-partite) in the Frari church this morning, and this afternoon we went to the Giovanelli palace, and saw Giorgione's "Storm" (of which I keep a reproduction in my bedroom). Marvellous! Unhuman. So rich and full and harmonious. Finer than I had hoped for. The palace has a tremendous series of communicating salons, with a huge ball-room. All heavily furnished, with much ugly stuff, but rich. The hundreds and hundreds of candles had been turned to electricity. We went in a 2-man gondola, and went home by the lagoon to the Piazzetta.

Sunday, September 12th.

I arose at 6, said good-bye to Dorothy 7.50, and caught the 9 a.m. train for Milan. I read Galsworthy's *Silver Spoon* most of the day, finishing it before dinner. It held me, and I thought it very good in its own limits. I think most of the press criticisms are too severe. The criticisms of Wells's *Clissold* are much too severe.

Tuesday, September 14th. 75 Cadogan Square, London.

Pauline (Smith) lunched here and rested and took advice, and then went back to the Royal Court Hotel to change for dinner. She dined here at 7.5, and I took her to the first night of Margaret Kennedy's and Basil Dean's *The Constant Nymph* at the New Theatre. Mary Moore (who takes some of the swag) was in a box. Literature was highly represented by Wells, Maugham, Galsworthy, and myself. The first act of the play was masterly; but Galsworthy insisted that it was all good, which it was not. 2nd act inferior to 1st, and 3rd inferior to 2nd. I liked best Coward, Mary Clare, and Helen Spencer (who played in *London Life*). The performance lasted three hours and a quarter at least, and the atmosphere of the theatre was stifling.

Friday, September 17th.

Jane Wells and the Swinnertons came for lunch, the same being a farewell lunch to the Swinnertons previous to their departure for United States tomorrow. All three were in the greatest form. F. S. told terrible stories of the literary world. He promised to correct his statement in the N.Y. *Bookman* to the effect that Max was the original of *Raingo*.

Rudolf Kommer dined with me at the Garrick Club. He told me that *The Great Adventure* was supposed to open with Pallenberg and a fine comedienne, in Berlin on 25th, but he had cabled and written urgently to get it postponed for a week in order to allow for more rehearsals. He said that the 16 days allowed for rehearsing was an average period in Germany, where runs are shorter than here, but that it wasn't enough for *The Great Adventure*. Kommer has done the translation himself. He is very keen on translating *The Pretty Lady,* to which he gave the very highest praise, and which he said would have a greater success in Germany than it had had in England or America.

Saturday, September 18. Cherkley Court, Leatherhead.

I left for Cherkley [1] at 2.45 in a car, and after various stoppages *en route* by thickness of traffic, and losing our way several times after passing Leatherhead—I arrived at 4.15. At first I found only Jean Norton, on the veranda. Then Max appeared. Only the three of us to dinner. I indulged in champagne and peaches and dozed during a film which Max inflicted on us. This film, entitled *The City of Sin,* is certainly the worst film, from the point of view of intelligence, that I ever saw. But it is worth seeing because of its deliberate exploitation of public ingenuous religious feeling and its own staggering ingenuousness. We saw only parts 1, 2, 3, and 6. But I wish we had seen it all. It has to be seen to be believed. After this I felt much better, and quite wakeful. A lot of newspaper talk, especially about journalists. I was undecided whether to go to bed or to wait up for Noel Coward, who was due to arrive (fast car) at 12.15. Time passed. I didn't go to bed. Coward arrived just after 12.30 quite fresh. At 12.50 I said: "Well, having glimpsed him, I'm going to bed." But we all went to bed at the same time. 2 a.m. This is twice this week that late bed has happened to me. I was vexed with myself. But I argued: Why not break out sometimes, and suffer a little! As a fact, I had quite a good night.

Sunday, September 19th.

Arose and ate apples and shaved and had breakfast in room. Noel Coward greeted me out of his window, and ultimately got downstairs. He and I had a long talk about personalities before the others appeared. Tea and talk. Talk afterwards. No exercise. No walking. No games. Lloyd George and Miss Stephenson, and Sir Warren Fisher (head of the Treasury, I think) and Lady Ebury came to dinner. But the *clou* of the evening was the Arnold Dolmetsch family, who came to play. We heard them playing while we were finishing dinner, and one by one we popped

---

[1] The country house of Lord Beaverbrook.

into the drawing-room to salute them. Father is just like a gnome, hair all over his face, and a strange, clear, pure, impish, masterful glance. Maureen is the sister of Sir Harry Johnston. Adolescent boy of about 19, girl of about ditto, and a younger boy who was much bored. They all play all the instruments; some of the instruments very beautiful. Music of the highest class—all 16th and 17th cent., admirably played. But the terrible feeling of a family ruled by a man who had only one idea in his head—an idea about one particular kind of music, and scornful of anything else on earth. Fanatic Lloyd George put his oar in all the time, and spoilt the atmosphere completely by his blasted all-knowing geniality and determination to show knowledge which he didn't possess at all.

Tuesday, September 21st. Eltham, Torquay.

I left at 11.30, and caught the noon express to Torquay. Shared a compartment with two middle-aged gentlemen with out-door faces, about which I propose to write an article. I had been rather gloomy and preoccupied before, but as soon as I had written down the notes for the short article I felt better. Emily Phillpotts met me, to my great surprise.

Adelaide was rather quieter than usual, but had little bursts of talking. We had a tremendous literary and social powwow—just as usual—interrupted by a short view of the garden. This powwow went on from 4 to 7, without a break, and it will certainly be continued tonight.

Wednesday, September 22nd.

I began to write an article about the journey yesterday at 7.30 a.m. after quite a fair night. I fear for my projected average of 1000 words a day for the year. I am already a day behind it.

Last evening, we listened extensively to the wireless. It soon gets boring, in fact as soon as one has got used to the marvel of it. All sounds are somewhat falsified—thickened. Still, it is all, very marvellous.

I wrote an article during the day, in three instalments of time. Talk with Eden in garden, about "shop" matters. He goes on working rather harder than ever. He says he has nothing else to do, and would vanish if he didn't work. Adelaide also is a great worker. She said that in London she goes to bed at 10.30 (and lies awake thinking) and gets up at 7.30. Works at desk most of morning, walks before tea, and works after tea.

Saturday, September 25th. 75 Cadogan Square, London.

I met Ida Miller, to whom I think I gave her first permanent job, on *Woman* about thirty or more years ago, this morning in Sloane Square. She seemed to have changed little. She must be sixty at least, and is still in full work. She asked me if I saw Mrs. Goddard at all. Mrs. Goddard was on my staff before she was married, and I remember her husband, a lawyer's clerk, standing me a lunch so as to get me to agree to a furlough for her while she had a baby. She was very young and very beautiful. "She's a grandmother now," said Ida Miller. "Twice a grandmother. And just the same sweet nature, and just as young." I was staggered, because I had always thought of her as a young girl.

Tuesday, September 28th.

I got out earlier than usual with the intention of walking about till I found the ideas for the story of which I had the germ. I walked to Hyde Park Corner, and then by bus to Piccadilly Circus. Then up Shaftesbury Avenue and down Charing Cross Road, where I bought three books, and thence to the National Gallery, of which I saw that the re-arrangement had been proceeding still further. The N.G. is now very fine indeed. I've seen no Gallery equal to it. In some rooms every picture is a masterpiece. By this time I had got quite sufficient ideas to enable me to start the story.

Wednesday, September 29th.

Michael Morton came by appointment to see me at 6.30. He said that *Riceyman Steps* had been refused by practically everyone in the West End, except Leon M. Lion. Lion was prepared to do it (as he was having a great success with Galsworthy's *Escape*); but he would only begin it by a series of six matinées, and he would get it into an evening bill if it succeeded at matinées. Lion instanced the case of *Tiger Cats*. He gave four matinées of this and lost £900; then, after an interval, put it into the evening bill and made £5000. Morton believes in him. He says he is sure he wants to do fine things. Lion has a brother in the City, who said to Morton: "I haven't read this *Riceyman Steps* play, but I believe it's a fine thing, and I'll back it with my money, and I don't care if I lose over it." Etc. Lion is to play the miser. A month ago I should have said that the notion of Lion playing the miser was absurd, but after seeing him in Galsworthy's *Escape,* I should say that he could play it very well indeed. I gave my consent to the scheme.

Monday, October 4th.

I was up at 6.15. I got into the streets about 10.10 and got back before 11, and finished my short story by noon. Then I did letters and organizing, and walked up to the Reform Club for lunch, and was greeted by the brothers Sitwell in Pall Mall; they stopped their taxi in order to smile on their uncle. Lunched with Page, Roch, Hedges, Cecil Harmsworth, and Spender. Spender and I startled the table by our interest in clothes and tailors. Spender said that there was nothing between a really high-class tailor and the ready-made people. I agreed.

Saturday, October 9th. Sanclu Hotel, Ramsgate.

I corrected two articles and a short story, and went for a walk in the morning, and felt that I had had an idle morning. I read about 50 pp. of Osbert Sitwell's first novel, *Before the Bombardment.* It is inscribed to "dear, good, uncle Arnold from a nephew." Well, it is difficult to read. Very brilliant, or perhaps "rather" brilliant; but it doesn't seem to have much form, and much individual interest. The man *describes* characters instead of showing them.

Several more criticisms of *Raingo* yesterday. Better than I expected, for I had expected a bad press, as there is no really "lovable" or "pure" character in the book.

Sunday, October 10th.

Drove to Sandwich. A really antique feeling about this place. Streets such as Delf Street. Most curious the moment you begin really to think about it inquisitively. Happily a few barges get there still, up the stream, and seem to live in fields. All churches round here are closed on Sunday. We got into the one at Sandwich because some unfortunate children were imprisoned there for the afternoon service, but the fine church at Minster was closed; reminding me of my Sunday visit to Truro to see the monstrosity of a cathedral there: which was closed entirely.

Monday, October 11th.

We stopped in Harbour Street, at Hyland's and at Woolworth's. I had long been in need of a new cigarette-case (second) and I got one here for 6*d*. Dorothy received from me a pink pearl necklace with earrings to match, and 1 hat pin and 2 morocco (?) books to hold snap-shots of Virginia—the whole costing 8*s*. 6*d*. No wonder that this shop has a great fascination for the majority of human beings.

We hired a car and drove to Canterbury. I was rather overwhelmed by the size and the grandeur of the Cathedral. Unfortunately we got in while a service was going on. This service, as far as I heard it, was un-accompanied choral, with bursts of organ. I never heard any other words but "Amen," and I must have heard this twenty or thirty times. The composer had made a speciality of sustained notes, and some of these were certainly droned for quite a minute at a time. The music seemed to me to be banal, but the singing good. The organ music played later was far more banal. As soon as the service was over, the people waiting to inspect the place were let loose, D. and I among them. Yes, I was much impressed. The choir is original (William of Sens). Stained glass often fine. Also the place is full of history. The town also is "pullulating" with history and antiquity. We got home just after six.

Thursday, October 14th. 75 Cadogan Square, London.

At 3.30 I was in the film world at Wardour Street, and I saw my titles for Part I of *Faust* roughly on the screen. T. told me that the Censor would not pass the word "damned," and when in another place, I altered a phrase to "Show me woman in the flesh," he said that the censor would not pass that either. It is a great and fearful world, the film-world.

I drove home in a taxi. This is the first time I have taken a taxi either to or from the film world. I am getting fonder and fonder of motor-bus riding.

Friday, October 15th.

After a bad night, I began to write the story "Murder," and did 1300 words before 12.30, and another 300 words in the afternoon. This was probably due to having an absolutely simple and clear plot, which I fashioned by myself and which is probably rather original. The idea of writing a story about a murder, however, came from Dorothy. I then went up to the Garrick Club for a luncheon given to William McFee. I expected only a few male authors, but there were several women authors —Margaret Kennedy and Marie Lowndes (between whom I sat) and Tennyson Jesse. McFee seemed quite a nice Englishman, a bit changed by residence in U.S.A.

Sunday, October 17th.

I printed the title page of the MS. of *Riceyman Steps*. I have no longer the interest keen enough to do an elaborate title page; but for a simple one the title page I did was not too bad. Then, as Dorothy was in her boudoir writing for her life, it occurred to me I needed exercise and would go out for a walk. So I walked smartly to Westminster Cathedral, and sat therein for a quarter of an hour while the evening service began. I got back at 7.40 and began to write notes.

Monday, October 18th.

The new nurse was very glum when I greeted her yesterday morning in Dorothy's bedroom. Later in the day she definitely gave notice. The new under housemaid also gave notice, saying she wouldn't have come if she had known there was a nurse and that she never could get on with nurses. Dorothy thinks the real reason is the absence of the marriage ceremony; but I don't. The first attack of neuralgia I've had since August 15, nine weeks' freedom. No wonder I have been able to work better and easier.

I finished reading *La Prodigeuse Vie d'Honoré de Balzac* by René Benjamin this morning. It is a very good book indeed. Strange that at the end he makes no reference to the (alleged) fact that Eve de Hanska's mother was in the house on the night of Balzac's death! I want this book to be translated into English. As regards *Lord Raingo*, 35,000 copies have now been printed (three editions) and 18,450 had been sold up to the end of last week. That is to say, within ten days of publication.

Tuesday, October 19th.

Dentist. I got a taxi in Portman Street and drove home and immediately wrote the last 400 words of my story "Murder." Then I boasted of this to Miss Nerney and walked and drove to the Reform Club for lunch—with Gardiner, Page, O'Brien, and Tudor Walters. Sachie Sitwell's book [1] came and I read a lot of it. Superb bricks out of ghastly straw. We didn't have much dinner as we were going to a supper party at the Lewises. Evening in Dorothy's bedroom reading. Arrived at 11.30. On arriving I was taken straight to talk to the Infanta of Spain. George Lewis was on the other side of her. I wondered whether I could leave her without outraging the *conte;* I stayed a long time while others were curtsying to her, etc.

Wednesday, October 20th.

No work today. I went out at 11 a.m. determined to think "up" an idea for a short novel, and I did gradually think of one. I went first of all to Charing Cross Road; but couldn't find any book that I really wanted to buy. I bought one or two little brochures on French and German painters, and a copy of the *Calendar* with a grotesque article by D. H. Lawrence in dispraise of Wells's *Clissold:* a terrible revelation of Lawrence's childish and spiteful disposition.

Thursday, October 21st.

The Wellses, the Robert Nicholses, Geoffrey Scott, and Alec Shepeler came for dinner. This party went off admirably well and was a great

---

[1] *All Summer in a Day.*

lark. Wells is quieter than he used to be, and Nichols is even noisier than he used to be. There was a lot of argument between him and H. G. Wells in which H. G. was quiet and effective. Geoffrey Scott is a very good talker, and very charming. He really has a brain, and isn't afraid to give its results to you at once. I turned out my light at one p.m., having read a bit of Ludwig's newly published life of the Kaiser.[1] This seems to me to be a pretty goodish sort of a kind of a book.

Friday, October 22nd.

I began to get one or two (I think) real ideas, for a short novel. I also finished reading Phillpotts's *Brunel's Tower,* in the afternoon. It is done in the classical manner and tradition, but needs a relief of which there is no indication. I now have two others to read before I can write the introduction to the *édition de luxe* of his novels. It is interesting to find, in the copy of *Brunel's Tower* which he lent me to read, how he has perceived ten years after writing the book, that it was too long and might be cut with advantage. This copy is marked in red ink for the printer of the new edition, and I should say that a good 50 pages have been cut out of it: which here and there makes it rather awkward to read.

Dorothy and I dined alone, and at 9.30 "Lulu" Powys[2] and wife (Alyse Gregory) called to see us. Handsome fellow, in a pinky red shirt and necktie. I only found out after a time that she had been editor of *The Dial.* We asked them to dinner. All the Powyses that I have seen have almost exactly the same manner. They are enthusiastic in pleasure. When I praised Dreiser's *American Tragedy,* three of them used exactly the same phrase with the same enthusiastic intonation. "Oh! I *am* glad. Dreiser *will* be honoured." Etc. But they are a highly brainy lot. We had a most interesting two hours of talk that was a bit more good than small talk.

Saturday, October 23rd.

A short walk. At 12.15 we drove down to Cherkley to lunch with Max

---

[1] *William the Second.*
[2] Llewelyn Powys's *Verdict of Bridlegoose* was published this year.

[Lord Beaverbrook]. Max asked me if I would write a weekly article on books under my own name for the *Evening Standard*. I didn't give a definite answer, but what I said and didn't say was not far short of a consent.

We were leaving about 5.10 when Mackenzie King, the Canadian Prime Minister, came in, for the week-end. He was very polite.

Sunday, October 24th.

I went out for a walk in bright sunshine a little before 11—down to the river, stared at the river, and returned, having heard congregational singing in a "conventicle" *en route*. I visualized the inside of the conventicle and hated the thought of my youth. Then I read *Nature*, profitably.

Monday, October 25th.

I found that my article in yesterday's *Sunday Pictorial* on British weights and measures must have created quite a stir, for I received three letters about it from strangers by first post this morning. I expect they will have lots at the offices of the *S.P.*, and I hope to God they won't send them on to me. It is just this kind of an article which does interest the sort of mind that writes to the papers or to authors.

We dined at the Galsworthys': the Herberts and the Margaret Kennedy Davieses were there; and it was a thoroughly good evening. Left at about 11.25, having of course meant to leave earlier; it was then snowing. Indeed there was about an inch of snow on the trees; but it had all gone by the time we were half-way down Hampstead Road. John Galsworthy was very quiet. He talks, but talks more quietly than ever. He is now enjoying a greater success than ever—far greater, he is the idol of Germany, the United States, and England (and I expect that tends to quietude of demeanour).

Tuesday, October 26th.

Went to Chekhov's *Three Sisters* at the Barnes Theatre. Well, I was bored frequently. Did I enjoy myself? No, not on the whole. Was I uplifted as I had been by an even gloomier play *Rosmersholm*? No. It seemed to me that often the author was wilfully pessimistic. He is certainly very monotonous, and all his plays that I've seen have the same tone. A decent Philistine man, sitting just behind us, said at the end of the second act that he had been disappointed and bored. But he liked Act III better, and Act IV still better. On the whole Chekhov had succeeded with him. When I got home I found a great letter from H. G. Wells about (1) *Raingo*, (2) Dorothy, (3) my "renewed" home, (4) my improved health. It was a fine letter.

Wednesday, October 27th.

At 6 o'clock Lewis Mannering came, to ask me to open the new establishment of Foyle the bookseller. He then asked me for a play for the Q. Theatre, and then we talked about religion and books. He is a great collector of folk-lore books. He got 20,000, was bored, and sold "every leaf" and then he began again and has now reached 5 or 6000. He is a firm rationalist. Not a bad sort. We had André Maurois, Ethel Sands, Jeanne de Casalis, Ruby Lindsay, Alfie Mason, and Arthur Waley to dinner, and it was a very good party. Maurois showed extraordinary charm. He spoke once more about doing a French very free adaptation of *Milestones*. I encouraged him.

Thursday, October 28th.

I read half of Carl Van Vechten's *Nigger Heaven*. A short book. Quite good, and interesting in its exoticism. Yet I fear that when I finish it I shall say that there is nothing in it, really. It is very nicely done. This is true of a number of American books. The difference between Van Vechten and Theodore Dreiser!

Saturday, October 30th.

I began to think more seriously about the plan of my new novel. I had already got the moral background for it: the dissatisfaction of a successful and rich man with his own secret state of discontent and with the evils of the age. I wanted a frame. I walked about three miles this morning, and about a mile after tea, without getting a really satisfactory idea; then as I was lolling in my "easy" about 6.30, I suddenly thought that I would extend the role of the *train de luxe,* which I had thought of for the scene of the opening of the story, to be the scene of the whole of the novel—so that the entire time-space of the novel will only be about thirty hours or so.[1] I didn't go any further than this; I had enough for the day. Then quite a lot of reading of Ludwig on the Kaiser. This seems to me to be rather a great book.

Sunday, October 31st.

At 12 Dorothy and I went for our Sunday morning walk in Hyde Park. We had a rendezvous with Nurse and Virginia inside the Stag gate, and lo! the rendezvous was kept punctually by all parties. Dorothy wanted to know whether I felt that it was "undignified" for me to walk by the perambulator in the crowded Sunday morning Park! I did, however, refuse to push the vehicle myself.

Tuesday, November 2nd.

Beaverbrook and Jean Norton came to lunch. I agreed with Max to do a series of book gossip articles for the *Evening Standard,* beginning next week. Then I rushed off to Wardour films, and spent a final 2¾ hours on *Faust,* finishing it except for passing proofs of titles and choosing some types. Thorpe asked me to do their next film, *Carmen,* and said I had done splendid work for them and been very patient. I said that I had lost money on *Faust,* in the sense that I could have earned more by other work in the same time. True. But the advantage of doing titles is that they involve no brain-strain.

Wednesday, November 3rd.

Dorothy and I dined at home, and we went to the first night of Eden and Adelaide Phillpotts's new comedy *Yellow Sands.* The first act was pretty good, but played nearly an hour. If half an hour had been cut out of it, the play would have *been* better and *gone* far better. I think it will

---

[1] His novel *Accident.*

be half a success. The mischief with it is that it is not dramatic. Every act stands almost still for about 90 per cent of its time.

Thursday, November 4th.

I walked to the Savoy Hotel for the luncheon given to Osbert Sitwell prior to his departure for America. 60 people at this lunch. It was exceedingly well done. Birrell, aged 76, was in the chair, and as lively as a boy. He made two excellent, informal speeches. I got home at 4 p.m., and did oddments and had tea, and then went to bed for two hours 5.15 to 7.15. We were ten minutes late for dinner at H. G. Wells's, and H. G. himself was eleven minutes late. The Shaws were there, and Frank Wells, and Marjorie Craig (H. G.'s morning secretary) and the Leonard Woolfs. Both gloomy, these two last. But I liked both of them in spite of their naughty treatment of me in the press. Shaw talked practically the whole time, which is the same thing as saying that he talked a damn sight too much. After dinner he and Dorothy and Virginia Woolf and H. G. formed a group and never moved. I formed another group with Charlotte Shaw and Jane Wells, and never moved either. I really wanted to have a scrap with Virginia Woolf; but got no chance.

Saturday, November 6th. Eastern Glebe near Dunmow.

I forgot to put down a thing I heard Edmund Gosse say at the Sitwell lunch on Thursday. He said, in reply to a remark: "Who is James Agate?" Considering that Agate is the dramatic critic on *The Sunday Times,* of which Gosse is the chief literary critic, and that they are both weekly contributors . . . ! André Gide sent me one of 25 author's copies of *Le Journal des Faux Monnayeurs.* This gave me the idea of keeping a journal of my next novel. I may do it. But I ought to have begun it a month ago.

We caught the 2.34 from Liverpool Street to Bishops Stortford where we were met by Jane Wells and Frank, and driven to Easton Glebe,[1] where H. G. Wells received us. Mr. and Mrs. C. R. W. Nevinson had already arrived.

---

[1] Residence of H. G. Wells.

Sunday, November 7th.

A lovely, a heavenly morning; very clear and sunshiny. But very damp underfoot. I breakfasted with Jane Wells at 9.15 and then others came down. Then H. G. and I and D. went for a walk in Easton Park and the grounds of Easton Lodge, and saw a heron on the lake, and heard from H. G. a *résumé* of Lady Warwick's political life, wrong in certain details. We came back, and H. G. and I changed, and all six of us (without the Nevinsons) played ball games for 50 minutes. Fine lunch, with 3 ducks and a hot apple pie. After which, sleep, which enabled me to miss the tennis. There was some tennis and some bridge and some Schubert trio on the gramophone, and some yacht talk, and some tea—with rose-leaf jam. The day (outdoor) was now over, and all we had to live for was the fireworks postponed from wet yesterday evening. H. G. disappeared for about 90 minutes after tea. We thought he was reading or asleep. But at midnight he told us that he had suddenly had the ideas for continuing a novel that he hadn't touched for a month, and so had gone on with it.

There was not much intellectual activity about the day, but there was a feeling of latent activity.

Monday, November 8th. 75 Cadogan Square, London.

The Wellses' house soon emptied this morning. First Frank Wells went off in his midget, then the Nevinsons went off in their 5-year-old Morris. And then we went off with H. G. and Jane in their Talbot, H. G. driving. He drives better than he used to do, but is still nervous, and cannot forbear from talking about his tactics. The drive as far as the South end of Epping Forest was delightful as regards autumn colour.

Wednesday, November 10th.

Ellery Sedgwick (editor of the *Atlantic Monthly* and now also a rich publisher) came to lunch. Sedgwick is a very agreeable and well-informed fellow, with a proper curiosity about the general situation in England, as to which he is rather pessimistic.

Saturday, November 13th.

Gale, rainy windy showers early. Rain all day till 8 o'clock. I drove in driving rain to the Tate Gallery, in order to think over my novel, and saw some good English pictures. There are indeed some fine ones. The elder of the two Tate lecturers was very good on both Blake and Rossetti. He pointed out the humour in Rossetti's water-colours, and he very well explained their origin. Then I wrote some more notes for my novel—to be called, pro tem, *Accident*. Also I found names for two of the characters.

We drove, still in rain—or had the rain just stopped?—to the Lyceum for the first night of the Russian ballet. The whole highbrow and snob world was there, with a good sprinkling of decent people. The spectacle was good. I liked *Petrouchka* as much as ever, and *The House Party* more than ever. I begin now to understand the latter. It is all Sodom and Gomorrah. The *Swan Lake* had much applause: a fine old-fashioned example of Petipas's work. Orchestra better than usual. Immense auditorium packed with the elect and with candidates for election.

Sunday, November 14th.

I corrected my article on E. Phillpotts, for his limited edition. I think very little of this critical exercise: I hope it will help to sell the edition; but I doubt whether anything will overcome the general public objection to peasants in fiction. This was always strongly against Hardy's success, too. If Phillpotts had dealt with the bourgeois, he would have been accepted as one of our leading psychologists. However, it doesn't matter, anyway he has made the public accept two bucolic comedies at once. Dorothy and I went out to meet Nurse and Virginia in the Park and we did meet them, punctually, and walked with them. Virginia was very wakeful and had a most mischievous, even dangerous look. There will be trouble with that child. Mrs. Belloc Lowndes, Dorothy Massingham, and the Bertie Powyses all came for tea and to behold the baby, and the baby behaved perfectly.

Monday, November 15th.

Duff Tayler and I lunched together and discussed his sick leg, and the

future of the Lyric, Hammersmith. He had an idea for burlesquely pro-
ducing one of the old melodramas, such as *Sweeney Todd*. So we walked
at once to French's and bought six old melodramas, of which we each
took three. I drove home, slept, and read *Sweeney Todd* and half of *Black-
Eyed Susan*. I decided *Sweeney* would do, but *B.-E. Susan* would not.
Elizabeth L. came to early dinner, and we took her to the first night of
The Would-Be Gentleman at the Lyric. This was rather less awful than
I had feared: but it was pretty amateurish, and the recommendations
of Duff and myself had not been carried out with any thoroughness.

Tuesday, November 16th.

After lunch at the Reform Club, upstairs, Sir George Paish came across
and talked to us about the world situation. I taxed him with being gloomy,
but he soon proved to us that he wasn't. He said it was highly dangerous;
but he thought the danger was so serious of a complete smash that the
bigwigs would never allow it to come to pass. He said that the head
Governor of the Bank of England, Montagu Norman, was first-rate, and
was also very courageous. Also that the finest banking mind in England
was Lord Revelstoke (a Baring); he was pessimistic because of his vast
knowledge—especially of history. He said that American bankers were
not to be named with European bankers: they had been only national
bankers: national banking was easy compared to international ditto.

Friday, November 19th.

We went to the Gaiety Theatre to see *Just a Kiss*. A rotten musical
play, with a terrible chorus, and not enough music. Ranalow, the chief
singer and a fine singer, had only one song to sing. Happily he is also a
fine actor (though untutored). It all seemed to me to be a bit sad. Generations of actors and actresses (in that same theatre, or in one on the
same site) always talking and singing of love and fornication and kisses
and drink, and always in a piffling childish way.

Saturday, November 20th.

Another day when rain prevented me from taking exercise. I taxied up to the Ambassadors Theatre for the rehearsal of Michael Morton's *Ricey-man Steps,* arriving at 10.40. We rehearsed until 3.5 p.m. and then ate a good snack of chicken, tongue, and salad, and admirable claret, in Leon M. Lion's dressing-room.

I got Leon to give up his terrific dying scene and to substitute a simple death; also to agree to Elsie and Joe being seen in the background at the end. He objected for a long time—"Believe me, my dear Bennett, I'm not thinking of myself and my part—I'm thinking only of the play," etc., etc., but gave in ultimately. Gwen ffrangcon-Davies showed charac-ter, both as a woman and as an actress. There was nothing really remark-able about the rehearsal. Just the usual display on the part of nearly everyone concerned; the failure to exercise imagination—to realize that in certain circumstances people could never do what the producers were making them do.

Tuesday, November 23rd.

Showery. Bleak. No rain later. Misty. Chilly evening. Chores in early morning. I wrote a letter to the *Daily Mail* in reply to Birkenhead's criti-cism of *Raingo* in that paper, and I signed it before I left home. After I left, the *Mail* telephoned that they would like an article at 2*s.* a word, as well as the letter. They said the letter was too good to lose. So, by tele-phone from the theatre, I agreed to both. I much enjoyed writing both the letter and the short article. I love a friendly scrap in the press.

Wednesday, November 24th.

Dress rehearsal of *Riceyman Steps* at Ambassadors Theatre. It actually began at 10.45. Rather good. It ended at 2 o'clock, and was on the whole satisfactory. Athene Seyler cried. Nicholas Hannen was impressed. A stout middle-aged man spoke to me afterwards and said: "I don't know you, Mr. Bennett, but your play is most moving and impressive, etc." I said: "But I haven't written a line of it." He said it was all my material. I learnt afterwards that this was Horace Hodges, the actor. I wanted to be alone (with the *Manchester Guardian*) and so I went to Arthur's restaurant (Leicester Square). It was full, but I got a table after a mo-

ment. I then returned to the theatre and had speech with various persons
and saw more bits of rehearsal, and then I slipped away and left everything to Michael Morton.

Thursday, November 25th.

Dorothy was at the 1st performance of *Riceyman Steps* at the Ambassadors Theatre. She arrived home shortly before 6, with a very gloomy
account of it. Said that the miserliness was far too much *insisted* upon
instead of being revealed, that the audience was chilled and not at all
responsive; in short, that the thing was a failure. Which did not surprise
me; though I think that Dorothy was perhaps a little over gloomy. She
also told me that the old nurse had run after our beautiful new nurse in
the street and told her something that made her think she ought to leave.
Wanton mischief-making. The new nurse said that she could not tell
Dorothy what the terrible thing was!!!

Friday, November 26th.

I began my novel *Accident* this morning at 11 o'clock. More about the
trouble with the nurse. Dorothy went out with her and the perambulated
Virginia, and came back hoarse with talking. Nurse said that anything
known to one or two nurses in the Park was soon known to all of them.
I expect that nurses live for this kind of gossip. Of course the previous
nurse must have told the great tidings. The present nurse said to Dorothy: "At first I couldn't understand why they looked at me in such a
queer way; I thought my petticoat must be coming down." I perceive
that the nurse world is a world of its own. Nurse told both her sisters,
and her mother and father know. She said: "Mother and father are
good-living people and they go to church." Strange—or not strange—
that all our friends accept the situation without a murmur, indeed with a
sort of eagerness, but the servant class does not seem able to accept it.

Saturday, November 27th.

Two good days' work. Dorothy and I dined at home. Afterwards came
in Eric Kennington and Mrs. ditto, Arthur Waley, and Alec Shepeler.

Eric K. is very shy, but he is a delightful man. Eric brought Lawrence's[1] £30 book *The Seven Pillars* to show me. It is not very good book-making; very *fine* illustrations in it, many of them coloured, and lots of lovely drawings by Roberts. But most of the illustrations are thoroughly out of place in the book and spoil the look of it. It seems that Lawrence has kept Kennington and Roberts, not to mention Wadsworth, pretty busy on it for several years. Arthur Waley has great knowledge and great charm. He went home on his bicycle—no overcoat, and a dank, chill night.

Monday, November 29th.

I didn't finally wake up till 7.58, very rare occurrence, as I had had very few breaks during the night. *Daily Mail* article by Birkenhead on me, in which he practically accused me of lying.

I went downstairs and wrote my reply to Birkenhead in the form of a letter to the *Mail*. When I took it to Miss Nerney, she said that the *Mail* had telephoned for an article: so I crossed out the Sir, and Yours truly, and called it an article and charged £60 for it.

Wednesday, December 1st.

When I opened the *Daily Mail* this morning I found that Birkenhead had made no further answer to me; so the incident is now, I suppose, closed. The press has been very generally in my favour. I had prepared some heavy artillery to kill him if he had continued the fight.

Mary Borden wrote an article in the *Standard* (as a retort to my criticisms of her) advising the young to take no notice of the work of H. G. Wells and myself. She is a clever woman, and was clever enough to ignore my criticisms of herself.

Thursday, December 2nd.

As I had not got my ideas clear for the next chapter of the novel, I went out for a walk after finishing correspondence and oddments, and

---

[1] *The Seven Pillars of Wisdom* by T. E. Lawrence (Aircraftsman Shaw), from which *Revolt in the Desert* was later published separately.

walked to the XXI Gallery in Durham House Street, Strand. I found my ideas on the way all right. The XXI is a very dark gallery. Exhibition of Cosmo Clark's pictures of Black Country. I wasn't awfully pleased with them, but I bought one because I'd known Cosmo as a baby and was an old friend of his father's.

I walked all the way to the Savoy Theatre for the dinner of the Other Club. Birkenhead came in, and we were very affable to one another, and everybody laughed about the just finished scrap between us in the *Daily Mail*. Afterwards he was most friendly and asked me to lunch with him alone. Reading was in the chair, and the dinner was the most agreeable that I remember of this Club. I sat next to Charles Masterman and opposite Alf Mason, and we had a great time. Afterwards I went and sat next to Jim Garvin. He talked exceedingly well, and is full of knowledge and ideas. Churchill and Jack Seeley came in very late, long after dinner. Churchill said to me: "Receive the congratulations of Tom Hogarth" (over my row with Birkenhead). There was a great deal of *Raingo* throughout the evening.

Sunday, December 5th. Royal Albion Hotel, Brighton.

Walter Sickert and wife (Thérèse Lessore) and Cobb and Schuster and Wylde dined with us at the Royal York. Sickert (now aged 66) was in great form, especially towards the end of the dinner and later when we all came over to this hotel and sat in our sitting-room. His wife was very quiet and dark and sweet, but far less quiet than when I sat next to her at dinner at Ethel Sands's a year or two ago. Sickert said some fine, sound things. He explained to us exactly why he liked Leader's pictures. But his pose is increasing of admiring the public as a judge of Hart. I said that what he said was only half true, and he said, "Yes, but there is a great deal in it."

Monday, December 13th. 75 Cadogan Square, London.

To the Hotel Cecil for the grand political Liberal party dinner in honour of Vivian Phillipps, chief whip and organizer of the said Party. Earl Grey in the chair. It was quite lively at our table. Grey made a very good and really weighty speech of 45 minutes. The others were all good, but in a class inferior to Grey. Grey very short-sighted. Nearly all the white-haired politicians behaved as usual at these things, just like kids—pleased to death at the slightest "hit" or comedy platitudes. Beaming all the time.

Wednesday, December 15th.

Lunched with Swinnerton and Sherwood Anderson. The latter outrageously untidy and long grey hair, all over his eyes, etc., blue shirt and darker blue silk necktie in the arty style of the 90's, with a pink-stoned ring to hold the tie; still it looked rather nice—save for its evil arty associations. He had sound sense on lots of things, and I liked him.

Sunday, December 19th.

I seemed to have forgotten all about my novel; but I had one gleam as to it in the middle of the night. Too much alcohol today. Stout, and a cocktail, and Rhine wine in the evening. This is a great error of conduct, and I don't care what anyone says to the contrary. So there.

Monday, December 20th.

I swore to write 365,000 words this year, and today I have reached the number. But of course I shall write still more.

Thursday, December 23rd.

It took me a long time making trifling Xmas arrangements before I could begin to think at all about *Accident*. Twice I started out for a reflection walk, and twice had to come back. Then down to the Reform Club, where I had 35 minutes to write down notes and have a glass of sherry before lunch. I had the necessary ideas by this time for the continuation of my chapter.

Saturday, December 25th.

This Xmas all right, though I did not have a good night before it. It was all organized by Dorothy, and she made it very successful. It was her first Christmas in charge of a household. The Dorans (our only guests) arrived at 7.55 instead of 8. The brandy sauce to the pudding (sauce made by Dorothy) was perfect.

Monday, December 27th.

I read *Jew Süss,* and am enjoying it more and more.[1] It gave colour and *height* to the ideas for my novel which I got during my walk.

Thursday, December 30th.

I went out for a preliminary walk at 10.30, about a mile and a half in Chelsea, and came back and wrote 500 words of *Accident.* Then I did chores quickly and walked quickly to the Reform Club, and lunched in the sweet society of Tyler (barrister), A. G. Gardiner, and Gardiner's son Gilbert, whom he had brought. Vivian Phillipps came later. Upstairs we talked about money, the comparative advantages of various careers, etc. In fact it soon became all money, and I was sorry that young Gilbert Gardiner (still at Cambridge) should hear his elders in this sordid mood.

Friday, December 31st.

I meant to have a good night last night in order to prepare for tonight, but I had a bad one. I went out for a longish walk (Oxford Circus, etc.) and got a few ideas for my first article for *Nash's Magazine,* but not really much. Lunch with Vivian Phillipps. Then afterwards I stayed talking with Sassoon and E. M. Forster. The latter said that he had not begun a new novel, and hadn't got any ideas for one. So I cursed him and urged him to get on with a novel; but of course I knew it would be no good.

We gave a dinner for New Year's Eve at the Gargoyle, joining with the A. P. Herberts, who also had a party at one big table. Place full.

---

[1] It was Arnold Bennett's enthusiastic championship of Feuchtwanger's *Jew Süss* (American title: *Power*) that started it towards its vast success in Great Britain.

1927

Saturday, January 1st.

I wrote 378,100 words last year, having contracted with myself to write, at first 300,000, and then 365,000. I make no contract with myself for 1927. I published 28 articles during 1926 and, apparently, only four short stories. I know I wrote more than four—I should think seven, eight, or ten.

Very feeble this morning, after the New Year's Eve carousing, and bed at 2.30. Towards noon I walked to South Kensington Museum to see the temporary exhibition of commercial printing and illustrations. I met D. S. McColl there. He told me that some time since Tonks had been "very much bitten with the idea" of illustrating *The Old Wives' Tale*. I never knew before. I remember that Sickert wanted to illustrate *Clayhanger*.

Monday, January 3rd.

Reception given by the Robert Mayers to the members of the jury which decides what new works shall be produced at the International Music Festival. They are here (5 of them) for a week, and have to weed out 200 modern works. Arthur Bliss was there, and very lively; also Calvocoressi; also Yelli d'Aranyi, looking most distinguished. But the chief draw for me was Bernard van Dieren, whom I had never met. Apparently about forty: looks frail and good-humoured and a bit sardonic. A marvellous brain. He indulged in an argumentative scrap with Bliss, who also is very intelligent, and beat him hollow. I was obliged to tell them that I never could argue. I liked van Dieren very much; or rather I admired him very much.

Tuesday, January 4th.

Freddie Lonsdale was due for tea at 4.30. I never expected him to come, but exactly at 4.30 I heard his voice in the drawing-room. He had really come to talk about his growing penchant for alcohol. He said it was all due to his desire to be social. He said: "Even if it means cirrhosis of the liver, I can't bear that a friend should pass a dull evening." He has a most delicious personality.

Wednesday, January 5th.

I bought *Treasure Island,* as I had lately heard such praise of it. All I remember of my first reading of it, many years ago, is that I liked it. I read a lot of it this afternoon, and all I can say is that I thought it wasn't so bad.

Friday, January 7th.

Set off to walk to the Royal Academy for the Belgian-Flemish picture show, calling on the way to look at a book-shop. A growing crowd at the R.A. The Belgian masters are magnificent, but none of them—not even Rubens—ranks with the biggest Italians. Memling, van Eyck, and Breughel are the best. I was sitting in front of the Breughels when Laurence Binyon came up and said: "Don't you think Breughel is the finest painter in the world?" He isn't, but I was very pleased, because I've been saying this ever since I saw the small Breughel seascapes and things in Rome. Then I went, Dorothy with me, to the Capitol to see the *Cinderella* film, of which I had heard very high praise. It lacks invention; but much of the photography was exceedingly fine. The melancholy of the thought that the organist is playing the organ all day. Began my preface for Agate's new book of dramatic criticism, and wrote 600 words.

Saturday, January 8th.

Gargoyle Club for dinner, the Crosby Gaiges and the Richmond Temples. The club was fuller than usual, and is evidently doing better and better: which is a pity. It will certainly become too popular, and that will be the end of that. Both Mrs. Gaige and Mrs. Temple, being Americans, had heavy colds in this English winter climate. Yet they were both cheerful, and didn't really make any fuss about going early. We danced a bit. We all danced. Not bad. I found more and more that Gaige is a real book-collector. He is severely bitten by the mania, and must have been bitten in early youth.

Monday, January 10th.

After discussing it with D., I decided to make over to her all the rights in all my performed plays—reserving those not performed. And when we got home at about 10.40 I at once wrote a letter to Geoffrey Russell on this great subject, giving instructions and asking advice.

Tuesday, January 11th.

I walked to the Carlton Hotel to meet Colonel Fitzhugh Minnegerode, Leader representative of the Magazine Section of the *New York Times*. Minnegerode had been twenty years in the American army, and had lost the greater part of his regiment at Verdun. He told me the funniest story I have ever heard about a writer. At d'Annunzio's place, somewhere in the north of Italy, the servants have the strictest orders when they meet the master in or about the house, to drop instantly whatever they may be carrying, and to put one hand and forearm over the other. Whatever it is—a teatray with glasses, e.g., must be dropped on the floor. So that now the servants have instituted a private "heralding" system. A man carrying anything is preceded by another, and if the former meets the master he crosses his arms, and the latter gets quickly out of the way. Minnegerode said also that in the architecture somewhere there is an unfinished column, and d'Annunzio says that that column will be finished after Ireland is completely free.

Sunday, January 16th.

Bernard van Dieren came for tea. He stayed two hours: talking about

75 per cent. of the time. He is a very fine talker, but he drones or chants, and his command of English, though marvellous, is that of a foreigner. He told us he had lived in London for twenty years. He is one of the most cultured men I ever met, and seemed very good in all the arts, and in at least 4 languages. He really came to consult me about the book of an opera he is writing on the subject of Caesar Borgia.

Monday, January 17th.

Walk, after chores. It was thick fog at 7.30. Then it cleared a bit, but was still foggy. Then, just as I was going out at 10.5, it began to rain. However, I went out and walked to South Kensington Museum and looked at a few good things to buck me up, including my favourite early 15th-century Virgin and Child and then walked home again. More chores, and then I went up by bus to the Carlton Grill to be the guest of Colonel Minnegerode.

Wednesday, January 19th.

Swinnerton told us that he found a very wide interest in my works in U.S.A. and curiosity about my doings. He said, what I have long thought, that the lecturing business does not help the sale of books. The Americans talk a lot about the value of "making contacts," but (said he) they make so many contacts that they spend all their time in contacts and get nothing done.

Thursday, January 20th. Hôtel Bristol, Paris.

Owing to the insufficiency of porters we did not have too much time to catch the Flèche d'Or train. However, we caught it by about 3 minutes. It is a great spectacle. Good coaches, black and gold. Wherever you are your meal is brought to you. At the Gare du Nord, all the hand stuff thrown out together and a man took Dorothy's valise in mistake for his own. Nothing could be more annoying. We searched platform, and then all cabs going off. Then Dorothy went back to the train, and frightened the car attendant, who came back with her. He took her to the Wagons-Lits office, where, the *man's* bag was found, with Central Hotel on it.

We drove with this bag and the attendant to the Central Hotel and got Dorothy's suit-case. All right. But the adventure was extremely exasperating while it lasted.

Saturday, January 22nd. Hotel Tyrol, Innsbruck.

Eventless journey. I talked with the Wagons-Lits conductor of our coach. He said that conductors depended solely on tips. He said it was all right when the train was full, but not otherwise. He said that 50 francs was a fine tip. People gave 30 and 20; even 10 and even 5. He said Americans demanded the most attention and gave the smallest tips. He had an idea that tips were not given in America.

We had breakfast and lunch on the train, in monotonous snow-laden landscapes with black rivers running through them, and tree-covered steep hill sides. A few skiers. Small villages.

Sunday, January 23rd. Hotel Savoy, Cortina.

We left Innsbruck in snow at 7.10. We reached Cortina at 8.40. Thick snow at Cortina. I had telegraphed to the Savoy that we couldn't arrive till Monday, but later, when the special had been altered, I telegraphed we should arrive. But the second telegram never reached Cortina. So that instead of a suite of three rooms and bathroom we had only one room and no bathroom. We were deprived of our sitting-room owing to all sorts of changes forcibly made in the hotel on account of the imminent visit of the Duke of Genoa, who wanted twelve rooms and could not be refused.

Monday, January 24th.

Magnificent morning. Pinkish, salmonish Dolomite peaks, grey rocks, white snow, blue sky, strong sunshine. The air is undoubtedly very tonic at this height, 4200 ft.

The Aldous Huxleys called on us. We talked with them for some time and then they took us to their house for tea, where several other people arrived.

Tuesday, January 25th.

First full, empty day of holiday. We met Aldous and Maria Huxley, who had been skiing. I stood about till I could risk the cold no longer, and then went for a walk, breaking often into a run. By this time (4 p.m.) all the tracks round here were in shadow. The Aldous Huxleys came for dinner and stayed till 11.55.

Wednesday, January 26th.

The Duke of Genoa, with his two sons, Dukes of Padua and Pistoia, had arrived, with certain ladies. The ducal party had a table in a corner of the restaurant, and were waited upon by the head waiter from the bar-room. They then sat in the ball-room, the National Anthem or something being played at their entrance therein, and the young dukes danced a bit, one of them with a hotel visitor. They seemed bored. The Duke of Genoa is very old, with a hatchet, sharp face, and he seems to chew all his food, at great length, with his front teeth. Gives the appearance of a rat eating at a piece of wood. But apparently a decent fellow.

Thursday, January 27th.

I began to have vague ideas about work today, partly due no doubt to Aldous Huxley's remark that he always began to pine away after only a few days of complete holiday from work.

At 3 p.m. we set off to see the finish of the bob-sleigh match. Nothing much to see at the end of the *"Pista da Bob,"* except the ducal party standing and sitting on a rough platform of boards. At intervals a "bob" swept round the corner and drew up past the winning post, where men sat at a table in the sharp frost writing down times and numbers in a book. The skiing practice of village boys on a neighbouring slope was much more amusing. Fortunately this spot was close to the Huxleys' cottage. We were bidden there for tea, and arrived before 4, and played make-believes with the two kids and Matthew's mother.

I read another 70 or 80 pages of Olive Schreiner's *From Man to Man;* which is still missing the first-rate.

Friday, January 28th.

I went off to catch the funicular up to the Belvedere on a hill 1000 feet higher than Cortina. We call it a funicular, but it isn't one. The carriage swings on a wire over the tree-tops etc. All the other passengers were skiers. The sensation of floating over the snowy slopes, and seeing fir trees from the top is rather amusing. The *trajet* takes only ten minutes.

Saturday, January 29th.

I had an idea for writing a series of *souvenirs d'enfance.* There is nothing about *souvenirs d'enfance* in Louis Aragon's *Paysan de Paris,* but this book is certainly stimulating me into a fresh creativeness. I must say that, though it is uneven, I should like to write a book like that—I mean about London. Only of course England would never tolerate the *belle franchise* of this French book. While Dorothy was dressing I went out for a walk. I wanted to be alone to think about a short story and about two articles and about my dimly projected *souvenirs,* but I came across Baroness F., acquaintance of the Huxleys. She would walk with me. And when I said I must turn she said she also must turn back. Then she took my photograph twice in the middle of the road, blazing sunshine screwing up eyes, etc. However, she did tell me one interesting thing. She knew Ibsen. She said she spent a whole season in the same hotel with him and his family somewhere. She sat at the next table to the Ibsens. They— father, mother, and boy—never spoke a word during the whole time. Ibsen (said Mme. F.) would talk freely to Madame F. afterwards. He told her that he wrote all his work four times. Also that he wrote *The Doll's House* in the open air, in tremendous sunshine, at Sorrento. He loved the greatest possible heat to work in.

Sunday, January 30th.

Disappointed at seeing no rosy sunrise effects on the peak opposite my window. We arrived with D.'s skis, and a hotel lunch for two in a paper bag, at the Teleferica station—the rendezvous with the Aldous Huxleys. They were there first. We discussed some time whether or not we should go to the top, as the peaks were already wreathed in clouds. But of course in the end we decided to go. And we were glad we did go. We ate our lunches in the restaurant of the little hotel at the top, and had soup and wine therewith. Also coffee. And everything was very good. Then the 3 skiers set off for the descent at 1.50, and I set off to walk down by the main road (which road I had failed to discover two days ago). It had begun to snow at 1 o'clock, and it was now snowing pretty thickly. I passed a middle-aged native with a spade, as drunk as anything. He reeled from side to side of the precipice-bounded path, and fell down once on his stomach. As I couldn't do anything I cheerfully left him. At the bridge where the ski-path crosses the road, no sign of the skiers. The whole mountainous landscape on every side is obscured by clouds. Snow ceased for a bit at 4 o'clock.

Dorothy got back at about 5.15. Maria brought her. They both said that the skiing down the mountain in the falling snow had been a very disagreeable experience. They all fell all the time, and Aldous H. had one severe fall.

Wednesday, February 2nd.

I was wakened at 5 by the Convent Hospital bell—a fearsome clangour. At 5.40 my day had begun, and although tired I felt rather jolly about starting so early. By 9 o'clock, or perhaps earlier, I had written the third section of my short story—over 1000 words. I went out at 10.30 so as to change my skates, which were too small for my new large uncomfortable boots. The demoiselle at the shop was most agreeable; she came to me almost at once, and gave me size 28 instead of 27, and I departed, content, except that I had no desire whatever to skate.

Thursday, February 3rd.

Il Principe Ereditario [of Italy] arrived about 11 this morning. Band and popular applause. Plenty of people in the street. Peasant girls staring at the hotel long after the Prince had definitely disappeared within. To-night the village is illuminated, and you can see illuminations far up the hillside. The church tower, quite lofty, is illuminated with quiet and effective taste. Secretaries or underlings of some sort, from one to six of them, are continuously standing on the first-floor landing in front of the Crown Prince's suite. You might almost think that he was more important than Mussolini, and that his uncles and cousins are as naught in comparison with him.

We sleighed to Huxleys' to dinner and back, and it was very cold, with marvellous stars. When we got back at 11.20 the hotel was in full swing. Ballroom crowded and the hall turned into a *vestiiaire*. Crown Prince, in uniform, dancing with various women.

Saturday, February 5th.

Today at last we made our excursion up to Tre Croci. A magnificent day. We took a 2-horse sleigh and the professor of skiing, and picked up the Huxleys at the Hotel Belleoni. Tre Croci is 600 metres higher than Cortina. As you rise, the sky seems to get bluer and the air clearer, and the craggy reddish mountains more grand. The beauty of the severe landscapes, and the quality of the air were exhilarating to the point of intoxication sometimes. All the way up—8 kilometres—the road was patrolled by gendarmes at a distance of about 200 yards apart, because the Crown Prince was going up there to lunch. Strange, to think of all those gendarmes standing nearly all day in the cold (only a few of them had boards to stand on—and remember it was freezing hard), well uniformed, barbered, cleaned, with wives and children probably—all so that the Crown Prince should see them as he drove up in his sleigh. We took lunch with us—against my advice—and a good thing we did, for the big hotel at the top was all sixes and sevens with excitement and preparations about and for the Prince. We had difficulty in getting cocktails. The head waiter was not polite. After the cocktails we took our food out into the open and ate in the sunshine. Rather messy, and my hands were soon very cold; but we enjoyed it.

The skiers started, under guidance of the professor, and I and Peter (Huxley's dog) kept near them in the sleigh. We met every now and then, and I saw several fine runs and several falls. Dorothy was doing very well. They were all enjoying themselves enormously. I got home first. Dorothy said it was the finest day she had ever had in all her life. Certainly a most marvellous day, even for me, with air, sunshine, superb landscapes, and a universal clarity. A Spanish costume ball at night, but only about two Spanish costumes and Dorothy's Spanish shawl.

Sunday, February 6th.

Didn't get out till 11.30 and we had lunch at noon, in order to go to the International Ski-Jumping Contest, two miles off. We took the Huxleys. Frost, overcast. We drove there in a small sleigh, but had to walk at the end up hill about half a mile to get to our *tribune,* upon which we got excellent seats.

The tribunes are built on poles down the 45° snow slopes of the jump. The Scandinavians were best and the Italians the worst, but there were exceptions. The first jump gives you a great thrill, but you soon get used to it, when you perceive that the chances of a serious accident are trifling. The swiftest of them you can hear hurtling through the air. I tried to watch the faces of the competitors as they flew past us and above me. On the whole they seemed fairly calm and set.

I read *The Times Lit. Suppl.* article on "Re-reading Walter Pater," and found in it no reason why I should re-read W. Pater. Huxley agrees with me on Pater.

Monday, February 7th.

Great feeling of health and energy this morning. I walked the hill about twice as high as the Hotel Cristallo, and walked down again because I could not find a circular tour. Lonely bare larch woods up there, and the forlorn spectacle of a hotel shut up for the winter. The views of the opposite mountains are very fine, but you can't look at them unless you stand still in the cold. Going up you have your back to them, and coming down you have to look where you are putting your feet— every step.

I found from my *Evening Standards* that my last week's article, re-ferring to young imaginative authors, had aroused the usual opposition. J. Drinkwater, Mrs. Lowndes, C. S. Evans, all defending the young. They don't see what a lark and what a desirable thing it is to give the young a flick now and then. No one has supported the young more violently than I have.

Wednesday, February 9th.

Today I read in the *Continental Daily Mail* that George Sturt [1] was dead. This death produced no effect of sadness on me at all. George had been ill and half-paralysed for many years, and I don't think I had seen him at all for about sixteen years. When I did see him I drove down to Farnham, and he asked me to keep my car and chauffeur out of the way lest it should constrain or frighten or embarrass, or something, his household. And I had to eat at the inn. I understood all this perfectly well, however, and I had about a couple of hours' fine time with him, chiefly in his garden. His later books, so far as I read them, were not as good as his earlier. I remember that when I started to keep a journal—it must be over thirty years ago—I made up and bound (in cardboard etc.) the volumes myself. (I had them bound in calf later.) I showed the first volume, scarcely written in, to George. George said: "If you'll bind me a volume like that, I'll keep a journal too." So I did. Afterwards he kept on keeping a journal, but in large volumes. I think that he had made notes before, but he had never kept a journal. Of course all these notes and journals were the material of his books in a quite exceptional degree.

Thursday, February 10th.

I have now read positively as much as I shall read of Fleuret's *Histoire de la Bienheureuse Fille Raton*. It contains a good idea—that of professional fornication for the love of God—and some excellent scenes. But it is not *quite* good enough, and much of its attraction depends on its extreme licentiousness. Indeed, you can see the author passing on from scene to scene, each exceeding the previous one in licentiousness, exactly in the manner of a merely bawdy book. I did not read by any means all the middle part of it. Still it is a book to examine.

---

[1] An old friend of Bennett's and author of various books under the pseudonym of G. Bourne.

I saw by chance in the *Nation* a wonderful description of a thunder and hailstorm at a popular resort on a mountain top, by D. H. Lawrence. He can do it sometimes. In fact he can d——d well do it sometimes.

Friday, February 11th.

Huxley told me a story of Wellington. When Wellington was asked, apropos of the mistakes of military commanders, what was the worst order he had ever heard of as being given by a G.O.C., he said it was: "Soldiers, remember that you are Portuguese."

I am enjoying Boni de Castellane's *Comment j'ai découvert l'Amérique* but there are parts that I skip, and a good deal of the book, I think, would hardly have been written by a man of nice taste. On the whole the French books I bought in Paris have panned out pretty well.

Saturday, February 12th.

I want to write one more article for the *Evening Standard* before we leave here; but I don't seem to be able to get a leading idea for it, except that of slating one or two of my young friends, such as William Gerhardi. I read a lot more of Castellane's Memoirs. There are still very good things in it, though some pages are tedious and even absurd. And all the criticisms of his wife are a mistake. After all, he lived with her for twelve years, and had two children by her. When you have done that you ought to leave a woman alone.

Sunday, February 13th.

Idle in the grand manner today. The Huxleys came for lunch shortly after 1 o'clock, and we had a very good lunch, and I drank beer, and it did me no harm. This is the first time I have drunk beer without suffering for it, for about eighteen years. The last time I drank it was at a restaurant at or near Baia; it made me ill instantly. The time before that was about sixteen or seventeen or eighteen years ago in a café in the *place* where are the Théâtres Sarah Bernhardt and Porte St.-Martin, after seeing Sarah Bernhardt in some rotten play; it made me quite ill for twenty-four hours.

But I was forgetting. I wasn't completely idle. I corrected the last three-quarters of the proofs of my 20,000-word short story *The Woman Who Stole Everything*. I thought this story one of the best I had ever done. I was so full of this idea that I wrote to Miss Nerney about it, and talked at some length with Dorothy about it, and wrote to Newman Flower about a special jacket for the book: which is to come out this Spring.

Dorothy is planning to come here again next winter, with a larger party. But I don't think that this will happen. She won't be able to get a larger party—perhaps no party at all. Interesting people aren't free. They have their own plans. However—the queer thing is that I simply don't mind where I go for a holiday—if there is a really good hotel on the spot. I can amuse myself and pass the time agreeably anywhere.

Monday, February 14th.

Aldous Huxley is getting more and more into the habit of using such words as "inconceivable," "incredible," "fantastic." These three are his favourite words, and one of them comes into nearly every sentence. His general knowledge is extraordinarily good. In fact it is inconceivable, incredible, and fantastic.

Saturday, February 19th. Hôtel Ruhl, Nice.

I read a lot of the book Robert Nichols specially recommended to me, *Neighbours* by Claude Houghton. I think there may be an idea in it, but up to p. 100 it is very amateurish. I have also read three acts of *Troilus and Cressida*. It is great stuff, as regards character and language and "closeness" of texture; and yet it takes the fellow nearly three acts to come to the real point of the plot.

Tuesday, February 22nd.

We were due at H. G. Wells's, Quartier St.-Mathieu, Grasse, for lunch. It soon began to rain. Nevertheless the continuously mounting drive to Grasse was very beautiful. Little seems to have changed in that region in the last five years. Nor at Grasse either. The rendezvous with H. G. was for noon in the *Cours* at Grasse. We arrived precisely at twelve, and he was there, signalling, in a big doggy overcoat with the collar turned up, in the rain. Plenty of mud. We left our car and got into his Citroën. Drive of about ten minutes, narrow curving, up and down, thoroughly bad little road. He has the *dépendance* of a larger house, but is building a house of his own on the opposite side of a little valley. Odette Keun came rapidly downstairs to greet us. She enveloped us in welcome. The "feminine touch" all over the place. Excellent lunch, Provençale, with appreciable garlic in it. An original lunch. We went over to see the new house in process of construction. Well, H. G. designed it himself and got an architect to "re-draw the plans." What he would call a jolly little house. But it wouldn't suit me. Rooms too small, and windows too large, and no tradition behind the design. Still the open-air rooms will be very "jolly" for eating and sitting about in. Much charm in the situation. We greatly enjoyed this visit. It was very invigorating in every way.

Thursday, February 24th. Hôtel Bristol, Paris.

We walked along the Rue du Faubourg St.-Honoré. Lovely shops. Beautifully arranged. Marvellously arranged. This fact strikes me more and more. You may wander afar off to see old quaint quarters of Paris; but they are not more artistic than these modern shops in the middle of the much-despised modern shopping Anglo-American quarter.

I read in Paul Morand's *Rien que la Terre*. This book does not seem to me to be anything very remarkable—at best you can call it remarkably bright, variegated journalism. This is the last of the six French books which I bought in Paris on the day we left for Cortina. I have now read or sampled them all. The best is certainly Aragon's *Paysan de Paris*. I gave it to the Aldous Huxleys. Boni de Castellane's *Comment j'ai découvert l'Amérique* is very interesting and alive for the most part, and contains a few rather profound things. But on the whole I haven't read anything really very startling since we left England. I doubt whether I am in fact very fond of reading. I always *look forward* to reading. But the realization is less satisfactory. I soon tire of it.

Monday, February 28th.

We dined at the Cheval Pie and then walked to the "Studio des Champs-Élysées" for a rendezvous with the Maurois and Maurice Baring, who had come over in the afternoon, to see *Maya*. We had the private directorial box, and it was very hot and hard, with a very side view. The play is drawing all Paris, because it is about the life of *grues* at Marseilles. It is very dull, and artistically is not a bit better than *Le Souris d'Hôtel* that we saw the other evening at the Édouard VII.

Tuesday, March 1st.

I got up at 6, to write this and do oddments, and I shall now go to bed again. I read a good bit of *Si le grain ne meurt* in the night. The *souvenirs d'enfance* are beautifully done. I am liking this book, of which Gide has sent me a copy of the special *tirage* (50 copies) of the *nouvelle édition*. Certainly I have learnt a little about the newest French literature since I left England. Gide said yesterday that he should speak to Gaston Gallimard to find out why the *N.R.F.* was so silly as to begin the French translations of my works with *The Ghost*.

Wednesday, March 2nd.

I did nothing else all morning, except take a short stroll to the Champs-Élysées and back. The André Maurois and Maurice Baring came to lunch at the hotel. They stayed till just 3 o'clock.

Walked up the Avenue Victor Emanuel III searching for stuffs and for a writing-desk for Dorothy. The stuffs were still dearer in this street than in the Rue du F. St.-Honoré. The writing desks averaged £60 to £70! I noticed that, though guaranteed *de l'époque,* they were all splashed with ink to make them still more *de l'époque*.

We dined well, at the Bœuf à la Mode. Excellent, but spoilt by the presence of accented and free-mannered Americans.

Alfred Savoir *Passy 22–85* play at the Potinière. A *childish* thing, as I knew it would be. All these fashionable things *are* childish. But Charlotte Lyses was admirable in it.

Thursday, March 3rd.

I drove down to the Institut de France along the quays, and then walked slowly back as far as the Rue du Bac, looking at the book-boxes. I only bought one book, *Les Moments Perdus de John Shag* by Gilbert de Voisins, which Gide had specially recommended me. It was marked *"Service de la Presse,"* 8 frs. instead of 12, and its transparent paper envelope had not been violated at all.

I then walked on to the Restaurant Lucas, where Maurice Baring gave a very good lunch to Dorothy and me and a Russian exile named Dimitriev Momonov, a sharp-nosed man with a good grey beard, speaking good English. Unfortunately he had not been reading the new Russian authors, except Leonid Leonov, whom he specially recommended to me. He said that *The Death of Simon Fuge* was in the Chekhov style, though probably written before I had read Chekhov. There is something in this. Maurice said I had never written the sort of plays I ought to write and could write. Something in this, too.

We entertained the whole five Godebski-Blaque Bellair crew to dinner. We had a most agreeable and chattering evening. Dorothy was at bottom very exhausted, yet she plotted with the others to force me to go to the Grand Écart on Friday night, and stay till 1 or 2 in the morning. Her dressmaking business is now fairly well concluded—or rather she thinks it is.

Friday, March 4th.

Tea at the Café de Madrid. All around there the *grand boulevard est très changé*—I mean where the Boulevard Haussmann now begins. I looked for the Taverne Pousset. It had gone. Great concourses of people. Vulgar shops. D. had insisted on going to the Grand Écart afterwards, the momentarily fashionable night-café of Montmartre (Rue Fromentin). The Grand Écart is *bien fréquenté,* but terrible. Met Léon-Paul Fargue, who was nearly bald, but otherwise little changed. After much trouble we got away about 1.15, having been terribly bored nearly all the time, and both of us dropping with exhaustion. Before 2 a.m. just as she was to go off to sleep, Dorothy began to admit how stupid she had been in insisting on going to this blasted café and how repentant she was. I read a lot more of *Si le grain ne meurt*. Fargue said he thought it is Gide's best book. I think so too.

Saturday, March 5th.

Dorothy wanted to see Geraldy's new play *Son Mari* ("only one act or at most two"). Happily no seats obtainable. So we got two for the Variétés (*L'Habit Vert* of Flers and Caillavet). Now Dorothy thought that she had been asking the theatre-man here for seats for *Variétés*, the German Jannings film—known as *Vaudeville* in England. It was not till we were driving along the boulevard that she discovered that she had misled two men, the theatre-man and me, as to what she really wanted.

Monday, March 7th. 75 Cadogan Square, London.

I read the sketch of Einstein's theory in Sullivan's *Aspects of Science*. It is not clear to me, but it is the least obscure description of the theory that I have yet seen. Sullivan has quite an exceptional mind—scientific and artistic at once. He has real, fundamental, scientific conceptions, and is extremely interesting.

Virginia has struck us as quite grown up. She is very active. Dorothy says she is plainer than she was; but I can't see this myself.

Tuesday, March 8th.

The Edgar Selwyns came to lunch. We talked chiefly about the proposed play on *Lord Raingo*. His ideas for it still seemed to me to be very good. He talked of the casting. Said he wanted George Arliss . . . just as if the play was all ready for production! He said that Arliss seldom played to less than $20,000 a week. Also that Arliss was almost the only star who would go "on the road."

I find that the *Evening Standard* weekly article is becoming rather a nuisance. It is attracting too much attention from the writing and publishing worlds. When an author, perfectly unknown to me, calls with a book . . . and editors and publishers are continually sending books to me personally, in the hope . . . !

Wednesday, March 9th.

This morning before noon I finished reading what I had done of *Accident* and I decidedly liked it. It seemed to me to be sound and interesting; of course, old-fashioned—at least I suppose so.

Then I walked up to the Reform, and got there early, I lunched with Page, Gardiner, Roch, and two others. Discussion of Churchill's book.[1] Everyone praised it as a *tour de force,* but said it was by no means always honest, and certainly wasn't history, inasmuch as it was obviously written to prove that Churchill had been right throughout the war. Personally, I think it is a bit better than that. I regard it as a remarkable achievement. I came home by bus and slept. I felt gloomy. I hadn't really begun to get my ideas into order for proceeding with my novel.

Then I read the newest fiction. Priestley's *Adam in Moonshine* and Romer Wilson's *Latter-Day Symphony,* and I at once wrote paragraphs about them to go into a future *Standard* article. Poor and pretentious stuff, *I* thought. Nothing original in them. But Elizabeth Madox Roberts's *The Time of Man* (American—sent to me by Doran) seems to me to be pretty good authentic fiction. A very different affair from the other two.

Thursday, March 10th.

Went to the dinner of the Other Club at the Savoy. It was a small but a particularly good meeting. I had Ned Lutyens on my left and Archie Sinclair on my right, and Churchill opposite me during the last and best part of the evening. I referred to Charlie Masterman's criticism of his rhetorical style, and in particular of the phrase about pistols drinking blood. Churchill at once said: "What about taking arms against a sea of troubles?" He said that when he wrote that phrase he had pistols actually by him (for some reason which I forget).

Friday, March 11th.

First thing after breakfast and seeing Dorothy I wrote a little article about Westminster Cathedral for the *Oxford and Cambridge* (illustrated

---

[1] *The World Crisis, 1916–18.*

weekly). I took the material from notes made on a visit. I've got a lot of these notes made within about twelve months. I shouldn't ever have written the article without the notes. Moral.

Unhappily I do this article gratis.

I spent a bit of time in miscellaneous reading. The Colefaxes, Alec Schepeler and Otto Kahn and Rudolf Kommer came for dinner. Kahn came through Kommer. Kahn wanted a nice bunch for his yachting cruise in the Greek Archipelago, and Kommer, who is very friendly with him, suggested me as one. Kahn is short and white and sturdy. Of course very assured in style. Stuffed with brains. Highly intelligent. Phrases his talk very well. I at once decided to sail with him. April 20th for a month. Kahn was never uninteresting, he gave a great deal of his attention to Dorothy. You can see he is efficient in everything. His information-giving talk with me about the projected cruise was excellently terse—couldn't have been better.

Saturday, March 12th.

We lunched with Beaverbrook at the Vineyard. He wanted various opinions on things from me, and some special information about a journalist. Max showed me a detailed alternative plan for his new yacht, and we all lay on the floor of his wretched little drawing-room to study them. He was most benevolent and charming, and flattering about my *Books and Persons*. He showed me two specimens of proposed publicity for Ethel M. Dell's serial in the *Evening Standard,* which I should have phrased very differently. I got him to alter one bit.

Sunday, March 13th.

I went out for a walk, along the Embankment past the old Clock House (now turned into flats and looking damned odd—what a change, only a year or two ago I met at dinner the woman who lived in Clock House all by herself), and past Oakley Street into Cheyne Row and past Carlyle's gloomy house, which I hadn't seen for a long time, and home by 12 o'clock. Whereupon, having got my ideas into order, I at once sat down and wrote 800 words of *Accident*. Lunch at home with Dorothy.

At night I resumed Sinclair Lewis's new novel.[1] At 3.25 we went forth by a 11 bus to the National Gallery, and saw a few fine things again, and the Hubert van Eyck thing that was in the Flemish Exhibition at the R.A. Good, but not, to my mind, in the same place as John van Eyck which is hanging close by. D. showed me a portrait of a man by (I forget —Italian, 15 cent.), and said that for her it was the finest portrait in the world. It was very fine, but perhaps she was as much attracted by the subject as by the painting.

D. and I dined alone together, and then we played four-hand bits out of the *Meistersinger*. This quiet day, without seeing *anyone,* was a pleasant change.

Monday, March 14th.

Lunch with Richmond Temple in a private room at the Savoy. I had asked him to the Reform, but he suggested the Savoy because we should be quieter. I wanted to get from Temple a few general ideas about hotel management here and on the continent, so that I could decide whether it would be practicable, artistically or otherwise, for me to write a "big" novel with a hotel organism, or two hotel organisms, as environment, and probably a hotel manager as hero. Temple has imagination and he abounds in general ideas and in 90 minutes or less he gave me all the ideas I wanted, and I practically decided to write the book.[2] He told me lots more interesting things. I make no mention here of his general ideas. Those are in my head only, and the impression they left is the only important thing to me. This alone decided me that I would write the novel.

Saturday, March 19th.

I went to the Goupil to see Stanley Spencer's big "Resurrection" (15 ft. long). It contains over 60 figures. It is a sincere and highly emotional

---

[1] *Elmer Gantry.*
[2] This was *Imperial Palace.*

affair. I respected it, liked bits of it, and was not pleased with it as a whole. Some of Spencer's sketches and smaller pictures were very original. "Resurrection" is the talk of London at the moment.

We reached the Savoy Café at 8.40 of the clock. The Savoy Grill Room seemed rather a gloomy place.

But considering that she was to have an operation tomorrow morning, Dorothy was quite cheerful.

Sunday, March 20th.

The nurse for Dorothy's operation was here about 8 o'clock, and soon D.'s bedroom was transformed into an operating-room.

I walked for about 40 minutes, saw Dorothy, and began to write my chapter at noon precisely. I wrote about 750 words. Saw Dorothy again and then at intervals I wrote more words. Nurse had been sitting in the drawing-room and elsewhere for a change. When she returned to the bedroom, I returned to my study, and finished my chapter, and counted the words. I had written a complete chapter of 1700 words, and was fairly assuaged and content. Then went and had my own dinner and drank some Burgundy, and read Sinclair Lewis's *Elmer Gantry,* which is acutely alive and readable. Then I saw Dorothy again, and came downstairs and had half of one of my new Partaga cigars. I saw Dorothy again, previous to her being arranged for the night. I came back to my study and finished my cigar, and read more *Elmer Gantry.* Finally I got to bed by 11 p.m. but with the expectancy of a disturbed night. I didn't spend one penny of petty cash all day. It was a satisfactory day, considering all circumstances, and I had done a day's work sufficient for even an absolutely free day.

Monday, March 21st.

I've written 20,000 words in the last twelve days. I had to order the meals and wrestle with the French cook this morning. Also I had a highly disturbing letter from F. C. B. about a wild project of his for coming to London; which upset me. So that by 10.30, after I had seen Dorothy twice, although I had had a very calm pre-prandial time (from 6.30 to

8.30), I was beginning to have a headache and felt *dans tous mes états*. I went out for an idea-finding walk, and got to the South Kensington Museum and sat down in a corner, and no sooner had I done so than four workmen came to disturb me by moving trestles. No sooner had they gone than the ideas came to me in a vague but satisfactory rush; and I walked straight out again. I saw Dorothy a third time, and exactly at 12 sat down to work and at 12.35 had actually written 700 words. It seems as if nothing can stop me from working just now.

Tuesday, March 22nd.

I went out to South Kensington Museum at 11.15 to find ideas, and got them, among English pictures of a second-rate kind, easily. I came home. And at 1 p.m. had written 400 words. Before 6 I had written another 1400 words of the novel: 1800 words in all, the complete chapter describing the railway accident. I wrote it at great speed, and was rather pleased with it.

Thursday, March 24th.

Finally awoke at 5.40. Very tired. I couldn't see the end of the last chapter of the first part of *Accident*.

Strange to say, after I had seen Dorothy again, and sat down in my easy chair in the study to think, I instantly saw the end of the chapter, with scarcely any cerebration, and went to the desk to write it. I did 800 words in about an hour. I then walked up to Fortnum and Mason, reflecting creatively.

During dinner I suddenly had the idea of not continuing *Accident* until after my return from the Greek cruise. I haven't got the ideas very clear yet for Part II, and there is no hurry. And I have heaps of other work to do. I might do two short stories beside all my articles by Good Friday. And I could return to the novel with a fresh mind on my return. I think it might make a radical difference to the end of the novel. This now decided. And yet three hours ago I hadn't the slightest notion of doing it. Now it seems to be the only right thing to do. I discussed various other literary businesses with Dorothy.

Saturday, March 26th.

Fair night, vitiated by over-smoking. However, at the end I received from God just over 2½ hours of unbroken sleep, and at 5.45 accordingly felt restored to health. Before dressing I wrote a little opinion, at the request of the *Sunday Express,* about the pirating of Joyce's *Ulysses* by one Samuel Roth. Into this I contrived to insinuate the opinion that Joyce is a very important figure in the evolution of the novel.

Tuesday, March 29th.

I went by bus to Trafalgar Square, and into the National Gallery, and stayed there for an hour, and greatly enjoyed Nicolas Poussin's "Nativity," which is the most amusing "Nativity" I have ever seen; and I came out with the required idea, which I shall begin to write tomorrow.

James O'Connor came in. I walked up to Piccadilly with him. He said: "I only heard indirectly of the change in your circumstances, my dear Arnold. My wife would much like to call. She is very fond of babies." We travelled by bus together to Sloane Street. Home at 2.45. Corrected a *Sunday Pictorial* article. Decent sleep. I then wrote 400 words of an *Evening Standard* article by 4 o'clock, when Michael Morton called by appointment. He told me that he thought he could sell the film rights of *Riceyman Steps* to the Gainsborough people (Hitchcock, producer) for £2500. I told him to go away and do it.

This morning I read a Russian short story before leaving the house on the idea-quest, to inspire me. It did inspire me. D. and I played Haydn after dinner.

Thursday, March 31st.

Bernard Shaw and wife, Molly MacCarthy, and Francis Birrell came to lunch. I was constrained, as always in the society of G. B. S. He talked a lot and well. He told us that X.'s parents were both deaf-mutes (Belfast) and that he used to attend a meeting-house for deaf-mutes as a child, and there amused himself by making as much noise as he liked, singing songs, etc. during the meetings, because nobody could hear him.

Saturday, April 2nd.

I had the idea of going up to Poland Street, and buying a ring for Dorothy. I bought three rings, two for her and one for myself, for which I paid cash. I had a chat with old Calipé. This shop does not seem to change. The two are still there with the old man, cheerful and spry and good-natured.

Sunday, April 3rd.

The Messmore Kendalls came for lunch. I showed them the picture of Hondecoeter of which I had got them the refusal. He would have bought it instantly, but there is a large peacock in the picture, and Messmore said that his mother held that peacocks (with certain other birds) were unlucky, and that if they had it in the house she would never be induced to come into the same. I felt at once that I could turn the peacock idea into a story.[1]

Monday, April 4th.

A fairly idle day. I went to South Kensington Museum, and looked at the De Wint oils. I searched for ideas; but not too seriously. However, I found enough. Yesterday I read a lot of Gorky's novel *Decadence*. It is very fine. The best thing of his that I have read.

Wednesday, April 6th.

Dorothy and I dined with Beaverbrook at the Vineyard. Masterman was there, but nobody else. A young blonde, Kitty Kinross, came in about 11. Max was in great form as a *raconteur* of scandals. Very great fun. We left at 11.50 to go to Syrie Maugham's house-warming party in King's Road. A large crowd.

Sunday, April 10th.

I went out for a stroll, both morning and afternoon, but it was chilly. In Sloane Square a mob-orator preaching against Socialism to a sparse audience and making a collection afterwards. I expect he partly lives on

---

[1] This story, "The Peacock,' was reprinted in *The Night Visitor*.

it. He looked conceited: all these mob orators do, even when they have no mob in front of them.

I finished reading Sullivan on Relativity, and I also read Montmorency's new little book *From Kant to Einstein,* in the evening. So that I now have enough instinct for my article—Relativity—for the *Evening Standard.* Dorothy and I dined at home. I read afterwards, though *éreinté,* and got her to play Beethoven to me.

Monday, April 11th.

I now began to feel as if my work was drawing to a close. I mean the work I have to do before going away. I wrote an article on Relativity for the *Evening Standard* this afternoon and this morning. I then found that I have five of these articles in hand. I might do another one to-morrow.

Sir George Lewis, Sir Roderick and Lady Jones, Olga Lynn, Gertrude Jennings, and Humbert Wolfe dined. This party was a rather noisy success. Everyone gabbled. Lewis was more ingratiatingly Oriental than ever.

Tuesday, April 12th.

Anthony Ellis wrote to me asking if he could do *Don Juan* with Ivor Novello as Don Juan. I wrote an answer, No, and then tore it up, having decided to talk to Dorothy about the affair.

I read two "art" books—T. Bodkin's *The Approach to Painting* and Clive Bell's *Landmarks in Nineteenth Century Painting,* for the purpose of writing an article about them for the *Evening Standard.* Then drove to Reform Club, and began lunch, by myself. H. G. Wells, who joined me, said that he had lost the art of reading. He got restless if he read for long. Perhaps his eyes—but I know it isn't his eyes. Because I'm just the same, and I know it isn't my eyes.

Dorothy and I dined at the Yacht Club. Not a very good dinner, but they had a new antique Italian chandelier which gave us much pleasure.

I was strangely depressed all day. I think it was purely physical, but I can't be sure.

At 5 a.m. (Wednesday) I came down to my study, and smoked a cigarette, and got *Monsieur Parent* to read. Maupassant is still wearing very well.

Friday, April 15th.

Left Victoria 9 a.m. for Rome and Taormina.

Saturday, April 16th. Grand Hotel Continentale, Rome.

Lovely morning. Environs of Turin 8 a.m. The journey passed without incident. The train was always punctual and arrived at Rome exactly at the appointed hour, 8.10 p.m. Not a bad achievement for an international train. I got a porter at once, and he carried my stuff across the Piazza to this hotel. I was served by a middle-aged kindly waiter evidently alcoholic, though not drunk at that moment.

Then put on my overcoat and went for a walk round the big church S. Maria degli Angeli close by. Squeaking trams on curves. Many hotels here near the station. Then I walked into the station, in which one of the chief departments was apparently the Militia *"Commando."* I went to bed at or before 11, having eaten a bit too much. Nothing much on the train journey here, except that I read *Brothers Karamazov.* Third or fourth time of reading. Yes, fourth time. I read it slowly to savour it. It is very great and masterful. An Englishwoman, fattish, sixtysh, very energetic, had the *cabine* next to mine. She talked at length to anyone she could get hold of about Mussolini and her interview with him and the greatness of Italy, rottenness of France, and muddledness of England. Loud voice, very tedious. A Fascist, carrying the insignia, and the official card with photograph. I had to sit opposite to her at lunch. She tried hard to get up a talk, but I beat her off. All her ideas were wrong. But if anything evil happened to her in Italy she might well change them all. Her acquaintance with Italian customs and Italian was such that when she got her lunch bill and saw "Tassa de Bollo" [Government Tax] at the foot of it, she called the waiter and said she hadn't had any *tassa.* She talked French volubly and not well.

The sunset round about Civita Vecchia was richly marvellous. Such a thing as you couldn't see in England. The whole day was lovely, and quite warm. Lovely bright leaves and blossoms on the trees everywhere. Especially after emerging from the Mont Cenis tunnel and later it was marvellous.

Sunday, April 17th. Rome–Taormina Train.

I had another good night, despite trams and other things outside. I hired a car, after lots of various letter-writing and note-making, and drove to Santa Maria Maggiore, St. Peter's, San Giovanni Lateran, and Santa Croce, and made notes on the same. I also drove up to the Garibaldi Monument (Monte Gianicolo). All this in two hours. I did not feel like lunching wholesale in the hotel, so I went out and found a little *trattoria*, and ate there. Then hired a horse cab, and went to the Pincio Gardens. Very dusty everywhere in Rome. Paid bill and made arrangements, and then went for a walk. The Terme, in front of the station, was closed, but the church (I forget the name) was open, and I went in there and found in the vast place a congregation evidently waiting for a sermon. When I looked at my watch it was 5.25. Train due at 6. I hurried off. I only caught the train by six minutes. It left one minute late, but got to Naples on time.

Monday, April 18th. San Domenico Palace Hotel, Taormina, Sicily.

No restaurant on the train between Naples and Sicily. The car-conductor made black coffee in a little kettle at the end of the corridor. I had two cups with great joy at 8 a.m.

We got to San Giovanni fairly on time (9.35), but fiddled about some time in getting carriages 3 abreast on the steamer-ferry. It was raining. I walked about on the steamer itself, unovercoated in the spitting rain. The crossing took exactly half an hour. We were 20 minutes late on leaving San Giovanni. But the restaurant had been hooked on, and a hungry lot of us rushed into it and began eating before the train left. I had already eaten two apples and an orange and I said to myself, I wouldn't eat much else. But could I resist eggs and bacon? I could not. I ate all there was. This was after 10.30. It didn't seem long before we were at Taormina, where nearly everybody got out. The San Domenico bus was soon full. The climb up to the hotel is terrific. I should say 5 or 600 feet, and when you are in the hotel dining-room you look down on the seat almost perpendicularly. The hotel seems really to have been a monastery. Kahn telegraphed saying "they" would arrive tomorrow afternoon. He is attentive.

Tuesday, April 19th.

Another incredibly good night. I got up at 6.30, feeling that I had had enough sleep. I felt in the humour for work. I decided the form of my cruise articles, namely, the disjointed note form—rather like Taine's *Notes sur l'Angleterre*. I wrote several such notes during the day, and I may do more before I go to bed.

The clerk at the reception told me that Otto K. and party would arrive at 6.30. They did, punctually, having come from Palermo—6 hours' travelling; Kahn being still full of energy. I met Dougherty the painter, and Jo Davidson the sculptor, and Frank Crowninshield after 15½ years, and didn't recognize any of them. There is also David Gray, playwright (part author of *The Best People*), and of course also Rudolf Kommer.

Wednesday, April 20th.

The whole band of us, Kahn, Kommer, Dougherty, Davidson, Gray, and Crowninshield, went out with the mayor, or *podestá*, of Taormina to see the Greek temple, which we saw, and had great fun listening to an Italian guide speaking cockney English to the populace. Then drinks on the *terrasse* of the Timeo Hotel.

A lovely day today, with a superlative moving view of Etna. Some clouds later, and never really hot.

Thursday, April 21st. Hôtel des Etrangers, Syracuse.

Lovely morning. We drove down to Taormina station and caught the 10.18 for Syracuse, which was ten minutes late. I saw a four-master as we entered the town. I said to Kahn: "She's here." But we couldn't be quite sure; I might have seen a four-master trading schooner. The guide awaiting us at the station said that no yacht had come in. We drove to the port, and there was the yacht all right—a magnificent object. Thrilling. We went on board and were greeted by Captain Davies (a Chester man), very young for the post, I thought. We looked over the staterooms and saloons. Highly satisfactory. Beautiful. The artists were thrilled by the yacht. So was I, only more so.

We went to the Hôtel des Etrangers (Casa Polliti) which overlooks the port, and Kahn engaged rooms there. I insisted on some of them having a cup of tea before we rushed off in a terrific haste and pother of dust to the Greek Theatre for a performance in the Greek convention of Aristophanes' *The Clouds*. I expected to be bored by this, but was not. It was very impressive as much by itself as by its surroundings. All classic, legendary, history. Good acting of the play. Clear enunciation heard at a great distance. Fine dancing. I understood all of a sudden the classicalness of the classic drama. We stayed about 100 minutes. It was getting a bit chilly after a blazing afternoon. We saw the quarry De Pasadora, and heard its echo, and saw the surroundings, all very impressive. Then to the Duomo—Greek, Moorish, and Christian—still more impressive. Then back to the hotel.

Friday, April 22nd. Yacht Flying Cloud. *Course about E.*

We all went out soon after ten to the Museum, and saw two fine statues, including the Venus Anadyomene, and a finer earlier one in bronze, and some vases, including a few Greek indecencies; then to the catacombs, very large, but not very interesting; they seemed to me, oddly, to have been made stuffy by the residence of Christians in them; then to the Latomia, the second one, finer even than the one we saw yesterday.

I forget now what time we were clear of the harbour but it must have been something after 5 p.m. When I took the log about 6, we were doing, according to me, 8.9 knots. I then came to my bunk and slept. I felt very tired and not like doing any work, though I had work in my head almost ready.

Saturday, April 23rd. Flying Cloud, *between Sicily and Cape Matapan.*

I didn't have a great deal of sleep, but felt that I had had enough sleep. Sore throat which I might have cured if I could have stopped smoking; but I couldn't. The thing would have to be much more serious to make me give up this habit even for a time. I thought about an article on Syracuse; so soon I was determined to write it today. I was chatting with the Chief Officer on the poop before 6 a.m. Perfect morning. Saw one sail, a brig, about ten miles to the north going westward. Saw nothing else all day. There was a slant of wind, and I reckon that the ship was making 3 or 4 knots under sail only. Four sails set, 2 topsails, 1 top stay-sail, the sky-sail, and three jibs. Bridge has been played nearly the whole day. And it has been a simply magnificent day. Captain Davies said that he was not a yacht-captain but a captain in a yacht. Well, the yacht shows it.

Monday, April 25th. Flying Cloud, *Nauplia.*

We left the yacht at Getheon at 8.3 a.m. and motored to Sparta and Mistra; thence by foot and by mule to the ruined Byzantine City of the Palæologues above Mistra. Lunch in nun's house by church. We left there at 2.30 and motored 100 miles through Arcadia and Argos to Nauplia, where we dined (very well) at the Hôtel Bretagne.

Wednesday, April 27th. Flying Cloud, *at sea between Milo and Crete.*

We anchored in Milo harbour at 7.40 a.m. I had then written 800 words. At 9.45 we went ashore and took mules to the little town on the opposite coast. Damnably uncomfortable riding. I determined to walk back, and did so, despite the considerable heat. We stopped at a curio shop and had wine and water and Turkish delight. The walk back was exhausting. Some of us "had a dip" off the ship before lunch. It all arose from me saying that if the Commodore bathed I should. Kahn replied: "This is a challenge which the Commodore will not reject." In five minutes he was undressed. In six minutes I was.

We weighed anchor for Crete at 1.20, being then 6 hours in front of

our schedule time. There was no object in staying longer at Milo. We
saw the place where the Venus was found. At about 5 p.m. we saw the
mountains of Crete, 60 or 70 miles off, the highest rising to over 8000
feet. The wind shifted westward and gave us a slant. Sail was made, but
by the time it was made, the wind had nearly died away.

Thursday, April 28th.

At 5.45 a.m., Crete seemed to be further off than it was yesterday
afternoon at tea time. In fact sometimes you couldn't see it at all. I
would not go up to the poop to talk to the officer of the watch because
I wanted to think of what I should write about Milo. I wrote the 400
words by 7 a.m. We dropped anchor in the Candia roadstead about
8.30 a.m. We went ashore at 9.30, and drove straight to the Knossos
excavations. Very wonderful, but I was disappointed in the size. Drove
to the Museum in the town. Not in the least disappointing. Got back to
the ship at 12.20, exhausted. Some of us bathed.

We left for Santorin at 6 p.m. Slight head wind. This morning when
I got up all plain sail was still set, and was drawing nicely.

Friday, April 29th. Flying Cloud, *near Paros.*

We anchored off the island of Santorin at 5.30 a.m., and shall proceed
inside the crater-harbour at 9 a.m. The harbour is too deep for anchorage.
Later we went into the crater-harbour. At 8.30 Kahn, Crowninshield,
and Gray walked up to the nearest town. Paul Dougherty, Davidson,
and I made sketches. The walkers returned at 11.30. Kahn said that he
was 60, and had never yet known the sensation of either mental or
physical fatigue. This I believe. He never *is* tired.

We anchored about 7, near Paros, for the night, instead of going on
to Delos as the skipper was not sure of the lying at Delos, and a N. wind
had sprung up. It died about 10.15.

Sunday, May 1st. Flying Cloud, *Piræus, off Athens.*

I corrected my *Sunday Pictorial* article and prepared things for post,
and read François Mauriac, and began to concoct a *conte libertin.—*

Indeed, idleness. I had my first view of the Parthenon and the Acropolis at 3 p.m. We must have anchored shortly before. I couldn't see it properly because of a smaller hill just above it, and rising higher. The harbour people who came aboard seemed a smartly dressed and fishy lot. No luggage was examined. We none of us went ashore except Kahn, who searched for me to go with him, but didn't disturb me because he thought I was asleep. As a fact I was writing the opening chapters of the *roman libertin* (I had enlarged it from the mere *conte* above referred to) which I had in mind. I wrote two chapters (3000 words in all) in a very short time. Shows what you can do when you really have something to say.

Kommer described the beauties of bridge to me very well indeed yesterday morning. He really did *show* its beauties, and made you feel his own pleasure in it as an art and a craft. He started to teach me piquet, but I gave it up, as it bewildered me. He still said that he could make me a *good* bridge player in ten days, if I would practise two hours a day. I declined to believe it, but he insisted. He said: "I'm sure of it, I know you could learn. In the first place *you* have *no* vanity—" However, I don't think I shall learn bridge all the same.

At dinner we talked about the causes of the war, and Kahn was very good on the subject, and showed both knowledge and sense and breadth. He is certainly a tremendous admirer of England's political wisdom.

Monday, May 2nd. Hôtel Petit Palais, Athens.

We left the yacht at 9.30 about, and after landing drove to this hotel. Not an attractive city; but a very good and very small hotel. The first person I saw was Arthur Rubinstein, in a bath-gown, just out of his bath. He joined us at lunch and talked all the time. Kommer called him a traveller in music, and enlarged on this definition very well indeed. We went to the National Museum. The pre-Phidias things were the best. I made up a theory out of this, which I shall use. We then drove to the Acropolis. Dust. Great heat. The Acropolis and the Parthenon fully sustained their reputation. The spectacle was really overwhelming. Also the Anterior room in the Acropolis Museum was equally overwhelming. What sensations! Extreme exhaustion. But after tea, despite this, Kommer and Dougherty and I went out shopping, but didn't get all the photos we wanted. They don't exist in Athens, being out of stock. We were recommended to get them in Florence!

Tuesday, May 3rd.

Sleep. Great discussions in the air throughout the day about a change of plans which would make Constantinople possible. The thing to be settled tonight, I hope. We saw a Byzantine small church after sleep. Intense heat. Then we went shopping in the "Shoe Street" (second-hand quarter). I bought a heavy gold, silver, and lace scarf-shawl for Dorothy. From Salamis; old. Then tea, to which came Mr. Hill, formerly head of the American archæological school here. He took us to the Acropolis, and was intensely interesting and brilliantly clear the whole time.

Saturday, May 7th. Lloyd Triestino Steamer Féodora *between Athens and Constantinople.*

After many delays, we drove to the town of Piræus. Quite a big town, with some streets terribly shabby and slatternly and badly paved, and others rather handsome. After quite a long time we reached the port, and it was quite a port, full of steamers. At last the launch fetched us to the *Féodora*, which had evidently only just arrived. Lovely afternoon and dusk. Smooth sea. Light wind. Lovely view of Piræus on leaving, and marvellous views of the Acropolis half an hour later.

The general atmosphere of the ship was *très sympathique*. A heavenly night. Our lot played just as much cards as usual.

Sunday, May 8th. Pera Palace Hotel, Constantinople.

The sight of the Dardanelles, which we entered about 8 a.m., had a strange solemnizing effect. Not, however, on those who were still in bed, or on those who stuck in a corner of the smoking-room and played bridge. Cooper, Kahn's valet, was the only person who mentioned to me his sensations on beholding Cape Helles and the monument to the slain.

We moored at about 7 p.m. and were kept in the boat till about 8.45 by passport delays, there being many officials and much fuss. Owing to bad staff work two of the three cars went to Yildiz Kiosque for dinner—miles out, when the rendezvous was at the Tokatlian Hotel. They were brought back by telephone. Good dinner at the Tokatlian.

Monday, May 9th.

At 10 we went forth in two cars and saw Santa Sophia, the Blue Mosque, the subterranean bath (Yerebatan Palace, as it is called), the Big Bazaar, and a mosque (unknown) where a service was going on. Lunch at the Turquoise Restaurant, which is Russian. Very good, and served by Russian girls, said by the proprietor to be wives or widows of Russian officers, etc.

The Big Bazaar is very good, and we wanted to go there again. I did very little in the afternoon in the way of seeing, but I wrote quite a lot both before and after tea. Dined at Yildiz Kiosque. A weak imitation of Monte Carlo as regards the gambling. Croupiers very quiet indeed. Petits Champs music-hall. A few women there. Nice auditorium. Among the audience, Polgar noticed a young man who had killed his wife, from jealousy, in Vienna. Bored. We got home at just after midnight.

Saturday, May 14th. Flying Cloud, *between Itea and Olympia.*

At 9.50 we went off in the launch, and three motor cars left at 10 a.m. precisely bearing us, and a luncheon, up to Delphi. Wondrous scenery. Eagles. Clouds. Craggy hillsides. Roads zigzagging upwards in the distance. Hill had charge of us, and Polemi, the regular guide, was worn down to a cipher. The Museum is excellently arranged. After seeing all we wanted to of the Delphic remains, we had tea by the plane tree on the spot where Agamemnon is said to have planted a plane tree, and drove back to Itea. I was on board again at 2 p.m. I got Hill to tell me more about the Delphic Oracle business. Then, determined not to write my impressions until after tea, I passed the time in wirelessing and writing to Dorothy, and in reading up about Delphi.

Sunday, May 15th. Flying Cloud, *between Kalakolo and Corfu.*

I learnt that the string of beads which so many men carry is used merely to employ the hands, apparently thus soothing the nerves. It has no religious significance. The village of Kalakolo was decorated for some fête of the Virgin, and on a high terrace we saw males dancing, and the sound of an instrument like a bagpipes came to us.

The moonlit scene, as the yacht passed between Cephalonia and Ithaca was marvellous, both in romantic quality and in beauty. I got all the card-players out to see it.

Monday, May 16th. Flying Cloud, *between Corfu and Cattars.*

I was on deck at 6.5. The ship was just approaching the S. end of Corfu. The hills of the mainland (? Albania) had a wonderful grey quality. Everybody was utterly and ravingly enthusiastic about the situation of Corfu, and its scenery. It seemed to be the real "earthly paradise." In the drive we saw lots of women in picturesque costume with large head-dresses arranged for burden-carrying, and we saw a vast deal of burden-carrying by women and none by men. Lots of women were working in the fields, and very few men. Every imaginable fruit and vegetable growing. We came aboard with large quantities of wood-strawberries, which are exquisite. The coast scenery of Albania is extremely wild and impressive.

Wednesday, May 18th.

I wrote a description of Cattaro, the ride to Ragusa, and Ragusa before 6 a.m. after only about four hours' sleep. After breakfast we went ashore, and visited monasteries, etc. under the direction of the head of a museum. Some of us left him early and sat in a café. Then rejoined the yacht at the small port and sailed to old Ragusa.

Thursday, May 19th. Flying Cloud. *Spalato.*

We arrived at Spalato about 8 a.m. Lunch on the yacht. Then off in three cars to see Trani, 17 or 18 miles. A rotten, dusty, noisy drive. First we saw the remains of a large Roman town, once the capital of Dalmatia, then a series of horrid cement works in clouds of smoke, and then suddenly we were in Trani, a perfectly preserved medieval town, with a marvellous church, with marvellous sculptures (especially an Adam and Eve on a porch) in a marvellous state of preservation.

Friday, May 20th. Flying Cloud, *at sea between Spalato and Venice.*

A magnificent morning. Flat calm sea. The departure of the yacht renewed all my ferocious desire to be running my own yacht. But now I want a better yacht, faster than the *Marie Marguerite*. By 11 o'clock I had written in all 1100 words of my article for Hearsts, and by 6.15 I had written over 2000 words of it.

At 11.30 we were at anchor within the narrow channel leading to a town beginning with S.,[1] rather medieval. We took the launch, without a pilot, up the river or inlet, to find a celebrated waterfall. We got lost, and ended in a *cul-de-sac*.

We regained the yacht at 2.15, and lunched. The yacht got under way instantly. A very hot afternoon. I had intervals on deck. We called at Zara about 7.30. The port authority would not let us land till the doctor had been on board. So we got out of the launch on to the yacht again. Whereupon the officer said we could land. Ashore military officers had heard of Kahn, and were very polite. Zara is a nice new-looking city, with a straight front right on the sea and many largish cafés on the front. Plenty of promenaders, including many girls, nice-looking. Narrow thronged streets behind, plenty of movement. Much Italianized—you can feel the clinch of the Italian protectorate—and a street called Gabriele d'Annunzio, etc.

Saturday, May 21st. Flying Cloud, *Venice.*

In the afternoon I went on with my own private novel about Arthur. We sailed all day, and got familiar with the lights of Venice about 9.30, feeling our way up and taking a cast at intervals, there was never less than nine fathoms. We flared for a pilot about 10.30, but none came.

---

[1] Sebenico.

About 11.30 we cast anchor; but where, I hadn't the slightest idea. A fine day, with a head wind the whole time, but not much of it.

Sunday, May 22nd.

I hired a two-man gondola after breakfast, and Jo Davidson and I went first to the Grand Hotel and then to the Piazza, and saw the cathedral with some others, and then he and I went off alone and we had a drink at Florian's, and then we resumed the gondola and went to the Belle Arti, and once more I was not particularly struck by it. Then we did a tour of some of the small canals and saw the Colleone statue and got back to the yacht at 12.30.

In the morning Davidson, Crowninshield, and I had ordered a dinner (to be given by the gang to Kahn) in the evening.

Monday, May 23rd.

Pouring with rain. Having nothing to do, I continued my short *Arthur* novel, and wrote about 1000 words. Then ashore at 12.50.

Tuesday, May 24th. Sacher Hotel, Vienna.

Captain Davies came with us to the station (Venice) in the launch. The Grand Canal was marvellously beautiful in the morning light. Train left sharp at 6.25 with Polgar, Kommer, and me in it. Scenery excellent all the way, and magnificent in places. Train arrived at Vienna, before time.

Wednesday, May 25th.

The Schlesingers and Mrs. Adler (Reinhardt's secretary) came to lunch on Kommer's invitation. Then I got my own room and unpacked. Tea with Kommer at a café. Then to station, where we met Dorothy. Diana Cooper and Iris Tree were in the train going to Budapest.

Thursday, May 26th.

We got out at 1 o'clock and then drove, against our judgment, to Hubertishof Restaurant. Wet. Took 35 minutes. A large place, chiefly

for outdoor work. We were the only customers. Good service. Rothschilds
and Chaliapine had been there the night before. At night, when full, it
must be a great sight. Got back into Vienna at 3.20. The Art Museum
was closed. We strolled around. Then to the *Rosenkavalier* at the Opera
House. Full house. Good performance. Olczewska as Ottavia was great.
They were all good. Met Count Kralich there. Music critic—*trés dis-
tingué*. Then to the fashionable supper place. The grill of the Bristol
Hotel. This day apart from my fatigue was very satisfactory.

Friday, May 27th.

My birthday.

We went to the Picture Gallery in the morning. Great sensations. I
was really astounded by the splendour of this gallery. Masterpieces all
over the place. We must have had lunch somewhere, but I can't remember where.

A snack at the Restaurant Sacher in the Ring (no connexion with the
hotel). Good. Then dress, to go to Hofmannsthal's play *Der Schwierige*.
Comedy. Superb production. Very fine acting by Gustav Waldau, Helene
Thimig, and Lili Darvas (wife of Molnar). But everyone acted well. The
whole affair thoroughly and soundly artistic. Reinhardt's secretary came
in and looked after us and explained to us. She is the soul of benevolence.

Monday, May 30th.

We saw the Prater, and went along the Danube a bit, and then had tea
at some place, and got back at 6.5. This was very agreeable. The Danube
is quite a stream. D. and I dined at an open-air restaurant near the
Theater an der Wien. Decent. Then to the said theatre to see Oscar
Strauss's *Die Königin,* supposed to be the rage of the moment. Vienna
is the centre and birthplace of musical comedy. Yet the show was very
poor. Music, on its own plane, not so awful, but the rest awful. Two
women and one man: three stars all well on in age, and without real
talent for either singing, dancing, or acting, and without voices. The
whole affair slack, inartistic, dull, and largely ugly to the eye. We stood
two acts.

Wednesday, June 1st.

Left Vienna at 9.5. Journey without any particular incident.

Monday, June 6th. 75 Cadogan Square, London.

I finished my *Evening Standard* article. It was only sixteen days since I had written anything; yet I felt as if I had not written for a long time, and I was strangely satisfied to have written something again. I then read "in" various poetries and novels.

Maurice Browne was in the drawing-room practising *Don Juan* scenes with Dorothy. By arrangement they came into my study for tea, and we discussed a change at the end of the play. I then drove off to visit Jane Wells. H. G. opened the door himself. Jane was lying on a broad sofa in the drawing-room. She looked ill, but not so ill as I had expected. Enlarged eyes. A sort of exhausted but determined wild cheerfulness in her. H. G. kept going in and out.

Tuesday, June 7th.

I went to Arts Theatre Club, where I found the St. John Ervines and dined at their table.

The Ervines and I went on to the Italian puppets at the Scala. This show, to my surprise, was very good, and I much enjoyed it. Home at 11.15.

Wednesday, June 8th.

I read through the whole of the second part of *Accident* in typescript in the morning, and was rather pleased with it. Miss Nerney is very pleased with it, and insists on its marked originality. Whereat I was well satisfied. Otto Kahn, H. G. Wells, Elinor Wylie, Jeanne de Casalis, and Maurice Browne came to lunch, and there was a vast amount of chatter. Otto was in lovely form.

Thursday, June 9th.

The Woman Who Stole Everything and Other Stories was published today, and was reviewed in the *Manchester Guardian* by Ivor Brown.

Sunday, June 12th.

Alone in the house until tonight. Telephone invitation from Syrie Maugham to dine at her house tonight. I accepted for us both.

Lunch alone, during which I finished reading the current number of *Nature.* Sleep. After which I read Wells's lecture at the Sorbonne, "Democracy under Revision," of which he gave me copy yesterday. Then I went again at my article, and I had finished it at 4.35. I read a lot of Graves's and Edith Sitwell's poetry, and two highbrow monthlies and year books, and most of Virginia Woolf's new novel *To the Lighthouse.* In fact, I had quite a day of writing and reading.

We did actually meet the Maughams at 8.31. Syrie was not down, but W. S. M. awaited us. The new house is now practically finished and looks very strange and agreeable. I saw Liza Maugham (aged 13) for the first time, after having heard of her for years and years. This evening was very agreeable. Just us four, and some nice talking.

I read a few pages of *Karamazov* before sleeping. The relief of a masterpiece after all the "current" stuff which I had been reading and writing during the day!

Tuesday, June 14th.

I drove to the Reform Club to lunch with Herbert Samuel and Gardiner about the project for a dinner of Liberal intellectuals to be held at the Reform. Samuel was late, and he hadn't engaged a table, which rather vexed me. However, his subsequent explanation that he had been at Lord Swaythling's funeral and couldn't avoid lateness placated and reassured me. Sir William Collins, secretary of the Political Committee of the Reform Club was also of the party. We made out a list of suitable guests, and all went well, and Samuel and Collins disappeared immediately the meal was over. In answer to my questions Gardiner told me that he had known Samuel for over twenty years, and that he was an honest man and a *good* man, and entirely dependable, and a tremendous worker.

George Middleton, chairman of the American Dramatists' Guild, called to see me about English authors joining the American Guild for their own protection in regard to American productions of their plays. I signed myself up at once.

We dined at the Julian Huxleys'.

Wednesday, June 15th.

I arose earlyish, ate fruit, and smoked a cigarette on my balcony. I had my earstops in my ears. Milkmen and newsboys and a few cyclists moving about in the Square, in perfect silence. Uncanny: romantic. I wrote about 800 words by 12.15, and then walked to the Reform Club, where I lunched. Home by bus. Sleep. A headache afterwards. Why? But I Coué-ed most of it away at once. Work on *Accident*.

Duff Tayler came to dinner and we went to see Constance Collier in an American play *Meet the Wife*. She was good, but the show as a whole was so awful that we left after the 2nd Act.

Thursday, June 16th.

Not a good night. I left the house at 8.43 by car to see houses at Rye, Winchelsea, and Littlestone-on-Sea. We had seen our first house at Rye before noon. I got back at 7.9, having driven 184.6 miles. Lovely day. Winchelsea heavenly. I think "The Retreat" there will be our choice.

Saturday, June 18th.

Duff Tayler dined with us at Ciro's, and we went to Seymour Hicks's *Mr. What's His Name* at Wyndham's. At second interval we went round to see him. Tears were in his eyes from the stress of the performance. He gave a marvellous show. In the third act he turns the farce into a tragedy, or at least into a highly emotional comedy—with the greatest convincingness.

Sunday, June 19th.

Maurice Browne and a man named Lewis (a B.B.C.[1] person) came

---

[1] British Broadcasting Company.

for tea. I left them at 5, and they proceeded to rehearse the 2nd Act of my *Don Juan* in the drawing-room.

Some fairly heavy showers.

Browne and Dorothy came into my study after the drawing-room rehearsal, and he and I discussed his misapprehension about me having given him an option on *Don Juan*. I told him plainly that all I could do was, if a big, established management took the play, to instruct the management to consider him, Browne, seriously as the producer of the play. Dorothy wanted air, and so we walked out and called at a chemist to get my finger dressed; I had cut it instead of my nails at 7.45 p.m. While it was being dressed, Dorothy chatted with a *grue* who was taking a pick-me-up in the shop. Then we returned to the Green Park, and I had the opportunity of watching the nervousness of the Russian danseuse before she ran into the restaurant for her turn.

Tuesday, June 21st.

Went to the Savoy to the luncheon given to Blumenfeld in honour of the completion of his 40th year in Fleet Street. A vast crowd of 400, including about 20 women, who seemed lost. I sat at table No. 1, and had one of Blumenfeld's daughters on my left, and George Lewis on my right. Lewis was unwell, overwork: he seemed a bit peevish beneath his amiable manner, and left before the speeches began. The others at the table were Burbidge, head of Harrods, and John Buchan (now M.P.)[1] and two whom I didn't know. These proved to be De Vere Stacpoole and Emil Ludwig (author of the recent books on the Kaiser and Napoleon). I had only a very little talk with him. H. G. Wells ought to have been at my table, but did not come. Churchill and Blumenfeld spoke; neither of them well. Then Birkenhead made a very amusing chaffing speech. I fled as it ended.

I got home at 4.25, and found a letter from Cochran asking me to do an "impression" of either Walker or Milligan (protagonists in the forth-

---

[1] Buchan was principal reader for the publishing firm of Bodley Head when Bennett first met him in 1896.

coming middle-weight championship). I replied and sent up the answer by car. Charles Cochran called about 10.30 by appointment, and I arranged to go with him tomorrow at about 3 to see Walker at the Karsino, Hampton Court, tomorrow.

Thursday, June 23rd.

I had a world article on Walker the boxer to write this morning, and to deliver typed by 1.30. So I began it at 7 a.m. and finished it at 10 a.m., and was able to leave the house shortly afterwards for a walk in a rough wind.

T. S. Eliot came to tea. He was very late after saying he wouldn't be. Talked about books and theatres, and I half promised to let him have a lot of my Florence "Journal" for use in the *New Criterion*. I dined at the Other Club. Small but lively company. Hilton Young sat opposite to me and was amusing. One or two new members: J. M. Keynes very agreeable and rather brilliant; and Salmond, the 2nd in command of the Air Force, very strong and silent. Talk drawn out. I should think he is stern but also agreeable. Looks like one born to great authority. Garvin talked all the evening. Locker Lampson was in the chair. Home at 11.15.

Friday, June 24th.

N. came to see me at 9.30 about his critical position. Can't get work. Only earned £23 last month. Has shaved off his beard in order to look younger, and so on. Even at this interview, which was supposed to be very serious, he could not keep to the point. He would fly off to odd, trivial matters which had nothing whatever to do with the point, and I had to bring him back to the point again and again. However it is very easy to criticize a man who has got himself into a mess. I gave him a few ideas for money-making to think over. He left at 10.10. After this my thoughts were miles off my work, and I scarcely hoped to do any. However, by tenacity, I got my thoughts back, and between 11.15 and 12.30 I wrote 600 words of a new chapter of *Accident*. I corrected two articles for Hearsts, and then had time to go out for a walk before Noel Coward came for tea. Noel was very bright and good and sensible, and talked much sagacity to Dorothy. He told me that he had started a novel and written 25,000 but had destroyed it because it was done too hastily and carelessly. He said he *had* to write a play quickly (and that he wrote *Hay Fever* in three days), but he had now found that this method wouldn't do in a novel. So he was going to start again. Sybil Colefax, Alf Mason, Lilian Braithwaite, Peter Colefax, Cynthia Noble, and Hubert Griffith dined. Terrific talking. In the drawing-room the company got split up too much into couples, though the talking was still as lively as ever. I haven't had a really good night for weeks. However, my work is now going a bit better. I got figures from Flower about book sales tonight. *Raingo* has sold over 29,900 copies, and *The Woman Who Stole* sold 548 copies last week—over 12,000 in all he told me yesterday. So that I was rather pleased. Apropos of my article in the *Daily Mail* today, practically everybody I met referred to it. There can be no doubt that no other paper gets into so many hands. In fact everybody seems to make a point of at any rate looking at it. The price of the English-speaking world rights for that 1200-word article is £270. Highest I ever got, I think.

Saturday, June 25th.

Lunch with Dorothy at home. Then we went off for a drive, nominally, but Dorothy landed me at the Tower of London, where I had never been. Very large. Restored to death. Regalia very ugly. Large crowds of people. I drove Dorothy to Edith Sitwell's and came home and had tea, and wrote 250 words more of *Accident* and actually finished the chapter.

In the City, on way to Tower of London, we had tea at a Lyons shop. Good tea. These Lyons and similar places always interest me. I *like* going into them for a tea or a snack and seeing life.

Sunday, June 26th.

I had a really great lark in writing my next Thursday's *Evening Standard* article about Oscar Wilde and other authors. I wrote it at great speed and with unusual verve. Bad weather. But I took a walk. We drove down to Bray, to Leo Schuster's Elgar concert at "The Long White

Cloud." Very heavy rain *en route*. A great crowd of cars and fashionable persons in the music-room and the purlieus thereof at Schuster's. The programme was entitled "Homage to Elgar." A nice thought of old Schuster's. We sat, among Sitwells, just outside the barn-like doors of the music-room, and I soon got cold. I spoke to Elgar and he said, when 1 praised his part of the entertainment: "The silences are good, anyhow." After a pianoforte and violin sonata and a quartet, we departed.

Monday, June 27th.

Ivor Novello, Gertrude Jennings, and the Julian Huxleys came for dinner. A great deal of talk between Novello and us about *Don Juan*. He argued that a long provincial tour would spoil it for London: also that the provinces, except the biggest towns, would not really care for it, would only care for him, and that provincial audiences would *force* him to play down to them. He was rather convincing. Novello made a favourable impression on me.

Wednesday, June 29th.

Eclipse morning. Began at 5.26 a.m. and finished at 7.18, I think. Rain the whole time. Up till nearly 6.30 (when eclipse supposed to be at its height). I perceived practically no diminution of light; but of course the light didn't increase as normally as it would have done. Eclipse was a complete wash-out. Also I had a thoroughly bad night. I wrote 500 words of *Accident* before lunch. I walked to the Reform Club to meet Swinnerton by appointment, and we lunched. Then I resumed the novel. I wasn't quite so fired up as in the morning. In the morning I made Alan[1] lose his temper, and I did it with such heat that I felt as if I had lost my own temper when I went down to see Miss Nerney and I felt called upon to explain to her the cause of my demeanour.

Thursday, June 30th.

We left in the car for Easton Glebe at 10.47, 17 minutes late, and got there at 12.40. Jane Wells was in an easy-chair and then walking about

---

[1] Character in *Accident*.

and she ate lunch with us. Said to be better. But when I asked H. G. privately: "*Is* she better?" he said "No." We sat in a summer-house after lunch, and had tea there at 3.20 and left at 4.5.

Harry Preston gave a dinner at the Green Park Hotel for the Walker-Milligan prize fight. About 22 covers. Michael Arlen and I had the two ends of the long table, and Harry sat in the middle, with Lord Grim-thorpe and Solly Joel on his right and left. I was surrounded by Grant Morden, George Sutton, Freddy Lonsdale, and George Nichols.[1] Grant Morden talked nearly all the time—too much—but he was very interest-ing about James White's suicide. He said that James lost his head in the end. The matter of finding money to take up the shares had been arranged; it then fell through; but it was picked up again, and X. Y. undertook to "find the difference." X. Y.'s secretary sat up all night waiting for W. to come, but White had gone down to his house at Swindon and fixed everything up for his suicide. Michael Arlen drove me and a man called "Mike" to the fight.

Desolate sight at Olympia. Thousands of empty seats. Charles Coch-ran gloomy. Harry Preston had been deceived in his seats and was *most* gloomy. However, Cochran changed them and we got magnificent seats. The world-championship fight—Walker *vs.* Milligan—was the most exciting I ever saw. Milligan was soon done in. Walker won tremendously. And yet he got scarcely a hand (being American) whereas Milligan, smashed to bits and tottering (with stitches in his lip), was terrifically cheered. This because of Milligan's mad pluck. Walker crossed himself before fighting. Arlen drove me home and came in for a drink. He said his new book had been a great frost.

Friday, July 1st.

Appointment for 6 o'clock with Edward Newton, the American biblio-phile, apropos of a suggested introduction by him to the reproduced MS. of *The Old Wives' Tale.* I was 25 minutes late. A shameful position, and inexcusable. Newton and I agreed that a preface by him seemed neither practicable nor useful, and we gave the idea up, especially as I had

---

[1] Bennett wrote an introduction to Nichols's book *London Town.*

already written an introduction myself and the sheets were already printed and signed by me. Dined at home with Dorothy and we went to Playroom Six, 6 New Compton Street, to see d'Annunzio's *The Honeysuckle*. The play had form, interest, and power in its voluptuous way, but the performance was simply terrible. The theatre only holds about 100 people. It has a nice atmosphere, and the bar, etc. is *sympathique*, especially the gas-ring lodged on a chair.

Saturday, July 2nd.

I wrote 400 words of *Accident* before going out; then forty minutes' activity in the streets of London; then another 300 words. Then lunch with Dorothy. Then a sleep—not deep or reposeful. Then another 400 words, finishing another chapter. I was then in a state of nerves. But having the scheme of the prefatory note which Bertie Sullivan and Newman Flower desired me to write for their biography of Arthur Sullivan, I decided to write it at once, and I did so, getting it off my chest. 400 words. Sprightly. I then went out for a walk in the fair but unsatisfactory weather. Returned by bus. Dined alone with Dorothy. We played the greater part of Schubert's Octette—pianoforte 4 *mains*. Great noise and fun, which did me much good, for I had been depressed.

Tuesday, July 5th.

London representative of the *Amsterdam Telegraaf* came to see me about Dutch rights of my *Evening Standard* articles. A short dark man, probably of Spanish descent, with a foolish short beard. Full of brains and awareness. We were most charming to one another. I said he could have the Dutch rights of the article for £5 a week. I didn't want to ask more.

Wednesday, July 6th.

I walked quickly, with perspiration, in hot sunshine, to get ideas for *Accident*, and reached the Tate Gallery. I thought I would look at the Conders. No sooner was I in the Conder room than Aitken, the director, came along, towing Lewis Hind and wife and two young men, one at least of whom was a son of Mitchell Kennerley. Then, when I had shaken myself free, Aitken, who is a very nice fellow, came along again to me and took me along to see the big wall decorations, by a young man named Whistler, aged 21, in the refreshment-room—decorations still far from finished. I enjoyed them. I got outside and walked around. Finally into a tram to Victoria and thence by bus to Sloane Square. By good chance I found the ideas I wanted, and wrote them for three-quarters of an hour.

We went on to Holland Park Hall to see Lenglen play tennis. Sparsely filled. The men's singles (Cozelin and Kinsey) were fine. Women's singles poor, because Lenglen (v. Dewhurst) had nothing to do. Cozelin is an exceedingly fine player. I should like to see him against Tilden. Another thing that I should like to see would be Lenglen against a man —I mean a really good one, a first-rate man. She would be beaten, but it would make a fine show, and would restore the public perspective. Lenglen is short and walks well, though with a rather peculiar step.

Friday, July 8th.

Crossing St. James's Square I was accosted by a smart military-bearing man of 60 or so, in white top hat, white waistcoat, etc. "Arnold Bennett?" "Yes," I said. "And you?" He was the second son of A. B. D. S., late of Hanley. He said he had been 30 years in the army. Quite a pleasant encounter. He said I was just like my photos. I didn't like that much.

Then D. and I played "in" the Grieg pianoforte concerto, and she and I played four hands first movement of a Schubert trio. I drove up to the Garrick Club to dine with Duff Tayler. James Whale was dining here with Dorothy. Quite a warm day. I was fantastically tired at tea time, after my work.

Saturday, July 9th.

I have the last few days been reading Prince Mirsky's volume on modern Russian literature. Better than I had expected, from memories of the reviews of it. I still have scores of books unopened which I ought to look at but shall not. They seem to come in at the rate of about two a day. I had three today.

Sunday, July 10th.

To Arts Theatre Club, where we sat next to Gerald Duckworth and wife. A curtain-raiser of Sudermann, one of his one-act plays about roses. Rotten, old-fashioned, untrue, purely silly thing. Why it was produced I cannot imagine. Then the *Histoire du Soldat* of Stravinsky. Nothing much in this. Childish re-telling of the old devil-story; very much out of proportion. Music its only *raison d'être* and the music not very distinguished.

Monday, July 11th.

George Arliss came at 4.30 for tea and to discuss Edgar Selwyn's scenario for *Lord Raingo*. He had been sufficiently interested to do a scenario of his own, and after much talk he said that he would re-write his own scenario. An attractive, very "sound" fellow of about 50 or 55, with the true actor's face. Quiet, firm, no frills, no theatrical gush whatever. He said he was frankly old-fashioned as to the art of the theatre. Liked the old. Thought the new no good. Didn't think there had been any progress, or ever would be. I liked him. He stayed till 6 p.m.

We went to the Russian ballet. Enormous crowd. We went chiefly to see Satie's *Mercury* which I rather liked. Mise-en-scène extremely odd and original. I also saw *Cimarosiana* and *The Cat* for the first time. All very original and striking. The Russian ballet is looking up a bit.

Wednesday, July 13th.

Mrs. Patrick Campbell came for lunch. She looked a bit younger, and referred all the time to her great age. She was extremely brilliant, and was magnificent with the baby. She was full of sense and very strongly dissuaded Dorothy from returning to the stage in small parts. She said, better and with more authority, all that I had been saying to Dorothy on this great matter.

Friday, July 15th.

Duff Tayler and I dined together and we went to the Russian ballet gala performance for the King of Spain, who raised his hands and applauded everything. I saw *The Cat* for the second time, and now am decided that it is beautiful. I saw *Prince Igor* again and thought it magnificent. *The Triumph of Neptune* I definitely did not care for. Vast crowd. The latter half of the Russian ballet season is a great success.

Saturday, July 16th.

At 11.10 we set off by car for Knole, to lunch with Edward Sackville-West. Eddie proved just as delightful as ever. After lunch, he took Dorothy to see the main part of the house—he lives over the main gateway, up turret-stairs and things. His rooms, very thick walls, etc., struck me as chill.

Sunday, July 17th.

I read on in Tolstoy's *A Confession* and slept. Then a longish walk along Chelsea Embankment. I stopped in Cadogan Street to see the start of the R. C. procession of "Our Lady of Ransom." Fairly picturesque. Two bands. Many young girls (kids) in veils, some holding banners, and all under the obvious influence of emotion. It just didn't rain.

Tuesday, July 19th.

I went on with *Accident* today morning and afternoon, and finished it about 6.30 p.m. I didn't care much for the last 300 words. Total length 67,300 words. I felt gloomy as usual when I had finished it.

George Arliss sent me his own scenario for *Lord Raingo*. This is the second one he has done. It has points, but as it stands is really quite useless. So is Edgar Selwyn's.

I drove with Dorothy up to Garrick Club, and she went on to dine at the Morrells'. At the Garrick Freddie Lonsdale gave a dinner to about 15 people. I was the chief guest. Very merry, this affair. Some great stories. It ended with bridge.

Wednesday, July 20th.

By way of holiday today, the day after finishing my novel, I wrote two *Evening Standard* articles, one in the morning and the other in the afternoon. I went for three walks, and my weight in the evening was less than it can have been for very many years: 10 st. 9 lb. 13 oz.

Thursday, July 21st.

I prepared the whole of the copy for my next book of essays. (I thought of a title *Gusto* for it, but I doubt if it will do.)[1] This was my second day's work after finishing my novel.

Friday, July 22nd.

I wrote the preface to my new book of essays during the morning, despite interruptions. Then I walked quickly to the Reform Club and lunched with Masterman, etc. Masterman was in great form. After lunch his description of the state of things in the East End inspired me to resolve to take politics more seriously in my future articles in *The World Today* than I had intended.

As I came home on the bus (top), a woman who had climbed up after me said: "I'm on the wrong bus, and I got on to it so that I would travel by the same bus as Arnold Bennett." She was a lady and seemed quite serious. She got off the bus before Hyde Park Corner. I was quite touched. I talked to her a bit.

Chalmers Mitchell dined with me at Reform. I spoke to Festing Jones, who was dining with Siegfried Sassoon. Chalmers Mitchell took me to the Zoo, the Geoffrey Russells and Lady Decies and a friend joined us, and C. Mitchell showed us the Reptile House and the Aquarium by night. Staggering.

Tuesday, July 26th.

Lunched at Sybil Colefax's. Rather learned. Balfour, Lewis Malet, Garvin, Julian Huxley. Women: Ruth Draper, Mrs. Garvin, Lady Edward Grosvenor. More men than women. I sat between Ruth and Mrs. Garvin. I talked to Ruth about the critical work she might do on men. She wanted ideas for this. Mrs. Garvin talked to me about *The*

---

[1] Published as *The Savour of Life*.

Price of Love, for which she has much affection. This pleased me.

Bishop of Liverpool [1] called to see me at 6 sharp. Wanted me to contribute to a series of little books which will be meant to help to show some sort of design, order, divine origin in the world, 5000 to 10,000 words each. I said I would contribute a booklet if he could suggest to me some subjects which appealed to me. Tall, dark, muscular chap, decided, clear tones and movements. A ready smile at a joke. I liked him. I saw him out. He had a dispatch-case and an umbrella. He wouldn't have a taxi. Set off to walk towards Paddington.

I then read the first pages of Wells's *Meanwhile,* which arrived this morning. Dorothy Massingham came to dinner, and we talked personalities about our friends. I took her to see Lonsdale's *On Approval* at the Fortune Theatre. Not a bad first act in a very old-fashioned "smart" way, with some very good jocular lines. In the first *entr'acte* in came Elizabeth Bibesco and a young man. She said she hoped the first act was not the best act. I said it would certainly be the best act. She had merely arrived one hour late for the play.

Wednesday, July 27th. Easton Glebe, near Dunmow.

H. G. Wells called for me and drove me down to Easton to see Jane. First part of the drive in heavy rain. When it cleared up we stopped and had a drink at a pub on the edge of the forest, gin and ginger-beer. We arrived at 12.6. Jane had just got downstairs. She is carried down, and wheeled everywhere; but she walks a few steps. H. G. had said she was better, stronger; but she didn't seem to me to be so. Jane keeps an eye on the house. She had just arranged for the servants' holidays. Several people came in during the afternoon. Bridge first. Then tennis. Wells joined in both. Nobody for dinner except 1 nurse. H. G. went upstairs to spend 15 minutes with Jane, and then came down and we talked till 11.10. At the end he made tea for himself. We discussed his wife, his servants, his sons. He was in favour of me politically running *The World Today,* and said that whatever I undertook I should succeed in.

---

[1] Dr. Albert David.

Thursday, July 28th. Royal Victoria Hotel, St. Leonards.

I saw Jane Wells in bed before I left Easton Glebe. Left in car for Winchelsea at 2.30. Arrived there 5.10. Tea with Dorothy, nurse, and baby.

Friday, July 29th.

We drove over to Winchelsea at 11.35. I walked down to Winchelsea beach, and lay on pebbles and read H. M. Tomlinson's *Gallions Reach*, which is not good. The rest of the family arrived later in bits. Great trouble over the tent—too flimsy. I went off and read more Tomlinson. Robert Nichols, who had brought me flowers yesterday, came in for tea.

Monday, August 1st.

Dorothy worked on a scenario of *Lord Raingo* in morning. We left for Winchelsea at 12.26.

Wednesday, August 3rd.

Went to see the *Metropolis* film at the Élite Theatre. Sickening sentimentality. Many good effects, spectacular, spoilt by over-insistence. A footling story. No understanding of psychology of either employers or workmen. "Adapted by Channing Pollock." Good God! What captions. Enough to make you give up the ghost. The theatre was very nearly empty.

Thursday, August 4th.

During the evening I finished reading Katherine Mayo's *Mother India*. This book is very remarkable.

I have spent hours of meditation on my new task of politically editing *The World Today*. I tried to read Chapman's Homer. Couldn't. Finally I resumed Gibbon.

Friday, August 5th.

I wrote part of an article in the morning for *Evening Standard*. Komisarzhevsky and wife came at 12.30. She is Austrian. They talk Russian when alone. She learnt it in nine months. Agreeable and pretty and melancholy. After five hours' acquaintance she told me all sorts of things about the disadvantages of her life in London. "Lost in Kommy," etc. They lunched with us. We drove over to Winchelsea.

We had tea at the Beach Café. Not bad. Sort of lady-waitresses. We asked for salt. The waitress cried: "Salt—whatever *for?*"

Sunday, August 7th.

Robert Nichols paid us three visits at the house during the day. We also saw him with his wife's brother-in-law, Sir Everard Digby Pauncefort Duncombe, on the beach. Robert said that this blond relative did nothing for a living. I said that a man with a great name like that was entitled to do nothing. We had tea on the beach, and I had some responsibilities with Virginia, who bathed like anything.

Wednesday, August 10th.

We drove over to Winchelsea at noon. Lunched with the Robert Nicholses to meet Arthur Symons and wife. We had met wife in Paris with the Sutros about 18 months ago. Arthur Symons, a little, very pale, white-haired man, prim. He is full of reminiscences of French and English authors, especially French. Verlaine and Baudelaire and Villon he considers to be the three greatest French poets,—the rest not comparable. I rather liked him. He is in every way a "little" man, but with real taste and refinement.

Tuesday, August 16th.

After dinner I went out for a walk on the beach at low tide. I got as far as Hastings Pier. Wonderful twilight effects of black figures against grey water and foam, and bits of cold blue sky, etc.

Wednesday, August 17th.

I left for Petworth at 10.45. We drove on the way to Midhurst, so as not to be too early for Alf Mason's lunch at his house New Grove. We got there well on time, and he came out to meet us on the gravel. Duff and Diana Cooper came later. Garden afterwards. A pleasing house, built in 3 periods: pre-Tudor, Tudor, and William and Mary. Not much architecturally, except the latest part. At my request Alfred gave me his new book *No Other Tiger*. First book of his I shall have read since (I think) *The Four Feathers*.

Friday, August 19th.

Reading of all the letters I have received from George Sturt. The scene begins in 1895. This is for the introduction which I am to write for his posthumous work. These letters are extremely good, and many of them ought to be printed in full. They made me feel sad, somehow; because I saw in them a reflection in commentary of the history of all my literary life—over thirty years.

Saturday, August 20th.

I read Ostrovsky's play *The Suitors,* which Komisarzhevsky wants to begin with at the Court Theatre. It is a good, quiet, old-fashioned, and very *Russian* comedy of manners, with all that damned Russian incapacity and financial corruption—which we are so sick of in Russian manners. It would have no chance whatever on the London stage. People would wonder what the hell it was all about. Dorothy agreed; in fact she was more severe than I was. So it will be turned down.

Sunday, August 21st.

Bernstein, the "business man" in Komisarzhevsky's and our "Sloane Productions Co. Ltd.," which is to run at the Court Theatre in the autumn, was to have come down for lunch today. He arrived—scarcely hoped for—at 3.25, and stayed for tea. He proved to be all right, *sympathique,* young, some artistic perceptions and some artistic blindnesses. Thus he could see *nothing* in *Malborough s'en va-t-en guerre.* Before dinner I read Merezhkovsky's *Paul I* and decided that it would do for the Court Theatre.

I have been very gloomy; I began to be gloomy yesterday. Dorothy pointed out to me that my liver is out of order, and I think it certainly is.

Thursday, August 25th.

Dorothy went to Winchelsea by bus. I walked on the front westwards and watched bowls and thought of the plot of my next story "Under the Hammer," [1] for about 1½ hours. By appointment Chalmers Roberts of Heinemanns came down for lunch and tea to discuss *The World Today* projects. He brought with him a young man named Longwell (of Doubledays) over on a holiday of inspection. Quite agreeable.

I finished reading *Coningsby* on Tuesday. It is a sad welter. No construction. Very little cohesion. Too much eloquence. But there are good things in it. It is very rich and varied. The big interview between Monmouth and his grandson Coningsby towards the end, written in a very inflated style, is excellent in force and effectiveness—the convention of it being once granted. Much of the political criticism is good, and much of it very epigrammatic and amusing.

Friday, August 26th.

We left for Wittersham soon after 12. We were 12 minutes late for lunch at the Arthur Symonses, who live at Island Cottage. "Quaint old place." Symons very proud of it, and began showing it off at once, garden and all. Mrs. Jowett (K.C.) was there.

It was a lively lunch. Symons pleased me by referring most enthusiastically to my old *Yellow Book* story, "A Letter Home." He said it was equal to de Maupassant. And so on.

Bed early. The secret of health and equanimity is to go to bed early.

Sunday, August 28th.

I meant to begin my short story "Under the Hammer" in the afternoon. Then I finished the Masterman thriller, and I couldn't concentrate on my own story, so I wrote an *Evening Standard* article on thrillers, etc.

Monday, August 29th.

During the afternoon and evening I was much held by Julian Green's

---

[1] Published in *The Night Visitor.*

Adrienne Mesurat.[1] This is a very fine novel—but I've read only half of it yet. It is the most "holding" French novel that I've read for years.

Wednesday, August 31st.

At 5 or so we drove into Goodwood Park and had tea at a sort of rendezvous with the famous "Shell House" near by; the last is good. I spoke to Lady Diana about her playing at the Court Theatre.

Sunday, September 4th. 75 Cadogan Square, London.

We left St. Leonards at 2.18, and did the first 50 miles in 90 minutes, which was some going.

We had an appointment with Komisarzhevsky and Bernstein here at 7 p.m. We decided that the 2nd production at the Court Theatre should be *Mr. Prohack*, subject to Golding Bright's approval on behalf of Knoblock. Komi and Bernstein only left at 8.20 when Dorothy happily turned them out.

Monday, September 5th.

Shortly after 6 I began on the book proofs of *The Vanguard*, and worked on them for 1¾ hours. Dorothy and I dined at Beaverbrook's office. Max invited me to go to Berlin with him on Friday. I said I would. Just the sort of holiday that I am after.

Thursday, September 8th.

Dorothy and the Swinnertons for lunch, and we settled our course of conduct—I mean F. S. and me—to be followed when Doran at last wrote to us to say that he had sold his business to Doubleday's.

Harriet Cohen came for tea—hadn't seen her for months. I had to leave her, and Dorothy had to leave her to see the actor Charles Laughton, whom I had to pass as a possible "Prohack." He passed with honours in about five minutes.

Geoffrey Russell dined with me. We had some talk afterwards with

---

[1] The English title was *The Closed Garden*.

Harold Nicolson, who said he was writing a work on biography.[1] He asked me what I thought was the best English biography. I said Lockhart's *Scott*. He said he thought so too.

Friday, September 9th. S.S. Deutschland, *English Channel.*

The excursion party consists of Beaverbrook, Venetia Montagu, Castlerosse, Diana Cooper, and me. Train punctual. Arrived at quay at 6.15. Found we had to go down to the Solent in a tender to join the *Deutschland*. Tender very slow in starting. And, having arrived in the Solent, had to wait about an hour for the *Deutschland* to turn up. The *Deutschland* is only a 20,000-ton ship, but looked enormous, endless, as we boarded her about 8.30 p.m.

Saturday, September 10th. S.S. Deutschland, *off Flemish and German coasts.*

Sailing all day. Never saw any land worth talking about. Ship not very interesting. Music three times a day. Dance at night. I read some of Mottram's *Our Mr. Dormer*. Good. Also the last pages of *Le Temps Retrouvé;* I got ideas for an article thereupon; they came to me. Otherwise, I purposely kept off all cerebration.

Sunday, September 11th. Hotel Adlon, Berlin.

No trouble with customs. Arrived at Berlin 4.40. Kommer was there. In fact he is staying here. Walk along Wilhelmstrasse. Rendezvous at bar with Diana and Kommer and Venetia Montagu at 7.30. Cocktail. Sandwich. Then to Grossesschauspielhaus to see German spectacular transmogrification of *The Mikado,* by Challer. Then, after 75 minutes of this, to a restaurant to dine.

Monday, September 12th.

At my request, before dinner, Max gave a full account of the rise of Baldwin. I wanted this for my first political article. It was a marvellous

---

[1] *Development of English Biography* was published in 1928.

narrative, and full of meat for me. All of us were enthralled. I wrote part of it in shorthand as he talked and more afterwards before dinner. Thus although we were not timed to leave the hotel for dinner till 9 p.m. we were still later—twenty minutes late.

Dined at a good restaurant in a suburb. I heard neither name nor place. Fine boulevards and plenty of electric signs here and there of restaurants, etc., etc. At 11.45 we set off to get hold of Sinclair Lewis (who had called at the hotel during day) so that he and Castlerosse and perhaps all of us might go and see night life. However, Sinclair's fiancée, Dorothy Thompson, correspondent of a Philadelphia paper, had a small party.

Tuesday, September 13th.

In morning, I went out with Kommer to Charlottenburg to buy books and things. I bought a few German books and some good coloured reproductions of Cézanne, Seurat, etc. very cheap. Lunch with Castlerosse, Sinclair Lewis, Bartsch (a director) of Ufa, and three American journalists—all very agreeable. No time for sleep. We went at 4 to Potsdam to see Sans Souci. Fine avenues thither, speed-roads, etc. Back at 6.25. The girls, Kommer, and I went to Piscator's Communistic play *Hoppla wir leben* at the Rollenplatz Theatre.[1]

Wednesday, September 14th.

Broken but good night. Didn't definitely awake till 9 a.m. Weyland (secretary) came in at 10.35, before I had begun to dress to say that Max had been after all forced to go to see the Ullstein establishment,[2] and would I go with him at 11? I dressed in 25 min. and went. We all went. 20 minutes' drive from the Adlon. Huge place. Finished this year. The visit to the Ufa establishment was dished at the last moment by Max having a sore throat and going to bed till dinner-time. Tea with Kommer and Venetia at the *chic* tea-place. The girls, Kommer, and I went to the opera at 7 p.m. *Tristan*. Frida Leider was superb as Isolde. Good orchestra. Kommer and Diana left at 8.20 to see Reinhardt.

---

[1] Erwin Piscator was the producer; the author was Ernst Toller.
[2] One of the largest German publishers of books and periodicals.

Thursday, September 15th. Train between Berlin and Cuxhaven.

Nothing in morning except a walk in Unter den Linden and Leipzigerstrasse with Castlerosse.

The Ufa people sent a car and a representative to take us to the Ufa studios, and the excursion took place which ought to have taken place yesterday. Usual screen stuff. We saw two films being done simultaneously. Back at 5.10.

Friday, September 16th. Hamburg-Amerika Liner New York.

We arrived at Cuxhaven only a few minutes late, and were on board the *New York* at about 11.30. This is a less uglily decorated ship than the *Deutschland,* and being a bit later, has a few new contraptions. Thus in the cabins there is wireless.

I am now near the end of Mottram's *Our Mr. Dormer.* It is all good, and the last third is the best. This man has an original mind.

Wednesday, September 21st. 75 Cadogan Square, London.

Trying to begin my first article for *The World Today,* but unable really to make up my mind to start. Nervousness, I suppose. I have most of the required ideas, however. I went out for a walk instead of working. And afterwards instead of working I read a "thesis" on myself, and the paper.

Thursday, September 22nd.

This morning came a cable from Doran announcing his amalgamation with Doubleday, Page & Co. Swinnerton and I had been wondering how he would break this news to us (seeing that he had always sworn such a thing was absolutely out of the question), and his cable solution is characteristically clever. To Apollo Theatre to see Strindberg's *The Father.* Met Nelson Keys there, who said he was still looking for a play and was going to America to look for one. Very disappointed with *The Father.* It is the work of a madman, inconsequent, loose, too quick, too slow, sort of shaking all the time.

Sunday, September 25th.

We drove down to Easton Glebe to see Jane Wells. Frank Wells was there with fiancée Peggy, and Gyp with wife Marjorie. Jane was too ill to come down or to see anyone. H. G. was visibly very much upset indeed. The Hugh Byngs came to lunch, too. I think H. G. likes a lot of people to distract him. We played a bit of ball game in the barn, but not H. G. nor Marjorie. Basil Dean and Lady Mercy [1] called in about 3.30. I read most of Jäckh's *The New Germany* in the afternoon and evening. Still going on with Gibbon.

Tuesday, September 27th.

Mrs. Patrick Campbell and Komisarzhevsky came for lunch—in order to meet each other. Komi said very little. Stella talked tremendously, and very well. Her ideas are exceedingly sound, and in spite of all that I have heard about her naughtiness, she seems to me to be fundamentally good-natured. She said more than once that she was unpleasant, whereas Dorothy was by nature courteous. These two like one another. Then I went over to the theatre to see a rehearsal, having previously learnt—but only by my own inquiries—that the directors' meeting supposed to be arranged for tonight had not been arranged at all. I was rather glad, as this would give me an extra 90 minutes at least for my work. I stayed at the rehearsal till after 5, hearing Mrs. Pat's excellent criticisms. I came back and finished my general political survey.

Friday, September 30th.

Chores. Walked up to Piccadilly Circus, in sunshine, thinking about my short story and getting a few ideas.

I went to the first dress rehearsal. It started an hour later. At 6.25 the last act was only just begun. I got home at 6.30. Dorothy came in soon after. Dined at home. We went to the Gate Theatre (held at the Ettlinger Theatre temporarily). 1st night of Paul Green's *The Field God*. Farmhouse stuff. Goodish dialogue but not *really* true. Anyhow a change from the West End drawing-room stuff. It had moments of truth. But the

---

[1] Dean's wife, *née* Lady Mercy Greville, daughter of the fifth Earl of Warwick.

thing is really nothing but a chronicle play. No genuine construction or artifice. Just a tale. Nicely produced. I rather liked the light being centred on the middle of the stage. So that people walking along down stage showed only like black silhouettes. But this of course was quite as untrue to life as any other form of lighting.

Tuesday, October 4th.

I went to a rehearsal of *Paul I* in the morning after a walk in Battersea Park.

Court Theatre crowded.[1] Good performance. Only fair reception. George Hayes, Charles Laughton, and Dorothy all admirable. Reception in Dorothy's dressing-room afterwards.

Sunday, October 9th.

I walked 2¾ miles in Battersea in the morning—lovely morning—and saw the aviary, which is rather poor, and then came home and began on Act III of *Mr. Prohack*. After lunch I attacked Act III again. I must have done three hours of really concentrated work on it during the day. I was very tired.

Monday, October 10th.

I finished the revision of Act III of *Mr. Prohack* before lunch, after a walk in the Park. As a fact it needed less work on it than I had feared. I then had to go at once to Jane Wells's funeral. Lots of people there, and only one man in full mourning. The Wells family and wives were not in mourning. Shaw had an amber handkerchief and no overcoat. Number of really A1. people present, very small; which shows how Wells kept out of the "great" world and how the great world is not practically interested in Wells. T. E. Page read the funeral oration (written by H. G. himself) very well.

Tuesday, October 11th.

Chores. I then attended part of a rehearsal of *Mr. Prohack*. Charles Laughton very fine as Mr. P. and Lydia Sherwood good as Sissie.

---

[1] The first night of *Paul I*.

I went to the Albert Hall, as guest of the Cochrans, to hear Chaliapine in Rimsky's *Mozart and Salieri* and in the new scene in *Boris*. The first is not very interesting. Chaliapine was tremendous and lovely as the monk in *Boris*. I met Ramsay MacDonald in the corridor, and was introduced to him by a man on the *Daily Herald* who only knew me by sight. "Well, Bennett," MacDonald began. I wonder what he will think when he reads my remarks on him in *The World Today*.

I walked both to and from the Albert Hall. When I got home I found A. J. Munnings here. He is an old friend of Dorothy's. A decent, chatty fellow. He said that Dorothy's brother [1] is the finest landscape painter in England and that a few people know it. At which Dorothy was justifiably much pleased.

Wednesday, October 12th.

H. G. Wells telephoned he would like to spend the afternoon with me. We went to see the film *Chang* at the Plaza. Very good. Then tea at Slater's in Piccadilly. Then I left him. Marjorie Gordon dined with me at the Yacht Club and I took her to *The Silver Cord* [2] at St. Martin's. Lilian Braithwaite, Clare Eames, and Marjorie Mars. I liked the play. It had one first-rate scene in 2nd Act between husband and wife. Some American clumsiness in the play.

Friday, October 14th.

Rehearsal of *Mr. Prohack* in the morning. I lunched at home, having had my little exercise. Then after a sleep I returned to the theatre for another rehearsal, till after 5 p.m. Then reading. I do not read enough, and have far too many books which ought to be read but aren't.

Saturday, October 15th.

Madame Komisarzhevsky was to arrive at 3.30 to play duets with me. I was fully awake at 3, and so I thought I would just begin my next week's *Evening Standard* article. She came at 4.15. By that time I had nearly finished my article. We played Haydn and Schubert. She read very well,

---

[1] C. S. Cheston, artist and etcher, member of New English Art Club.
[2] By Sidney Howard. It was produced in New York in 1926.

and said that she had never had a lesson in her life. She said that Englishmen were not interesting. I contradicted her, and offered to show her lots of interesting Englishmen. She said she much wanted to see them.

On the first full week of *Paul I* we have paid off £150 towards production expenses. This is very good, for a thoroughly gloomy play.

I finished my *Evening Standard* article before dinner, all by utilizing spare moments. This is the secret of doing more work than you can in the time at your disposal.

Monday, October 17th.

Rehearsal of *Prohack* at Court at 11. Nearly everybody late. However, I saw the 1st part of Act III gone through for the first time, and decided that, with cutting, it would do very well indeed. Komisarzhevsky came for tea, and we went through Act III except the end; all right except cutting. But he wanted a change of construction in Act II, which rather troubled me.

Dinner given by his friends to Harry Preston at the Piccadilly Hotel. I sat between Cochran and Lucas, with Sickert next to Lucas. Dewar was the star orator, and far from as good as usual. Harry P. made a perfect speech in reply. This dinner was organized by Lord Decies.

Wednesday, October 19th. Queen's Hotel, Manchester.

Came to Manchester by 11.50 a.m. arriving at 3.40 for performance of *Flora*[1] at Rusholme.

The *Manchester Guardian* man came to the hotel, and I gave him tea. Then he took me out to see architecture. Damned little to see. I got a car to drive to Rusholme. Theatre full except two back rows. Theatre quite decent, considering that it was once the stable of the Tramway Company (in horse days). I was pleased on the whole with the play. It certainly has holding power, and this power survived even the acting.

Thursday, October 20th.

I took the 12.5 back to London, which went through the Potteries. The sight of this district gave me a shudder.

---

[1] Bennett's play, not as yet produced except at this theatre.

Sunday, October 23rd.

Went 2½ mile walk in Battersea Park to find ideas for short story "The Wind." [1] I found them. I wrote 800 words of "The Wind," read various things, went for a short walk, had tea alone, and played on the floor with the infant in the nursery.

Monday, October 24th.

Lydia Sherwood (in the cast of *Mr. Prohack*) came for lunch and was most agreeable. She had been out shopping with Dorothy for theatre clothes. Sleep, after they had gone. I then went over to the rehearsal for a bit. Dorothy had got me the script of Act II. After tea I re-wrote, in the form desired by Komi and Dorothy, the beginning of the act. It was posted to Komi at night.

Tuesday, October 25th.

To first night of Coward's *Home Chat*. Not good; but Noel's best play up to date. I told him so. I then called for Dorothy at Court Theatre, and we went to Syrie Maugham's party in honour of Noel's first night. Many people. A very good party.

Thursday, October 27th.

I went to South Kensington Museum to think, and I thought. Then I wrote the penultimate section of my story "The Wind" in about an hour. I dined with Geoffrey Russell at the Reform, and we went to the Lener concert together at Queen's Hall. Fine concert. All Mozart. I thought that exclusive Mozart would be trying, but it wasn't.

Monday, October 31st.

I wrote the Russian part of my next *World Today* article, so that it might be vetted by a lawyer as being "safe" from the Official Secrets Act. Then I drove to the Court Theatre and assisted at a rehearsal of *Prohack* for an hour. At 2.30 I flew over to Sybil Colefax's at her special request, to show me to Granville Barker and wife. G. B. has become prim. I got

---

[1] Short story reprinted in *The Night Visitor*.

across him on the subject of a French play *Maya*, which he liked and I did not.

Saturday, November 5th.

I took Dorothy to the Court Theatre, and went off to hear Poushinoff give the last of his six pianoforte recitals of Chopin. Quite a good audience. What fame—Chopin's—to stand six consecutive evenings after 100 years!

Friday, November 11th.

I walked out and "saw" the Two Minutes Silence from inside the lobby of the Court Theatre. When I saw old gents standing two minutes in that perishing wind, hatless, I was glad I'd come inside. Rehearsal of *Prohack* 11.10 to 1.15. Then rush to Bernard Shaws' to lunch at their new flat in Whitehall Court, to meet Trebitsch the original author of *Jitta's Atonement*. Trebitsch, who pleased me, was pleased with Dorothy for Jitta. The St. John Ervines also present. All very agreeable.

Wednesday, November 16th.

I dressed, and went off to entertain Major and Mrs. Whittall at the Yacht Club. It is a fact that between 8.15 and 10.15 or 10.20 I never once remembered that the first performance of *Mr. Prohack* was going on at the Court Theatre. The Whittalls left about 10.35. I smoked a cigarette, after a cigar, and then drove down to the theatre. The curtain had just fallen. It kept going up again while I was in the wings or near the wings. Much satisfaction in the wings, on the staircases, and in the dressing-rooms. Charles Laughton very pleased with himself, as he had the right to be, seeing he had had a great triumph. Everybody who "came round" professed the greatest enjoyment of the play. I almost believed in a success. Especially as, going into the theatre, I saw Komisarzhevsky outside in the dark entry. I said: "Is it all right?" He said: "Oh yes, it's all right." Dorothy said she had not played very well, but she was not depressed.

She said: "You and I are great adventurers."

Thursday, November 17th.

I read all the morning press notices of *Prohack* at breakfast. *Express* good. Most of the others gently praising, tepid. *The Times* most depreciatory. Board Meeting of Sloane Productions, Ltd., at 2.30. Bernstein, who had not liked the play when he read it, was really very enthusiastic about the play in performance. Dorothy had bought the afternoon papers, all of which were encomiastic.

I escorted D. to the theatre, came back home, which felt empty, and drove by taxi to the Reform Club and met Geoffrey Russell on the steps as I was entering. He said I was going with him to hear Liszt's *Faust Symphony* at the Philharmonic concert. So I went. Heard the last movements of a Brahms pianoforte concerto played by Arthur Schnabel. He is a very fine player.

I got back to the Court Theatre before the performance was over, and heard the end of the play from the Royal Box with Whitaker, the manager. The public laughter was very reassuring, and I felt more optimistic about the future of the play.

In the afternoon I had written a character sketch of Masterman the news of whose death I had had in the morning.

Friday, November 18th.

I walked up to the National Gallery, partly to think up an idea for a story, and partly to find Poussin pictures on classical subjects which I could use for illustrating my book of Greek travel.

Monday, November 21st.

Disturbed night; dreamed much. I seldom dream. I did some work to-day for a change. I began my new short story at 10.30 after a walk, and wrote 600 words of it in about an hour. I then set off in the rain to St. Margaret's for the funeral service of Charles Masterman. A lot of people there. Ll. George following the coffin. I didn't like the sight of him there. At 9 I was at Mrs. Masterman's discussing her affairs with her. I promised to set on foot a scheme for collecting £4000 for education of the three children, all of whom I saw.

Tuesday, November 22nd.

I wrote another 500 words of short story, and then wrote six letters to friends of mine and the late Masterman about a fund for the education of his children. This took some time. I walked then to Embassy Club, and lunched with Harry Preston. Pat Thompson was the only other guest. They wanted advice from me as to how Pat's help to Harry in the writing of his book of reminiscences could best be acknowledged.[1] I turned down their own scheme and gave them a new one, which they heartily accepted.

Thence with Sidney Bernstein to the Wardour Films private theatre to see a German film about health-culture, as cut by the Film Society. I am to arbitrate between the Film Society and Wardour about their respective versions of this film. I am to see the Wardour (fuller version) next Tuesday. Dorothy and I and Marjorie Gordon dined at Queen's Restaurant, and I took Marjorie on to the opening of the new Gate Theatre in Villiers Street. An English version of the French prostitute play *Maya* played by prim English actresses with 'Varsity and Kensingtonian accents.

Thursday, November 24th.

Went to the Savoy for the Other Club dinner, 15 minutes late. Alfred Mason in the chair. I had some sparring with Birkenhead, rather loud and abusive, but good-natured. However, I could be just as abusive as he could.

Friday, November 25th.

I went to the Reform Club to dine. I there met Raymond Mortimer and Francis Birrell, who were going to second night of Coward's *Sirocco*. So I said I would go. I did go. Goodish 1st Act. Putrid 2nd. And trying and hysterical third. On the whole a trying evening.

Sunday, November 27th.

We lunched at Norman Wilkinson's. He lives alone at Strawberry House, Chiswick Mall. Very nice and tasteful. Several old harpsichords

---

[1] This was *Memories*, published in 1928.

and similar instruments, in perfect order, on which he plays nicely. He is charming, sensible, and has taste.

We dined at the Ivy, and saw there the St. John Ervines, Hutchinsons, Lytton Strachey, the Basil Deans, etc., etc. Then to first night of the Sitwell entertainment, *First-Class Passengers Only,* at the Theatre Arts Club. Packed. Some parts amusing. More parts tedious. Some fine acting. Some rotten. It was a sort of revue in backchat.

Monday, November 28th.

Doran, Jules Godby, Ellery Sedgwick and daughter Henrietta, Humbert Wolfe, and Mrs. Belloc Lowndes came to tea and baby. Baby and gramophone do nothing whatever to promote highbrow conversation.

I dined at the Piccadilly Hotel restaurant with Harry Preston, to meet the Prince of Wales. Very affable. He spoke with approval of my soft shirt at dinner. Afterwards he said: "I don't know you very well, but can I tell you a story?" He told me one. Then to National Sporting Club, to see Moody beat Moore. A goodish fight.

Thursday, December 1st.

Lady Beaverbrook died at 5 a.m. today. This was a damned shame. I say no more. Dorothy said that between 3 and 4 a.m. when she couldn't sleep, she was full of the idea of death. Although I had had a good night's sleep I couldn't work.

Saturday, December 3rd.

I decided at early morn to go to Gladys Beaverbrook's funeral today. I drove off in the car at 1.40, and got to Mickleham, scene of the funeral, at 2.25. So I drove on to Dorking and through Dorking and came back, the car having taken a wrong turning, just as the hearse and procession was arriving at the lych-gate of the churchyard. I went in and Castlerosse joined me, and I saw Baxter, Blumenfeld, James Dunn, Raymond Thompson, and a whole lot of Max's secretaries, clerks, etc., etc. The entrance of the coffin, covered with really magnificent wreaths, was moving. Max was leaning on young Max's arm, and looked quite old.

Chopin's funeral march—not equal to Handel's. "Abide With Me" at the end. This hymn is quite a good poem. Then the coffin goes out again, and a scene of terrible damp cold at the graveside, and our hats off, and Lord Ashfield only just up that day from a chill. These funeral rites in an English winter are absolutely barbaric. I met Max at the gate, and was so moved, unknown to myself till the moment came, that I could not speak to him.

Sunday, December 4th.

I had written my *Evening Standard* article by 11.10. I then went out for a walk in darkness and mist.

We walked to the Albert Hall for the Furtwängler concert. Fine concert, marvellous band and conductor, with an unsatisfactory programme.

Dined at the Savoy in the Pinafore Room. George Doran's party: Colefaxes, Noel Coward, Joan Sutherland, Ethel Mannin, Humbert Wolfe, O. Sitwell (sardonic), Rebecca West, Clemence Dane (highly ingenious). Fine dinner. I was too tired and gloomy to enjoy it much.

Tuesday, December 6th.

I attended the dinner of the P.E.N. club to Lion Feuchtwanger, and sat next to him, and was pleased with his personality. He is evidently well used to publicity. He said that his Berlin secretary said that he spent one hour in writing and the rest of the day in business, making contracts, and seeing people. Rebecca West was in the chair, and she didn't say enough. Feuchtwanger spoke very satisfactorily in very bad English. I went over and talked to May Sinclair, whom I hadn't seen for sixteen or seventeen years. Her last great tragedy was the death of a cat. I also went over to Mrs. Aria. She said: "You haven't kissed me." So I kissed her—for the first time.

Thursday, December 8th.

Feuchtwanger came for tea at 4.40. Also Hugh Walpole. Dorothy came in at 4.45 from her matinée. Feuchtwanger looks just like a cat. He is certainly very intelligent.

Saturday, December 10th.

Rotten night. No work. I went to Professor Theremine's demonstration of "Music from the Ether" at noon at the Savoy Hotel under direction of Charlie Cochran, Edwin Evans being the lecturer. Lots of notorieties. Rather good. Then lunch at the Shaws', to meet Feuchtwanger again. St. John Ervine and Dorothy the other guests. Shaw has flashes, but not many. Charlotte Shaw is quiet and sweet. Ervine is fine company. Feuchtwanger was agreeable and intelligent, with a sense of humour.

Sunday, December 11th.

Mrs. P. Campbell came for tea at 5.30 and made a terrific outpouring. She said: "If you want to keep me quiet give me a cigar." So I gave her one. Later, she went out into the Square smoking it. Her energy seems quite unimpaired. She now wants to produce and play in *Flora*. She arrived with a great scheme all complete. She read the play about a year ago or more, and saw nothing in it. Now she reads it again and sees everything in it. I discussed a few things with her and left the rest to Pinkers.

I finished *Monte Cristo* at 11.30. On the whole this is a wonderful book. The end is too hurried, especially considering the immense leisureliness of all that precedes it. Many explanations are lacking.

Thursday, December 15th.

Grand dinner and presentation of portrait (by Clive Gardiner) to Dr. T. E. Page. 30 people. The dinner was offered to the company by Tudor Walters, who was in the chair. Old Sir Walter Runciman sang two or three sea-chanties. Over 80. Also the French chef was called in, and complimented, and asked to sing a verse of the Marseillaise; which he did.

Wednesday, December 21st.

Nothing doing this morning with my short story. So that before breakfast I had already come to the decision that I would leave it for today, and write my next week's *Evening Standard* article instead. Which I did. Then at 3.30 Saville, together with a scenario writer, came to discuss a scenario for *The Pretty Lady*. I made it absolutely clear that Christine must remain absolutely a prostitute.

Tuesday, December 27th.

Forty minutes' talk with Dorothy about the fortunes of *Mr. Prohack*. Then I walked in snowy Battersea Park. At 12.15 I sat down to draft a letter to authors urging them to subscribe to the National Book Council. It is suggested that this appeal should be signed by Hardy, Shaw, Wells, me, and two or three others. I shall send it tomorrow to Willie Maxwell for his consideration.

Wednesday, December 28th.

At 8.15 I heard Harry Lauder on the wireless. He was mediocre, but knew his job perfectly. Dorothy left for theatre. I was fantastically bored, and could think of nothing better to do than visit the *Cinderella* panto-mime at the Chelsea Palace. I stood it for one hour; then came home. At 10.35, after a few more chores, I went to bed. I wrote to J. B. Priestley today about his novel *Benighted,* which I finished in the night. I read a lot of Iris Barry's book on Lady Mary Wortley Montagu.[1] Mannered, but goodish. Also some of André Siegfried's *America Comes of Age.* It seems to be very good. This is the third successive evening that I have spent alone. I can stand almost anything better than a solitary evening. I can't tolerate many more.

Thursday, December 29th.

Splendid health. I have now cut my breakfast down to four or five kinds of fruit (raisins, orange, apple, lemon, and prunes) plus two cups of tea and two pieces of rye bread. And little or no meat for lunch. After chores, I saw Dorothy, apropos chiefly of a cable from Estelle Winwood asking for American rights of *Flora.* I then walked along the Embank-ment to the next bridge West and down along King's Road, and then wrote 750 words of my "Millionaire" article in 1¼ hours at most. Then by bus to Piccadilly. Lunch at Reform Club. Talk about our own defects,

---

[1] *Portrait of Lady Mary Montagu,* published in 1928.

and about the characters of politicians. I came to the conclusion that what Liberal statesmen lacked is courage. This applies to Walter Runciman, Herbert Samuel, and Asquith, and John Burns. Most of them seem also to lack charm.

Friday, December 30th.

We went to lunch with Ruth Draper, who has a little house in Charles Street, belonging to an American named Chubb. Present: the Alan Herberts, and Mrs. Phipps, sister of Lady Astor. She was full of Bernard Shaw's conversational liveliness. She is very lively herself and I liked her. Ruth Draper again talked to me about writing a play for her, and I promised to write to her about such a play.

I have now cleared up all the work I have to do this year. In actual production it has not been quite as large as last year, but it has been quite large enough. And the financial results have been the best for many years; also the financial prospects for next year are good.

Saturday, December 31st.

I have now got my weight down again. So long as it keeps at 11 [stone] or under I'm content. A month ago it was at 11 st. 2 lb. I walked to the Army and Navy and back to get some clean pocket notebooks. I got six— 1d. each.

I read in Sarton's *Introduction to the History of Science*, Vol. 1, and decided to write an article on it for the *Evening Standard*. At 10.40 I went off to the Gargoyle Club, where we entertained A. P. Herbert and wife at supper. Few people we knew. The spectacle as a whole was degrading. And I think that not many were really enjoying themselves. Many drunks. I drove up there in snow and sleet. We danced but little. I was in bed at 2.35 and slept in all nearly six hours, which was an excellent introduction to the New Year, considering that I had eaten a quite hearty supper and drunk quite enough champagne—preceded by a cocktail.

1928

Sunday, January 1st.

After dinner we played bits and pieces out of the *Meistersinger*. Then I began to analyse myself for Dorothy's distraction. She was very interested, said I didn't do half enough of it. Lastly I read myself to sleep with *Peter Simple*. Yes, it is very good, but it seems to be all the same— the old picaresque stuff. Oddly, Marryat brings in another quite long story told by another young naval officer to Peter, about his life, a few years earlier. There is no contrast between the two. Just an idea that occurred to the author, I suppose, when he was hard up for an idea.

I have made only one good resolution: to write more legibly.

When I met Barry Jackson this morning on the Embankment in the snow, he was wearing snow-boots, as I was, but no overcoat. "Ah!" he said, pointing to my boots, "we're the same." He is the blandest person I ever met, I think. A sort of veiled voice—*voix blanche*. He said how well I looked. I said how well *he* looked. "That's my glass of orange juice," said he, beaming. He did look very well. He admitted that he had not of late been losing money in the theatre. Even after deducting the losses of his various failures, Phillpotts's two great successes showed him a profit. About his forthcoming production of *Macbeth* in modern clothes, he said he was afraid it would, so, prove too *grim* for modern audiences. He said he was having the greatest difficulty in getting a Macbeth. He had tried every star in London except Du Maurier and they all jibbed at it—asked to have time to read the play and think it over. He said some of them

993

hadn't read the play for years. I said that some of them had never read it at all.

Monday, January 2nd.

It is now difficult for me to begin "writing" before 11 o'clock. Chores seem to increase. Tea with Dorothy. The infant Virginia continues to make a devil of a fuss if the gramophone is not started for her. She lies down on the floor and sobs or weeps quietly. When the music begins she puts up her arms to be carried about with rhythmic motions of the carrier's feet. Strange! Dorothy keeps insisting that she is no ordinary child. I took Mrs. Masterman to dine at Sovrani's new restaurant in Jermyn Street. Lucy Masterman told me a lot about Charles, their children, and the Asquiths. She has a pleasingly sardonic yet affectionate tongue. She said to me once again: "Charles always said: 'If you're really in a hole, go to A. B. He's the one.'"

Wednesday, January 4th.

Francis Hackett and his wife (who sticks to her maiden Danish name of Toksvig) came to dinner. Dorothy had to leave at 8.30 for the theatre. We three remaining talked interested and interesting without stopping till 11 p.m. *She* is full of brains. *He* has brains and plenty of keenness. Irish, not American.

Thursday, January 5th.

I corrected typescripts for one hour, and then walked up to Piccadilly Circus and back, thinking further over my scheme for a play for Ruth Draper. I got this scheme into order, and wrote to Ruth about it immediately after lunch. I find I can think best when I am in a street of shops, now. I like more and more looking at shop-windows.

Friday, January 6th.

The core of the morning spent at the barber's, who wanted to see my wireless; so I told him to come along any evening. He is a man of quiet but extreme likes and dislikes. He loathes "jazz." He said he had been to see skate-waltzing on the rink in Grosvenor Road, and how it was the loveliest thing in movement he had ever seen. He said that Jellicoe was there, and Jellicoe had "passed a remark about how nice it was to see," etc. "Passed a remark" is a great phrase of his class. I love it.

Walked all along King's Road nearly to World's End, and got a few good ideas for my short story. I also observed the interiors of the scores and scores of small shops. The majority of them had customers within (5.15 to 6 p.m.) more customers on the return journey than on the outward.

Saturday, January 7th.

At Dorothy's urgent request, I went over to the Court Theatre. Atmosphere of the last night of a run, but, although no other theatre has yet been obtained, we trust it is not the last night of the run. Evelyn Cochran came round after the performance, and Charles was *really* enthusiastic about the play. He said he hadn't liked a play so much for years. Evelyn said she had never seen Charlie so happy in a theatre. He also liked the acting. It seemed impossible not to believe that this play, in the West End, and *kept* on for a bit, should not develop into a very great success. All the packing up had to be finished in Dorothy's dressing-room. More good-byes. Sally, the dresser, is really a very nice old woman, with a voice as thin as a piece of paper. We got home at midnight. Then searchings in larder for food for Dorothy.

Sunday, January 8th.

Enfeebled, gloomy. I wrote a lot more of my story, and then supplanted the cook in Dorothy's audience chamber, and arranged to go for a walk with her at noon. Part of Grosvenor Road, the interesting part near the Tate Gallery, was barricaded. Crowds of gazers. We went on to Vauxhall Bridge. Nothing to be seen anywhere, except mud on the footpath of Grosvenor Road, and the damp interior of the Riviera Club, which had been flooded out.

Monday, January 9th.

We went to the first night of Barry Jackson's new Court season, *The Adding Machine,* by Elmer Rice (American). I feared the worst for this play; but it turned out quite well. It has the misfortune of having two subjects—first one and then another, and it is under-produced. But the writing and satire, and some of the expressionist stuff are quite decent. I enjoyed myself.

Tuesday, January 10th.

I received the big Funk & Wagnall's big standard Dictionary as a gift from F. & W., because I had boomed their smaller dictionary in the *Evening Standard.* On examining it, I found that whereas my name is in the smaller ed., (1922), it is not in the larger edition (1927—but is it really 1927?). I felt hurt. I told Dorothy and her first remark was, eagerly: "And is Wells in both?" I pointed this thing out to F. & W.; but I am not sure if they will appreciate my humour. We went to the Victoria Palace to see "The World's Master Juggler"—Salerno. He was good, but not sublime. Arthur Prince was sublime. Not a bad evening. We came home by bus. I am now getting to the end of *Peter Simple.* There is a wonderfully sly bit of social satire in this work; comic description of a Negro religious meeting in Barbados, followed immediately by a comic letter from an Irish priest. The juxtaposition shows that there is nothing to choose between the nigger parson and the Irish priest.

Wednesday, January 11th.

Ivor Nicholson came for tea at 5.15, and wanted six more articles for Hearsts: but only the English rights thereof. So I refused. I said I would write for 2s. a word and return to Hearsts all I received by selling the articles on my own in U.S.A. He offered me a Hearst luncheon, grand and celebritous, to celebrate my 40th year in London, 1929. I said: "You couldn't give it me."

The *Daily News* rang up to say that Hardy was dead, and would I say something. I wouldn't. But I decided that I must get up early tomor-

row, and write a *Standard* article on Hardy to take the place of the one
on Gilbert Murray.

Friday, January 13th.

There was some of the best talking I have heard even at the Reform
Club, especially in appraising the characters of John Simon, Herbert
Samuel, etc. T. S. Eliot and Humbert Wolfe came for a later tea to discuss with me the future of the *New Criterion*. Their real object was to
find out whether I would help to find capital.

Robert Nichols came in after dinner bearing a book for me from
Jacques Blanche. We heard the Symphony Concert on the wireless, and
it was very good. Harty conducting. Nichols was in a swearing mood.
Nurse was present. He said, of Wagner: "Blast his bloody eyes. I rage
against him, but he always gets me."

Saturday, January 14th.

I walked to the Leicester Galleries and on the way thought of a great
idea for a modernized version of *Faust*. I mean I thought it out in some
detail. I had thought of it yesterday. Today I ordered a literal translation
of Goethe's *Faust*.

At Leicester Galleries a show of drawings and lithographs by Matisse.
Compared to the price of his paintings the drawings were very low
priced. I bought one drawing, 25 guineas, and two lithographs. Also a
show of paintings by John Armstrong, which are causing some stir. I
wasn't quite startled by their excellence. I had a talk with Armstrong,
who was looking quite spick and span in relatively new clothes. He said,
in reply to my questions, that he had been chiefly influenced by Carpaccio
(a Venetian painting of which he had never seen the original) and Sig-
norelli. Also Picasso.

Sunday, January 15th.

To the Green Room Rag performance of Alfred Savoir's *Sexes and
Sevens*, which play had been banned by the Censor, and for which I had

written a programme-foreword, and Orpen had done a cover design. The play had goodish points, but on the whole was lifeless, despite good acting by stars.

Monday, January 16th.

I had to lunch early to go to Hardy's funeral at Westminster Abbey. It was all done very smoothly and calmly. Music good. South transept not full. In the morning I had written a letter to the *Daily Express* animadverting upon the distribution of tickets for this affair.

Tuesday, January 17th.

Formerly in my life I was always preoccupied by my insomnia and my digestion. I only rarely think about my digestion now—it is so good—but I am still terribly preoccupied with my sleeping. I walked to the Metropole for the Dramatists' Club. Pinero in the chair. Quite a muster of members because Pinero had been ill. Coward and Malleson appeared for the first time—new members. Coward said to me: "Don't leave me, Arnold. I feel so strange here. I'm on the verge of hysteria among all these people." He sat on Pinero's right with Barrie next to him.

When Barth was reading the minutes at the end, I said: "Bad grammar, I regret to say." The sin was "None . . . were." But Barth couldn't see it, and others couldn't. I think only Barrie saw it. Yet all were authors.

Saturday, January 21st.

I walked to South Kensington Museum, and had a look at the British Water Colours, which I had not examined before as a whole. Well, I think that Cotman is the best of them, easily. Peter de Wint I like less than I did. He gets pretty and his colour is often not agreeable. Brabazon, clumsy and groping, is still the most interesting of the moderns. Indeed, I couldn't see anybody else who aroused any emotion in me.

After dinner I read a lot of the sixth series of H. L. Mencken's *Prejudices*. This fellow is getting better. He has a general basis of common sense, and really writes very well for a journalist. To the Trocadero Grill for the cabaret show, as the guests of Charles Cochran. Tilly Losch

(formerly *première danseuse* at the Vienna Opera House) and Mrs. C.
B. C. were there. Tilly Losch was very simple and sound and very pretty.
She is doing the dances for C. B.'s new revue. The cabaret show was
extremely lively.

I had gone specially to see Hayes, the juggler, of whom I had heard
fine accounts. He was very skilled, imaginative, and comic; but his turn
was too short. Slept for five hours without a break. It is years since I did
this great feat.

Sunday, January 22nd.

I read more of *Faust* and spent a lot of time in loose reflection—vaguely
on a new play and on my next *Evening Standard* article. I went for a
walk right down over Chelsea Bridge and along Battersea Park Road,
and home by Albert Bridge Road, and King's Road home. Then I filled
up the time in writing to Phillpotts about Hardy's funeral.

Battersea is a different world. I saw on a *Sunday Express* poster:
"Hardy's last novel, by Sir Edmund Gosse." It seemed terribly absurd
there. How many people in Battersea Bridge had heard of Hardy, or of
Gosse, or could get up any interest whatever in a last novel though it
were written by God himself? It is a gloomy, drab street, with most
repulsive tenements, a big technical institute, an open gramophone shop
(with a machine grinding out a tune and a song) and an open "Fun
Fair" sort of place (a shop with the front taken out) and a few small
boys therein amusing themselves with penny-in-the-slot machines. We
dined at Mrs. Patrick Campbell's, across the Square.

Tuesday, January 24th.

To the first night of Behrman's (American) *The Second Man* at the
Playhouse, in which Noel Coward is playing. Good first act. Noel
Coward was admirable.

Wednesday, February 1st.

I went out for a long walk and got really quite a decent few ideas for
my play during this walk, which took just under two hours. Lambreth

was the most interesting part of it. Had tea at the Express Dairy in King's Road. I always enjoy this place. Total cost: 3*d*. Dorothy and I dined and danced at the Savoy which is still the best restaurant in London.

The only man I knew was F. B. Characteristically, he got the professional *danseuse* at his table (two other men with him) in about ten seconds and was immediately dancing with her. This typical London *roué* looked very grey (in the face) and is showing age. Home at 11. Dorothy's great tragic news was that Eadie had offered her the Royalty Theatre, almost at once, but she couldn't take it now because Charles Laughton had gone. This was really bad luck. Had she known a week earlier, she might have gone on with her season and the play.

Thursday, February 2nd.

X. came for tea and talk about her affairs and her children. Rather wearing, these visits from relatives whom you scarcely ever see, and whose course of existence is separating more widely from you every year, and has been so doing for over 30 years. It is in fact desolating.

Saturday, February 4th.

Bernard Shaw came for lunch. He and Dorothy talked theatre all the time. He said that the first preliminary to her going in for theatrical management and acting was a divorce between us. He was very quiet, chatty, sensible, and agreeable. He went up with us to Harriet Cohen's Henry Wood orchestral concert at Wigmore Hall, and by chance had got a seat next to ours. We all enjoyed this concert. The hall was full. I dozed off twice, being very fatigued and sleepy, but still I enjoyed it. We drove home in rain. Shaw left us to get exercise on foot. Dined at the St. John Hutchinsons: Ethel Sands, Roger Fry, and W. Gerhardi. Fry was in great form. His latest notion is that Delacroix, though a great man, was not a great artist.

Sunday, February 5th.

Dined at the Ivy Restaurant. Then to Alec Rea's invitation performance of dances and episodes by the American Angna Enters. Good,

Rather distinguished, but not self-expressive enough. I liked it, but was not really moved.

Tuesday, February 7th.

I was just going out on a secret mission when Dorothy came in so that I had to hurry like anything to my destination, which was in Eaton Place, and even then arrived after Father Vincent McNabb, O.C. had begun his "spiritual conference" in a West End drawing-room to a pretty full audience in which I was the only man. I liked Father McNabb. He looked about 50. Very refined face and voice. Good enunciation, with unembarrassed pauses for a word or a sentence. Very soft-toned. Rather restless. Subject: Parable of the Vineyard. He said some good things; but his chief effect is that his bearing and mood compel you to think about spiritual values. I was certainly impressed. It was Maurice Baring who told me to go and hear him. Lasted half an hour. Then the Father came down from his low rostrum and passed along the front row, where I was, and I saw that he was much older than I had thought. Everyone remained seated till he had gone. He went out as it were furtively, as if self-conscious. He was in a monk's dress.

I finished *Tess* yesterday. It is really a very impressive masterpiece; and its faults are quite trifling. I was wrong to say in the *Evening Standard* that it is not among Hardy's five best.

Friday, February 17th.

I was determined to begin my play [1] this morning, and I did at 11 o'clock, after various chores and a fair night, which did not definitely finish till 8.15 a.m. I wrote just the little preliminary scene with the maidservant, introducing the young male character. It was enough. It gave me a start.

Monday, February 20th.

I walked to the Garrick Club to lunch with Duff Tayler and Knoblock. Knoblock is just back from America, with horrible tales of the

---

[1] *The Return Journey.*

noise and the slow traffic of New York, and the harshness and the enterprise of theatrical managers there. We dined at 7.30 and went to Van Druten's *Young Woodley* at the Theatre Arts Club.

All you can say about *Young Woodley*, which has been extravagantly praised, is that it is a very good play for a boy of 23 or 24. The construction and movements are clumsy; the theme seems to be in two separate halves; the dialogue is very good indeed. Most of the acting, especially Kathleen O'Regan's and Frank Lawton's, was beautiful. The big scenes were rather moving. Several people cried.

Wednesday, February 22nd.

I lunched at the Reform. Spender (just back from U.S.A.) was full of Los Angeles as a deliberately "planned" city. He said he would as soon talk to Douglas Fairbanks, on *any* topic, as to any man in America. Spender had a very low opinion of American politicians. After lunch I went over to E. M. Forster, who had had Lowes Dickinson to lunch, and talked to them about Russian novelists.

Saturday, February 25th.

I went by bus to Colefaxes; Sam Courtauld and Eliz. Lewis. All of us except Arthur Colefax went to see *The Unknown Warrior* by Raynal at the Little Theatre. First act false and awful, and all the three players, including Maurice Browne, awful. But 2nd and 3rd Acts quite good and rather moving, and Maurice was better—much better.

Tuesday, February 28th. Midland Hotel, Manchester.

A walk in town with Cochran. First night of *Cochran's 1928 Revue* at 7.30. Packed. Atmosphere of success. Glimpse of stage afterwards. Cochran gave a supper.

Thursday, March 1st. 75 Cadogan Square, London.

I dined with Beaverbrook at the Vineyard, Fulham. He has given up his office on the top floor of the *Express* building. Nobody but me and

Max. We grew rather intimate again. I stayed till 11.53, and arranged to go down to Cherkley on Sunday for the night.

Friday, March 2nd.

Mildred Temple, Ray Long's London representative, told me that Pauline Smith's story, "Desolation," was very fine, and she personally loved it, etc., etc., all the usual stuff—it was a little too gloomy for them. I reasoned seriously with her; told her she had spoilt my evening and refused to dance with her.

Wednesday, March 7th.

John Buchan, invited for tea at 4.30, arrived at 4.27. He is a thoroughly organized man. He had a Committee Meeting for 5.30. And at 5.15 he simply got up and left. I then, fatigued somehow—but not by Buchan, who is most brisk—rested a bit, and then took up the play again, and reeled it off with strange ease.

Saturday, March 10th.

I went out for a walk in order to get ideas, found that I had them already, and came back at once accordingly, and started on the new scene in Act II and wrote 500 words of it in about 80 minutes.

George Doran came to lunch, and after lunch in my study he began talking about the idea he had given me last year for a novel based on the tragic life of Ernest Hodder-Williams.[1] I said I liked it, but couldn't handle it yet, as I was more attracted by a scheme for a realistic novel about a big luxury hotel.[2] Then I saw that I might combine the two schemes and that one would strengthen the other. From that moment I seemed to see my next novel as a complete entity, and I shall probably begin it as soon as I have finished my play.

Wednesday, March 14th.

Went to see Chaplin's film *The Circus* at the New Gallery, where I

---

[1] Sir Ernest Hodder-Williams, the publisher and author of books on the Red Cross and the Y. M. C. A.

[2] *Imperial Palace.*

joined a party. Fairly good film: a few fine moments in it, really funny, and some dull parts; the end had pathos with distinction. Then all of us in three or four cabs to Sybil Colefax's for supper. A lot of stage nobs came in: Coward, Du Maurier, Leslie Faber, Oliver Messel. Wells came. Victor Beigal sang Viennese popular songs superbly; Noel Coward sang his own songs extremely cleverly. Viola Tree and Oliver Messel gave side-splitting imitations, and I concluded the programme.

Thursday, March 29th.

I read a great deal more of Madame de Rémusat's Memoirs. This is a really absorbing book. Aldous and Maria Huxley came for lunch and were very agreeable, vivacious, and original. I promised to subscribe to the private edition of D. H. Lawrence's new indecent novel, to be printed in Florence.[1]

Tuesday, April 3rd.

I read "in" Azevedo's Portuguese novel *A Brazilian Tenement* sent to me by Cassells. It is like so many translations from the less important languages—imitative and fairish. You say to yourself: it is very good for a Portuguese. About 30 or 50 years behind the times. Still, it seems to be pretty true stuff. At 3.30 a clerk from Braby & Waller, my solicitors, with a notary public, called to attend to the formalities of my signature to a document giving Marguerite power to handle her own securities and manage her own affairs. The French law is terribly behind the English in its attitude to women. Also a female witness to a signature is inadmissible in French law. Tania Cohen came for dinner, and I took her to *The Spider* at the Winter Garden Theatre. Not a bad entertainment for children, and the production showed much imaginative attention to detail and to mood.

Wednesday, April 4th.

We lunched with Marie Tempest and Graham Browne in Regents

---

[1] *Lady Chatterley's Lover.*

Park. A charmingly arranged house. Marie is still surprisingly young in looks and gestures; but she talks old—about *"today," "modern," "there's nothing"*—etc., etc. I offered her my play *Flora*.

Wednesday, April 11th.

During the holiday [at Sidmouth] I read all the 520 pp. of *The Moonstone*. It is a very good detective novel, one of the best. It holds you throughout, and it has some fun in it. The method of narration—personal narration—is unsatisfactory, because all the narratives are so obviously written by Wilkie Collins. A few failures in *vraisemblance*—e.g., how could an officer of the police force be *paid* for his services by a private person (Lady Verinder)? Still, a good book, though entirely *terre-à-terre*. Collins has some good observations about life, and some hard things to say about women. One narrator says: "Women have no principles." This is misleading but true. He ought to have said "general principles." To which he might retort that every principle, by the very nature of it, is "general."

Walked up Sloane Street. Meant to walk to National Gallery, but took a bus at Knightsbridge. I got to the N.G. at 11.30. I chose the Ansidei Room, and looked for 20 minutes at the "Coronation of the Virgin" by Orcagna, and the ditto by Gaddi. Also the "Immaculate Conception" by Cuvelli. All these pictures are more interesting to me than the Ansidei Madonna of Raphael. They lifted up the plane of my thought of my play (Act III) and I got a few notions.

Thursday, April 12th.

Bad night. Thorpe, of British International Films, and Dupont, the German producer of *Vaudeville* and *Moulin Rouge*, came to see me about writing a film story about Piccadilly, under the title *Piccadilly*, for Dupont to produce; I agreed to write, and promised the first sketch for Tuesday.

Lunch with Sir Lawrence Weaver and an American named Littauer (fiction editor of *Collier's Weekly*). He asked if he could buy the American rights of my *Standard* articles. I said he could. He had decided views. He challenged me to stick to my printed view that *The Bridge of San Luis Rey* is "absolutely first-rate."

We dined at 7.35 and went to *A Man with Red Hair,* with Charles Laughton in it. We arranged beforehand that I should leave after the second act in order to go to bed early. So I did, though with reluctance, because the 2nd Act interested me, and I had a desire to see the 3rd.

Friday, April 13th.

I got away early, and began to think about my Dupont film *Piccadilly*. Then I walked to Dent's in Cockspur Street, where yesterday I had seen a bed-table watch, which I had the notion of giving to Dorothy. The price, £15, annoyed and repelled me, but in the end I yielded to the d . . . d thing and bought it. Dorothy called for me at the Club, and at 3.50 I began to write my sketch for the film story. It was interrupted by a grand nursery-tea, this being Virginia's second birthday. It was all over at 5.30, after which I finished all the preliminary part of my film story. I hope to write the actual sequence of events tomorrow morning.

Saturday, April 14th.

I had a bad night, very, but I was determined to write the story of the film for Dupont, and I wrote practically all day. I never went out of the house till night, and didn't dress until I dressed for dinner. I finished the thing by about 5.30.

Friday, April 20th.

I walked to Dr. Griffin's to have my heart examined. He told me he had "no fault whatever to find" with my heart. Also that my arteries were those of a man of 40, and my blood pressure just a trifle below normal. I had this examination solely to satisfy Dorothy.

Monday, April 23rd.

I went out, and in Hyde Park I met W. J. Turner. He said that life could and did "maim" a man. I replied: "Very rarely." I said that it was well to remember that nothing happened to a man outside his own head, and that therefore if the mind was under control, etc., etc. I left him suddenly, saying that though apparently idle I was busy working.

Tuesday, April 24th.

We went to see skittles played in the open-air alley of the Black Lion, close by. This was very amusing and quaint. Dorothy and I both played a bit.

Sunday, April 29th.

I wore my new house-suit from Sulka's. As I wanted to wear it all morning, I decided not to go out. It is so magnificent that I felt rather shy about showing it to the nurses. However, they gave no sign of stupefaction. I wrote my *Evening Standard* article, finishing it at just 1 o'clock; but before that I had done chores. Virginia came down to lunch with me. I am told that Virginia now strongly objects to being put in her pen. She made a fantastic noise this morning. I read *Le Collier de la Reine*, and pieces of Woodforde's *Diary of a Parson*, given to me by Humphrey Milford of the Oxford University Press. I dressed and went out. Sat in the Park a bit, and listened to the band under Charles Godfrey. Then I walked on to the Park orators. Socialist and Anti-Socialist. The Socialist was the best; he held his audience and made me laugh. Salvation Army lass preaching Jesus. Awful. A speaker of the "Catholic Evidence" society. Large crowds at each pulpit. I walked back, and read the typescript of a Biblical novel by a dissenting parson in Somerset. His claim on me was that he had once been stationed in Tunstall. The book is worthless. I wrote to him at once, more or less to that effect. Then I read my third Act. I couldn't judge it fairly, because when you have read a bad thing, anything that you read immediately afterwards always seems to be bad. I drove to Victoria to meet Dorothy's train, which was 25 minutes late.

Monday, May 7th.

Board meeting of Pugh's Film Enterprises, Ltd. Hoyt, the film producer, was really most enthusiastic about my novels as subjects for films. He said that *The Grand Babylon Hotel* was absolutely perfect for the film.

Saturday, May 12th.

I wanted some tea, so I went out with the *Manchester Guardian* and had two cups of China at the Express Dairy in King's Road. I like that place; it is rather romantic for me.

Sinclair Lewis, his second bride-to-be (on Monday), Miss Thompson, and Harriet Cohen came to dinner. Stayed till 12.25. We had a fine time. Sinclair did too many imitations.

Thursday, May 17th.

I asked Crosby Gaige to lunch at the Yacht Club. We decided that he should issue between 30 and 40,000 words from the first volume of my journal, and terms were fixed. I went out for a walk to get ideas for my next film scene and didn't get them. Newman Flower came to tea.

Tuesday, May 22nd.

I wrote another 2700 words of my film, at terrific speed. I had two promenades. Aldous Huxley came for lunch.

Thursday, May 24th.

Finished the whole film story, just under 17,000 words, at 12.30. I began a fortnight ago exactly. This has been the most strenuous fortnight I've had for years.

Monday, June 4th.

I worked in the morning on proofs and instructions concerning my Mediterranean book. Good sleep after lunch. I went on with work on the Mediterranean book. At last decided on a title for the book, *Mediterranean Scenes.*[1] Then I finished up the proofs, illustrations, etc.

I've been reading *Endymion*. Opening too descriptive and too *gen-*

---

[1] This was published in a limited edition of 1000 copies.

erally narrative, not *individual* enough in event and description. But it can be read.

Tuesday, June 5th.

Pauline Smith came at 3 and we drove down to Dulwich Gallery. Curious semi-sylvan surroundings. Only three or four people in it. An old servitor at the gate. You have to sign your name in a book. A few very fine pictures, especially a Watteau, a Velasquez, and a Murillo. Also the place almost makes you like Cuyp. Some of the famous Poussins are not fearfully good. But two are. What a waste to have this gallery in Dulwich.

Wednesday, June 13th.

I was at the Memorial Service to Dennis Eadie at St. Martin's in the Fields at 12.30. Sat with Mason and Miss Stevens. Then Viola Tree drove me to the Garrick Club so that I could see Gerald Du Maurier about my (Faust) play. Gerald offered to accept my play without seeing it. I refused the offer; but promised to do the play as quickly as I could.

Saturday, June 16th.

I messed about in the morning and went to South Kensington Museum; but I did not get any good ideas for my last act. Kitty Roberts and Dorothy and I played tennis in the Square [1] from 12.15 to 1.15. Cynthia Noble came for lunch. Then I had a heavy sleep. I started out for a walk to get ideas but felt too tired and read *La Princesse de Clèves,* which has the classic feel.

Eugene Goossens and Alec Shepeler came for dinner. Eugene began to play and sing our opera *Judith.* He has evidently set out to do something not too incomprehensible. Better than I had expected. Dramatic. Effective. My libretto seemed quite good. He talked of a production at Covent Garden next year.

A young girl from Liverpool called yesterday afternoon, with a packet

---

[1] Cadogan Square.

which an uncle in Peking had charged her to deliver to me personally. So she had come from Liverpool on purpose, though some weeks ago I had told her she mustn't. She seemed resentful against her uncle; said she knew nothing about the matter and couldn't understand her uncle. I opened the packet. It contained simply the documents of a British government official at Peking deeply possessed of a grievance about being dismissed from the Salt Administration, and an appeal to me to see that Justice was done. Pathetic.

Monday, June 18th.

I proceeded with the play. I don't feel convinced of its excellence as a show for a large public. And I really doubt whether I will ever do another. Career as a dramatist closing!

Wednesday, June 20th.

I went to the Spender dinner at the Reform Club. Hugh Bell and John Simon spoke briefly and badly. Walter Runciman spoke briefly and very well, and Spender made a very excellent and rather long discourse on America. Old Sir Walter Runciman then, by request, began to sing sea-chanties.

Thursday, June 21st.

I finished writing the (unnamed) play on the Faust theme about 11 a.m. I was very exhausted. Lucas came to lunch, and was rather sardonic and very witty.

Thursday, June 28th.

I walked to Garrick Club to see Gerald Du Maurier, who at once told me that he accepted with enthusiasm my unnamed Faust play, and would produce it in August.

Saturday, June 30th. Hôtel Westminster, Le Touquet.

Dorothy and I left Victoria at 9 a.m. Arrived at Étaples for Le Touquet at 2.43 instead of 1.30. Drove in the Westminster Hotel omnibus about the wastes of sands of the north end of Le Touquet-Paris Plage to find our villa and, ultimately, found it.

Thursday, July 5th. Villa Ma Coquille, Le Touquet.

The Swinnertons left Étaples and installed themselves at the Hôtel Métropole close by here.

Friday, July 6th. 75 Cadogan Square, London.

I went to London at Du Maurier's urgent request, by 11.35 boat. I was at St. James's Theatre at 4 and saw Gilbert Miller, Du Maurier not being there. They wanted a change at the end of Act II of play. I got home at 6. I went to see Gerald after show at St. James's. The dressing-room full, including Tallulah Bankhead and Hunter (the tennis player). At something after 12, Gerald and his daughter and I went by appointment to a supper-party at Viola Tree's, where were Ivor Novello, Bobby Andrews, Lady Du Maurier, and both her daughters. Gerald and I had some talk in another room. He wanted a character altered (and complicated). I refused.

Saturday, July 7th. Villa Ma Coquille, Le Touquet.

I had written a new scheme for end of Act II of play before 10 a.m. Julian Huxley called to see me about a new magazine at 10.20. I was at St. James's Theatre at 11.30 and had a full palaver with Gilbert Miller and Gerald and arranged to alter end of Act II at once, definitely.

Sunday, July 8th.

I worked off and on all day in altering Act II of play, and finished it at 6 p.m. I had had a thinking-walk, two miles on beach, in the morning, and I walked again after 6 p.m. After dinner Dorothy and I went to see the film *Casanova* at the Casino de la Plage. It was rotten.

Monday, July 9th.

At 10.30 we went off in our car, with the Swinnertons in a hired car, to Amiens. We went through Abbeville and Picquigny. No possible restaurant at Picquigny, or at Ailly—nothing indeed between Abbeville and Amiens. Relative barbarism of French provincial towns (*pavé,* etc., dullness). We had a fine lunch at the Petit Vatel. Rather disappointed with the Cathedral—except the west front. Some lovely bits of architecture in the town. We came home via Doullens and Frévent—war country.

Friday, July 13th.

We drove over to Hardelot (Pré-Catalan) about half a mile inland, for dinner. First we saw Hardelot Plage itself. A small place, with one hotel and many villas, all packed together, like a town. Fine sands, otherwise awful. The dust on all the roads, including those through the forest, was blinding, and choking. I wouldn't stay at Hardelot for quite a lot of money. We dined in the large garden at the Pré-Catalan farm—sort of restaurant. Plain but excellent. We got home about 10.30.

Sunday, July 15th.

Dorothy and I drove off to the races. Just a nice crowd, with a few *chic* women. Dorothy gambled and I joined her and we lost 350 francs between us. But we forgot to collect a won bet at the end. Otherwise we should have lost under 300 francs. Small sum, but I hate losing; it makes me depressed. The absence of a noisy crowd of bookmakers makes a French race meeting strangely agreeable. We didn't see a single person who was obviously a scoundrel. A modiste brought a hat at 9 p.m., and this the Sunday after the biggest fête of the year! Imagine such a call in England!

Monday, July 16th.

I finished my *Evening Standard* article and finished also the revision of Dorothy's translation of Bourdet's play *Vient de Paraître* in the morning; and then walked to the beach. I walked up to the fashionable Le Touquet at 6 p.m. and bought a book *Lucienne* by Jules Romains. My serial *Train de Luxe* (*Accident*) began in the *Daily Express* today. Not badly presented.

Wednesday, July 18th.

I finished re-reading *Mansfield Park*.[1] This is a fine novel. One or two pages of Zola's or rather Huysmans's realism in it. Also at the end she refrains from killing Edmund's elder brother so that Edmund may come into the money, and the title.

Monday, July 23rd.

It took me a long time to do my correspondence, after London visit. I walked down to the beach. Some wind there. Visitors increasing. Kites more and better. After lunch and sleep I went down to the beach again.

Tuesday, July 24th.

After dinner, I began to re-read Baudelaire. I was much struck in Baudelaire by the recurrence of the word *"ennui."* In one place he says that it is the child of "incuriosity." Something in this, but not everything. I am apt to get bored here myself sometimes; sitting on the beach in a wind, for instance; watching the wickedness of Virginia, for instance. She has a complex which often prevents her from doing what she really wants to do. One of her most-used words is "No! *No!*" used with apparently the deepest conviction, when asked to do something which she wants to do. I have two desires here. One is to perambulate, and eat in, the fashionable (forest) part of the town, and the other is to go for excursions (of which there are not many). What I enjoy most is lounging about in my dressing-gown after breakfast, smoking a cigar, talking to Dorothy and others.

Saturday, August 4th. Grand Hôtel, Le Touquet.

I spent most of the morning in the bar of the Restaurant de la Forêt, writing letters. We lunched with Robert Horne at the Hermitage. A Mrs. Christie (Toronto) was the fourth. Tea with Lili d'Alvarez at Westminster. She seems to be living a secret intellectual life, and writing a book on the world, time, space, etc. An egoist. Attractive, young.

---

[1] By Jane Austen.

Monday, August 6th.

I finished my *Standard* article in the morning. Then messing about and to beach. Reading. Down to beach, where Virginia, while really wanting to bathe, protested against bathing, though Dorothy and nurse were with her. Then Dorothy went off driving and I walked up to the tennis club to see d'Alvarez, Ryan, Norman Brookes, and another play a friendly match. After that the two women played the two men and beat them. Dorothy and I dined here. Then to the gaming-rooms, where I met Gilbert Miller, Hore-Belisha, and others, and Dorothy had a long lesson in baccarat from Robert Horne. Horne, Dorothy, and I drank and talked. Horne had been to Paris this day for a board meeting of the Suez Canal, and back, leaving Le Touquet at 7 a.m. And yet he seemed quite fresh at 1.30 a.m. Dorothy and I walked home.

Tuesday, August 7th.

I read Coward's play *The Queen Was in the Parlour* and had already begun to think about the preface which I had promised to write for a volume of this and two other plays. Then we all drove off to have a picnic tea in the woods.

Monday, August 13th.

Felt as if I had a serious chill (but I hadn't). I stayed in bed nearly all morning. Just walked out to look at the sea and buy cigarettes. I passed casually into the *boule* room and made 1000 francs net which I took away complete. We had a rendezvous with Lili d'Alvarez and a young man at 6.30 for cocktails and port in the Restaurant de la Forêt, and we talked for 1½ hours.

Tuesday, August 14th. 75 Cadogan Square, London.

We left the Grand Hôtel Le Touquet at 9.55 and reached No. 75 at 3.45 p.m. Comfortable journey throughout. The purser fellow on the boat got us through the Customs without examination and saw to all other arrangements. All because I gave him an autographed book. I daren't give him a tip. Infant in perfect form, and a very good traveller. Immediately on arrival I set to work to clear up things, and before I went to bed had done four hours' concentrated work. Also I had searched Bible and Shakespeare concordances for a title for the play.

Wednesday, August 15th.

I walked all the way to the Garrick Club for lunch; hot, close, sunny day; 2½ miles and I really felt no fatigue whatever. Talked to Pinero. He came up and asked me how my rehearsals were going on. I said I hated rehearsals, dealing with a lot of hypersensitive and sometimes conceited persons; watching what they did, etc. Pinero said: "Yes, and watching what they don't do, and you want 'em to do, and what they leave out." Pinero is the most charming old man I know. Met Marie Tempest and spouse in a car just outside the Club. She asked me to go and see her in the new play. Another charmer, but capable of ferocity.

Thursday, August 16th.

I am reading Lawrence's *Lady Chatterley's Lover*. He is the most original novelist now writing, except James Joyce.

Sunday, August 19th.

Alfred Mason called for us in his car at 10.30, and at 10.45 we set off for Aldwick (Diana Cooper's), his car following ours. We found Maurice Baring in the garden; then Diana's mother, the Duchess of Rutland. At lunch there were only these and we and the host and hostess. Duff Cooper turns out to be a very considerable reader. It was a good gossiping, scandal-talking, literature-discussing lunch, which lasted till after 3. A number of younger cousins and things came in after lunch and sat on cushions on the small lawn, and people tried to remember the first lines of Shakespeare's plays. Diana and Maurice were very good at this.

Monday, August 20th.

I wrote pieces of an article. Lunch at home. I felt drowsy after it, and so went to the romantic Express Dairy in King's Road and had some China tea. Came back in a shower, and by 4.30 had finished my article.

We dined at home and then, Dorothy having a sudden desire to see a film, we went and saw Douglas Fairbanks's *The Gaucho*. Vast house, quite full—a wonderful sight. Goodish film on its pseudo-romantic plane. Fairbanks really admirable. On the whole tolerable.

Tuesday, August 21st.

During the morning I put down 11 titles for the play, and in the end everyone agreed on one title *The Return Journey*. Whereupon this title was officially given out to Louis Nethersole, the press-agent. The rehearsals went quite well: three acts out of four nearly done. I gave lunch to Gerald at the Green Park. He insists on a particular cocktail, anchovies, cold roast beef, no sweet, no cheese, beer, and a couple of ports, and then goes off and works again like the devil.

Friday, August 24th.

Rehearsal all day. I made enormous cuts in last Act, which went much better. I think the play will be rather short. I went alone to lunch at the Garrick, and saw James Douglas and Chartres Biron together in the lounge, so I set violently on Jimmy at once about his attack on Radclyffe Hall's sapphic novel.[1] Jimmy was very quiet and restrained but Biron defended Jimmy with *real* heat; so I went on attacking. I told Jimmy to come in and lunch with me. He did. He said there was an imp in me. We dined at home and then Dorothy worked and I read. Bed early.

I got and began to read Freud's pamphlet about religion[2] and H. G. Wells's new book.[3]

Saturday, August 25th.

Rehearsals at St. James's Theatre all day. I walked to the theatre, trying to think of my religious book,[4] and failing.

We dined with Lionel Feilding (of the B.B.C.) to meet Thornton

---

[1] *The Well of Loneliness.*
[2] *The Future of an Illusion.*
[3] Wells published four books this year: *The Book of Catherine Wells; The Way the World Is Going; The Open Conspiracy; Mr. Blettsworthy on Rampole Island.*
[4] For the Bishop of Liverpool's Affirmation series.

Wilder, who came with his sister [1] (a theatre enthusiast "qualifying" in U.S.A. as a "director"). André Maurois and wife arrived late. Edith Evans was to come, but didn't turn up at all. Wilder, a nice modest dark young man, had to go off for 20 minutes to broadcast.

Wednesday, August 29th.

Walked to Garrick Club and lunch with Chartres Biron, Sutro, and Jacobs. Jacobs very witty. Rehearsal (dress) at 2.30. At 7.30 I dressed at the theatre (rehearsal still going on) and dined at Piccadilly as guest of Harry Preston and sat next to Gene Tunney, the guest of honour. About thirty people. He is agreeable to talk to. He made a good speech, but too long.

Saturday, September 1st.

I walked to the St. James's Theatre [2] but seeing a crowd still in front, I walked round St. James's parish for a bit, and entered the stage door at 11.27. I found Gerald Du M. alone in his dressing-room. He seemed fairly content, but not enthusiastic at all, about the reception. Reception on the stage, champagne, etc.

Monday, September 3rd.

After chores I reached the St. James's Theatre at 11 a.m. Everyone was pretty gloomy, except me. They pretend to despise critics but they attach extraordinary importance to everything the critics say. Gilbert Miller was cheerful, and he and I upraised their spirits. By 5 p.m. they were quite cheerful, and dreaming of an "enormous success"; and so on. I was on the stage for six hours during the day, making minor alterations, and changing the business at the end of the last act, and rehearsing the same.

Tuesday, September 4th. Train between Paris and Aix les Bains.

We left Victoria for Annecy at 2 p.m. In the French train Dorothy and I discussed my *Punch and Judy* film at some length.

---

[1] Isabel Wilder, whose first novel, *Mother and Three,* was published in 1933.
[2] This was the first night of *The Return Journey.*

Wednesday, September 5th. Imperial Palace Hotel, Annecy.

We got to Annecy half an hour late. First impressions very agreeable. Situation of hotel on lake very agreeable. Hotel *sympathique*. But the great shadow lay over us of our big baggage not having turned up—for it hadn't turned up. Discussions. Telegrams and things. Also I had left my eyeglasses in the bed in the train. I telegraphed to Rome instantly about these. When we came down to dinner the luggage had mysteriously come. My original theory that the delay had had nothing to do with the Customs and that the stuff had merely missed the train at Paris was confirmed. I began to read Plutarch's life of Alexander the Great. Good stuff.

Thursday, September 6th.

Too idle to shave myself. I employed the hotel barber, who had little to say, even about the weather. Lunch a bit late, and then we dashed off in a taxi to catch the 2.10 steamer *France* for the *tour du lac*. There are one or two fine mountains in full view (7000 ft. or so) but I found it impossible to be enthusiastic about lake scenery. It is like living in a picture postcard, especially when there is full sunshine. The steamer calls at all sorts of places, little places. Menthon was the best. We stepped off at Duingt because Noel Coward had given such an enthusiastic account of it to Dorothy. Not bad, but suffering from the disadvantage of being seriously cut off by hills from the sun both east and west. Noel must have been there in love, some hot August. After tea, we climbed a little way up the hill below the church and sat, and I made a slight sketch of a lake-and-mountain composition (the first interesting one I had seen). Then another steamer back, arriving at 6.30 at Annecy. I then reflected for one hour on my film and I got a real notion or two. After dinner I read about 50 pages of Keyserling's *Europe*. I was prepared to disdain it, but did not utterly.

Friday, September 7th.

We drove into Chambéry. Not very good scenery. Chambéry *est très sympathique*. We began by going into the Chapel of the Dukes of Savoy in mistake for the Cathedral. The arcaded street is good architecture and unspoilt. Rousseau must have seen it just like that, and the people the same, too—except for their clothes. Provincial ceremoniousness when friends meet on footpath. I doubt if you could see it in England. A rather "petty" people, I thought; but naturally so. How could they be otherwise? We liked it all. The cathedral itself is not much, roof good—Genoese-decorated walls not good. But it is nice and small, and one has a pleasant change from big cathedrals. The elephant fountain is not *sympathique*. Quantities of old architecture, corners, squares, little old shops. We came back by the mountain route, etc. Very fine scenery, good roads, full of hairpin turns; vast vision of a wall of cloud (and a rainbow above it or in it) hiding the highest mountain. Scarcely were we reposing in our rooms than there was outcry at Dorothy's door. "Afraid you've made a mistake," said Dorothy. "No, I haven't," said a voice. "Arnold. Dorothy." I then recognized Diana Cooper's voice. She had just arrived from Chambéry.

Saturday, September 8th.

This was our hottest day so far. I began a rough preliminary sketch of my new film and I did about a third of it in the morning before a bathe. We bathed with Diana Cooper, Lady Horner, who had her two granddaughters, Lady Helen and Lady Perdita Asquith, in the water with her, and the boy, Lord Oxford. I talked to the old lady while on the raft. The Diana-Horner party went off to lunch at Talloires. Duff Cooper had arrived in the early afternoon from Geneva. He and Diana were returning from a rowing excursion (and reading Wells's new novel aloud to one another on the lake) just as Dorothy and I were finishing tea on the terrace.

Monday, September 10th.

Lunch with Duff Cooper and Diana at the Restaurant du Parc des Eaux Vives, Geneva. Apparently Geneva is "full." Flags of strange new designs, of new nations, hanging about on all the big hotels. At the Beaurivage the clientele seems to be rather earnest, movement-y, and narrow-minded. The other guest at the luncheon was a middle-aged Italian *flaneur,* named Piacci (or some such name) who knew everybody in Italy, Belgium, France, Switzerland, and England (except Beaverbrook, whom he thought was a brother of Rothermere). He is a type one meets in Paris; apparently kindly, broad-minded, a bit cynical, with no ambition. Friend of many authors, statesmen, princesses, etc. The Queen of Belgium had done his portrait three times. Ojetti has written his portrait in *Cose Viste,* etc., etc. A good talker, but a bit too much of a solo performer. Still it was all very good.

We then drove to the hotel and Dorothy and I walked back to the Hall of the League of Nations for the afternoon session. It is a biggish hall, absolutely awful acoustics, in the ex-Hôtel Victoria. Atmosphere (mental) rather like the House of Commons. Physical atmosphere simply terrible; hot, stuffy, odorous of people in the *première galerie*, for which Duff had got us tickets. Briand had orated in the morning, and they all said it was *marvellous.* But in the afternoon we saw nothing marvellous. We saw him record his vote—he is now a hunchback—on the admission of new nations to the Council. These were Persia, Venezuela—I forget the third. This business of voting on new admissions took a long time. Before that there had been statements about new rules. At the end of the declaration of the vote, the Chairman declared an interval of ten minutes. On the floor of the big Chamber, delegates and secretaries moving about and coming in and going out (especially at the back of the platform) the whole time. My general impression of the League was that something is being done there, despite the appearances of tedium and slackness.

Thursday, September 20th. 75 Cadogan Square, London.

Dorothy and I went to see my play at the St. James's. Full house. An ordeal. The play seemed to me to be very harrowing. The upper circle and the dress circle liked it better than the stalls, or showed their liking more. We talked to Gerald afterwards in his dressing-room. Bed 12.30. Exhausted. Goodish night last night.

Friday, September 21st.

I walked about and got ideas for "God" book. I wrote a lot of them before lunch. Wells came for lunch: his 62nd birthday. Dorothy arrived late for lunch, but with a gardenia for him. Agreeable lunch. He left before 3.

Ivor Nicholson and Miss Head, of *Hearst's Magazine,* London Branch, gave a dinner to Marion Davies and Hearst. Marion was the guest of honour, of course. She praised Hollywood tremendously. Then I met Hearst, who made a very nice, mild, good speech, in which he said that a *rapprochement* between Britain and U.S.A. was his chief desire and he should do all he could to promote it. He is a very agreeable man of about 58, urbane, smiles easily, and listens well. He seemed to me to have a lot of character. In fact I liked him. I said to him: "The foundation of good health and hard work is going to bed early. So I must go." He didn't agree. He said that as a morning newspaper man, 5 a.m. had been his time for going to bed and that often he and a pal of his, who ran an evening newspaper, used to have supper and breakfast together.

Monday, September 24th.

I walked to the Garrick to lunch with Maurice Marston, who explained to me his new "Readers' Guide" scheme (on behalf of the National Book Council) for selling more books. He wanted me to boom it. I said I would. Young Hamilton (of Harpers) wanted me to be chief judge of a novel competition arranged jointly by Jonathan Cape and Harpers. There would be six MS. novels to read. I refused.

Wednesday, September 26th.

My ideas for continuation of "God" book being not quite in order, I wanted a romantic change, and went off by Underground eastwards and got off at the Monument, and walked about the City for an hour, and came home through Holborn in a 22 bus. The City is continually changing architecturally, growing grander and more ornamental; and banks seem to be increasing their premises more and more. The City is a symbol of the domination of the banks. Expense has not been spared in financial architecture in the City. There is grandeur, despite the lack of space.

I have at last finished D. H. Lawrence's *Lady Chatterley's Lover*. It is *foncièrement* indecent, but not pornographic. Some of it is very good, and some awful in dryness. Generally speaking, the lechery scenes are the best.

Thursday, September 27th.

Lunch at the Reform. H. G. Wells came upstairs later and Gardiner being rather boastful I offered to play him a tennis match on the hard court in Cadogan Square for a quid. He took it on. He also offered to play Wells after he had played me, and Wells took that on, too. The matches are to take place on Wednesday at 3.

Friday, September 28th.

Noel Coward telephoned he couldn't come to lunch. Reginald Turner telephoned he was in bed with a cold and couldn't come to lunch so that only the Bernard Shaws and Jeanne de Casalis came. This lunch was very successful and Shaw was in better form than I have seen him for a long time past. Charlotte Shaw plays the role of the super-celebrity's wife with much tact.

Saturday, September 29th.

Charles Laughton came by appointment at 10.40 (for 10.30) to consult me about his most private affairs. He stayed till 12. He would have left earlier but I wouldn't let him. Towards the end he said he wanted to play Shakespeare. He said little on this subject but what he said was good.

Tuesday, October 2nd.

I walked three miles round Battersea and Beaufort St. to get my ideas for the next section of the religious booklet. I got them and began at once to write. Noel Coward and Jeanne de Casalis and her father and mother came to lunch. Noel was in the greatest form. Papa de Casalis was a good and lively talker and arguer. Jeanne was appropriately daughterly in the presence of her parents, and the lunch was a great success.

Wednesday, October 3rd.

I walked three miles around Battersea Park, forgetting that I had to play tennis in the afternoon, and came home and worked on the penultimate section of my religious booklet. Preparations for tennis with Gardiner and H. G. Wells in Square. Gardiner came shortly after 3 and Wells a little before his appointed time, 3.30. Both middle-aged, grave, jocular, voluble. They changed their clothes up in my room. Our ages, A. G. G. 63, H. G. W. 62, and me 61. I beat Gardiner 6–5, and then he thought he should only play one set with me as he had to play Wells. He beat Wells 6–2. He then played Wells again and beat him 6–2. The last was only a fun set. I was told that there was betting at the Club—all against me. I took £1 off Gardiner and Gardiner took £1 off Wells. A man had been sitting on a bench watching us throughout the games. At the end he came up to us. He was a *Daily Mail* man. In the morning the *Mail* had telephoned me to allow a photographer to come down and take us at tennis. I said no. I don't know how the news of the great match reached the *Mail*.

Thursday, October 18th.

Enfeebled after neuralgia, and bad night. I did little in the morning, except prepare. Then, though still very neuralgic, I wrote 600 words of short story.

We arrived last at Sybil Colefax's dinner. Margaret Kennedy and husband, Desmond MacCarthy and wife, Oliver Brett and wife, Rudolf Kommer and Anita Loos—charming. I had neuralgia and was silent and indiscreetly talkative by turns.

Friday, October 19th.

I wrote 1000 words of short story before noon. I then walked two miles and then drove to the Garrick Club, where Du Maurier lunched with me. He practically wanted me to rewrite Acts II and III of *The Return*

Journey. I told him I couldn't, but gave him leave to fool around with the play.

We reached the Ravel Concert at the Aeolian Hall 20 minutes late, and Ravel himself came into the vestibule. We talked a bit.[1] This concert was extremely satisfactory. It seemed to me to be *all* good music.

Saturday, October 20th.

I spent most of the morning out of doors, down Battersea way, railways with streets down each side of them, and signal box coming out across pavement, and so on. Three big lines crossing over or under one another. Smuts, steam, noise. Heavy shower as I was getting home. I had my ideas in order. I wrote 1100 words of my story during the afternoon.

Wednesday, October 24th.

To Hunterbridge near King's Langley to dine with Gilda Gray on her birthday. A quiet young man who looked me steadily in the eye and said he had come over with Gilda Gray, was there. And Dupont and his German actress wife were the only other guests. Evening very decent, and showing a decent lack of taste. The birthday cake which had been ordered from Lyons was very enormous and characteristic. The whole thing was a bit of Hollywood transported into Hertfordshire.

Tuesday, October 30th.

I went alone to *The Power of Darkness,* arranged by the Tolstoy Society. Rotten but earnest production. Sad spectacle of third-rate West End actors with their West End voices trying to play Russian peasants. Pathetic. Comic. Yet the play came through as a majestic and vast work. No wonder it has been played all over Europe. It goes so largely and so smoothly that you can't easily find any fault with it.

Thursday, November 1st.

I walked out in the morning—Chelsea Embankment, and got a few ideas for completing a scene of *Punch and Judy,* and finished the scene

---

[1] They were old friends from Bennett's Paris days.

before lunch. With Dorothy to Eliz. Lewis's (now Wansborough's) wedding reception at Bryanston Square. Father dead; mother in a nursing home—brother educating in Germany. What a sadness! Crowds of people. I talked to lots and embraced several. I left just after the bride and bridegroom, and walked to Yacht Club and thought. Then to South Kensington museum and thought. Then home and thought. But didn't get my next scene absolutely clear after all.

Friday, November 2nd.

Worried by my film *Punch and Judy* I walked out for an hour and got ideas and came back and wrote another scene. Then at 2.15 I drove in a studio car to Elstree to see some shooting of the *Piccadilly* film. Full crowd. 300 guests in the famous club. The colouring of the dresses was not at all distinguished; but this doesn't matter on the screen. Each item was filmed five or six times. Endless trouble taken. Considerable heat from *terrific* blaze of electric lamps. I talked with Gilda Gray. The Denison Rosses, the Colefaxes, Muriel Foster, Humbert Wolfe, and H. G. Wells came to dinner and the uproariousness of the whole evening was terrific.

Monday, November 5th.

Took one of the new 6-wheel buses, just to try it, to the Ritz, and walked up Bond Street to the Queen's Hall to look at programmes.

At 3 p.m. I was at the Board Meeting of the *New Statesman* to discuss scheme for getting a push on sales. I promised to write a booklet, to sign it, and to find £200 towards the outlay required for the push, such sum and any further sums to have a prior claim on previous loans.

Wednesday, November 7th.

I went by bus to the Embassy Club to lunch with Harry Preston; Marconi, Harry McGowan, Humphrey de Trafford, Lord Knebworth (boxer), Beverley Baxter, and Charles Graves (*Daily Mail* gossip man). I sat next to Marconi. A quiet man, without a lot to say.

Inspected Victoria Station at 6.30 and the surroundings.

Saturday, November 10th.

I walked three miles to get ideas and didn't get them. Julian Huxley and Professor Church came to see me at noon about their proposed magazine *The Realist*, and I poured wisdom into them, of which they were very receptive, for one hour.

I saw the Quintero brothers' little piece in three scenes, *Fortunata*, at the Court, with O. B. Clarence in the principal role. I went to see this because Dorothy had praised it so highly. A very good, picturesque little comedy, and well played. I met A. P. Herbert there. The remainder of the afternoon I chiefly wasted—I think because I had felt a chill going out in the wet to the theatre. Henry Williamson, author of *The Pathway*, came to dinner. I'd never seen him before. 32, dark. Highly strung. Bit by bit we got on better and better, and he left at 11.15 much touched by the contact. I liked him. Married. Two children. Seems to be very fond of his wife, and admires her. She is the original of "Mary" in *The Pathway;* so she must be fine. He told me lots of autobiography.

Sunday, November 11th.

I read the *Memoirs of Max of Baden*, and learned something about Germany in the war. Then to Stornoway House to dine with Beaverbrook. Dean Inge and wife, Churchill and McKenna, were the other guests. The gloomy dean was not at all gloomy. In argument on finance McKenna knocked Churchill to bits. We all went to the Armistice Festival organized by the *Express* at the Albert Hall; we had the box next to King, Queen, and Co. This affair was very impressive indeed.

The financial debate between the Chancellor and the ex-Chancellor was very diverting. I left at midnight. I enjoyed this evening. It woke me up.

Wednesday, November 14th.

I wrote more of *Punch and Judy*. Then walked to the Reform Club, round by Piccadilly Circus. I met Paul Nash in Coventry Street, and he told me about the case of C., an author (esteemed by Galsworthy) on his beam-ends, to the fund for whom I subscribed last week through Nash. Nash is a kindly fellow. Then I corrected over 60 pages of the pianoforte score of the new Goossen's opera *Judith*. Lots of errors in the text. Then Dr. Griffin called to see me, so that I could get from him medical details for *Punch and Judy*.

To the Lyric, Hammersmith, where there was a great concourse of cars, to see *The Critic* and A. P. Herbert's *Two Gentlemen of Soho*. *The Critic* wears very well and Playfair has produced it quite well. A. P. Herbert's little piece (30 minutes' play) has little or no dramatic quality, but very many marvellously funny lines—in fact many as good as Sheridan's.

Sunday, November 18th.

Michael Arlen and wife and William Gerhardi came to lunch; all stayed till 3.15, and Gerhardi stayed till 3.40. I liked Mrs. Arlen. If she doesn't see a joke she doesn't pretend to see it and doesn't laugh. She speaks very fluent and correct English, with an accent. Arlen was full of common sense.

Wednesday, November 21st.

1st night of Quintero's play *100 Years Old* at Hammersmith. Lovely 1st Act. Other acts not so good. Then we all four went to Dorothy Warren's and Philip Trotter's pre-nuptial supper at Boulestin's. About 200 I should think. I sat next to Lady Raleigh and opposite the betrothed couple, Anna May Wong, and Harold Baker. Got home in taxi at about 1.30. Good evening.

Saturday, November 24th.

I began to read Zweig's *The Case of Sergeant Grischa*. Goodish and good and sometimes very good; but marred by too much allusiveness and periphrasis, and by confused, overcharged writing. Then we went to see O'Neill's *All God's Chillun* at the Gate Theatre. Packed. First act sentimental, patchy, and not clear. Second Act (in three scenes—the 1st act was in four) very much better, and the last scene of it very good, and rather moving. This is the best bit of O'Neill that I have seen, and rather alters my opinion of him. I was almost tragically, fatally, exhausted. I can't remember ever having felt more exhausted. I read more of *Grischa*.

Monday, November 26th.

One of the Cartes telephoned me early in the morning that Bertie Sullivan had just died of heart failure. This upset me. At the Garrick Club, where I dined with Duff Tayler, everybody was talking of this death.

Thursday, November 29th.

I read a great deal of Blunden's *Undertones of War*. A very fine book.

Friday, November 30th.

We had a lunch. Max Beerbohm and MacCarthy and I stayed talking. Beerbohm was very strong against the Russians as a thoroughly inferior race, and he said he simply could not read their novels (except Tolstoy). I think what he objects to is their inefficiency.

Monday, December 3rd.

Walk round Shaftesbury Avenue, etc. to Reform Club to get ideas for *Punch and Judy*. I got some, and I got more at the Club between 12.30 and 1. I did a little writing of the film between 5 and 6.30. Dined at home, and we dashed off to see Tallulah Bankhead in *Her Cardboard Lover*, a French farce by Deval, anglicized by P. G. Wodehouse and another. This was quite a good boulevard farce in the traditional manner, well played by Tallulah and Leslie Howard. The rest very mediocre. Wodehouse had handled it with some skill. Tallulah has great resource, and so has Leslie Howard. We got home by 11.15, after learning that the King was *slightly* better. Crowds continually in front of the Palace. I read some of J. W. N. Sullivan's *Beethoven*, and wasn't much struck by it. Then 100 pages of *Alice in Wonderland*. Quite readable, though confined to one set of fanciful invention. Tenniel's pictures very ugly.

Tuesday, December 4th.

I walked by roundabout ways to Garrick Club. *En route* I met and was stopped by four people, including one who didn't know me but thought he would like to be sure that I was I, and an old lady whom I had met once at Monte·Carlo about seven years ago for a few minutes.

Geoffrey Russell suggested I should go with him to Bach's B Minor Mass at St. Margaret's. I did. I ate oysters with him at the Reform hastily, first. Church full. The whole thing marvellous. It seems that the Mass was not performed for many years after it was written and delivered, and Bach delivered it mainly as a proof to his sovereign that he was fitted for a post of Kappelmeister! Good performance. The effect was terrific; also uplifting, despite dowdiness of every woman in the congregation.

Monday, December 10th.

Went to see Max Beerbohm's caricatures at the Leicester Galleries. They are just as fine as ever. I bought a caricature of G. B. Shaw, not included in the exhibition, one of the finest Max drawings I ever saw, for 25 guineas. Couldn't resist.

Read Osbert Sitwell's witty book on London statues,[1] read the *Manchester Guardian*, hated to start work, did start, and in 90 minutes had written a chapter of *Punch and Judy*. We dined at the McKnight Kauffers'. The only other guest was Alfred A. Knopf, the New York publisher.

Sunday, December 16th.

Terrific day. The best I have done for years. Nearly 5000 words. I dined at the Savoy. The millionaire owner of a number of papers, came up to me and I didn't know him. I asked him: "Who are you?" He said he wanted some *really* good stuff for *X*. He said my article in the first issue had done them a great deal of harm, and asked why I had attacked Lloyd George, and Ll. George wanted to know. Considering that I had not mentioned him, or indicated him in any way, or any other politician,

---

[1] *The People's Album of London Statues.*

I said that this was a bit thick. I said I didn't know whether I could think of any subjects; I had too much to do. He said he worked harder than I did. I said: "You don't!" "Don't?" said he. "Don't," said I. "Don't?" said he. "Don't," said I. I gazed at him. His eye fell.

Tuesday, December 18th.

Today I finished correcting typescript of *Punch and Judy* film. Geoffrey Russell, F. Swinnerton came to lunch on business; also Elena Sullivan, our first view of her since Bertie's death about three weeks ago. She behaved with Latin calm and dignity. Exactly the right touch.

After lunch I formally gave to Dorothy 47 volumes of my MSS. (34 of Journal, 2 *Old Wives' Tale*, 1 *Riceyman Steps*, 1 *Elsie*, and 9 *Clayhanger Family*) in the presence of Miss Nerney, Fred Harvey, Swinnerton, and Geoffrey Russell.

Monday, December 31st.

This year I have written 304,000 words; 1 play, 2 films, 1 small book on religion, and about 80 or 81 articles. Also I lost a full month in rehearsals, and a full month, no, six weeks, on holidays.

[This concludes the three volumes of Arnold Bennett's Journals. The volume for 1929 he published, greatly abridged, during his life-time. He died in London on March 27, 1931, of typhoid fever contracted in France.]

INDEX

INDEX

NOTE: Wherever possible, the Index includes some brief explanatory reference to the names, titles, etc., mentioned in the text.